NCERT SOLUTIONS

with Chapterwise **Study Notes**

MATHEMATICS 12th

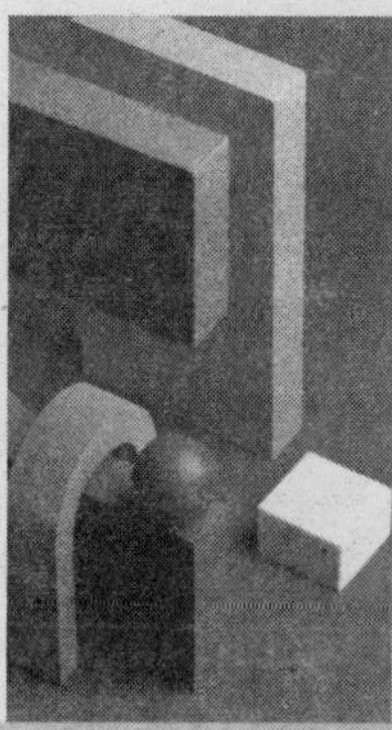

Fully Updated as per
Latest NCERT Textbook

NCERT SOLUTIONS

with Chapterwise **Study Notes**

MATHEMATICS 12th

Author
Somesh Jain

ARIHANT PRAKASHAN (Series), MEERUT

卐 **Administrative & Production Offices**

Regd. Office

'Ramchhaya' 4577/15, Agarwal Road, Darya Ganj, New Delhi -110002
Tele: 011- 47630600, 43518550

卐 **Head Office**

Kalindi, TP Nagar, Meerut (UP) - 250002
Tel: 0121-7156203, 7156204

卐 **Sales & Support Offices**

Agra, Ahmedabad, Bengaluru, Bareilly, Chennai, Delhi, Guwahati, Hyderabad, Jaipur, Jhansi, Kolkata, Lucknow, Nagpur & Pune.

卐 **PRICE** ₹455.00

卐 **PO No. :** TXT-59-T070793-5-26

Published by Arihant Publications (India) Ltd.

For further information about the books published by Arihant, log on to www.arihantbooks.com or e-mail at info@arihantbooks.com

Follow us on   

Preface

Feeling the immense importance and value of NCERT books, we are presenting this book, having the **NCERT Exercises Solutions**. For the overall benefit of the students we have made this book unique in such a way that it presents not only solutions but also detailed explanations. Through these detailed and through explanations, students can learn the concepts which will enhance their thinking and learning abilities.

We have introduced some Additional Features with the solutions which are given below:

- **Explanatory Solutions** Along with the solutions to questions we have given all the points that tell how to approach to solve a problem. Here we have tried to cover all those loopholes which may lead to confusion. All formulae and hints are discussed in full detail.
- Also included **Thinking Process** and **Mistake Alert** to understanding 'How to solve question' and points of mistakes.
- **Note** We have provided notes also to solutions in which special points are mentioned which are of great value for the students.

Apart from all those who helped in the compilation of this book a special note of thanks to all. With the hope that this book will be of great help to the students, we wish great success to our readers.

Somesh Jain

Contents

1. Relations and Functions 1-27
2. Inverse Trigonometric Functions 28-55
3. Matrices 56-100
4. Determinants 101-151
5. Continuity and Differentiability 152-237
6. Application of Derivatives 238-314
7. Integrals 315-453
8. Application of integrals 454-466
9. Differential Equations 467-535
10. Vector Algebra 536-578
11. Three Dimensional Geometry 579-600
12. Linear Programming 601-618
13. Probability 619-664

Relations and Functions

CHAPTER 01

Important Points

Relation

Let A be a non-empty set and let $R \subseteq A \times A$. Then, R is called a relation on A.

If $(a, b) \in R$, then we say that a is related to b and we write it as aRb.

01 Empty Relation A relation R on a set A is called empty relation, if no element of A is related to any element of A *i.e.*, $R = \phi \subset A \times A$ is the empty relation.

For example, Let $A = \{1,2,3\}$ and R be a relation is A by $R = \{(a,b) : a + b = 8\}$. Then, no element of A is related to any element of A. So, R is an empty relation.

02 Universal Relation A relation R on a set is called universal relation, if each element of A is related to every element of A. Thus, $R = A \times A$ is the universal relation.

Let $A = \{1,2,3\}$ and R be a relation given by $R = \{(a,b) : a + b \leq 6\}$, then all ordered pairs $(a,b) \in A \times A$ satisfy $a + b \leq 6$. So, R is a universal relation A.

03 A relation R on a set A is called

(i) reflexive, if $(a,a) \in R$ for every $a \in A$

(ii) symmetric, if $(a,b) \in R \Rightarrow (b,a) \in R$ for all $a, b, c \in A$.

(iii) transitive, if $(a,b) \in R$ and $(b,c) \in R \Rightarrow (a,c) \in R$, for all $a, b, c \in A$

04 Equivalence Relation A relation R on set A is called an equivalence relation, if it is reflexive, symmetric and transitive.

05 Equivalence Class Let R be an equivalence relation on a non-empty set A and let $a \in A$. Then, $[a]$ is the equivalence class determined by a and defined as $[a] = \{x \in A : (a,x) \in R\}$.

Function

Let A and B be two non-empty sets. Then, a function f from A to B is rule which associates each element of set A to a unique element of set B

and we write, $f: A \to B$.

A is called the domain of f and we write, dom $(f) = A$.

B is called the co-domain of f.

Also, $\{f(x): x \in A\} \subseteq B$ is called the range of f, written as range (f).

01 One-one (or Injective) Function A function $f: A \to B$ is said to be one-one function, if distinct elements of A have distinct images in B. Mathematically, for every $x_1, x_2 \in A$, if $x_1 \neq x_2$, then $f(x_1) \neq f(x_2)$ and if $f(x_1) = f(x_2)$, then $x_1 = x_2$.

02 Many-one Function A function $f: A \to B$ is said to be many-one, if two or more than two elements in A have the same image in B.

03 Onto (or surjective) Function A function $f: A \to B$ is said to be onto, if every element in B has its pre-image in A. *i.e.*, for each $y \in B$, there exists an element $x \in A$ such that $f(x) = y$. This happens when range $(f) = B$.

04 Into Function A function $f: A \to B$ is said to be into, if there exists one element is B, which have no pre-image in A.

05 Bijective Function A function $f: A \longrightarrow B$ is said to be bijective, if f is both one-one and onto.

Exercise 1.1

Question 1 Determine whether each of the following relations are reflexive, symmetric and transitive :

(i) Relation R in the set $A = \{1, 2, 3, \ldots\ldots, 13, 14\}$ defined as $R = \{(x, y): 3x - y = 0\}$

(ii) Relation R in set N of natural numbers defined as $R = \{(x, y): y = x + 5 \text{ and } x < 4\}$

(iii) Relation R in the set $A = \{1, 2, 3, 4, 5, 6\}$ as $R = \{(x, y): y \text{ is divisible by } x\}$

(iv) Relation R in the set Z of all integers defined as $R = \{(x, y): x - y$ is an integer$\}$

(v) Relation R in set A of human beings in a town at a particular time given by

(a) $R=\{(x,y): x$ and y work to the same place$\}$

(b) $R=\{(x,y): x$ and y live in the same locality$\}$

(c) $R=\{(x,y): x$ is exactly 7 cm taller than $y\}$

(d) $R=\{(x,y): x$ is wife of $y\}$

(e) $R=\{(x,y): x$ is father of $y\}$

Sol.

(i) (a) Given that, $A=\{1, 2, 3, 4, \ldots\ldots, 12, 13, 14\}$ and $R=\{(x,y): 3x-y=0\}$ for reflexive relation $(x, x) \in R\ \forall\ x \in A$

$\therefore$ If $y=x$, $3x-y=0 \Rightarrow 2x \neq 0 \Rightarrow (x, x) \notin R$.

So, R is not reflexive.

(b) Given $R=\{(x,y): 3x-y=0\}$ for symmetric relation $(x, y) \in R \Rightarrow (y,x) \in R$

If $(x, y) \in R \Rightarrow 3x-y=0$, then $3y-x \neq 0 \Rightarrow (y,x) \notin R$, so R is not symmetric.

For example; if $x=1, y=3, 3\times 1-3=0, 3\times 3-1=9-1=8 \neq 0$

(c) For transitive, if $(x,y) \in R \Rightarrow 3x-y=0$, $(y, z) \in R \Rightarrow 3y-z=0$, then $3x-z \neq 0$. So, R is not transitive.

For example, when, $x=1, y=3, z=9$, then

$$3\times 1-3=0, 3\times 3-9=0, 3\times 1-9 \neq 0$$

Quick Solution

Given, $A=\{1, 2, 3 \ldots, 14\}$

$$R=\{(x,y): 3x-y=0\} \Rightarrow R=\{(1,3)(2,6)(3,9),(4,12)\}$$

(a) Since, $(1, 1) \notin R$, so $(a,a) \notin R \forall a \in A$. So, R is not reflexive

(b) Since, $(1, 3) \in R$ but $(3, 1) \notin R$, thus $(a,b) \in R$ but $(b, a) \notin R\ \forall\ a, b$. So, R is not symmetric.

(c) $(1, 3) \in R$ and $(3, 9) \in R$ but $(1, 9) \notin R$, thus $(a, b) \in R$ and $(b, c) \in R$ but $(a,c) \notin R \forall a, b, c$. Hence R is not transitive.

(ii) Here, $A=N$, the set of natural numbers and

$$R=\{(x, y): y=x+5, x<4\}$$
$$=\{(x,x+5): x \in N \text{ and } x<4\}=\{(1, 6),(2, 7), (3, 8)\}$$

(a) For reflexive $(x,x) \in R\ \forall\ x \in A$ putting $y=x$, $x \neq y+5 \Rightarrow (1, 1) \notin R$. So, R is not reflexive.

(b) For symmetrical $(x,y) \in R \Rightarrow (y,x) \in R$ putting $y=x+5$, then $x \neq y+5 \Rightarrow (1, 6) \in R$ but $(6, 1) \notin R$. So, R is not symmetric.

(c) For transitivity $(x,y) \in R, (y,z) \in R \Rightarrow (x,z) \in R$ if $y=x+5$, $z=y+5$, then $z \neq x+5$. Since, $(1, 6) \in R$ and there is no order pair in R which has 6 as the first element same in the case for $(2, 7)$ and $(3, 8)$. So, R is transitive.

(iii) (a) For reflexive, we know that x is divisible by x for all $x \in A$.

$\therefore$ $(x, x) \in R$ for all $x \in R$. So, R is reflexive.

(b) For symmetric we observe that 6 is divisible by 2 but 2 is not divisible by 6. This means that $(2, 6) \in R$ but $(6, 2) \notin R$. So, R is not symmetric.

(c) For transitivity, let $(x, y) \in R$ and $(y, z) \in R$, then z is divisible by x.

$\Rightarrow$ $(x, z) \in R$

For example, 2 is divisible by 1and 4 is divisible by 2

So, 4 is divisible by 1. So, R is transitive.

(iv) (a) For reflexive put $y = x, x - x = 0$ which is an integer for all $x \in Z$. So, R is reflexive on Z.

(b) For symmetry let $(x,y) \in R$, then $(x - y)$ is an integer λ and also $y - x = -\lambda$ $[\because \lambda \in Z \Rightarrow -\lambda \in Z]$

$\therefore$ $y - x$ is an integer $\Rightarrow (y, x) \in R$. So, R is symmetric.

(c) For transitivity, let $(x,y) \in R$ and $(y, z) \in R$

$\therefore$ $x - y =$ integer and $y - z =$ integers, then $x - z$ is also an integer $y - z = u$. Let us say $x - y = \lambda,\ y - z = u$.

$\Rightarrow x - z = \lambda + \mu$

[if λ and μ are integers, then $\lambda + \mu$ will also be a integer]

$\therefore$ $(x, z) \in R$. So, R is transitive.

(v) (a) Here, R is reflexive as x and x will be the same person and same person always work in the same place.

$\Rightarrow$ $(x,x) \in R$

R is symmetric also as if x and y work at the same place, then it is obvious that y and x work at the same place. $(x,y) \in R \Rightarrow (y,x) \in R$.

R is transitive as x and y work at the same place and y and z work at the same place, then x and z also work at the same place.

$$(x,y) \in R, (y,z) \in R \Rightarrow (x,z) \in R$$

(b) Here, R is reflexive as x and x are the same person and same person lives in the same locality.

$$(x,x) \in R$$

R is symmetric as if x and y live in same locality, then y and x also live in the same locality. $(x,y) \in R \Rightarrow (y,x) \in R$.

R is transitive as if x and y live in the same locality and y and z live in the same locality, then it is obvious that x and z live in the same locality

$$(x,y) \in R, (y,z) \in R \Rightarrow (x,z) \in R$$

(c) Here, R is not reflexive as x is not 7 cm taller than x.

R is not symmetric as if x is exactly 7 cm taller than y, then y cannot be 7 cm taller than x and R is not transitive as if x is exactly 7 cm taller than y and y is exactly 7 cm taller than z, then x is exactly 14 cm taller than z.

(d) Here, R is not reflexive as x is not wife of x. R is not symmetric, as if x is wife of y, then y is husband (not wife) of x and R is transitive as transitivity is not contradicted in this case. Whenever $(x, y) \in R$, then $(y, z) \notin R$ for any z as if x is wife of y, then y is a male and a male cannot be a wife.

(e) Here, R is not reflexive; as x cannot be father of x. For any x, R is not symmetric as if x is father of y, then y cannot be father of x. R is not transitive as if x is father of y and y is father of z, then x is grandfather (not father) of z.

Mistake Alert If x is father of y and y is father of z, then students will assume that x is also father of z, which will give the incorrect result.

Question 2 Show that the relation R in the set R of real numbers, defined as $R=\{(a, b): a \le b^2\}$ is neither reflexive nor symmetric nor transitive.

Thinking Process In these type of question, we will take the ordered pair as an examples according to the condition, then we will chek the conditions of reflexive, symmetric and transitive.

Sol. We have $R=\{(a, b): a \le b^2\}$, where $a, b \in R$

For reflexivity, we observe that $\frac{1}{2} \le \left(\frac{1}{2}\right)^2$ is not true.

So, R is not reflexive as $\left(\frac{1}{2}, \frac{1}{2}\right) \notin R \Rightarrow (a,a) \notin R \forall a$

For symmetry, we observe that $-1 \le 3^2$ but $3 \not\le (-1)^2$

$\therefore$ $(-1, 3) \in R$ but $(3, -1) \notin R$.

$\Rightarrow$ $(a, b) \in R$ but $(b,a) \notin R \forall a,b$

So, R is not symmetric.

For transitivity, we observe that $2 \le (-3)^2$ and $-3 \le (1)^2$ but $2 \not\le (1)^2$

$\therefore$ $(2, -3) \in R$ and $(-3, 1) \in R$ but $(2, 1) \notin R$.

$\Rightarrow$ $(a,b) \in R, (b,c) \in R$ but $(a, c) \notin R \forall a,b,c$

So, R is not transitive.

Hence, R is neither reflexive, nor symmetric and nor transitive.

Question 3 Check whether the relation R defined in the set $\{1, 2, 3, 4, 5, 6\}$ as $R=\{(a, b): b=a+1\}$ is reflexive, symmetric or transitive.

Sol. Let $A=\{1, 2, 3, 4, 5, 6\}$

A relation R is defined on set A is

$R=\{(a, b): b=a+1\}$. Therefore, $R=\{(1, 2), (2, 3) (3, 4), (4, 5), (5, 6)\}$

Now, $6 \in A$ but $(6, 6) \notin R. \Rightarrow (a, a) \notin R \forall a$

Therefore, R is not reflexive.

It can be observed that $(1, 2) \in R$ but $(2, 1) \notin R$. Therefore, R is not symmetric.

Now, $(1, 2)$ and $(2, 3) \in R$ but $(1, 3) \notin R$. Therefore, R is not transitive.

Hence, R is neither reflexive nor symmetric nor transitive.

Question 4 Show that the relation R in R defined as $R = \{a, b) : a \le b\}$, is reflexive and transitive but not symmetric.

Sol. We have $R = \{(a, b) : a \le b\}$. Let $a, b \in R$.

Reflexive For any $a \in R$ we have $a \le a$. So, R is reflexive.

Symmetric We observe that $(2, 3) \in R$ but $(3, 2) \notin R$. So, R is not symmetric.

Transitivity $(a, b) \in R$ and $(b, c) \in R \Rightarrow a \le b$ and $b \le c \Rightarrow a \le c \Rightarrow (a, c) \in R$

So, R is transitive. Hence, R is reflexive and transitive but not symmetric.

Question 5 Check whether the relation R in R defined by $R = \{(a, b): a \le b^3\}$ is reflexive, symmetric or transitive.

Sol. Given that $R = \{(a, b): a \le b^3\}$

It is observed that $\left(\frac{1}{2}, \frac{1}{2}\right) \in R$ as $\frac{1}{2} < \left(\frac{1}{2}\right)^3 = \frac{1}{8} \Rightarrow (a, a) \notin R \, \forall a$

So, R is not reflexive.

Now, $(1, 2) \in R \; (\quad 1 < 2^3 = 8)$

But $(2, 1) \notin R (\quad 2^3 > 1) \Rightarrow (a, b) \in R$, but $(b, a) \notin R \, \forall \, a, b$

So, R is not symmetric.

We have $\left(3, \frac{3}{2}\right), \left(\frac{3}{2}, \frac{6}{5}\right) \in R$ as $3 < \left(\frac{3}{2}\right)^3$ and $\frac{3}{2} < \left(\frac{6}{5}\right)^3$

But $\left(3, \frac{6}{5}\right) \notin R$ as $3 > \left(\frac{6}{5}\right)^3 \Rightarrow (a, b) \in R, (b, c) \in R$ but $(a, c) \notin R \forall \, a, b, c$

Therefore, R is not transitive.

Hence, R is neither reflexive nor symmetric nor transitive.

Question 6 Show that the relation R in the set $\{1, 2, 3\}$ given by $R = \{(1, 2), (2, 1)\}$ is symmetric but neither reflexive nor transitive.

Sol. Given that $A = \{1, 2, 3\}$

A relation R on A is defined as $R = \{(1, 2), \{2, 1)\}$

It is seen that $(1, 1) (2, 2), (3, 3) \notin R$.

Therefore, R is not reflexive.

Now, $(1,2) \in R$ and $(2, 1) \in R$. So, R is symmetric.

Now, $(1, 2)$ and $(2, 1) \in R$ but $(1, 1) \notin R$. So, R is not transitive.

Hence, R is symmetric but neither reflexive nor transitive.

Question 7 Show that the relation R in the set A of all the books in a library of a college, given by $R = \{(x, y): x$ and y have same number of pages$\}$, is an equivalence relation.

Sol. Here, set A is the set of all books in the library of a college and $R = \{(x, y): x$ and y have the same number of pages$\}$

Now , R is reflexive, since $(x, x) \in R$ as x and x has the same number of pages.

Let $(x, y) \in R$

$\Rightarrow$ x and y have the same number of pages.

$\Rightarrow$ y and x have the same number of pages.

$\Rightarrow$ $(y,x) \in R$. So, R is symmetric.

Now, let $(x,y) \in R$ and $(y,z) \in R$.

$\Rightarrow$ x and y and have the same number of pages and y and z have the same number of pages.

$\Rightarrow$ x and z have the same number of pages $\Rightarrow$ $(x,z) \in R$

Therefore, R is transitive. Hence, R is an equivalence relation.

Question 8 Show that the relation R in the set $A = \{1, 2, 3, 4, 5\}$ is given by $R = \{(a, b): |a - b| \text{ is even }\}$, is an equivalence relation. Show that all the elements of $\{1, 3, 5\}$ are related to each other and all the elements of $\{2, 4\}$ are related to each other, but no element of $\{1, 3, 5\}$ is related to any element of $\{2, 4\}$.

Sol. Given that $A = \{1, 2, 3, 4, 5\}$, $R = \{(a,b) : |a - b| \text{ is even }\}$

Let $a \in A \Rightarrow |a - a| = 0$ (which is even) $\forall\, a$

So, R is reflexive.

Let $(a, b) \in R \Rightarrow |a - b|$ is even

$\Rightarrow$ $|-(b - a)| = |b - a|$ is also even

$\Rightarrow$ $(b,a) \in R$. So, R is symmetric.

Now, let $(a,b) \in R$ and $(b,c) \in R$

$\Rightarrow$ $|a - b|$ is even and $|b - c|$ is even

$\Rightarrow$ $(a - b)$ is even and $(b - c)$ is even

$\Rightarrow$ $(a - c) = (a - b) + (b - c)$ is even [sum of two even integers is even]

$\Rightarrow$ $|a - c|$ is even $\Rightarrow$ $(a, c) \in R$.

So, R is transitive. Hence, R is an equivalence relation.

Now, all elements of the set $\{1, 3, 5\}$ are related to each other as all the elements of this set are odd. So, the modulus of the difference between any two elements will be even.

Similarly, all elements of the set $\{2, 4\}$ are related to each other as all the elements of this set are even. So, the modulus of the difference between any two elements will be even.

Also, no element of the $\{1, 3, 5\}$ can be related to any element of $\{2, 4\}$ as all elements of $\{1, 3, 5\}$ are odd and all elements of $\{2, 4\}$ are even. So, the modulus of the difference between the two elements (from each of these two subsets) will not be even.

Question 9 Show that each of the relation R in the set $A = \{x \in Z : 0 \le x \le 12\}$, given by

(i) $R = \{(a, b) : |a - b| \text{ is a multiple of } 4\}$

(ii) $R = \{(a, b) : a = b\}$, are equivalence relations. Find the set of all elements related to 1 in the each case.

Sol. Given that $A = \{x \in Z : 0 \le x \le 12\} = \{0, 1, 2, 3, 4, 5, 6, 7, 8, 9, 10, 11, 12\}$

(i) $R = \{(a, b) : |a - b| \text{ is a multiple of } 4\}$

For any element $a \in A$, we have $(a, a) \in R$ as $|a - a| = 0$ is a multiple of 4. Therefore, R is reflexive.

Now, let $(a, b) \in R$

$\Rightarrow |a - b|$ is a multiple of $4 \Rightarrow |b - a| = |-(a - b)|$ is also a multiple of 4

$\Rightarrow (b, a) \in R$ Therefore, R is symmetric.

Now, let $(a, b), (b, c) \in R$

So, $|a - b|$ and $|b - c|$ is multiple of 4.

$\Rightarrow |a - c|$ is also multiple of 4 $\Rightarrow (a, c) \in R$

Therefore, R is transitive.

Hence, R is an equivalence relation.

$\Rightarrow$ The set of elements related to 1 is $\{1, 5, 9\}$, since

$|1 - 1| = 0$ is multiple of 4

$|5 - 1| = 4$ is a multiple of 4 and

$|9 - 1| = 8$ is a multiple of 4

(ii) $R = \{(a, b) : a = b\}$

For any element $a \in A$, we have $(a, a) \in R$, as $a = a$. Therefore, R is reflexive.

Now, let $(a, b) \in R \Rightarrow a = b \Rightarrow b = a \Rightarrow (b, a) \in R$

Therefore, R is symmetric.

Now, let $(a, b) \in R$ and $(b, c) \in R$

$\Rightarrow \quad a = b$ and $b = c \Rightarrow a = c \Rightarrow (a, c) \in R$. Therefore, R is transitive.

Hence, R is an equivalence relation.

The elements in R that are related to 1 will be those elements from set A, which are equal to 1.

Hence, the set of elements related to 1 is $\{1\}$.

Question 10 Given an example of a relation which is

(i) symmetric but neither reflexive nor transitive.
(ii) transitive but neither reflexive nor symmetric.
(iii) reflexive and symmetric but not transitive.
(iv) reflexive and transitive but not symmetric.
(v) symmetric and transitive but not reflexive.

Sol.

(i) Let $A = \{5, 6, 7\}$

Defined a relation R on A as $R = \{(5, 6), (6, 5)\}$

Relation R is not reflexive as $(5, 5), (6, 6), (7, 7) \notin R$.

Now, as $(5, 6) \in R$ and also $(6, 5) \in R$. So, R is symmetric.

Also $(5, 6)$ and $(6, 5) \in R$ but $(5, 5) \notin R$. Therefore, R is not transitive.

Hence, relation R is symmetric but neither reflexive nor transitive.

(ii) Consider a relation R in R defined as

$$R = \{(a, b): a < b\}$$

For any $a \in R$, we have $(a, a) \notin R$, since a cannot be strictly less than a itself. Therefore, R is not reflexive. $[\because a = a]$

Now, $(1, 2) \in R$ (as $1 < 2$)

But $(2,1) \notin R$ as 2 is not less than 1.

$\Rightarrow (a, b) \in R$ but $(b, a) \in R$.

Therefore, R is not symmetric.

Now, let (a, b) and $(b, c) \in R$

$\Rightarrow \qquad a < b$ and $b < c$

$\Rightarrow \qquad a < c \Rightarrow (a, c) \in R$

Therefore, R is transitive.

Hence, relation R is transitive but neither symmetric nor reflexive.

(iii) Let $A = \{4, 6, 8\}$

Defined a relation R on A as A

$$= \{(4, 4), (6, 6), (8, 8), (4, 6), (6, 4), (6, 8), (8, 6)\}$$

Relation R is reflexive, since for every $a \in A, (a, a) \in R$ *i.e.*, $(4, 4), (6, 6), (8, 8) \in R$.

Relation R is symmetric since $(a, b) \in R \Rightarrow (b, a) \in R$ for all $a, b \in R$.

Relation R is not transitive, since $(4, 6), (6, 8) \in R$, but $(4, 8) \notin R$.

Hence, relation R is reflexive and symmetric but not transitive.

(iv) Define a relation R in R as $R = \{(a, b) : a^3 \geq b^3\}$

Clearly $(a, a) \in R$ as $a^3 = a^3$. Therefore, R is reflexive.

Now, $(2,1) \in R$ (as $2^3 \geq 1^3$) But, $(1, 2) \notin R$ (as $1^3 < 2^3$)

$\Rightarrow (a,b) \in R$ but $(b, a) \notin R$.

Therefore, R is not symmetric.

Now, let $(a, b), (b, c) \in R$

$\Rightarrow a^3 \geq b^3$ and $b^3 \geq c^3 \Rightarrow a^3 \geq c^3 \Rightarrow (a,c) \in R$. Therefore, R is transitive.

Hence, relation R is reflexive and transitive but not symmetric.

(v) Let $A = \{-5, -6\}$

Define a relation R on A as: $R = \{(-5, -6), (-6, -5), (-5, -5)\}$

Relation R is not reflexive as $(-6, -6) \notin R$

Relation R is symmetric as $(-5, -6) \in R$ and $(-6, -5) \in R$

Now, $(-5, -6), (-6, -5) \in R \Rightarrow (-5, -5) \in R$.

Therefore, the relation R is transitive.

Hence, relation R is symmetric and transitive but not reflexive.

Question 11 Show that the relation R in the set A of points in a plane, given by $R = \{(P, Q)$: distance of the point P from the origin is same as the distance of the point Q from the origin$\}$, is an equivalence relation. Further, show that the set of all points related to a point $P \neq (0,0)$ is the circle passing through P with origin as centre.

Sol. Here, $R = \{(P, Q)$: distance of point P from the origin is same as the distance of point Q from the origin$\}$. Clearly, $(P, P) \in R$, since the distance of point P from the origin is always the same as the distance of the same point P from the origin. Therfore, R is reflexive.

Now, let $(P, Q) \in R$

$\Rightarrow$ The distance of point P from the origin is same as the distance of point Q from the origin.

$\Rightarrow$ The distance of point Q from the origin is same as the distance of point P from the origin.

$\Rightarrow$ $(Q, P) \in R$

Therefore, R is symmetric.

Now, let $(P, Q), (Q, S) \in R$

$\Rightarrow$ The distance of point P from the origin is same as the distance of point Q from the origin and the distance of point Q from the origin is same as the distance of point S from the origin.

$\Rightarrow$ The distance of point P from the origin is same as the distance of point S from the origin.

$\Rightarrow$ $(P, S) \in R$

Therefore, R is transitive. Therefore, R is an equivalence relation.

The set of all points related to $P \neq (0, 0)$ will be those points whose distance from the origin is the same as the distance of point P from the origin.

In other words, if $O(0, 0)$ is the origin and $OP = k$, then the set of all points related to P is at a distance of k from the origin.

Hence, this set of points forms a circle with the centre as the origin and this circle passes through point P.

Question 12 Show that the relation R, defined in the set of A all triangles as $R = \{(T_1, T_2) : T_1$ is similar to $T_2\}$, is equivalence relation. Consider three right angle triangles T_1 with sides $3, 4, 5$; T_2 with sides $5, 12, 13$ and T_3 with sides $6, 8, 10$. Which triangle among T_1, T_2 and T_3 are related ?

◎ ***Thinking Process*** To prove equivalence relation, we have to prove reflexive, symmetric and transitive relation.

Sol. Here, $R = \{(T_1, T_2) : T_1$ is similar to $T_2\}$

R is reflexive; since every triangle is similar to itself.

Further, if $(T_1, T_2) \in R$, then T_1 is similar to T_2.

$\Rightarrow$ T_2 is similar to $T_1 \Rightarrow (T_2, T_1) \in R$

Therefore, R is symmetric.

Now, let $(T_1, T_2), (T_2, T_3) \in R$.

$\Rightarrow T_1$ is similar to T_2 and T_2 is similar to T_3.

$\Rightarrow T_1$ is similar to $T_3 \Rightarrow (T_1, T_3) \in R$

Therefore, R is transitive. Thus, R is an equivalence relation.

Now, we can observe that $\frac{3}{6} = \frac{4}{8} = \frac{5}{10} = \left(\frac{1}{2}\right)$

Therefore, the corresponding sides of triangles T_1 and T_3 are in the same ratio. Then, triangle T_1 is similar to triangle T_3.

Hence, T_1 is related to T_3.

Question 13 Show that the relation R, defined in the set A of all polygons as $R = \{(P_1, P_2): P_1$ and P_2 have same number of sides$\}$, is an equivalence relation. What is the set of all elements in A related to the right angle triangle T with sides 3, 4 and 5?

Sol. Here, $R = \{(P_1, P_2)$; P_1 and P_2 have the same number of sides$\}$.

R is reflexive, since $(P_1, P_1) \in R$ as the same polygon has the same number of sides with itself.

Let $(P_1, P_2) \in R$

$\Rightarrow$ P_1 and P_2 have the same number of sides

$\Rightarrow$ P_2 and P_1 have the same number of sides.

$\Rightarrow$ $(P_2, P_1) \in R$

Therefore, R is symmetric.

Now, let $(P_1, P_2), (P_2, P_3) \in R$

$\Rightarrow$ P_1 and P_2 have the same number of sides. Also, P_2 and P_3 have the same number of sides. Therefore P_1 and P_3 have the same number of sides.

$\Rightarrow$ $(P_1, P_3) \in R$

Therefore R is transitive. Hence, R is an equivalence relation.

The elements in A related to the right-angled triangle (T) with sides 3, 4 and 5 are those polygons which have 3 sides, (since T is a polygon with 3 sides).

Hence, the set of all elements in A related to triangle T is the set of all triangles.

Question 14 Let L be the set of all lines in XY-plane and R be the relation in L defined as $R = \{(L_1, L_2): L_1$ is parallel to $L_2\}$. Show that R is an equivalence relation. Find the set of all lines related to the line $y = 2x + 4$.

Sol. Here, $R = \{(L_1, L_2): L_1$ is parallel to $L_2\}$

R is reflexive as any line L_1 is parallel to itself *i.e.*, $(L_1, L_1) \in R$.

Now, let $(L_1, L_2) \in R$

$\Rightarrow$ L_1 is parallel to $L_2 \Rightarrow L_2$ is parallel to L_1 $\Rightarrow$ $(L_2, L_1) \in R$

Therefore, R is symmetric.

Now, let $(L_1, L_2), (L_2, L_3) \in R$

$\Rightarrow$ L_1 is parallel to L_2, also L_2 is parallel to L_3.

$\Rightarrow$ L_1 is parallel to L_3

$\Rightarrow$ $(L_1, L_3) \in R$. Therefore, R is transitive.

Hence, R is an equivalence relation.

The set of all lines related to the line $y = 2x + 4$ is the set of all lines that are parallel to the line $y = 2x + 4$.

Slope of line $y = 2x + 4$ is $m = 2$ $[\because y = mx + c$ *i.e.*, slope of line $= m]$

It is known that parallel lines have the same slope.

The line parallel to the given line is of the form $y = 2x + c$, where $c \in R$.

Hence, the set of all lines related to the given line is given by $y = 2x + c$, where $c \in R$.

Question 15 Let R be the relation in the set $\{1,2,3,4\}$ given by $R=\{(1,2),(2,2),(1,1),(4,4),(1,3),(3,3),(3,2)\}$. Choose the correct answer.

(a) R is reflexive and symmetric but not transitive
(b) R is reflexive and transitive but not symmetric
(c) R is symmetric and transitive but not reflexive
(d) R is an equivalence relation

Sol. (b) Here, $R = \{(1, 2), (2, 2), (1, 1), (4, 4), (1, 3), (3, 3), (3, 2)\}$

Since, $(a, a) \in R$., for every $a \in \{1, 2, 3, 4\}$. Therefore, R is reflexive.

Now, since $(1, 2) \in R$ but $(2, 1) \notin R$. *i.e.*, $(a, b) \in R$ but $(b, a) \notin R$. Therefore, R is not symmetric.

Also, it is observed that $(a, b), (b, c) \in R$

$\Rightarrow$ $(a, c) \in R$. For all $a, b, c \in \{1, 2, 3, 4\}$

Therefore, R is transitive. Hence, R is reflexive and transitive but not symmetric.

Question 16 Let R be the relation in the set N given by $R=\{(a,b): a=b-2, b>6\}$. Choose the correct answer

(a) $(2, 4) \in R$ (b) $(3, 8) \in R$
(c) $(6, 8) \in R$ (d) $(8, 7) \in R$

Sol. (c) Given, $R = \{(a, b) : a = b - 2, b>6\}$

Now, since, $b>6$ $(2, 4) \notin R$. Also, as $3 \neq 8 - 2$ $(3, 8) \notin R$ and as $8 \neq 7 - 2$
Therefore, $(8, 7) \notin R$

Now, consider $(6, 8)$. We have $8 >6$ and also, $6 = 8 - 2$

Therefore, $(6, 8) \in R$.

Exercise 1.2

Question 1 Show that the function $f: R_* \rightarrow R_*$ defined by $f(x)=\dfrac{1}{x}$ is one-one, where R_* is the set of all non-zero real numbers. Is the result true, if the domain R_* is replaced by N with co-domain being same as R_*?

Sol. It is given that $f: R_* \rightarrow R_*$ defined by $f(x) = \dfrac{1}{x}$.

For one-one, $f(x) = f(y) \Rightarrow \dfrac{1}{x} = \dfrac{1}{y} \Rightarrow x = y$

Therefore, f is one-one.

For onto,

It is clear that for $y \in R_*$, there exists $x = \dfrac{1}{y} \in R_*$ (as $y \neq 0$) such that

$$f(x) = \frac{1}{\left(\frac{1}{y}\right)} = y$$

Therefore, f is onto. Thus, the given function (f) is one-one and onto.

Now, consider function $g : N \to R_*$ defined by $g(x) = \frac{1}{x}$.

We have, $$g(x_1) = g(x_2) \Rightarrow \frac{1}{x_1} = \frac{1}{x_2} \Rightarrow x_1 = x_2$$

Therefore, g is one-one.

Further, it is clear that g is not onto as for $5 \in R_*$, therefore does not exist any x in N such that $g(x) = \frac{1}{5}$ because $\frac{1}{5} \notin N$.

Hence, function g is one-one but not onto.

Mistake Alert Student may assume that domain of g is R_* instead of N, leading to incorrect results.

Question 2 Check the injectivity and surjectivity of the following functions :

(i) $f : N \to N$ given by $f(x) = x^2$ (ii) $f : Z \to Z$ given by $f(x) = x^2$

(iii) $f : R \to R$ given by $f(x) = x^2$ (iv) $f : N \to N$ given by $f(x) = x^3$

(v) $f : Z \to Z$ given by $f(x) = x^3$

Sol.

(i) $f : N \to N$ is given by $f(x) = x^2$

It is seen that for $x, y \in N, f(x) = f(y)$

$\Rightarrow$ $x^2 = y^2 \Rightarrow x = y$ ($\because$ x and y are positive numbers)

Therefore, f is injective.

Now, $2 \in N$ (co-domain) but there does not exist any x in N such that $f(x) = x^2 = 2$.

It means there is some element in co-domain in which do not have any pre-images. Therefore, f is not surjective.

Hence, function f is injective but not surjective.

(ii) $f : Z \to Z$ is given by $f(x) = x^2$

It is seen that $f(-1) = f(1) = 1$ but $-1 \neq 1$

Therefore f is not injective

Now, $-2 \in Z$ (co-domain). But there does not exist any elements $x \in Z$ such that $f(x) = x^2 = -2$. It means all negative integers in co-domain do not have pre-image.

Therefore, f is not surjective.

Hence, function f is neither injective nor surjective.

(iii) $f : R \to R$ is given by $f(x) = x^2$. It is seen that $f(-1) = f(1) = 1$ but $-1 \neq 1$.

Therefore, f is not injective.

Now, $-2 \in R$ (co-domain) . But there does not exist any element $x \in R$ such that $f(x) = x^2 = -2$. It means all negative real numbers do not have any pre-images. Therefore, f is not surjective.

Hence, function f is neither injective nor surjective.

(iv) $f : N \to N$ given by, $f(x) = x^3$

It is seen that for $x, y \in N$, $f(x) = f(y) \Rightarrow x^3 = y^3 \Rightarrow x = y$

Therefore, f is injective. Now, $2 \in N$ (co-domain). But, there does not exist any element x in domain N such that $f(x) = x^3 = 2$.

Therefore, f is not surjective.

Hence, function f is injective but not surjective.

(v) $f : Z \to Z$ is given by, $f(x) = x^3$

It is seen that for $x, y \in Z$, $f(x) = f(y) \Rightarrow x^3 = y^3 \Rightarrow x = y$

Therefore, f is injective.

Now, $2 \in Z$ (co-domain). But, there does not exist any element x in domain Z such that $f(x) = x^3 = 2$. Therefore, f is not surjective.

Hence, function f is injective but not surjective.

Question 3 Prove that the greatest integer function $f : R \to R$, given by $f(x) = [x]$, is neither one-one nor onto, where $[x]$ denotes the greatest integer less than or equal to x.

Sol. Here, $f : R \to R$ is given by, $f(x) = [x]$

It is seen that $f(1.2) = [1.2] = 1$, $f(1.9) = [1.9] = 1$

Therefore, $f(1.2) = f(1.9)$, but $1.2 \neq 1.9$

Therefore, f is not one-one.

Now, consider $0.7 \in R$. It is known that $f(x) = [x]$ is always an integer.

Thus, there does not exist any element $x \in R$ such that $f(x) = 0.7$.

Means every non integral elements in co-domain do not have preimages.

Therefor, f is not onto.

Hence, the greatest integer function is neither one-one nor onto.

Question 4 Show that the modulus function $f : R \to R$, given by $f(x) = |x|$, is neither one-one nor onto, where $|x|$ is x, if x is positive or 0 and $|x|$ is $-x$, if x is negative.

Sol. Here, $f : R \to R$ is given by $f(x) = |x| = \begin{cases} x, & \text{if } x \geq 0 \\ -x, & \text{if } x < 0 \end{cases}$

It is seen that $f(-1) = |-1| = 1$, $f(1) = |1| = 1$

Therefore, $f(-1) = f(1)$ but $-1 \neq 1$

Therefore, f is not one-one.

Now, consider $-1 \in R$

It is known that $f(x) = |x|$ is always non-negative.

Thus, there does not exist any element x in domain R such that

$$f(x) = |x| = -1.$$

Therefore, f is not onto.

Hence, the modulus functions is neither one-one nor onto.

Question 5 Show that the Signum function $f: R \to R$, given by $f(x)=\begin{cases}1, & \text{if } x>0\\ 0, & \text{if } x=0\\ -1, & \text{if } x<0\end{cases}$ is neither one-one nor onto.

Thinking Process To prove not one-one, show that atleast two elements have the same image and to prove not onto, show that atleast one element of co-domain is not the image of any element of domain.

Sol. We have, $f: R \to R$, $f(x)=\begin{cases}1, & x>0\\ 0, & x=0\\ -1, & x<0\end{cases}$

It is seen that $f(1) = f(2) = 1$ but $1 \neq 2$. Therefore, f is not one-one.

Now, as $f(x)$ takes only three values (1, 0 or -1) for the element -2 in co-domain R, there does not exist any x in domain R such that $f(x) = -2$.

Therefore, f is not onto.

Hence, the Signum function is neither one-one nor onto.

Question 6 Let $A=\{1,2,3\}$, $B=\{4,5,6,7\}$ and let $f=\{(1,4),(2,5),(3,6)\}$ be a function from A to B. Show that f is one-one.

Sol. Given that $A = \{1, 2, 3\}$ and $B = \{4, 5, 6, 7\}$

Now, $f: A \to B$ is defined as $f = \{(1, 4), (2, 5), (3, 6)\}$

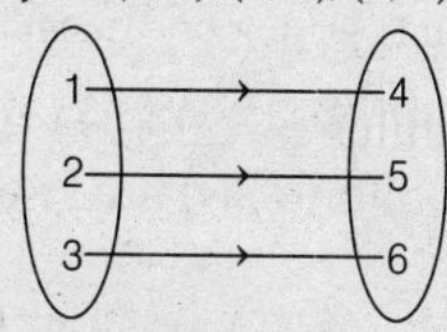

Therefore, $f(1) = 4$, $f(2) = 5$, $f(3) = 6$

It is seen that the images of distinct elements of A under f are distinct.

Hence, function f is one-one.

Question 7 In each of the following cases, state whether the functions is one-one, onto or bijective. Justify answer.

(i) $f: R \to R$ defined by $f(x) = 3 - 4x$

(ii) $f: R \to R$ defined by $f(x) = 1 + x^2$

Sol.

(i) Here, $f: R \to R$ is defined by $f(x) = 3 - 4x$

Let $x_1, x_2 \in R$ such that $f(x_1) = f(x_2)$

$\Rightarrow \quad 3 - 4x_1 = 3 - 4x_2 \Rightarrow -4x_1 = -4x_2 \Rightarrow x_1 = x_2$

Therefore, f is one-one.

For any real number y in R, there exists $\frac{3-y}{4}$ in R such that

$$f\left(\frac{3-y}{4}\right) = 3 - 4\left(\frac{3-y}{4}\right) = y$$

Therefore, f is onto. Hence, f is bijective.

(ii) Here $f: R \to R$ is defined as

$$f(x) = 1 + x^2$$

Let $x_1, x_2 \in R$ such that $f(x_1) = f(x_2)$

$\Rightarrow \quad 1 + x_1^2 = 1 + x_2^2 \Rightarrow x_1^2 = x_2^2 \Rightarrow x_1 = \pm x_2$

For instance, $f(1) = f(-1) = 2$

Therefore, $f(x_1) = f(x_2)$ does not imply that $x_1 = x_2$

Therefore, f is not one-one.

Consider an element -2 in co-domain R.

It is seen that $f(x) = 1 + x^2$ is positive for all $x \in R$.

Thus, there does not exist any x in domain R such that $f(x) = -2$.

Therefore, f is not onto. Hence, f is neither one-one nor onto.

Quick Solution

$$f(x) = 1 + x^2$$

$$f(1) = 1 + 1^2 = 2, \; f(-1) = 1 = (-1)^2 = 2$$

$\therefore \quad f(1) = f(-1)$ but $1 \neq -1$

So, f is not one-one

We have $f(x) = 1 + x^2$ with co-domain $= R$

Let $\quad y = 1 + x^2 \Rightarrow x = \sqrt{y-1}$

The value of x exist only when $y - 1 \geq 0$

$\Rightarrow \quad y \geq 0 \Rightarrow y \in [1, \infty)$

Now, we can see that,

Co-domain $(R) \neq$ Range $([1, \infty))$

Thus, $f(x)$ is not onto.

Question 8 Let A and B be sets. Show that $f: A \times B \to B \times A$ such that $f(a, b) = (b, a)$ is bijective function.

Sol. Here, $f: A \times B \to B \times A$ is defined as $f(a, b) = (b, a)$

Let $\quad (a_1, b_1), (a_2, b_2) \in A \times B$

Such that $\quad f(a_1, b_1) = f(a_2, b_2) \Rightarrow (b_1, a_1) = (b_2, a_2)$

$\Rightarrow \quad b_1 = b_2$ and $a_1 = a_2 \Rightarrow (a_1, b_1) = (a_2, b_2)$

Therefore, f is one-one. Now, let $(b, a) \in B \times A$ of any element.
Then, there exist $(a, b) \in A \times B$ such that $f(a, b) = (b, a)$ [definition of f]
Therefore, f is onto. Hence, f is bijective.

Question 9 Let $f : N \to N$ be defined by $f(n) = \begin{cases} \frac{n+1}{2}, & \text{if } n \text{ is odd} \\ \frac{n}{2}, & \text{if } n \text{ is even} \end{cases}$

for all $n \in N$.
State whether the function f is bijective. Justify your answer.

Sol. Here, $f : N \to N$ is defined as, $f(n) = \begin{cases} \frac{n+1}{2}, & \text{if } n \text{ is odd} \\ \frac{n}{2}, & \text{if } n \text{ is even} \end{cases}$ for all $n \in N$.

It can be observed that

$$f(1) = \frac{1+1}{2} = 1 \text{ and } f(2) = \frac{2}{2} = 1 \quad \text{[By definition of } f\text{]}$$

$\therefore \quad f(1) = f(2)$ but $1 \neq 2$.

Therefore, f is not one-one. Consider a natural number n in co-domain N.

Case **I** When n is odd.

Therefore, $n = 2r + 1$ for some $r \in N$.

Then, there exists $4r + 1 \in N$ such that $f(4r + 1) = \frac{4r + 1 + 1}{2} = 2r + 1$.

Therefore, f is onto.

Case **II** When n is even

Therefore, $n = 2r$ for some $r \in N$

Then, there exists $4r \in N$ such that $f(4r) = \frac{4r}{2} = 2r$

Therefore, f is onto. Hence, f is not a bijective function.

Mistake Alert Do not forget the following cases.
(i) When n_1 is odd and n_2 is even.
(ii) When n_1 is even and n_2 is odd.

Question 10 Let $A = R - \{3\}$ and $B = R - \{1\}$. Consider the function $f : A \to B$ defined by $f(x) = \left(\frac{x-2}{x-3}\right)$. Is f one-one and onto ? Justify your answer.

Sol. Here, $A = R - \{3\}, B = R - \{1\}$

and $f : A \to B$ is defined as $f(x) = \left(\frac{x-2}{x-3}\right)$

Let $x, y \in A$ such that $f(x) = f(y)$

$\Rightarrow \quad \dfrac{x-2}{x-3} = \dfrac{y-2}{y-3} \Rightarrow (x-2)(y-3) = (y-2)(x-3)$

$\Rightarrow \quad xy - 3x - 2y + 6 = xy - 3y - 2x + 6 \Rightarrow -3x - 2y = -3y - 2x$

$\Rightarrow \quad 3x - 2x = 3y - 2y \Rightarrow x = y$

Therefore, f is one- one.

Let $y \in B = R - \{1\}$. Then, $y \neq 1$

The function f is onto if there exists $x \in A$ such that $f(x) = y$.

Now, $f(x) = y$

$\Rightarrow \quad \dfrac{x-2}{x-3} = y \Rightarrow x - 2 = xy - 3y \Rightarrow x(1-y) = -3y + 2$

$\Rightarrow \quad x = \dfrac{2-3y}{1-y} \in A (y \neq 1)$

Thus, for any $y \in B$, there exists $\dfrac{2-3y}{1-y} \in A$ such that

$$f\left(\frac{2-3y}{1-y}\right) = \frac{\left(\frac{2-3y}{1-y}\right) - 2}{\left(\frac{2-3y}{1-y}\right) - 3} = \frac{2-3y-2+2y}{2-3y-3+3y} = \frac{-y}{-1} = y$$

Therefore, f is onto. Hence, function f is one-one and onto.

Quick Solution

We have $f(x) = \dfrac{x-2}{x-3}$ with co-domain $R - \{1\}$

Let $\quad y = \dfrac{x-2}{x-3} \Rightarrow x = \dfrac{2-3y}{1-y}$

Value of x exist only when $1 - y \neq 0 \Rightarrow y \neq 1 \Rightarrow y \in R - \{1\}$

We can clearly see that co-domain = Range

Thus, $f(x)$ is onto.

Question 11 Let $f: R \to R$ be defined as $f(x) = x^4$. Choose the correct answer.

(a) f is one-one onto

(b) f is many-one onto

(c) f is one-one but not onto

(d) f is neither one-one nor onto

Sol. (d) Function $f: R \to R$ is defined as $f(x) = x^4$

Let $x, y \in R$ such that $f(x) = f(y)$

$\Rightarrow \quad x^4 = y^4$

$\Rightarrow \quad x = \pm y$

Therefore, $f(x_1) = f(x_2)$ does not imply that $x_1 = x_2$

For instance, $\quad f(1) = f(-1) = 1$

Therefore, f is not one-one.

Consider an element 2 in co-domain R. It is clear that there does not exist any x in domain R such that $f(x) = -2 \Rightarrow x^4 = -2$, so x is imaginary

Therefore, f is not onto. Hence, function f is neither one-one nor onto.

Question 12 Let $f: R \to R$ be defined as $f(x) = 3x$. Choose the correct answer.

(a) f is one-one onto (b) f is many-one onto

(c) f in one-one but not onto (d) f is neither one-one nor onto.

Thinking Process

(i) A function f is one-one or injective, if every element x in the domain has only one image y in the co-domain.

(ii) A function is onto or surjective, if every element of the co-domain has a pre-image in the domain.

(iii) If a function is both injective and surjective, then it is said to be bijective.

Sol. (a) We have, $f: R \to R$ is defined as $f(x) = 3x$

Let $x, y \in R$ such that $f(x) = f(y)$.

$$\Rightarrow \quad 3x = 3y \Rightarrow x = y$$

Therefore, f is one-one.

Also, for any real number (y) in co-domain R, there exists $\frac{y}{3}$ in R such that

$$f\left(\frac{y}{3}\right) = 3\left(\frac{y}{3}\right) = y$$

Therefore, f is onto. Hence, function f is one-one and onto.

Miscellaneous Exercise

Question 1 Show that the function $f: R \to \{x \in R: -1 < x < 1\}$ defined by $f(x) = \frac{x}{x + |x|}$, $x \in R$ is one-one and onto function.

Sol. It is given that $f: R \to \{x \in R: -1 < x < 1\}$ is defined as $f(x) = \frac{x}{1 + |x|}$, $x \in R$.

Suppose, $f(x) = f(y)$, where $x, y \in R \Rightarrow \frac{x}{1 + |x|} = \frac{y}{1 + |y|}$

It can be observed that if x is positive and y is negative, then we have

$$\frac{x}{1 + x} = \frac{y}{1 - y} \Rightarrow 2xy = x - y$$

Since, x is positive and y is negative, then

$$x > y \Rightarrow x - y > 0$$

But, $2xy$ is negative. Then, $2xy \neq x - y$.

Thus, the case of x being positive and y being negative can be ruled out.

Under a similar argument, x being negative and y being positive can also be ruled out. Therefore, x and y have to be either positive or negative.

When x and y are both positive, we have

$$f(x) = f(y) \Rightarrow \frac{x}{1+x} = \frac{y}{1+y} \Rightarrow x + xy = y + xy \Rightarrow x = y$$

When x and y are both negative, we have

$$f(x) = f(y) \Rightarrow \frac{x}{1-x} = \frac{y}{1-y} \Rightarrow x - xy = y - yx \Rightarrow x = y$$

Therefore, f is one-one.

Now, let $y \in R$ such that $-1 < y < 1$.

If y is negative, then there exists $x = \frac{y}{1+y} \in R$ such that

$$f(x) = f\left(\frac{y}{1+y}\right) = \frac{\left(\frac{y}{1+y}\right)}{1 + \left|\frac{y}{1+y}\right|} = \frac{\frac{y}{1+y}}{1 + \left(\frac{-y}{1+y}\right)} = \frac{y}{1+y-y} = y$$

If y is positive, then there exists $x = \frac{y}{1-y} \in R$ such that

$$f(x) = f\left(\frac{y}{1-y}\right) = \frac{\left(\frac{y}{1-y}\right)}{1 + \left|\left(\frac{y}{1-y}\right)\right|} = \frac{\frac{y}{1-y}}{1 + \frac{y}{1-y}} = \frac{y}{1-y+y} = y$$

Therefore, f is onto. Hence, f is one-one and onto.

Question 2 Show that the function $f: R \rightarrow R$ given by $f(x) = x^3$ is injective.

Thinking Process Injective (one-one) function can be proved in two ways.

(i) $f(x_1) = f(x_2) \Rightarrow x_1 = x_2$ or (ii) $x_1 \neq x_2 \Rightarrow f(x_1) \neq f(x_2)$.

Here, the second method is useful *i.e.*, $x \neq y$, hence $x^3 \neq y^3$

Sol. Here, $f: R \rightarrow R$ is given as $f(x) = x^3$.

Suppose, $f(x) = f(y)$, where $x, y \in R \Rightarrow x^3 = y^3$ ...(i)

Now, we need to show that $x = y$

Suppose, $x \neq y$, their cubes will also not be equal.

$$x^3 \neq y^3$$

However, this will be a contradiction to Eq. (i).

Therefore, $x = y$. Hence, f is injective.

Question 3 Given a non-empty set X. Consider $P(X)$, which is the set of all subset of X. Defined the relation R in $P(X)$ as follows :
For subsets A and B in $P(X)$, ARB if and only if $A \subset B$. Is R an equivalence relation on $P(X)$? Justify your answer.

Sol. Since, every set is a subset of itself, ARA for all $A \in P(X)$.

Therefore, R is reflexive.

Let $\quad ARB \Rightarrow A \subset B$

This cannot be implied to $B \subset A$.
For instance, if $A = \{1,2\}$ and $B = \{1,2,3\}$, then it cannot be implied that B is related to A.

$\Rightarrow \quad (A, B) \in R$ but $(B, A) \notin R$

Therefore, R is not symmetric.
Further, if ARB and BRC, then $A \subset B$ and $B \subset C$.

$$(A, B) \in R, (B, C) \in R$$

$\Rightarrow \quad (A, C) \in R$

$\Rightarrow \quad A \subset C \Rightarrow ARC$. Therefore, R is transitive.

Hence, R is not an equivalence relation since, it is not symmetric.

Question 4 Find the number of all onto functions from the set $\{1,2,3,\ldots,n\}$ to itself.

Sol. Onto function from the set $\{1,2,3,\ldots,n)$ to itself is simply a permutation on n symbol $1,2,\ldots n$.
Thus, the total number of onto maps from $\{1,2,\ldots.,n\}$ to itself is the same as the total number of permutations on symbols $1, 2, \ldots..,n$, which is $n!$.

Quick Solution

As f is onto, every so element of {1, 2, 3........} will have a unique pre-image

Element	Number of possible pairs
1	n
2	$n-1$
3	$n-2$
⋮	⋮
⋮	⋮
⋮	⋮
$n-1$	2
n	1

So total number of onto function $= n \times (n-1) \times (n-2) \ldots\ldots.2 \times 1 = n!$

Question 5 Let $A=\{-1,0,1,2\}$, $B=\{-4,-2,0,2\}$ and $f,g: A \to B$ be the function defined by $f(x)=x^2-x, x \in A$ and $g(x)=2\left|x-\frac{1}{2}\right|-1, x \in A$.

Are f and g equal? Justify your answer.

◎ ***Thinking Process*** One may note that two functions $f: A \to B$ and $g: A \to B$ such that $f(a)=g(a)\ \forall a \in A$, are called equal functions.

Sol. Given that $A=\{-1, 0, 1, 2\}$, $B=\{-4, -2, 0, 2\}$.

Also, it is given that $f, g: A \to B$ are defined by $f(x)=x^2-x, x \in A$ and $g(x)=2\left|x-\frac{1}{2}\right|-1, x \in A$.

It is observed that $f(-1)=(-1)^2-(-1)=1+1=2$

and $g(-1)=2\left|(-1)-\frac{1}{2}\right|-1=2\left(\frac{3}{2}\right)-1=3-1=2 \Rightarrow f(-1)=g(-1)$

Next $f(0)=(0)^2-0=0$ and $g(0)=2\left|0-\frac{1}{2}\right|-1=2\left(\frac{1}{2}\right)-1=1-1=0$

$\Rightarrow$ $f(0)=g(0)$

Next, $f(1)=(1)^2-1=1-1=0$

and $g(1)=2\left|1-\frac{1}{2}\right|-1=2\left(\frac{1}{2}\right)-1=1-1=0 \Rightarrow f(1)=g(1)$

Next, $f(2)=(2)^2-2=4-2=2$

and $g(2)=2\left|2-\frac{1}{2}\right|-1=2\left(\frac{3}{2}\right)-1=3-1=2$

$\Rightarrow$ $f(2)=g(2)$

$\therefore$ $f(a)=g(a)\ \forall\ a \in A$.

Hence, the functions f and g are equal.

Question 6 Let $A=\{1,2,3\}$. Then, number of relations containing $(1,2)$ and $(1,3)$ which are reflexive and symmetric but not transitive is

(a) 1 (b) 2
(c) 3 (d) 4

Sol. (a) This is because relation R is reflexive as $(1, 1), (2, 2), (3, 3) \in R$.

Relations R is symmetric since $(1, 2), (2, 1) \in R$ and $(1, 3), (3, 1) \in R$.

But relation R is not transitive as $(3, 1), (1, 2) \in R$ but $(3, 2) \notin R$.

Now, if we add any one of the two pairs $(3, 2)$ and $(2, 3)$ or both to relation R, then relation R will become transitive.

Hence, the total number of desired relations is one.

Question 7 Let $A=\{1,2,3\}$. Then, number of equivalence relations containing $(1,2)$ is

(a) 1 (b) 2
(c) 3 (d) 4

Sol. (b) It is given that $A = \{1, 2, 3\}$.

An equivalence relation is reflexive, symmetric and transitive.
The smallest equivalence relation containing (1, 2) is given by,

$$R_1 = \{(1, 1), (2, 2), (3, 3), (1, 2), (2, 1)\}$$

Now, we are left with only four pairs *i.e.*, (2, 3), (3, 2), (1, 3), and (3, 1).
If we add any one pair [say (2, 3)] to R_1, then for symmetry we must add (3, 2).
Also, for transitivity we are required to add (1, 3) and (3, 1).
Hence, the only equivalence relation (bigger than R_1) is the universal relation.

$\Rightarrow$ $R_2 = \{(1, 1), (2, 2), (3, 3), (1, 2), (2, 1), (1, 3), (3, 1), (2, 3), (3, 2)\}$

This shows that the total number of equivalence relations containing (1, 2) is two.

DIKSHA APP Questions

☐ Multiple Choice Questions

Q.1 Given, set $A=\{1,2,3\}$ and a relation $R=\{(1,2),(2,1)\}$, the relation R will be

(a) reflexive if (1, 1) is added (b) symmetric if (2, 3) is added
(c) transitive if (1, 1) is added (d) symmetric if (3, 2) is added

Sol. (c) We have, $R = \{(1,2),(2,1)\}$

On adding (1, 1) it will not be reflexive because we have to add (2, 2) and (3, 3) also.

On adding (2, 3) it will not be symmetric because we have to add (3, 2) also.

On adding (1, 1) it will be transitive because $(1, 2) \in R, (2,1) \in R \Rightarrow (1,1) \in R$.

Q.2 Given set $A=\{a,b,c\}$, then identity relation in set A is

(a) $R=\{(a,b),(a,c)\}$
(b) $R=\{(a,a),(b,b),(c,c)\}$
(c) $R=\{(a,a),(c,c),(b,b),(a,c)\}$
(d) $R=\{(b,a),(c,a),(a,a)\}$

Sol. (b) Identity relation on $A = \{a,b,c\}$ is a set of ordered pairs $(a,a),(b,b),(c,c)$.

Q.3 Let R be a relation the set L of line defined by $l_1 R l_2$, if l_1 is perpendicular to l_2 then relation R is

(a) reflexive and symmetric (b) symmetric and transitive

(c) equivalence relation (d) symmetric

Sol. (d) We have $R = \{(l_1, l_2) : l_1 \perp l_2\}$

For reflexive l_1 is not perpendicular to l_1

$\therefore \quad (l_1, l_1) \notin R$

So, R is not reflexive

For symmetric : Let $(l_1, l_2) \in R$, then $l_1 \perp l_2 \Rightarrow l_2 \perp l_1 \Rightarrow (l_2, l_1) \in R$

So, R is symmetric.

For transitive : Let $(l_1, l_2) \in R$ and $(l_2, l_3) \in R$, then $l_1 \perp l_2$ and $l_2 \perp l_3$

$\Rightarrow l_1$ is not perpendicular to l_3

$\therefore \quad (l_1, l_3) \notin R$

So, R is not transitive.

Q.4 The maximum number of equivalence relation on set $A = \{a, b, c\}$ are

(a) 2 (b) 1

(c) 5 (d) 3

Sol. (c) Given that $A = \{a, b, c\}$. Now the possible equivalence relation on A are

$R_1 = \{(a,a),(b,b),(c,c)\}$

$R_2 = \{(a,a),(b,b),(c,c),(a,b),(b,a)\}$

$R_3 = \{(a,a),(b,b),(c,c),(a,c),(c,a)\}$

$R_4 = \{(a,a),(b,b),(c,c),(b,c),(c,b)\}$

$R_5 = \{(a,a),(b,b),(c,c),(a,b),(b,c),(a,c),(c,a),(b,a)(c,b)\}$

Thus total number of equivalence relations is 5.

Q.5 Let A be a non empty set, then identity function on set A is

(a) injective (b) surjective

(c) bijective (d) None of these

Sol. (c) If $f : A \to A$ is identity function

Then, $f(x) = x \ \forall \ x \in A$

For one-one $f(x_1) = f(x_2)$

$\Rightarrow \quad x_1 = x_2$

So, f is one-one.

For onto

To prove that f is onto, we need to prove that for every $y \in A$, there exists $x \in A$ such that $f(x) = y$

Let y be an arbitrary element of A and we can choose $x = y$, the $f(x) = f(y) = y$

So, f is onto.

Hence, $f(x)$ is bijective

Q.6 Let the function $f : N \rightarrow N$ defined by $f(x) = 2x$ is

(a) one-one (b) bijective
(c) one-one but not onto (d) None of these

Sol. (c) We have $f(x) = 2x$.

For one-one $f(x_1) = f(x_2)$

$\Rightarrow \quad 2x_1 = 2x_2$

$\Rightarrow \quad x_1 = x_2$

So, f is one-one.

For onto

Let $y \in N$ be any element, then there exist $x \in N$ such that $f(x) = y$

$\Rightarrow \quad 2x = y \Rightarrow x = \dfrac{y}{2}$

If $y = 1$, then $x = \dfrac{1}{2} = 0.5$ which is not possible as $x \in N$.

So, f is not onto.

Q.7 Set A has 3 elements and the set B has 4 elements, then number of injective function that can be defined from set A to B is

(a) 120 (b) 24
(c) 144 (d) 64

Thinking Process If set A has n elements and set B has m elements, $m \geq n$, then number of injective function is given by $\dfrac{m!}{(m-n)!}$.

Sol. (b) We have $n(A) = 3$ and $n(B) = 4$

Number of injective functions $= \dfrac{m!}{(m-n)!} = \dfrac{4!}{(4-3)!} = \dfrac{4!}{1!} = 24.$

Q.8 If $f : R \rightarrow B$ given $f(x) = \sin x$ is onto function, then set B will be

(a) real numbers (b) $[-1, 1]$
(c) $(-1, 1)$ (d) None of these

Sol. (c) $f : R \rightarrow B$ given by $f(x) = \sin x$

We have domain $= R$.

Graph of $\sin x$ is

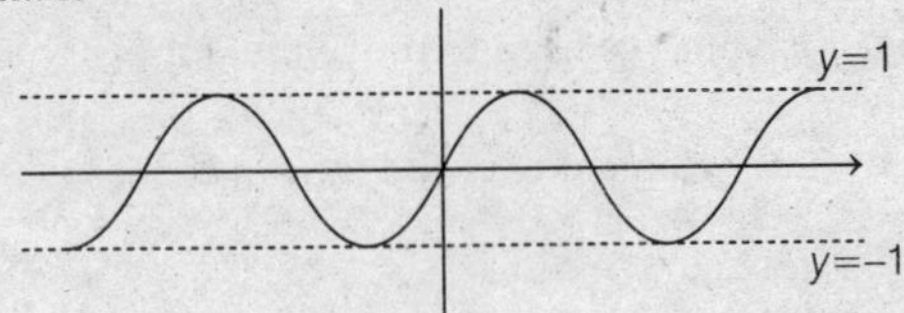

Clearly we can see that the value of $\sin x \in [-1, 1]$ for all real value of x, so set B must be [-1, 1] for which $f(x)$ is onto.

Q.9 Which of the following function Z into Z is bijective?

(a) $f(x) = x^3$ (b) $f(x) = x + 2$ (c) $f(x) = 2x + 1$ (d) $f(x) = x^2 + 1$

Thinking Process A function $f : A \to B$ is said to be bijective, if f is both one-one and onto

Sol. (b)

(a) We have $f(x) = x^3$

In co-domain elements which are not perfect cube for *eg*. {2, 3, 5....} do not have pre-image. So, $f(x) = x^3$ is not onto

Hence, f is not bijective.

(b) We have $f(x) = x + 2$

For one-one $f(x_1) = f(x_2)$

$\Rightarrow \quad x_1 + 2 = x_2 + 2 \Rightarrow x_1 = x_2$

Thus, f is one-one.

For onto

If $x \in Z \Rightarrow x + 2 \in Z$

So, $f(x)$ is onto also. Hence, it is bijective.

(c) We have $f(x) = 2x + 1$

Let $f(x) = y, y \in z$

$\Rightarrow y = 2x + 1 \Rightarrow x = \dfrac{y-1}{2}$

If put $y = 0$, then $x = -\dfrac{1}{2} \notin Z$

$\therefore y = 0 \in Z$ does not have pre image in Z.

So, f is not onto.

Hence f is not bijective.

(d) We have $f(x) = x^2 + 1$

Let $f(x_1) = f(x_2) \Rightarrow x_1^2 + 1 = x_2^2 + 1 = 1 \Rightarrow x_1^2 = x_2^2 \Rightarrow x_1 = \pm x_2$

For e.g. $f(-1) = (-1)^2 + 1 = 2$ and $f(1) = (1)^2 + 1 = 2$

$\therefore f(-1) = f(1)$ but $-1 \neq -1$

So, f is not one-one

Hence, f is not bijective.

Q.10 Let R be a relation defined on Z as following $(x, y) \in R \Leftrightarrow |x - y| \le 1$, then R is

(a) reflexive and transitive (b) reflexive and symmetric
(c) symmetric and transitive (d) an equivalence relation

Sol. (b) We have, $R = \{(x,y) : |x - y| \le 1\}$

For reflexive

We know that $|x - x| = 0 \le 1$.

Thus $(x,x) \in R$, So, R is reflexive

For symmetric

If $(x, y) \in R \Rightarrow |x - y| \le 1 \Rightarrow |-(x - y)| \le 1$

$\Rightarrow \quad |y - x| \le 1$

$\Rightarrow \quad (y,x) \in R$

Hence, R is symmetric.

For transitive let $a = 1, b = 2, c = 3$

$|a - b| = |1 - 2| = 1 \le 1$ which is true

$|b - c| = |2 - 3| = 1 \le 1$ which is true

but $|a - c| = |1 - 3| = 2 \le 1$ which is not true

So, $(a,b) \in R, (b,c) \in R$ but $(a,c) \notin R$

Hence, R is not transitive.

Q.11 Let $A = \{1, 2, 3\}$ and $B = \{1, 5, 7, 9\}$ and R is the relation from A to B by 'x is greater than y' then range of R is given by

(a) {1, 5, 7, 9} (b) {5, 7, 9}
(c) {1} (d) None of these

Sol. (c) We have, $A = \{1,2,3\}, B = \{1,5,7,9\}$

$R = \{(x,y) : x$ is greater that $y, x \in A, y \in B\}$

For '1' in A, 1 is not greater than any of element in B.

For '2' in A, 2 is greater than only 1 element in B.

For '3' in A, 3 is greater than only 1 element in B.

$\therefore R = \{(2,1),(3,1)\}$

Hence, range of $R = \{1\}$.

Inverse Trigonometric Functions

CHAPTER 02

Important Points

01 Domain, Range (Principal value branch) of Inverse Trigonometric Functions

Function	Domain	Range (Principal value branch)
$\sin^{-1}x$	$[-1, 1]$	$\left[-\frac{\pi}{2}, \frac{\pi}{2}\right]$
$\cos^{-1}x$	$[-1, 1]$	$[0, \pi]$
$\tan^{-1}x$	R	$\left(-\frac{\pi}{2}, \frac{\pi}{2}\right)$
$\operatorname{cosec}^{-1}x$	$R-(-1, 1)$	$\left[-\frac{\pi}{2}, \frac{\pi}{2}\right]-\{0\}$
$\sec^{-1}x$	$R-(-1, 1)$	$[0, \pi]-\left\{\frac{\pi}{2}\right\}$
$\cot^{-1}x$	R	$(0, \pi)$

02 Properties of Inverse Trigonometric Functions

- $\sin^{-1}(\sin\theta)=\theta,\ \theta\in\left[-\frac{\pi}{2},\frac{\pi}{2}\right]$
- $\cos^{-1}(\cos\theta)=\theta,\ \theta\in[0,\pi]$
- $\tan^{-1}(\tan\theta)=\theta,\ \theta\in\left(-\frac{\pi}{2},\frac{\pi}{2}\right)$
- $\cot^{-1}(\cot\theta)=\theta,\ \theta\in(0,\pi)$
- $\sec^{-1}(\sec\theta)=\theta,\ \theta\in[0,\pi]-\left\{\frac{\pi}{2}\right\}$
- $\operatorname{cosec}^{-1}(\operatorname{cosec}\theta)=\theta,\ \theta\in\left[-\frac{\pi}{2},\frac{\pi}{2}\right]-\{0\}$

03 Formulae of Trigonmetry Functions

- $\sin x = \dfrac{1}{\text{cosec}\, x}$, $\cos x = \dfrac{1}{\sec x}$, $\tan x = \dfrac{1}{\cot x} = \dfrac{\sin x}{\cos x}$,

  $\cot x = \dfrac{1}{\tan x} = \dfrac{\cos x}{\sin x}$
- $\sin^2 x + \cos^2 x = 1$, $\sec^2 x - \tan^2 x = 1$, $\text{cosec}^2 x - \cot^2 x = 1$

04 Graphs of Inverse Trigonometric Functions

(a) $\sin^{-1} x$

Domain $= [-1, 1]$ Range $= \left[-\dfrac{\pi}{2}, \dfrac{\pi}{2}\right]$

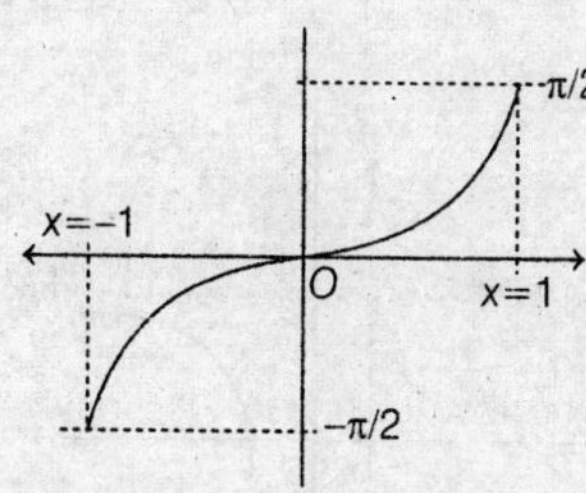

(b) $\cos^{-1} x$

Domain $= [-1, 1]$ Range $= [0, \pi]$

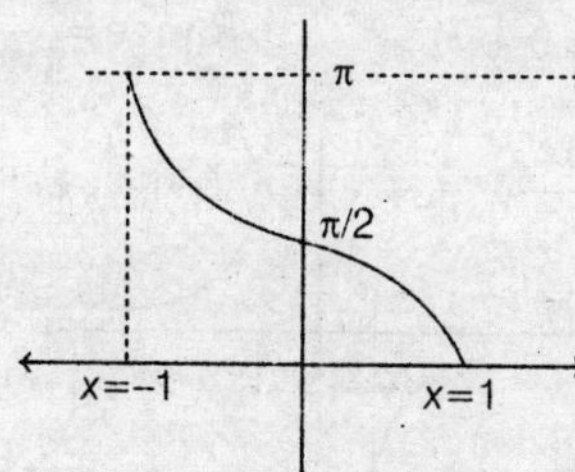

(c) $\tan^{-1} x$

Domain $= R$ Range $= \left(-\dfrac{\pi}{2}, \dfrac{\pi}{2}\right)$

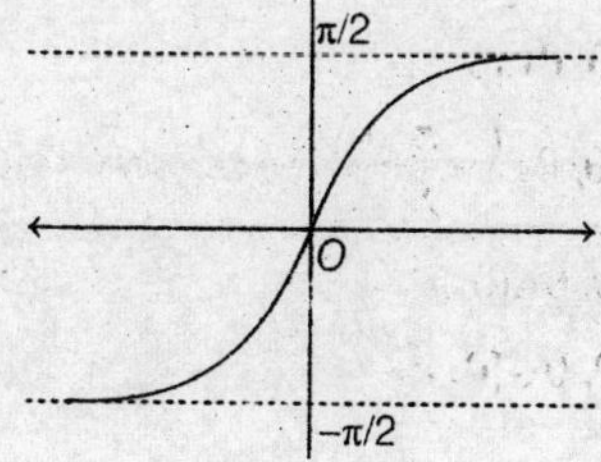

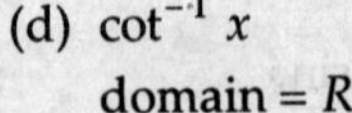

(d) $\cot^{-1} x$

domain $= R$ 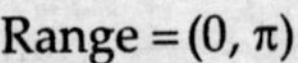 Range $= (0, \pi)$

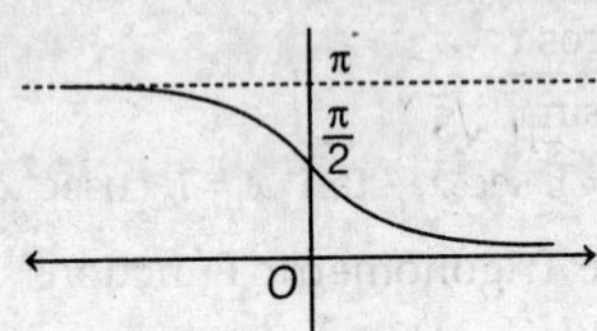

(e) $\sec^{-1} x$

Domain $= R - (-1, 1)$ Range $= [0, \pi] - \left\{\frac{\pi}{2}\right\}$

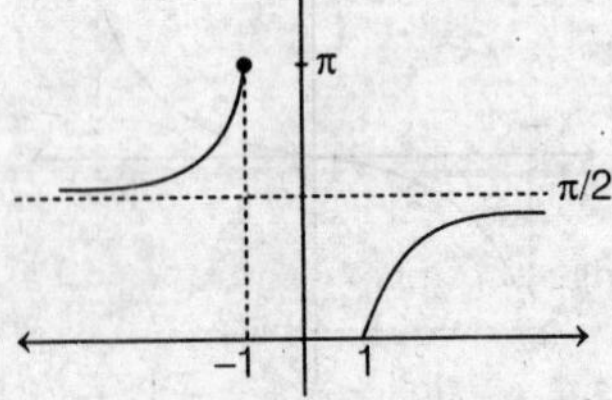

(f) $\text{cosec}^{-1} x$

Domain $= R - (-1, 1)$ Range $= \left[-\frac{\pi}{2}, \frac{\pi}{2}\right] - \{0\}$

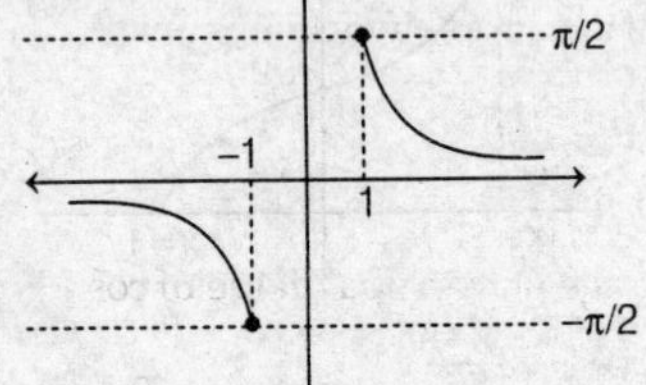

Exercise 2.1

Direction (Q. Nos. 1 to 10) Find the principal values of the following questions

1. $\sin^{-1}\left(-\frac{1}{2}\right)$ **2.** $\cos^{-1}\left(\frac{\sqrt{3}}{2}\right)$ **3.** $\text{cosec}^{-1}(2)$ **4.** $\tan^{-1}(-\sqrt{3})$

5. $\cos^{-1}\left(-\frac{1}{2}\right)$ **6.** $\tan^{-1}(-1)$ **7.** $\sec^{-1}\left(\frac{2}{\sqrt{3}}\right)$ **8.** $\cot^{-1}(\sqrt{3})$

9. $\cos^{-1}\left(-\frac{1}{\sqrt{2}}\right)$ **10.** $\text{cosec}^{-1}(-\sqrt{2})$

Solutions for Q. Nos. 1-10

1. Let $\sin^{-1}\left(-\frac{1}{2}\right) = \theta \Rightarrow \sin\theta = -\frac{1}{2}$

We know that the range of principal value of $\sin^{-1}\theta$ is $\left[-\frac{\pi}{2}, \frac{\pi}{2}\right]$.

$\therefore \quad \sin\theta = -\frac{1}{2} = -\sin\frac{\pi}{6} = \sin\left(-\frac{\pi}{6}\right) \quad [\because \sin(-\theta) = -\sin\theta]$

$\Rightarrow \quad \theta = -\frac{\pi}{6}$, where $\theta \in \left[-\frac{\pi}{2}, \frac{\pi}{2}\right] \Rightarrow \sin^{-1}\left(-\frac{1}{2}\right) = -\frac{\pi}{6}$

Hence, the principal value of $\sin^{-1}\left(-\frac{1}{2}\right)$ is $-\frac{\pi}{6}$.

Note Principal value of any inverse function is unique.

2. Let $\cos^{-1}\left(\frac{\sqrt{3}}{2}\right) = \theta \Rightarrow \cos\theta = \frac{\sqrt{3}}{2}$

We know that the range of principal value of $\cos^{-1}\theta$ is $[0, \pi]$.

$\therefore \cos\theta = \frac{\sqrt{3}}{2} = \cos\frac{\pi}{6} \Rightarrow \theta = \frac{\pi}{6}$, where $\theta \in [0, \pi] \Rightarrow \cos^{-1}\left(\frac{\sqrt{3}}{2}\right) = \frac{\pi}{6}$

Hence, the principal value of $\cos^{-1}\left(\frac{\sqrt{3}}{2}\right)$ is $\frac{\pi}{6}$.

3. Let $\text{cosec}^{-1} 2 = \theta \Rightarrow \text{cosec}\,\theta = 2$.

We know that the range of principal value of $\text{cosec}^{-1}\theta$ is $\left[-\frac{\pi}{2}, \frac{\pi}{2}\right] - \{0\}$.

$\therefore \text{cosec}\,\theta = 2 = \text{cosec}\frac{\pi}{6} \Rightarrow \theta = \frac{\pi}{6}$, where $\theta \in \left[-\frac{\pi}{2}, \frac{\pi}{2}\right] - \{0\} \Rightarrow \text{cosec}^{-1}(2) = \frac{\pi}{6}$

Hence, the principal value of $\text{cosec}^{-1}(2)$ is $\frac{\pi}{6}$.

4. Let $\tan^{-1}(-\sqrt{3}) = \theta \Rightarrow \tan\theta = -\sqrt{3}$

We know that the range of principal value of $\tan^{-1}\theta$ $\left(-\frac{\pi}{2}, \frac{\pi}{2}\right)$.

$\therefore \quad \tan\theta = -\sqrt{3} = -\tan\frac{\pi}{3} = \tan\left(-\frac{\pi}{3}\right)$ $\quad [\because \tan(-\theta) = -\tan\theta]$

$\Rightarrow \quad \theta = -\frac{\pi}{3}$, where $\theta \in \left(-\frac{\pi}{2}, \frac{\pi}{2}\right) \Rightarrow \tan^{-1}(-\sqrt{3}) = -\frac{\pi}{3}$

Hence, principal value of $\tan^{-1}(-\sqrt{3})$ is $-\frac{\pi}{3}$.

5. Let $\cos^{-1}\left(-\frac{1}{2}\right) = \theta \Rightarrow \cos\theta = -\frac{1}{2}$

We know that the range of principal value of $\cos^{-1}\theta$ is $[0, \pi]$.

$\therefore \quad \cos\theta = -\frac{1}{2} = -\cos\frac{\pi}{3} = \cos\left(\pi - \frac{\pi}{3}\right)$ $\quad [\because \cos(\pi - \theta) = -\cos\theta]$

$= \cos\frac{2\pi}{3}$

$\Rightarrow \quad \theta = \frac{2\pi}{3}$, where $\theta \in [0, \pi] \Rightarrow \cos^{-1}\left(-\frac{1}{2}\right) = \frac{2\pi}{3}$

Hence, principal value of $\cos^{-1}\left(-\frac{1}{2}\right)$ is $\frac{2\pi}{3}$.

Mistake Alert $\cos^{-1}(-\theta) \neq -\cos^{-1}\theta$

6. Let $\tan^{-1}(-1) = \theta \Rightarrow \tan\theta = -1$

We know that the range of principal value of $\tan^{-1}\theta$ is $\left(-\frac{\pi}{2}, \frac{\pi}{2}\right)$.

$\therefore \quad \tan\theta = -1 = -\tan\frac{\pi}{4} = \tan\left(-\frac{\pi}{4}\right)$ $\quad (\because \tan(-\theta) = -\tan\theta)$

$\Rightarrow \quad \theta = -\frac{\pi}{4}$; where $\theta \in \left(-\frac{\pi}{2}, \frac{\pi}{2}\right)$

Hence, the principal value of $\tan^{-1}(-1)$ is $-\frac{\pi}{4}$.

7. Let $\sec^{-1}\left(\frac{2}{\sqrt{3}}\right) = \theta \Rightarrow \sec\theta = \frac{2}{\sqrt{3}}$

We know that the range of principal value of $\sec^{-1}\theta$ is $[0, \pi] - \left\{\frac{\pi}{2}\right\}$.

$\therefore \quad \sec\theta = \frac{2}{\sqrt{3}} = \sec\frac{\pi}{6} \Rightarrow \theta = \frac{\pi}{6}$, where $\theta \in [0, \pi] - \left\{\frac{\pi}{2}\right\}$

$\Rightarrow \quad \sec^{-1}\left(\frac{2}{\sqrt{3}}\right) = \frac{\pi}{6}$

Hence, the principal value of $\sec^{-1}\left(\frac{2}{\sqrt{3}}\right)$ is $\frac{\pi}{6}$.

8. Let $\cot^{-1}(\sqrt{3}) = \theta \Rightarrow \cot\theta = \sqrt{3}$

We know that the range of principal value of $\cot^{-1}\theta$ is $(0, \pi)$.

$\therefore\ \cot\theta = \sqrt{3} = \cot\frac{\pi}{6} \Rightarrow \theta = \frac{\pi}{6}$; where $\theta \in (0, \pi) \Rightarrow \cot^{-1}(\sqrt{3}) = \frac{\pi}{6}$

Hence, the principal value of $\cot^{-1}(\sqrt{3})$ is $\frac{\pi}{6}$.

9. Let $\cos^{-1}\left(-\frac{1}{\sqrt{2}}\right) = \theta \Rightarrow \cos\theta = -\frac{1}{\sqrt{2}}$

We know that the range of principal value of $\cos^{-1}\theta$ is $[0, \pi]$.

$$\therefore\quad \cos\theta = -\frac{1}{\sqrt{2}} = -\cos\frac{\pi}{4} = \cos\left(\pi - \frac{\pi}{4}\right) \quad [\because \cos(\pi - \theta) = -\cos\theta)]$$

$$\Rightarrow\quad \theta = \frac{3\pi}{4}, \text{ where } \theta \in [0, \pi] \Rightarrow \cos^{-1}\left(-\frac{1}{\sqrt{2}}\right) = \frac{3\pi}{4}$$

Hence, the principal value of $\cos^{-1}\left(-\frac{1}{\sqrt{2}}\right)$ is $\frac{3\pi}{4}$.

10. Let $\text{cosec}^{-1}(-\sqrt{2}) = \theta \Rightarrow \text{cosec}\,\theta = -\sqrt{2}$

We know that the range of principal value of $\text{cosec}^{-1}\theta$ is $\left[-\frac{\pi}{2}, \frac{\pi}{2}\right] - \{0\}$.

$$\therefore\ \text{cosec}\,\theta = -\sqrt{2} = -\text{cosec}\frac{\pi}{4} = \text{cosec}\left(-\frac{\pi}{4}\right) \quad (\because \text{cosec}(-\theta) = -\text{cosec}\,\theta)$$

$$\Rightarrow\quad \theta = -\frac{\pi}{4}, \text{ where } \theta \in \left[-\frac{\pi}{2}, \frac{\pi}{2}\right] - \{0\} \Rightarrow \text{cosec}^{-1}(-\sqrt{2}) = -\frac{\pi}{4}$$

Hence, the principal value of $\text{cosec}^{-1}(-\sqrt{2})$ is $-\frac{\pi}{4}$.

Direction (Q. Nos. 11 to 14) Find the values of the following questions.

Question 11 $\tan^{-1}(1) + \cos^{-1}\left(-\frac{1}{2}\right) + \sin^{-1}\left(-\frac{1}{2}\right)$

◎ ***Thinking Process*** Given expression is not a standard identity, so we separately find the value of $\tan^{-1}(1)$, $\cos^{-1}\left(-\frac{1}{2}\right)$, $\sin^{-1}\left(-\frac{1}{2}\right)$ and simplify it.

Sol. Let $\tan^{-1}(1) = x \Rightarrow \tan x = 1 = \tan\frac{\pi}{4} \Rightarrow x = \frac{\pi}{4}$

where principal value $x \in \left(-\frac{\pi}{2}, \frac{\pi}{2}\right)$

$$\therefore\quad \tan^{-1}(1) = \frac{\pi}{4}$$

Let $\cos^{-1}\left(-\frac{1}{2}\right) = y \Rightarrow \cos y = -\frac{1}{2} = -\cos\left(\frac{\pi}{3}\right) = \cos\left(\pi - \frac{\pi}{3}\right) = \cos\left(\frac{2\pi}{3}\right)$

$[\because \cos(\pi - \theta) = -\cos\theta]$

$$\Rightarrow\quad y = \frac{2\pi}{3}, \text{ where principal value } y \in [0, \pi]$$

$$\therefore\quad \cos^{-1}\left(-\frac{1}{2}\right) = \frac{2\pi}{3}$$

Let $\sin^{-1}\left(-\frac{1}{2}\right) = z \Rightarrow \sin z = -\frac{1}{2} = -\sin\left(\frac{\pi}{6}\right) = \sin\left(-\frac{\pi}{6}\right)$

$\Rightarrow$ $z = -\frac{\pi}{6}$, where principal value $z \in \left[-\frac{\pi}{2}, \frac{\pi}{2}\right]$

$\therefore$ $$\sin^{-1}\left(-\frac{1}{2}\right) = -\frac{\pi}{6}$$

$\therefore$ $$\tan^{-1}(1) + \cos^{-1}\left(-\frac{1}{2}\right) + \sin^{-1}\left(-\frac{1}{2}\right) = x + y + z = \frac{\pi}{4} + \frac{2\pi}{3} - \frac{\pi}{6}$$
$$= \frac{3\pi + 8\pi - 2\pi}{12} = \frac{9\pi}{12} = \frac{3\pi}{4}$$

Question 12 $\cos^{-1}\left(\frac{1}{2}\right) + 2\sin^{-1}\left(\frac{1}{2}\right)$

◎ *Thinking Process* We can find the value of given expression by simplifying the individual terms.

Sol. Let $\cos^{-1}\left(\frac{1}{2}\right) = x \Rightarrow \cos x = \frac{1}{2} = \cos\frac{\pi}{3} \Rightarrow x = \frac{\pi}{3} \in [0, \pi]$

Again, let $\sin^{-1}\left(\frac{1}{2}\right) = y \Rightarrow \sin y = \frac{1}{2} = \sin\frac{\pi}{6}$

$\Rightarrow$ $y = \frac{\pi}{6} \in \left[-\frac{\pi}{2}, \frac{\pi}{2}\right]$

$\therefore$ $$\cos^{-1}\left(\frac{1}{2}\right) + 2\sin^{-1}\left(\frac{1}{2}\right) = x + 2y = \frac{\pi}{3} + 2 \times \frac{\pi}{6} = \frac{2\pi}{3}$$

Question 13 If $\sin^{-1} x = y$, then

(a) $0 \le y \le \pi$ (b) $-\frac{\pi}{2} \le y \le \frac{\pi}{2}$ (c) $0 < y < \pi$ (d) $-\frac{\pi}{2} < y < \frac{\pi}{2}$

Sol. (b) As, range of $\sin^{-1} x$ is $\left[-\frac{\pi}{2}, \frac{\pi}{2}\right]$, therefore $-\frac{\pi}{2} \le y \le \frac{\pi}{2}$.

Question 14 $\tan^{-1}\sqrt{3} - \sec^{-1}(-2)$ is equal to

(a) π (b) $-\frac{\pi}{3}$ (c) $\frac{\pi}{3}$ (d) $\frac{2\pi}{3}$

Sol. (b) Let $\tan^{-1}\sqrt{3} = x \Rightarrow \tan x = \sqrt{3} \Rightarrow \tan x = \tan\frac{\pi}{3}$

$\Rightarrow$ $x = \frac{\pi}{3} \in \left(-\frac{\pi}{2}, \frac{\pi}{2}\right)$

Let $\sec^{-1}(-2) = y \Rightarrow \sec y = -2$

$\Rightarrow$ $\sec y = -\sec\frac{\pi}{3} \Rightarrow \sec y = \sec\left(\pi - \frac{\pi}{3}\right)$ $[\because \sec(\pi - \theta) = -\sec\theta]$

$\Rightarrow$ $\sec y = \sec\left(\frac{2\pi}{3}\right) \Rightarrow y = \frac{2\pi}{3} \in [0, \pi] - \left\{\frac{\pi}{2}\right\}$

$\therefore$ $$\tan^{-1}\sqrt{3} - \sec^{-1}(-2) = x - y = \frac{\pi}{3} - \frac{2\pi}{3} = -\frac{\pi}{3}$$

Exercise 2.2

Direction (Q. Nos. 1 to 2) Prove the following questions :

Question 1 $3\sin^{-1}x = \sin^{-1}(3x - 4x^3),\ x \in \left[-\frac{1}{2}, \frac{1}{2}\right]$

◎ ***Thinking Process*** The right hand side of a given expression can be converted into a standard formula $\sin 3\theta$ when we substitute $\sin^{-1}x$ as θ and then applying the formula $\sin 3\theta = 3\sin\theta - 4\sin^3\theta$.

Sol. Let $\sin^{-1}x = \theta \Rightarrow x = \sin\theta$

Now, LHS $= 3\sin^{-1}x = 3\sin^{-1}(\sin\theta) = 3\theta$ $\quad [\because \sin^{-1}(\sin x) = x]$

RHS $= \sin^{-1}(3x - 4x^3) = \sin^{-1}[3\sin\theta - 4\sin^3\theta] = \sin^{-1}[\sin 3\theta] = 3\theta$

$[\because \sin 3\theta = 3\sin\theta - 4\sin^3\theta]$

$\therefore$ LHS = RHS **Hence Proved.**

Question 2 $3\cos^{-1}x = \cos^{-1}(4x^3 - 3x),\ x \in \left[\frac{1}{2}, 1\right]$.

◎ ***Thinking Process*** The right hand side of a given expression can be converted into a standard formula $\cos 3\theta$ when we substitute $\cos^{-1}x$ as θ and then applying the formula $\cos 3\theta = 4\cos^3\theta - 3\cos\theta$.

Sol. Let $\cos^{-1}x = \theta \Rightarrow x = \cos\theta$

Now, LHS $= 3\cos^{-1}x = 3\cos^{-1}(\cos\theta) = 3\theta$ $\quad [\because \cos^{-1}(\cos x) = x]$

RHS $= \cos^{-1}(4x^3 - 3x) = \cos^{-1}[4\cos^3\theta - 3\cos\theta] = \cos^{-1}[\cos 3\theta] = 3\theta$

$[\because \cos 3\theta = 4\cos^3\theta - 3\cos\theta]$

$\therefore$ LHS = RHS **Hence Proved**

Direction (Q. Nos. 3 to 7) Write the following functions in the simplest form.

Question 3 $\tan^{-1}\dfrac{\sqrt{1+x^2}-1}{x},\ x \neq 0$

◎ ***Thinking Process*** To remove the square root sign, we substituting x as $\tan\theta$ and simplify it.

Sol. Let $x = \tan\theta$, then $\theta = \tan^{-1}x$ $\quad \ldots(i)$

$$\therefore \quad \tan^{-1}\frac{\sqrt{1+x^2}-1}{x} = \tan^{-1}\left(\frac{\sqrt{1+\tan^2\theta}-1}{\tan\theta}\right) = \tan^{-1}\left(\frac{\sqrt{\sec^2\theta}-1}{\tan\theta}\right)$$

$[\because 1 + \tan^2\theta = \sec^2\theta]$

$$= \tan^{-1}\left[\frac{\sec\theta - 1}{\tan\theta}\right]$$

$$= \tan^{-1}\left[\frac{\dfrac{1}{\cos\theta}-1}{\dfrac{\sin\theta}{\cos\theta}}\right] = \tan^{-1}\left[\frac{\dfrac{1-\cos\theta}{\cos\theta}}{\dfrac{\sin\theta}{\cos\theta}}\right] = \tan^{-1}\left[\frac{1-\cos\theta}{\cos\theta}\times\frac{\cos\theta}{\sin\theta}\right]$$

$$= \tan^{-1}\left[\frac{1-\cos\theta}{\sin\theta}\right] = \tan^{-1}\left[\frac{2\sin^2\frac{\theta}{2}}{2\sin\frac{\theta}{2}\cos\frac{\theta}{2}}\right] \qquad \left[\because 1-\cos\theta = 2\sin^2\frac{\theta}{2},\ \sin\theta = 2\sin\frac{\theta}{2}\cos\frac{\theta}{2}\right]$$

$$= \tan^{-1}\left[\frac{2\sin\frac{\theta}{2}}{2\cos\frac{\theta}{2}}\right] = \tan^{-1}\left[\tan\frac{\theta}{2}\right] = \frac{\theta}{2} = \frac{\tan^{-1}x}{2} \qquad \text{[from Eq. (i)]}$$

Question 4 $\tan^{-1}\left(\sqrt{\dfrac{1-\cos x}{1+\cos x}}\right),\ 0 < x < \pi$

◎ *Thinking Process* Applying the formula $1-\cos x = 2\sin^2(x/2)$ and $1+\cos x = 2\cos^2(x/2)$ to remove the square root sign and simplify it.

Sol. We have, $\tan^{-1}\left(\sqrt{\dfrac{1-\cos x}{1+\cos x}}\right) = \tan^{-1}\left(\sqrt{\dfrac{2\sin^2(x/2)}{2\cos^2(x/2)}}\right)$

$$\left(\because \begin{array}{l} 1-\cos x = 2\sin^2(x/2) \\ 1+\cos x = 2\cos^2(x/2) \end{array}\right)$$

$$= \tan^{-1}\left(\sqrt{\tan^2\frac{x}{2}}\right) = \tan^{-1}\left(\tan\frac{x}{2}\right) = \frac{x}{2}$$

Note If x is positive, then $\sqrt{\tan^2\frac{x}{2}} = \tan\frac{x}{2}$ and if x is negative, then $\sqrt{\tan^2\frac{x}{2}} = -\tan\frac{x}{2}$. If $x \in (0,\pi) \Rightarrow \frac{x}{2} \in \left(0, \frac{\pi}{2}\right) \Rightarrow \tan\frac{x}{2} > 0$

Question 5 $\tan^{-1}\left(\dfrac{\cos x - \sin x}{\cos x + \sin x}\right),\ -\dfrac{\pi}{4} < x < \dfrac{3\pi}{4}$

◎ *Thinking Process* First we convert the angle of given function in $\tan\theta$, so that we use the identity. For this we have change the angle of numerator and denominator in terms of $\tan x$ and then using the formula

$$\tan(a-b) = \frac{\tan a - \tan b}{1+\tan a\tan b}$$

Sol. We have, $\tan^{-1}\left(\dfrac{\cos x - \sin x}{\cos x + \sin x}\right) = \tan^{-1}\left(\dfrac{\dfrac{\cos x}{\cos x} - \dfrac{\sin x}{\cos x}}{\dfrac{\cos x}{\cos x} + \dfrac{\sin x}{\cos x}}\right)$

[inside the bracket dividing numerator and denominator by $\cos x$]

$$= \tan^{-1}\left(\frac{1-\tan x}{1+\tan x}\right) = \tan^{-1}\left[\tan\left(\frac{\pi}{4}-x\right)\right]$$

$$\left[\because \tan\left(\frac{\pi}{4}-x\right) = \frac{\tan\frac{\pi}{4}-\tan x}{1+\tan\frac{\pi}{4}\cdot\tan x} = \frac{1-\tan x}{1+\tan x}\right]$$

$$= \frac{\pi}{4} - x$$

Question 6 $\tan^{-1}\dfrac{x}{\sqrt{a^2-x^2}}, |x| < a$

◎ *Thinking Process* Substitute x as $a \sin\theta$ to remove the squrare root sign and then use the identity.

Sol. Let $x = a\sin\theta \Rightarrow \frac{x}{a} = \sin\theta \Rightarrow \sin^{-1}\left(\frac{x}{a}\right) = \theta$ ...(i)

$$\therefore \quad \tan^{-1}\frac{x}{\sqrt{a^2-x^2}} = \tan^{-1}\left(\frac{a\sin\theta}{\sqrt{a^2-a^2\sin^2\theta}}\right)$$

$$= \tan^{-1}\left(\frac{a\sin\theta}{a\sqrt{1-\sin^2\theta}}\right) = \tan^{-1}\left(\frac{\sin\theta}{\cos\theta}\right)$$

$$\left(\because \begin{array}{l}\sin^2 x + \cos^2 x = 1\\ \Rightarrow \cos x = \sqrt{1-\sin^2 x}\end{array}\right)$$

$$= \tan^{-1}(\tan\theta) = \theta = \sin^{-1}\left(\frac{x}{a}\right) \quad \text{[from Eq. (i)]}$$

Question 7 $\tan^{-1}\left(\dfrac{3a^2x - x^3}{a^3 - 3ax^2}\right), a > 0; \dfrac{-a}{\sqrt{3}} \le x \le \dfrac{a}{\sqrt{3}}$

◎ *Thinking Process* The angle of given function can be converted into standard result of $\tan 3\theta$ by putting $x = a\tan\theta$, so that we use the identity $\tan^{-1}(\tan\theta) = \theta$, where $\tan 3\theta = \dfrac{3\tan\theta - \tan^3\theta}{1-3\tan^2\theta}$

Sol. Let $x = a\tan\theta$

$$\Rightarrow \quad \frac{x}{a} = \tan\theta \Rightarrow \theta = \tan^{-1}\left(\frac{x}{a}\right) \quad \text{...(i)}$$

$$\therefore \quad \tan^{-1}\left(\frac{3a^2x - x^3}{a^3 - 3ax^2}\right) = \tan^{-1}\left(\frac{3a^2(a\tan\theta) - (a\tan\theta)^3}{a^3 - 3a(a\tan\theta)^2}\right)$$

$$= \tan^{-1}\left(\frac{a^3(3\tan\theta - \tan^3\theta)}{a^3(1-3\tan^2\theta)}\right)$$

$$= \tan^{-1}\left(\frac{3\tan\theta - \tan^3\theta}{1-3\tan^2\theta}\right) = \tan^{-1}(\tan 3\theta)$$

$$\left(\because \tan 3\theta = \frac{3\tan\theta - \tan^3\theta}{1-3\tan^2\theta}\right)$$

$$= 3\theta = 3\tan^{-1}\left(\frac{x}{a}\right) \quad \text{[from Eq.(i)]}$$

Direction (Q. Nos. 8-9) Find the value of each of the following:

Question 8 $\tan^{-1}\left[2\cos\left(2\sin^{-1}\frac{1}{2}\right)\right]$.

Sol. We have, $\tan^{-1}\left[2\cos\left(2\sin^{-1}\frac{1}{2}\right)\right] = \tan^{-1}\left[2\cos\left\{2\sin^{-1}\left(\sin\frac{\pi}{6}\right)\right\}\right]$

$$\left[\because \sin\frac{\pi}{6} = \frac{1}{2}\right]$$

$$= \tan^{-1}\left[2\cos\left(2\times\frac{\pi}{6}\right)\right] = \tan^{-1}\left[2\cos\frac{\pi}{3}\right]$$

$$= \tan^{-1}\left[2\times\frac{1}{2}\right] = \tan^{-1}(1) \quad \left[\because \cos\frac{\pi}{3} = \frac{1}{2}\right]$$

$$= \tan^{-1}\left(\tan\frac{\pi}{4}\right) = \frac{\pi}{4} \quad \left[\because \tan\frac{\pi}{4} = 1\right]$$

Question 9 $\tan\frac{1}{2}\left[\sin^{-1}\frac{2x}{1+x^2} + \cos^{-1}\frac{1-y^2}{1+y^2}\right]$, $|x|<1$, $y>0$ and $xy<1$

Sol. Let $x = \tan\alpha$, $y = \tan\beta$

$$\therefore \tan\frac{1}{2}\left[\sin^{-1}\frac{2x}{1+x^2} + \cos^{-1}\frac{1-y^2}{1+y^2}\right]$$

$$= \tan\frac{1}{2}\left[\sin^{-1}\frac{2\tan\alpha}{1+\tan^2\alpha} + \cos^{-1}\frac{1-\tan^2\beta}{1+\tan^2\beta}\right]$$

$$= \tan\frac{1}{2}[\sin^{-1}(\sin 2\alpha) + \cos^{-1}(\cos 2\beta)]$$

$$= \tan\frac{1}{2}[2\alpha + 2\beta] = \tan(\alpha+\beta)$$

$$= \frac{\tan\alpha + \tan\beta}{1-\tan\alpha\tan\beta} = \frac{x+y}{1-xy}$$

Direction (Q. Nos. 10 to 12) Find the values of each of the expressions.

Question 10 $\sin^{-1}\left(\sin\frac{2\pi}{3}\right)$

◎ ***Thinking Process*** Since, the range of $\sin^{-1} x$ is $\left[-\frac{\pi}{2}, \frac{\pi}{2}\right]$ so, firstly we write $\sin\frac{2\pi}{3} = \sin\left(\pi - \frac{\pi}{3}\right)$ and then use the identity $\sin^{-1}(\sin\theta) = \theta$.

Sol. We have, $\sin^{-1}\left(\sin\frac{2\pi}{3}\right) = \sin^{-1}\left[\sin\left(\pi - \frac{\pi}{3}\right)\right] = \sin^{-1}\left(\sin\frac{\pi}{3}\right)$

$[\because \sin(\pi - \theta) = \sin\theta]$

$= \frac{\pi}{3}$ which lies in the range $\left[-\frac{\pi}{2}, \frac{\pi}{2}\right]$.

Note $\sin^{-1}(\sin\theta) = \theta$ is only when $\theta \in \left[-\frac{\pi}{2}, \frac{\pi}{2}\right]$.

Question 11 $\tan^{-1}\left(\tan\frac{3\pi}{4}\right)$

Sol. We have, $\tan^{-1}\left(\tan\frac{3\pi}{4}\right) = \tan^{-1}\left[\tan\left(\pi - \frac{\pi}{4}\right)\right] = \tan^{-1}\left(-\tan\frac{\pi}{4}\right)$

$[\because \tan(\pi - \theta) = -\tan\theta]$

$= \tan^{-1}\left[\tan\left(-\frac{\pi}{4}\right)\right]$ $[\because -\tan\theta = \tan(-\theta)]$

$= -\frac{\pi}{4}$ which lies in the range $\left(-\frac{\pi}{2}, \frac{\pi}{2}\right)$.

Mistake Alert Do not take $\tan^{-1}(\tan x) = x$ without checking x lies in the principal value range.

Question 12 $\tan\left(\sin^{-1}\frac{3}{5} + \cot^{-1}\frac{3}{2}\right)$

Sol. Let $\sin^{-1}\frac{3}{5} = x$

$\Rightarrow \quad \sin x = \frac{3}{5}$

Now, $\tan x = \frac{\sin x}{\cos x} = \frac{\sin x}{\sqrt{1 - \sin^2 x}}$ $[\therefore \sin^2 x + \cos^2 x = 1]$

$\Rightarrow \quad \tan x = \frac{\frac{3}{5}}{\sqrt{1 - \frac{9}{25}}} = \frac{\frac{3}{5}}{\frac{4}{5}} = \frac{3}{4}$

Let $\cot^{-1}\frac{3}{2} = y \Rightarrow \cot y = \frac{3}{2} \Rightarrow \tan y = \frac{2}{3}$ $\left[\because \cot\theta = \frac{1}{\tan\theta}\right]$

$$\therefore \tan\left(\sin^{-1}\frac{3}{5} + \cos^{-1}\frac{3}{2}\right) = \tan(x+y)$$

$$= \frac{\tan x + \tan y}{1 - \tan x \cdot \tan y}$$

$$= \frac{\frac{3}{4} + \frac{2}{3}}{1 - \frac{3}{4}\cdot\frac{2}{3}} = \frac{\frac{9+8}{12}}{\frac{12-6}{12}} = \frac{17}{6}$$

Question 13 $\cos^{-1}\left(\cos\frac{7\pi}{6}\right)$ is equal to

(a) $\frac{7\pi}{6}$ (b) $\frac{5\pi}{6}$ (c) $\frac{\pi}{3}$ (d) $\frac{\pi}{6}$

◎ ***Thinking Process*** First we reduce the quantity $\frac{7\pi}{6}$ according to the interval $[0, \pi]$ *i.e., by* using $\cos\theta = \cos(2\pi - \theta)$ and then use the identity $\cos^{-1}(\cos\theta) = \theta$.

Sol. (b) We have, $\cos^{-1}\left(\cos\frac{7\pi}{6}\right) = \cos^{-1}\left[\cos\left(2\pi - \frac{7\pi}{6}\right)\right]$

$$\therefore \quad = \cos^{-1}\left[\cos\left(\frac{5\pi}{6}\right)\right] = \frac{5\pi}{6} \quad [\because \cos(2\pi - \theta) = \cos\theta]$$

Question 14 $\sin\left[\frac{\pi}{3} - \sin^{-1}\left(-\frac{1}{2}\right)\right]$ is equal to

(a) $\frac{1}{2}$ (b) $\frac{1}{3}$

(c) $\frac{1}{4}$ (d) 1

Sol. (d) We have, $\sin\left[\frac{\pi}{3} - \sin^{-1}\left(-\frac{1}{2}\right)\right] = \sin\left[\frac{\pi}{3} - \sin^{-1}\left(-\sin\frac{\pi}{6}\right)\right]$ $\left[\because \sin\frac{\pi}{6} = \frac{1}{2}\right]$

$$= \sin\left[\frac{\pi}{3} - \sin^{-1}\left\{\sin\left(-\frac{\pi}{6}\right)\right\}\right] \quad (\because \sin(-x) = -\sin x)$$

$$= \sin\left[\frac{\pi}{3} - \left(-\frac{\pi}{6}\right)\right]$$

$$= \sin\left[\frac{\pi}{3} + \frac{\pi}{6}\right]$$

$$= \sin\frac{\pi}{2} = 1$$

Question 15 $\tan^{-1}\sqrt{3}-\cot^{-1}(-\sqrt{3})$ is equal to

(a) π (b) $-\frac{\pi}{2}$ (c) 0 (d) $2\sqrt{3}$

Sol. (b) We have, $\tan^{-1}\sqrt{3}-\cot^{-1}(-\sqrt{3})$

Let $\tan^{-1}\sqrt{3}=x \Rightarrow \tan x=\sqrt{3}$

$\Rightarrow \tan x=\tan\frac{\pi}{3} \Rightarrow x=\frac{\pi}{3}$

Now, let $\cot^{-1}(-\sqrt{3})=y$

$\Rightarrow \cot y = -\sqrt{3} = -\cot\frac{\pi}{6}$

$\Rightarrow \cot y=\cot\left(\pi-\frac{\pi}{6}\right) \Rightarrow \cot y=\cot\frac{5\pi}{6} \Rightarrow y=\frac{5\pi}{6}$

$\therefore \tan^{-1}\sqrt{3}-\cot^{-1}(-\sqrt{3})=\frac{\pi}{3}-\frac{5\pi}{6}=\frac{2\pi-5\pi}{6}=-\frac{\pi}{2}$

Miscellaneous Exercsie

Direction (Q. Nos. 1 and 2) Find the value of following:

Question 1 $\cos^{-1}\left(\cos\frac{13\pi}{6}\right)$.

Sol. We have, $\cos^{-1}\left(\cos\frac{13\pi}{6}\right)=\cos^{-1}\left[\cos\left(2\pi+\frac{\pi}{6}\right)\right]$; where $\frac{\pi}{6}\in[0,\pi]$

$=\cos^{-1}\left[\cos\left(\frac{\pi}{6}\right)\right]=\frac{\pi}{6}$ $[\because \cos(2\pi+\theta)=\cos\theta]$

Mistake Alert Student may take $\cos^{-1}\left(\cos\frac{13\pi}{6}\right)=\frac{13\pi}{6}$ instead of $\cos\left(\cos\frac{13\pi}{6}\right)=\frac{\pi}{6}$ without checking the range of $\cos^{-1}x$ which in $[0,\pi]$.

Question 2 $\tan^{-1}\left(\tan\frac{7\pi}{6}\right)$

Thinking Process The given angle does not lie in the principal interval *i.e.,* $\left(-\frac{\pi}{2},\frac{\pi}{2}\right)$, so we convert it such that it lies in $\left(-\frac{\pi}{2},\frac{\pi}{2}\right)$.

Sol. We have, $\tan^{-1}\left(\tan\frac{7\pi}{6}\right)=\tan^{-1}\left[\tan\left(\pi+\frac{\pi}{6}\right)\right]$; where $\frac{\pi}{6}\in\left(-\frac{\pi}{2},\frac{\pi}{2}\right)$

$=\tan^{-1}\left[\tan\frac{\pi}{6}\right]=\frac{\pi}{6}$ $[\because \tan(\pi+\theta)=\tan\theta]$

Direction (Q. Nos. 3 to 10) Prove that

Question 3 $2\sin^{-1}\frac{3}{5}=\tan^{-1}\frac{24}{7}$

Sol. Let $2\sin^{-1}\frac{3}{5}=x \Rightarrow \frac{x}{2}=\sin^{-1}\frac{3}{5} \Rightarrow \sin\frac{x}{2}=\frac{3}{5}$ ...(i)

Now, $\tan x=\frac{\sin x}{\cos x}=\frac{2\sin\frac{x}{2}\cos\frac{x}{2}}{1-2\sin^2\frac{x}{2}}$ $\left[\because \sin A=2\sin\frac{A}{2}\cos\frac{A}{2} \text{ and } \cos A=1-2\sin^2\frac{A}{2}\right]$

$=\frac{2\sin\frac{x}{2}\sqrt{1-\sin^2\frac{x}{2}}}{1-2\sin^2\frac{x}{2}}$ $\left[\because \cos^2\frac{A}{2}=\sqrt{1-\sin^2\frac{A}{2}}\right]$

$=\frac{2\times\frac{3}{5}\times\sqrt{1-\frac{9}{25}}}{1-2\times\frac{9}{25}}$ [using Eq. (i)]

$\Rightarrow \quad \tan x=\frac{2\times\frac{3}{5}\times\frac{4}{5}}{\frac{7}{25}}=\frac{24}{7}$

$\Rightarrow \quad x=\tan^{-1}\frac{24}{7}$

$\therefore \quad 2\sin^{-1}\frac{3}{5}=\tan^{-1}\frac{24}{7}$ **Hence Proved.**

Question 4 $\sin^{-1}\frac{8}{17}+\sin^{-1}\frac{3}{5}=\tan^{-1}\frac{77}{36}$

Sol. Let $\sin^{-1}\frac{8}{17}=x \Rightarrow \sin x=\frac{8}{17}$

$\therefore \quad \tan x=\frac{\sin x}{\cos x}=\frac{\sin x}{\sqrt{1-\sin^2 x}}=\frac{\frac{8}{17}}{\sqrt{1-\frac{64}{289}}}=\frac{\frac{8}{17}}{\frac{15}{17}}=\frac{8}{15}$

and $\sin^{-1}\frac{3}{5}=y \Rightarrow \sin y=\frac{3}{5}$

$\therefore \tan y=\frac{\sin y}{\cos y}=\frac{\sin y}{\sqrt{1-\sin^2 y}}=\frac{\frac{3}{5}}{\sqrt{1-\frac{9}{25}}}=\frac{\frac{3}{5}}{\frac{4}{5}}=\frac{3}{4}$

Now, $\tan(x+y)=\frac{\tan x+\tan y}{1-\tan x\cdot\tan y}=\frac{\frac{8}{15}+\frac{3}{4}}{1-\frac{8}{15}\cdot\frac{3}{4}}=\frac{32+45}{60-24}=\frac{77}{36}$

$\Rightarrow \quad x + y = \tan^{-1}\dfrac{77}{36}$

$\therefore \quad \sin^{-1}\dfrac{8}{17} + \sin^{-1}\dfrac{3}{5} = \tan^{-1}\dfrac{77}{36}$ **Hence Proved.**

Question 5 $\cos^{-1}\dfrac{4}{5} + \cos^{-1}\dfrac{12}{13} = \cos^{-1}\dfrac{33}{65}$.

Sol. Let $\cos^{-1}\dfrac{4}{5} = x \Rightarrow \cos x = \dfrac{4}{5}$

$\therefore \quad \sin x = \sqrt{1-\cos^2 x} = \sqrt{1-\left(\dfrac{4}{5}\right)^2} = \sqrt{1-\dfrac{16}{25}} = \dfrac{3}{5}$

and $\quad \cos^{-1}\dfrac{12}{13} = y \Rightarrow \cos y = \dfrac{12}{13}$

$\therefore \quad \sin y = \sqrt{1-\cos^2 y} = \sqrt{1-\dfrac{144}{169}} = \dfrac{5}{13}$

Now, $\cos(x+y) = \cos x \cos y - \sin x \sin y$

$= \dfrac{4}{5}\times\dfrac{12}{13} - \dfrac{3}{5}\times\dfrac{5}{13} = \dfrac{48-15}{65} = \dfrac{33}{65}$

$\Rightarrow \quad x + y = \cos^{-1}\dfrac{33}{65} \Rightarrow \cos^{-1}\dfrac{4}{5} + \cos^{-1}\dfrac{12}{13} = \cos^{-1}\dfrac{33}{65}$ **Hence Proved.**

Mistake Alert Students may incorrectly apply the identity as $\sin\theta = 1-\cos^2\theta$ instead of $\sin\theta = \sqrt{1-\cos^2\theta}$

Question 6 $\cos^{-1}\dfrac{12}{13} + \sin^{-1}\dfrac{3}{5} = \sin^{-1}\dfrac{56}{65}$

Sol. Let $\cos^{-1}\dfrac{12}{13} = x \Rightarrow \cos x = \dfrac{12}{13}$

$\therefore \quad \sin x = \sqrt{1-\cos^2 x} = \sqrt{1-\dfrac{144}{169}} = \dfrac{5}{13}$

and $\quad \sin^{-1}\dfrac{3}{5} = y \Rightarrow \sin y = \dfrac{3}{5}$

$\therefore \quad \cos y = \sqrt{1-\sin^2 y} = \sqrt{1-\dfrac{9}{25}} = \dfrac{4}{5}$

Now, $\quad \sin(x+y) = \sin x \cos y + \cos x \sin y$

$= \dfrac{5}{13}\times\dfrac{4}{5} + \dfrac{12}{13}\times\dfrac{3}{5} = \dfrac{20+36}{65} = \dfrac{56}{65} \Rightarrow x + y = \sin^{-1}\dfrac{56}{65}$

$\Rightarrow \cos^{-1}\dfrac{12}{13} + \sin^{-1}\dfrac{3}{5} = \sin^{-1}\dfrac{56}{65}$ **Hence Proved.**

Question 7 $\tan^{-1}\frac{63}{16} = \sin^{-1}\frac{5}{13} + \cos^{-1}\frac{3}{5}$.

Sol. Let $\sin^{-1}\frac{5}{13} = x \Rightarrow \sin x = \frac{5}{13}$

$$\therefore \quad \tan x = \frac{\sin x}{\cos x} = \frac{\sin x}{\sqrt{1-\sin^2 x}} = \frac{\frac{5}{13}}{\sqrt{1-\frac{25}{169}}} = \frac{\frac{5}{13}}{\frac{12}{13}} = \frac{5}{12}$$

and $\cos^{-1}\frac{3}{5} = y \Rightarrow \cos y = \frac{3}{5}$

$$\therefore \quad \tan y = \frac{\sin y}{\cos y} = \frac{\sqrt{1-\cos^2 y}}{\cos y} = \frac{\sqrt{1-\frac{9}{25}}}{\frac{3}{5}} = \frac{\frac{4}{5}}{\frac{3}{5}} = \frac{4}{3}$$

Now, $\tan(x+y) = \frac{\tan x + \tan y}{1 - \tan x \cdot \tan y}$

$$= \frac{\frac{5}{12}+\frac{4}{3}}{1-\frac{5}{12}\times\frac{4}{3}} = \frac{15+48}{36-20} = \frac{63}{16}$$

$$\Rightarrow \quad x + y = \tan^{-1}\frac{63}{16}$$

$$\therefore \quad \sin^{-1}\frac{5}{13} + \cos^{-1}\frac{3}{5} = \tan^{-1}\frac{63}{16}$$ **Hence Proved.**

Question 8 $\tan^{-1}\sqrt{x} = \frac{1}{2}\cos^{-1}\left(\frac{1-x}{1+x}\right), x \in [0, 1]$.

Sol. Let $x = \tan^2\theta \Rightarrow \tan\theta = \sqrt{x} \Rightarrow \theta = \tan^{-1}\sqrt{x}$

$$\text{RHS} = \frac{1}{2}\cos^{-1}\left(\frac{1-\tan^2}{1+\tan^2\theta}\right)$$

$$= \frac{1}{2}\cos^{-1}(\cos 2\theta) \qquad \left[\because \frac{1-\tan^2\theta}{1+\tan^2\theta} = \cos 2\theta\right]$$

$$= \frac{1}{2}\times 2\theta \qquad [\cos^{-1}(\cos x) = x]$$

$$= \theta = \tan^{-1}\sqrt{x} = \text{LHS}$$ **Hence Proved.**

Question 9 $\cot^{-1}\left(\dfrac{\sqrt{1+\sin x}+\sqrt{1-\sin x}}{\sqrt{1+\sin x}-\sqrt{1-\sin x}}\right)=\dfrac{x}{2}, x\in\left(0,\dfrac{\pi}{4}\right)$

◎ *Thinking Process* To remove the square root sign, we use the identity $1=\sin^2\dfrac{x}{2}+\cos^2\dfrac{x}{2}$ and the relation $\sin x=2\sin\dfrac{x}{2}\cdot\cos\dfrac{x}{2}$ and also use the identities $(a+b)^2=a^2+b^2+2ab$ and $(a-b)^2=a^2+b^2-2ab$.

Sol. We have to prove that, $\cot^{-1}\left(\dfrac{\sqrt{1+\sin x}+\sqrt{1-\sin x}}{\sqrt{1+\sin x}-\sqrt{1-\sin x}}\right)=\dfrac{x}{2}, x\in\left(0,\dfrac{\pi}{4}\right)$

$$\text{LHS}=\cot^{-1}\left(\frac{\sqrt{1+\sin x}+\sqrt{1-\sin x}}{\sqrt{1+\sin x}-\sqrt{1-\sin x}}\right) \quad \text{...(i)}$$

Now, we can write

$$\sqrt{1+\sin x}=\sqrt{\sin^2\frac{x}{2}+\cos^2\frac{x}{2}+2\sin\frac{x}{2}\cos\frac{x}{2}}=\sqrt{\left(\sin\frac{x}{2}+\cos\frac{x}{2}\right)^2}$$

$$\left[\because \sin^2\frac{x}{2}+\cos^2\frac{x}{2}=1 \quad \sin x=2\sin\frac{x}{2}\cos\frac{x}{2}\right]$$

$$\Rightarrow \quad \sqrt{1+\sin x}=\sin\frac{x}{2}+\cos\frac{x}{2}$$

Similarly, we can get $\sqrt{1-\sin x}=\cos\dfrac{x}{2}-\sin\dfrac{x}{2}$

On substituting above two values in Eq. (i), we get

$$\text{LHS}=\cot^{-1}\left(\frac{\sin\frac{x}{2}+\cos\frac{x}{2}+\cos\frac{x}{2}-\sin\frac{x}{2}}{\sin\frac{x}{2}+\cos\frac{x}{2}+\sin\frac{x}{2}-\cos\frac{x}{2}}\right)=\cot^{-1}\left(\frac{2\cos\frac{x}{2}}{2\sin\frac{x}{2}}\right)$$

$$=\cot^{-1}\left(\cot\frac{x}{2}\right)=\frac{x}{2}= \quad \left[\text{If } x\in\left(0,\frac{\pi}{4}\right)\Rightarrow\frac{x}{2}\in\left(0,\frac{\pi}{8}\right)\right]$$ **Hence Proved.**

Quick Solution

$$\text{LHS}=\cot^{-1}\left[\frac{\sqrt{1+\sin x}+\sqrt{1-\sin x}}{\sqrt{1+\sin x}-\sqrt{1-\sin x}}\right]$$

$$=\cot^{-1}\left[\frac{\sqrt{1+\sin x}+\sqrt{1-\sin x}}{\sqrt{1+\sin x}-\sqrt{1-\sin x}}\times\frac{\sqrt{1+\sin x}+\sqrt{1-\sin x}}{\sqrt{1+\sin x}+\sqrt{1-\sin x}}\right]$$

[by rationalising denominator]

$$=\cot^{-1}\left[\frac{1+\sin x+1-\sin x+2\sqrt{1-\sin^2 x}}{1+\sin x-1+\sin x}\right]$$

$$=\cot^{-1}\left[\frac{2+2\cos x}{2\sin x}\right] \quad [\because \cos x=\sqrt{1-\sin^2 x}]$$

$$= \cot^{-1}\left[\frac{1+\cos x}{\sin x}\right] = \cot^{-1}\left[\frac{2\cos^2 x/2}{2\sin x/2 \cos x/2}\right]$$

$$\left[\because 1+\cos x = 2\cos^2\frac{x}{2} \qquad \sin x = 2\sin\frac{x}{2}\cos\frac{x}{2}\right]$$

$$= \cot^{-1}\left[\cot\frac{x}{2}\right] = \frac{x}{2} = \text{RHS} \qquad \left[\text{If } x \in \left(0, \frac{\pi}{4}\right) \Rightarrow \frac{x}{2} \in \left(0, \frac{\pi}{8}\right)\right]$$

Hence Proved.

Note If $x \in \left(0, \frac{\pi}{2}\right)$, then $\sqrt{1-\sin x} = \cos\frac{x}{2} - \sin\frac{x}{2}$ and if $x \in \left(\frac{\pi}{2}, \pi\right)$, then

$$\sqrt{1-\sin x} = \sin\frac{x}{2} - \cos\frac{x}{2}$$

Question 10 $\tan^{-1}\left(\frac{\sqrt{1+x}-\sqrt{1-x}}{\sqrt{1+x}+\sqrt{1-x}}\right) = \frac{\pi}{4} - \frac{1}{2}\cos^{-1} x, \frac{-1}{\sqrt{2}} \le x \le 1$

◎ ***Thinking Process*** To remove the square root sign, first substitute $x = \cos\theta$, then use the relation $1+\cos\theta = 2\cos^2(\theta/2)$ and $1-\cos\theta = 2\sin^2(\theta/2)$.

Sol. Let $x = \cos\theta$ so that $\cos^{-1} x = \theta$

$$\text{LHS} = \tan^{-1}\left(\frac{\sqrt{1+x}-\sqrt{1-x}}{\sqrt{1+x}+\sqrt{1-x}}\right) = \tan^{-1}\left(\frac{\sqrt{1+\cos\theta}-\sqrt{1-\cos\theta}}{\sqrt{1+\cos\theta}+\sqrt{1-\cos\theta}}\right)$$

$$= \tan^{-1}\left(\frac{\sqrt{2\cos^2\frac{\theta}{2}}-\sqrt{2\sin^2\frac{\theta}{2}}}{\sqrt{2\cos^2\frac{\theta}{2}}+\sqrt{2\sin^2\frac{\theta}{2}}}\right)$$

$$\left[\because 1+\cos\theta = 2\cos^2\frac{\theta}{2} \text{ and } 1-\cos\theta = 2\sin^2\frac{\theta}{2}\right]$$

$$= \tan^{-1}\left(\frac{\sqrt{2}\cos\frac{\theta}{2}-\sqrt{2}\sin\frac{\theta}{2}}{\sqrt{2}\cos\frac{\theta}{2}+\sqrt{2}\sin\frac{\theta}{2}}\right)$$

$$= \tan^{-1}\left(\frac{\cos\frac{\theta}{2}-\sin\frac{\theta}{2}}{\cos\frac{\theta}{2}+\sin\frac{\theta}{2}}\right) = \tan^{-1}\left(\frac{1-\tan\frac{\theta}{2}}{1+\tan\frac{\theta}{2}}\right)$$

(inside the bracket dividing numerator and denominator by $\cos\theta/2$)

$$= \tan^{-1}\left(\tan\left(\frac{\pi}{4}-\frac{\theta}{2}\right)\right) \qquad \left[\because \tan(A-B) = \frac{\tan A - \tan B}{1+\tan A \tan B}\right]$$

$$= \frac{\pi}{4} - \frac{\theta}{2} = \frac{\pi}{4} - \frac{1}{2}\cos^{-1} x$$

Hence Proved.

Direction (Q. Nos. 11 to 12) Solve the following equations for x :

Question 11 $2\tan^{-1}(\cos x) = \tan^{-1}(2\operatorname{cosec} x)$

Sol. We have, $2\tan^{-1}(\cos x) = \tan^{-1}(2\operatorname{cosec} x)$ ...(i)

Let $2\tan^{-1}(\cos x) = \theta \Rightarrow \tan^{-1}(\cos x) = \frac{\theta}{2} \Rightarrow \cos x = \tan\frac{\theta}{2}$

From Eq. (i),

$$2\tan^{-1}(\cos x) = \tan^{-1}(2\operatorname{cosec} x)$$

$$\Rightarrow \theta = \tan^{-1}(2\operatorname{cosec} x) \Rightarrow \tan\theta = 2\operatorname{cosec} x$$

$$\Rightarrow \frac{2\tan\frac{\theta}{2}}{1-\tan^2\frac{\theta}{2}} = 2\operatorname{cosec} x \qquad \left[\because \tan\theta = \frac{2\tan\theta}{1-\tan^2\frac{\theta}{2}}\right]$$

$$\Rightarrow \frac{2\cos x}{1-\cos^2 x} = 2\operatorname{cosec} x \Rightarrow \frac{\cos x}{\sin^2 x} = \frac{1}{\sin x} \Rightarrow \frac{\cos x}{\sin x} = 1$$

$$\Rightarrow \tan x = 1 = \tan\frac{\pi}{4} \Rightarrow x = \frac{\pi}{4}$$

Mistake Alert Students may incorrectly apply the identity as $\tan 2\theta = \frac{\tan\theta}{1+\tan^2\theta}$ instead of $\tan 2\theta = \frac{2\tan\theta}{1-\tan^2\theta}$

Question 12 $\tan^{-1}\frac{1-x}{1+x} = \frac{1}{2}\tan^{-1} x, (x > 0).$

Sol. We have, $\tan^{-1}\left(\frac{1-x}{1+x}\right) = \frac{1}{2}\tan^{-1} x, (x > 0)$ ...(i)

Let $x = \tan\theta, \Rightarrow \theta = \tan^{-1} x$

Then Eq. (i) becomes

$$\tan^{-1}\left(\frac{1-\tan\theta}{1+\tan\theta}\right) = \frac{1}{2}\tan^{-1}(\tan\theta) \Rightarrow \tan^{-1}\left(\frac{\tan\frac{\pi}{4}-\tan\theta}{1+\tan\frac{\pi}{4}\tan\theta}\right) = \frac{\theta}{2}$$

$$\Rightarrow \tan^{-1}\left(\tan\left(\frac{\pi}{4}-\theta\right)\right) = \frac{\theta}{2}$$

$$\Rightarrow \frac{\pi}{4} - \theta = \frac{\theta}{2}$$

$$\Rightarrow \frac{3\theta}{2} = \frac{\pi}{4}$$

$$\Rightarrow \theta = \frac{\pi}{6}$$

$$\Rightarrow \tan^{-1} x = \frac{\pi}{6}$$

$$\Rightarrow x = \tan\frac{\pi}{6}$$

$$\Rightarrow x = \frac{1}{\sqrt{3}}$$

Question 13 $\sin(\tan^{-1} x), |x|<1$ is equal to

(a) $\frac{x}{\sqrt{1-x^2}}$ (b) $\frac{1}{\sqrt{1-x^2}}$ (c) $\frac{1}{\sqrt{1+x^2}}$ (d) $\frac{x}{\sqrt{1+x^2}}$

Sol. (d) Let $\tan^{-1} x = \theta \Rightarrow \tan\theta = x$

Now, $\sin(\tan^{-1} x) = \sin\theta = \sqrt{1-\cos^2\theta} = \sqrt{1-\frac{1}{\sec^2\theta}}$ $\left[\because \cos A = \frac{1}{\sec A}\right]$

$= \sqrt{1-\frac{1}{1+\tan^2\theta}}$ $[\because \sec^2 A = 1 + \tan^2 A]$

$= \sqrt{1-\frac{1}{1+x^2}} = \sqrt{\frac{x^2}{1+x^2}}$

$\therefore$ $\sin(\tan^{-1} x) = \frac{x}{\sqrt{1+x^2}}$ $[\because \theta = \tan^{-1} x]$

Question 14 $\sin^{-1}(1-x) - 2\sin^{-1} x = \frac{\pi}{2}$, then x is equal to

(a) $0, \frac{1}{2}$ (b) $1, \frac{1}{2}$

(c) 0 (d) $\frac{1}{2}$

Sol. (c) Given, $\sin^{-1}(1-x) - 2\sin^{-1} x = \frac{\pi}{2}$

Let $x = \sin\theta \Rightarrow \theta = \sin^{-1} x$,

$\therefore$ $\sin^{-1}(1-x) - 2\sin^{-1} x = \frac{\pi}{2} \Rightarrow \sin^{-1}(1-\sin\theta) - 2\theta = \frac{\pi}{2}$

$\Rightarrow$ $\sin^{-1}(1-\sin\theta) = \frac{\pi}{2} + 2\theta$

$\Rightarrow$ $1-\sin\theta = \sin\left(\frac{\pi}{2}+2\theta\right) \Rightarrow 1-\sin\theta = \cos 2\theta$ $\left[\because \sin\left(\frac{\pi}{2}+\theta\right) = \cos\theta\right]$

$\Rightarrow$ $1-\sin\theta = 1-2\sin^2\theta$ $[\because \cos 2\theta = 1-2\sin^2\theta]$

$\Rightarrow$ $2\sin^2\theta - \sin\theta = 0 \Rightarrow \sin\theta(2\sin\theta - 1) = 0$

Either $\sin\theta = 0$ or $2\sin\theta - 1 = 0$

$\Rightarrow$ $x = 0$ or $2x - 1 = 0$ $[\because \sin\theta = x]$

$\Rightarrow$ $x = 0$ or $x = \frac{1}{2}$

But $x = \frac{1}{2}$ does not satisfy the given equation. So, $x = 0$.

To check your answer

On putting $x = 0$ in the given equation,

$\therefore$ $\sin^{-1}(1-0) - 2\sin^{-1} 0 = \frac{\pi}{2} \Rightarrow \frac{\pi}{2} - 2\times 0 = \frac{\pi}{2}$

$\Rightarrow$ $\frac{\pi}{2} = \frac{\pi}{2}$

On putting $x = \frac{1}{2}$ in the given equation,

$$\therefore \quad \sin^{-1}\left(1-\frac{1}{2}\right) - 2\sin^{-1}\frac{1}{2} = \frac{\pi}{2}$$

$$\Rightarrow \quad \sin^{-1}\frac{1}{2} - 2\sin^{-1}\frac{1}{2} = \frac{\pi}{2} \Rightarrow \frac{\pi}{6} - 2\times\frac{\pi}{6} = \frac{\pi}{2}$$

$$\Rightarrow \quad \frac{\pi - 2\pi}{6} = \frac{\pi}{2} \Rightarrow \frac{-\pi}{6} = \frac{\pi}{2} \quad \text{(false)}$$

So $x = \frac{1}{2}$ is not possible.

DIKSHA APP Questions

☐ Multiple Choice Questions

Q.1 Principal value of the expression value of $\cos^{-1}\cos(-680°)$ is

(a) $\frac{2\pi}{9}$ (b) $-\frac{2\pi}{9}$ (c) $\frac{34\pi}{9}$ (d) $\frac{\pi}{9}$

Sol. (a) We have, $\cos^{-1}(\cos(-680°))$

$= \cos^{-1}\cos(680°)$ $\quad [\because \cos(-\theta) = \cos\theta]$

$= \cos^{-1}\cos(720° - 40°)$

$= \cos^{-1}(\cos 40°)$ $\quad [\because \cos(720° - \theta) = \cos\theta]$

$= 40°$

$= \frac{2\pi}{9}$

Q.2 If $\tan^{-1} x = \frac{\pi}{4} - \tan^{-1}\frac{1}{3}$, then the value of x is

(a) $\frac{1}{2}$ (b) $\frac{1}{4}$ (c) $\frac{1}{6}$ (d) None of these

Sol. (a) We have, $\tan^{-1} x = \frac{\pi}{4} - \tan^{-1}\frac{1}{3}$ ...(i)

We know that $\tan\frac{\pi}{4} = 1$

$$\Rightarrow \quad \frac{\pi}{4} = \tan^{-1} 1$$

On putting the value of $\frac{\pi}{4}$ in Eq. (i), we get

$$\tan^{-1} x = \tan^{-1} 1 - \tan^{-1}\frac{1}{3}$$

Now, let $\tan^{-1}x = \alpha \Rightarrow x = \tan\alpha$

and $\tan^{-1}\frac{1}{3} = \beta \Rightarrow \frac{1}{3} = \tan\beta$

$\therefore\ \tan^{-1}x = \tan^{-1}1 - \tan^{-1}\frac{1}{3} \Rightarrow \alpha = \tan^{-1}1 - \beta$

$\Rightarrow \quad \alpha + \beta = \tan^{-1}1$

$\Rightarrow \quad \tan(\alpha+\beta) = 1 \Rightarrow \frac{\tan\alpha + \tan\beta}{1 - \tan\alpha\tan\beta} = 1$

$\Rightarrow \quad \frac{x + \frac{1}{3}}{1 - x \times \frac{1}{3}} = 1 \Rightarrow \frac{3x+1}{3-x} = 1 \Rightarrow 4x = 2 \Rightarrow x = \frac{1}{2}$

Q.3 Find the value of $\cos^{-1}\left(\cos\frac{5\pi}{3}\right) + \sin^{-1}\left(\sin\frac{5\pi}{3}\right)$

(a) $\frac{\pi}{2}$ (b) $\frac{5\pi}{3}$

(c) $\frac{10\pi}{3}$ (d) 0

Sol. (d) We have, $\cos^{-1}\cos\left(\frac{5\pi}{3}\right) + \sin^{-1}\sin\left(\frac{5\pi}{3}\right)$

$= \cos^{-1}\cos\left(2\pi - \frac{\pi}{3}\right) + \sin^{-1}\sin\left(2\pi - \frac{\pi}{3}\right)$

$= \cos^{-1}\left(\cos\frac{\pi}{3}\right) + \sin^{-1}\left(-\sin\frac{\pi}{3}\right)$ $\left[\because \cos(2\pi-\theta) = \cos\theta \text{ and } \sin(2\pi-\theta) = -\sin\theta\right]$

Let $\sin^{-1}\left(-\sin\frac{\pi}{3}\right) = \theta \Rightarrow -\sin\frac{\pi}{3} = \sin\theta \Rightarrow \sin\left(-\frac{\pi}{3}\right) = \sin\theta \Rightarrow \theta = -\frac{\pi}{3}$

$\therefore \cos^{-1}\left(\cos\frac{\pi}{3}\right) + \sin^{-1}\left(-\sin\frac{\pi}{3}\right) = \frac{\pi}{3} - \frac{\pi}{3} = 0$

Q.4 If $\tan^{-1}(\cot x) = 2x$, then what is the value of x?

(a) $\pm\frac{\pi}{3}$ (b) $\pm\frac{\pi}{4}$

(c) $\pm\frac{\pi}{6}$ (d) None of these

Sol. (c) We have, $\tan^{-1}(\cot x) = 2x$

$\Rightarrow \quad \tan^{-1}\left[\tan\left(\pm\frac{\pi}{2} - x\right)\right] = 2x$ $\left(\because \tan\left(\frac{\pi}{2} - \theta\right) = \cot\theta\right)$

$\Rightarrow \quad \pm\frac{\pi}{2} - x = 2x$ $[\tan^{-1}(\tan x) = x]$

$\Rightarrow \quad \pm\frac{\pi}{2} = 3x \Rightarrow x = \pm\frac{\pi}{6}$

Q.5 What is the value of $\sin^{-1}\left(\cos\frac{33\pi}{5}\right)$

(a) $-\frac{\pi}{10}$ (b) $\frac{3\pi}{5}$

(c) $\frac{\pi}{10}$ (d) $\frac{7\pi}{5}$

Sol. (a) We have, $\sin^{-1}\cos\left(\frac{33\pi}{5}\right) = \sin^{-1}\cos\left(7\pi - \frac{2\pi}{5}\right)$

$= \sin^{-1}\left(-\cos\frac{2\pi}{5}\right)$ $[\because \cos(7\pi - \theta) = -\cos\theta]$

Now, let $\sin^{-1}\left(-\cos\frac{2\pi}{5}\right) = \theta$

$\Rightarrow -\cos\frac{2\pi}{5} = \sin\theta \Rightarrow -\sin\theta = \cos\frac{2\pi}{5}$

$\Rightarrow \sin(-\theta) = \sin\left(\frac{\pi}{2} - \frac{2\pi}{5}\right)$ $\left[\because \sin(-\theta) = -\sin\theta \text{ and } \sin\left(\frac{\pi}{2} - \theta\right) = \cos\theta\right]$

$\Rightarrow -\theta = \frac{\pi}{2} - \frac{2\pi}{5} = \frac{\pi}{10}$

$\Rightarrow \theta = -\frac{\pi}{10}$

$\therefore \sin^{-1}\left(\cos\frac{33\pi}{5}\right) = -\frac{\pi}{10}$

Q.6 If $x = \sin^{-1} k$ and $y = \cos^{-1} k$, $k \in [-1, 1]$, then relation between x and y is

(a) $x + y = 2$ (b) $x - y = 2$

(c) $x - y = \frac{\pi}{2}$ (d) $x + y = \frac{\pi}{2}$

Sol. (d) We have $x = \sin^{-1} k \Rightarrow k = \sin x$ ...(i)

and $y = \cos^{-1} k \Rightarrow k = \cos y$ ...(ii)

From Eqs. (i) and (ii), we have

$\sin x = \cos y \Rightarrow \sin x = \sin\left(\frac{\pi}{2} - y\right)$ $\left[\therefore \sin\left(\frac{\pi}{2} - \theta\right) = \cos\theta\right]$

$\Rightarrow x = \frac{\pi}{2} - y \Rightarrow x + y = \frac{\pi}{2}$

Q.7 What is the value of $\cot\left(\sec^{-1} x + \sin^{-1}\frac{1}{x}\right)$?

(a) 2 (b) – 1

(c) 0 (d) 1

Sol. (c) We have, $\cot\left(\sec^{-1}x+\sin^{-1}\frac{1}{x}\right)$

Let $\sec^{-1}x=\alpha$

$\Rightarrow$ $x=\sec\alpha$

$\therefore$ $\tan^2\alpha=\sec^2\alpha-1=x^2-1$ $[\because 1+\tan^2\theta=\sec^2\theta]$

$\Rightarrow$ $\tan\alpha=\sqrt{x^2-1}$

$\Rightarrow$ $\cot\alpha=\frac{1}{\sqrt{x^2-1}}$

Now, let $\sin^{-1}\frac{1}{x}=\beta$

$\Rightarrow$ $\text{cosec}\beta=x$

$\therefore$ $\cot^2\beta=\text{cosec}^2\beta-1=x^2-1$ $[\because 1+\cot^2\theta=\text{cosec}^2\theta]$

$\Rightarrow$ $\cot\beta=\sqrt{x^2-1}$

Now, $\cot\left(\sec^{-1}x+\sin^{-1}\frac{1}{x}\right)=\cot(\alpha+\beta)=\frac{\cot\alpha\cot\beta-1}{\cot\beta+\cot\alpha}$

$$=\frac{\frac{1}{\sqrt{x^2-1}}\times\sqrt{x^2-1}-1}{\sqrt{x^2-1}+\frac{1}{\sqrt{x^2-1}}}=\frac{1-1}{\frac{x^2-1+1}{\sqrt{x^2-1}}}=0$$

Q.8 Domain of $\cos^{-1}(x^2-4)$ is

(a) [3, 5]
(b) [5, π]
(c) $[-\sqrt{5},-\sqrt{3}]\cup[-\sqrt{5},3]$
(d) $[-\sqrt{5},-\sqrt{3}]\cup[\sqrt{3},\sqrt{5}]$

Sol. (d) We know that domain of $\cos^{-1}x$ is [– 1, 1].

So, $-1\le x^2-4\le 1$

Case I $x^2-4\le 1$

$\Rightarrow$ $x^2-5\le 0$

$\Rightarrow$ $(x-\sqrt{5})(x+\sqrt{5})\le 0$

$\Rightarrow$ $x\in[-\sqrt{5},\sqrt{5}]$ ...(i)

Case II $x^2-4\ge -1$

$\Rightarrow$ $x^2-3\ge 0$

$\Rightarrow$ $(x-\sqrt{3})(x+\sqrt{3})\ge 0$

$\Rightarrow$ $x\in(-\infty,-\sqrt{3}]\cup[\sqrt{3},\infty)$ ...(ii)

Taking intersection of Eqs. (i) and (ii), we get

$x\in[-\sqrt{5},-\sqrt{3}]\cup[\sqrt{3},\sqrt{5}]$

Q.9 The value of $\tan^{-1}\left(\sin\left(-\frac{\pi}{2}\right)\right)$ is

(a) -1 (b) $-\frac{\pi}{4}$

(c) $\frac{\pi}{4}$ (d) None of these

Sol. (b) We have, $\tan^{-1}\left(\sin\left(-\frac{\pi}{2}\right)\right)$

$= \tan^{-1}\left(-\sin\frac{\pi}{2}\right)$ $[\sin(-x) = -\sin x]$

$= \tan^{-1}(-1)$ $\left[\sin\frac{\pi}{2} = 1\right]$

Let $\tan^{-1}(-1) = \theta \Rightarrow \tan\theta = -1$

$\Rightarrow \tan\theta = -\tan\frac{\pi}{4}$

$\Rightarrow \tan\theta = \tan\left(-\frac{\pi}{4}\right)$ $[\because \tan(-\theta) = -\tan\theta]$

$\Rightarrow \theta = -\frac{\pi}{4}$

$\therefore \tan^{-1}\left(\sin\left(-\frac{\pi}{2}\right)\right) = -\frac{\pi}{4}$

□ Subjective Type Questions

Q.1 Find the value of $\cos^{-1}\left(\frac{1}{2}\right) - 2\sin^{-1}\left(-\frac{1}{2}\right)$.

Sol. We have, $\cos^{-1}\left(\frac{1}{2}\right) - 2\sin^{-1}\left(-\frac{1}{2}\right)$

Let $2\sin^{-1}\left(-\frac{1}{2}\right) = \theta \Rightarrow \sin^{-1}\left(\frac{-1}{2}\right) = \frac{\theta}{2}$

$\Rightarrow \sin\frac{\theta}{2} = -\frac{1}{2} \Rightarrow \sin\frac{\theta}{2} = -\sin\frac{\pi}{6}$

$\Rightarrow \sin\frac{\theta}{2} = \sin\left(-\frac{\pi}{6}\right)$

$\Rightarrow \frac{\theta}{2} = \frac{-\pi}{6} \Rightarrow \theta = -\frac{\pi}{3}$

$\therefore \cos^{-1}\left(\frac{1}{2}\right) - 2\sin^{-1}\left(-\frac{1}{2}\right) = \cos^{-1}\left(\cos\frac{\pi}{3}\right) - \left(-\frac{\pi}{3}\right)$

$= \frac{\pi}{3} + \frac{\pi}{3}$ $[\cos^{-1}(\cos x) = x]$

$= \frac{2\pi}{3}$

Q.2 Prove that $2\tan^{-1}\frac{1}{2}+\tan^{-1}\frac{1}{7}=\tan^{-1}\frac{31}{17}$.

Sol. Let $2\tan^{-1}\frac{1}{2}=x$

$$\Rightarrow \quad \tan^{-1}\frac{1}{2}=\frac{x}{2}$$

$$\Rightarrow \quad \tan\frac{x}{2}=\frac{1}{2}$$

$$\therefore \tan x=\frac{2\tan\frac{x}{2}}{1-\left(\tan\frac{x}{2}\right)^2}=\frac{2\times\frac{1}{2}}{1-\left(\frac{1}{2}\right)^2}=\frac{1}{3/4}=\frac{4}{3}$$

Now, let $\tan^{-1}\frac{1}{7}=y$

$$\Rightarrow \quad \tan y=\frac{1}{7}$$

$$\therefore \tan(x+y)=\frac{\tan x+\tan y}{1-\tan x\tan y}=\frac{\frac{4}{3}+\frac{1}{7}}{1-\frac{4}{3}\times\frac{1}{7}}=\frac{\frac{28+3}{21}}{\frac{21-4}{21}}=\frac{31}{17}$$

$$\Rightarrow x+y=\tan^{-1}\frac{31}{17}\Rightarrow 2\tan^{-1}\frac{1}{2}+\tan^{-1}\frac{1}{7}=\tan^{-1}\frac{31}{17}$$ **Hence Proved.**

Q.3 Find the value of $\sec^2(\tan^{-1}2)+\text{cosec}^2(\cot^{-1}3)$.

Sol. We have, $\sec^2(\tan^{-1}2)+\text{cosec}^2(\cos^{-1}3)$

$$=1+\tan^2(\tan^{-1}2)+1+\cot^2(\cot^{-1}3)$$

$[\because 1+\tan^2\theta=\sec^2\theta,\ 1+\cot^2\theta=\text{cosec}^2\theta]$

$$=1+[\tan(\tan^{-1}2)]^2+1+[\cot(\cot^{-1}3)]^2$$

$$=1+2^2+1+3^2 \qquad \left[\begin{array}{l}\tan(\tan^{-1}x)=x\\ \cot(\cot^{-1}x)=x\end{array}\right]$$

$$=1+4+1+9=15$$

Q.4 Find the value of $\tan\left(2\tan^{-1}\frac{1}{5}-\frac{\pi}{4}\right)$.

◎ ***Thinking Process*** First use the identity $\tan(x-y)=\frac{\tan x-\tan y}{1+\tan x\tan y}$, then use the identity $\tan x=\frac{2\tan x/2}{1-\tan^2\frac{x}{2}}$ to get the required value.

Sol. Let $2\tan^{-1}\frac{1}{5} = x \Rightarrow \tan^{-1}\frac{1}{5} = \frac{x}{2}$

$$\Rightarrow \qquad \tan\frac{x}{2} = \frac{1}{5}$$

$$\therefore \tan\left(2\tan^{-1}\frac{1}{5} - \frac{\pi}{4}\right) = \tan\left(x - \frac{\pi}{4}\right)$$

$$= \frac{\tan x - \tan\frac{\pi}{4}}{1 + \tan x \tan\frac{\pi}{4}} = \frac{\tan x - 1}{1 + \tan x} \qquad \ldots\text{(i)}$$

Now, $\tan x = \dfrac{2\tan\frac{x}{2}}{1 - \tan^2\frac{x}{2}}$ $\qquad \left[\because \tan 2x = \dfrac{2\tan x}{1 - \tan^2 x}\right]$

$$= \frac{2 \times \frac{1}{5}}{1 - \left(\frac{1}{5}\right)^2} = \frac{\frac{2}{5}}{\frac{24}{25}} = \frac{5}{12}$$

On putting the value of $\tan x$ in Eq. (i), we get

$$\tan\left(2\tan^{-1}\frac{1}{5} - \frac{\pi}{4}\right) = \frac{\frac{5}{12} - 1}{1 + \frac{5}{12}} = \frac{-7}{17}$$

Matrices

CHAPTER 03

Important Points

01 A matrix of order $m \times n$ is of the form

$$A = \begin{bmatrix} a_{11} & a_{12} & a_{13} & \dots & a_{1n} \\ a_{21} & a_{22} & a_{23} & \dots & a_{2n} \\ \dots & \dots & \dots & \dots & \dots \\ a_{m1} & a_{m2} & a_{m3} & \dots & a_{mn} \end{bmatrix}$$

Its element in the ith row and jth column is a_{ij}.

If $m = n$, the matrix is a square matrix. $\begin{pmatrix} m = \text{no. of rows} \\ n = \text{no. of column} \end{pmatrix}$

02 Type of Matrices Some types of matrices are given below

(i) **Row Matrix** A matrix having only one row is called a row matrix. eg. $[1, \ 2, \ 5,], [-1, 0]$

(ii) **Column Matrix** A matrix having only one column is called a column matrix.

$e.g., \begin{bmatrix} 1 \\ 2 \\ 5 \end{bmatrix}, \begin{bmatrix} 4 \\ \sqrt{5} \end{bmatrix}$

(iii) **Square Matrix** A matrix having equal number of rows and columns called square matrix i.e. $m \times m$ is known as a square matrix of order 'm'.

(iv) **Diagonal Matrix** A square matrix $A = [a_{ij}]_{m \times m}$ is said to be diagonal matrix if all the elements except those in the principal diagonal are zero. *i.e.* $a_{ij} = 0$ when $i \neq j$.

e.g. $\begin{bmatrix} 1 & 0 & 0 \\ 0 & 2 & 0 \\ 0 & 0 & 3 \end{bmatrix}$

It can be written as diagonal (1 2 3) or diagonal [1 2 3]

Note 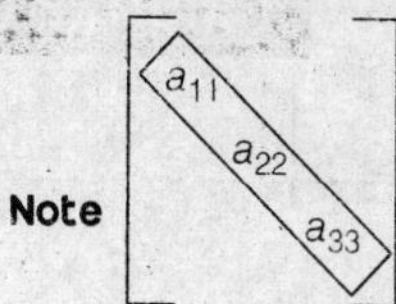

only this is called principal diagonal 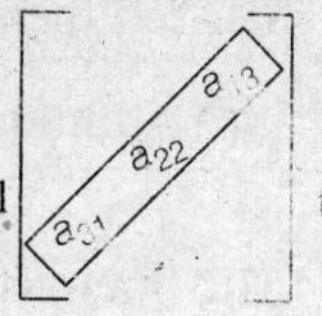

this is not principal diagonal.

(v) **Scalar Matrix** A diagonal matrix $A = [a_{ij}]_{m \times m}$ is said to be scalar matrix if its diagonal elements are equal.

i.e., $a_{ij} = \begin{cases} 0 & i \neq j \\ p & i = j \end{cases}$ for some constant p.

e.g. $\begin{bmatrix} 5 & 0 & 0 \\ 0 & 5 & 0 \\ 0 & 0 & 5 \end{bmatrix}$

(vi) **Unit or Identity Matrix** A square matrix, in which every non-diagonal element is zero and every diagonal element is 1, is called unit matrix or an identity matrix, *i.e.*

$a_{ij} = \begin{cases} 0, \text{when } i \neq j \\ 1, \text{when } i = j \end{cases}$

e.g. $\begin{bmatrix} 1 & 0 & 0 \\ 0 & 1 & 0 \\ 0 & 0 & 1 \end{bmatrix}_3$ or $\begin{bmatrix} 1 & 0 \\ 0 & 1 \end{bmatrix}_2$

(vii) **Zero (Null) Matrix** A matrix is said to be zero or null matrix if each of its elements is '0'.

e.g. = $\begin{bmatrix} 0 & 0 & 0 \\ 0 & 0 & 0 \end{bmatrix}, \begin{bmatrix} 0 \\ 0 \end{bmatrix}$

Equality of matrices

Two matrices $A = [a_{ij}]$ and $B = [b_{ij}]$ are said to be equal if

(i) they are of the same order,

(ii) each element of A is equal to the corresponding element of B, that is $a_{ij} = b_{ij} \forall$ i and j.

03 Operations on Matrices Let $A = \begin{bmatrix} a & b \\ c & d \end{bmatrix}$ and $B = \begin{bmatrix} e & f \\ g & h \end{bmatrix}$ are two matrices, then

(i) Addition of matrices, $A + B = \begin{bmatrix} a+e & b+f \\ c+g & d+h \end{bmatrix}$

(ii) Subtraction of matrices, $A - B = \begin{bmatrix} a-e & b-f \\ c-g & d-h \end{bmatrix}$

(iii) Multiplication of a matrix by a scalar:

$$kA = k\begin{bmatrix} a & b \\ c & d \end{bmatrix} = \begin{bmatrix} ka & kb \\ kc & kd \end{bmatrix}.$$

Where, k is scalar matrix.

(iv) Multiplication of matrices, $A \times B = \begin{bmatrix} ae+bg & af+bh \\ ce+dg & cf+dh \end{bmatrix}$

04 Properties of Addition of Matrices If A, B and C are three matrices of order $m \times n$, then

(i) **Commutative law** $A + B = B + A$

(ii) **Associative law** $(A + B) + C = A + (B + C)$

(iii) **Existence of additive Identity** A zero matrix of order $m \times n$, is addition identity, if $A + O = A = O + A$

(iv) **Existance of additive Inverse** If A is *a* square matrix, then the matrix $(-A)$ is called additive inverse, if

$A + (-A) = O = (-A) + A$

(v) **Cancellation Law**

$A + B = A + C \Rightarrow B = C$ (Left cancellation law)

$B + A = C + A \Rightarrow B = C$ (Right cancellation law)

05 Properties of Scalar Multiplication If A and B are two matrices of order $m \times n$, then

(i) $k(A + B) = kA + kB$

(ii) $(k_1 + k_2)A = k_1A + k_2A$

(iii) $k_1k_2A = k_1(k_2A) = k_2(k_1A)$

(iv) $(-kA) = -(kA) = k(-A)$

Where k, k_1 and k_2 are scalers

06 Properties of Multiplication of Matrices If A, B and C are three matrices such that their products are defined, then

(i) $(AB)C = A(BC)$ (ii) $A(B+C) = AB + AC$

(iii) $(A+B)C = AC + BC$ (iv) $IA = AI = A$

07 Transpose of a Matrix The matrix obtained by interchanging the rows and columns of a given matrix A is called the transpose of A and is denoted by A' or A^T.

08 Properties of Transpose of the Matrices

(i) $(A+B)' = A' + B'$ (ii) $(kA)' = kA'$

(iii) $(AB)' = B'A'$ (iv) $(A')' = A$

09 (i) **Symmetric matrix** A square matrix A is called symmetric, if $A' = A$.

(ii) **Skew-symmetric matrix** A square matrix A is called skew-symmetric, if $A' = -A$.

Note (i) All the diagonal elements of a skew-symmetric matrix are zero.
(ii) If a square matrix is both symmetric and skew symmetric then it will be null matrix.

10 Properties of symmetric and Skew-symmetric matrices

(i) For any square matrix A with real number enteries, $A + A'$ is a symmetric matrix and $A - A'$ is a skew symmetric matrix.

(ii) Any square matrix can be expressed as the sum of a symmetric and a skew-symmetric matrix.

i.e., Matrix A can be written as $\frac{1}{2}(A+A') + \frac{1}{2}(A-A')$.

Where $\frac{1}{2}(A+A')$ is symmetric matrix.

and $\frac{1}{2}(A-A')$ is skew-symmetric matrix.

11 Invertible Matrices

If A is a square matrix of order m and if there exist another square matrix B of the same order m, such that $AB = BA = I$, then B is called the inverse matrix of A and it is denoted by A^{-1}. In that case A is said to be invertible.

12 Properties of Inverse

(i) $AA^{-1} = A^{-1}A = I$ (ii) $(AB)^{-1} = B^{-1}A^{-1}$

(iii) $(A^{-1})^{-1} = A$ (iv) $|A^{-1}| = \frac{1}{|A|}$

(v) $(A')^{-1} = (A^{-1})'$ or $(A^T)^{-1} = (A^{-1})^T$, where A' or A^T is transpose of a matrix A.

Exercise 3.1

Question 1 In the matrix $A=\begin{bmatrix} 2 & 5 & 19 & -7 \\ 35 & -2 & \frac{5}{2} & 12 \\ \sqrt{3} & 1 & -5 & 17 \end{bmatrix}$, write:

(i) The order of the matrix

(ii) The number of elements,

(iii) The elements $a_{13}, a_{21}, a_{33}, a_{24}, a_{23}$.

Sol.

(i) In the given matrix, the number of rows is 3 and the number of columns is 4. Therefore, the order of the matrix is 3×4.

(ii) Since, the order of the matrix is 3×4, so there are $3 \times 4 = 12$ elements in it.

(iii) Let $\begin{bmatrix} 2 & 5 & 19 & -7 \\ 35 & -2 & \frac{5}{2} & 12 \\ \sqrt{3} & 1 & -5 & 17 \end{bmatrix} = \begin{bmatrix} a_{11} & a_{12} & a_{13} & a_{14} \\ a_{21} & a_{22} & a_{23} & a_{24} \\ a_{31} & a_{32} & a_{33} & a_{34} \end{bmatrix}$

On comparing the corresponding elements, we get

$$a_{13} = 19; a_{21} = 35; a_{33} = -5;$$

$$a_{24} = 12; a_{23} = \frac{5}{2}.$$

Question 2 If a matrix has 24 elements, what are the possible orders it can have? What, if it has 13 elements?

Sol. We know that if a matrix is of the order $m \times n$, it has mn elements. Hence, a matrix containing 24 elements can have any one of the following orders :

$$1 \times 24,\ 2 \times 12,\ 3 \times 8,\ 4 \times 6,\ 6 \times 4,\ 8 \times 3,\ 12 \times 2 \text{ or } 24 \times 1$$

Similarly, a matrix containing 13 elements can have order 1×13 or 13×1.

Question 3 If a matrix has 18 elements, what are the possible orders it can have? What, if it has 5 elements?

Sol. A matrix containing 18 elements can have any one of the following orders

$$1 \times 18,\ 18 \times 1,\ 2 \times 9,\ 9 \times 2,\ 3 \times 6, 6 \times 3$$

Similarly, a matrix containing 5 elements can have order 1×5 or 5×1.

Question 4 Construct 2×2 matrix, $A=[a_{ij}]$ whose elements are given by

(i) $a_{ij} = \frac{(i+j)^2}{2}$ (ii) $a_{ij} = \frac{i}{j}$ (iii) $a_{ij} = \frac{(i+2j)^2}{2}$.

Sol.

(i) The order of the given matrix is 2×2, so, $A = \begin{bmatrix} a_{11} & a_{12} \\ a_{21} & a_{22} \end{bmatrix}_{2 \times 2}$, where

$a_{ij} = \frac{(i+j)^2}{2}$. To find a_{11}, put $i=1$ and $j=1$

$$\therefore \quad a_{11} = \frac{(1+1)^2}{2} = 2$$

Similarly, $$a_{12} = \frac{(1+2)^2}{2} = \frac{9}{2},$$

$$a_{21} = \frac{(2+1)^2}{2} = \frac{9}{2} \quad \text{and} \quad a_{22} = \frac{(2+2)^2}{2} = 8$$

Hence, the required matrix is $A = \begin{bmatrix} 2 & 9/2 \\ 9/2 & 8 \end{bmatrix}_{2 \times 2}$.

(ii) Here, $A = \begin{bmatrix} a_{11} & a_{12} \\ a_{21} & a_{22} \end{bmatrix}_{2 \times 2}$, where $a_{ij} = \frac{i}{j}$.

$$\therefore \quad a_{11} = \frac{1}{1} = 1, a_{12} = \frac{1}{2}, \quad a_{21} = \frac{2}{1} = 2 \quad \text{and} \quad a_{22} = \frac{2}{2} = 1$$

Hence, the required matrix is $A = \begin{bmatrix} 1 & 1/2 \\ 2 & 1 \end{bmatrix}_{2 \times 2}$.

(iii) Here, $A = \begin{bmatrix} a_{11} & a_{12} \\ a_{21} & a_{22} \end{bmatrix}_{2 \times 2}$, where $a_{ij} = \frac{(i+2j)^2}{2}$

$$\therefore \quad a_{11} = \frac{(1+2)^2}{2} = \frac{9}{2}, \quad a_{12} = \frac{(1+4)^2}{2} = \frac{25}{2},$$

$$a_{21} = \frac{(2+2)^2}{2} = 8 \quad \text{and} \quad a_{22} = \frac{(2+4)^2}{2} = 18$$

Hence, the required matrix is $A = \begin{bmatrix} 9/2 & 25/2 \\ 8 & 18 \end{bmatrix}_{2 \times 2}$.

Question 5 Construct a 3×4 matrix whose elements are given by

(i) $a_{ij} = \frac{1}{2} |-3i + j|$ (ii) $a_{ij} = 2i - j$.

Sol.

(i) The order of given matrix is 3×4, so let the required matrix is

$$A = \begin{bmatrix} a_{11} & a_{12} & a_{13} & a_{14} \\ a_{21} & a_{22} & a_{23} & a_{24} \\ a_{31} & a_{32} & a_{33} & a_{34} \end{bmatrix}_{3 \times 4}, \text{ where } a_{ij} = \frac{1}{2}|-3i + j|.$$

Putting the values in place of i and j, we will find all the elements of matrix A.

Now, $a_{11} = \frac{1}{2}|-3+1| = 1,\quad a_{12} = \frac{1}{2}|-3+2| = \frac{1}{2}$

$a_{13} = \frac{1}{2}|-3+3| = 0,\quad a_{14} = \frac{1}{2}|-3+4| = \frac{1}{2}$

$a_{21} = \frac{1}{2}|-6+1| = \frac{5}{2},\quad a_{22} = \frac{1}{2}|-6+2| = 2$

$a_{23} = \frac{1}{2}|-6+3| = \frac{3}{2},\quad a_{24} = \frac{1}{2}|-6+4| = 1$

$a_{31} = \frac{1}{2}|-9+1| = 4,\quad a_{32} = \frac{1}{2}|-9+2| = \frac{7}{2}$

$a_{33} = \frac{1}{2}|-9+3| = 3$ and $a_{34} = \frac{1}{2}|-9+4| = \frac{5}{2}$

Hence, the required matrix is $A = \begin{bmatrix} 1 & 1/2 & 0 & 1/2 \\ 5/2 & 2 & 3/2 & 1 \\ 4 & 7/2 & 3 & 5/2 \end{bmatrix}_{3 \times 4}$

(ii) Let $A = \begin{bmatrix} a_{11} & a_{12} & a_{13} & a_{14} \\ a_{21} & a_{22} & a_{23} & a_{24} \\ a_{31} & a_{32} & a_{33} & a_{34} \end{bmatrix}_{3 \times 4}$, where $a_{ij} = 2i - j$

$\therefore$ $a_{11} = 2 - 1 = 1,\quad a_{12} = 2 - 2 = 0,$

$a_{13} = 2 - 3 = -1,\quad a_{14} = 2 - 4 = -2,$

$a_{21} = 4 - 1 = 3,\quad a_{22} = 4 - 2 = 2,$

$a_{23} = 4 - 3 = 1,\quad a_{24} = 4 - 4 = 0$

$a_{31} = 6 - 1 = 5,\quad a_{32} = 6 - 2 = 4,$

$a_{33} = 6 - 3 = 3$ and $a_{34} = 6 - 4 = 2$

Hence, the required matrix is $A = \begin{bmatrix} 1 & 0 & -1 & -2 \\ 3 & 2 & 1 & 0 \\ 5 & 4 & 3 & 2 \end{bmatrix}_{3 \times 4}$.

Question 6 Find the values of x, y and z from the following equations

(i) $\begin{bmatrix} 4 & 3 \\ x & 5 \end{bmatrix} = \begin{bmatrix} y & z \\ 1 & 5 \end{bmatrix}$ (ii) $\begin{bmatrix} x+y & 2 \\ 5+z & xy \end{bmatrix} = \begin{bmatrix} 6 & 2 \\ 5 & 8 \end{bmatrix}$ (iii) $\begin{bmatrix} x+y+z \\ x+z \\ y+z \end{bmatrix} = \begin{bmatrix} 9 \\ 5 \\ 7 \end{bmatrix}$

Sol.

(i) Given, $\begin{bmatrix} 4 & 3 \\ x & 5 \end{bmatrix} = \begin{bmatrix} y & z \\ 1 & 5 \end{bmatrix}$. By definition of equality of matrix as the given matrices are equal, their corresponding elements are equal.

Comparing the corresponding elements, we get

$4 = y,\ 3 = z$ and $x = 1 \Rightarrow x = 1,\ y = 4$ and $z = 3$

(ii) Given, $\begin{bmatrix} x + y & 2 \\ 5 + z & xy \end{bmatrix} = \begin{bmatrix} 6 & 2 \\ 5 & 8 \end{bmatrix}$. By definition of equality of matrix as the given matrices are equal, their corresponding elements are equal.

On comparing the corresponding elements, we get

$$x + y = 6 \quad \text{...(i)}$$

$$5 + z = 5 \quad \text{...(ii)}$$

and $$xy = 8 \quad \text{...(iii)}$$

From Eq. (ii), we get $z = 0$,

From Eq. (i), $y = 6 - x$ ...(iv)

On substituting the value of y in Eq. (iii), we get

$$x(6 - x) = 8 \Rightarrow x^2 - 6x + 8 = 0$$

$$\Rightarrow (x - 2)(x - 4) = 0$$

$$\Rightarrow x = 2$$

or $$x = 4$$

When $x = 2$, then from Eq. (iv), $y = 6 - 2 = 4$ and

when $x = 4$, then from Eq.(iv), $y = 6 - 4 = 2$.

So, either $x = 2,\ y = 4$ and $z = 0$

or $x = 4,\ y = 2$ and $z = 0$

(iii) Given, $\begin{bmatrix} x + y + z \\ x + z \\ y + z \end{bmatrix} = \begin{bmatrix} 9 \\ 5 \\ 7 \end{bmatrix}$. By definition of equality of matrix as the given matrices are equal, their corresponding elements are equal.

On comparing the corresponding elements, we get

$$x + y + z = 9 \quad \text{...(i)}$$

$$x + z = 5 \quad \text{...(ii)}$$

$$y + z = 7 \quad \text{...(iii)}$$

Subtracting Eq. (ii) from Eq. (i), we get $y = 4$

Subtracting Eq. (iii) from Eq. (i), we get $x = 2$

Substituting $y = 4$ in Eq. (iii), we get

$$4 + z = 7$$

$$\Rightarrow z = 7 - 4 = 3$$

Hence, $x = 2,\ y = 4,\ z = 3$

Question 7 Find the values of a, b, c and d from the equation
$$\begin{bmatrix} a-b & 2a+c \\ 2a-b & 3c+d \end{bmatrix} = \begin{bmatrix} -1 & 5 \\ 0 & 13 \end{bmatrix}.$$

◎ ***Thinking Process*** If two matrices are equal then their corresponding elements are equal. So, to find the values of a, b and c, equate the elements and frame the equations and solve them.

Sol. Given, $\begin{bmatrix} a-b & 2a+c \\ 2a-b & 3c+d \end{bmatrix} = \begin{bmatrix} -1 & 5 \\ 0 & 13 \end{bmatrix}$

By definition of equality of matrix as the given matrices are equal, their corresponding elements are equal.
On comparing the corresponding elements, we get

$$a - b = -1 \quad \text{...(i)}$$
$$2a - b = 0 \quad \text{...(ii)}$$
$$2a + c = 5 \quad \text{...(iii)}$$

and $$3c + d = 13 \quad \text{...(iv)}$$

On subtracting Eq.(i) from Eq.(ii), we get $a = 1$
Putting $a = 1$ in Eq. (i) and Eq. (iii), we get

$$1 - b = -1 \text{ and } 2 + c = 5$$
$$\Rightarrow \quad b = 2 \text{ and } c = 3$$

Substituting $c = 3$ in Eq. (iv), we get

$$3 \times 3 + d = 13$$
$$\Rightarrow \quad d = 13 - 9 = 4$$

Hence, $a = 1$, $b = 2$, $c = 3$ and $d = 4$.

Question 8 $A = [a_{ij}]_{m \times n}$ is an square matrix, if

(a) $m < n$ (b) $m > n$
(c) $m = n$ (d) None of these

Sol. (c) Since, in an square matrix, the number of rows is equal to the number of columns, therefore, we must have $m = n$.

Question 9 Which of the given values of x and y make the following pairs of matrices equal $\begin{bmatrix} 3x+7 & 5 \\ y+1 & 2-3x \end{bmatrix}, \begin{bmatrix} 0 & y-2 \\ 8 & 4 \end{bmatrix}$?

(a) $x = \frac{-1}{3}, y = 7$ (b) Not possible to find
(c) $y = 7, x = \frac{-2}{3}$ (d) $x = \frac{-1}{3}, y = \frac{-2}{3}$

Sol. (b) Given, $\begin{bmatrix} 3x+7 & 5 \\ y+1 & 2-3x \end{bmatrix} = \begin{bmatrix} 0 & y-2 \\ 8 & 4 \end{bmatrix}$

By definition of equality of matrices, we get

$$3x + 7 = 0 \quad \ldots(i)$$
$$5 = y - 2 \quad \ldots(ii)$$
$$y + 1 = 8 \quad \ldots(iii)$$
$$2 - 3x = 4 \quad \ldots(iv)$$

From Eq. (ii), $y = 7$

From Eq. (i), $3x + 7 = 0 \Rightarrow x = \frac{-7}{3}$

From Eq. (iv), $2 - 3x = 4 \Rightarrow x = \frac{-2}{3}$

Since, x can have only one value at a time. Hence, it is not possible to find the values of x and y for which the given matrices are equal.

> **Note** Sometimes on solving an equation, we get more than one values of the variables. This means that such a matrix does not exist.

Question 10 The number of all possible matrices of order 3×3 with each entry 0 to 1 is

(a) 27 (b) 18 (c) 81 (d) 512

Sol. (d) As order of 3×3 matrix contains 9 elements. Each element can be selected in 2 ways (it can be either 0 or 1).

Hence, all the nine entries can be chosen in $2^9 = 512$ ways

(By the multiplication principle)

$\therefore$ Required number of matrices is 512.

Exercise 3.2

Question 1 Let $A = \begin{bmatrix} 2 & 4 \\ 3 & 2 \end{bmatrix}$, $B = \begin{bmatrix} 1 & 3 \\ -2 & 5 \end{bmatrix}$, $C = \begin{bmatrix} -2 & 5 \\ 3 & 4 \end{bmatrix}$. Find each of the following:

(i) $A + B$ (ii) $A - B$

(iii) $3A - C$ (iv) AB (v) BA

Sol.

(i) $A + B = \begin{bmatrix} 2 & 4 \\ 3 & 2 \end{bmatrix} + \begin{bmatrix} 1 & 3 \\ -2 & 5 \end{bmatrix} = \begin{bmatrix} 2+1 & 4+3 \\ 3+(-2) & 2+5 \end{bmatrix} = \begin{bmatrix} 3 & 7 \\ 1 & 7 \end{bmatrix}$

(ii) $A - B = \begin{bmatrix} 2 & 4 \\ 3 & 2 \end{bmatrix} - \begin{bmatrix} 1 & 3 \\ -2 & 5 \end{bmatrix} = \begin{bmatrix} 2-1 & 4-3 \\ 3-(-2) & 2-5 \end{bmatrix} = \begin{bmatrix} 1 & 1 \\ 5 & -3 \end{bmatrix}$

(iii) $3A - C = 3\begin{bmatrix} 2 & 4 \\ 3 & 2 \end{bmatrix} - \begin{bmatrix} -2 & 5 \\ 3 & 4 \end{bmatrix} = \begin{bmatrix} 6 & 12 \\ 9 & 6 \end{bmatrix} - \begin{bmatrix} -2 & 5 \\ 3 & 4 \end{bmatrix}$

$$= \begin{bmatrix} 6-(-2) & 12-5 \\ 9-3 & 6-4 \end{bmatrix} = \begin{bmatrix} 8 & 7 \\ 6 & 2 \end{bmatrix}$$

(iv) $AB = \begin{bmatrix} 2 & 4 \\ 3 & 2 \end{bmatrix}\begin{bmatrix} 1 & 3 \\ -2 & 5 \end{bmatrix} = \begin{bmatrix} 2\times 1 + 4\times(-2) & 2\times 3 + 4\times 5 \\ 3\times 1 + 2\times(-2) & 3\times 3 + 2\times 5 \end{bmatrix} = \begin{bmatrix} -6 & 26 \\ -1 & 19 \end{bmatrix}$

(v) $BA = \begin{bmatrix} 1 & 3 \\ -2 & 5 \end{bmatrix}\begin{bmatrix} 2 & 4 \\ 3 & 2 \end{bmatrix} = \begin{bmatrix} 1\times 2 + 3\times 3 & 1\times 4 + 3\times 2 \\ (-2)\times 2 + 5\times 3 & (-2)\times 4 + 5\times 2 \end{bmatrix} = \begin{bmatrix} 11 & 10 \\ 11 & 2 \end{bmatrix}$

Note If two matrices have different orders then we can neither add nor subtract the matrices but we can multiply the matrices either the orders are same or number of columns of first matrix is equal to the number of rows of second matrix.

Question 2 Compute the following

(i) $\begin{bmatrix} a & b \\ -b & a \end{bmatrix} + \begin{bmatrix} a & b \\ b & a \end{bmatrix}$

(ii) $\begin{bmatrix} a^2+b^2 & b^2+c^2 \\ a^2+c^2 & a^2+b^2 \end{bmatrix} + \begin{bmatrix} 2ab & 2bc \\ -2ac & -2ab \end{bmatrix}$

(iii) $\begin{bmatrix} -1 & 4 & -6 \\ 8 & 5 & 16 \\ 2 & 8 & 5 \end{bmatrix} + \begin{bmatrix} 12 & 7 & 6 \\ 8 & 0 & 5 \\ 3 & 2 & 4 \end{bmatrix}$

(iv) $\begin{bmatrix} \cos^2 x & \sin^2 x \\ \sin^2 x & \cos^2 x \end{bmatrix} + \begin{bmatrix} \sin^2 x & \cos^2 x \\ \cos^2 x & \sin^2 x \end{bmatrix}$

Sol.

(i) We have, $\begin{bmatrix} a & b \\ -b & a \end{bmatrix} + \begin{bmatrix} a & b \\ b & a \end{bmatrix} = \begin{bmatrix} a+a & b+b \\ -b+b & a+a \end{bmatrix} = \begin{bmatrix} 2a & 2b \\ 0 & 2a \end{bmatrix}$.

(ii) We have, $\begin{bmatrix} a^2+b^2 & b^2+c^2 \\ a^2+c^2 & a^2+b^2 \end{bmatrix} + \begin{bmatrix} 2ab & 2bc \\ -2ac & -2ab \end{bmatrix}$

$$= \begin{bmatrix} a^2+b^2+2ab & b^2+c^2+2bc \\ a^2+c^2-2ac & a^2+b^2-2ab \end{bmatrix}$$

$$= \begin{bmatrix} (a+b)^2 & (b+c)^2 \\ (a-c)^2 & (a-b)^2 \end{bmatrix} \quad \left[\because \begin{array}{l} (a+b)^2 = a^2+2ab+b^2 \\ (a-b)^2 = a^2-2ab+b^2 \end{array}\right]$$

(iii) We have, $\begin{bmatrix} -1 & 4 & -6 \\ 8 & 5 & 16 \\ 2 & 8 & 5 \end{bmatrix} + \begin{bmatrix} 12 & 7 & 6 \\ 8 & 0 & 5 \\ 3 & 2 & 4 \end{bmatrix} = \begin{bmatrix} -1+12 & 4+7 & -6+6 \\ 8+8 & 5+0 & 16+5 \\ 2+3 & 8+2 & 5+4 \end{bmatrix}$

$$= \begin{bmatrix} 11 & 11 & 0 \\ 16 & 5 & 21 \\ 5 & 10 & 9 \end{bmatrix}.$$

(iv) We have, $\begin{bmatrix} \cos^2 x & \sin^2 x \\ \sin^2 x & \cos^2 x \end{bmatrix} + \begin{bmatrix} \sin^2 x & \cos^2 x \\ \cos^2 x & \sin^2 x \end{bmatrix}$

$$= \begin{bmatrix} \cos^2 x + \sin^2 x & \sin^2 x + \cos^2 x \\ \sin^2 x + \cos^2 x & \cos^2 x + \sin^2 x \end{bmatrix} = \begin{bmatrix} 1 & 1 \\ 1 & 1 \end{bmatrix} \quad [\because \sin^2 A + \cos^2 A = 1]$$

Question 3 Compute the indicated products.

(i) $\begin{bmatrix} a & b \\ -b & a \end{bmatrix}\begin{bmatrix} a & -b \\ b & a \end{bmatrix}$ (ii) $\begin{bmatrix} 1 \\ 2 \\ 3 \end{bmatrix}[2 \quad 3 \quad 4]$

(iii) $\begin{bmatrix} 1 & -2 \\ 2 & 3 \end{bmatrix}\begin{bmatrix} 1 & 2 & 3 \\ 2 & 3 & 1 \end{bmatrix}$ (iv) $\begin{bmatrix} 2 & 3 & 4 \\ 3 & 4 & 5 \\ 4 & 5 & 6 \end{bmatrix}\begin{bmatrix} 1 & -3 & 5 \\ 0 & 2 & 4 \\ 3 & 0 & 5 \end{bmatrix}$

(v) $\begin{bmatrix} 2 & 1 \\ 3 & 2 \\ -1 & 1 \end{bmatrix}\begin{bmatrix} 1 & 0 & 1 \\ -1 & 2 & 1 \end{bmatrix}$ (vi) $\begin{bmatrix} 3 & -1 & 3 \\ -1 & 0 & 2 \end{bmatrix}\begin{bmatrix} 2 & -3 \\ 1 & 0 \\ 3 & 1 \end{bmatrix}$

Sol.

(i) We have, $\begin{bmatrix} a & b \\ -b & a \end{bmatrix}\begin{bmatrix} a & -b \\ b & a \end{bmatrix} = \begin{bmatrix} a \times a + b \times b & a \times (-b) + b \times a \\ (-b) \times a + a \times b & (-b) \times (-b) + a \times a \end{bmatrix}$

$$= \begin{bmatrix} a^2 + b^2 & -ab + ab \\ -ab + ab & b^2 + a^2 \end{bmatrix} = \begin{bmatrix} a^2 + b^2 & 0 \\ 0 & b^2 + a^2 \end{bmatrix}$$

(ii) $\begin{bmatrix} 1 \\ 2 \\ 3 \end{bmatrix}_{3 \times 1} [2 \quad 3 \quad 4]_{1 \times 3} = \begin{bmatrix} 1 \times 2 & 1 \times 3 & 1 \times 4 \\ 2 \times 2 & 2 \times 3 & 2 \times 4 \\ 3 \times 2 & 3 \times 3 & 3 \times 4 \end{bmatrix}_{3 \times 3} = \begin{bmatrix} 2 & 3 & 4 \\ 4 & 6 & 8 \\ 6 & 9 & 12 \end{bmatrix}$

(iii) $\begin{bmatrix} 1 & -2 \\ 2 & 3 \end{bmatrix}\begin{bmatrix} 1 & 2 & 3 \\ 2 & 3 & 1 \end{bmatrix} = \begin{bmatrix} 1 \times 1 + (-2) \times 2 & 1 \times 2 + (-2) \times 3 & 1 \times 3 + (-2) \times 1 \\ 2 \times 1 + 3 \times 2 & 2 \times 2 + 3 \times 3 & 2 \times 3 + 3 \times 1 \end{bmatrix}$

$$= \begin{bmatrix} -3 & -4 & 1 \\ 8 & 13 & 9 \end{bmatrix}$$

(iv) $\begin{bmatrix} 2 & 3 & 4 \\ 3 & 4 & 5 \\ 4 & 5 & 6 \end{bmatrix}\begin{bmatrix} 1 & -3 & 5 \\ 0 & 2 & 4 \\ 3 & 0 & 5 \end{bmatrix} = \begin{bmatrix} 2+0+12 & -6+6+0 & 10+12+20 \\ 3+0+15 & -9+8+0 & 15+16+25 \\ 4+0+18 & -12+10+0 & 20+20+30 \end{bmatrix}$

$= \begin{bmatrix} 14 & 0 & 42 \\ 18 & -1 & 56 \\ 22 & -2 & 70 \end{bmatrix}$

(v) $\begin{bmatrix} 2 & 1 \\ 3 & 2 \\ -1 & 1 \end{bmatrix}\begin{bmatrix} 1 & 0 & 1 \\ -1 & 2 & 1 \end{bmatrix} = \begin{bmatrix} 2-1 & 0+2 & 2+1 \\ 3-2 & 0+4 & 3+2 \\ -1-1 & 0+2 & -1+1 \end{bmatrix} = \begin{bmatrix} 1 & 2 & 3 \\ 1 & 4 & 5 \\ -2 & 2 & 0 \end{bmatrix}$

(vi) $\begin{bmatrix} 3 & -1 & 3 \\ -1 & 0 & 2 \end{bmatrix}\begin{bmatrix} 2 & -3 \\ 1 & 0 \\ 3 & 1 \end{bmatrix} = \begin{bmatrix} 6-1+9 & -9+0+3 \\ -2+0+6 & 3+0+2 \end{bmatrix} = \begin{bmatrix} 14 & -6 \\ 4 & 5 \end{bmatrix}$

Question 4 If $A = \begin{bmatrix} 1 & 2 & -3 \\ 5 & 0 & 2 \\ 1 & -1 & 1 \end{bmatrix}$, $B = \begin{bmatrix} 3 & -1 & 2 \\ 4 & 2 & 5 \\ 2 & 0 & 3 \end{bmatrix}$ and $C = \begin{bmatrix} 4 & 1 & 2 \\ 0 & 3 & 2 \\ 1 & -2 & 3 \end{bmatrix}$

then compute $(A+B)$ and $(B-C)$. Also verify that $A+(B-C)=(A+B)-C$.

Sol. We have, $A+B = \begin{bmatrix} 1 & 2 & -3 \\ 5 & 0 & 2 \\ 1 & -1 & 1 \end{bmatrix} + \begin{bmatrix} 3 & -1 & 2 \\ 4 & 2 & 5 \\ 2 & 0 & 3 \end{bmatrix} = \begin{bmatrix} 4 & 1 & -1 \\ 9 & 2 & 7 \\ 3 & -1 & 4 \end{bmatrix}$

and $B-C = \begin{bmatrix} 3 & -1 & 2 \\ 4 & 2 & 5 \\ 2 & 0 & 3 \end{bmatrix} - \begin{bmatrix} 4 & 1 & 2 \\ 0 & 3 & 2 \\ 1 & -2 & 3 \end{bmatrix} = \begin{bmatrix} -1 & -2 & 0 \\ 4 & -1 & 3 \\ 1 & 2 & 0 \end{bmatrix}$

$\therefore \quad (A+B)-C = \begin{bmatrix} 4 & 1 & -1 \\ 9 & 2 & 7 \\ 3 & -1 & 4 \end{bmatrix} - \begin{bmatrix} 4 & 1 & 2 \\ 0 & 3 & 2 \\ 1 & -2 & 3 \end{bmatrix} = \begin{bmatrix} 0 & 0 & -3 \\ 9 & -1 & 5 \\ 2 & 1 & 1 \end{bmatrix}$

and $A+(B-C) = \begin{bmatrix} 1 & 2 & -3 \\ 5 & 0 & 2 \\ 1 & -1 & 1 \end{bmatrix} + \begin{bmatrix} -1 & -2 & 0 \\ 4 & -1 & 3 \\ 1 & 2 & 0 \end{bmatrix} = \begin{bmatrix} 0 & 0 & -3 \\ 9 & -1 & 5 \\ 2 & 1 & 1 \end{bmatrix}$

Hence, $(A+B)-C = A+(B-C)$ is verified.

Question 5 If $A = \begin{bmatrix} 2/3 & 1 & 5/3 \\ 1/3 & 2/3 & 4/3 \\ 7/3 & 2 & 2/3 \end{bmatrix}$ and $B = \begin{bmatrix} 2/5 & 3/5 & 1 \\ 1/5 & 2/5 & 4/5 \\ 7/5 & 6/5 & 2/5 \end{bmatrix}$, then compute $3A-5B$.

◎ ***Thinking Process*** Firstly, multiply each element of A by 3 and each element of B by 5, then subtract.

Sol. We have, $3A - 5B$

$$= 3\begin{bmatrix} 2/3 & 1 & 5/3 \\ 1/3 & 2/3 & 4/3 \\ 7/3 & 2 & 2/3 \end{bmatrix} - 5\begin{bmatrix} 2/5 & 3/5 & 1 \\ 1/5 & 2/5 & 4/5 \\ 7/5 & 6/5 & 2/5 \end{bmatrix}$$

$$= \begin{bmatrix} 2 & 3 & 5 \\ 1 & 2 & 4 \\ 7 & 6 & 2 \end{bmatrix} - \begin{bmatrix} 2 & 3 & 5 \\ 1 & 2 & 4 \\ 7 & 6 & 2 \end{bmatrix} = \begin{bmatrix} 0 & 0 & 0 \\ 0 & 0 & 0 \\ 0 & 0 & 0 \end{bmatrix}$$

Question 6 Simplify $\cos\theta\begin{bmatrix} \cos\theta & \sin\theta \\ -\sin\theta & \cos\theta \end{bmatrix} + \sin\theta\begin{bmatrix} \sin\theta & -\cos\theta \\ \cos\theta & \sin\theta \end{bmatrix}$.

Sol. We have, $\cos\theta\begin{bmatrix} \cos\theta & \sin\theta \\ -\sin\theta & \cos\theta \end{bmatrix} + \sin\theta\begin{bmatrix} \sin\theta & -\cos\theta \\ \cos\theta & \sin\theta \end{bmatrix}$

$$= \begin{bmatrix} \cos^2\theta & \sin\theta\cos\theta \\ -\cos\theta\sin\theta & \cos^2\theta \end{bmatrix} + \begin{bmatrix} \sin^2\theta & -\sin\theta\cos\theta \\ \cos\theta\sin\theta & \sin^2\theta \end{bmatrix}$$

$$= \begin{bmatrix} \cos^2\theta + \sin^2\theta & \cos\theta\sin\theta - \sin\theta\cos\theta \\ -\cos\theta\sin\theta + \sin\theta\cos\theta & \cos^2\theta + \sin^2\theta \end{bmatrix}$$

$$= \begin{bmatrix} 1 & 0 \\ 0 & 1 \end{bmatrix}. \qquad [\because \cos^2 A + \sin^2 A = 1]$$

Question 7 Find X and Y if

(i) $X + Y = \begin{bmatrix} 7 & 0 \\ 2 & 5 \end{bmatrix}$ and $X - Y = \begin{bmatrix} 3 & 0 \\ 0 & 3 \end{bmatrix}$

(ii) $2X + 3Y = \begin{bmatrix} 2 & 3 \\ 4 & 0 \end{bmatrix}$ and $3X + 2Y = \begin{bmatrix} 2 & -2 \\ -1 & 5 \end{bmatrix}$

Sol.

(i) Given, $X + Y = \begin{bmatrix} 7 & 0 \\ 2 & 5 \end{bmatrix}$ ...(i)

and $X - Y = \begin{bmatrix} 3 & 0 \\ 0 & 3 \end{bmatrix}$ ...(ii)

On adding Eqs. (i) and (ii), we get

$$2X = \begin{bmatrix} 7 & 0 \\ 2 & 5 \end{bmatrix} + \begin{bmatrix} 3 & 0 \\ 0 & 3 \end{bmatrix} = \begin{bmatrix} 10 & 0 \\ 2 & 8 \end{bmatrix} \Rightarrow X = \frac{1}{2}\begin{bmatrix} 10 & 0 \\ 2 & 8 \end{bmatrix} = \begin{bmatrix} 5 & 0 \\ 1 & 4 \end{bmatrix}$$

On subtracting Eq. (ii) from Eq. (i), we get

$$2Y = \begin{bmatrix} 7 & 0 \\ 2 & 5 \end{bmatrix} - \begin{bmatrix} 3 & 0 \\ 0 & 3 \end{bmatrix} = \begin{bmatrix} 4 & 0 \\ 2 & 2 \end{bmatrix} \Rightarrow Y = \frac{1}{2}\begin{bmatrix} 4 & 0 \\ 2 & 2 \end{bmatrix} = \begin{bmatrix} 2 & 0 \\ 1 & 1 \end{bmatrix}$$

(ii) Given, $2X + 3Y = \begin{bmatrix} 2 & 3 \\ 4 & 0 \end{bmatrix}$ ...(i)

and $3X + 2Y = \begin{bmatrix} 2 & -2 \\ -1 & 5 \end{bmatrix}$ ...(ii)

On multiplying Eq. (i) by 2, Eq. (ii) by 3 and then subtracting, we get

$$2(2X + 3Y) - 3(3X + 2Y) = 2\begin{bmatrix} 2 & 3 \\ 4 & 0 \end{bmatrix} - 3\begin{bmatrix} 2 & -2 \\ -1 & 5 \end{bmatrix}$$

$$\Rightarrow \quad 4X + 6Y - 9X - 6Y = \begin{bmatrix} 4 & 6 \\ 8 & 0 \end{bmatrix} - \begin{bmatrix} 6 & -6 \\ -3 & 15 \end{bmatrix}$$

$$\Rightarrow \quad -5X = \begin{bmatrix} 4-6 & 6+6 \\ 8+3 & 0-15 \end{bmatrix} = \begin{bmatrix} -2 & 12 \\ 11 & -15 \end{bmatrix}$$

$$\Rightarrow \quad X = -\frac{1}{5}\begin{bmatrix} -2 & 12 \\ 11 & -15 \end{bmatrix} = \begin{bmatrix} 2/5 & -12/5 \\ -11/5 & 3 \end{bmatrix}$$

Then, from Eq. (i), $3Y = \begin{bmatrix} 2 & 3 \\ 4 & 0 \end{bmatrix} - 2X = \begin{bmatrix} 2 & 3 \\ 4 & 0 \end{bmatrix} - 2\begin{bmatrix} 2/5 & -12/5 \\ -11/5 & 3 \end{bmatrix}$

$$= \begin{bmatrix} 2 - \frac{4}{5} & 3 + \frac{24}{5} \\ 4 + \frac{22}{5} & 0 - 6 \end{bmatrix} = \begin{bmatrix} 6/5 & 39/5 \\ 42/5 & -6 \end{bmatrix}$$

$$\therefore \quad Y = \frac{1}{3}\begin{bmatrix} 6/5 & 39/5 \\ 42/5 & -6 \end{bmatrix} = \begin{bmatrix} 2/5 & 13/5 \\ 14/5 & -2 \end{bmatrix}$$

Question 8 Find X, if $Y = \begin{bmatrix} 3 & 2 \\ 1 & 4 \end{bmatrix}$ and $2X + Y = \begin{bmatrix} 1 & 0 \\ -3 & 2 \end{bmatrix}$.

Sol. Given, $2X + Y = \begin{bmatrix} 1 & 0 \\ -3 & 2 \end{bmatrix}$ and $Y = \begin{bmatrix} 3 & 2 \\ 1 & 4 \end{bmatrix}$

$$\Rightarrow \quad 2X = \begin{bmatrix} 1 & 0 \\ -3 & 2 \end{bmatrix} - Y = \begin{bmatrix} 1 & 0 \\ -3 & 2 \end{bmatrix} - \begin{bmatrix} 3 & 2 \\ 1 & 4 \end{bmatrix} = \begin{bmatrix} 1-3 & 0-2 \\ -3-1 & 2-4 \end{bmatrix} = \begin{bmatrix} -2 & -2 \\ -4 & -2 \end{bmatrix}$$

$$\Rightarrow \quad X = \frac{1}{2}\begin{bmatrix} -2 & -2 \\ -4 & -2 \end{bmatrix} = \begin{bmatrix} -1 & -1 \\ -2 & -1 \end{bmatrix}$$

Question 9 Find x and y, if $2\begin{bmatrix} 1 & 3 \\ 0 & x \end{bmatrix} + \begin{bmatrix} y & 0 \\ 1 & 2 \end{bmatrix} = \begin{bmatrix} 5 & 6 \\ 1 & 8 \end{bmatrix}$.

Sol. Given, $2\begin{bmatrix} 1 & 3 \\ 0 & x \end{bmatrix} + \begin{bmatrix} y & 0 \\ 1 & 2 \end{bmatrix} = \begin{bmatrix} 5 & 6 \\ 1 & 8 \end{bmatrix} \Rightarrow \begin{bmatrix} 2+y & 6+0 \\ 0+1 & 2x+2 \end{bmatrix} = \begin{bmatrix} 5 & 6 \\ 1 & 8 \end{bmatrix}$

By definition of equality of matrix as the given matrices are equal, their corresponding elements are equal.

On comparing the corresponding elements, we get

$$2 + y = 5 \quad \text{...(i)}$$

and

$$2x + 2 = 8 \quad \text{...(ii)}$$

$\Rightarrow \quad y = 5 - 2 = 3$ and $2x = 8 - 2$

$\Rightarrow \quad y = 3$ and $x = \dfrac{6}{2} = 3$

Question 10 Solve the equation of x, y, z and t, if

$$2\begin{bmatrix} x & z \\ y & t \end{bmatrix} + 3\begin{bmatrix} 1 & -1 \\ 0 & 2 \end{bmatrix} = 3\begin{bmatrix} 3 & 5 \\ 4 & 6 \end{bmatrix}.$$

Sol. Given, $2\begin{bmatrix} x & z \\ y & t \end{bmatrix} + 3\begin{bmatrix} 1 & -1 \\ 0 & 2 \end{bmatrix} = 3\begin{bmatrix} 3 & 5 \\ 4 & 6 \end{bmatrix}$

$$\Rightarrow \begin{bmatrix} 2x & 2z \\ 2y & 2t \end{bmatrix} + \begin{bmatrix} 3 & -3 \\ 0 & 6 \end{bmatrix} = \begin{bmatrix} 9 & 15 \\ 12 & 18 \end{bmatrix}$$

$$\Rightarrow \begin{bmatrix} 2x + 3 & 2z - 3 \\ 2y + 0 & 2t + 6 \end{bmatrix} = \begin{bmatrix} 9 & 15 \\ 12 & 18 \end{bmatrix}$$

By definition of equality of matrix as the given matrices are equal, their corresponding elements are equal.

On comparing the corresponding elements, we get

$$2x + 3 = 9, \quad 2y + 0 = 12, \quad 2z - 3 = 15 \quad \text{and} \quad 2t + 6 = 18$$

$$\Rightarrow \quad x = \frac{9-3}{2}, \quad y = \frac{12}{2}, \quad z = \frac{15+3}{2} \quad \text{and} \quad t = \frac{18-6}{2}$$

$$\Rightarrow \quad x = 3, \quad y = 6, \quad z = 9 \quad \text{and} \quad t = 6.$$

Question 11 If $x\begin{bmatrix} 2 \\ 3 \end{bmatrix} + y\begin{bmatrix} -1 \\ 1 \end{bmatrix} = \begin{bmatrix} 10 \\ 5 \end{bmatrix}$, find the values of x and y.

Sol. Given, $x\begin{bmatrix} 2 \\ 3 \end{bmatrix} + y\begin{bmatrix} -1 \\ 1 \end{bmatrix} = \begin{bmatrix} 10 \\ 5 \end{bmatrix} \Rightarrow \begin{bmatrix} 2x + y(-1) \\ 3x + y \end{bmatrix} = \begin{bmatrix} 10 \\ 5 \end{bmatrix}$

By definition of equality of matrix as the given matrices are equal, their corresponding elements are equal.

On comparing the corresponding elements, we get

$$2x - y = 10 \quad \text{...(i)}$$

and

$$3x + y = 5 \quad \text{...(ii)}$$

On adding Eqs. (i) and (ii), we get

$$5x = 15$$

$$\Rightarrow \quad x = 3$$

On substituting $x = 3$ in Eq. (i), we get

$$2 \times 3 - y = 10$$

$$\Rightarrow \quad y = 6 - 10 = -4$$

Question 12 If $3\begin{bmatrix} x & y \\ z & w \end{bmatrix} = \begin{bmatrix} x & 6 \\ -1 & 2w \end{bmatrix} + \begin{bmatrix} 4 & x+y \\ z+w & 3 \end{bmatrix}$, find the values of x, y, z and w.

Sol. Given, $3\begin{bmatrix} x & y \\ z & w \end{bmatrix} = \begin{bmatrix} x & 6 \\ -1 & 2w \end{bmatrix} + \begin{bmatrix} 4 & x+y \\ z+w & 3 \end{bmatrix}$

$$\Rightarrow \quad \begin{bmatrix} 3x & 3y \\ 3z & 3w \end{bmatrix} = \begin{bmatrix} x+4 & 6+x+y \\ -1+z+w & 2w+3 \end{bmatrix}$$

By definition of equality of matrix as the given matrices are equal, their corresponding elements are equal.

On comparing the corresponding elements, we get

$$3x = x + 4 \Rightarrow 2x = 4 \Rightarrow x = 2$$

$$3y = 6 + x + y \Rightarrow 2y = 6 + x \Rightarrow y = \frac{6+x}{2}$$

$$\Rightarrow \quad y = \frac{6+2}{2} \quad [\because x = 2]$$

$$\Rightarrow \quad y = 4$$

$$3z = -1 + z + w \Rightarrow 2z = -1 + w$$

$$\Rightarrow \quad z = \frac{-1+w}{2} \quad \text{...(i)}$$

and $\quad 3w = 2w + 3 \Rightarrow w = 3$

Putting the value of w in Eq. (i), we get

$$z = \frac{-1+3}{2} = \frac{2}{2} = 1$$

Hence, the values of x, y, z and w are 2, 4, 1 and 3 respectively.

Question 13 If $F(x) = \begin{bmatrix} \cos x & -\sin x & 0 \\ \sin x & \cos x & 0 \\ 0 & 0 & 1 \end{bmatrix}$, then show that $F(x)F(y) = F(x+y)$.

◎ **Thinking Process** For $F(y)$, replace x in $F(x)$ by y. and for $F(x+y)$, replace x in $F(x)$ by $(x+y)$. Now, multiply $F(x)$ and $F(y)$ using matrix multiplication and solve it to get the desired result.

Sol. We have, $F(x)F(y) = F(x+y)$

$$\text{LHS} = F(x)\,F(y) = \begin{bmatrix} \cos x & -\sin x & 0 \\ \sin x & \cos x & 0 \\ 0 & 0 & 1 \end{bmatrix}\begin{bmatrix} \cos y & -\sin y & 0 \\ \sin y & \cos y & 0 \\ 0 & 0 & 1 \end{bmatrix}$$

$$= \begin{bmatrix} \cos x \cos y - \sin x \sin y & -\sin y \cos x - \sin x \cos y & 0 \\ \sin x \cos y + \cos x \sin y & -\sin x \sin y + \cos x \cos y & 0 \\ 0 & 0 & 1 \end{bmatrix}$$

$$= \begin{bmatrix} \cos(x+y) & -\sin(x+y) & 0 \\ \sin(x+y) & \cos(x+y) & 0 \\ 0 & 0 & 1 \end{bmatrix} \quad \begin{bmatrix} \because \cos(A+B) = \cos A \cos B - \sin A \sin B \\ \sin(A+B) = \sin A \cos B + \sin B \cos A \end{bmatrix}$$

$= F(x+y) =$ RHS. **Hence Proved.**

Question 14 Show that

(i) $\begin{bmatrix} 5 & -1 \\ 6 & 7 \end{bmatrix}\begin{bmatrix} 2 & 1 \\ 3 & 4 \end{bmatrix} \neq \begin{bmatrix} 2 & 1 \\ 3 & 4 \end{bmatrix}\begin{bmatrix} 5 & -1 \\ 6 & 7 \end{bmatrix}$

(ii) $\begin{bmatrix} 1 & 2 & 3 \\ 0 & 1 & 0 \\ 1 & 1 & 0 \end{bmatrix}\begin{bmatrix} -1 & 1 & 0 \\ 0 & -1 & 1 \\ 2 & 3 & 4 \end{bmatrix} \neq \begin{bmatrix} -1 & 1 & 0 \\ 0 & -1 & 1 \\ 2 & 3 & 4 \end{bmatrix}\begin{bmatrix} 1 & 2 & 3 \\ 0 & 1 & 0 \\ 1 & 1 & 0 \end{bmatrix}$

Sol.

(i) We have, $\begin{bmatrix} 5 & -1 \\ 6 & 7 \end{bmatrix}\begin{bmatrix} 2 & 1 \\ 3 & 4 \end{bmatrix} = \begin{bmatrix} 10-3 & 5-4 \\ 12+21 & 6+28 \end{bmatrix} = \begin{bmatrix} 7 & 1 \\ 33 & 34 \end{bmatrix}$

and $\begin{bmatrix} 2 & 1 \\ 3 & 4 \end{bmatrix}\begin{bmatrix} 5 & -1 \\ 6 & 7 \end{bmatrix} = \begin{bmatrix} 10+6 & -2+7 \\ 15+24 & -3+28 \end{bmatrix} = \begin{bmatrix} 16 & 5 \\ 39 & 25 \end{bmatrix}$

Hence, $\begin{bmatrix} 5 & -1 \\ 6 & 7 \end{bmatrix}\begin{bmatrix} 2 & 1 \\ 3 & 4 \end{bmatrix} \neq \begin{bmatrix} 2 & 1 \\ 3 & 4 \end{bmatrix}\begin{bmatrix} 5 & -1 \\ 6 & 7 \end{bmatrix}$

(ii) Here, $\begin{bmatrix} 1 & 2 & 3 \\ 0 & 1 & 0 \\ 1 & 1 & 0 \end{bmatrix}\begin{bmatrix} -1 & 1 & 0 \\ 0 & -1 & 1 \\ 2 & 3 & 4 \end{bmatrix} = \begin{bmatrix} -1+0+6 & 1-2+9 & 0+2+12 \\ 0+0+0 & 0+(-1)+0 & 0+1+0 \\ -1+0+0 & 1-1+0 & 0+1+0 \end{bmatrix}$

$$= \begin{bmatrix} 5 & 8 & 14 \\ 0 & -1 & 1 \\ -1 & 0 & 1 \end{bmatrix}$$

and $\begin{bmatrix} -1 & 1 & 0 \\ 0 & -1 & 1 \\ 2 & 3 & 4 \end{bmatrix}\begin{bmatrix} 1 & 2 & 3 \\ 0 & 1 & 0 \\ 1 & 1 & 0 \end{bmatrix}$

$$= \begin{bmatrix} -1+0+0 & -2+1+0 & -3+0+0 \\ 0+0+1 & 0-1+1 & 0+0+0 \\ 2+0+4 & 4+3+4 & 6+0+0 \end{bmatrix} = \begin{bmatrix} -1 & -1 & -3 \\ 1 & 0 & 0 \\ 6 & 11 & 6 \end{bmatrix}$$

Hence, the required result is verified.

Question 15 Find $A^2 - 5A + 6I$, if $A = \begin{bmatrix} 2 & 0 & 1 \\ 2 & 1 & 3 \\ 1 & -1 & 0 \end{bmatrix}$

Sol. Given, $A = \begin{bmatrix} 2 & 0 & 1 \\ 2 & 1 & 3 \\ 1 & -1 & 0 \end{bmatrix}$

Here, $A^2 = A \times A = \begin{bmatrix} 2 & 0 & 1 \\ 2 & 1 & 3 \\ 1 & -1 & 0 \end{bmatrix}\begin{bmatrix} 2 & 0 & 1 \\ 2 & 1 & 3 \\ 1 & -1 & 0 \end{bmatrix}$

$$= \begin{bmatrix} 4+0+1 & 0+0-1 & 2+0+0 \\ 4+2+3 & 0+1-3 & 2+3+0 \\ 2-2+0 & 0-1+0 & 1-3+0 \end{bmatrix} = \begin{bmatrix} 5 & -1 & 2 \\ 9 & -2 & 5 \\ 0 & -1 & -2 \end{bmatrix}$$

$$\therefore \quad A^2 - 5A + 6I = \begin{bmatrix} 5 & -1 & 2 \\ 9 & -2 & 5 \\ 0 & -1 & -2 \end{bmatrix} - 5\begin{bmatrix} 2 & 0 & 1 \\ 2 & 1 & 3 \\ 1 & -1 & 0 \end{bmatrix} + 6\begin{bmatrix} 1 & 0 & 0 \\ 0 & 1 & 0 \\ 0 & 0 & 1 \end{bmatrix}$$

$$= \begin{bmatrix} 5 & -1 & 2 \\ 9 & -2 & 5 \\ 0 & -1 & -2 \end{bmatrix} - \begin{bmatrix} 10 & 0 & 5 \\ 10 & 5 & 15 \\ 5 & -5 & 0 \end{bmatrix} + \begin{bmatrix} 6 & 0 & 0 \\ 0 & 6 & 0 \\ 0 & 0 & 6 \end{bmatrix}$$

$$= \begin{bmatrix} 5-10+6 & -1+0+0 & 2-5+0 \\ 9-10+0 & -2-5+6 & 5-15+0 \\ 0-5+0 & -1+5+0 & -2+0+6 \end{bmatrix} = \begin{bmatrix} 1 & -1 & -3 \\ -1 & -1 & -10 \\ -5 & 4 & 4 \end{bmatrix}$$

Question 16 If $A = \begin{bmatrix} 1 & 0 & 2 \\ 0 & 2 & 1 \\ 2 & 0 & 3 \end{bmatrix}$, prove that $A^3 - 6A^2 + 7A + 2I = O$.

Sol. Given, $A = \begin{bmatrix} 1 & 0 & 2 \\ 0 & 2 & 1 \\ 2 & 0 & 3 \end{bmatrix}$

Now, $\quad A^2 = A \times A = \begin{bmatrix} 1 & 0 & 2 \\ 0 & 2 & 1 \\ 2 & 0 & 3 \end{bmatrix}\begin{bmatrix} 1 & 0 & 2 \\ 0 & 2 & 1 \\ 2 & 0 & 3 \end{bmatrix}$

$$= \begin{bmatrix} 1+0+4 & 0+0+0 & 2+0+6 \\ 0+0+2 & 0+4+0 & 0+2+3 \\ 2+0+6 & 0+0+0 & 4+0+9 \end{bmatrix} = \begin{bmatrix} 5 & 0 & 8 \\ 2 & 4 & 5 \\ 8 & 0 & 13 \end{bmatrix}$$

and $\quad A^3 = A^2 \times A = \begin{bmatrix} 5 & 0 & 8 \\ 2 & 4 & 5 \\ 8 & 0 & 13 \end{bmatrix}\begin{bmatrix} 1 & 0 & 2 \\ 0 & 2 & 1 \\ 2 & 0 & 3 \end{bmatrix}$

$$= \begin{bmatrix} 5+0+16 & 0+0+0 & 10+0+24 \\ 2+0+10 & 0+8+0 & 4+4+15 \\ 8+0+26 & 0+0+0 & 16+0+39 \end{bmatrix} = \begin{bmatrix} 21 & 0 & 34 \\ 12 & 8 & 23 \\ 34 & 0 & 55 \end{bmatrix}$$

$$\therefore \quad A^3 - 6A^2 + 7A + 2I = \begin{bmatrix} 21 & 0 & 34 \\ 12 & 8 & 23 \\ 34 & 0 & 55 \end{bmatrix} - 6\begin{bmatrix} 5 & 0 & 8 \\ 2 & 4 & 5 \\ 8 & 0 & 13 \end{bmatrix} + 7\begin{bmatrix} 1 & 0 & 2 \\ 0 & 2 & 1 \\ 2 & 0 & 3 \end{bmatrix} + 2\begin{bmatrix} 1 & 0 & 0 \\ 0 & 1 & 0 \\ 0 & 0 & 1 \end{bmatrix}$$

$$= \begin{bmatrix} 21 & 0 & 34 \\ 12 & 8 & 23 \\ 34 & 0 & 55 \end{bmatrix} - \begin{bmatrix} 30 & 0 & 48 \\ 12 & 24 & 30 \\ 48 & 0 & 78 \end{bmatrix} + \begin{bmatrix} 7 & 0 & 14 \\ 0 & 14 & 7 \\ 14 & 0 & 21 \end{bmatrix} + \begin{bmatrix} 2 & 0 & 0 \\ 0 & 2 & 0 \\ 0 & 0 & 2 \end{bmatrix}$$

$$= \begin{bmatrix} 21-30+7+2 & 0-0+0+0 & 34-48+14+0 \\ 12-12+0+0 & 8-24+14+2 & 23-30+7+0 \\ 34-48+14+0 & 0-0+0+0 & 55-78+21+2 \end{bmatrix} = \begin{bmatrix} 0 & 0 & 0 \\ 0 & 0 & 0 \\ 0 & 0 & 0 \end{bmatrix} = O$$

Hence Proved.

Question 17 If $A = \begin{bmatrix} 3 & -2 \\ 4 & -2 \end{bmatrix}$ and $I = \begin{bmatrix} 1 & 0 \\ 0 & 1 \end{bmatrix}$, then find k so that $A^2 = kA - 2I$.

Sol. Given, $A = \begin{bmatrix} 3 & -2 \\ 4 & -2 \end{bmatrix}$ and $I = \begin{bmatrix} 1 & 0 \\ 0 & 1 \end{bmatrix}$

Now, $\quad A^2 = kA - 2I \Rightarrow AA = kA - 2I$

$$\Rightarrow \begin{bmatrix} 3 & -2 \\ 4 & -2 \end{bmatrix}\begin{bmatrix} 3 & -2 \\ 4 & -2 \end{bmatrix} = k\begin{bmatrix} 3 & -2 \\ 4 & -2 \end{bmatrix} - 2\begin{bmatrix} 1 & 0 \\ 0 & 1 \end{bmatrix}$$

$$\Rightarrow \begin{bmatrix} 9-8 & -6+4 \\ 12-8 & -8+4 \end{bmatrix} = \begin{bmatrix} 3k & -2k \\ 4k & -2k \end{bmatrix} - \begin{bmatrix} 2 & 0 \\ 0 & 2 \end{bmatrix}$$

$$\Rightarrow \begin{bmatrix} 1 & -2 \\ 4 & -4 \end{bmatrix} = \begin{bmatrix} 3k-2 & -2k \\ 4k & -2k-2 \end{bmatrix}$$

By definition of equality of matrix as the given matrices are equal, their corresponding elements are equal.
On comparing the corresponding elements, we get

$$3k - 2 = 1 \Rightarrow k = 1$$
$$-2k = -2 \Rightarrow k = 1$$
$$4k = 4 \Rightarrow k = 1$$
$$-4 = -2k - 2 \Rightarrow k = 1 \qquad \text{Hence, } k = 1$$

Question 18 If $A = \begin{bmatrix} 0 & -\tan\frac{\alpha}{2} \\ \tan\frac{\alpha}{2} & 0 \end{bmatrix}$ and I is the identity matrix of order 2, show that $I + A = (I - A)\begin{bmatrix} \cos\alpha & -\sin\alpha \\ \sin\alpha & \cos\alpha \end{bmatrix}$

Sol. Here, $A = \begin{bmatrix} 0 & -t \\ t & 0 \end{bmatrix}$, where $t = \tan\left(\frac{\alpha}{2}\right)$

Now, $\quad \cos\alpha = \dfrac{1 - \tan^2\left(\frac{\alpha}{2}\right)}{1 + \tan^2\left(\frac{\alpha}{2}\right)} = \dfrac{1 - t^2}{1 + t^2}$ and $\sin\alpha = \dfrac{2\tan\left(\frac{\alpha}{2}\right)}{1 + \tan^2\left(\frac{\alpha}{2}\right)} = \dfrac{2t}{1 + t^2}$

$$\text{RHS} = (I - A)\begin{bmatrix}\cos\alpha & -\sin\alpha \\ \sin\alpha & \cos\alpha\end{bmatrix} = \left[\begin{pmatrix}1 & 0 \\ 0 & 1\end{pmatrix} - \begin{pmatrix}0 & -t \\ t & 0\end{pmatrix}\right]\begin{bmatrix}\frac{1-t^2}{1+t^2} & \frac{-2t}{1+t^2} \\ \frac{2t}{1+t^2} & \frac{1-t^2}{1+t^2}\end{bmatrix}$$

$$= \begin{bmatrix}1 & t \\ -t & 1\end{bmatrix}\begin{bmatrix}\frac{1-t^2}{1+t^2} & \frac{-2t}{1+t^2} \\ \frac{2t}{1+t^2} & \frac{1-t^2}{1+t^2}\end{bmatrix} = \begin{bmatrix}\frac{1-t^2+2t^2}{1+t^2} & \frac{-2t+t(1-t^2)}{1+t^2} \\ \frac{-t(1-t^2)+2t}{1+t^2} & \frac{2t^2+1-t^2}{1+t^2}\end{bmatrix}$$

$$= \begin{bmatrix}\frac{1+t^2}{1+t^2} & \frac{-2t+t-t^3}{1+t^2} \\ \frac{-t+t^3+2t}{1+t^2} & \frac{1+t^2}{1+t^2}\end{bmatrix}$$

$$= \begin{bmatrix}1 & \frac{-t(1+t^2)}{1+t^2} \\ \frac{t(1+t^2)}{1+t^2} & 1\end{bmatrix} = \begin{bmatrix}1 & -t \\ t & 1\end{bmatrix}$$

$$\text{LHS} = \begin{bmatrix}1 & 0 \\ 0 & 1\end{bmatrix} + \begin{bmatrix}0 & -t \\ t & 0\end{bmatrix}$$

$$= \begin{bmatrix}0+1 & -t+0 \\ t+0 & 0+1\end{bmatrix} = \begin{bmatrix}1 & -t \\ t & 1\end{bmatrix} = \text{RHS}$$

Hence Proved.

Quick Solution

Here, $A = \begin{bmatrix}0 & -\tan\left(\frac{\alpha}{2}\right) \\ \tan\left(\frac{\alpha}{2}\right) & 0\end{bmatrix}$

$$\therefore\ I + A = \begin{bmatrix}1 & 0 \\ 0 & 1\end{bmatrix} + \begin{bmatrix}0 & -\tan\left(\frac{\alpha}{2}\right) \\ \tan\left(\frac{\alpha}{2}\right) & 0\end{bmatrix} = \begin{bmatrix}1 & -\tan\left(\frac{\alpha}{2}\right) \\ \tan\left(\frac{\alpha}{2}\right) & 0\end{bmatrix}$$

and $I - A = \begin{bmatrix}1 & 0 \\ 0 & 1\end{bmatrix} - \begin{bmatrix}0 & -\tan\left(\frac{\alpha}{2}\right) \\ \tan\left(\frac{\alpha}{2}\right) & 0\end{bmatrix} = \begin{bmatrix}1 & \tan\left(\frac{\alpha}{2}\right) \\ -\tan\left(\frac{\alpha}{2}\right) & 1\end{bmatrix}$

$$\therefore\ (I - A)\begin{bmatrix}\cos\alpha & -\sin\alpha \\ \sin\alpha & \cos\alpha\end{bmatrix} = \begin{bmatrix}1 & \tan\left(\frac{\alpha}{2}\right) \\ -\tan\left(\frac{\alpha}{2}\right) & 1\end{bmatrix}\begin{bmatrix}\cos\alpha & -\sin\alpha \\ \sin\alpha & \cos\alpha\end{bmatrix}$$

$$=\begin{bmatrix} \cos\alpha + \tan(\alpha/2)\sin\alpha & -\sin\alpha + \tan(\alpha/2)\cos\alpha \\ -\tan(\alpha/2)\cos\alpha + \sin\alpha & \tan(\alpha/2)\sin\alpha + \cos\alpha \end{bmatrix}$$

$$=\begin{bmatrix} \dfrac{\cos\alpha\cos(\alpha/2) + \sin(\alpha/2)\sin\alpha}{\cos(\alpha/2)} & \dfrac{-\sin\alpha\cos(\alpha/2) + \sin(\alpha/2)\cos\alpha}{\cos(\alpha/2)} \\ \dfrac{-\sin(\alpha/2)\cos\alpha + \cos(\alpha/2)\sin\alpha}{\cos(\alpha/2)} & \dfrac{\sin(\alpha/2)\sin\alpha + \cos(\alpha/2)\cos\alpha}{\cos(\alpha/2)} \end{bmatrix}$$

$$=\begin{bmatrix} \dfrac{\cos\left(\alpha - \frac{\alpha}{2}\right)}{\cos\left(\frac{\alpha}{2}\right)} & \dfrac{-\sin\left(\alpha - \frac{\alpha}{2}\right)}{\cos\left(\frac{\alpha}{2}\right)} \\ \dfrac{\sin\left(\alpha - \frac{\alpha}{2}\right)}{\cos\left(\frac{\alpha}{2}\right)} & \dfrac{\cos\left(\alpha - \frac{\alpha}{2}\right)}{\cos\left(\frac{\alpha}{2}\right)} \end{bmatrix} = \begin{bmatrix} \dfrac{\cos\left(\frac{\alpha}{2}\right)}{\cos\left(\frac{\alpha}{2}\right)} & \dfrac{-\sin\left(\frac{\alpha}{2}\right)}{\cos\left(\frac{\alpha}{2}\right)} \\ \dfrac{\sin\left(\frac{\alpha}{2}\right)}{\cos\left(\frac{\alpha}{2}\right)} & \dfrac{\cos\left(\frac{\alpha}{2}\right)}{\cos\left(\frac{\alpha}{2}\right)} \end{bmatrix}$$

$$\left(\begin{array}{l} \because \cos(A - B) = \cos A\cos B + \sin A\sin B \\ \text{and } \sin(A - B) = \sin A\cos B - \cos A\sin B \end{array}\right)$$

$$=\begin{bmatrix} 1 & -\tan\left(\frac{\alpha}{2}\right) \\ \tan\left(\frac{\alpha}{2}\right) & 1 \end{bmatrix} = I + A$$

Thus, $I + A = (I - A)\begin{bmatrix} \cos\alpha & -\sin\alpha \\ \sin\alpha & \cos\alpha \end{bmatrix}$ **Hence Proved.**

Question 19 A trust fund has ₹ 30000 that must be invested in two different types of bonds. The first bond pays 5% interest per year and the second bond pays 7% interest per year. Using matrix multiplication, determine how to divide ₹ 30000 among the two types of bonds, if the trust fund must obtain an annual total interest of

(a) ₹ 1800 (b) ₹ 2000.

Sol. Let the amount invested in first type of bonds is ₹ x, then that invested in second type of bonds will be ₹ $(30000 - x)$.

(a) According to given condition,

$$[x \quad 30000 - x]\begin{bmatrix} \dfrac{5}{100} \\ \dfrac{7}{100} \end{bmatrix} = [1800]$$

$$\Rightarrow \quad \left[\frac{5x}{100} + \frac{(30000 - x)7}{100}\right] = [1800]$$

On comparing the corresponding elements, we get

$$\frac{5x + 210000 - 7x}{100} = 1800$$

$$\Rightarrow \quad 210000 - 2x = 180000$$
$$\Rightarrow \quad 30000 = 2x$$
$$\Rightarrow \quad x = 15000$$

Hence, the amounts invested in the two types of bonds are respectively ₹ 15000 and ₹ (30000 – 15000) = ₹ 15000.

(b) According to the given condition, $[x \quad 30000 - x]\begin{bmatrix} \frac{5}{100} \\ \frac{7}{100} \end{bmatrix} = [2000]$

$$\Rightarrow \quad \left[\frac{5x}{100} + \frac{(30000 - x)7}{100}\right] = [2000]$$

$$\Rightarrow \quad \left[\frac{5x + 210000 - 7x}{100}\right] = [2000]$$

On comparing the corresponding elements, we get

$$-2x + 210000 = 200000$$
$$\Rightarrow \quad 2x = 10000$$
$$\Rightarrow \quad x = 5000$$

Hence, the amounts invested in two types of bonds are respectively ₹ 5000 and ₹ (30000 – 5000) = ₹ 25000.

Mistake Alert Some students get wrong with the order while forming matrices.

Question 20 The bookshop of a particular school has 10 dozen chemistry books, 8 dozen physics books, 10 dozen economics books. Their selling prices are ₹ 80, ₹ 60 and ₹ 40 each subject respectively. Find the total amount the bookshop will receive from selling the books using matrix algebra.

Sol. Let $A = [10 \times 12 \quad 8 \times 12 \quad 10 \times 12] = [120 \quad 96 \quad 120]$

and $$B = \begin{bmatrix} 80 \\ 60 \\ 40 \end{bmatrix}$$

Amount received by the bookseller on selling the types of books can be computed by evaluating the product AB.

Now, $$AB = [120 \quad 96 \quad 120]\begin{bmatrix} 80 \\ 60 \\ 40 \end{bmatrix}$$

$$= [120 \times 80 + 96 \times 60 + 120 \times 40]_{1 \times 1}$$
$$= [9600 + 5760 + 4800]_{1 \times 1} = [20160]_{1 \times 1}$$

∴ Amount recieved by the bookseller = ₹ 20160

Direction (Q. Nos. 21 and 22) Assume X, Y, Z, W and P are matrices of orders $2 \times n, 3 \times k, 2 \times p, n \times 3$ and $p \times k$ respectively. Choose the correct answer in Q. 21 and Q. 22.

Question 21 The restrictions on n, k and p so that $PY + WY$ will be defined are

(a) $k = 3, p = n$

(b) k is arbirary, $p = 2$

(c) p is arbitrary

(d) $k = 2, p = 3$

Sol. (a) Matrices P and Y are of the orders $p \times k$ and $3 \times k$ respectively.

In matrix multiplication $A \cdot B$ is possible only when no. of columns of A = no. of rows of B.

Therefore, matrix PY will be defined if $k = 3$. Consequently, PY will be of the order $p \times k$. Matrices W and Y are of the orders $n \times 3$ and $3 \times k$ respectively.

Since, the number of columns in W is equal to the number of rows in Y, matrix WY is well-defined and is of the order $n \times k$.

Matrices PY and WY can be added only where their orders are the same. However, PY is of the order $p \times k$ and WY is of the order $n \times k$, therefore we must have $p = n$. Thus, $k = 3$ and $p = n$ are the restrictions on n, k and p so that $PY + WY$ will be defined.

Question 22 If $n = p$, then the order of the matrix $7X - 5Z$ is

(a) $p \times 2$ (b) $2 \times n$

(c) $n \times 3$ (d) $p \times n$

Sol. (b) Matrix X is of the order $2 \times n$.

Therefore, matrix $7X$ is also of the same order.

Matrix Z is of the order $2 \times p$ i.e., $2 \times n$. [Since, $n = p$]

Therefore, matrix $5Z$ is also of the same order .

Now, both the matrices $7X$ and $5Z$ are of the order $2 \times n$.

Thus, matrix $7X - 5Z$ is well-defined and is of the order $2 \times n$.

Exercise 3.3

Question 1 Find the transpose of each of the following matrices.

(i) $\begin{bmatrix} 5 \\ 1/2 \\ -1 \end{bmatrix}$ (ii) $\begin{bmatrix} 1 & -1 \\ 2 & 3 \end{bmatrix}$ (iii) $\begin{bmatrix} -1 & 5 & 6 \\ \sqrt{3} & 5 & 6 \\ 2 & 3 & -1 \end{bmatrix}$

Sol. (i) Let $A = \begin{bmatrix} 5 \\ 1/2 \\ -1 \end{bmatrix}_{3\times 1}$, then, $A' = [5 \quad 1/2 \quad -1]_{1\times 3}$

(ii) Let $A = \begin{bmatrix} 1 & -1 \\ 2 & 3 \end{bmatrix}$, then $A' = \begin{bmatrix} 1 & 2 \\ -1 & 3 \end{bmatrix}$

(iii) Let $A = \begin{bmatrix} -1 & 5 & 6 \\ \sqrt{3} & 5 & 6 \\ 2 & 3 & -1 \end{bmatrix}$, then $A' = \begin{bmatrix} -1 & \sqrt{3} & 2 \\ 5 & 5 & 3 \\ 6 & 6 & -1 \end{bmatrix}$

Question 2 If $A = \begin{bmatrix} -1 & 2 & 3 \\ 5 & 7 & 9 \\ -2 & 1 & 1 \end{bmatrix}$ and $B = \begin{bmatrix} -4 & 1 & -5 \\ 1 & 2 & 0 \\ 1 & 3 & 1 \end{bmatrix}$, then verify that

(i) $(A + B)' = A' + B'$ (ii) $(A - B)' = A' - B'$

Sol.

(i) Here, $A + B = \begin{bmatrix} -1 & 2 & 3 \\ 5 & 7 & 9 \\ -2 & 1 & 1 \end{bmatrix} + \begin{bmatrix} -4 & 1 & -5 \\ 1 & 2 & 0 \\ 1 & 3 & 1 \end{bmatrix} = \begin{bmatrix} -5 & 3 & -2 \\ 6 & 9 & 9 \\ -1 & 4 & 2 \end{bmatrix}$

$\therefore \quad (A + B)' = \begin{bmatrix} -5 & 6 & -1 \\ 3 & 9 & 4 \\ -2 & 9 & 2 \end{bmatrix}$ ...(i)

Also $A' + B' = \begin{bmatrix} -1 & 2 & 3 \\ 5 & 7 & 9 \\ -2 & 1 & 1 \end{bmatrix}' + \begin{bmatrix} -4 & 1 & -5 \\ 1 & 2 & 0 \\ 1 & 3 & 1 \end{bmatrix}'$

$= \begin{bmatrix} -1 & 5 & -2 \\ 2 & 7 & 1 \\ 3 & 9 & 1 \end{bmatrix} + \begin{bmatrix} -4 & 1 & 1 \\ 1 & 2 & 3 \\ -5 & 0 & 1 \end{bmatrix} = \begin{bmatrix} -5 & 6 & -1 \\ 3 & 9 & 4 \\ -2 & 9 & 2 \end{bmatrix}$ ...(ii)

From Eqs. (i) and (ii), it is verified that $(A + B)' = A' + B'$.

(ii) Here, $A - B = \begin{bmatrix} -1 & 2 & 3 \\ 5 & 7 & 9 \\ -2 & 1 & 1 \end{bmatrix} - \begin{bmatrix} -4 & 1 & -5 \\ 1 & 2 & 0 \\ 1 & 3 & 1 \end{bmatrix}$

$$= \begin{bmatrix} -1+4 & 2-1 & 3+5 \\ 5-1 & 7-2 & 9-0 \\ -2-1 & 1-3 & 1-1 \end{bmatrix} = \begin{bmatrix} 3 & 1 & 8 \\ 4 & 5 & 9 \\ -3 & -2 & 0 \end{bmatrix}$$

$$\Rightarrow \qquad (A - B)' = \begin{bmatrix} 3 & 4 & -3 \\ 1 & 5 & -2 \\ 8 & 9 & 0 \end{bmatrix} \qquad \ldots(\text{i})$$

Also, $A' - B' = \begin{bmatrix} -1 & 5 & -2 \\ 2 & 7 & 1 \\ 3 & 9 & 1 \end{bmatrix} - \begin{bmatrix} -4 & 1 & 1 \\ 1 & 2 & 3 \\ -5 & 0 & 1 \end{bmatrix} = \begin{bmatrix} -1+4 & 5-1 & -2-1 \\ 2-1 & 7-2 & 1-3 \\ 3-(-5) & 9-0 & 1-1 \end{bmatrix}$

$$= \begin{bmatrix} 3 & 4 & -3 \\ 1 & 5 & -2 \\ 8 & 9 & 0 \end{bmatrix} \qquad \ldots(\text{ii})$$

From Eqs. (i) and (ii), it is verified that $(A - B)' = A' - B'$.

Question 3 If $A' = \begin{bmatrix} 3 & 4 \\ -1 & 2 \\ 0 & 1 \end{bmatrix}$ and $B = \begin{bmatrix} -1 & 2 & 1 \\ 1 & 2 & 3 \end{bmatrix}$, then verify that

(i) $(A + B)' = A' + B'$ (ii) $(A - B)' = A' - B'$.

Sol. Given, $A' = \begin{bmatrix} 3 & 4 \\ -1 & 2 \\ 0 & 1 \end{bmatrix}$

$$\therefore \qquad A = (A')' = \begin{bmatrix} 3 & 4 \\ -1 & 2 \\ 0 & 1 \end{bmatrix}' = \begin{bmatrix} 3 & -1 & 0 \\ 4 & 2 & 1 \end{bmatrix}$$

and $B = \begin{bmatrix} -1 & 2 & 1 \\ 1 & 2 & 3 \end{bmatrix}$

$$\therefore \quad B' = \begin{bmatrix} -1 & 1 \\ 2 & 2 \\ 1 & 3 \end{bmatrix}$$

(i) Here, $\quad + \quad = \begin{bmatrix} 3 & -1 & 0 \\ 4 & 2 & 1 \end{bmatrix} + \begin{bmatrix} -1 & 2 & 1 \\ 1 & 2 & 3 \end{bmatrix} = \begin{bmatrix} 2 & 1 & 1 \\ 5 & 4 & 4 \end{bmatrix}$

$$\therefore \text{LHS} = (A + B)' = \begin{bmatrix} 2 & 1 & 1 \\ 5 & 4 & 4 \end{bmatrix}' = \begin{bmatrix} 2 & 5 \\ 1 & 4 \\ 1 & 4 \end{bmatrix} \qquad \ldots(\text{i})$$

and $\quad \text{RHS} = A' + B' = \begin{bmatrix} 3 & 4 \\ -1 & 2 \\ 0 & 1 \end{bmatrix} + \begin{bmatrix} -1 & 1 \\ 2 & 2 \\ 1 & 3 \end{bmatrix} = \begin{bmatrix} 2 & 5 \\ 1 & 4 \\ 1 & 4 \end{bmatrix}$ ...(ii)

From Eqs. (i) and (ii), it is verified that $(A+B)' = A' + B'$.

(ii) Here,

$$\text{RHS} = A' - B' = \begin{bmatrix} 3 & 4 \\ -1 & 2 \\ 0 & 1 \end{bmatrix} - \begin{bmatrix} -1 & 1 \\ 2 & 2 \\ 1 & 3 \end{bmatrix} = \begin{bmatrix} 3+1 & 4-1 \\ -1-2 & 2-2 \\ 0-1 & 1-3 \end{bmatrix} = \begin{bmatrix} 4 & 3 \\ -3 & 0 \\ -1 & -2 \end{bmatrix} \quad ...(i)$$

and LHS $(A-B)' = \left(\begin{bmatrix} 3 & -1 & 0 \\ 4 & 2 & 1 \end{bmatrix} - \begin{bmatrix} -1 & 2 & 1 \\ 1 & 2 & 3 \end{bmatrix} \right)'$

$$= \begin{bmatrix} 3+1 & -1-2 & 0-1 \\ 4-1 & 2-2 & 1-3 \end{bmatrix}' = \begin{bmatrix} 4 & -3 & -1 \\ 3 & 0 & -2 \end{bmatrix}' = \begin{bmatrix} 4 & 3 \\ -3 & 0 \\ -1 & -2 \end{bmatrix} \quad ...(ii)$$

So, verified that $(A-B)' = A' - B'$. [from Eqs. (i) and (ii)]

Question 4 If $A' = \begin{bmatrix} -2 & 3 \\ 1 & 2 \end{bmatrix}$ and $B = \begin{bmatrix} -1 & 0 \\ 1 & 2 \end{bmatrix}$, then find $(A + 2B)'$.

Sol. Given, $A' = \begin{bmatrix} -2 & 3 \\ 1 & 2 \end{bmatrix}$

$\Rightarrow \quad A - (A')' = \begin{bmatrix} -2 & 3 \\ 1 & 2 \end{bmatrix}' = \begin{bmatrix} -2 & 1 \\ 3 & 2 \end{bmatrix}$ $[\because (A')' = A]$

and $\quad B = \begin{bmatrix} -1 & 0 \\ 1 & 2 \end{bmatrix} \Rightarrow 2B = 2\begin{bmatrix} -1 & 0 \\ 1 & 2 \end{bmatrix} = \begin{bmatrix} -2 & 0 \\ 2 & 4 \end{bmatrix}$

$\therefore \quad A + 2B = \begin{bmatrix} -2 & 1 \\ 3 & 2 \end{bmatrix} + \begin{bmatrix} -2 & 0 \\ 2 & 4 \end{bmatrix} = \begin{bmatrix} -4 & 1 \\ 5 & 6 \end{bmatrix} \Rightarrow (A+2B)' = \begin{bmatrix} -4 & 1 \\ 5 & 6 \end{bmatrix}' = \begin{bmatrix} -4 & 5 \\ 1 & 6 \end{bmatrix}$

Question 5 For the matrices A and B, verify that $(AB)' = B'A'$, where

(i) $A = \begin{bmatrix} 1 \\ -4 \\ 3 \end{bmatrix}$, $B = [-1 \quad 2 \quad 1]$ (ii) $A = \begin{bmatrix} 0 \\ 1 \\ 2 \end{bmatrix}$, $B = [1 \quad 5 \quad 7]$.

Sol.

(i) Here, $\quad AB = \begin{bmatrix} 1 \\ -4 \\ 3 \end{bmatrix} [-1 \quad 2 \quad 1] = \begin{bmatrix} -1 & 2 & 1 \\ 4 & -8 & -4 \\ -3 & 6 & 3 \end{bmatrix}$

$$\therefore \quad (AB)' = \begin{bmatrix} -1 & 2 & 1 \\ 4 & -8 & -4 \\ -3 & 6 & 3 \end{bmatrix}' = \begin{bmatrix} -1 & 4 & -3 \\ 2 & -8 & 6 \\ 1 & -4 & 3 \end{bmatrix} \quad ...(i)$$

Also, $B'A' = [-1 \ \ 2 \ \ 1]' \begin{bmatrix} 1 \\ -4 \\ 3 \end{bmatrix}' = \begin{bmatrix} -1 \\ 2 \\ 1 \end{bmatrix} [1 \ \ -4 \ \ 3] = \begin{bmatrix} -1 & 4 & -3 \\ 2 & -8 & 6 \\ 1 & -4 & 3 \end{bmatrix}$ ...(ii)

From Eqs. (i) and (ii), it is verified that $(AB)' = B'A'$.

(ii) Here, $AB = \begin{bmatrix} 0 \\ 1 \\ 2 \end{bmatrix} [1 \ \ 5 \ \ 7] = \begin{bmatrix} 0 & 0 & 0 \\ 1 & 5 & 7 \\ 2 & 10 & 14 \end{bmatrix}$

$\therefore \ (AB)' = \begin{bmatrix} 0 & 0 & 0 \\ 1 & 5 & 7 \\ 1 & 10 & 14 \end{bmatrix}' = \begin{bmatrix} 0 & 1 & 2 \\ 0 & 5 & 10 \\ 0 & 7 & 14 \end{bmatrix}$ ...(i)

Also, $B'A' = [1 \ \ 5 \ \ 7]' \begin{bmatrix} 0 \\ 1 \\ 2 \end{bmatrix}' = \begin{bmatrix} 1 \\ 5 \\ 7 \end{bmatrix} [0 \ \ 1 \ \ 2] = \begin{bmatrix} 0 & 1 & 2 \\ 0 & 5 & 10 \\ 0 & 7 & 14 \end{bmatrix}$ ...(ii)

From Eqs. (i) and (ii), it is verified that $(AB)' = B'A'$.

Question 6 If (i) $A = \begin{bmatrix} \cos\alpha & \sin\alpha \\ -\sin\alpha & \cos\alpha \end{bmatrix}$, then verify that $A' A = I$.

(ii) $A = \begin{bmatrix} \sin\alpha & \cos\alpha \\ -\cos\alpha & \sin\alpha \end{bmatrix}$, then verify that $A' A = I$.

Sol.

(i) Here, $A = \begin{bmatrix} \cos\alpha & \sin\alpha \\ -\sin\alpha & \cos\alpha \end{bmatrix}$

$\therefore \quad A' = \begin{bmatrix} \cos\alpha & \sin\alpha \\ -\sin\alpha & \cos\alpha \end{bmatrix}' = \begin{bmatrix} \cos\alpha & -\sin\alpha \\ \sin\alpha & \cos\alpha \end{bmatrix}$

Now, $A'A = \begin{bmatrix} \cos\alpha & -\sin\alpha \\ \sin\alpha & \cos\alpha \end{bmatrix} \begin{bmatrix} \cos\alpha & \sin\alpha \\ -\sin\alpha & \cos\alpha \end{bmatrix}$

$= \begin{bmatrix} (\cos\alpha)(\cos\alpha) + (\sin\alpha)(\sin\alpha) & (\cos\alpha)(\sin\alpha) + (-\sin\alpha)(\cos\alpha) \\ (\sin\alpha)(\cos\alpha) + (\cos\alpha)(-\sin\alpha) & (\cos\alpha)(\cos\alpha) + (\sin\alpha)(\sin\alpha) \end{bmatrix}$

$= \begin{bmatrix} \cos^2\alpha + \sin^2\alpha & \cos\alpha\sin\alpha - \sin\alpha\cos\alpha \\ \sin\alpha\cos\alpha - \cos\alpha\sin\alpha & \sin^2\alpha + \cos^2\alpha \end{bmatrix} = \begin{bmatrix} 1 & 0 \\ 0 & 1 \end{bmatrix} = I \cdot$

$[\because \sin^2 A + \cos^2 A = 1]$ **Hence, verified.**

(ii) Here, $A = \begin{bmatrix} \sin\alpha & \cos\alpha \\ -\cos\alpha & \sin\alpha \end{bmatrix} \quad \therefore A' = \begin{bmatrix} \sin\alpha & \cos\alpha \\ -\cos\alpha & \sin\alpha \end{bmatrix}' = \begin{bmatrix} \sin\alpha & -\cos\alpha \\ \cos\alpha & \sin\alpha \end{bmatrix}$

Now, $A'A = \begin{bmatrix} \sin\alpha & -\cos\alpha \\ \cos\alpha & \sin\alpha \end{bmatrix} \begin{bmatrix} \sin\alpha & \cos\alpha \\ -\cos\alpha & \sin\alpha \end{bmatrix}$

$= \begin{bmatrix} (\sin\alpha)(\sin\alpha) + (-\cos\alpha)(-\cos\alpha) & (\sin\alpha)(\cos\alpha) + (-\cos\alpha)(\sin\alpha) \\ (\sin\alpha)(\cos\alpha) + (\sin\alpha)(-\cos\alpha) & (\cos\alpha)(\cos\alpha) + (\sin\alpha)(\sin\alpha) \end{bmatrix}$

$$= \begin{bmatrix} \sin^2\alpha + \cos^2\alpha & \sin\alpha\cos\alpha - \cos\alpha\sin\alpha \\ \sin\alpha\cos\alpha - \sin\alpha\cos\alpha & \cos^2\alpha + \sin^2\alpha \end{bmatrix} = \begin{bmatrix} 1 & 0 \\ 0 & 1 \end{bmatrix} = I.$$

$[\because \sin^2 A + \cos^2 A = 1]$ **Hence verified.**

Question 7 (i) Show that the matrix, $A = \begin{bmatrix} 1 & -1 & 5 \\ -1 & 2 & 1 \\ 5 & 1 & 3 \end{bmatrix}$ is a symmetric matrix.

(ii) Show that the matrix, $A = \begin{bmatrix} 0 & 1 & -1 \\ -1 & 0 & 1 \\ 1 & -1 & 0 \end{bmatrix}$ is a skew-symmetric matrix.

◎ *Thinking Process* For symmetric matrix we have to prove $A' = A$ and for skew-symmetric matrix we have to prove $A' = -A$

Sol.

(i) Here, $A' = \begin{bmatrix} 1 & -1 & 5 \\ -1 & 2 & 1 \\ 5 & 1 & 3 \end{bmatrix}' = \begin{bmatrix} 1 & -1 & 5 \\ -1 & 2 & 1 \\ 5 & 1 & 3 \end{bmatrix} = A$

Hence, A is a symmetric matrix.

(ii) Now, $A' = \begin{bmatrix} 0 & 1 & -1 \\ -1 & 0 & 1 \\ 1 & -1 & 0 \end{bmatrix}' = \begin{bmatrix} 0 & -1 & 1 \\ 1 & 0 & -1 \\ -1 & 1 & 0 \end{bmatrix} = -\begin{bmatrix} 0 & 1 & -1 \\ -1 & 0 & 1 \\ 1 & -1 & 0 \end{bmatrix} = -A$

Hence, A is skew-symmetric matrix.

Question 8 For the matrix, $A = \begin{bmatrix} 1 & 5 \\ 6 & 7 \end{bmatrix}$, verify that

(i) $(A + A')$ is a symmetric matrix.

(ii) $(A - A')$ is a skew-symmetric matrix.

◎ *Thinking Process*

(i) To verify $(A + A')$ is a symmetric matrix, find transpose of $(A + A')$ and use the property that if A is a symmetric matrix, then $A' = A$.

(ii) To verify $(A - A')$ is a skew-symmetric matrix, find transpose of $(A - A')$ and also use the property that if A is a skew-symmetric matrix, then $A' = -A$.

Sol.

(i) Here, $A + A' = \begin{bmatrix} 1 & 5 \\ 6 & 7 \end{bmatrix} + \begin{bmatrix} 1 & 5 \\ 6 & 7 \end{bmatrix}' = \begin{bmatrix} 1 & 5 \\ 6 & 7 \end{bmatrix} + \begin{bmatrix} 1 & 6 \\ 5 & 7 \end{bmatrix} = \begin{bmatrix} 2 & 11 \\ 11 & 14 \end{bmatrix}$

$\therefore \quad (A + A')' = \begin{bmatrix} 2 & 11 \\ 11 & 14 \end{bmatrix}' = \begin{bmatrix} 2 & 11 \\ 11 & 14 \end{bmatrix} = A + A'$

Hence, $(A + A')$ is a symmetric matrix.

(ii) Here, $A - A' = \begin{bmatrix} 1 & 5 \\ 6 & 7 \end{bmatrix} - \begin{bmatrix} 1 & 5 \\ 6 & 7 \end{bmatrix}' = \begin{bmatrix} 1 & 5 \\ 6 & 7 \end{bmatrix} - \begin{bmatrix} 1 & 6 \\ 5 & 7 \end{bmatrix} = \begin{bmatrix} 0 & -1 \\ 1 & 0 \end{bmatrix}$

$$\Rightarrow \quad A - A' = \begin{bmatrix} 0 & -1 \\ 1 & 0 \end{bmatrix}$$

$$\therefore \quad (A - A')' = \begin{bmatrix} 0 & -1 \\ 1 & 0 \end{bmatrix}' = \begin{bmatrix} 0 & 1 \\ -1 & 0 \end{bmatrix} = -\begin{bmatrix} 0 & -1 \\ 1 & 0 \end{bmatrix} = -(A - A')$$

Hence, $(A - A')$ is a skew-symmetric matrix.

Mistake Alert Some students commits error in solving the problems based on symmetric and skew-symmetric matrices.

Question 9 Find $\frac{1}{2}(A + A')$ and $\frac{1}{2}(A - A')$, when $A = \begin{bmatrix} 0 & a & b \\ -a & 0 & c \\ -b & -c & 0 \end{bmatrix}$.

Sol. Here, $\frac{1}{2}(A + A') = \frac{1}{2}\left(\begin{bmatrix} 0 & a & b \\ -a & 0 & c \\ -b & -c & 0 \end{bmatrix} + \begin{bmatrix} 0 & a & b \\ -a & 0 & c \\ -b & -c & 0 \end{bmatrix}'\right)$

$$= \frac{1}{2}\left(\begin{bmatrix} 0 & a & b \\ -a & 0 & c \\ -b & -c & 0 \end{bmatrix} + \begin{bmatrix} 0 & -a & -b \\ a & 0 & -c \\ b & c & 0 \end{bmatrix}\right) = \frac{1}{2}\begin{bmatrix} 0 & 0 & 0 \\ 0 & 0 & 0 \\ 0 & 0 & 0 \end{bmatrix} = \begin{bmatrix} 0 & 0 & 0 \\ 0 & 0 & 0 \\ 0 & 0 & 0 \end{bmatrix}$$

and $\quad \frac{1}{2}(A - A') = \frac{1}{2}\left(\begin{bmatrix} 0 & a & b \\ -a & 0 & c \\ -b & -c & 0 \end{bmatrix} - \begin{bmatrix} 0 & a & b \\ -a & 0 & c \\ -b & -c & 0 \end{bmatrix}'\right)$

$$= \frac{1}{2}\left(\begin{bmatrix} 0 & a & b \\ -a & 0 & c \\ -b & -c & 0 \end{bmatrix} - \begin{bmatrix} 0 & -a & -b \\ a & 0 & -c \\ b & c & 0 \end{bmatrix}\right)$$

$$= \frac{1}{2}\begin{bmatrix} 0 & 2a & 2b \\ -2a & 0 & 2c \\ -2b & -2c & 0 \end{bmatrix} = \begin{bmatrix} 0 & a & b \\ -a & 0 & c \\ -b & -c & 0 \end{bmatrix}$$

Question 10 Express the following matrices as the sum of a symmetric and a skew-symmetric matrices

(i) $\begin{bmatrix} 3 & 5 \\ 1 & -1 \end{bmatrix}$ (ii) $\begin{bmatrix} 6 & -2 & 2 \\ -2 & 3 & -1 \\ 2 & -1 & 3 \end{bmatrix}$

(iii) $\begin{bmatrix} 3 & 3 & -1 \\ -2 & -2 & 1 \\ -4 & -5 & 2 \end{bmatrix}$ (iv) $\begin{bmatrix} 1 & 5 \\ -1 & 2 \end{bmatrix}$

Thinking Process To express any matrix A as a sum of symmetric matrix, $P = \frac{1}{2}(A + A')$ and a skew-symmetric matrix, $Q = \frac{1}{2}(A - A')$.

Sol.

(i) Let $A = \begin{bmatrix} 3 & 5 \\ 1 & -1 \end{bmatrix}$, then $A = P + Q$

where, $P = \frac{1}{2}(A + A')$ and $Q = \frac{1}{2}(A - A')$

Now, $P = \frac{1}{2}(A + A') = \frac{1}{2}\left(\begin{bmatrix} 3 & 5 \\ 1 & -1 \end{bmatrix} + \begin{bmatrix} 3 & 1 \\ 5 & -1 \end{bmatrix}\right) = \frac{1}{2}\begin{bmatrix} 6 & 6 \\ 6 & -2 \end{bmatrix} = \begin{bmatrix} 3 & 3 \\ 3 & -1 \end{bmatrix}$

$\therefore \quad P' = \begin{bmatrix} 3 & 3 \\ 3 & -1 \end{bmatrix}' = \begin{bmatrix} 3 & 3 \\ 3 & -1 \end{bmatrix} = P$

Thus, $P = \frac{1}{2}(A + A')$ is a symmetric matrix.

Now, $Q = \frac{1}{2}(A - A') = \frac{1}{2}\left(\begin{bmatrix} 3 & 5 \\ 1 & -1 \end{bmatrix} - \begin{bmatrix} 3 & 1 \\ 5 & -1 \end{bmatrix}\right)$

$= \frac{1}{2}\begin{bmatrix} 0 & 4 \\ -4 & 0 \end{bmatrix} = \begin{bmatrix} 0 & 2 \\ -2 & 0 \end{bmatrix}$

$\therefore \quad Q' = \begin{bmatrix} 0 & 2 \\ -2 & 0 \end{bmatrix}' = \begin{bmatrix} 0 & -2 \\ 2 & 0 \end{bmatrix} = -Q$

Thus, $Q = \frac{1}{2}(A - A')$ is a skew-symmetric matrix.

Representing A as the sum of P and Q,

$P + Q = \begin{bmatrix} 3 & 3 \\ 3 & -1 \end{bmatrix} + \begin{bmatrix} 0 & 2 \\ -2 & 0 \end{bmatrix}$

$= \begin{bmatrix} 3 & 5 \\ 1 & -1 \end{bmatrix} = A.$

(ii) Let $A = \begin{bmatrix} 6 & -2 & 2 \\ -2 & 3 & -1 \\ 2 & -1 & 3 \end{bmatrix}$, then $A' = \begin{bmatrix} 6 & -2 & 2 \\ -2 & 3 & -1 \\ 2 & -1 & 3 \end{bmatrix}' = \begin{bmatrix} 6 & -2 & 2 \\ -2 & 3 & -1 \\ 2 & -1 & 3 \end{bmatrix}$

Now, $A + A' = \begin{bmatrix} 6 & -2 & 2 \\ -2 & 3 & -1 \\ 2 & -1 & 3 \end{bmatrix} + \begin{bmatrix} 6 & -2 & 2 \\ -2 & 3 & -1 \\ 2 & -1 & 3 \end{bmatrix} = \begin{bmatrix} 12 & -4 & 4 \\ -4 & 6 & -2 \\ 4 & -2 & 6 \end{bmatrix}$

Let $P = \frac{1}{2}(A + A') = \frac{1}{2}\begin{bmatrix} 12 & -4 & 4 \\ -4 & 6 & -2 \\ 4 & -2 & 6 \end{bmatrix} = \begin{bmatrix} 6 & -2 & 2 \\ -2 & 3 & -1 \\ 2 & -1 & 3 \end{bmatrix}$

Now, $P' = \begin{bmatrix} 6 & -2 & 2 \\ -2 & 3 & -1 \\ 2 & -1 & 3 \end{bmatrix}' = \begin{bmatrix} 6 & -2 & 2 \\ -2 & 3 & -1 \\ 2 & -1 & 3 \end{bmatrix} = P$

Thus, $P = \frac{1}{2}(A + A')$ is a symmetric matrix.

Now, $A - A' = \begin{bmatrix} 6 & -2 & 2 \\ -2 & 3 & -1 \\ 2 & -1 & 3 \end{bmatrix} - \begin{bmatrix} 6 & -2 & 2 \\ -2 & 3 & -1 \\ 2 & -1 & 3 \end{bmatrix} = \begin{bmatrix} 0 & 0 & 0 \\ 0 & 0 & 0 \\ 0 & 0 & 0 \end{bmatrix}$

Let $Q = \frac{1}{2}(A - A') = \frac{1}{2}\begin{bmatrix} 0 & 0 & 0 \\ 0 & 0 & 0 \\ 0 & 0 & 0 \end{bmatrix} = \begin{bmatrix} 0 & 0 & 0 \\ 0 & 0 & 0 \\ 0 & 0 & 0 \end{bmatrix}$

Now, $Q' = \begin{bmatrix} 0 & 0 & 0 \\ 0 & 0 & 0 \\ 0 & 0 & 0 \end{bmatrix} = -Q$

Thus, $Q = \frac{1}{2}(A - A')$ is a skew-symmetric matrix.

Representing A as the sum of P and Q,

$P + Q = \begin{bmatrix} 6 & -2 & 2 \\ -2 & 3 & -1 \\ 2 & -1 & 3 \end{bmatrix} + \begin{bmatrix} 0 & 0 & 0 \\ 0 & 0 & 0 \\ 0 & 0 & 0 \end{bmatrix} = \begin{bmatrix} 6 & -2 & 2 \\ -2 & 3 & -1 \\ 2 & -1 & 3 \end{bmatrix} = A$

(iii) Let $A = \begin{bmatrix} 3 & 3 & -1 \\ -2 & -2 & 1 \\ -4 & -5 & 2 \end{bmatrix}$, then $A' = \begin{bmatrix} 3 & -2 & -4 \\ 3 & -2 & -5 \\ -1 & 1 & 2 \end{bmatrix}$

Now, $A + A' = \begin{bmatrix} 3 & 3 & -1 \\ -2 & -2 & 1 \\ -4 & -5 & 2 \end{bmatrix} + \begin{bmatrix} 3 & -2 & -4 \\ 3 & -2 & -5 \\ -1 & 1 & 2 \end{bmatrix} = \begin{bmatrix} 6 & 1 & -5 \\ 1 & -4 & -4 \\ -5 & -4 & 4 \end{bmatrix}$

Let $P = \frac{1}{2}(A + A') = \frac{1}{2}\begin{bmatrix} 6 & 1 & -5 \\ 1 & -4 & -4 \\ -5 & -4 & 4 \end{bmatrix} = \begin{bmatrix} 3 & 1/2 & -5/2 \\ 1/2 & -2 & -2 \\ -5/2 & -2 & 2 \end{bmatrix}$

Now, $P' = \begin{bmatrix} 3 & 1/2 & -5/2 \\ 1/2 & -2 & -2 \\ -5/2 & -2 & 2 \end{bmatrix}' = \begin{bmatrix} 3 & 1/2 & -5/2 \\ 1/2 & -2 & -2 \\ -5/2 & -2 & 2 \end{bmatrix} = P$

Thus, $P = \frac{1}{2}(A + A')$ is a symmetric matrix.

Now, $A - A' = \begin{bmatrix} 3 & 3 & -1 \\ -2 & -2 & 1 \\ -4 & -5 & 2 \end{bmatrix} - \begin{bmatrix} 3 & -2 & -4 \\ 3 & -2 & -5 \\ -1 & 1 & 2 \end{bmatrix} = \begin{bmatrix} 0 & 5 & 3 \\ -5 & 0 & 6 \\ -3 & -6 & 0 \end{bmatrix}$

Let $Q = \frac{1}{2}(A - A') = \frac{1}{2}\begin{bmatrix} 0 & 5 & 3 \\ -5 & 0 & 6 \\ -3 & -6 & 0 \end{bmatrix} = \begin{bmatrix} 0 & 5/2 & 3/2 \\ -5/2 & 0 & 3 \\ -3/2 & -3 & 0 \end{bmatrix}$

Now, $Q' = \begin{bmatrix} 0 & 5/2 & 3/2 \\ -5/2 & 0 & 3 \\ -3/2 & -3 & 0 \end{bmatrix}' = \begin{bmatrix} 0 & -5/2 & -3/2 \\ 5/2 & 0 & -3 \\ 3/2 & 3 & 0 \end{bmatrix} = -Q$

Thus, $Q = \frac{1}{2}(A - A')$ is a skew-symmetric matrix.

Representing A as the sum of P and Q,

$$P + Q = \begin{bmatrix} 3 & 1/2 & -5/2 \\ 1/2 & -2 & -2 \\ -5/2 & -2 & 2 \end{bmatrix} + \begin{bmatrix} 0 & 5/2 & 3/2 \\ -5/2 & 0 & 3 \\ -3/2 & -3 & 0 \end{bmatrix}$$

$$= \begin{bmatrix} 3 & 3 & -1 \\ -2 & -2 & 1 \\ -4 & -5 & 2 \end{bmatrix} = A$$

(iv) Let $A = \begin{bmatrix} 1 & 5 \\ -1 & 2 \end{bmatrix}$. Then, $A' = \begin{bmatrix} 1 & 5 \\ -1 & 2 \end{bmatrix}' = \begin{bmatrix} 1 & -1 \\ 5 & 2 \end{bmatrix}$

Now, $A + A' = \begin{bmatrix} 1 & 5 \\ -1 & 2 \end{bmatrix} + \begin{bmatrix} 1 & -1 \\ 5 & 2 \end{bmatrix} = \begin{bmatrix} 2 & 4 \\ 4 & 4 \end{bmatrix}$

Let $P = \frac{1}{2}(A + A') = \frac{1}{2}\begin{bmatrix} 2 & 4 \\ 4 & 4 \end{bmatrix} = \begin{bmatrix} 1 & 2 \\ 2 & 2 \end{bmatrix}$.

Now, $P' = \begin{bmatrix} 1 & 2 \\ 2 & 2 \end{bmatrix}' = \begin{bmatrix} 1 & 2 \\ 2 & 2 \end{bmatrix} = P$

Thus, $P = \frac{1}{2}(A + A')$ is a symmetric matrix.

Now, $A - A' = \begin{bmatrix} 1 & 5 \\ -1 & 2 \end{bmatrix} - \begin{bmatrix} 1 & -1 \\ 5 & 2 \end{bmatrix} = \begin{bmatrix} 0 & 6 \\ -6 & 0 \end{bmatrix}$

Let $Q = \frac{1}{2}(A - A') = \frac{1}{2}\begin{bmatrix} 0 & 6 \\ -6 & 0 \end{bmatrix} = \begin{bmatrix} 0 & 3 \\ -3 & 0 \end{bmatrix}$

Now, $$Q' = \begin{bmatrix} 0 & 3 \\ -3 & 0 \end{bmatrix}' = \begin{bmatrix} 0 & -3 \\ 3 & 0 \end{bmatrix} = -Q$$

Thus, $Q = \frac{1}{2}(A - A')$ is a skew-symmetric matrix.

Representing A as the sum of P and Q,

$$P + Q = \begin{bmatrix} 1 & 2 \\ 2 & 2 \end{bmatrix} + \begin{bmatrix} 0 & 3 \\ -3 & 0 \end{bmatrix} = \begin{bmatrix} 1 & 5 \\ -1 & 2 \end{bmatrix} = A$$

Directions (Q. Nos. 11 and 12) Choose the correct answer in the following questions :

Question 11 If A, B are symmetric matrices of same order, then $AB - BA$ is a

(a) skew-symmetric matrix (b) symmetric matrix
(c) zero matrix (d) identity matrix

◎ **Thinking Process** If A and B are symmetric matrices, then $A' = A$ and $B = B'$. Using these results and verify the option.

Sol. (a) Given, A and B are symmetric matrices.

$\therefore$ $A' = A$ and $B' = B$

Now, $(AB - BA)' = (AB)' - (BA)'$ $[\because (A - B)' = A' - B']$

$= B'A' - A'B'$ $[\because (AB)' = B'A']$

$= BA - AB$ $[\because A' = A \text{ and } B' = B]$

$= -(AB - BA)$

Thus, $(AB - BA)$ is a skew-symmetric matrix.

Question 12 If $A = \begin{bmatrix} \cos\alpha & -\sin\alpha \\ \sin\alpha & \cos\alpha \end{bmatrix}$, then $A + A' = I$, if the value of α is

(a) $\pi/6$ (b) $\pi/3$ (c) π (d) $3\pi/2$

Sol. (b) Here, $A = \begin{bmatrix} \cos\alpha & -\sin\alpha \\ \sin\alpha & \cos\alpha \end{bmatrix}$ and $A' = \begin{bmatrix} \cos\alpha & -\sin\alpha \\ \sin\alpha & \cos\alpha \end{bmatrix}' = \begin{bmatrix} \cos\alpha & \sin\alpha \\ -\sin\alpha & \cos\alpha \end{bmatrix}$

Given, $A + A' = I$

$$\Rightarrow \begin{bmatrix} \cos\alpha & -\sin\alpha \\ \sin\alpha & \cos\alpha \end{bmatrix} + \begin{bmatrix} \cos\alpha & \sin\alpha \\ -\sin\alpha & \cos\alpha \end{bmatrix} = \begin{bmatrix} 1 & 0 \\ 0 & 1 \end{bmatrix}$$

$$\Rightarrow \begin{bmatrix} 2\cos\alpha & 0 \\ 0 & 2\cos\alpha \end{bmatrix} = \begin{bmatrix} 1 & 0 \\ 0 & 1 \end{bmatrix}$$

On comparing the corresponding elements of the above matrices, we get

$$2\cos\alpha = 1 \Rightarrow \cos\alpha = \frac{1}{2} = \cos\frac{\pi}{3} \Rightarrow \alpha = \frac{\pi}{3}.$$

Exercise 3.4

Question 1 Matrices A and B will be inverse of each other only if

(a) $AB = BA$ (b) $AB = BA = O$
(c) $AB = O, BA = I$ (d) $AB = BA = I$

Sol. (d) We know that if A is a square matirx of order m and if there exists another square matrix B of the same order m, such that $AB = BA = I$, then B is said to be the inverse of A.

In this case, it is clear that A is the inverse of B.

Thus, matrices A and B will be inverse of each other only if $AB = BA = I$

Miscellaneous Exercise

Question 1 If A and B are symmetric matrices, prove that $AB - BA$ is a skew-symmetric matrix.

Sol. Given, A and B are symmetric matrices.

$\therefore \quad A' = A$ and $B' = B$.

Now, $(AB - BA)' = (AB)' - (BA)'$ $\quad (\because (A - B)' = A' - B')$

$= B'A' - A'B'$ $\quad [\because (AB)' = B'A']$

$= BA - AB$ $\quad (\because B' = B$ and $A' = A)$

$= -(AB - BA)$

Thus, $(AB - BA)$ is a skew-symmetric matrix.

Question 2 Show that the matrix $B'AB$ is symmetric or skew-symmetric according as A is symmetric or skew-symmetric.

Sol. Let A is a symmetric matrix, then $A' = A$.

Consider $(B'AB)' = \{B'(AB)\}' = (AB)'(B')'$ $\quad [\because (AB)' = B'A']$

$= B'A'(B)$ $\quad [\because (B')' = B]$

$= B'(A'B) = B'(AB)$ $\quad [\because A' = A]$

$\therefore \quad (B'AB)' = B'AB$

which shows that $B'AB$ is a symmetric matrix.

Now, we suppose that A is a skew-symmetric matrix.

Then, $A' = -A$

Consider $(B'AB)' = [B'(AB)]' = (AB)'(B')'$ $\quad [\because (AB)' = B'A'$ and $(A')' = A]$

$= (B'A')B = B'(-A)B = -B'AB$ $\quad [\because A' = -A]$

$\therefore$ $(B'AB)' = -B'AB$ which shows that $B'AB$ is a skew-symmetric matrix.

Question 3 Find the values of x, y and z if the matrix $A=\begin{bmatrix}0 & 2y & z\\ x & y & -z\\ x & -y & z\end{bmatrix}$ satisfies the equation $A'A=I$.

Sol. Given, $A'A=I$

$$\Rightarrow \begin{bmatrix}0 & 2y & z\\ x & y & -z\\ x & -y & z\end{bmatrix}'\begin{bmatrix}0 & 2y & z\\ x & y & -z\\ x & -y & z\end{bmatrix}=I \Rightarrow \begin{bmatrix}0 & x & x\\ 2y & y & -y\\ z & -z & z\end{bmatrix}\begin{bmatrix}0 & 2y & z\\ x & y & -z\\ x & -y & z\end{bmatrix}=\begin{bmatrix}1 & 0 & 0\\ 0 & 1 & 0\\ 0 & 0 & 1\end{bmatrix}$$

$$\Rightarrow \begin{bmatrix}0+x^2+x^2 & 0+xy-xy & 0-xz+xz\\ 0+yx-yx & 4y^2+y^2+y^2 & 2yz-yz-yz\\ 0-zx+zx & 2yz-yz-yz & z^2+z^2+z^2\end{bmatrix}=\begin{bmatrix}1 & 0 & 0\\ 0 & 1 & 0\\ 0 & 0 & 1\end{bmatrix}$$

$$\Rightarrow \begin{bmatrix}2x^2 & 0 & 0\\ 0 & 6y^2 & 0\\ 0 & 0 & 3z^2\end{bmatrix}=\begin{bmatrix}1 & 0 & 0\\ 0 & 1 & 0\\ 0 & 0 & 1\end{bmatrix}$$

On comparing the corresponding elements, we get

$$2x^2=1,\quad 6y^2=1,\quad 3z^2=1$$

$$\Rightarrow \quad x^2=\frac{1}{2},\quad y^2=\frac{1}{6},\quad z^2=\frac{1}{3}$$

$$\Rightarrow \quad x=\pm\frac{1}{\sqrt{2}},\quad y=\pm\frac{1}{\sqrt{6}},\quad z=\pm\frac{1}{\sqrt{3}}$$

Question 4 For what value of x, $[1\ \ 2\ \ 1]\begin{bmatrix}1 & 2 & 0\\ 2 & 0 & 1\\ 1 & 0 & 2\end{bmatrix}\begin{bmatrix}0\\ 2\\ x\end{bmatrix}=O$?

Sol. Given, $[1\ \ 2\ \ 1]\left(\begin{bmatrix}1 & 2 & 0\\ 2 & 0 & 1\\ 1 & 0 & 2\end{bmatrix}\begin{bmatrix}0\\ 2\\ x\end{bmatrix}\right)=O$

$$\Rightarrow \quad [1\ \ 2\ \ 1]\begin{bmatrix}1 & 2 & 0\\ 2 & 0 & 1\\ 1 & 0 & 2\end{bmatrix}\begin{bmatrix}0\\ 2\\ x\end{bmatrix}=O$$

$$\Rightarrow \quad [1\ \ 2\ \ 1]\begin{bmatrix}0+4+0\\ 0+0+x\\ 0+0+2x\end{bmatrix}=O$$

$$\Rightarrow \quad [1\ \ 2\ \ 1]\begin{bmatrix}4\\ x\\ 2x\end{bmatrix}=O \Rightarrow [4+2x+2x]=[O]$$

$$\Rightarrow \quad 4+4x=0 \Rightarrow x=-1.$$

Question 5 If $A=\begin{bmatrix}3 & 1\\ -1 & 2\end{bmatrix}$, show that $A^2-5A+7I=O$.

Solution Given, $A=\begin{bmatrix}3 & 1\\ -1 & 2\end{bmatrix}$

$$\therefore \quad A^2=AA=\begin{bmatrix}3 & 1\\ -1 & 2\end{bmatrix}\begin{bmatrix}3 & 1\\ -1 & 2\end{bmatrix}=\begin{bmatrix}9-1 & 3+2\\ -3-2 & -1+4\end{bmatrix}=\begin{bmatrix}8 & 5\\ -5 & 3\end{bmatrix}$$

Now, $$A^2-5A+7I=\begin{bmatrix}8 & 5\\ -5 & 3\end{bmatrix}-5\begin{bmatrix}3 & 1\\ -1 & 2\end{bmatrix}+7\begin{bmatrix}1 & 0\\ 0 & 1\end{bmatrix}$$

$$=\begin{bmatrix}8 & 5\\ -5 & 3\end{bmatrix}-\begin{bmatrix}15 & 5\\ -5 & 10\end{bmatrix}+\begin{bmatrix}7 & 0\\ 0 & 7\end{bmatrix}$$

$$=\begin{bmatrix}8-15+7 & 5-5+0\\ -5+5+0 & 3-10+7\end{bmatrix}=\begin{bmatrix}0 & 0\\ 0 & 0\end{bmatrix}=O$$

Hence Proved.

Question 6 Find x, if $\begin{bmatrix}x & -5 & -1\end{bmatrix}\begin{bmatrix}1 & 0 & 2\\ 0 & 2 & 1\\ 2 & 0 & 3\end{bmatrix}\begin{bmatrix}x\\ 4\\ 1\end{bmatrix}=O$.

Sol. Given, $[x \quad -5 \quad -1]\begin{bmatrix}1 & 0 & 2\\ 0 & 2 & 1\\ 2 & 0 & 3\end{bmatrix}\begin{bmatrix}x\\ 4\\ 1\end{bmatrix}=O$

$$\Rightarrow \quad [x \quad -5 \quad -1]\left(\begin{bmatrix}1 & 0 & 2\\ 0 & 2 & 1\\ 2 & 0 & 3\end{bmatrix}\begin{bmatrix}x\\ 4\\ 1\end{bmatrix}\right)=O$$

$$\Rightarrow \quad [x \quad -5 \quad -1]\begin{bmatrix}x+0+2\\ 0+8+1\\ 2x+0+3\end{bmatrix}=O$$

$\Rightarrow \quad [x(x+2)+(-5)(9)+(-1)(2x+3)]=[O]$

$\Rightarrow \quad x^2-48=0 \Rightarrow x^2=48 \Rightarrow x=\pm\sqrt{48}=\pm 4\sqrt{3}$

Question 7 A manufacturer sells the products x, y, z in two markets, annual sales are indicated below.

Market	Products		
I	10,000	2,000	18,000
II	6,000	20,000	8,000

(a) If unit sale prices of x, y and z are ₹ 2.50, ₹ 1.50 and ₹ 1.00 respectively. Find the total revenue in each market with the help of matrix algebra.

(b) If the unit costs of the above three commodities are ₹ 2.00, ₹ 1.00 and 50 paise respectively. Find the gross profit.

Sol. Let the matrix representing the sales be $A = \begin{bmatrix} 10000 & 2000 & 18000 \\ 6000 & 20000 & 8000 \end{bmatrix}$

(a) Let the matrix representing the sale price per unit be $B = \begin{bmatrix} 2.50 \\ 1.50 \\ 1.00 \end{bmatrix}$

Total revenue in each market is given by the product AB

$$= \begin{bmatrix} 10000 & 2000 & 18000 \\ 6000 & 20000 & 8000 \end{bmatrix} \begin{bmatrix} 5/2 \\ 3/2 \\ 1 \end{bmatrix}$$

$$= \begin{bmatrix} 10000 \times \frac{5}{2} + 2000 \times \frac{3}{2} + 18000 \times 1 \\ 6000 \times \frac{5}{2} + 20000 \times \frac{3}{2} + 8000 \times 1 \end{bmatrix} = \begin{bmatrix} 46000 \\ 53000 \end{bmatrix}$$

Hence, total revenue in market I is ₹ 46000 and that in market II is ₹ 53000.

(b) Let the matrix representing the cost price per unit be $C = \begin{bmatrix} 2.00 \\ 1.00 \\ 0.50 \end{bmatrix}$

∴ Total cost in the two markets is given by the product AC

$$= \begin{bmatrix} 10000 & 2000 & 18000 \\ 6000 & 20000 & 8000 \end{bmatrix} \begin{bmatrix} 2 \\ 1 \\ 1/2 \end{bmatrix}$$

$$\Rightarrow \quad AC = \begin{bmatrix} 10000 \times 2 + 2000 \times 1 + 18000 \times \frac{1}{2} \\ 6000 \times 2 + 20000 \times 1 + 8000 \times \frac{1}{2} \end{bmatrix} = \begin{bmatrix} 31000 \\ 36000 \end{bmatrix}$$

Profit in market I =₹46000 – 31000) = ₹ 15000

and profit in market II = ₹(53000 – 36000) =₹ 17000

∴ The gross profit = ₹ (15000 + 17000) = ₹ 32000.

Question 8 Find the matrix X so that, $X \begin{bmatrix} 1 & 2 & 3 \\ 4 & 5 & 6 \end{bmatrix} = \begin{bmatrix} -7 & -8 & -9 \\ 2 & 4 & 6 \end{bmatrix}$.

Sol. Given, $X \begin{bmatrix} 1 & 2 & 3 \\ 4 & 5 & 6 \end{bmatrix} = \begin{bmatrix} -7 & -8 & -9 \\ 2 & 4 & 6 \end{bmatrix}$

The matrix given on the RHS of the equation is a 2×3 matrix and the one given on the LHS of the equation is as a 2×3 matrix. Therefore, X has to be a 2×2 matrix. Now, let $X = \begin{bmatrix} a & c \\ b & d \end{bmatrix}$

Therefore,

$$\begin{bmatrix} a & c \\ b & d \end{bmatrix}\begin{bmatrix} 1 & 2 & 3 \\ 4 & 5 & 6 \end{bmatrix} = \begin{bmatrix} -7 & -8 & -9 \\ 2 & 4 & 6 \end{bmatrix}$$

$$\Rightarrow \quad \begin{bmatrix} a+4c & 2a+5c & 3a+6c \\ b+4d & 2b+5d & 3b+6d \end{bmatrix} = \begin{bmatrix} -7 & -8 & -9 \\ 2 & 4 & 6 \end{bmatrix}$$

On equating the corresponding elements of the two matrices, we get

$$a + 4c = -7, \quad 2a + 5c = -8, \quad 3a + 6c = -9$$

$$b + 4d = 2, \quad 2b + 5d = 4, \quad 3b + 6d = 6$$

Now, $\quad a + 4c = -7 \Rightarrow a = -7 - 4c$

$$2a + 5c = -8 \Rightarrow -14 - 8c + 5c = -8 \Rightarrow -3c = 6 \Rightarrow c = -2$$

$\therefore \quad a = -7 - 4(-2) = -7 + 8 = 1$

Now, $\quad b + 4d = 2 \Rightarrow b = 2 - 4d$

and $\quad 2b + 5d = 4 \Rightarrow 4 - 8d + 5d = 4$

$\Rightarrow \quad -3d = 0 \Rightarrow d = 0$

$\therefore \quad b = 2 - 4(0) = 2$

Thus, $\quad a = 1, b = 2, \quad c = -2, \quad d = 0$

Hence, the required matrix X is $\begin{bmatrix} 1 & -2 \\ 2 & 0 \end{bmatrix}$.

Direction (Q. Nos. 9 to 11) Choose the correct answer in the following questions:

Question 9 If $A = \begin{bmatrix} \alpha & \beta \\ \gamma & -\alpha \end{bmatrix}$ is such that $A^2 = I$, then

(a) $1 + \alpha^2 + \beta\gamma = 0$ (b) $1 - \alpha^2 + \beta\gamma = 0$

(c) $1 - \alpha^2 - \beta\gamma = 0$ (d) $1 + \alpha^2 - \beta\gamma = 0$

Thinking Process

(i) Find A^2 and use the given equation $A^2 = I$ as given in question.

(ii) Equate the respective elements of A^2 and I to find out the correct option.

Sol. (c) Given, $A^2 = I$

$$\therefore AA = I \Rightarrow \begin{bmatrix} \alpha & \beta \\ \gamma & -\alpha \end{bmatrix}\begin{bmatrix} \alpha & \beta \\ \gamma & -\alpha \end{bmatrix} = \begin{bmatrix} 1 & 0 \\ 0 & 1 \end{bmatrix}$$

$$\Rightarrow \begin{bmatrix} \alpha^2 + \beta\gamma & \alpha\beta - \alpha\beta \\ \alpha\gamma - \gamma\alpha & \gamma\beta + \alpha^2 \end{bmatrix} = \begin{bmatrix} 1 & 0 \\ 0 & 1 \end{bmatrix} \Rightarrow \begin{bmatrix} \alpha^2 + B\gamma & 0 \\ 0 & \gamma\beta + \alpha^2 \end{bmatrix} = \begin{bmatrix} 1 & 0 \\ 0 & 1 \end{bmatrix}$$

On comparing the corresponding elements, we get

$$\alpha^2 + \beta\gamma = 1 \quad \Rightarrow \alpha^2 + \beta\gamma - 1 = 0$$

$$\Rightarrow \quad 1 - \alpha^2 - \beta\gamma = 0$$

Question 10 If a matrix A is both symmetric and skew-symmetric matrix, then

(a) A is a diagonal matrix
(b) A is zero matrix
(c) A is a square matrix
(d) None of the above

Sol. (b) Let A be a square matrix such that A is both symmetric and skew-symmetric matrix.

$\Rightarrow$ $A' = A$ ($\because A$ is symmetric)

and $A' = -A$ ($\because A$ is skew-symmetric)

$\therefore$ $A = -A$

$\Rightarrow$ $A + A = O \Rightarrow 2A = O \Rightarrow A = O$

Question 11 If A is square matrix such that $A^2 = A$, then $(I + A)^3 - 7A$ is equal to

(a) A
(b) $I - A$
(c) I
(d) $3A$

Sol. (c) Here, $(I + A)^3 = (I + A)(I + A)(I + A)$

$= (I^2 + IA + AI + A^2)(I + A)$

$= (I + A + A + A)(I + A)$ $\left(\begin{array}{l} \because I^n = I \\ I \cdot A = A = A \cdot I \\ A^2 = A \text{ (given)} \end{array}\right)$

$= (I + 3A)(I + A)$

$= I^2 + IA + 3AI + 3A^2$

$= I + A + 3A + 3A$

$= I + 7A$

Now, $(I + A)^3 - 7A = I + 7A - 7A = I$

Mistake Alert For matrices $(A + B)^3 \neq A^3 + B^3 + 3A^2B + 3AB^2$. We have to multiply $(A + B)(A + B)(A + B)$. Because $AB \neq BA$.

DIKSHA APP Questions

☐ Multiple Choice Questions

Q.1 If $a_{ij} = |2i + 3j^2|$, then matrix $A_{2\times 2} = [a_{ij}]$ is

(a) $\begin{bmatrix} 5 & -14 \\ 7 & 16 \end{bmatrix}$ (b) $\begin{bmatrix} 5 & 14 \\ -7 & 16 \end{bmatrix}$ (c) $\begin{bmatrix} 5 & 14 \\ 7 & 16 \end{bmatrix}$ (d) $\begin{bmatrix} 5 & 14 \\ 7 & -16 \end{bmatrix}$

Sol. (c) We have, $a_{ij} = |2i + 3j^2|$ ...(i)

Now, $A_{2\times 2} = [a_{ij}] \Rightarrow A = \begin{bmatrix} a_{11} & a_{12} \\ a_{21} & a_{22} \end{bmatrix}$

Here, $a_{11} = |2 + 3| = 5$ (Put $i = 1, j = 1$)

$a_{12} = |2 + 12| = 14$ (Put $i = 1, j = 2$)

$a_{21} = |4 + 3| = 7$ (Put $i = 2, j = 1$)

$a_{22} = |4 + 12| = 16$ (Put $i = 2, j = 2$)

So, $A = \begin{bmatrix} 5 & 14 \\ 7 & 16 \end{bmatrix}$

Q.2 Horizontally arranged elements in a matrix are called

(a) column (b) rows (c) transpose (d) none

Sol. (b) If we have, $A = \begin{bmatrix} a_{11} & a_{12} & \cdots & a_{1n} \\ a_{21} & \cdots & \cdots & \cdots \\ \vdots & \cdots & \cdots & \cdots \\ a_{m_1} & \cdots & \cdots & a_{mn} \end{bmatrix}$

Horizontally arranged elements are $a_{11}\ a_{12} \cdots a_{1n}$ and it is called row.

Q.3 Who is the father of matrices.

(a) Arthur Cayley (b) James Sylevester

(c) JP Morgan (d) Gauss

Sol. (a) Arthur Cayley is the father of matrices.

Q.4 If $A = \begin{bmatrix} 0 & x & y \\ 2 & 0 & 5 \\ -6 & -5 & z \end{bmatrix}$ is a skew-symmetric matrix then value of $x + y^2 + z$ is

(a) -34 (b) 38

(c) 34 (d) 35

Sol. (c) We have, $A = \begin{bmatrix} 0 & x & y \\ 2 & 0 & 5 \\ 6 & -5 & z \end{bmatrix}$

$$\therefore \quad A^T = \begin{bmatrix} 0 & 2 & 6 \\ x & 0 & -5 \\ y & 5 & z \end{bmatrix}$$

It is given that A is skew symmetric matrix, so

$$\Rightarrow \quad A^T = -A$$

$$\Rightarrow \quad \begin{bmatrix} 0 & 2 & 6 \\ x & 0 & -5 \\ y & 5 & z \end{bmatrix} = -\begin{bmatrix} 0 & x & y \\ 2 & 0 & 5 \\ 6 & -5 & z \end{bmatrix}$$

$$\Rightarrow \quad \begin{bmatrix} 0 & 2 & 6 \\ x & 0 & -5 \\ y & 5 & z \end{bmatrix} = \begin{bmatrix} 0 & -x & -y \\ -2 & 0 & -5 \\ -6 & 5 & -z \end{bmatrix}$$

On comparing the corresponding elements, we get

$$x = -2, y = -6, z = -z$$

$$\Rightarrow \quad z + z = 0 \Rightarrow z = 0$$

So, $\quad x + y^2 + z = (-2) + (-6)^2 + 0 = -2 + 36 + 0 = 34$

Q.5 If $A = \begin{bmatrix} 5 & 1 & 0 \\ 6 & 2 & -1 \end{bmatrix}$ and $B^T = \begin{bmatrix} 2 & 1 \\ -2 & 0 \\ 1 & 3 \end{bmatrix}$ then BA^T is

(a) $\begin{bmatrix} 8 & 7 \\ 5 & 3 \end{bmatrix}$ (b) $\begin{bmatrix} 8 & 5 \\ 7 & 3 \end{bmatrix}$ (c) $\begin{bmatrix} 3 & 7 \\ 5 & 8 \end{bmatrix}$ (d) $\begin{bmatrix} 3 & 5 \\ 7 & 8 \end{bmatrix}$

Sol. (a) Given, $A = \begin{bmatrix} 5 & 1 & 0 \\ 6 & 2 & -1 \end{bmatrix}$ and $B^T = \begin{bmatrix} 2 & 1 \\ -2 & 0 \\ 1 & 3 \end{bmatrix}$

$$\therefore \quad A^T = \begin{bmatrix} 5 & 6 \\ 1 & 2 \\ 0 & -1 \end{bmatrix} \text{ and } B = (B^T)^T = \begin{bmatrix} 2 & -2 & 1 \\ 1 & 0 & 3 \end{bmatrix}$$

Now, $\quad BA^T = \begin{bmatrix} 2 & -2 & 1 \\ 1 & 0 & 3 \end{bmatrix} \begin{bmatrix} 5 & 6 \\ 1 & 2 \\ 0 & -1 \end{bmatrix}$

$$= \begin{bmatrix} 10-2+0 & 12-4-1 \\ 5+0+0 & 6+0-3 \end{bmatrix} = \begin{bmatrix} 8 & 7 \\ 5 & 3 \end{bmatrix}$$

Q.6 If $\begin{bmatrix}4\\2\\3\end{bmatrix}[1 \quad 3 \quad -3]\begin{bmatrix}x\\y\\z\end{bmatrix} = O$, then $x+3y-3z$ is

(a) 1 (b) 3

(c) 4 (d) 0

Sol. (d) Given, $\begin{bmatrix}4\\2\\3\end{bmatrix}[1 \quad 3 \quad -3]\begin{bmatrix}x\\y\\z\end{bmatrix} = O$

$$\Rightarrow \begin{bmatrix}4 & 12 & -12\\2 & 6 & -6\\3 & 9 & -9\end{bmatrix}\begin{bmatrix}x\\y\\z\end{bmatrix} = O$$

$$\Rightarrow \begin{bmatrix}4x+12y-12z\\2x+6y-6z\\3x+9y-9z\end{bmatrix} = O = \begin{bmatrix}0\\0\\0\end{bmatrix}$$

On comparing both sides, we get

$$\Rightarrow \quad 4x+12y-12z = 0 \Rightarrow x+3y-3z = 0$$

Q.7 If $\begin{bmatrix}2 & -5\\4 & 6\end{bmatrix} + 3X = \begin{bmatrix}8 & 4\\1 & 0\end{bmatrix}$ then X is

(a) $\begin{bmatrix}2 & 3\\-1 & -2\end{bmatrix}$ (b) $\begin{bmatrix}2 & 3\\1 & -2\end{bmatrix}$ (c) $\begin{bmatrix}2 & 3\\-1 & 2\end{bmatrix}$ (d) $\begin{bmatrix}2 & 3\\1 & 2\end{bmatrix}$

Sol. (a) Given, $\begin{bmatrix}2 & -5\\4 & 6\end{bmatrix} + 3X = \begin{bmatrix}8 & 4\\1 & 0\end{bmatrix}$

$$\Rightarrow \quad 3X = \begin{bmatrix}8 & 4\\1 & 0\end{bmatrix} - \begin{bmatrix}2 & -5\\4 & 6\end{bmatrix} \Rightarrow 3X = \begin{bmatrix}8-2 & 4-(-5)\\1-4 & 0-6\end{bmatrix}$$

$$\Rightarrow \quad 3X = \begin{bmatrix}6 & 9\\-3 & -6\end{bmatrix} \Rightarrow X = \begin{bmatrix}\frac{6}{3} & \frac{9}{3}\\-\frac{3}{3} & -\frac{6}{3}\end{bmatrix} = \begin{bmatrix}2 & 3\\-1 & -2\end{bmatrix}$$

Q.8 If A and B are symmetric matrix then $(BA)^T$ is

(a) AB (b) BA (c) A (d) B

Sol. (a) Given, A and B are symmetric matrices.

So, $A^T = A, B^T = B$

Now, $(BA)^T = A^T \cdot B^T$ $\quad ((AB)^T = B^T \cdot A^T)$

$= AB$

☐ Subjective Type Questions

Q.1 Find $A^3 - 2A^2 + 3A - I$ where, I is a unit matrix and

$$A = \begin{bmatrix} 1 & 3 & 2 \\ 2 & 0 & 3 \\ 1 & -1 & 1 \end{bmatrix}.$$

Sol. We have, $A = \begin{bmatrix} 1 & 3 & 2 \\ 2 & 0 & 3 \\ 1 & -1 & 1 \end{bmatrix}$

$$\therefore A^2 = A \cdot A = \begin{bmatrix} 1 & 3 & 2 \\ 2 & 0 & 3 \\ 1 & -1 & 1 \end{bmatrix}\begin{bmatrix} 1 & 3 & 2 \\ 2 & 0 & 3 \\ 1 & -1 & 1 \end{bmatrix}$$

$$= \begin{bmatrix} 1+6+2 & 3+0-2 & 2+9+2 \\ 2+0+3 & 6+0-3 & 4+0+3 \\ 1-2+1 & 3+0-1 & 2-3+1 \end{bmatrix} = \begin{bmatrix} 9 & 1 & 13 \\ 5 & 3 & 7 \\ 0 & 2 & 0 \end{bmatrix}$$

and $\quad A^3 = A^2 \cdot A$

$$= \begin{bmatrix} 9 & 1 & 13 \\ 5 & 3 & 7 \\ 0 & 2 & 0 \end{bmatrix}\begin{bmatrix} 1 & 3 & 2 \\ 2 & 0 & 3 \\ 1 & -1 & 1 \end{bmatrix}$$

$$= \begin{bmatrix} 9+2+13 & 27+0-13 & 18+3+13 \\ 5+6+7 & 15+0-7 & 10+9+7 \\ 0+4+0 & 0+0+0 & 0+6+0 \end{bmatrix} = \begin{bmatrix} 24 & 14 & 34 \\ 18 & 8 & 26 \\ 4 & 0 & 6 \end{bmatrix}$$

Now, $\quad A^3 - 2A^2 + 3A - I$

$$= \begin{bmatrix} 24 & 14 & 34 \\ 18 & 8 & 26 \\ 4 & 0 & 6 \end{bmatrix} - 2\begin{bmatrix} 9 & 1 & 13 \\ 5 & 3 & 7 \\ 0 & 2 & 0 \end{bmatrix} + 3\begin{bmatrix} 1 & 3 & 2 \\ 2 & 0 & 3 \\ 1 & -1 & 1 \end{bmatrix} - \begin{bmatrix} 1 & 0 & 0 \\ 0 & 1 & 0 \\ 0 & 0 & 1 \end{bmatrix}$$

$$= \begin{bmatrix} 24 & 14 & 34 \\ 18 & 8 & 26 \\ 4 & 0 & 6 \end{bmatrix} - \begin{bmatrix} 18 & 2 & 26 \\ 10 & 6 & 14 \\ 0 & 4 & 0 \end{bmatrix} + \begin{bmatrix} 3 & 9 & 6 \\ 6 & 0 & 9 \\ 3 & -3 & 3 \end{bmatrix} - \begin{bmatrix} 1 & 0 & 0 \\ 0 & 1 & 0 \\ 0 & 0 & 1 \end{bmatrix}$$

$$= \begin{bmatrix} 24-18+3-1 & 14-2+9-0 & 34-26+6-0 \\ 18-10+6-0 & 8-6+0-1 & 26-14+9-0 \\ 4-0+3-0 & 0-4-3-0 & 6-0+3-1 \end{bmatrix}$$

$$= \begin{bmatrix} 8 & 21 & 14 \\ 14 & 1 & 21 \\ 7 & -7 & 8 \end{bmatrix}$$

Q.2 If $A=\begin{bmatrix}1 & 2 & 3\\ 4 & 1 & 5\\ 3 & 6 & 6\end{bmatrix}$, then prove that A can be expressed as sum of symmetric and skew symmetric matrices.

Sol. Given, $A=\begin{bmatrix}1 & 2 & 3\\ 4 & 1 & 5\\ 3 & 6 & 6\end{bmatrix}$ $\therefore A^T=\begin{bmatrix}1 & 4 & 3\\ 2 & 1 & 6\\ 3 & 5 & 6\end{bmatrix}$

Let $P=\dfrac{A+A^T}{2}=\dfrac{1}{2}\left[\begin{bmatrix}1 & 2 & 3\\ 4 & 1 & 5\\ 3 & 6 & 6\end{bmatrix}+\begin{bmatrix}1 & 4 & 3\\ 2 & 1 & 6\\ 3 & 5 & 6\end{bmatrix}\right]$

$$=\frac{1}{2}\begin{bmatrix}2 & 6 & 6\\ 6 & 2 & 11\\ 6 & 11 & 12\end{bmatrix}=\begin{bmatrix}1 & 3 & 3\\ 3 & 1 & \frac{11}{2}\\ 3 & \frac{11}{2} & 6\end{bmatrix}$$

and $Q=\dfrac{A-A^T}{2}=\dfrac{1}{2}\left[\begin{bmatrix}1 & 2 & 3\\ 4 & 1 & 5\\ 3 & 6 & 6\end{bmatrix}-\begin{bmatrix}1 & 4 & 3\\ 2 & 1 & 6\\ 3 & 5 & 6\end{bmatrix}\right]=\dfrac{1}{2}\begin{bmatrix}0 & -2 & 0\\ 2 & 0 & -1\\ 0 & 1 & 0\end{bmatrix}$

$$=\begin{bmatrix}0 & -1 & 0\\ 1 & 0 & -\frac{1}{2}\\ 0 & \frac{1}{2} & 0\end{bmatrix} \quad \therefore P^{T}=\begin{bmatrix}1 & 3 & 3\\ 3 & 1 & \frac{11}{2}\\ 3 & \frac{11}{2} & 6\end{bmatrix}=P$$

Hence P is symmetric

and $Q^T=\begin{bmatrix}0 & 1 & 0\\ -1 & 0 & \frac{1}{2}\\ 0 & -\frac{1}{2} & 0\end{bmatrix}=-Q$

Hence, Q is skew-symmetric

Now $P+Q=\begin{bmatrix}1 & 3 & 3\\ 3 & 1 & \frac{11}{2}\\ 3 & \frac{11}{2} & 6\end{bmatrix}+\begin{bmatrix}0 & -1 & 0\\ 1 & 0 & -\frac{1}{2}\\ 0 & \frac{1}{2} & 0\end{bmatrix}=\begin{bmatrix}1 & 2 & 3\\ 4 & 1 & 5\\ 3 & 6 & 6\end{bmatrix}=A$

Hence, A can be expressed as a sum of symmetric and skew-symmetric matrix.

Determinants

CHAPTER 04

Important Points

Every square matrix A is associated with a number called its determinant and it is denoted by $|A|$ and det(A) or Δ. Only square matrices have determinants.

01 Expansion of determinant of order 1 $|a| = a$

02 Expansion of determinant of order (2×2)

$$\begin{vmatrix} a_{11} & a_{12} \\ a_{21} & a_{22} \end{vmatrix} = (a_{11}\, a_{22} - a_{21}\, a_{12})$$

03 Expansion of determinant of order (3×3)

$$\begin{vmatrix} a_{11} & a_{12} & a_{13} \\ a_{21} & a_{22} & a_{23} \\ a_{31} & a_{32} & a_{33} \end{vmatrix} = a_{11}\,(a_{22}\, a_{33} - a_{32}\, a_{23}) - a_{12}(a_{21}\, a_{33} - a_{31}\, a_{23})$$

$$+ a_{13}(a_{21}\, a_{32} - a_{31}\, a_{22})$$

Note Similarly, we can expand the above determinant corresponding to any row or column.

04 **Area of a Triangle** Let $A(x_1, y_1)$, $B(x_2, y_2)$ and $C(x_3, y_3)$ be the vertices of a $\Delta\, ABC$. Then, its area is given by

$$\Delta = \frac{1}{2}\begin{vmatrix} x_1 & y_1 & 1 \\ x_2 & y_2 & 1 \\ x_3 & y_3 & 1 \end{vmatrix} = \frac{1}{2} \cdot \{x_1(y_2 - y_3) + x_2(y_3 - y_1) + x_3\,(y_1 - y_2)\}$$

05 **Collinearity** Three points $A\,(x_1, y_1)$, $B\,(x_2, y_2)$ and $C\,(x_3, y_3)$ are collinear when $\Delta = 0$.

i.e.
$$\begin{vmatrix} x_1 & y_1 & 1 \\ x_2 & y_2 & 1 \\ x_3 & y_3 & 1 \end{vmatrix} = 0$$

06 Minor of an element a_{ij} of a matrix is the determinant obtained by deleting i^{th} row and j^{th} column in which a_{ij} lies. Minor of a_{ij} is denoted by M_{ij}.

$$\text{If } A = \begin{vmatrix} a_{11} & a_{12} & a_{13} \\ a_{21} & a_{22} & a_{23} \\ a_{31} & a_{32} & a_{33} \end{vmatrix}, \text{ then}$$

(i) Minors of A are $M_{11} = \begin{vmatrix} a_{22} & a_{23} \\ a_{32} & a_{33} \end{vmatrix}$, $M_{12} = \begin{vmatrix} a_{21} & a_{23} \\ a_{31} & a_{33} \end{vmatrix}$

$$M_{13} = \begin{vmatrix} a_{21} & a_{22} \\ a_{31} & a_{32} \end{vmatrix}, M_{21} = \begin{vmatrix} a_{12} & a_{13} \\ a_{32} & a_{33} \end{vmatrix}$$

$$M_{22} = \begin{vmatrix} a_{11} & a_{13} \\ a_{31} & a_{33} \end{vmatrix}, M_{23} = \begin{vmatrix} a_{11} & a_{12} \\ a_{31} & a_{32} \end{vmatrix}$$

$$M_{31} = \begin{vmatrix} a_{12} & a_{13} \\ a_{22} & a_{23} \end{vmatrix}, M_{32} = \begin{vmatrix} a_{11} & a_{13} \\ a_{21} & a_{23} \end{vmatrix}, \quad M_{33} = \begin{vmatrix} a_{11} & a_{12} \\ a_{21} & a_{22} \end{vmatrix}$$

07 Cofactors of an element a_{ij} denote by A_{ij} is defined by $A_{ij} = (-1)^{i+j} \cdot M_{ij}$, where M_{ij} is minor of a_{ij} and $i = 1, 2, 3, \ldots\ldots$, $j = 1, 2, 3 \ldots\ldots$

08 **Adjoint of a Square Matrix** Let $A = [a_{ij}]$ be a square matrix. Also assume $B = [A_{ij}]$, where A_{ij} is the cofactor of element a_{ij} in matrix A.

Then the transpose of B (*i.e.*, B^T) is called adjoint of a matrix and denoted by adj(A).

09 Some Properties Associated with Matrices and Determinant

(i) $AB \neq BA$

(ii) $AI = IA = A$

(iii) $(A^T)^{-1} = (A^{-1})^T$

(iv) $(AB)^{-1} = B^{-1}A^{-1}$

(v) $A \operatorname{adj}(A) = \operatorname{adj}(A) A = |A| I$

(vi) $\operatorname{adj}(AB) = \operatorname{adj}(B) \operatorname{adj}(A)$

(vii) $\operatorname{adj}(A^T) = (\operatorname{adj} A)^T$

(viii) $\operatorname{adj}(A^{-1}) = (\operatorname{adj} A)^{-1}$

(ix) $|\operatorname{adj} A| = |A|^{n-1}$, if $|A| \neq 0$ and n is the order of A.

(x) $|AB| = |A||B|$

(xi) $|kA| = k^n |A|$, where n is order of A.

(xii) $|A \text{ adj } A| = |A|^n$, where n is order of A.

(xiii) $|A^{-1}| = \dfrac{1}{|A|}$

(xiv) $\text{adj}(\text{adj} A) = |A|^{n-2} A$. If A is non-singular and n is the order of A.

(xv) $|A^K| = |A|^K$

(xvi) If $AB = BA = I$ then $A^{-1} = B$ or $B^{-1} = A$ and hence $(A^{-1})^{-1} = A$

10 Let the system of equations is

$a_1x + b_1y + c_1z = d_1, \quad a_2x + b_2y + c_2z = d_2, \quad a_3x + b_3y + c_3z = d_3,$

then, this system of equations can be written as $AX = B$, where

$$A = \begin{bmatrix} a_1 & b_1 & c_1 \\ a_2 & b_2 & c_2 \\ a_3 & b_3 & c_3 \end{bmatrix}, X = \begin{bmatrix} x \\ y \\ z \end{bmatrix} \text{ and } B = \begin{bmatrix} d_1 \\ d_2 \\ d_3 \end{bmatrix}$$

A system of equations is consistent or inconsistent according as its solution exists or not.

(a) For a square matrix A in matrix equation $AX = B$

(i) $|A| \neq 0$, then system of equations is consistent and has unique solution.

(ii) $|A| = 0$ and (adj A) $B \neq 0$, then there exists no solution, *i.e.*, inconsistent.

(iii) $|A| = 0$ and (A) $B = 0$, then system of equations is consistent and has an infinite number of solutions.

(b) When $B = \begin{bmatrix} 0 \\ 0 \\ 0 \end{bmatrix}$.

In such cases, we have

(i) $|A| \neq 0 \Rightarrow$ system has only trivial solution *i.e.*, $x = 0, y = 0, z = 0$

(ii) $|A| = 0 \Rightarrow$ system has infinitely many solutions.

Exercise 4.1

Direction (Q. Nos. 1 and 2) Evaluate the determinants.

Question 1 $\begin{vmatrix} 2 & 4 \\ -5 & -1 \end{vmatrix}$.

Sol. We hae, $\begin{vmatrix} 2 & 4 \\ -5 & -1 \end{vmatrix}, = 2 \times (-1) - (-5) \times 4 = -2 + 20 = 18$

Question 2 (i) $\begin{vmatrix} \cos\theta & -\sin\theta \\ \sin\theta & \cos\theta \end{vmatrix}$ (ii) $\begin{vmatrix} x^2 - x + 1 & x - 1 \\ x + 1 & x + 1 \end{vmatrix}$

Sol.

(i) We have, $\begin{vmatrix} \cos\theta & -\sin\theta \\ \sin\theta & \cos\theta \end{vmatrix} = (\cos\theta)(\cos\theta) - (\sin\theta)(-\sin\theta)$

$= \cos^2\theta + \sin^2\theta = 1$ $(\because \sin^2 A + \cos^2 A = 1)$

(ii) We have, $\begin{vmatrix} x^2 - x + 1 & x - 1 \\ x + 1 & x + 1 \end{vmatrix} = (x^2 - x + 1)(x + 1) - (x + 1)(x - 1)$

$= x^3 - x^2 + x + x^2 - x + 1 - (x^2 - 1)$

$= x^3 + 1 - (x^2 - 1) = x^3 - x^2 + 2$

Question 3 If $A = \begin{bmatrix} 1 & 2 \\ 4 & 2 \end{bmatrix}$, then show that $|2A| = 4|A|$.

Sol. Given, $A = \begin{bmatrix} 1 & 2 \\ 4 & 2 \end{bmatrix}$ $\therefore$ $2A = 2\begin{bmatrix} 1 & 2 \\ 4 & 2 \end{bmatrix} = \begin{bmatrix} 2 \times 1 & 2 \times 2 \\ 2 \times 4 & 2 \times 2 \end{bmatrix} = \begin{bmatrix} 2 & 4 \\ 8 & 4 \end{bmatrix}$

$\text{LHS} = |2A| = \begin{vmatrix} 2 & 4 \\ 8 & 4 \end{vmatrix} = 2 \times 4 - 8 \times 4 = -24$

Now, $|A| = \begin{vmatrix} 1 & 2 \\ 4 & 2 \end{vmatrix} = 1 \times 2 - 4 \times 2 = -6$

$\therefore$ $\text{RHS} = 4|A| = 4 \times (-6) = -24$

$\therefore$ LHS = RHS

Note If A is a square matrix of order n, then $|kA| = k^n |A|$.

Question 4 $A=\begin{bmatrix}1&0&1\\0&1&2\\0&0&4\end{bmatrix}$, then show that $|3A|=27|A|$.

Sol. Given, $A=\begin{bmatrix}1&0&1\\0&1&2\\0&0&4\end{bmatrix}$

It can be observed that in the first column, two entries are zero. Thus, we expand the matrix A along the first column (C_1) for finding $|A|$.

$$\therefore \quad |A|=1\begin{vmatrix}1&2\\0&4\end{vmatrix}-0\begin{vmatrix}0&1\\0&4\end{vmatrix}+0\begin{vmatrix}0&1\\1&2\end{vmatrix}=1(1\times4-0\times2)=4$$

$$\therefore \quad 27|A|=27\times4=108 \quad \ldots(i)$$

Now,
$$3A=3\begin{bmatrix}1&0&1\\0&1&2\\0&0&4\end{bmatrix}=\begin{bmatrix}3&0&3\\0&3&6\\0&0&12\end{bmatrix}$$

$$\therefore \quad |3A|=\begin{vmatrix}3&0&3\\0&3&6\\0&0&12\end{vmatrix}$$

It can be observed that in the first column, two entries are zero. Thus, we expand the determinant along the first column (C_1) for easier calculation.

$$|3A|=3\begin{vmatrix}3&6\\0&12\end{vmatrix}-0\begin{vmatrix}0&3\\0&12\end{vmatrix}+0\begin{vmatrix}0&3\\3&6\end{vmatrix}=3(3\times12-0\times6)$$

$$\Rightarrow \quad |3A|=3(36)=108 \quad \ldots(ii)$$

From Eqs. (i) and (ii), we get

$$|3A|=27|A|$$

Hence, the given result is proved.

Question 5 Evaluate the determinants.

(i) $\begin{vmatrix}3&-1&-2\\0&0&-1\\3&-5&0\end{vmatrix}$ (ii) $\begin{vmatrix}3&-4&5\\1&1&-2\\2&3&1\end{vmatrix}$

(iii) $\begin{vmatrix}0&1&2\\-1&0&-3\\-2&3&0\end{vmatrix}$ (iv) $\begin{vmatrix}2&-1&-2\\0&2&-1\\3&-5&0\end{vmatrix}$

◎ ***Thinking Process*** Determinant can be easily expand either corresponding to a row or column which have maximum number of zero as.

Sol.

(i) Let $A = \begin{vmatrix} 3 & -1 & -2 \\ 0 & 0 & -1 \\ 3 & -5 & 0 \end{vmatrix}$

It can be observed that in the second row, two entries are zero. Thus, we expand the determinant along the second row for easier calculation.

$$|A| = -0\begin{vmatrix} -1 & -2 \\ -5 & 0 \end{vmatrix} + 0\begin{vmatrix} 3 & -2 \\ 3 & 0 \end{vmatrix} - (-1)\begin{vmatrix} 3 & -1 \\ 3 & -5 \end{vmatrix}$$

$$= \{3 \times (-5) - 3 \times (-1)\}$$

$$= -15 + 3 = -12$$

(ii) We have, $\begin{vmatrix} 3 & -4 & 5 \\ 1 & 1 & -2 \\ 2 & 3 & 1 \end{vmatrix}$

By expanding along R_1 (first row), we get

$$= 3\begin{vmatrix} 1 & -2 \\ 3 & 1 \end{vmatrix} - (-4)\begin{vmatrix} 1 & -2 \\ 2 & 1 \end{vmatrix} + 5\begin{vmatrix} 1 & 1 \\ 2 & 3 \end{vmatrix}$$

$$= 3(1 + 6) + 4(1 + 4) + 5(3 - 2)$$

$$= 3(7) + 4(5) + 5(1)$$

$$= 21 + 20 + 5 = 46$$

(iii) We have, $\begin{vmatrix} 0 & 1 & 2 \\ -1 & 0 & -3 \\ -2 & 3 & 0 \end{vmatrix}$

By expanding along R_1 (first row), we get

$$0\begin{vmatrix} 0 & -3 \\ 3 & 0 \end{vmatrix} - 1\begin{vmatrix} -1 & -3 \\ -2 & 0 \end{vmatrix} + 2\begin{vmatrix} -1 & 0 \\ -2 & 3 \end{vmatrix}$$

$$= -1(0 - 6) + 2(-3 - 0)$$

$$= -1(-6) + 2(-3) = 6 - 6 = 0$$

(iv) We have, $\begin{vmatrix} 2 & -1 & -2 \\ 0 & 2 & -1 \\ 3 & -5 & 0 \end{vmatrix}$

By expanding along R_2 (second row), we get

$$-0\begin{vmatrix} -1 & -2 \\ -5 & 0 \end{vmatrix} + 2\begin{vmatrix} 2 & -2 \\ 3 & 0 \end{vmatrix} - (-1)\begin{vmatrix} 2 & -1 \\ 3 & -5 \end{vmatrix}$$

$$= 0 + 2(0 + 6) + (-10 + 3)$$

$$= 12 - 7 = 5$$

Question 6 If $A=\begin{bmatrix}1 & 1 & -2\\ 2 & 1 & -3\\ 5 & 4 & -9\end{bmatrix}$, find $|A|$

Sol. Given, $A=\begin{bmatrix}1 & 1 & -2\\ 2 & 1 & -3\\ 5 & 4 & -9\end{bmatrix}$

By expanding along R_1 (first row), we get

$$|A| = 1\begin{vmatrix}1 & -3\\ 4 & -9\end{vmatrix} - 1\begin{vmatrix}2 & -3\\ 5 & -9\end{vmatrix} + (-2)\begin{vmatrix}2 & 1\\ 5 & 4\end{vmatrix}$$

$$= 1(-9+12) - 1(-18+15) - 2(8-5)$$

$$= 1(3) - 1(-3) - 2(3) = 3 + 3 - 6 = 0$$

Question 7 Find the values of x, if

(i) $\begin{vmatrix}2 & 4\\ 5 & 1\end{vmatrix} = \begin{vmatrix}2x & 4\\ 6 & x\end{vmatrix}$ (ii) $\begin{vmatrix}2 & 3\\ 4 & 5\end{vmatrix} = \begin{vmatrix}x & 3\\ 2x & 5\end{vmatrix}$

Thinking Process Expand both the determinants which gives an equation in x and then solve that equation for finding the value of x.

Sol.

(i) Given, $\begin{vmatrix}2 & 4\\ 5 & 1\end{vmatrix} = \begin{vmatrix}2x & 4\\ 6 & x\end{vmatrix}$

On expanding both determinants, we get

$$2 \times 1 - 5 \times 4 = 2x \times x - 6 \times 4$$

$\Rightarrow$ $$2 - 20 = 2x^2 - 24$$

$\Rightarrow$ $$2x^2 = -18 + 24$$

$\Rightarrow$ $$x^2 = \frac{6}{2} = 3$$

$\Rightarrow$ $$x = \pm\sqrt{3}$$

(ii) Given, $\begin{vmatrix}2 & 3\\ 4 & 5\end{vmatrix} = \begin{vmatrix}x & 3\\ 2x & 5\end{vmatrix}$

On expanding both determinants, we get

$$2 \times 5 - 4 \times 3 = 5 \times x - 3 \times 2x$$

$\Rightarrow$ $$10 - 12 = 5x - 6x$$

$\Rightarrow$ $$-2 = -x$$

$\Rightarrow$ $$x = 2$$

Mistake Alert We cannot compare corresponding elements of determinant. we can do it in matrix.

Question 8 If $\begin{vmatrix} x & 2 \\ 18 & x \end{vmatrix} = \begin{vmatrix} 6 & 2 \\ 18 & 6 \end{vmatrix}$, then x is equal to

(a) 6 (b) ± 6
(c) – 6 (d) 0

Sol. (b) Given, $\begin{vmatrix} x & 2 \\ 18 & x \end{vmatrix} = \begin{vmatrix} 6 & 2 \\ 18 & 6 \end{vmatrix}$

On expanding both determinants, we get

$$x \times x - 18 \times 2 = 6 \times 6 - 18 \times 2 \Rightarrow x^2 - 36 = 36 - 36$$

$$\Rightarrow \quad x^2 - 36 = 0 \Rightarrow x^2 = 36 \Rightarrow x = \pm 6$$

Exercise 4.2

Question 1 Find area of the triangle with vertices at the points given in each of the following

(i) (1, 0), (6, 0), (4, 3) (ii) (2, 7), (1, 1), (10, 8)
(iii) (–2, –3), (3, 2), (–1, – 8)

◎ *Thinking Process* If $(x_1, y_1), (x_2, y_2)$ and (x_3, y_3) are vertices of a triangle, then area of triangle is $\frac{1}{2}\begin{vmatrix} x_1 & y_1 & 1 \\ x_2 & y_2 & 1 \\ x_3 & y_3 & 1 \end{vmatrix}$. Now put the values and get the area.

Sol. We know that, if $(x_1, y_1), (x_2, y_2)$ and (x_3, y_3) are vertices of a triangle, then area of triangle is $\frac{1}{2}\begin{vmatrix} x_1 & y_1 & 1 \\ x_2 & y_2 & 1 \\ x_3 & y_3 & 1 \end{vmatrix}$.

(i) Required area $= \frac{1}{2}\begin{vmatrix} 1 & 0 & 1 \\ 6 & 0 & 1 \\ 4 & 3 & 1 \end{vmatrix} = \frac{1}{2}|1(0-3) - 0(6-4) + 1(18-0)|$

$$= \frac{1}{2}|-3+18| = \frac{15}{2} \text{ sq. unit}$$

(ii) Required area $= \frac{1}{2}\begin{vmatrix} 2 & 7 & 1 \\ 1 & 1 & 1 \\ 10 & 8 & 1 \end{vmatrix} = \frac{1}{2}|2(1-8) - 7(1-10) + 1(8-10)|$

$$= \frac{1}{2}|2(-7) - 7(-9) + 1(-2)|$$

$$= \frac{1}{2}|-14 + 63 - 2| = \frac{47}{2} \text{ sq. unit}$$

(iii) Required area $= \frac{1}{2}\begin{vmatrix} -2 & -3 & 1 \\ 3 & 2 & 1 \\ -1 & -8 & 1 \end{vmatrix} = \frac{1}{2}|-2(2+8)+3(3+1)+1(-24+2)|$

$$= \frac{1}{2}|-20+12-22| = \frac{1}{2}|-30| = 15 \text{ sq. unit}$$

Note Area of triangle is always positive.

Question 2 Show that points $A(a, b+c)$, $B(b, c+a)$, $C(c, a+b)$ are collinear.

◎ *Thinking Process* Three points are said to be collinear if area of triangle generated by these three points is equal to zero.

Sol. Area of $\Delta ABC = \frac{1}{2}\begin{vmatrix} a & b+c & 1 \\ b & c+a & 1 \\ c & a+b & 1 \end{vmatrix} = \frac{1}{2}|a\{(c+a)\times 1-(a+b)\times 1\}$

$$-(b+c)\{b\times 1-1\times c\}+1\{b\times(a+b)-(c+a)\times c\}|$$

$$= \frac{1}{2}|a(c+a-a-b)-(b+c)(b-c)+1(ab+b^2-c^2-ac)|$$

$$= \frac{1}{2}|ac-ab-b^2+c^2+ab+b^2-c^2-ac| = \frac{1}{2}\times 0 = 0$$

Since, area of $\Delta ABC = 0$

Hence, points $A(a, b+c)$, $B(b, c+a)$ and $C(c, a+b)$ are collinear.

Question 3 Find the value of k, if area of triangle is 4 sq. units and vertices are

(i) $(k,0),(4,0)(0,2)$ (ii) $(-2,0),(0,4),(0,k)$

Sol. Area of triangle $= \frac{1}{2}\begin{vmatrix} x_1 & y_1 & 1 \\ x_2 & y_2 & 1 \\ x_3 & y_3 & 1 \end{vmatrix}$

(i) Given, $\frac{1}{2}\begin{vmatrix} k & 0 & 1 \\ 4 & 0 & 1 \\ 0 & 2 & 1 \end{vmatrix} = \pm 4$

$\Rightarrow \quad k(0-2)+1(8-0) = \pm 8$

$\Rightarrow \quad -2k+8 = \pm 8$

On taking positive sign $-2k+8=8$

$\Rightarrow \quad -2k=0 \Rightarrow k=0$

On taking negative sign $-2k+8=-8$

$\Rightarrow \quad -2k=-16$

$\Rightarrow \quad k=8$

$\therefore \quad k=0, 8$

(ii) Given, $\frac{1}{2}\begin{vmatrix} -2 & 0 & 1 \\ 0 & 4 & 1 \\ 0 & k & 1 \end{vmatrix} = \pm 4$

$\Rightarrow \quad -2(4-k) + 1(0-0) = \pm 8$

$\Rightarrow \quad [-8 + 2k] = \pm 8$

On taking positive sign, $2k - 8 = 8 \Rightarrow 2k = 16 \Rightarrow k = 8$

On taking negative sign, $2k - 8 = -8 \Rightarrow 2k = 0 \Rightarrow k = 0$

$\therefore \quad k = 0, 8$

Mistake Alert Remember that if area of triangle is given then always use $\pm$ $\pm$ ive signs for finding the value of given unknown.

Question 4 (i) Find the equation of the line joining (1, 2) and (3, 6) using determinants.

(ii) Find the equation of the line joining (3, 1) and (9, 3) using determinants.

Thinking Process Use the relation $\frac{1}{2}\begin{vmatrix} x_1 & y_1 & 1 \\ x_2 & y_2 & 1 \\ x_3 & y_3 & 1 \end{vmatrix} = 0$ for finding the equation of line. Make (x_1, y_1) as (1, 2) and (x_2, y_2) as (3, 6) and (x_3, y_3) as (x, y) solve to get equation of line.

Sol.

(i) Let $P(x, y)$ be any point on the line joining $A(1, 2)$ and $B(3, 6)$. If the points A, B and P are collinear, then the area of triangle ABP will be zero.

$\therefore \quad \frac{1}{2}\begin{vmatrix} 1 & 2 & 1 \\ 3 & 6 & 1 \\ x & y & 1 \end{vmatrix} = 0 \Rightarrow \frac{1}{2}[1(6-y) - 2(3-x) + 1(3y - 6x)] = 0$

$\Rightarrow \quad 6 - y - 6 + 2x + 3y - 6x = 0$

$\Rightarrow \quad 2y - 4x = 0 \Rightarrow y = 2x$

Hence, the equation of the line joining the given points is $y = 2x$.

(ii) Let $P(x, y)$ be any point on the line joining $A(3, 1)$ and $B(9, 3)$. Then, the points A, B and P are collinear. Therefore, the area of triangle ABP will be zero.

$\therefore \quad \frac{1}{2}\begin{vmatrix} 3 & 1 & 1 \\ 9 & 3 & 1 \\ x & y & 1 \end{vmatrix} = 0$

$\Rightarrow \quad \frac{1}{2}|3(3-y) - 1(9-x) + 1(9y - 3x)| = 0$

$\Rightarrow \quad 9 - 3y - 9 + x + 9y - 3x = 0$

$\Rightarrow \quad 6y - 2x = 0 \Rightarrow x - 3y = 0$

Hence, the equation of the line joining the given points is $x - 3y = 0$.

Question 5 If area of a triangle is 35 sq units with vertices $(2,-6),(5,4)$ and $(k,4)$, then k is

(a) 12 (b) -2

(c) $-12,-2$ (d) $12,-2$

Sol. (d) Given, $\frac{1}{2}\begin{vmatrix} 2 & -6 & 1 \\ 5 & 4 & 1 \\ k & 4 & 1 \end{vmatrix} = \pm 35$

$\Rightarrow \quad 2(4-4)+6(5-k)+1(20-4k) = \pm 70$

$\Rightarrow \quad 30-6k+20-4k = \pm 70$

$\Rightarrow \quad -10k+50 = \pm 70$

On taking positive sign, $-10k+50=70 \Rightarrow -10k=20 \Rightarrow k=-2$

On taking negative sign, $-10k+50=-70 \Rightarrow -10k=-120 \Rightarrow k=12$

$\therefore k = 12, -2$

Exercise 4.3

Direction (Q. Nos. 1 and 2) Write Minors and Cofactors of the elements of following determinants:

Question 1 (i) $\begin{vmatrix} 2 & -4 \\ 0 & 3 \end{vmatrix}$ (ii) $\begin{vmatrix} a & c \\ b & d \end{vmatrix}$

Sol.

(i) Here, $\begin{vmatrix} 2 & -4 \\ 0 & 3 \end{vmatrix}$

$\therefore$ Minors, $M_{11}=3$, $M_{12}=0$, $M_{21}=-4$ and $M_{22}=2$

Also cofactors, $A_{11}=(-1)^{1+1}M_{11}=1\times 3=3$

$A_{12}=(-1)^{1+2}M_{12}=(-1)\times 0=0$

$A_{21}=(-1)^{2+1}M_{21}=(-1)\times(-4)=4$

and $A_{22}=(-1)^{2+2}M_{22}=1\times 2=2$

(ii) Here, $\begin{vmatrix} a & c \\ b & d \end{vmatrix}$ $\therefore$ Minors, $M_{11}=d$, $M_{12}=b$, $M_{21}=c$ and $M_{22}=a$

Also cofactors, $A_{11}=(-1)^{1+1}M_{11}=1\times d=d$

$A_{12}=(-1)^{1+2}M_{12}=(-1)\times b=-b$

$A_{21}=(-1)^{2+1}M_{21}=(-1)\times c=-c$

$A_{22}=(-1)^{2+2}M_{22}=1\times a=a$

Question 2 (i) $\begin{vmatrix} 1 & 0 & 0 \\ 0 & 1 & 0 \\ 0 & 0 & 1 \end{vmatrix}$ (ii) $\begin{vmatrix} 1 & 0 & 4 \\ 3 & 5 & -1 \\ 0 & 1 & 2 \end{vmatrix}$

Sol.

(i) Here, $\begin{vmatrix} 1 & 0 & 0 \\ 0 & 1 & 0 \\ 0 & 0 & 1 \end{vmatrix}$

Minors of elements of first row are

$$M_{11} = \begin{vmatrix} 1 & 0 \\ 0 & 1 \end{vmatrix} = 1 - 0 = 1,$$

$$M_{12} = \begin{vmatrix} 0 & 0 \\ 0 & 1 \end{vmatrix} = 0 - 0 = 0$$

and $$M_{13} = \begin{vmatrix} 0 & 1 \\ 0 & 0 \end{vmatrix} = 0 - 0 = 0$$

Minors of elements of second row are

$$M_{21} = \begin{vmatrix} 0 & 0 \\ 0 & 1 \end{vmatrix} = 0 - 0 = 0$$

$$M_{22} = \begin{vmatrix} 1 & 0 \\ 0 & 1 \end{vmatrix} = 1 - 0 = 1$$

and $$M_{23} = \begin{vmatrix} 1 & 0 \\ 0 & 0 \end{vmatrix} = 0 - 0 = 0$$

Minors of elements of third row are

$$M_{31} = \begin{vmatrix} 0 & 0 \\ 1 & 0 \end{vmatrix} = 0 - 0 = 0$$

$$M_{32} = \begin{vmatrix} 1 & 0 \\ 0 & 0 \end{vmatrix} = 0 - 0 = 0$$

and $$M_{33} = \begin{vmatrix} 1 & 0 \\ 0 & 1 \end{vmatrix} = 1 - 0 = 1$$

Hence, cofactors of elements of first row are

$$A_{11} = (-1)^{1+1} M_{11} = 1 \times 1 = 1, \quad A_{12} = (-1)^{1+2} M_{12} = -1 \times 0 = 0$$

$$A_{13} = (-1)^{1+3} M_{13} = 1 \times 0 = 0$$

Cofactors of elements of second row are

$$A_{21} = (-1)^{2+1} M_{21} = -1 \times 0 = 0, A_{22} = (-1)^{2+2} M_{22} = 1 \times 1 = 1$$

$$A_{23} = (-1)^{2+3} M_{23} = -1 \times 0 = 0$$

Cofactors of elements of third row are

$$A_{31} = (-1)^{3+1} M_{31} = 1 \times 0 = 0,$$
$$A_{32} = (-1)^{3+2} M_{32} = -1 \times 0 = 0$$
$$A_{33} = (-1)^{3+3} M_{33} = 1 \times 1 = 1$$

(ii) Here, $\begin{vmatrix} 1 & 0 & 4 \\ 3 & 5 & -1 \\ 0 & 1 & 2 \end{vmatrix}$

Minors of elements of first row are

$$M_{11} = \begin{vmatrix} 5 & -1 \\ 1 & 2 \end{vmatrix} = 10 + 1 = 11,$$

$$M_{12} = \begin{vmatrix} 3 & -1 \\ 0 & 2 \end{vmatrix} = 6 - 0 = 6$$

and $$M_{13} = \begin{vmatrix} 3 & 5 \\ 0 & 1 \end{vmatrix} = 3 - 0 = 3$$

Minors of elements of second row are

$$M_{21} = \begin{vmatrix} 0 & 4 \\ 1 & 2 \end{vmatrix} = 0 - 4 = -4,$$

$$M_{22} = \begin{vmatrix} 1 & 4 \\ 0 & 2 \end{vmatrix} = 2 - 0 = 2$$

and $$M_{23} = \begin{vmatrix} 1 & 0 \\ 0 & 1 \end{vmatrix} = 1 - 0 = 1$$

Minors of elements of third row are

$$M_{31} = \begin{vmatrix} 0 & 4 \\ 5 & -1 \end{vmatrix} = 0 - 20 = -20,$$

$$M_{32} = \begin{vmatrix} 1 & 4 \\ 3 & -1 \end{vmatrix} = -1 - 12 = -13$$

and $$M_{33} = \begin{vmatrix} 1 & 0 \\ 3 & 5 \end{vmatrix} = 5 - 0 = 5$$

Hence, cofactors of elements of first row are

$$A_{11} = (-1)^{1+1} M_{11} = 1 \times 11 = 11, \quad A_{12} = (-1)^{1+2} M_{12} = -1 \times 6 = -6$$
$$A_{13} = (-1)^{1+3} M_{13} = 1 \times 3 = 3$$

Cofactors of elements of second row are

$$A_{21} = (-1)^{2+1} M_{21} = -1 \times -4 = 4$$
$$A_{22} = (-1)^{2+2} M_{22} = 1 \times 2 = 2$$
$$A_{23} = (-1)^{2+3} M_{23} = -1 \times 1 = -1$$

Cofactors of elements of third row are

$$A_{31} = (-1)^{3+1} M_{31} = 1 \times -20 = -20$$
$$A_{32} = (-1)^{3+2} M_{32} = -1 \times -13 = 13$$
$$A_{33} = (-1)^{3+3} M_{33} = 1 \times 5 = 5$$

Question 3 Using cofactors of the elements of second row, evaluate

$$\Delta = \begin{vmatrix} 5 & 3 & 8 \\ 2 & 0 & 1 \\ 1 & 2 & 3 \end{vmatrix}.$$

◎ ***Thinking Process*** In this question we expand the given determinant corresponding to second row.

Sol. Given, $\Delta = \begin{vmatrix} 5 & 3 & 8 \\ 2 & 0 & 1 \\ 1 & 2 & 3 \end{vmatrix}$

Cofactors of the elements of second row

$$A_{21} = (-1)^{2+1} \begin{vmatrix} 3 & 8 \\ 2 & 3 \end{vmatrix} = -(9 - 16) = 7, \qquad [\because A_{ij} = (-1)^{i+j} M_{ij}]$$

$$A_{22} = (-1)^{2+2} \begin{vmatrix} 5 & 8 \\ 1 & 3 \end{vmatrix} = 15 - 8 = 7$$

and $$A_{23} = (-1)^{2+3} \begin{vmatrix} 5 & 3 \\ 1 & 2 \end{vmatrix} = -(10 - 3) = -7$$

Now, expansion of Δ using cofactors of elements of second row is given by

$$\Delta = a_{21}A_{21} + a_{22}A_{22} + a_{23}A_{23} = 2 \times 7 + 0 \times 7 + 1(-7) = 14 - 7 = 7$$

Question 4 Using cofactors of elements of third column, evaluate

$$\Delta = \begin{vmatrix} 1 & x & yz \\ 1 & y & zx \\ 1 & z & xy \end{vmatrix}.$$

◎ ***Thinking Process*** In this question we expand the given determinant corresponding to C_3.

Sol. Given, $\Delta = \begin{vmatrix} 1 & x & yz \\ 1 & y & zx \\ 1 & z & xy \end{vmatrix}$

Cofactors of the elements of third column are

$$A_{13} = (-1)^{1+3} \begin{vmatrix} 1 & y \\ 1 & z \end{vmatrix} = 1(z - y) = z - y,$$

$$A_{23} = (-1)^{2+3} \begin{vmatrix} 1 & x \\ 1 & z \end{vmatrix} = -1(z - x) = x - z$$

and $$A_{33} = (-1)^{3+3} \begin{vmatrix} 1 & x \\ 1 & y \end{vmatrix} = 1(y - x) = y - x$$

Now, expansion of Δ using cofactors of elements of third column is given by

$$\Delta = a_{13}A_{13} + a_{23}A_{23} + a_{33}A_{33} = yz(z - y) + zx(x - z) + xy(y - x)$$

$$= yz^2 - y^2z + zx^2 - z^2x + xy^2 - x^2y = x^2(z - y) + x(y^2 - z^2) + yz(z - y)$$

$$= (z - y)\{x^2 - x(y + z) + yz\} = (z - y)\{x^2 - xy - xz + yz\}$$

$= (z-y)[x(x-y) - z(x-y)] = (y-z)(x-y)(z-x) = (x-y)(y-z)(z-x)$

Question 5 If $\Delta = \begin{vmatrix} a_{11} & a_{12} & a_{13} \\ a_{21} & a_{22} & a_{23} \\ a_{31} & a_{32} & a_{33} \end{vmatrix}$ and A_{ij} is cofactor of a_{ij}, then value of Δ is given by

(a) $a_{11}A_{31} + a_{12}A_{32} + a_{13}A_{33}$ (b) $a_{11}A_{11} + a_{12}A_{21} + a_{13}A_{31}$

(c) $a_{21}A_{11} + a_{22}A_{12} + a_{23}A_{13}$ (d) $a_{11}A_{11} + a_{21}A_{21} + a_{31}A_{31}$

Sol. (d) Δ is equal to the sum of the products of the elements of a row (or a column) with their corresponding cofactors.

$\Delta = a_{11}A_{11} + a_{12}A_{12} + a_{13}A_{13}$ or $a_{21}A_{21} + a_{22}A_{22} + a_{23}A_{23}$

or $a_{31}A_{31} + a_{32}A_{32} + a_{33}A_{33}$ or $a_{11}A_{11} + a_{21}A_{21} + a_{31}A_{31}$

or $a_{12}A_{12} + a_{22}A_{22} + a_{32}A_{32}$ or $a_{13}A_{13} + a_{23}A_{23} + a_{33}A_{33}$

Sum of the products of the elements of first column with their corresponding cofactors is $\Delta = a_{11}A_{11} + a_{21}A_{21} + a_{31}A_{31}$

Note Sum of the product of elements of any row (or column) with corresponding cofactors of another row (or column) is equal to zero.

i.e. $a_{11}c_{21} + a_{12}c_{22} + a_{13}c_{23} = 0$

or $a_{11}c_{13} + a_{21}c_{23} + a_{31}c_{33} = 0$

Exercise 4.4

Direction (Q. No. 1 and 2) Find adjoint of each of the matrices.

Question 1 $\begin{bmatrix} 1 & 2 \\ 3 & 4 \end{bmatrix}$

Sol. Let $A = \begin{bmatrix} 1 & 2 \\ 3 & 4 \end{bmatrix}$

Here, $A_{11} = 4$, $A_{12} = -3$, $A_{21} = -2$ and $A_{22} = 1$

$\therefore$ $\text{adj } A = \begin{bmatrix} A_{11} & A_{12} \\ A_{21} & A_{22} \end{bmatrix}^T = \begin{bmatrix} 4 & -3 \\ -2 & 1 \end{bmatrix}^T = \begin{bmatrix} 4 & -2 \\ -3 & 1 \end{bmatrix}$

Note There is a short cut to find adjoint of any 2×2 matrix $A = \begin{bmatrix} a_{11} & a_{12} \\ a_{21} & a_{22} \end{bmatrix}$

Change the place of a_{11} and a_{22}

Change the sign of a_{12} and a_{21}

i.e. $\text{adj}(A) = \begin{bmatrix} a_{22} & -a_{12} \\ -a_{21} & a_{11} \end{bmatrix}$

Question 2 $\begin{bmatrix} 1 & -1 & 2 \\ 2 & 3 & 5 \\ -2 & 0 & 1 \end{bmatrix}$

Sol. Let $A = \begin{bmatrix} 1 & -1 & 2 \\ 2 & 3 & 5 \\ -2 & 0 & 1 \end{bmatrix}$

Cofactors of elements of first row are $A_{11} = \begin{vmatrix} 3 & 5 \\ 0 & 1 \end{vmatrix} = 3 - 0 = 3,$

$$A_{12} = -\begin{vmatrix} 2 & 5 \\ -2 & 1 \end{vmatrix} = -(2 + 10) = -12, \; A_{13} = \begin{vmatrix} 2 & 3 \\ -2 & 0 \end{vmatrix} = 0 - (-6) = 6$$

Cofactors of elements of second row are

$$A_{21} = -\begin{vmatrix} -1 & 2 \\ 0 & 1 \end{vmatrix} = -(-1 - 0) = 1, \; A_{22} = \begin{vmatrix} 1 & 2 \\ -2 & 1 \end{vmatrix} = (1 + 4) = 5,$$

$$A_{23} = -\begin{vmatrix} 1 & -1 \\ -2 & 0 \end{vmatrix} = -(0 - 2) = 2$$

Cofactors of elements of third row are

$$A_{31} = \begin{vmatrix} -1 & 2 \\ 3 & 5 \end{vmatrix} = (-5 - 6) = -11, \; A_{32} = -\begin{vmatrix} 1 & 2 \\ 2 & 5 \end{vmatrix} = -(5 - 4) = -1,$$

$$A_{33} = \begin{vmatrix} 1 & -1 \\ 2 & 3 \end{vmatrix} = 3 + 2 = 5$$

Hence, $$\text{adj}(A) = \begin{bmatrix} 3 & -12 & 6 \\ 1 & 5 & 2 \\ -11 & -1 & 5 \end{bmatrix}^T = \begin{bmatrix} 3 & 1 & -11 \\ -12 & 5 & -1 \\ 6 & 2 & 5 \end{bmatrix}$$

Mistake Alert Students should remember that value of cofactor is – ve and + ve when $(i + j)$ is odd and even, respectively.

Direction (Q. Nos. 3 and 4) Verify $A(\text{adj } A) = (\text{adj } A)\, A = |A|\, I$

Question 3 $\begin{bmatrix} 2 & 3 \\ -4 & -6 \end{bmatrix}$

Sol. Let $A = \begin{bmatrix} 2 & 3 \\ -4 & -6 \end{bmatrix}$, then $|A| = \begin{vmatrix} 2 & 3 \\ -4 & -6 \end{vmatrix} = -12 - (-12) = -12 + 12 = 0$

$$\therefore \quad |A|\, I = 0 \begin{bmatrix} 1 & 0 \\ 0 & 1 \end{bmatrix} = \begin{bmatrix} 0 & 0 \\ 0 & 0 \end{bmatrix} = O$$

Cofactors of A are $A_{11} = -6$, $A_{12} = 4$, $A_{21} = -3$, $A_{22} = 2$

$$\therefore \quad \text{adj}(A) = \begin{bmatrix} -6 & 4 \\ -3 & 2 \end{bmatrix}^T = \begin{bmatrix} -6 & -3 \\ 4 & 2 \end{bmatrix}$$

Now, $(\text{adj } A)A = \begin{bmatrix} -6 & -3 \\ 4 & 2 \end{bmatrix}\begin{bmatrix} 2 & 3 \\ -4 & -6 \end{bmatrix} = \begin{bmatrix} -12+12 & -18+18 \\ 8-8 & 12-12 \end{bmatrix} = \begin{bmatrix} 0 & 0 \\ 0 & 0 \end{bmatrix} = O$

Also, $A(\quad A) = \begin{bmatrix} 2 & 3 \\ -4 & -6 \end{bmatrix}\begin{bmatrix} -6 & -3 \\ 4 & 2 \end{bmatrix}$

$$= \begin{bmatrix} -12+12 & -6+6 \\ 24-24 & 12-12 \end{bmatrix} = \begin{bmatrix} 0 & 0 \\ 0 & 0 \end{bmatrix} = O$$

Hence, $A(\quad A) = (\quad A)A = |A|I.$

Question 4 $\begin{bmatrix} 1 & -1 & 2 \\ 3 & 0 & -2 \\ 1 & 0 & 3 \end{bmatrix}$

Sol. Let $A = \begin{bmatrix} 1 & -1 & 2 \\ 3 & 0 & -2 \\ 1 & 0 & 3 \end{bmatrix}$

Now, $|A| = \begin{vmatrix} 1 & -1 & 2 \\ 3 & 0 & -2 \\ 1 & 0 & 3 \end{vmatrix} = 1(0-0) - (-1)(9+2) + 2(0-0) = 0 + 11 + 0 = 11$

$\therefore \quad |A|I = 11\begin{bmatrix} 1 & 0 & 0 \\ 0 & 1 & 0 \\ 0 & 0 & 1 \end{bmatrix} = \begin{bmatrix} 11 & 0 & 0 \\ 0 & 11 & 0 \\ 0 & 0 & 11 \end{bmatrix}$

Cofactors of A are

$A_{11} = 0$, $A_{12} = -(9+2) = -11$, $A_{13} = 0$, $A_{21} = -(-3-0) = 3$, $A_{22} = 3-2 = 1$,
$A_{23} = -(0+1) = -1$, $A_{31} = 2-0 = 2$, $A_{32} = -(-2-6) = 8$,
$A_{33} = 0+3 = 3$

$\therefore \quad \text{adj}(A) = \begin{bmatrix} 0 & -11 & 0 \\ 3 & 1 & -1 \\ 2 & 8 & 3 \end{bmatrix}^T = \begin{bmatrix} 0 & 3 & 2 \\ -11 & 1 & 8 \\ 0 & -1 & 3 \end{bmatrix}$

Now, $A(\text{adj } A) = \begin{bmatrix} 1 & -1 & 2 \\ 3 & 0 & -2 \\ 1 & 0 & 3 \end{bmatrix}\begin{bmatrix} 0 & 3 & 2 \\ -11 & 1 & 8 \\ 0 & -1 & 3 \end{bmatrix}$

$$= \begin{bmatrix} 0+11+0 & 3-1-2 & 2-8+6 \\ 0+0+0 & 9+0+2 & 6+0-6 \\ 0+0+0 & 3+0-3 & 2+0+9 \end{bmatrix} = \begin{bmatrix} 11 & 0 & 0 \\ 0 & 11 & 0 \\ 0 & 0 & 11 \end{bmatrix}$$

Also, $(\text{adj } A)A = \begin{bmatrix} 0 & 3 & 2 \\ -11 & 1 & 8 \\ 0 & -1 & 3 \end{bmatrix}\begin{bmatrix} 1 & -1 & 2 \\ 3 & 0 & -2 \\ 1 & 0 & 3 \end{bmatrix}$

$$= \begin{bmatrix} 0+9+2 & 0+0+0 & 0-6+6 \\ -11+3+8 & 11+0+0 & -22-2+24 \\ 0-3+3 & 0+0+0 & 0+2+9 \end{bmatrix}$$

$$= \begin{bmatrix} 11 & 0 & 0 \\ 0 & 11 & 0 \\ 0 & 0 & 11 \end{bmatrix}$$

Hence, $A(\text{adj } A) = (\text{adj } A)A = |A|I$

Direction (Q. Nos. 5 to 11) Find the inverse of each of the matrices (if it exists) .

Question 5 $\begin{bmatrix} 2 & -2 \\ 4 & 3 \end{bmatrix}$

◎ *Thinking Process* Inverse of a matrix is possible only when it is non-singular (i.e. det $\neq 0$). If (det $= 0$) it is called singular matrix and then inverse does not exist.

Sol. Let $A = \begin{bmatrix} 2 & -2 \\ 4 & 3 \end{bmatrix}$. Now, $|A| = \begin{vmatrix} 2 & -2 \\ 4 & 3 \end{vmatrix} = 6-(-8) = 14 \neq 0$

$\therefore A^{-1}$ exist.

Cofactors of A are $A_{11} = 3,\ A_{12} = -4,\ A_{21} = 2,\ A_{22} = 2$

$$\therefore \quad \text{adj}(A) = \begin{bmatrix} 3 & -4 \\ 2 & 2 \end{bmatrix}^T = \begin{bmatrix} 3 & 2 \\ -4 & 2 \end{bmatrix}$$

Now,
$$A^{-1} = \frac{1}{|A|}(\text{adj } A) = \frac{1}{14}\begin{bmatrix} 3 & 2 \\ -4 & 2 \end{bmatrix} = \begin{bmatrix} \frac{3}{14} & \frac{2}{14} \\ -\frac{4}{14} & \frac{2}{14} \end{bmatrix} = \begin{bmatrix} \frac{3}{14} & \frac{1}{7} \\ -\frac{2}{7} & \frac{1}{7} \end{bmatrix}$$

Question 6 $\begin{bmatrix} -1 & 5 \\ -3 & 2 \end{bmatrix}$

Sol. Let $A = \begin{bmatrix} -1 & 5 \\ -3 & 2 \end{bmatrix}$. Now, $|A| = \begin{vmatrix} -1 & 5 \\ -3 & 2 \end{vmatrix} = -2-(-15) = 13 \neq 0$

$\therefore A^{-1}$ exist.

Now, cofactors of A are $A_{11} = 2,\ A_{12} = 3,\ A_{21} = -5,\ A_{22} = -1$

$$\therefore \quad \text{adj}(A) = \begin{bmatrix} 2 & 3 \\ -5 & -1 \end{bmatrix}^T = \begin{bmatrix} 2 & -5 \\ 3 & -1 \end{bmatrix}$$

Now,
$$A^{-1} = \frac{1}{|A|}(\text{adj } A) = \frac{1}{13}\begin{bmatrix} 2 & -5 \\ 3 & -1 \end{bmatrix} = \begin{bmatrix} \frac{2}{13} & -\frac{5}{13} \\ \frac{3}{13} & -\frac{1}{13} \end{bmatrix}$$

Question 7 $\begin{bmatrix} 1 & 2 & 3 \\ 0 & 2 & 4 \\ 0 & 0 & 5 \end{bmatrix}$

Sol. Let $A = \begin{bmatrix} 1 & 2 & 3 \\ 0 & 2 & 4 \\ 0 & 0 & 5 \end{bmatrix}$

Now, $|A| = 1(10-0) - 2(0-0) + 3(0-0) = 10 \neq 0$

$\therefore A^{-1}$ exist.

Now, cofactors of A are

$A_{11} = 10 - 0 = 10, A_{12} = -(0-0) = 0, A_{13} = 0 - 0 = 0,$

$A_{21} = -(10-0) = -10, A_{22} = 5 - 0 = 5, A_{23} = -(0-0) = 0$

$A_{31} = 8 - 6 = 2, A_{32} = -(4-0) = -4, \quad A_{33} = 2 - 0 = 2$

$$\therefore \quad \text{adj}(A) = \begin{bmatrix} 10 & 0 & 0 \\ -10 & 5 & 0 \\ 2 & -4 & 2 \end{bmatrix}^T = \begin{bmatrix} 10 & -10 & 2 \\ 0 & 5 & -4 \\ 0 & 0 & 2 \end{bmatrix}$$

Now, $$A^{-1} = \frac{1}{|A|}(\text{adj } A) = \frac{1}{10}\begin{bmatrix} 10 & -10 & 2 \\ 0 & 5 & -4 \\ 0 & 0 & 2 \end{bmatrix} = \begin{bmatrix} 1 & -1 & \frac{1}{5} \\ 0 & \frac{1}{2} & -\frac{2}{5} \\ 0 & 0 & \frac{1}{5} \end{bmatrix}$$

Question 8 $\begin{bmatrix} 1 & 0 & 0 \\ 3 & 3 & 0 \\ 5 & 2 & -1 \end{bmatrix}$

Sol. Let $A = \begin{bmatrix} 1 & 0 & 0 \\ 3 & 3 & 0 \\ 5 & 2 & -1 \end{bmatrix}$. Now, $|A| = \begin{vmatrix} 1 & 0 & 0 \\ 3 & 3 & 0 \\ 5 & 2 & -1 \end{vmatrix}$

$$= 1(-3-0) - 0 + 0 = -3 \neq 0$$

$\therefore A^{-1}$ exist.

Cofactors of A are

$A_{11} = -3 - 0 = -3, \quad A_{12} = -(-3-0) = 3, \quad A_{13} = 6 - 15 = -9$

$A_{21} = -(0-0) = 0, \quad A_{22} = -1 - 0 = -1, \quad A_{23} = -(2-0) = -2$

$A_{31} = 0 - 0 = 0, \quad A_{32} = -(0-0) = 0, \quad A_{33} = 3 - 0 = 3$

$$\therefore \quad \text{adj}(A) = \begin{bmatrix} -3 & 3 & -9 \\ 0 & -1 & -2 \\ 0 & 0 & 3 \end{bmatrix}^T = \begin{bmatrix} -3 & 0 & 0 \\ 3 & -1 & 0 \\ -9 & -2 & 3 \end{bmatrix}$$

Now, $$A^{-1} = \frac{1}{|A|}(\text{adj } A) = \frac{1}{-3}\begin{bmatrix} -3 & 0 & 0 \\ 3 & -1 & 0 \\ -9 & -2 & 3 \end{bmatrix}$$

$$= \begin{bmatrix} 1 & 0 & 0 \\ -1 & \frac{1}{3} & 0 \\ 3 & \frac{2}{3} & -1 \end{bmatrix}$$

Question 9 $\begin{bmatrix} 2 & 1 & 3 \\ 4 & -1 & 0 \\ -7 & 2 & 1 \end{bmatrix}$

Sol. Let $A = \begin{bmatrix} 2 & 1 & 3 \\ 4 & -1 & 0 \\ -7 & 2 & 1 \end{bmatrix}$

Now, $$|A| = \begin{vmatrix} 2 & 1 & 3 \\ 4 & -1 & 0 \\ -7 & 2 & 1 \end{vmatrix}$$

$$= 2(-1-0) - 1(4-0) + 3(8-7) = -2-4+3 = -3 \neq 0$$

$\therefore A^{-1}$ exist.

Cofactors of A are

$A_{11} = -1-0 = -1,\quad A_{12} = -(4-0) = -4,\quad A_{13} = 8-7 = 1$

$A_{21} = -(1-6) = 5,\quad A_{22} = 2+21 = 23,\quad A_{23} = -(4+7) = -11$

$A_{31} = 0+3 = 3,\quad A_{32} = -(0-12) = 12,\quad A_{33} = -2-4 = -6$

$$\therefore \quad \text{adj}(A) = \begin{bmatrix} -1 & -4 & 1 \\ 5 & 23 & -11 \\ 3 & 12 & -6 \end{bmatrix}^T = \begin{bmatrix} -1 & 5 & 3 \\ -4 & 23 & 12 \\ 1 & -11 & -6 \end{bmatrix}$$

Now, $$A^{-1} = \frac{1}{|A|}(\text{adj } A) = \frac{1}{-3}\begin{bmatrix} -1 & 5 & 3 \\ -4 & 23 & 12 \\ 1 & -11 & -6 \end{bmatrix}$$

$$= \begin{bmatrix} \frac{1}{3} & -\frac{5}{3} & -1 \\ \frac{4}{3} & -\frac{23}{3} & -4 \\ -\frac{1}{3} & \frac{11}{3} & 2 \end{bmatrix}$$

Question 10 $\begin{bmatrix} 1 & -1 & 2 \\ 0 & 2 & -3 \\ 3 & -2 & 4 \end{bmatrix}$

Sol. Let $A = \begin{bmatrix} 1 & -1 & 2 \\ 0 & 2 & -3 \\ 3 & -2 & 4 \end{bmatrix}$

Now, $|A| = \begin{vmatrix} 1 & -1 & 2 \\ 0 & 2 & -3 \\ 3 & -2 & 4 \end{vmatrix} = 1(8-6) - (-1)(0+9) + 2(0-6)$

$= 2 + 9 - 12 = -1 \neq 0$

$\therefore A^{-1}$ exist.

Cofactors of A are

$A_{11} = 8 - 6 = 2, \quad A_{12} = -(0+9) = -9, \quad A_{13} = 0 - 6 = -6$
$A_{21} = -(-4+4) = 0, \quad A_{22} = 4 - 6 = -2, \quad A_{23} = -(-2+3) = -1$
$A_{31} = 3 - 4 = -1, \quad A_{32} = -(-3-0) = 3, \quad A_{33} = 2 - 0 = 2$

$\therefore \qquad \text{adj}(A) = \begin{bmatrix} 2 & -9 & -6 \\ 0 & -2 & -1 \\ -1 & 3 & 2 \end{bmatrix}^T = \begin{bmatrix} 2 & 0 & -1 \\ -9 & -2 & 3 \\ -6 & -1 & 2 \end{bmatrix}$

Now, $A^{-1} = \frac{1}{|A|}(\text{adj } A) = \frac{1}{-1}\begin{bmatrix} 2 & 0 & -1 \\ -9 & -2 & 3 \\ -6 & -1 & 2 \end{bmatrix}$

$= \begin{bmatrix} -2 & 0 & 1 \\ 9 & 2 & -3 \\ 6 & 1 & -2 \end{bmatrix}$

Question 11 $\begin{bmatrix} 1 & 0 & 0 \\ 0 & \cos\alpha & \sin\alpha \\ 0 & \sin\alpha & -\cos\alpha \end{bmatrix}$

Sol. Let $A = \begin{bmatrix} 1 & 0 & 0 \\ 0 & \cos\alpha & \sin\alpha \\ 0 & \sin\alpha & -\cos\alpha \end{bmatrix}$

Now, $|A| = \begin{vmatrix} 1 & 0 & 0 \\ 0 & \cos\alpha & \sin\alpha \\ 0 & \sin\alpha & -\cos\alpha \end{vmatrix} = 1(-\cos^2\alpha - \sin^2\alpha)$

$= -(\cos^2\alpha + \sin^2\alpha) = -1 \neq 0 \qquad [\because \cos^2\theta + \sin^2\theta = 1]$

$\therefore A^{-1}$ exist.

Cofactors of A are

$A_{11} = -\cos^2\alpha - \sin^2\alpha = -1,\quad A_{12} = -(0-0) = 0,\quad A_{13} = 0 - 0 = 0$

$A_{21} = -(0-0) = 0,\quad A_{22} = -\cos\alpha - 0 = -\cos\alpha,\quad A_{23} = -(\sin\alpha - 0) = -\sin\alpha$

$A_{31} = 0 - 0 = 0,\quad A_{32} = -(\sin\alpha - 0) = -\sin\alpha,\quad A_{33} = \cos\alpha - 0 = \cos\alpha$

$$\therefore \quad \text{adj}(A) = \begin{bmatrix} -1 & 0 & 0 \\ 0 & -\cos\alpha & -\sin\alpha \\ 0 & -\sin\alpha & \cos\alpha \end{bmatrix}^T = \begin{bmatrix} -1 & 0 & 0 \\ 0 & -\cos\alpha & -\sin\alpha \\ 0 & -\sin\alpha & \cos\alpha \end{bmatrix}$$

Now, $$A^{-1} = \frac{1}{|A|}(\text{adj } A)$$

$$= \frac{1}{-1}\begin{bmatrix} -1 & 0 & 0 \\ 0 & -\cos\alpha & -\sin\alpha \\ 0 & -\sin\alpha & \cos\alpha \end{bmatrix} = \begin{bmatrix} 1 & 0 & 0 \\ 0 & \cos\alpha & \sin\alpha \\ 0 & \sin\alpha & -\cos\alpha \end{bmatrix}$$

Question 12 Let $A = \begin{bmatrix} 3 & 7 \\ 2 & 5 \end{bmatrix}$ and $B = \begin{bmatrix} 6 & 8 \\ 7 & 9 \end{bmatrix}$ verify that $(AB)^{-1} = B^{-1}A^{-1}$.

Sol. Given, $A = \begin{bmatrix} 3 & 7 \\ 2 & 5 \end{bmatrix}$. Now, $|A| = \begin{vmatrix} 3 & 7 \\ 2 & 5 \end{vmatrix} = 15 - 14 = 1 \neq 0$

$\therefore A^{-1}$ exist.

Cofactors of A are $A_{11} = 5,\ A_{12} = -2,\ A_{21} = -7,\ A_{22} = 3$

$$\therefore \quad \text{adj}(A) = \begin{bmatrix} 5 & -2 \\ -7 & 3 \end{bmatrix}^T = \begin{bmatrix} 5 & -7 \\ -2 & 3 \end{bmatrix}$$

Now, $$A^{-1} = \frac{1}{|A|}(\text{adj}(A)) = \frac{1}{1}\begin{bmatrix} 5 & -7 \\ -2 & 3 \end{bmatrix}$$

Here, $$B = \begin{bmatrix} 6 & 8 \\ 7 & 9 \end{bmatrix}$$

$$\therefore \quad |B| = \begin{vmatrix} 6 & 8 \\ 7 & 9 \end{vmatrix} = 54 - 56 = -2 \neq 0$$

So, A^{-1} exist.

Cofactors of B are $B_{11} = 9,\ B_{12} = -7,\ B_{21} = -8,\ B_{22} = 6$

$$\text{adj}(B) = \begin{bmatrix} 9 & -7 \\ -8 & 6 \end{bmatrix}^T = \begin{bmatrix} 9 & -8 \\ -7 & 6 \end{bmatrix}$$

$$\therefore \quad B^{-1} = \frac{1}{|B|}(\text{adj } B) = \frac{1}{-2}\begin{bmatrix} 9 & -8 \\ -7 & 6 \end{bmatrix}$$

Now, $$B^{-1}A^{-1} = \frac{1}{-2}\begin{bmatrix} 9 & -8 \\ -7 & 6 \end{bmatrix}\begin{bmatrix} 5 & -7 \\ -2 & 3 \end{bmatrix}$$

$$= \frac{1}{-2}\begin{bmatrix} 45 + 16 & -63 - 24 \\ -35 - 12 & 49 + 18 \end{bmatrix}$$

$$= \frac{1}{-2}\begin{bmatrix} 61 & -87 \\ -47 & 67 \end{bmatrix} = \begin{bmatrix} -\frac{61}{2} & \frac{87}{2} \\ \frac{47}{2} & -\frac{67}{2} \end{bmatrix} \quad \ldots(i)$$

Now, $AB = \begin{bmatrix} 3 & 7 \\ 2 & 5 \end{bmatrix}\begin{bmatrix} 6 & 8 \\ 7 & 9 \end{bmatrix} = \begin{bmatrix} 18+49 & 24+63 \\ 12+35 & 16+45 \end{bmatrix} = \begin{bmatrix} 67 & 87 \\ 47 & 61 \end{bmatrix}$

$\therefore$ $|AB| = \begin{vmatrix} 67 & 87 \\ 47 & 61 \end{vmatrix} = 67 \times 61 - 47 \times 87 = 4087 - 4089 = -2 \neq 0$

So, $(AB)^{-1}$ exist.

Cofactors of AB are $A_{11} = 61$, $A_{12} = -47$, $A_{21} = -87$, $A_{22} = 67$

$$\text{adj}(AB) = \begin{bmatrix} 61 & -47 \\ -87 & 67 \end{bmatrix}^T = \begin{bmatrix} 61 & -87 \\ -47 & 67 \end{bmatrix}$$

$\therefore$ $(AB)^{-1} = \frac{1}{|AB|}(\text{adj } AB) = \frac{1}{-2}\begin{bmatrix} 61 & -87 \\ -47 & 67 \end{bmatrix} = \begin{bmatrix} -\frac{61}{2} & \frac{87}{2} \\ \frac{47}{2} & -\frac{67}{2} \end{bmatrix} \quad \ldots(ii)$

From Eqs. (i) and (ii), we get $(AB)^{-1} = B^{-1}A^{-1}$

Hence, the given result is proved.

Question 13 If $A = \begin{bmatrix} 3 & 1 \\ -1 & 2 \end{bmatrix}$, show that $A^2 - 5A + 7I = O$. Hence, find A^{-1}.

◎ ***Thinking Process*** Firstly we proved $A^2 - 5A + 7I = O$, then we take $7I$ to the other side and multiply both sides by A^{-1} to find it. As we know that $AA^{-1} = A^{-1}A = I$.

Sol. Given, $A = \begin{bmatrix} 3 & 1 \\ -1 & 2 \end{bmatrix}$

$\therefore$ $A^2 = AA = \begin{bmatrix} 3 & 1 \\ -1 & 2 \end{bmatrix}\begin{bmatrix} 3 & 1 \\ -1 & 2 \end{bmatrix} = \begin{bmatrix} 9-1 & 3+2 \\ -3-2 & -1+4 \end{bmatrix} = \begin{bmatrix} 8 & 5 \\ -5 & 3 \end{bmatrix}$

Now, $A^2 - 5A + 7I$

$$= \begin{bmatrix} 8 & 5 \\ -5 & 3 \end{bmatrix} - 5\begin{bmatrix} 3 & 1 \\ -1 & 2 \end{bmatrix} + 7\begin{bmatrix} 1 & 0 \\ 0 & 1 \end{bmatrix} = \begin{bmatrix} 8 & 5 \\ -5 & 3 \end{bmatrix} - \begin{bmatrix} 15 & 5 \\ -5 & 10 \end{bmatrix} + \begin{bmatrix} 7 & 0 \\ 0 & 7 \end{bmatrix}$$

$$= \begin{bmatrix} 8-15+7 & 5-5+0 \\ -5+5+0 & 3-10+7 \end{bmatrix} = \begin{bmatrix} 0 & 0 \\ 0 & 0 \end{bmatrix} = O$$

$\therefore$ $A^2 - 5A + 7I = O$

$\because$ $|A| = \begin{vmatrix} 3 & 1 \\ -1 & 2 \end{vmatrix} = 6 + 1 = 7 \neq 0.$

$\therefore$ A^{-1} exists.

Now, $A \cdot A - 5A = -7I$

Post multiplying by A^{-1} on both sides, we get

$$A \cdot (AA^{-1}) - 5AA^{-1} = -7\, IA^{-1}$$

$\Rightarrow$ $AI - 5I = -7A^{-1}$ (using $AA^{-1} = I$ and $IA^{-1} = A^{-1}$)

$\Rightarrow$ $A^{-1} = -\frac{1}{7}(A - 5I) \Rightarrow A^{-1} = \frac{1}{7}(5I - A)$

$$= \frac{1}{7}\left(\begin{bmatrix} 5 & 0 \\ 0 & 5 \end{bmatrix} - \begin{bmatrix} 3 & 1 \\ -1 & 2 \end{bmatrix}\right) = \frac{1}{7}\begin{bmatrix} 2 & -1 \\ 1 & 3 \end{bmatrix}$$

$\therefore$ $A^{-1} = \frac{1}{7}\begin{bmatrix} 2 & -1 \\ 1 & 3 \end{bmatrix}$

Note (i) If we are multiplying A^{-1}, after each element of equation it is called post multiplying and if we are multiplying A^{-1} before each element of equation then it is called pre-multiplying.

(ii) When we multiply by A^{-1} in the given equation, it is necessary that $|A| \neq 0$. *If* $|A| = 0$, *then* A^{-1} *does not exist.*

Question 14 For the matrix $A = \begin{bmatrix} 3 & 2 \\ 1 & 1 \end{bmatrix}$, find the numbers a and b such that $A^2 + aA + bI = O$.

Sol. Given, $A = \begin{bmatrix} 3 & 2 \\ 1 & 1 \end{bmatrix}$

Now, $A^2 = AA = \begin{bmatrix} 3 & 2 \\ 1 & 1 \end{bmatrix}\begin{bmatrix} 3 & 2 \\ 1 & 1 \end{bmatrix} = \begin{bmatrix} 9+2 & 6+2 \\ 3+1 & 2+1 \end{bmatrix} = \begin{bmatrix} 11 & 8 \\ 4 & 3 \end{bmatrix}$

Also, given $A^2 + aA + bI = O$

On putting the values of A^2, A and I, we get

$$\begin{bmatrix} 11 & 8 \\ 4 & 3 \end{bmatrix} + a\begin{bmatrix} 3 & 2 \\ 1 & 1 \end{bmatrix} + b\begin{bmatrix} 1 & 0 \\ 0 & 1 \end{bmatrix} = O \Rightarrow \begin{bmatrix} 11 + 3a + b & 8 + 2a + 0 \\ 4 + a + 0 & 3 + a + b \end{bmatrix} = O$$

$\Rightarrow$ $\begin{bmatrix} 11 + 3a + b & 8 + 2a \\ 4 + a & 3 + a + b \end{bmatrix} = \begin{bmatrix} 0 & 0 \\ 0 & 0 \end{bmatrix}$

If two matrices are equal, then their corresponding elements are equal.

$\therefore$ $11 + 3a + b = 0,$ ...(i)

$8 + 2a = 0,$ ...(ii)

$4 + a = 0$ ...(iii)

and $3 + a + b = 0$ ...(iv)

On solving Eqs. (iii) and (iv), we get

$$4 + a = 0 \Rightarrow a = -4$$

and $3 + a + b = 0$

$\Rightarrow \quad 3-4+b=0$

$\Rightarrow \quad b=1$

Thus, $\quad a=-4$ and $b=1$

Question 15 For the matrix $A=\begin{bmatrix}1&1&1\\1&2&-3\\2&-1&3\end{bmatrix}$. Show that $A^3-6A^2+5A+11I=O$. Hence, find A^{-1}.

Sol. Given, $A=\begin{bmatrix}1&1&1\\1&2&-3\\2&-1&3\end{bmatrix}$

$$\therefore \quad A^2=AA=\begin{bmatrix}1&1&1\\1&2&-3\\2&-1&3\end{bmatrix}\begin{bmatrix}1&1&1\\1&2&-3\\2&-1&3\end{bmatrix}$$

$$=\begin{bmatrix}1+1+2&1+2-1&1-3+3\\1+2-6&1+4+3&1-6-9\\2-1+6&2-2-3&2+3+9\end{bmatrix}=\begin{bmatrix}4&2&1\\-3&8&-14\\7&-3&14\end{bmatrix}$$

and $\quad A^3=A^2A=\begin{bmatrix}4&2&1\\-3&8&-14\\7&-3&14\end{bmatrix}\begin{bmatrix}1&1&1\\1&2&-3\\2&-1&3\end{bmatrix}$

$$=\begin{bmatrix}4+2+2&4+4-1&4-6+3\\-3+8-28&-3+16+14&-3-24-42\\7-3+28&7-6-14&7+9+42\end{bmatrix}=\begin{bmatrix}8&7&1\\-23&27&-69\\32&-13&58\end{bmatrix}$$

$$\therefore \quad A^3-6A^2+5A+11I$$

$$=\begin{bmatrix}8&7&1\\-23&27&-69\\32&-13&58\end{bmatrix}-6\begin{bmatrix}4&2&1\\-3&8&-14\\7&-3&14\end{bmatrix}+5\begin{bmatrix}1&1&1\\1&2&-3\\2&-1&3\end{bmatrix}+11\begin{bmatrix}1&0&0\\0&1&0\\0&0&1\end{bmatrix}$$

$$=\begin{bmatrix}8&7&1\\-23&27&-69\\32&-13&58\end{bmatrix}-\begin{bmatrix}24&12&6\\-18&48&-84\\42&-18&84\end{bmatrix}+\begin{bmatrix}5&5&5\\5&10&-15\\10&-5&15\end{bmatrix}+\begin{bmatrix}11&0&0\\0&11&0\\0&0&11\end{bmatrix}$$

$$=\begin{bmatrix}8-24+5+11&7-12+5+0&1-6+5+0\\-23+18+5+0&27-48+10+11&-69+84-15+0\\32-42+10+0&-13+18-5+0&58-84+15+11\end{bmatrix}=\begin{bmatrix}0&0&0\\0&0&0\\0&0&0\end{bmatrix}$$

$=O$

Now, $A^3-6A^2+5A+11I=O$

$$\Rightarrow \quad (AAA)A^{-1}-6(AA)A^{-1}+5AA^{-1}+11IA^{-1}=O$$

(Post-multiplying by A^{-1} as $|A|\neq 0$)

$$\left[\because |A| = \begin{vmatrix} 1 & 1 & 1 \\ 1 & 2 & -3 \\ 2 & -1 & 3 \end{vmatrix} = 1(6-3) - 1(3+6) + 1(-1-4) = 3 - 9 - 5 = -11 \neq 0\right]$$

$\Rightarrow$ $$AA(AA^{-1}) - 6A(AA^{-1}) + 5(AA^{-1}) + 11(IA^{-1}) = O$$

$\Rightarrow$ $$AAI - 6AI + 5I + 11A^{-1} = O$$

(using $AA^{-1} = I$ and $IA^{-1} = A^{-1}$)

$\Rightarrow$ $$A^2 - 6A + 5I = -11A^{-1}$$ (using $AAI = A^2$ and $AI = A$)

$\Rightarrow$ $A^{-1} = -\frac{1}{11}(A^2 - 6A + 5I) \Rightarrow A^{-1} = \frac{1}{11}(-A^2 + 6A - 5I)$

$$= \frac{1}{11}\left\{-\begin{bmatrix} 4 & 2 & 1 \\ -3 & 8 & -14 \\ 7 & -3 & 14 \end{bmatrix} + 6\begin{bmatrix} 1 & 1 & 1 \\ 1 & 2 & -3 \\ 2 & -1 & 3 \end{bmatrix} - 5\begin{bmatrix} 1 & 0 & 0 \\ 0 & 1 & 0 \\ 0 & 0 & 1 \end{bmatrix}\right\}$$

$$= \frac{1}{11}\left\{\begin{bmatrix} -4 & -2 & -1 \\ 3 & -8 & 14 \\ -7 & 3 & -14 \end{bmatrix} + \begin{bmatrix} 6 & 6 & 6 \\ 6 & 12 & -18 \\ 12 & -6 & 18 \end{bmatrix} - \begin{bmatrix} 5 & 0 & 0 \\ 0 & 5 & 0 \\ 0 & 0 & 5 \end{bmatrix}\right\}$$

$$= \frac{1}{11}\begin{bmatrix} -4+6-5 & -2+6-0 & -1+6-0 \\ 3+6-0 & -8+12-5 & 14-18-0 \\ -7+12-0 & 3-6+0 & -14+18-5 \end{bmatrix} = \frac{1}{11}\begin{bmatrix} -3 & 4 & 5 \\ 9 & -1 & -4 \\ 5 & -3 & -1 \end{bmatrix}$$

Question 16 If $A = \begin{bmatrix} 2 & -1 & 1 \\ -1 & 2 & -1 \\ 1 & -1 & 2 \end{bmatrix}$ verify that $A^3 - 6A^2 + 9A - 4I = O$ and hence find A^{-1}.

Sol. Given, $A = \begin{bmatrix} 2 & -1 & 1 \\ -1 & 2 & -1 \\ 1 & -1 & 2 \end{bmatrix}$

$$\therefore \quad A^2 = AA = \begin{bmatrix} 2 & -1 & 1 \\ -1 & 2 & -1 \\ 1 & -1 & 2 \end{bmatrix}\begin{bmatrix} 2 & -1 & 1 \\ -1 & 2 & -1 \\ 1 & -1 & 2 \end{bmatrix}$$

$$= \begin{bmatrix} 4+1+1 & -2-2-1 & 2+1+2 \\ -2-2-1 & 1+4+1 & -1-2-2 \\ 2+1+2 & -1-2-2 & 1+1+4 \end{bmatrix} = \begin{bmatrix} 6 & -5 & 5 \\ -5 & 6 & -5 \\ 5 & -5 & 6 \end{bmatrix}$$

and $$A^3 = A^2A = \begin{bmatrix} 6 & -5 & 5 \\ -5 & 6 & -5 \\ 5 & -5 & 6 \end{bmatrix}\begin{bmatrix} 2 & -1 & 1 \\ -1 & 2 & -1 \\ 1 & -1 & 2 \end{bmatrix}$$

$$= \begin{bmatrix} 12+5+5 & -6-10-5 & 6+5+10 \\ -10-6-5 & 5+12+5 & -5-6-10 \\ 10+5+6 & -5-10-6 & 5+5+12 \end{bmatrix} = \begin{bmatrix} 22 & -21 & 21 \\ -21 & 22 & -21 \\ 21 & -21 & 22 \end{bmatrix}$$

$\therefore \quad A^3 - 6A^2 + 9A - 4I$

$$= \begin{bmatrix} 22 & -21 & 21 \\ -21 & 22 & -21 \\ 21 & -21 & 22 \end{bmatrix} - 6\begin{bmatrix} 6 & -5 & 5 \\ -5 & 6 & -5 \\ 5 & -5 & 6 \end{bmatrix} + 9\begin{bmatrix} 2 & -1 & 1 \\ -1 & 2 & -1 \\ 1 & -1 & 2 \end{bmatrix} - 4\begin{bmatrix} 1 & 0 & 0 \\ 0 & 1 & 0 \\ 0 & 0 & 1 \end{bmatrix}$$

$$= \begin{bmatrix} 22 & -21 & 21 \\ -21 & 22 & -21 \\ 21 & -21 & 22 \end{bmatrix} - \begin{bmatrix} 36 & -30 & 30 \\ -30 & 36 & -30 \\ 30 & -30 & 36 \end{bmatrix} + \begin{bmatrix} 18 & -9 & 9 \\ -9 & 18 & -9 \\ 9 & -9 & 18 \end{bmatrix} - \begin{bmatrix} 4 & 0 & 0 \\ 0 & 4 & 0 \\ 0 & 0 & 4 \end{bmatrix}$$

$$= \begin{bmatrix} 22-36+18-4 & -21+30-9-0 & 21-30+9-0 \\ -21+30-9-0 & 22-36+18-4 & -21+30-9-0 \\ 21-30+9-0 & -21+30-9-0 & 22-36+18-4 \end{bmatrix} = \begin{bmatrix} 0 & 0 & 0 \\ 0 & 0 & 0 \\ 0 & 0 & 0 \end{bmatrix} = O$$

$\therefore \quad A^3 - 6A^2 + 9A - 4I = O$

$\Rightarrow \quad (AAA)A^{-1} - 6(AA)A^{-1} + 9AA^{-1} - 4\,IA^{-1} = O$

(Post-multiplying by A^{-1} as $|A| \neq 0$)

$$\left[\because |A| = \begin{vmatrix} 2 & -1 & 1 \\ -1 & 2 & -1 \\ 1 & -1 & 2 \end{vmatrix} = 2(4-1) + 1(-2+1) + 1(1-2) = 6 - 1 - 1 = 4 \neq 0\right]$$

$\Rightarrow \quad AA(AA^{-1}) - 6A(AA^{-1}) + 9(AA^{-1}) - 4(IA^{-1}) = O$

$\Rightarrow \quad AAI - 6AI + 9I - 4A^{-1} = O$ (using $AA^{-1} = I$ and $IA^{-1} = A^{-1}$)

$\Rightarrow \quad A^2 - 6A + 9I = 4A^{-1}$ (using $A^2 I = A^2$ and $AI = A$)

$\Rightarrow \quad A^{-1} = \frac{1}{4}(A^2 - 6A + 9I)$

$$= \frac{1}{4}\left\{\begin{bmatrix} 6 & -5 & 5 \\ -5 & 6 & -5 \\ 5 & -5 & 6 \end{bmatrix} - 6\begin{bmatrix} 2 & -1 & 1 \\ -1 & 2 & -1 \\ 1 & -1 & 2 \end{bmatrix} + 9\begin{bmatrix} 1 & 0 & 0 \\ 0 & 1 & 0 \\ 0 & 0 & 1 \end{bmatrix}\right\}$$

$$= \frac{1}{4}\left\{\begin{bmatrix} 6 & -5 & 5 \\ -5 & 6 & -5 \\ 5 & -5 & 6 \end{bmatrix} - \begin{bmatrix} 12 & -6 & 6 \\ -6 & 12 & -6 \\ 6 & -6 & 12 \end{bmatrix} + \begin{bmatrix} 9 & 0 & 0 \\ 0 & 9 & 0 \\ 0 & 0 & 9 \end{bmatrix}\right\}$$

$$= \frac{1}{4}\begin{bmatrix} 6-12+9 & -5+6+0 & 5-6+0 \\ -5+6+0 & 6-12+9 & -5+6+0 \\ 5-6+0 & -5+6+0 & 6-12+9 \end{bmatrix} = \frac{1}{4}\begin{bmatrix} 3 & 1 & -1 \\ 1 & 3 & 1 \\ -1 & 1 & 3 \end{bmatrix}$$

Question 17 Let A be a non-singular square matrix of order 3×3, then $|\text{adj } A|$ is equal to

(a) $|A|$ (b) $|A|^2$

(c) $|A|^3$ (d) $3|A|$

Sol. (b) We know that (adj A) $A = |A|\, I$

$$= |A| \begin{bmatrix} 1 & 0 & 0 \\ 0 & 1 & 0 \\ 0 & 0 & 1 \end{bmatrix} = \begin{bmatrix} |A| & 0 & 0 \\ 0 & |A| & 0 \\ 0 & 0 & |A| \end{bmatrix}$$

$$\Rightarrow \quad |(\text{adj } A)\, A| = \begin{vmatrix} |A| & 0 & 0 \\ 0 & |A| & 0 \\ 0 & 0 & |A| \end{vmatrix}$$

$$\Rightarrow \quad |(\text{adj } A)\, A| = |A|^3 \begin{vmatrix} 1 & 0 & 0 \\ 0 & 1 & 0 \\ 0 & 0 & 1 \end{vmatrix} = |A|^3 |I|$$

$$\Rightarrow \quad |\text{adj } A||A| = |A|^3 \qquad (\because |I| = 1)$$

$$\therefore \quad |(\text{adj } A)| = |A|^2$$

Question 18 If A is an invertible matrix of order 2, then det (A^{-1}) is equal to

(a) det (A) (b) $\frac{1}{\det(A)}$ (c) 1 (d) zero

Sol. (b) Since, A is an invertible matrix, A^{-1} exists and $A^{-1} = \frac{1}{|A|}$ adj (A)

As matrix A is of order 2,

Let $A = \begin{bmatrix} a & b \\ c & d \end{bmatrix}$, then $|A| = ad - bc$ and adj $(A) = \begin{bmatrix} d & -b \\ -c & a \end{bmatrix}$

Now, $A^{-1} = \frac{1}{|A|}$ adj $(A) = \frac{1}{|A|} \begin{bmatrix} d & -b \\ -c & a \end{bmatrix} = \begin{bmatrix} \frac{d}{|A|} & -\frac{b}{|A|} \\ -\frac{c}{|A|} & \frac{a}{|A|} \end{bmatrix}$

$$\therefore \quad |A^{-1}| = \begin{vmatrix} \frac{d}{|A|} & -\frac{b}{|A|} \\ -\frac{c}{|A|} & \frac{a}{|A|} \end{vmatrix} = \frac{1}{|A|} \times \frac{1}{|A|} \begin{vmatrix} d & -b \\ -c & a \end{vmatrix} = \frac{1}{|A|^2}(ad - bc)$$

$$= \frac{1}{|A|^2} \cdot |A| \qquad (\because |A| = ad - bc)$$

$$= \frac{1}{|A|}$$

$\therefore$ det $(A^{-1}) = \frac{1}{\det(A)}$.

Quick Solution

We know that $AA^{-1} = I$

$\therefore |AA^{-1}| = |I| \Rightarrow |A||A^{-1}| = 1$ (using $|AA^{-1}| = |A||A^{-1}|$ and $|I| = 1$)

$\Rightarrow |A^{-1}| = \frac{1}{|A|} = \frac{1}{\det(A)}$.

Exercise 4.5

Direction (Q. Nos. 1 to 6) Examine the consistency of the system of equations.

Question 1 $x + 2y = 2,\ 2x + 3y = 3.$

◎ *Thinking Process* The system of equations of the form $AX = B$ is consistent, if $|A| \neq 0$. If $|A| = 0$, then if (adj A)$B = 0$ then system of equations is consistent and if (adj A)$B \neq 0$ then inconsistent.

Sol. The given system of equations can be written as $AX = B$, where

$$A = \begin{bmatrix} 1 & 2 \\ 2 & 3 \end{bmatrix}, X = \begin{bmatrix} x \\ y \end{bmatrix} \text{ and } B = \begin{bmatrix} 2 \\ 3 \end{bmatrix}$$

$$\therefore \quad |A| = \begin{vmatrix} 1 & 2 \\ 2 & 3 \end{vmatrix} = 1(3) - 2(2) = 3 - 4 = -1 \neq 0$$

$\therefore A$ is non-singular. Therefore, A^{-1} exists.

Hence, the given system of equations is consistent and has unique solution.

Question 2 $2x - y = 5,\quad x + y = 4.$

Sol. The given system of equation can be written as $AX = B$, where

$$A = \begin{bmatrix} 2 & -1 \\ 1 & 1 \end{bmatrix}, X = \begin{bmatrix} x \\ y \end{bmatrix} \text{ and } B = \begin{bmatrix} 5 \\ 4 \end{bmatrix}$$

Here,
$$|A| = \begin{vmatrix} 2 & -1 \\ 1 & 1 \end{vmatrix} = 2(1) - (-1)(1) = 2 + 1 = 3 \neq 0$$

$\therefore A$ is non-singular. Therefore, A^{-1} exists.

Hence, the given system of equations is consistent and has unique solution.

Question 3 $x + 3y = 5,\ 2x + 6y = 8.$

Sol. The given of equations system can be written as $AX = B$, where

$$A = \begin{bmatrix} 1 & 3 \\ 2 & 6 \end{bmatrix}, X = \begin{bmatrix} x \\ y \end{bmatrix} B = \begin{bmatrix} 5 \\ 8 \end{bmatrix}$$

Here,
$$|A| = \begin{vmatrix} 1 & 3 \\ 2 & 6 \end{vmatrix} = 1(6) - 3(2) = 6 - 6 = 0$$

$\therefore A$ is singular matrix.

Nothing can be said about consistency as yet. We compute

$$(\text{adj } A)\, B = \begin{bmatrix} 6 & -3 \\ -2 & 1 \end{bmatrix} \begin{bmatrix} 5 \\ 8 \end{bmatrix} \qquad \left[\because \text{adj} \begin{bmatrix} a_{11} & a_{12} \\ a_{21} & a_{22} \end{bmatrix} = \begin{bmatrix} a_{22} & -a_{12} \\ -a_{21} & a_{11} \end{bmatrix}\right]$$

$$= \begin{bmatrix} 30 - 24 \\ -10 + 8 \end{bmatrix} = \begin{bmatrix} 6 \\ -2 \end{bmatrix} \neq 0$$

Thus, the solution of the given system of equations does not exist. Hence, the system of equations is inconsistent.

Question 4 $x + y + z = 1, \quad 2x + 3y + 2z = 2, \quad ax + ay + 2az = 4.$

Sol. The given system of equations can be written as $AX = B$, where

$$A = \begin{bmatrix} 1 & 1 & 1 \\ 2 & 3 & 2 \\ a & a & 2a \end{bmatrix}, X = \begin{bmatrix} x \\ y \\ z \end{bmatrix} B = \begin{bmatrix} 1 \\ 2 \\ 4 \end{bmatrix}$$

Here, $|A| = \begin{vmatrix} 1 & 1 & 1 \\ 2 & 3 & 2 \\ a & a & 2a \end{vmatrix} = 1(6a - 2a) - 1(4a - 2a) + 1(2a - 3a)$

$$= 4a - 2a - a = 4a - 3a = a \neq 0$$

$\therefore$ A is non-singular.
Therefore, A^{-1} exists.
Hence, the given system of equations is consistent and has unique solution.

Question 5 $3x - y - 2z = 2, 2y - z = -1, 3x - 5y = 3.$

Sol. The given system of equations is $3x - y - 2z = 2$,

$$0x + 2y - z = -1 \quad \text{and} \quad 3x - 5y + 0z = 3,$$

which can be written as $AX = B$, where

$$A = \begin{bmatrix} 3 & -1 & -2 \\ 0 & 2 & -1 \\ 3 & -5 & 0 \end{bmatrix}, X = \begin{bmatrix} x \\ y \\ z \end{bmatrix} \text{ and } B = \begin{bmatrix} 2 \\ -1 \\ 3 \end{bmatrix}$$

Here, $|A| = \begin{vmatrix} 3 & -1 & -2 \\ 0 & 2 & -1 \\ 3 & -5 & 0 \end{vmatrix} = 3(0 - 5) + 1(0 + 3) - 2(0 - 6)$

$$= -15 + 3 + 12 = 0$$

$\therefore$ A is a singular matrix.

Therefore, nothing can be said about consistency as yet. So, we compute (A) B.

Cofactors of A are

$A_{11} = -5, A_{12} = -3, A_{13} = -6, \quad A_{21} = 10, A_{22} = 6, A_{23} = 12$

$A_{31} = 5, A_{32} = 3, A_{33} = 6$

$$(A) = \begin{bmatrix} -5 & -3 & -6 \\ 10 & 6 & 12 \\ 5 & 3 & 6 \end{bmatrix}^T = \begin{bmatrix} -5 & 10 & 5 \\ -3 & 6 & 3 \\ -6 & 12 & 6 \end{bmatrix}$$

$$\therefore \quad (\text{adj } A)B = \begin{bmatrix} -5 & 10 & 5 \\ -3 & 6 & 3 \\ -6 & 12 & 6 \end{bmatrix} \begin{bmatrix} 2 \\ -1 \\ 3 \end{bmatrix}$$

$$= \begin{bmatrix} -10-10+15 \\ -6-6+9 \\ -12-12+18 \end{bmatrix} = \begin{bmatrix} -5 \\ -3 \\ -6 \end{bmatrix} \neq 0$$

Thus, the solution of the given system of equations does not exist.
Hence, the system of equations is inconsistent.

Question 6 $5x - y + 4z = 5, \quad 2x + 3y + 5z = 2, 5x - 2y + 6z = -1.$

Sol. The given system of equations can be written as $AX = B$, where

$$A = \begin{bmatrix} 5 & -1 & 4 \\ 2 & 3 & 5 \\ 5 & -2 & 6 \end{bmatrix}, X = \begin{bmatrix} x \\ y \\ z \end{bmatrix} \text{ and } B = \begin{bmatrix} 5 \\ 2 \\ -1 \end{bmatrix}$$

Here, $$|A| = \begin{vmatrix} 5 & -1 & 4 \\ 2 & 3 & 5 \\ 5 & -2 & 6 \end{vmatrix}$$

$$= 5(18+10) - (-1)(12-25) + 4(-4-15)$$

$$= 140 - 13 - 76 = 51 \neq 0$$

$\therefore$ A is non-singular. Therefore, A^{-1} exists.

Hence, the given system of equations is consistent.

Direction (Q. Nos. 7 to 14) Solve the following system of linear equations, using matrix method.

Question 7 $5x + 2y = 4, \quad 7x + 3y = 5.$

Sol. The given system of equation can be written as $AX = B$, where

$$A = \begin{bmatrix} 5 & 2 \\ 7 & 3 \end{bmatrix}, X = \begin{bmatrix} x \\ y \end{bmatrix} \text{ and } B = \begin{bmatrix} 4 \\ 5 \end{bmatrix}$$

Here, $$|A| = \begin{vmatrix} 5 & 2 \\ 7 & 3 \end{vmatrix} = 15 - 14 = 1 \neq 0$$

Thus, A is non-singular. Therefore, its inverse exists.

Therefore, the given system is consistent and has a unique solution given by

$$A^{-1}(AX) = A^{-1}B \Rightarrow X = A^{-1}B \quad \ldots\text{(i)}$$

Cofactors of A are, $A_{11} = 3, A_{12} = -7, A_{21} = -2, A_{22} = 5$

$$\therefore \quad \text{adj}(A) = \begin{bmatrix} 3 & -7 \\ -2 & 5 \end{bmatrix}^T = \begin{bmatrix} 3 & -2 \\ -7 & 5 \end{bmatrix}$$

and $$A^{-1} = \frac{1}{|A|}(\text{adj } A) = \frac{1}{1}\begin{bmatrix} 3 & -2 \\ -7 & 5 \end{bmatrix} = \begin{bmatrix} 3 & -2 \\ -7 & 5 \end{bmatrix}$$

Now, $$X = A^{-1}B = \begin{bmatrix} 3 & -2 \\ -7 & 5 \end{bmatrix}\begin{bmatrix} 4 \\ 5 \end{bmatrix}$$

$$= \begin{bmatrix} 3 \times 4 + (-2) \times 5 \\ -7 \times 4 + 5 \times 5 \end{bmatrix} = \begin{bmatrix} 2 \\ -3 \end{bmatrix} \Rightarrow \begin{bmatrix} x \\ y \end{bmatrix} = \begin{bmatrix} 2 \\ -3 \end{bmatrix}$$

Hence, $x = 2$ and $y = -3$.

Question 8 $2x - y = -2, \quad 3x + 4y = 3.$

Sol. The given system of equation can be written as $AX = B$, where

$$A = \begin{bmatrix} 2 & -1 \\ 3 & 4 \end{bmatrix}, X = \begin{bmatrix} x \\ y \end{bmatrix}, B = \begin{bmatrix} -2 \\ 3 \end{bmatrix}$$

Here, $$|A| = \begin{vmatrix} 2 & -1 \\ 3 & 4 \end{vmatrix} = 2 \times 4 - (-3) \times 1 = 11 \neq 0$$

Thus, A is non-singular. Therefore, its inverse exists.

Therefore, the given system of equation is consistent and has a unique solution given by

$$X = A^{-1}B$$

Cofactors of A are $A_{11} = 4$, $A_{12} = -3$, $A_{21} = 1$, $A_{22} = 2$

$$\therefore \quad (A) = \begin{bmatrix} 4 & -3 \\ 1 & 2 \end{bmatrix}^T = \begin{bmatrix} 4 & 1 \\ -3 & 2 \end{bmatrix} \text{ and } A^{-1} = \frac{1}{|A|}(\quad A) = \frac{1}{11}\begin{bmatrix} 4 & 1 \\ -3 & 2 \end{bmatrix}$$

Now, $$X = A^{-1}B = \frac{1}{11}\begin{bmatrix} 4 & 1 \\ -3 & 2 \end{bmatrix}\begin{bmatrix} -2 \\ 3 \end{bmatrix}$$

$$= \frac{1}{11}\begin{bmatrix} -8 + 3 \\ 6 + 6 \end{bmatrix} = \frac{1}{11}\begin{bmatrix} -5 \\ 12 \end{bmatrix} = \begin{bmatrix} -\frac{5}{11} \\ \frac{12}{11} \end{bmatrix} \Rightarrow \begin{bmatrix} x \\ y \end{bmatrix} = \begin{bmatrix} \frac{-5}{11} \\ \frac{12}{11} \end{bmatrix}$$

Hence, $$x = \frac{-5}{11} \text{ and } y = \frac{12}{11}.$$

Question 9 $4x - 3y = 3, 3x - 5y = 7.$

Sol. The given system of equation can be written as $AX = B$, where

$$A = \begin{bmatrix} 4 & -3 \\ 3 & -5 \end{bmatrix}, X = \begin{bmatrix} x \\ y \end{bmatrix}, B = \begin{bmatrix} 3 \\ 7 \end{bmatrix}$$

Here, $$|A| = \begin{vmatrix} 4 & -3 \\ 3 & -5 \end{vmatrix} = 4(-5) - 3(-3) = -20 + 9 = -11 \neq 0$$

Thus, A is non-singular. Therefore, its inverse exists.

Therefore, the given system of equation is consistent and has a unique solution given by $X = A^{-1}B$

Cofactors of A are

$$A_{11} = -5, A_{12} = -3\ A_{21} = 3, A_{22} = 4$$

$$\therefore \quad \text{adj}(A) = \begin{bmatrix} -5 & -3 \\ 3 & 4 \end{bmatrix}^T = \begin{bmatrix} -5 & 3 \\ -3 & 4 \end{bmatrix}$$

and $$A^{-1} = \frac{1}{|A|}(\text{adj } A) = \frac{1}{-11}\begin{bmatrix} -5 & 3 \\ -3 & 4 \end{bmatrix}$$

Now, $$X = A^{-1}B = \frac{1}{-11}\begin{bmatrix} -5 & 3 \\ -3 & 4 \end{bmatrix}\begin{bmatrix} 3 \\ 7 \end{bmatrix} = \frac{1}{-11}\begin{bmatrix} -15+21 \\ -9+28 \end{bmatrix} = \frac{1}{-11}\begin{bmatrix} 6 \\ 19 \end{bmatrix}$$

$$\Rightarrow \quad \begin{bmatrix} x \\ y \end{bmatrix} = \begin{bmatrix} \frac{-6}{11} \\ \frac{-19}{11} \end{bmatrix}.$$

Hence, $x = -\frac{6}{11}$ and $y = -\frac{19}{11}$.

Question 10 $5x + 2y = 3, \quad 3x + 2y = 5.$

Sol. The given system of equations can be written as $AX = B$, where

$$A = \begin{bmatrix} 5 & 2 \\ 3 & 2 \end{bmatrix}, X = \begin{bmatrix} x \\ y \end{bmatrix} \text{ and } B = \begin{bmatrix} 3 \\ 5 \end{bmatrix}. \quad \text{Here, } |A| = \begin{vmatrix} 5 & 2 \\ 3 & 2 \end{vmatrix} = 10 - 6 = 4 \neq 0,$$

Thus, A is non-singular. Therefore, its inverse exists.

Therefore, the given system of equation is consistent and has a unique solution given by $X = A^{-1}B$.

Cofactors of A are,

$$A_{11} = 2,\ A_{12} = -3,\quad A_{21} = -2,\ A_{22} = 5$$

$$\therefore \quad \text{adj}(A) = \begin{bmatrix} 2 & -3 \\ -2 & 5 \end{bmatrix}^T = \begin{bmatrix} 2 & -2 \\ -3 & 5 \end{bmatrix}$$

and $$A^{-1} = \frac{1}{|A|}(\text{adj } A) = \frac{1}{4}\begin{bmatrix} 2 & -2 \\ -3 & 5 \end{bmatrix}$$

Now, $$X = A^{-1}B = \frac{1}{4}\begin{bmatrix} 2 & -2 \\ -3 & 5 \end{bmatrix}\begin{bmatrix} 3 \\ 5 \end{bmatrix} = \frac{1}{4}\begin{bmatrix} 6-10 \\ -9+25 \end{bmatrix} = \frac{1}{4}\begin{bmatrix} -4 \\ 16 \end{bmatrix} = \begin{bmatrix} -1 \\ 4 \end{bmatrix}$$

$\Rightarrow \quad \begin{bmatrix} x \\ y \end{bmatrix} = \begin{bmatrix} -1 \\ 4 \end{bmatrix}$. Hence, $x = -1$ and $y = 4$.

Question 11 $2x + y + z = 1, \quad x - 2y - z = \frac{3}{2}, \quad 3y - 5z = 9$

Sol. The given system of equations can be written as $AX = B$, where

$$A = \begin{bmatrix} 2 & 1 & 1 \\ 2 & -4 & -2 \\ 0 & 3 & -5 \end{bmatrix}, X = \begin{bmatrix} x \\ y \\ z \end{bmatrix} \text{ and } B = \begin{bmatrix} 1 \\ 3 \\ 9 \end{bmatrix}$$

Here, $|A| = \begin{vmatrix} 2 & 1 & 1 \\ 2 & -4 & -2 \\ 0 & 3 & -5 \end{vmatrix} = 2(20+6) - 1(-10-0) + 1(6-0)$

$$= 52 + 10 + 6 = 68 \neq 0$$

Thus, A is non-singular. Therefore, its inverse exists.

Therefore, the given system of equations is consistent and has a unique solution given by $X = A^{-1}B$.

Cofactors of A are

$A_{11} = 20 + 6 = 26, \quad A_{12} = -(-10+0) = 10, \quad A_{13} = 6 + 0 = 6$

$A_{21} = -(-5-3) = 8, \quad A_{22} = -10 - 0 = -10, \quad A_{23} = -(6-0) = -6$

$A_{31} = (-2+4) = 2, \quad A_{32} = -(-4-2) = 6, \quad A_{33} = -8 - 2 = -10$

$$\therefore \quad (A) = \begin{bmatrix} 26 & 10 & 6 \\ 8 & -10 & -6 \\ 2 & 6 & -10 \end{bmatrix}^T = \begin{bmatrix} 26 & 8 & 2 \\ 10 & -10 & 6 \\ 6 & -6 & -10 \end{bmatrix}$$

and
$$A^{-1} = \frac{1}{|A|}(\quad A) = \frac{1}{68}\begin{bmatrix} 26 & 8 & 2 \\ 10 & -10 & 6 \\ 6 & -6 & 10 \end{bmatrix}$$

Now,
$$X = A^{-1}B \Rightarrow \begin{bmatrix} x \\ y \\ z \end{bmatrix} = \frac{1}{68}\begin{bmatrix} 26 & 8 & 2 \\ 10 & -10 & 6 \\ 6 & -6 & -10 \end{bmatrix}\begin{bmatrix} 1 \\ 3 \\ 9 \end{bmatrix}$$

$$\Rightarrow \begin{bmatrix} x \\ y \\ z \end{bmatrix} = \frac{1}{68}\begin{bmatrix} 26 + 24 + 18 \\ 10 - 30 + 54 \\ 6 - 18 - 90 \end{bmatrix} = \frac{1}{68}\begin{bmatrix} 68 \\ 34 \\ -102 \end{bmatrix} \Rightarrow \begin{bmatrix} x \\ y \\ z \end{bmatrix} = \begin{bmatrix} 1 \\ \frac{1}{2} \\ \frac{-3}{2} \end{bmatrix}$$

Hence,
$$x = 1, y = \frac{1}{2} \text{ and } z = \frac{-3}{2}.$$

Question 12 $x - y + z = 4, \quad 2x + y - 3z = 0, \quad x + y + z = 2.$

Sol. The given system of equations can be written as $AX = B$, where

$$A = \begin{bmatrix} 1 & -1 & 1 \\ 2 & 1 & -3 \\ 1 & 1 & 1 \end{bmatrix}, X = \begin{bmatrix} x \\ y \\ z \end{bmatrix} \text{ and } B = \begin{bmatrix} 4 \\ 0 \\ 2 \end{bmatrix}$$

Here, $|A| = \begin{vmatrix} 1 & -1 & 1 \\ 2 & 1 & -3 \\ 1 & 1 & 1 \end{vmatrix} = 1(1+3) - (-1)(2+3) + 1(2-1) = 4 + 5 + 1 = 10 \neq 0$

Thus, A is non-singular. Therefore, its inverse exists.

Therefore, the given system of equation is consistent and has a unique solution given by $X = A^{-1} B$.

Cofactors of A are

$$A_{11} = 1 + 3 = 4, \quad A_{12} = -(2+3) = -5, \quad A_{13} = 2 - 1 = 1,$$
$$A_{21} = -(-1-1) = 2, \quad A_{22} = 1 - 1 = 0, \quad A_{23} = -(1+1) = -2,$$
$$A_{31} = 3 - 1 = 2, \quad A_{32} = -(-3-2) = 5, \quad A_{33} = 1 + 2 = 3$$

$$\therefore \quad (A) = \begin{bmatrix} 4 & -5 & 1 \\ 2 & 0 & -2 \\ 2 & 5 & 3 \end{bmatrix}^T = \begin{bmatrix} 4 & 2 & 2 \\ -5 & 0 & 5 \\ 1 & -2 & 3 \end{bmatrix}$$

and $$A^{-1} = \frac{1}{|A|}(\quad A) = \frac{1}{10}\begin{bmatrix} 4 & 2 & 2 \\ -5 & 0 & 5 \\ 1 & -2 & 3 \end{bmatrix}$$

Now, $$X = A^{-1}B \Rightarrow \begin{bmatrix} x \\ y \\ z \end{bmatrix} = \frac{1}{10}\begin{bmatrix} 4 & 2 & 2 \\ -5 & 0 & 5 \\ 1 & -2 & 3 \end{bmatrix}\begin{bmatrix} 4 \\ 0 \\ 2 \end{bmatrix}$$

$$\Rightarrow \begin{bmatrix} x \\ y \\ z \end{bmatrix} = \frac{1}{10}\begin{bmatrix} 16+0+4 \\ -20+0+10 \\ 4+0+6 \end{bmatrix} \Rightarrow \begin{bmatrix} x \\ y \\ z \end{bmatrix} = \frac{1}{10}\begin{bmatrix} 20 \\ -10 \\ 10 \end{bmatrix} = \begin{bmatrix} 2 \\ -1 \\ 1 \end{bmatrix}$$

Hence, $x = 2$, $y = -1$ and $z = 1$.

Question 13 $2x + 3y + 3z = 5, x - 2y + z = -4, 3x - y - 2z = 3.$

Sol. The given system of equations can be written as $AX = B$, where

$$A = \begin{bmatrix} 2 & 3 & 3 \\ 1 & -2 & 1 \\ 3 & -1 & -2 \end{bmatrix}, X = \begin{bmatrix} x \\ y \\ z \end{bmatrix} \text{ and } B = \begin{bmatrix} 5 \\ -4 \\ 3 \end{bmatrix}$$

Here, $$|A| = \begin{vmatrix} 2 & 3 & 3 \\ 1 & -2 & 1 \\ 3 & -1 & -2 \end{vmatrix} = 2(4+1) - 3(-2-3) + 3(-1+6)$$

$$= 10 + 15 + 15 = 40 \neq 0$$

Thus, A is non-singular. Therefore, its inverse exists. Therefore, the given system of equations is consistent and has a unique solution given by $X = A^{-1}B$

Cofactors of A are

$$A_{11} = 4 + 1 = 5, \quad A_{12} = -(-2-3) = 5, \quad A_{13} = (-1+6) = 5,$$
$$A_{21} = -(-6+3) = 3, \quad A_{22} = (-4-9) = -13, \quad A_{23} = -(-2-9) = 11,$$
$$A_{31} = 3 + 6 = 9, \quad A_{32} = -(2-3) = 1, \quad A_{33} = -4 - 3 = -7$$

$$\therefore \quad (A) = \begin{bmatrix} 5 & 5 & 5 \\ 3 & -13 & 11 \\ 9 & 1 & -7 \end{bmatrix}^T = \begin{bmatrix} 5 & 3 & 9 \\ 5 & -13 & 1 \\ 5 & 11 & -7 \end{bmatrix}$$

and $$A^{-1} = \frac{1}{|A|}(\text{adj } A) = \frac{1}{40}\begin{bmatrix} 5 & 3 & 9 \\ 5 & -13 & 1 \\ 5 & 11 & -7 \end{bmatrix}$$

Now, $X = A^{-1}B$

$$\Rightarrow \begin{bmatrix} x \\ y \\ z \end{bmatrix} = \frac{1}{40}\begin{bmatrix} 5 & 3 & 9 \\ 5 & -13 & 1 \\ 5 & 11 & -7 \end{bmatrix}\begin{bmatrix} 5 \\ -4 \\ 3 \end{bmatrix} = \frac{1}{40}\begin{bmatrix} 25 - 12 + 27 \\ 25 + 52 + 3 \\ 25 - 44 - 21 \end{bmatrix}$$

$$= \frac{1}{40}\begin{bmatrix} 40 \\ 80 \\ -40 \end{bmatrix} = \begin{bmatrix} 1 \\ 2 \\ -1 \end{bmatrix}$$

Hence, $x = 1, y = 2$ and $z = -1$.

Question 14 $x - y + 2z = 7, \quad 3x + 4y - 5z = -5, \quad 2x - y + 3z = 12.$

Sol. The given system of equations can be written as $AX = B$, where

$$A = \begin{bmatrix} 1 & -1 & 2 \\ 3 & 4 & -5 \\ 2 & -1 & 3 \end{bmatrix}, X = \begin{bmatrix} x \\ y \\ z \end{bmatrix} \text{ and } B = \begin{bmatrix} 7 \\ -5 \\ 12 \end{bmatrix}$$

Here, $$|A| = \begin{vmatrix} 1 & -1 & 2 \\ 3 & 4 & -5 \\ 2 & -1 & 3 \end{vmatrix}$$

$$= 1(12 - 5) - (-1)(9 + 10) + 2(-3 - 8)$$
$$= 7 + 19 - 22 = 4 \neq 0$$

Thus, A is non-singular. Therefore, its inverse exists.

Therefore, the given system of equations is consistent and has a unique solution given by $X = A^{-1} B$

Cofactors of A are

$A_{11} = 12 - 5 = 7$, $A_{12} = -(9 + 10) = -19$, $A_{13} = -3 - 8 = -11$,
$A_{21} = -(-3 + 2) = 1$, $A_{22} = 3 - 4 = -1$, $A_{23} = -(-1 + 2) = -1$,
$A_{31} = 5 - 8 = -3$, $A_{32} = -(-5 - 6) = 11$, $A_{33} = 4 + 3 = 7$

$$\therefore \quad (\text{adj } A) = \begin{bmatrix} 7 & -19 & -11 \\ 1 & -1 & -1 \\ -3 & 11 & 7 \end{bmatrix}^T = \begin{bmatrix} 7 & 1 & -3 \\ -19 & -1 & 11 \\ -11 & -1 & 7 \end{bmatrix}$$

and $$A^{-1} = \frac{1}{|A|}(\text{adj } A) = \frac{1}{4}\begin{bmatrix} 7 & 1 & -3 \\ -19 & -1 & 11 \\ -11 & -1 & 7 \end{bmatrix}$$

Now, $X = A^{-1}B$

$$\Rightarrow \begin{bmatrix} x \\ y \\ z \end{bmatrix} = \frac{1}{4}\begin{bmatrix} 7 & 1 & -3 \\ -19 & -1 & 11 \\ -11 & -1 & 7 \end{bmatrix}\begin{bmatrix} 7 \\ -5 \\ 12 \end{bmatrix} = \frac{1}{4}\begin{bmatrix} 49-5-36 \\ -133+5+132 \\ -77+5+84 \end{bmatrix}$$

$$\Rightarrow \begin{bmatrix} x \\ y \\ z \end{bmatrix} = \frac{1}{4}\begin{bmatrix} 8 \\ 4 \\ 12 \end{bmatrix} = \begin{bmatrix} 2 \\ 1 \\ 3 \end{bmatrix}.$$

Hence, $x = 2$, $y = 1$ and $z = 3$.

Question 15 If $A = \begin{bmatrix} 2 & -3 & 5 \\ 3 & 2 & -4 \\ 1 & 1 & -2 \end{bmatrix}$, find A^{-1}. Using A^{-1} solve the system of equations $2x - 3y + 5z = 11$, $3x + 2y - 4z = -5$, $x + y - 2z = -3$.

Sol. Given, $A = \begin{bmatrix} 2 & -3 & 5 \\ 3 & 2 & -4 \\ 1 & 1 & -2 \end{bmatrix}$

$$\therefore \quad |A| = \begin{vmatrix} 2 & -3 & 5 \\ 3 & 2 & -4 \\ 1 & 1 & -2 \end{vmatrix} = 2(-4+4) - (-3)(-6+4) + 5(3-2)$$

$$= 0 - 6 + 5 = -1 \neq 0$$

Thus, A is non-singular. Therefore, its inverse exists.

Therefore, the given system of equations is consistent and has a unique solution given by $X = A^{-1}B$

Cofactors of A are

$A_{11} = -4 + 4 = 0$, $A_{12} = -(-6+4) = 2$, $A_{13} = 3 - 2 = 1$,

$A_{21} = -(6-5) = -1$, $A_{22} = -4 - 5 = -9$, $A_{23} = -(2+3) = -5$,

$A_{31} = (12 - 10) = 2$, $A_{32} = -(-8-15) = 23$, $A_{33} = 4 + 9 = 13$

$$\therefore \quad \text{adj}(A) = \begin{bmatrix} 0 & 2 & 1 \\ -1 & -9 & -5 \\ 2 & 23 & 13 \end{bmatrix}^T = \begin{bmatrix} 0 & -1 & 2 \\ 2 & -9 & 23 \\ 1 & -5 & 13 \end{bmatrix}$$

and $$A^{-1} = \frac{1}{|A|}(\text{adj } A) = \frac{1}{-1}\begin{bmatrix} 0 & -1 & 2 \\ 2 & -9 & 23 \\ 1 & -5 & 13 \end{bmatrix} = \begin{bmatrix} 0 & 1 & -2 \\ -2 & 9 & -23 \\ -1 & 5 & -13 \end{bmatrix}$$

The given system of equations can be written as $AX = B$, where

$$A = \begin{bmatrix} 2 & -3 & 5 \\ 3 & 2 & -4 \\ 1 & 1 & -2 \end{bmatrix}, X = \begin{bmatrix} x \\ y \\ z \end{bmatrix} \text{ and } B = \begin{bmatrix} 11 \\ -5 \\ -3 \end{bmatrix}$$

Now, $X = A^{-1}B \Rightarrow \begin{bmatrix} x \\ y \\ z \end{bmatrix} = \begin{bmatrix} 0 & 1 & -2 \\ -2 & 9 & -23 \\ -1 & 5 & -13 \end{bmatrix} \begin{bmatrix} 11 \\ -5 \\ -3 \end{bmatrix}$

$\Rightarrow \begin{bmatrix} x \\ y \\ z \end{bmatrix} = \begin{bmatrix} 0 - 5 + 6 \\ -22 - 45 + 69 \\ -11 - 25 + 39 \end{bmatrix} = \begin{bmatrix} 1 \\ 2 \\ 3 \end{bmatrix}$. Hence, $x = 1$, $y = 2$ and $z = 3$.

Question 16 The cost of 4 kg onion, 3 kg wheat and 2 kg rice is ₹ 60. The cost of 2 kg onion, 4 kg wheat and 6 kg rice is ₹ 90. The cost of 6 kg onion, 2 kg wheat and 3 kg rice is ₹ 70. Find cost of each item per kg by matrix method.

◎ ***Thinking Process*** Consider ₹x, ₹y, ₹ z be the costs of onion, wheat and rice and frame the three equations.

(i) Frame matrix A using the coefficients of x, y and z from the three equations.

(ii) Frame 3×1 matrix X using variables x, y, z.

(iii) Frame matrix B using constants involved in the equation.

(iv) Using the relation $AX = B$ to find the variables x, y and z.

Sol. Let the prices (per kg) of onion, wheat and rice be ₹ x, ₹ y and ₹ z, respectively then according to given statement, we have following equations.

$$4x + 3y + 2z = 60, \quad 2x + 4y + 6z = 90, \quad 6x + 2y + 3z = 70$$

This system of equations can be written as $AX = B$, where

$$A = \begin{bmatrix} 4 & 3 & 2 \\ 2 & 4 & 6 \\ 6 & 2 & 3 \end{bmatrix}, X = \begin{bmatrix} x \\ y \\ z \end{bmatrix} \text{ and } B = \begin{bmatrix} 60 \\ 90 \\ 70 \end{bmatrix}$$

Here, $|A| = \begin{vmatrix} 4 & 3 & 2 \\ 2 & 4 & 6 \\ 6 & 2 & 3 \end{vmatrix} = 4(12 - 12) - 3(6 - 36) + 2(4 - 24)$

$$= 0 + 90 - 40 = 50 \neq 0$$

Thus, A is non-singular. Therefore, its inverse exists. Therefore, the given system of equations is consistent and has a unique solution given by $X = A^{-1}B$

Cofactors of A are,

$$A_{11} = 12 - 12 = 0, \quad A_{12} = -(6 - 36) = 30, \quad A_{13} = 4 - 24 = -20,$$
$$A_{21} = -(9 - 4) = -5, \; A_{22} = 12 - 12 = 0, \; A_{23} = -(8 - 18) = 10,$$
$$A_{31} = (18 - 8) = 10, \; A_{32} = -(24 - 4) = -20, \; A_{33} = 16 - 6 = 10$$

$$\therefore \quad \text{adj}(A) = \begin{bmatrix} 0 & 30 & -20 \\ -5 & 0 & 10 \\ 10 & -20 & 10 \end{bmatrix}^T = \begin{bmatrix} 0 & -5 & 10 \\ 30 & 0 & -20 \\ -20 & 10 & 10 \end{bmatrix}$$

and
$$A^{-1} = \frac{1}{|A|}(\text{adj } A) = \frac{1}{50}\begin{bmatrix} 0 & -5 & 10 \\ 30 & 0 & -20 \\ -20 & 10 & 10 \end{bmatrix}$$

Now,
$$X = A^{-1}B$$

$$\Rightarrow \quad \begin{bmatrix} x \\ y \\ z \end{bmatrix} = \frac{1}{50}\begin{bmatrix} 0 & -5 & 10 \\ 30 & 0 & -20 \\ -20 & 10 & 10 \end{bmatrix}\begin{bmatrix} 60 \\ 90 \\ 70 \end{bmatrix} = \frac{1}{50}\begin{bmatrix} 0 - 450 + 700 \\ 1800 + 0 - 1400 \\ -1200 + 900 + 700 \end{bmatrix}$$

$$\Rightarrow \quad \begin{bmatrix} x \\ y \\ z \end{bmatrix} = \frac{1}{50}\begin{bmatrix} 250 \\ 400 \\ 400 \end{bmatrix} = \begin{bmatrix} 5 \\ 8 \\ 8 \end{bmatrix}$$

$\therefore \quad x = 5, y = 8$ and $z = 8$.

Hence, price of onion per kg is ₹ 5, price of wheat per kg is ₹ 8 and that of rice per kg is ₹ 8.

Miscellaneous Exercise

Question 1 Prove that the determinant $\begin{vmatrix} x & \sin\theta & \cos\theta \\ -\sin\theta & -x & 1 \\ \cos\theta & 1 & x \end{vmatrix}$ is independent of θ.

Sol. Let $\Delta = \begin{vmatrix} x & \sin\theta & \cos\theta \\ -\sin\theta & -x & 1 \\ \cos\theta & 1 & x \end{vmatrix}$

Expanding to corresponding first row, we get

$$\Delta = x\begin{vmatrix} -x & 1 \\ 1 & x \end{vmatrix} - \sin\theta\begin{vmatrix} -\sin\theta & 1 \\ \cos\theta & x \end{vmatrix} + \cos\theta\begin{vmatrix} -\sin\theta & -x \\ \cos\theta & 1 \end{vmatrix}$$

$$= x(-x^2 - 1) - \sin\theta(-x\sin\theta - \cos\theta) + \cos\theta(-\sin\theta + x\cos\theta)$$

$$= -x^3 - x + x\sin^2\theta + \sin\theta\cos\theta - \sin\theta\cos\theta + x\cos^2\theta$$

$$= -x^3 - x + x(\sin^2\theta + \cos^2\theta) = -x^3 - x + x \qquad (\because \sin^2 A + \cos^2 A = 1)$$

$$= -x^3.$$

Hence, Δ is independent of θ.

Question 2 Evaluate $\begin{vmatrix} \cos\alpha\cos\beta & \cos\alpha\sin\beta & -\sin\alpha \\ -\sin\beta & \cos\beta & 0 \\ \sin\alpha\cos\beta & \sin\alpha\sin\beta & \cos\alpha \end{vmatrix}$.

Sol. Given, determinant $= \begin{vmatrix} \cos\alpha\cos\beta & \cos\alpha\sin\beta & -\sin\alpha \\ -\sin\beta & \cos\beta & 0 \\ \sin\alpha\cos\beta & \sin\alpha\sin\beta & \cos\alpha \end{vmatrix}$,

Expanding to corresponding R_1, we get

$= \cos\alpha\cos\beta(\cos\alpha\cos\beta - 0) - \cos\alpha\sin\beta(-\cos\alpha\sin\beta - 0)$
$\quad - \sin\alpha(-\sin^2\beta\sin\alpha - \cos^2\beta\sin\alpha)$

$= \cos^2\alpha\cos^2\beta + \cos^2\alpha\sin^2\beta + \sin^2\alpha(\sin^2\beta + \cos^2\beta)$

$= \cos^2\alpha(\cos^2\beta + \sin^2\beta) + \sin^2\alpha(\sin^2\beta + \cos^2\beta)$

$= \cos^2\alpha(1) + \sin^2\alpha(1) = \cos^2\alpha + \sin^2\alpha = 1.$ $[\because \sin^2\theta + \cos^2\theta = 1]$

Question 3 If $A^{-1} = \begin{bmatrix} 3 & -1 & 1 \\ -15 & 6 & -5 \\ 5 & -2 & 2 \end{bmatrix}$ and $B = \begin{bmatrix} 1 & 2 & -2 \\ -1 & 3 & 0 \\ 0 & -2 & 1 \end{bmatrix}$, find $(AB)^{-1}$.

◎ ***Thinking Process*** Firstly, find the B^{-1} and using the formula $(AB)^{-1} = B^{-1}A^{-1}$ and simplify it.

Sol. We know that, $(AB)^{-1} = B^{-1}A^{-1}$ and A^{-1} is known, therefore we proceed to find B^{-1}.

Here, $|B| = \begin{vmatrix} 1 & 2 & -2 \\ -1 & 3 & 0 \\ 0 & -2 & 1 \end{vmatrix} = 1(3-0) - 2(-1-0) - 2(2-0) = 3 + 2 - 4 = 1 \neq 0$

$\therefore$ B^{-1}exists.

Cofactors of B are

$B_{11} = (3-0) = 3, B_{12} = -(-1-0) = 1, B_{13} = (2-0) = 2,$
$B_{21} = -(2-4) = 2, \; B_{22} = 1 - 0 = 1, B_{23} = -(-2-0) = 2,$
$B_{31} = (0+6) = 6, B_{32} = -(0-2) = 2, B_{33} = 3 + 2 = 5,$

$\therefore$ $\text{adj}(B) = \begin{bmatrix} 3 & 1 & 2 \\ 2 & 1 & 2 \\ 6 & 2 & 5 \end{bmatrix}^T = \begin{bmatrix} 3 & 2 & 6 \\ 1 & 1 & 2 \\ 2 & 2 & 5 \end{bmatrix}$

and $B^{-1} = \frac{1}{|B|}\text{adj}(B) = \frac{1}{1}\begin{bmatrix} 3 & 2 & 6 \\ 1 & 1 & 2 \\ 2 & 2 & 5 \end{bmatrix} = \begin{bmatrix} 3 & 2 & 6 \\ 1 & 1 & 2 \\ 2 & 2 & 5 \end{bmatrix}$

Now, $(AB)^{-1} = B^{-1} A^{-1} = \begin{bmatrix} 3 & 2 & 6 \\ 1 & 1 & 2 \\ 2 & 2 & 5 \end{bmatrix} \begin{bmatrix} 3 & -1 & 1 \\ -15 & 6 & -5 \\ 5 & -2 & 2 \end{bmatrix}$

$$= \begin{bmatrix} 9-30+30 & -3+12-12 & 3-10+12 \\ 3-15+10 & -1+6-4 & 1-5+4 \\ 6-30+25 & -2+12-10 & 2-10+10 \end{bmatrix} = \begin{bmatrix} 9 & -3 & 5 \\ -2 & 1 & 0 \\ 1 & 0 & 2 \end{bmatrix}.$$

Question 4 Let $A = \begin{bmatrix} 1 & -2 & 1 \\ -2 & 3 & 1 \\ 1 & 1 & 5 \end{bmatrix}$, verify that

(a) $[\text{adj } A]^{-1} = \text{adj}(A^{-1})$ (b) $(A^{-1})^{-1} = A$.

Solution Given, $A = \begin{bmatrix} 1 & -2 & 1 \\ -2 & 3 & 1 \\ 1 & 1 & 5 \end{bmatrix} \therefore |A| = \begin{vmatrix} 1 & -2 & 1 \\ -2 & 3 & 1 \\ 1 & 1 & 5 \end{vmatrix}$

$= 1(15-1) - (-2)(-10-1) + 1(-2-3)$

$= 14 - 22 - 5 = -13 \neq 0$

Cofactors of A are

$A_{11} = 15 - 1 = 14,\ A_{12} = -(-10-1) = 11,\ A_{13} = -2-3 = -5,$

$A_{21} = -(-10-1) = 11,\ A_{22} = 5 - 1 = 4,\ A_{23} = -(1+2) = -3,$

$A_{31} = (-2-3) = -5,\ A_{32} = -(1+2) = -3,\ A_{33} = 3-4 = -1$

$\therefore \quad \text{adj}(A) = \begin{bmatrix} 14 & 11 & -5 \\ 11 & 4 & -3 \\ -5 & -3 & -1 \end{bmatrix}^T = \begin{bmatrix} 14 & 11 & -5 \\ 11 & 4 & -3 \\ -5 & -3 & -1 \end{bmatrix}$

and $\quad A^{-1} = \dfrac{1}{|A|}(\text{adj } A) = \dfrac{1}{-13}\begin{bmatrix} 14 & 11 & -5 \\ 11 & 4 & -3 \\ -5 & -3 & -1 \end{bmatrix} = \begin{bmatrix} -\frac{14}{13} & -\frac{11}{13} & \frac{5}{13} \\ -\frac{11}{13} & -\frac{4}{13} & \frac{3}{13} \\ \frac{5}{13} & \frac{3}{13} & \frac{1}{13} \end{bmatrix}$

(a) Here, $\text{adj}(A) = \begin{bmatrix} 14 & 11 & -5 \\ 11 & 4 & -3 \\ -5 & -3 & -1 \end{bmatrix} = B$ (let)

$\therefore \quad |B| = |\text{adj } A| = \begin{vmatrix} 14 & 11 & -5 \\ 11 & 4 & -3 \\ -5 & -3 & -1 \end{vmatrix}$

$= 14(-4-9) - 11(-11-15) - 5(-33+20)$

$= -182 + 286 + 65 = 169 \neq 0$

Cofactors of B are

$B_{11} = (-4-9) = -13$, $B_{12} = -(-11-15) = 26$, $B_{13} = (-33+20) = -13$,
$B_{21} = -(-11-15) = 26$, $B_{22} = -14-25 = -39$, $B_{23} = -(-42+55) = -13$,
$B_{31} = (-33+20) = -13$, $B_{32} = -(-42+55) = -13$, $B_{33} = 56-121 = -65$,

$$\therefore \quad \text{adj}(B) = \text{adj}(\text{adj } A) = \begin{bmatrix} -13 & 26 & -13 \\ 26 & -39 & -13 \\ -13 & -13 & -65 \end{bmatrix}^T = \begin{bmatrix} -13 & 26 & -13 \\ 26 & -39 & -13 \\ -13 & -13 & -65 \end{bmatrix}$$

and $$B^{-1} = [\text{adj } A]^{-1} = \frac{1}{|\text{adj}A|}\{\text{adj (adj } A)\}$$

$$\Rightarrow \quad [\text{adj } A]^{-1} = \frac{1}{169}\begin{bmatrix} -13 & 26 & -13 \\ 26 & -39 & -13 \\ -13 & -13 & -65 \end{bmatrix} = \frac{1}{13}\begin{bmatrix} -1 & 2 & -1 \\ 2 & -3 & -1 \\ -1 & -1 & -5 \end{bmatrix} \quad \ldots\text{(i)}$$

Cofactors of A^{-1} are

$$A_{11} = \frac{-13}{169}, A_{12} = \frac{26}{169}, A_{13} = \frac{-13}{169}, \quad A_{21} = \frac{26}{169}, A_{22} = \frac{-39}{169}, A_{23} = \frac{-13}{169}$$

$$A_{31} = \frac{-13}{169}, A_{32} = -\frac{13}{169}, A_{33} = -\frac{65}{169}$$

Now, adj (A^{-1})

$$= \begin{bmatrix} -\frac{13}{169} & \frac{26}{169} & -\frac{13}{169} \\ \frac{26}{169} & -\frac{39}{169} & -\frac{13}{169} \\ -\frac{13}{169} & -\frac{13}{169} & -\frac{65}{169} \end{bmatrix}^T = \begin{bmatrix} -\frac{13}{169} & \frac{26}{169} & -\frac{13}{169} \\ \frac{26}{169} & -\frac{39}{169} & -\frac{13}{169} \\ -\frac{13}{169} & -\frac{13}{169} & -\frac{65}{169} \end{bmatrix}$$

$$\Rightarrow \quad \text{adj}(A^{-1}) = \frac{1}{13}\begin{bmatrix} -1 & 2 & -1 \\ 2 & -3 & -1 \\ -1 & -1 & -5 \end{bmatrix} \quad \ldots\text{(ii)}$$

From Eqs. (i) and (ii), we get that adj $(A^{-1}) = (\text{adj } A)^{-1}$

(b) We have, $$A^{-1} = \begin{bmatrix} -\frac{14}{13} & -\frac{11}{13} & \frac{5}{13} \\ -\frac{11}{13} & -\frac{4}{13} & \frac{3}{13} \\ \frac{5}{13} & \frac{3}{13} & \frac{1}{13} \end{bmatrix}$$

$$|A^{-1}| = -\frac{14}{13}\left(-\frac{4}{169} - \frac{9}{169}\right) + \frac{11}{13}\left(-\frac{11}{169} - \frac{15}{169}\right) + \frac{5}{13}\left(-\frac{33}{169} + \frac{20}{169}\right)$$

$$= -\frac{14}{13}\left(-\frac{13}{169}\right) + \frac{11}{13}\left(-\frac{26}{169}\right) + \frac{5}{13}\left(-\frac{13}{169}\right)$$

$$= \frac{14}{169} - \frac{22}{169} - \frac{5}{169} = -\frac{13}{169} = -\frac{1}{13}$$

and $\text{adj}(A^{-1}) = \dfrac{1}{13}\begin{bmatrix} -1 & 2 & -1 \\ 2 & -3 & -1 \\ -1 & -1 & -5 \end{bmatrix}$

$$\therefore \quad (A^{-1})^{-1} = \frac{1}{|A^{-1}|}(\text{adj } A^{-1})$$

$$= \frac{1}{-\frac{1}{13}} \times \frac{1}{13}\begin{bmatrix} -1 & 2 & -1 \\ 2 & -3 & -1 \\ -1 & -1 & -5 \end{bmatrix} = \begin{bmatrix} 1 & -2 & 1 \\ -2 & 3 & 1 \\ 1 & 1 & 5 \end{bmatrix} = A$$

Question 5 Evaluate $\begin{vmatrix} x & y & x+y \\ y & x+y & x \\ x+y & x & y \end{vmatrix}$.

Sol. We have, $\begin{vmatrix} x & y & x+y \\ y & x+y & x \\ x+y & x & y \end{vmatrix}$

Expanding along R_1 we get

$= x(y(x+y) - x \cdot x) - y(y \cdot y - x(x+y)) + (x+y)(xy - (x+y)(x+y))$

$= x(xy + y^2 - x^2) - y(y^2 - x^2 - xy) + (x+y)(xy - x^2 - y^2 - 2xy)$

$= x^2y + xy^2 - x^3 - y^3 + x^2y + xy^2 + (x+y)(-xy - x^2 - y^2)$

$= 2x^2y + 2xy^2 - x^3 - y^3 - x^2y - x^3 - xy^2 - xy^2 - yx^2 - y^3$

$= 2x^2y + 2xy^2 - 2x^3 - 2y^3 - 2x^2y - 2xy^2 = -2(x^3 + y^3).$

Question 6 Evaluate $\begin{vmatrix} 1 & x & y \\ 1 & x+y & y \\ 1 & x & x+y \end{vmatrix}$.

Sol. We have, $\begin{vmatrix} 1 & x & y \\ 1 & x+y & y \\ 1 & x & x+y \end{vmatrix}$

Expanding along C_1

$= 1((x+y)^2 - xy) - 1(x \cdot (x+y) - xy) + 1(xy - y(x+y))$

$= (x^2 + y^2 + 2xy - xy) - (x^2 + xy - xy) + (xy - xy - y^2)$

$= x^2 + y^2 + xy - x^2 - y^2 = xy$

Question 7 Solve the system of equations

$$\frac{2}{x} + \frac{3}{y} + \frac{10}{z} = 4, \frac{4}{x} - \frac{6}{y} + \frac{5}{z} = 1 \text{ and } \frac{6}{x} + \frac{9}{y} - \frac{20}{z} = 2.$$

◎ ***Thinking Process*** Consider $\frac{1}{x} = p, \frac{1}{y} = q, \frac{1}{z} = r$ to make a standard form of system of equations and use the matrix method to solve the three equations in p, q and r.

Sol. Let $\frac{1}{x} = p, \frac{1}{y} = q$ and $\frac{1}{z} = r$, then the given equations become

$$2p + 3q + 10r = 4, \quad 4p - 6q + 5r = 1, \quad 6p + 9q - 20r = 2$$

This system of equations can be written as $AX = B$, where

$$A = \begin{bmatrix} 2 & 3 & 10 \\ 4 & -6 & 5 \\ 6 & 9 & -20 \end{bmatrix}, X = \begin{bmatrix} p \\ q \\ r \end{bmatrix}, B = \begin{bmatrix} 4 \\ 1 \\ 2 \end{bmatrix}$$

Here, $|A| = \begin{vmatrix} 2 & 3 & 10 \\ 4 & -6 & 5 \\ 6 & 9 & -20 \end{vmatrix} = 2(120 - 45) - 3(-80 - 30) + 10(36 + 36)$

$$= 150 + 330 + 720 = 1200 \neq 0$$

Thus, A is non-singular. Therefore, its inverse exists.

Therefore, the above system of equations is consistent and has a unique solution given by $X = A^{-1}B$

Cofactors of A are

$A_{11} = 120 - 45 = 75, \ A_{12} = -(-80 - 30) = 110, A_{13} = (36 + 36) = 72,$

$A_{21} = -(-60 - 90) = 150, \quad A_{22} = (-40 - 60) = -100, A_{23} = -(18 - 18) = 0,$

$A_{31} = 15 + 60 = 75, \quad A_{32} = -(10 - 40) = 30, A_{33} = -12 - 12 = -24$

$$\therefore \quad \text{adj}(A) = \begin{bmatrix} 75 & 110 & 72 \\ 150 & -100 & 0 \\ 75 & 30 & -24 \end{bmatrix}^T = \begin{bmatrix} 75 & 150 & 75 \\ 110 & -100 & 30 \\ 72 & 0 & -24 \end{bmatrix}$$

and $$A^{-1} = \frac{1}{|A|}(\text{adj } A) = \frac{1}{1200}\begin{bmatrix} 75 & 150 & 75 \\ 110 & -100 & 30 \\ 72 & 0 & -24 \end{bmatrix}$$

Now, $$X = A^{-1}B \Rightarrow \begin{bmatrix} p \\ q \\ r \end{bmatrix} = \frac{1}{1200}\begin{bmatrix} 75 & 150 & 75 \\ 110 & -100 & 30 \\ 72 & 0 & -24 \end{bmatrix}\begin{bmatrix} 4 \\ 1 \\ 2 \end{bmatrix}$$

$$= \frac{1}{1200}\begin{bmatrix} 300 + 150 + 150 \\ 440 - 100 + 60 \\ 288 + 0 - 48 \end{bmatrix} = \frac{1}{1200}\begin{bmatrix} 600 \\ 400 \\ 240 \end{bmatrix} = \begin{bmatrix} \frac{1}{2} \\ \frac{1}{3} \\ \frac{1}{5} \end{bmatrix}$$

$$\Rightarrow \quad p = \frac{1}{2}, q = \frac{1}{3}, r = \frac{1}{5}$$

$$\Rightarrow \quad \frac{1}{x} = \frac{1}{2}, \frac{1}{y} = \frac{1}{3}, \frac{1}{z} = \frac{1}{5}$$

$\Rightarrow \quad x = 2, y = 3$ and $z = 5$.

Direction (Q. Nos. 8-9) Choose the correct answer in the following question:

Question 8 If x, y, z are non-zero real numbers, then the inverse of matrix $A = \begin{bmatrix} x & 0 & 0 \\ 0 & y & 0 \\ 0 & 0 & z \end{bmatrix}$ is

(a) $\begin{bmatrix} x^{-1} & 0 & 0 \\ 0 & y^{-1} & 0 \\ 0 & 0 & z^{-1} \end{bmatrix}$ (b) $xyz \begin{bmatrix} x^{-1} & 0 & 0 \\ 0 & y^{-1} & 0 \\ 0 & 0 & z^{-1} \end{bmatrix}$

(c) $\frac{1}{xyz} \begin{bmatrix} x & 0 & 0 \\ 0 & y & 0 \\ 0 & 0 & z \end{bmatrix}$ (d) $\frac{1}{xyz} \begin{bmatrix} 1 & 0 & 0 \\ 0 & 1 & 0 \\ 0 & 0 & 1 \end{bmatrix}$

Sol. (a) Given, $A = \begin{bmatrix} x & 0 & 0 \\ 0 & y & 0 \\ 0 & 0 & z \end{bmatrix}$

$$|A| = \begin{vmatrix} x & 0 & 0 \\ 0 & y & 0 \\ 0 & 0 & z \end{vmatrix} = x(yz - 0) = xyz \neq 0 \qquad (\because x, y \text{ and } z \text{ are non -zero})$$

Cofactors of A are

$A_{11} = (yz - 0) = yz,\ A_{12} = -(0 - 0) = 0,\ A_{13} = 0 - 0 = 0,$
$A_{21} = -(0 - 0) = 0,\ A_{22} = xz - 0 = xz,\ A_{23} = -(0 - 0) = 0,$
$A_{31} = 0 - 0 = 0,\ A_{32} = -(0 - 0) = 0,\ A_{33} = (xy - 0) = xy,$

$$\therefore \quad \text{adj}(A) = \begin{bmatrix} yz & 0 & 0 \\ 0 & xz & 0 \\ 0 & 0 & xy \end{bmatrix}^T = \begin{bmatrix} yz & 0 & 0 \\ 0 & xz & 0 \\ 0 & 0 & xy \end{bmatrix}$$

Now, $\quad A^{-1} = \frac{1}{|A|}(\text{adj } A)$

$$= \frac{1}{xyz}\begin{bmatrix} yz & 0 & 0 \\ 0 & xz & 0 \\ 0 & 0 & xy \end{bmatrix} = \begin{bmatrix} \frac{1}{x} & 0 & 0 \\ 0 & \frac{1}{y} & 0 \\ 0 & 0 & \frac{1}{z} \end{bmatrix} = \begin{bmatrix} x^{-1} & 0 & 0 \\ 0 & y^{-1} & 0 \\ 0 & 0 & z^{-1} \end{bmatrix}$$

Question 9 Let $A=\begin{bmatrix} 1 & \sin\theta & 1 \\ -\sin\theta & 1 & \sin\theta \\ -1 & -\sin\theta & 1 \end{bmatrix}$, where $0 \le \theta \le 2\pi$, then

(a) det $A = 0$
(b) det $A \in (2, \infty)$
(c) det $A \in (2, 4)$
(d) det $A \in [2, 4]$.

Sol. (d) Given, $A=\begin{bmatrix} 1 & \sin\theta & 1 \\ -\sin\theta & 1 & \sin\theta \\ -1 & -\sin\theta & 1 \end{bmatrix}$

$$\therefore \quad |A| = \begin{vmatrix} 1 & \sin\theta & 1 \\ -\sin\theta & 1 & \sin\theta \\ -1 & -\sin\theta & 1 \end{vmatrix}$$

$$= 1(1+\sin^2\theta) - \sin\theta(-\sin\theta + \sin\theta) + 1(\sin^2\theta + 1)$$

$$= 2 + 2\sin^2\theta$$

For $0 \le \theta \le 2\pi$,

$$-1 \le \sin\theta \le 1 \Rightarrow 0 \le \sin^2\theta \le 1$$

$$\Rightarrow \quad 1 \le 1 + \sin^2\theta \le 2 \Rightarrow 2 \le 2(1+\sin^2\theta) \le 4$$

$\therefore$ det (A) $\in [2, 4]$

DIKSHA APP Questions

☐ Multiple Choice Questions

Q.1 The system of linear equations $x+y+z=2$, $2x+y-z=3$ and $3x+2y+kz=4$ unique solution, then

(a) $k \ne 0$
(b) $-1 < k < 1$
(c) $-1 > k > 1$
(d) $k = 0$

Sol. (a) We have, $x + y + z = 2$

$$2x + y - z = 3$$

$$3x + 2y + kz = 4$$

If equation have unique solution then,

$$|A| \ne 0 \text{ where } A = \begin{bmatrix} 1 & 1 & 1 \\ 2 & 1 & -1 \\ 3 & 2 & k \end{bmatrix}$$

$$\Rightarrow \quad |A| = \begin{vmatrix} 1 & 1 & 1 \\ 2 & 1 & -1 \\ 3 & 2 & k \end{vmatrix} \ne 0$$

$\Rightarrow \quad 1(k+2)-1(2k+3)+1(4-3) \neq 0$ [Expanding along R_1]

$\Rightarrow \quad k+2-2k-3+1 \neq 0$

$\Rightarrow \quad -k \neq 0$

$\Rightarrow \quad k \neq 0$

Q.2 If $A = \begin{bmatrix} a & 0 & 0 \\ 0 & a & 0 \\ 0 & 0 & a \end{bmatrix}$ then value of $|\operatorname{adj}(A)|$ is

(a) a^{27} (b) a^9
(c) a^6 (d) a^2

Sol. (c) Given, $A = \begin{bmatrix} a & 0 & 0 \\ 0 & a & 0 \\ 0 & 0 & a \end{bmatrix}$

$\therefore \quad |A| = \begin{vmatrix} a & 0 & 0 \\ 0 & a & 0 \\ 0 & 0 & a \end{vmatrix}$

$|A| = a(a^2-0) = a^3$ [Expanding along, R_1]

We know that $|\operatorname{adj} A| = |A|^{n-1}$

$\therefore \quad |\operatorname{adj} A| = |A|^2 = (a^3)^2 = a^6$ [$\because n = 3$ (order of A)]

Q.3 If A is an invertible matrix of order n then $|\operatorname{adj}(A)| =$

(a) $|A|^n$ (b) $|A|^{n+1}$
(c) $|A|^{n-1}$ (d) $|A|^{n+2}$

Sol. (c) We know that $|\operatorname{adj} A| = |A|^{n-1}$ where n is order.

Q.4 If the area of the triangle is 4 square unit and vertices are $(k, 0)$, $(4, 0)$ and $(0, 2)$ then $k =$

(a) 6 (b) 4
(c) 0 (d) 2

Sol. (c) Let the vertices of a triangle be $A(x_1, y_1) = (k, 0)$, $B(x_2, y_2) = (4, 0)$ and $C(x_3, y_3) = (0, 2)$

Given, area of triangle = 4 sq units.

$\therefore \quad \frac{1}{2}\begin{vmatrix} k & 0 & 1 \\ 4 & 0 & 1 \\ 0 & 2 & 1 \end{vmatrix} = \pm 4$ $\left[\because \text{Area of triangle} = \frac{1}{2}\begin{vmatrix} x_1 & y_1 & 1 \\ x_2 & y_2 & 1 \\ x_3 & y_3 & 1 \end{vmatrix}\right]$

$$\Rightarrow \quad \begin{vmatrix} k & 0 & 1 \\ 4 & 0 & 1 \\ 0 & 2 & 1 \end{vmatrix} = \pm 8$$

Expanding along c_2

$\Rightarrow \quad -2(k-4) = \pm 8$

$\Rightarrow \quad -2k + 8 = \pm 8$

$\Rightarrow \quad -2k + 8 = 8$ or $-2k + 8 = -8$

$\Rightarrow \quad k = 0$ or $k = 8$

Q.5 If $A = \begin{bmatrix} 0 & 3 & 2x \\ 2 & 0 & 1 \\ 4 & -1 & 6 \end{bmatrix}$ is a singular matrix then $x =$

(a) -3 (b) 3

(c) -6 (d) 6

Sol. (c) Given, $A = \begin{bmatrix} 0 & 3 & 2x \\ 2 & 0 & 1 \\ 4 & -1 & 6 \end{bmatrix}$

If a matrix is singular, then $|A| = 0$

$$\therefore \quad |A| = \begin{vmatrix} 0 & 3 & 2x \\ 2 & 0 & 1 \\ 4 & -1 & 6 \end{vmatrix} = 0$$

$\Rightarrow \quad 0(0+1) - 3(12-4) + 2x(-2-0) = 0$ [Expanding along R_1]

$\Rightarrow \quad -24 - 4x = 0$

$\Rightarrow \quad 4x = -24$

$\Rightarrow \quad x = -6$

Q.6 The sum of the product of the elements of any row of a determinant A with the cofactors of other row is always equal to

(a) $|A|$ (b) 0

(c) $\frac{1}{2}|A|$ (d) 1

Sol. (b) Sum of the product of the element of any row of a determinant with the cofactor of other row is always zero.

i.e., $a_{11}A_{21} + a_{12}A_{22} + a_{13}A_{23} = 0$

Where a_{ij} is element and A_{ij} is cofactor.

Q.7 The sum of the product of the elements of any row of a determinant A with the cofactors of same row is always equal to

(a) $|A|$ (b) 0

(c) $\frac{1}{2}|A|$ (d) 1

Sol. (a) Sum of the product of the element of any row of a determinant A with the cofactor of same row is equal to $|A|$

i.e., $a_{11}A_{11} + a_{12}A_{12} + a_{13}A_{13} = |A|$

Q.8 The minors of – 4 and 9 and cofactors of – 4 and 9 in the determinant $A = \begin{vmatrix} -1 & -2 & 3 \\ -4 & -5 & -6 \\ -7 & 8 & 9 \end{vmatrix}$ are respectively.

(a) (42, 3; – 42, 3) (b) (– 42, – 3; 42, – 3)

(c) (42, 3; – 42, – 3) (d) (42, 3; 42, 3)

Sol. (b) We have, $A = \begin{vmatrix} -1 & -2 & 3 \\ -4 & -5 & -6 \\ -7 & 8 & 9 \end{vmatrix}$

Minor of (– 4) *i.e.*, $M_{21} = -2 \times 9 - 8 \times 3$

$= -18 - 24 = -42$

Minor of (9) *i.e.*, $M_{33} = -1 \times -5 - (-4) \times (-2)$

$= 5 - 8 = -3$

Cofactor of (– 4) *i.e.*, $A_{21} = (-1)^{2+1} M_{21} = -(-42) = 42$

Cofactor of (9) *i.e.*, $A_{33} = (-1)^{3+3} M_{33} = -3$

Hence, the minor and cofactor of – 4 and 9 are (– 42, – 3) and (42, – 3) respectively.

Q.9 If $A = \begin{bmatrix} a & 4 \\ 4 & a \end{bmatrix}$ and $|A|^3 = 729$ then $a =$

(a) ± 6 (b) ± 3 (c) ± 4 (d) ± 5

Sol. (d) Given, $A = \begin{bmatrix} a & 4 \\ 4 & a \end{bmatrix}$

$\therefore \quad |A| = a \cdot a - 4 \cdot 4 = a^2 - 16$ ...(i)

Also, given $|A|^3 = 729$

$\Rightarrow \quad |A| = 9$ ...(ii)

From Eqs. (i) and (ii), we get $a^2 - 16 = 9 \Rightarrow a^2 - 16 = 9$

$\Rightarrow \quad a^2 = 25 \Rightarrow a = \pm 5$

☐ Subjective Type Questions

Q.1 Using adjoint, find the inverse of matrix $A = \begin{bmatrix} 2 & 0 & -1 \\ 5 & 1 & 0 \\ 0 & 1 & 3 \end{bmatrix}$.

Sol. We have, $A = \begin{bmatrix} 2 & 0 & -1 \\ 5 & 1 & 0 \\ 0 & 1 & 3 \end{bmatrix}$

Here, $|A| = 2(3-0) - 0 - 1(5-0) = 6 - 5 = 1 \neq 0$

So, A^{-1} exists

Cofactors of A are

$$A_{11} = (-1)^{1+1}(3-0) = 3$$
$$A_{12} = (-1)^{1+2}(15-0) = -15$$
$$A_{13} = (-1)^{1+3}(5-0) = 5$$
$$A_{21} = (-1)^{2+1}(0+1) = -1$$
$$A_{22} = (-1)^{2+2}(6-0) = 6$$
$$A_{23} = (-1)^{2+3}(2-0) = -2$$
$$A_{31} = (-1)^{3+1}(0+1) = 1$$
$$A_{32} = (-1)^{3+2}(0+5) = -5$$
$$A_{33} = (-1)^{3+3}(2-0) = 2$$

$$\therefore \text{adj } A = \begin{bmatrix} A_{11} & A_{12} & A_{13} \\ A_{21} & A_{22} & A_{23} \\ A_{31} & A_{32} & A_{33} \end{bmatrix}^T$$

$$= \begin{bmatrix} 3 & -15 & 5 \\ -1 & 6 & -2 \\ 1 & -5 & 2 \end{bmatrix}^T = \begin{bmatrix} 3 & -1 & 1 \\ -15 & 6 & -5 \\ 5 & -2 & 2 \end{bmatrix}$$

Now, $$A^{-1} = \frac{1}{|A|}(\text{adj } A)$$

$$= 1\begin{vmatrix} 3 & -1 & 1 \\ -15 & 6 & -5 \\ 5 & -2 & 2 \end{vmatrix}$$

$$= \begin{vmatrix} 3 & -1 & 1 \\ -15 & 6 & -5 \\ 5 & -2 & 2 \end{vmatrix}$$

Q.2 Prove theat a, b, c are in GP, if $\begin{vmatrix} a & b & ak+b \\ b & c & bk+c \\ ak+b & bk+c & 0 \end{vmatrix} = 0$

Sol. Given, $\begin{vmatrix} a & b & ak+b \\ b & c & bk+c \\ ak+b & bk+c & 0 \end{vmatrix} = 0$

On expanding along R_3, we get

$(ak+b)(b^2k+bc-cak-bc)-(bk+c)(abk+ca-abk-b^2)+0=0$

$\Rightarrow ab^2k^2+abck-a^2ck^2-abck+b^3k+b^2c-abck-b^2c$

$-(ab^2k^2+abck-ab^2k^2-b^3k+abck+ac^2-abck-b^2c)=0$

$\Rightarrow -a^2ck^2-2abck+2b^3k+b^2c+ab^2k^2-c^2a=0$

$\Rightarrow -a^2ck^2+ab^2k^2-2abck+2b^3k+b^2c-c^2a=0$

$\Rightarrow \quad ak^2(b^2-ca)+2bk(b^2-ac)+c(b^2-ca)=0$

$\Rightarrow \quad (b^2-ca)(ak^2+2bk+c)=0$

Now, $\quad ak^2+2bk+c=0$ or $b^2-ca=0$

$b^2=ca$

Hence, a, b, c are in GP.

Continuity and Differentiability

CHAPTER 05

Important Points

Continuity

01 (i) **Right Hand Limit** $\lim_{x \to a^+} f(x)$ or $f(a+0)$

Rule Replace x by $(a+h)$ and take the limit as $h \to 0$

(ii) **Left Hand Limit** $\lim_{x \to a^-} f(x)$ or $f(a-0)$

Rule Replace x by $(a-h)$ and take the limit as $h \to 0$

02 **Test for Continuity** If $f(a) = \lim_{x \to a^+} f(x) = \lim_{x \to a^-} f(x)$, then $f(x)$ is continuous at $x = a$ otherwise, $f(x)$ is discontinuous at $x = a$.

If $f(x)$ is continuous at every point into domain D, then $f(x)$ is said to be continuous in D.

Note If domain of f is a singleton then f is a continuous function.

03 (i) **Right Hand Derivative** $Rf'(a) = \lim_{h \to 0} \frac{f(a+h) - f(a)}{h}$

(ii) **Left Hand Derivative** $Lf'(a) = \lim_{h \to 0} \frac{f(a-h) - f(a)}{-h}$

04 **Test for Differentiability**

$f(x)$ is differentiable at $x = a$ if $Rf'(a) = L\,f'(a)$, otherwise $f(x)$ is not differentiable at $x = a$.

If f is differentiable at every point of its domain then f is said to be differentiable function.

05 Properties of Continuity

(i) Every constant function is continuous.

(ii) Every identity function is continuous.

(iii) Every polynomial function is continuous.

(iv) If f and g be two continuous functions in domain D, then

(a) $(f+g)$ is continuous (b) $(f-g)$ is continuous

(c) cf is continuous (d) fg is continuous

(e) $\frac{f}{g}$ is continuous in D except at the points where $g(x)=0$.

(v) If f is continuous, then $|f|$ is continuous.

06 Every differentiable function is continuous. But a continuous function need not be differentiable.

07 Suppose f and g are real valued functions such that (fog) is defined at c. If g is continous at c and if f is contionus at $g(c)$, then (fog) is continous at c.

08 Standard Results

(i) $\lim_{x\to a}\frac{x^n-a^n}{x-a}=na^{n-1}$ (ii) $\lim_{x\to 0}\frac{\sin x}{x}=1$ (iii) $\lim_{x\to 0}\frac{\tan x}{x}=1$

(iv) $\lim_{x\to 0}\frac{\sin^{-1}x}{x}=1$ (v) $\lim_{x\to 0}\frac{\tan^{-1}x}{x}=1$ (vi) $\lim_{x\to 0}\frac{e^x-1}{x}=1$

(vii) $\lim_{x\to 0}\frac{a^x-1}{x}=\log_e a$ (viii) $\lim_{x\to 0}\frac{\log(1+x)}{x}=1$

(ix) $\lim_{x\to 0}(1+x)^{1/x}=e$ (x) $\lim_{x\to\infty}\left(1+\frac{1}{x}\right)^x=e$ (xi) $\lim_{x\to\infty}\frac{\sin x}{x}=0$

Differentiation

01 Derivatives of standard functions

(i) $\frac{d}{dx}(x^n)=nx^{n-1}$ (ii) $\frac{d}{dx}(\text{constant})=0$

(iii) $\frac{d}{dx}(cx^n)=c\frac{d}{dx}(x^n)$ (iv) $\frac{d}{dx}(\sin x)=\cos x$

(v) $\frac{d}{dx}(\cos x)=-\sin x$ (vi) $\frac{d}{dx}(\tan x)=\sec^2 x$

(vii) $\frac{d}{dx}(\sec x)=\sec x\tan x$ (viii) $\frac{d}{dx}(\cot x)=-\operatorname{cosec}^2 x$

(ix) $\frac{d}{dx}(\text{cosec}\, x) = -\text{cosec}\, x \cot x$

(x) $\frac{d}{dx}(e^x) = e^x$

(xi) $\frac{d}{dx} a^x = a^x \log a,\ a > 0$ (xii) $\frac{d}{dx}(\log_e x) = \frac{1}{x},\ x > 0$

(xiii) $\frac{d}{dx}(\log_a x) = \frac{1}{x \log_e a},\ a > 0,\ a \neq 1$

(xiv) $\frac{d}{dx}(\sin^{-1} x) = \frac{1}{\sqrt{1-x^2}}$ (xv) $\frac{d}{dx}(\cos^{-1} x) = -\frac{1}{\sqrt{1-x^2}}$

(xvi) $\frac{d}{dx}(\tan^{-1} x) = \frac{1}{1+x^2}$ (xvii) $\frac{d}{dx}(\cot^{-1} x) = \frac{-1}{1+x^2}$

(xviii) $\frac{d}{dx}(\sec^{-1} x) = \frac{1}{|x|\sqrt{x^2-1}}$ (xxi) $\frac{d}{dx}(\text{cosec}^{-1} x) = \frac{-1}{|x|\sqrt{x^2-1}}$

These two formulae will be handy

$$\frac{d}{dx}(\sqrt{x}) = \frac{1}{2\sqrt{x}} \quad \text{and} \quad \frac{d}{dx}\left(\frac{1}{x}\right) = -\frac{1}{x^2}$$

02 Derivative's rules

(i) $\frac{d}{dx}(u \pm v) = \frac{du}{dx} \pm \frac{dv}{dx}$

(ii) $\frac{d}{dx}(u \pm v \pm w \pm \ldots) = \frac{du}{dx} \pm \frac{dv}{dx} \pm \frac{dw}{dx} \pm \ldots$

(iii) $\frac{d}{dx} u \cdot v = u \frac{d}{dx} v + v \frac{d}{dx} u$ (Product rule)

(iv) $\frac{d}{dx}\left(\frac{u}{v}\right) = \frac{v \frac{d}{dx} u - u \frac{d}{dx} v}{v^2}$ where $v \neq 0$ (Quotient rule)

(v) $y = [f(x)]^{g(x)} \Rightarrow \frac{dy}{dx} = [f(x)]^{g(x)} \left[\frac{g(x)}{f(x)} f'(x) + \log f(x) \cdot g'(x)\right]$

[Logarithmic differential]

(vi) If $x = f(t)$ and $y = g(t)$, then $\frac{dy}{dx} = \frac{\left(\frac{dy}{dt}\right)}{\left(\frac{dx}{dt}\right)}$ [For parametric form]

(vii) If $y = f(g(x))$, then $\frac{dy}{dx} = f'(g(x))\, g'(x)$ [Chain rule]

03 Suitable substitutions

Function	Substitution	Function	Substitution
$\sqrt{a^2-x^2}$	$x = a\sin\theta$ or $a\cos\theta$	$\sqrt{\dfrac{x}{a+x}}$	$x = a\tan^2\theta$
$\sqrt{x^2-a^2}$	$x = a\sec\theta$ or $a\operatorname{cosec}\theta$	$\sqrt{\dfrac{a-x}{a+x}}$	$x = \cos 2\theta$
$\sqrt{(x-a)(b-x)}$	$x = a\sec^2\theta + b\sin^2\theta$	$\sqrt{ax-x^2}$	$x = a\sin^2\theta$
$\sqrt{(x-a)(x-b)}$	$x = a\sec^2\theta - b\tan^2\theta$	$\sqrt{\dfrac{x}{a-x}}$	$x = a\sin^2\theta$
$\sqrt{x^2+a^2}$	$x = a\tan\theta$ or $a\cot\theta$	$\sqrt{a^2-x^2}$	$x^2 = a^2\cos 2\theta$

04 Differentiation of a determinant

If $y = \begin{vmatrix} p & q & r \\ u & v & w \\ l & m & n \end{vmatrix}$, then

$$\frac{dy}{dx} = \begin{vmatrix} \frac{dp}{dx} & \frac{dq}{dx} & \frac{dr}{dx} \\ u & v & w \\ l & m & n \end{vmatrix} + \begin{vmatrix} p & q & r \\ \frac{du}{dx} & \frac{dv}{dx} & \frac{dw}{dx} \\ l & m & n \end{vmatrix} + \begin{vmatrix} p & q & r \\ u & v & w \\ \frac{dl}{dx} & \frac{dm}{dx} & \frac{dn}{dx} \end{vmatrix}$$

05 Useful logarithmic formulae (in differentiation)

(i) $\log_a mn = \log_a m + \log_a n$ (ii) $\log_a \dfrac{m}{n} = \log_a m - \log_a n$

(iii) $\log_a m^n = n\log_a m$ (iv) $\log_a a = 1$

(v) $\log_a m = \log_b m \times \log_a b$ (vi) $\log_a m \times \log_m a = 1$

(vii) $\log_{b^m} a = \dfrac{1}{m}\log_b a$ (viii) $\log_b a = \dfrac{1}{\log_a b}$

(ix) $\log_b a = \dfrac{\log_m a}{\log_m b}$ (x) $a^{\log_a m} = m$

06 Second order derivative

The second-order derivative is the derivative of the first derivative. It is computed by differentiating $\dfrac{dy}{dx}$ to get $\dfrac{d^2y}{dx^2}$ and it is denoted by $\dfrac{d^2y}{dx^2}$ or $f''(x)$ or D^2y or y'' or y_2 if $y = f(x)$.

Exercise 5.1

Question 1 Prove that the function $f(x) = 5x - 3$ is continuous at $x = 0$, at $x = -3$ and at $x = 5$.

◎ *Thinking Process* (Q. Nos. 1 to 2) For $f(x)$ to be continuous at any point at $x = a$, then $\lim_{x \to a} f(x) = f(a)$.

Sol. Here, $f(x) = 5x - 3$

At $x = 0$, $\lim_{x \to 0} f(x) = \lim_{x \to 0} (5x - 3) = 5 \times 0 - 3 = 0 - 3 = -3$

and $f(0) = 5 \times 0 - 3 = -3$

$\therefore$ $\lim_{x \to 0} f(x) = f(0)$. Thus, $f(x)$ is continuous at $x = 0$.

At $x = -3$, $\lim_{x \to -3} f(x) = \lim_{x \to -3} (5x - 3) = 5 \times (-3) - 3 = -15 - 3 = -18$

and $f(-3) = 5 \times -3 - 3 = -18$

$\therefore$ $\lim_{x \to -3} f(x) = f(-3)$. Thus, $f(x)$ is continuous at $x = -3$.

At $x = 5$, $\lim_{x \to 5} f(x) = \lim_{x \to 5} (5x - 3) = 5 \times 5 - 3 = 25 - 3 = 22$

and $f(5) = 5 \times 5 - 3 = 25 - 3 = 22$

$\therefore$ $\lim_{x \to 5} f(x) = f(5)$. Thus, $f(x)$ is continuous at $x = 5$.

Question 2 Examine the continuity of the function $f(x) = 2x^2 - 1$ at $x = 3$.

Sol. Here, $f(x) = 2x^2 - 1$

At $x = 3$, $\lim_{x \to 3} f(x) = \lim_{x \to 3} (2x^2 - 1) = 2 \times (3)^2 - 1 = 18 - 1 = 17$

and $f(3) = 2 \times (3)^2 - 1 = 18 - 1 = 17$

$\therefore$ $\lim_{x \to 3} f(x) = f(3)$. Thus, $f(x)$ is continuous at $x = 3$.

Question 3 Examine the following functions for continuity

(a) $f(x) = x - 5$ (b) $f(x) = \dfrac{1}{x - 5}, x \neq 5$

(c) $f(x) = \dfrac{x^2 - 25}{x + 5}, x \neq -5$ (d) $f(x) = |x - 5|$

Sol.

(a) $f(x) = x - 5$ is a polynomial functions, so $f(x)$ is continuous for all values of x.

(b) $f(x) = \dfrac{1}{x-5}$ is a quotient function of two polynomial functions, so $f(x)$ is continuous for all values of x provided $x \neq 5$.

(c) $f(x) = \dfrac{x^2 - 25}{x+5} = \dfrac{(x+5)(x-5)}{x+5} = x - 5$

$\therefore$ $f(x) = x - 5$ is a polynomial function, so $f(x)$ is continuous at all values of x, provided $x \neq -5$

(d) $f(x) = |x - 5| = \begin{cases} x - 5, & \text{for } x \geq 5 \\ 5 - x, & \text{for } x < 5 \end{cases}$

For $x \to 5^+$, $\lim\limits_{x \to 5^+} f(x) = \lim\limits_{h \to 0} f(5+h) = \lim\limits_{h \to 0} (5+h) - 5 = \lim\limits_{h \to 0} h = 0$

For $x \to 5^-$, $\lim\limits_{x \to 5^-} f(x) = \lim\limits_{h \to 0} f(5-h) = \lim\limits_{h \to 0} 5 - (5-h) = \lim\limits_{h \to 0} h = 0$

Also, $f(5) = 5 - 5 = 0$

$\because$ LHL = RHL = $f(5)$. Therefore, the function is continuous at $x = 5$.

Note In any rational function $f(x) = \dfrac{p(x)}{q(x)}$ and if $p(x)$ and $q(x)$ are polynomials and $q(x)$ is zero at any value of x and $p(x) \neq 0$, then $f(x)$ is not continuous at that point.

Question 4 Prove that the function $f(x) = x^n$ is continuous at $x = n$, where n is a positive integer.

Sol. Here, $f(x) = x^n$

$\therefore$ $\lim\limits_{x \to n} f(x) = \lim\limits_{x \to n} x^n = n^n$

and $f(n) = n^n$ $\quad [\because f(x) = x^n]$

$\because$ $\lim\limits_{x \to n} f(x) = f(n)$

Thus, $f(x)$ is continuous at $x = n$, where n is a positive integer.

Question 5 Is the function f defined by $f(x) = \begin{cases} x, & \text{if } x \leq 1 \\ 5, & \text{if } x > 1 \end{cases}$ continuous at $x = 0$? At $x = 1$? At $x = 2$?

Thinking Process $f(0-h)$ and $f(0+h)$ both will satisfy $x \leq 1$

$f(2+h)$ and $f(2-h)$ both will satisfy $x > 1$

Sol. Here, $f(x) = \begin{cases} x, \text{if } x \leq 1 \\ 5, \text{if } x > 1 \end{cases}$

At $x = 0$, LHL $= \lim_{x \to 0^-} f(x) = \lim_{x \to 0^-} (x)$

Putting $x = 0 - h$ as $x \to 0^-$ when $h \to 0 = \lim_{h \to 0} (0 - h) = 0 - 0 = 0$

RHL $= \lim_{x \to 0^+} f(x) = \lim_{x \to 0^+} (x)$

Putting $x = 0 + h$ as $x \to 0^+$ when $h \to 0$, $\lim_{h \to 0} (0 + h) = 0 + 0 = 0$

Also, $f(0) = 0$ $[\because f(x) = x]$

$\therefore$ LHL = RHL $= f(0)$

Thus, $f(x)$ is continuous at $x = 0$.

At $x = 1$, LHL $= \lim_{x \to 1^-} f(x) = \lim_{x \to 1^-} (x)$

Putting $x = 1 - h$ as $x \to 1^-$ when $h \to 0$, $\lim_{h \to 0} (1 - h) = 1 - 0 = 1$

and RHL $= \lim_{x \to 1^+} f(x) = 5$

$\therefore$ LHL $\neq$ RHL

Thus, $f(x)$ is discontinuous at $x = 1$.

At $x = 2$, $\lim_{x \to 2^-} f(x) = \lim_{h \to 0}(5) = 5$

and $\lim_{x \to 2^+} f(x) = \lim_{h \to 0} (5) = 5$

Also, $f(2) = 5$. $\therefore$ LHL = RHL $= f(2)$. Thus, $f(x)$ is continuous at $x = 2$.

Direction (Q. Nos. 6 to 12) Find all points of discontinuity of f, where f is defined in the question.

Question 6 $f(x) = \begin{cases} 2x + 3, & \text{if } x \leq 2 \\ 2x - 3 & \text{if } x > 2. \end{cases}$

◎ ***Thinking Process*** Every polynomial function is continuous. So, the discontinuity of given function may be occur at $x = 2$.

Sol Here, $f(x) = \begin{cases} 2x + 3, \text{if } x \leq 2 \\ 2x - 3, \text{if } x > 2 \end{cases}$

LHL $= \lim_{x \to 2^-} f(x) = \lim_{x \to 2^-} (2x + 3)$

Putting $x = 2 - h$ as $x \to 2^-$ when $h \to 0$

$\therefore \lim_{h \to 0} [2(2 - h) + 3] = \lim_{h \to 0} (7 - 2h) = 7 - 2 \times 0 = 7$

and RHL $= \lim_{x \to 2^+} f(x) = \lim_{x \to 2^+} (2x - 3)$

Putting $x = 2 + h$ as $x \to 2^+$ when $h \to 0$

$\therefore \lim_{h \to 0} [2(2 + h) - 3] = \lim_{h \to 0} (1 + 2h) = 1 + 2 \times 0 = 1$

$\therefore$ LHL $\neq$ RHL. Thus, $f(x)$ is discontinuous at $x = 2$.

Question 7 $f(x)=\begin{cases}|x|+3, & \text{if } x\le -3\\ -2x, & \text{if } -3<x<3\\ 6x+2, & \text{if } x\ge 3\end{cases}$

◎ *Thinking Process* A polynomial and modulus function is always continuous. So, we have to check the continuity only at $x = -3$ and 3.

Sol. Here, $f(x)=\begin{cases}|x|+3, & x\le -3\\ -2x, & -3<x<3\\ 6x+2, & x\ge 3\end{cases}$

For $x < -3$, $f(x) = |x| + 3 = -x + 3$

$$-3<x<3,\ f(x)=-2x \text{ and } x>3,\ f(x)=6x+2$$

is a polynomial function, so it is continuous in a given interval. So, we have to check the continuity only at $x=-3$ and 3.

At $x = -3$, $\quad \text{LHL} = \lim_{x\to -3^-} f(x) = \lim_{x\to -3^-}(-x+3)$

Putting $x = (-3 - h)$ as $x \to -3^-$ when $h \to 0$

$\therefore \quad \lim_{h\to 0}[-(-3-h)+3] = \lim_{h\to 0}(6+h) = 6 + 0 = 6$

$$\text{RHL} = \lim_{x\to 3^+} f(x) = \lim_{x\to 3^+}(-2x)$$

Putting $x = -3 + h$ as $x \to -3^+$ when $h \to 0$

$\therefore \quad \lim_{h\to 0} -2(-3+h) = \lim_{h\to 0}(6-2h) = 6 - 2\times 0 = 6$

Also, $\quad f(-3) = |-3| + 3 = 3 + 3 = 6 \quad [\because f(x) = |x| + 3]$

$\therefore \quad \text{LHL} = \text{RHL} = f(-3)$

Thus, $f(x)$ is continuous at $x = -3$.

At $x = 3$, $\quad \text{LHL} = \lim_{x\to 3^-} f(x) = \lim_{x\to 3^-}(-2x)$

Putting $x = 3 - h$ as $x \to 3^-$ when $h \to 0$

$\therefore \quad \lim_{h\to 0} -2(3-h) = \lim_{h\to 0}(-6+2h) = -6 + 2\times 0 = -6$

$$\text{RHL} = \lim_{x\to 3^+} f(x) = \lim_{x\to 3^+}(6x+2)$$

Putting $x = 3 + h$ as $x \to 3^+$ when $h \to 0$

$\therefore \lim_{h\to 0}[6(3+h)+2] = \lim_{h\to 0}(18+6h+2) = \lim_{h\to 0}(20+6h) = 20 + 6\times 0 = 20$

$\therefore$ LHL $\ne$ RHL. Thus, $f(x)$ is discontinuous at $x = 3$.

Note $|x|=\begin{cases}x, & x\ge 0\\ -x, & x<0\end{cases}$

Question 8 $f(x)=\begin{cases}\dfrac{|x|}{x}, & \text{if } x\neq 0\\ 0, & \text{if } x=0\end{cases}$

Sol. Here, $f(x)=\begin{cases}\dfrac{|x|}{x}, & \text{if } x\neq 0\\ 0, & \text{if } x=0\end{cases}$

$$\text{LHL}=\lim_{x\to 0^-} f(x)=\lim_{x\to 0^-}\frac{|x|}{x}$$

Putting $x = 0 - h$ as $x \to 0^-$ when $h \to 0$

$\therefore$ $$\lim_{h\to 0}\frac{|0-h|}{0-h}=\lim_{h\to 0}\frac{h}{-h}=-1 \qquad [\because |-h|=h]$$

and $$\text{RHL}=\lim_{x\to 0^+} f(x)=\lim_{x\to 0^+}\frac{|x|}{x}$$

Putting $x = 0 + h$ as $x \to 0^+$; $h \to 0$

$\therefore$ $$\lim_{h\to 0}\frac{|0+h|}{0+h}=\lim_{h\to 0}\frac{h}{h}=1 \qquad (\because |h|=h)$$

$\therefore$ LHL $\neq$ RHL. Thus, $f(x)$ is discontinuous at $x = 0$.

Note $|f(x)|=\begin{cases}f(x) & \text{when } f(x)\geq 0\\ -f(x) & \text{when } f(x)<0\end{cases}$

Question 9 $f(x)=\begin{cases}\dfrac{x}{|x|}, & \text{if } x<0\\ -1, & \text{if } x\geq 0\end{cases}$

Sol. Here, $f(x)=\begin{cases}\dfrac{x}{|x|}, & \text{if } x<0\\ -1, & \text{if } x\geq 0\end{cases}$

$$\text{LHL}=\lim_{x\to 0^-} f(x)=\lim_{x\to 0^-}\frac{x}{|x|}$$

Putting $x = 0 - h$ as $x \to 0^-$, when $h \to 0$

$\therefore$ $$\lim_{h\to 0}\frac{0-h}{|0-h|}=\lim_{h\to 0}\frac{-h}{h}=-1 \qquad (\because |-h|=h)$$

$$\text{RHL}=\lim_{x\to 0^+} f(x)=-1$$

Also, $f(0) = -1$

$\therefore$ $$\text{LHL}=\text{RHL}=f(0)$$

Thus, $f(x)$ is continuous at $x = 0$. There is no point of discontinuity for this function $f(x)$.

Question 10 $f(x)=\begin{cases} x+1, & \text{if } x \ge 1 \\ x^2+1, & \text{if } x<1 \end{cases}$

◎ *Thinking Process* If each piece of a piecewise-defined function is continous within its respective domain, then to check the continuity of the entire function, it is sufficient to verify the continuity at the boundary points of the sub domains.

Sol. Here, $$f(x)=\begin{cases} x+1, \text{ if } x \ge 1 \\ x^2+1, \text{if } x<1 \end{cases}$$

For $x>1$, $f(x)=x+1$ and $x<1$, $f(x)=x^2+1$ is a polynomial function, so $f(x)$ is a continuous in the given interval. Therefore, we have to check the continuity at $x=1$.

$$\text{LHL} = \lim_{x \to 1^-} f(x) = \lim_{x \to 1^-} (x^2+1)$$

Putting $x=1-h$ as $x \to 1^-$ when $h \to 0$

$\therefore \lim_{h \to 0} [(1-h)^2+1] = \lim_{h \to 0} [1+h^2-2h+1] = \lim_{h \to 0} [2+h^2-2h] = 2+0-0=2$

$$\text{RHL} = \lim_{x \to 1^+} f(x) = \lim_{x \to 1^+} (x+1)$$

Putting $x=1+h$ as $x \to 1^+$ when $h \to 0$

$\therefore$ $$\lim_{h \to 0} (1+h+1) = \lim_{h \to 0} (2+h) = 2+0=2$$

Also $$f(1)=1+1=2 \qquad [\because f(x)=x+1]$$

$\therefore$ LHL = RHL = $f(1)$. Thus, $f(x)$ is continuous at $x=1$.

Hence, there is no point of discontinuity for this function $f(x)$.

Question 11 $f(x)=\begin{cases} x^3-3, & \text{if } x \le 2 \\ x^2+1, & \text{if } x>2. \end{cases}$

Sol. Here, $$f(x)=\begin{cases} x^3-3, & x \le 2 \\ x^2+1, & x>2 \end{cases}$$

For $x<2$, $f(x)=x^2-3$ and for $x>2$, $f(x)=x^2+1$ in both case these are polynomial functions, so f is continuous in the above interval. Therefore, we have to check the continuity at $x=2$.

$$\text{LHL} = \lim_{x \to 2^-} f(x) = \lim_{x \to 2^-} (x^3-3)$$

Putting $x=2-h$ as $x \to 2^-$ when $h \to 0$

$\therefore$ $$\lim_{h \to 0} [(2-h)^3-3] = \lim_{h \to 0} [8-h^3-12h+6h^2-3]$$

$$= \lim_{h \to 0} (5-h^3-12h+6h^2) = 5$$

and $$\text{RHL} = \lim_{x \to 2^+} f(x) = \lim_{x \to 2^+} (x^2+1)$$

Putting $x = 2 + h$ as $x \to 2^+$ when $h \to 0$

$\therefore \quad \lim_{h \to 0} [(2+h)^2 + 1] = \lim_{h \to 0} (4 + h^2 + 4h + 1) = \lim_{h \to 0} (5 + h^2 + 4h) = 5$

Also, $\quad f(2) = (2)^3 - 3 = 8 - 3 = 5 \quad [\because f(x) = x^3 - 3]$

$\therefore \quad \text{LHL} = \text{RHL} = f(2).$

Thus, $f(x)$ is continuous at $x = 2$.

Hence, there is no point of discontinuity for this function $f(x)$.

Question 12 $f(x) = \begin{cases} x^{10} - 1, \text{ if } x \le 1 \\ x^2 \quad , \quad \text{if } x > 1. \end{cases}$

Sol. Here, $f(x) = \begin{cases} x^{10} - 1, \text{if } x \le 1 \\ x^2, \quad \text{if } x > 1 \end{cases}$

For $x < 1$, $f(x) = x^{10} - 1$ and $x > 1$, $f(x) = x^2$ in both case these are polynomial functions, so f is continuous in the above intervals. Therefore, we have to check the continuity at $x = 1$.

$$\text{LHL} = \lim_{x \to 1^-} f(x) = \lim_{x \to 1^-} (x^{10} - 1)$$

Putting $x = 1 - h$ as $x \to 1^-$ when $h \to 0$

$\therefore \quad \lim_{h \to 0} [(1-h)^{10} - 1] = (1-0)^{10} - 1 = 1 - 1 = 0$

and $\quad \text{RHL} = \lim_{x \to 1^+} f(x) = \lim_{x \to 1^+} (x^2)$

Putting $x = 1 + h$ as $x \to 1^+$ when $h \to 0$

$\therefore \quad \lim_{h \to 0} (1+h)^2 = \lim_{h \to 0} (1 + h^2 + 2h) = 1$

$\therefore \quad \text{LHL} \ne \text{RHL}$

Thus, $f(x)$ is discontinuous at $x = 1$.

Question 13 Is the function defined by $f(x) = \begin{cases} x + 5, \text{ if } x \le 1 \\ x - 5, \text{ if } x > 1 \end{cases}$, a continuous function?

Sol. Here, $\quad f(x) = \begin{cases} x + 5, \text{if } x \le 1 \\ x - 5, \text{if } x > 1 \end{cases}$

$$\text{LHL} = \lim_{x \to 1^-} f(x) = \lim_{x \to 1} (x + 5)$$

Putting $x = 1 - h$ as $x \to 1^-$ when $h \to 0$

$\therefore \quad \lim_{h \to 0} [1 - h + 5] = \lim_{h \to 0} (6 - h) = 6 - 0 = 6$

$$\text{RHL} = \lim_{x \to 1^+} f(x) = \lim_{x \to 1^+} (x - 5)$$

Putting $x = 1 + h$ as $x \to 1^+$ when $h \to 0$

$\therefore \quad \lim_{h \to 0} (1 + h - 5) = \lim_{h \to 0} (h - 4) = 0 - 4 = -4$

$\therefore$ LHL $\ne$ RHL. Thus, $f(x)$ is not continuous at $x = 1$.

Direction (Q. Nos. 14 to 16) Discuss the continuity of the function defined in the question.

Question 14. $f(x)=\begin{cases}3, \text{ if } 0\le x\le 1\\ 4, \text{ if } 1<x<3\\ 5, \text{ if } 3\le x\le 10.\end{cases}$

◎ ***Thinking Process*** Constant functions are always continuous. We only need to check the continuity at the break points of the domain.

Sol. Here, $f(x)=\begin{cases}3, \text{if } 0\le x\le 1\\ 4, \text{if } 1<x<3\\ 5, \text{if } 3\le x\le 10\end{cases}$

For $0\le x<1$, $f(x)=3$; $1<x<3$; $f(x)=4$ and $3<x\le 10$, $f(x)=5$ are constant functions, so f is continuous in the above interval, so we have to check the continuity at $x=1$ and 3.

At $x=1$, LHL $=\lim\limits_{x\to 1^-} f(x)=\lim\limits_{x\to 1^-}(3)=3$, RHL $=\lim\limits_{x\to 1^+} f(x)=\lim\limits_{x\to 1^+}(4)=4$

$\therefore$ LHL $\ne$ RHL

Thus, $f(x)$ is discontinuous at $x=1$.

At $x=3$, LHL $=\lim\limits_{x\to 3^-} f(x)=\lim\limits_{x\to 3^-}(4)=4$,

RHL $=\lim\limits_{x\to 3^+} f(x)=\lim\limits_{x\to 3^+}(5)=5$

$\therefore$ LHL $\ne$ RHL. Thus, $f(x)$ is continuous everywhere except at $x=1$ and 3.

Question 15 $f(x)=\begin{cases}2x, \text{ if } x<0\\ 0, \text{ if } 0\le x\le 1\\ 4x, \text{ if } x>1.\end{cases}$

Sol. Here, $f(x)=\begin{cases}2x, \text{if } x<0\\ 0, \text{if } 0\le x\le 1\\ 4x, \text{if } x>1\end{cases}$

For $x<0$, $f(x)=2x$; $0<x<1$, $f(x)=0$ and $x>1$, $f(x)=4x$ are polynomials and constant function, so f is continuous in the given intervals. So, we have to check the continuity at $x=0, 1$.

At $x=0$, LHL $=\lim\limits_{x\to 0^-} f(x)=\lim\limits_{x\to 0^-}(2x)$

Putting $x=0-h$ as $x\to 0^-$ when $h\to 0$

$\therefore \lim\limits_{h\to 0}[2(0-h)]=\lim\limits_{h\to 0}(-2h)=-2\times 0=0$

RHL $=\lim\limits_{x\to 0^+} f(x)=\lim\limits_{x\to 0^+}(0)=0$

Also, $f(0)=0$

$\therefore$ LHL $=$ RHL $=f(0)$

Thus, $f(x)$ is continuous for all values of x.

At $x = 1$, LHL $= \lim_{x \to 1^-} f(x) = \lim_{x \to 1^-} (0) = 0$

RHL $= \lim_{x \to 1^+} f(x) = \lim_{x \to 1^+} (4x)$

Putting $x = 1 + h$ as $x \to 1^+$ when $h \to 0$

$$\lim_{h \to 0} [4(1+h)] = \lim_{h \to 0} (4 + 4h) = 4 + 4 \times 0 = 4$$

$\therefore$ LHL $\neq$ RHL. Thus, $f(x)$ is continuous everywhere except at $x = 1$.

Question 16 $f(x) = \begin{cases} -2, & \text{if } x \le -1 \\ 2x, & \text{if } -1 < x \le 1 \\ 2, & \text{if } x > 1 \end{cases}$

Sol. Here, $f(x) = \begin{cases} -2, \text{if} & x \le -1 \\ 2x, \text{if} & -1 < x \le 1 \\ 2, \text{if} & x > 1 \end{cases}$

We have to check the continuity only at $x = -1$ and 1.

At $x = -1$, LHL $= \lim_{x \to -1^-} f(x) = \lim_{x \to -1^-} (-2) = -2$

and RHL $= \lim_{x \to -1^+} f(x) = \lim_{x \to -1^+} (2x)$

Putting $x = -1 + h$ as $x \to -1^+$ when $h \to 0$

$\therefore$ $\lim_{h \to 0} 2(-1 + h) = \lim_{h \to 0} (-2 + 2h) = -2 + 0 = -2$

Also, $f(-1) = -2$

$\therefore$ LHL = RHL = $f(-1)$. Thus, $f(x)$ is continuous at $x = -1$.

At $x = 1$, LHL $= \lim_{x \to 1^-} f(x) = \lim_{x \to 1^-} (2x)$

Putting $x = 1 - h$ as $h \to 1^-$ when $h \to 0$

$\therefore$ $\lim_{h \to 0} [2(1 - h)] = \lim_{h \to 0} (2 - 2h) = 2 - 2 \times 0 = 2$

and RHL $= \lim_{x \to 1^+} f(x) = \lim_{x \to 1^+} (2) = 2$

Also, $f(1) = 2 \times 1 = 2$ $[\because f(x) = 2x]$

$\therefore$ LHL = RHL = $f(1)$

Thus, $f(x)$ is continuous at $x = 1$.

Hence, $f(x)$ is continuous for every value of x.

Question 17 Find the values of a and b so that the function defined by $f(x) = \begin{cases} ax + 1, \text{if } x \le 3 \\ bx + 3, \text{if } x > 3 \end{cases}$ is continuous at $x = 3$.

Soln Here, $f(x) = \begin{cases} ax + 1, \text{if } x \le 3 \\ bx + 3, \text{if } x > 3 \end{cases}$

At $x = 3$, LHL $= \lim_{x \to 3^-} f(x) = \lim_{x \to 3^-} (ax + 1)$

Putting $x = 3 - h$ as $x \to 3^-$ when $h \to 0$

$\therefore$ $$\lim_{h\to 0}[a(3-h)+1] = \lim_{h\to 0}(3a - ah + 1) = 3a + 1$$

and $$\text{RHL} = \lim_{x\to 3^+} f(x) = \lim_{x\to 3^+}(bx+3)$$

Putting $x = 3 + h$ as $x \to 3^+$ when $h \to 0$

$\therefore$ $$\lim_{h\to 0}[b(3+h)+3] = \lim_{h\to 0}(3b + bh + 3) = 3b + 3$$

Also, $f(3) = 3a + 1$ $\quad [\because f(x) = ax + 1]$

Since, $f(x)$ is continuous at $x = 3$.

$\therefore$ LHL = RHL = $f(3)$

$\Rightarrow$ $$3a + 1 = 3b + 3 \Rightarrow 3a = 3b + 2 \Rightarrow a = b + \frac{2}{3}$$

Question 18 For what value of λ is the function defined by

$f(x) = \begin{cases} \lambda(x^2 - 2x) & \text{if } x \le 0 \\ 4x + 1, & \text{if } x > 0 \end{cases}$ continuous at $x = 0$? What about continuity at $x = 1$?

Sol. Here, $$f(x) = \begin{cases} \lambda(x^2 - 2x), \text{if } x \le 0 \\ 4x + 1, \quad \text{if } x > 0 \end{cases}$$

At $x = 0$, $$\text{LHL} = \lim_{x\to 0^-} f(x) = \lim_{x\to 0^-}\lambda(x^2 - 2x)$$

Putting $x = 0 - h$ as $x \to 0^-$ when $h \to 0$

$\therefore$ $$\lim_{h\to 0}\lambda[(0-h)^2 - 2(0-h)] = \lim_{h\to 0}[\lambda(h^2 + 2h)] = 0$$

and $$\text{RHL} = \lim_{x\to 0^+} f(x) = \lim_{x\to 0^+}(4x+1)$$

Putting $x = 0 + h$ as $x \to 0^+$ when $h \to 0$

$\therefore$ $$\lim_{h\to 0}[4(0+h)+1] = \lim_{h\to 0}[4h+1] = 0 + 1 = 1$$

$\therefore$ LHL $\neq$ RHL. Thus, $f(x)$ is not continuous at $x = 0$ for any value of λ. Hence here is no value of λ.

At $x = 1$, $$\text{LHL} = \lim_{x\to 1^-} f(x) = \lim_{x\to 1^-}(4x+1)$$

Putting $x = 1 - h$ as $x \to 1^-$ when $h \to 0$

$\therefore$ $$\lim_{h\to 0}[4(1-h)+1] = \lim_{h\to 0}[5 - 4h] = 5 - 0 = 5$$

and $$\text{RHL} = \lim_{x\to 1^+} f(x) = \lim_{x\to 1^+}(4x+1)$$

Putting $x = 1 + h$ as $x \to 1^+$ when $h \to 0$

$\therefore$ $$\lim_{h\to 0}[4(1+h)+1] = \lim_{h\to 0}(5 + 4h) = 5 + 0 = 5$$

Also, $f(1) = 4 \times 1 + 1 = 5$ $\quad [\because f(x) = 4x + 1]$

Thus, $f(x)$ is continuous at $x = 1$ for all values of λ.

Mistake Alert Be aware $f(1+h)$ and $f(1-h)$ both satisfy $f(x) = 4x + 1$, $x > 0$

Question 19 Show that the function defined by $g(x) = x - [x]$ is discontinuous at all integral points. Here, $[x]$ denotes the greatest integer less than or equal to x.

Sol. Here, $g(x) = x - [x]$

Let a be an integer, then $[a - h] = a - 1$, $[a + h] = a$ and $[a] = a$, where $0 < h < 1$

At $= a$, $\quad \text{LHL} = \lim_{x \to a^-} g(x) = \lim_{x \to a^-} (x - [x])$

Putting $x = a - h$ as $x \to a^-$ when $h \to 0$

$\therefore \lim_{h \to 0} (a - h - [a - h]) = \lim_{h \to 0} [a - h - (a - 1)] = \lim_{h \to 0} [-h + 1] = 1 \qquad (\because [a - h] = a - 1)$

$$\text{RHL} = \lim_{x \to a^+} g(x) = \lim_{x \to a^+} (x - [x])$$

Putting $x = a + h$ as $x \to a^+$ when $h \to 0$

$$\lim_{h \to 0} (a + h - [a + h]) = \lim_{h \to 0} (a + h - a) = \lim_{h \to 0} h = 0 \quad (\because [a + h] = a)$$

$\therefore \qquad \text{LHL} \neq \text{RHL}$

Thus, $g(x)$ is discontinuous at all integral points.

Note The greatest integer function is continuous at all points except at integer points.

Question 20 Is the function defined by $x^2 - \sin x + 5$ continuous at $x = \pi$?

Sol. Let $f(x) = x^2 - \sin x + 5$

$$\text{LHL} = \lim_{x \to \pi^-} f(x) = \lim_{x \to \pi^-} (x^2 - \sin x + 5)$$

Putting $x = \pi - h$ as $x \to \pi^-$ when $h \to 0$

$\therefore \qquad \lim_{h \to 0} ((\pi - h)^2 - \sin(\pi - h) + 5)$

$= \lim_{h \to 0} (\pi^2 + h^2 - 2\pi h - \sin h + 5) \qquad (\because \sin(\pi - h) = \sinh)$

$= \pi^2 + 0 - 0 - \sin(0) + 5 = \pi^2 + 5$

$$\text{RHL} = \lim_{x \to \pi^+} f(x) = \lim_{x \to \pi^+} (x^2 - \sin x + 5)$$

Putting $\qquad x = \pi + h$ as $x \to \pi^+$ when $h \to 0$

$\therefore \qquad \lim_{h \to 0} [(\pi + h)^2 - \sin(\pi + h) + 5]$

$= \lim_{h \to 0} [\pi^2 + h^2 + 2\pi h + \sin h + 5] = \pi^2 + 5$

$[\because \sin(\pi + h) = -\sin h]$

Also, $\qquad f(\pi) = \pi^2 - \sin \pi + 5 = \pi^2 + 5$

$\therefore \qquad \text{LHL} = \text{RHL} = f(\pi).$

Hence, function is continuous at $x = \pi$.

Question 21 Discuss the continuity of the following functions

(a) $f(x)=\sin x+\cos x$ (b) $f(x)=\sin x-\cos x$ (c) $f(x)=\sin x\cos x$

◎ *Thinking Process* Firstly simplify the given function in simplest form and then check the continuity general point.

Sol. (a) $f(x)=\sin x+\cos x=\sqrt{2}\left(\frac{1}{\sqrt{2}}\sin x+\frac{1}{\sqrt{2}}\cos x\right)$

$$=\sqrt{2}\left(\sin x\cos\frac{\pi}{4}+\cos x\sin\frac{\pi}{4}\right)=\sqrt{2}\sin\left(x+\frac{\pi}{4}\right)$$

At $x=a$, where $a\in R$

$$\text{LHL}=\lim_{x\to a^-}f(x)=\lim_{x\to a^-}\sqrt{2}\sin\left(x+\frac{\pi}{4}\right)=\lim_{h\to 0}\sqrt{2}\sin\left(a-h+\frac{\pi}{4}\right)$$

$$=\sqrt{2}\lim_{h\to 0}\left[\sin\left(a+\frac{\pi}{4}\right)\cos h-\cos\left(a+\frac{\pi}{4}\right)\sin h\right]$$

$[\because \sin(A-B)=\sin A\cos B-\cos A\sin B]$

$$=\sqrt{2}\sin\left(a+\frac{\pi}{4}\right)\cos 0-\sqrt{2}\cos\left(a+\frac{\pi}{4}\right)\sin 0=\sqrt{2}\sin\left(a+\frac{\pi}{4}\right)$$

$$\text{RHL}=\lim_{x\to a^+}f(x)=\lim_{x\to a^+}\sqrt{2}\sin\left(x+\frac{\pi}{4}\right)=\lim_{h\to 0}\sqrt{2}\sin\left(a+h+\frac{\pi}{4}\right)$$

$$=\sqrt{2}\lim_{h\to 0}\left[\sin\left(a+\frac{\pi}{4}\right)\cos h+\sin h\cos\left(a+\frac{\pi}{4}\right)\right]$$

$[\because \sin(A+B)=\sin A\cos B+\cos A\sin B]$

$$=\sqrt{2}\sin\left(a+\frac{\pi}{4}\right)\cos 0+\sin 0\cos\left(a+\frac{\pi}{4}\right)$$

Also, $f(a)=\sqrt{2}\sin\left(a+\frac{\pi}{4}\right)$

$\therefore$ LHL = RHL = $f(a)$

Hence, $f(x)$ is continuous at all points.

(b) Here, $f(x)=\sin x-\cos x$

$$=\sqrt{2}\left(\frac{1}{\sqrt{2}}\sin x-\frac{1}{\sqrt{2}}\cos x\right)=\sqrt{2}\left(\sin x\cos\frac{\pi}{4}-\cos x\sin\frac{\pi}{4}\right)$$

$$=\sqrt{2}\sin\left(x-\frac{\pi}{4}\right)$$

At $x=a$, where $a\in R$

$$\text{LHL}=\lim_{x\to a^-}f(x)=\lim_{x\to a^-}\sqrt{2}\sin\left(x-\frac{\pi}{4}\right)=\lim_{h\to 0}\sqrt{2}\sin\left(a-h-\frac{\pi}{4}\right)$$

$$=\lim_{h\to 0}\sqrt{2}\left[\sin\left(a-\frac{\pi}{4}\right)\cos h-\cos\left(a-\frac{\pi}{4}\right)\sin h\right]$$

$$=\sqrt{2}\left[\sin\left(a-\frac{\pi}{4}\right)\right]\cos 0-\sqrt{2}\cos\left(a-\frac{\pi}{4}\right)\sin 0=\sqrt{2}\sin\left(a-\frac{\pi}{4}\right)$$

$$\text{RHL} = \lim_{x \to a^+} \sqrt{2}\ \sin\left(x - \frac{\pi}{4}\right) = \lim_{h \to 0} \sqrt{2}\sin\left(a + h - \frac{\pi}{4}\right)$$

$$= \lim_{h \to 0} \sqrt{2}\left[\sin\left(a - \frac{\pi}{4}\right)\cos h + \cos\left(a - \frac{\pi}{4}\right)\sin h\right]$$

$$= \sqrt{2}\left[\sin\left(a - \frac{\pi}{4}\right)\right]\cos 0 + \cos\left(a - \frac{\pi}{4}\right)\sin 0 = \sqrt{2}\sin\left(a - \frac{\pi}{4}\right)$$

Also, $f(a) = \sqrt{2}\sin\left(a - \frac{\pi}{4}\right)$

$\therefore$ LHL = RHL = $f(a)$.

Hence, $f(x)$ is continuous at all points.

(c) Here, $f(x) = \sin x \cos x$

$$= \frac{1}{2} \times 2\sin x \cos x = \frac{1}{2}\sin 2x$$

At x = a, where $a \in R$

$$\text{LHL} = \lim_{x \to a^-} f(x) = \lim_{x \to a^-} \frac{1}{2}\sin 2x = \lim_{h \to 0} \frac{1}{2}\sin 2(a - h)$$

$$= \lim_{h \to 0} \frac{1}{2}[\sin 2a \cos 2h - \cos 2a \sin 2h]$$

$$= \frac{1}{2}[\sin 2a \cos 0 - \cos 2a \sin 0] = \frac{1}{2}\sin 2a$$

$$\text{RHL} = \lim_{x \to a^+} f(x) = \lim_{x \to a^+} \frac{1}{2}\sin 2x = \lim_{h \to 0} \frac{1}{2}\sin 2(a + h)$$

$$= \lim_{h \to 0} \frac{1}{2}[\sin 2a \cos 2h + \cos 2a \sin 2h]$$

$$= \lim_{h \to 0} \frac{1}{2}[\sin(2a + 2h)] = \frac{1}{2}\sin 2a$$

Also, $f(a) = \frac{1}{2}\sin 2a$

$\therefore$ LHL = RHL = $f(a)$.

Hence, $f(x)$ is continuous at all points.

Note Trigonometric functions are always continuous in their domain and sum, difference and product of two continuous functions always continuous.

Question 22 Discuss the continuity of the cosine, cosecant, secant and cotangent functions.

Thinking Process Trigonometric functions are always continuous in their domain.

Sol.

(i) Let $f(x) = \cos x$

At $x = a$, where $a \in R$

$$\lim_{x \to a} f(x) = \lim_{x \to a} \cos x = \cos a \qquad [\because f(x) = \cos x]$$

$$f(a) = \cos a$$

$$\therefore \qquad \lim_{x \to a} f(x) = f(a)$$

Thus, $f(x)$ is continuous at $x = a$. But a is an arbitrary points so $f(x)$ is continuous at all points.

So, $f(x)$ is continuous at all points.

(ii) Let $f(x) = \text{cosec } x$. Since, $f(x)$ is not defined at $x = n\pi$, $n \in Z$.

Thus, $f(x)$ is continuous at all points except $x = n\pi$, $n \in Z$

(iii) Let $f(x) = \sec x$

Since, $f(x)$ is not defined at $x = (2n + 1)\dfrac{\pi}{2}$, $n \in Z$. (odd multiple of $\dfrac{\pi}{2}$)

Thus, $f(x)$ is continuous at all points except $x = (2n + 1)\dfrac{\pi}{2}$, $n \in Z$.

(iv) Let, $f(x) = \cot x$

Since, $f(x)$ is not defined at $x = n\pi$, $n \in Z$.

Thus, $f(x)$ is continuous at all points except $x = n\pi$, $n \in Z$.

Question 23 Find all the points of discontinuity of f, where

$$f(x) = \begin{cases} \dfrac{\sin x}{x}, & \text{if } \quad x < 0 \\ x + 1, & \text{if } \quad x \geq 0. \end{cases}$$

Thinking Process Suppose $f(x) = \dfrac{h(x)}{g(x)}$, if $h(x)$ and $g(x)$ are continuous and $g(x) \neq 0$, then $f(x)$ is continuous.

Sol. Here, $f(x) = \begin{cases} \dfrac{\sin x}{x}, & \text{if } \quad x < 0 \\ x + 1, & \text{if } \quad x \geq 0 \end{cases}$

$\text{LHL} = \lim\limits_{x \to 0^-} f(x) = \lim\limits_{x \to 0^-} \dfrac{\sin x}{x}$. Putting $x = 0 - h$ as $x \to 0^-$ when $h \to 0$

$$\therefore \quad \lim_{h \to 0} \frac{\sin(0 - h)}{(0 - h)} = \lim_{h \to 0} \frac{-\sin h}{-h} = \lim_{h \to 0} \frac{\sin h}{h} = 1 \qquad (\because \sin(-h) = -\sin h)$$

and $\qquad \text{RHL} = \lim\limits_{x \to 0^+} f(x) = \lim\limits_{x \to 0^+} (x + 1)$

Putting $x = 0 + h$ as $x \to 0^+$ when $h \to 0$

$\therefore \lim\limits_{h \to 0} (0 + h + 1) = 0 + 1 = 1, \quad f(0) = 0 + 1 = 1 \qquad [\because f(x) = x + 1]$

$\therefore \qquad \text{LHL} = \text{RHL} = f(0)$

Thus, $f(x)$ is continuous at $x = 0$.

When $x < 0$, $\sin x$ and x both are continuous.

Therefore, $\dfrac{\sin x}{x}$ is also continuous. When $x > 0$, $f(x) = x + 1$ is a polynomial.

Therefore f is continuous.

Hence, there is no point of discontinuity for this function $f(x)$.

Question 24 Determine if f defined by $f(x)=\begin{cases} x^2 \sin\frac{1}{x}, & \text{if } x \neq 0 \\ 0, & \text{if } x=0 \end{cases}$ is a continuous function?

Solution Here, $f(x)=\begin{cases} x^2 \sin\frac{1}{x}, & \text{if } x \neq 0 \\ 0, & \text{if } x=0 \end{cases}$

LHL $= \lim_{x \to 0^-} f(x) = \lim_{x \to 0^-} x^2 \sin\frac{1}{x}$. Putting $x = 0 - h$ as $x \to 0^-$ when $h \to 0$

($\lim_{h \to 0} \sin\frac{1}{h}$ is a finite value between -1 and 1 but it is not a definite value)

$$\therefore \quad \lim_{h \to 0} (0-h)^2 \sin\frac{1}{(0-h)} = \lim_{h \to 0} \left(-h^2 \sin\frac{1}{h}\right) \qquad (\because \sin(-\theta) = -\sin\theta)$$

$$= -0 \times \sin(\infty) = 0 \qquad (\because -1 \le \sin x \le 1, \forall x \in R)$$

$$\text{RHL} = \lim_{x \to 0^+} f(x) = \lim_{x \to 0^+} x^2 \sin\frac{1}{x}$$

Putting $x = 0 + h$ as $x \to 0^+$ when $h \to 0$

$$\therefore \lim_{h \to 0} (0+h)^2 \sin\frac{1}{0+h} = \lim_{h \to 0} h^2 \sin\frac{1}{h} = 0 \times (\text{finite value}) = 0$$

$$(\because -1 \le \sin x \le 1, \forall x \in R)$$

$\therefore$ LHL = RHL = $f(0)$. Thus, $f(x)$ is continuous at $x = 0$.

When $x < 0$ and $x > 0$, x^2 and $\sin\frac{1}{x}$ are continuous functions. So $x^2 \sin\frac{1}{x}$ is also continuous. Therefore f is continuous.

Question 25 Examine the continuity of f, where f is defined by

$$f(x)=\begin{cases} \sin x - \cos x, & \text{if } x \neq 0 \\ -1, & \text{if } x = 0. \end{cases}$$

Thinking Process If $f(x)$ and $g(x)$ are continuous functions then $f(x) \pm g(x)$ is also continuous function.

Sol. Here, $f(x)=\begin{cases} \sin x - \cos x, & \text{if } x \neq 0 \\ -1, & \text{if } x = 0 \end{cases}$

$$\text{LHL} = \lim_{x \to 0^-} f(x) = \lim_{x \to 0^-} (\sin x - \cos x)$$

Putting $x = 0 - h$ as $x \to 0^-$ when $h \to 0$

$$\therefore \quad \lim_{h \to 0} [\sin(0-h) - \cos(0-h)] = \lim_{h \to 0} (-\sin h - \cos h) = 0 - 1 = -1$$

$$\text{RHL} = \lim_{x \to 0^+} f(x) = \lim_{x \to 0^+} (\sin x - \cos x)$$

Putting $x = 0 + h$ as $x \to 0^+$ when $h \to 0$

$$\therefore \quad \lim_{h \to 0} [\sin(0+h) - \cos(0+h)] = \lim_{h \to 0} (\sin h - \cos h) = 0 - 1 = -1$$

$\therefore$ LHL = RHL = $f(0)$. Thus, $f(x)$ is continuous at $x = 0$.

We know at $x<0$, $f(x)=\sin x-\cos x$ is continuous and at $x>0$, $f(x)=\sin x-\cos x$ is also continuous.
Hence, $f(x)$ is continuous for all values of x.

Direction (Q. Nos. 26 to 29) Find the values of k so that the function f is continuous at the indicated point

Question 26 $f(x)=\begin{cases}\dfrac{k\cos x}{\pi-2x}, & \text{if } x\neq\dfrac{\pi}{2}\\ 3, & \text{if } x=\dfrac{\pi}{2}.\end{cases}$ at $x=\dfrac{\pi}{2}$

Thinking Process If f is continuous at $x=a$, then LHL = RHL = $f(a)$

Sol. Here, $f(x)=\begin{cases}\dfrac{k\cos x}{\pi-2x}, & \text{if } x\neq\dfrac{\pi}{2}\\ 3, & \text{if } x=\dfrac{\pi}{2}\end{cases}$

At $x=\dfrac{\pi}{2}$, $\quad$ LHL $=\lim\limits_{x\to\frac{\pi^-}{2}} f(x)=\lim\limits_{x\to\frac{\pi^-}{2}}\dfrac{k\cos x}{\pi-2x}$

Putting $x=\dfrac{\pi}{2}-h$ as $x\to\dfrac{\pi}{2}$ when $h\to 0$

$$\therefore \lim_{h\to 0}\frac{k\cos\left(\frac{\pi}{2}-h\right)}{\pi-2\left(\frac{\pi}{2}-h\right)}=\lim_{h\to 0}\frac{k\sin h}{2h} \qquad \left(\because \cos\left(\frac{\pi}{2}-h\right)=\sin h\right)$$

$$=\lim_{h\to 0}\frac{k}{2}\times\frac{\sin h}{h}=\frac{k}{2}\times 1=\frac{k}{2} \qquad \left[\because \lim_{x\to 0}\frac{\sin x}{x}=1\right]$$

$$\text{RHL}=\lim_{x\to\frac{\pi^+}{2}} f(x)=\lim_{x\to\frac{\pi^+}{2}}\frac{k\cos x}{\pi-2x}$$

Putting $x=\dfrac{\pi}{2}+h$ as $x\to\dfrac{\pi^+}{2}$ when $h\to 0$

$$\therefore \lim_{h\to 0}\frac{k\cos\left(\frac{\pi}{2}+h\right)}{\pi-2\left(\frac{\pi}{2}+h\right)}=\lim_{h\to 0}\frac{-k\sin h}{-2h} \qquad \left(\because \cos\left(\frac{\pi}{2}+h\right)=-\sin h\right)$$

$$=\lim_{h\to 0}\frac{k}{2}\times\frac{\sin h}{h}=\frac{k}{2}\times 1=\frac{k}{2} \qquad \left[\because \lim_{x\to 0}\frac{\sin x}{x}=1\right]$$

Also, $f\left(\dfrac{\pi}{2}\right)=3$. Since, $f(x)$ is continuous at $x=\dfrac{\pi}{2}$.

$$\therefore \quad \text{LHL}=\text{RHL}=f\left(\frac{\pi}{2}\right)\Rightarrow\frac{k}{2}=3\Rightarrow k=6$$

Question 27 The function is defined by $f(x)=\begin{cases} kx^2, \text{if } x \le 2 \\ 3, \ \text{if } x>2 \end{cases}$ at $x=2$.

Sol. Here, $f(x)=\begin{cases} kx^2, \text{if } x \le 2 \\ 3, \ \text{if } x>2 \end{cases}$

At $x = 2$, $\text{LHL} = \lim_{x \to 2^-} f(x) = \lim_{x \to 2^-} kx^2.$

Putting $x = 2 - h$ as $x \to 2^-$ when $h \to 0$

$$\therefore \quad \lim_{h \to 0} k(2-h)^2 = \lim_{h \to 0} k(4 + h^2 - 4h) = 4k$$

$$\text{RHL} = \lim_{x \to 2^+} f(x) = \lim_{x \to 2^+} (3) = 3$$

Also, $f(2) = k \times (2)^2 = 4k$ $\quad [\because f(x) = kx^2]$

Since, $f(x)$ is continuous at $x = 2$.

$$\therefore \quad \text{LHL} = \text{RHL} = f(2) \Rightarrow 4k = 3 \Rightarrow k = \frac{3}{4}$$

Question 28 The function is defined by $f(x)=\begin{cases} \text{k}x+1, \text{if } x \le \pi \\ \cos x, \ \text{if } x>\pi \end{cases}$ at $x=\pi$.

Sol. Here, $f(x)=\begin{cases} kx+1, \text{if } x \le \pi \\ \cos x, \ \text{if } x>\pi \end{cases}$

At $x = \pi$, $\text{LHL} = \lim_{x \to \pi^-} f(x) = \lim_{x \to \pi^-} (kx + 1)$

Putting $x = \pi - h$ as $x \to \pi^-$ when $h \to 0$

$$\therefore \quad \lim_{h \to 0} k(\pi - h) + 1 = \lim_{h \to 0} k\pi - kh + 1 = k\pi + 1$$

$\text{RHL} = \lim_{x \to \pi^+} f(x) = \lim_{x \to \pi^+} \cos x.$

Putting $x = \pi + h$ as $x \to \pi^+$ when $h \to 0$

$$\therefore \quad \lim_{h \to 0} \cos(\pi + h) = \lim_{h \to 0} -\cos h = -1$$

Also, $f(\pi) = k\pi + 1$ $\quad [\because f(x) = kx + 1]$

$\therefore$ Since, $f(x)$ is continuous at $x = \pi$.

$\therefore \quad \text{LHL} = \text{RHL} = f(\pi)$

$\Rightarrow \quad k\pi + 1 = -1$

$\Rightarrow \quad k = \dfrac{-2}{\pi}$

Question 29 The function is defined by $f(x)=\begin{cases} kx+1, \text{if } x \le 5 \\ 3x-5, \text{if } x>5 \end{cases}$ at $x=5$.

Sol. Here, $f(x)=\begin{cases} kx+1, \text{if } x \le 5 \\ 3x-5, \quad x>5 \end{cases}$

At $x = 5$, $\text{LHL} = \lim_{x \to 5^-} f(x) = \lim_{x \to 5^-} (kx+1)$

Putting $x = 5 - h$ as $x \to 5^-$ when $h \to 0$

$\therefore$ $\lim_{h \to 0} [k(5-h)+1] = \lim_{h \to 0} [5k - kh + 1] = 5k+1$

$\text{RHL} = \lim_{x \to 5^+} f(x) = \lim_{x \to 5^+} (3x-5)$

Putting $x = 5 + h$ as $x \to 5^+$ when $h \to 0$

$\therefore$ $\lim_{h \to 0} [3(5+h)-5] = \lim_{h \to 0} (10+3h) = 10$

Also, $f(5) = 5k+1$ $\quad [\because f(x) = kx+1]$

Since, $f(x)$ is continuous at $x = 5$.

$\therefore$ $\text{LHL} = \text{RHL} = f(5) \Rightarrow 5k+1 = 10 \Rightarrow k = \frac{9}{5}$

Question 30 Find the values of a and b such that the function defined by $f(x)=\begin{cases} 5, & \text{if } x \le 2 \\ ax+b, & \text{if } 2<x<10 \\ 21, & \text{if } x \ge 10 \end{cases}$ is a continuous function.

Sol. Here, $f(x)=\begin{cases} 5, & \text{if } x \le 2 \\ ax+b, & \text{if } 2<x<10 \\ 21, & \text{if } x \ge 10 \end{cases}$

At $x = 2$, $\text{LHL} = \lim_{x \to 2^-} f(x) = \lim_{x \to 2^-} (5) = 5$

$\text{RHL} = \lim_{x \to 2^+} f(x) = \lim_{x \to 2^+} (ax+b)$

Putting $x = 2 + h$ as $x \to 2^+$ when $h \to 0$

$\therefore$ $\lim_{h \to 0} [a(2+h)+b] = \lim_{h \to 0} (2a+ah+b) = 2a+b$

Also, $f(2) = 5$

Since, $f(x)$ is continuous at $x = 2$.

$\therefore$ $\text{LHL} = \text{RHL} = f(2) \Rightarrow 2a+b = 5$ $\quad \ldots$(i)

At $x = 10$, $\text{LHL} = \lim_{x \to 10^-} f(x) = \lim_{x \to 10^-} (ax+b)$

Putting $x = 10 - h$ as $x \to 10^-$ when $h \to 0$

$\therefore$ $\lim_{h \to 0} [a(10-h)+b] = \lim_{h \to 0} (10a - ah + b) = 10a+b$

$\text{RHL} = \lim_{x \to 10^+} f(x) = \lim_{x \to 10^+} (21) = 21$

Also, $f(10) = 21$

Since, $f(x)$ is continuous at $x = 10$.

$$\text{LHL} = \text{RHL} = f(10) \Rightarrow 10a + b = 21 \qquad \ldots(\text{ii})$$

Subtracting Eq. (i) from Eq. (ii), we get $8a = 16 \Rightarrow a = 2$

Put $a = 2$ in Eq. (i), we get $2 \times 2 + b = 5 \Rightarrow b = 1$

Question 31 Show that the function defined by $f(x) = \cos x^2$ is a continuous function.

◎ **Thinking Process** (Q. Nos. 31 to 33) If $f(x)$ and $g(x)$ are two continuous functions, then composition function $f(g(x))$ is always continuous function.

Sol. Let $h(x) = x^2$ and $g(x) = \cos x$

Now, $h(x)$ is a polynomial function, so it is continuous for all $x \in R$.

$g(x)$ is a cosine function, so it is continuous function in its domain *i.e.*, $x \in R$.

$$\therefore \qquad (goh)(x) = g[h(x)] = g(x^2) = \cos x^2$$

Since, $g(x)$ and $h(x)$ are both continuous functions for all $x \in R$, so composition of $g(x)$ and $h(x)$ is also a continuous function for all $x \in R$.

Thus, $f(x) = \cos(x^2)$ is a continuous function for all $x \in R$.

Question 32 Show that the function defined by $f(x) = |\cos x|$ is a continuous function.

Sol. Let $g(x) = \cos x$ and $h(x) = |x|$

Now, $g(x)$ is a cosine function, so it is continuous function in its domain *i.e.*, $x \in R$.

and $h(x) = |x|$ is the absolute valued function, so it is continuous function for all $x \in R$.

$$\therefore \qquad (hog)(x) = h[g(x)] = h(\cos x) = |\cos x|$$

Since, $g(x)$ and $h(x)$ are both continuous functions for all $x \in R$, so composition of $g(x)$ and $h(x)$ is also a continuous function for all $x \in R$.

Thus, $f(x) = |\cos x|$ is a continuous function for all $x \in R$.

Note If $f(x)$ is continuous then $|f(x)|$ is also continuous.

Question 33 Examine that $\sin |x|$ is a continuous function.

Sol. Let $g(x) = |x|$ and $h(x) = \sin x$

Now, $g(x) = |x|$ is the absolute valued function, so it is continuous function for all $x \in R$.

$h(x) = \sin x$ is the sine function, so it is a continuous function for all $x \in R$.

$$\therefore \qquad (hog)(x) = h[g(x)] = h(|x|) = \sin |x|$$

Since, $g(x)$ and $h(x)$ are both continuous functions for all $x \in R$, so composition of $g(x)$ and $h(x)$ is also a continuous function for all $x \in R$.

Thus, $f(x) = \sin |x|$ is a continuous function.

Question 34 Find all the points of discontinuity of f defined by $f(x) = |x| - |x+1|$.

Sol. Let $g(x) = |x|$ and $h(x) = |x + 1|$

Now, $g(x) = |x|$ is the absolute valued function, so it is a continuous function for all $x \in R$.

$h(x) = |x + 1|$ is the absolute valued function, so it is a continuous function for all $x \in R$.

Since, $g(x)$ and $h(x)$ are both continuous functions for all $x \in R$, so difference of two continuous function is a continuous function for all $x \in R$.

thus, $f(x) = |x| - |x + 1|$ is a continuous function at all points.

Hence, there is no point at which $f(x)$ is discontinuous.

Exercise 5.2

Direction (Q. Nos. 1 to 8) Differentiate the following functions with respect to x.

Thinking Process Given differentiation is not a standard differentiation, so chain rule is used to differentiate the function easily.

Question 1 $\sin(x^2 + 5)$.

Sol. Let $y = \sin(x^2 + 5)$

On differentiating both sides w.r.t. x, we get

$$\frac{dy}{dx} = \frac{d}{dx}(\sin(x^2 + 5)) = \cos(x^2 + 5)\frac{d}{dx}(x^2 + 5) \quad \text{(By using chain rule)}$$

$$= \cos(x^2 + 5)(2x + 0) = 2x\cos(x^2 + 5)$$

Mistake Alert $\frac{d}{dx}\sin(x^2 + 5) \neq \cos(x^2 + 5)$

Question 2 $\cos(\sin x)$.

Sol. Let $y = \cos(\sin x)$

On differentiating both sides w.r.t. x, we get

$$\frac{dy}{dx} = \frac{d}{dx}(\cos(\sin x)) = -\sin(\sin x)\frac{d}{dx}(\sin x) \quad \text{(By using chain rule)}$$

$$= -\sin(\sin x)\cos x = -\cos x \sin(\sin x).$$

Question 3 $\sin(ax+b)$.

Sol. Let $y = \sin(ax+b)$

On differentiating both sides w.r.t. x, we get

$$\frac{dy}{dx} = \frac{d}{dx}\sin(ax+b) = \cos(ax+b)\frac{d}{dx}(ax+b) \quad \text{(By chain rule)}$$

$$= \cos(ax+b)\{a \times 1 + 0\} = a\cos(ax+b).$$

Note Chain rule If $h(x) = f(g(x))$ then $h'(x) = f'(g(x)\cdot g'(x)$

Question 4 $\sec(\tan\sqrt{x})$.

Sol. Let $y = \sec(\tan\sqrt{x})$

On differentiating both sides w.r.t. x, we get

$$\frac{dy}{dx} = \frac{d}{dx}(\sec(\tan\sqrt{x})) = \sec(\tan\sqrt{x})\tan(\tan\sqrt{x})\frac{d}{dx}(\tan\sqrt{x})$$

(By chain rule)

$$= \sec(\tan\sqrt{x})\tan(\tan\sqrt{x})\sec^2\sqrt{x}\frac{d}{dx}(\sqrt{x})$$

$$= \sec(\tan\sqrt{x})\tan(\tan\sqrt{x})(\sec^2\sqrt{x})\left(\frac{1}{2\sqrt{x}}\right)$$

$$= \frac{1}{2\sqrt{x}}\sec(\tan\sqrt{x})\cdot\tan(\tan\sqrt{x})(\sec^2\sqrt{x})$$

Mistake Alert By careful, while using chain rule sometimes students forget to differentiate some functions.

Question 5 $\dfrac{\sin(ax+b)}{\cos(cx+d)}$.

Thinking Process Since, the given function is in u/v form.

So, applying the quotient rule *i.e.*, $\dfrac{d}{dx}\left(\dfrac{u}{v}\right) = \dfrac{v\dfrac{d}{dx}u - u\dfrac{d}{dx}v}{v^2}$

Sol. Let $y = \dfrac{\sin(ax+b)}{\cos(cx+d)}$

On differentiating both sides w.r.t. x, we get

$$\frac{dy}{dx} = \frac{d}{dx}\left(\frac{\sin(ax+b)}{\cos(cx+d)}\right)$$

$$= \frac{\cos(cx+d)\dfrac{d}{dx}\{\sin(ax+b)\} - \sin(ax+b)\dfrac{d}{dx}\{\cos(cx+d)\}}{\{\cos(cx+d)\}^2}$$

(By Quotient rule)

$$= \frac{\cos(cx+d)\cos(ax+b).(a+0) + \sin(ax+b)\sin(cx+d)(c+0)}{\cos^2(cx+d)}$$

[applying chain rule in numerator]

$$= \frac{a\cos(cx+d)\cos(ax+b) + c\sin(ax+b)\sin(cx+d)}{\cos^2(cx+d)}$$

$$= \frac{a\cos(cx+d)\cos(ax+b)}{\cos^2(cx+d)} + \frac{c\sin(ax+b)\sin(cx+d)}{\cos^2(cx+d)}$$

$$= \frac{a\cos(ax+b)}{\cos(cx+d)} + \frac{c\sin(ax+b)\sin(cx+d)}{\cos(cx+d)\cos(cx+d)}$$

$$= a\cos(ax+b)\sec(cx+d) + c\sin(ax+b)\tan(cx+d)\sec(cx+d)$$

Question 6 $\cos x^3 \sin^2(x^5)$

Thinking Process Since, the given function is a product of two different functions.

So, using the product rule *i.e.*,

$$\frac{d}{dx}(uv) = u\frac{d}{dx}(v) + v\frac{d}{dx}(u)$$

Sol. Let $y = \cos x^3 \sin^2(x^5)$

On differentiating both sides w.r.t. x, we get

$$\frac{dy}{dx} = \frac{d}{dx}\{\cos x^3 \sin^2(x^5)\}$$

$$= \cos x^3 \frac{d}{dx}\sin^2(x^5) + \sin^2(x^5)\frac{d}{dx}(\cos x^3)$$

[using product rule]

$$= (\cos x^3)(2\sin x^5)\frac{d}{dx}(\sin x^5) + \sin^2(x^5)(-\sin x^3)\frac{d}{dx}(x^3)$$

[using chain rule]

$$= (\cos x^3)(2\sin x^5)(\cos x^5)\frac{d}{dx}(x^5) + \sin^2(x^5)(-\sin x^3)(3x^2)$$

[using chain rule]

$$= (\cos x^3)(2\sin x^5)(\cos x^5)(5x^4) - \sin^2(x^5)(\sin x^3)(3x^2)$$

$$= 10x^4(\sin x^5)(\cos x^5)(\cos x^3) - 3x^2\sin x^3 \sin^2 x^5$$

$$= 5x^4 \sin 2x^5 \cdot \cos x^3 - 3x^2 \sin x^3 \sin^2 x^5 \quad [\because 2\sin A\cos A = \sin 2A]$$

Question 7 $2\sqrt{\cot(x^2)}$.

Sol. Let $y = 2\sqrt{\cot(x^2)}$

On differentiating both sides w.r.t. x, we get

$$\frac{dy}{dx} = \frac{d}{dx} 2(\cot x^2)^{1/2}$$

$$= 2.\frac{1}{2}\{\cot(x^2)\}^{\frac{1}{2}-1} \frac{d}{dx}\cot(x^2) \qquad \text{[using chain rule]}$$

$$= \frac{1}{\sqrt{\cot(x^2)}}[-\operatorname{cosec}^2 x^2] \frac{d}{dx}(x^2) \qquad \text{[using chain rule]}$$

$$= -\frac{\operatorname{cosec}^2(x^2)\, 2x}{\sqrt{\cot(x^2)}}$$

$$= \frac{-2x \operatorname{cosec}^2(x^2)}{\sqrt{\cot(x^2)}}$$

$$= \frac{-2x}{\sin^2 x^2 \sqrt{\cot x^2}} \qquad \left(\because \operatorname{cosec}\theta = \frac{1}{\sin\theta}\right)$$

$$= \frac{-2x}{\sin^2 x^2 \sqrt{\frac{\cos x^2}{\sin x^2}}} \qquad \left(\because \cot\theta = \frac{\cos\theta}{\sin\theta}\right)$$

$$= \frac{-2x}{\sin x^2 \sqrt{\sin x^2 \cos x^2}}$$

$$= \frac{-2\sqrt{2}x}{\sin x^2 \sqrt{2\sin x^2 \cos x^2}} \qquad \text{(multiply and divide by } \sqrt{2}\text{)}$$

$$= \frac{-2\sqrt{2}x}{\sin x^2 \sqrt{\sin 2x^2}}$$

Question 8 $\cos(\sqrt{x})$.

Sol. Let $y = \cos(\sqrt{x})$

On differentiating both sides w.r.t. x, we get

$$\frac{dy}{dx} = \frac{d}{dx}\cos(\sqrt{x})$$

$$= -\sin\sqrt{x} \frac{d}{dx}(\sqrt{x}) \qquad \text{[using chain rule]}$$

$$= -\sin\sqrt{x} \frac{1}{2\sqrt{x}}$$

$$= -\frac{\sin\sqrt{x}}{2\sqrt{x}}$$

Question 9 Prove that the function f is given by $f(x)=|x-1|, x \in R$ is not differentiable at $x=1$.

◎ *Thinking Process* Any function is not differentiable if LHD $\neq$ RHD
i.e., $Lf'(x) \neq Rf'(x)$

Sol. Given, $f(x) = |x-1| = \begin{cases} x-1, & \text{if } x-1 \geq 0 \\ -(x-1), & x-1 < 0 \end{cases} = \begin{cases} x-1, \text{if } x-1 \geq 0 \\ 1-x, \quad x-1<0 \end{cases}$

We have to check the differentiability at $x=1$

Here, $f(1) = 1-1 = 0$

$$Lf'(1) = \lim_{h \to 0^-} \frac{f(1-h)-f(1)}{-h}$$

$$= \lim_{h \to 0^-} \frac{1-(1-h)-0}{-h} = \lim_{h \to 0^-} \frac{h}{-h} = -1$$

[$\because$ when $x<1 \Rightarrow f(x) = 1-x$]

and $$Rf'(1) = \lim_{h \to 0^+} \frac{f(1+h)-f(1)}{h}$$

$$= \lim_{h \to 0^+} \frac{(1+h)-1-0}{h} = \lim_{h \to 0^+} \frac{h}{h} = 1$$

[$\because$ when $x>1 \Rightarrow f(x) = x-1$]

$\therefore Lf'(1) \neq Rf'(1)$.

Hence, $f(x)$ is not differentiable at $x=1$.

Question 10 Prove that the greatest integer function defined by $f(x)=[x], 0<x<3$ is not differentiable at $x=1$ and $x=2$.

Sol. Given $f(x)=[x]$,

(i) RHD of $f(x)$ at $x=1$;

Putting $x=1+h$ as $x \to 1^+ \Rightarrow h \to 0$

$$Rf'(1) = \lim_{h \to 0} \frac{[1+h]-[1]}{h} = \lim_{h \to 0} \frac{1-1}{h} = 0 \qquad \left(\because Rf'(x)=\frac{f(x+h)-f(x)}{h}\right)$$

$([a+h] = a \text{ for } a \in I)$

LHD of $f(x)$ at $x=1$; putting $x=1-h$ as $x \to 1^- \Rightarrow h \to 0$

$$Lf'(1) = \lim_{h \to 0} \frac{[1-h]-[1]}{-h} = \lim_{h \to 0} \frac{0-1}{-h} = \lim_{h \to 0} \frac{1}{h} = \infty.$$

$(\because [a-h] = a-1, \forall a \in I)$

$$\left(\because Lf'(x)=\frac{f(x-h)-f(x)}{-h}\right)$$

$\therefore$ LHD $\neq$ RHD. Thus, $f(x)$ is not differentiable at $x=1$.

(ii) At $x = 2$

$$\text{RHD} = Rf'(2) = \lim_{h \to 0} \frac{f(2+h) - f(2)}{h} \qquad \left(\because Rf'(x) = \frac{f(x+h) - f(x)}{h}\right)$$

$$= \lim_{h \to 0} \frac{[2+h] - 2}{h}$$

$$= \lim_{h \to 0} \frac{2-2}{h} = 0 \qquad (\because [2+h] = 2)$$

$$\text{LHD} = Lf'(2) = \lim_{h \to 0} \frac{f(2-h) - f(2)}{-h} \qquad \left(\therefore Lf'(x) = \frac{f(x-h) - f(x)}{-h}\right)$$

$$= \lim_{h \to 0} \frac{[2-h] - [2]}{-h}$$

$$= \lim_{h \to 0} \frac{1-2}{-h} = \infty \qquad (\because [2-h] = 1)$$

$\therefore$ RHD $\neq$ LHD

Thus, $f(x)$ is not differentiable at $x = 2$. **Hence Proved.**

Mistake Alert Student make error while putting the value of greatest integer function

Exercise 5.3

Direction (Q. Nos. 1 to 15) Find $\frac{dy}{dx}$ in the following questions:

Question 1 $2x + 3y = \sin x$.

Thinking Process (Q. Nos. 1 to 8) It is not a standard differentiation, so differentiate each term separately.

Sol. Given, $2x + 3y = \sin x$

On differentiating both sides w.r.t. x, we get

$$\frac{d}{dx}(2x + 3y) = \frac{d}{dx}(\sin x)$$

$$2 + 3\frac{dy}{dx} = \cos x$$

$$\Rightarrow \quad 3\frac{dy}{dx} = \cos x - 2$$

$$\Rightarrow \quad \frac{dy}{dx} = \frac{\cos x - 2}{3}$$

Question 2 $2x+3y=\sin y.$

Sol. Given, $2x+3y=\sin y$

On differentiating both sides w.r.t. x, we get

$$\frac{d}{dx}(2x+3y)=\frac{d}{dx}(\sin y)$$

$$\Rightarrow \quad 2+3\frac{dy}{dx}=\cos y\frac{dy}{dx} \Rightarrow 3\frac{dy}{dx}-\cos y\frac{dy}{dx}=-2$$

$$\Rightarrow \quad (3-\cos y)\frac{dy}{dx}=-2 \Rightarrow \frac{dy}{dx}=\frac{2}{\cos y-3}$$

Mistake Alert $\frac{d}{dx}\sin y \neq \cos y$

Question 3 $ax+by^2=\cos y.$

Sol. Given, $ax+by^2=\cos y$

On differentiating both sides w.r.t. x, we get

$$\frac{d}{dx}(ax+by^2)=\frac{d}{dx}(\cos y)$$

$$a+2by\frac{dy}{dx}=-\sin y\frac{dy}{dx}$$

$$\Rightarrow \quad 2by\frac{dy}{dx}+\sin y\frac{dy}{dx}=-a$$

$$\Rightarrow \quad \frac{dy}{dx}(2by+\sin y)=-a$$

$$\Rightarrow \quad \frac{dy}{dx}=\frac{-a}{2by+\sin y}$$

Question 4 $xy+y^2=\tan x+y.$

Sol. Given, $xy+y^2=\tan x+y$

On differentiating both sides w.r.t. x, we get

$$\frac{d}{dx}(xy+y^2)=\frac{d}{dx}(\tan x+y)$$

$$\frac{d}{dx}(xy)+\frac{d}{dx}(y^2)=\sec^2 x+\frac{dy}{dx}$$

$$\Rightarrow \quad x\frac{dy}{dx}+y\cdot 1+2y\frac{dy}{dx}=\sec^2 x+\frac{dy}{dx} \qquad \text{(using product rule)}$$

$$\Rightarrow \quad x\frac{dy}{dx}+2y\frac{dy}{dx}-\frac{dy}{dx}=\sec^2 x-y$$

$$\Rightarrow \quad (x+2y-1)\frac{dy}{dx}=\sec^2 x-y$$

$$\Rightarrow \quad \frac{dy}{dx}=\frac{\sec^2 x-y}{x+2y-1}$$

Question 5 $x^2 + xy + y^2 = 100.$

Sol. Given, $x^2 + xy + y^2 = 100$

On differentiating both sides w.r.t. x, we get

$$\frac{d}{dx}(x^2 + xy + y^2) = 0$$

$$\Rightarrow \quad 2x + \left(x\frac{dy}{dx} + y \cdot 1\right) + 2y\frac{dy}{dx} = 0 \quad \text{(using product rule)}$$

$$\Rightarrow \quad \frac{dy}{dx}(x + 2y) = -2x - y$$

$$\Rightarrow \quad \frac{dy}{dx} = -\frac{(2x + y)}{x + 2y}$$

Question 6 $x^3 + x^2y + xy^2 + y^3 = 81.$

Sol. Given, $x^3 + x^2y + xy^2 + y^3 = 81$

On differentiating both sides w.r.t x, we get

$$\frac{d}{dx}(x^3 + x^2y + xy^2 + y^3) = 81$$

$$\Rightarrow \quad 3x^2 + \frac{d}{dx}(x^2y) + \frac{d}{dx}(xy^2) + 3y^2\frac{dy}{dx} = 0$$

$$\Rightarrow 3x^2 + x^2\frac{dy}{dx} + y(2x) + x\left(2y\frac{dy}{dx}\right) + y^2.1 + 3y^2\frac{dy}{dx} = 0 \quad \text{(using product rule)}$$

$$\Rightarrow \quad (x^2 + 2xy + 3y^2)\frac{dy}{dx} = -3x^2 - 2xy - y^2$$

$$\Rightarrow \quad \frac{dy}{dx} = -\frac{(3x^2 + 2xy + y^2)}{x^2 + 2xy + 3y^2}$$

Question 7 $\sin^2 y + \cos xy = k.$

Sol. Given, $\sin^2 y + \cos xy = k$

On differentiating both sides w.r.t. x, we get

$$\frac{d}{dx}(\sin^2 y + \cos xy) = \frac{d}{dx}(k)$$

$$\Rightarrow \quad \frac{d}{dx}(\sin^2 y) + \frac{d}{dx}(\cos xy) = 0$$

$$\Rightarrow \quad 2\sin y\cos y\frac{dy}{dx} + (-\sin xy)\frac{d}{dx}(xy) = 0 \quad \text{(using chain rule)}$$

$$\Rightarrow \quad \sin 2y\frac{dy}{dx} - \sin xy\left(x\frac{dy}{dx} + y.1\right) = 0 \quad (\because \sin 2x = 2\sin x \cdot \cos x)$$

$$\Rightarrow \quad \sin 2y\frac{dy}{dx} - x\sin xy\frac{dy}{dx} = y\sin xy$$

$$\Rightarrow \quad \frac{dy}{dx} = \frac{y\sin(xy)}{\sin 2y - x\sin(xy)}$$

Question 8 $\sin^2 x + \cos^2 y = 1$.

Sol. Given, $\sin^2 x + \cos^2 y = 1$

On differentiating both sides w.r.t. x, we get

$$\frac{d}{dx}(\sin^2 x + \cos^2 y) = \frac{d}{dx}(1)$$

$$2\sin x\cos x + 2\cos y\left(-\sin y\frac{dy}{dx}\right) = 0 \qquad \text{(using chain rule)}$$

$$\Rightarrow \quad -2\sin y\cos y\frac{dy}{dx} = -2\sin x\cos x \Rightarrow \frac{dy}{dx} = \frac{-\sin 2x}{-\sin 2y} = \frac{\sin 2x}{\sin 2y}$$

$(\because \sin 2A = 2\sin A.\cos A)$

Question 9 $y = \sin^{-1}\left(\frac{2x}{1+x^2}\right)$.

◎ *Thinking Process* Substitute $x = \tan\theta$ and make inside bracket in terms of sine, so as to simplify the expression and then differentiate it.

Sol. Given, $y = \sin^{-1}\left(\frac{2x}{1+x^2}\right)$

Putting $\theta = \tan^{-1} x$ *i.e.,* $x = \tan\theta$

Then, $y = \sin^{-1}\left(\frac{2\tan\theta}{1+\tan^2\theta}\right) = \sin^{-1}(\sin 2\theta) = 2\theta = 2\tan^{-1} x \quad \left[\because \sin 2A = \frac{2\tan A}{1+\tan^2 A}\right]$

On differentiating both sides w.r.t. x, we get

$$\frac{dy}{dx} = \frac{d}{dx}(2\tan^{-1} x)$$

$$\frac{dy}{dx} = 2\cdot\frac{1}{1+x^2} = \frac{2}{1+x^2} \qquad \left[\because \frac{d}{dx}\tan^{-1} x = \frac{1}{1+x^2}\right]$$

Question 10 $y = \tan^{-1}\left(\frac{3x-x^3}{1-3x^2}\right), -\frac{1}{\sqrt{3}} < x < \frac{1}{\sqrt{3}}$.

Sol. Given, $y = \tan^{-1}\left(\frac{3x-x^3}{1-3x^2}\right)$

Substitute $\tan^{-1} x = \theta$ *i.e.,* $x = \tan\theta$,

$$\therefore \quad y = \tan^{-1}\left(\frac{3x-x^3}{1-3x^2}\right) = \tan^{-1}\left(\frac{3\tan\theta - \tan^3\theta}{1-3\tan^2\theta}\right)$$

$$\Rightarrow \quad y = \tan^{-1}(\tan 3\theta) = 3\theta = 3\tan^{-1} x \qquad \left[\because \tan 3A = \frac{3\tan A - \tan^3 A}{1-3\tan^2 A}\right]$$

On differentiating both sides w.r.t. x, we get

$$\Rightarrow \quad \frac{dy}{dx} = 3\frac{d}{dx}(\tan^{-1} x) = \frac{3}{1+x^2} \qquad \left[\because \frac{d}{dx}(\tan^{-1} x) = \frac{1}{1+x^2}\right]$$

Question 11 $y = \cos^{-1}\left(\frac{1-x^2}{1+x^2}\right), 0 < x < 1.$

◎ ***Thinking Process*** (Q. Nos. 11 to 15) Firstly put x is equal to some trigonometric value, so that it becomes the some standard trigonometric function. So, as to simplify the expression and then differentiate.

Sol. Given, $y = \cos^{-1}\left(\frac{1-x^2}{1+x^2}\right)$

Let $\tan^{-1} x = \theta$ *i.e.*, $x = \tan\theta$

$$\therefore \quad y = \cos^{-1}\left(\frac{1-x^2}{1+x^2}\right) = \cos^{-1}\left(\frac{1-\tan^2\theta}{1+\tan^2\theta}\right) \quad \left(\because \frac{1-\tan^2 A}{1+\tan^2 A} = \cos 2A\right)$$

$$\Rightarrow \quad y = \cos^{-1}(\cos 2\theta) = 2\theta = 2\tan^{-1} x$$

On differentiating both sides w.r.t. x, we get

$$\frac{dy}{dx} = 2\frac{d}{dx}(\tan^{-1} x) = \frac{2}{1+x^2} \quad \left(\because \frac{d}{dx}\tan^{-1} x = \frac{1}{1+x^2}\right)$$

Question 12 $y = \sin^{-1}\left(\frac{1-x^2}{1+x^2}\right), 0 < x < 1.$

Sol. Given, $y = \sin^{-1}\left(\frac{1-x^2}{1+x^2}\right)$

Substitute $x = \tan\theta \Rightarrow \tan^{-1} x = \theta$

$$\therefore \quad y = \sin^{-1}\left(\frac{1-\tan^2\theta}{1+\tan^2\theta}\right) = \sin^{-1}(\cos 2\theta)$$

$$\Rightarrow \quad y = \sin^{-1}\left[\sin\left(\frac{\pi}{2} - 2\theta\right)\right] \quad \left[\because \sin\left(\frac{\pi}{2} - x\right) = \cos x\right]$$

$$\Rightarrow \quad y = \frac{\pi}{2} - 2\theta \Rightarrow y = \frac{\pi}{2} - 2\tan^{-1} x$$

On differentiating both sides, w.r.t. x we get

$$\frac{dy}{dx} = \frac{d}{dx}\left(\frac{\pi}{2}\right) - 2\frac{d}{dx}(\tan^{-1} x)$$

$$\frac{dy}{dx} = 0 - \frac{2}{1+x^2} \Rightarrow \frac{dy}{dx} = \frac{-2}{1+x^2} \quad \left(\because \frac{d}{dx}(\tan^{-1} x) = \frac{1}{1+x^2}\right)$$

Question 13 $y = \cos^{-1}\left(\frac{2x}{1+x^2}\right), -1 < x < 1.$

Sol. Given, $y = \cos^{-1}\left(\frac{2x}{1+x^2}\right)$

Substitute $x = \tan\theta \Rightarrow \theta = \tan^{-1} x$

$\therefore \quad y = \cos^{-1}\left(\frac{2\tan\theta}{1+\tan^2\theta}\right) \Rightarrow y = \cos^{-1}(\sin 2\theta) \quad \left[\because \sin 2A = \frac{2\tan A}{1+\tan^2 A}\right]$

$\Rightarrow \quad y = \cos^{-1}\left[\cos\left(\frac{\pi}{2} - 2\theta\right)\right] \quad \left[\because \sin 2A = \cos\left(\frac{\pi}{2} - 2A\right)\right]$

$\Rightarrow \quad y = \frac{\pi}{2} - 2\theta \Rightarrow y = \frac{\pi}{2} - 2\tan^{-1} x \quad [\because \theta = \tan^{-1} x]$

On differentiating both sides w.r.t. x, we get

$$\frac{dy}{dx} = 0 - \frac{2}{1+x^2} \Rightarrow \frac{dy}{dx} = \frac{-2}{1+x^2} \quad \left[\because \frac{d}{dx}(\tan^{-1} x) = \frac{1}{1+x^2}\right]$$

Question 14 $y = \sin^{-1}(2x\sqrt{1-x^2}), \ -\frac{1}{\sqrt{2}} < x < \frac{1}{\sqrt{2}}.$

Sol. Given, $y = \sin^{-1}(2x\sqrt{1-x^2})$

Let $\sin^{-1} x = \theta$, then $x = \sin\theta$

$\therefore \quad y = \sin^{-1}(2\sin\theta\sqrt{1-\sin^2\theta})$

$\Rightarrow \quad y = \sin^{-1}(2\sin\theta\cos\theta) = \sin^{-1}(\sin 2\theta)$

$[\because 1 - \sin^2 A = \cos^2 A \text{ and } \sin 2A = 2\sin A\cos A]$

$\Rightarrow \quad y = 2\theta \Rightarrow y = 2\sin^{-1} x$

On differentiating both sides w.r.t. x, we get

$$\Rightarrow \quad \frac{dy}{dx} = \frac{2}{\sqrt{1-x^2}} \quad \left(\because \frac{d}{dx}\sin^{-1} x = \frac{1}{\sqrt{1-x^2}}\right)$$

Question 15 $y = \sec^{-1}\left(\frac{1}{2x^2-1}\right), 0 < x < \frac{1}{\sqrt{2}}.$

Sol. Given, $y = \sec^{-1}\left(\frac{1}{2x^2-1}\right)$

Let $\cos^{-1} x = \theta$ *i.e.*, $x = \cos\theta$

$\therefore \quad y = \sec^{-1}\left(\frac{1}{2\cos^2\theta - 1}\right) \Rightarrow y = \sec^{-1}\left(\frac{1}{\cos 2\theta}\right) \quad (\because \cos 2A = 2\cos^2 A - 1)$

$\Rightarrow \quad y = \sec^{-1}(\sec 2\theta)$

$\Rightarrow \quad y = 2\theta$

$\Rightarrow \quad y = 2\cos^{-1} x$

On differentiating both sides w.r.t. x, we get

$$\Rightarrow \quad \frac{dy}{dx} = 2\frac{d}{dx}(\cos^{-1} x) = \frac{-2}{\sqrt{1-x^2}} \quad \left(\because \frac{d}{dx}(\cos^{-1} x) = \frac{-1}{\sqrt{1-x^2}}\right)$$

Exercise 5.4

Direction (Q. Nos. 1 to 10) Differentiate the following questions w.r.t. x.

Question 1 $\dfrac{e^x}{\sin x}$.

◎ *Thinking Process* It is not a standard differentiation, So applying quotient rule *i.e.*, $\dfrac{d}{dx}\left(\dfrac{u}{v}\right)=\dfrac{v\dfrac{d}{dx}u-u\dfrac{d}{dx}v}{v^2}$. Which will be easy to solve it.

Sol. Let $y=\dfrac{e^x}{\sin x}$.

On differentiating both sides w.r.t. x, we get

$$\frac{dy}{dx}=\frac{d}{dx}\left(\frac{e^x}{\sin x}\right) \quad \text{(using quotient rule)}$$

$$=\frac{\sin x\dfrac{d}{dx}e^x-e^x\dfrac{d}{dx}\sin x}{\sin^2 x}$$

$$=\frac{\sin x\, e^x-e^x\cos x}{\sin^2 x} \quad \left[\because \frac{d}{dx}e^x=e^x\right]$$

$$=\frac{e^x(\sin x-\cos x)}{\sin^2 x},\ x\neq n\pi,\ n\in Z.$$

Question 2 $e^{\sin^{-1}x}$.

◎ *Thinking Process* (Q. Nos. 2 to 5) It is not a standard differentiation, so applying chain rule, to get the required result.

Sol. Let $y=e^{\sin^{-1}x}$

On differentiating both sides w.r.t. x, we get

$$\frac{dy}{dx}=\frac{d}{dx}(e^{\sin^{-1}x})=e^{\sin^{-1}x}\frac{d}{dx}\sin^{-1}x \quad \text{(using chain rule)}$$

$$=e^{\sin^{-1}x}\frac{1}{\sqrt{1-x^2}}=\frac{e^{\sin^{-1}x}}{\sqrt{1-x^2}},\ x\in(-1,1)$$

$$\left[\because \frac{1}{\sqrt{1-x^2}} \text{ is defined for } x\in(-1,1)\right]$$

Question 3 e^{x^3}.

Sol. Let $y = e^{x^3}$

On differentiating both sides w.r.t. x, we get

$$\Rightarrow \quad \frac{dy}{dx} = \frac{d}{dx}(e^{x^3}) = e^{x^3}\frac{d}{dx}(x^3) = e^{x^3}(3x^2) = 3x^2 e^{x^3}$$

(using chain rule)

Question 4 $\sin(\tan^{-1} e^{-x})$.

Sol. Let $y = \sin(\tan^{-1} e^{-x})$

On differentiating both sides w.r.t. x, we get

$$\Rightarrow \quad \frac{dy}{dx} = \frac{d}{dx}[\sin(\tan^{-1}(e^{-x})]$$

$$= \cos\{\tan^{-1}(e^{-x})\}\frac{d}{dx}\{\tan^{-1}(e^{-x})\} \quad \text{(using chain rule)}$$

$$= \cos\{\tan^{-1}(e^{-x})\}\frac{1}{1+(e^{-x})^2}\frac{d}{dx}(e^{-x}) = \cos(\tan^{-1}(e^{-x}))\frac{1}{1+e^{-2x}}\cdot(-e^{-x})$$

$$= -\frac{e^{-x}\cos(\tan^{-1} e^{-x})}{1+e^{-2x}}$$

Question 5 $\log(\cos e^x)$.

Sol. Let $y = \log(\cos e^x)$

On differentiating both sides w.r.t. x, we get

$$\frac{dy}{dx} = \frac{d}{dx}[\log\{\cos(e^x)\}] = \frac{1}{\cos(e^x)}\frac{d}{dx}\{\cos(e^x)\} \quad \text{(using chain rule)}$$

$$= \frac{1}{\cos(e^x)}\{-\sin(e^x)\}\frac{d}{dx}(e^x)$$

$$= -\tan(e^x)\cdot e^x = -e^x\tan(e^x)$$

Note $\frac{d}{dx}(\log_e x) = \frac{1}{x}$

Question 6 $e^x + e^{x^2} + \ldots\ldots + e^{x^5}$.

Sol. Let $y = e^x + e^{x^2} + \ldots\ldots + e^{x^5}$

On differentiating both sides w.r.t. x, we get

$$\frac{dy}{dx} = \frac{d}{dx}\{e^x + e^{x^2} + e^{x^3} + e^{x^4} + e^{x^5}\}$$

$$= \frac{d}{dx}(e^x) + \frac{d}{dx}(e^{x^2}) + \frac{d}{dx}(e^{x^3}) + \frac{d}{dx}(e^{x^4}) + \frac{d}{dx}(e^{x^5})$$

$$= e^x + e^{x^2}\frac{d}{dx}(x^2) + e^{x^3}\frac{d}{dx}(x^3) + e^{x^4}\frac{d}{dx}(x^4) + e^{x^5}\frac{d}{dx}(x^5)$$

(   )

$$= e^x + e^{x^2}(2x) + e^{x^3}(3x^2) + e^{x^4}(4x^3) + e^{x^2}(5x^4)$$

$$= e^x + 2xe^{x^2} + 3x^2e^{x^3} + 4x^3e^{x^4} + 5x^4e^{x^5}$$

Question 7 $\sqrt{e^{\sqrt{x}}}, x>0$

◎ *Thinking Process* Write $\sqrt{e^{\sqrt{x}}}$ as $(e^{\sqrt{x}})^{1/2}$ and then use the rule $\frac{d}{dx}(x^n) = nx^{n-1}$.

Sol. Let $y = (e^{\sqrt{x}})^{1/2}$

On differentiating both sides w.r.t. x, we get

$$\frac{dy}{dx} = \frac{1}{2}(e^{\sqrt{x}})^{\frac{1}{2}-1}\frac{d}{dx}e^{\sqrt{x}}$$

$$\Rightarrow \quad \frac{dy}{dx} = \frac{1}{2}(e^{\sqrt{x}})^{-\frac{1}{2}}.e^{\sqrt{x}}.\frac{d}{dx}(\sqrt{x})$$

$$\Rightarrow \quad \frac{dy}{dx} = \frac{1}{2}\frac{e^{\sqrt{x}}}{\sqrt{e^{\sqrt{x}}}} \times \frac{1}{2\sqrt{x}} = \frac{e^{\sqrt{x}}}{4\sqrt{x}\sqrt{e^{\sqrt{x}}}} = \frac{\sqrt{e^{\sqrt{x}}}}{4\sqrt{x}}, x>0$$

Question 8 $\log(\log x), x>1.$

Sol. Let $y = \log(\log x)$

On differentiating both sides w.r.t. x, we get

$$\frac{dy}{dx} = \frac{d}{dx}(\log(\log x)) = \frac{1}{\log x}\left\{\frac{d}{dx}(\log x)\right\} \qquad \left[\because \frac{d}{dx}\log_e x = \frac{1}{x}\right]$$

$$\Rightarrow \quad \frac{dy}{dx} = \frac{1}{\log x}.\frac{1}{x} = \frac{1}{x\log x}, x>1$$

Question 9 $\frac{\cos x}{\log x}, x>0.$

◎ *Thinking Process* The given expression is in $\frac{u}{v}$ form, so applying the quotient rule and solve it.

Sol. Let $y = \frac{\cos x}{\log x}$

On differentiating both sides w.r.t. x, we get

$$\frac{dy}{dx} = \frac{d}{dx}\left(\frac{\cos x}{\log x}\right), x>0$$

$$\Rightarrow \quad \frac{dy}{dx} = \frac{(\log x)\frac{d}{dx}(\cos x) - \cos x \frac{d}{dx}(\log x)}{(\log x)^2}$$

$$\left(\because \frac{d}{dx}\left(\frac{u}{v}\right) = \frac{v\frac{d}{dx}(u) - u\frac{d}{dx}(v)}{v^2}\right)$$

$$\Rightarrow \quad \frac{dy}{dx} = \frac{(\log x)(-\sin x) - (\cos x)\frac{1}{x}}{(\log x)^2}$$

$$\Rightarrow \quad \frac{dy}{dx} = -\frac{x \sin x \log x + \cos x}{x(\log x)^2}, x > 0$$

Question 10 $\cos(\log x + e^x), x > 0$

Sol. Let $y = \cos(\log x + e^x)$

On differentiating both sides w.r.t. x, we get

$$\frac{dy}{dx} = \frac{d}{dx}\{\cos(\log x + e^x)\}$$

$$\Rightarrow \quad \frac{dy}{dx} = -\sin(\log x + e^x)\frac{d}{dx}(\log x + e^x) \qquad \text{(Using chain rule)}$$

$$\Rightarrow \quad \frac{dy}{dx} = -\sin(\log x + e^x)\left(\frac{1}{x} + e^x\right)$$

$$\Rightarrow \quad \frac{dy}{dx} = \frac{-(xe^x + 1)\sin(\log x + e^x)}{x}, x > 0$$

Note In the above questions, we have to consider the base of the logarithm as e.

Exercise 5.5

Direction (Q. Nos. 1 to 11) Differentiate the given functions w.r.t. x.

Question 1 $\cos x \cos 2x \cos 3x$.

Thinking Process (i) Since, it is difficult to differentiate by applying product rule to a product of more than two functions.

(ii) Take log on both sides of $y = \cos x \cos 2x \cos 3x$ and use the rule $\log(m \cdot n) = \log m + \log n$ and then differentiate.

Sol. Let $y = \cos x \cos 2x \cos 3x$,

Taking log on both sides, we get

$$\log y = \log(\cos x \cos 2x \cos 3x) \qquad [\because \log m \times n \times l = \log m + \log n + \log l]$$

$$\Rightarrow \log y = \log(\cos x) + \log(\cos 2x) + \log(\cos 3x)$$

On differentiating both sides w.r.t. x, we get

$$\frac{d}{dx}\log y = \frac{d}{dx}\log(\cos x) + \frac{d}{dx}\log(\cos 2x) + \frac{d}{dx}\log(\cos 3x)$$

$$\frac{1}{y}\frac{dy}{dx} = \frac{1}{\cos x}(-\sin x) + \frac{1}{\cos 2x}\left(-\sin 2x \frac{d}{dx}(2x)\right)$$

$$+ \frac{1}{\cos 3x}\left(-\sin 3x \cdot \frac{d}{dx}(3x)\right) \text{ [by chain rule]}$$

$$\Rightarrow \quad \frac{dy}{dx} = y\{-\tan x - 2\tan 2x - 3\tan 3x\}$$

$$= -y\{\tan x + 2\tan 2x + 3\tan 3x\}$$

$$= -\cos x \cos 2x \cos 3x\{\tan x + 2\tan 2x + 3\tan 3x\}$$

Question 2 $\sqrt{\dfrac{(x-1)(x-2)}{(x-3)(x-4)(x-5)}}$.

◎ ***Thinking Process*** Take log on both sides of the given equation and use the rules $\log(m^n) = n\log m, \log(m\cdot n) = \log m + \log n$ and $\log\left(\dfrac{m}{n}\right) = \log m - \log n$ further it differentiate.

Sol. Let $y = \sqrt{\dfrac{(x-1)(x-2)}{(x-3)(x-4)(x-5)}}$

Taking log on both sides, we get

$$\log y = \log\left\{\frac{(x-1)(x-2)}{(x-3)(x-4)(x-5)}\right\}^{1/2}$$

$$= \frac{1}{2}\left[\log(x-1)(x-2) - \log(x-3)(x-4)(x-5)\right]$$

$$= \frac{1}{2}\{\log(x-1) + \log(x-2) - \log(x-3) - \log(x-4) - \log(x-5)\}$$

On differentiating both sides w.r.t. x, we get

$$\frac{1}{y}\frac{dy}{dx} = \frac{1}{2}\left[\frac{d}{dx}\log(x-1) + \frac{d}{dx}\log(x-2) - \frac{d}{dx}\log(x-3) - \frac{d}{dx}\log(x-4) - \frac{d}{dx}\log(x-5)\right]$$

$$= \frac{1}{2}\left\{\frac{1}{x-1}(1-0) + \frac{1}{x-2}(1-0) - \frac{1}{x-3}(1-0) - \frac{1}{x-4}(1-0) - \frac{1}{x-5}(1-0)\right\}$$

[by chian rule]

$$\Rightarrow \quad \frac{dy}{dx} = \frac{y}{2}\left\{\frac{1}{x-1} + \frac{1}{x-2} - \frac{1}{x-3} - \frac{1}{x-4} - \frac{1}{x-5}\right\}$$

$$= \frac{1}{2}\sqrt{\frac{(x-1)(x-2)}{(x-3)(x-4)(x-5)}}\left\{\frac{1}{x-1} + \frac{1}{x-2} - \frac{1}{x-3} - \frac{1}{x-4} - \frac{1}{x-5}\right\}$$

Question 3 $(\log x)^{\cos x}$.

Sol. Let $y = (\log x)^{\cos x}$

On taking log both sides, we get

$$\log y = \log \{(\log x)^{\cos x}\}$$

$$\Rightarrow \quad \log y = \cos x \log (\log x) \qquad [\because \log m^n = n \log m]$$

On differentiating both sides w.r.t. x, we get

$$\frac{1}{y}\frac{dy}{dx} = \frac{d}{dx}\{\cos x \log(\log x)\}$$

$$\Rightarrow \quad \frac{1}{y}\frac{dy}{dx} = \cos x \frac{1}{\log x}.\frac{1}{x} + \log(\log x)(-\sin x) \quad \text{(using product rule)}$$

$$\Rightarrow \quad \frac{dy}{dx} = y\left\{\frac{\cos x}{x \log x} - \sin x \log(\log x)\right\}$$

$$= (\log x)^{\cos x}\left\{\frac{\cos x}{x \log x} - \sin x \log(\log x)\right\}.$$

Note In a log function, if base is not given then, it is consider as e, then $\frac{d}{dx}(\log x) = \frac{1}{x}$. If base is other than e. Then, $\frac{d}{dx}(\log_a x) = \log_a e \cdot \frac{1}{x}$

Question 4 $x^x - 2^{\sin x}$.

◎ ***Thinking Process*** Separately assume $u = x^x$ and $v = 2^{\sin x}$.

(i) Rewrite the equation $y = x^x - 2^{\sin x}$ in terms of u and v and differentiate w.r.t. x.

(ii) Separately find $\frac{du}{dx}$ and $\frac{dv}{dx}$ and substitute in the above framed equation.

Sol. Let $y = x^x - 2^{\sin x}$

Again, let $\quad u = x^x$ and $v = 2^{\sin x}$

$\therefore \quad y = u - v$

On differentiating both sides w.r.t. x, we get

$$\frac{dy}{dx} = \frac{du}{dx} - \frac{dv}{dx} \qquad \text{...(i)}$$

Now, $\quad u = x^x$

Taking log on both sides, we get

$$\log u = \log x^x$$

$$\Rightarrow \quad \log u = x \log x$$

$$\Rightarrow \quad \frac{1}{u}\frac{du}{dx} = x \frac{d}{dx}\log x + \log x \frac{d}{dx} x \qquad \text{(differentiate w.r.t. } x\text{)}$$

$$\Rightarrow \quad \frac{1}{u}\frac{du}{dx} = x \times \frac{1}{x} + \log x$$

$$\Rightarrow \quad \frac{1}{u}\frac{du}{dx} = 1 + \log x \Rightarrow \frac{du}{dx} = x^x(1 + \log x)$$

and $\quad v = 2^{\sin x}$

Taking log on both sides, we get

$$\log v = \log(2^{\sin x})$$

$$\Rightarrow \quad \log v = (\sin x)\log 2$$

$$\Rightarrow \quad \frac{1}{v}\frac{dv}{dx} = \cos x(\log 2) \qquad \text{(Differentiate w.r.t. } x\text{)}$$

$$\Rightarrow \quad \frac{dv}{dx} = v[\cos x \log 2] = 2^{\sin x}[\cos x \log 2]$$

Now, putting the values of $\frac{du}{dx}$ and $\frac{dv}{dx}$ in Eq. (i),

$$\frac{dy}{dx} = x^x\,[1 + \log x] - 2^{\sin x}\,[\cos x \log 2]$$

Mistake Alert If $y = f_1(x) \pm f_2(x)$

We will not take log because

$$\log(f_1(x) \pm f_2(x)) \neq \log f_1(x) \pm \log f_2(x)$$

Be aware $\frac{d}{dx}x^x \neq x^{x-1}$

Question 5 $(x+3)^2\,(x+4)^3\,(x+5)^4$.

Sol. Let $y = (x+3)^2\,(x+4)^3\,(x+5)^4$

Taking log on both sides, we get

$$\log y = \log\{(x+3)^2\,(x+4)^3\,(x+5)^4\}$$

or $\quad \log y = 2\log(x+3) + 3\log(x+4) + 4\log(x+5)$

$$(\because \log(lmn) = \log l + \log m + \log n)$$

On differentiating both sides w.r.t. x, we get

$$\frac{d}{dx}(\log y) = 2\frac{d}{dx}\log(x+3) + 3\frac{d}{dx}\log(x+4) + 4\frac{d}{dx}\log(x+5)$$

$$\frac{1}{y}\frac{dy}{dx} = 2\left(\frac{1}{x+3}\right)(1+0) + 3\left(\frac{1}{x+4}\right)(1+0) + 4\left(\frac{1}{x+5}\right)(1+0)$$

$$\Rightarrow \quad \frac{dy}{dx} = y\left\{\left(\frac{2}{x+3}\right) + \left(\frac{3}{x+4}\right) + \left(\frac{4}{x+5}\right)\right\}$$

$$\Rightarrow \quad \frac{dy}{dx} = (x+3)^2\,(x+4)^3\,(x+5)^4\left\{\left(\frac{2}{x+3}\right) + \left(\frac{3}{x+4}\right) + \left(\frac{4}{x+5}\right)\right\}$$

$$= (x+3)^2 (x+4)^3 (x+5)^4 \left\{\frac{2(x+4)(x+5) + 3(x+3)(x+5) + 4(x+3)(x+4)}{(x+3)(x+4)(x+5)}\right\}$$

$$= (x+3)(x+4)^2 (x+5)^3 [2(x^2+9x+20) + 3(x^2+8x+15) + 4(x^2+7x+12)]$$

$$= (x+3)(x+4)^2 (x+5)^3 (9x^2+70x+133)$$

Question 6 $\left(x+\frac{1}{x}\right)^x + x^{\left(1+\frac{1}{x}\right)}$

Sol. Let $y = \left(x+\frac{1}{x}\right)^x + x^{\left(1+\frac{1}{x}\right)}$

Again, let $u = \left(x+\frac{1}{x}\right)^x$ and $v = x^{\left(1+\frac{1}{x}\right)}$

$\therefore \quad y = u + v$

On differentiating w.r.t. x, we get

$$\frac{dy}{dx} = \frac{du}{dx} + \frac{dv}{dx} \quad \ldots\text{(i)}$$

Now, $\quad u = \left(x+\frac{1}{x}\right)^x$

On taking log both sides, we get

$$\log u = \log\left(x+\frac{1}{x}\right)^x \Rightarrow \log u = x\log\left(x+\frac{1}{x}\right) \quad [\because \log m^n = n\log m]$$

On differentiating both sides w.r.t. x, we get

$$\frac{1}{u}\frac{du}{dx} = x\frac{d}{dx}\log\left(x+\frac{1}{x}\right) + \log\left(x+\frac{1}{x}\right)\frac{d}{dx}(x) \quad \text{[using chain rule]}$$

$$\Rightarrow \frac{1}{u}\frac{du}{dx} = \frac{x\times 1}{\left(x+\frac{1}{x}\right)}\left[1-\frac{1}{x^2}\right] + \log\left(x+\frac{1}{x}\right)$$

$$\left(\because \frac{d}{dx}\left(\frac{1}{x}\right) = \frac{d}{dx}(x^{-1}) = -1x^2 = \frac{-1}{x^2}\right)$$

$$\Rightarrow \frac{1}{u}\frac{du}{dx} = \frac{x}{\frac{(x^2+1)}{x}}\left[\frac{x^2-1}{x^2}\right] + \log\left(x+\frac{1}{x}\right)$$

$$\Rightarrow \frac{1}{u}\frac{du}{dx} = \left[\frac{(x^2-1)}{(x^2+1)} + \log\left(x+\frac{1}{x}\right)\right]$$

$$\Rightarrow \frac{du}{dx} = u\left[\frac{(x^2-1)}{(x^2+1)} + \log\left(x+\frac{1}{x}\right)\right]$$

$$\Rightarrow \frac{du}{dx} = \left(x+\frac{1}{x}\right)^x\left[\frac{(x^2-1)}{(x^2+1)} + \log\left(x+\frac{1}{x}\right)\right]$$

and $v = x^{\left(1+\frac{1}{x}\right)}$

On taking log both sides, we get

$$\Rightarrow \quad \log v = \log x^{\left(1+\frac{1}{x}\right)} \Rightarrow \log v = \left(1+\frac{1}{x}\right)\log x$$

On differentiating both sides w.r.t. x, we get

$$\Rightarrow \quad \frac{1}{v}\frac{dv}{dx} = \left(1+\frac{1}{x}\right)\frac{d}{dx}(\log x) + \log x \frac{d}{dx}\left(1+\frac{1}{x}\right) \quad \text{(using chain rule)}$$

$$\Rightarrow \quad \frac{1}{v}\frac{dv}{dx} = \left(1+\frac{1}{x}\right)\times\frac{1}{x} + \log x\left[0-\frac{1}{x^2}\right]$$

$$\Rightarrow \quad \frac{1}{v}\frac{dv}{dx} = \left[\frac{x+1}{x^2}\right] - \frac{1}{x^2}\log x$$

$$\Rightarrow \quad \frac{1}{v}\frac{dv}{dx} = \left[\frac{x+1-\log x}{x^2}\right] \Rightarrow \frac{dv}{dx} = v\left[\frac{x+1-\log x}{x^2}\right]$$

$$\Rightarrow \quad \frac{dv}{dx} = x^{\left(1+\frac{1}{x}\right)}\left[\frac{x+1-\log x}{x^2}\right]$$

Putting the values of $\frac{du}{dx}$ and $\frac{dv}{dx}$ in Eq. (i),

$$\therefore \quad \frac{dy}{dx} = \left(x+\frac{1}{x}\right)^x\left[\frac{(x^2-1)}{(x^2+1)} + \log\left(x+\frac{1}{x}\right)\right] + x^{\left(1+\frac{1}{x}\right)}\left[\frac{x+1-\log x}{x^2}\right]$$

Mistake Alert If $y = f(x) \pm g(x)$

We will not take log as $\log y \neq \log f(x) \pm \log g(x)$

Question 7 $(\log x)^x + x^{\log x}$.

Sol. Let $y = (\log x)^x + x^{\log x}$

Again, let $u = (\log x)^x, v = x^{\log x}$ ...(i)

$\therefore \quad y = u + v$

On differentiating both sides w.r.t. x, we get $\frac{dy}{dx} = \frac{du}{dx} + \frac{dv}{dx}$

Now, $u = (\log x)^x$

Taking log on both sides,

$$\Rightarrow \quad \log u = \log(\log x)^x \Rightarrow \log u = x\log(\log x)$$

On differentiating both sides w.r.t. x, we get

$$\frac{1}{u}\frac{du}{dx} = x\frac{d}{dx}\log(\log x) + \log(\log x)\frac{d}{dx}(x) \quad \text{(using chain rule)}$$

$$\Rightarrow \quad \frac{1}{u}\frac{du}{dx} = \frac{x}{\log x}\times\frac{1}{x} + \log(\log x) \Rightarrow \frac{du}{dx} = u\left[\frac{1}{\log x} + \log(\log x)\right]$$

$$\Rightarrow \quad \frac{du}{dx} = (\log x)^x \left[\frac{1}{\log x} + \log(\log x)\right]$$

and $\quad v = x^{\log x}$

Taking log on both sides,

$\Rightarrow \quad \log v = \log x^{\log x} \Rightarrow \log v = (\log x)(\log x) \Rightarrow \log v = (\log x)^2$

On differentiating both sides w.r.t. x, we get

$$\frac{1}{v}\frac{dv}{dx} = 2\log x \frac{d}{dx}(\log x) = 2\log x \times \frac{1}{x} \qquad \left(\because \frac{d}{dx}[f(x)]^2 = 2f(x)\frac{d}{dx}f(x)\right)$$

$$\Rightarrow \quad \frac{dv}{dx} = v\left[\frac{2\log x}{x}\right] \Rightarrow \frac{dv}{dx} = x^{\log x}\left[\frac{2\log x}{x}\right]$$

Now, putting the values of $\frac{du}{dx}$ and $\frac{dv}{dx}$ in Eq. (i), we get

$$\frac{dy}{dx} = (\log x)^x\left[\frac{1}{\log x} + \log(\log x)\right] + x^{\log x}\left[\frac{2\log x}{x}\right]$$

$$\Rightarrow \quad \frac{dy}{dx} = (\log x)^{x-1}\left[1 + \log x \log(\log x)\right] + 2x^{\log x - 1} \cdot \log x$$

Question 8 $(\sin x)^x + \sin^{-1}\sqrt{x}$.

Sol. Let $y = (\sin x)^x + \sin^{-1}\sqrt{x}$

Again, let $\quad u = (\sin x)^x$ and $v = \sin^{-1}\sqrt{x}$

$\therefore \quad y = u + v$

On differentiating both sides w.r.t. x, we get

$$\frac{dy}{dx} = \frac{du}{dx} + \frac{dv}{dx} \qquad \ldots(i)$$

Now, $\quad u = (\sin x)^x$

Taking log on both sides, $\log u = \log(\sin x)^x \Rightarrow \log u = x\log(\sin x)$

On differentiating both sides w.r.t. x, we get

$$\frac{1}{u}\frac{du}{dx} = x\frac{d}{dx}\log(\sin x) + \log(\sin x)\frac{d}{dx}(x) \quad \text{(using product rule)}$$

$$= \frac{x}{\sin x}\cos x + \log(\sin x)$$

$$\Rightarrow \quad \frac{du}{dx} = u[x\cot x + \log\sin x] = (\sin x)^x[x\cot x + \log\sin x]$$

and $\quad v = \sin^{-1}\sqrt{x}$

On differentiating both sides w.r.t. x, we get

$$\frac{dv}{dx} = \frac{1}{\sqrt{1-(\sqrt{x})^2}}\frac{d}{dx}x^{1/2} = \frac{1}{\sqrt{1-x}}\frac{1}{2}x^{-1/2} \quad \text{(using chain rule)}$$

$$\Rightarrow \quad \frac{dv}{dx} = \frac{1}{\sqrt{1-x}} \times \frac{1}{2\sqrt{x}}$$

$$\Rightarrow \quad = \frac{1}{2\sqrt{x}\sqrt{1-x}} \Rightarrow \frac{dv}{dx} = \frac{1}{2\sqrt{x-x^2}}$$

Putting the values of $\frac{du}{dx}$ and $\frac{dv}{dx}$ in Eq. (i), we get

$$\frac{dy}{dx}=(\sin x)^x\,[x\cot x+\log\sin x]+\frac{1}{2\sqrt{x-x^2}}$$

Question 9 $x^{\sin x}+\sin x^{\cos x}$.

Thinking Process Assume separately $u=x^{\sin x}$ and $v=(\sin x)^{\cos x}$ and write the equation $y=x^{\sin x}+\sin x^{\cos x}$ in terms of u and v and differentiate it.

Sol. Let $y=x^{\sin x}+(\sin x^{\cos x})$

Again, let $u=x^{\sin x}$ and $v=\sin x^{\cos x}$

$\therefore \quad y=u+v$

On differentiating both sides w.r.t. x, we get

$$\frac{dy}{dx}=\frac{du}{dx}+\frac{dv}{dx} \qquad \ldots(\text{i})$$

Now, $\quad u=x^{\sin x}$

Taking log on both sides, $\log u=(\sin x)\log x$

On differentiating both sides w.r.t. x, we get

$$\frac{d}{dx}(\log u)=\sin x\frac{d}{dx}(\log x)+\log x\frac{d}{dx}(\sin x) \qquad \text{(using the product rule)}$$

$$\Rightarrow \quad \frac{1}{u}\frac{du}{dx}=\left[\sin x\times\frac{1}{x}+\log x\cos x\right]$$

$$\Rightarrow \quad \frac{du}{dx}=u\left[\frac{\sin x}{x}+\cos x\log x\right]$$

$$\Rightarrow \quad \frac{du}{dx}=x^{\sin x}\left[\frac{\sin x}{x}+\cos x\log x\right]$$

and $\quad v=\sin x^{\cos x}$

Taking log on both sides, $\log v=\cos x\log(\sin x)$

On differentiating both sides w.r.t. x, we get

$$\frac{d}{dx}(\log v)=\cos x\frac{d}{dx}\log(\sin x)+\log\sin x\frac{d}{dx}\cos x$$

$$\Rightarrow \quad \frac{1}{v}\frac{dv}{dx}=\left[\cos x\times\frac{1}{\sin x}\times\cos x+\log\sin x\,(-\sin x)\right]$$

$$\Rightarrow \quad \frac{dv}{dx}=v\,[\cot x\cos x-\sin x\log(\sin x)]$$

$$\Rightarrow \quad \frac{dv}{dx}=\sin x^{\cos x}\,[\cot x\cos x-\sin x\log(\sin x)]$$

Now, putting the values of $\frac{du}{dx}$ and $\frac{dv}{dx}$ in Eq.(i)

$$\frac{dy}{dx}=x^{\sin x}\left[\frac{\sin x}{x}+\cos x\log x\right]+\sin x^{\cos x}[\cot x\cos x-\sin x\log(\sin x)]$$

Question 10 $x^{x\cos x} + \dfrac{x^2+1}{x^2-1}$.

Sol. Let $y = x^{x\cos x} + \dfrac{x^2+1}{x^2-1}$

Again, let $u = x^{x\cos x}$, $v = \dfrac{x^2+1}{x^2-1}$

$\therefore \quad y = u + v$

On differentiating both sides w.r.t. x, we get

$$\frac{dy}{dx} = \frac{du}{dx} + \frac{dv}{dx}$$

Now, $\quad u = x^{x\cos x}$

Taking log on both sides, $\log u = x\cos x \log x$

On differentiating both sides w.r.t. x, we get

$$\frac{d}{dx}(\log u) = x\cos x\frac{d}{dx}(\log x) + \log x\frac{d}{dx}(x\cos x)$$

$$\Rightarrow \quad \frac{1}{u}\frac{du}{dx} = x\cos x \times \frac{1}{x} + \log x\left[x\frac{d}{dx}\cos x + \cos x\frac{d}{dx}(x)\right]$$

$$\Rightarrow \quad \frac{1}{u}\frac{du}{dx} = x\cos x \times \frac{1}{x} + \log x\,[(-x\sin x) + \cos x]$$

$$\Rightarrow \quad \frac{du}{dx} = u\,[\cos x - x\sin x\log x + \cos x.\log x]$$

$$\Rightarrow \quad \frac{du}{dx} = x^{x\cos x}\,[\cos x - x\sin x\log x + \cos x \cdot \log x]$$

and $\quad v = \dfrac{x^2+1}{x^2-1}$

You can use direct

$$\frac{d}{dx}\left(\frac{u}{v}\right) = \frac{v\frac{d}{dx}u - u\frac{d}{dx}v}{v^2}$$

$$\frac{d}{dx}\left(\frac{x^2+1}{x^2-1}\right) = \frac{(x^2-1)\cdot 2x - (x^2+1)\cdot 2x}{(x^2-1)^2} = \frac{-4x}{(x^2-1)^2}$$

Taking log on both sides, $\log v = \log(x^2+1) - \log(x^2-1)$

On differentiating both sides w.r.t. x, we get

$$\Rightarrow \quad \frac{d}{dx}\log v = \frac{d}{dx}\log(x^2+1) - \frac{d}{dx}\log(x^2-1)$$

$$\Rightarrow \quad \frac{1}{v}\frac{dv}{dx} = \frac{1}{(x^2+1)}\frac{d}{dx}(x^2+1) - \frac{1}{(x^2-1)}\frac{d}{dx}(x^2-1)$$

$$\Rightarrow \quad \frac{1}{v}\frac{dv}{dx} = \frac{2x}{(x^2+1)} - \frac{2x}{(x^2-1)} = 2x\left[\frac{(x^2-1)-(x^2+1)}{(x^2+1)(x^2-1)}\right]$$

$$\Rightarrow \quad \frac{dv}{dx} = v\left[\frac{-4x}{x^4-1}\right] = \frac{x^2+1}{x^2-1}\left[\frac{-4x}{x^4-1}\right]$$

Now, putting the values of $\frac{du}{dx}$ and $\frac{dv}{dx}$ in Eq. (i),

$$\therefore \quad \frac{dy}{dx} = x^{x\cos x}\,[\cos x - x\sin x\log x + \cos x.\log x] + \frac{x^2+1}{x^2-1}\left[\frac{-4x}{x^4-1}\right]$$

$$= x^{x\cos x}\,[\cos x.(1+\log x) - x\sin x\log x] - \frac{4x}{(x^2-1)^2}$$

Question 11 $(x\cos x)^x + (x\sin x)^{\frac{1}{x}}$.

Sol. Let $y = (x\cos x)^x + (x\sin x)^{1/x}$,

Again, let $u = (x\cos x)^x$, $v = (x\sin x)^{1/x}$

$\therefore \quad y = u + v$

On differentiating both sides w.r.t. x, we get $\frac{dy}{dx} = \frac{du}{dx} + \frac{dv}{dx}$ ...(i)

Now, $u = (x\cos x)^x$

On taking log both sides, $\log u = x\log(x\cos x)$

On differentiating both sides w.r.t. x, we get

$$\frac{d}{dx}(\log u) = x\frac{d}{dx}\log(x\cos x) + \log(x\cos x)\frac{d}{dx}(x)$$

$$\Rightarrow \quad \frac{1}{u}\frac{du}{dx} = x \times \frac{1}{x\cos x}\frac{d}{dx}(x\cos x) + \log(x\cos x)\times 1$$

$$\Rightarrow \quad \frac{1}{u}\frac{du}{dx} = \frac{1}{\cos x}\left(x\frac{d}{dx}\cos x + \cos x\frac{d}{dx}x\right) + \log(x\cos x)$$

$$\Rightarrow \quad \frac{1}{u}\frac{du}{dx} = \frac{1}{\cos x}[x(-\sin x) + \cos x] + \log(x\cos x)$$

$$= \frac{1}{\cos x}[-x\sin x + \cos x] + \log(x\cos x)$$

$$\Rightarrow \quad \frac{1}{u}\frac{du}{dx} = -x\tan x + 1 + \log(x\cos x)$$

$$\Rightarrow \quad \frac{du}{dx} = u[-x\tan x + 1 + \log(x\cos x)]$$

$$\Rightarrow \quad \frac{du}{dx} = (x\cos x)^x[-x\tan x + 1 + \log(x\cos x)]$$

and $v = (x\sin x)^{1/x}$

Taking log on both sides, $\log v = \frac{1}{x}\log(x\sin x)$

On differentiating both sides w.r.t. x, we get

$$\frac{1}{v}\frac{dv}{dx} = \frac{1}{x}\frac{d}{dx}(\log(x\sin x)) + \log(x\sin x)\frac{d}{dx}\left(\frac{1}{x}\right)$$

$$\Rightarrow \quad \frac{1}{v}\frac{dv}{dx} = \frac{1}{x}\left[\frac{1}{x\sin x}\frac{d}{dx}(x\sin x)\right] + \log(x\sin x)\left(-\frac{1}{x^2}\right)$$

$$= \frac{1}{x}\left[\frac{1}{x\sin x}\left\{x\frac{d}{dx}\sin x + \sin x\frac{d}{dx}x\right\}\right] - \left(\frac{1}{x^2}\right)\log(x\sin x)$$

$$\Rightarrow \quad \frac{1}{v}\frac{dv}{dx} = \frac{1}{x}\,\frac{1}{x\sin x}[x\cos x + \sin x] + \log(x\sin x)\left(\frac{-1}{x^2}\right)$$

$$= \frac{x\cos x}{x^2\sin x} + \frac{\sin x}{x^2\sin x} + \left(\frac{-1}{x^2}\right)\log(x\sin x)$$

$$\Rightarrow \quad \frac{dv}{dx} = v\left[\frac{\cot x}{x} + \frac{1}{x^2} - \frac{1}{x^2}\log(x\sin x)\right]$$

$$\Rightarrow \quad \frac{dv}{dx} = v\left[\frac{x\cot x + 1 - \log(x\sin x)}{x^2}\right]$$

$$\Rightarrow \quad \frac{dv}{dx} = (x\sin x)^{1/x}\left[\frac{x\cot x + 1 - \log(x\sin x)}{x^2}\right]$$

Now, putting the values of $\frac{du}{dx}$ and $\frac{dv}{dx}$ in Eq.(i),

$$\frac{dy}{dx} = (x\cos x)^x\,[-x\tan x + 1 + \log(x\cos x)] + (x\sin x)^{1/x}\left[\frac{x\cot x + 1 - \log(x\sin x)}{x^2}\right]$$

Direction (Q. Nos. 12 to 15) Find $\frac{dy}{dx}$ of the functions given in question.

Question 12 $x^y + y^x = 1$.

Sol. Given $x^y + y^x = 1$

Let $u = x^y$, $v = y^x$

$\therefore \quad u + v = 1$

On differentiating both sides w.r.t. x, $\frac{du}{dx} + \frac{dv}{dx} = 0$ ...(i)

Now, $\quad u = x^y$

Taking log on both sides, we get $\log u = y\log x$

On differentiating both sides w.r.t. x, we get

$$\frac{1}{u}\frac{du}{dx} = y \times \frac{1}{x} + \log x\frac{dy}{dx} \quad \text{(using product rule)}$$

$$\Rightarrow \quad \frac{du}{dx} = u\left[\frac{y}{x} + \log x\frac{dy}{dx}\right]$$

$$\Rightarrow \quad \frac{du}{dx} = x^y\left[\frac{y}{x} + \log x\frac{dy}{dx}\right]$$

$$\Rightarrow \quad \frac{du}{dx} = yx^{y-1} + x^y.\log x\frac{dy}{dx}$$

and $\quad v = y^x$

Taking log on both sides, we get

$\Rightarrow \quad \log v = x \log y$

On differentiating both sides w.r.t. x, we get

$\Rightarrow \quad \frac{1}{v}\frac{dv}{dx} = x \times \frac{1}{y}\frac{dy}{dx} + \log y$ (using product rule)

$\Rightarrow \quad \frac{dv}{dx} = v\left[\frac{x}{y}\frac{dy}{dx} + \log y\right] \Rightarrow \frac{dv}{dx} = y^x\left[\frac{x}{y}\frac{dy}{dx} + \log y\right]$

$\Rightarrow \quad \frac{dv}{dx} = xy^{x-1}\frac{dy}{dx} + y^x \log y$

Now, putting the values of $\frac{du}{dx}$ and $\frac{dv}{dx}$ in Eq. (i),

$$yx^{y-1} + x^y.\log x\frac{dy}{dx} + xy^{x-1}\frac{dy}{dx} + y^x \log y = 0$$

$\Rightarrow \quad \frac{dy}{dx}[x^y \log x + xy^{x-1}] = -y^x \log y - yx^{y-1}$

$\Rightarrow \quad \frac{dy}{dx} = -\frac{y^x \log y + yx^{y-1}}{x^y \log x + xy^{x-1}}$

Question 13 $y^x = x^y$.

Sol. Given, $y^x = x^y$

Taking log on both sides, we get $\log y^x = \log x^y \Rightarrow x \log y = y \log x$

On differentiating both sides w.r.t. x, we get

$$\frac{d}{dx}(x \log y) = \frac{d}{dx}(y \log x)$$

$\Rightarrow \quad x\left(\frac{1}{y}\right)\frac{dy}{dx} + (\log y) = y\frac{1}{x} + (\log x)\frac{dy}{dx}$ (using product rule)

$\Rightarrow \quad \frac{x}{y}\frac{dy}{dx} - (\log x)\frac{dy}{dx} = \frac{y}{x} - \log y$

$\Rightarrow \quad \left(\frac{x}{y} - \log x\right)\frac{dy}{dx} = \frac{y}{x} - \log y$

$\Rightarrow \quad \left(\frac{x - y\log x}{y}\right)\frac{dy}{dx} = \frac{y - x\log y}{x} \Rightarrow \frac{dy}{dx} = \frac{y}{x}\left(\frac{y - x\log y}{x - y\log x}\right)$

Question 14 $(\cos x)^y = (\cos y)^x$.

Sol. Given, $(\cos x)^y = (\cos y)^x$

Taking log on both sides, we get

$\log\{(\cos x)^y\} = \log\{(\cos y)^x\}$ or $y \log(\cos x) = x \log(\cos y)$

On differentiating both sides w.r.t.x, we get

$$y\frac{d}{dx}(\log \cos x) + \log \cos x\frac{d}{dx}y = x\frac{d}{dx}(\log \cos y) + \log \cos y\frac{d}{dx}x$$

(using product rule)

$$y\left(\frac{1}{\cos x}\right)(-\sin x) + \log(\cos x)\frac{dy}{dx} = x\left(\frac{1}{\cos y}\right)(-\sin y)\frac{dy}{dx} + \log(\cos y).1$$

$$\Rightarrow \quad \log(\cos x)\frac{dy}{dx} + x\tan y\frac{dy}{dx} = \log(\cos y) + y\tan x$$

$$\Rightarrow \quad (\log(\cos x) + x\tan y)\frac{dy}{dx} = \log(\cos y) + y\tan x$$

$$\Rightarrow \quad \frac{dy}{dx} = \frac{\log(\cos y) + y(\tan x)}{\log(\cos x) + x\tan y}$$

Question 15 [illegible] $= e^{(x-y)}$.

Sol. Given, [illegible] $= e^{(x-y)}$

On differentiating both sides w.r.t. x, we get

$$\frac{d}{dx}(xy) = \frac{d}{dx}(e^{x-y}) \Rightarrow x\frac{dy}{dx} + y.1 = e^{x-y}\frac{d}{dx}(x-y)$$

(using product rule in LHS and chain rule in RHS)

$$\Rightarrow \quad x\frac{dy}{dx} + y = e^{x-y}\left(1 - \frac{dy}{dx}\right) \Rightarrow x\frac{dy}{dx} + e^{x-y}\frac{dy}{dx} = e^{x-y} - y$$

$$\Rightarrow \quad (x + e^{x-y})\frac{dy}{dx} = e^{x-y} - y \Rightarrow \frac{dy}{dx} = \frac{e^{x-y} - y}{x + e^{x-y}} = \frac{xy - y}{x + xy}$$

($\because e^{x-y} = xy$ is given)

$$= \frac{y(x-1)}{x(1+y)}$$

Question 16 Find the derivative of the function given by $f(x) = (1+x)(1+x^2)(1+x^4)(1+x^8)$ and hence find $f'(1)$.

◎ **Thinking Process** Take logarithm on both sides of the equation and use the rule $\log(m\,n) = \log m + \log n$ and then differentiate the equation.

Sol. Given, $f(x) = (1+x)(1+x^2)(1+x^4)(1+x^8)$

On taking log both sides, we get

$$\log(f(x)) = \log\{(1+x)(1+x^2)(1+x^4)(1+x^8)\}$$

$$\Rightarrow \quad \log(f(x)) = \log(1+x) + \log(1+x^2) + \log(1+x^4) + \log(1+x^8)$$

On differentiating both sides, w.r.t. x, we get

$$\frac{d}{dx}\log(f(x)) = \frac{d}{dx}\log(1+x) + \frac{d}{dx}\log(1+x^2)$$
$$+ d/dx\log(1+x^4) + d/dx\log(1+x^8)$$

$$\Rightarrow \quad \frac{1}{f(x)}f'(x) = \frac{1}{1+x}(0+1) + \frac{1}{1+x^2}(0+2x)$$
$$+ \frac{1}{1+x^4}(0+4x^3) + \frac{1}{1+x^8}(0+8x^7)$$

$$\Rightarrow f'(x) = f(x)\left\{\frac{1}{1+x} + \frac{2x}{1+x^2} + \frac{4x^3}{1+x^4} + \frac{8x^7}{1+x^8}\right\}$$

$$= (1+x)(1+x^2)(1+x^4)(1+x^8)\left\{\frac{1}{1+x} + \frac{2x}{1+x^2} + \frac{4x^3}{1+x^4} + \frac{8x^7}{1+x^8}\right\}$$

$$\therefore \quad f'(1) = (1+1)(1+1)(1+1)(1+1)\left\{\frac{1}{1+1} + \frac{2}{1+1} + \frac{4}{1+1} + \frac{8}{1+1}\right\}$$

$$= 2^4\left\{\frac{1}{2} + 1 + 2 + 4\right\} = 16\left(\frac{15}{2}\right) = 120$$

Question 17 Differentiate $(x^2 - 5x + 8)(x^3 + 7x + 9)$ in three ways mentioned below.

(a) By using product rule.

(b) By expanding the product to obtain a single polynomial.

(c) By logarithmic differentiation.

Do they all give the same answer?

Sol. Let $y = (x^2 - 5x + 8)(x^3 + 7x + 9)$ ...(i)

(a) Using product rule,

$$\frac{dy}{dx} = (x^2 - 5x + 8)\frac{d}{dx}(x^3 + 7x + 9) + (x^3 + 7x + 9)\frac{d}{dx}(x^2 - 5x + 8)$$

$$= (x^2 - 5x + 8)(3x^2 + 7) + (x^3 + 7x + 9)(2x - 5)$$

$$= 3x^4 - 15x^3 + 24x^2 + 7x^2 - 35x + 56 + 2x^4 + 14x^2 + 18x - 5x^3 - 35x - 45$$

$$= 5x^4 - 20x^3 + 45x^2 - 52x + 11 \quad \text{...(ii)}$$

(b) Writing y as a single polynomial,

$y = (x^2 - 5x + 8)(x^3 + 7x + 9) = x^5 - 5x^4 + 15x^3 - 26x^2 + 11x + 72$

On differentiating both sides w.r.t. x, we get

$$\therefore \quad \frac{dy}{dx} = \frac{d}{dx}(x^5 - 5x^4 + 15x^3 - 26x^2 + 11x + 72)$$

$$= 5x^4 - 20x^3 + 45x^2 - 52x + 11 \quad \text{...(iii)}$$

(c) Taking logarithms on both sides of Eq. (i), we get

$$\log y = \log\{(x^2 - 5x + 8)(x^3 + 7x + 9)\}$$

$$\Rightarrow \quad \log y = \log(x^2 - 5x + 8) + \log(x^3 + 7x + 9)$$

$[\because \log mn = \log m + \log n]$

On differentiating both sides w.r.t. x, we get

$$\frac{1}{y}\frac{dy}{dx} = \frac{1}{x^2 - 5x + 8}\frac{d}{dx}(x^2 - 5x + 8) + \frac{1}{x^3 + 7x + 9}\frac{d}{dx}(x^3 + 7x + 9)$$

(using chain rule)

$$\Rightarrow \quad \frac{1}{y}\frac{dy}{dx} = \frac{2x - 5}{x^2 - 5x + 8} + \frac{3x^2 + 7}{x^3 + 7x + 9}$$

$$\Rightarrow \quad \frac{dy}{dx} = y\left(\frac{2x-5}{x^2-5x+8} + \frac{3x^2+7}{x^3+7x+9}\right)$$

$$= (x^2-5x+8)(x^3+7x+9)\left(\frac{2x-5}{x^2-5x+8} + \frac{3x^2+7}{x^3+7x+9}\right)$$

$$= (2x-5)(x^3+7x+9) + (3x^2+7)(x^2-5x+8)$$

$$= 2x^4 + 14x^2 + 18x - 5x^3 - 35x - 45 + 3x^4 - 15x^3 + 24x^2 + 7x^2 - 35x + 56$$

$$= 5x^4 - 20x^3 + 45x^2 - 52x + 11 \quad \ldots\text{(iv)}$$

From Eqs. (ii), (iii) and (iv), we find that result is same in every case.

Question 18 If u, v and w are functions of x, then show that

$$\frac{d}{dx}(u \cdot v \cdot w) = \frac{du}{dx} v \cdot w + u \cdot \frac{dv}{dx} \cdot w + u \cdot v \frac{dw}{dx}$$

In two ways-first by repeated application of product rule, second by logarithmic differentiation.

Sol. First, we use product rule and find that

$$\frac{d}{dx}(uvw) = \frac{d}{dx}\{(uv)w\}$$

$$= (uv)\frac{dw}{dx} + w\frac{d}{dx}(uv)$$

(consider hare uv as one function and w as another function)

$$= uv\frac{dw}{dx} + w\left(u\frac{dv}{dx} + v\frac{du}{dx}\right) = uv\frac{dw}{dx} + wu\frac{dv}{dx} + wv\frac{du}{dx} \quad \ldots\text{(i)}$$

Next, we use logarithmic differentiation to obtain $d/dx\,(uvw)$.

Let $y = uvw \Rightarrow \log y = \log(uvw)$

$$\Rightarrow \quad \log y = \log u + \log v + \log w$$

On differentiating both sides w.r.t x, we get

$$\frac{1}{y}\frac{dy}{dx} = \frac{1}{u}\frac{du}{dx} + \frac{1}{v}\frac{dv}{dx} + \frac{1}{w}\frac{dw}{dx}$$

$$\Rightarrow \quad \frac{dy}{dx} = y\left\{\frac{1}{u}\frac{du}{dx} + \frac{1}{v}\frac{dv}{dx} + \frac{1}{w}\frac{dw}{dx}\right\}$$

$$= (uvw)\left\{\frac{1}{u}\frac{du}{dx} + \frac{1}{v}\frac{dv}{dx} + \frac{1}{w}\frac{dw}{dx}\right\}$$

$$= (vw)\frac{du}{dx} + (uw)\frac{dv}{dx} + (uv)\frac{dw}{dx}$$

$$= uv\frac{dw}{dx} + uw\frac{dv}{dx} + wv\frac{du}{dx} \quad \ldots\text{(ii)}$$

From Eqs. (i) and (ii), we find that the result obtained is same in the two cases.

Exercise 5.6

Direction (Q. Nos. 1 to 10) Find $\frac{dy}{dx}$, if x and y are connected parametrically by the equations given in questions without eliminating the parameter.

Question 1 $x = 2at^2, y = at^4$.

◎ *Thinking Process* Firstly, differentiate the parametric equations x and y separately with respect to t and then determine $\frac{dy}{dx}$.

Sol. Given, $x = 2at^2, y = at^4$

On differentiating both sides w.r.t. t, we get

$$\frac{dx}{dt} = (2a)(2t) \text{ and } \frac{dy}{dt} = a(4t^3) = 4at^3$$

$$\therefore \quad \frac{dy}{dx} = \frac{\frac{dy}{dt}}{\frac{dx}{dt}} = \frac{4at^3}{4at} = t^2 \qquad \left(\because \frac{dy}{dx} = \frac{dy/dt}{dx/dt}\right)$$

Question 2 $x = a\cos\theta, y = b\cos\theta$.

Sol. Given, $x = a\cos\theta, y = b\cos\theta$

On differentiating both sides w.r.t. θ, we get

$$\frac{dx}{d\theta} = a(-\sin\theta) \text{ and } \frac{dy}{d\theta} = b(-\sin\theta)$$

$$\Rightarrow \quad \frac{dx}{d\theta} = -a\sin\theta \text{ and } \frac{dy}{d\theta} = -b\sin\theta$$

$$\therefore \quad \frac{dy}{dx} = \frac{\frac{dy}{d\theta}}{\frac{dx}{d\theta}} = \frac{-b\sin\theta}{-a\sin\theta} = \frac{b}{a} \qquad \left(\because \frac{dy}{dx} = \frac{dy/dt}{dx/dt}\right)$$

Question 3 $x = \sin t, y = \cos 2t$.

Sol. Given, $x = \sin t, y = \cos 2t$

On differentiating both sides w.r.t. t, we get

$$\therefore \quad \frac{dx}{dt} = \cos t \text{ and } \frac{dy}{dt} = -(\sin 2t)\, 2 = -2\sin 2t$$

$$\therefore \quad \frac{dy}{dx} = \frac{\frac{dy}{dt}}{\frac{dx}{dt}} = \frac{dy}{dt} \times \frac{dt}{dx} \qquad \left(\because \frac{dy}{dx} = \frac{dy/dt}{dx/dt}\right)$$

$$= \frac{-2\sin 2t}{\cos t} = \frac{-2(2\sin t\cos t)}{\cos t} = -4\sin t \quad (\because \sin 2\theta = 2\sin\theta\cos\theta)$$

Question 4 $x = 4t, y = \dfrac{4}{t}$.

Sol. Given, $x = 4t,\ y = \dfrac{4}{t}$

On differentiating both sides w.r.t. t, we get

$$\frac{dx}{dt} = 4 \text{ and } \frac{dy}{dt} = 4(-1)t^{-2} = -4t^{-2}$$

$$\therefore \quad \frac{dy}{dx} = \frac{\frac{dy}{dt}}{\frac{dx}{dt}} = \frac{-4t^{-2}}{4} = -\frac{1}{t^2} \qquad \left(\because \frac{dy}{dx} = \frac{dy/dt}{dx/dt}\right)$$

Question 5 $x = \cos\theta - \cos 2\theta,\ y = \sin\theta - \sin 2\theta$.

Sol. Given, $x = \cos\theta - \cos 2\theta, \quad y = \sin\theta - \sin 2\theta$

On differentiating both sides w.r.t. θ, we get

$$\therefore \quad \frac{dx}{d\theta} = \frac{d}{d\theta}(\cos\theta - \cos 2\theta)$$

$$= -\sin\theta - (-\sin 2\theta)\,2 = -\sin\theta + 2\sin 2\theta$$

$$\text{and} \quad \frac{dy}{d\theta} = \frac{d}{d\theta}(\sin\theta - \sin 2\theta)$$

$$= \cos\theta - (\cos 2\theta)2 = \cos\theta - 2\cos 2\theta$$

$$\therefore \quad \frac{dy}{dx} = \frac{\frac{dy}{d\theta}}{\frac{dx}{d\theta}} = \frac{\cos\theta - 2\cos 2\theta}{2\sin 2\theta - \sin\theta}$$

Question 6 $x = a(\theta - \sin\theta),\ y = a(1 + \cos\theta)$.

Sol. Given, $x = a(\theta - \sin\theta),\ y = a(1 + \cos\theta)$,

On differenting both sides w.r.t. θ, we get

$$\therefore \quad \frac{dx}{d\theta} = \frac{d}{d\theta}a(\theta - \sin\theta) = a(1 - \cos\theta)$$

$$\text{and} \quad \frac{dy}{d\theta} = \frac{d}{d\theta}a(1 + \cos\theta) = a(0 - \sin\theta) = -a\sin\theta$$

$$\therefore \quad \frac{dy}{dx} = \frac{\frac{dy}{d\theta}}{\frac{dx}{d\theta}}$$

$$= \frac{-a\sin\theta}{a(1 - \cos\theta)} = \frac{-2\sin\frac{\theta}{2}\cos\frac{\theta}{2}}{2\sin^2\left(\frac{\theta}{2}\right)} = -\cot\left(\frac{\theta}{2}\right) \qquad \left[\begin{array}{l}\because \sin 2A = 2\sin A\cos A \\ 1 - \cos A = 2\sin^2\frac{A}{2}\end{array}\right]$$

Question 7 $x = \dfrac{\sin^3 t}{\sqrt{\cot 2t}}, y = \dfrac{\cos^3 t}{\sqrt{\cos 2t}}.$

Thinking Process Since, both x and y are in $\dfrac{u}{v}$ form, so

(i) find $\dfrac{dx}{dt}$ and $\dfrac{dy}{dt}$ by simply using rule $\dfrac{d}{dx}\left(\dfrac{u}{v}\right) = \dfrac{v\dfrac{du}{dx} - u\dfrac{dv}{dx}}{v^2}$.

(ii) then, use $\dfrac{dy}{dx} = \dfrac{dy}{dt} \times \dfrac{dt}{dx}$.

Sol. Given, $x = \dfrac{\sin^3 t}{\sqrt{\cos 2t}}, y = \dfrac{\cos^3 t}{\sqrt{\cos 2t}}$

On differentiating both sides w.r.t. t, we get

$$\frac{dx}{dt} = \frac{d}{dt}\left(\frac{\sin^3 t}{\sqrt{\cos 2t}}\right) = \frac{\sqrt{\cos 2t}\,(3\sin^2 t\cos t) - \sin^3 t\left(\dfrac{-2\sin 2t}{2\sqrt{\cos 2t}}\right)}{(\sqrt{\cos 2t})^2}$$

(using quotient rule)

$$= \frac{3(\cos 2t)\sin^2 t\cos t + \sin 2t\sin^3 t}{\cos 2t\sqrt{\cos 2t}}$$

$$= \frac{3(1 - 2\sin^2 t)\sin^2 t\cos t + (2\sin t\cos t)\sin^3 t}{\cos 2t\sqrt{\cos 2t}}$$

$(\because \cos 2A = 1 - 2\sin^2 A$ and $\sin 2A = 2\sin A\cos A)$

$$= \frac{3\sin^2 t\cos t - 4\sin^4 \cos t}{\cos 2t\sqrt{\cos 2t}}$$

and $$\frac{dy}{dt} = \frac{d}{dt}\left(\frac{\cos^3 t}{\sqrt{\cos 2t}}\right) = \frac{\sqrt{\cos 2t}\,(-3\cos^2 t\sin t) - \cos^3 t\left(\dfrac{-2\sin 2t}{2\sqrt{\cos 2t}}\right)}{(\sqrt{\cos 2t})^2}$$

(using quotient rule)

$$= \frac{-3(\cos 2t)\cos^2 t\sin t + \sin 2t\cos^3 t}{\cos 2t\sqrt{\cos 2t}}$$

$$= \frac{-3(2\cos^2 t - 1)\cos^2 t\sin t + \cos^3 t(2\sin t\cos t)}{\cos 2t\sqrt{\cos 2t}} \quad \left[\because \begin{array}{l}\cos 2A = 2\cos^2 A - 1\\ \sin 2A = 2\sin A\cos A\end{array}\right]$$

$$= \frac{3\cos^2 t\sin t - 4\cos^4 t\sin t}{\cos 2t\sqrt{\cos 2t}}$$

$$\therefore \frac{dy}{dx} = \frac{\dfrac{dy}{dt}}{\dfrac{dx}{dt}} = \frac{dy}{dt} \times \frac{dt}{dx} = \frac{3\cos^2 t\sin t - 4\cos^4 t\sin t}{\cos 2t\sqrt{\cos 2t}} \times \frac{\cos 2t\sqrt{\cos 2t}}{3\sin^2 t\cos t - 4\sin^4 t\cos t}$$

$$= \frac{3\cos^2 t\sin t - 4\cos^4 t\sin t}{3\sin^2 t\cos t - 4\sin^4 t\cos t}$$

$$= \frac{\cos^2 t \sin t\,(3-4\cos^2 t)}{\sin^2 t \cos t\,(3-4\sin^2 t)} = \frac{\cos t\,(3-4\cos^2 t)}{\sin t\,(3-4\sin^2 t)} = \frac{3\cos t - 4\cos^3 t}{3\sin t - 4\sin^3 t}$$

$$= \frac{-\cos 3t}{\sin 3t} = -\cot 3t \qquad \left[\because \begin{array}{l}\cos 3A = 4\cos^3 A - 3\cos A\\ \sin 3A = 3\sin A - 4\sin^3 A\end{array}\right]$$

Quick Solution

We have $x = \frac{\sin^3 t}{\sqrt{\cos 2t}}$

On taking log both sides, we get $\log x = 3\log\sin t - \frac{1}{2}\log\cos 2t$

On differentiating both sides w.r.t t, we get

$$\frac{1}{x}\cdot\frac{dx}{dt} = 3\cdot\frac{1}{\sin t}\cdot\frac{d}{dt}(\sin t) - \frac{1}{2\cos 2t}\cdot\frac{d}{dt}(\cos 2t)$$

$$= 3\frac{1}{\sin t}\cdot\cos t - \frac{1}{2\cos 2t}(-\sin 2t)2 \Rightarrow \frac{dx}{dt} = x(3\cot t + \tan 2t)$$

and $y = \frac{\cos^3 t}{\sqrt{\cos 2t}} \Rightarrow \log y = 3\log\cos t - \frac{1}{2}\log\cos 2t$ (taking log both side)

$$\Rightarrow \frac{1}{y}\cdot\frac{dy}{dt} = \frac{3}{\cos t}\cdot\frac{d}{dt}(\cos t) - \frac{1}{2\cos 2t}\cdot\frac{d}{dt}(\cos 2t) \quad \text{(on differentiating)}$$

$$= \frac{3}{\cos t}(-\sin t) - \frac{1}{2\cos 2t}(-\sin 2t)2 \Rightarrow \frac{dy}{dt} = y(-3\tan t + \tan 2t)$$

$$\therefore \frac{dy}{dx} = \frac{\frac{dy}{dt}}{\frac{dx}{dt}} = \frac{y(-3\tan t + \tan 2t)}{x(3\cot t + \tan 2t)} = \frac{\cos^3 t\left(-3\tan t + \frac{2\tan t}{1-\tan^2 t}\right)}{\sin^3 t\cdot\left(\frac{3}{\tan t} + \frac{2\tan t}{1-\tan^2 t}\right)}$$

$$= \frac{1}{\tan^2 t}\left(\frac{-3\tan t + 3\tan^3 t + 2\tan t}{3 - 3\tan^2 t + 2\tan^2 t}\right) = \frac{1}{\tan t}\left(\frac{3\tan^2 t - 1}{3 - \tan^2 t}\right)$$

$$= \frac{3\tan^2 t - 1}{3\tan t - \tan^3 t} = -\left(\frac{1 - 3\tan^2 t}{3\tan t - \tan^3 t}\right) \Rightarrow \frac{dy}{dx} = \frac{1}{\tan 3t} = -\cot 3t$$

Question 8 $x = a\left(\cos t + \log\tan\frac{t}{2}\right), y = a\sin t.$

Sol. Given, $x = a\left(\cos t + \log\tan\frac{t}{2}\right), y = a\sin t$

On differentiating both sides w.r.t. t, we get

$$\frac{dx}{dt} = a\left\{-\sin t + \frac{1}{\tan\frac{t}{2}}.\sec^2\frac{t}{2}.\frac{1}{2}\right\} \qquad \left[\because \frac{d}{dx}(\log|x|) = \frac{1}{x}\right]$$

$$= a\left\{-\sin t + \frac{1}{2\sin\frac{t}{2}\cos\frac{t}{2}}\right\}$$

$$= a\left\{-\sin t + \frac{1}{\sin t}\right\} = a\left\{\frac{1-\sin^2 t}{\sin t}\right\} \quad \left(\because \sin t = 2\sin\frac{t}{2}\cos\frac{t}{2}\right)$$

$\Rightarrow$ $$\frac{dx}{dt} = \frac{a\cos^2 t}{\sin t} \quad (\because 1-\sin^2 t = \cos^2 t) \ldots\text{(i)}$$

and $$\frac{dy}{dt} = a\cos t \quad \ldots\text{(ii)}$$

$\therefore$ $$\frac{dy}{dx} = \frac{\frac{dy}{dt}}{\frac{dx}{dt}} \Rightarrow \frac{dy}{dx} = \frac{a\cos t}{\frac{a\cos^2 t}{\sin t}} = \tan t$$

Question 9 $x = a\sec\theta,\ y = b\tan\theta.$

Sol. Given, $x = a\sec\theta,\ y = b\tan\theta$

On differentiating both sides w.r.t.. θ, we get

$$\frac{dx}{d\theta} = a\sec\theta\tan\theta \text{ and } \frac{dy}{d\theta} = b\sec^2\theta$$

$\therefore$ $$\frac{dy}{dx} = \frac{\frac{dy}{d\theta}}{\frac{dx}{d\theta}} = \frac{b\sec^2\theta}{a\sec\theta\tan\theta} = \frac{b}{a}\left(\frac{\sec\theta}{\tan\theta}\right) = \frac{b}{a}\operatorname{cosec}\theta$$

Question 10 $x = a(\cos\theta + \theta\sin\theta),\ y = a(\sin\theta - \theta\cos\theta).$

Sol. Given, $x = a(\cos\theta + \theta\sin\theta),\ y = a(\sin\theta - \theta\cos\theta)$

On differentiating both sides w.r.t. θ, we get

$\therefore$ $$\frac{dx}{d\theta} = a\frac{d}{d\theta}(\cos\theta + \theta\sin\theta) = a\left\{\frac{d}{d\theta}(\cos\theta) + \frac{d}{d\theta}(\theta\sin\theta)\right\}$$

$$= a\{-\sin\theta + (\theta\cos\theta + \sin\theta.1)\} = a\theta\cos\theta$$

(using product rule in $\frac{d}{d\theta}(\theta\sin\theta)$)

and $$\frac{dy}{d\theta} = a\frac{d}{d\theta}(\sin\theta - \theta\cos\theta) = a\left\{\frac{d}{d\theta}(\sin\theta) - \frac{d}{d\theta}(\theta\cos\theta)\right\}$$

$$= a[\cos\theta - \{\theta(-\sin\theta) + \cos\theta.1\}] = a\theta\sin\theta$$

(using product rule in $\frac{d}{d\theta}(\theta\cos\theta)$)

$\therefore$ $$\frac{dy}{dx} = \frac{\frac{dy}{d\theta}}{\frac{dx}{d\theta}} = \frac{a\theta\sin\theta}{a\theta\cos\theta} = \tan\theta$$

Question 11 If $x = \sqrt{a^{\sin^{-1}t}},\ y = \sqrt{a^{\cos^{-1}t}}$, then show that $\frac{dy}{dx} = -\frac{y}{x}$.

Sol. Given, $x = \sqrt{a^{\sin^{-1}t}},\ y = \sqrt{a^{\cos^{-1}t}}$

i.e., $$x = a^{\frac{1}{2}\sin^{-1}t} \text{ and } y = a^{\frac{1}{2}\cos^{-t}t} \quad [\because (a^b)^c = a^{bc}]$$

On differentiating both sides w.r.t. t, we get

$$\frac{dx}{dt} = a^{\frac{1}{2}\sin^{-1}t} \log a \frac{d}{dt}\left(\frac{1}{2}\sin^{-1}t\right) \qquad \left[\because \frac{d}{dx}a^x = a^x \log a\right]$$

$$= a^{\frac{1}{2}\sin^{-1}t} \log a\left(\frac{1}{2\sqrt{1-t^2}}\right) = \frac{a^{\frac{1}{2}\sin^{-1}t}\log a}{2\sqrt{1-t^2}}$$

and $$\frac{dy}{dt} = a^{\frac{1}{2}\cos^{-1}t} \log a \frac{d}{dt}\left(\frac{1}{2}\cos^{-1}t\right) \qquad \text{(using chain rule)}$$

$$= a^{\frac{1}{2}\cos^{-1}t} \log a\left(\frac{-1}{2\sqrt{1-t^2}}\right) = \frac{-a^{\frac{1}{2}\cos^{-1}t}\log a}{2\sqrt{1-t^2}}$$

$$\Rightarrow \quad \frac{dy}{dx} = \frac{\frac{dy}{dt}}{\frac{dx}{dt}} = \frac{-a^{\frac{1}{2}\cos^{-1}t}}{a^{\frac{1}{2}\sin^{-1}t}} = -\frac{\sqrt{a^{\cos^{-1}t}}}{\sqrt{a^{\sin^{-1}t}}} = -\frac{y}{x}$$

Quick Solution

Given, $$x = \sqrt{a^{\sin^{-1}t}}$$

Taking log on both sides, $\log x = \log(a^{\sin^{-1}t})^{1/2} \Rightarrow \log x = \frac{1}{2}\log a^{\sin^{-1}t}$

$$\Rightarrow \quad \log x = \frac{1}{2}\sin^{-1}t \log a \Rightarrow \log x = \frac{1}{2}\log a \sin^{-1}t$$

On differentiating both sides w.r.t. t, we get

$$\frac{1}{x}.\frac{dx}{dt} = \frac{1}{2}\log a \frac{d}{dt}(\sin^{-1}t) = \frac{1}{2}\log a \frac{1}{\sqrt{1-t^2}}$$

$$\Rightarrow \quad \frac{dx}{dt} = \frac{x\log a}{2} \times \frac{1}{\sqrt{1-t^2}}$$

and $$y = \sqrt{a^{\cos^{-1}t}}$$

Taking log on both sides, $\log y = \log(a^{\cos^{-1}t})^{1/2}$

$$\Rightarrow \quad \log y = \frac{1}{2}\log a^{\cos^{-1}t} \Rightarrow \log y = \frac{1}{2}\cos^{-1}t \cdot \log a$$

On differentiating both sides w.r.t. t, we get

$$\frac{1}{y}.\frac{dy}{dt} = \frac{1}{2}\log a \times \left[\frac{-1}{\sqrt{1-t^2}}\right] \Rightarrow \frac{dy}{dt} = -\frac{y\log a}{2} \times \frac{1}{\sqrt{1-t^2}}$$

We know that

$$\frac{dy}{dx} = \frac{dy}{dt} \times \frac{dt}{dx} \Rightarrow \frac{dy}{dx} = \frac{-y\log a}{2} \times \frac{1}{\sqrt{1-t^2}} \times \frac{2 \times \sqrt{1-t^2}}{x\log a}$$

$$\Rightarrow \quad \frac{dy}{dx} = \frac{-y}{x}$$

Exercise 5.7

Direction (Q. Nos. 1 to 10) Find the second order derivative of the given functions.

◎ ***Thinking Process*** Find the first derivative $f'(x)$ of the function then differentiate $f'(x)$ again to obtain the second order derivative $f''(x)$.

Question 1 $x^2 + 3x + 2.$

Sol. Let $y = x^2 + 3x + 2,$

On differentiating both sides twice w.r.t. x, we get

$$\frac{dy}{dx} = 2x + 3$$

and
$$\frac{d^2y}{dx^2} = \frac{d}{dx}(2x + 3) = 2$$

Question 2 $x^{20}.$

Sol. Let $y = x^{20}$

On differentiating both sides twice w.r.t. x, we get $\frac{dy}{dx} = 20x^{19}$

and
$$\frac{d^2y}{dx^2} = \frac{d}{dx}(20x^{19}) = 20(19x^{18}) = 380x^{18}$$

Question 3 $x \cos x.$

Sol. Let $y = x\cos x$

On differentiating both sides twice w.r.t. x, we get

$$\frac{dy}{dx} = \frac{d}{dx}(x\cos x) = x\frac{d}{dx}\cos x + \cos x\frac{d}{dx}(x)$$

$$= x(-\sin x) + \cos x.\ 1 = -x\sin x + \cos x$$

(using product rule)

and
$$\frac{d^2y}{dx^2} = \frac{d}{dx}(-x\sin x + \cos x) = -\frac{d}{dx}(x\sin x) + \frac{d}{dx}(\cos x)$$

$$= -\{x\cos x + \sin x.\ 1\} - \sin x = -x\cos x - 2\sin x$$

(using product rule)

Question 4 $\log x.$

Sol. Let $y = \log x$

On differentiating both sides twice w.r.t. x, we get

$$\frac{dy}{dx} = \frac{1}{x} \text{ and } \frac{d^2y}{dx^2} = \frac{d}{dx}\left(\frac{1}{x}\right) = \frac{-1}{x^2}$$

Question 5 $x^3 \log x$.

Sol. Let $y = x^3 \log x$.

On differentiating both sides twice w.r.t. x, we get

$$\frac{dy}{dx} = \frac{d}{dx}(x^3 \log x) = x^3 \frac{d}{dx}(\log x) + \log x \frac{d}{dx}(x^3)$$

$$= x^3 \left(\frac{1}{x}\right) + (\log x)(3x^2) = x^2 (1 + 3\log x) \quad \text{(using product rule)}$$

and $$\frac{d^2y}{dx^2} = \frac{d}{dx}\{x^2 (1 + 3\log x)\} = x^2 \left(0 + \frac{3}{x}\right) + (1 + 3\log x)(2x)$$

$$= 3x + 2x(1 + 3\log x) = x(5 + 6\log x)$$

Question 6 $e^x \sin 5x$.

Sol. Let $y = e^x \sin 5x$.

On differentiating both sides twice w.r.t. x, we get

$$\frac{dy}{dx} = \frac{d}{dx}(e^x \sin 5x) = e^x \frac{d}{dx}(\sin 5x) + \sin 5x \frac{d}{dx}(e^x)$$

$$= e^x \cos 5x.5 + \sin 5x\, e^x \quad \text{(using product rule)}$$

$$= e^x (5\cos 5x + \sin 5x)$$

and $$\frac{d^2y}{dx^2} = \frac{d}{dx}\{e^x (5\cos 5x + \sin 5x)\}$$

$$= e^x \frac{d}{dx}(5\cos 5x + \sin 5x) + (5\cos 5x + \sin 5x)\frac{d}{dx} e^x \quad \text{(using product rule)}$$

$$= e^x \{-5\sin 5x \cdot 5 + \cos 5x \cdot 5\} + (5\cos 5x + \sin 5x)\, e^x$$

$$= e^x \{10\cos 5x - 24 \sin 5x\} = 2e^x (5\cos 5x - 12\sin 5x)$$

Question 7 $e^{6x} \cos 3x$.

Sol. Let $y = e^{6x} \cos 3x$

On differentiating both sides twice w.r.t.x, we get

$$\frac{dy}{dx} = \frac{d}{dx}(e^{6x} \cos 3x) = e^{6x} \frac{d}{dx}(\cos 3x) + \cos 3x \frac{d}{dx}(e)^{6x} \quad \text{(using product rule)}$$

$$= e^{6x}(-\sin 3x \cdot 3) + (\cos 3x)\, e^{6x} \cdot 6 = e^{6x} \{-3\sin 3x + 6\cos 3x\}$$

and $$\frac{d^2y}{dx^2} = \frac{d}{dx}\{e^{6x}(-3\sin 3x + 6\cos 3x)\}$$

$$= e^{6x} \frac{d}{dx}(-3\sin 3x + 6\cos 3x) + (-3\sin 3x + 6\cos 3x)\frac{d}{dx} e^{6x}$$

(using product rule)

$$= e^{6x}(-3\cos 3x \cdot 3 - 6\sin 3x \cdot 3) + (-3\sin 3x + 6\cos 3x)\, e^{6x} \cdot 6$$

$$= e^{6x} \{-9\cos 3x - 18\sin 3x - 18\sin 3x + 36\cos 3x\}$$

$$= e^{6x} \{27\cos 3x - 36 \sin 3x\} = 9e^{6x} \{3\cos 3x - 4\sin 3x\}$$

Question 8 $\tan^{-1} x$.

Sol. Let $y = \tan^{-1} x$

On differentiating both sides twice w.r.t. x, we get

$$\frac{dy}{dx} = \frac{d}{dx}(\tan^{-1} x) = \frac{1}{1+x^2}$$

and
$$\frac{d^2y}{dx^2} = \frac{d}{dx}\left(\frac{1}{1+x^2}\right) = \frac{d}{dx}(1+x^2)^{-1}$$

$$= -1(1+x^2)^{-2}\frac{d}{dx}(1+x^2)$$

$$= -1(1+x^2)^{-2}(0+2x) = \frac{-2x}{(1+x^2)^2}$$

Question 9 $\log(\log x)$.

Sol. Let $y = \log(\log x)$

On differentiating both sides twice w.r.t. x, we get

$$\frac{dy}{dx} = \frac{1}{\log x}\frac{d}{dx}(\log x) = \frac{1}{\log x}\cdot\frac{1}{x} = \frac{1}{x\log x}$$

and
$$\frac{d^2y}{dx^2} = \frac{d}{dx}\left(\frac{1}{x\log x}\right) = \frac{d}{dx}(x\log x)^{-1} = -1(x\log x)^{-2}\frac{d}{dx}(x\log x)$$

$$= -\frac{1}{(x\log x)^2}\left[x\frac{d}{dx}\log x + \log x\frac{d}{dx}(x)\right]$$

$$= \frac{-1}{(x\log x)^2}\left(x.\frac{1}{x} + \log x \,.\, 1\right) = \frac{-(1+\log x)}{(x\log x)^2}$$

Question 10 $\sin(\log x)$.

Sol. Let $y = \sin(\log x)$

On differentiating both sides twice w.r.t. x, we get

$$\frac{dy}{dx} = \cos(\log x)\frac{d}{dx}(\log x) = \cos(\log x)\frac{1}{x} = \frac{\cos(\log x)}{x}$$

and
$$\frac{d^2y}{dx^2} = \frac{d}{dx}\left(\frac{\cos(\log x)}{x}\right) = \frac{x\frac{d}{dx}(\cos(\log x)) - \cos(\log x)\frac{d}{dx}(x)}{x^2}$$

(using quotient rule)

$$= \frac{x\left\{-\sin(\log x)\cdot\frac{1}{x}\right\} - \cos(\log x)\,.\,1}{x^2}$$

$$= -\frac{\sin(\log x) + \cos(\log x)}{x^2}$$

Question 11 If $y = 5\cos x - 3\sin x$, prove that $\frac{d^2y}{dx^2} + y = 0$.

Sol. Given, $y = 5\cos x - 3\sin x$

On differentiating both sides twice w.r.t. x, we get

$$\frac{dy}{dx} = -5\sin x - 3\cos x$$

and $$\frac{d^2y}{dx^2} = \frac{d}{dx}(-5\sin x - 3\cos x) = -5\cos x + 3\sin x$$

$$= -(5\cos x - 3\sin x) = -y$$

$\Rightarrow \quad \frac{d^2y}{dx^2} + y = 0.$ **Hence proved.**

Question 12 If $y = \cos^{-1} x$, then find $\frac{d^2y}{dx^2}$ in terms of y alone.

Sol. We have, $y = \cos^{-1} x$

$$\frac{dy}{dx} = \frac{-1}{\sqrt{1-x^2}} = -(1-x^2)^{-\frac{1}{2}} \quad \text{(on differentiating w.r.t. } x\text{)}$$

$$\frac{d^2y}{dx} = -\left(-\frac{1}{2}(1-x^2)^{\frac{-3}{2}}\right)\frac{d}{dx}(1-x^2) \quad \text{(by chain rule)}$$

$$= \frac{1}{2(1-x^2)^{\frac{3}{2}}}(-2x) = \frac{-x}{(1-x^2)^{\frac{3}{2}}} \quad \text{...(i)}$$

We have, $y = \cos^{-1} x \Rightarrow x = \cos y$ put in (i)

$$\frac{d^2y}{dx^2} = \frac{-\cos y}{(1-\cos^2 y)^{\frac{3}{2}}} = \frac{-\cos y}{(\sin^2 y)^{\frac{3}{2}}} = \frac{-\cos y}{\sin^3 y}$$

$$= -\frac{\cos y}{\sin y \cdot \sin^2 y} = -\cot y \operatorname{cosec}^2 y$$

Quick Solution

Given, $y = \cos^{-1} x \Rightarrow x = \cos y$

On differentiating both sides w.r.t. y, we get

$$\frac{dx}{dy} = -\sin y \Rightarrow \frac{dy}{dx} = -\operatorname{cosec} y \quad \text{...(i)}$$

Again, on differentiating both sides w.r.t. x, we get

$$\frac{d^2y}{dx^2} = \frac{d}{dx}(-\operatorname{cosec} y) = -(-\operatorname{cosec} y \cot y)\frac{dy}{dx}$$

$$= \operatorname{cosec} y \cot y(-\operatorname{cosec} y) = -\cot y \cdot \operatorname{cosec}^2 y \quad \text{[from Eq. (i)]}$$

Question 13 If $y = 3\cos(\log x) + 4\sin(\log x)$, show that $x^2 y_2 + xy_1 + y = 0$.

Sol. Given, $y = 3\cos(\log x) + 4\sin(\log x)$ ...(i)

On differentiating both sides w.r.t. x, we get

$$\frac{dy}{dx} = y_1 = -3\sin(\log x)\frac{d}{dx}(\log x) + 4\cos(\log x)\frac{d}{dx}\log x \quad \left(\because \frac{dy}{dx} = y_1\right)$$

$$= -3\sin(\log x)\frac{1}{x} + 4\cos(\log x)\frac{1}{x}$$

Multiplying by x, we get

$$xy_1 = -3\sin(\log x) + 4\cos(\log x) \quad \text{...(ii)}$$

Again, on differentiating both sides w.r.t. x, we obtain

$$xy_2 + y_1 \cdot 1 = -3\cos(\log x)\frac{d}{dx}(\log x) - 4\sin(\log x)\frac{d}{dx}\log x$$

$$= -3\cos(\log x)\frac{1}{x} - 4\sin(\log x)\frac{1}{x}$$

Multiplying throughout by x, we have

$$x^2 y_2 + xy_1 = -(3\cos(\log x) + 4\sin(\log x)) \quad \text{[from Eq. (i)]}$$

$\Rightarrow$ $$x^2 y_2 + xy_1 = -y$$

$\Rightarrow$ $$x^2 y_2 + xy_1 + y = 0$$

Question 14 If $y = Ae^{mx} + Be^{nx}$, show that

$$\frac{d^2y}{dx^2} - (m+n)\frac{dy}{dx} + mny = 0.$$

Sol. Given, $y = Ae^{mx} + Be^{nx}$ ...(i)

On differentiating both sides twice w.r.t. x, we get

$$\frac{dy}{dx} = Ae^{mx}\frac{d}{dx}(mx) + Be^{nx}\frac{d}{dx}(nx) = Ae^{mx}m + Be^{nx}n \quad \text{...(ii)}$$

and $$\frac{d^2y}{dx^2} = m^2 Ae^{mx} + n^2 Be^{nx} \quad \text{...(iii)}$$

Using Eqs. (i), (ii) and (iii), we have

$$\frac{d^2y}{dx^2} - (m+n)\frac{dy}{dx} + mny$$

$$= m^2 Ae^{mx} + n^2 Be^{nx} - (m+n)\{Ame^{mx} + nBe^{nx}\} + mn\{Ae^{mx} + Be^{nx}\}$$

$$= m^2 Ae^{mx} + n^2 Be^{nx} - m^2 Ae^{mx} - mnBe^{nx} - mnAe^{mx} - n^2 Be^{nx} + mnAe^{mx} + mnBe^{nx}$$

i.e., $$\frac{d^2y}{dx^2} - (m+n)\frac{dy}{dx} + mny = 0.$$

Hence Proved.

Question 15 If $y = 500\, e^{7x} + 600\, e^{-7x}$, show that $\frac{d^2y}{dx^2} = 49\, y$.

Sol. Given, $y = 500\, e^{7x} + 600\, e^{-7x}$ ...(i)

On differentiating both sides twice w.r.t. x, we get

$$\frac{dy}{dx} = 500 e^{7x} \frac{d}{dx}(7x) + 600 e^{-7x} \frac{d}{dx}(-7x) = 500\, e^{7x} .7 + 600 e^{-7x} .(-7)$$

and $$\frac{d^2y}{dx^2} = (7 \times 500) e^{7x} .7 - (7 \times 600) e^{-7x}\,(-7)$$

$$= 49\,\{500 e^{7x} + 600 e^{-7x}\} \Rightarrow \frac{d^2y}{dx^2} = 49\, y.$$ **Hence Proved.**

Question 16 If $e^y\,(x+1) = 1$, show that $\frac{d^2y}{dx^2} = \left(\frac{dy}{dx}\right)^2$.

Sol. Given, $e^y\,(x + 1) = 1$

$$\Rightarrow \quad e^y = \frac{1}{x+1}$$

On differentiating both sides w.r.t. x, we get

$$e^y \frac{dy}{dx} = -\frac{1}{(x+1)^2} \Rightarrow \left(\frac{1}{x+1}\right)\frac{dy}{dx} = -\frac{1}{(x+1)^2} \qquad \left(\because e^y = \frac{1}{x+1}\right)$$

$$\Rightarrow \quad \frac{dy}{dx} = -\frac{x+1}{(x+1)^2} = -\frac{1}{x+1}$$

Again, on differentiating both sides w.r.t. x, we get

$$\frac{d^2y}{dx^2} = \frac{1}{(x+1)^2} \quad \text{or} \quad \frac{d^2y}{dx^2} = \left(-\frac{1}{x+1}\right)^2 = \left(\frac{dy}{dx}\right)^2$$

Question 17 If $y = (\tan^{-1} x)^2$, show that $(x^2 + 1)^2 y_2 + 2x\,(x^2 + 1)\, y_1 = 2$.

Sol. Given, $y = (\tan^{-1} x)^2$

On differentiating both siedes w.r.t. x, we get

$$\frac{dy}{dx} = 2\tan^{-1} x \frac{d}{dx}(\tan^{-1} x) = 2\,(\tan^{-1} x)\frac{1}{1+x^2}$$

or $$(1 + x^2)\, y_1 = 2\tan^{-1} x \qquad \left(\because \frac{dy}{dx} = y_1\right)$$

Again, on differentiating both sides w.r.t. x, we get

$$(1 + x^2)\frac{dy_1}{dx} + y_1 \frac{d}{dx}(1 + x^2) = \frac{2}{1+x^2} \Rightarrow (1 + x^2) y_2 + y_1\,(0 + 2x) = \frac{2}{1+x^2}$$

$$\left(\because \frac{d}{dx}(y_1) = y_2\right)$$

$$\Rightarrow \quad (1 + x^2)^2 y_2 + 2x\,(1 + x^2) y_1 = 2$$ **Hence Proved.**

Miscellaneous Exercise

Direction (Q. Nos. 1 to 11) Differentiate given problems w.r.t. x.

Question 1 $(3x^2 - 9x + 5)^9$.

Sol. Let $y = (3x^2 - 9x + 5)^9$

On differentiating both sides w.r.t. x, we get

$$\frac{dy}{dx} = 9(3x^2 - 9x + 5)^8 \frac{d}{dx}(3x^2 - 9x + 5) \quad \text{(by chain Rule)}$$

$$= 9(3x^2 - 9x + 5)^8 (6x - 9)$$

$$= 9 \times 3(2x - 3)(3x^2 - 9x + 5)^8$$

$$= 27(2x - 3)(3x^2 - 9x + 5)^8$$

Question 2 $\sin^3 x + \cos^6 x$.

Sol. Let $y = \sin^3 x + \cos^6 x$

On differentiating both sides w.r.t. x, we get

$$\frac{dy}{dx} = \frac{d}{dx}(\sin^3 x + \cos^6 x) = \frac{d}{dx}(\sin x)^3 + \frac{d}{dx}(\cos x)^6$$

$$= 3(\sin x)^{3-1} \frac{d}{dx}(\sin x) + 6(\cos x)^{6-1} \frac{d}{dx}(\cos x) \quad \text{(by chain Rule)}$$

$$= 3\sin^2 x \cos x + 6\cos^5 x(-\sin x)$$

$$= 3\sin^2 x \cos x - 6\sin x \cos^5 x$$

$$= 3\sin x \cos x(\sin x - 2\cos^4 x)$$

Question 3 $(5x)^{3\cos 2x}$.

Sol. Let $y = (5x)^{3\cos 2x}$

Taking log on both sides, we get $\log y = \log(5x)^{3\cos 2x} = 3\cos 2x(\log 5x)$

On differentiating both sides w.r.t x, we get

$$\frac{1}{y}\frac{dy}{dx} = 3\cos 2x \frac{d}{dx}(\log 5x) + \log 5x \frac{d}{dx}(3\cos 2x) \quad \text{[using product rule]}$$

$$= (3\cos 2x)\left(\frac{1}{5x}.5\right) + (\log 5x)\{3(-\sin 2x).2\} \quad \text{(by chain Rule)}$$

$$\Rightarrow \frac{dy}{dx} = y\left\{\frac{3\cos 2x}{x} - 6(\sin 2x)(\log 5x)\right\}$$

$$\Rightarrow \frac{dy}{dx} = (5x)^{3\cos 2x}\left\{\frac{3\cos 2x}{x} - 6\sin 2x \log 5x\right\}$$

Question 4 $\sin^{-1}(x\sqrt{x}), 0 \le x \le 1.$

Sol. Let $y = \sin^{-1}(x\sqrt{x})$

On differentiating both sides w.r.t. x, we get

$$\Rightarrow \quad \frac{dy}{dx} = \frac{d}{dx}(\sin^{-1} x\sqrt{x})$$

$$\Rightarrow \quad \frac{dy}{dx} = \frac{1}{\sqrt{1-(x\sqrt{x})^2}}\frac{d}{dx}(x^{3/2})$$

$$\Rightarrow \quad \frac{dy}{dx} = \frac{\frac{3}{2}x^{1/2}}{\sqrt{1-x^3}}$$

$$\Rightarrow \quad \frac{dy}{dx} = \frac{3}{2}\frac{\sqrt{x}}{\sqrt{1-x^3}}$$

Question 5 $\dfrac{\cos^{-1}\frac{x}{2}}{\sqrt{2x+7}}, -2 < x < 2.$

Sol. Let $y = \dfrac{\cos^{-1}\frac{x}{2}}{\sqrt{2x+7}}, -2 < x < 2$

On differentiating both sides w.r.t. x, we get

$$\frac{dy}{dx} = \frac{\sqrt{2x+7}\,\frac{d}{dx}\left(\cos^{-1}\frac{x}{2}\right) - \cos^{-1}\frac{x}{2}\,\frac{d}{dx}(\sqrt{2x+7})}{2x+7}$$

$$\left[\because \frac{d}{dx}\left(\frac{u}{v}\right) = \frac{v\frac{d}{dx}(u) - u\frac{d}{dx}(v)}{v^2}\right]$$

$$= \frac{\sqrt{2x+7}\,\frac{-1}{\sqrt{1-\left(\frac{x^2}{4}\right)}}\cdot\frac{1}{2} - \cos^{-1}\left(\frac{x}{2}\right)\cdot\frac{2}{2\sqrt{2x+7}}}{2x+7}$$

$$= \frac{-\frac{\sqrt{2x+7}}{\sqrt{4-x^2}} - \frac{\cos^{-1}\left(\frac{x}{2}\right)}{\sqrt{2x+7}}}{2x+7} = \frac{-\left\{2x+7+\cos^{-1}\left(\frac{x}{2}\right)\sqrt{4-x^2}\right\}}{\sqrt{4-x^2}\,(2x+7)^{3/2}}$$

$$= -\left[\frac{1}{\sqrt{4-x^2}\,\sqrt{2x+7}} + \frac{\cos^{-1}\frac{x}{2}}{(2x+7)^{3/2}}\right]$$

Question 6 $\cot^{-1}\left[\dfrac{\sqrt{1+\sin x}+\sqrt{1-\sin x}}{\sqrt{1+\sin x}-\sqrt{1-\sin x}}\right], 0<x<\dfrac{\pi}{2}.$

◎ *Thinking Process* Use the indentities $\sin^2 x+\cos^2 x=1$, $\sin x = 2\sin\dfrac{x}{2}\cos\dfrac{x}{2}$ and the identities $(a+b)^2=a^2+b^2+2ab$ and $(a-b)^2=a^2+b^2-2ab$ to simplify inside the bracket.

Sol. Let $y=\cot^{-1}\left[\dfrac{\sqrt{1+\sin x}+\sqrt{1-\sin x}}{\sqrt{1+\sin x}-\sqrt{1-\sin x}}\right]$

$$=\cot^{-1}\left[\frac{\left(\sin\frac{x}{2}+\cos\frac{x}{2}\right)+\left(\cos\frac{x}{2}-\sin\frac{x}{2}\right)}{\left(\sin\frac{x}{2}+\cos\frac{x}{2}\right)-\left(\cos\frac{x}{2}-\sin\frac{x}{2}\right)}\right]$$

$$\left[\begin{array}{l}\because 1+\sin x=\sin^2\frac{x}{2}+\cos^2\frac{x}{2}+2\sin\frac{x}{2}.\cos\frac{x}{2}=\left(\sin\frac{x}{2}+\cos\frac{x}{2}\right)^2\\ \text{and } 1-\sin x=\sin\ \frac{x}{2}+\cos^2\frac{x}{2}-2\sin\frac{x}{2}\cos\frac{x}{2}=\left(\cos\frac{x}{2}-\sin\frac{x}{2}\right)^2\end{array}\right]$$

$$=\cot^{-1}\left(\frac{2\cos(x/2)}{2\sin(x/2)}\right)=\cot^{-1}\left(\cot\left(\frac{x}{2}\right)\right)=\frac{x}{2}\Rightarrow\frac{dy}{dx}=\frac{1}{2}$$

Note If $\dfrac{\pi}{2}<x<\pi$, then $\sqrt{1-\sin x}=\sin\dfrac{x}{2}-\cos\dfrac{x}{2}$.

Question 7 $(\log x)^{\log x}, x>1$

◎ *Thinking Process* Take logarithm on both sides of the given equation $y=(\log x)^{\log x}$ and then differentiate w.r.t. x.

Sol. Let $y=(\log x)^{\log x}$

Taking log on both sides, we get $\log y=\log[(\log x)^{\log x}]$

$\Rightarrow$ $\log y=\log x\log(\log x)$ $(\because \log m^n = n\log m)$

On differentiating both sides w.r.t. x, we have

$$\frac{1}{y}\frac{dy}{dx}=(\log x)\frac{d}{dx}\log(\log x)+\log\log(x)\frac{d}{dx}\log(x) \quad \text{[by product rule]}$$

$$=(\log x)\frac{1}{\log x}\cdot\frac{1}{x}+\log(\log x)\frac{1}{x}=\frac{1}{x}\{1+\log(\log x)\} \quad \text{[by Chain rule]}$$

$$\Rightarrow \frac{dy}{dx}=\frac{y}{x}\{1+\log(\log x)\}$$

$$=\frac{(\log x)^{\log x}}{x}(1+\log(\log x))=(\log x)^{\log x}\left[\frac{1}{x}+\frac{\log(\log x)}{x}\right]$$

Question 8 $\cos(a\cos x + b\sin x)$, for some constants a and b.

Sol. Let $y = \cos(a\cos x + b\sin x)$

On differentiating both sides w.r.t. x, we get

$$\frac{dy}{dx} = \frac{d}{dx}\{\cos(a\cos x + b\sin x) = -\sin(a\cos x + b\sin x)\frac{d}{dx}(a\cos x + b\sin x)$$

(by chain Rule)

$$= -\sin(a\cos x + b\sin x)\{-a\sin x + b\cos x\}$$
$$= \{a\sin x - b\cos x\}\sin(a\cos x + b\sin x)$$

Question 9 $(\sin x - \cos x)^{(\sin x - \cos x)}, \frac{\pi}{4} < x < \frac{3\pi}{4}$

Sol. Let $y = (\sin x - \cos x)^{(\sin x - \cos x)}$

Taking log on both sides w.r.t. x, we get

$$\log y = \log\{(\sin x - \cos x)^{(\sin x - \cos x)}\}$$

$\Rightarrow$ $\log y = (\sin x - \cos x)\log(\sin x - \cos x)$ $(\because \log m^n = n\log m)$

On differentiating both sides w.r.t. x, we obtain

$$\frac{1}{y}\frac{dy}{dx} = (\sin x - \cos x).\frac{\cos x + \sin x}{\sin x - \cos x} + \{\log(\sin x - \cos x)\}(\cos x + \sin x)$$

$$\Rightarrow \frac{dy}{dx} = y(\cos x + \sin x)\{1 + \log(\sin x - \cos x)\}$$

$$= (\cos x + \sin x)(\sin x - \cos x)^{(\sin x - \cos x)}\{1 + \log(\sin x - \cos x)\}$$

Question 10 $x^x + x^a + a^x + a^a$, for some fixed $a > 0$ and $x > 0$.

◎ *Thinking Process* Use the formulae $\frac{d}{dx}(u^v) = u^v\frac{d}{dx}(v\log u)$ and $\frac{d}{dx}a^x = a^x\log a$ to find $\frac{dx^x}{dx}$ and $\frac{da^x}{dx}$.

Sol. Let $y = x^x = x^a + a^x + a^a$

On differentiating both sides w.r.t. x, we get

$$\frac{dy}{dx} = \frac{d}{dx}(x^x + x^a + a^x + a^a)$$

$$\Rightarrow \frac{d}{dx}(x^x) + \frac{d}{dx}(x^a) + \frac{d}{dx}(a^x) + \frac{d}{dx}(a^a)$$

$$= x^x\frac{d}{dx}(x\log x) + ax^{a-1} + a^x\log a + 0 \quad \left(\because \frac{d}{dx}(u^v) = u^v\frac{d}{dx}(v\log u)\right)$$

$$= x^x\left(x\frac{1}{x} + \log x.1\right) + ax^{a-1} + a^x\log a$$

$$= x^x(1 + \log x) + ax^{a-1} + a^x\log a$$

Question 11 $x^{x^2-3}+(x-3)^{x^2}$, for $x>3$.

Sol. Let $y = x^{x^2-3} + (x-3)^{x^2}$

Again, let $u = x^{x^2-3}$

and $v = (x-3)^{x^2}$

$\therefore$ $y = u + v$

On differentiating both sides w.r.t.x, we get

$$\frac{dy}{dx} = \frac{du}{dx} + \frac{dv}{dx} \quad \text{...(i)}$$

and $u = x^{x^2-3}$

Taking log on both sides, we get

$$\log u = \log (x)^{x^2-3} = (x^2 - 3)\log x \quad (\because \log m^n = n \log m)$$

On differentiating both sides w.r.t. x, we get

$$\frac{1}{u}\cdot\frac{du}{dx} = (x^2-3)\cdot\frac{1}{x} + 2x\log x$$

$$\Rightarrow \frac{du}{dx} = u\left[\frac{x^2-3}{x} + 2x\log x\right]$$

$$\Rightarrow \frac{du}{dx} = x^{x^2-3}\left[\frac{x^2-3}{x} + 2x\log x\right]$$

and $v = (x-3)^{x^2}$

Taking log on both sides, we get

$$\log v = \log (x-3)^{x^2}$$

$$= x^2 \log (x-3)$$

On differentiating both sides w.r.t.x, we get

$$\frac{1}{v}\frac{dv}{dx} = x^2\frac{d}{dx}\log (x-3) + \log (x-3)\frac{d}{dx}x^2$$

$$\Rightarrow = x^2\cdot\frac{1}{x-3} + 2x\log (x-3)$$

$$\Rightarrow \frac{dv}{dx} = v\left[\frac{x^2}{x-3} + 2x.\log (x-3)\right]$$

$$\Rightarrow \frac{dv}{dx} = (x-3)^{x^2}\left[\frac{x^2}{x-3} + 2x.\log (x-3)\right]$$

Putting the values of $\frac{du}{dx}$ and $\frac{dv}{dx}$ in Eq. (i), we get

$$\frac{dy}{dx} = x^{x^2-3}\left[\frac{x^2-3}{x} + 2x\log x\right] + (x-3)^{x^2}\left[\frac{x^2}{x-3} + 2x\log (x-3)\right]$$

Question 12 Find $\frac{dy}{dx}$, if $y = 12(1-\cos t)$,

$$x = 10(t - \sin t), -\frac{\pi}{2} < t < \frac{\pi}{2}.$$

Sol. Given, $y = 12(1-\cos t)$, $x = 10(t - \sin t)$

On differentiating both equations w.r.t. t, we get

$$\frac{dy}{dt} = 12(0 + \sin t) = 12\sin t$$

and
$$\frac{dx}{dt} = 10(1 - \cos t)$$

$\therefore$
$$\frac{dy}{dx} = \frac{\frac{dy}{dt}}{\frac{dx}{dt}}$$

$$= \frac{12\sin t}{10(1-\cos t)}$$

$$= \frac{12 \times 2\sin(t/2)\cos(t/2)}{10\{2\sin^2(t/2)\}}$$

$$= \frac{6}{5}\cot\left(\frac{t}{2}\right)$$

$(\because \sin 2A = 2\sin A\cos A \text{ and } \cos 2A = 1 - 2\sin^2 A)$

Question 13 Find $\frac{dy}{dx}$, if $y = \sin^{-1} x + \sin^{-1}\sqrt{1-x^2}$, $-1 \le x \le 1$.

Sol. Given, $y = \sin^{-1} x + \sin^{-1}\sqrt{1-x^2}$

On putting $\sin^{-1} x = \theta$

$\Rightarrow$ $x = \sin\theta$, we get

$$y = \theta + \sin^{-1}\sqrt{1-\sin^2\theta}$$

$\Rightarrow$ $y = \theta + \sin^{-1}(\cos\theta)$ $[\because 1 - \sin^2\theta = \cos^2\theta]$

$\Rightarrow$ $y = \theta + \sin^{-1}\sin\left(\frac{\pi}{2} - \theta\right)$

$\Rightarrow$ $y = \theta + \frac{\pi}{2} - \theta = \frac{\pi}{2}$ $\left(\therefore \sin\left(\frac{\pi}{2} - A\right) = \cos A\right)$

$\Rightarrow$ $y = \frac{\pi}{2}$

On differentiating both sides w.r.t. x, we get $\frac{dy}{dx} = 0$

Question 14 If $x\sqrt{1+y}+y\sqrt{1+x}=0$, for $-1<x<1$, prove that $\frac{dy}{dx}=-\frac{1}{(1+x)^2}$.

Sol. Given, $x\sqrt{1+y}+y\sqrt{1+x}=0$

$\Rightarrow$ $x\sqrt{1+y}=-y\sqrt{1+x}$ ...(i)

On squaring both sides of Eq.(i), we get

$$x^2(1+y)=y^2(1+x)$$

$\Rightarrow$ $x^2-y^2+x^2y-y^2x=0 \Rightarrow (x-y)(x+y)+xy(x-y)=0$

$\Rightarrow$ $(x-y)\{x+y+xy\}=0 \Rightarrow x-y=0$ or $x+y+xy=0$

$\Rightarrow$ $y=x$ or $y\cdot(1+x)=-x \Rightarrow y=x$ or $y=\frac{-x}{1+x}$

But $y=x$ does not satisfy the given equation.

So, we consider only $y=-\frac{x}{1+x}$

On differentiating both sides w.r.t. x, we get

$$\frac{dy}{dx}=\frac{d}{dx}\left(\frac{-x}{1+x}\right)=-\frac{(1+x)\frac{d}{dx}(x)-x\frac{d}{dx}(1+x)}{(1+x)^2}$$

$$=-\frac{(1+x).1-x(0+1)}{(1+x)^2}=-\frac{1}{(1+x)^2}$$ **Hence Proved.**

Question 15 If $(x-a)^2+(y-b)^2=c^2$, for some $c>0$, prove that $\frac{\left[1+\left(\frac{dy}{dx}\right)^2\right]^{\frac{3}{2}}}{\frac{d^2y}{dx^2}}$ is a constant independent of a and b.

Sol. Given, $(x-a)^2+(y-b)^2=c^2$ ...(i)

On differentiating both sides w.r.t. x, we get

$$2(x-a)+2(y-b)\frac{dy}{dx}=0 \Rightarrow \frac{dy}{dx}=-\frac{x-a}{y-b}$$ ...(ii)

Again, on differentiating both sides w.r.t. x, we get

$$\frac{d^2y}{dx^2}=-\frac{(y-b).1-(x-a)\frac{dy}{dx}}{(y-b)^2}$$ $\left(\because \frac{d}{dx}\left(\frac{u}{v}\right)=\frac{v\frac{du}{dx}-u\frac{dv}{dx}}{v^2}\right)$

$$=-\frac{(y-b).1-(x-a)\left(-\frac{x-a}{y-b}\right)}{(y-b)^2}$$ (using Eq. (ii))

$$= -\frac{(y-b)^2+(x-a)^2}{(y-b)^3} = -\frac{c^2}{(y-b)^3}$$

Now, $$\frac{\left[1+\left(\frac{dy}{dx}\right)^2\right]^{3/2}}{\frac{d^2y}{dx^2}} = \frac{\left[1+\left(\frac{x-a}{y-b}\right)^2\right]^{3/2}}{-\frac{c^2}{(y-b)^3}} = \frac{\{(y-b)^2+(x-a)^2\}^{3/2}}{\{(y-b)^2\}^{3/2}\frac{(-c^2)}{(y-b)^3}}$$

$$= \frac{(c^2)^{3/2}}{-c^2} = \frac{c^3}{-c^2} = -c,$$

which is independent of a and b. **Hence Proved.**

Question 16 If $\cos y = x\cos(a+y)$, with $\cos a \neq \pm 1$, prove that $\frac{dy}{dx} = \frac{\cos^2(a+y)}{\sin a}$.

Sol. Given, $\cos y = x\cos(a+y)$

$$\Rightarrow \quad x = \frac{\cos y}{\cos(a+y)}$$

On differentiating both sides w.r.t. y, we get

$$\frac{dx}{dy} = \frac{d}{dy}\left\{\frac{\cos y}{\cos(a+y)}\right\}$$

$$= \frac{\cos(a+y)(-\sin y) - \cos y(-\sin(a+y).1)}{\cos^2(a+y)}$$

(using quotient rule)

$$= \frac{\sin(a+y)\cos y - \cos(a+y)\sin y}{\cos^2(a+y)}$$

$$= \frac{\sin(a+y-y)}{\cos^2(a+y)} = \frac{\sin a}{\cos^2(a+y)}$$

$(\because \sin(A-B) = \sin A\cos B - \cos A\sin B)$

$$\therefore \quad \frac{dy}{dx} = \frac{1}{\frac{dx}{dy}} = \frac{\cos^2(a+y)}{\sin a}.$$ **Hence Proved.**

Question 17 If $x = a(\cos t + t\sin t)$ and $y = a(\sin t - t\cos t)$, find $\frac{d^2y}{dx^2}$.

mention the domain in which it is valid.

Sol. Given, $x = a(\cos t + t\sin t)$ and $y = a(\sin t - t\cos t)$

On differtiating both sides w.r.t. t, we get

$$\frac{dx}{dt} = a\left[\frac{d}{dt}\cos t + \left(t\frac{d}{dt}(\sin t) + \sin t\frac{d}{dt}(t)\right)\right]$$

$$\Rightarrow \quad \frac{dx}{dt} = a\{-\sin t + (t\cos t + \sin t.\ 1)\} = at\cos t$$

and
$$\frac{dy}{dt} = a\left[\frac{d}{dt}\sin t - \left(t\frac{d}{dt}\cos t + \cos t.1\right)\right]$$

$$\Rightarrow \quad \frac{dy}{dt} = a\ \{\cos t - (t(-\sin t) + \cos t.\ 1)\} = at\sin t$$

$$\therefore \quad \frac{dy}{dx} = \frac{\frac{dy}{dt}}{\frac{dx}{dt}} = \frac{at\sin t}{at\cos t} = \tan t \quad i.e., \quad \frac{dy}{dx} = \tan t \qquad \ldots(i)$$

On differentiating again both sides w.r.t. x, we get

$$\frac{d^2y}{dx^2} = \frac{d}{dx}(\tan t) = \frac{d}{dt}(\tan t)\frac{dt}{dx} = \frac{\sec^2 t}{at\cos t} \qquad \left\{\because \frac{dx}{dt} = at\cos t\right\}$$

$$= \frac{1}{at}\sec^3 t$$

The result is valid for all real t except 0 and odd multiples of $\frac{\pi}{2}$.

Mistake Alert If $\frac{dy}{dx} = f(t)$

Then $\frac{d^2y}{dx^2} = f'(t)\cdot\frac{dt}{dx}$

Question 18 If $f(x) = |x|^3$, show that $f''(x)$ exists for all x and find it.

Sol. Here,
$$f(x) = |x|^3 = \begin{cases} x^3, & x \geq 0 \\ -x^3, & x < 0 \end{cases}$$

When $x > 0$, $\quad f(x) = |x|^3 = x^3$

On differentiating both sides w.r.t.x, we get

$$\frac{d}{dx}[f(x)] = \frac{d}{dx}(x^3) \Rightarrow f'(x) = 3x^2$$

Again, on differentiating both sides w.r.t. x, we get

$$\frac{d}{dx}[f'(x)] = \frac{d}{dx}(3x^2) \Rightarrow f''(x) = 6x$$

Hence, $f''(x)$ exists for $x > 0$

When $x < 0$,

$$f(x) = |x|^3 = -x^3$$

On differentiating both sides w.r.t. x, we get

$$\frac{d}{dx}[f(x)] = \frac{d}{dx}(-x^3) \Rightarrow f'(x) = -3x^2$$

Again, on differentiating both sides w.r.t.x, we get

$$\frac{d}{dx}[f'(x)] = \frac{d}{dx}(-3x^2) = -6x$$

$\Rightarrow \quad f''(x) = -6x$. Hence, $f''(x)$ exists for $x < 0$

We need to check differentiability of $f(x)$ at $x = 0$

Now, $Lf'(0) = \lim_{h\to 0} \dfrac{f(0-h)-f(0)}{-h} = \lim_{h\to 0} \dfrac{-h^3-0}{-h} = 0$

and $Rf'(0) = \lim_{h\to 0} \dfrac{f(0+h)-f(0)}{h} = \lim_{h\to 0} \dfrac{h^3-0}{h} = 0$

$\therefore$ $Lf'(0) = Rf'(0)$, so $f(x)$ is differentiable at $x = 0$ and derivative of $f(x)$ is given by

$$f'(x) = \begin{cases} 3x^2, & x \geq 0 \\ -3x^2, & x < 0 \end{cases}$$

Now, we need to check differentiability of $f'(x)$ at $x = 0$

$$\because \quad Lf''(0) = \lim_{h\to 0} \frac{f'(0-h)-f'(0)}{-h}$$

$$= \lim_{h\to 0} \frac{-3(-h)^2 - 3(0)^2}{-h} = \lim_{h\to 0} \frac{-3h^2}{0-h} = 0$$

and $Rf''(0) = \lim_{h\to 0} \dfrac{f'(0+h)-f'(0)}{h}$

$$= \lim_{h\to 0} \frac{3(h)^2 - 3(0)^2}{h} = \lim_{h\to 0} \frac{3h^2}{h} = 0$$

$\therefore$ $Lf''(0) = Rf'(0)$, so $f'(x)$ is differentiable at $x = 0$

Hence, $f'(x)$ exists for $x = 0$.

Therefore, $f'(x)$ exists for all real values of x and $f'(x) = \begin{cases} 6x, & x \geq 0 \\ -6x, & x < 0 \end{cases}$

Question 19 Using the fact that $\sin(A+B) = \sin A \cos B + \cos A \sin B$ and differentiation, obtain the sum formula for cosines.

Sol. We have, $\sin(A+B) = \sin A \cos B + \cos A \sin B$

On differentiating both sides w.r.t. x, we get

$$\cos(A+B)\left(\frac{dA}{dx} + \frac{dB}{dx}\right) = \left(\sin A \frac{d}{dx}\cos B + \cos B \frac{d}{dx}\sin A\right) + \left(\cos A \frac{d}{dx}\sin B + \sin B \frac{d}{dx}\cos A\right)$$

(using product rule)

$$= \sin A(-\sin B)\frac{dB}{dx} + \cos B \cos A \frac{dA}{dx} + \cos A \cos B \frac{dB}{dx} + \sin B(-\sin A)\frac{dA}{dx}$$

$$= \frac{dA}{dx}(\cos A \cos B - \sin A \sin B) + \frac{dB}{dx}(\cos A \cos B - \sin A \sin B)$$

$$\Rightarrow \cos(A+B)\left(\frac{dA}{dx} + \frac{dB}{dx}\right) = (\cos A + \cos B - \sin A \sin B)\left(\frac{dB}{dx} + \frac{dA}{dx}\right)$$

$$\Rightarrow \qquad \cos(A+B) = \cos A \cos B - \sin A \sin B$$

Question 20 Does there exist a function which is continuous every where but not differentiable at exactly two points? Justify your answer.

Sol. Yes, we have the continuous function $f(x) = |x - 1| + |x - 2|$, which is continuous at all $x \in R$ but differentiable at all x except 1, 2.

Here, $$f(x) = |x-1| + |x-2| = \begin{cases} -(x-1)-(x-2), & \text{if } x<1 \\ x-1-(x-2), & \text{if } 1 \le x \le 2 \\ x-1+x-2, & \text{if } x>2 \end{cases}$$

i.e., $$f(x) = \begin{cases} -2x+3, & \text{if } x<1 \\ 1, & \text{if } 1 \le x \le 2 \\ 2x-3, & \text{if } x>2 \end{cases}$$

Since, polynomial function is continuous, so it is clear that for these intervals, f is continuous. We only need to check for continuity at $x = 1,2$

At $x = 1$ $f(1) = 1$,

$$\text{LHL} = \lim_{x \to 1^-} f(x) = \lim_{x \to 1^-} (-2x+3) = \lim_{h \to 0} (-2(1-h)+3) = -2+3 = 1$$

$$\text{RHL} = \lim_{x \to 1^+} f(x) = \lim_{x \to 1^+} 1 = 1$$

$\Rightarrow$ $f(1) = \lim_{x \to 1^-} f(x) = \lim_{x \to 1^+} f(x) \Rightarrow f$ is continuous at $x = 1$

At $x=2$ $f(2)=1$

$$\text{LHL} = \lim_{x \to 2^-} f(x) = \lim_{x \to 2^-} (1) = 1$$

$$\text{RHL} = \lim_{x \to 2^+} f(x) = \lim_{x \to 2^+} (2x-3) = \lim_{h \to 0} (2(2+h)-3) = 2 \times 2 - 3 = 1$$

$\Rightarrow$ $f(x) = \lim_{x \to 2^-} f(x) = \lim_{x \to 2^+} f(x)$

So, f is continuous at $x = 2$. Thus, f is continuous at all $x \in R$.

Also, $$f'(x) = \begin{cases} -2, & x<1 \\ 0, & 1<x<2 \\ 2, & x>2 \end{cases}$$

We check the differentiability at 1, 2

$$Lf'(1) = \lim_{h \to 0} \frac{f(1-h) - f(1)}{-h} = \lim_{h \to 0} \frac{-2(1-h)+3-1}{-h} = -2$$

and $$Rf'(1) = \lim_{h \to 0} \frac{f(1+h) - f(1)}{h} = \lim_{h \to 0} \frac{1-1}{h} = 0$$

$\therefore$ $L f'(1) \ne f'(1)$.

So, f is not differentiable at 1.

Further,

$\Rightarrow$ $$Lf'(2) = \lim_{h \to 0} \frac{f(2-h) - f(2)}{-h} = \lim_{h \to 0} \frac{1-1}{-h} = 0$$

and $\quad R\,f'(2) = \lim_{h \to 0} \frac{f(2+h) - f(2)}{h}$

$$= \lim_{h \to 0} \frac{2(2+h) - 3 - 1}{h} = 2$$

$\therefore \quad L\,f'(2) \neq R\,f'(2)$

$\Rightarrow$ f is not differentiable at 2.

Thus, we see that $f(x) = |x-1| + |x-2|$ is continuous everywhere and differentiable also at all $x \in R$ except at 1, 2.

Note If $f(x) = |x-a| + |x-b| + |x-c|$ then f is continous everywhere and differentiable everywhere except at $x = a, b$ and c.

Question 21 If $y = \begin{vmatrix} f(x) & g(x) & h(x) \\ l & m & n \\ a & b & c \end{vmatrix}$, prove that $\frac{dy}{dx} = \begin{vmatrix} f'(x) & g'(x) & h'(x) \\ l & m & n \\ a & b & c \end{vmatrix}$.

Sol. Given, $y = \begin{vmatrix} f(x) & g(x) & h(x) \\ l & m & n \\ a & b & c \end{vmatrix}$

Expand along R_1

$$\Rightarrow \quad y = (mc - nb) f(x) + (na - lc)\, g(x) + (lb - ma) h(x)$$

On differentiating both sides w.r.t. x, we get

$$\Rightarrow \quad \frac{dy}{dx} = (mc - nb)\, f'(x) + (na - lc)\, g'(x) + (lb - ma) h'(x) = \begin{vmatrix} f'(x) & g'(x) & h'(x) \\ l & m & n \\ a & b & c \end{vmatrix}$$

Alternative to differentiate a determinant, we differentiate one row or one column) at a time, keeping other unchange.

$$\therefore \quad y = \begin{vmatrix} f(x) & g(x) & h(x) \\ l & m & n \\ a & b & c \end{vmatrix}$$

Differentiating w.r.t. x, we get in determinant. If any row or any column is zero then whole determinant is zero.

$$\frac{dy}{dx} = \begin{vmatrix} f'(x) & g'(x) & h'(x) \\ l & m & n \\ a & b & c \end{vmatrix} + \begin{vmatrix} f(x) & g(x) & h(x) \\ 0 & 0 & 0 \\ a & b & c \end{vmatrix} + \begin{vmatrix} f(x) & g(x) & h(x) \\ l & m & n \\ 0 & 0 & 0 \end{vmatrix}$$

$$= \begin{vmatrix} f'(x) & g'(x) & h'(x) \\ l & m & n \\ a & b & c \end{vmatrix}$$

Question 22 $y = e^{a\cos^{-1}x}$, $-1 \le x \le 1$ show that

$$(1-x^2)\frac{d^2y}{dx^2} - x\frac{dy}{dx} - a^2y = 0.$$

Sol. Given, $y = e^{a\cos^{-1}x}$ ...(i)

On differentiating both sides w.r.t. x, we get

$$\Rightarrow \quad \frac{dy}{dx} = e^{a\cos^{-1}x}\frac{d}{dx}a\cos^{-1}x = e^{a\cos^{-1}x}\cdot\frac{-a}{\sqrt{1-x^2}}$$

$$\Rightarrow \quad \frac{dy}{dx} = \frac{-ay}{\sqrt{1-x^2}} \qquad (\because e^{a\cos^{-1}x} = y)$$

$$\Rightarrow \quad \sqrt{1-x^2}\frac{dy}{dx} = -ay \qquad \text{...(ii)}$$

Again differentiating both sides w.r.t. x, we get

$$\sqrt{1-x^2}\frac{d^2y}{dx^2} + \frac{dy}{dx}\cdot\frac{-2x}{2\sqrt{1-x^2}} = -a\frac{dy}{dx}$$

$$\Rightarrow \quad \sqrt{1-x^2}\frac{d^2y}{dx^2} + \left(\frac{-x}{\sqrt{1-x^2}}\right)\frac{dy}{dx} = \frac{-a(-ay)}{\sqrt{1-x^2}} \qquad \text{(Using Eq.(ii))}$$

Multiplying throughout by $\sqrt{1-x^2}$, we get $(1-x^2)\frac{d^2y}{dx^2} - x\frac{dy}{dx} - a^2y = 0$

Hence Proved.

DIKSHA APP Questions

☐ Multiple Choice Questions

Q.1 If $x = at^2$, $y = 2at$, then $\frac{d^2y}{dx^2} =$

(a) $-\frac{1}{t^2}$ (b) $\frac{1}{2at^3}$

(c) $-\frac{1}{t^3}$ (d) $-\frac{1}{2at^3}$

Sol. (d) We have, $x = at^2$

$$\Rightarrow \quad \frac{dx}{dt} = a(2t) = 2at \qquad \text{(on differentiating w.r.t. '}t\text{')}$$

and $\quad y = 2at$ ...(i)

$\Rightarrow \quad \dfrac{dy}{dt} = 2a$ (on differentiating w.r.t. 't')

Now, $\dfrac{dy}{dx} = \dfrac{\dfrac{dy}{dt}}{\dfrac{dx}{dt}} = \dfrac{2a}{2at} = \dfrac{1}{t}$

Again, on differentiating both sides w.r.t. x, we get

$$\frac{d^2y}{dx^2} = -\frac{1}{t^2}\cdot\frac{dt}{dx}$$

$$= -\frac{1}{t^2}\cdot\frac{1}{\left(\dfrac{dx}{dt}\right)}$$

$$= -\frac{1}{t^2}\times\frac{1}{2at} = -\frac{1}{2at^3} \quad \text{(by Eq. (i))}$$

Q.2 If $y = a\sin mx + b\cos mx$ then $\dfrac{d^2y}{dx^2} =$

(a) $-m^2y$
(b) m^2y
(c) $-my$
(d) my

Sol. (a) We have, $y = a\sin mx + b\cos mx$ ..(i)

On differentiating both sides w.r.t. x, we get

$$\frac{dy}{dx} = a\cos mx\,\frac{d}{dx}(mx) + b(-\sin(mx))\,\frac{d}{dx}(mx) \text{ (by chain rule)}$$

$$= am\cos(mx) - bm\sin(mx)$$

Again, on differentiating both sides w.r.t. x, we get

$$\frac{d^2y}{dx^2} = am\cdot(-\sin(mx))\frac{d}{dx}mx - bm\cos mx\cdot\frac{d}{dx}(mx)$$

$$= -am^2\sin mx - bm^2\cos mx$$

$$\frac{d^2y}{dx^2} = -m^2(a\sin mx + b\cos mx)$$

$$= -m^2y \quad \text{(by Eq. (i))}$$

Q.3 If $x = 2\cos t - \cos 2t$, $y = 2\sin t - \sin 2t$ then $\dfrac{dy}{dx} =$

(a) 1
(b) $\tan\dfrac{t}{2}$
(c) $-\tan\dfrac{3t}{2}$
(d) $\tan\dfrac{3t}{2}$

Sol. (d) Given, $x = 2\cos t - \cot 2t$

$\Rightarrow \quad \dfrac{dx}{dt} = 2(-\sin t) - (-\sin 2t)\cdot 2$ (on differentiating w.r.t. 't')

$$= 2\sin 2t - 2\sin t = 2(\sin 2t - \sin t)$$

$$= 2\cdot\left(2\cos\frac{2t+t}{2}\cdot\sin\frac{2t-t}{2}\right)$$

$$\left(\because \sin C - \sin D = 2\cos\frac{C+D}{2}\sin\frac{C-D}{2}\right)$$

$$= 4\cos\frac{3t}{2}\sin\frac{t}{2}$$

and $\quad y = 2\sin t - \sin 2t$

$\Rightarrow \quad \dfrac{dy}{dt} = 2\cos t - \cos 2t\cdot 2 \quad$ (on differentiating w.r.t. 't')

$$= 2(\cos t - \cos 2t)$$

$$= 2\left(2\sin\frac{t+2t}{2}\cdot\sin\frac{2t-t}{2}\right)$$

$$\left(\because \cos C - \cos D = 2\sin\frac{C+D}{2}\sin\frac{D-C}{2}\right)$$

$$= 4\sin\frac{3t}{2}\cdot\sin\frac{t}{2}$$

Now, $\quad \dfrac{dy}{dx} = \dfrac{\frac{dy}{dt}}{\frac{dx}{dt}} = \dfrac{4\sin\frac{3t}{2}\cdot\sin\frac{t}{2}}{4\cos\frac{3t}{2}\sin\frac{t}{2}} = \tan\dfrac{3t}{2} \quad \left(\because \dfrac{\sin\theta}{\cos\theta} = \tan\theta\right)$

Q.4 If $x = \dfrac{a}{1+m^3}$, $y = \dfrac{am}{1+m^3}$ then $\dfrac{dy}{dx} =$

(a) $\dfrac{1+2m^3}{3m^2}$ (b) $\dfrac{1-2m^3}{3m^2}$

(c) $\dfrac{-1+2m^3}{3m^2}$ (d) 1

Sol. (c) Given, $x = \dfrac{a}{1+m^3}$

$\Rightarrow \quad \dfrac{dx}{dm} = \dfrac{(1+m^3)\frac{d}{dx}(a) - a\frac{d}{dx}(1+m^3)}{(1+m^3)^2} \quad$ (on differentiating w.r.t. 'm')

$$= \frac{0 - a(3m^2)}{(1+m^3)^2} = \frac{-3m^2a}{(1+m^3)^2}$$

and $\quad y = \dfrac{am}{1+m^3}$

$\dfrac{dy}{dm} = \dfrac{(1+m^3)\frac{d}{dx}(am) - am\frac{d}{dx}(1+m^3)}{(1+m^3)^2} \quad$ (on differentiating w.r.t. 'm')

$$= \frac{(1+m^3)a - am(3m^2)}{(1+m^3)^2}$$

$$= \frac{a + am^3 - 3am^3}{(1+m^3)^2} = \frac{a - 2am^3}{(1+m^3)^2}$$

Now,
$$\frac{dy}{dx} = \frac{\frac{dy}{dm}}{\frac{dx}{dm}} = \frac{\frac{a-2am^3}{(1+m^3)^2}}{\frac{-3m^2a}{(1+m^3)^2}}$$

$$= \frac{a - 2am^3}{-3am^2} = \frac{-1+2m^3}{3m^2}$$

Q.5 If $y = 10^{10^x}$ then $\frac{dy}{dx} =$

(a) $10^{10^x} \log 10$ (b) $10^{10^x} (\log 10)^2$

(c) $10^{10^x} \cdot 10^x (\log 10)^2$ (d) $10^{10^x} \cdot 10^x \cdot \log 10$

Sol. (c) Given, $y = 10^{10^x}$

On differentiating both sides w.r.t. x, we get

$$\frac{dy}{dx} = 10^{10^x} \log 10 \frac{d}{dx}(10^x) \qquad \left(\because \frac{d}{dx} a^x = a^x \log a\right)$$

$$= 10^{10^x} \log 10(10^x \log 10) = 10^{10^x} \cdot 10^x (\log 10)^2$$

Q.6 Derivative of $e^{x \log x}$ is

(a) $x \log x$ (b) x^x

(c) $x^x(1 + \log x)$ (d) $x(x)^{x-1}$

Sol. (c) Given, $y = e^{x \log x}$

$$y = e^{\log x^x} \qquad (\because \log a^b = b \log a)$$

$$y = x^x \qquad (\because e^{\log f(x)} = f(x))$$

On taking log both sides

$$\log y = x \log x$$

On differentiating both sides w.r.t. x, we get

$$\frac{1}{y}\frac{dy}{dx} = x \cdot \frac{d}{dx}(\log x) + \log x \frac{d}{dx}(x) \qquad \text{(using product rule)}$$

$$\Rightarrow \quad \frac{1}{y}\frac{dy}{dx} = \left(x \cdot \frac{1}{x} + \log x\right)$$

$$\Rightarrow \quad \frac{dy}{dx} = y(1 + \log x) = x^x(1 + \log x)$$

Q.7 If $\sin(x+y) = \log(x+y)$, then $\frac{dy}{dx} =$

(a) 2 (b) – 2

(c) 1 (d) – 1

Sol. (d) We have, $\sin(x+y) = \log(x+y)$

On differentiating both sides w.r.t. x, we get

$$\cos(x+y)\frac{d}{dx}(x+y) = \frac{1}{x+y}\frac{d}{dx}(x+y) \quad \text{(using chain rule)}$$

$$\Rightarrow \quad \cos(x+y)\left(1+\frac{dy}{dx}\right) = \frac{1}{x+y}\left(1+\frac{dy}{dx}\right)$$

$$\Rightarrow \quad \cos(x+y)\left(1+\frac{dy}{dx}\right) - \frac{1}{x+y}\left(1+\frac{dy}{dx}\right) = 0$$

$$\Rightarrow \quad \left(1+\frac{dy}{dx}\right)\left(\cos(x+y) - \frac{1}{x+y}\right) = 0$$

$$\because \quad \cos(x+y) - \frac{1}{x+y} \text{ can not be zero.}$$

So, $$1 + \frac{dy}{dx} = 0 \Rightarrow \frac{dy}{dx} = -1$$

Q.8 If $y = e^{-x^2}\sin(\log x)$, then $\frac{dy}{dx} =$

(a) $e^{-2x}\cos(\log x)$

(b) $e^{-x^2}\cos(\log x)$

(c) $e^{-x}\cos(\log x)$

(d) $-2xe^{-x^2}\sin(\log x) + e^{-x^2}\cos(\log x)\cdot\frac{1}{x}$

Sol. (d) Given, $y = e^{-x^2}\sin(\log x)$

On differentiating both sides w.r.t. x, we get (using product rule)

$$\frac{dy}{dx} = e^{-x^2}\frac{d}{dx}(\sin\log x) + \sin(\log x)\frac{d}{dx}e^{-x^2}$$

$$= e^{-x^2}\cdot\cos(\log x)\frac{d}{dx}(\log x) + \sin\log x\cdot e^{-x^2}\cdot\frac{d}{dx}(-x^2)$$

(using chain rule)

$$= e^{-x^2}\cos(\log x)\cdot\frac{1}{x} + \sin(\log x)\cdot e^{-x^2}\cdot(-2x)$$

$$= -2xe^{-x^2}\sin(\log x) + e^{-x^2}\cos(\log x)\cdot\frac{1}{x}$$

Q.9 If $y=\sqrt{\sin x+y}$, then $\frac{dy}{dx}=$

(a) $\frac{\sin x}{2y-1}$ (b) $\frac{\sin x}{1-2y}$

(c) $\frac{\cos x}{1-2y}$ (d) $\frac{\cos x}{2y-1}$

Sol. (d) Given, $y=\sqrt{\sin x+y}$

On squaring both side, we get

$$y^2=\sin x+y$$

On differentiating both sides w.r.t. x, we get

$$2y\frac{dy}{dx}=\cos x+\frac{dy}{dx}$$

$$\Rightarrow \quad 2y\frac{dy}{dx}-\frac{dy}{dx}=\cos x \Rightarrow \frac{dy}{dx}(2y-1)=\cos x$$

$$\Rightarrow \quad \frac{dy}{dx}=\frac{\cos x}{2y-1}$$

Q.10 Derivative of $x\log x$ is

(a) 1 (b) $1+\frac{1}{x}$ (c) $\log x+1$ (d) $\frac{1}{x}$

Sol. (c) Let $y=x\log x$

On differentiating both sides w.r.t. x, we get

$$\frac{dy}{dx}=x\cdot\frac{d}{dx}(\log x)+(\log x)\frac{d}{dx}(x) \qquad \text{(using product rule)}$$

$$=x\cdot\frac{1}{x}+\log x\,(1)$$

$$=1+\log x$$

Q.11 For what value of k will the function $f(x)=\begin{cases}\frac{x^2-25}{x-5} & x\neq 5\\ k & x=5\end{cases}$

is continuous function.

(a) 10 (b) 0

(c) not defined (d) 5

Sol. (a) We have, $f(x)=\begin{cases}\frac{x^2-25}{x-5} & x\neq 5\\ k & x=5\end{cases}$

If $f(x)$ is a continuous function than it will be continuous at $x=5$

L.H.L $=\lim\limits_{x\to 5^-} f(x)=\lim\limits_{h\to 0} f(5-h)$

$$= \lim_{h \to 0} \frac{(5-h)^2 - 25}{5 - h - 5} = \lim_{h \to 0} \frac{25 + h^2 - 10h - 25}{-h}$$

$$= \lim_{h \to 0} \frac{h(h-10)}{-h} = \lim_{h \to 0} (10 - h) = 10$$

$$\text{R.H.L} = \lim_{x \to 5^+} f(x) = \lim_{h \to 0} f(5+h) = \lim_{h \to 0} \frac{(5+h)^2 - 25}{5 + h - 5}$$

$$= \lim_{h \to 0} \frac{25 + h^2 + 10h - 25}{h} = \lim_{h \to 0} \frac{h(h+10)}{h}$$

$$= \lim_{h \to 0} (h + 10) = 10$$

Also, $f(5) = k$

Now if $f(x)$ is continuous at $x = 5$ then

L.H.L = R.H.L = $f(5)$

$\therefore\ 10 = 10 = k$

So, $k = 10$

Q.12 For what value of x will the function $f(x) = \begin{cases} \dfrac{x+4}{x+4} & x \neq -4 \\ 1 & x = -4 \end{cases}$

is discontinuous?

(a) -4 (b) 4

(c) 1 (d) no point of discontinuity

Sol. (d) We have, $f(x) = \begin{cases} \dfrac{x+4}{x+4} & x \neq -4 \\ 1 & x = -4 \end{cases}$

When $x \neq -4$, $f(x) = \dfrac{x+4}{x+4} = 1$

As it is a constant function so it will be continuous at $x \neq -4$.

Now, for $x = -4$

$$\text{L.H.L} = \lim_{x = -4^-} f(x) = \lim_{h \to 0} f(-4-h)$$

$$= \lim_{h \to 0} \frac{-4 - h + 4}{-4 - h + 4} = 1$$

$$\text{R.H.L} = \lim_{x = -4^+} f(x) = \lim_{h \to 0} f(-4+h)$$

$$= \lim_{h \to 0} \frac{-4 + h + 4}{-4 + h + 4} = 1$$

Also, $f(-4) = 1$

So, L.H.L = R.H.L = $f(-4)$

Thus, $f(x)$ is continuous at $x = -4$

Hence, there is no point of discontinuity.

☐ Subjective Type Questions

Q.1 If $y=\cos^{-1}\left(\dfrac{3x+4\sqrt{1-x^2}}{5}\right)$ find $\dfrac{dy}{dx}$

Sol. We have, $y=\cos^{-1}\left(\dfrac{3x+4\sqrt{1-x^2}}{5}\right)$

Let $x=\cos\theta \Rightarrow \theta=\cos^{-1}x$

$$\therefore \quad y=\cos^{-1}\left[\frac{3\cos\theta+4\sqrt{1-\cos^2\theta}}{5}\right]$$

$$=\cos^{-1}\left[\frac{3}{5}\cos\theta+\frac{4}{5}\sin\theta\right] \quad (\because 1-\cos^2 A=\sin^2 A) \qquad \text{...(i)}$$

Again, let $\dfrac{3}{5}=\cos\alpha$

Then, $\dfrac{4}{5}=\sin\alpha$

$\therefore$ From Eq. (i), $y=\cos^{-1}[\cos\alpha\cos\theta+\sin\alpha\sin\theta]$

$$\Rightarrow \quad y=\cos^{-1}[\cos(\theta-\alpha)]=\theta-\alpha$$

$$\Rightarrow \quad y=\cos^{-1}x-\cos^{-1}\frac{3}{5}$$

On differentiating both sides w.r.t. x, we get

$$\frac{dy}{dx}=-\frac{1}{\sqrt{1-x^2}}$$

Q.2 If $y=\tan^{-1}\left(\dfrac{\sqrt{1+x^2}-\sqrt{1-x^2}}{\sqrt{1+x^2}+\sqrt{1-x^2}}\right)$ find $\dfrac{dy}{dx}$.

Sol. We have, $y=\tan^{-1}\left[\dfrac{\sqrt{1+x^2}-\sqrt{1-x^2}}{\sqrt{1+x^2}+\sqrt{1-x^2}}\right]$

Let us assume $x^2=\cos\theta \Rightarrow \theta=\cos^{-1}x^2$

$$\therefore \quad y=\tan^{-1}\left[\frac{\sqrt{1+\cos\theta}-\sqrt{1-\cos\theta}}{\sqrt{1+\cos\theta}+\sqrt{1-\cos\theta}}\right]$$

$$=\tan^{-1}\left[\frac{\sqrt{2\cos^2\frac{\theta}{2}}-\sqrt{2\sin^2\frac{\theta}{2}}}{\sqrt{2\cos\frac{\theta}{2}}+\sqrt{2\sin^2\frac{\theta}{2}}}\right] \quad \left[\begin{array}{l}\because 1-\cos A=2\sin^2\frac{A}{2}\\ \text{and } 1+\cos A=2\cos^2\frac{A}{2}\end{array}\right]$$

$$= \tan^{-1}\left[\frac{\sqrt{2}\cos\frac{\theta}{2} - \sqrt{2}\sin\frac{\theta}{2}}{\sqrt{2}\cos\frac{\theta}{2} + \sqrt{2}\sin\frac{\theta}{2}}\right]$$

On dividing numerator and denominator by $\sqrt{2}\cos\frac{\theta}{2}$, we get

$$y = \tan^{-1}\left[\frac{1 - \tan\frac{\theta}{2}}{1 + \tan\frac{\theta}{2}}\right]$$

$$= \tan^{-1}\left(\tan\left(\frac{\pi}{4} - \frac{\theta}{2}\right)\right) \qquad \left(\because \frac{1 - \tan A}{1 + \tan A} = \tan\left(\frac{\pi}{4} - A\right)\right)$$

$$= \frac{\pi}{4} - \frac{\theta}{2}$$

$$\Rightarrow \qquad y = \frac{\pi}{4} - \frac{1}{2}\cos^{-1} x^2$$

On differentiating both sides w.r.t. x, we get

$$\frac{dy}{dx} = 0 - \frac{1}{2}\cdot\frac{-1}{\sqrt{1-(x^2)^2}}\frac{d}{dx}(x^2) \qquad \text{(by chain rule)}$$

$$= \frac{1(2x)}{2\sqrt{1-x^4}} = \frac{x}{\sqrt{1-x^4}}$$

Q.3 Find $\frac{dy}{dx}$, when $y = \cot^{-1}\left(\frac{\sqrt{1+x^2} - 1}{x}\right)$

Sol. Given, $y = \cot^{-1}\left(\frac{\sqrt{1+x^2} - 1}{x}\right)$

Let $x = \tan\theta$

$\Rightarrow \quad \theta = \tan^{-1} x$

$$\therefore \qquad y = \cot^{-1}\left(\frac{\sqrt{1+\tan^2\theta} - 1}{\tan\theta}\right)$$

$$= \cot^{-1}\left(\frac{\sqrt{\sec^2\theta} - 1}{\tan\theta}\right) \qquad (\because 1 + \tan^2 A = \sec^2 A)$$

$$= \cot^{-1}\left(\frac{\sec\theta - 1}{\tan\theta}\right)$$

$$= \cot^{-1}\left(\frac{\frac{1}{\cos\theta}-1}{\frac{\sin\theta}{\cos\theta}}\right) \qquad \left(\because \sec A = \frac{1}{\cos A}, \tan A = \frac{\sin A}{\cos A}\right)$$

$$= \cot^{-1}\left(\frac{1-\cos\theta}{\sin\theta}\right)$$

$$= \cot^{-1}\left(\frac{2\sin^2\frac{\theta}{2}}{2\sin\frac{\theta}{2}\cos\frac{\theta}{2}}\right) \qquad \left(\because 1-\cos A = 2\sin^2\frac{A}{2}, \sin A = 2\sin\frac{A}{2}\cos\frac{A}{2}\right)$$

$$= \cot^{-1}\left(\tan\frac{\theta}{2}\right)$$

$$= \cot^{-1}\cot\left(\frac{\pi}{2}-\frac{\theta}{2}\right) \qquad \left(\because \cot\left(\frac{\pi}{2}-A\right) = \tan A\right)$$

$$\Rightarrow \quad y = \frac{\pi}{2}-\frac{\theta}{2} = \frac{\pi}{2}-\frac{1}{2}\tan^{-1}x$$

On differentiating both sides w.r.t. x, we get

$$\frac{dy}{dx} = 0 - \frac{1}{2}\cdot\frac{1}{1+x^2} = \frac{-1}{2(1+x^2)}$$

Q.4 If $x\sqrt{1+y} = -y\sqrt{1+x}$ find $\frac{dy}{dx}$.

Sol. We have, $x\sqrt{1+y} = -y\sqrt{1+x}$

On squaring both sides, we get

$$x^2(1+y) = y^2(1+x)$$

$$\Rightarrow \quad x^2 + x^2y = y^2 + y^2x$$

$$\Rightarrow \quad x^2 - y^2 = y^2x - x^2y$$

$$\Rightarrow \quad (x-y)(x+y) = xy(y-x) \qquad (\because x^2-y^2 = (x+y)(x-y))$$

$$\Rightarrow (x-y)(x+y) + xy(x-y) = 0$$

$$\Rightarrow \quad (x-y)(x+y+xy) = 0$$

$$\because \quad x \neq y \qquad \text{(question does not exist)}$$

$$\therefore \quad x+y+xy = 0$$

$$\Rightarrow \quad y(1+x) = -x$$

$$\Rightarrow \quad y = \frac{-x}{1+x}$$

On differentiating both sides w.r.t. x, we get

$$\frac{dy}{dx} = -\left[\frac{(1+x)\frac{d}{dx}x - x\frac{d}{dx}(1+x)}{(1+x)^2}\right] = -\left[\frac{1+x-x}{(1+x)^2}\right] = -\frac{1}{(1+x)^2}$$

Application of Derivatives

CHAPTER 06

Important Points

Rate of Change of Quantities

01 Average rate of change of y w.r.t. $x = \dfrac{\Delta y}{\Delta x}$.

02 Instantaneous rate of change of y w.r.t. $x = \dfrac{dy}{dx}$.

03 Related rate of change $= \dfrac{dy}{dx} = \dfrac{dy/dt}{dx/dt}$ if $\dfrac{dx}{dt} \neq 0$.

04 **Marginal Cost** Marginal cost is the rate of change of total cost with respect to the output.

05 **Marginal Revenue** Marginal revenue is the rate of change of total revenue with respect to the number unit sold.

Increasing and Decreasing Functions

01 **Increasing Functions** Let I be an interval contained in the domain of a real valued function f. Then, f is said to be

(i) increasing on I, if $x_1 < x_2 \Rightarrow f(x_1) \le f(x_2)\ \forall\ x_1, x_2 \in I$

(ii) strictly increasing on I, if $x_1 < x_2 \Rightarrow f(x_1) < f(x_2)\ \forall x_1, x_2 \in I$

02 **Decreasing Functions** Let I be an interval contained in the domain of a real valued function f. Then, f is said to be

(i) decreasing on I, if $x_1 < x_2 \Rightarrow f(x_1) \ge f(x_2)\ \forall\ x_1, x_2 \in I$

(ii) strictly decreasing on I, if $x_1 < x_2 \Rightarrow f(x_1) > f(x_2)\ \forall x_1, x_2 \in I$

03 Let f be continuous on $[a, b]$ and differentiable on (a, b). Then,

(i) If $f'(x) > 0$ for each $x \in (a, b)$, then $f(x)$ is said to be increasing in $[a, b]$ and strictly increasing in (a, b).

(ii) If $f'(x) < 0$ for each $x \in (a, b)$, then $f(x)$ is said to be decreasing in $[a, b]$ and strictly decreasing in (a, b).

(iii) If $f'(x) = 0$ for each $x \in (a, b)$, then f is said to be a constant function in $[a, b]$.

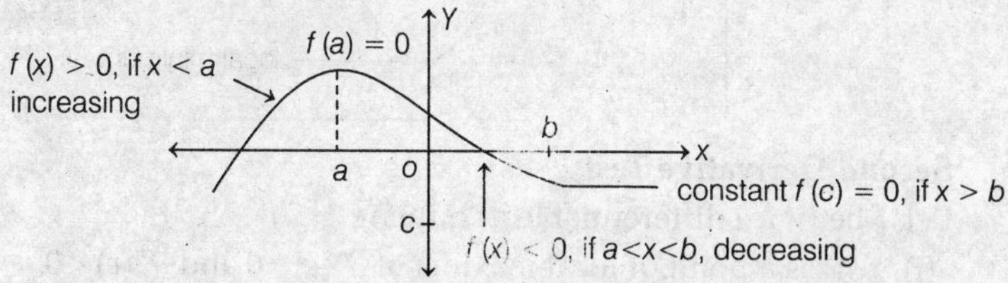

Monotonic Function

A function $f(x)$ is said to be monotonic on an interval (a,b) if it is either increasing or decreasing on (a, b)

Maxima and Minima

Let f be a real valued function and let c be an interior point in the domain of f. Then,

Local Maxima

Point c is called a local maxima, if there is a $h > 0$ such that

$$f(c) \geq f(x) \text{ for all } x \text{ in } (c - h, c + h)$$

Local Minima

Point c is called a point of local minima if there is a $h > 0$ such that

$$f(c) \leq f(x) \text{ for all } x \text{ in } (c - h, c + h)$$

Note If f has a local maxima or a local minima at $x = c$, then either $f'(c) = 0$ or f is not differentiable at $x = c$.

First Derivative Test

(i) If $f'(x) > 0$ to closely left of c and $f'(x) < 0$ to closely right of c, then c is a point of local maxima.

(ii) If $f'(x) < 0$ to closely left of c and $f'(x) > 0$ to closely right of c, then c is a point of local minima.

(iii) If $f'(x)$ does not change sign as x increases through c, then c is neither a point of local maxima nor a point of local minima. This point is called a point of inflection.

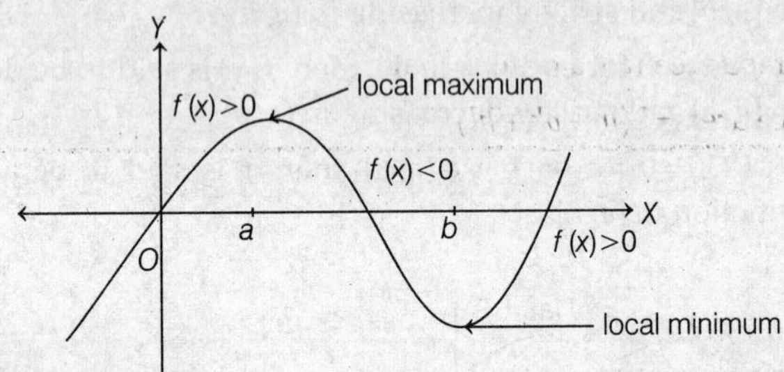

Second Derivative Test

Let f be twice differentiable at c, then

(i) $x = c$ is a point of local maxima, if $f'(c) = 0$ and $f''(c) < 0$. Then, $f(c)$ is local maximum value of f.

(ii) $x = c$ is a point of local minima, if $f'(c) = 0$ and $f''(c) > 0$ Then, $f(c)$ is local minimum value of f.

(iii) If $f'(c) = 0$ and $f''(c) = 0$, then the test fails.

Function in a Closed Interval [*a*, *b*]

Let f be a differentiable function on $[a, b]$ and let c be a point in $[a, b]$ such that $f'(c) = 0$. Then, find $f(a)$, $f(b)$ and $f(c)$.
The maximum of these values gives a maxima or absolute maxima and minimum of these values gives a minima or absolute minima.

Some Useful Formula of Mensuration

Triangle

Area $= \frac{1}{2} \times$ base $\times$ height

Area of equilateral triangle $= \frac{\sqrt{3}}{4}$ side^2

Area $= \sqrt{s(s-a)(s-b)(s-c)}$ where $s = \frac{a+b+c}{2}$

Pythagoras theorem $(AC)^2 = (AB)^2 + (BC)^2$ in ΔABC where $\angle B = 90°$

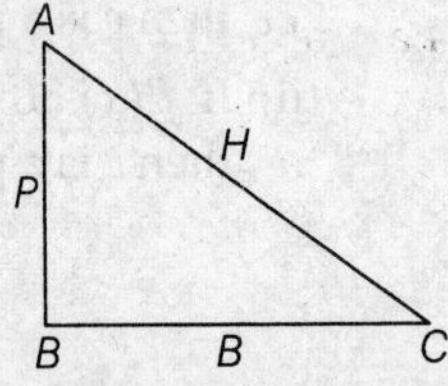

Rectangle Area = length $\times$ breadth

Perimeter = 2(length + breadth)

Square Area = (side)^2

Perimeter = 4 $\times$ side

Circle Area $= \pi r^2$

Perimeter $= 2\pi r$

Cuboid Volume $= l \times b \times h$

Lateral surface area (area of four walls) $= 2h(l + b)$

Total surface area $= 2(lb + bh + hl)$

Longest pole $= \sqrt{l^2 + b^2 + h^2}$

Cube volume $=$ (side)^3

Lateral surface area $= 4(side)^2$

Total surface area $= 6$ (side)^2

Cylinder Volume $= \pi r^2 h$

Lateral surface area $= 2\pi rh$

Total surface area $= 2\pi r(r + h)$

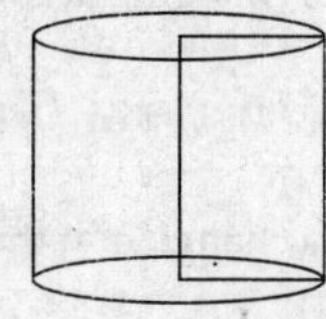

Cone Volume $= \frac{1}{3}\pi r^2 h$

Lateral surface area $= \pi rl$

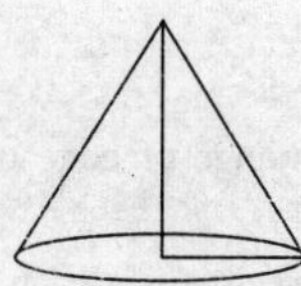

Total surface area $= \pi r(l + r)$

Sphere Volume $= \frac{4}{3}\pi r^3$

Surface area $= 4\pi r^2$

Hemisphere Volume $= \frac{2}{3}\pi r^3$

Lateral Surface Area $= 2\pi r^2$

Total surface area $= 3\pi r^2$

Exercise 6.1

Question 1 Find the rate of change of the area of a circle with respect to its radius r when

(a) $r = 3$ cm (b) $r = 4$ cm

◎ ***Thinking Process*** Write area A in terms of radius r using $A = \pi r^2$ and then differentiate it w.r.t. r to find the rate of change.

Sol. Let A denotes the area of the circle when its radius is r, then $A = \pi r^2$.
Now, the rate of change of the area with respect to its radius is given by,

$$\frac{dA}{dr} = \frac{d}{dr}(\pi r^2) = 2\pi r$$

(a) When $r = 3$ cm, $\left(\frac{dA}{dr}\right)_{r=3} = 2\pi(3) = 6\pi \text{ cm}^2$ per

Hence, the area of the circle is changing at the rate of 6π cm^2/cm when its radius is 3 cm.

(b) When $r = 4$ cm, $\left(\frac{dA}{dr}\right)_{r=4} = 2\pi(4) = 8\pi \text{ cm}^2$ per cm

Hence, the area of the circle is changing at the rate of 8π cm^2/cm when its radius is 4 cm.

Question 2 The volume of a cube is increasing at the rate of 8 cm^3/s. How fast is the surface area increasing when the length of an edge is 12 cm ?

◎ ***Thinking Process***

(i) Find out the rate of change of edge of cube (a) by differentiating the relation $V = a^3$.

(ii) Use the relation between surface area and edge of cube (a) then differentiate it and substitute $\frac{dA}{dt}$ to find rate of change of surface area.

Sol. Let x be the length of a side (edge), V be the volume and S be the surface area of the cube.

$\therefore$ $V = x^3$ and $S = 6x^2$ ($\because$ cube has six square faces, each of side x.)

where, x is a function of time t.

It is given that $\frac{dV}{dt} = 8 \text{ cm}^3/\text{s}$.

Then, by using the chain rule, we get

$$8 = \frac{dV}{dt} = \frac{d}{dt}(x^3) = 3x^2 \cdot \frac{dx}{dt} \Rightarrow \frac{dx}{dt} = \frac{8}{3x^2} \quad \ldots\text{(i)}$$

Now, $$\frac{dS}{dt} = \frac{d}{dt}(6x^2) = 12x\frac{dx}{dt} = 12x\left(\frac{8}{3x^2}\right) = \frac{32}{x} \quad \text{[from Eq. (i)]}$$

Thus, when $x = 12$ cm, $\frac{dS}{dt} = \frac{32}{12}$ cm^2/s $= \frac{8}{3}$ cm^2/s.

Hence, if the length of the edge of a cube is 12 cm, then the surface area is increasing at the rate of $\frac{8}{3}$ cm^2/s.

Mistake Alert $\frac{dx^3}{dt} = 3x^2 \frac{dx}{dt} \neq 3x^2$

Here, x is a dependent variable of t.

Question 3 The radius of a circle is increasing uniformly at the rate of 3 cm/s. Find the rate at which the area of the circle is increasing when the radius is 10 cm.

Sol. Let r be the radius of circle and A be the area of circle at any time t. Area of circle $A = \pi r^2$.

Now, the rate of change of area A with respect to time t is given by

$$\frac{dA}{dt} = \frac{d}{dt}(\pi r^2) = 2\pi r \frac{dr}{dt} \qquad \text{(by chain rule)}$$

It is given that radius of circle is increasing at the rate of 3 cm/s, so $\frac{dr}{dt} = 3$ cm / s.

$$\therefore \quad \frac{dA}{dt} = 2\pi r(3) = 6\pi r \text{ cm}^2\text{/s}$$

Thus, when $r = 10$ cm, $\frac{dA}{dt} = 6\pi(10) = 60\pi$ cm^2/s

Hence, the rate at which the area of the circle is increasing, when the radius is 10 cm, is 60π cm^2/s.

Question 4 An edge of a variable cube is increasing at the rate of 3 cm/s. How fast is the volume of the cube increasing when the edge is 10 cm long?

Sol. Let x be the length of an edge of cube and V be the volume of the cube. Then, $V = x^3$

$\therefore$ Rate of change of volume w.r.t. time

$$\frac{dV}{dt} = \frac{d}{dt}(x^3) = 3x^2 \frac{dx}{dt} \qquad \text{(by chain rule)}$$

It is given that edge of the cube is increasing at the rate of 3 cm/s, so $\frac{dx}{dt} = 3$ cm/s.

$$\therefore \quad \frac{dV}{dt} = 3x^2(3) = 9x^2 \text{ cm}^3\text{/s}$$

Thus, when $x = 10$ cm, $\frac{dV}{dt} = 9(10)^2 = 900$ cm^3/s

Hence, the volume of the cube is increasing at the rate of 900 cm^3/s when the edge is 10 cm long.

Question 5 A stone is dropped into a quiet lake and waves move in circles at the speed of 5 cm/s. At the instant when the radius of the circular wave is 8 cm, how fast is the enclosed area increasing?

◎ *Thinking Process* Use the relation between area of a circle and its radius *i.e.*, $A = \pi r^2$. Differentiate both sides w.r.t. time t and find out how fast is the enclosed area changing.

Sol. Let r be the radius of the circular wave and A be the area, then $A = \pi r^2$

Therefore, the rate of change of area (A) with respect to time (t) is given by

$$\frac{dA}{dt} = \frac{d}{dt}(\pi r^2) \Rightarrow \frac{dA}{dt} = 2\pi r\frac{dr}{dt} \qquad \text{(By chain rule)}$$

It is given that waves move in circles at the speed of 5 cm/s.

So, $\frac{dr}{dt} = 5 \text{ cm/s}$

$\therefore \quad \frac{dA}{dt} = 2\pi r \times 5 = 10\pi r \text{ cm}^2/\text{s}$

Thus, when $r = 8$ cm, $\frac{dA}{dt} = 10\pi(8) = 80\pi \text{ cm}^2/\text{s}$

Hence, when the radius of the circular wave is 8 cm, the enclosed area is increasing at the rate of $80\pi \text{ cm}^2/\text{s}$.

Question 6 The radius of a circle is increasing at the rate of 0.7 cm/s. What is the rate of increase of its circumference?

◎ *Thinking Process* Using the formula for perimeter and area of a rectangle in terms of its length and breadth. By differentiating these two relations we can get the required result.

Sol. At any instant of time t, let the radius of the circle be r and its circumference be C, then $C = 2\pi r$

$\Rightarrow$ Rate of increase of circumference, $\frac{dC}{dt} = 2\pi\frac{dr}{dt}$

(Differentiating w.r.t. t, by chain rule)

where, $\frac{dr}{dt}$ is rate of increase of radius, so $\frac{dr}{dt} = 0.7$ cm/s

$$\therefore \quad \frac{dC}{dt} = 2\pi\,(0.7)\text{ cm/s} = 1.4\pi \text{ cm/s} \qquad \left(\because \frac{dr}{dt} = 0.7 \text{ cm/s}\right)$$

Hence, rate of increase of circumference is 1.4π cm/s.

Question 7 The length x of a rectangle is decreasing at the rate of 5 cm/min and the width y is increasing at the rate of 4 cm/min. When $x = 8$ cm and $y = 6$ cm, find the rate of change of

(a) the perimeter. (b) the area of the rectangle.

Sol. At any instant of time t, let length, breadth, perimeter and area of the rectangle are x, y, P and A respectively, then

$$P = 2(x + y) \text{ and } A = xy \quad \ldots(i)$$

(Perimeter of rectangle = 2 (length + breadth) and area = length × breadth

It is given that $\frac{dx}{dt} = -5$ cm/min and $\frac{dy}{dt} = 4$ cm/min

(–ve sign shows that the length is decreasing)

(a) Now, $P = 2(x + y)$.

On differentiating both sides w.r.t. t, we get

Rate of change of perimeter, $\frac{dP}{dt} = 2\left(\frac{dx}{dt} + \frac{dy}{dt}\right)$

$= 2\{-5 + 4\}$ cm/min

$= -2$ cm/min

Hence, perimeter of the rectangle is decreasing at the rate of 2 cm/min.

(b) Here, area of rectangle $A = xy$.

On differentiating both sides w.r.t. t, we get

Rate of change of area, $\frac{dA}{dt} = x\frac{dy}{dt} + y\frac{dx}{dt} = 8 \times 4 + 6 \times (-5)$

(using product rule)

$= 32 - 30 = 2 \text{ cm}^2/\text{min}$

Hence, area of the rectangle is increasing at the rate of $2 \text{ cm}^2/\text{min}$.

Note If rate of change is increasing, we take positive sign and if rate of change is decreasing, then we take negative sign.

Question 8 A balloon which always remains spherical on inflation, is being inflated by pumping in 900 cubic cm of gas per second. Find the rate at which the radius of the balloon increases when the radius is 15 cm.

Sol. At any instant of time t, let the radius of the balloon be r and its volume be V, then volume of balloon, $V = \left(\frac{4}{3}\right)\pi r^3$

The balloon is being inflated at 900 cubic cm/s *i.e.*, the rate of change of volume with respect to time is $900 \text{ cm}^3/\text{s}$.

On differentiating both sides w.r.t. t, we get

Rate of change of volume $\frac{dV}{dt} = \left(\frac{4}{3}\pi\right)\left(3r^2\frac{dr}{dt}\right)$ (by chain rule)

Thus, when $r = 15$ cm, then $900 = \left(\frac{4}{3}\pi\right)\left\{3(15)^2\frac{dr}{dt}\right\}$

$$\Rightarrow \quad \frac{dr}{dt} = \frac{900}{3 \times (15)^2} \times \frac{3}{4\pi}$$

$\Rightarrow$ Rate of change of radius r, $\dfrac{dr}{dt} = \dfrac{900}{4\pi \times (15)^2} = \dfrac{225}{\pi \times 225} = \dfrac{1}{\pi}$ cm/s

Hence, the rate at which the radius of the balloon increases when the radius is 15 cm is $\dfrac{1}{\pi}$ cm/s.

Question 9 A balloon which remains spherical has a variable radius. Find the rate at which its volume is increasing with the radius when the radius is 10 cm.

Sol. Let r be the radius of spherical balloon and V be its volume. Then, $r = 10$ cm and $V = \dfrac{4}{3}\pi r^3$,

Rate of change of volume w.r.t. radius r, $\dfrac{dV}{dr} = \left(\dfrac{4}{3}\pi\right) 3r^2$ (differentiating w.r.t. r)

$$= 4\pi r^2 = 4\pi (10)^2 = 400\,\pi \quad (\because r = 10 \text{ cm})$$

Hence, the volume of the balloon is increasing at the rate of 400π cm^3/cm.

Question 10 A ladder 5 m long is leaning against a wall. The bottom of the ladder is pulled along the ground, away from the wall, at the rate of 2 cm/s. How fast is its height on the wall decreasing when the foot of the ladder is 4 m away from the wall?

◎ *Thinking Process* The leader when against leaving the wall form a right angled triangle. Here, hypotenuse is length of ladder, base is distance between foot of ladder and wall and altitude is the height of the wall at which ladder touches.

Sol. Let $AB = 5$ m $= 500$ cm be the ladder and y be the height of the wall at which the ladder touches. Also, let the foot of the ladder be at B whose distance from the wall is x.

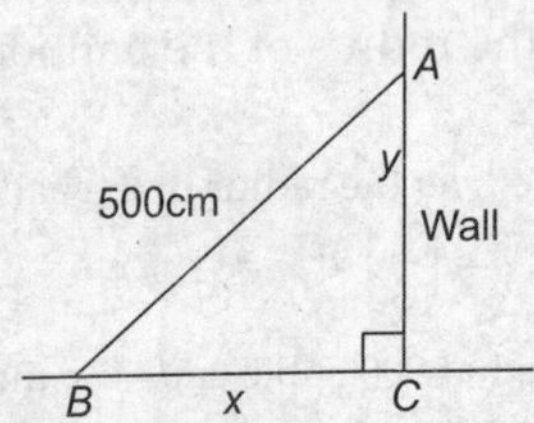

Given that the bottom of ladder is pulled along the ground at 2 cm/s,

so $\dfrac{dx}{dt} = 2$ cm/s

As we know that ΔABC is right angled, so by Pythagoras theorem, we have

$$x^2 + y^2 = 500^2 \qquad \ldots(i)$$

when $x = 400$, then

$$y^2 = 500^2 - 400^2$$

$\Rightarrow \quad y = \sqrt{250000 - 160000}$

$\Rightarrow \quad y = 300$ cm

Differentiating Eq. (i) w.r.t. time t on both sides, we get

$$2x\frac{dx}{dt} + 2y\frac{dy}{dt} = 0$$

$$\Rightarrow \quad x\frac{dx}{dt} + y\frac{dy}{dt} = 0$$

$$\Rightarrow \quad 400 \times 2 + 300 \times \frac{dy}{dt} = 0 \qquad \left[\because x = 400 \text{ and } \frac{dx}{dt} = 2\right]$$

$\Rightarrow$ The rate of fall of height on the wall, $\frac{dy}{dt} = -\frac{8}{3}$ cm/s

[Negative sign shows that height of ladder on the wall is decreasing at the rate of $\frac{8}{3}$ cm/s.]

Question 11 A particle move along the curve $6y = x^3 + 2$. Find the points on the curve at which the y-coordinate is changing 8 times as fast as the x-coordinate.

Thinking Process The rate of change of x and y coordinates w.r.t. t, is $\frac{dx}{dt}$ and $\frac{dy}{dt}$ and also use the relation $\frac{dy}{dt} = \frac{8dx}{dt}$ as y-coordinate is changing 8 times as fast as the x-coordinate.

Sol. Given, $6y = x^3 + 2$ ...(i)

and $\frac{dy}{dt} = 8\frac{dx}{dt}$ ...(ii)

On differentiating Eq. (i) both sides w.r.t. t, we get

$$6\frac{dy}{dt} = 3x^2\frac{dx}{dt}$$

$$\Rightarrow \quad 6 \times 8\frac{dx}{dt} = 3x^2\frac{dx}{dt} \qquad \text{[using Eq. (ii)]}$$

$$\Rightarrow \quad 3x^2 = 48$$

$$\Rightarrow \quad x^2 = 16$$

$$\Rightarrow \quad x = \pm 4$$

When $x = 4$, then $6y = (4)^3 + 2$

$$\Rightarrow \quad 6y = 64 + 2$$

$$\Rightarrow \quad y = \frac{66}{6} = 11$$

When $x = -4$, then $6y = (-4)^3 + 2 \Rightarrow 6y = -64 + 2$

$$\Rightarrow \quad y = \frac{-62}{6} = \frac{-31}{3}$$

Hence, the required points on the curve are (4, 11) and $\left(-4, \frac{-31}{3}\right)$.

Question 12 The radius of an air bubble is increasing at the rate of $\frac{1}{2}$ cm/s. At what rate is the volume of the bubble increasing when the radius is 1 cm?

Sol. The air bubble is in the shape of a sphere.

Let r be the radius of bubble and V be the volume of bubble at any time t.

Then, rate of change of radius, $\frac{dr}{dt} = \frac{1}{2}$ cm/s and $r = 1$ cm (given)

Now, volume of the bubble $V = \frac{4}{3}\pi r^3$

On differentiating both sides w.r.t. t, we get

Rate of volume increasing, $\frac{dV}{dt} = \left(\frac{4}{3}\pi\right)\left(3r^2 \frac{dr}{dt}\right)$

$$= 4\pi r^2 \frac{dr}{dt} = 4\pi(1)^2 \frac{1}{2} \quad \left(\text{On putting } r = 1 \text{ and } \frac{dr}{dt} = \frac{1}{2}\right)$$

$$= 2\pi \text{ cm}^3/\text{s}$$

Hence, the rate at which the volume of the bubble increases is 2π cm^3/s.

Question 13 A balloon, which always remains spherical, has a variable diameter 3/2 $(2x + 1)$. Find the rate of change of its volume with respect to x.

◎ ***Thinking Process*** Use the relation, volume of sphere $= \frac{4}{3}\pi\,(\text{radius})^3 = \frac{4}{3}\pi\left(\frac{\text{Diameter}}{2}\right)^3$. Differentiating w.r.t. x and get the required result.

Sol. Given, the diameter of the balloon $= \frac{3}{2}(2x + 1)$

$\therefore$ Radius of the balloon $= \frac{\text{Diameter}}{2} = \frac{1}{2}\left[\frac{3}{2}(2x + 1)\right] = \frac{3}{4}(2x + 1)$

For the volume V, the balloon is given by

$$V = \frac{4}{3}\pi\,(\text{radius})^3 = \frac{4}{3}\pi\left[\frac{3}{4}(2x + 1)\right]^3 = \frac{9\pi}{16}(2x + 1)^3$$

For the rate of change of volume, differentiate both sides w.r.t. x, we get

$$\frac{dV}{dx} = \frac{9\pi}{16} \times 3(2x + 1)^2 \times 2$$

$$= \frac{27\pi}{8}(2x + 1)^2$$

Thus, rate of change of volume is $\frac{27\pi}{8}(2x + 1)^2$.

Quick Solution

Let r be the radius and v be the volume of the spherical balloon, then

$$V = \frac{4}{3}\pi r^3 \text{ and } r = \frac{\text{diameter}}{2} = \frac{3}{4}(2x+1)$$

$$\therefore \quad \frac{dV}{dx} = \frac{4}{3}\pi\left(3r^2\frac{dr}{dx}\right) = 4\pi r^2\frac{dr}{dx} \quad \text{... (i)}$$

and $\quad \frac{dr}{dx} = \frac{3}{4} \times 2 = \frac{3}{2}$

Put $\frac{dr}{dx}$ and r in Eq. (i)

$$\frac{dV}{dx} = 4\pi\left[\frac{3}{4}(2x+1)\right]^2 \frac{3}{2} = \frac{27\pi}{8}(2x+1)^2$$

Question 14 Sand is pouring from a pipe at the rate of 12 cm^3/s. The falling sand forms a cone on the ground in such a way that the height of the cone is always one-sixth of the radius of the base. How is fast the height of the sand cone increasing when the height is 4 cm?

Sol. Let r be the radius, h be the height and V be the volume of sand cone at any time t.

It is given that $\frac{dV}{dt} = 12$ cm³/s and $h = \frac{1}{6}r \Rightarrow r = 6h$

$$\therefore \quad V = \frac{1}{3}\pi r^2 h = \frac{1}{3}\pi(6h)^2 h = 12\pi h^3$$

On differentiating both sides w.r.t. t, we get

$$\frac{dV}{dt} = (12\pi)\left(3h^2\frac{dh}{dt}\right) = 36\pi h^2\frac{dh}{dt}$$

$$\Rightarrow \quad 12 = 36\pi(4)^2\frac{dh}{dt} \quad \left(\because h = 4 \text{ cm and } \frac{dV}{dt} = 12 \text{ cm}^3/\text{s}\right)$$

$$\Rightarrow \quad \frac{dh}{dt} = \frac{12}{36\pi \times 16} = \frac{1}{48\pi} \text{ cm/s}$$

Hence, when the height of the sand cone is 4 cm, its height is increasing at the rate of $\frac{1}{48\pi}$ cm/s.

Question 15 The total cost $C(x)$ in rupees associated with the production of x units of an item is given by $C(x) = 0.007x^3 - 0.003x^2 + 15x + 4000$. Find the marginal cost when $x = 17$ units are produced.

Thinking Process Marginal cost is the rate of change of total cost with respect to output.

Sol. Given, total cost, $C(x) = 0.007x^3 - 0.003x^2 + 15x + 4000$

$$\text{Marginal Cost (MC)} = \frac{dC}{dx} = 0.007(3x^2) - 0.003(2x) + 15$$

$$= 0.021x^2 - 0.006x + 15$$

When $x = 17$, $MC = 0.021(17)^2 - 0.006(17) + 15$

$= 0.021(289) - 0.006(17) + 15$

$= 6.069 - 0.102 + 15$

$= 20.967$

Hence, when 17 units are produced, the marginal cost is ₹ 20.967.

Question 16 The total revenue in rupees received from the sale of x units of a product is given by $R(x) = 13x^2 + 26x + 15$. Find the marginal revenue when $x = 7$.

◎ *Thinking Process* Marginal revenue is the rate of change of total revenue with respect to the number of units sold.

Sol. Given, total revenue, $R(x) = 13x^2 + 26x + 15$

$\therefore$ Marginal Revenue (MR) $= \dfrac{dR}{dx} = \dfrac{d}{dx}(13x^2 + 26x + 15)$

$= 13 \times 2x + 26 = 26x + 26$

When $x = 7$, $MR = 26(7) + 26 = 182 + 26 = 208$

Hence, the required marginal revenue is ₹ 208.

Direction (Q. Nos. 17 and 18) Choose the correct answer.

Question 17 The rate of change of the area of a circle with respect to its radius r at $r = 6$ cm is

(a) 10π (b) 12π (c) 8π (d) 11π

Sol. (b) If A is the area of the circle corresponding to radius r, then $A = \pi r^2$

On differentiating both sides w.r.t. r, we get

$$\frac{dA}{dr} = 2\pi r$$

On putting $r = 6$, we get $\left(\dfrac{dA}{dr}\right) = 2\pi(6) = 12\pi \text{ cm}^2/\text{cm}$

Hence, the required rate of change of the area of a circle is 12π cm^2 per cm.

Question 18 The total revenue in rupees received from the sale of x units of a product is given by $R(x) = 3x^2 + 36x + 5$. The marginal revenue, when $x = 15$ is

(a) 116 (b) 96
(c) 90 (d) 126

Sol. (d) Given, $R(x) = 3x^2 + 36x + 5$

$\therefore$ Marginal Revenue (MR) $= \dfrac{dR}{dx} = \dfrac{d}{dx}(3x^2 + 36x + 5) = 6x + 36$

When $x = 15$, $MR = 6 \times 15 + 36 = 126$

Hence, the required marginal revenue is ₹ 126.

Exercise 6.2

Question 1 Show that the function given by $f(x)=3x+17$ is strictly increasing on R.

◎ *Thinking Process* When $f(x)$ is increasing, then $f'(x)\geq 0$ and when $f(x)$ is strictly increasing, then $f'(x)>0$.

Sol. Let x_1 and x_2 be any two numbers in R.

Such that $x_1 < x_2$.

Then, $3x_1 < 3x_2 \Rightarrow 3x_1 + 17 < 3x_2 + 17$

i.e. $f(x_1) < f(x_2)$

Now, we see that if $x_1 < x_2 \Rightarrow f(x_1) < f(x_2)\ \forall x_1 x_2 \in R$. Hence, f is increasing on R.

Quick Solution

Given, $f(x) = 3x + 17$.

On differentiating both sides w.r.t. x, we get

$f'(x) = 3 > 0$, in every interval of R.

Thus, the function is strictly increasing on R.

Question 2 Show that the function given by $f(x)=e^{2x}$ is strictly increasing on R.

Sol. Let x_1 and x_2 be any two numbers in R, where $x_1 < x_2$.

Given, $f(x) = e^{2x}$

Then, we have $x_1 < x_2 \Rightarrow 2x_1 < 2x_2 \Rightarrow e^{2x_1} < e^{2x_2} \Rightarrow f(x_1) < f(x_2)$

Hence, f is strictly increasing on R.

Quick Solution

Given, $f(x) = e^{2x}$

On differentiating both sides w.r.t. x, we get

$$\frac{d}{dx} f(x) = \frac{d}{dx}(e^{2x}) \Rightarrow f'(x) = 2e^{2x}$$

Since, the value of e^{2x} is always positive for any real value of x.

$\therefore$ $f'(x) > 0$

Hence, $f(x)$ is strictly increasing function on R.

Question 3 Show that the function given by $f(x)=\sin x$ is

(a) strictly increasing in $\left(0, \frac{\pi}{2}\right)$.

(b) strictly decreasing in $\left(\frac{\pi}{2}, \pi\right)$.

(c) neither increasing nor decreasing in $(0, \pi)$.

◎ *Thinking Process* $f(x)$ is strictly increasing in (a, b), if $f'(x)>0$ and strictly decreasing in (a, b), if $f'(x)<0$.

Sol. The given function is $f(x) = \sin x$

On differentiating both sides w.r.t. x, we get $f'(x) = \cos x$

(a) Since, for each $x \in \left(0, \frac{\pi}{2}\right)$, $\cos x > 0$; we have $f'(x) > 0$

($\because \cos x$ in Ist quadrant is positive).

Hence, f is strictly increasing in $\left(0, \frac{\pi}{2}\right)$.

(b) Since, for each $x \in \left(\frac{\pi}{2}, \pi\right)$, $\cos x < 0$, we have $f'(x) < 0$

($\because \cos x$ in IInd quadrant is negative).

Hence, f is strictly decreasing in $\left(\frac{\pi}{2}, \pi\right)$.

(c) When $x \in (0, \pi)$. We see that $f'(x) > 0$ in $\left(0, \frac{\pi}{2}\right)$ and $f'(x) < 0$ in $\left(\frac{\pi}{2}, \pi\right)$

So, $f'(x)$ is positive and negative in $(0, \pi)$.

Thus, $f(x)$ is neither increasing nor decreasing in $(0, \pi)$.

Question 4 Find the intervals in which the function f given by $f(x) = 2x^2 - 3x$ is

(a) strictly increasing (b) strictly decreasing.

Thinking Process (i) Find $f'(x)$

(ii) Solve $f'(x) = 0$ for critical points.

(iii) Divide the domain using critical points and test the sign of $f'(x)$ in each internal

(iv) If $f'(x) > 0$, then f will be strictly increasing on that interval.

(v) If $f'(x) < 0$, then f will be strictly decreasing on that interval.

Sol. Given, $f(x) = 2x^2 - 3x$

On differentiating both sides w.r.t. x, we get

$$f'(x) = 4x - 3$$

On putting $f'(x) = 0$, we get $4x - 3 = 0 \Rightarrow x = 3/4$

The point $x = 3/4$ divides the real line into two disjoint intervals namely $\left(-\infty, \frac{3}{4}\right)$ and $\left(\frac{3}{4}, \infty\right)$.

$-\infty$ − $\frac{3}{4}$ + ∞

Intervals	Sign of $f'(x)$	Nature of $f(x)$
$\left(-\infty, \frac{3}{4}\right)$	(−) negative ($\because x < 3/4$)	Strictly decreasing
$\left(\frac{3}{4}, \infty\right)$	(+) positive ($\because x > 3/4$)	Strictly increasing

Hence, $f(x)$ is strictly increasing on $\left(\frac{3}{4}, \infty\right)$ and strictly decreasing on $\left(-\infty, \frac{3}{4}\right)$.

Question 5 Find the intervals in which the function f given by $f(x)=2x^3-3x^2-36x+7$ is
(a) strictly increasing, (b) strictly decreasing?

Sol. Given, $f(x) = 2x^3 - 3x^2 - 36x + 7$

On differentiating both sides w.r.t. x, we get $f'(x) = \frac{d}{dx}(2x^3 - 3x^2 - 36x + 7)$

$$= 2 \times 3x^2 - 3 \times 2x - 36 \times 1 + 0$$
$$= 6x^2 - 6x - 36 = 6(x^2 - x - 6)$$

$\Rightarrow \quad f'(x) = 6(x-3)(x+2)$

On putting $f'(x) = 0$, we get $6(x-3)(x+2) = 0 \Rightarrow x = 3$ and -2 which divides real line into three intervals namely $(-\infty, -2)$, $(-2, 3)$ and $(3, \infty)$.

$-\infty$ + -2 – 3 + ∞

Intervals	Sign of $f'(x)$	Nature of $f(x)$
$(-\infty, -2)$	$(-)(-) = +$ ve ($\because x < -2$ *i.e.*, x is $-3, -4, -5$ ... for these values, $(x-3)$ and $(x-2)$ both will be negative)	Strictly increasing
$(-2, 3)$	$(-)(+) = -$ ve ($\because 3 > x < -2$ *i.e.*, x is $1, 2, 0, -1$ ... for these values $(x-3)$ will be negative and $(x+2)$ will be positive)	Strictly decreasing
$(3, \infty)$	$(+)(+) = +$ ve ($\because x > 3$ *i.e.*, x is $4, 5, 6$, ... for these values $(x-3)$ and $(x+2)$ both are positive)	Strictly increasing

Hence, the given function f is strictly increasing in intervals $(-\infty, -2)$ and $(3, \infty)$, while function f is strictly decreasing in the interval $(-2, 3)$.

Question 6 Find the interval in which the following functions are strictly increasing or decreasing :

(a) $x^2 + 2x - 5$ (b) $10 - 6x - 2x^2$

(c) $-2x^3 - 9x^2 - 12x + 1$ (d) $6 - 9x - x^2$

(e) $(x+1)^3 (x-3)^3$

Sol.

(a) Let $f(x) = x^2 + 2x - 5 \Rightarrow f'(x) = 2x + 2$ (by differentiating w.r.t. x)
Putting $f'(x) = 0$, we get $2x + 2 = 0 \Rightarrow 2x = -2 \Rightarrow x = -1$

$-\infty$ – -1 + ∞

$x = -1$ divides real line into two intervals namely $(-\infty, -1)$ and $(-1, \infty)$.

Intervals	Sign of $f'(x)$	Nature of $f(x)$
$(-\infty, -1)$	–ve	Strictly decreasing
$(-1, \infty)$	+ve	Strictly increasing

Therefore, $f(x)$ is strictly increasing when $x > -1$ and strictly decreasing when $x < -1$.

(b) Let $f(x) = 10 - 6x - 2x^2 \Rightarrow f'(x) = 0 - 6 - 2 \times 2x = -6 - 4x$

On putting $f'(x) = 0$, we get $-6 - 4x = 0 \Rightarrow x = \frac{-3}{2}$

which divides real line into two intervals namely $\left(-\infty, \frac{-3}{2}\right)$ and $\left(\frac{-3}{2}, \infty\right)$.

$-\infty$ + −3/2 − ∞

Intervals	Sign of $f'(x)$	Nature of $f(x)$
$\left(-\infty, -\frac{3}{2}\right)$	+ ve	Strictly increasing
$\left(-\frac{3}{2}, \infty\right)$	– ve	Strictly decreasing

Hence, f is strictly increasing for $x < -\frac{3}{2}$ and strictly decreasing for $x > -\frac{3}{2}$

(c) Let $f(x) = -2x^3 - 9x^2 - 12x + 1$,

On differentiating both sides w.r.t. x, we get

$$f'(x) = -2 \times 3x^2 - 9 \times 2x - 12 = -6x^2 - 18x - 12$$
$$= -6(x + 2)(x + 1)$$

On putting $f'(x) = 0$, we get

$\Rightarrow$ $x = -2, -1$

which divides real line into three intervals $(-\infty, -2)$, $(-2, -1)$ and $(-1, \infty)$

$-\infty$ − −2 + −1 − ∞

Intervals	Sign of $f'(x)$	Nature of $f(x)$
$(-\infty, -2)$	$(-)(-)(-) = -$ ve	Strictly decreasing
$(-2, -1)$	$(-)(+)(-) = +$ ve	Strictly increasing
$(-1, \infty)$	$(-)(+)(+) = -$ ve	Strictly decreasing

Therefore, $f(x)$ is strictly increasing in $-2 < x < -1$ and strictly decreasing for $x < -2$ and $x > -1$.

(d) Let $f(x) = 6 - 9x - x^2$

On differentiating both sides w.r.t. x, we get

$$f'(x) = -9 - 2x$$

On putting $f'(x) = 0$, we get $-9 - 2x = 0 \Rightarrow x = -\frac{9}{2}$

which divides the real line in two disjoint intervals $\left(-\infty, \frac{-9}{2}\right)$ and $\left(-\frac{9}{2}, \infty\right)$.

$-\infty$ + − ∞

−9/2

Intervals	Sign of $f'(x)$	Nature of $f(x)$
$(-\infty, -9/2)$	+ ve	Strictly increasing
$(-9/2, \infty)$	− ve	Strictly decreasing

Therefore, $f(x)$ is strictly increasing when $x < -\frac{9}{2}$ and strictly decreasing when $x > -\frac{9}{2}$.

(e) Let $f(x) = (x+1)^3 (x-3)^3$

On differentiating both sides w.r.t. x, we get

$$f'(x) = (x+1)^3 \cdot 3(x-3)^2 \cdot 1 + (x-3)^3 \cdot 3(x+1)^2 \cdot 1$$
$$= 3(x-3)^2 (x+1)^2 \{(x+1) + (x-3)\}$$
$$= 3(x-3)^2 (x+1)^2 (2x-2)$$
$$= 6(x-3)^2 (x+1)^2 (x-1)$$

On putting $f'(x) = 0$, we get $x = -1, 1, 3$ which divides real line into four disjoint intervals namely $(-\infty, -1)$, $(-1, 1)$, $(1,3)$ and $(3, \infty)$.

$-\infty$ − − + + ∞

−1 1 3

Intervals	Sign of $f'(x)$	Nature of $f(x)$
$-\infty < x < -1$	(+) (+) (−) = − ve	Strictly decreasing
$-1 < x < 1$	(+) (+) (−) = − ve	Strictly decreasing
$1 < x < 3$	(+) (+) (+) = + ve	Strictly increasing
$3 < x < \infty$	(+) (+) (+) = + ve	Strictly increasing

Therefore, $f(x)$ is strictly increasing in $(1, 3)$ and $(3, \infty)$ and strictly decreasing in $(-\infty, -1)$ and $(-1, 1)$.

Note • If $a > 0$ and $b > 0$ or $a < 0$ and $b < 0$ then $ab > 0$.

• If $a > 0$ and $b < 0$ or $a < 0$ and $b > 0$ then $ab < 0$

Question 7 Show that $y = \log(1+x) - \dfrac{2x}{2+x}$, $x > -1$, is an increasing function of x throughout its domain.

◎ *Thinking Process* y is an increasing function throughout its domain if $y' > 0$ throught out the domain.

Sol. Given, $y = \log(1+x) - \dfrac{2x}{(2+x)}$.

$-\infty$ 0 1 2 ∞

On differentiating both sides w.r.t. x, we get $\dfrac{dy}{dx} = \dfrac{d}{dx}\left[\log(1+x) - \dfrac{2x}{2+x}\right]$

$$= \frac{1}{1+x} - \frac{(2+x)\frac{d}{dx}(2x) - 2x\frac{d}{dx}(2+x)}{(2+x)^2}$$

$$= \frac{1}{1+x} - \frac{4+2x-2x}{(2+x)^2} = \frac{1}{1+x} - \frac{4}{(2+x)^2}$$

$$= \frac{(2+x)^2 - 4(1+x)}{(1+x)(2+x)^2} = \frac{4+x^2+4x-4-4x}{(1+x)(2+x)^2} = \frac{x^2}{(1+x)(2+x)^2}$$

When, $x \in (-1, \infty)$, then $\dfrac{x^2}{(2+x)^2} > 0$ and $(1+x) > 0$

$\therefore \dfrac{dy}{dx} > 0$ when $x > -1$

Hence, y is an increasing function of $x(x > -1)$ throughout its domain.

Question 8 Find the values of x for which $y = [x(x-2)]^2$ is an increasing function.

Sol. Given, $y = [x(x-2)]^2 = [x^2 - 2x]^2$

On differentiating both sides w.r.t. x, we get

$$\frac{dy}{dx} = 2(x^2 - 2x)\frac{d}{dx}(x^2 - 2x) = 2(x^2 - 2x)(2x - 2) = 4x(x-2)(x-1)$$

On putting $\dfrac{dy}{dx} = 0$, we get $x = 0, 1$ and 2

which divides real line into four disjoint intervals namely $(-\infty, 0)$, $(0, 1)$, $(1, 2)$ and $(2, \infty)$.

Intervals	Sign of $y'(x)$	Nature of $y(x)$
$(-\infty, 0)$	$(-)(-)(-) = -$ ve	Strictly decreasing
$(0, 1)$	$(+)(-)(-) = +$ ve	Strictly increasing
$(1, 2)$	$(+)(-)(+) = -$ ve	Strictly decreasing
$(2, \infty)$	$(+)(+)(+) = +$ ve	Strictly increasing

Therefore, $y(x)$ is increasing in $(0, 1)$ and $(2, \infty)$.

Question 9 Prove that $y = \dfrac{4\sin\theta}{(2+\cos\theta)} - \theta$ is an increasing on θ in $\left[0, \dfrac{\pi}{2}\right]$.

Sol. We have, $y = \dfrac{4\sin\theta}{(2+\cos\theta)} - \theta$

On differentiating both sides w.r.t. θ, we get

$$\frac{dy}{d\theta} = \frac{d}{d\theta}\left[\frac{4\sin\theta}{2+\cos\theta} - \theta\right] = \frac{(2+\cos\theta)\frac{d}{d\theta}(4\sin\theta) - 4\sin\theta\frac{d}{d\theta}(2+\cos\theta)}{(2+\cos\theta)^2} - 1$$

$$= \frac{4\cos\theta(2+\cos\theta) - 4\sin\theta(-\sin\theta)}{(2+\cos\theta)^2} - 1$$

$$= \frac{8\cos\theta + 4\cos^2\theta + 4\sin^2\theta}{(2+\cos\theta)^2} - 1 = \frac{8\cos\theta + 4(\cos^2\theta + \sin^2\theta)}{(2+\cos\theta)^2} - 1$$

$$= \frac{8\cos\theta + 4}{(2+\cos\theta)^2} - 1 = \frac{8\cos\theta + 4 - (2+\cos\theta)^2}{(2+\cos\theta)^2} \qquad [\because \sin^2 A + \cos^2 A = 1]$$

$$= \frac{8\cos\theta + 4 - 4 - \cos^2\theta - 4\cos\theta}{(2+\cos\theta)^2} = \frac{4\cos\theta - \cos^2\theta}{(2+\cos\theta)^2} = \frac{\cos\theta(4-\cos\theta)}{(2+\cos\theta)^2}$$

In interval $\left[0, \dfrac{\pi}{2}\right]$, we have $\cos\theta \ge 0$. Also, $4 > \cos\theta$ $\quad (\because \cos\theta \in [-1, 1])$

$\Rightarrow (4 - \cos\theta) > 0.$

$\therefore \quad \cos\theta\,(4-\cos\theta) \ge 0$ and also $(2+\cos\theta)^2 > 0$

$\Rightarrow \quad \dfrac{\cos\theta(4-\cos\theta)}{(2+\cos\theta)^2} \ge 0 \Rightarrow \dfrac{dy}{d\theta} \ge 0$

Hence, given function is increasing in interval $\left[0, \dfrac{\pi}{2}\right]$.

Note Since, it is a continuous function,
(i) for increasing function, $f' \ge 0$. (ii) for strictly increasing function, $f' > 0$

Question 10 Prove that the logarithmic function is strictly increasing on $(0, \infty)$.

Sol. Let $f(x) = \log x \Rightarrow \quad f'(x) = \dfrac{1}{x}$ (Differentiate w.r.t. x)

When $x \in (0, \infty)$, $f'(x) > 0$. Therefore, $f(x)$ is strictly increasing in $(0, \infty)$.

Question 11 Prove that the function f given by $f(x) = x^2 - x + 1$ is neither increasing nor decreasing strictly on $(-1, 1)$.

Sol. Given, $f(x) = x^2 - x + 1$

On differentiating both sides w.r.t. x, we get $f'(x) = 2x - 1$

On putting $f'(x) = 0$, we get $x = 1/2$

which divides the given interval into two intervals as $\left(-1, \frac{1}{2}\right)$ and $\left(\frac{1}{2}, 1\right)$.

– + (number line: −1, 1/2, 1)

Intervals	Sign of $f'(x)$	Nature of $f(x)$
$\left(-1, \frac{1}{2}\right)$	– ve	Strictly decreasing
$\left(\frac{1}{2}, 1\right)$	+ ve	Strictly increasing

$\therefore$ $f'(x)$ does not have same sign throughout the interval $(-1, 1)$.
Thus, $f(x)$ is neither increasing nor decreasing strictly in the interval $(-1, 1)$.

Question 12 Which of the following functions are strictly decreasing on $\left(0, \frac{\pi}{2}\right)$.

(a) $\cos x$ (b) $\cos 2x$ (c) $\cos 3x$ (d) $\tan x$

Sol.

(a) Let $f(x) = \cos x$, then $f'(x) = -\sin x$. (Differentiate w.r.t. x)

In interval $\left(0, \frac{\pi}{2}\right)$, $f'(x) < 0$ $\left[\because \sin x > 0, \forall x \in \left(0, \frac{\pi}{2}\right)\right]$

Therefore, $f(x)$ is strictly decreasing on $\left(0, \frac{\pi}{2}\right)$.

(b) Let $f(x) = \cos 2x \Rightarrow f'(x) = -2\sin 2x$. (Differentiate w.r.t. x)

In interval $\left(0, \frac{\pi}{2}\right)$, $f'(x) < 0$

Because $\sin 2x$ will either lie in the first or second quadrant which will give a positive value. Therefore, $f(x)$ is strictly decreasing on $\left(0, \frac{\pi}{2}\right)$.

(c) Let $f(x) = \cos 3x \Rightarrow f'(x) = -3\sin 3x$. (Differentiate w.r.t. x)

In interval $\left(0, \frac{\pi}{3}\right)$, $f'(x) < 0$

Because $\sin 3x$ will either lie in the first or second quadrant which will give a positive value. Therefore, $f(x)$ is strictly decreasing on $\left(0, \frac{\pi}{3}\right)$.

When $x \in \left(\frac{\pi}{3}, \frac{\pi}{2}\right)$, then $f'(x) > 0$

Because $\sin 3x$ will lie in the third quadrant which will give a negative value.

Therefore, $f(x)$ is not strictly decreasing on $\left(0, \frac{\pi}{2}\right)$.

(d) Let $f(x) = \tan x \Rightarrow f'(x) = \sec^2 x$. (Differentiate w.r.t. x)

In interval $x \in \left(0, \frac{\pi}{2}\right)$, $f'(x) > 0$

Therefore, $f(x)$ is not strictly decreasing on $\left(0, \frac{\pi}{2}\right)$.

Question 13 On which of the following intervals is the function f given by $f(x) = x^{100} + \sin x - 1$ strictly decreasing?

(a) (0, 1) (b) $\left(\frac{\pi}{2}, \pi\right)$

(c) $\left(0, \frac{\pi}{2}\right)$ (d) None of these

Sol. (d) Given, $f(x) = x^{100} + \sin x - 1 \Rightarrow f'(x) = 100x^{99} + \cos x$

(Differentiate w.r.t. x)

(a) In interval (0, 1), $\cos x > 0$ and $100x^{99} > 0$

$\therefore \quad f'(x) > 0 \quad [\because \text{In } \left(0, \frac{\pi}{2}\right), \cos x > 0]$

Thus, function f is strictly increasing in interval (0, 1).

(b) In interval $\left(\frac{\pi}{2}, \pi\right)$, $\cos x < 0$ and $100x^{99} > 0$. Also, $100x^{99} > \cos x$

If $x \in \left(\frac{\pi}{2}, \pi\right) \Rightarrow \cos x \in [-1, 0]$ but $100x^{99}$ is a very large quantity.

$\therefore \quad f'(x) > 0 \text{ in } \left(\frac{\pi}{2}, \pi\right)$

Thus, function f is strictly increasing in interval $\left(\frac{\pi}{2}, \pi\right)$.

(c) In interval $\left(0, \frac{\pi}{2}\right)$, $\cos x > 0$ and $100x^{99} > 0$.

$\therefore \quad 100x^{99} + \cos x > 0$

$\Rightarrow \quad f'(x) > 0 \text{ in } \left(0, \frac{\pi}{2}\right)$

Thus, f is strictly increasing in interval $\left(0, \frac{\pi}{2}\right)$.

Hence, function f is not strictly decreasing in the given intervals.

Question 14. Find the least value of a such that the function f given by $f(x) = x^2 + ax + 1$ is strictly increasing on (1, 2).

◎ ***Thinking Process*** Firstly, we find $f'(x)$, then for $1 < x < 2$, put $f'(x) > 0$ and find the required least value of a.

Sol. Given, $f(x) = x^2 + ax + 1 \Rightarrow f'(x) = 2x + a$ (Differentiate w.r.t. x)

In interval (1, 2), $1 < x < 2 \Rightarrow 2 < 2x < 4$

$\Rightarrow \quad (2 + a) < (2x + a) < (4 + a)$

Since, $f(x)$ is strictly increasing function, then $(2x + a) > 0$

[For this $f'(x) > 0$ and $(2x + a) > (2 + a)$]

$\therefore$ Minimum value of $f'(x)$ is $2 + a$ and maximum value is $4 + a$

For least value, $2 + a > 0 \Rightarrow a > -2$

Hence, the least value of a is -2.

Question 15 Let I be any interval disjoint from $(-1, 1)$. Prove that the function f given by $f(x) = x + \frac{1}{x}$ is strictly increasing on I.

Sol. Given, $f(x) = x + \frac{1}{x} \Rightarrow f'(x) = 1 - \frac{1}{x^2} = \frac{x^2 - 1}{x^2}$ (Differentiate w.r.t. x)

Since, intervals are disjoint from $(-1, 1)$. Therefore,

If $x < -1$, then $f'(x) > 0$. If $x > 1$, then $f'(x) > 0$

$\therefore$ $f(x)$ is strictly increasing on interval I disjoint from $(-1, 1)$.

Question 16 Prove that the function f given by $f(x) = \log(\sin x)$ is strictly increasing on $\left(0, \frac{\pi}{2}\right)$ and strictly decreasing on $\left(\frac{\pi}{2}, \pi\right)$.

Sol. Given, $f(x) = \log(\sin x) \Rightarrow f'(x) = \frac{1}{\sin x}(\cos x) = \cot x$

(Differentiate w.r.t. x)

In interval $\left(0, \frac{\pi}{2}\right)$, $f'(x) = \cot x > 0$ [$\because \cot x$ is positive in the Ist quadrant]

$\therefore$ f is strictly increasing in $\left(0, \frac{\pi}{2}\right)$. Also, in interval $\left(\frac{\pi}{2}, \pi\right)$, $f'(x) = \cot x < 0$

[$\because \cot x$ is negative in the IInd quadrant]

$\therefore$ f is strictly decreasing on $\left(\frac{\pi}{2}, \pi\right)$.

Question 17 Prove that function f given by $f(x) = \log|\cos x|$ is strictly decreasing on $\left(0, \frac{\pi}{2}\right)$ and strictly increasing on $\left(\frac{3\pi}{2}, 2\pi\right)$.

Sol. Given, $f(x) = \log|\cos x|$

$$\Rightarrow \quad f'(x) = \frac{1}{\cos x} . (-\sin x) = -\tan x \quad \text{(Differentiate w.r.t. } x)$$

In interval $\left(0, \frac{\pi}{2}\right)$, $\tan x > 0$ ($\because \tan x$ is in Ist quadrant)

$$\Rightarrow \quad -\tan x < 0$$

$$\therefore \quad f'(x) < 0 \text{ in } \left(0, \frac{\pi}{2}\right)$$

Hence, f is strictly decreasing in $\left(0, \frac{\pi}{2}\right)$.

Also, in interval $\left(\frac{3\pi}{2}, 2\pi\right)$, $\tan x < 0 \Rightarrow -\tan x > 0$ ($\because \tan x$ is in IVth quadrant)

$$\therefore \quad f'(x) > 0 \text{ in } \left(\frac{3\pi}{2}, 2\pi\right)$$

Hence, f is strictly increasing in $\left(\frac{3\pi}{2}, 2\pi\right)$.

Hence Proved.

Question 18 Prove that the function given by $f(x) = x^3 - 3x^2 + 3x - 100$ is increasing in R.

Sol. Given, $f(x) = x^3 - 3x^2 + 3x - 100$

$\Rightarrow \quad f'(x) = 3x^2 - 6x + 3$ (Differentiate w.r.t. x)

$= 3(x^2 - 2x + 1) = 3(x - 1)^2$

For any $x \in R$, $(x - 1)^2 > 0$ since, a perfect square cannot be negative.

Then, $f'(x) \geq 0$. Hence, the given function f is an increasing function on R.

Note The square of any real number is always greater than or equal to zero.

Question 19 The interval in which $y = x^2 e^{-x}$ is increasing with respect to x is

(a) $(-\infty, \infty)$ (b) $(-2, 0)$

(c) $(2, \infty)$ (d) $(0, 2)$

Sol. Given, $y = x^2 e^{-x} \Rightarrow \dfrac{dy}{dx} = x^2 e^{-x}(-1) + e^{-x}(2x)$ (Differentiate w.r.t. x)

$= x e^{-x}(-x + 2) = x(2 - x) e^{-x}$

For increasing function, $\dfrac{dy}{dx} > 0 \Rightarrow xe^{-x}(2 - x) > 0$

Since, e^{-x} is always positive.

$\therefore \quad f'(x) > 0$ If $x > 0$ and $2 - x > 0$

$\Rightarrow \quad x > 0$ and $x < 2 \Rightarrow x \in (0, 2)$

or $\quad x < 0$ and $2 - x < 0$

$x < 0$ and $x > 2$ which is not possible.

Exercise 6.3

Question 1 Find the maximum and minimum values, if any, of the following functions given by

(a) $f(x) = (2x - 1)^2 + 3$ (b) $f(x) = 9x^2 + 12x + 2$

(c) $f(x) = -(x - 1)^2 + 10$ (d) $g(x) = x^3 + 1$

Sol

(a) Given, function is $f(x) = (2x - 1)^2 + 3$

It can be observed that $(2x - 1)^2 \geq 0$ for every $x \in R$

[Since, it is perfect square for any real number]

Therefore, $f(x) = (2x - 1)^2 + 3 \geq 3$ for every $x \in R$

The minimum value of f is attained when $2x - 1 = 0$

i.e., $\quad 2x - 1 = 0 \Rightarrow x = \dfrac{1}{2}$

$\therefore$ Minimum value of $f = f\left(\frac{1}{2}\right) = \left(2 \times \frac{1}{2} - 1\right)^2 + 3 = 3$

For any value of x, value of $f(x)$ will always be greater than 3, hence function f does not have particular maximum value.

(b) Given, function is $f(x) = 9x^2 + 12x + 2 = 9x^2 + 12x + 4 - 2$

$$= (9x^2 + 6x + 6x + 4) - 2$$
$$= [3x(3x + 2) + 2(3x + 2)] - 2$$
$$= [(3x + 2)(3x + 2)] - 2 = (3x + 2)^2 - 2$$

It can be observed that $(3x + 2)^2 \geq 0$ for every $x \in R$

Therefore, $f(x) = (3x + 2)^2 - 2 \geq -2$ for every $x \in R$

The minimum value of f is attained when $3x + 2 = 0$

i.e., $3x + 2 = 0$

$\Rightarrow$ $x = \frac{-2}{3}$

$\therefore$ Minimum value of $f = f\left(\frac{-2}{3}\right) = \left(3 \times \frac{-2}{3} + 2\right)^2 - 2 = -2$

For any value of x, value of $f(x)$ will always be greater than -2, hence, function of does not have particular maximum value.

Quick Solution

$$f(x) = 9x^2 + 12x + 2$$
$$f'(x) = 18x + 12 \quad \text{(Differentiating w.r.t. '}x\text{')}$$

For maxima and minima $f'(x) = 0$

$\Rightarrow$ $18x + 12 = 0$

$\Rightarrow$ $x = \frac{-2}{3}$

$f''(x) = 18 > 0$ thus $f(x)$ is minimum at $x = -\frac{2}{3}$

$\therefore$ Minimum value $= f\left(\frac{-2}{3}\right) = 9\left(\frac{-2}{3}\right)^2 + 12\left(\frac{-2}{3}\right) + 2 = -2$

For any value of x, $f(x) \geq -2$, hence function f does not have a particular maximum value.

(c) Given, function is $f(x) = -(x - 1)^2 + 10$.

It can be observed that $(x - 1)^2 \geq 0$ for all $x \in R$

$\Rightarrow$ $-(x - 1)^2 \leq 0$ for every $x \in R$

Therefore, $f(x) = -(x - 1)^2 + 10 \leq 10$ for every $x \in R$

The maximum value of f is attained when $(x - 1) = 0$

i.e., $(x - 1) = 0 \Rightarrow x = 1$

$\therefore$ Maximum value of $f = f(1) = -(1 - 1)^2 + 10 = 10$

For any value of x, $f(x) \leq 10$, hence function f does not have a particular minimum value.

(d) Given, function is $g(x) = x^3 + 1$.
We observe that the value of $f(x)$ increases when the value of x increase and $f(x)$ can be made as large as we please by giving large value to x. So, $f(x)$ does not have the maximum value. Similarly, $f(x)$ can be made as small as we please by giving smaller values of x. So, $f(x)$ does not have the minimum value.

Quick Solution

Here, $g(x) = x^3 + 1$, $g'(x) = 3x^2$, $g''(x) = 6x$

For maxima or minima put $g'(x) = 0$

$\Rightarrow \quad 3x^2 = 0$

$\Rightarrow \quad x = 0$

At $x = 0$, $\quad g''(0) = 6 \times 0 = 0$

Hence at $x = 0$, $g'(x)$ does not change sign as x increases through $x = 0$.
$\therefore$ It is a point of inflexion.

Note If the second order derivative test fails, we need to apply the first order derivative test.

Question 2 Find the maximum and minimum values, if any of the following functions given by:

(a) $f(x) = |x + 2| - 1$ (b) $g(x) = -|x + 1| + 3$ (c) $h(x) = \sin(2x) + 5$
(d) $f(x) = |\sin 4x + 3|$ (e) $h(x) = x + 1, x \in (-1, 1)$

Sol.

(a) Given, function is $f(x) = |x + 2| - 1$
We know that $|x + 2| \geq 0$ for all $x \in R$.
Therefore, $f(x) = |x + 2| - 1 \geq -1$ for every $x \in R$.
The minimum value of f is attained when $|x + 2| = 0$.

i.e., $\quad |x + 2| = 0 \Rightarrow x = -2$

$\therefore$ Minimum value of $f = f(-2) = |-2 + 2| - 1 = 0 - 1 = -1$
Hence, $f(x)$ has minimum value -1 at $x = 2$ but $f(x)$ has no maximum value.

Note The modulus value of a function is always ≥ 0.

(b) Given function is $g(x) = -|x + 1| + 3$
We know that $|x + 1| \geq 0$ for all $x \in R$
$\Rightarrow -|x + 1| \leq 0$ for all $x \in R \Rightarrow -|x + 1| + 3 \leq 3$ for all $x \in R$
The maximum value of g is attained when $|x + 1| = 0$.

i.e., $\quad |x + 1| = 0$

$\Rightarrow \quad x = -1$

$\therefore$ Maximum value of $g = g(-1) = -|-1 + 1| + 3 = 3$.
Hence, $g(x)$ has maximum value 3 at $x = -1$ but $g(x)$ has no minimum value.

(c) Given function is $h(x) = \sin 2x + 5$

We know that, $-1 \le \sin x \le 1 \Rightarrow -1 \le \sin 2x \le 1$

$\Rightarrow \quad -1 + 5 \le \sin 2x + 5 \le 1 + 5 \Rightarrow 4 \le \sin 2x + 5 \le 6$

Hence, maximum value of $h(x)$ is 6 and minimum value of $h(x)$ is 4.

(d) Given function is $f(x) = |\sin 4x + 3|$

We know that $-1 \le \sin 4x \le 1 \Rightarrow 3 - 1 \le \sin 4x + 3 \le 1 + 3$

$\Rightarrow \quad 2 \le \sin 4x + 3 \le 4$

$\Rightarrow \quad 2 \le |\sin 4x + 3| \le 4$

Hence, maximum value of $f(x)$ is 4 and minimum value of $f(x)$ is 2.

Mistake Alert Becarefull where trigonometry function is given in mod.

Ex. $f(x) = |3 \sin x - 2|$ if you put

$\sin x = -1 \Rightarrow f(x) = 5$

$\sin x = 1 \Rightarrow f(x) = 1$

(e) Given function is $h(x) = x + 1, -1 < x < 1$

Now, $\quad -1 < x < 1 \Leftrightarrow -1 + 1 < x + 1 < 1 + 1 \Leftrightarrow 0 < x + 1 < 2$

Here, on the point (0,2), f has neither a maximum nor a minimum value.

Quick Solution

Given, $h(x) = x + 1$

$\therefore \quad h'(x) = 1$ exists at all $x \in (-1, 1)$

Also, $h'(x) \ne 0$ for any $x \in (-1, 1)$.

Further $h(x)$ is defined on an open interval.

So, there is no point for which $f(x)$ may have a minimum or a maximum value.

Note We can apply the second order derivative test only if the function differentiate twice in the given interval.

Question 3 Find the local maxima and local minima, if any of the following functions. Also, find the local maximum and the local minimum values, as the case may be as follows:

(i) $f(x) = x^2$

(ii) $g(x) = x^3 - 3x$

(iii) $h(x) = \sin x + \cos x, \ 0 < x < \dfrac{\pi}{2}$

(iv) $f(x) = \sin x - \cos x, \ 0 < x < 2\pi$

(v) $f(x) = x^3 - 6x^2 + 9x + 15$

(vi) $g(x) = \dfrac{x}{2} + \dfrac{2}{x}, \ x > 0$

(vii) $g(x) = \dfrac{1}{x^2 + 2}$

(viii) $f(x) = x\sqrt{1 - x}, \ 0 < x < 1$

Thinking Process Use second derivative test to find local minima and local maxima. Putting first derivative equal to zero to find the value of variable and for that value check second derivative, if value is greater than zero, then the point, will be of local minimum, if value is less than zero, then the points will be of local maximum.

Sol.

(i) Given function is $f(x) = x^2$

On differentiating both sides w.r.t. x, we get $f'(x) = 2x$

and again differentiating both sides w.r.t. x, we get $f''(x) = 2$

For maxima or minima, put $f'(x) = 0$

$\therefore \quad 2x = 0 \Rightarrow x = 0$

Thus, $x = 0$ is the only critical point which could be possible the point of local maxima or local minima of f.

We have $f''(0) = 2 > 0$ (which is positive)

Therefore, by second derivative test, $x = 0$ is a point of local minima and local minimum value of f at $x = 0$ is $f(0) = x^2 = 0^2 = 0$.

(ii) Given function is $g(x) = x^3 - 3x$

$\therefore \quad g'(x) = 3x^2 - 3$ and $g''(x) = 6x$ (Differentiate w.r.t. x)

For maxima or minima put $g'(x) = 0$

$\therefore \quad 3x^2 - 3 = 0 \Rightarrow x^2 = 1 \Rightarrow x = \pm 1$

Thus, we expect extremum only at two points -1 and 1.

At $x = -1$, $\quad g''(-1) = 6(-1) = -6 < 0$

$\therefore$ g has a local maxima at $x = -1$ and local maximum value $= g(-1)$

$= (-1)^3 - 3(-1) = -1 + 3 = 2$

At $x = 1$, $\quad g''(1) = 6 \times 1 = 6 > 0$

$\therefore$ g has a local minima at $x = 1$ and local minimum value $= g(1)$

$= 1^3 - 3 \times 1 = -2$

(iii) Given function is $h(x) = \sin x + \cos x,\ 0 < x < \dfrac{\pi}{2}$

$\therefore \quad h'(x) = \cos x - \sin x$ and $h''(x) = -\sin x - \cos x$ (Differentiate w.r.t. x)

For maxima or minima put $h'(x) = 0$

$\Rightarrow \sin x = \cos x \Rightarrow \dfrac{\sin x}{\cos x} = 1 \Rightarrow \tan x = 1 \Rightarrow x = \dfrac{\pi}{4} \in \left(0, \dfrac{\pi}{2}\right)$

At $x = \dfrac{\pi}{4}$, $h''\left(\dfrac{\pi}{4}\right) = -\sin\dfrac{\pi}{4} - \cos\dfrac{\pi}{4} = -\dfrac{1}{\sqrt{2}} - \dfrac{1}{\sqrt{2}} = -\dfrac{2}{\sqrt{2}} = -\sqrt{2} < 0$

Therefore, by second derivative test $x = \dfrac{\pi}{4}$ is a point of local maxima and the local maximum value of h at $x = \dfrac{\pi}{4}$ is

$$h\left(\frac{\pi}{4}\right) = \sin\frac{\pi}{4} + \cos\frac{\pi}{4} = \frac{1}{\sqrt{2}} + \frac{1}{\sqrt{2}} = \frac{2}{\sqrt{2}} = \sqrt{2}$$

(iv) Given function is $f(x) = \sin x - \cos x \quad 0 < x < 2\pi$

$\therefore \quad f'(x) = \cos x + \sin x$ and $f''(x) = -\sin x + \cos x$

(Differentiate w.r.t. x)

For maxima or minima put $f'(x) = 0$

$$\Rightarrow \quad \cos x + \sin x = 0 \Rightarrow \frac{\sin x}{\cos x} = -1 \Rightarrow \tan x = -1$$

$\tan x$ is -ve in second and fourth quadrant.

$$\Rightarrow \quad x = \pi - \frac{\pi}{4}, 2\pi - \frac{\pi}{4} \Rightarrow x = \frac{3\pi}{4}, \frac{7\pi}{4}; x \in (0, 2\pi)$$

$\therefore$ The points at which extremum may occur are $\frac{3\pi}{4}$ and $\frac{7\pi}{4}$.

At $x = \frac{3\pi}{4}$, $f''\left(\frac{3\pi}{4}\right) = -\sin\frac{3\pi}{4} + \cos\frac{3\pi}{4} = -\sin\left(\pi - \frac{\pi}{4}\right) + \cos\left(\pi - \frac{\pi}{4}\right)$

$[\because \sin(\pi - \theta)) = \sin\theta$ and $\cos(\pi - \theta) = -\cos\theta]$

$$= -\sin\frac{\pi}{4} - \cos\frac{\pi}{4} = -\frac{1}{\sqrt{2}} - \frac{1}{\sqrt{2}} = -\sqrt{2} < 0$$

$\therefore x = \frac{3\pi}{4}$ is a point of maxima.

and maximum value $= f\left(\frac{3\pi}{4}\right) = \sin\frac{3\pi}{4} - \cos\frac{3\pi}{4}$

$$= \sin\left(\pi - \frac{\pi}{4}\right) - \cos\left(\pi - \frac{\pi}{4}\right) = \sin\frac{\pi}{4} + \cos\frac{\pi}{4}$$

$$= \frac{1}{\sqrt{2}} + \frac{1}{\sqrt{2}} = \frac{2}{\sqrt{2}} = \sqrt{2}$$

At $x = \frac{7\pi}{4}$, $f''\left(\frac{7\pi}{4}\right) = -\sin\frac{7\pi}{4} + \cos\frac{7\pi}{4} = -\sin\left(2\pi - \frac{\pi}{4}\right) + \cos\left(2\pi - \frac{\pi}{4}\right)$

$[\because \sin(2\pi - \theta) = -\sin\theta$ and $\cos(2\pi - \theta) = \cos\theta]$

$$= \sin\frac{\pi}{4} + \cos\frac{\pi}{4} = \frac{1}{\sqrt{2}} + \frac{1}{\sqrt{2}} = \sqrt{2} > 0$$

$\therefore \quad x = \frac{7\pi}{4}$ is a point of minima.

and minimum value $= f\left(\frac{7\pi}{4}\right) = \sin\frac{7\pi}{4} - \cos\frac{7\pi}{4}$

$$= \sin\left(2\pi - \frac{\pi}{4}\right) - \cos\left(2\pi - \frac{\pi}{4}\right)$$

$$= -\sin\frac{\pi}{4} - \cos\frac{\pi}{4}$$

$$= -\frac{1}{\sqrt{2}} - \frac{1}{\sqrt{2}} = -\sqrt{2}$$

Mistake Alert In trigonometre function.
When $f'(x) = 0$ we have to take all possible values of x in the given interval.

(v) Given function is $f(x) = x^3 - 6x^2 + 9x + 15$

$\therefore \quad f'(x) = 3x^2 - 12x + 9$ and $f''(x) = 6x - 12$

(Differentiate w.r.t. x)

For maxima or minima put $f'(x) = 0$

$\Rightarrow \quad 3x^2 - 12x + 9 = 0 \Rightarrow 3(x^2 - 4x + 3) = 0$

$\Rightarrow \quad 3(x^2 - 3x - x + 3) = 0 \Rightarrow 3[x(x-3) - 1(x-3)] = 0$

$\Rightarrow \quad 3(x-1)(x-3) = 0 \Rightarrow \quad x = 1 \text{ or } x = 3$

At $x = 1$, $f''(1) = 6 \times 1 - 12 = 6 - 12 = -6 < 0$

$\therefore x = 1$ is a point of maxima.

and maximum value $= f(1) = (1)^3 - 6(1)^2 + 9(1) + 15 = 1 - 6 + 9 + 15 = 19$

At $x = 3$, $\quad f''(3) = 6 \times 3 - 12 = 18 - 12 = 6 > 0$

$\therefore x = 3$ is a point of minima

and minimum value $= f(3) = 3^3 - 6 \times 3^2 + 9 \times 3 + 15$

$= 27 - 54 + 27 + 15 = 15$

(vi) Given function is $g(x) = \frac{x}{2} + \frac{2}{x}, x > 0$

$\therefore g'(x) = \frac{1}{2} + 2\left(-\frac{1}{x^2}\right) = \frac{1}{2} - \frac{2}{x^2}$ and $g''(x) = -2(-2)x^{-3} = \frac{4}{x^3}$

(Differentiate w.r.t. x)

For maxima or minima put, $g'(x) = 0$

$\Rightarrow \quad \frac{1}{2} - \frac{2}{x^2} = 0 \Rightarrow \frac{1}{2} = \frac{2}{x^2} \Rightarrow x^2 = 4 \Rightarrow x = 2, -2$

$\Rightarrow \quad x = 2 \qquad [\because x > 0 \; (\qquad) \text{ so neglect } x = -2]$

At $x = 2$, $\quad g''(2) = \frac{4}{2^3} = \frac{4}{8} = \frac{1}{2} > 0$

$\therefore x = 2$ is a point of minima.

and minimum value, $g(2) = \frac{2}{2} + \frac{2}{2} = 1 + 1 = 2$

(vii) Given function is $g(x) = \frac{1}{x^2 + 2} = (x^2 + 2)^{-1}$

On differentiating both sides w.r.t. x, we get

$$g'(x) = -1(x^2 + 2)^{-1-1} \times 2x = \frac{-2x}{(x^2 + 2)^2}$$

Again, on differentiating both sides w.r.t. x we get

$$g''(x) = \frac{(x^2 + 2)^2 \cdot (-2) - (-2x) \cdot 2(x^2 + 2) \cdot 2x}{(x^2 + 2)^4}$$

$$= \frac{-2(x^2 + 2)^2 + 8x^2(x^2 + 2)}{(x^2 + 2)^4} = \frac{(x^2 + 2)[-2x^2 - 4 + 8x^2]}{(x^2 + 2)^4}$$

$$= \frac{6x^2 - 4}{(x^2 + 2)^3} = \frac{2(3x^2 - 2)}{(x^2 + 2)^3}$$

For maxima or minima put $g'(x) = 0 \Rightarrow \dfrac{-2x}{(x^2+2)^2} = 0 \Rightarrow -2x = 0 \Rightarrow x = 0$

At $x = 0$, $\quad g''(0) = \dfrac{2[3(0)^2 - 2]}{[(0)^2 + 2]^3} = \dfrac{-4}{8} = -\dfrac{1}{2} < 0$

$\therefore$ $x = 0$ is a point of maxima and maximum value, $g(0) = \dfrac{1}{(0)^2 + 2} = \dfrac{1}{2}$

(viii) Given function is $f(x) = x\sqrt{1-x}$

On differentiating both sides w.r.t. x, we get

$$f'(x) = \frac{x(-1)}{2\sqrt{1-x}} + \sqrt{1-x} = \frac{-x + 2(1-x)}{2\sqrt{1-x}} = \frac{2-3x}{2\sqrt{1-x}}$$

Again, on differentiating both sides w.r.t. x, we get

$$f''(x) = \frac{1}{2}\left[\frac{\sqrt{1-x}(-3) - (2-3x)\left(\dfrac{-1}{2\sqrt{1-x}}\right)}{(1-x)}\right]$$

$$= \frac{\sqrt{1-x}(-3) - (2-3x)\left(\dfrac{-1}{2\sqrt{1-x}}\right)}{2(1-x)}$$

$$= \frac{-6(1-x) + (2-3x)}{4(1-x)^{3/2}}$$

$$= \frac{3x-4}{4(1-x)^{3/2}}$$

For maxima or minima put $f'(x) = 0$

$\therefore \quad \dfrac{2-3x}{2\sqrt{1-x}} = 0$

$\Rightarrow \quad 2 - 3x = 0$

$\Rightarrow \quad x = \dfrac{2}{3}$

At $x = \dfrac{2}{3}$, $\quad f''\left(\dfrac{2}{3}\right) = \dfrac{3\left(\dfrac{2}{3}\right) - 4}{4\left(1 - \dfrac{2}{3}\right)^{3/2}} = \dfrac{2-4}{4\left(\dfrac{1}{3}\right)^{3/2}} = \dfrac{-1}{2\left(\dfrac{1}{3}\right)^{3/2}} < 0$

$\therefore x = \dfrac{2}{3}$ is a point of maxima.

and maximum value $= f\left(\dfrac{2}{3}\right) = \dfrac{2}{3}\sqrt{1 - \dfrac{2}{3}} = \dfrac{2}{3} \times \sqrt{\dfrac{1}{3}}$

$$= \frac{2}{3\sqrt{3}} = \frac{2\sqrt{3}}{9}$$

Quick Solution

$$f(x) = x\sqrt{1-x}$$

$$\Rightarrow \quad (f(x))^2 = x^2(1-x) = x^2 - x^3$$

If $f(x)$ is maximum or minimum, then $(f(x)^2)$ will be also maximum or minimum.

Now, $\frac{d}{dx}(f(x)^2) = 2x - 3x^2$ and $\frac{d^2}{dx^2}(f(x)^2) = 2 - 6x$ (on differentiation)

For maxima and minima, put $\frac{d}{dx}(f(x))^2 = 0 \Rightarrow 2x - 3x^2 = 0 \Rightarrow x = \frac{2}{3}, 0$

$$\Rightarrow \quad x = \frac{2}{3} \qquad (\because x > 0, \text{ given, ignore } x = 0)$$

At $x = \frac{2}{3}, 0 \qquad f''(x) = 2 - 6x \Rightarrow f''\left(\frac{2}{3}\right) = -2 < 0$

$\therefore x = \frac{2}{3}$ is a point of maxima.

and maximum value $= f\left(\frac{2}{3}\right) = \frac{2}{3}\sqrt{1-\frac{2}{3}} = \frac{2}{3\sqrt{3}} = \frac{2\sqrt{3}}{9}$

Question 4 Prove that the following functions do not have maxima or minima

(a) $f(x) = e^x$ (b) $g(x) = \log x$ (c) $h(x) = x^3 + x^2 + x + 1$

Sol.

(a) Given function is $f(x) = e^x$

$$\therefore \quad f'(x) = e^x \qquad \text{(Differentiate w.r.t. } x)$$

Now, if $f'(x) = 0$, then $e^x = 0$. But, the exponential function can never assume 0 for any value of x.

Therefore, there does not exist any $x \in R$ such that $f'(x) = 0$

Hence, function f does not have maxima or minima.

(b) Given function is $g(x) = \log x$

$$\therefore \quad g'(x) = \frac{1}{x} \qquad \text{(Differentiate w.r.t. } x)$$

Since, log x is defined for a positive number x, then $g'(x) > 0$ for any x.

Therefore, there does not exist any $x \in R$ such that $g'(x) = 0$

Hence, function g does not have maxima or minima.

(c) Given function is $h(x) = x^3 + x^2 + x + 1$

$$\therefore \quad h'(x) = 3x^2 + 2x + 1 \qquad \text{(Differentiate w.r.t. } x)$$

Now, put $h'(x) = 0 \Rightarrow 3x^2 + 2x + 1 = 0$

$$\Rightarrow \quad x = \frac{-2 \pm \sqrt{4 - 4 \times 3 \times 1}}{6} = \frac{-2 \pm \sqrt{-8}}{6} \qquad \left[\text{u} \quad x \quad \frac{-b \pm \sqrt{b^2 - 4ac}}{2a}\right]$$

$$\Rightarrow \quad x = \frac{-2 \pm 2\sqrt{2}\,i}{6} = \frac{2(-1 \pm \sqrt{2}\,i)}{6} = \frac{-1 \pm \sqrt{2}\,i}{3} \notin R$$

Therefore, there does not exist any $x \in R$ such that $h'(x) = 0$

Hence, function h does not have maxima or minima.

Question 5 Find the absolute maximum value and the absolute minimum value of the following functions in the given intervals :

◎ ***Thinking Process*** The maximum or minimum value of a function in a closed interval is called absolute maximum or absolute minimum value of the function. To find the absolute maximum or absolute minimum, evaluate the value of f at critical point and at end points of the interval.

(a) $f(x)=x^3, x\in[-2,2]$ (b) $f(x)=\sin x+\cos x, x\in[0,\pi]$

(c) $f(x)=4x-\frac{1}{2}x^2, x\in\left[-2,\frac{9}{2}\right]$ (d) $f(x)=(x-1)^2+3, x\in[-3,1]$

Sol.

(a) Given function is $f(x)=x^3$

$\therefore$ $$f'(x)=3x^2 \quad \text{(Differentiate w.r.t. } x)$$

For maxima or minima put $f'(x)=0 \Rightarrow 3x^2=0 \Rightarrow x=0\in[-2,2]$

Now, we evaluate the value of f at critical point $x=0$ and at end points of the interval $[-2, 2]$.

At $x=0$, $f(0)=0^3=0$

At $x=-2$, $f(-2)=(-2)^3=-8$

At $x=2$, $f(2)=(2)^3=8$

Thus, absolute maximum value is 8 at $x=2$ and absolute minimum value is -8 at $x=-2$.

(b) Given function is $f(x)=\sin x+\cos x$

$\therefore$ $$f'(x)=\cos x-\sin x \quad \text{(Differentiate w.r.t. } x)$$

For maxima or minima put $f'(x)=0 \Rightarrow \cos x-\sin x=0 \Rightarrow \frac{\sin x}{\cos x}=1$

$\Rightarrow$ $$\tan x=1\Rightarrow x=\frac{\pi}{4}\in[0,\pi]$$

Now, we evaluate the value of f at critical point $x=\frac{\pi}{4}$ and at the end points of the interval $[0,\pi]$.

At $x=\frac{\pi}{4}$, $f\left(\frac{\pi}{4}\right)=\sin\frac{\pi}{4}+\cos\frac{\pi}{4}=\frac{1}{\sqrt{2}}+\frac{1}{\sqrt{2}}=\sqrt{2}$

At $x=0$, $f(0)=\sin 0+\cos 0=0+1=1$

At $x=\pi$, $f(\pi)=\sin\pi+\cos\pi=0-1=-1$

Thus, absolute maximum value is $\sqrt{2}$ at $x=\frac{\pi}{4}$ and absolute minimum value is -1 at $x=\pi$.

(c) Given function is $f(x)=4x-\frac{1}{2}x^2$

$\therefore$ $$f'(x)=4-\frac{1}{2}(2x)=4-x \quad \text{(Differentiate w.r.t. } x)$$

For maxima or minima put $f'(x)=0$, $4-x=0\Rightarrow x=4\in\left[-2,\frac{9}{2}\right]$

Now, we evaluate the value of f at critical point $x=4$ and at the end points of the interval $\left[-2,\frac{9}{2}\right]$.

At $x = 4$, $\quad f(4) = 4(4) - \frac{1}{2}(4)^2 = 16 - 8 = 8$

At $x = -2$, $\quad f(-2) = 4(-2) - \frac{1}{2}(-2)^2 = -8 - 2 = -10$

At $x = \frac{9}{2}$, $\quad f\left(\frac{9}{2}\right) = 4\left(\frac{9}{2}\right) - \frac{1}{2}\left(\frac{9}{2}\right)^2 = 18 - \frac{81}{8} = \frac{63}{8} = 7.875$

Thus, absolute maximum value is 8 at $x = 4$ and absolute minimum value is -10 at $x = -2$.

(d) Given function is $f(x) = (x-1)^2 + 3$

$\therefore \quad f'(x) = 2(x-1)$ (Differentiate w.r.t x)

For maxima or minima put $f'(x) = 0 \Rightarrow 2(x-1) = 0 \Rightarrow x = 1$

Now, we evaluate the value of f at critical point $x = 1$ and at the end points of the interval $[-3, 1]$.

At $x = 1$, $\quad f(1) = (1-1)^2 + 3 = 3$

At $x = -3$, $\quad f(-3) = (-3-1)^2 + 3 = 19$

Thus, absolute maximum value is 19 at $x = -3$ and absolute minimum value is 3 at $x = 1$.

Note If $f'(x) = 0$ gives value outside the given interval then that will be neglected.

Question 6 Find the maximum profit that a company can make, if the profit function is given by $p(x) = 41 - 72x - 18x^2$.

◎ ***Thinking Process*** Firstly, differentiate given equation and put $\frac{dp}{dx} = 0$ and solve it to get value of x and check $\frac{d^2p}{dx^2}$ at different values of x. If $\frac{d^2y}{dx^2}$ is negative at any particular value of x, then put that value of x in given equation, to get the maximum value.

Sol. The profit function is given as $p(x) = 41 - 72x - 18x^2$

On differentiating both sides w.r.t. x, we get $\quad p'(x) = -72 - 36x = -36(2 + x)$

and again differentiating both sides w.r.t. x, we get $p''(x) = -36$

For maxima or minima put $p'(x) = 0$

$\Rightarrow \quad -36(2 + x) = 0 \Rightarrow x + 2 = 0 \Rightarrow x = -2$

At $x = -2$, $\quad p''(-2) = -36 < 0$

$\therefore x = -2$ is a point of maxima.

$\therefore$ Maximum profit, $p(-2) = 41 - 72(-2) - 18(-2)^2 = 41 + 144 - 72 = 113$

Question 7 Find both the maximum value and the minimum value of $3x^4 - 8x^3 + 12x^2 - 48x + 25$ on the interval $[0, 3]$.

Sol. Let $f(x) = 3x^4 - 8x^3 + 12x^2 - 48x + 25$

On differentiating both sides w.r.t. x, we get

$$f'(x) = 12x^3 - 24x^2 + 24x - 48 = 12(x^3 - 2x^2 + 2x - 4)$$

$= 12\{x^2(x-2) + 2(x-2)\} = 12(x-2)(x^2+2)$

For maxima or minima put $f'(x) = 0$

$\Rightarrow 12(x-2)(x^2+2) = 0 \Rightarrow$ if $x - 2 = 0 \Rightarrow x = 2 \in [0, 3]$

and if, $\quad x^2 + 2 = 0 \Rightarrow x^2 = -2 \Rightarrow x = \sqrt{-2}$ (which is not real)

Hence, the only real root is $x = 2$ which is considered as critical point.

Now, we evaluate the value of f at critical point $x = 2$ and at the end points of the interval [0, 3].

At $x = 2$, $\quad f(2) = 3 \times 2^4 - 8 \times 2^3 + 12 \times 2^2 - 48 \times 2 + 25$

$= 48 - 64 + 48 - 96 + 25 = -39$

At $x = 0$, $\quad f(0) = 0 - 0 + 0 - 0 + 25 = 25$

At $x = 3$, $\quad f(3) = 3 \times 3^4 - 8 \times 3^3 + 12 \times 3^2 - 48 \times 3 + 25$

$= 243 - 216 + 108 - 144 + 25 = 16$

Hence, we can conclude that the absolute maximum value of f is 25 at $x = 0$ and the absolute minimum value of f is -39 at $x = 2$.

Question 8 At what points in the interval $[0, 2\pi]$, does the function $\sin 2x$ attain its maximum value?

Sol. Let $f(x) = \sin 2x$

$\therefore \quad f'(x) = 2\cos 2x$ (Differentiate w.r.t. x)

For maxima or minima put $f'(x) = 0$

$\Rightarrow \quad 2\cos 2x = 0 \Rightarrow \cos 2x = 0$

$\Rightarrow \quad 2x = \frac{\pi}{2}, \frac{3\pi}{2}, \frac{5\pi}{2}, \frac{7\pi}{2} \Rightarrow x = \frac{\pi}{4}, \frac{3\pi}{4}, \frac{5\pi}{4}, \frac{7\pi}{4}$

Thus, we evaluate the values of f at critical points $x = \frac{\pi}{4}, \frac{3\pi}{4}, \frac{5\pi}{4}, \frac{7\pi}{4}$ and at the end points of the interval $[0, 2\pi]$.

At $x = 0$, $\quad f(0) = \sin(2 \times 0) = 0$

At $x = 2\pi$, $\quad f(2\pi) = \sin(2 \times 2\pi) = 0$

At $x = \frac{\pi}{4}$, $\quad f\left(\frac{\pi}{4}\right) = \sin\left(2 \times \frac{\pi}{4}\right) = \sin\frac{\pi}{2} = 1$

At $x = \frac{3\pi}{4}$, $\quad f\left(\frac{3\pi}{4}\right) = \sin\left(2 \times \frac{3\pi}{4}\right) = \sin\frac{3\pi}{2} = \sin\left(\pi + \frac{\pi}{2}\right) = -\sin\frac{\pi}{2} = -1$

At $x = \frac{5\pi}{4}$, $\quad f\left(\frac{5\pi}{4}\right) = \sin\left(2 \times \frac{5\pi}{4}\right) = \sin\frac{5\pi}{2} = \sin\left(2\pi + \frac{\pi}{2}\right) = \sin\frac{\pi}{2} = 1$

At $x = \frac{7\pi}{4}$, $\quad f\left(\frac{7\pi}{4}\right) = \sin\left(2 \times \frac{7\pi}{4}\right) = \sin\frac{7\pi}{2} = \sin\left(2\pi + \frac{3\pi}{2}\right) = \sin\frac{3\pi}{2} = -1$

Hence, we can conclude that absolute maximum value of f on $[0, 2\pi]$ is 1 occurring at $x = \frac{\pi}{4}$ and $x = \frac{5\pi}{4}$.

Mistake Alert We have take all values of x in the given interval.

Question 9 What is the maximum value of the function $\sin x + \cos x$?

Sol. Let $f(x) = \sin x + \cos x$ $\therefore$ $f'(x) = \cos x - \sin x$ (Differentiate w.r.t x)

and $f''(x) = -\sin x - \cos x = -(\sin x + \cos x)$ (again, differentiate w.r.t.x)

For maxima or minima put $f'(x) = 0$

$\Rightarrow$ $\cos x - \sin x = 0 \Rightarrow \sin x = \cos x$

$\Rightarrow$ $\dfrac{\sin x}{\cos x} = 1 \Rightarrow \tan x = 1$

$\because$ $x = \dfrac{\pi}{4}, \dfrac{5\pi}{4}, \ldots\ldots\ldots,$

$\tan x$ is + ve in first and third quardant.

Now, $f''(x)$ will be negative when $(\sin x + \cos x)$ is positive *i.e.*, when $\sin x$ and $\cos x$ are both positive. Also, we know that $\sin x$ and $\cos x$ both are positive in the first quadrant.

Then, $f''(x)$ will be negative when $x \in \left(0, \dfrac{\pi}{2}\right)$.

Thus, we consider $x = \dfrac{\pi}{4}$.

$$f''\left(\frac{\pi}{4}\right) = -\left(\sin\frac{\pi}{4} + \cos\frac{\pi}{4}\right) = -\left(\frac{1}{\sqrt{2}} + \frac{1}{\sqrt{2}}\right) = -\frac{2}{\sqrt{2}} = -\sqrt{2} < 0$$

$\therefore$ By second derivative test, f will be maximum at $x = \dfrac{\pi}{4}$ and the maximum value of f is $f\left(\dfrac{\pi}{4}\right) = \sin\dfrac{\pi}{4} + \cos\dfrac{\pi}{4} = \dfrac{1}{\sqrt{2}} + \dfrac{1}{\sqrt{2}} = \dfrac{2}{\sqrt{2}} = \sqrt{2}$

Question 10 Find the maximum value of $2x^3 - 24x + 107$ in the interval $[1, 3]$. Find the maximum value of the same function in $[-3, -1]$.

Sol. Let $f(x) = 2x^3 - 24x + 107$

$\therefore$ $f'(x) = 6x^2 - 24 = 6(x^2 - 4) = 6(x + 2)(x - 2)$ (Differentiate w.r.t. x)

For maxima or minima put $f'(x) = 0 \Rightarrow 6(x + 2)(x - 2) = 0$

$\Rightarrow$ $x = 2, -2$

We first consider the interval $[1, 3]$.

So, we have to evaluate the value of f at the critical point $x = 2 \in [1, 3]$ and at the end points of $[1, 3]$.

At $x = 1$, $f(1) = 2 \times 1^3 - 24 \times 1 + 107 = 85$

At $x = 2$, $f(2) = 2 \times 2^3 - 24 \times 2 + 107 = 75$

At $x = 3$, $f(3) = 2 \times 3^3 - 24 \times 3 + 107 = 89$

Hence, the absolute maximum value of $f(x)$ in the interval $[1, 3]$ is 89 occurring at $x = 3$.

Next, we consider the function in the interval $[-3, -1]$, then evaluate the value of f at the critical point $x = -2 \in [-3, -1]$ and at the end points of the interval $[-3, -1]$.

At $x = -1$, $\quad f(-1) = 2(-1)^3 - 24(-1) + 107 = -2 + 24 + 107 = 129$

At $x = -2$, $\quad f(-2) = 2(-2)^3 - 24(-2) + 107 = -16 + 48 + 107 = 139$

At $x = -3$, $\quad f(-3) = 2(-3)^3 - 24(-3) + 107 = -54 + 72 + 107 = 125$

Hence, the absolute maximum value of $f(x)$ in the interval $[-3, -1]$ is 139 occurring at $x = -2$.

Question 11 It is given that at $x = 1$, the function $x^4 - 62x^2 + ax + 9$ attains its maximum value, on the interval $[0, 2]$. Find the value of a.

Sol. Let $f(x) = x^4 - 62x^2 + ax + 9$

$\therefore \quad f'(x) = 4x^3 - 124x + a$ (Differentiate w.r.t. x)

It is given that function f attains its maximum value on the interval [0, 2] at $x = 1$.

$\therefore \quad f'(1) = 0 \Rightarrow 4 \times 1^3 - 124 \times 1 + a = 0$

$\Rightarrow \quad 4 - 124 + a = 0 \Rightarrow a = 120$

Hence, the value of a is 120.

Question 12 Find the maximum and minimum values of $x + \sin 2x$ on $[0, 2\pi]$.

Sol. Let $\quad f(x) = x + \sin 2x$,

$\therefore \quad f'(x) = 1 + 2\cos 2x$ (Differentiate w.r.t. x)

For maxima or minima put $f'(x) = 0$

$\Rightarrow 1 + 2\cos 2x = 0 \Rightarrow \cos 2x = -\frac{1}{2} \Rightarrow \cos 2x = -\cos\frac{\pi}{3} = \cos\frac{2\pi}{3}$

If $x \in [0, 2\pi] \Rightarrow 2x \in [0, 4\pi]$

$\Rightarrow \quad \cos 2x = \cos\left(\pi - \frac{\pi}{3}\right), \cos\left(\pi + \frac{\pi}{3}\right), \cos\left(3\pi - \frac{\pi}{3}\right), \cos\left(3\pi + \frac{\pi}{3}\right)$

($\because$ We know that $\cos x$ is negative in second and third quadrant)

Then, $\quad 2x = 2n\pi \pm \frac{2\pi}{3}, n \in Z$

$\Rightarrow \quad 2x = \frac{2\pi}{3}, \frac{4\pi}{3}, \frac{8\pi}{3}, \frac{10\pi}{3}$

$\Rightarrow \quad x = \frac{\pi}{3}, \frac{2\pi}{3}, \frac{4\pi}{3}, \frac{5\pi}{3} \in [0, 2\pi]$

Then, we evaluate the value of f at critical points $x = \frac{\pi}{3}, \frac{2\pi}{3}, \frac{4\pi}{3}, \frac{5\pi}{3}$ and at the end points of the interval $[0, 2\pi]$.

At $x = 0$, $\quad f(0) = 0 + \sin 0 = 0$

At $x = \frac{\pi}{3}$, $\quad f\left(\frac{\pi}{3}\right) = \frac{\pi}{3} + \sin\frac{2\pi}{3} = \frac{\pi}{3} + \sin\frac{\pi}{3} = \frac{\pi}{3} + \frac{\sqrt{3}}{2}$

At $x = \frac{2\pi}{3}$, $\quad f\left(\frac{2\pi}{3}\right) = \frac{2\pi}{3} + \sin\frac{4\pi}{3} = \frac{2\pi}{3} - \sin\frac{\pi}{3} = \frac{2\pi}{3} - \frac{\sqrt{3}}{2}$

At $x = \frac{4\pi}{3}$, $\quad f\left(\frac{4\pi}{3}\right) = \frac{4\pi}{3} + \sin\frac{8\pi}{3} = \frac{4\pi}{3} + \sin\frac{2\pi}{3} = \frac{4\pi}{3} + \frac{\sqrt{3}}{2}$

At $x = \frac{5\pi}{3}$, $f\left(\frac{5\pi}{3}\right) = \frac{5\pi}{3} + \sin\frac{10\pi}{3} = \frac{5\pi}{3} - \sin\frac{2\pi}{3} = \frac{5\pi}{3} - \frac{\sqrt{3}}{2}$

At $x = 2\pi$, $f(2\pi) = 2\pi + \sin 4\pi = 2\pi + 0 = 2\pi$

Thus, maximum value is 2π at $x = 2\pi$ and minimum value is 0 at $x = 0$.

Question 13 Find two numbers whose sum is 24 and whose product is large as possible.

◎ *Thinking Process* First we need to establish a relation; so assume one number to be x, then the other is $(24 - x)$. Assume $y = x(24 - x)$. Using differentiation, find the required two numbers.

Sol. Let one number be x. Then, the other number is $(24 - x)$.

($\because$ Sum of the two numbers is 24)

Let y denotes the product of the two numbers. Thus, we have

$$y = x(24 - x) = 24x - x^2$$

On differentiating both sides twice w.r.t. x, we get

$$\frac{dy}{dx} = 24 - 2x \text{ and } \frac{d^2y}{dx^2} = -2$$

Now, put $\frac{dy}{dx} = 0 \Rightarrow 24 - 2x = 0 \Rightarrow x = 12$

At $x = 12$, $\frac{d^2y}{dx^2} = -2 < 0$

$\therefore$ By second derivative test, $x = 12$ is the point of local maxima of y. Thus, the product of the number is maximum when the numbers are 12 and $24 - 12 = 12$.

Hence, the numbers are 12 and 12.

Question 14 Find two positive numbers x and y such that $x + y = 60$ and xy^3 is maximum.

◎ *Thinking Process* Firstly, assume $P = xy^3$ and reduce P in terms of one variable. By using second derivative test, find the required numbers.

Sol. Let $P = xy^3$

Given $x + y = 60 \Rightarrow x = 60 - y$

On putting this value in $P = xy^3$, we get

$$P = (60 - y)y^3 \Rightarrow P = 60y^3 - y^4$$

On differentiating both sides twice w.r.t. y, we get

$$\frac{dP}{dy} = 180y^2 - 4y^3$$

and $$\frac{d^2P}{dy^2} = 360y - 12y^2$$

For maxima, put $\frac{dP}{dy} = 0$

$\Rightarrow \quad 180y^2 - 4y^3 = 0 \Rightarrow 4y^2(45 - y) = 0 \Rightarrow y = 0, 45$

But $y \neq 0$, so $y = 45$ because x and y are positive

At $y = 45$, $\left(\frac{d^2P}{dy^2}\right)_{y=45} = 360 \times 45 - 12 \times (45)^2 = 16200 - 24300 = -8100 < 0$

$\Rightarrow$ P has a local maxima at $y = 45$

$\therefore$ By second derivative test, $y = 45$ is a point of local maxima of P. Thus, function xy^3 is maximum when $y = 45$ and $x = 60 - 45 = 15$.

Hence, the required numbers are 15 and 45.

Question 15 Find two positive numbers x and y such that their sum is 35 and the product x^2y^5 is a maximum.

Sol. Let $P = x^2y^5$.

Given, $x + y = 15 \Rightarrow x = 35 - y$, $\therefore P = (35 - y)^2 y^5$

On differentiating both sides twice w.r.t. y, we get

$$\frac{dP}{dy} = (35 - y)^2 \times 5y^4 + y^5 \times 2(35 - y)(-1)$$

$$= y^4(35 - y)[5(35 - y) - 2y] = y^4(35 - y)(175 - 5y - 2y)$$

$$= y^4(35 - y)(175 - 7y) = (35y^4 - y^5)(175 - 7y)$$

and

$$\frac{d^2P}{dy^2} = (35y^4 - y^5)(-7) + (175 - 7y)(4 \times 35 \times y^3 - 5y^4)$$

$$= -7y^4(35 - y) + 7(25 - y) \times 5y^3(28 - y)$$

$$= -7y^4(35 - y) + 35y^3(25 - y)(28 - y)$$

For maxima put $\frac{dP}{dy} = 0$

$\Rightarrow \quad y^4(35 - y)(175 - 7y) = 0 \Rightarrow y = 0, 35 - y = 0, 175 - 7y = 0$

$\Rightarrow \quad y = 0, y = 25, y = 35$

When $y = 0$, $x = 35 - 0 = 35$ and the product x^2y^5 will be 0.

When $y = 35$ and $x = 35 - 35 = 0$. This will make the product x^2y^5 equal to 0.

$\therefore$ $y = 0$ and $y = 35$ cannot be the possible value of y.

When $y = 25$,

$$\left(\frac{d^2P}{dy^2}\right)_{y=25} = -7 \times (25)^4 \times (35 - 25) + 35 \times (25)^3 \times (25 - 25)(28 - 25)$$

$$= -7 \times 390625 \times 10 + 35 \times 15625 \times 0 \times 3$$

$$= -27343750 + 0 = -27343750 < 0$$

$\therefore$ By second derivative test, P will be the maximum when $y = 25$ and $x = 35 - 25 = 10$.

Hence, the required numbers are 10 and 25.

Question 16 Find two positive numbers whose sum is 16 and the sum of whose cubes is minimum.

Sol. Let one number is x. Then, the other number will be $(16 - x)$.

Let the sum of the cubes of these numbers be denoted by S.

Then, $S = x^3 + (16 - x)^3$

On differentiating both sides twice w.r.t. x, we get

$$\frac{dS}{dx} = 3x^2 + 3(16 - x)^2 (-1)$$
$$= 3x^2 - 3(16 - x)^2$$

and $$\frac{d^2S}{dx^2} = 6x + 6(16 - x)$$

For minima, put $\frac{dS}{dx} = 0$

$\Rightarrow$ $3x^2 - 3(16 - x)^2 = 0$

$\Rightarrow$ $x^2 - (256 + x^2 - 32x) = 0$

$\Rightarrow$ $32x = 256 \Rightarrow x = 8$

At $x = 8$, $\left(\frac{d^2S}{dx^2}\right)_{x=8} = 96 > 0$

$\therefore$ By second derivative test, $x = 8$ is the point of local minima of S.

Thus, the sum of the cubes of the numbers is the minimum when the numbers are 8 and $16 - 8 = 8$.

Hence, the required numbers are 8 and 8.

Question 17 A square piece of tin of side 18 cm is to be made into a box without top, by cutting-off square from each corner and folding up the flaps of the box. What should be the side of the square to be cut off so that the volume of the box is maximum possible.

◎ ***Thinking Process*** First of all, draw the figure of square piece. Establish a relation between volume V and the side of the box formed, differentiate it. Put $\frac{dV}{dx} = 0$. Find the critical points and apply the second derivative test to find the required side of the square.

Sol. Let the side of the square to be cut-off be x cm $(0 < x < 9)$. Then, the length and the breadth of the box will be $(18 - 2x)$ cm each and the height of the box is x cm.

Let V be the volume of the open box formed by folding up the flaps, then

$$V = x(18 - 2x)(18 - 2x)$$
$$= 4x(9 - x)^2 = 4x(81 + x^2 - 18x)$$

$$= 4(x^3 - 18x^2 + 81x)$$

On differentiating both sides twice w.r.t. x, we get

$$\frac{dV}{dx} = 4(3x^2 - 36x + 81) = 12(x^2 - 12x + 27)$$

and $$\frac{d^2V}{dx^2} = 12(2x - 12) = 24(x - 6)$$

For maxima put $\frac{dV}{dx} = 0 \Rightarrow 12(x^2 - 12x + 27) = 0$

$\Rightarrow$ $x^2 - 12x + 27 = 0 \Rightarrow (x-3)(x-9) = 0$

$\Rightarrow$ $x = 3, 9$

But $x = 9$ is not possible. (If $x = 9$, box is not possible.)

$\because$ $2x = 2 \times 9 = 18$ which is equal to side of square piece.

At $x = 3$, $\left(\frac{d^2V}{dx^2}\right)_{x=3} = 24(3-6) = -72 < 0$

$\therefore$ By second derivative test, $x = 3$ is the point of maxima.

Hence, if we cut off the side 3 cm from each corner of the square tin and make a box from the remaining sheet, then the volume of the box obtained is the largest possible.

Question 18 A rectangular sheet of tin 45 cm by 24 cm is to be made into a box without top, by cutting-off square from each corner and folding up the flaps. What should be the side of the square to be cut-off so that the volume of the box is maximum?

Sol. Let the side of the square to be cut off be x cm. Then, the height of the box is x, the length is $45 - 2x$ and the breadth is $24 - 2x$.

Let V be the corresponding volume of the box then,

$$V = x(24 - 2x)(45 - 2x)$$

$\Rightarrow$ $$V = x(4x^2 - 138x + 1080)$$

$$= 4x^3 - 138x^2 + 1080x$$

On differentiating both sides twice w.r.t. x, we get

$$\frac{dV}{dx} = 12x^2 - 276x + 1080$$

and $$\frac{d^2V}{dx^2} = 24x - 276$$

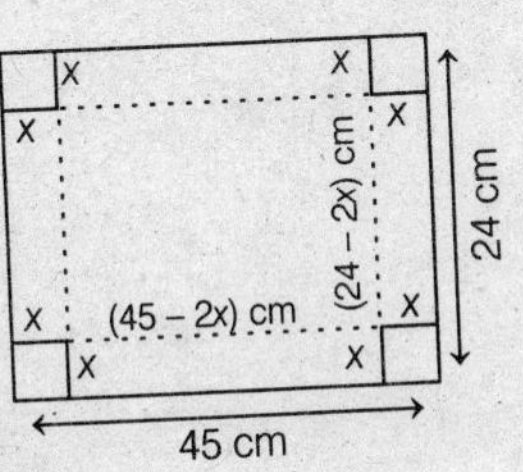

For maxima put $\frac{dV}{dx} = 0$

$$\Rightarrow \quad 12x^2 - 276x + 1080 = 0$$

$$\Rightarrow \quad x^2 - 23x + 90 = 0$$

$$\Rightarrow \quad (x - 18)(x - 5) = 0$$

$$\Rightarrow \quad x = 5, 18$$

It is not possible to cut-off a square of side 18 cm from each corner of the rectangular sheet. Thus, x cannot be equal to 18.

At $x = 5$, $\left(\frac{d^2V}{dx^2}\right)_{x=5} = 24 \times 5 - 276 = 120 - 276 = -156 < 0$

$\therefore$ By second derivative test, $x = 5$ is the point of maxima.

Hence, the side of the square to be cut-off to make the volume of the box maximum possible is 5 cm.

Question 19 Show that of all the rectangles inscribed in a given fixed circle, the square has the maximum area.

◎ ***Thinking Process*** The diagonal of the rectangle is equal to the diameter of the circle. So, area of the rectangle can be expressed in terms of radius of the circle and simplify it.

Sol. Let $ABCD$ be a rectangle inscribed in the given circle of radius r having centre at O.

Let $\quad \angle CEB = \theta$

Then, $\quad EC = 2r,\ EB = 2r\cos\theta$ and $BC = 2r\sin\theta$

Let A be the area of rectangle $BCDE$.

Then, $A = EB \times BC = 4r^2 \sin\theta\cos\theta = 2r^2 \sin 2\theta$ $\quad [\because 2\sin A\cos A = \sin 2A]$

Thus, $\quad A = 2r^2 \sin 2\theta$ where, r is constant.

On differentiating both sides twice w.r.t. θ, we get

$$\frac{dA}{d\theta} = 4r^2\cos 2\theta \text{ and } \frac{d^2A}{d\theta^2} = -8r^2\sin 2\theta$$

Now, put $\quad \frac{dA}{d\theta} = 0$

$$\Rightarrow \quad 4r^2\cos 2\theta = 0 \Rightarrow \cos 2\theta = 0$$

$$\Rightarrow \quad 2\theta = \frac{\pi}{2}, \frac{3\pi}{2}, \ldots$$

$$\Rightarrow \quad \theta = \frac{\pi}{4}, \frac{3\pi}{4}, \ldots$$

But θ can not be greater tan $\frac{\pi}{4}$.

So, $\quad \theta = \frac{\pi}{4}$

At $\theta = \frac{\pi}{4}, \left(\frac{d^2A}{d\theta^2}\right)_{\theta=\frac{\pi}{4}} = -8r^2 \sin\frac{\pi}{2} = -8r^2 < 0$

$\therefore \quad \theta = \frac{\pi}{4}$ is a point of maxima.

Thus, area is maximum when $\theta = \frac{\pi}{4}$

In this case, $EB = 2r\cos\frac{\pi}{4} = r\sqrt{2}$ and $BC = 2r\sin\frac{\pi}{4} = r\sqrt{2}$

Thus, $EB = BC$ and therefore, $BCDE$ is a square.

Quick Solution

We have $ABCD$ is rectangle and r is the radius of given circle so r is constant.

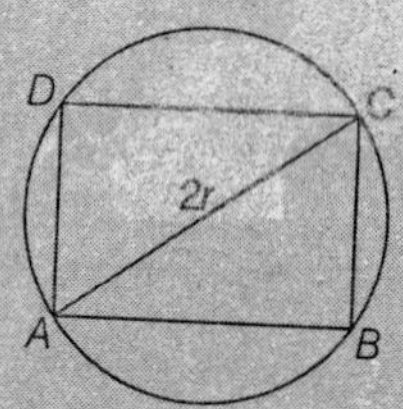

Let, $BC = x$

Then by Pythagoras theorem, $AB = \sqrt{(2r)^2 - x^2}$ ... (i)

Now, area of rectangle $ABCD$, $A = \text{Length} \times \text{Breadth}$

$= BC \times AB$

$\Rightarrow \quad A = x\sqrt{4r^2 - x^2}$ ... (ii)

$\Rightarrow \quad A^2 = x^2(4r^2 - x^2) = (4r^2x^2 - x^4)$ (squaring both sides)

If A is maximum then A^2 will also be maximum.

On differentiating both sides twice w.r.t. x, we get

$$\frac{d}{dx}(A^2) = 8r^2x - 4x^3$$

and $\frac{d^2}{dx^2}(A^2) = 8r^2 - 12x^2$

For maxima, put $\frac{d}{dx}(A^2) = 0$

$\Rightarrow \quad 8r^2x - 4x^3 = 0 \Rightarrow 4x(2r^2 - x^2) = 0$

$\Rightarrow \quad x = 0, x = \sqrt{2}r$

$x = 0$ is not possible

At $x = \sqrt{2}r \quad \frac{d^2}{dx^2}(A^2)_{(at\ x = \sqrt{2}r)} = 8r^2 - 24r^2 = -16r^2 < 0$

Thus A^2 is maximum at $x = \sqrt{2}r$

From Eq. (i), $\quad AB = \sqrt{4r^2 - 2r^2} = \sqrt{2}r$

So, $\quad AB = BC$

Hence it is a square.

Question 20 Show that the closed right circular cylinder of given surface and maximum volume is such that its height is equal to the diameter of the base.

◎ **Thinking Process** Hence, we have two independent variable r and h, so we eliminate one variable. For this, find the value of h in terms of r and S and put in volume, then use the second derivative test.

Sol. Let r and h be the radius and height of the cylinder respectively.
Then, the surface area S of the cylinder is

$$S = 2\pi r^2 + 2\pi rh$$

$$\Rightarrow \quad 2\pi rh = S - 2\pi r^2 \Rightarrow h = \frac{S - 2\pi r^2}{2\pi r} \quad \dots(i)$$

Also, volume of the cylinder, $V = \pi r^2 h$ ...(ii)

On putting the value of h from Eq. (i) in Eq. (ii), we get

$$V = \pi r^2 \left(\frac{S - 2\pi r^2}{2\pi r}\right) = \frac{Sr}{2} - \pi r^3 \quad \dots(iii)$$

On differentiating Eq. (iii) twice w.r.t. r, we get

$$\frac{dV}{dr} = \frac{S}{2} - 3\pi r^2$$

and $$\frac{d^2V}{dr^2} = -6\pi r$$

For maxima or minima put $\frac{dV}{dr} = 0$

$$\Rightarrow \quad \frac{S}{2} - 3\pi r^2 = 0 \Rightarrow S = 6\pi r^2 \Rightarrow r^2 = \frac{S}{6\pi} \quad \dots(iv)$$

At $r^2 = \frac{S}{6\pi}$, $\left(\frac{d^2V}{dr^2}\right)_{r=\sqrt{\frac{S}{6\pi}}} = -6\pi\left(\sqrt{\frac{S}{6\pi}}\right) < 0$

[$\because r > 0$ as it represents measure of distance]

By second derivative test, the volume is maximum when $r^2 = \frac{S}{6\pi}$.

when $$r^2 = \frac{S}{6\pi}$$

or $$S = 6\pi r^2$$

Then, $$h = \frac{6\pi r^2 - 2\pi r^2}{2\pi r} \quad \text{[using Eq. (i)]}$$

$$= \frac{4\pi r^2}{2\pi r} = 2r$$

Hence, the volume is maximum when the height is twice the radius *i.e.*, when the height is equal to the diameter.

Question 21 Of all the closed cylindrical cans (right circular), of a given volume of 100 cubic centimeters, find the diamensions of the can which has the minimum surface area?

Thinking Process Hence, we have two independent variable r and h. Since, here surface area is minimum so find the value of h in terms of r by using $V = \pi r^2 h$ and put in surface area for eliminating h. Then, apply second derivative test.

Sol. Let r cm be the radius of base and h cm be the height of the cylindrical can. Let its volume be V and S its total surface area.

Then, $V = 100 \text{ cm}^3$

$\Rightarrow \quad \pi r^2 h = 100$ (given)

$\Rightarrow \quad h = \dfrac{100}{\pi r^2}$ ...(i)

Also, $S = 2\pi r^2 + 2\pi rh$ ...(ii)

In Eq. (ii), there are two independent variables r and h. We eliminate h, by putting the value of h in Eq. (ii) from Eq. (i), we get

$$S = 2\pi r^2 + 2\pi r\left(\frac{100}{\pi r^2}\right) = 2\pi r^2 + \frac{200}{r} \quad \text{...(iii)}$$

On differentiating Eq. (iii) w.r.t. r, we get $\dfrac{dS}{dr} = 4\pi r - \dfrac{200}{r^2}$ ...(iv)

Now, for maxima or minima put $\dfrac{dS}{dr} = 0 \Rightarrow 4\pi r = \dfrac{200}{r^2}$

$$\Rightarrow \quad r^3 = \frac{200}{4\pi} \Rightarrow r = \left(\frac{50}{\pi}\right)^{1/3}$$

On differentiating Eq. (iv) w.r.t. r, we get $\dfrac{d^2S}{dr^2} = 4\pi + \dfrac{400}{r^3}$

At $r = \left(\dfrac{50}{\pi}\right)^{1/3}$, $\quad \dfrac{d^2S}{dr^2} = \dfrac{400}{\left(\dfrac{50}{\pi}\right)} + 4\pi = \dfrac{400}{50} \times \pi + 4\pi = 8\pi + 4\pi = 12\pi > 0$

$\therefore$ By second derivative test, the surface area is minimum when the radius of the cylinder is $\left(\dfrac{50}{\pi}\right)^{1/3}$. Hence, S is minimum when $r = \left(\dfrac{50}{\pi}\right)^{1/3}$

On putting value of r in Eq. (i), we get

$$h = \frac{100}{\pi\left(\frac{50}{\pi}\right)^{2/3}} = 2\left(\frac{50}{\pi}\right)\left(\frac{50}{\pi}\right)^{-2/3}$$

$$= 2\left(\frac{50}{\pi}\right)^{1/3}$$

Question 22 A wire of length 28 m is to be cut into two pieces. One of the pieces is to be made into a square and the other into a circle. What should be the length of the two pieces so that the combined area of the square and the circle is minimum?

Thinking Process First, we divide the wire into two parts, x and $28 - x$. Then, we calculate the areas of the circle and square, using x as the circumference of the circle and $28 - x$ as the perimeter of the square. Next, we express the total area as a function of x and use the second derivative test to find the minimum area.

Sol. Let the length of the piece bent into the shape of a circle be x (units) so that the length of the other piece bent into the shape of a square is $(28 - x)$ units.
If we are bending a wire into a circle or square then perimeter of shape will be equal to length of the wire.

Now, radius of the circle $= \dfrac{\text{Circumference}}{2\pi} = \dfrac{x}{2\pi}$

Area of the circle $= \pi\,(\text{radius})^2 = \pi\left(\dfrac{x}{2\pi}\right)^2 = \dfrac{x^2}{4\pi}$

Also, the length of each side of the square $= \dfrac{\text{Perimeter}}{4} = \dfrac{28 - x}{4}$

Area of the square $= (\text{Side})^2 = \left(\dfrac{28 - x}{4}\right)^2 = \dfrac{(28 - x)^2}{16}$

Let $f(x)$ be the sum of the areas of the two figures, then

$$f(x) = \frac{x^2}{4\pi} + \frac{(28 - x)^2}{16} \quad \text{...(i)}$$

On differentiating Eq. (i) twice w.r.t. x, we get

$$f'(x) = \frac{2x}{4\pi} + \frac{2(28 - x)(-1)}{16} = \frac{x}{2\pi} - \frac{28 - x}{8}$$

and $$f''(x) = \frac{1}{2\pi} - \frac{(-1)}{8} = \frac{1}{2\pi} + \frac{1}{8}$$

Now put $f'(x) = 0 \Rightarrow \dfrac{x}{2\pi} - \dfrac{28 - x}{8} = 0$

$\Rightarrow$ $4x - \pi(28 - x) = 0$

$\Rightarrow$ $4x + \pi x - 28\pi = 0$

$\Rightarrow$ $x(4 + \pi) = 28\pi$

$\Rightarrow$ $x = \dfrac{28\pi}{4 + \pi}$

and for this value of x, $f''(x) = \dfrac{1}{2\pi} + \dfrac{1}{8} > 0$

$\therefore f(x)$ has a local minima at $x = \dfrac{28\pi}{4 + \pi}$

Since, f is continuous in (0, 28) and has only one extreme point at $\frac{28\pi}{4+\pi} \in (0, 28)$,

therefore, $f(x)$ is absolutely minimum for $x = \frac{28\pi}{4+\pi}$.

Hence, the length of circular piece $= \frac{28\pi}{4+\pi}$.

and square piece $= 28 - \frac{28\pi}{4+\pi} = \frac{112}{4+\pi}$.

Question 23 Prove that the volume of the largest cone that can be inscribed in a sphere of radius R is $\frac{8}{27}$ of the volume of the sphere.

Sol. Let $OC = x, CQ = r$

Now, $OA = R$ (given)

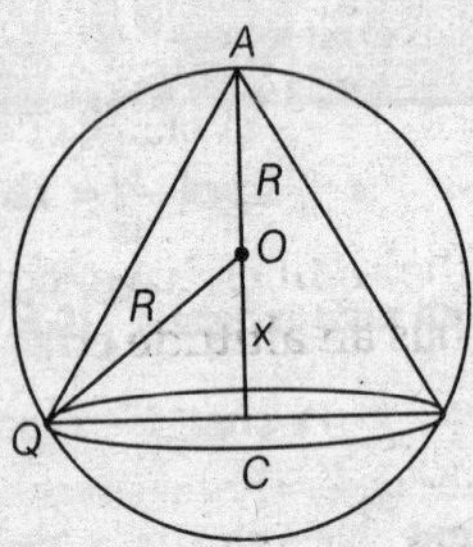

Height of the cone $= h = x + R \Rightarrow x = h - R$

$\therefore$ Volume of the cone $= V = \frac{1}{3}\pi r^2 h$ ...(i)

Also, from right angled ΔOCQ

$$OC^2 + CQ^2 = OQ^2 \Rightarrow x^2 + r^2 = R^2 \Rightarrow r^2 = R^2 - x^2$$

$$\Rightarrow \quad r^2 = R^2 - (h-R)^2$$

$$= R^2 - h^2 - R^2 + 2hR$$

$$\Rightarrow \quad r^2 = 2hR - h^2 \quad \text{... (ii)}$$

From Eqs. (i) and (ii), we have

$$V = \frac{1}{3}\pi(2hR - h^2)\cdot h$$

$$\Rightarrow \quad V = \frac{1}{3}\pi(2h^2R - h^3) \quad \text{...... (iii)}$$

On differentiating both sides twice w.r.t. h, we get

$$\frac{dV}{dh} = \frac{1}{3}\pi(4hR - 3h^2)$$

and $$\frac{d^2V}{dh^2} = \frac{1}{3}\pi(4R - 6h)$$

For maxima or minima, put $\frac{dV}{dh} = 0$

$\Rightarrow$ $$\frac{1}{3}\pi(4hR - 3h^2) = 0$$

$\Rightarrow$ $$h = \frac{4R}{3}$$

Now, $$\left(\frac{d^2V}{dh^2}\right)_{h=\frac{4R}{3}} = \frac{1}{3}\pi\left(4R - 6 \times \frac{4R}{3}\right)$$

$$= \frac{1}{3}\pi(-4R) < 0$$

$\therefore V$ has local maxima at $h = \frac{4R}{3}$

Put the value of h in Eq. (iii) we get

$$V = \frac{1}{3}\pi\left(2\left(\frac{4R}{3}\right)^2 R - \left(\frac{4R}{3}\right)^3\right)$$

$$= \frac{8}{27}\left(\frac{4}{3}\pi R^3\right) = \frac{8}{27} \text{ (Volume of sphere)}$$ **Hence Proved.**

Question 24 Show that the right circular cone of least curved surface area and given volume has an altitude equal to $\sqrt{2}$ times the radius of the base.

Sol. Let r be the radius of the base, h be the height, V be the volume and S be the curved surface area of the cone. Then,

$$V = \frac{1}{3}\pi r^2 h \Rightarrow 3V = \pi r^2 h$$

$\Rightarrow$ $$9V^2 = \pi^2 r^4 h^2 \Rightarrow h^2 = \frac{9V^2}{\pi^2 r^4} \quad \text{...(i)}$$

and $$S = \pi r l \Rightarrow S = \pi r\sqrt{r^2 + h^2} \quad (\because l = \sqrt{h^2 + r^2})$$

$\Rightarrow$ $$S^2 = \pi^2 r^2 (r^2 + h^2) = \pi^2 r^2\left(\frac{9V^2}{\pi^2 r^4} + r^2\right) \quad \text{[using Eq. (i)]}$$

$\Rightarrow$ $$S^2 = \frac{9V^2}{r^2} + \pi^2 r^4 \quad \text{...(ii)}$$

When S is least, S^2 is also least.

On differentiating Eq. (ii) w.r.t. r, we get

$$\frac{d}{dr}(S^2) = -\frac{18V^2}{r^3} + 4\pi^2 r^3 \quad \text{...(iii)}$$

For minima, put $$\frac{d}{dr}(S^2) = 0$$

$\Rightarrow$ $$-\frac{18V^2}{r^3} + 4\pi^2 r^3 = 0$$

$\Rightarrow$ $$18V^2 = 4\pi^2 r^6 \Rightarrow 9V^2 = 2\pi^2 r^6 \quad \text{...(iv)}$$

Again, differentiating Eq. (iii) w.r.t. r, we get

$$\frac{d^2}{dr^2}(S^2) = \frac{54V^2}{r^4} + 12\pi^2 r^2$$

At $9V^2 = 2\pi^2 r^6$, $\frac{d^2}{dr^2}(S^2) = \frac{54}{r^4}\left(\frac{2\pi^2 r^6}{9}\right) + 12\,\pi^2 r^2$

$$= \frac{12\pi^2 r^6}{r^4} + 12\pi^2 r^2 = 24\pi^2 r^2 > 0$$

Hence, S^2 and therefore S is minimum when $9V^2 = 2\pi^2 r^6$

On putting $9V^2 = 2\pi^2 r^6$ in Eq. (i), we get

$$h^2 = \frac{2\pi^2 r^6}{\pi^2 r^4} \Rightarrow h^2 = 2r^2 \Rightarrow h = \sqrt{2}\, r$$

Hence, altitude of right circular cone is $\sqrt{2}$ times the radius of the base. Hence proved.

Question 25 Show that the semi-vertical angle of the cone of the maximum volume and of given slant height is $\tan^{-1}\sqrt{2}$.

Sol. Let θ be the semi-vertical angle of the cone.

It is clear that $\theta \in \left(0, \frac{\pi}{2}\right)$.

Let r, h and l be the radius, height and the slant height of the cone respectively.

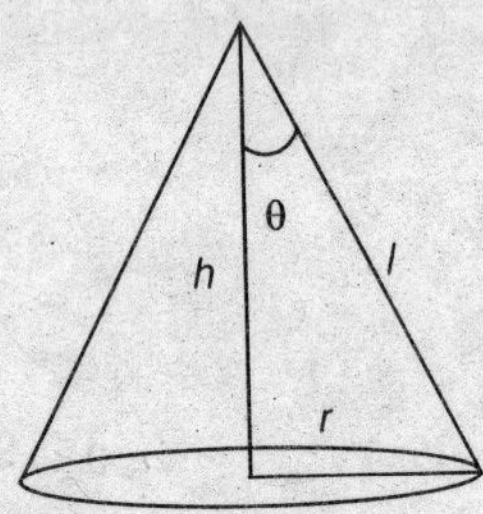

The slant height of the cone is given *i.e.*, consider as constant.

Now, $r = l\sin\theta$ and $h = l\cos\theta$

Let V be the volume of the cone; $V = \frac{1}{3}\pi r^2 h$

$$\Rightarrow \quad V = \frac{1}{3}\pi(l^2\sin^2\theta)(l\cos\theta) = \frac{1}{3}\pi l^3 \sin^2\theta\cos\theta$$

On differentiating both sides twice w.r.t. θ, we get

$$\frac{dV}{d\theta} = \frac{l^3\pi}{3}[\sin^2\theta(-\sin\theta) + \cos\theta(2\sin\theta\cos\theta)]$$

$$= \frac{l^3\pi}{3}(-\sin^3\theta + 2\sin\theta\cos^2\theta)$$

and $$\frac{d^2V}{d\theta^2} = \frac{l^3\pi}{3}(-3\sin^2\theta\cos\theta + 2\cos^3\theta - 4\sin^2\theta\cos\theta)$$
$$= \frac{l^3\pi}{3}(2\cos^3\theta - 7\sin^2\theta\cos\theta)$$

For maxima put $\frac{dV}{d\theta} = 0$

$\Rightarrow$ $$\sin^3\theta = 2\sin\theta\cos^2\theta \Rightarrow \tan^2\theta = 2$$
$\Rightarrow$ $$\tan\theta = \sqrt{2} \Rightarrow \theta = \tan^{-1}\sqrt{2}$$

Now, when $\theta = \tan^{-1}\sqrt{2}$, then $\tan^2\theta = 2$ or $\sin^2\theta = 2\cos^2\theta$

Then, we have
$$\frac{d^2V}{d\theta^2} = \frac{l^3\pi}{3}(2\cos^3\theta - 14\cos^3\theta) = -4\pi l^3\cos^3\theta < 0 \text{ for } \theta \in \left(0, \frac{\pi}{2}\right)$$

$\therefore$ By second derivative test, the volume V is maximum when $\theta = \tan^{-1}\sqrt{2}$

Hence, for a given slant height, the semi-vertical angle of the cone of the maximum volume is $\tan^{-1}\sqrt{2}$.

Question 26 Show that the semi-vertical angle of right circular cone of given surface area and maximum volume is $\sin^{-1}\left(\frac{1}{3}\right)$.

Sol. With usual notation, given that total surface area $S = \pi rl + \pi r^2$

$\Rightarrow$ $$S = \pi r\sqrt{r^2 + h^2} + \pi r^2 \qquad [\because l = \sqrt{r^2 + h^2}]$$

$\Rightarrow$ $$\frac{S}{\pi r} - r = \sqrt{r^2 + h^2} \Rightarrow \left(\frac{S}{\pi r} - r\right)^2 = r^2 + h^2 \Rightarrow \frac{S^2}{\pi^2 r^2} - \frac{2S}{\pi} = h^2$$

$\Rightarrow$ $$h = \sqrt{\frac{S^2}{\pi^2 r^2} - \frac{2S}{\pi}}, \qquad \left(\because \frac{S^2}{\pi^2 r^2} > \frac{2S}{\pi}\right) \quad \ldots\text{(i)}$$

and volume $$V = \frac{1}{3}\pi r^2 h = \frac{1}{3}\pi r^2\sqrt{\frac{S^2}{\pi^2 r^2} - \frac{2S}{\pi}}$$

$\Rightarrow$ $$V = \frac{r}{3}\sqrt{S^2 - 2S\pi r^2},\ r^2 < \frac{S}{2\pi} \text{ i.e., } 0 < r < \sqrt{\frac{S}{2\pi}}$$

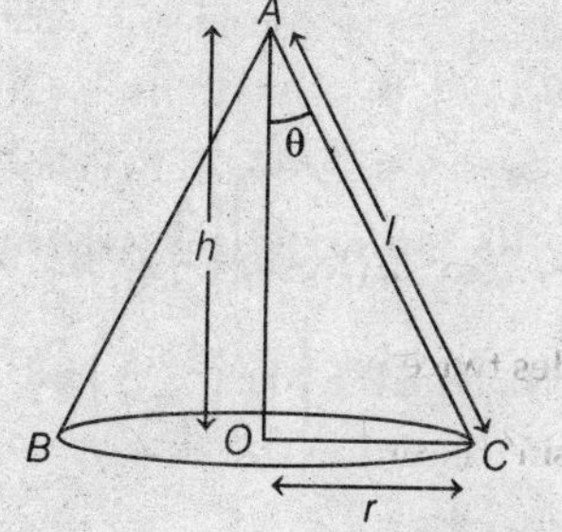

Since, V is maximum, then V^2 is maximum

Now, $$V^2 = \frac{S^2r^2}{9} - \frac{2S\pi r^4}{9}, 0 < r < \sqrt{\frac{S}{2\pi}}$$

On differentiating both sides twice w.r.t. r, we get

$$\therefore \quad \frac{d}{dr}(V^2) = \frac{2rS^2}{9} - \frac{8S\pi r^3}{9}$$

and $$\frac{d^2}{dr^2}(V^2) = \frac{2S^2}{9} - \frac{24S\pi r^2}{9}$$

For maxima put $$\frac{dV^2}{dr} = 0$$

$$\Rightarrow \quad \frac{2rS^2}{9} - \frac{8S\pi r^3}{9} = 0 \Rightarrow r^2 = \frac{S}{4\pi} \Rightarrow r = \sqrt{\frac{S}{4\pi}}$$

$$\Rightarrow \quad S = 4\pi r^2$$

$$\Rightarrow \quad \pi rl + \pi r^2 = 4\pi r^2$$

$$\Rightarrow \quad \pi rl = 3\pi r^2$$

$$\Rightarrow \quad l = 3r$$

$$\Rightarrow \quad \frac{r}{l} = \frac{1}{3}$$

Here, $$\frac{d^2(V^2)}{dr^2} < 0 \quad \text{for} \quad r = \sqrt{\frac{S}{4\pi}}$$

So, V^2 and hence, V is maximum, when $r = \sqrt{\frac{S}{4\pi}}$

If θ is the semi-vertical angle of the cone when the volume is maximum, then in right triangle AOC,

$$\sin\theta = \frac{r}{l} = \frac{1}{3} \Rightarrow \theta = \sin^{-1}\frac{1}{3}$$

Direction (Q. Nos. 27 to 29) Choose the correct answer.

Question 27 The point on the curve $x^2 = 2y$ which is nearest to the point (0, 5) is

(a) $(2\sqrt{2}, 4)$ (b) $(2\sqrt{2}, 0)$ (c) (0, 0) (d) (2, 2)

Thinking Process Firstly, consider any point (x, y) on the curve and use the formula of distance between two points and adjust them in one variable and simplify it.

Sol. (a) Let d be the distance of the point (x, y) on $x^2 = 2y$ from the point (0, 5), then

$$d = \sqrt{(y-4)^2 + 9}$$

$$\Rightarrow \quad d^2 = (y-4)^2 + 9 \qquad \text{...(i)}$$

If d is minimum than d^2 will be minimum.

On differentiating Eq. (i) w.r.t. y, we get

$$\frac{d}{dy}(d^2) = 2(y-4) \quad \text{...(ii)}$$

For minima, put $\frac{d}{dy}(d^2) = 0 \Rightarrow 2(y-4) = 0 \Rightarrow y = 4$

On differentiating Eq. (ii) w.r.t. y, we get

$$\frac{d^2}{dy^2}(d)^2 = 2 > 0. \text{ Thus, } d^2 \text{ is minimum at } y = 4$$

Since, d^2 is minimum then d will also be minimum at $y = 4$

$\therefore \quad x^2 = 2y \Rightarrow x^2 = 8 \Rightarrow x = \pm 2\sqrt{2}$

Hence, the point $(2\sqrt{2}, 4)$ and $(-2\sqrt{2}, 4)$ on the given curve are nearest to the point (0, 5).

Quick Solution

Let d be the distance of the point (x, y) on $x^2 = 2y$ from the point (0, 5), then

$$d = \sqrt{(x-0)^2 + (y-5)^2} = \sqrt{x^2 + (y-5)^2} \quad \text{...(i)}$$

$$= \sqrt{2y + (y-5)^2} \quad (\text{Putting } x^2 = 2y)$$

$$= \sqrt{y^2 - 8y + 25} = \sqrt{y^2 - 8y + 4^2 + 9} = \sqrt{(y-4)^2 + 9}$$

Here, d is least when $(y-4)^2 = 0$ *i.e.*, when $y = 4$

When $y = 4$ then, $x^2 = 2 \times 4 \Rightarrow x = \pm\sqrt{8} = \pm 2\sqrt{2}$

$\therefore$ The points $(2\sqrt{2}, 4)$ and $(-2\sqrt{2}, 4)$ on the given curve are nearest to the point (0, 5).

Question 28 For all real values of x, the minimum value of $\frac{1-x+x^2}{1+x+x^2}$ is

(a) zero (b) 1 (c) 3 (d) 1/3

Sol. (d) Let $y = \frac{1-x+x^2}{1+x+x^2}$

On differentiating both sides twice w.r.t. x, we get

$$\frac{dy}{dx} = \frac{(1+x+x^2)(-1+2x) - (1-x+x^2)(1+2x)}{(1+x+x^2)^2}$$

$$= \frac{-1+2x-x+2x^2-x^2+2x^3-1-2x+x+2x^2-x^2-2x^3}{(1+x+x^2)^2}$$

$$= \frac{-2+2x^2-2x^2+2x^2}{(1+x+x^2)^2} = \frac{2x^2-2}{(1+x+x^2)^2} = \frac{2(x^2-1)}{(1+x+x^2)^2}$$

and $$\frac{d^2y}{dx^2} = \frac{2[(1+x+x^2)^2(2x) - (x^2-1)(2)(1+x+x^2)(1+2x)]}{(1+x+x^2)^4}$$

$$= \frac{4(1+x+x^2)[(1+x+x^2)x-(x^2-1)(1+2x)]}{(1+x+x^2)^4}$$

$$= \frac{4[x+x^2+x^3-x^2-2x^3+1+2x]}{(1+x+x^2)^3} = \frac{4(1+3x-x^3)}{(1+x+x^2)^3}$$

For minima or maxima put $\frac{dy}{dx} = 0 \Rightarrow x^2 = 1 \Rightarrow x = \pm 1$

At $x = 1$, $\left(\frac{d^2y}{dx^2}\right)_{x=1} = \frac{4[1+3(1)-1^3]}{(1+1+1^2)^3} = \frac{4(3)}{3^3} = \frac{4}{9} > 0$

At $x = -1$, $\left(\frac{d^2y}{dx^2}\right)_{x=-1} = \frac{4[1+3(-1)-(-1)^3]}{[1+(-1)+(-1)^2]^3} = \frac{4(1-3+1)}{(1-1+1)^3} = 4(-1) = -4 < 0$

$\therefore$ By second derivative test, f is minimum at $x = 1$ and the minimum value is given by $y = \frac{1-1+1}{1+1+1} = \frac{1}{3}$

Question 29 The maximum value of $[x(x-1)+1]^{1/3}, 0 \le x \le 1$ is

(a) $\left(\frac{1}{3}\right)^{1/3}$ (b) $\frac{1}{2}$ (c) 1 (d) zero

Sol. (c) Let $f(x) = [x(x-1)+1]^{1/3}, \quad 0 \le x \le 1$

$$= (x^2 - x + 1)^{1/3}$$

On differentiating both sides w.r.t. x, we get

$$f'(x) = \frac{1}{3}(x^2 - x + 1)^{\frac{1}{3}-1}(2x-1) = \frac{1(2x-1)}{3(x^2-x+1)^{2/3}}$$

Now, put $f'(x) = 0 \Rightarrow 2x - 1 = 0 \Rightarrow x = \frac{1}{2} \in [0, 1]$.

So, $x = \frac{1}{2}$ is a critical point.

Now, we evaluate the value of f at critical point $x = \frac{1}{2}$ and at the end points of the interval [0, 1].

At $x = 0$, $f(0) = (0 - 0 + 1)^{1/3} = 1$

At $x = 1$, $f(1) = (1 - 1 + 1)^{1/3} = 1$

At $x = \frac{1}{2}$, $f\left(\frac{1}{2}\right) = \left(\frac{1}{4} - \frac{1}{2} + 1\right)^{1/3} = \left(\frac{3}{4}\right)^{1/3}$

$\therefore$ Maximum value of $f(x)$ is 1 at $x = 0, 1$.

Miscellaneous Exercise

Question 1 Show that the function given by $f(x)=\frac{\log x}{x}$ has maximum at $x=e$.

Sol. Given, $f(x)=\frac{\log x}{x}$

On differentiating both sides w.r.t. x, we get $f'(x)=\frac{x\left(\frac{1}{x}\right)-(\log x).1}{x^2}=\frac{1-\log x}{x^2}$

Again, on differentiating both sides we get $f''(x)=\frac{x^2\left(-\frac{1}{x}\right)-(1-\log x).2x}{(x^2)^2}$

$$=\frac{-x-2x+2x\log x}{x^4}=\frac{x(2\log x-3)}{x^4}=\frac{2\log x-3}{x^3}$$

For maximum put $f'(x)=0 \Rightarrow \frac{1-\log x}{x^2}=0$

$\Rightarrow \quad \log x=1 \Rightarrow x=e \quad [\because \log_b a=c \Rightarrow a=b^c]$

At $x=e$, $f''(e)=\frac{2\log e-3}{e^3}=\frac{2\cdot 1 \; 2}{e^3}=\frac{-1}{e^3}<0$

Therefore, by second derivative test, f is maximum at $x=e$.

Note In calculus if base of log is not given than it is implied to be 'e'.

Question 2 The two equal sides of an isosceles triangle with fixed base b are decreasing at the rate of 3 cm/s. How fast is the area decreasing when the two equal sides are equal to the base?

Sol. Let ΔABC be isosceles triangle where BC is the base of fixed length b.

Let the length of two equal sides of ΔABC be x.

Draw $AD \perp BC$ in figure.

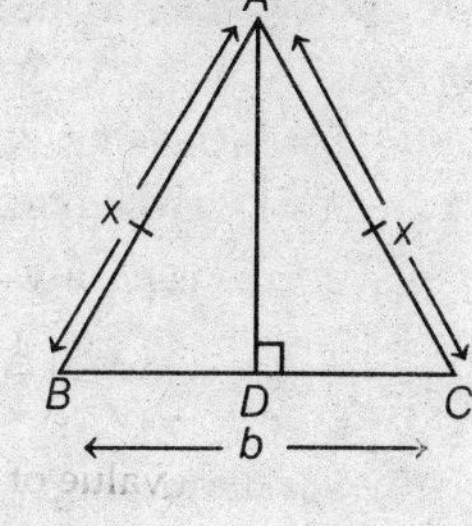

Now, in ΔADC, by applying the Pythagoras theorem,

we have $AD=\sqrt{x^2-\left(\frac{b}{2}\right)^2}=\sqrt{x^2-\frac{b^2}{4}}$

$\therefore$ Area of triangle $(A)=\frac{1}{2}\times \text{base}\times\text{height}$

$$=\frac{b}{2}\sqrt{x^2-\frac{b^2}{4}}$$

The rate of change of the area A w.r.t. time t is given by

$$\frac{dA}{dt}=\frac{1}{2}b\times\frac{1}{2}\frac{2x}{\sqrt{x^2-\frac{b^2}{4}}}\times\frac{dx}{dt}=\frac{xb}{\sqrt{4x^2-b^2}}\frac{dx}{dt}$$

It is given that the two equal sides of the triangle are deceasing at the rate of 3 cm/s.

$\therefore \quad \dfrac{dx}{dt} = -3$ cm/s (Negative sign use for decreasing)

$$\therefore \quad \frac{dA}{dt} = \frac{-3xb}{\sqrt{4x^2 - b^2}} \text{cm}^2/\text{s}$$

When $x = b$, we have $\dfrac{dA}{dt} = \dfrac{-3b^2}{\sqrt{3b^2}} = -\sqrt{3}\,b\,\text{cm}^2/\text{s}$

Hence, if the two equal sides are equal to the base, then the area of the triangle is decreasing at the rate of $\sqrt{3}\,b\,\text{cm}^2/\text{s}$.

Question 3 Find the intervals in which the function f given by $f(x) = \dfrac{4\sin x - 2x - x\cos x}{2 + \cos x}$ is

(a) increasing (b) decreasing

Sol. Given, $f(x) = \dfrac{4\sin x - 2x - x\cos x}{2+\cos x}$

$$= \frac{4\sin x - x(2+\cos x)}{2+\cos x} = \frac{4\sin x}{2+\cos x} - \frac{x(2+\cos x)}{2+\cos x} = \frac{4\sin x}{2+\cos x} - x$$

On differentiating both sides w.r t. x, we get

$$f'(x) = 4\left\{\frac{(2+\cos x)\cos x - \sin x\,(0-\sin x)}{(2+\cos x)^2}\right\} - 1 = 4\left\{\frac{2\cos x + \cos^2 x + \sin^2 x}{(2+\cos x)^2}\right\} - 1$$

$$= \frac{8\cos x + 4}{(2+\cos x)^2} - 1 = \frac{8\cos x + 4 - (2+\cos x)^2}{(2+\cos x)^2} \qquad (\because \cos^2\theta + \sin^2\theta = 1)$$

$$= \frac{8\cos x + 4 - 4 - \cos^2 x - 4\cos x}{(2+\cos x)^2} = \frac{4\cos x - \cos^2 x}{(2+\cos x)^2} = \frac{\cos x(4-\cos x)}{(2+\cos x)^2}$$

We know that $-1 \le \cos x \le 1$

$\Rightarrow \quad 4 - \cos x > 0$ and $(2+\cos x)^2 > 0$

(a) **For increasing**

$f'(x) > 0$ when $\cos x > 0$

$\because$ $\cos x$ is positive in 1st and 4th quadrant

$\therefore$ $f(x)$ is increasing in the interval $\left(0, \dfrac{\pi}{2}\right)$ and $\left(\dfrac{3\pi}{2}, 2\pi\right)$.

(b) **For decreasing**

$f'(x) < 0$ when $\cos x < 0$

$\because$ $\cos x$ is negative in 2nd and 3rd quadrant

$\therefore$ $f(x)$ is decreasing in the interval $\left(\dfrac{\pi}{2}, \dfrac{3\pi}{2}\right)$.

Question 4 Find the intervals in which the function f given by $f(x)=x^3+\dfrac{1}{x^3}, x \neq 0$ is

(a) increasing (b) decreasing

Sol. Given, $f(x) = x^3 + \dfrac{1}{x^3}$

On differentiating both sides w.r.t. x, we get $f'(x) = 3x^2 - \dfrac{3}{x^4}$

(a) $f(x)$ is increasing, if $f'(x) \geq 0$

$\Rightarrow \quad 3x^2 - \dfrac{3}{x^4} \geq 0 \Rightarrow x^6 \geq 1 \Rightarrow (x^2)^3 \geq 1$

$\Rightarrow \quad x^2 \geq 1 \Rightarrow x \in (-\infty, -1] \cup [1, \infty]$

Hence, f is increasing in $(-\infty, -1] \cup [1, \infty)$ or $x < -1$ and $x > 1$.

(b) $f(x)$ is decreasing, if $f'(x) \leq 0$

$\Rightarrow \quad 3x^2 - \dfrac{3}{x^4} \leq 0 \Rightarrow x^6 \leq 1$

$\Rightarrow \quad (x^2)^3 \leq 1 \Rightarrow x^2 \leq 1$

$\Rightarrow \quad -1 \leq x \leq 1$ but $x \neq 0 \Rightarrow [-1, 0) \cup (0, 1]$

$\therefore$ f is decreasing in $[-1, 0) \cup (0, 1]$.

Question 5 Find the maximum area of an isosceles triangle inscribed in the ellipse $\dfrac{x^2}{a^2}+\dfrac{y^2}{b^2}=1$ with its vertex at one end of the major axis.

Sol. Given the equation of an ellipse be $\dfrac{x^2}{a^2}+\dfrac{y^2}{b^2}=1$, then any point P on the ellipse is $(a\cos\theta, b\sin\theta)$.

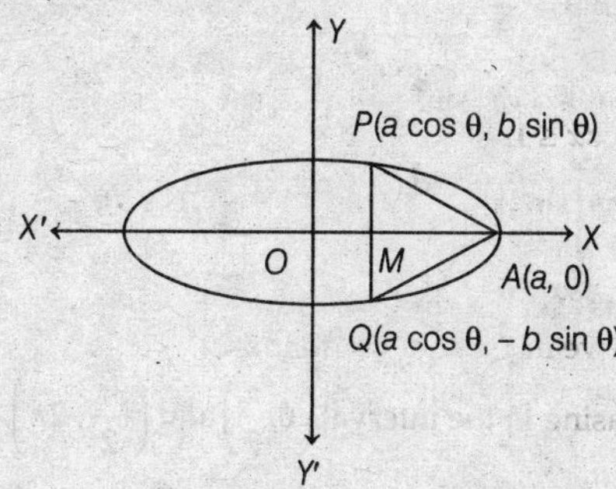

From P, draw $PM \perp OX$ and produce it to meet the ellipse at Q, then APQ is an isosceles triangle.

Let S be its area, then

$$S = 2 \times \frac{1}{2} \times AM \times MP = (OA - OM) \times MP = (a - a\cos\theta) \cdot b\sin\theta$$

$$\Rightarrow \quad S = ab(\sin\theta - \sin\theta\cos\theta) = ab\left(\sin\theta - \frac{1}{2}\sin 2\theta\right)$$

On differentiating both sides w.r.t. θ, we get

$$\frac{dS}{d\theta} = ab(\cos\theta - \cos 2\theta)$$

Again, differentiating both sides w.r.t. θ, we get

$$\frac{d^2S}{d\theta^2} = ab(-\sin\theta + 2\sin 2\theta)$$

For maxima or minima, put $\frac{dS}{d\theta} = 0$

$$\Rightarrow \quad \cos\theta = \cos 2\theta$$

$$\Rightarrow \quad \cos\theta = \cos(2\pi - 2\theta)$$

$$\Rightarrow \quad \theta = 2\pi - 2\theta$$

$$\Rightarrow \quad \theta = \frac{2\pi}{3}$$

At $\theta = \frac{2\pi}{3}$, $\left(\frac{d^2S}{d\theta^2}\right)_{\theta = \frac{2\pi}{3}} = ab\left[-\sin\frac{2\pi}{3} + 2\sin\left(2 \times \frac{2\pi}{3}\right)\right]$

$$= ab\left[-\sin\left(\pi - \frac{\pi}{3}\right) + 2\sin\left(\pi + \frac{\pi}{3}\right)\right]$$

$$= ab\left(-\sin\frac{\pi}{3} - 2\sin\frac{\pi}{3}\right) \qquad \left[\begin{array}{l}\because \sin(\pi - \theta) = \sin\theta \\ \sin(\pi + \theta) = -\sin\theta\end{array}\right]$$

$$= ab\left(-\frac{\sqrt{3}}{2} - \frac{2\sqrt{3}}{2}\right)$$

$$= ab\left(\frac{-3\sqrt{3}}{2}\right) = \frac{-3\sqrt{3}ab}{2} < 0$$

$\therefore$ S is maximum, when $\theta = \frac{2\pi}{3}$

and maximum value of $S = ab\left(\sin\frac{2\pi}{3} - \frac{1}{2}\cdot 2\sin\frac{2\pi}{3}\cos\frac{2\pi}{3}\right)$ $[\because \sin 2\theta = 2\sin\theta\cos\theta]$

$$= ab\left[\sin\left(\pi - \frac{\pi}{3}\right) - \sin\left(\pi - \frac{\pi}{3}\right)\cos\left(\pi - \frac{\pi}{3}\right)\right]$$

$$= ab\left(\sin\frac{\pi}{3} - \sin\frac{\pi}{3} \times \left(-\cos\frac{\pi}{3}\right)\right)$$

$$= ab\left(\sin\frac{\pi}{3} + \sin\frac{\pi}{3}\cos\frac{\pi}{3}\right)$$

$$= ab\left(\frac{\sqrt{3}}{2} + \frac{\sqrt{3}}{2} \times \frac{1}{2}\right)$$

$$= ab\left(\frac{2\sqrt{3} + \sqrt{3}}{4}\right) = \frac{3\sqrt{3}}{4}\,ab \text{ sq unit}$$

Thus, maximum area of isosceles triangle is $\frac{3\sqrt{3}}{4}ab$ sq unit.

Quick Solution

Let point $B = (x, y)$

Then, area of $\Delta ABC = \frac{1}{2}$ Base $\times$ height $= \frac{1}{2}(BC)(AD)$

$$= \frac{1}{2}(2y)(x + a) = y(x + a) \quad \ldots \text{(i)}$$

Given equation is $\frac{x^2}{a^2} + \frac{y^2}{b^2} = 1 \Rightarrow y = \frac{b}{a}\sqrt{a^2 - x^2}$

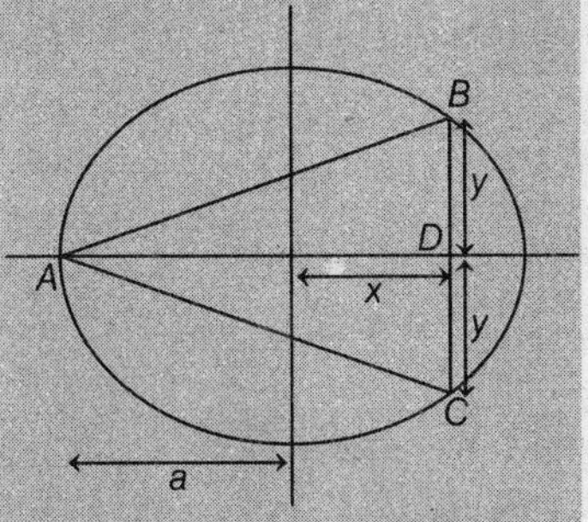

Put the value of y in Eq. (i)

$$A = \frac{b}{a}\sqrt{a^2 - x^2}\,(x + a)$$

$$\Rightarrow \quad A^2 = \frac{b^2}{a^2}(a^2 - x^2)(x + a)^2$$

(squaring both side)

$$= \frac{b^2}{a^2}(a + x)(a - x)(x + a)^2$$

$$\Rightarrow \quad A^2 = \frac{b^2}{a^2}(a + x)^3(a - x)$$

On differentiating both sides twice w.r.t. x, we get

$$\frac{d}{dx}(A^2) = \frac{b^2}{a^2}[(a + x)^3(-1) + (a - x)\,3(a + x)^2]$$

$$= \frac{b^2}{a^2}(a + x)^2[-a - x + 3a - 3x] = \frac{b^2}{a^2}(a + x)^2\,[2a - 4x]$$

and $\frac{d^2}{dx^2}(A^2) = \frac{b^2}{a^2}[(a + x)^2(-4) + (2a - 4x)\cdot 2(a + x)]$

$$= \frac{b^2}{a^2}(a + x)(-4a - 4x + 4a - 8x) = \frac{b^2}{a^2}(a + x)(-12x)$$

For maxima, put $\frac{d}{dx}(A^2) = 0$

$$\Rightarrow \quad \frac{b^2}{a^2}(a + x)^2(2a - 4x) = 0$$

$$\Rightarrow \quad x = -a,\ x = \frac{a}{2}$$

$x = -a$ is not possible. So $x = \frac{a}{2}$

$$\left(\frac{d^2}{dx^2}(A^2)\right)_{at\ x = \frac{a}{2}} = \frac{b^2}{a^2}\left(-\frac{12a}{2}\left(a + \frac{a}{2}\right)\right) < 0$$

So, maxima at $x = \frac{a}{2}$

Maximum area $= \frac{b}{a}\sqrt{a^2 - \frac{a^2}{4}}\left(\frac{a}{2} + a\right) = \frac{b}{a}\sqrt{\frac{3a^2}{4}}\left(\frac{3a}{2}\right) = \frac{3\sqrt{3}}{4}\,ab$ sq. unit

Question 6 A tank with rectangular base and rectangular sides, open at the top is to be constructed so that its depth is 2 m and volume is 8 m^3. If building of tank costs ₹ 70 per sq metre for the base and ₹ 45 per sq metre for sides. What is the cost of least expensive tank?

Sol. Let the length and breadth of the tank be x metre and y metre, respectively.

Given, depth (height) = 2 m and volume of tank = $8m^3$

$\therefore$ Volume of tank $= 2 \times x \times y \Rightarrow 2xy = 8$

$$\Rightarrow \qquad xy = 4$$

$$\Rightarrow \qquad y = \frac{4}{x} \qquad \ldots\text{(i)}$$

Also, area of the base $= xy = x \times \frac{4}{x} = 4$

and area of the four sides $= 2x + 2y + 2x + 2y = 4x + 4y = 4(x + y)$

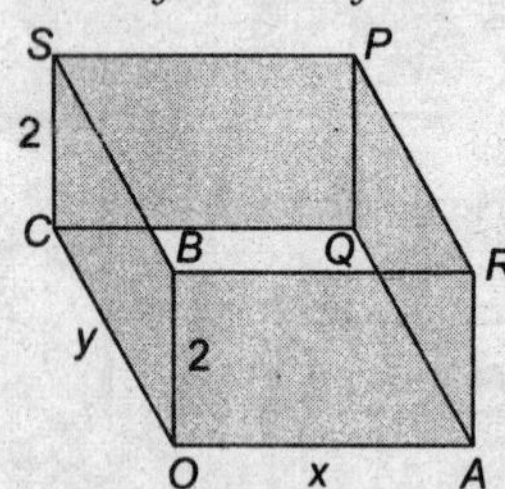

It is given that, the cost of construction on base is ₹ 70 per sq. metre and for side is ₹ 45 per sq metre.

So, cost of construction, $C = ₹[70 \times xy + 45 \times 4(x + y)]$

$$= ₹[70xy + 180(x + y)] \qquad \ldots\text{(ii)}$$

On putting value of y in Eq. (ii) from Eq. (i), we get

$$C = 70 \times 4 + 180\left(x + \frac{4}{x}\right)$$

$$= 280 + 180\left(x + \frac{4}{x}\right) \qquad \ldots\text{(iii)}$$

On differentiating both sides w.r.t. x, we get

$$\frac{dC}{dx} = 0 + 180\left(1 - \frac{4}{x^2}\right) = 180\left(\frac{x^2 - 4}{x^2}\right)$$

For least expensive, put $\frac{dC}{dx} = 0$

$$\Rightarrow \qquad 180\left(\frac{x^2 - 4}{x^2}\right) = 0 \Rightarrow x^2 = 4 \Rightarrow x = \pm 2$$

$\frac{dC}{dx}$ changes sign from negative to positive at $x = 2$.

$\therefore$ C is minimum at $x = 2$

[length of the tank cannot be negative. So, $x = -2$ is not consider]

So, $x = 2$ and $y = \frac{4}{x} = \frac{4}{2} = 2$

Thus, tank is a cube of side 2 m.

Now, least cost of construction [from Eq. (iii)]

$$= ₹\left[280 + 180\left(2 + \frac{4}{2}\right)\right] = ₹\,[280 + 720] = ₹\,1000$$

Question 7 The sum of the perimeter of a circle and square is k, where k is some constant. Prove that the sum of their areas is least when the side of square is double the radius of the circle.

Sol. Let x be the side of square and r be the radius of circle.

$\therefore$ Perimeter of a circle $= 2\pi r$ and perimeter of a square $= 4x$

Given, $2\pi r + 4x = k \Rightarrow x = \frac{k - 2\pi r}{4}$ ...(i)

Now, area, $A = x^2 + \pi r^2 = \left[\frac{k - 2\pi r}{4}\right]^2 + \pi r^2 = \left(\frac{1}{16}\right)(k^2 - 4k\pi r + 4\pi^2 r^2) + \pi r^2$

On differentiating both sides w.r.t. r, we get $\frac{dA}{dr} = \left(\frac{1}{16}\right)(-4k\pi + 8\pi^2 r) + 2\pi r$

Again, on differentiating both sides w.r. t. r, we get

$$\frac{d^2 A}{dr^2} = \frac{1}{16}[0 + 8\pi^2] + 2\pi = 2\pi + \frac{\pi^2}{2} > 0$$

For maximum or minimum, put $\frac{dA}{dr} = 0$

$$\Rightarrow 2\pi r - \frac{4k\pi}{16} + \frac{8\pi^2 r}{16} = 0 \Rightarrow r\left(2\pi + \frac{\pi^2}{2}\right) = \frac{k\pi}{4} \Rightarrow r = \frac{\left(\frac{k\pi}{4}\right)}{2\pi + \frac{\pi^2}{2}} = \frac{k}{8 + 2\pi} \quad \text{...(ii)}$$

Now, $\left(\frac{d^2 A}{dr^2}\right)_{r = \frac{k}{8+2\pi}} = 2\pi + \frac{\pi^2}{2}$ value

$\therefore$ A is least when $r = \frac{k}{8 + 2\pi}$ and put this value in Eq. (i), we get

$$x = \frac{k - 2\pi r}{4} = \frac{1}{4}\left(k - 2\pi \times \frac{k}{8 + 2\pi}\right)$$

$$= \frac{1}{4}\left[\frac{8k + 2\pi k - 2\pi k}{8 + 2\pi}\right]$$

$$= \frac{2k}{8 + 2\pi} = 2\left(\frac{k}{8 + 2\pi}\right) = 2r \quad \text{[using Eq. (ii)]}$$

Hence, S is least when side of the square is double the radius of the circle.

Question 8 A window is in the form of a rectangle surmounted by a semi-circle opening. The perimeter of the window is 10 m. Find the dimensions of the window to admit maximum light through the whole opening.

Sol. Let radius of semi-circle = r

$\therefore$ One side of rectangle = $2r$. Let other side = x

Given, perimeter = 10 m

$\Rightarrow \quad 2x + 2r + \frac{1}{2}(2\pi r) = 10 \Rightarrow 2x = 10 - r(\pi + 2) \quad$ ...(i)

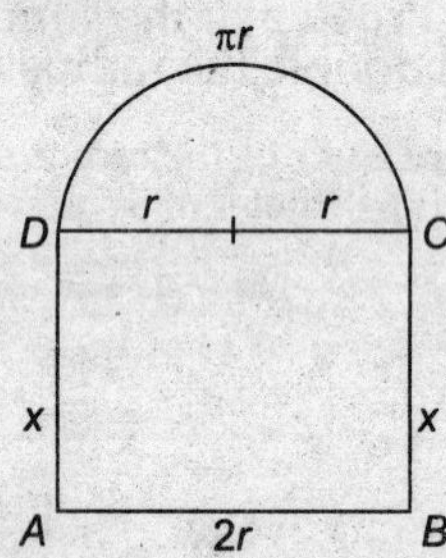

Let A be area of the figure, then

A = Area of semi-circle + Area of rectangle = $\frac{1}{2}\pi r^2 + 2rx$

$\Rightarrow \quad A = \frac{1}{2}(\pi r^2) + r[10 - r(\pi + 2)] \quad$ [Using Eq. (i)]

$= \frac{1}{2}(\pi r^2) + 10r - r^2\pi - 2r^2 = 10r - \frac{\pi r^2}{2} - 2r^2$

On differentiating both sides twice w.r.t. r, we get

$$\frac{dA}{dr} = 10 - \pi r - 4r \quad \text{...(ii)}$$

and $$\frac{d^2A}{dr^2} = -\pi - 4 \quad \text{...(iii)}$$

For maxima or minima, put $\frac{dA}{dr} = 0 \Rightarrow 10 - \pi r - 4r = 0$

$\Rightarrow \quad 10 = (4 + \pi)r \Rightarrow r = \frac{10}{4 + \pi}$

On putting $r = \frac{10}{4 + \pi}$ in Eq. (iii), we get $\frac{d^2A}{dr^2} = -\pi - 4$ = negative value

Thus, A has local maximum when $r = \frac{10}{4 + \pi} \quad$ ...(iv)

$\therefore \quad$ Radius of semi-circle = $\frac{10}{4 + \pi}$,

one side of rectangle = $2r = \frac{2 \times 10}{4 + \pi} = \frac{20}{4 + \pi}$

and other side of rectangle *i.e.,* x from Eq. (i) is given by

$$x = \frac{1}{2}[10 - r(\pi + 2)] = \frac{1}{2}\left[10 - \left(\frac{10}{\pi + 4}\right)(\pi + 2)\right] \quad \text{[from Eq. (iv)]}$$

$$= \frac{10\pi + 40 - 10\pi - 20}{2(\pi + 4)} = \frac{20}{2(\pi + 4)} = \frac{10}{\pi + 4}$$

Light is maximum when area is maximum.

So, dimensions of the window are length $= 2r = \dfrac{20}{\pi + 4}$ and breadth $= x = \dfrac{10}{\pi + 4}$.

Mistake Alert When perimeter of window will be taken then side DC will not be included.

Question 9 A point on the hypotenuse of a triangle is at distance a and b from the sides of the triangle. Show that the minimum length of the hypotenuse is $(a^{2/3} + b^{2/3})^{3/2}$.

Thinking Process With the help of trigonometry, write the length of the hypotenuse in terms of a and b. Follow second derivative test to prove that required result.

Sol. Let P be a point on the hypotenuse AC of right angled ΔABC.

Such that $PL \perp AB = a$ and $PM \perp BC = b$

Let $\angle APL = \angle ACB = \theta$ (say) (Corresponding angles)

Then, $AP = a\sec\theta,\ PC = b\,\text{cosec}\,\theta$

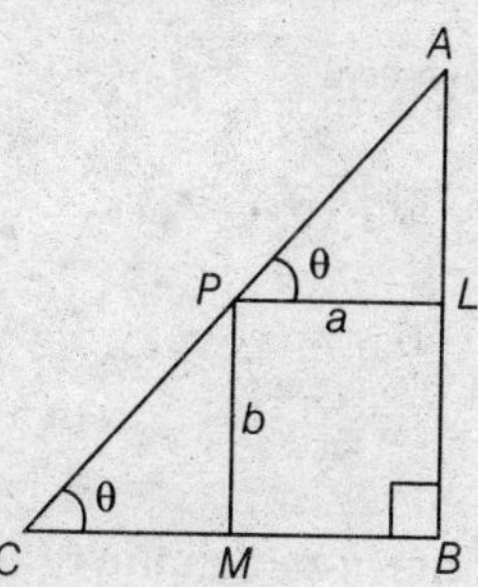

Let l be the length of the hypotenuse, then

$$l = AP + PC \Rightarrow l = a \quad \theta + b \quad \theta,\ 0 < \theta < \frac{\pi}{2}$$

On differentiating both sides w.r.t. θ, we get

$$\frac{dl}{d\theta} = a \cdot \quad \theta\tan\theta - b \cdot \quad \theta\cot\theta$$

For maxima or minima put $\dfrac{dl}{d\theta} = 0$

$$\Rightarrow \quad a\sec\theta\tan\theta = b \quad \theta\cot\theta$$

$$\Rightarrow \quad \frac{a\sin\theta}{\cos^2\theta} = \frac{b\cos\theta}{\sin^2\theta} \Rightarrow \frac{\sin^3\theta}{\cos^3\theta} = \frac{b}{a}$$

$$\Rightarrow \qquad \tan^3\theta = \frac{b}{a} \Rightarrow \tan\theta = \left(\frac{b}{a}\right)^{1/3}$$

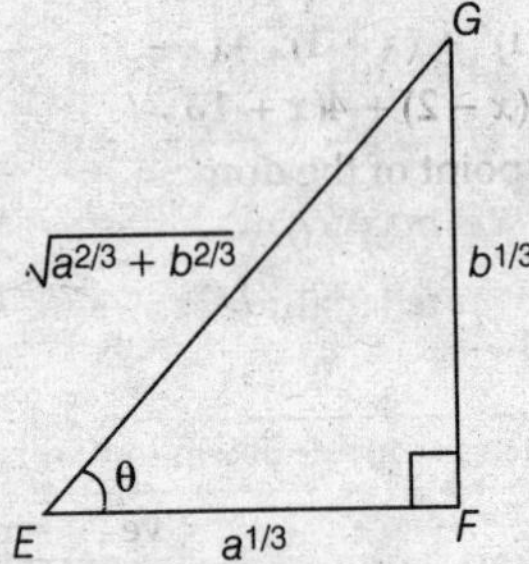

Now, $\frac{d^2l}{d\theta^2} = a(\quad \theta \times \sec^2\theta + \tan\theta \times \sec\theta\tan\theta]$

$$- b[\text{cosec}\,\theta(-\text{cosec}^2\theta) + \cot\theta(-\text{cosec}\,\theta\cot\theta)]$$

$$= a\sec\theta(\sec^2\theta + \tan^2\theta) + b\,\text{cosec}\,\theta(\text{cosec}^2\theta + \cot^2\theta)$$

Since, $0 < \theta < \frac{\pi}{2}$, so, trigonometric ratios are positive.

Also, $a > 0$ and $b > 0$.

$\therefore \qquad \frac{d^2l}{d\theta^2}$ is positive.

$\Rightarrow \qquad l$ is least when $\tan\theta = \left(\frac{b}{a}\right)^{1/3}$

$\therefore$ Least value of $l = a\sec\theta + b\,\text{cosec}\,\theta$

$$= a\frac{\sqrt{a^{2/3}+b^{2/3}}}{a^{1/3}} + b\frac{\sqrt{a^{2/3}+b^{2/3}}}{b^{1/3}}$$

$\left[\because \text{In } \Delta EFG, \sec\theta = \frac{\sqrt{a^{2/3}+b^{2/3}}}{a^{1/3}} \text{ and cosec}\,\theta = \frac{\sqrt{a^{2/3}+b^{2/3}}}{b^{1/3}}\right]$

$= \sqrt{a^{2/3}+b^{2/3}}\,(a^{2/3}+b^{2/3}) = (a^{2/3}+b^{2/3})^{3/2}$ **Hence Proved.**

Question 10 Find the points at which the function f given by $f(x) = (x-2)^4(x+1)^3$ has

(a) local maxima (b) local minima (c) point of inflexion

◎ ***Thinking Process***

(i) If at any point $f'(x)$ changes sign from negative to positive, then $f(x)$ has a point of local minima at that point.

(ii) If at any point, $f'(x)$ changes sign from positive to negative, then $f(x)$ has a point of local maxima.

(iii) If at any point, $f'(x)$ does not change the sign than $f(x)$ has a point of inflection.

Sol. The given equation is $f(x) = (x-2)^4 (x+1)^3$

On differentiating both sides w.r.t. x, we get

$$f'(x) = (x-2)^4\, 3(x+1)^2 + (x+1)^3\, 4(x-2)^3$$
$$= (x-2)^3 (x+1)^2 \{3(x-2) + 4(x+1)\} = (x-2)^3 (x+1)^2 \{7x-2\}$$

Clearly, $f'(x)$ exists at every point of the domain.

For maximum or minimum put $f'(x) = 0$

$\Rightarrow \quad (x-2)^3 (x+1)^2 (7x-2) = 0$

$\Rightarrow \quad x = 2, -1, \dfrac{2}{7}$

At $x = 2$,

$f'(x)$	$(x-2)^3$	$(x+1)^2$	$(7x-2)$	Result
x slightly < 2	– ve	+ ve	+ ve	– ve
x slightly > 2	+ ve	+ ve	+ ve	+ ve

$\therefore$ $f'(x)$ change sign from – ve to + ve. Thus, $x = 2$ is a point of local minima.

At $x = -1$,

$f'(x)$	$(x-2)^3$	$(x+1)^2$	$(7x-2)$	Result
x slightly < -1	– ve	+ ve	– ve	+ ve
x slightly > -1	– ve	+ ve	– ve	+ ve

$\therefore$ $f'(x)$ does not change the sign. Thus, $x = -1$ is a point of inflexion.

At $x = \dfrac{2}{7}$,

$f'(x)$	$(x-2)^3$	$(x+1)^2$	$(7x-2)$	Result
x slightly $< \dfrac{2}{7}$	– ve	+ ve	– ve	+ ve
x slightly $> \dfrac{2}{7}$	– ve	+ ve	+ ve	– ve

$\therefore$ $f'(x)$ changes sign from + ve to – ve. Thus, $x = 2/7$ is a point of local maxima.

So, we can say as the value of x varies through -1, $f'(x)$ does not changes its sign. Thus, $x = -1$ is the point of inflexion.

Question 11 Find the absolute maximum and minimum values of the function f given by $f(x) = \cos^2 x + \sin x,\ x \in [0, \pi]$.

Sol. Given, $f(x) = \cos^2 x + \sin x,\ x \in [0, \pi]$

Now, $f'(x) = 2\cos x(-\sin x) + \cos x = -2\sin x\cos x + \cos x$

For maximum or minimum put $f'(x) = 0 \Rightarrow -2\sin x\cos x + \cos x = 0$

$\Rightarrow \quad \cos x(-2\sin x + 1) = 0$

$\Rightarrow \quad \cos x = 0$ or $\sin x = \dfrac{1}{2}$

$\Rightarrow \quad x = \dfrac{\pi}{6}, \dfrac{5\pi}{6}, \dfrac{\pi}{2}$

For absolute maximum and absolute minimum, we have to evaluate

$$f(0),\ f\left(\frac{\pi}{6}\right),\ f\left(\frac{\pi}{2}\right),\ f(\pi),\ f\left(\frac{5\pi}{6}\right)$$

At $x = 0$, $\quad f(0) = \cos^2 0 + \sin 0 = 1^2 + 0 = 1$

At $x = \frac{\pi}{6}$, $f\left(\frac{\pi}{6}\right) = \cos^2\left(\frac{\pi}{6}\right) + \sin\frac{\pi}{6} = \left(\frac{\sqrt{3}}{2}\right)^2 + \frac{1}{2} = \frac{5}{4} =$

At $x = \frac{\pi}{2}$, $f\left(\frac{\pi}{2}\right) = \cos^2\left(\frac{\pi}{2}\right) + \sin\frac{\pi}{2} = 0^2 + 1 = 1$

At $x = \pi$, $\quad f(\pi) = \cos^2\pi + \sin\pi = (-1)^2 + 0 = 1$

At $x = \frac{5\pi}{6}$, $f\left(\frac{5\pi}{6}\right) = \cos^2\frac{5\pi}{6} + \sin\frac{5\pi}{6}$

$$= \cos^2\frac{\pi}{6} + \sin^2\frac{\pi}{6} = \frac{3}{4} + \frac{1}{2} = \frac{5}{4} = 1.25$$

Hence, the absolute maximum value of f is 1.25 occurring at $x = \frac{\pi}{6}$ and $\frac{5\pi}{6}$ and the absolute minimum value of f is 1 occurring at $x = 0, \frac{\pi}{2}$ and π.

Note If close interval is given, to determine absolute maximum (minimum), check the value at all critical points as well as end points of a given interval.

Question 12 Show that the altitude of the right circular cone of maximum volume that can be inscribed in a sphere of radius r is $\frac{4r}{3}$.

Sol. Let R be the radius and h be the height of cone.

$\therefore \quad OA = h - r$

In ΔOAB, $r^2 = R^2 + (h-r)^2 \Rightarrow r^2 = R^2 + h^2 + r^2 - 2rh$

$\Rightarrow \quad R^2 = 2rh - h^2$

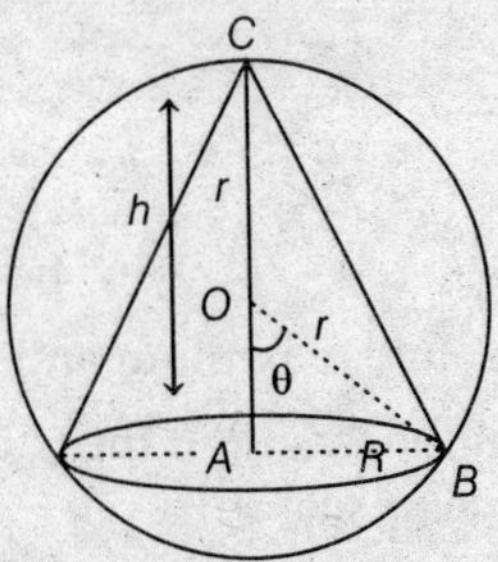

The volume V of the cone is given by $V = \frac{1}{3}\pi R^2 h$

$$= \frac{1}{3}\pi h(2rh - h^2) = \frac{1}{3}\pi(2rh^2 - h^3)$$

On differentiating both sides w.r.t. h, we get

$$\frac{dV}{dh} = \frac{1}{3}\pi(4rh - 3h^2)$$

For maximum or minimum put $\frac{dV}{dh} = 0$

$\Rightarrow \quad 4rh = 3h^2 \Rightarrow 4r = 3h$

$$\therefore \qquad h = \frac{4r}{3} \qquad (h \neq 0)$$

Now, $\dfrac{d^2V}{dh^2} = \dfrac{1}{3}\pi(4r - 6h)$

At $h = \dfrac{4r}{3}$, $\left(\dfrac{d^2V}{dh^2}\right)_{h=\frac{4r}{3}} = \dfrac{1}{3}\pi\left(4r - 6 \times \dfrac{4r}{3}\right) = \dfrac{\pi}{3}(4r - 8r) = \dfrac{-4r\pi}{3} < 0$

$\Rightarrow V$ is maximum when $h = \dfrac{4r}{3}$. Hence, volume of the cone is maximum when $h = \dfrac{4r}{3}$, which is the altitude of cone.

Question 13 Let f be a function defined on $[a, b]$ such that $f'(x) > 0$, for all $x \in (a, b)$. Then prove that f is an increasing function on (a, b).

Sol. Given, $f'(x) > 0$ on (a, b)

$\therefore$ f is a differentiable function on (a, b)

Also, every differentiable function is continuous, therefore f is continuous on (a, b).

Let $x_1, x_2 \in (a, b)$ and $x_2 > x_1$, consider the subinterval $[x_1, x_2]$.

Since, $f(x)$ is differentiable on (a, b) then also differentiable on $(x_1, x_2) \subset (a, b)$ then by LMV theorem, there exist $c \in (x_1, x_2)$ such that

$$f'(c) = \frac{f(x_2) - f(x_1)}{x_2 - x_1}$$

$$\Rightarrow \qquad f(x_2) - f(x_1) = (x_2 - x_1)\, f'(c)$$

$$\Rightarrow \qquad f(x_2) - f(x_1) > 0 \text{ as } x_2 > x_1$$

and $\qquad f'(x) > 0$

$$\Rightarrow \qquad f(x_2) > f(x_1)$$

Since, x_1, x_2 are arbitrary points in (a, b)

$\therefore$ Therefore $x_1 < x_2 \Rightarrow f(x_1) < f(x_2)$ for all $x_1, x_2 \in (a, b))$

Hence, f is an increasing function on (a, b).

Question 14 Show that the height of the cylinder of maximum volume that can be inscribed in a sphere of radius R is $\dfrac{2R}{\sqrt{3}}$. Also, find the maximum volume.

◎ ***Thinking Process*** Draw the diagram of a cylinder of height h and radius r inscribed in a sphere of radius R. Now, express volume V in terms of R and h and then apply second derivative test to prove the required results.

Sol. Given radius of the sphere $= R$

Let h be the height and x be the diameter of the base of the inscribed cylinder.

Then, $h^2 + x^2 = (2R)^2 \Rightarrow h^2 + x^2 = 4R^2$ ...(i)

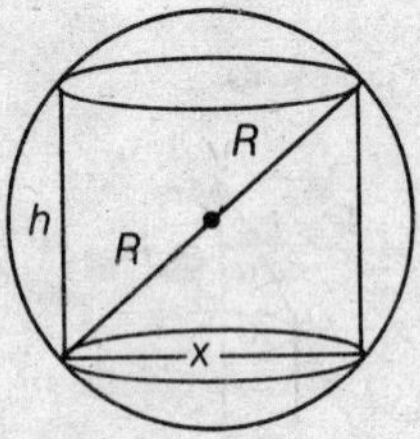

Now, volume of the cylinder = π (radius)^2 × height

$\Rightarrow$ $V = \pi\left(\frac{x}{2}\right)^2 \cdot h = \frac{1}{4}\pi x^2 h \Rightarrow V = \frac{1}{4}\pi h(4R^2 - h^2)$ ...(ii)

[from Eq. (i), $x^2 = 4R^2 - h^2$]

$\Rightarrow$ $V = \pi R^2 h - \frac{1}{4}\pi h^3$

On differentiating both sides w.r.t. h, we get

$$\frac{dV}{dh} = \pi R^2 - \frac{3}{4}\pi h^2 = \pi\left(R^2 - \frac{3}{4}h^2\right)$$

Put $\frac{dV}{dh} = 0 \Rightarrow R^2 = \frac{3}{4}h^2 \Rightarrow h = \frac{2R}{\sqrt{3}}$

Also, $\frac{d^2V}{dh^2} = -\frac{3}{4} \times 2\pi h$

At $h = \frac{2R}{\sqrt{3}}$, $\frac{d^2V}{dh^2} = -\frac{3}{4} \times 2\pi\left(\frac{2R}{\sqrt{3}}\right) = -\sqrt{3}\pi R = -$ ve

$\Rightarrow V$ is maximum at $h = \frac{2R}{\sqrt{3}}$

Maximum volume at $h = \frac{2R}{\sqrt{3}}$ is $V = \frac{1}{4}\pi\left(\frac{2R}{\sqrt{3}}\right)\left(4R^2 - \frac{4R^2}{3}\right)$ [using Eq (ii)]

$$= \frac{\pi R}{2\sqrt{3}}\left(\frac{8R^2}{3}\right) = \frac{4\pi R^3}{3\sqrt{3}} \text{ sq unit.}$$

Thus, volume of the cylinder is maximum when $h = \frac{2R}{\sqrt{3}}$.

Question 15 Show that the height of the cylinder of greatest volume which can be inscribed in a right circular cone of height h and semi-vertical angle α is one-third that of the cone and the greatest volume of cylinder is $\frac{4}{27}\pi h^3 \tan^2 \alpha$.

Sol. Let VAB be the cone of height h, semi-vertical angle α and let x be the radius of the base of the cylinder $A'B'DC$ which is inscribed in the cone VAB. Then, OO' is the height of the cylinder = $VO - VO' = h - x\cot\alpha$

Volume of the cylinder,

$V = \pi x^2 (h - x\cot\alpha)$ ...(i) [$\because v = \pi r^2 h$]

On differentiating both sides w.r.t. x, we get

$$\frac{dV}{dx} = 2\pi xh - 3\pi x^2 \cot\alpha$$

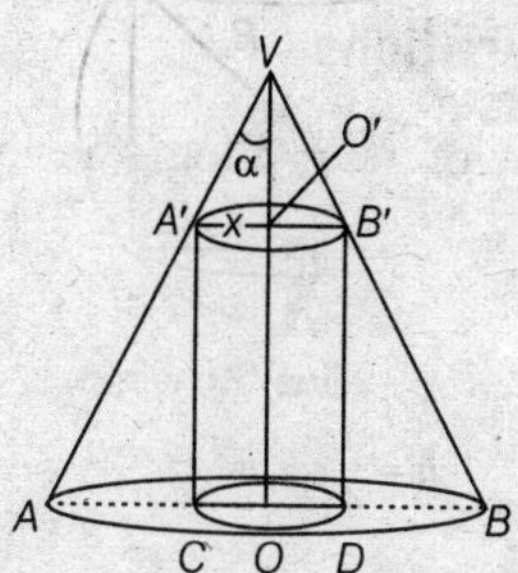

For maxima or minima put $\frac{dV}{dx} = 0$

$\Rightarrow \quad 2\pi xh - 3\pi x^2 \cot\alpha = 0$

$\Rightarrow \quad x = \frac{2h}{3}\tan\alpha \qquad (\because x \neq 0)$

Now, $\quad \frac{d^2V}{dx^2} = 2\pi h - 6\pi x \cot\alpha$

At $x = \frac{2h}{3}\tan\alpha$, $\quad \frac{d^2V}{dx^2} = \pi(2h - 4h) = -2\pi h < 0$

$\Rightarrow V$ is maximum, when $x = \frac{2h}{3}\tan\alpha$. Now $OO' = h - x\cot\alpha = h - \frac{2h}{3} = \frac{h}{3}$

$\therefore$ The maximum volume of the cylinder is

$$V = \pi\left(\frac{2h}{3}\tan\alpha\right)^2\left(\frac{h}{3}\right) = \frac{4}{27}\pi h^3 \tan^2\alpha$$

Question 16. A cylindrical tank of radius 10 m is being filled with wheat at the rate 314 cubic m per h. Then, the depth of the wheat is increasing at the rate of

(a) 1 m/h
(b) 0.1 m/h
(c) 1.1 m/h
(d) 0.5 m/h

Sol. (a) Let at any instant of time t h the depth of the wheat in the cylinder be h m, then the volume V m^3 of the wheat at any instant is given by $V = \pi r^2 h = \pi(10)^2 h = 100\pi h$

On differentiating both sides w.r.t. t, we get

$$\frac{dV}{dt} = 100\pi\frac{dh}{dt} \Rightarrow 314 = 100\pi\frac{dh}{dt} \quad \left(\text{Given, } \frac{dV}{dt} = 314\right)$$

$$\Rightarrow \frac{dh}{dt} = \frac{314}{100(3.14)} = 1 \text{ m/h}$$

Hence, the depth of wheat is increasing at the rate of 1 m/h.

DIKSHA APP Questions

Multiple Choice Questions

Q.1 The minimum value of $f(x) = x \log_e x$ is equal to

(a) e (b) $\frac{1}{e}$

(c) $-\frac{1}{e}$ (d) $2e$

Sol. (c) We have $f(x) = x \log_e x$

On differentiating both sides w.r.t x, we get

$$f'(x) = x \cdot \frac{d}{dx} \log_e x + \log_e x \frac{d}{dx} x \quad \text{(Using product rule)}$$

$$\Rightarrow \quad f'(x) = x \cdot \frac{1}{x} + \log_e x$$

$$\Rightarrow \quad f'(x) = 1 + \log_e x$$

For maxima and minima put $f'(x) = 0$

$$\Rightarrow \quad 1 + \log_e x = 0$$

$$\Rightarrow \quad \log_e x = -1$$

$$\Rightarrow \quad x = e^{-1} = \frac{1}{e}$$

Now $\quad f''(x) = \frac{1}{x}$

$$\Rightarrow \quad f''\left(\frac{1}{e}\right) = e > 0$$

$\therefore x = \frac{1}{e}$ is a point of minima.

and minimum value $= f\left(\frac{1}{e}\right) = \frac{1}{e} \cdot \log_e \frac{1}{e}$

$$= \frac{1}{e} \log_e e^{-1} = \frac{-1}{e} \quad [\because \log_e e = 1]$$

Q.2 If $x + y = 8$, then maximum value of xy is

(a) 8 (b) 16

(c) 20 (d) 24

Sol. (b) Given, $x + y = 8 \Rightarrow y = (8 - x)$ ... (i)

Let $\quad f(x) = x \cdot y$

$$\Rightarrow \quad f(x) = x(8 - x) \quad \text{[From Eq. (i)]}$$

$$\Rightarrow \quad f(x) = 8x - x^2$$

On differentiating both sides w.r.t. x, we get $f'(x) = 8 - 2x$

For maxima and minima, put $f'(x) = 0$

$\Rightarrow \quad 8 - 2x = 0$

$\Rightarrow \quad x = 4$

Now $\quad f''(x) = -2 < 0$

$\therefore$ $x = 4$ is point of maxima.

and maximum value = $f(4) = 4(8 - 4) = 16$

Q.3 If the function $f(x) = x^3 - 9kx^2 + 27x + 30$ is increasing on R, then

(a) $-1 \le k \le 1$ (b) $k < -1$ or $k > 1$
(c) $0 < k < 1$ (d) $-1 < k < 0$

Sol. (a) We have $f(x) = x^3 - 9kx^2 + 27x + 30$

On differentiating both sides w.r.t. x, we get $f'(x) = 3x^2 - 18kx + 27$

$= 3(x^2 - 6kx + 9)$

For increasing $f'(x) \ge 0$

$x^2 - 6kx + 9 \ge 0$

If any quadratic $ax^2 + bx + c \ge 0$

Then, $a > 0$, $D \le 0 (D = b^2 - 4ac)$

So, $\quad (-6k)^2 - 4 \times 9 \times 1 \le 0$

$\Rightarrow \quad 36k^2 - 36 \le 0$

$\Rightarrow \quad k^2 - 1 \le 0$

$\Rightarrow \quad (k + 1)(k - 1) \le 0 \Rightarrow -1 \le k \le 1$

Q.4 If the function $f(x) = 2x^2 - kx + 5$ is increasing on [1, 2], then k lies in the interval

(a) $(-\infty, 4)$ (b) $(4, \infty)$
(c) $(-\infty, 8)$ (d) $(8, \infty)$

Sol. (a) We have $f(x) = 2x^2 - kx + 5$

On differentiating both sides twice w.r.t. x, we get $f'(x) = 4x - k$.

and $\quad f''(x) = 4$

Now, $f''(x) = 4 > 0 \; \forall \; x \notin [1, 2)$

Thus, $f'(1)$ is the least value of $f(x)$

Now, $\quad f'(1) > 0$

$\Rightarrow \quad 4 - k > 0$

$\Rightarrow \quad k < 4$

$\Rightarrow \quad k \in (-\infty, 4)$

Q.5 A man 2 meter tall walks away from a lamp post 5 meters high at the rate of 4.8 km/ hr. The rate of increase of length of shadow is

(a) 1.6 km/hr (b) 6.3 km/hr (c) 5 km/hr (d) 3.2 km/hr

Sol. (d) Let AB be the lamp post and PQ be the man.

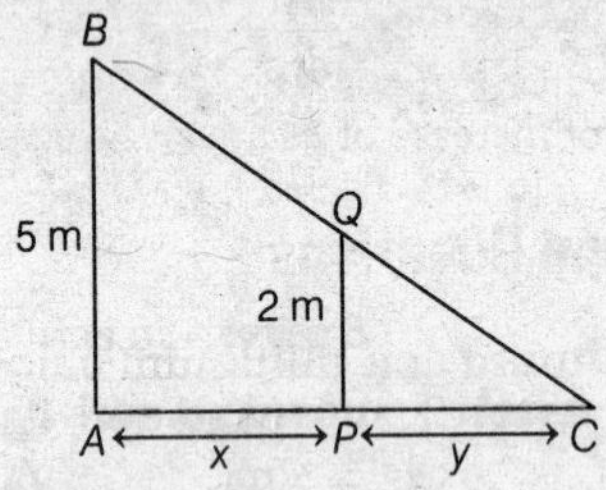

Let the distance of man from lamp post is x and length of shadow is y.

Now, if man is walking away from lamp post then x is increasing.

$$\therefore \quad \frac{dx}{dt} = 4.8 \text{ km/hr}$$

In ΔABC and ΔPQC

$$\angle A = \angle P \quad \text{(each } 90°)$$

$$\angle C = \angle C \quad \text{(common)}$$

So $\Delta ABC \sim \Delta PQC$ (AA similarity criteria)

$$\Rightarrow \quad \frac{AB}{PQ} = \frac{AC}{PC} \Rightarrow \frac{5}{2} = \frac{x+y}{y}$$

$$\Rightarrow \quad 5y = 2x + 2y \Rightarrow 3y = 2x$$

On differentiating both sides w.r.t. t, we get $3\frac{dy}{dt} = 2\frac{dx}{dt}$

$$\Rightarrow \quad 3\frac{dy}{dt} = 2 \times 4.8 \quad \left(\frac{dx}{dt} = 4.8 \text{ km/hr}\right)$$

$$\Rightarrow \quad \frac{dy}{dt} = 3.2 \text{ km/h}$$

Hence, the rate of increase of length is 3.2 km/h.

Q.6 Each side of an equilateral triangle is increasing at the rate of 8 cm/hr. The rate of increase of its area when side is 2 cm is

(a) $8\sqrt{3}$ cm^2 / hr (b) $4\sqrt{4}$ cm^2 / hr

(c) $\frac{\sqrt{3}}{8}$cm^2 / hr (d) None of these

Sol. (a) Let x be the side of equilateral triangle and side is increasing at the rate of 8 cm/hr.

So, $$\frac{dx}{dt} = 8 \text{ cm/hr.}$$

Let A be the area, then $A = \frac{\sqrt{3}}{4} \cdot x^2$

On differentiating both sides w.r.t. t, we get $\frac{dA}{dt} = \frac{\sqrt{3}}{4} \cdot 2 \cdot x \cdot \frac{dx}{dt}$

On putting $x = 2$ (given) and $\frac{dx}{dt} = 8$ cm/h, we get

$$\frac{dA}{dt} = \frac{\sqrt{3}}{4} \times 2 \times 2 \times 8 = 8\sqrt{3} \text{ cm}^2\text{/hr}$$

Hence, the rate of increase of its area is $8\sqrt{3}$ cm^2/hr.

☐ Subjective Type Questions

Q.1 Find the maximum and minimum values of $f(x) = \sin x$ in the interval $[\pi, 2\pi]$.

Sol. Given, $f(x) = \sin x$

On differentiating both sides w.r.t. x, we get $f'(x) = \cos x$

For maxima or minima, put $f'(x) = 0$

$$\Rightarrow \quad \cos x = 0 \Rightarrow \cos x = \cos\frac{3\pi}{2} \Rightarrow x = \frac{3\pi}{2}$$

For absolute maximum and absolute minimum, we have to evalute

$$f(\pi),\ f\left(\frac{3\pi}{2}\right),\ f(2\pi)$$

At $\quad x = \pi,\ f(x) = \sin \pi = 0$

At $\quad x = \frac{3\pi}{2},\ f\left(\frac{3\pi}{2}\right) = \sin\frac{3\pi}{2} = -1$

At $\quad x = 2\pi,\ f(2\pi) = \sin 2\pi = 0$

Hence, the maximum value is 0 and minimum value is -1.

Q.2 Of all the rectangle each of which has perimeter 40 mt., find one which has maximum area, find the area also.

Sol. Let x be the length and y be the breadth of rectangle.

Perimeter of rectangle $= 2(x + y) = 40$ (given)

$$\Rightarrow \quad x + y = 20 \Rightarrow y = (20 - x)$$

Now, let $f(x) = \text{Area} = x \cdot y$

$$\Rightarrow \quad f(x) = x(20 - x)$$

$$\Rightarrow \quad f(x) = 20x - x^2$$

On differentiating both sides twice w.r.t. x, we get

$$f'(x) = 20 - 2x \text{ and } f''(x) = -2$$

For maxima and minima, put $f'(x) = 0$

$$\Rightarrow \quad 20 - 2x = 0 \Rightarrow x = 10$$

At $x = 10$, $f''(10) = -2 < 0$

$\therefore$ $x = 10$ is the point of maxima.

and maximum area $= f(10) = 10(20-10)$

$$= 10 \times 10$$

$$= 100 \text{ m}^2$$

Q.3 Find the values of k for which $f(x) = kx^3 - 9kx^2 + 9x + 3$ is increasing on R.

Sol. We have $f(x) = kx^3 - 9kx^2 + 9x + 3$

On differentiating both sides w.r.t. x, we get

$$f'(x) = 3kx^2 - 18kx + 9.$$

If $f(x)$ is increasing on R, then

$$f'(x) \geq 0$$

$\Rightarrow$ $3kx^2 - 18kx + 9 \geq 0$

When a quadratic $ax^2 + bx + c \geq 0$

then $a > 0$ and $D \leq 0$

So $3k > 0$ and $(-18k)^2 - 4 \times 9 \times 3k \leq 0$

$$k > 0 \text{ and } 324k^2 - 108k \leq 0$$

$\Rightarrow$ $108k(3k-1) \leq 0$

$\Rightarrow$ $0 \leq k \leq \frac{1}{3}$

So, $k \in \left[0, \frac{1}{3}\right]$

Q.4 Show that the function $f(x) = \frac{3}{x} + 7$ is decreasing for $x \in R - \{0\}$.

Sol. We have $f(x) = \frac{3}{x} + 7$ $(x \neq 0)$

On differentiating both sides w.r.t. x, we get

$$f'(x) = \frac{-3}{x^2}$$

We know that $x^2 \geq 0$

$\therefore$ $\frac{1}{x^2} > 0$ $(x \neq 0)$

$\Rightarrow$ $\frac{-3}{x^2} < 0$

So, $f'(x) < 0$ for $x \neq 0$

So $f(x)$ is decreasing for $R - \{0\}$.

Q.5 A man is walking at the rate of 6.5 km/hr towards the foot of the tower 120m high. At what rate is he approaching the top of the tower when he is 50m away from the tower?

Sol. Let AB be the tower and C is the man.
Height of the man will be negligible as compare to the tower.

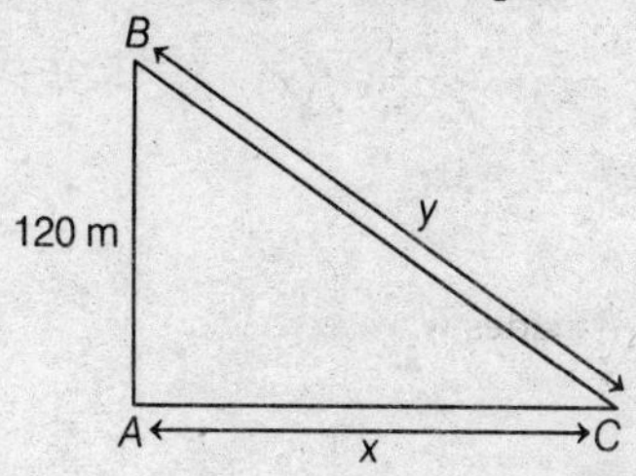

If the man is walking towards the tower, then x is decreasing

$$\therefore \frac{dx}{dt} = -6.5 \text{ km/hr.}$$

Applying Pythagoras in ΔABC

$$y^2 = (120)^2 + x^2$$

$$\Rightarrow \quad y = \sqrt{(120)^2 + x^2}$$

On differentiating both sides w.r.t. t, we get

$$\frac{dy}{dt} = \frac{1}{2\sqrt{(120)^2 + (x^2)}} \frac{d}{dt}((120)^2 + x^2)$$

$$= \frac{1}{2\sqrt{(120)^2 + x^2}} 2x \cdot \frac{dx}{dt} = \frac{x}{\sqrt{(120)^2 + x^2}} \frac{dx}{dt}$$

Put $x = 50$ m and $\frac{dx}{dt} = -6.5$ km/hr.

$$\frac{dy}{dt} = \frac{50}{\sqrt{(120)^2 + (50)^2}}(-6.5)$$

$$= \frac{50}{130} \times (-6.5)\text{km/hr.}$$

$$= -2.5 \text{ km/hr.}$$

Q.6 The volume of a cube is increasing at constant rate. Prove that the increase in surface area varies inversely as the length of the edge of the cube.

Sol. Volume of cube increasing at constant rate.

$$\therefore \quad \frac{dV}{dt} = k$$

Let x be the side of cube, then

Surface Area, $S = 6x^2$

On differentiating both sites w.r.t. t, we get $\frac{ds}{dt} = 12x \cdot \frac{dx}{dt}$ ... (i)

Now, volume $V = x^3$

On differentiating both sides w.r.t. t, we get

$$\frac{dV}{dt} = 3x^2 \frac{dx}{dt}$$

$\Rightarrow$ $k = 3x^2 \frac{dx}{dt}$

$\Rightarrow$ $\frac{dx}{dt} = \frac{k}{3x^2}$

Put the value of $\frac{dx}{dt}$ in Eq. (i) we get

$$\frac{dS}{dt} = 12 \cdot x \cdot \frac{k}{3x^2} = \frac{4k}{x}$$

Let $4k = m$

$\therefore$ $\frac{dS}{dt} = \frac{m}{x}$

$\Rightarrow$ $\frac{dS}{dt} \alpha \frac{1}{x}$

Q.7 Find all the points of local maxima and minima and corresponding maximum and minimum values of the function $f(x) = 2x^3 - 21x^2 + 36x - 20$.

Sol. We have $f(x) = 2x^3 - 21x^2 + 36x - 20$

On differentiating both sides twice w.r.t, x, we get

$$f'(x) = 6x^2 - 42x + 36 \text{ and } f''(x) = 12x - 42$$

For maxima and minima, put $f'(x) = 0$

$\Rightarrow$ $6x^2 - 42x + 36 = 0$

$\Rightarrow$ $x^2 - 7x + 6 = 0$

$\Rightarrow$ $x^2 - 6x - x + 6 = 0$

$\Rightarrow$ $(x - 6)(x - 1) = 0$

$\Rightarrow$ $x = 1, 6$

At $x = 1$, $f''(1) = 12 - 42 = -30 < 0$

$\therefore x = 1$ is the point of maxima.

and at $x = 6$, $f''(6) = 72 - 42 = +30 > 0$

$\therefore$ $x = 6$ is the point of minima.

Now, on maximum value $= f(1) = 2(1)^3 - 21(1)^2 + 36(1) - 20$

$= 2 - 21 + 36 - 20$

$= -3$

and minimum value = $f(6) = 2(6)^3 - 21(6)^2 + 36(6) - 20$

$$= 432 - 756 + 216 - 20$$

$$= -128$$

Q.8 Find the intervals in which $f(x) = x^2 - 2x + 15$ is increasing or decreasing.

Sol. We have, $f(x) = x^2 - 2x + 15$

On differentiating both sides w.r.t. x, we get

$$f'(x) = 2x - 2$$

On putting $f'(x) = 0$, we get $x = 1$, which divides real line into two disjoint interval namely $(-\infty, 1)$ and $(1, \infty)$.

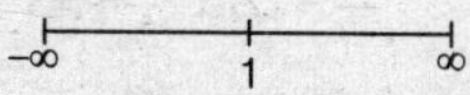

Intervals	Sign of $f'(x)$	Nature of $f(x)$
$(-\infty, 1)$	$-ve$	Decreasing
$(1, \infty)$	$+ve$	Increasing

Therefore, $f(x)$ is increasing on $(1, \infty)$ and $f(x)$ is decreasing on $(-\infty\ 1)$

Q.9 The surface area of a special bubble is increasing at the rate of $2\ \text{cm}^2/\text{s}$. When the radius of the bubble is 6 cm, at what rate is the volume of the bubble increasing?

Sol. Given, surface area (S) is increasing at $2\ \text{cm}^2/\text{s}$

$$\therefore \quad \frac{dS}{dt} = 2\ \text{cm}^2/\text{s}$$

and $\quad r = 6$ cm

Now, $\quad S = 4\pi r^2$

On differentiating both sides w.r.t. t, we get

$$\frac{dS}{dt} = 8\pi r \frac{dr}{dt}$$

$$\Rightarrow \quad 2 = 8\pi r \frac{dr}{dt}$$

$$\Rightarrow \quad \frac{dr}{dt} = \frac{1}{4\pi r} \quad \text{...(i)}$$

Now, volume $V = \frac{4}{3}\pi r^3$

On differentiating both sides w.r.t. t, we get

$$\frac{dV}{dt} = 4\pi r^2 \frac{dr}{dt}$$

On Putting $r = 6$ cm and $\frac{dr}{dt} = \frac{1}{4\pi r}$, we get

$$\frac{dV}{dt} = 4\pi(6)^2 \frac{1}{4\pi(6)} = 6 \text{ cm}^3/\text{s} \qquad \text{[using Eq. (i)]}$$

Q.10 Show that the right circular cylinder of given volume open at the top minimum surface area, provided its height is equal to radius of its base.

Sol. We have a cylinder open at top.

Let h and r be the height and radius of the cylinder, respectively.

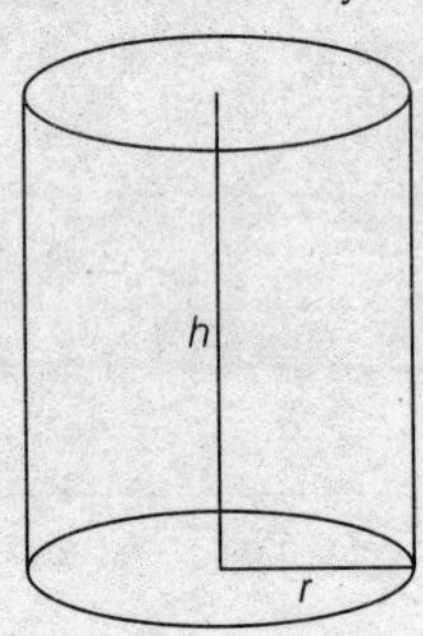

$\therefore$ Volume of cylinder,

$$V = \pi r^2 h$$

$$\Rightarrow \quad h = \frac{V}{\pi r^2} \qquad \text{... (i)}$$

Now, $$S = 2\pi rh + \pi r^2 \qquad (\because \text{ open at the top})$$

On putting the value of h from Eq. (i), we get

$$S = 2\pi r \frac{V}{\pi r^2} + \pi r^2 \Rightarrow S = \frac{2V}{r} + \pi r^2$$

On differentiating both sides w.r.t. r, we get

$$\frac{dS}{dr} = \frac{-2V}{r^2} + 2\pi r$$

For maxima and minima, put $\frac{dS}{dr} = 0$

$$\Rightarrow \quad \frac{-2V}{r^2} + 2\pi r = 0 \Rightarrow 2\pi r = \frac{2V}{r^2}$$

$$\Rightarrow \quad \pi r^3 = V$$

$$\Rightarrow \quad \pi r^3 = \pi r^2 h \qquad (\because V = \pi r^2 h)$$

$$\Rightarrow \quad r = h$$

Now, $$\frac{d^2S}{dr^2} = \frac{4V}{r^3} + 2\pi > 0$$

So $h = r$ is the point of minima. **Hence Proved.**

Integrals

CHAPTER 07

Important Points

Integration

Integration is reverse process of differentiation. If the derivative of $F(x)$, is $f(x)$, then we say that the integral (anti-derivative) of $f(x)$ is $F(x)$ and we write

$$\int f(x)\, dx = F(x) + C$$

where, C is an arbitrary constant known as constant of integration.

01 (i) $\int x^n dx = \frac{x^{n+1}}{(n+1)} + C, n \neq -1$ (ii) $\int \frac{1}{x}\, dx = \log|x| + C, x \neq 0$

(iii) $\int e^x dx = e^x + C$ (iv) $\int a^x dx = \frac{a^x}{\log a} + C$

02 (i) $\int \sin x\, dx = -\cos x + C$

(ii) $\int \cos x\, dx = \sin x + C$

(iii) $\int \tan x\, dx = \log|\sec x| + C = -\log|\cos x| + C$

(iv) $\int \cot x dx = \log|\sin x| + C$

(v) $\int \sec x\, dx = \log|\sec x + \tan x| + C = \log|\tan(\pi/4 + x/2)| + C$

(vi) $\int \operatorname{cosec} x\, dx = \log|\operatorname{cosec} x - \cot x| + C = \log|\tan(x/2)| + C$

(vii) $\int \sec^2 x dx = \tan x + C$

(viii) $\int \operatorname{cosec} \;\; x\, dx = -\cot x + C$

(ix) $\int \sec x \tan x dx = \sec x + C$

(x) $\int \operatorname{cosec} x \cot x dx = -\operatorname{cosec} x + C$

03 (i) $\int \frac{dx}{\sqrt{1-x^2}} = \sin^{-1} x + C$ (ii) $\int \frac{-1}{\sqrt{1-x^2}}\, dx = \cos^{-1} x + C$

(iii) $\int \frac{dx}{1+x^2} = \tan^{-1} x + C$ (iv) $\int \frac{-1}{1+x^2}\, dx = \cot^{-1} x + C$

(v) $\int \frac{dx}{x\sqrt{x^2-1}} = \sec^{-1} x + C$

(vi) $\int \frac{-1}{x\sqrt{x^2-1}}\, dx = \operatorname{cosec}^{-1} x + C$

04 $\int (ax+b)^n\, dx = \frac{1}{a}\frac{(ax+b)^{n+1}}{(n+1)} + C$

05 **Integration by Substitution** The method of reducing a given integral into one of the standard integrals by a proper substitution is called method of substitution.

Suppose, in the integral $I = \int f(x) dx$, $f(x)$ is not in any standard form.

Now, $\int f(x)\, dx$ can be transformed to another form by changing the independent variable x to other variable t by substituting $x = g(t)$.

$\therefore \quad \frac{dx}{dt} = g'(t)$ or $dx = g'(t)\, dt$

Now, putting the value of dx in the above integral, we get

$$\int f(x)\, dx = \int g'(t)\, dt$$

06 (i) $\int \frac{dx}{(x^2-a^2)} = \frac{1}{2a}\log\left|\frac{x-a}{x+a}\right| + C$ (ii) $\int \frac{dx}{(a^2-x^2)} = \frac{1}{2a}\log\left|\frac{a+x}{a-x}\right| + C$

(iii) $\int \frac{dx}{(x^2+a^2)} = \frac{1}{a}\tan^{-1}\frac{x}{a} + C$

07 (i) $\int \frac{dx}{\sqrt{a^2-x^2}} = \sin^{-1}\frac{x}{a} + C$ (ii) $\int \frac{dx}{\sqrt{x^2-a^2}} = \log\left|x + \sqrt{x^2-a^2}\right| + C$

(iii) $\int \frac{dx}{\sqrt{x^2+a^2}} = \log\left|x + \sqrt{x^2+a^2}\right| + C$

08 (i) $\int \sqrt{a^2-x^2}\, dx = \frac{x}{2}\sqrt{a^2-x^2} + \frac{a^2}{2}\sin^{-1}\frac{x}{a} + C$

(ii) $\int \sqrt{x^2-a^2}\, dx = \frac{x}{2}\sqrt{x^2-a^2} - \frac{a^2}{2}\log\left|x + \sqrt{x^2-a^2}\right| + C$

(iii) $\int \sqrt{x^2+a^2}\, dx = \frac{x}{2}\sqrt{x^2+a^2} + \frac{a^2}{2}\log\left|x + \sqrt{x^2+a^2}\right| + C$

09 (i) Integrals of the form $\int \frac{dx}{\sqrt{(ax^2+bx+c)}}$

Method Put the denominator in the form $a[(x+\alpha)^2+\beta^2]$ and then integrate.

(ii) Integrals of the form $\int \frac{dx}{(ax^2+bx+c)}$

Method Put (ax^2+bx+c) in the form $a[(x+\alpha)^2+\beta^2]$ and then integrate.

10 (i) Integrals of the form $\int (px+q)\sqrt{(ax^2+bx+c)}dx$

Method Put $(px+q)=A\cdot\frac{d}{dx}(ax^2+bx+c)+B.$

Comparing the coefficients of like powers of x on both sides and find A and B. The integrands are now easily integrable.

(ii) Integrals of the form $\int \frac{(px^2+qx+r)}{(ax^2+bx+c)}dx$

Method Put $(px^2+qx+r)=A(ax^2+bx+c)+B\cdot\frac{d}{dx}(ax^2+bx+c)+C$

Comparing the coefficients of like powers of x on both sides and find A, B and C. The integrands are now easily integrable.

11 Integrals of the form $\int \frac{dx}{P\sqrt{Q}}$, where P and Q are linear or quadratic expressions in x.

Method (i) When Q is linear, put $Q=t^2$

(ii) When Q is quadratic and P is linear, put $P=\frac{1}{t}$.

(iii) When Q and P are both purely quadratic, put $x=\frac{1}{t}$.

12 Integrals of the form $\int \frac{dx}{(a\sin^2 x+b\cos^2 x)}$.

Method Divide numerator and denominator by $\cos^2 x$, then put $\tan x=t$ and integrate.

13 Integrals of the form $\int \frac{dx}{(a+b\cos x)}$ or $\int \frac{dx}{(a+b\sin x)}$

Method Put $\cos x=\frac{1-\tan^2(x/2)}{1+\tan^2(x/2)}$ and $\sin x=\frac{2\tan(x/2)}{1+\tan^2(x/2)}$

Now, put $\tan(x/2)=t$.

14 Integrals of the form $\int \frac{a\sin x + b\cos x}{c\sin x + d\cos x}$

Method Let numerator $= A$ (denominator) + B. (Derivative of denominator)
Equating the coefficients of $\sin x$ and $\cos x$ on both sides, we get A and B and then integrate.

15 **Integration by Partial Fractions** Rational functions are of the form $\frac{P(x)}{Q(x)}$, where $P(x)$ and $Q(x)$ are polynomials in x and $Q(x) \neq 0$. If degree of $Q(x)$ is less than or equal to the degree of $P(x)$, then divide $P(x)$ by $Q(x)$ by using long division method till the degree of new $P(x)$ (*i.e.*, quotient) is less than the degree of $Q(x)$. Now, use the following cases :

(i) If $Q(x)$ is the product of linear factors, then
$$\frac{P(x)}{(x+a)(x+b)} = \frac{A}{x+a} + \frac{B}{x+b}$$

(ii) If $Q(x)$ is the product of repeated linear factors, then
$$\frac{P(x)}{(x+a)(x+b)^2} = \frac{A}{x+a} + \frac{B}{x+b} + \frac{C}{(x+b)^2}$$

(iii) If $Q(x)$ is the product of linear and quadratic factors, then
$$\frac{P(x)}{(x+a)(px^2+qx+r)} = \frac{A}{x+a} + \frac{Bx+C}{px^2+qx+r}$$

(iv) If $Q(x)$ is the product of quadratic factors, then
$$\frac{P(x)}{(ax^2+bx+c)(px^2+qx+r)} = \frac{Ax+B}{ax^2+bx+c} + \frac{Cx+D}{px^2+qx+r}$$

16 **Integration by Parts** (Integral of the product of two functions)
$\int (uv)\,dx = u\int v dx - \int\left[\frac{d}{dx}(u).\int v dx\right] dx$ = (First function × Integration of IInd function)
$-\int$[(Differential coefficient of I[st] function)
× (Integration of IInd function)]dx

Note • We can also choose the first function as the function which comes first in the word ILATE, where
I = Inverse trigonometric function, L = Logarithmic function
A = Algebraic function T = Trigonometric function
E = Exponential function

• If both the functions are trigonometrical, then take that function as v whose integral is simpler.

• If both the functions are algebraic, then take that function as u whose differentiation is simpler.

17 Integral of the Type $\int e^x[f(x)+f'(x)]dx$

In this type of integral, integrand is the product of two functions. One is in exponential form and second function is the sum of two functions in which one is derivative of other function. Then, to evaluate such integrals, we directly use the following formula,

$$\int e^x[f(x)+f'(x)]\,dx = e^x f(x) + C$$

18 Definite Integrals

Let $f(x)$ be a continuous function defined on an interval $[a, b]$ and having anti-derivative $F(x)$. Then, its definite integral over $[a, b]$ is denoted by $\int_a^b f(x)dx$, which is defined as

$\int_a^b f(x)dx = [F(x)]_a^b = F(b) - F(a)$, where a and b are known as lower limit and upper limit respectively.

Definite integral by substitution method:

To evaluate $\int_a^b f(x)dx$ by substitution, we follow the following steps

(i) First, make suitable substitution, so that given integral reduces to a known form.

(ii) Change the upper and lower limits corresponding to the new variable.

(iii) Integrate the new integral with respect to the new variable.

Properties of Definite Integrals.

(i) $\int_a^b f(x)\,dx = \int_a^b (t)\,dt$ (ii) $\int_a^b f(x)dx = -\int_b^a f(x)dx$

(iii) $\int_a^b f(x)dx = \int_a^c f(x)dx + \int_c^b f(x)dx$, where $a < c < b$

(iv) $\int_a^b f(x)dx = \int_a^b f(a+b-x)dx$

(v) $\int_0^a f(x)dx = \int_0^a f(a-x)dx$

(vi) $\int_0^{2a} f(x)dx = \int_0^a f(x)dx + \int_0^a f(2a-x)dx$

(vii) $\int_0^{2a} f(x)dx = \begin{cases} 2\cdot\int_0^a f(x)dx, & \text{when } f(2a-x) = f(x) \\ 0, & \text{when } f(2a-x) = -f(x) \end{cases}$

(viii) $\int_{-a}^a f(x)dx = \begin{cases} 2\cdot\int_0^a f(x)dx, & \text{when } f(x) \text{ is an even function i.e., } f(-x) = f(x) \\ 0, & \text{when } f(x) \text{ is an odd function i.e., } f(-x) = -f(x) \end{cases}$

Exercise 7.1

Direction (Q. No. 1 to 5) Find the anti-derivative (or integral) of the following by the method of inspection.

Question 1 $\sin 2x$

Sol. $\int \sin 2x\, dx = -\frac{1}{2}\cos 2x + C$ $\left[\because \frac{d}{dx}\left(-\frac{1}{2}\cos 2x\right) = -\frac{1}{2}(-\sin 2x)\,2 = \sin 2x\right]$

Mistake Alert Do not forget to add the constant C after integration.

Question 2 $\cos 3x$

Sol. $\int \cos 3x\, dx = \frac{1}{3}\sin 3x + C$ $\left[\because \frac{d}{dx}\left(\frac{1}{3}\sin 3x\right) = \frac{1}{3}(\cos 3x)\,3 = \cos 3x\right]$

Question 3 e^{2x}

Sol. $\int e^{2x}\, dx = \frac{1}{2}e^{2x} + C$ $\left[\because \frac{d}{dx}\left(\frac{1}{2}e^{2x}\right) = \frac{1}{2}e^{2x}.2 = e^{2x}\right]$

Question 4 $(ax+b)^2$

Sol. $\int (ax+b)^2\, dx = \frac{1}{3a}(ax+b)^3 + C$ $\left[\because \frac{d}{dx}\left(\frac{1}{3a}(ax+b)^3\right) = \frac{1}{3a}.\,3(ax+b)^2 a = (ax+b)^2\right]$

Question 5 $\sin 2x - 4e^{3x}$.

Sol. $\int (\sin 2x - 4e^{3x})\, dx$

$$= \int \sin 2x\, dx - 4\int e^{3x}\, dx = \frac{-\cos 2x}{2} - \frac{4e^{3x}}{3}$$

$$\left[\because \frac{d}{dx}\left\{-\frac{1}{2}\cos 2x\right\} = -\frac{1}{2}(-\sin 2x)2 = \sin 2x \quad \frac{d}{dx}\left(\frac{4}{3}e^{3x}\right) = \frac{4}{3}(e^{3x}\,3) = 4e^{3x}\right]$$

Direction (Q. No. 6 to 20) Find the following integrals.

Question 6 $\int (4e^{3x} + 1)dx$.

Sol. $\int (4e^{3x} + 1)\, dx = 4\int e^{3x}\, dx + \int 1dx$

$$= \frac{4e^{3x}}{3} + x + C \qquad \left[\therefore \int e^{nx}\, dx = \frac{e^{nx}}{n} + C\right]$$

Mistake Alert Do not assume $\int k\, dx = k + C$ instead of $\int k\, dx = kx + C$

Question 7 $\int x^2\left(1-\frac{1}{x^2}\right)dx.$

Sol. $\int x^2\left(1-\frac{1}{x^2}\right)dx = \int\left(x^2-\frac{x^2}{x^2}\right)dx$

$$= \int(x^2-1)\,dx = \int x^2 dx - \int 1\,dx = \frac{x^3}{3} - x + C$$

Question 8 $\int(ax^2+bx+c)dx.$

Sol. $\int(ax^2+bx+c)\,dx = \int ax^2\,dx + \int bx\,dx + c\int 1\,dx$

$$= \frac{ax^3}{3} + \frac{bx^2}{2} + cx + K \text{ (where, } K \text{ is a constant of integration)}$$

Question 9 $\int(2x^2+e^x)\,dx.$

Sol. $\int(2x^2+e^x)\,dx = 2\int x^2\,dx + \int e^x\,dx = \frac{2x^3}{3} + e^x + C$

Question 10 $\int\left(\sqrt{x}-\frac{1}{\sqrt{x}}\right)^2 dx.$

Sol. $\int\left(\sqrt{x}-\frac{1}{\sqrt{x}}\right)^2 dx = \int\left[(\sqrt{x})^2 + \left(\frac{1}{\sqrt{x}}\right)^2 - 2\sqrt{x}\times\frac{1}{\sqrt{x}}\right]dx$

$[\because (a-b)^2 = a^2+b^2-2ab]$

$$= \int\left(x+\frac{1}{x}-2\right)dx = \int x\,dx + \int\frac{1}{x}\,dx - 2\int 1\,dx$$

$$= \frac{x^2}{2} + \log|x| - 2x + C$$

Question 11 $\int\frac{x^3+5x^2-4}{x^2}\,dx.$

◎ **Thinking Process** Here, the integrand cannot integrate directly, so we will break the integrand into three terms by taking x^2 as denominator of each term of numerator and then integrate each term separately.

Sol. $\int\frac{x^3+5x^2-4}{x^2}\,dx = \int\frac{x^3}{x^2}\,dx + 5\int\frac{x^2}{x^2}\,dx - 4\int\frac{1}{x^2}\,dx$

$$= \int x\,dx + 5\int 1\cdot dx - 4\int x^{-2}\,dx$$

$$= \frac{x^2}{2} + 5x - 4\left(\frac{x^{-2+1}}{-2+1}\right) + C$$

$$= \frac{x^2}{2} + 5x - 4\left(\frac{x^{-1}}{-1}\right) + C \qquad \left[\because \int x^n dx = \frac{x^{n+1}}{n+1} + C\right]$$

$$= \frac{x^2}{2} + 5x + \frac{4}{x} + C$$

Question 12 $\int \frac{x^3+3x+4}{\sqrt{x}}\,dx.$

Sol. $\int \frac{x^3+3x+4}{\sqrt{x}}\,dx = \int \frac{x^3}{\sqrt{x}}\,dx + 3\int \frac{x}{\sqrt{x}}\,dx + 4\int \frac{1}{\sqrt{x}}\,dx$

$$= \int x^3 \times x^{-1/2}\,dx + 3\int x^{1/2}\,dx + 4\int x^{-1/2}\,dx$$

$$= \int x^{(6-1)/2}\,dx + 3\int x^{1/2}\,dx + 4\int x^{-1/2}\,dx$$

$$= \int x^{5/2}\,dx + 3\int x^{1/2}\,dx + 4\int x^{-1/2}\,dx$$

$$= \frac{x^{(5/2)+1}}{(5/2)+1} + \frac{3x^{(1/2)+1}}{(1/2)+1} + \frac{4x^{(-1/2)+1}}{(-1/2)+1} + C$$

$$\left(\because \int x^n\,dx = \frac{x^{n+1}}{n+1} + C\right)$$

$$= \frac{x^{7/2}}{7/2} + \frac{3x^{3/2}}{3/2} + \frac{4x^{1/2}}{1/2} + C = \frac{2}{7}x^{7/2} + 2\cdot x^{3/2} + 8x^{1/2} + C$$

Question 13 $\int \frac{x^3-x^2+x-1}{(x-1)}\,dx$

◎ *Thinking Process* Here, first we factorise the numerator and cancel the common term from numerator and denominator and then integrate it.

Sol. $\int \frac{x^3-x^2+x-1}{(x-1)}\,dx = \int \frac{x^2(x-1)+1(x-1)}{(x-1)}\,dx$

$$= \int \frac{(x^2+1)(x-1)}{(x-1)}\,dx = \int (x^2+1)\,dx = \frac{x^3}{3} + x + C$$

Question 14 $\int (1-x)\sqrt{x}\,dx.$

Sol. $\int (1-x)\sqrt{x}\,dx = \int \left(\sqrt{x} - x^{\frac{3}{2}}\right) dx$

$$= \frac{x^{(1/2)+1}}{(1/2)+1} - \frac{x^{(3/2)+1}}{(3/2)+1} + C = \frac{x^{(3/2)}}{(3/2)} - \frac{x^{(5/2)}}{(5/2)} + C$$

$$\left(\because \int x^n\,dx = \frac{x^{n+1}}{n+1} + C\right)$$

$$= \frac{2}{3}x^{3/2} - \frac{2}{5}x^{5/2} + C$$

Question 15 $\int \sqrt{x}(3x^2+2x+3)dx.$

◎ *Thinking Process* Here, the given integrand is written as the product of two functions, so first, we multiply both functions and then integrate.

Sol. $\int \sqrt{x}(3x^2 + 2x + 3)\, dx = 3\int x^{5/2}\, dx + 2\int x^{3/2}\, dx + 3\int x^{1/2}\, dx$

$$= \frac{3 \cdot x^{(5/2)+1}}{(5/2)+1} + \frac{2 \cdot x^{(3/2)+1}}{(3/2)+1} + \frac{3 \cdot x^{(1/2)+1}}{(1/2)+1} + C$$

$$= \frac{3x^{7/2}}{7/2} + \frac{2x^{5/2}}{5/2} + \frac{3x^{3/2}}{3/2} + C = \frac{6}{7}x^{7/2} + \frac{4}{5}x^{5/2} + 2x^{3/2} + C$$

Question 16 $\int (2x - 3\cos x + e^x)\, dx.$

Sol. $\int (2x - 3\cos x + e^x)dx = 2\int x dx - 3\int \cos x\, dx + \int e^x\, dx$

$$= \frac{2x^2}{2} - 3\sin x + e^x + C = x^2 - 3\sin x + e^x + C$$

Mistake Alert Students can take integration as differentiation, so they will take $\int \cos x\, dx = -\sin x + C$ instead of $\int \cos x\, dx = \sin x + C$

Question 17 $\int (2x^2 - 3\sin x + 5\sqrt{x})\, dx.$

Sol. $\int (2x^2 - 3\sin x + 5\sqrt{x})\, dx = 2\int x^2\, dx - 3\int \sin x\, dx + 5\int x^{1/2}\, dx$

$$= \frac{2x^3}{3} - 3(-\cos x) + 5\frac{x^{(1/2)+1}}{(1/2)+1} + C$$

$$= \frac{2}{3}x^3 + 3\cos x + \frac{5 \times 2}{3}x^{3/2} + C = \frac{2}{3}x^3 + 3\cos x + \frac{10}{3}x^{3/2} + C$$

Question 18 $\int \sec x(\sec x + \tan x)\, dx.$

Sol. $\int \sec x(\sec x + \tan x)\, dx = \int (\sec^2 x + \sec x \cdot \tan x)\, dx$

$$= \int \sec^2 x\, dx + \int \sec x \cdot \tan x\, dx = \tan x + \sec x + C$$

Question 19 $\int \frac{\sec^2 x}{\csc^2 x}\, dx.$

Thinking Process Here, we can convert given integrand into simple form by using trigonometric identities and then integrate it easily.

Sol. $\int \frac{\sec^2 x}{\csc^2 x} dx = \int \frac{\sin^2 x}{\cos^2 x} dx$ $\qquad \left(\because \frac{1}{\csc^2\theta} = \sin^2\theta \text{ and } \sec^2\theta = \frac{1}{\cos^2\theta}\right)$

$$= \int \tan^2 x\, dx = \int (\sec^2 x - 1)\, dx$$

$$= \int \sec^2 x\, dx - \int 1 dx = \tan x - x + C$$

Question 20 $\int \frac{2 - 3\sin x}{\cos^2 x}\, dx.$

Sol. $\int \frac{2 - 3\sin x}{\cos^2 x}\, dx = \int \frac{2}{\cos^2 x} dx - 3\int \frac{\sin x}{\cos^2 x} dx$

$$= 2\int \sec^2 x\, dx - 3\int \tan x \cdot \sec x\, dx$$

$$= 2\tan x - 3\sec x + C \qquad \left[\because \frac{\sin\theta}{\cos^2\theta} = \frac{\sin\theta}{\cos\theta} \cdot \frac{1}{\cos\theta} = \sec\theta\tan\theta\right]$$

Question 21 The anti-derivative of $\left(\sqrt{x}+\frac{1}{\sqrt{x}}\right)$ equals

(a) $\frac{1}{3}x^{\frac{1}{3}}+2x^{\frac{1}{2}}+C$ (b) $\frac{2}{3}x^{\frac{2}{3}}+\frac{1}{2}x^2+C$

(c) $\frac{2}{3}x^{\frac{3}{2}}+2x^{\frac{1}{2}}+C$ (d) $\frac{3}{2}x^{\frac{3}{2}}+\frac{1}{2}x^{\frac{1}{2}}+C$

Sol. (c) $\int\left(\sqrt{x}+\frac{1}{\sqrt{x}}\right)dx=\int\sqrt{x}\,dx+\int\frac{1}{\sqrt{x}}dx$

$$=\int x^{1/2}dx+\int x^{-1/2}dx=\frac{x^{3/2}}{3/2}+\frac{x^{1/2}}{1/2}+C=\frac{2}{3}x^{3/2}+2x^{1/2}+C$$

Question 22 If $\frac{d}{dx}f(x)=4x^3-\frac{3}{x^4}$ such that $f(2)=0$. Then, $f(x)$ is

(a) $x^4+\frac{1}{x^3}-\frac{129}{8}$ (b) $x^3+\frac{1}{x^4}+\frac{129}{8}$

(c) $x^4+\frac{1}{x^3}+\frac{129}{8}$ (d) $x^3+\frac{1}{x^4}-\frac{129}{8}$

◎ *Thinking Process* It is an anti-derivative of $f(x)$, so we integrate both sides and use the given condition to find the value of constant of integration.

Sol. (a) Given, $\frac{d}{dx}f(x)=4x^3-\frac{3}{x^4}$

$\Rightarrow$ Anti-derivative of $\left(4x^3-\frac{3}{x^4}\right)=f(x)$

$\therefore$ $$f(x)=\int\left(4x^3-\frac{3}{x^4}\right)dx=4\int x^3dx-3\int x^{-4}dx$$

$\Rightarrow$ $$f(x)=4\left(\frac{x^4}{4}\right)-3\left(\frac{x^{-3}}{-3}\right)+C=x^4+\frac{1}{x^3}+C$$

Also, $$f(2)=0\Rightarrow(2)^4+\frac{1}{(2)^3}+C=0$$

$\Rightarrow$ $$16+\frac{1}{8}+C=0\Rightarrow C=-\left(16+\frac{1}{8}\right)$$

$\Rightarrow$ $$C=-\frac{129}{8}$$

$\therefore$ $$f(x)=x^4+\frac{1}{x^3}-\frac{129}{8}.$$

Exercise 7.2

Direction (Q. No. 1 to 37) *Integrate the following functions.*

Question 1 $\frac{2x}{1+x^2}$.

Sol. Let $I=\int \frac{2x}{1+x^2}dx$

Let $1+x^2=t$

On differentiating both sides w.r.t. x, we get $2x\,dx=dt \Rightarrow dx=\frac{dt}{2x}$

$$\therefore \quad I=\int \frac{2x}{t}\frac{dt}{2x}=\int \frac{1}{t}dt=\log|t|+C=\log|1+x^2|+C$$

Mistake Alert Do not confuse $\int \frac{1}{x}dx=\log|x|+C$ with power rule *i.e.*, $\int \frac{1}{x^n}dx=\int x^{-n}dx$, where $n\neq -1$.

Question 2 $\frac{(\log x)^2}{x}$

Sol. Let $I=\int \frac{(\log x)^2}{x}dx$

Let $\log x=t$

On differentiating both sides w.r.t. x, we get $\frac{1}{x}=\frac{dt}{dx} \Rightarrow dx=x\,dt$

$$\therefore \quad I=\int \frac{t^2}{x}x\,dt=\int t^2dt=\frac{t^3}{3}+C=\frac{(\log x)^3}{3}+C$$

Question 3 $\frac{1}{x+x\log x}$

Sol. Let $I=\int \frac{1}{x+x\log x}dx=\int \frac{1}{x(1+\log x)}dx$

Let $1+\log x=t$

On differentiating both sides w.r.t. x, we get $\frac{1}{x}=\frac{dt}{dx} \Rightarrow dx=x\,dt$

$$\therefore \quad I=\int \frac{1}{x(t)}x\,dt=\int \frac{1}{t}dt=\log|t|+C$$

$$=\log|1+\log x|+C$$

Question 4 $\sin x \sin(\cos x)$.

◎ *Thinking Process* The differentiation of $\cos x$ is $\sin x$ which is given in the integral. So, solve it by substitution method.

Sol. Let $I = \int \sin x \sin(\cos x)\, dx$

Let $\quad \cos x = t$

On differentiating both sides w.r.t. x, we get $-\sin x = \dfrac{dt}{dx}$

$$\Rightarrow \quad dx = \frac{dt}{-\sin x}$$

$$\therefore \quad I = \int \sin x \sin(t) \frac{dt}{-\sin x} = -\int \sin t\, dt = -[-\cos t] + C = \cos(\cos x) + C$$

Question 5 $\sin(ax+b)\cos(ax+b)$.

Sol. Let $I = \int \sin(ax+b)\cos(ax+b)\, dx$

Let $\sin(ax+b) = t$

On differentiating both sides w.r.t. x, we get $a\cos(ax+b) = \dfrac{dt}{dx}$

$$\Rightarrow \quad dx = \frac{dt}{a\cos(ax+b)}$$

$$\therefore \quad I = \int t\cos(ax+b)\frac{dt}{a\cos(ax+b)}$$

$$= \frac{1}{a}\int t\, dt = \frac{1}{a}\cdot\frac{t^2}{2} + C$$

$$= \frac{[\sin(ax+b)]^2}{2a} + C$$

$$= \frac{\sin^2(ax+b)}{2a} + C$$

Question 6 $\sqrt{ax+b}$

Sol. Let $I = \int \sqrt{ax+b}\, dx = \int (ax+b)^{1/2} dx$

$$= \frac{(ax+b)^{(1/2)+1}}{a\left(\frac{1}{2}+1\right)} + C \quad \left[\because \int (ax+b)^n dx = \frac{(ax+b)^{n+1}}{a(n+1)} + C\right]$$

$$= \frac{(ax+b)^{3/2}}{a\left(\frac{3}{2}\right)} + C$$

$$= \frac{2}{3a}(ax+b)^{3/2} + C$$

Question 7 $x\sqrt{x+2}$

Sol. Let $I = \int x\sqrt{x+2}\,dx = \int (x+2-2)\sqrt{x+2}\,dx$

$$= \int (x+2)\sqrt{x+2}\,dx - 2\int \sqrt{x+2}\,dx$$

$$= \int (x+2)^{3/2}dx - 2\int (x+2)^{1/2}dx$$

$$= \frac{(x+2)^{(3/2)+1}}{(3/2)+1} - 2\frac{(x+2)^{(1/2)+1}}{(1/2)+1} + C \qquad \left[\because \int x\,dx = \frac{x^{n+1}}{n+1} + C\right]$$

$$= \frac{2}{5}(x+2)^{5/2} - \frac{2\times 2}{3}(x+2)^{3/2} + C$$

$$= \frac{2}{5}(x+2)^{5/2} - \frac{4}{3}(x+2)^{3/2} + C$$

Quick Solution

Let $x+2 = t$ or $x = (t-2) \Rightarrow 1 = \frac{dt}{dx} \Rightarrow dx = dt$

Then, $\int x\sqrt{x+2}\,dx = \int (t-2)\sqrt{t}\,dt = \int (t^{3/2} - 2t^{1/2})\,dt$

$$= \frac{t^{(3/2)+1}}{(3/2)+1} - 2\frac{t^{(1/2)+1}}{(1/2)+1} + C$$

$$= \frac{2}{5}t^{5/2} - \frac{4}{3}t^{3/2} + C = \frac{2}{5}(x+2)^{5/2} - \frac{4}{3}(x+2)^{3/2} + C$$

Question 8 $x\sqrt{1+2x^2}$

Sol. Let $I = \int x\sqrt{1+2x^2}\,dx$

Let $1+2x^2 = t$

On differentiating both sides w.r.t. x, we get $4x = \frac{dt}{dx} \Rightarrow dx = \frac{dt}{4x}$

$$\therefore \quad I = \int x\sqrt{t}\,\frac{dt}{4x} = \frac{1}{4}\int \sqrt{t}\,dt = \frac{1}{4}\int t^{1/2}dt = \frac{1}{4}\frac{t^{(1/2)+1}}{(1/2)+1} + C = \frac{1}{6}(1+2x^2)^{3/2} + C$$

Note In these type of integrals, it is better to substitute the root function, so that it may be converted into a standard integral.

Question 9 $(4x+2)\sqrt{x^2+x+1}$

Sol. Let $I = \int (4x+2)\sqrt{x^2+x+1}\,dx.$

Let $x^2+x+1 = t$

On differentiating both sides w.r.t. x, we get $2x+1 = \frac{dt}{dx} \Rightarrow dx = \frac{dt}{(2x+1)}$

$$\therefore \quad I = \int (4x+2)\sqrt{t}\,\frac{dt}{(2x+1)} = \int 2(2x+1)\sqrt{t}\,\frac{dt}{(2x+1)} = 2\int \sqrt{t}\,dt$$

$$= 2\frac{t^{(1/2)+1}}{(1/2)+1} + C = \frac{4}{3}(x^2+x+1)^{3/2} + C$$

Question 10 $\dfrac{1}{x-\sqrt{x}}$

Sol. Let $I = \int \dfrac{1}{x-\sqrt{x}}\,dx = \int \dfrac{1}{\sqrt{x}(\sqrt{x}-1)}\,dx$

Let $\sqrt{x} - 1 = t \Rightarrow \dfrac{1}{2\sqrt{x}} = \dfrac{dt}{dx} \Rightarrow dx = 2\sqrt{x}\,dt$

$\therefore$ $$\int \frac{1}{\sqrt{x}(\sqrt{x}-1)}\,dx = \int \frac{1}{\sqrt{x}\,t} 2\sqrt{x}\,dt$$

$$= \int \frac{2}{t}\,dt = 2\cdot \log|t| + C = 2\log|\sqrt{x}-1| + C$$

Question 11 $\dfrac{x}{\sqrt{x+4}}, x > 0.$

Sol. Let $I = \int \dfrac{x}{\sqrt{x+4}}\,dx = \int \dfrac{x+4-4}{\sqrt{x+4}}\,dx$

$$= \int \frac{x+4}{\sqrt{x+4}}\,dx - 4\int \frac{1}{\sqrt{x+4}}\,dx$$

$$= \int (x+4)^{1/2}\,dx - 4\int (x+4)^{-1/2}\,dx$$

$$= \frac{(x+4)^{(1/2)+1}}{(1/2)+1} - 4\,\frac{(x+4)^{(-1/2)+1}}{(-1/2)+1} + C$$

$$= \frac{2}{3}(x+4)^{3/2} - 8\,(x+4)^{1/2} + C$$

Quick Solution

Let $I = \int \dfrac{x}{\sqrt{x+4}}\,dx$

Let $x + 4 = t^2$

$\Rightarrow$ $x = t^2 - 4$

On differentiating both sides w.r.t 'x', we get

$$1 = 2t\,\frac{dt}{dx}$$

$\Rightarrow$ $dx = 2t\,dt$

$\therefore$ $$I = \int \frac{(t^2-4)}{t}\cdot 2t\,dt = 2\int (t^2-4)\,dt$$

$$= 2\left(\frac{t^3}{3} - 4t\right) + C$$

$$= \frac{2}{3}(x+4)^{\frac{3}{2}} - 8\,(x+4)^{\frac{1}{2}} + C$$

Question 12 $(x^3-1)^{1/3}x^5$

Sol. Let $I=\int(x^3-1)^{1/3}x^5\,dx=\int(x^3-1)^{1/3}x^3\cdot x^2\,dx$

Let $x^3-1=t \Rightarrow x^3=t+1$

On differentiating both sides w.r.t. x, we get $3x^2=\frac{dt}{dx} \Rightarrow dx=\frac{dt}{3x^2}$

$$\therefore \quad I=\int(x^3-1)^{1/3}x^3\cdot x^2\,dx=\int t^{1/3}(t+1)x^2\frac{dt}{3x^2}=\frac{1}{3}\int(t^{4/3}+t^{1/3})\,dt$$

$$=\frac{1}{3}\left[\frac{t^{7/3}}{\frac{7}{3}}+\frac{t^{4/3}}{\frac{4}{3}}\right]+C=\frac{1}{3}\left[\frac{3}{7}t^{7/3}+\frac{3}{4}t^{4/3}\right]+C$$

$$=\frac{1}{7}t^{7/3}+\frac{1}{4}t^{4/3}+C=\frac{1}{7}(x^3-1)^{7/3}+\frac{1}{4}(x^3-1)^{4/3}+C$$

$$=(x^3-1)^{\frac{4}{3}}\left[\frac{x^3-1}{7}+\frac{1}{4}\right]+C=(x^3-1)^{\frac{4}{3}}\left[\frac{4x^3+3}{28}\right]+C$$

Question 13 $\frac{x^2}{(2+3x^3)^3}$

Sol. Let $I=\int\frac{x^2}{(2+3x^3)^3}dx$

Let $2+3x^3=t \Rightarrow 9x^2=\frac{dt}{dx} \Rightarrow dx=\frac{dt}{9x^2}$

$$\therefore \quad \int\frac{x^2}{(2+3x^3)^3}dx=\int\frac{x^2}{t^3}\cdot\frac{dt}{9x^2}=\frac{1}{9}\int\frac{1}{t^3}dt=\frac{1}{9}\int t^{-3}dt=\frac{1}{9}\left(\frac{t^{-3+1}}{-3+1}\right)+C$$

$$=\frac{1}{9}\times\frac{1}{-2}t^{-2}+C=\frac{-1}{18t^2}+C=\frac{-1}{18(2+3x^3)^2}+C$$

Question 14 $\frac{1}{x(\log x)^m}, x>0, m\neq 1$

Thinking Process Here, given integrand is not in a standard form. So, we convert it in a standard form by substitution method and then integrate it.

Sol. Let $I=\int\frac{1}{x(\log x)^m}dx$

Let $\log x=t \Rightarrow \frac{1}{x}=\frac{dt}{dx} \Rightarrow dx=x\,dt$

$$\therefore \quad I=\int\frac{1}{x(\log x)^m}dx=\int\frac{1}{x(t)^m}x\,dt=\int t^{-m}dt$$

$$=\frac{t^{-m+1}}{-m+1}+C=\frac{(\log x)^{1-m}}{1-m}+C$$

Question 15 $\dfrac{x}{9-4x^2}$

Sol. Let $I = \int \dfrac{x}{9-4x^2}\,dx$

Let $9-4x^2 = t \Rightarrow -8x = \dfrac{dt}{dx} \Rightarrow dx = \dfrac{dt}{-8x}$

$\therefore$ $I = \int \dfrac{x}{9-4x^2}\,dx = \int \dfrac{x}{t}\,\dfrac{dt}{-8x} = \dfrac{1}{-8}\int \dfrac{1}{t}\,dt = \dfrac{1}{-8}\log|t| + C$

$= -\dfrac{1}{8}\log|9-4x^2| + C = \dfrac{1}{8}\log\left|\dfrac{1}{9-4x^2}\right| + C$

$\left[\because -a\log b = a\log b^{-1} = a\log\dfrac{1}{b}\right]$

Question 16 $e^{(2x+3)}$.

Sol. Let $I = \int e^{(2x+3)}dx$

Let $2x+3 = t \Rightarrow 2 = \dfrac{dt}{dx} \Rightarrow dx = \dfrac{dt}{2}$

$\therefore$ $I = \int e^{(2x+3)}dx = \int e^t\,\dfrac{dt}{2} = \dfrac{1}{2}\int e^t dt = \dfrac{1}{2}e^t + C = \dfrac{1}{2}e^{(2x+3)} + C$

Question 17 $\dfrac{x}{e^{x^2}}$

Sol. Let $I = \int \dfrac{x}{e^{x^2}}\,dx$

Let $x^2 = t \Rightarrow 2x = \dfrac{dt}{dx} \Rightarrow dx = \dfrac{dt}{2x}$

$\therefore$ $I = \int \dfrac{x}{e^{x^2}}\,dx = \int \dfrac{x}{e^t}\,\dfrac{dt}{2x} = \dfrac{1}{2}\int e^{-t}dt = -\dfrac{1}{2}e^{-t} + C = -\dfrac{1}{2}e^{-(x^2)} + C$

Question 18 $\dfrac{e^{\tan^{-1}x}}{1+x^2}$.

◎ *Thinking Process* Here, the given integrand is of the form $\dfrac{e^{f(x)}}{f'(x)}$, so we use substitution method to integrate it.

Sol. Let $I = \int \dfrac{e^{\tan^{-1}x}}{1+x^2}\,dx$

Let $\tan^{-1}x = t \Rightarrow \dfrac{1}{1+x^2} = \dfrac{dt}{dx} \Rightarrow dx = (1+x^2)\,dt$

$\therefore$ $I = \int \dfrac{e^{\tan^{-1}x}}{1+x^2}\,dx = \int \dfrac{e^t}{1+x^2}(1+x^2)\,dt$

$= \int e^t dt = e^t + C = e^{\tan^{-1}x} + C$

Question 19 $\dfrac{e^{2x}-1}{e^{2x}+1}$

Sol. Let $I = \int \frac{e^{2x}-1}{e^{2x}+1}dx = \int \frac{(e^x.e^x-1)}{(e^x.e^x+1)}dx = \int \frac{e^x\left(e^x - \frac{1}{e^x}\right)}{e^x\left(e^x + \frac{1}{e^x}\right)}dx = \int \frac{(e^x - e^{-x})}{(e^x + e^{-x})}dx$

Let $\quad e^x + e^{-x} = t \Rightarrow e^x - e^{-x} = \frac{dt}{dx} \Rightarrow dx = \frac{dt}{e^x - e^{-x}}$

$\therefore \quad I = \int \frac{e^{2x}-1}{e^{2x}+1}dx = \int \frac{(e^x - e^{-x})}{t} \frac{dt}{e^x - e^{-x}} = \int \frac{1}{t}dt = \log|t| + C = \log|e^x + e^{-x}| + C$

Question 20 $\dfrac{e^{2x}-e^{-2x}}{e^{2x}+e^{-2x}}$.

Sol. Let $I = \int \frac{e^{2x}-e^{-2x}}{e^{2x}+e^{-2x}}dx$

Let $\quad e^{2x} + e^{-2x} = t \Rightarrow 2e^{2x} - 2e^{-2x} = \frac{dt}{dx} \Rightarrow dx = \frac{dt}{2(e^{2x} - e^{-2x})}$

$\therefore \quad I = \int \frac{e^{2x}-e^{-2x}}{e^{2x}+e^{-2x}}dx = \int \frac{e^{2x}-e^{-2x}}{t} \frac{dt}{2[e^{2x}-e^{-2x}]}$

$= \frac{1}{2}\int \frac{1}{t}dt = \frac{1}{2}\log|t| + C = \frac{1}{2}\log|e^{2x} + e^{-2x}| + C$

Question 21 $\tan^2(2x-3)$

◎ ***Thinking Process*** Firstly, the integrand is converted into some standard integrand by substitution method and then integrate it.

Sol. Let $I = \int \tan^2(2x-3)\,dx = \int \sec^2(2x-3)\,dx - \int 1dx \quad [\because \tan^2\theta = \sec^2\theta - 1]$

Let $\quad 2x - 3 = t$

$\Rightarrow \quad 2dx = dt \Rightarrow dx = \frac{1}{2}dt$

$\therefore \quad \int \sec^2(2x-3)\,dx - \int 1dx = \frac{1}{2}\int(\sec^2 t)\,dt - \int 1dx$

$= \frac{1}{2}\tan t - x + C = \frac{1}{2}\tan(2x-3) - x + C$

Question 22 Let $I = \sec^2(7-4x)$.

Sol. Let $I = \int \sec^2(7-4x)\,dx$

Let $\quad 7 - 4x = t \Rightarrow -4 = \frac{dt}{dx} \Rightarrow dx = \frac{dt}{-4}$

$\therefore \quad \int \sec^2(7-4x)\,dx = \int \sec^2 t.\frac{dt}{-4}$

$= -\frac{1}{4}\tan t + C = -\frac{1}{4}\tan(7-4x) + C$

Question 23 $\dfrac{\sin^{-1} x}{\sqrt{1-x^2}}$

Sol. Let $I=\int \dfrac{\sin^{-1} x}{\sqrt{1-x^2}}\,dx$

Let $\sin^{-1} x = t$

$\Rightarrow \quad \dfrac{1}{\sqrt{1-x^2}} = \dfrac{dt}{dx} \Rightarrow dx = \sqrt{1-x^2}\,dt$

$\therefore \quad I = \int \dfrac{t}{\sqrt{1-x^2}}\sqrt{1-x^2}\,dt$

$$= \int t\,dt = \frac{t^2}{2} + C = \frac{(\sin^{-1} x)^2}{2} + C$$

Question 24 $\dfrac{2\cos x - 3\sin x}{6\cos x + 4\sin x}$

Sol. Let $I = \int \dfrac{2\cos x - 3\sin x}{6\cos x + 4\sin x}\,dx = \int \dfrac{2\cos x - 3\sin x}{2(3\cos x + 2\sin x)}\,dx$

Let $3\cos x + 2\sin x = t$

$\Rightarrow \quad -3\sin x + 2\cos x = \dfrac{dt}{dx} \quad \Rightarrow \quad dx = \dfrac{dt}{2\cos x - 3\sin x}$

$\therefore \quad \int \dfrac{2\cos x - 3\sin x}{2(3\cos x + 2\sin x)}\,dx = \int \dfrac{2\cos x - 3\sin x}{2(t)} \dfrac{dt}{2\cos x - 3\sin x}$

$$= \frac{1}{2}\int \frac{1}{t}\,dt = \frac{1}{2}\log|t| + C$$

$$= \frac{1}{2}\log|3\cos x + 2\sin x| + C$$

Question 25 $\dfrac{1}{\cos^2 x(1-\tan x)^2}$

Sol. Let $I = \int \dfrac{1}{\cos^2 x(1-\tan x)^2}\,dx = \int \dfrac{\sec^2 x}{(1-\tan x)^2}\,dx$

Let $1 - \tan x = t$

$\Rightarrow \quad -\sec^2 x = \dfrac{dt}{dx} \Rightarrow dx = \dfrac{dt}{-\sec^2 x}$

$\therefore \quad \int \dfrac{\sec^2 x}{(1-\tan x)^2}\,dx = \int \dfrac{\sec^2 x}{t^2} \dfrac{dt}{(-\sec^2 x)}$

$$= -\int t^{-2} \quad = -\left(\frac{t^{-2+1}}{-2+1}\right) + C$$

$$= \frac{1}{t} + C = \frac{1}{1-\tan x} + C$$

Question 26 $\dfrac{\cos\sqrt{x}}{\sqrt{x}}$

Sol. Let $I = \int \dfrac{\cos\sqrt{x}}{\sqrt{x}}\,dx$

Let $\sqrt{x} = t \Rightarrow \dfrac{1}{2\sqrt{x}} = \dfrac{dt}{dx} \Rightarrow dx = 2\sqrt{x}\,dt$

$\therefore \int \dfrac{\cos\sqrt{x}}{\sqrt{x}}\,dx = \int \dfrac{\cos t}{\sqrt{x}} 2\sqrt{x}\,dt = 2\int \cos t\,dt = 2\sin t + C = 2\sin\sqrt{x} + C$

Question 27 $\sqrt{\sin 2x}\cos 2x$

Sol. Let $I = \int \sqrt{\sin 2x}\cos 2x\,dx$

Let $\sin 2x = t \Rightarrow 2\cos 2x = \dfrac{dt}{dx} \Rightarrow dx = \dfrac{dt}{2\cos 2x}$

$\therefore \int \sqrt{\sin 2x}\cos 2x\,dx = \int \sqrt{t}\cos 2x \dfrac{dt}{2\cos 2x} = \dfrac{1}{2}\int \sqrt{t}\,dt$

$= \dfrac{1}{2}\dfrac{t^{1/2+1}}{\left(\dfrac{1}{2}+1\right)} + C = \dfrac{1}{3}t^{3/2} + C = \dfrac{1}{3}(\sin 2x)^{3/2} + C$

Question 28 $\dfrac{\cos x}{\sqrt{1+\sin x}}$

Sol. Let $I = \int \dfrac{\cos x}{\sqrt{1+\sin x}}\,dx = \int (1+\sin x)^{-1/2}\cos x\,dx$

Let $1+\sin x = t \Rightarrow \cos x = \dfrac{dt}{dx} \Rightarrow dx = \dfrac{dt}{\cos x}$

$\therefore \int (1+\sin x)^{-1/2}\cos x\,dx = \int (t)^{-1/2}\cos x \dfrac{dt}{\cos x} = \dfrac{t^{-1/2+1}}{\left(-\dfrac{1}{2}+1\right)} + C$

$= 2t^{1/2} + C = 2\sqrt{1+\sin x} + C$

Question 29 $\cot x \log \sin x$

Sol. Let $I = \int \cot x \log \sin x\,dx$

Let $\log \sin x = t \Rightarrow \dfrac{1}{\sin x} \times \cos x = \dfrac{dt}{dx}$

$\Rightarrow \cot x = \dfrac{dt}{dx} \Rightarrow dx = \dfrac{dt}{\cot x}$

$\therefore \int \cot x \log \sin x\,dx = \int \cot x \cdot t \dfrac{dt}{\cot x}$

$= \int t\,dt = \dfrac{t^2}{2} + C = \dfrac{(\log \sin x)^2}{2} + C$

Question 30 $\dfrac{\sin x}{1+\cos x}$

Sol. Let $I=\int\dfrac{\sin x}{1+\cos x}dx$

Let $1+\cos x=t \Rightarrow -\sin x=\dfrac{dt}{dx}\Rightarrow dx=\dfrac{dt}{-\sin x}$

$\therefore$ $I=\int\dfrac{\sin x}{t}\times\dfrac{dt}{-\sin x}=-\int\dfrac{1}{t}dt=-\log|t|+C=-\log|1+\cos x|+C$

$=\log\left|\dfrac{1}{1+\cos x}\right|+C$ $\left(\because -\log a=\log\dfrac{1}{a}\right)$

Question 31 $\dfrac{\sin x}{(1+\cos x)^2}$

Sol. Let $I=\int\dfrac{\sin x}{(1+\cos x)^2}dx$

Let $1+\cos x=t \Rightarrow -\sin x=\dfrac{dt}{dx}\Rightarrow dx=\dfrac{dt}{-\sin x}$

$\therefore$ $I=\int\dfrac{\sin x}{(1+\cos x)^2}dx=\int\dfrac{\sin x}{t^2}\times\dfrac{dt}{-\sin x}=-\int\dfrac{1}{t^2}dt$

$=-\int t^{-2}dt=\dfrac{-t^{-2+1}}{-2+1}+C=\dfrac{1}{t}+C=\dfrac{1}{1+\cos x}+C$

Question 32 $\dfrac{1}{(1+\cot x)}$

◎ ***Thinking Process*** Here, the given integrand cannot integrate directly. So, use the trigonometric ratios to convert it into simplest form and then apply substitution method to integrate it.

Sol. Let $I=\int\dfrac{1}{(1+\cot x)}dx=\int\dfrac{1}{1+\dfrac{\cos x}{\sin x}}dx$

$=\int\dfrac{1}{\dfrac{\sin x+\cos x}{\sin x}}dx=\int\dfrac{\sin x}{(\sin x+\cos x)}dx$

$=\dfrac{1}{2}\int\dfrac{2(\sin x)}{\sin x+\cos x}dx=\dfrac{1}{2}\int\dfrac{\sin x+\sin x+\cos x-\cos x}{\sin x+\cos x}dx$

[add and subtract $\cos x$ in numerator]

$=\dfrac{1}{2}\int\dfrac{(\sin x+\cos x)+(\sin x-\cos x)}{(\sin x+\cos x)}dx$

$=\dfrac{1}{2}\left[\int\dfrac{(\sin x+\cos x)}{(\sin x+\cos x)}dx+\int\dfrac{(\sin x-\cos x)}{(\sin x+\cos x)}dx\right]$

$$= \frac{1}{2}\left[\int 1 dx + \int \frac{(\sin x - \cos x)}{(\sin x + \cos x)} dx\right]$$

Let $\quad \sin x + \cos x = t \Rightarrow \cos x - \sin x = \frac{dt}{dx}$

$\Rightarrow \quad dx = \frac{dt}{-[\sin x - \cos x]}$

$\therefore \quad I = \frac{1}{2}\left[\int 1\, dx + \int \frac{(\sin x - \cos x)}{t} \frac{dt}{-[\sin x - \cos x]}\right] = \frac{1}{2}\left[\int 1 dx - \int \frac{1}{t} dt\right]$

$$= \frac{1}{2}[x - \log |t|] + C = \frac{1}{2}[x - \log |\sin x + \cos x|] + C$$

Question 33 $\frac{1}{1 - \tan x}$

Sol. Let $I = \int \frac{1}{1 - \tan x} dx = \int \frac{1}{1 - \frac{\sin x}{\cos x}} dx = \int \frac{1}{\frac{\cos x - \sin x}{\cos x}} dx$

$$= \frac{1}{2}\int \frac{2(\cos x) dx}{(\cos x - \sin x)} = \frac{1}{2}\int \frac{\cos x + \cos x + \sin x - \sin x}{(\cos x - \sin x)} dx$$

[add and subtract $\sin x$ in numerator]

$$= \frac{1}{2}\left[\int \frac{(\cos x - \sin x)}{(\cos x - \sin x)} dx + \int \frac{(\cos x + \sin x)}{(\cos x - \sin x)} dx\right]$$

$$= \frac{1}{2}\left[\int 1 dx + \int \frac{(\cos x + \sin x)}{(\cos x - \sin x)} dx\right]$$

Let $\quad \cos x - \sin x = t$

$\Rightarrow \quad -\sin x - \cos x = \frac{dt}{dx}$

$\Rightarrow \quad -[\sin x + \cos x] = \frac{dt}{dx}$

$\Rightarrow \quad dx = \frac{dt}{-[\sin x + \cos x]}$

$\therefore \quad I = \frac{1}{2}\left[\int 1\, dx + \int \frac{\cos x + \sin x}{t} \frac{dt}{-[\sin x + \cos x]}\right]$

$$= \frac{1}{2}\left[\int 1\, dx - \int \frac{1}{t} dt\right]$$

$$= \frac{1}{2}[x - \log |t|] + C$$

$$= \frac{1}{2}[x - \log |\cos x - \sin x|] + C$$

Question 34 $\dfrac{\sqrt{\tan x}}{\sin x \cdot \cos x}$

Sol. Let $I = \int \frac{\sqrt{\tan x}}{\sin x \cos x} dx = \int \frac{\sqrt{\tan x}}{\sin x \cos x \times \frac{\cos x}{\cos x}} dx$

[multiply and divide by $\cos x$ in denominator]

$$= \int \frac{\sqrt{\tan x}}{\tan x . \cos^2 x} dx = \int \frac{\sqrt{\tan x}}{\tan x} . \sec^2 x\, dx = \int \frac{\sec^2 x\, dx}{\sqrt{\tan x}}$$

Let $\tan x = t \Rightarrow \sec^2 x = \frac{dt}{dx} \Rightarrow dx = \frac{dt}{\sec^2 x}$

$\therefore$ $$= \int \frac{1}{\sqrt{t}} dt = \int t^{-1/2} dt = \frac{t^{-1/2+1}}{\left(-\frac{1}{2}+1\right)} + C = 2\sqrt{t} + C = 2\sqrt{\tan x} + C$$

Quick Solution

Let $I = \int \frac{\sqrt{\tan x}}{\sin x \cos x} dx$

Let $\tan x = t^2$

On differentiating both sides w.r.t. 'x', we get

$$\sec^2 x = 2t \frac{dt}{dx}$$

$\Rightarrow$ $$dx = \frac{2t}{\sec^2 x} dt = 2t \cos^2 x dt$$

$$I = \int \frac{t}{\sin x \cos x} \cdot 2t \cos^2 x\, dt$$

$$= \int \frac{2t^2}{\frac{\sin x}{\cos x}} dt = \int \frac{2t^2}{\tan x} dt$$

$$= \int \frac{2t^2}{t^2} dt = 2\int dt$$

$$= 2t + C = 2\sqrt{\tan x} + C \quad [\because \tan x = t^2 \Rightarrow t = \sqrt{\tan x}]$$

Question 35 $\dfrac{(1+\log x)^2}{x}$

Sol. Let $I = \int \frac{(1+\log x)^2}{x} dx$

Let $1 + \log x = t \Rightarrow \frac{1}{x} = \frac{dt}{dx} \Rightarrow dx = x\, dt$

$\therefore$ $$\int \frac{(1+\log x)^2}{x} dx = \int \frac{t^2}{x} x\, dt$$

$$= \int t^2 dt = \frac{t^3}{3} + C = \frac{(1+\log x)^3}{3} + C$$

Question 36 $\dfrac{(x+1)(x+\log x)^2}{x}$

Sol. Let $I = \int \dfrac{(x+1)(x+\log x)^2}{x} dx = \int (x+\log x)^2 \left(\dfrac{x+1}{x}\right) dx$

$$= \int (x+\log x)^2 \left(1+\frac{1}{x}\right) dx$$

Let $x + \log x = t \Rightarrow \left(1+\dfrac{1}{x}\right) dx = dt$

$\therefore \int \left(1+\dfrac{1}{x}\right)(x+\log x)^2 dx = \int t^2 dt = \dfrac{t^3}{3} + C = \dfrac{(x+\log x)^3}{3} + C$

Question 37 $\dfrac{x^3 \sin(\tan^{-1} x^4)}{(1+x^8)}$.

Sol. Let $I = \int \dfrac{x^3 \sin(\tan^{-1} x^4)}{(1+x^8)} dx$

Let $\tan^{-1} x^4 = t \Rightarrow \dfrac{1}{1+x^8}.4x^3 = \dfrac{dt}{dx} \Rightarrow dx = \dfrac{(1+x^8)}{4x^3} dt$

$\therefore I = \int \dfrac{x^3 \sin t}{(1+x^8)}.\dfrac{(1+x^8)dt}{4x^3} = \dfrac{1}{4}\int \sin t \, dt = -\dfrac{1}{4}\cos t + C$

$$= -\frac{1}{4}\cos(\tan^{-1} x^4) + C$$

Direction (Q. No. 38 and 39) Choose the correct answer.

Question 38 $\int \left(\dfrac{10x^9 + 10^x \log_e 10}{x^{10} + 10^x}\right) dx$ equals

(a) $10^x - x^{10} + C$ (b) $10^x + x^{10} + C$

(c) $(10^x - x^{10})^{-1} + C$ (d) $\log|10^x + x^{10}| + C$

Sol. (d) Let $I = \int \left(\dfrac{10x^9 + 10^x \log_e 10}{x^{10} + 10^x}\right) dx$

Let $x^{10} + 10^x = t \Rightarrow (10x^9 + 10^x \log_e 10)\, dx = dt$

$\Rightarrow dx = \dfrac{dt}{10x^9 + 10^x \log_e 10}$

$\therefore \int \left(\dfrac{10x^9 + 10^x \log_e 10}{x^{10} + 10^x}\right) dx = \int \dfrac{10x^9 + 10^x \log_e 10}{t} \times \dfrac{dt}{10x^9 + 10^x \log_e 10}$

$$= \int \frac{dt}{t} = \log|t| + C$$

$$= \log|10^x + x^{10}| + C$$

Question 39 $\int \frac{dx}{\sin^2 x \cos^2 x}$ equals

(a) $\tan x + \cot x + C$ (b) $\tan x - \cot x + C$
(c) $\tan x \cot x + C$ (d) $\tan x - \cot 2x + C$

Sol. (b) Let $I = \int \frac{dx}{\sin^2 x \cos^2 x} = \int \frac{\sin^2 x + \cos^2 x}{\sin^2 x . \cos^2 x} dx$ $[\because \sin^2 x + \cos^2 x = 1]$

$$= \int \frac{\sin^2 x}{\sin^2 x . \cos^2 x} dx + \int \frac{\cos^2 x}{\sin^2 x . \cos^2 x} dx = \int \frac{1}{\cos^2 x} dx + \int \frac{1}{\sin^2 x} dx$$

$$= \int \sec^2 x \, dx + \int \text{cosec}^2 x \, dx = \tan x - \cot x + C$$

Exercise 7.3

Direction (Q. No. 1 to 22) Find the integrals of the functions.

Question 1. $\sin^2 (2x + 5)$.

◎ *Thinking Process* There is no standard integral formula for $\sin^2 x$. So, we use the relation $\sin^2 x = \frac{1 - \cos 2x}{2}$ to convert it into simple form and then integrate it.

Sol. Let $I = \int \sin^2 (2x + 5) \, dx = \int \frac{1 - \cos 2(2x + 5)}{2} dx$

$$= \int \frac{1 - \cos(4x + 10)}{2} dx \quad \left(\because \sin^2 x = \frac{1 - \cos 2x}{2}\right)$$

$$= \int \frac{1}{2} dx - \frac{1}{2} \int \cos(4x + 10) \, dx$$

$$= \frac{1}{2} x - \frac{1}{2} \frac{\sin(4x + 10)}{4} + C \quad \left[\because \int \cos(ax + b) dx = \frac{\sin(ax + b)}{a} + C\right]$$

$$= \frac{1}{2} x - \frac{\sin(4x + 10)}{8} + C$$

Question 2 $\sin 3x \cos 4x$.

Sol. Let $I = \int \sin 3x \cos 4x \, dx = \frac{1}{2} \int 2 \sin 3x \cos 4x \, dx$ [multiply and divide by 2]

$$= \frac{1}{2} \int \{\sin 7x + \sin(3x - 4x)\} \, dx \quad [\because 2 \sin A \cos B = \sin(A + B) + \sin(A - B)]$$

$$= \frac{1}{2} \int \{\sin 7x - \sin x)\} \, dx \quad [\because \sin(-\theta) = -\sin \theta]$$

$$= \frac{1}{2}\left(\frac{-\cos 7x}{7} + \cos x\right) + C \quad \left[\because \int \sin ax \, dx = \frac{-\cos ax}{a} + C\right]$$

$$= \frac{-\cos 7x}{14} + \frac{\cos x}{2} + C$$

Question 3 $\cos 2x \cos 4x \cos 6x$

◎ *Thinking Process* There is no standard integral formula for given integrand. So, we simplify the function by using the formula, $2\cos A \cos B = [\cos(A+B) + \cos(A-B)]$ and then integrate it.

Sol.

$$\text{Let } I = \int \cos 2x \cos 4x \cos 6x \, dx = \int \cos 2x \left[\frac{1}{2}\{\cos(4x+6x) + \cos(4x-6x)\}\right] dx$$

$$[\because 2\cos A \cos B = \cos(A+B) + \cos(A-B)]$$

$$= \frac{1}{2}\int [\cos 2x \cos 10x + \cos 2x \cos(-2x)]\, dx$$

$$= \frac{1}{2}\int [\cos 2x \cos 10x + \cos^2 2x]\, dx \qquad [\because \cos(-\theta) = \cos\theta]$$

$$= \frac{1}{2}\int \left[\frac{1}{2}\{\cos(2x+10x) + \cos(2x-10x)\} + \left(\frac{1+\cos 4x}{2}\right)\right] dx$$

$$\left(\because \cos^2\theta = \frac{1+\cos 2\theta}{2}\right)$$

$$= \frac{1}{4}\int [\cos 12x + \cos 8x + 1 + \cos 4x]\, dx$$

$$= \frac{1}{4}\left[\frac{\sin 12x}{12} + \frac{\sin 8x}{8} + x + \frac{\sin 4x}{4}\right] + C$$

Question 4 $\sin^3(2x+1)$

Sol. Let $I = \int \sin^3(2x+1)\, dx = \int \sin^2(2x+1).\sin(2x+1)\, dx$

$$= \int [1 - \cos^2(2x+1)] \sin(2x+1)\, dx \qquad [\because \sin^2\theta = 1 - \cos^2\theta]$$

Let $\cos(2x+1) = t \Rightarrow -2\sin(2x+1)\, dx = dt \Rightarrow \sin(2x+1)\, dx = -\frac{dt}{2}$

$$\therefore \int \sin^3(2x+1)\, dx = \frac{-1}{2}\int (1-t^2)\, dt = \frac{-1}{2}\left(t - \frac{t^3}{3}\right) + C$$

$$= \frac{-1}{2}\left(\cos(2x+1) - \frac{\cos^3(2x+1)}{3}\right) + C = \frac{-\cos(2x+1)}{2} + \frac{\cos^3(2x+1)}{6} + C$$

Quick Solution

Let $I = \int \sin^3(2x+1)\, dx$

We know that, $\sin 3\theta = 3\sin\theta - 4\sin^3\theta$

$$\Rightarrow \sin^3\theta = \frac{3\sin\theta - \sin 3\theta}{4}$$

$$\Rightarrow \sin^3(2x+1) = \frac{3\sin(2x+1) - \sin(6x+3)}{4}$$

$$\int \sin^3(2x+1)\, dx = \frac{1}{4}\int [3\sin(2x+1) - \sin(6x+3)]\, dx$$

$$= \frac{1}{4}\left[-\frac{3\cos(2x+1)}{2} - \frac{-\cos(6x+3)}{6}\right] + C$$

$$= \frac{-3}{8}\cos(2x+1) + \frac{1}{24}\cos[3(2x+1)] + C$$

$$= \frac{-3}{8}\cos(2x+1) + \frac{1}{24}[4\cos^3(2x+1) - 3\cos(2x+1)] + C$$

$[\because \cos 3\theta = 4\cos^3\theta - 3\cos\theta]$

$$= \frac{-3}{8}\cos(2x+1) + \frac{1}{6}\cos^3(2x+1) - \frac{1}{8}\cos(2x+1) + C$$

$$= \frac{-1}{2}\cos(2x+1) + \frac{1}{6}\cos^3(2x+1) + C$$

Question 5 $\sin^3 x \cdot \cos^3 x$

Sol. Let $I = \int \sin^3 x \cdot \cos^3 x \, dx$

Let $\cos x = t \Rightarrow -\sin x = \frac{dt}{dx} \Rightarrow dx = \frac{dt}{-\sin x}$

$\therefore$ $\int \sin^3 x \cos^3 x \, dx = \int \sin^3 x \cdot t^3 \frac{dt}{-\sin x}$

$$= -\int \sin^2 x . t^3 dt = -\int t^3 (1 - \cos^2)\, dt = -\int t^3 \cdot (1 - t^2)\, dt$$

$$= -\int [t^3 - t^5]\, dt = -\left[\frac{t^4}{4} - \frac{t^6}{6}\right] + C = \frac{\cos^6 x}{6} - \frac{\cos^4 x}{4} + C$$

Question 6 $\sin x \sin 2x \sin 3x.$

◎ ***Thinking Process*** There is no standard integral formula for given integrand so we simplify it by using the formula $2\sin A \sin B = \cos(A-B) - \cos(A+B)$ and then integrate it.

Sol. Let $I = \int \sin x \sin 2x \sin 3x \, dx = \frac{1}{2}\int (2\sin 3x \sin x) \sin 2x \, dx$

$= \frac{1}{2}\int \{\cos 2x - \cos 4x\} \sin 2x \, dx$ $\quad [\because 2\sin A \sin B = \cos(A-B) - \cos(A+B)]$

$$= \frac{1}{4}\int \{2\sin 2x \cos 2x - 2\cos 4x \sin 2x\}\, dx$$

$$= \frac{1}{4}\int \{(\sin 4x - \sin 0) - (\sin 6x - \sin 2x)\}\, dx$$

$$\left[\begin{array}{l}\because 2\sin A \cos B = \sin(A+B) + \sin(A-B) \\ 2\cos A \sin B = \sin(A+B) - \sin(A-B)\end{array}\right]$$

$$= \frac{1}{4}\int (\sin 4x - \sin 6x + \sin 2x)\, dx$$

$= \frac{1}{4}\left\{\frac{-\cos 4x}{4} - \frac{(-\cos 6x)}{6} + \frac{(-\cos 2x)}{2}\right\} + C$ $\quad \left[\because \int \sin ax \, dx = -\frac{\cos ax}{a} + C\right]$

$$= \frac{-\cos 4x}{16} + \frac{\cos 6x}{24} - \frac{\cos 2x}{8} + C$$

Question 7 $\sin 4x \sin 8x$

Sol. Let $I = \int \sin 4x \sin 8x\, dx = \frac{1}{2}\int 2\sin 8x \sin 4x\, dx$

$$= \frac{1}{2}\int (\cos 4x - \cos 12x)\, dx \quad [\because 2\sin A \sin B = \cos(A-B) - \cos(A+B)]$$

$$= \frac{1}{2}\left[\frac{\sin 4x}{4} - \frac{\sin 12x}{12}\right] + C = \frac{\sin 4x}{8} - \frac{\sin 12x}{24} + C$$

Question 8 $\dfrac{(1-\cos x)}{(1+\cos x)}$

◎ *Thinking Process* The given integrand cannot integrate directly. So, simplify it by using the relation $1-\cos x = 2\sin^2\frac{x}{2}$ and $1+\cos x = 2\cos^2\frac{x}{2}$, then integrate it.

Sol. Let $I = \int \frac{(1-\cos x)}{(1+\cos x)} dx = \int \frac{2\sin^2\frac{x}{2}}{2\cos^2\frac{x}{2}} dx = \int \tan^2\frac{x}{2} dx$

$$\left[\because 1-\cos\theta = 2\sin^2\frac{\theta}{2} \text{ and } 1+\cos\theta = 2\cos^2\frac{\theta}{2}\right]$$

$$= \int\left(\sec^2\frac{x}{2} - 1\right) dx \quad [\because \tan^2\theta = \sec^2\theta - 1]$$

$$= \int \sec^2\frac{x}{2} dx - \int 1\, dx = \frac{\tan\frac{x}{2}}{\frac{1}{2}} - x + C \quad \left(\because \int \sec^2 ax\, dx = \frac{\tan ax}{a} + C\right)$$

$$= 2\tan\frac{x}{2} - x + C$$

Question 9 $\dfrac{\cos x}{1+\cos x}$

Sol. Let $I = \int \frac{\cos x}{1+\cos x} dx = \int \frac{1-1+\cos x}{1+\cos x} dx$ [add and subtract 1 in numerator]

$$= \int \frac{1+\cos x}{1+\cos x} dx - \int \frac{1}{1+\cos x} dx$$

$$= \int 1\, dx - \int \frac{1}{2\cos^2\frac{x}{2}} dx = \int 1\, dx - \frac{1}{2}\int \sec^2\frac{x}{2} dx$$

$$= x - \frac{1}{2}\cdot 2\tan\frac{x}{2} + C = x - \tan\frac{x}{2} + C \quad \left(\because \int \sec^2 ax\, dx = \frac{\tan ax}{a} + C\right)$$

Question 10 $\sin^4 x$

Sol. Let $I = \int \sin^4 x\, dx = \int (\sin^2 x)^2\, dx = \int \left(\frac{1-\cos 2x}{2}\right)^2 dx \quad \left(\because \sin^2\theta = \frac{1-\cos 2\theta}{2}\right)$

$$= \frac{1}{4}\int (1-\cos 2x)^2 dx = \frac{1}{4}\int (1+\cos^2 2x - 2\cos 2x)\, dx$$

$$= \frac{1}{4}[\int 1\,dx + \int \cos^2 2x\,dx - 2\int \cos 2x\,dx]$$

$$= \frac{1}{4}\left[\int 1\,dx + \int \frac{1+\cos 4x}{2}\,dx - 2\int \cos 2x\,dx\right]\left[\because \cos^2\theta = \frac{1+\cos 2\theta}{2}\right]$$

$$= \frac{1}{4}\left[\int 1\,dx + \frac{1}{2}\{\int 1\,dx + \int \cos 4x\,dx\} - 2\int \cos 2x\,dx\right]$$

$$= \frac{1}{4}\left[x + \frac{1}{2}\left\{x + \frac{\sin 4x}{4}\right\} - \frac{2\sin 2x}{2}\right] + C$$

$$= \frac{1}{4}x + \frac{x}{8} + \frac{\sin 4x}{32} - \frac{\sin 2x}{4} + C = \left(\frac{2x+x}{8}\right) + \frac{\sin 4x}{32} - \frac{\sin 2x}{4} + C$$

$$= \frac{3x}{8} + \frac{\sin 4x}{32} - \frac{\sin 2x}{4} + C$$

Question 11 $\cos^4 2x$

Sol. Let $I = \int \cos^4 2x\,dx = \int (\cos^2 2x)^2\,dx = \int \left(\frac{1+\cos 4x}{2}\right)^2 dx$

$$= \frac{1}{4}\int (1+\cos 4x)^2\,dx = \frac{1}{4}\int (1+\cos^2 4x + 2\cos 4x)\,dx$$

$$= \frac{1}{4}\left[\int 1\,dx + \int \cos^2 4x\,dx + 2\int \cos 4x\,dx\right]$$

$$= \frac{1}{4}\left[\int 1\,dx + \int \frac{1+\cos 8x}{2}\,dx + 2\int \cos 4x\,dx\right]\left[\because \cos^2\theta = \frac{1+\cos 2\theta}{2}\right]$$

$$= \frac{1}{4}\left[\int 1\,dx + \frac{1}{2}\{\int 1\,dx + \int \cos 8x\,dx\} + 2\int \cos 4x\,dx\right]$$

$$= \frac{1}{4}\left[x + \frac{1}{2}\left\{x + \frac{\sin 8x}{8}\right\} + \frac{2\sin 4x}{4}\right] + C$$

$$= \frac{1}{4}x + \frac{x}{8} + \frac{\sin 8x}{64} + \frac{\sin 4x}{8} + C = \frac{3x}{8} + \frac{\sin 8x}{64} + \frac{\sin 4x}{8} + C$$

Mistake Alert Students may incorrectly apply the identity as $\cos^2 x = \frac{1-\cos 2x}{2}$ instead of $\cos^2 x = \frac{1+\cos 2x}{2}$

Question 12 $\dfrac{\sin^2 x}{(1+\cos x)}$

Sol. Let $I = \int \frac{\sin^2 x}{(1+\cos x)}\,dx = \int \frac{(1-\cos^2 x)}{(1+\cos x)}\,dx$ $\quad [\because \sin^2\theta = 1-\cos^2\theta]$

$$= \int \frac{(1+\cos x)(1-\cos x)}{(1+\cos x)}\,dx = \int (1-\cos x)\,dx$$

$$= \int 1\,dx - \int \cos x\,dx = x - \sin x + C$$

Question 13 $\dfrac{\cos 2x - \cos 2\alpha}{\cos x - \cos \alpha}$

Sol. Let $I = \int \dfrac{\cos 2x - \cos 2\alpha}{\cos x - \cos \alpha} dx$

$$= \int \frac{(2\cos^2 x - 1) - (2\cos^2 \alpha - 1)}{(\cos x - \cos \alpha)} dx \qquad [\because \cos 2\theta = 2\cos^2\theta - 1]$$

$$= \int \frac{2\cos^2 x - 1 - 2\cos^2 \alpha + 1}{(\cos x - \cos \alpha)} dx = \int \frac{2(\cos^2 x - \cos^2 \alpha)}{(\cos x - \cos \alpha)} dx$$

$$= 2\int \frac{(\cos x - \cos \alpha)(\cos x + \cos \alpha)}{(\cos x - \cos \alpha)} dx \qquad [\because a^2 - b^2 = (a+b)(a-b)]$$

$$= 2\left[\int \cos x\, dx + \cos\alpha \int 1\, dx\right]$$

$$= 2[\sin x + \cos\alpha \cdot x] + C = 2\sin x + 2x\cos\alpha + C$$

Question 14 $\dfrac{\cos x - \sin x}{1 + \sin 2x}$

Sol. Let $I = \int \dfrac{\cos x - \sin x}{1 + \sin 2x} dx = \int \dfrac{\cos x - \sin x}{\sin^2 x + \cos^2 x + 2\sin x \cos x} dx$

$$[\because \sin^2\theta + \cos^2\theta = 1;\ \sin 2\theta = 2\sin\theta\cos\theta]$$

$$= \int \frac{\cos x - \sin x}{(\sin x + \cos x)^2} dx$$

Let $\cos x + \sin x = t \Rightarrow -\sin x + \cos x = \dfrac{dt}{dx}$

$\Rightarrow \quad dx = \dfrac{dt}{(\cos x - \sin x)}$

$\therefore \quad I = \int \dfrac{\cos x - \sin x}{t^2} \cdot \dfrac{dt}{(\cos x - \sin x)}$

$$= \int \frac{1}{t^2} dt = \int t^{-2} dt$$

$$= \frac{t^{-2+1}}{-2+1} + C = \frac{-1}{\cos x + \sin x} + C$$

Question 15 $\tan^3 2x \sec 2x$

Sol. Let $I = \int \tan^3 2x \sec 2x\, dx$

$$= \int \tan^2 2x \cdot \tan 2x \cdot \sec 2x\, dx$$

$$= \int (\sec^2 2x - 1)\tan 2x . \sec 2x\, dx \qquad [\because 1 + \tan^2\theta = \sec^2\theta]$$

Put $\sec 2x = t \Rightarrow 2\tan 2x \sec 2x = \dfrac{dt}{dx}$

$\Rightarrow \quad dx = \dfrac{dt}{2\tan 2x \sec 2x}$

$\therefore \qquad I = \int (t^2 - 1)\tan 2x \cdot \sec 2x \times \frac{dt}{2\tan 2x \sec 2x}$

$$= \frac{1}{2}\int (t^2 - 1)dt = \frac{1}{2}\left[\frac{t^3}{3} - t\right] + C$$

$$= \frac{1}{2}\left[\frac{\sec^3 2x}{3} - \sec 2x\right] + C$$

$$= \frac{1}{6}\sec^3 2x - \frac{1}{2}\sec 2x + C$$

Question 16 $\tan^4 x$

Sol. Let $I = \int \tan^4 x\, dx = \int (\tan^2 x)(\tan^2 x)\, dx$

$$= \int (\sec^2 x - 1)(\tan^2 x)\, dx = \int \sec^2 x \tan^2 x\, dx - \int \tan^2 x\, dx$$

$$= \int \sec^2 x \tan^2 x\, dx - \int [\sec^2 x - 1]\, dx$$

$$= \int \sec^2 x \tan^2 x dx - \left[\int \sec^2 x\, dx - \int 1\, dx\right]$$

Now, let $I_1 = \int \sec^2 x \tan^2 x\, dx$ and $I_2 = \int \sec^2 x dx - \int 1 dx$

Then, $\qquad I = I_1 - I_2 \qquad \ldots$(i)

In I_1, put $\qquad \tan x = t \Rightarrow \sec^2 x = \frac{dt}{dx} \Rightarrow dx = \frac{dt}{\sec^2 x}$

$\therefore \qquad I_1 = \int \sec^2 x\, t^2 . \frac{dt}{\sec^2 x}$

$\Rightarrow \qquad I_1 = \int t^2\, dt = \frac{t^3}{3} + C_1 = \frac{\tan^3 x}{3} + C_1$

Now, $\qquad I_2 = \int \sec^2 x\, dx - \int 1\, dx = \tan x - x + C_2$

$\therefore$ Putting the values of I_1 and I_2 in Eq. (i), we get

$$I = \frac{\tan^3 x}{3} + C_1 - (\tan x - x) + C_2$$

$\Rightarrow \qquad I = \frac{\tan^3 x}{3} - \tan x + x + C$

($\because$ constant + constant = constant $\therefore C_1 + C_2 = C$)

Question 17 $\dfrac{\sin^3 x + \cos^3 x}{\sin^2 x \cos^2 x}$

Sol. Let $I = \int \frac{\sin^3 x + \cos^3 x}{\sin^2 x \cos^2 x} dx = \int \frac{\sin^3 x}{\sin^2 x \cos^2 x} dx + \int \frac{\cos^3 x}{\sin^2 x \cos^2 x} dx$

$$= \int \frac{\sin x}{\cos x \cos x} dx + \int \frac{\cos x}{\sin x \sin x} dx$$

$$= \int \tan x \cdot \sec x\, dx + \int \cot x \cdot \operatorname{cosec} x\, dx$$

$$= \sec x - \operatorname{cosec} x + C$$

Question 18 $\dfrac{\cos 2x + 2\sin^2 x}{\cos^2 x}$

Sol. Let $I = \int \dfrac{\cos 2x + 2\sin^2 x}{\cos^2 x}\, dx = \int \dfrac{1 - 2\sin^2 x + 2\sin^2 x}{\cos^2 x}\, dx$

$[\because \cos 2\theta = 1 - 2\sin^2 \theta]$

$$= \int \frac{1}{\cos^2 x}\, dx = \int \sec^2 x\, dx = \tan x + C$$

Question 19 $\dfrac{1}{\sin x \cos^3 x}$

◎ *Thinking Process* Here, we can convert the given integrand in the terms of tan x and $\sec^2 x$. Thn, put $\tan x = t$ to convert integrand in term of t and then integrate easily.

Sol. Let $= \int \dfrac{1}{\sin x \cos^3 x}\, dx = \int \dfrac{\cos x}{\sin x} \sec^4 x\, dx$

$= \int \dfrac{\sec^2 x \sec^2 x}{\tan x}\, dx = \int \dfrac{(1 + \tan^2 x)\sec^2 x}{\tan x}\, dx$ $\quad (\because \sec^2 \theta = 1 + \tan^2 \theta)$

Put $\tan x = t \Rightarrow \sec^2 x = \dfrac{dt}{dx} \Rightarrow dx = \dfrac{dt}{\sec^2 x}$

$\therefore$
$$= \int \left[\frac{1 + t^2}{t}\right] \sec^2 x \frac{dt}{\sec^2 x} = \int \frac{1 + t^2}{t}\, dt = \int \left[\frac{1}{t} + t\right] dt$$

$$= \log |t| + \frac{t^2}{2} + C = \log |\tan x| + \frac{\tan^2 x}{2} + C$$

Question 20 $\dfrac{\cos 2x}{(\cos x + \sin x)^2}$

Sol. Let $I = \int \dfrac{\cos 2x}{(\cos x + \sin x)^2}\, dx = \int \dfrac{\cos^2 x - \sin^2 x}{(\cos x + \sin x)^2}\, dx$

$[\because \cos 2\theta = \cos^2 \theta - \sin^2 \theta]$

$$= \int \frac{(\cos x - \sin x)(\cos x + \sin x)}{(\cos x + \sin x)^2}\, dx = \int \frac{\cos x - \sin x}{\cos x + \sin x}\, dx$$

$[\because (a^2 - b^2) = (a - b)(a + b)]$

Put $\cos x + \sin x = t \Rightarrow -\sin x + \cos x = \dfrac{dt}{dx} \Rightarrow dx = \dfrac{dt}{\cos x - \sin x}$

$\therefore$
$$I = \int \frac{\cos x - \sin x}{t} \cdot \frac{dt}{\cos x - \sin x}$$

$$= \int \frac{1}{t}\, dt = \log |t| + C = \log |\cos x + \sin x| + C$$

Question 21 $\sin^{-1}(\cos x)$

Sol. Let $I = \sin^{-1}(\cos x)dx = \int \sin^{-1}\left[\sin\left(\frac{\pi}{2} - x\right)\right]dx$

$$= \int \left(\frac{\pi}{2} - x\right) dx = \frac{\pi x}{2} - \frac{x^2}{2} + C$$

Question 22 $\frac{1}{\cos(x-a)\cos(x-b)}$.

Sol. Let $I = \int \frac{1}{\cos(x-a)\cos(x-b)}dx = \frac{1}{\sin(b-a)}\int \frac{\sin\{(x-a)-(x-b)\}}{\cos(x-a)\cos(x-b)}dx$

[Multiply by $\sin(b-a)$ in numerator and denominator both and $\sin(b-a) = \sin[(x-a)-(x-b)]$.

$$= \frac{1}{\sin(b-a)}\int \frac{\sin(x-a)\cos(x-b) - \cos(x-a)\sin(x-b)}{\cos(x-a)\cos(x-b)}dx$$

$[\because \sin(C-D) = \sin C\cos D - \cos C\sin D]$

$$= \frac{1}{\sin(b-a)}\int \left[\frac{\sin(x-a)\cos(x-b)}{\cos(x-a)\cos(x-b)} - \frac{\cos(x-a)\sin(x-b)}{\cos(x-a)\cos(x-b)}\right]dx$$

$$= \frac{1}{\sin(b-a)}\int \{\tan(x-a) - \tan(x-b)\}\,dx$$

$$= \frac{1}{\sin(b-a)}.\{-\log|\cos(x-a)| + \log|\cos(x-b)|\} + C$$

$[\because \int \tan x\,dx = -\log|\cos x| + C]$

$$= \frac{1}{\sin(b-a)}\log\left|\frac{\cos(x-b)}{\cos(x-a)}\right| + C$$

Direction (Q. No. 23 and 24) Choose the correct answer.

Question 23 $\int \frac{\sin^2 x - \cos^2 x}{\sin^2 x\cos^2 x}dx$ is equal to

(a) $\tan x + \cot x + C$

(b) $\tan x + \text{cosec}\, x + C$

(c) $-\tan x + \cot x + C$

(d) $\tan x + \sec x + C$

Sol. (a) Let $I = \int \frac{\sin^2 x - \cos^2 x}{\sin^2 x\cos^2 x}dx = \int\left(\frac{1}{\cos^2 x} - \frac{1}{\sin^2 x}\right)dx$

$$= \int(\sec^2 x - \text{cosec}^2 x)\,dx$$

$$= \tan x + \cot x + C$$

Question 24 $\int \frac{e^x(1+x)}{\cos^2(e^x x)} dx$ equals

(a) $-\cot(ex^x)+C$ (b) $\tan(xe^x)+C$
(c) $\tan(e^x)+C$ (d) $\cot(e^x)+C$

Sol. (b) Let $I = \int \frac{e^x(1+x)}{\cos^2(e^x x)} dx$

Let $xe^x = t \Rightarrow (xe^x + e^x) = \frac{dt}{dx} \Rightarrow dx = \frac{dt}{e^x(x+1)}$

$\therefore$ $\int \frac{e^x(1+x)}{\cos^2(e^x x)} dx = \int \frac{e^x(1+x)}{\cos^2 t} \times \frac{dt}{e^x(1+x)}$

$= \int \frac{1}{\cos^2 t} dt = \int \sec^2 t\, dt = \tan t + C = \tan(xe^x) + C$

Exercise 7.4

Direction (Q. Nos. 1 to 23) Integrate the following functions.

Question 1 $\frac{3x^2}{x^6+1}$

◎ *Thinking Process* It is not a standard form of integration. So, we put $x^3 = t$ and convert it into standard form of integration and then integrate.

Sol. Let $I = \int \frac{3x^2}{x^6+1} dx = \int \frac{3x^2}{(x^3)^2+1} dx$

Let $x^3 = t \Rightarrow 3x^2 = \frac{dt}{dx} \Rightarrow dx = \frac{dt}{3x^2}$

$\therefore$ $\int \frac{3x^2}{(x^3)^2+1} dx = \int \frac{3x^2}{t^2+1} \cdot \frac{dt}{3x^2} = \int \frac{dt}{t^2+1}$

$= \frac{1}{1}\tan^{-1}\left(\frac{t}{1}\right) + C = \tan^{-1}(x^3) + C$

Question 2 $\frac{1}{\sqrt{1+4x^2}}$

Sol. Let $I = \int \frac{dx}{\sqrt{1+4x^2}} = \int \frac{dx}{\sqrt{4\left(\left(\frac{1}{2}\right)^2 + x^2\right)}}$

$= \frac{1}{2}\int \frac{dx}{\sqrt{x^2 + \left(\frac{1}{2}\right)^2}}$

$$= \frac{1}{2} \log \left| x + \sqrt{x^2 + \left(\frac{1}{2}\right)^2} \right| + C$$

$$\left(\because \int \frac{1}{\sqrt{x^2 + a^2}} dx = \log \left| x + \sqrt{x^2 + a^2} \right| + C \right)$$

$$= \frac{1}{2} \log \left| x + \frac{\sqrt{4x^2 + 1}}{2} \right| + C$$

$$= \frac{1}{2} \log | 2x + \sqrt{4x^2 + 1} | - \frac{1}{2} \log 2 + C$$

$$\left[\because \log\left(\frac{m}{n}\right) = \log m - \log n \right]$$

$$= \frac{1}{2} \log | 2x + \sqrt{4x^2 + 1} | + C$$

$$\left[\because \frac{1}{2} \log 2 \text{ is constant and constant + constant} = C \right]$$

Quick Solution

Let $I = \int \frac{dx}{\sqrt{1 + 4x^2}} = \int \frac{dx}{\sqrt{1 + (2x)^2}}$

Put $2x = t$

On differentiating both sides w.r.t. x, we get

$$2 = \frac{dt}{dx} \Rightarrow dx = \frac{1}{2} dt$$

$$\therefore \quad I = \frac{1}{2} \int \frac{dt}{\sqrt{1 + t^2}} = \frac{1}{2} \log \left| t + \sqrt{t^2 + 1} \right| + C$$

$$= \frac{1}{2} \log \left| 2x + \sqrt{4x^2 + 1} \right| + C$$

Question 3 $\dfrac{1}{\sqrt{(2 - x)^2 + 1}}$

Sol. Let $I = \int \frac{1}{\sqrt{(2 - x)^2 + 1}} dx = \int \frac{1}{\sqrt{(x - 2)^2 + 1}} dx$

$$= \log \left| (x - 2) + \sqrt{(x - 2)^2 + 1} \right| + C$$

$$\left[\because \int \frac{dx}{\sqrt{x^2 + a^2}} = \log \left| x + \sqrt{x^2 + a^2} \right| + C \right]$$

Question 4 $\dfrac{1}{\sqrt{9-25x^2}}$

Sol. Let $I = \int \dfrac{1}{\sqrt{9-25x^2}}\,dx = \int \dfrac{1}{\sqrt{25\left[\left(\frac{3}{5}\right)^2 - x^2\right]}}\,dx = \dfrac{1}{5}\int \dfrac{1}{\sqrt{\left(\frac{3}{5}\right)^2 - x^2}}\,dx$

$$= \frac{1}{5}\sin^{-1}\left(\frac{x}{\frac{3}{5}}\right) + C \qquad \left[\because \int \frac{dx}{\sqrt{a^2 - x^2}} = \sin^{-1}\left(\frac{x}{a}\right) + C\right]$$

$$= \frac{1}{5}\sin^{-1}\left(\frac{5x}{3}\right) + C$$

Quick Solution

Let $I = \int \dfrac{1}{\sqrt{9-(5x)^2}}\,dx$

Let $5x = t$

On differentiating both sides w.r.t x, we get $5 = \dfrac{dt}{dx}$

$\Rightarrow \quad dx = \dfrac{1}{5}dt$

$\therefore \quad I = \dfrac{1}{5}\int \dfrac{dt}{\sqrt{3^2 - t^2}}$

$$= \frac{1}{5}\sin^{-1}\frac{t}{3} + C \qquad \left(\because \int \frac{dx}{\sqrt{a^2 - x^2}} = \sin^{-1}\frac{x}{a} + C\right)$$

$$= \frac{1}{5}\sin^{-1}\left(\frac{5x}{3}\right) + C$$

Question 5 $\dfrac{3x}{1+2x^4}$

Sol. Let $I = \int \dfrac{3x}{1+2x^4}\,dx = \dfrac{3}{2}\int \dfrac{x\,dx}{\frac{1}{2} + x^4} = \dfrac{3}{2}\int \dfrac{x\,dx}{\frac{1}{2} + (x^2)^2}$

Let $\quad x^2 = t \Rightarrow 2x = \dfrac{dt}{dx} \Rightarrow dx = \dfrac{dt}{2x}$

$\therefore \quad I = \dfrac{3}{2}\int \dfrac{x\,dx}{\frac{1}{2} + (x^2)^2} = \dfrac{3}{2}\int \dfrac{x}{\left[\frac{1}{2} + (t)^2\right]}\dfrac{dt}{2x}$

$$= \frac{3}{4}\int \frac{dt}{t^2 + \left(\frac{1}{\sqrt{2}}\right)^2} = \frac{3}{4} \times \frac{1}{\frac{1}{\sqrt{2}}}\tan^{-1}\left(\frac{t}{\frac{1}{\sqrt{2}}}\right) + C$$

$$= \frac{3}{2\sqrt{2}} \tan^{-1}(\sqrt{2}t) + C \qquad \left[\because \int \frac{dx}{a^2 + x^2} = \frac{1}{a} \tan^{-1}\left(\frac{x}{a}\right) + C\right]$$

$$= \frac{3}{2\sqrt{2}} \tan^{-1}(\sqrt{2}x^2) + C \qquad [\because t = x^2]$$

Question 6 $\frac{x^2}{1-x^6}$

Sol. Let $I = \int \frac{x^2}{1 - x^6}\, dx = \int \frac{x^2}{1 - (x^3)^2}\, dx$

Let $x^3 = t \Rightarrow 3x^2 = \frac{dt}{dx} \Rightarrow dx = \frac{dt}{3x^2}$

$\therefore$ $I = \int \frac{x^2}{1 - t^2} \frac{dt}{3x^2} = \frac{1}{3}\int \frac{dt}{1 - t^2}$

$$= \frac{1}{3} \cdot \frac{1}{2} \log\left|\frac{1 + t}{1 - t}\right| + C \qquad \left[\because \int \frac{dx}{a^2 - x^2} = \frac{1}{2a} \log\left|\frac{a + x}{a - x}\right| + C\right]$$

$$= \frac{1}{6} \log\left|\frac{1 + x^3}{1 - x^3}\right| + C \qquad [\because t = x^3]$$

Question 7 $\frac{x-1}{\sqrt{x^2 - 1}}$.

Sol. Let $I = \int \frac{x - 1}{\sqrt{x^2 - 1}}\, dx = \int \frac{x}{\sqrt{x^2 - 1}}\, dx - \int \frac{1}{\sqrt{x^2 - 1}}\, dx = I_1 - I_2$ (say) ...(i)

Now, $I_1 = \int \frac{x}{\sqrt{x^2 - 1}}\, dx,$

Let $x^2 - 1 = t \Rightarrow 2x = \frac{dt}{dx} \Rightarrow dx = \frac{dt}{2x}$

$\therefore$ $I_1 = \int \frac{x}{\sqrt{t}} \frac{dt}{2x} = \frac{1}{2}\int \frac{dt}{\sqrt{t}} = \frac{1}{2}\int t^{-\frac{1}{2}} dt = \frac{1}{2}\left[\frac{t^{\frac{1}{2}}}{1/2}\right] + C_1$

$$= \sqrt{t} + C_1 = \sqrt{x^2 - 1} + C_1 \qquad [\because t = x^2 - 1]$$

Now, $I_2 = \int \frac{1}{\sqrt{x^2 - 1}} dx$

$$= \log\left|x + \sqrt{x^2 - 1}\right| + C_2 \qquad \left[\because \int \frac{dx}{\sqrt{x^2 - a^2}} = \log\left|x + \sqrt{x^2 - a^2}\right| + C\right]$$

On putting the values of I_1 and I_2 in Eq. (i), we get

$$\int \frac{x-1}{\sqrt{x^2-1}} dx = \sqrt{x^2-1} - \log|x + \sqrt{x^2-1}| + C \qquad [\text{where, } C = C_1 - C_2]$$

Question 8 $\dfrac{x^2}{\sqrt{x^6+a^6}}$

Sol. Let $I = \int \dfrac{x^2}{\sqrt{x^6+a^6}}\,dx = \int \dfrac{x^2}{\sqrt{(x^3)^2+a^6}}\,dx$

Let $\quad x^3 = t \Rightarrow 3x^2 = \dfrac{dt}{dx} \Rightarrow dx = \dfrac{dt}{3x^2}$

$\therefore \quad \int \dfrac{x^2}{\sqrt{(x^3)^2+a^6}}\,dx = \int \dfrac{x^2}{\sqrt{t^2+a^6}}\dfrac{dt}{3x^2}$

$$= \frac{1}{3}\int \frac{dt}{\sqrt{t^2+(a^3)^2}} = \frac{1}{3}\log\left|t+\sqrt{t^2+a^6}\right| + C$$

$$\left[\because \int \frac{dx}{\sqrt{x^2+a^2}} = \log\left|x+\sqrt{x^2+a^2}\right| + C\right]$$

$$= \frac{1}{3}\log\left|x^3+\sqrt{x^6+a^6}\right| + C \qquad [\because t = x^3]$$

Question 9 $\dfrac{\sec^2 x}{\sqrt{\tan^2 x+4}}$

Sol. Let $I = \int \dfrac{\sec^2 x}{\sqrt{\tan^2 x+4}}\,dx$

Let $\quad \tan x = t \Rightarrow \sec^2 x = \dfrac{dt}{dx} \Rightarrow dx = \dfrac{dt}{\sec^2 x}$

$\therefore \quad \int \dfrac{\sec^2 x}{\sqrt{\tan^2 x+4}}\,dx = \int \dfrac{\sec^2 x}{\sqrt{t^2+4}}\dfrac{dt}{\sec^2 x} = \int \dfrac{dt}{\sqrt{t^2+2^2}}$

$$= \log\left|t+\sqrt{t^2+4}\right| + C \quad \left[\because \int \frac{dx}{\sqrt{x^2+a^2}} = \log\left|x+\sqrt{x^2+a^2}\right| + C\right]$$

$$= \log\left|\tan x+\sqrt{\tan^2 x+4}\right| + C \qquad [\because t = \tan x]$$

Question 10 $\dfrac{1}{\sqrt{x^2+2x+2}}$.

Thinking Process The given integrand is of the form $\left(\dfrac{1}{\sqrt{ax^2+bx+c}}\right)$, so, express the denominator in the form $a[(x+\alpha)^2+\beta^2]$ and then integrate.

Sol. Let $\quad I = \int \dfrac{1}{\sqrt{x^2+2x+2}}\,dx = \int \dfrac{1}{\sqrt{(x^2+2x+1)+1}}\,dx$

$$= \int \frac{1}{\sqrt{(x+1)^2+1}}\,dx$$

Let $\quad x+1 = t \Rightarrow dx = dt$

$$\therefore I = \int \frac{1}{\sqrt{t^2+1}}dt = \log\left|t + \sqrt{t^2+1}\right| + C \quad \left[\because \int \frac{dx}{\sqrt{x^2+a^2}} = \log\left|x + \sqrt{x^2+a^2}\right| + C\right]$$

$$= \log|(x+1) + \sqrt{(x+1)^2+1}| + C \qquad [\because t = x+1]$$

$$= \log|(x+1) + \sqrt{x^2+2x+2}| + C$$

Question 11 $\dfrac{1}{9x^2+6x+5}$

Sol. Let $I = \int \frac{1}{9x^2+6x+5}dx = \frac{1}{9}\int \frac{1}{x^2+\frac{2}{3}x+\frac{5}{9}}dx$

$$= \frac{1}{9}\int \frac{1}{x^2 + 2\cdot\frac{1}{3}\cdot x + \left(\frac{1}{3}\right)^2 + \frac{5}{9} - \left(\frac{1}{3}\right)^2}dx$$

$$= \frac{1}{9}\int \frac{1}{x^2+\frac{2}{3}x+\left(\frac{1}{3}\right)^2+\frac{5}{9}-\frac{1}{9}}dx = \frac{1}{9}\int \frac{1}{\left(x+\frac{1}{3}\right)^2+\left(\frac{2}{3}\right)^2}dx$$

$$= \frac{1}{9}\left(\frac{1}{\frac{2}{3}}\right)\tan^{-1}\left(\frac{x+\frac{1}{3}}{\frac{2}{3}}\right) + C \quad \left[\because \int \frac{dx}{a^2+x^2} = \frac{1}{a}\tan^{-1}\left(\frac{x}{a}\right)+C\right]$$

$$= \frac{1}{6}\tan^{-1}\left(\frac{3x+1}{2}\right) + C$$

Quick Solution

Let $I = \int \frac{1}{9x^2+6x+5}dx = \int \frac{1}{(3x)^2 + 2\times 3x + 1 + 4}dx$

$$= \int \frac{1}{(3x+1)^2+2^2}dx$$

Put $3x+1 = t$

On differentiating both sides w.r.t x, we get $3 = \frac{dt}{dx}$

$\Rightarrow \quad dx = \frac{1}{3}dt$

$\therefore \quad I = \frac{1}{3}\int \frac{dt}{t^2+2^2}$

$$= \frac{1}{3}\cdot\frac{1}{2}\tan^{-1}\frac{t}{2} + C \qquad \left(\because \int \frac{dx}{x^2+a^2} = \frac{1}{a}\tan^{-1}\frac{x}{a} + C\right)$$

$$= \frac{1}{6}\tan^{-1}\left(\frac{3x+1}{2}\right) + C$$

Question 12 $\dfrac{1}{\sqrt{7-6x-x^2}}$

Sol. Let $I=\int \dfrac{1}{\sqrt{7-6x-x^2}}dx=\int \dfrac{1}{\sqrt{7-(x^2+6x)}}dx$

$$=\int \frac{1}{\sqrt{7-[x^2+2\times 3x+(3)^2-(3)^2]}}dx=\int \frac{1}{\sqrt{7-[x^2+6x+3^2-9]}}dx$$

$$=\int \frac{1}{\sqrt{7-[(x+3)^2-9]}}dx=\int \frac{1}{\sqrt{4^2-(x+3)^2}}dx$$

Let $x+3=t \Rightarrow dx=dt$

$\therefore$ $$I=\int \frac{1}{\sqrt{4^2-t^2}}dt=\sin^{-1}\left(\frac{t}{4}\right)+C \qquad \left[\because \int \frac{dx}{\sqrt{a^2-x^2}}=\sin^{-1}\left(\frac{x}{a}\right)+C\right]$$

$$=\sin^{-1}\left(\frac{x+3}{4}\right)+C \qquad (\because t=x+3)$$

Question 13 $\dfrac{1}{\sqrt{(x-1)(x-2)}}$.

Sol. Let $I=\int \dfrac{1}{\sqrt{(x-1)(x-2)}}dx=\int \dfrac{1}{\sqrt{x^2-3x+2}}dx$

$$=\int \frac{1}{\sqrt{x^2-3x+\left(\frac{3}{2}\right)^2-\left(\frac{3}{2}\right)^2+2}}dx$$

$$=\int \frac{1}{\sqrt{\left(x-\frac{3}{2}\right)^2+\frac{(-9)+8}{4}}}=\int \frac{1}{\sqrt{\left(x-\frac{3}{2}\right)^2-\left(\frac{1}{2}\right)^2}}dx$$

Let $x-\dfrac{3}{2}=t \Rightarrow dx=dt$

$\therefore$ $$I=\int \frac{1}{\sqrt{t^2-\left(\frac{1}{2}\right)^2}}dt$$

$$=\log\left|t+\sqrt{t^2-\frac{1}{4}}\right|+C \quad \left[\because \int \frac{dx}{\sqrt{x^2-a^2}}=\log\left|x+\sqrt{x^2-a^2}\right|+C\right]$$

$$=\log\left|x-\frac{3}{2}+\sqrt{\left(x-\frac{3}{2}\right)^2-\frac{1}{4}}\right|+C$$

$$=\log\left|\left(x-\frac{3}{2}\right)+\sqrt{x^2-3x+2}\right|+C$$

Mistake Alert Students may use method of partial fraction in these type of questions.

Question 14 $\frac{1}{\sqrt{8+3x-x^2}}$

Sol. Let $I=\int \frac{1}{\sqrt{8+3x-x^2}}dx=\int \frac{1}{\sqrt{8-\left[x^2-3x+\left(\frac{3}{2}\right)^2-\left(\frac{3}{2}\right)^2\right]}}dx$

$$=\int \frac{1}{\sqrt{8-\left[\left(x-\frac{3}{2}\right)^2-\frac{9}{4}\right]}}dx$$

$$=\int \frac{1}{\sqrt{8+\frac{9}{4}-\left(x-\frac{3}{2}\right)^2}}dx=\int \frac{1}{\sqrt{\left(\frac{\sqrt{41}}{2}\right)^2-\left(x-\frac{3}{2}\right)^2}}dx$$

Let $x-\frac{3}{2}=t \Rightarrow dx=dt$

$\therefore \quad I=\int \frac{1}{\sqrt{\left(\frac{\sqrt{41}}{2}\right)^2-t^2}}dt=\sin^{-1}\left(\frac{t}{\frac{\sqrt{41}}{2}}\right)+C \qquad \left[\because \int \frac{dx}{\sqrt{a^2-x^2}}=\sin^{-1}\left(\frac{x}{a}\right)+C\right]$

$$=\sin^{-1}\left(\frac{x-\frac{3}{2}}{\frac{\sqrt{41}}{2}}\right)+C=\sin^{-1}\left(\frac{2x-3}{\sqrt{41}}\right)+C \qquad \left(\because t=x-\frac{3}{2}\right)$$

Question 15 $\frac{1}{\sqrt{(x-a)(x-b)}}$

Sol. Let $I=\int \frac{1}{\sqrt{(x-a)(x-b)}}dx=\int \frac{1}{\sqrt{x^2-(a+b)x+ab}}dx$

$$=\int \frac{1}{\sqrt{\left[x^2-(a+b)x+\left(\frac{a+b}{2}\right)^2-\left(\frac{a+b}{2}\right)^2+ab\right]}}dx$$

$$=\int \frac{1}{\sqrt{\left[x-\left(\frac{a+b}{2}\right)\right]^2+ab-\left(\frac{a+b}{2}\right)^2}}dx$$

$$=\int \frac{1}{\sqrt{\left[x-\left(\frac{a+b}{2}\right)\right]^2+ab-\left(\frac{a^2+b^2+2ab}{4}\right)}}dx$$

$$= \int \frac{1}{\sqrt{\left[x - \left(\frac{a+b}{2}\right)\right]^2 + \frac{4ab - a^2 - b^2 - 2ab}{4}}} dx$$

$$= \int \frac{1}{\sqrt{\left[x - \left(\frac{a+b}{2}\right)\right]^2 + \frac{2ab - a^2 - b^2}{4}}} dx$$

$$= \int \frac{1}{\sqrt{\left[x - \left(\frac{a+b}{2}\right)\right]^2 - \left(\frac{a^2 + b^2 - 2ab}{4}\right)}} dx$$

$$= \int \frac{1}{\sqrt{\left(x - \frac{a+b}{2}\right)^2 - \left(\frac{a-b}{2}\right)^2}} dx$$

Let $x - \frac{a+b}{2} = t \Rightarrow dx = dt$

$$\therefore \quad I = \int \frac{1}{\sqrt{t^2 - \left(\frac{a-b}{2}\right)^2}} dt$$

$$= \log \left| t + \sqrt{t^2 - \left(\frac{a-b}{2}\right)^2} \right| + C \quad \left[\because \int \frac{dx}{\sqrt{x^2 - a^2}} = \log \left| x + \sqrt{x^2 - a^2} \right| + C\right]$$

$$= \log \left| \left(x - \frac{a+b}{2}\right) + \sqrt{\left(x - \frac{a+b}{2}\right)^2 - \left(\frac{a-b}{2}\right)^2} \right| + C \left(\because t = x - \frac{(a+b)}{2}\right)$$

$$= \log \left| \left(x - \frac{a+b}{2}\right) + \sqrt{(x-a)(x-b)} \right| + C$$

Question 16 $\dfrac{4x+1}{\sqrt{2x^2 + x - 3}}$

◎ **Thinking Process** The given integral is of the form $\int \frac{px+q}{\sqrt{ax^2 + bx + c}}$ and differential coefficient of $(2x^2 + x - 3)$ is in numerator. So, we solve it by substitution method.

Sol. Let $I = \int \frac{4x+1}{\sqrt{2x^2 + x - 3}} dx$

Let $2x^2 + x - 3 = t \Rightarrow 4x + 1 = \frac{dt}{dx} \Rightarrow dx = \frac{dt}{4x+1}$

$$\therefore \int \frac{4x+1}{\sqrt{2x^2 + x - 3}} dx = \int \frac{4x+1}{\sqrt{t}} \times \frac{dt}{4x+1} = \int \frac{1}{\sqrt{t}} dt = \frac{t^{-\frac{1}{2}+1}}{\frac{-1}{2}+1} + C = 2\sqrt{t} + C$$

$$= 2\sqrt{2x^2 + x - 3} + C \quad [\because t = 2x^2 + x - 3]$$

Question 17 $\dfrac{x+2}{\sqrt{x^2-1}}$

Sol. Let $I = \int \dfrac{x+2}{\sqrt{x^2-1}}\,dx = \int \dfrac{x}{\sqrt{x^2-1}}\,dx + \int \dfrac{2}{\sqrt{x^2-1}}\,dx = I_1 + I_2$ (say) ...(i)

Now, $I_1 = \int \dfrac{x}{\sqrt{x^2-1}}\,dx,$

Let $x^2 - 1 = t \Rightarrow 2x\,dx = dt \Rightarrow dx = \dfrac{dt}{2x}$

$$\therefore \quad I_1 = \int \frac{x}{\sqrt{t}} \times \frac{dt}{2x} = \frac{1}{2}\int \frac{dt}{\sqrt{t}}$$

$$= \frac{1}{2}\int t^{-1/2}dt = \frac{1}{2}[2t^{1/2}] = \sqrt{t} = \sqrt{x^2-1} + C_1 \qquad [\because t = x^2 - 1]$$

Now, $I_2 = 2\int \dfrac{1}{\sqrt{x^2-1}}\,dx = 2\log|x + \sqrt{x^2-1}| + C_2$

$$\left[\because \int \frac{dx}{\sqrt{x^2-a^2}} = \log|x + \sqrt{x^2-a^2}| + C\right]$$

On putting the values of I_1 and I_2 in Eq. (i), we get

$$I = \sqrt{x^2-1} + 2\log|x + \sqrt{x^2-1}| + C$$

where, $C = C_1 + C_2$

Question 18 $\dfrac{5x-2}{1+2x+3x^2}$

◎ **Thinking Process** The given integral is of the form $\int \dfrac{px+q}{ax^2+bx+c}\,dx$, so put $px + q = A\dfrac{d}{dx}(ax^2+bx+c) + B$. Then, find the values of A and B by comparing the coefficients of like powers of x and constant.

Sol. Let $I = \int \dfrac{5x-2}{1+2x+3x^2}\,dx$

Let $\quad 5x - 2 = A\dfrac{d}{dx}(1+2x+3x^2) + B$

$\Rightarrow \quad 5x - 2 = A(2+6x) + B \Rightarrow 5x - 2 = 6Ax + (2A + B)$

On equating the coefficient of x and constant term both sides, we get

$$5 = 6A \Rightarrow A = \frac{5}{6} \text{ and } 2A + B = -2 \Rightarrow B = -\frac{11}{3}$$

$$\therefore \quad 5x - 2 = \frac{5}{6}(2+6x) + \left(-\frac{11}{3}\right)$$

Now, $\quad I = \int \dfrac{5x-2}{1+2x+3x^2}\,dx = \int \dfrac{\frac{5}{6}(2+6x) - \frac{11}{3}}{1+2x+3x^2}\,dx$

$$= \frac{5}{6}\int \frac{2 + 6x}{1 + 2x + 3x^2}dx - \frac{11}{3}\int \frac{1}{1 + 2x + 3x^2}dx$$

Let $I_1 = \int \frac{2 + 6x}{1 + 2x + 3x^2}dx$ and $I_2 = \int \frac{1}{1 + 2x + 3x^2}dx$

$\therefore$ $$I = \frac{5}{6}I_1 - \frac{11}{3}I_2 \quad \text{...(i)}$$

Now, $$I_1 = \int \frac{2 + 6x}{1 + 2x + 3x^2}dx$$

Let $1 + 2x + 3x^2 = t$

$\Rightarrow$ $(2 + 6x)\,dx = dt$

$\therefore$ $$I_1 = \int \frac{dt}{t} = \log|t| + C_1$$

$\Rightarrow$ $$I_1 = \log|1 + 2x + 3x^2| + C_1 \quad \text{...(ii)}$$

Also, $$I_2 = \int \frac{1}{1 + 2x + 3x^2}dx$$

$1 + 2x + 3x^2$ can be written as $1 + 3\left(x^2 + \frac{2}{3}x\right)$

Therefore, $1 + 3\left(x^2 + \frac{2}{3}x\right) = 1 + 3\left(x^2 + \frac{2}{3}x + \frac{1}{9} - \frac{1}{9}\right)$

$$= 1 + 3\left(x + \frac{1}{3}\right)^2 - \frac{1}{3} = \frac{2}{3} + 3\left(x + \frac{1}{3}\right)^2$$

$$= 3\left[\left(x + \frac{1}{3}\right)^2 + \frac{2}{9}\right] = 3\left[\left(x + \frac{1}{3}\right)^2 + \left(\frac{\sqrt{2}}{3}\right)^2\right]$$

$\therefore$ $$I_2 = \frac{1}{3}\int \frac{dx}{\left[\left(x + \frac{1}{3}\right)^2 + \left(\frac{\sqrt{2}}{3}\right)^2\right]} = \frac{1}{3}\left[\frac{1}{\frac{\sqrt{2}}{3}}\tan^{-1}\left(\frac{x + \frac{1}{3}}{\frac{\sqrt{2}}{3}}\right)\right] + C_2$$

$$\left[\because \int \frac{dx}{a^2 + x^2} = \frac{1}{a}\tan^{-1}\left(\frac{x}{a}\right) + C\right]$$

$$= \frac{1}{3}\left[\frac{3}{\sqrt{2}}\tan^{-1}\left(\frac{3x + 1}{\sqrt{2}}\right)\right] + C_2 = \frac{1}{\sqrt{2}}\tan^{-1}\left(\frac{3x + 1}{\sqrt{2}}\right) + C_2 \quad \text{...(iii)}$$

On substituting the values of I_1 and I_2 from Eqs.(ii) and (iii) in Eq. (i), we get

$$I = \frac{5}{6}[\log|1 + 2x + 3x^2|] - \frac{11}{3}\left[\frac{1}{\sqrt{2}}\tan^{-1}\left(\frac{3x + 1}{\sqrt{2}}\right)\right] + C \quad \left[\because \frac{5}{6}C_1 - \frac{11}{3}C_2 = C\right]$$

$$= \frac{5}{6}\log|1 + 2x + 3x^2| - \frac{11}{3\sqrt{2}}\tan^{-1}\left(\frac{3x + 1}{\sqrt{2}}\right) + C$$

Question 19 $\dfrac{6x+7}{\sqrt{(x-5)(x-4)}}$

Sol. Let $I = \int \dfrac{6x+7}{\sqrt{(x-5)(x-4)}}\,dx = \int \dfrac{6x+7}{\sqrt{x^2-9x+20}}\,dx$

Let $6x + 7 = A\dfrac{d}{dx}(x^2 - 9x + 20) + B$

$\Rightarrow$ $6x + 7 = A(2x-9) + B \Rightarrow 6x + 7 = 2Ax + (-9A + B)$

On equating the coefficients of x and constant term both sides, we get

$2A = 6 \Rightarrow A = 3$

and $-9A + B = 7 \Rightarrow B = 34$

$\Rightarrow$ $6x + 7 = 3(2x-9) + 34$

$\therefore$ $\int \dfrac{6x+7}{\sqrt{x^2-9x+20}}\,dx = \int \dfrac{3(2x-9)+34}{\sqrt{x^2-9x+20}}\,dx$

$= 3\int \dfrac{2x-9}{\sqrt{x^2-9x+20}}\,dx + 34\int \dfrac{1}{\sqrt{x^2-9x+20}}\,dx$

Let $I_1 = \int \dfrac{2x-9}{\sqrt{x^2-9x+20}}\,dx$ and $I_2 = \int \dfrac{1}{\sqrt{x^2-9x+20}}\,dx$

$\therefore$ $\int \dfrac{6x+7}{\sqrt{x^2-9x+20}}\,dx = 3I_1 + 34I_2$ ...(i)

Now, $I_1 = \int \dfrac{2x-9}{\sqrt{x^2-9x+20}}\,dx$

Let $x^2 - 9x + 20 = t$

$\Rightarrow$ $(2x-9)\,dx = dt$

$\therefore$ $I_1 = \int \dfrac{dt}{\sqrt{t}} = 2\sqrt{t} + C_1 = 2\sqrt{x^2-9x+20} + C_1$ ...(ii)

And $I_2 = \int \dfrac{1}{\sqrt{x^2-9x+20}}\,dx$

$x^2 - 9x + 20$ can be written as $x^2 - 9x + 20 + \dfrac{81}{4} - \dfrac{81}{4}$

Therefore, $x^2 - 9x + 20 + \dfrac{81}{4} - \dfrac{81}{4} = \left(x - \dfrac{9}{2}\right)^2 - \dfrac{1}{4} = \left(x - \dfrac{9}{2}\right)^2 - \left(\dfrac{1}{2}\right)^2$

$\therefore$ $I_2 = \int \dfrac{1}{\sqrt{\left(x-\frac{9}{2}\right)^2 - \left(\frac{1}{2}\right)^2}}\,dx = \log\left|\left(x - \dfrac{9}{2}\right) + \sqrt{\left(x-\dfrac{9}{2}\right)^2 - \dfrac{1}{4}}\right| + C_2$

$\left[\because \int \dfrac{dx}{\sqrt{x^2-a^2}} = \log\left|x + \sqrt{x^2-a^2}\right| + C\right]$

$= \log\left|\left(x - \dfrac{9}{2}\right) + \sqrt{x^2-9x+20}\right| + C_2$ ...(iii)

On substituting the values of I_1 and I_2 from Eqs.(ii) and (iii) in Eq. (i), we get

$$\int \frac{6x+7}{\sqrt{x^2-9x+20}}\,dx = 3[2\sqrt{x^2-9x+20}]$$

$$+ 34\log\left|\left(x-\frac{9}{2}\right)+\sqrt{x^2-9x+20}\right| + C\,[\because 3C_1 + 34C_2 = C]$$

$$= 6\sqrt{x^2-9x+20} + 34\log\left|\left(x-\frac{9}{2}\right)+\sqrt{x^2-9x+20}\right| + C$$

Question 20 $\dfrac{x+2}{\sqrt{4x-x^2}}$

Sol. Let $I = \int \frac{x+2}{\sqrt{4x-x^2}}\,dx$

Let $x+2 = A\frac{d}{dx}(4x-x^2)+B \Rightarrow x+2 = A(4-2x)+B$

$$\Rightarrow \quad x+2 = -2Ax + (4A+B)$$

On equating the coefficients of x and constant term both sides, we get

$$-2A = 1 \Rightarrow A = -\frac{1}{2} \quad \text{and} \quad 4A+B = 2 \Rightarrow B = 4$$

$$\Rightarrow \quad (x+2) = -\frac{1}{2}(4-2x)+4$$

$$\therefore \int \frac{x+2}{\sqrt{4x-x^2}}\,dx = \int \frac{-\frac{1}{2}(4-2x)+4}{\sqrt{4x-x^2}}\,dx = -\frac{1}{2}\int \frac{4-2x}{\sqrt{4x-x^2}}\,dx + 4\int \frac{dx}{\sqrt{4x-x^2}}$$

Let $\quad I_1 = \int \frac{4-2x}{\sqrt{4x-x^2}}\,dx$ and $I_2 = \int \frac{dx}{\sqrt{4x-x^2}}$

Then $\quad \int \frac{x+2}{\sqrt{4x-x^2}}\,dx = -\frac{1}{2}I_1 + 4I_2 \quad$ ...(i)

Now, $\quad I_1 = \int \frac{4-2x}{\sqrt{4x-x^2}}\,dx$

Let $\quad 4x - x^2 = t \Rightarrow (4-2x)\,dx = dt$

$$\therefore \quad I_1 = \int \frac{dt}{\sqrt{t}} = 2\sqrt{t}+C_1$$

$$= 2\sqrt{4x-x^2}+C_1 \quad \text{...(ii)}$$

And $\quad I_2 = \int \frac{dx}{\sqrt{4x-x^2}}$

Now, $\quad 4x - x^2 = -(x^2-4x) = -\{(x-2)^2 - 4\} = (2)^2 - (x-2)^2$

$$\therefore \quad I_2 = \int \frac{1}{\sqrt{(2)^2-(x-2)^2}}\,dx = \sin^{-1}\left(\frac{x-2}{2}\right)+C_2 \quad \text{...(iii)}$$

$$\left[\because \int \frac{dx}{\sqrt{a^2-x^2}} = \sin^{-1}\left(\frac{x}{a}\right)+C\right]$$

On substituting the values of I_1 and I_2 from Eqs. (ii) and (iii) in Eq. (i), we get

$$\int \frac{x+2}{\sqrt{4x-x^2}}dx = -\frac{1}{2}[2\sqrt{4x-x^2}] + 4\sin^{-1}\left(\frac{x-2}{2}\right) + C \qquad \left[\because -\frac{1}{2}C_1 + 4C_2 = C\right]$$

$$= -\sqrt{4x-x^2} + 4\sin^{-1}\left(\frac{x-2}{2}\right) + C$$

Question 21 $\dfrac{x+2}{\sqrt{x^2+2x+3}}dx$

Sol. Let $I = \int \frac{x+2}{\sqrt{x^2+2+3}}dx$

Let $I = x+2 = A\frac{d}{dx}(x^2+2x+3) + B \Rightarrow x+2 = A(2x+2) + B$

$\Rightarrow \quad x+2 = 2Ax + (2A+B)$

On equating the coefficient of x and constant term both sides, we get

$2A = 1 \Rightarrow A = \frac{1}{2}$ and $2A + B = 2 \Rightarrow 2\times\frac{1}{2} + B = 2 \Rightarrow B = 2-1 = 1$

$$\Rightarrow \quad x+2 = \frac{1}{2}(2x+2) + 1$$

$$\therefore \quad \int \frac{x+2}{\sqrt{x^2+2x+3}}dx = \int \frac{\frac{1}{2}(2x+2)+1}{\sqrt{x^2+2x+3}}dx$$

$$= \frac{1}{2}\int \frac{2x+2}{\sqrt{x^2+2x+3}}dx + \int \frac{dx}{\sqrt{x^2+2x+3}}$$

Let $\quad I_1 = \int \frac{2x+2}{\sqrt{x^2+2x+3}}dx$ and $I_2 = \int \frac{dx}{\sqrt{x^2+2x+3}}$

Then, $\quad \int \frac{x+2}{\sqrt{x^2+2x+3}}dx = \frac{1}{2}I_1 + I_2 \quad$ ...(i)

Now, $\quad I_1 = \int \frac{2x+2}{\sqrt{x^2+2x+3}}dx$

Let $\quad x^2+2x+3 = t \Rightarrow (2x+2)\,dx = dt$

$$\therefore \quad I_1 = \int \frac{dt}{\sqrt{t}} = \int t^{-1/2}dt = \frac{t^{(-1/2)+1}}{-\frac{1}{2}+1} + C_1$$

$$= 2\sqrt{t} + C_1 = 2\sqrt{x^2+2x+3} + C_1$$

and $\quad I_2 = \int \frac{dx}{\sqrt{x^2+2x+3}} = \int \frac{dx}{\sqrt{x^2+2x+(1)^2+3-(1)^2}}$

$$= \int \frac{dx}{\sqrt{(x+1)^2+(\sqrt{2})^2}}$$

Let $\quad x+1 = t \Rightarrow dx = dt$

$\therefore \quad I_2 = \int \frac{dt}{\sqrt{t^2 + (\sqrt{2})^2}}$

$= \log|t + \sqrt{t^2 + 2}| + C_2 \quad \left[\because \int \frac{dx}{\sqrt{x^2 + a^2}} = \log|x + \sqrt{x^2 + a^2}| + C\right]$

$= \log|x + 1 + \sqrt{(x+1)^2 + 2}| + C_2$

$= \log|x + 1 + \sqrt{x^2 + 2x + 3}| + C_2$

On putting the values of I_1 and I_2 in Eq. (i), we get

$$\int \frac{x + 2}{\sqrt{x^2 + 2x + 3}} dx = \frac{1}{2}[2\sqrt{x^2 + 2x + 3}] + \log|x + 1 + \sqrt{x^2 + 2x + 3}| + C$$

$$\left[\because \frac{1}{2}C_1 + C_2 = C\right]$$

$$= \sqrt{x^2 + 2x + 3} + \log\left|x + 1 + \sqrt{x^2 + 2x + 3}\right| + C$$

Question 22 $\frac{x+3}{x^2 - 2x - 5}$

Sol. Let $I = \int \frac{x + 3}{x^2 - 2x - 5} dx$

Let $(x + 3) = A\frac{d}{dx}(x^2 - 2x - 5) + B$

$\Rightarrow \quad (x + 3) = A(2x - 2) + B \Rightarrow x + 3 = 2Ax - 2A + B$

On equating the coefficients of x and constant term both sides, we get

$$2A = 1 \Rightarrow A = \frac{1}{2} \quad \text{and} \quad -2A + B = 3 \Rightarrow B = 4$$

$\Rightarrow \quad (x + 3) = \frac{1}{2}(2x - 2) + 4$

$\therefore \quad \int \frac{x + 3}{x^2 - 2x - 5} dx = \int \frac{\frac{1}{2}(2x - 2) + 4}{x^2 - 2x - 5} dx$

$= \frac{1}{2}\int \frac{(2x - 2)}{x^2 - 2x - 5} dx + 4\int \frac{1}{x^2 - 2x - 5} dx$

Let $\quad I_1 = \int \frac{2x - 2}{x^2 - 2x - 5} dx$

and $\quad I_2 = \int \frac{1}{x^2 - 2x - 5} dx$

$\therefore \quad \int \frac{x + 3}{x^2 - 2x - 5} dx = \frac{1}{2} I_1 + 4I_2 \quad \text{...(i)}$

Now, $\quad I_1 = \int \frac{2x - 2}{x^2 - 2x - 5} dx$

Let $\quad x^2 - 2x - 5 = t \Rightarrow (2x - 2)\, dx = dt$

$\therefore \quad I_1 = \int \frac{dt}{t} = \log|t| + C_1 = \log|x^2 - 2x - 5| + C_1 \quad \text{...(ii)}$

and $$I_2 = \int \frac{1}{x^2 - 2x - 5}\,dx = \int \frac{1}{(x^2 - 2x + 1) - 6}\,dx$$

$$= \int \frac{1}{(x-1)^2 - (\sqrt{6})^2}\,dx$$

$$= \frac{1}{2\sqrt{6}} \log\left|\frac{x - 1 - \sqrt{6}}{x - 1 + \sqrt{6}}\right| \quad \text{...(iii)}$$

$$\left[\because \int \frac{dx}{x^2 - a^2} = \frac{1}{2a}\log\left|\frac{x-a}{x+a}\right| + C\right]$$

On substituting the values I_1 and I_2 from Eqs. (ii) and (iii) in Eq. (i), we get

$$\int \frac{x+3}{x^2 - 2x - 5}\,dx = \frac{1}{2}\log|x^2 - 2x - 5| + 4\left[\frac{1}{2\sqrt{6}}\log\left|\frac{x - 1 - \sqrt{6}}{x - 1 + \sqrt{6}}\right|\right] + C$$

$$\left[\because \frac{1}{2}C_1 + 4C_2 = C\right]$$

$$= \frac{1}{2}\log|x^2 - 2x - 5| + \frac{2}{\sqrt{6}}\log\left|\frac{x - 1 - \sqrt{6}}{x - 1 + \sqrt{6}}\right| + C$$

Question 23 $\dfrac{5x+3}{\sqrt{x^2 + 4x + 10}}$

Sol. Let $I = \int \frac{5x+3}{\sqrt{x^2 + 4x + 10}}\,dx$

Let $5x + 3 = A\frac{d}{dx}(x^2 + 4x + 10) + B$

$\Rightarrow$ $$5x + 3 = A(2x + 4) + B \Rightarrow 5x + 3 = 2Ax + 4A + B$$

On equating the coefficients of x and constant term both sides, we get

$$A = \frac{5}{2}$$

and $$4A + B = 3 \Rightarrow B = -7$$

$\therefore$ $$5x + 3 = \frac{5}{2}(2x + 4) - 7$$

$$\therefore \int \frac{5x+3}{\sqrt{x^2 + 4x + 10}}\,dx = \int \frac{\frac{5}{2}(2x+4) - 7}{\sqrt{x^2 + 4x + 10}}\,dx$$

$$= \frac{5}{2}\int \frac{2x+4}{\sqrt{x^2 + 4x + 10}}\,dx - 7\int \frac{1}{\sqrt{x^2 + 4x + 10}}\,dx$$

Let $$I_1 = \int \frac{2x+4}{\sqrt{x^2 + 4x + 10}}\,dx \text{ and } I_2 = \int \frac{1}{\sqrt{x^2 + 4x + 10}}\,dx$$

$\therefore$ $$\int \frac{5x+3}{\sqrt{x^2 + 4x + 10}}\,dx = \frac{5}{2}I_1 - 7I_2 \quad \text{...(i)}$$

Now, $$I_1 = \int \frac{2x+4}{\sqrt{x^2+4x+10}}\,dx$$

Let $x^2 + 4x + 10 = t$

$\Rightarrow$ $(2x+4)\,dx = dt$

$\Rightarrow$ $dx = \frac{dt}{2x+4}$

$$\therefore\ I_1 = \int \frac{2x+4}{\sqrt{t}} \times \frac{dt}{2x+4} = \int \frac{dt}{\sqrt{t}} = 2\sqrt{t} + C_1 = 2\sqrt{x^2+4x+10} + C_1 \quad \text{...(ii)}$$

And, $$I_2 = \int \frac{1}{\sqrt{x^2+4x+10}}\,dx = \int \frac{1}{\sqrt{(x^2+4x+4)+6}}\,dx$$

$$= \int \frac{1}{\sqrt{(x+2)^2+(\sqrt{6})^2}}\,dx = \log\left|(x+2)+\sqrt{(x+2)^2+6}\right| + C_2 \quad \text{...(iii)}$$

$$\left[\because \int \frac{dx}{\sqrt{x^2+a^2}} = \log\left|x+\sqrt{x^2+a^2}\right| + C\right]$$

$$= \log|x+2+\sqrt{x^2+4x+10}| + C_2$$

On substituting the values of I_1 and I_2 from Eqs. (ii) and (iii) in Eq. (i), we get

$$\int \frac{5x+3}{\sqrt{x^2+4x+10}}\,dx = \frac{5}{2}[2\sqrt{x^2+4x+10}] - 7\log|x+2+\sqrt{x^2+4x+10}| + C$$

$$\left[\because \frac{5}{2}C_1 - 7C_2 = C\right]$$

$$= 5\sqrt{x^2+4x+10} - 7\log|x+2+\sqrt{x^2+4x+10}| + C$$

Direction (For Q. No. 24 and 25) Choose the correct answer.

Question 24 $\int \frac{1}{x^2+2x+2}\,dx$ equals

(a) $x\tan^{-1}(x+1)+C$ (b) $\tan^{-1}(x+1)+C$

(c) $(x+1)\tan^{-1}x+C$ (d) $\tan^{-1}x+C$

Sol. (b) Let $I = \int \frac{1}{x^2+2x+2}\,dx = \int \frac{1}{(x+1)^2+1^2}\,dx$

Let $x+1 = t$

$\Rightarrow$ $dx = dt$

$$\therefore\ I = \int \frac{1}{t^2+1^2}\,dt = \frac{1}{1}\tan^{-1}\left(\frac{t}{1}\right) + C \quad \left[\because \int \frac{dx}{a^2+x^2} = \frac{1}{a}\tan^{-1}\left(\frac{x}{a}\right) + C\right]$$

$$= \tan^{-1}(x+1) + C$$

Question 25 $\int \frac{1}{\sqrt{9x-4x^2}}\, dx$ equals

(a) $\frac{1}{9}\sin^{-1}\left(\frac{9x-8}{8}\right)+C$ (b) $\frac{1}{2}\sin^{-1}\left(\frac{8x-9}{9}\right)+C$

(c) $\frac{1}{3}\sin^{-1}\left(\frac{9x-8}{8}\right)+C$ (d) $\frac{1}{2}\sin^{-1}\left(\frac{9x-8}{9}\right)+C$

Sol. (b) Let $I=\int \frac{1}{\sqrt{9x-4x^2}}\,dx=\frac{1}{\sqrt{4}}\int \frac{1}{\sqrt{\frac{9}{4}x-x^2}}\,dx$

$$=\frac{1}{2}\int \frac{1}{\sqrt{-\left[x^2-\frac{9}{4}x+\left(\frac{9}{8}\right)^2\right]+\left(\frac{9}{8}\right)^2}}\,dx=\frac{1}{2}\int \frac{1}{\sqrt{\left(\frac{9}{8}\right)^2-\left(x-\frac{9}{8}\right)^2}}\,dx$$

$$=\frac{1}{2}\sin^{-1}\left(\frac{x-\frac{9}{8}}{\frac{9}{8}}\right)+C \qquad \left[\because \int \frac{dx}{\sqrt{a^2-x^2}}=\sin^{-1}\left(\frac{x}{a}\right)+C\right]$$

$$=\frac{1}{2}\sin^{-1}\left(\frac{8x-9}{9}\right)+C$$

Exercise 7.5

Direction (Q. No. 1 to 21) Integrate the rational functions.

Question 1 $\frac{x}{(x+1)(x+2)}$

◎ *Thinking Process* The given integrand is not in standard form, so we use the partial fraction and then integrate it.

Sol. Let $I=\int \frac{x}{(x+1)(x+2)}\,dx$

Let $\frac{x}{(x+1)(x+2)}=\frac{A}{(x+1)}+\frac{B}{(x+2)}$

$\Rightarrow \qquad \frac{x}{(x+1)(x+2)}=\frac{A(x+2)+B(x+1)}{(x+1)(x+2)}$

$\Rightarrow \qquad x=Ax+2A+Bx+B \Rightarrow x=x(A+B)+2A+B$

On equating the coefficients of x and constant term both sides, we get

$$A+B=1 \qquad \text{...(i)}$$

and $\qquad 2A+B=0\Rightarrow B=-2A$

$\therefore \qquad A-2A=1\Rightarrow A=-1$

Now, on putting the value of A in Eq.(i), we get $-1 + B = 1 \Rightarrow B = 2$

$$\therefore \quad I = \int \frac{x}{(x+1)(x+2)}\,dx = \int \frac{(-1)}{x+1}\,dx + \int \frac{2}{x+2}\,dx$$

$$= -\log(x+1) + 2\log(x+2) + C = -\log(x+1) + \log(x+2)^2 + C$$

$[\because b\log a = \log a^b]$

$$= \log\left|\frac{(x+2)^2}{x+1}\right| + C \qquad \left[\because \log b - \log a = \log\frac{b}{a}\right]$$

Question 2 $\dfrac{1}{x^2-9}$

Sol. Let $I = \int \frac{1}{x^2-9}\,dx = \int \frac{1}{x^2-3^2}\,dx = \int \frac{1}{(x+3)(x-3)}\,dx$

Let
$$\frac{1}{(x+3)(x-3)} = \frac{A}{(x+3)} + \frac{B}{(x-3)}$$

$$\Rightarrow \quad 1 = A(x-3) + B(x+3) \Rightarrow 1 = x(A+B) + (-3A+3B)$$

On equating the coefficients of x and constant term both sides, we get

$$A + B = 0 \quad \text{and} \quad -3A + 3B = 1$$

On solving, we get $A = -\dfrac{1}{6}$ and $B = \dfrac{1}{6}$

$$\therefore \quad \int \frac{1}{(x+3)(x-3)}\,dx = \int \frac{(-1)}{6(x+3)}\,dx + \int \frac{1}{6(x-3)}\,dx$$

$$= -\frac{1}{6}\log|x+3| + \frac{1}{6}\log|x-3| + C$$

$$= \frac{1}{6}\log\left|\frac{x-3}{x+3}\right| + C \qquad \left[\because \log b - \log a = \log\frac{b}{a}\right]$$

Quick Solution

Let $I = \int \frac{1}{x^2-9}\,dx = \int \frac{1}{x^2-3^2}\,dx$

$$= \frac{1}{6}\log\left|\frac{x-3}{x+3}\right| + C \qquad \left[\because \int \frac{1}{x^2-a^2}\,dx = \frac{1}{2a}\log\left|\frac{x-a}{x+a}\right| + C\right]$$

Question 3 $\dfrac{3x-1}{(x-1)(x-2)(x-3)}$

Let $I = \int \dfrac{3x-1}{(x-1)(x-2)(x-3)}$

Sol. Let $\dfrac{3x-1}{(x-1)(x-2)(x-3)} = \dfrac{A}{(x-1)} + \dfrac{B}{(x-2)} + \dfrac{C}{(x-3)}$

$$\Rightarrow \frac{3x-1}{(x-1)(x-2)(x-3)} = \frac{A(x-2)(x-3)+B(x-1)(x-3)+C(x-1)(x-2)}{(x-1)(x-2)(x-3)}$$

$\Rightarrow \quad 3x - 1 = A[x^2 - 5x + 6] + B[x^2 - 4x + 3] + C[x^2 - 3x + 2]$

$\Rightarrow \quad 3x - 1 = x^2(A + B + C) + x(-5A - 4B - 3C) + (6A + 3B + 2C)$

On equating the coefficients of x^2, x and constant term both sides, we get

$$A + B + C = 0 \quad \ldots(i)$$
$$-5A - 4B - 3C = 3 \quad \ldots(ii)$$
and $$6A + 3B + 2C = -1 \quad \ldots(iii)$$

From Eq. (i), we get $A = -(B + C)$

On putting the value of A in Eqs. (ii) and (iii), we get

$$-5\{-(B + C)\} - 4B - 3C = 3 \Rightarrow 5B + 5C - 4B - 3C = 3$$

$\Rightarrow \quad B + 2C = 3 \quad \ldots(iv)$

and $\quad 6\{-(B + C)\} + 3B + 2C = -1$

$\Rightarrow \quad -6B - 6C + 3B + 2C = -1$

$\Rightarrow \quad -3B - 4C = -1 \quad \ldots(v)$

On solving Eqs. (iv) and (v), we get $\Rightarrow C = 4$

On putting the value of C in Eq. (iv), we get $B + 2 \times 4 = 3 \Rightarrow B = -5$

Now, put the values of B and C in Eq. (i), we get $A + (-5) + 4 = 0 \Rightarrow A = 1$

$\therefore \quad A = 1, B = -5, C = 4$

Now, $$\int \frac{3x-1}{(x-1)(x-2)(x-3)}dx = \int \left(\frac{A}{(x-1)} + \frac{B}{(x-2)} + \frac{C}{(x-3)}\right)dx$$

$$= \int \frac{1}{(x-1)}dx + \int \frac{(-5)}{(x-2)}dx + \int \frac{4}{(x-3)}dx$$

$$= \log|x-1| - 5\log|x-2| + 4\log|x-3| + C \quad \left(\because \int \frac{1}{x}dx = \log x + C\right)$$

Question 4 $\dfrac{x}{(x-1)(x-2)(x-3)}$

Sol. Let $I = \int \frac{x}{(x-1)(x-2)(x-3)}dx$

Let $$\frac{x}{(x-1)(x-2)(x-3)} = \frac{A}{(x-1)} + \frac{B}{(x-2)} + \frac{C}{(x-3)}$$

$$\Rightarrow \frac{x}{(x-1)(x-2)(x-3)} = \frac{A(x-2)(x-3)+B(x-1)(x-3)+C(x-1)(x-2)}{(x-1)(x-2)(x-3)}$$

$\Rightarrow \quad x = A[x^2 - 2x - 3x + 6] + B[x^2 - 4x + 3] + C[x^2 - x - 2x + 2]$

$\Rightarrow \quad x = x^2(A + B + C) + x(-5A - 4B - 3C) + (6A + 3B + 2C)$

On comparing the coefficients of x^2, x and constant term both sides, we get

$$A + B + C = 0 \Rightarrow A = -(B + C) \quad \ldots(i)$$
$$-5A - 4B - 3C = 1 \quad \ldots(ii)$$
and $$6A + 3B + 2C = 0 \quad \ldots(iii)$$

On putting the value of A in Eqs. (ii) and (iii), we get

$$-5\{-(B+C)\} - 4B - 3C = 1$$

$\Rightarrow$ $$5B + 5C - 4B - 3C = 1$$

$\Rightarrow$ $$B + 2C = 1 \qquad \text{...(iv)}$$

and $$6\{-(B+C)\} + 3B + 2C = 0 \Rightarrow -3B - 4C = 0 \qquad \text{...(v)}$$

Multiplying by 3 in Eq. (iv) and then adding with Eq. (v), we get $C = \frac{3}{2}$

On putting the value of C in Eq. (iv), we get $B + 2 \times \frac{3}{2} = 1 \Rightarrow B = -2$.

Now, put the values of B and C in Eq. (i), we get

$$A = 2 - \frac{3}{2} \Rightarrow A = \frac{4-3}{2} = \frac{1}{2}$$

$\therefore$ $$A = \frac{1}{2}, B = -2 \text{ and } C = \frac{3}{2}$$

Now, $$\int \frac{x}{(x-1)(x-2)(x-3)} dx = \int \frac{A}{(x-1)} dx + \int \frac{B}{(x-2)} dx + \int \frac{C}{(x-3)} dx$$

$$= \frac{1}{2}\int \frac{1}{(x-1)} dx - 2\int \frac{1}{(x-2)} dx + \frac{3}{2}\int \frac{1}{(x-3)} dx$$

$$= \frac{1}{2}\log |x-1| - 2\log |x-2| + \frac{3}{2}\log |x-3| + C$$

Question 5 $\dfrac{2x}{x^2+3x+2}$

◎ ***Thinking Process*** Here, the denominator can be factorise, so put it into the product of linear factors and then use partial fractions to convert it into simple form and then integrate.

Sol. Ler $I = \int \frac{2x}{x^2+3x+2} dx$

Now, $$\frac{2x}{x^2+3x+2} = \frac{2x}{x^2+2x+x+2}$$

$$= \frac{2x}{x(x+2)+1(x+2)} = \frac{2x}{(x+2)(x+1)}$$

Let $$\frac{2x}{(x+2)(x+1)} = \frac{A}{(x+2)} + \frac{B}{(x+1)}$$

$\Rightarrow$ $$\frac{2x}{(x+2)(x+1)} = \frac{A(x+1)+B(x+2)}{(x+2)(x+1)}$$

$\Rightarrow$ $$2x = Ax + A + Bx + 2B$$

$\Rightarrow$ $$2x = x(A+B) + (A+2B).$$

On comparing the coefficients of x and constant term both sides, we get

$$A + B = 2 \qquad \text{... (i)}$$

and $$A + 2B = 0 \qquad \text{...(ii)}$$

On subtracting Eq. (ii) form Eq. (i), we get $-B = 2 \Rightarrow B = -2$

On putting the value of B in Eq. (i), we get $A - 2 = 2 \Rightarrow A = 4$

$$\therefore \quad \int \frac{2x}{(x+2)(x+1)} dx = \int \frac{A}{(x+2)} dx + \int \frac{B}{(x+1)} dx$$

$$= \int \frac{4}{(x+2)} dx + \int \frac{(-2)}{(x+1)} dx = 4 \log |x+2| - 2 \log |x+1| + C$$

Question 6 $\dfrac{1-x^2}{x(1-2x)}$

Thinking Process In rational algebraic functions if the degree of numerator is greater than or equal to the degree of denominator, then always divide the numerator by denominator and use the result.

$$\frac{\text{Numerator}}{\text{Denominator}} = \text{Quotient} + \frac{\text{Remainder}}{\text{Denominator}}$$

Thus, we can convert the given integrand into simple form and then integrate easily.

Sol. Let $I = \int \frac{1-x^2}{x(1-2x)} dx$. Here, degree of numerator is equal to degree of denominator, so divide the numerator by denominator.

$$2x^2 - x)x^2 - 1(1/2$$
$$x^2 - x/2$$
$$- \quad +$$
$$x/2 - 1$$

Thus,
$$\frac{1-x^2}{x(1-2x)} = \frac{x^2-1}{2x^2-x} = \frac{1}{2} + \frac{\frac{1}{2}x - 1}{2x^2 - x}$$

$$\therefore \quad I = \int \frac{1}{2} dx + \int \frac{\frac{1}{2}x - 1}{(2x^2 - x)} dx \Rightarrow I = I_1 + I_2 \quad \ldots(i)$$

where,
$$I_1 = \int \frac{1}{2} dx \text{ and } I_2 = \int \frac{\frac{1}{2}x - 1}{(2x^2 - x)} dx$$

Now,
$$I_1 = \int \frac{1}{2} dx = \frac{1}{2}x + C_1 \text{ and } I_2 = \int \frac{\frac{1}{2}x - 1}{2x^2 - x} dx$$

Let
$$\frac{\frac{1}{2}x - 1}{(2x^2 - x)} = \frac{A}{x} + \frac{B}{(2x-1)} \Rightarrow \frac{\frac{1}{2}x - 1}{(2x^2 - x)} = \frac{A(2x-1) + Bx}{x(2x-1)}$$

$$\Rightarrow \quad \frac{1}{2}x - 1 = 2Ax - A + Bx$$

$$\Rightarrow \quad \frac{1}{2}x - 1 = x(2A + B) - A$$

On comparing the coefficient of x and constant term both sides, we get

$$2A + B = \frac{1}{2} \quad \text{...(i)}$$

and $\quad -A = -1 \Rightarrow A = 1 \quad$ ...(ii)

From Eq. (i), $\quad 2 \times 1 + B = \frac{1}{2}$

$\Rightarrow \quad B = \frac{1}{2} - 2 = \frac{-3}{2}$

$\therefore \quad I_2 = \int \left[\frac{1}{x} - \frac{3}{2(2x-1)}\right] dx = \int \frac{1}{x} dx - \frac{3}{2}\int \frac{1}{2x-1} dx$

$\Rightarrow \quad I_2 = \log x - \frac{3}{2} \frac{\log|2x-1|}{2} + C_2$

On putting the values of I_1 and I_2 in Eq (i), we get

$$I = \frac{1}{2}x + \log x - \frac{3}{4}\log|2x-1| + C \quad [C_1 + C_2 = C]$$

Question 7 $\dfrac{x}{(x^2+1)(x-1)}$

Sol. Let $I = \int \frac{x}{(x^2+1)(x-1)} dx$

First, we resolve the given integrand into partial fractions.

Let $\quad \frac{x}{(x^2+1)(x-1)} = \frac{A}{x-1} + \frac{Bx+C}{x^2+1} \quad$ ....(i)

$\Rightarrow \quad x = A(x^2+1) + (Bx+C)(x-1) \quad$ ....(ii)

Substituting $x = 1$ and 0 in Eq. (ii), we get

$$1 = A(2) \text{ and } 0 = A - C \Rightarrow A = \frac{1}{2} \text{ and } C = A = \frac{1}{2}$$

On equating the coefficient of x^2 both sides in Eq. (ii), we get

$$0 = A + B \Rightarrow B = -A = -\frac{1}{2}$$

$\therefore \quad \int \frac{x}{(x^2+1)(x-1)} dx = \int \left\{\frac{\frac{1}{2}}{x-1} + \frac{\left(-\frac{1}{2}x + \frac{1}{2}\right)}{x^2+1}\right\} dx$

$$= \frac{1}{2}\int \frac{1}{x-1} dx + \frac{1}{2}\int \frac{(-x+1)}{x^2+1} dx$$

$$= \frac{1}{2}\int \frac{1}{x-1} dx - \frac{1}{2}\int \frac{x}{x^2+1} dx + \frac{1}{2}\int \frac{1}{x^2+1} dx$$

$$= \frac{1}{2}\log|x-1| - \frac{1}{4}I_1 + \frac{1}{2}\tan^{-1}x + C_1 \quad \text{....(iii)}$$

where, $\quad I_1 = \int \frac{2x}{x^2+1} dx$

Let $x^2 + 1 = t \Rightarrow 2x\,dx = dt$

$\therefore$ $$I_1 = \int \frac{dt}{t} = \log|t| + C_2 = \log|x^2 + 1| + C_2$$

On putting the value of I_1 in Eq. (iii), we get

$$\int \frac{x}{(x^2 + 1)(x - 1)}\,dx = \frac{1}{2}\log|x - 1| - \frac{1}{4}\log|x^2 + 1| + \frac{1}{2}\tan^{-1}x + C$$

$[\because C = C_1 + C_2]$

Question 8 $\dfrac{x}{(x-1)^2(x+2)}$

Let $I = \int \dfrac{x}{(x-1)^2(x+2)}\,dx$

Sol. Let $$\frac{x}{(x-1)^2(x+2)} = \frac{A}{x-1} + \frac{B}{(x-1)^2} + \frac{C}{x+2} \quad \text{...(i)}$$

$$\Rightarrow \quad x = A(x-1)(x+2) + B(x+2) + C(x-1)^2 \quad \text{...(ii)}$$

On substituting $x = 1, -2$ in Eq. (ii), we get

$$1 = B(1+2) \text{ and } -2 = C(-2-1)^2 \Rightarrow B = \frac{1}{3} \text{ and } C = \frac{-2}{9}$$

On equating the coefficient of x^2 both sides in Eq. (ii), we get

$$0 = A + C \Rightarrow A = -C = \frac{2}{9}$$

$\therefore$ $$\int \frac{x}{(x-1)^2(x+2)}\,dx = \int \left\{ \frac{\frac{2}{9}}{x-1} + \frac{\frac{1}{3}}{(x-1)^2} + \frac{\left(-\frac{2}{9}\right)}{x+2} \right\} dx \quad \text{[from Eq. (i)]}$$

$$\Rightarrow \int \frac{x}{(x-1)^2(x+2)}\,dx = \frac{2}{9}\int \frac{1}{x-1}\,dx + \frac{1}{3}\int \frac{1}{(x-1)^2}\,dx - \frac{2}{9}\int \frac{1}{x+2}\,dx$$

$$= \frac{2}{9}\log|x-1| + \frac{1}{3}\frac{(x-1)^{-2+1}}{(-2+1)} - \frac{2}{9}\log|x+2| + C$$

$$= \frac{2}{9}\log\left|\frac{x-1}{x+2}\right| - \frac{1}{3}\left(\frac{1}{x-1}\right) + C \quad \left[\because \log b - \log a = \log\left(\frac{b}{a}\right)\right]$$

Question 9 $\dfrac{3x+5}{x^3 - x^2 - x + 1}$

Sol. Let $$I = \int \frac{3x+5}{x^3 - x^2 - x + 1}\,dx = \int \frac{3x+5}{(x^2-1)(x-1)}\,dx$$

$$= \int \frac{3x+5}{(x-1)(x+1)(x-1)}\,dx = \int \frac{3x+5}{(x-1)^2(x+1)}\,dx$$

Let $$\frac{3x+5}{(x-1)^2(x+1)} = \frac{A}{x-1} + \frac{B}{(x-1)^2} + \frac{C}{x+1}$$

$$\Rightarrow \quad \frac{3x+5}{(x-1)^2(x+1)} = \frac{A(x-1)(x+1) + B(x+1) + C(x-1)^2}{(x-1)^2(x+1)}$$

$\Rightarrow \quad 3x+5 = A(x^2-1)+Bx+B+C(x^2+1-2x)$

$\Rightarrow \quad 3x+5 = x^2(A+C)+x(B-2C)+(-A+B+C)$

On comparing the coefficients of x^2, x and constant term both sides, we get

$$A+C=0 \Rightarrow A=-C \quad \text{...(i)}$$

$$B-2C=3 \quad \text{...(ii)}$$

and $$-A+B+C=5 \quad \text{...(iii)}$$

On putting the value of A from Eq. (i) in Eq. (iii), we get

$$-(-C)+B+C=5 \Rightarrow B+2C=5 \quad \text{...(iv)}$$

On adding Eq. (ii) and Eq. (iv), we get $2B=8 \Rightarrow B=4$

On putting the value of B in Eq. (ii), we get $4-2C=3 \Rightarrow 1=2C \Rightarrow C=\frac{1}{2}$

Also, $$A=-C=-\frac{1}{2}$$

$$\therefore \quad \int \frac{3x+5}{(x-1)^2(x+1)}dx = \int \left(\frac{-\frac{1}{2}}{x-1} + \frac{4}{(x-1)^2} + \frac{\frac{1}{2}}{x+1} \right) dx$$

$$= -\frac{1}{2}\int \frac{1}{x-1}dx + 4\int \frac{1}{(x-1)^2}dx + \frac{1}{2}\int \frac{1}{x+1}dx$$

$$= -\frac{1}{2}\log|x-1| + 4\frac{(x-1)^{-2+1}}{(-2+1)} + \frac{1}{2}\log|x+1| + C$$

$$= \frac{1}{2}\log\left|\frac{x+1}{x-1}\right| - \frac{4}{x-1} + C \quad \left[\because \log b - \log a = \log\left(\frac{b}{a}\right)\right]$$

Question 10 $\dfrac{2x-3}{(x^2-1)(2x+3)}$

Sol. Let $I = \int \frac{2x-3}{(x^2-1)(2x+3)}dx = \int \frac{2x-3}{(x-1)(x+1)(2x+3)}dx$

Let $$\frac{2x-3}{(x-1)(x+1)(2x+3)} = \frac{A}{(x-1)} + \frac{B}{(x+1)} + \frac{C}{(2x+3)}$$

$$\Rightarrow \quad \frac{2x-3}{(x-1)(x+1)(2x+3)} = \frac{A(2x+3)(x+1)+B(x-1)(2x+3)+C(x-1)(x+1)}{(x-1)(x+1)(2x+3)}$$

$\Rightarrow 2x-3 = A(2x^2+3x+2x+3)+B(2x^2-2x+3x-3)+C(x^2-1)$

$\Rightarrow 2x-3 = x^2(2A+2B+C)+x(5A+B)+(3A-3B-C)$

On comparing the coefficients of x^2, x and constant term both sides, we get

$$2A+2B+C=0 \quad \text{...(i)}$$

$$5A+B=2$$

$$\Rightarrow \quad B=2-5A \quad \text{...(ii)}$$

and $$3A - 3B - C = -3 \quad \text{...(iii)}$$

On putting the value of B in Eqs. (i) and (iii), we get

$$2A + 2(2 - 5A) + C = 0 \Rightarrow 2A + 4 - 10A + C = 0$$

$$\Rightarrow \quad -8A + C = -4 \quad \text{...(iv)}$$

and $$3A - 3(2 - 5A) - C = -3 \Rightarrow 3A - 6 + 15A - C = -3$$

$$\Rightarrow \quad 18A - C = 3 \quad \text{...(v)}$$

On adding Eqs. (iv) and (v), we get

$$10A = -1 \Rightarrow A = \frac{-1}{10}$$

On putting the value of A in Eq. (ii), we get

$$B = 2 - 5\left(-\frac{1}{10}\right) \Rightarrow B = 2 + \frac{1}{2} = \frac{5}{2}$$

On putting the values of A and B in Eq. (i), we get

$$2\left(-\frac{1}{10}\right) + 2\left(\frac{5}{2}\right) + C = 0 \Rightarrow -\frac{1}{5} + 5 + C = 0 \Rightarrow C = -\frac{24}{5}$$

$$\therefore \quad A = -\frac{1}{10}, B = \frac{5}{2} \text{ and } C = -\frac{24}{5}$$

$$\therefore \quad \int \frac{2x - 3}{(x^2 - 1)(2x + 3)} dx = \int \frac{(-1)}{10(x - 1)} dx + \frac{5}{2}\int \frac{1}{x + 1} dx - \frac{24}{5}\int \frac{1}{2x + 3} dx$$

$$= -\frac{1}{10}\log|x - 1| + \frac{5}{2}\log|x + 1| - \frac{24}{5}\frac{\log|2x + 3|}{2} + C$$

$$= \frac{5}{2}\log|x + 1| - \frac{1}{10}\log|x - 1| - \frac{12}{5}\log|2x + 3| + C$$

Mistake Alert Do not consider $(x^2 - 1)$ as an irreducible quadratic factor. It can be factorised as $(x + 1)(x - 1)$.

Question 11 $\dfrac{5x}{(x+1)(x^2 - 4)}$.

Sol. Let $I = \int \frac{5x}{(x + 1)(x^2 - 4)} dx = \int \frac{5x}{(x + 1)(x + 2)(x - 2)} dx$

Let $$\frac{5x}{(x + 1)(x - 2)(x + 2)} = \frac{A}{(x + 1)} + \frac{B}{(x + 2)} + \frac{C}{(x - 2)} \quad \text{...(i)}$$

$$= \frac{A(x + 2)(x - 2) + B(x + 1)(x - 2) + C(x + 1)(x + 2)}{(x + 1)(x + 2)(x - 2)}$$

$$\Rightarrow \quad 5x = A(x^2 - 4) + B(x^2 + x - 2x - 2) + C(x^2 + x + 2x + 2)$$

$$\Rightarrow \quad 5x = x^2(A + B + C) + x(-B + 3C) + (-4A - 2B + 2C)$$

On comparing the coefficients of x^2, x and constant term both sides, we get

$$A + B + C = 0 \quad \text{...(ii)}$$

$$-B + 3C = 5 \quad \text{...(iii)}$$

and $$-4A - 2B + 2C = 0 \quad \text{...(iv)}$$

Multiply by 4 in Eq. (ii) and then adding with Eq. (iv), we get

$$2(B + 3C) = 0 \Rightarrow B + 3C = 0 \quad \text{...(v)}$$

On adding Eqs. (iii) and (v), we get $C = \frac{5}{6}$

On putting the value of C in Eq. (v), we get $B = -\frac{5}{2}$

On putting the values of B and C in Eq. (ii), we get $A = \frac{5}{3}$

$$\therefore \int \frac{5x}{(x+1)(x-2)(x+2)} dx = \int \frac{5}{3(x+1)} dx - \int \frac{5}{2(x+2)} dx + \int \frac{5}{6(x-2)} dx$$

$$= \frac{5}{3}\int \frac{1}{(x+1)} dx - \frac{5}{2}\int \frac{1}{(x+2)} dx + \frac{5}{6}\int \frac{1}{(x-2)} dx$$

$$= \frac{5}{3}\log|x+1| - \frac{5}{2}\log|x+2| + \frac{5}{6}\log|x-2| + C$$

Question 12 $\frac{x^3 + x + 1}{x^2 - 1}$

Sol. Let $I = \int \frac{x^3 + x + 1}{x^2 - 1} dx$

$$x^2 - 1 \overline{)x^3 + x + 1}(x$$

$$\frac{x^3 - x}{\quad - \quad +}$$

$$2x + 1$$

$$\therefore \quad I = \int \frac{x^3 + x + 1}{x^2 - 1} dx = \int x\,dx + \int \frac{2x + 1}{x^2 - 1} dx$$

$$= \int x\,dx + \int \frac{2x}{(x-1)(x+1)} dx$$

Let $$\frac{2x + 1}{(x+1)(x-1)} = \frac{A}{(x+1)} + \frac{B}{(x-1)}$$

$$\Rightarrow \quad \frac{2x + 1}{(x+1)(x-1)} = \frac{A(x-1) + B(x+1)}{(x+1)(x-1)}$$

$$\Rightarrow \quad 2x + 1 = x(A + B) - A + B$$

On comparing the coefficients of x and constant term both sides, we get

$$A + B = 2 \quad \text{and} \quad -A + B = 1$$

On adding above equations, we get $2B = 3 \Rightarrow B = \frac{3}{2}$ and then $A = \frac{1}{2}$

$$\therefore \int \frac{x^2 + x + 1}{x^2 - 1} dx = \int x\,dx + \int \frac{A}{(x+1)} dx + \int \frac{B}{(x-1)} dx$$

$$= \int x\,dx + \frac{1}{2}\int \frac{1}{(x+1)}dx + \frac{3}{2}\int \frac{1}{(x-1)}dx$$

$$= \frac{x^2}{2} + \frac{1}{2}\log|x+1| + \frac{3}{2}\log|x-1| + C$$

Question 13 $\dfrac{2}{(1-x)(1+x^2)}$

Sol. Let $I = \int \frac{2}{(1-x)(1+x^2)}dx$

Let $\frac{2}{(1-x)(1+x^2)} = \frac{A}{1-x} + \frac{Bx+C}{1+x^2}$

$$\therefore \quad \frac{2}{(1-x)(1+x^2)} = \frac{A(1+x^2) + (Bx+C)(1-x)}{(1-x)(1+x^2)}$$

$$\Rightarrow \quad 2 = A + Ax^2 + Bx + C - Bx^2 - Cx$$

$$\Rightarrow \quad 2 = x^2(A-B) + x(B-C) + (A+C)$$

On comparing the coefficients of x^2, x and constant term both sides, we get

$$A - B = 0 \Rightarrow A = B \qquad \ldots\text{(i)}$$

$$B - C = 0 \Rightarrow B = C \qquad \ldots\text{(ii)}$$

and $$A + C = 2 \qquad \ldots\text{(iii)}$$

From Eqs. (i) and (ii), we get $A = C$

Put this value in Eq. (iii), we get

$$2A = 2 \Rightarrow A = 1$$

Put the value of A in Eqs. (i) and (iii), we get $B = 1$ and $C = 1$

$$\therefore \quad \int \frac{2}{(1-x)(1+x^2)}dx = \int \left\{\frac{1}{1-x} + \frac{x+1}{x^2+1}\right\}dx$$

$$= \int \frac{1}{1-x}dx + \frac{1}{2}\int \frac{2x}{x^2+1}dx + \int \frac{1}{x^2+1}dx$$

$$= -\log|1-x| + \frac{1}{2}\log(1+x^2) + \tan^{-1}x + C$$

$$\left[\text{let } x^2 + 1 = t \Rightarrow 2x\,dx = dt \;\therefore \int \frac{2x}{x^2+1}dx = \int \frac{1}{t}dt = \log t\right]$$

Question 14 $\dfrac{3x-1}{(x+2)^2}$

Sol. Let $$I = \int \frac{3x-1}{(x+2)^2}dx$$

Let $$\frac{3x-1}{(x+2)^2} = \frac{A}{(x+2)} + \frac{B}{(x+2)^2}$$

$$\Rightarrow \quad 3x - 1 = A(x+2) + B$$

$$= Ax + (2A + B)$$

On equating the coefficients of x and constant term both sides, we get

$$A = 3 \quad \text{and} \quad 2A + B = -1$$

$$\Rightarrow \quad 2(3) + B = -1 \Rightarrow B = -7$$

$$\therefore \quad \frac{3x-1}{(x+2)^2} = \frac{3}{(x+2)} - \frac{7}{(x+2)^2}$$

$$\therefore \quad \int \frac{3x-1}{(x+2)^2} = 3\int \frac{1}{(x+2)} dx - 7\int \frac{1}{(x+2)^2} dx = 3 \log|x+2| - 7\left(\frac{-1}{x+2}\right) + C$$

$$= 3 \log|x+2| + \frac{7}{x+2} + C$$

Quick Solution

Let $I = \int \frac{3x-1}{(x+2)^2} dx = \int \frac{3x-1+6-6}{(x+2)^2} dx$

[adding and subtracting 6 in numerator]

$$= \int \left(\frac{3x+6}{(x+2)^2} - \frac{7}{(x+2)^2}\right) dx = 3\int \frac{1dx}{x+2} - 7\int \frac{dx}{(x+2)^2}$$

$$= 3 \log(x+2) - 7\frac{(x+2)^{-2+1}}{-2+1} + C = 3 \log(x+2) + \frac{7}{(x+2)} + C$$

Question 15 $\frac{1}{(x^4-1)}$

Sol. Let $I = \int \frac{1}{x^4-1} dx = \int \frac{1}{(x^2-1)(x^2+1)} dx$ $\quad [\because a^2 - b^2 = (a+b)(a-b)]$

$$= \int \frac{1}{(x+1)(x-1)(x^2+1)} dx$$

Let $\frac{1}{(x+1)(x-1)(x^2+1)} = \frac{A}{x+1} + \frac{B}{x-1} + \frac{(Cx+D)}{(x^2+1)}$ ...(i)

$$\Rightarrow \quad 1 = A(x-1)(x^2+1) + B(x+1)(x^2+1) + (Cx+D)(x+1)(x-1)$$

Put $x = -1$, we get $1 = A(-1-1)((-1)^2+1) \Rightarrow 1 = A(-2)(2) \Rightarrow A = \frac{-1}{4}$

Put $x = 1$, we get $1 = B(1+1)(1+1) \Rightarrow 1 = 4B$

$$\Rightarrow \quad B = \frac{1}{4}$$

Comparing coefficients of x^3 and constant both sides, we get

$$A + B + C = 0 \quad \text{and} \quad -A + B - D = 1$$

$$\therefore \quad \frac{-1}{4} + \frac{1}{4} + C = 0 \Rightarrow C = 0$$

and $\quad -\left(-\frac{1}{4}\right) + \frac{1}{4} - D = 1$

$$\Rightarrow \quad \frac{1}{2} - D = 1 \Rightarrow D = -\frac{1}{2}$$

From Eq (i)

$$\frac{1}{(x+1)(x-1)(x^2+1)} = \frac{-1}{4(x+1)} + \frac{1}{4(x-1)} + \frac{-1}{2(x^2+1)}$$

$$\therefore \quad I = \frac{-1}{4}\int \frac{1}{x+1}dx + \frac{1}{4}\int \frac{1}{x-1}dx - \frac{1}{2}\int \frac{1}{x^2+1}dx$$

$$= \frac{-1}{4}\log|x+1| + \frac{1}{4}\log|x-1| - \frac{1}{2}\tan^{-1}x + C$$

$$= \frac{1}{4}\log\left|\frac{x-1}{x+1}\right| - \frac{1}{2}\tan^{-1}x + C$$

Quick Solution

Let $\quad I = \int \frac{1}{x^4-1}dx = \int \frac{1}{(x^2-1)(x^2+1)}dx$

Put $x^2 = t$,

$$\therefore \quad \frac{1}{(x^2-1)(x^2+1)} = \frac{1}{(t-1)(t+1)}$$

Now, $\quad \frac{1}{(t-1)(t+1)} = \frac{A}{(t-1)} + \frac{B}{(t+1)}$ [by partial fraction]...(i)

$$\Rightarrow \quad \frac{1}{(t-1)(t+1)} = \frac{A(t+1) + B(t-1)}{(t-1)(t+1)}$$

$$\Rightarrow \quad 1 = At + A + Bt - B$$

$$\Rightarrow \quad 1 = t(A+B) + (A-B)$$

On comparing the coefficients of t and constant term both sides, we get

$A + B = 0$ ...(ii)

$A - B = 1$ ...(iii)

On adding Eqs. (ii) and (iii), we get

$$A = \frac{1}{2},$$

and from Eq. (iii), we get $B = -\frac{1}{2}$

On putting the values of A and B in Eq. (i), we get

$$\frac{1}{(t-1)(t+1)} = \frac{\frac{1}{2}}{t-1} + \frac{-\frac{1}{2}}{t+1}$$

$\Rightarrow \quad \frac{1}{(x^2-1)(x^2+1)} = \frac{1}{2}\times\frac{1}{x^2-1} - \frac{1}{2}\times\frac{1}{x^2+1}$ [put $t = x^2$]

$$\therefore \quad \int \frac{dx}{(x^2-1)(x^2+1)} = -\frac{1}{2}\int \frac{1}{x^2+1}dx + \frac{1}{2}\int \frac{1}{x^2-1}dx$$

$$= -\frac{1}{2}\tan^{-1}x + \frac{1}{2}\cdot\frac{1}{2}\log\left|\frac{x-1}{x+1}\right| + C$$

$$= -\frac{1}{2}\tan^{-1}x + \frac{1}{4}\log\left|\frac{x-1}{x+1}\right| + C$$

Question 16 $\dfrac{1}{x(x^n+1)}$

◎ *Thinking Process* Here, partial fractions of given integrand cannot find easily, so we convert it into easy form for partial fractions by multiply x^{n-1} in both numerator and denominator and then put $x^n = t$. Now, apply partial fractions method and then integrate.

Sol. Let $I = \int \dfrac{1}{x(x^n+1)}dx = \int \dfrac{x^{n-1}}{x^n(x^n+1)}dx$

Put $x^n = t \Rightarrow nx^{n-1}dx = dt \Rightarrow x^{n-1}dx = \dfrac{1}{n}dt$

$\therefore$ $I = \int \dfrac{x^{n-1}}{x^n(x^n+1)}dx = \dfrac{1}{n}\int \dfrac{1}{t(t+1)}dt$ ...(i)

Now, let $\dfrac{1}{t(t+1)} = \dfrac{A}{t} + \dfrac{B}{(t+1)} \Rightarrow 1 = A(1+t) + Bt$ ...(ii)

On substituting $t = 0, -1$ in Eq. (ii), we get $A = 1$ and $B = -1$

$\therefore$ $\dfrac{1}{t(t+1)} = \dfrac{1}{t} - \dfrac{1}{(t+1)}$

$\therefore$ $I = \dfrac{1}{n}\int\left(\dfrac{1}{t} - \dfrac{1}{(t+1)}\right)dt$ [from Eq. (i)]

$= \dfrac{1}{n}[\log|t| - \log|t+1|] + C$

$= \dfrac{1}{n}[\log|x^n| - \log|x^n+1|] + C$ [put $t = x^n$]

$= \dfrac{1}{n}\log\left|\dfrac{x^n}{x^n+1}\right| + C$

Question 17 $\dfrac{\cos x}{(1-\sin x)(2-\sin x)}$.

◎ *Thinking Process* Here, the given integrand contains trigonometric ratios, so we convert it into algebraic form by putting $\sin x = t$ and then use partial fractions to convert it into simple form and then integrate.

Sol. Let $I = \int \dfrac{\cos x}{(1-\sin x)(2-\sin x)}dx$

Put $\sin x = t \Rightarrow \cos x = \dfrac{dt}{dx} \Rightarrow dx = \dfrac{dt}{\cos x}$

$\therefore$ $I = \int \dfrac{\cos x}{(1-t)(2-t)}\dfrac{dt}{\cos x} = \int \dfrac{1}{(1-t)(2-t)}dt$

Let $\dfrac{1}{(1-t)(2-t)} = \dfrac{A}{1-t} + \dfrac{B}{2-t} = \dfrac{A(2-t)+B(1-t)}{(1-t)(2-t)}$ ...(i)

$\Rightarrow$ $1 = 2A - tA + B - Bt$

$$\Rightarrow \quad 1 = 1(2A + B) + t(-A - B)$$

On comparing the coefficients of t and constant term both sides, we get

$$2A + B = 1 \quad \text{and} \quad -A - B = 0$$

On adding above equations, we get

$$A = 1 \quad \text{and } B = -1$$

$$\therefore \quad I = \int \left(\frac{1}{1-t} - \frac{1}{2-t} \right) dt \qquad \text{[from Eq. (i)]}$$

$$= \int \frac{1}{(1-t)} dt - \int \frac{1}{(2-t)} dt = \frac{\log|1-t|}{(-1)} - \frac{\log|2-t|}{(-1)} + C$$

$$= \log\left|\frac{2-t}{1-t}\right| + C = \log\left|\frac{2-\sin x}{1-\sin x}\right| + C \qquad [\text{put } t = \sin x]$$

Question 18 $\dfrac{(x^2+1)(x^2+2)}{(x^2+3)(x^2+4)}$

Sol. Let $I = \int \dfrac{(x^2+1)(x^2+2)}{(x^2+3)(x^2+4)} dx$

Here, the degree of numerator and denominator are 4. So, we convert it into simple form by putting $x^2 = t$.

$$\therefore \quad \frac{(x^2+1)(x^2+2)}{(x^2+3)(x^2+4)} = \frac{(t+1)(t+2)}{(t+3)(t+4)} = \frac{t^2+3t+2}{t^2+7t+12}$$

Since, degree of numerator and denominator is same, so it can be written as

$$1 - \frac{4t+10}{t^2+7t+12}$$

Now, $$\int \frac{(x^2+1)(x^2+2)}{(x^2+3)(x^2+4)} dx = \int 1 dx - \int \frac{(4t+10)}{t^2+7t+12} dx$$

$$= \int 1 dx - \int \frac{4t+10}{(t+3)(t+4)} dx \qquad \text{....(i)}$$

Let $\dfrac{4t+10}{(t+4)(t+3)} = \dfrac{A}{(t+4)} + \dfrac{B}{(t+3)} \Rightarrow \dfrac{4t+10}{(t+3)(t+4)} = \dfrac{A(t+3)+B(t+4)}{(t+4)(t+3)}$

$\Rightarrow \; 4t + 10 = At + 3A + Bt + 4B \;\Rightarrow\; 4t + 10 = t(A+B) + (3A+4B)$

On comparing the coefficients of t and constant term both sides, we get

$$A + B = 4 \Rightarrow 3A + 3B = 12 \qquad \text{...(ii)}$$

and $$3A + 4B = 10 \qquad \text{...(iii)}$$

On subtracting Eq. (iii) from Eq. (ii), we get

$$-B = 2 \Rightarrow B = -2$$

On substituting the value of B in Eq. (ii), we get $A = 6$

$$\therefore \quad \frac{4t+10}{(t+4)(t+3)} = \frac{6}{t+4} - \frac{2}{t+3}$$

On putting this value in Eq. (i) we get

$$\int \frac{(x^2+1)(x^2+2)}{(x^2+3)(x^2+4)}dx = \int 1dx - \int\left[\frac{6}{t+4} - \frac{2}{t+3}\right]dx$$

$$= \int 1dx - \int\left(\frac{6}{(x^2+4)} - \frac{2}{(x^2+3)}\right)dx \qquad \text{[put } t = x^2]$$

$$\Rightarrow \int \frac{(x^2+1)(x^2+2)}{(x^2+3)(x^2+4)}dx = \int 1dx - \int\left(\frac{6}{x^2+2^2} - \frac{2}{x^2+(\sqrt{3})^2}\right)dx$$

$$\Rightarrow \int \frac{(x^2+1)(x^2+2)}{(x^2+3)(x^2+4)}dx = x - 6\left(\frac{1}{2}\tan^{-1}\frac{x}{2}\right) + 2\left(\frac{1}{\sqrt{3}}\tan^{-1}\frac{x}{\sqrt{3}}\right) + C$$

$$\left(\because \int \frac{1}{a^2+x^2}dx = \frac{1}{a}\tan^{-1}\frac{x}{a} + C\right)$$

$$= x - 3\tan^{-1}\frac{x}{2} + \frac{2}{\sqrt{3}}\tan^{-1}\frac{x}{\sqrt{3}} + C$$

Question 19 $\dfrac{2x}{(x^2+1)(x^2+3)}$

Sol. Let $I = \int \frac{2x}{(x^2+1)(x^2+3)}dx$

Put $x^2 = t \Rightarrow 2x = \frac{dt}{dx} \Rightarrow dx = \frac{dt}{2x}$

$\therefore \quad I = \int \frac{2x}{(t+1)(t+3)}\frac{dt}{2x} = \int \frac{1}{(t+1)(t+3)}dt$

Let $\frac{1}{(t+1)(t+3)} = \frac{A}{t+1} + \frac{B}{t+3} \Rightarrow \frac{1}{(t+1)(t+3)} = \frac{At+3A+Bt+B}{(t+1)(t+3)}$

$\Rightarrow \quad 1 = (A+B)t + (3A+B)$

On comparing the coefficients of t and constant terms both sides, we get

$$A + B = 0 \qquad \ldots\text{(i)}$$

and $$3A + B = 1 \qquad \ldots\text{(ii)}$$

On subtracting Eq. (i) from Eq. (ii), we get

$$2A = 1 \Rightarrow A = \frac{1}{2}$$

On putting the value of A in Eq. (i), we get $B = -\frac{1}{2}$

$$\therefore \quad I = \frac{1}{2}\int\frac{1}{t+1}dt - \frac{1}{2}\int\frac{1}{t+3}dt = \frac{1}{2}\log|t+1| - \frac{1}{2}\log|t+3| + C$$

$$= \frac{1}{2}\log\left|\frac{t+1}{t+3}\right| + C = \frac{1}{2}\log\left|\frac{x^2+1}{x^2+3}\right| + C \qquad \text{[put } t = x^2]$$

Question 20 $\dfrac{1}{x(x^4-1)}$

◎ *Thinking Process* Here, partial fractions of given integrand cannot find easily, so we multiply both numerator and denominator by x^3 and then put $x^4=t$ and then use partial fractions to convert it into simple form . After integration put $t=x^4$.

Sol. Let $I=\int\frac{1}{x(x^4-1)}dx=\int\frac{x^3}{x^4(x^4-1)}dx=\frac{1}{4}\int\frac{4x^3}{x^4(x^4-1)}dx$

Put $x^4=t \Rightarrow 4x^3=\frac{dt}{dx} \Rightarrow dx=\frac{dt}{4x^3}$

$$\therefore \quad I=\frac{1}{4}\int\frac{4x^3}{t(t-1)}\frac{dt}{4x^3}=\frac{1}{4}\int\frac{dt}{t(t-1)}$$

Let $\frac{1}{t(t-1)}=\frac{A}{t}+\frac{B}{(t-1)} \Rightarrow 1=A(t-1)+Bt$ ...(i)

On substituting $t=0$ and 1 in Eq. (i), we get

$$A=-1 \text{ and } B=1$$

$$\therefore \quad \frac{1}{t(t-1)}=\frac{-1}{t}+\frac{1}{t-1}$$

$$\therefore \quad I=\frac{1}{4}\int\left(-\frac{1}{t}+\frac{1}{t-1}\right)dt=\frac{1}{4}\{-\log|t|+\log|t-1|\}+C$$

$$=\frac{1}{4}\log\left|\frac{t-1}{t}\right|+C=\frac{1}{4}\log\left|\frac{x^4-1}{x^4}\right|+C \quad [\text{put } t=x^4]$$

Quick Solution

Let $I=\int\frac{1}{x(x^4-1)}dx=\frac{1}{4}\int\frac{4x^3}{x^4(x^4-1)}dx$

Put $x^4=t \Rightarrow dx=\frac{dt}{4x^3}$

$$\therefore \quad I=\frac{1}{4}\int\frac{dt}{t(t-1)}=\frac{1}{4}\int\frac{dt}{t^2-t}$$

$$=\frac{1}{4}\int\frac{dt}{t^2-t+\left(\frac{1}{2}\right)^2-\left(\frac{1}{2}\right)^2}=\frac{1}{4}\int\frac{dt}{\left(t-\frac{1}{2}\right)-\left(\frac{1}{2}\right)^2}$$

$$=\frac{1}{4}\frac{1}{\left(2\cdot\frac{1}{2}\right)}\log\left|\frac{t-\frac{1}{2}-\frac{1}{2}}{t-\frac{1}{2}+\frac{1}{2}}\right|+C \quad \left[\because \int\frac{1}{x^2-a^2}dx=\frac{1}{2a}\log\left|\frac{x-a}{x-a}\right|+C\right]$$

$$=\frac{1}{4}\log\left|\frac{t-1}{t}\right|+C=\frac{1}{4}\log\left(\frac{x^4-1}{x^4}\right)+C$$

Question 21 $\dfrac{1}{e^x - 1}$

Sol. Let $I = \int \dfrac{1}{e^x - 1}\, dx$

Put $\quad e^x = t \Rightarrow e^x = \dfrac{dt}{dx} \Rightarrow dx = \dfrac{dt}{e^x}$

$\therefore \quad I = \int \dfrac{1}{t-1} \times \dfrac{dt}{e^x} = \int \dfrac{1}{t(t-1)}\, dt$

Let $\quad \dfrac{1}{t(t-1)} = \dfrac{A}{t} + \dfrac{B}{t-1}$

$\Rightarrow \quad 1 = A(t-1) + Bt \Rightarrow 1 = (A+B)t - A$

On comparing the coefficient of t and constant terms both sides, we get

$A + B = 0$ and $-A = 1 \Rightarrow A = -1$

$\Rightarrow \quad -1 + B = 0 \Rightarrow B = 1$

$\therefore \quad I = \int \left(\dfrac{-1}{t} + \dfrac{1}{t-1} \right) dt = -\log|t| + \log|t-1| + C$

$$= \log\left|\frac{t-1}{t}\right| + C = \log\left|\frac{e^x - 1}{e^x}\right| + C$$

Quick Solution

Let $\quad I = \int \dfrac{1}{e^x - 1}\, dx$

On multiplying numerator and denominator by e^{-x}, we get

$$I = \int \frac{e^{-x}}{1 - e^{-x}}\, dx$$

Put $\quad 1 - e^{-x} = t \Rightarrow -e^{-x}(-1) = \dfrac{dt}{dx} \Rightarrow e^{-x} dx = dt$

$\therefore \quad I = \int \dfrac{dt}{t} = \log|t| + C = \log|1 - e^{-x}| + C$

$$= \log\left|\frac{e^x - 1}{e^x}\right| + C$$

Direction (Q. No. 22 and 23) Choose the correct answer in each of the question.

Question 22 $\int \dfrac{x}{(x-1)(x-2)}\, dx$ equals

(a) $\log\left|\dfrac{(x-1)^2}{x-2}\right| + C$

(b) $\log\left|\dfrac{(x-2)^2}{x-1}\right| + C$

(c) $\log\left|\left(\dfrac{x-1}{x-2}\right)^2\right|$

(d) $\log|(x-1)(x-2)| + C$

Sol. (b) Let $\frac{x}{(x-1)(x-2)} = \frac{A}{(x-1)} + \frac{B}{(x-2)}$

$\Rightarrow \qquad x = A(x-2) + B(x-1) \qquad \ldots(i)$

On substituting $x = 1$ and $x = 2$ in Eq. (i), we get $A = -1$ and $B = 2$

$\therefore \qquad \frac{x}{(x-1)(x-2)} = -\frac{1}{(x-1)} + \frac{2}{(x-2)}$

$\therefore \int \frac{x}{(x-1)(x-2)} dx = \int \frac{(-1)}{x-1} dx + \int \frac{2}{x-2} dx$

$= -\log|x-1| + 2\log|x-2| + C = -\log|x-1| + \log|(x-2)^2| + C$

$= \log\left|\frac{(x-2)^2}{x-1}\right| + C \qquad \left[\because \log b - \log a = \log\frac{b}{a}\right]$

Question 23 $\int \frac{dx}{x(x^2+1)}$ equals

(a) $\log|x| - \frac{1}{2}\log(x^2+1) + C$

(b) $\log|x| + \frac{1}{2}\log(x^2+1) + C$

(c) $-\log|x| + \frac{1}{2}\log(x^2+1) + C$

(d) $\frac{1}{2}\log|x| + \log(x^2+1) + C$

Sol. (a) Let $\frac{1}{x(x^2+1)} = \frac{A}{x} + \frac{Bx+C}{x^2+1}$

$\Rightarrow \qquad 1 = A(x^2+1) + (Bx+C)x \Rightarrow 1(A+B)x^2 + (x+A)$

On equating the coefficients of x^2, x and constant term both sides, we get

$A + B = 0, \quad C = 0$ and $A = 1$

On solving these equations, we get

$A = 1, B = -1$ and $C = 0$

$\therefore \qquad \frac{1}{x(x^2+1)} = \frac{1}{x} + \frac{-x}{x^2+1}$

$\therefore \qquad \int \frac{1}{x(x^2+1)} dx = \int \left\{\frac{1}{x} - \frac{x}{x^2+1} dx\right\}$

Let $\qquad x^2 + 1 = t \Rightarrow 2x dx = dt \Rightarrow x dx = \frac{dt}{2}$

$\therefore \qquad I = \int \frac{1}{x} dx - \int \frac{1}{t} \cdot \frac{dt}{2} = \log|x| - \frac{1}{2}\log + |t| + C$

$= \log|x| - \frac{1}{2}\log(x^2+1) + C$

Quick Solution

Let $$I = \int \frac{dx}{x(x^2+1)}$$

Multiply and divide by x, we get

$$I = \int \frac{x}{x^2(x^2+1)}\,dx$$

Put $x^2 = t$

$\Rightarrow$ $2x\,dx = dt$

$$x\,dx = \frac{1}{2}\,dt$$

$\therefore$ $$I = \frac{1}{2}\int \frac{dt}{t(t+1)} = \frac{1}{2}\int \frac{dt}{t^2+t}$$

$$= \frac{1}{2}\int \frac{dt}{t^2 + t + \left(\frac{1}{2}\right)^2 - \left(\frac{1}{2}\right)^2}$$

$$= \frac{1}{2}\int \frac{dt}{\left(t+\frac{1}{2}\right)^2 - \left(\frac{1}{2}\right)^2}$$

$$= \frac{1}{2}\cdot\frac{1}{\left(2\cdot\frac{1}{2}\right)}\log\left(\frac{t+\frac{1}{2}-\frac{1}{2}}{t+\frac{1}{2}+\frac{1}{2}}\right) + C$$

$$\left[\because \int \frac{1\,dx}{x^2-a^2} = \frac{1}{2a}\log\left(\frac{x-a}{x+a}\right) + C\right]$$

$$= \frac{1}{2}\log\left(\frac{t}{t+1}\right) + C$$

$$= \frac{1}{2}\log|t| - \frac{1}{2}\log(t+1) + C$$

$$= \frac{1}{2}\log|x^2| - \frac{1}{2}\log(x^2+1) + C$$

$$= \log|x| - \frac{1}{2}\log(x^2+1) + C \qquad [\because \log x^n = n\log x]$$

Exercise 7.6

Direction (Q. No. 1 to 22) Integrate the functions.

Question 1 $x \sin x$

◎ *Thinking Process* In this exercise, the integrands are given as product of two functions, so we integrate them by using integration by parts *i.e.*, use the formula

$$\int \underset{I}{u} \cdot \underset{II}{v}\, dx = u \int v\, dx - \int \left[\frac{d}{dx}(u) \int v dx \right] dx$$

Here, we choose u (first function) as the function which comes first in the word ILATE.

Sol. Let $I = \int \sin x \cdot x\, dx$

On taking x as first function and $\sin x$ as second function and integrating by parts, we get

$$I = x \int \sin x\, dx - \int \left[\frac{d}{dx}(x) \int \sin x\, dx \right] dx$$

$$= -x \cos x + \int 1 \cdot \cos x\, dx$$

$$\Rightarrow \quad I = -x \cos x + \sin x + C$$

Question 2 $x \sin 3x$

Sol. Let $I = \int x \sin 3x\, dx$

On taking x as first function and $\sin 3x$ as second function and integrating by parts, we get

$$I = x \int \sin 3x\, dx - \int \left[\frac{d}{dx}(x) \int \sin 3x\, dx \right] dx$$

$$= \frac{-x \cos 3x}{3} + \int \frac{\cos 3x}{3} dx \qquad \left(\because \int \sin ax\, dx = \frac{-\cos ax}{a} + C \right)$$

$$\Rightarrow \quad I = \frac{-x \cos 3x}{3} + \frac{1}{9} \sin 3x + C$$

Question 3 $x^2 e^x$

Sol. Let $I = \int x^2 e^x dx$

On taking x^2 as first function and e^x as second function and integrating by parts, we get $I = x^2 \int e^x dx - \int \left[\frac{d}{dx}(x^2) \int e^x dx \right] dx = x^2 e^x - \int [2xe^x] dx$

Again, integrating by parts, we get

$$I = x^2 e^x - \left\{ 2x \int e^x dx - 2 \int \left[\frac{d}{dx}(x) \int e^x dx \right] dx \right\} = x^2 e^x - 2xe^x + 2 \int e^x dx$$

$$= x^2 e^x - 2xe^x + 2e^x + C \Rightarrow I = e^x (x^2 - 2x + 2) + C$$

Question 4 $x \log x$

Sol. Let $I = \int x \log x \, dx$.

On taking $\log x$ as first function and x as second function and integrating by parts, we get [$\because$ log function comes before algebraic function in ILATE]

$$I = \log x \int x\,dx - \int \left[\frac{d}{dx}(\log x) \int x\,dx\right] dx$$

$$= \frac{x^2 \log x}{2} - \frac{1}{2}\int \frac{1}{x} x^2 dx = \frac{x^2 \log x}{2} - \frac{1}{2}\int x\,dx \Rightarrow I = \frac{x^2 \log x}{2} - \frac{1}{4}x^2 + C$$

Question 5 $x \log 2x$

Sol. Let $I = \int x \log 2x \, dx$

On taking $\log 2x$ as first function and x as second function and integrating by parts, we get [$\because$ log function comes before algebraic function in ILATE]

$$I = \int x \log 2x \, dx = \log 2x \int x\,dx - \int \left[\frac{d}{dx}(\log 2x) \int x\,dx\right] dx$$

$$= \frac{x^2}{2} \log 2x - \int \left[\frac{1}{2x} \times 2 \times \frac{x^2}{2} \, dx\right] = \frac{x^2 \log 2x}{2} - \frac{1}{2}\int x\,dx$$

$$\Rightarrow \quad I = \frac{x^2}{2} \log 2x - \frac{1}{4}x^2 + C$$

Question 6 $x^2 \log x$

Sol. Let $I = \int x^2 \log x \, dx$

On taking $\log x$ as first function and x^2 as second function and integrating by parts, we get

[$\because$ log function comes before algebraic function in ILATE]

$$I = \int x^2 \log x \, dx = \log x \int x^2 dx - \int \left[\frac{d}{dx}(\log x) \int x^2 dx\right] dx$$

$$= \frac{x^3}{3} \log x - \int \left[\frac{1}{x} \cdot \frac{x^3}{3}\right] dx = \frac{x^3}{3} \log x - \frac{1}{3}\int x^2 dx = \frac{x^3}{3} \log x - \frac{x^3}{9} + C$$

Question 7 $x \sin^{-1} x$

Sol. Let $I = \int x \sin^{-1} x \, dx$

On taking $\sin^{-1} x$ as first function and x as second function and integrating by parts, we get

[$\because$ Inverse functions comes before algebraic functions in ILATE]

$$I = \sin^{-1} x \int x\,dx - \int \left[\frac{d}{dx}(\sin^{-1} x) \int x\,dx\right] dx$$

$$= \sin^{-1} x \cdot \frac{x^2}{2} - \int \left[\frac{1}{\sqrt{1-x^2}} \cdot \frac{x^2}{2}\right] dx = \frac{x^2}{2} \cdot \sin^{-1} x + \int \left[\frac{1 - 1 - x^2}{\sqrt{1-x^2}} \cdot \frac{1}{2}\right] dx$$

(Add and subtract 1 in numerator of second term)

$$= \frac{x^2}{2} \cdot \sin^{-1} x - \frac{1}{2}\int \frac{1}{\sqrt{1-x^2}} dx + \frac{1}{2}\int \frac{1-x^2}{\sqrt{1-x^2}} dx$$

$$= \frac{x^2}{2} \cdot \sin^{-1} x - \frac{1}{2}\sin^{-1} x + \frac{1}{2}\int \sqrt{1-x^2}\, dx$$

$$\Rightarrow \quad I = \frac{x^2}{2} \cdot \sin^{-1} x - \frac{1}{2}\sin^{-1} x + \frac{1}{2}\left[\frac{1}{2}x\sqrt{1-x^2} + \frac{1}{2}\sin^{-1} x\right] + C$$

$$\Rightarrow \quad I = \sin^{-1} x\left[\frac{x^2}{2} - \frac{1}{4}\right] + \frac{1}{4}x\sqrt{1-x^2} + C$$

$$\Rightarrow \quad I = \frac{\sin^{-1} x}{4}(2x^2 - 1) + \frac{1}{4}x\sqrt{1-x^2} + C$$

Quick Solution

Let $\quad I = \int x \sin^{-1} x\, dx$

Put $\quad \sin^{-1} x = t$

$\Rightarrow \quad x = \sin t$

$dx = \cos t\, dt$ [on differentiating]

$\therefore \quad I = \int \sin t \cdot t \cdot \cos t\, dt$

$= \frac{1}{2}\int 2\sin t \cos t \cdot t \cdot dt$ [Multiply and divide by 2]

$= \frac{1}{2}\int t \sin 2t\, dt$ [$\because \sin 2\theta = 2\sin\theta\cos\theta$]

On taking t as first function and $\sin 2t$ as second function and integrating by parts, we get

$$= \frac{1}{2}\left[t \cdot \int \sin 2t\, dt - \int\left(\frac{d}{dt}(t)\int \sin 2t\, dt\right) dt\right]$$

$$= \frac{1}{2}\left[t \cdot \frac{-\cos 2t}{2} - \int 1 \cdot \frac{(-\cos 2t)}{2} dt\right] + C$$

$$= -\frac{1}{4}t\cos 2t + \frac{1}{4}\int \cos 2t\, dt$$

$$= \frac{-1}{4}t\cos 2t + \frac{1}{8}\sin 2t + C$$

$$= -\frac{1}{4}t \cdot (1 - 2\sin^2 t) + \frac{1}{8} \cdot 2\sin t\cos t + C \quad \left(\begin{array}{l}\because \cos 2\theta = 1 - 2\sin^2\theta \\ \text{and } \sin 2\theta = 2\sin\theta\cos\theta\end{array}\right)$$

$$= -\frac{1}{4}\sin^{-1} x\,(1 - 2x^2) + \frac{1}{4}x\sqrt{1-\sin^2 t} + C \quad [\because \cos^2\theta = 1 - \sin^2\theta]$$

$$= \frac{\sin^{-1} x(2x^2 - 1)}{4} + \frac{x\sqrt{1-x^2}}{4} + C$$

Question 8 $x \tan^{-1} x$

Sol. Let $I = \int x \tan^{-1} x \, dx$

On taking $\tan^{-1} x$ as first function and x as second function and integrating by parts, we get

[$\because$ inverse trigonometric functions comes before algebraic functions in ILATE]

$$\therefore \quad I = \tan^{-1} x \int x\,dx - \int \left[\frac{d}{dx}(\tan^{-1} x) \int x\,dx \right] dx$$

$$= \tan^{-1} x \cdot \frac{x^2}{2} - \int \left[\frac{1}{1+x^2} \cdot \frac{x^2}{2} \right] dx = \frac{x^2}{2} \cdot \tan^{-1} x - \frac{1}{2} \int \left[\frac{x^2 + 1 - 1}{1+x^2} \right] dx$$

[Add and subtract 1 in numerator of second term]

$$= \frac{x^2}{2} \cdot \tan^{-1} x - \frac{1}{2} \left[\int \frac{1+x^2}{1+x^2} dx - \int \frac{1}{1+x^2} dx \right]$$

$$= \frac{x^2}{2} \tan^{-1} x - \frac{1}{2} \left[\int 1\,dx - \int \frac{1}{1+x^2} dx \right]$$

$$= \frac{x^2}{2} \cdot \tan^{-1} x - \frac{1}{2} x + \frac{1}{2} \tan^{-1} x + C = \left(\frac{x^2 + 1}{2} \right) \tan^{-1} x - \frac{1}{2} x + C$$

Question 9 $x \cos^{-1} x$

Sol. Let $I = \int x \cos^{-1} x \, dx$

Put $\quad \cos^{-1} x = t \;\Rightarrow\; x = \cos t \;\Rightarrow\; dx = -\sin t\,dt$

$$\therefore \quad I = \int x \cos^{-1} x\,dx = -\int t \cos t \cdot \sin t\,dt$$

$$= -\frac{1}{2} \int t \cdot 2 \sin t \cos t\,dt = -\frac{1}{2} \int t \cdot \sin 2t\,dt$$

[$\because 2 \sin x \cos x = \sin 2x$]

On taking t as first function and $\sin 2t$ as second function and integrating by parts, we get

$$I = -\frac{1}{2} \left[t \int \sin 2t\,dt - \int \left\{ \frac{d}{dt}(t) \cdot \int \sin 2t\,dt \right\} dt \right]$$

$$= -\frac{1}{2} \left[t \frac{(-\cos 2t)}{2} + \int 1 \cdot \frac{\cos 2t}{2} dt \right]$$

$$= \frac{1}{4} t \cos 2t - \frac{1}{4} \int \cos 2t\,dt$$

$$= \frac{1}{4} t \cos 2t - \frac{1}{4} \frac{\sin 2t}{2} + C$$

$$= \frac{1}{4} t \cos 2t - \frac{1}{8} \sin 2t + C$$

$$= \frac{1}{4} t (2 \cos^2 t - 1) - \frac{1}{8} \cdot 2 \sin t \cos t + C$$

[$\because \cos 2x = 2\cos^2 x - 1$ and $\sin 2x = 2 \sin x \cos x$]

$$= \frac{1}{4}t(2\cos^2 t - 1) - \frac{1}{4}(1-\cos^2 t)^{1/2}\cos t + C$$

$$[\because \sin^2 x + \cos^2 x = 1 \Rightarrow \sin x = \sqrt{1-\cos^2 x}]$$

$\therefore$ $$\int x\cos^{-1}x\,dx = \frac{1}{4}\cos^{-1}x(2x^2-1) - \frac{1}{4}(1-x^2)^{1/2}x + C$$

$$[\text{put } \cos^{-1}x = t \text{ and } \cos t = x]$$

$$= \frac{1}{4}(2x^2-1)\cos^{-1}x - \frac{1}{4}x\sqrt{1-x^2} + C$$

Question 10 $(\sin^{-1}x)^2$

Sol. Let $I = \int(\sin^{-1}x)^2\,dx$

Put $\sin^{-1}x = \theta \Rightarrow x = \sin\theta \Rightarrow dx = \cos\theta\,d\theta$

$\therefore$ $$I = \int(\sin^{-1}x)^2\,dx = \int\theta^2\cos\theta\,d\theta$$

On taking θ^2 as first function and $\cos\theta$ as second function and integrating by parts, we get

$$I = \theta^2\int\cos\theta\,d\theta - \int\left[\frac{d}{d\theta}(\theta^2)\int\cos\theta\,d\theta\right]d\theta = \theta^2\sin\theta - \int 2\theta\sin\theta\,d\theta$$

Again integrating by parts, we get

$$I = \theta^2\sin\theta - 2[\theta(-\cos\theta) - \int 1(-\cos\theta)\,d\theta]$$

$$= \theta^2\sin\theta + 2\theta\cos\theta - 2\int\cos\theta\,d\theta + C$$

$$= \theta^2\sin\theta + 2\theta\cos\theta - 2\sin\theta + C$$

$$= (\sin^{-1}x)^2\,x + 2\sin^{-1}x\sqrt{1-\sin^2\theta} - 2x + C$$

$$[\text{put } \theta = \sin^{-1}x, \sin\theta = x \text{ and } \cos\theta = \sqrt{1-\sin^2\theta}]$$

$$= x(\sin^{-1}x)^2 + 2\sqrt{1-x^2}\sin^{-1}x - 2x + C$$

Question 11 $\dfrac{x\cos^{-1}x}{\sqrt{1-x^2}}$

Sol. Let $I = \int\frac{x\cos^{-1}x}{\sqrt{1-x^2}}dx \Rightarrow I = \int\cos^{-1}x\cdot\frac{x}{\sqrt{1-x^2}}dx$

Consider $\cos^{-1}x$ as first function and $\dfrac{x}{\sqrt{1-x^2}}$ as second function and integrating by parts, we get

$$I = \cos^{-1}x\int\frac{x}{\sqrt{1-x^2}}dx - \int\left[\frac{d}{dx}(\cos^{-1}x)\int\frac{x}{\sqrt{1-x^2}}dx\right]dx$$

Let $$1-x^2 = t^2 \Rightarrow -2x = 2t\frac{dt}{dx} \Rightarrow dx = -\frac{t}{x}dt$$

$\therefore$ $$I = \cos^{-1}x\int\frac{x}{t}\left(\frac{-t}{x}\right)dt - \int\left[\frac{d}{dx}(\cos^{-1}x)\int\frac{x}{t}\left(\frac{-t}{x}\right)dt\right]dx$$

$$= \cos^{-1} x\,(-t) - \int \left[\frac{(-1)}{\sqrt{1-x^2}} (-t)\, dt \right] dx$$

$$= -\sqrt{1-x^2} \cdot \cos^{-1} x - \int \left[\frac{\sqrt{1-x^2}}{\sqrt{1-x^2}} \right] dx$$

$$[\because 1 - x^2 = t^2 \Rightarrow t = \sqrt{1-x^2}]$$

$$= -\sqrt{1-x^2} \cdot \cos^{-1} x - \int 1\, dx = -\sqrt{1-x^2} \cdot \cos^{-1} x - x + C$$

Quick Solution

Let $I = \int \frac{x \cos^{-1} x}{\sqrt{1-x^2}}\, dx$

Put $\cos^{-1} x = t$ ...(i)

$\Rightarrow \quad x = \cos t$

On differentiating both sides of Eq. (i), we get

$$\frac{-1}{\sqrt{1-x^2}} = \frac{dt}{dx}$$

$$\Rightarrow \quad \frac{1}{\sqrt{1-x^2}}\, dx = -dt$$

$$\therefore \quad I = -\int \cos t \cdot t\, dt$$

On taking t as first function and $\cos t$ as second function and integrating by parts, we get

$$I = -\left[t \cdot \int \cos t\, dt - \int \left(\frac{d}{dt} t \int \cos t \right) dt \right]$$

$$= -[t \cdot \sin t - \int \sin t\, dt]$$

$$= -t \sin t - \cos t + C$$

$$= -t \cdot \sqrt{1 - \cos^2 t} - \cos t + C$$

$$= -\cos^{-1} x \sqrt{1-x^2} - x + C \quad [\text{put } t = \cos^{-1} x \text{ and } \cos t = x]$$

Question 12 $x \sec^2 x$

Sol. Let $I = \int x \sec^2 x\, dx$.

On taking x as first function and $\sec^2 x$ as second function and integrating by parts, we get

$$I = x \int \sec^2 x\, dx - \int \left[\frac{d}{dx}(x) \int \sec^2 x\, dx \right] dx$$

$$= x \tan x - \int \tan x\, dx = x \tan x - \log|\sec x| + C$$

$$\Rightarrow \quad I = x \tan x + \log|\cos x| + C$$

$$\left[\because \log|\sec x| = \log\left|\frac{1}{\cos x}\right| = \log 1 - \log|\cos x| = -\log|\cos x| \; (\because \log 1 = 0) \right]$$

Question 13 $\tan^{-1} x$

◎ *Thinking Process* There is no standard integration for $\tan^{-1} x$. So, take $\tan^{-1} x$ as first function and 1 as second function and integrating by parts.

Sol. Let $I = \int 1 \cdot \tan^{-1} x \, dx$

$$\Rightarrow I = \tan^{-1} x \int 1\, dx - \int \left[\frac{d}{dx}(\tan^{-1} x) \int 1\, dx\right] dx = x \tan^{-1} x - \int \frac{1}{1+x^2} \cdot x\, dx$$

Let $\qquad 1 + x^2 = t \Rightarrow 2x = \frac{dt}{dx} \Rightarrow dx = \frac{dt}{2x}$

$$\therefore \qquad I = x \tan^{-1} x - \int \frac{x}{t} \cdot \frac{dt}{2x} = x \tan^{-1} x - \frac{1}{2} \int \frac{1}{t} dt$$

$$= x \tan^{-1} x - \frac{1}{2} \log |t| + C = x \tan^{-1} x - \frac{1}{2} \log |1 + x^2| + C$$

Question 14 $x(\log x)^2$

Sol. Let $I = \int x (\log x)^2 dx$

On taking $(\log x)^2$ as first function and x as second function and integrating by parts, we get

$$I = (\log x)^2 \int x\, dx - \int \left[\frac{d}{dx}(\log x)^2 \int x\, dx\right] dx$$

$$= (\log x)^2 \cdot \frac{x^2}{2} - \int \left[\frac{2 \log x}{x} \cdot \frac{x^2}{2}\right] dx = \frac{x^2}{2} (\log x)^2 - \int x \log x\, dx$$

Again integrating by parts, we get

$$I = \frac{x^2}{2} (\log x)^2 - \left[\log x \int x\, dx - \int \left\{\left(\frac{d}{dx} \log x\right) \int x\, dx\right\} dx\right]$$

[$\log x$ be first function and x be second]

$$= \frac{x^2}{2} (\log x)^2 - \left[\frac{x^2}{2} \log x - \int \frac{1}{x} \cdot \frac{x^2}{2} dx\right]$$

$$= \frac{x^2}{2} (\log x)^2 - \frac{x^2}{2} \log x + \frac{1}{2} \int x\, dx = \frac{x^2}{2} (\log x)^2 - \frac{x^2}{2} \log x + \frac{x^2}{4} + C$$

Question 15 $(x^2 + 1) \log x$

Sol. Let $I = \int (x^2 + 1) \log x\, dx$

On taking $\log x$ as first function and $(x^2 + 1)$ as second function and integrating by parts, we get

$$I = \log x \int (x^2 + 1) dx - \int \left[\frac{d}{dx} (\log x) \int (x^2 + 1)\, dx\right] dx$$

$$\Rightarrow \qquad I = \log x \left(\frac{x^3}{3} + x\right) - \int \frac{1}{x} \cdot \left(\frac{x^3}{3} + x\right) dx$$

$$\Rightarrow \qquad I = \left(\frac{x^3}{3} + x\right) \log x - \int \left(\frac{x^2}{3} + 1\right) dx = \left(\frac{x^3}{3} + x\right) \log x - \frac{x^3}{9} - x + C$$

Question 16 $e^x(\sin x + \cos x)$

Sol. Let $I = \int e^x(\sin x + \cos x)dx$

Let $f(x) = \sin x \Rightarrow f'(x) = \cos x$

We know that, $\int e^x(f(x) + f'(x))\,dx = e^x\, f(x) + C$

$\therefore \quad I = e^x \sin x + C$

Question 17 $\dfrac{xe^x}{(1+x)^2}$

Sol. Let $I = \int \dfrac{xe^x}{(1+x)^2}dx = \int e^x \dfrac{(x+1)-1}{(1+x)^2}dx$

$$= \int e^x \left[\frac{1}{(1+x)} - \frac{1}{(1+x)^2}\right]dx$$

Let $f(x) = \dfrac{1}{1+x} \Rightarrow f'(x) = -\dfrac{1}{(1+x)^2}$

We know that, $\int e^x(f(x) + f'(x))\,dx = e^x\, f(x) + C$

$\Rightarrow \quad I = \int e^x \left\{\dfrac{1}{1+x} - \dfrac{1}{(1+x)^2}\right\}dx = \dfrac{e^x}{1+x} + C$

Question 18 $e^x\left(\dfrac{1+\sin x}{1+\cos x}\right)$

Sol. Let $I = \int e^x\left(\dfrac{1+\sin x}{1+\cos x}\right)dx = \int e^x\left(\dfrac{1}{1+\cos x} + \dfrac{\sin x}{1+\cos x}\right)dx$

$$= \int e^x\left(\frac{1}{2\cos^2\frac{x}{2}} + \frac{2\sin\frac{x}{2}\cos\frac{x}{2}}{2\cos^2\frac{x}{2}}\right)dx$$

$[\because \cos 2\theta = 2\cos^2\theta - 1 \text{ and } \sin 2\theta = 2\sin\theta\cos\theta]$

$$= \int e^x\left(\frac{\sec^2\frac{x}{2}}{2} + \tan\frac{x}{2}\right)dx$$

$$= \int e^x\left(\tan\frac{x}{2} + \frac{1}{2}\sec^2\frac{x}{2}\right)dx$$

Let $f(x) = \tan\dfrac{x}{2} \Rightarrow f'(x) = \dfrac{\sec^2\frac{x}{2}}{2}$

$\therefore \quad \int e^x\left(\tan\dfrac{x}{2} + \dfrac{\sec^2\frac{x}{2}}{2}\right)dx = e^x\tan\dfrac{x}{2} + C \quad [\because \int e^x[f(x) + f'(x)]dx = e^x f(x) + C]$

Question 19 $e^x\left(\frac{1}{x}-\frac{1}{x^2}\right)$

Sol. Let $I=\int e^x\left(\frac{1}{x}-\frac{1}{x^2}\right)dx$

Let $f(x)=\frac{1}{x} \Rightarrow f'(x)=-\frac{1}{x^2}$

Here, given integral is of the form $\int e^x[f(x)+f'(x)]dx=e^x f(x)+C$

$$\therefore \quad I=\frac{e^x}{x}+C$$

Question 20 $\frac{x-3}{(x-1)^3}e^x$

Sol. Let $I=\int \frac{x-3}{(x-1)^3}e^x\,dx=\int \frac{x-1-2}{(x-1)^3}e^x\,dx$

$$=\int e^x\left(\frac{x-1}{(x-1)^3}-\frac{2}{(x-1)^3}\right)dx=\int e^x\left(\frac{1}{(x-1)^2}-\frac{2}{(x-1)^3}\right)dx$$

Let $f(x)=\frac{1}{(x-1)^2} \Rightarrow f'(x)=\frac{-2}{(x-1)^3}$

$$\therefore \quad I=\frac{e^x}{(x-1)^2}+C \qquad [\because \int e^x(f(x)+f'(x))\,dx=e^x f(x)+C]$$

Question 21 $e^{2x}\sin x$

Sol. Let $I=\int e^{2x}\sin x\,dx$

On taking $\sin x$ as first function and e^{2x} as second function and integrating by parts, we get

$$I=\int e^{2x}\sin x\,dx=\sin x\cdot\int e^{2x}\,dx-\int\left[\frac{d}{dx}(\sin x)\cdot\int e^{2x}\,dx\right]dx$$

$$=\sin x\cdot\frac{e^{2x}}{2}-\int\cos x\cdot\frac{e^{2x}}{2}dx=\sin x\cdot\frac{e^{2x}}{2}-\frac{1}{2}\int e^{2x}\cos x\,dx$$

$$\Rightarrow \quad \int e^{2x}\sin x\,dx=\sin x\cdot\frac{e^{2x}}{2}-\frac{1}{2}I_1 \qquad \text{...(i)}$$

where, $I_1=\int e^{2x}\cos x\,dx$

On taking $\cos x$ as first function and e^{2x} as second function and integrating by parts, we get

$$I_1=\cos x\cdot\int e^{2x}\,dx-\int\left[\frac{d}{dx}(\cos x)\cdot\int e^{2x}\,dx\right]dx$$

$$=\cos x\cdot\frac{e^{2x}}{2}-\int(-\sin x)\cdot\frac{e^{2x}}{2}\,dx+C_1=\frac{e^{2x}\cos x}{2}+\frac{1}{2}\int e^{2x}\sin x\,dx+C_1$$

Putting the value of I_1 in Eq. (i), we get

$$\int e^{2x}\sin x\,dx=\frac{e^{2x}\sin x}{2}-\frac{1}{2}\left[\frac{e^{2x}\cos x}{2}+\frac{1}{2}\int e^{2x}\sin x\,dx+C_1\right]$$

$$\Rightarrow \quad \int e^{2x} \sin x\, dx = \frac{e^{2x} \sin x}{2} - \frac{e^{2x} \cos x}{4} - \frac{1}{4}\int e^{2x} \sin x\, dx - \frac{1}{2} C_1$$

$$\Rightarrow \quad \int e^{2x} \sin x\, dx + \frac{1}{4}\int e^{2x} \sin x\, dx = \frac{e^{2x} \sin x}{2} - \frac{e^{2x} \cos x}{4} - \frac{1}{2} C_1$$

$$\Rightarrow \quad \frac{5}{4}\int e^{2x} \sin x\, dx = \frac{e^{2x} \sin x}{2} - \frac{e^{2x} \cos x}{4} - \frac{1}{2} C_1$$

$$\Rightarrow \quad \int e^{2x} \sin x\, dx = \frac{4}{5}\left[\frac{e^{2x} \sin x}{2} - \frac{e^{2x} \cos x}{4} - \frac{1}{2} C_1\right]$$

$$= \frac{2}{5} e^{2x} \sin x - \frac{1}{5} e^{2x} \cos x - \frac{2}{5} C_1$$

$$= \frac{2}{5} e^{2x} \sin x - \frac{1}{5} e^{2x} \cos x + C \text{ where, } C = -\frac{2}{5} C_1$$

$$= \frac{e^{2x}}{5}(2 \sin x - \cos x) + C$$

Question 22 $\sin^{-1}\left(\dfrac{2x}{1+x^2}\right)$

Sol. Let $\quad I = \int \sin^{-1}\left(\dfrac{2x}{1+x^2}\right) dx$

On putting $x = \tan\theta$, we get $I = \int \sin^{-1}\left(\dfrac{2\tan\theta}{1+\tan^2\theta}\right) dx$

$$= \int \sin^{-1}(\sin 2\theta)\, dx \qquad \left(\because \sin 2\theta = \frac{2\tan\theta}{1+\tan^2\theta}\right)$$

$$= 2\int \theta\, dx = 2\int \tan^{-1} x\, dx \qquad [\because x = \tan\theta \Rightarrow \theta = \tan^{-1} x]$$

$$= 2\int \underset{\text{II}}{1} \cdot \underset{\text{I}}{\tan^{-1} x}\, dx$$

$$= 2\tan^{-1} x \int 1\, dx - 2\int\left[\frac{d}{dx}\tan^{-1} x \int 1\, dx\right] dx$$

(using integration by parts)

$$\Rightarrow \quad I = 2\tan^{-1} x \cdot x - 2\int\left[\frac{1}{1+x^2}\cdot x\right] dx$$

Put $\quad 1 + x^2 = t \Rightarrow 2x = \dfrac{dt}{dx} \Rightarrow dx = \dfrac{dt}{2x}$

$$\therefore \quad I = 2x\tan^{-1} x - 2\int\left[\frac{x}{t}\cdot\frac{dt}{2x}\right]$$

$$= 2x\tan^{-1} x - \int \frac{1}{t}\, dt$$

$$= 2x\tan^{-1} x - \log|t| + C$$

$$\Rightarrow \quad I = 2x\tan^{-1} x - \log|1 + x^2| + C$$

Direction (Q. No. 23 and 24) Choose the correct answer in the given question.

Question 23 $\int x^2 e^{x^3} dx$ equals

(a) $\frac{1}{3} e^{x^3} + C$ (b) $\frac{1}{3} e^{x^2} + C$

(c) $\frac{1}{2} e^{x^3} + C$ (d) $\frac{1}{2} e^{x^2} + C$

◎ *Thinking Process* Here, we convert the integrand into simplest form by substitution method *i.e.*, put $x^3 = t$ and then integrate it.

Sol. (a) Let $I = \int x^2 e^{x^3} dx$

Put $x^3 = t \Rightarrow 3x^2 = \frac{dt}{dx} \Rightarrow dx = \frac{dt}{3x^2}$

$\therefore$ $I \int x^2 e^t \cdot \frac{dt}{3x^2} = \frac{1}{3} \int e^t dt \Rightarrow I = \frac{1}{3} e^t + C = \frac{1}{3} e^{x^3} + C$

Question 24 $\int e^x \sec x (1 + \tan x) dx$ equals

(a) $e^x \cos x + C$ (b) $e^x \sec x + C$

(c) $e^x \sin x + C$ (d) $e^x \tan x + C$

Sol. (b) Let $I = \int e^x \sec x (1 + \tan x) dx$

$\Rightarrow$ $I = \int e^x \sec x\, dx + \int e^x \sec x \tan x\, dx$ ...(i)

Now, $\int e^x \sec x\, dx = \sec x \int e^x dx - \int \left[\frac{d}{dx} (\sec x) \int e^x dx \right] dx$

$= e^x \sec x - \int \text{sex } x \tan x\, e^x dx$ ...(ii)

On putting the value from Eq. (ii) in Eq. (i), we get

$I = e^x \sec x - \int e^x \text{ sex } x \tan x\, dx + \int \sec x \tan x\, e^x dx + C$

$\Rightarrow$ $I = e^x \text{sex } x + C.$

Quick Solution

$I = \int e^x (\sec x + \sec x \tan x) dx$

Let $f(x) = \sec x$

$\Rightarrow$ $f'(x) = \sec x \tan x$

Here, given integral is of the form

$\int e^x (f(x) + f'(x)) dx = e^x f(x) + C$

$\therefore$ $I = e^x \cdot \sec x + C$

Exercise 7.7

Direction (Q. Nos. 1 to 9) Integrate the functions.

Question 1 $\sqrt{4-x^2}$

Sol. Let $I = \int \sqrt{4-x^2}\, dx = \int \sqrt{2^2 - x^2}\, dx$

$$= \frac{x}{2}\sqrt{2^2 - x^2} + \frac{4}{2}\sin^{-1}\frac{x}{2} + C$$

$$\left[\because \int \sqrt{a^2 - x^2}\, dx = \frac{x}{2}\sqrt{a^2 - x^2} + \frac{a^2}{2}\sin^{-1}\frac{x}{a} + C\right]$$

$\Rightarrow$ $$I = \frac{x}{2}\sqrt{4-x^2} + 2\sin^{-1}\frac{x}{2} + C$$

Question 2 $\sqrt{1-4x^2}$

Sol. Let $I = \int \sqrt{1-4x^2}\, dx$

$$= \int \sqrt{4\left(\frac{1}{4} - x^2\right)}\, dx = 2\int \sqrt{\left(\left(\frac{1}{2}\right)^2 - x^2\right)}\, dx$$

$$= 2 \cdot \frac{x}{2}\sqrt{\left(\frac{1}{2}\right)^2 - x^2} + \frac{1}{4}\cdot\frac{2}{2}\sin^{-1}\frac{x}{1/2} + C$$

$$\left[\because \int \sqrt{a^2 - x^2}\, dx = \frac{x}{2}\sqrt{a^2 - x^2} + \frac{a^2}{2}\sin^{-1}\frac{x}{a} + C\right]$$

$\Rightarrow$ $$I = \frac{x}{2}\sqrt{1-4x^2} + \frac{1}{4}\sin^{-1}(2x) + C$$

Quick Solution

Let $I = \int \sqrt{1-4x^2}\, dx = \int \sqrt{1-(2x)^2}\, dx$

Put $2x = t$

$\Rightarrow$ $$2dx = dt$$

$\Rightarrow$ $$dx = \frac{1}{2}dt$$

$\therefore$ $$I = \frac{1}{2}\int \sqrt{1-t^2}\, dt$$

$$= \frac{1}{2}\left[\frac{t}{2}\sqrt{1-t^2} + \frac{1}{2}\sin^{-1} t\right] + C$$

$$= \frac{1}{2}x\sqrt{1-4x^2} + \frac{1}{4}\sin^{-1} 2x + C$$

Question 3 $\sqrt{x^2+4x+6}$

◎ *Thinking Process* Here, we can convert the integrand into some standard integrand of the form $\sqrt{x^2 \pm a^2}$ and then integrate.

Sol. Let $I = \int \sqrt{x^2+4x+6}\,dx = \int \sqrt{x^2+4x+2^2+6-2^2}\,dx$

$$= \int \sqrt{(x+2)^2+(\sqrt{2})^2}\,dx$$

$$= \frac{x+2}{2}\sqrt{(x+2)^2+(\sqrt{2})^2} + \frac{2}{2}\log\left|(x+2)+\sqrt{(x+2)^2+(\sqrt{2})^2}\right| + C$$

$$\left[\because \int \sqrt{x^2+a^2}\,dx = \frac{x}{2}\sqrt{x^2+a^2} + \frac{a^2}{2}\log\left|x+\sqrt{x^2+a^2}\right| + C\right]$$

$$\Rightarrow \quad I = \frac{x+2}{2}\sqrt{x^2+4x+6} + \log\left|(x+2)+\sqrt{x^2+4x+6}\right| + C$$

Question 4 $\sqrt{x^2+4x+1}$

Sol. Let $I = \int \sqrt{x^2+4x+1}\,dx = \int \sqrt{x^2+4x+1-2^2+2^2}\,dx$

$$= \int \sqrt{(x+2)^2-(\sqrt{3})^2}\,dx$$

$$\Rightarrow \quad I = \frac{x+2}{2}\sqrt{(x+2)^2-(\sqrt{3})^2} - \frac{(\sqrt{3})^2}{2}\log\left|(x+2)+\sqrt{(x+2)^2-(\sqrt{3})^2}\right| + C$$

$$\left[\because \int \sqrt{x^2-a^2}\,dx = \frac{x}{2}\sqrt{x^2-a^2} - \frac{a^2}{2}\log\left|x+\sqrt{x^2-a^2}\right| + C\right]$$

$$\Rightarrow \quad I = \frac{x+2}{2}\sqrt{x^2+4x+1} - \frac{3}{2}\log\left|x+2+\sqrt{x^2+4x+1}\right| + C$$

Question 5 $\sqrt{1-4x-x^2}$

◎ *Thinking Process* Here, we can convert the integrand in the standard form $\sqrt{a^2-x^2}$ and then apply the formula of integration.

Sol. Let $I = \int \sqrt{1-4x-x^2}\,dx = \int \sqrt{-(x^2+4x-1-2^2+2^2)}\,dx$

$$= \int \sqrt{-[(x+2)^2-(\sqrt{5})^2]}\,dx$$

$$= \int \sqrt{(\sqrt{5})^2-(x+2)^2}\,dx$$

$$= \frac{x+2}{2}\sqrt{(5)^2-(x+2)^2} + \frac{(\sqrt{5})^2}{2}\sin^{-1}\left(\frac{x+2}{\sqrt{5}}\right) + C$$

$$\left[\because \int \sqrt{a^2-x^2}\,dx = \frac{x}{2}\sqrt{a^2-x^2} + \frac{a^2}{2}\sin^{-1}\frac{x}{a} + C\right]$$

$$\Rightarrow \quad I = \frac{x+2}{2}\sqrt{1-4x-x^2} + \frac{5}{2}\sin^{-1}\left(\frac{x+2}{\sqrt{5}}\right) + C$$

Question 6 $\sqrt{x^2+4x-5}$

Sol. Let $I = \int \sqrt{x^2 + 4x - 5}\, dx$

Let $I = \int \sqrt{x^2 + 4x - 5 - 2^2 + 2^2}\, dx = \int \sqrt{(x+2)^2 - 5 - 4}\, dx$

$$= \int \sqrt{(x+2)^2 - (3)^2}\, dx$$

$$= \frac{x+2}{2}\sqrt{(x+2)^2 - (3)^2} - \frac{(3)^2}{2}\log\left|(x+2) + \sqrt{(x+2)^2 - (3)^2}\right| + C$$

$$\left[\because \int \sqrt{x^2 - a^2}\, dx = \frac{x}{2}\sqrt{x^2 - a^2} - \frac{a^2}{2}\log\left|x + \sqrt{x^2 - a^2}\right| + C\right]$$

$$\Rightarrow \quad I = \frac{x+2}{2}\sqrt{x^2 + 4x - 5} - \frac{9}{2}\log\left|(x+2) + \sqrt{x^2 + 4x - 5}\right| + C$$

Question 7 $\sqrt{1+3x-x^2}$

Sol. Let $I = \int \sqrt{1 + 3x - x^2}\, dx$

$$= \int \sqrt{-(x^2 - 3x - 1)}\, dx$$

$$= \int \sqrt{-\left(x^2 - 3x + \left(\frac{3}{2}\right)^2 - \left(\frac{3}{2}\right)^2 - 1\right)}\, dx$$

$$= \int \sqrt{-\left(\left(x - \frac{3}{2}\right)^2 - \frac{9}{4} - 1\right)}\, dx$$

$$= \int \sqrt{-\left(\left(x - \frac{3}{2}\right)^2 - \frac{9+4}{4}\right)}\, dx$$

$$= \int \sqrt{-\left(\left(x - \frac{3}{2}\right)^2 - \frac{13}{4}\right)}\, dx = \int \sqrt{\left(\frac{\sqrt{13}}{2}\right)^2 - \left(x - \frac{3}{2}\right)^2}\, dx$$

$$\therefore \quad I = \frac{x - \frac{3}{2}}{2}\sqrt{\left(\frac{\sqrt{13}}{2}\right)^2 - \left(\frac{x-3}{2}\right)^2} + \frac{13}{4 \times 2}\sin^{-1}\left(\frac{x - \frac{3}{2}}{\frac{\sqrt{13}}{2}}\right)$$

$$\left[\because \int \sqrt{a^2 - x^2}\, dx = \frac{x}{2}\sqrt{a^2 - x^2} + \frac{a^2}{2}\sin^{-1}\frac{x}{a} + C\right]$$

$$\Rightarrow \quad I = \frac{2x-3}{4}\sqrt{1 + 3x - x^2} + \frac{13}{8}\sin^{-1}\left(\frac{2x-3}{\sqrt{13}}\right) + C$$

Question 8 $\sqrt{x^2+3x}$

Sol. Let $I = \int \sqrt{x^2 + 3x}\, dx = \int \sqrt{x^2 + 3x - \left(\frac{3}{2}\right)^2 + \left(\frac{3}{2}\right)^2}\, dx$

$$= \int \sqrt{\left(x + \frac{3}{2}\right)^2 - \left(\frac{3}{2}\right)^2}\, dx$$

$$\Rightarrow \quad I = \frac{x + \frac{3}{2}}{2} \sqrt{\left(x + \frac{3}{2}\right)^2 - \left(\frac{3}{2}\right)^2} - \frac{9}{4 \times 2} \log \left| \left(x + \frac{3}{2}\right) + \sqrt{\left(x + \frac{3}{2}\right)^2 - \left(\frac{3}{2}\right)^2} \right| + C$$

$$\left[\because \int \sqrt{x^2 - a^2}\, dx = \frac{x}{2}\sqrt{x^2 - a^2} - \frac{a^2}{2} \log \left| x + \sqrt{x^2 - a^2} \right| + C\right]$$

$$\Rightarrow \quad I = \frac{2x + 3}{4} \sqrt{x^2 + 3x} - \frac{9}{8} \log \left| \left(\frac{2x + 3}{2}\right) + \sqrt{x^2 + 3x} \right| + C$$

Question 9 $\sqrt{1 + \frac{x^2}{9}}$

Sol. Let $I = \int \sqrt{1 + \frac{x^2}{9}}\, dx = \int \sqrt{\frac{9 + x^2}{9}}\, dx = \frac{1}{3} \int \sqrt{(3)^2 + x^2}\, dx$

$$= \frac{1}{3} \cdot \frac{x}{2} \sqrt{(3)^2 + x^2} + \frac{9}{2 \times 3} \log \left| x + \sqrt{9 + x^2} \right| + C$$

$$\left[\because \int \sqrt{a^2 + x^2}\, dx = \frac{1}{2} x \sqrt{a^2 + x^2} + \frac{1}{2} a^2 \log \left| x + \sqrt{a^2 + x^2} \right| + C\right]$$

$$= \frac{x}{6} \sqrt{x^2 + 9} + \frac{3}{2} \log \left| x + \sqrt{9 + x^2} \right| + C$$

Direction (Q. No. 10 and 11) Choose the correct answer in the given question.

Question 10 $\int \sqrt{1 + x^2}\, dx$ is equal to

(a) $\frac{x}{2} \sqrt{1 + x^2} + \frac{1}{2} \log \left| x + \sqrt{1 + x^2} \right| + C$

(b) $\frac{2}{3} (1 + x^2)^{\frac{3}{2}} + C$

(c) $\frac{2}{3} x (1 + x^2)^{\frac{3}{2}} + C$

(d) $\frac{x^2}{2} \sqrt{1 + x^2} + \frac{1}{2} x^2 \log \left| x + \sqrt{1 + x^2} \right| + C$

Sol. (a) Let $I = \int \sqrt{1 + x^2}\, dx$

$$\Rightarrow \quad I = \frac{x}{2} \sqrt{1 + x^2} + \frac{1}{2} \log \left| x + \sqrt{1 + x^2} \right| + C$$

$$\left[\because \int \sqrt{x^2 + a^2}\, dx = \frac{x}{2} \sqrt{x^2 + a^2} + \frac{a^2}{2} \log \left| x + \sqrt{x^2 + a^2} \right| + C\right]$$

Question 11 $\int \sqrt{x^2 - 8x + 7}\, dx$ is equal to

(a) $\frac{1}{2}(x-4)\sqrt{x^2 - 8x + 7} + 9 \log |x - 4 + \sqrt{x^2 - 8x + 7}| + C$

(b) $\frac{1}{2}(x+4)\sqrt{x^2 - 8x + 7} + 9 \log |x + 4 + \sqrt{x^2 - 8x + 7}| + C$

(c) $\frac{1}{2}(x-4)\sqrt{x^2 - 8x + 7} - 3\sqrt{2} \log |x - 4 + \sqrt{x^2 - 8x + 7}| + C$

(d) $\frac{1}{2}(x-4)\sqrt{x^2 - 8x + 7} - \frac{9}{2} \log |x - 4 + \sqrt{x^2 - 8x + 7}| + C$

Sol. (d) Let $I = \int \sqrt{x^2 - 8x + 7}\, dx$

$\Rightarrow$ $$I = \int \sqrt{x^2 - 8x + 7 + (4)^2 - (4)^2}\, dx$$
$$= \int \sqrt{(x-4)^2 + 7 - 16}\, dx$$
$$= \int \sqrt{(x-4)^2 - (3)^2}\, dx$$

$\Rightarrow$ $$I = \frac{x-4}{2}\sqrt{x^2 - 8x + 7} - \frac{9}{2} \log |x - 4 + \sqrt{x^2 - 8x + 7}| + C$$

$$\left[\because \int \sqrt{x^2 - a^2}\, dx = \frac{x}{2}\sqrt{x^2 - a^2} - \frac{a^2}{2} \log \left|x + \sqrt{x^2 - a^2}\right| + C\right]$$

Exercise 7.8

Direction (Q. No. 1 to 20) Evaluate the definite integrals.

Question 1 $\int_{-1}^{1} (x+1)\, dx$

◎ *Thinking Process* To find the value of definite integral, we simply integrate the integrand and then put the limits.

Sol. Let $I = \int_{-1}^{1} (x+1)\, dx = \left[\frac{x^2}{2} + x\right]_{-1}^{1} = \left[\frac{1^2}{2} + 1\right] - \left[\frac{(-1)^2}{2} - 1\right]$

$\Rightarrow$ $$I = \frac{3}{2} + \frac{1}{2} = \frac{4}{2} = 2$$

Question 2. $\int_{2}^{3} \frac{1}{x}\, dx$

Sol. Let $I = \int_{2}^{3} \frac{1}{x}\, dx = [\log x]_2^3 = \log 3 - \log 2 = \log \frac{3}{2}$ $\left(\because \log a - \log b = \log \frac{a}{b}\right)$

Question 3 $\int_1^2 (4x^3 - 5x^2 + 6x + 9)\,dx$

Sol. Let $I = \int_1^2 (4x^3 - 5x^2 + 6x + 9)\,dx$

$$= \left[\frac{4x^4}{4} - \frac{5x^3}{3} + \frac{6x^2}{2} + 9x\right]_1^2 = \left[x^4 - \frac{5x^3}{3} + 3x^2 + 9x\right]_1^2$$

$$= \left[(2)^4 - \frac{5(2)^3}{3} + 3(2)^2 + 9(2)\right] - \left[(1)^4 - \frac{5(1)^3}{3} + 3(1)^2 + 9(1)\right]$$

$$= \left[16 - \frac{40}{3} + 12 + 18\right] - \left[1 - \frac{5}{3} + 3 + 9\right]$$

$$= \left[46 - \frac{40}{3}\right] - \left[13 - \frac{5}{3}\right] = \left[\frac{138 - 40}{3}\right] - \left[\frac{39 - 5}{3}\right] = \frac{98}{3} - \frac{34}{3} = \frac{64}{3}$$

Question 4 $\int_0^{\pi/4} \sin 2x\,dx$

Sol. Let $I = \int_0^{\pi/4} \sin 2x\,dx = \int_0^{\pi/4} 2\sin x \cos x\,dx$ $\quad [\because \sin 2x = 2\sin x \cos x]$

Put $\sin x = t \Rightarrow \cos x = \frac{dt}{dx} \Rightarrow dx = \frac{dt}{\cos x}$

For limit, when $x = \frac{\pi}{4} \Rightarrow t = \sin\frac{\pi}{4} = \frac{1}{\sqrt{2}}$

and when $x = 0 \Rightarrow t = \sin 0 = 0$

$$\therefore \quad I = 2\int_0^{1/\sqrt{2}} t\cos x \frac{dt}{\cos x} = 2\int_0^{1/\sqrt{2}} t\,dt = 2\left[\frac{t^2}{2}\right]_0^{1/\sqrt{2}} = \left(\frac{1}{\sqrt{2}}\right)^2 = \frac{1}{2}$$

Quick Solution

Let $I = \int_0^{\frac{\pi}{4}} \sin 2x\,dx = \left[\frac{-\cos 2x}{2}\right]_0^{\frac{\pi}{4}}$ $\quad \left(\because \int \sin(ax) = \frac{-\cos(ax)}{a} + C\right)$

$$= -\frac{1}{2}\left[\cos 2\cdot\frac{\pi}{4} - \cos 2\cdot 0\right] = -\frac{1}{2}\left[\cos\frac{\pi}{2} - \cos 0\right]$$

$$= -\frac{1}{2}[0 - 1] = \frac{1}{2}$$ $\quad \left(\because \cos\frac{\pi}{2} = 0 \text{ and } \cos 0 = 1\right)$

Mistake Alert If we change the integral function by considerable another variable, then remember to change the limit or after integration change into the given variable and then apply the limit.

Question 5 $\int_0^{\pi/2} \cos 2x\,dx$

Sol. Let $I = \int_0^{\pi/2} \cos 2x\,dx = \left[\frac{\sin 2x}{2}\right]_0^{\pi/2}$ $\quad \left(\because \int \cos ax\,dx = \frac{\sin ax}{a} + C\right)$

$$= \frac{1}{2}\left[\left(\sin 2\times\frac{\pi}{2}\right) - \sin(0)\right] = \frac{1}{2}[0 - 0] = 0$$

Question 6 $\int_4^5 e^x\, dx$

Sol. Let $I = \int_4^5 e^x\, dx = [e^x]_4^5 = [e^5 - e^4] = e^4\,[e-1]$

Question 7 $\int_0^{\pi/4} \tan x\, dx$

Sol. Let $I = \int_0^{\pi/4} \tan x\, dx = [-\log|\cos x|]_0^{\pi/4} = -\log\left|\cos\frac{\pi}{4}\right| - (-\log|\cos 0|)$

$= -\log\left(\frac{1}{\sqrt{2}}\right) + \log 1 = -\log 2^{-1/2} + 0$ $[\because \log 1 = 0]$

$= \frac{1}{2}\log 2$ $[\log m^n = n\log m]$

Question 8 $\int_{\pi/6}^{\pi/4} \operatorname{cosec} x\, dx$

Sol. Let $I = \int_{\pi/6}^{\pi/4} \operatorname{cosec} x\, dx = [\log|\operatorname{cosec} x - \cot x|]_{\pi/6}^{\pi/4}$

$= \log\left|\operatorname{cosec}\frac{\pi}{4} - \cot\frac{\pi}{4}\right| - \log\left|\operatorname{cosec}\frac{\pi}{6} - \cot\frac{\pi}{6}\right|$

$= \log|\sqrt{2} - 1| - \log|2 - \sqrt{3}| = \log\left|\frac{\sqrt{2}-1}{2-\sqrt{3}}\right|$ $\left(\because \log a - \log b = \log\frac{a}{b}\right)$

Question 9 $\int_0^1 \frac{1}{\sqrt{1-x^2}}\, dx$

Sol. Let $I = \int_0^1 \frac{1}{\sqrt{1-x^2}}\, dx = [\sin^{-1} x]_0^1$ $\left(\because \int \frac{dx}{\sqrt{1-x^2}} = \sin^{-1} x + C\right)$

$= \sin^{-1} 1 - \sin^{-1} 0 = \frac{\pi}{2} - 0 = \frac{\pi}{2}$

Question 10 $\int_0^1 \frac{1}{1+x^2}\, dx$

Sol. Let $I = \int_0^1 \frac{1}{1+x^2}\, dx = [\tan^{-1} x]_0^1$ $\left(\because \int \frac{dx}{1+x^2} = \tan^{-1} x + C\right)$

$= \tan^{-1} 1 - \tan^{-1} 0 = \frac{\pi}{4}$

Question 11 $\int_2^3 \frac{1}{x^2-1}\, dx$

Sol. Let $I = \int_2^3 \frac{1}{x^2-1} dx = \left[\frac{1}{2}\log\left|\frac{x-1}{x+1}\right|\right]_2^3$ $\left[\because \int \frac{dx}{x^2-a^2} = \frac{1}{2a}\log\left|\frac{x-a}{x+a}\right| + C\right]$

$$= \frac{1}{2}\log\left|\frac{3-1}{3+1}\right| - \frac{1}{2}\log\left|\frac{2-1}{2+1}\right| = \frac{1}{2}\log\left|\frac{2}{4}\right| - \frac{1}{2}\log\left|\frac{1}{3}\right|$$

$$= \frac{1}{2}[\log(1) - \log(2) - \log(1) + \log(3)]$$

$$\left[\because \log\left(\frac{a}{b}\right) = \log a - \log b\right]$$

$$= \frac{1}{2}\log\left(\frac{3}{2}\right)$$

Question 12 $\int_0^{\pi/2} \cos^2 x\, dx$

◎ ***Thinking Process*** There is no standard integration of $\cos^2 x$, therefore we convert it in standard form by using the relation $\frac{\cos 2x + 1}{2}$, then integrate and put the limits.

Sol. Let $I = \int_0^{\pi/2} \cos^2 x\, dx = \int_0^{\pi/2}\left(\frac{\cos 2x + 1}{2}\right) dx$ $\quad (\because \cos 2x = 2\cos^2 x - 1)$

$$= \frac{1}{2}\int_0^{\pi/2} \cos 2x\, dx + \frac{1}{2}\int_0^{\pi/2} 1\, dx$$

$$= \frac{1}{2}\left[\frac{\sin 2x}{2}\right]_0^{\pi/2} + \frac{1}{2}[x]_0^{\pi/2}$$

$$= \frac{1}{2}\left[\left(\frac{\sin \pi}{2} - \frac{\sin 0}{2}\right) + \left(\frac{\pi}{2} - 0\right)\right] = \frac{0}{4} + \frac{\pi}{4} = \frac{\pi}{4}$$

Question 13 $\int_2^3 \frac{x}{x^2+1} dx$

Sol. Let $I = \int_2^3 \frac{x}{x^2+1} dx$

Put $\quad x^2 + 1 = t \Rightarrow 2x = \frac{dt}{dx} \Rightarrow dx = \frac{dt}{2x}$

$$\therefore \quad I = \int_2^3 \frac{x}{t}\frac{dt}{2x} = \frac{1}{2}\int_2^3 \frac{1}{t} dt$$

$$= \frac{1}{2}[\log |t|]_2^3 = \frac{1}{2}[\log |x^2 + 1|]_2^3 \qquad [\because t = x^2 + 1]$$

$$= \frac{1}{2}[\log |3^2 + 1| - \log |2^2 + 1|]$$

$$= \frac{1}{2}[\log |10| - \log |5|] = \frac{1}{2}\log\left|\frac{10}{5}\right| = \frac{1}{2}\log 2$$

$$\left(\because \log a - \log b = \log \frac{a}{b}\right)$$

Quick Solution

Let $I = \int \frac{x\,dx}{x^2+1}$

Put $\quad x^2 + 1 = t \Rightarrow 2x = \frac{dt}{dx} \Rightarrow xdx = \frac{1}{2}dt$

Now, if $\quad x = 2 \Rightarrow t = 2^2 + 1 = 5$

and if $\quad x = 3 \Rightarrow t = 3^2 + 1 = 10$

$\therefore \quad I = \frac{1}{2}\int_5^{10}\frac{dt}{t} = \frac{1}{2}(\log t)_5^{10} = \frac{1}{2}(\log 10 - \log 5) = \frac{1}{2}\log\frac{10}{5} = \frac{1}{2}\log 2$

$$\left(\because \log a - \log b = \log\frac{a}{b}\right)$$

Question 14 $\int_0^1 \frac{2x+3}{(5x^2+1)}dx$

◎ ***Thinking Process*** Here, the given integrand cannot integrate directly. So, we break it into terms and then integrate both terms by using suitable method and then put the limits.

Sol. Let $I = \int_0^1 \frac{2x+3}{(5x^2+1)}dx = \int_0^1 \frac{2x}{(5x^2+1)}dx + 3\int_0^1 \frac{1}{(5x^2+1)}dx$

Put $\quad 5x^2 + 1 = t \Rightarrow 10x = \frac{dt}{dx} \Rightarrow dx = \frac{dt}{10x}$

$$\therefore \quad I = \int_0^1 \frac{2x}{t}\frac{dt}{10x} + \frac{3}{5}\int_0^1 \frac{1}{x^2 + \left(\frac{1}{\sqrt{5}}\right)^2}dx$$

$$= \frac{1}{5}\int_0^1 \frac{1}{t}dt + \frac{3}{5}\int_0^1 \frac{1}{x^2 + \left(\frac{1}{\sqrt{5}}\right)^2}dx$$

$$= \frac{1}{5}[\log t]_0^1 + \frac{3}{5}\times\frac{1}{\frac{1}{\sqrt{5}}}\left[\tan^{-1}\frac{x}{\frac{1}{\sqrt{5}}}\right]_0^1 \quad \left(\because \int\frac{dx}{a^2+x^2} = \frac{1}{a}\tan^{-1}\frac{x}{a} + C\right)$$

$$= \frac{1}{5}[\log|5x^2+1|]_0^1 + \frac{3}{5}\sqrt{5}\,[\tan^{-1}(\sqrt{5}x)]_0^1$$

$$= \frac{1}{5}[\log|5+1| - \log|0+1|] + \frac{3}{\sqrt{5}}[\tan^{-1}\sqrt{5}(1) - \tan^{-1}\sqrt{5}(0)]$$

$$= \frac{1}{5}\log 6 + \frac{3}{\sqrt{5}}\tan^{-1}\sqrt{5} \quad [\because \log 1 = 0 \text{ and } \tan^{-1}(0) = 0]$$

Question 15 $\int_0^1 xe^{x^2}\, dx$

Sol. Let $I = \int_0^1 xe^{x^2}\, dx$

Put $\quad x^2 = t \Rightarrow 2x = \frac{dt}{dx} \Rightarrow dx = \frac{dt}{2x}$

For limits, when $x = 0 \Rightarrow t = 0$ and when $x = 1 \Rightarrow t = 1$

$\therefore \quad I = \int_0^1 xe^t \frac{dt}{2x} = \frac{1}{2}\int_0^1 e^t\, dt = \frac{1}{2}[e^t]_0^1 = \frac{1}{2}[e^1 - e^0] = \frac{1}{2}[e-1]$

Question 16 $\int_1^2 \frac{5x^2}{x^2+4x+3}\, dx$

Sol. Let $\quad I = \int_1^2 \frac{5x^2}{x^2+4x+3}\, dx$

Here, the degree of numerator and denominator is same, so on dividing numerator by denominator, we get

$$\frac{5x^2}{x^2+4x+3} = 5 - \frac{20x+15}{x^2+4x+3}$$

$$\therefore \quad I = \int_1^2 \left[5 - \frac{20x+15}{x^2+4x+3}\right] dx = \int_1^2 5\, dx - \int_1^2 \frac{20x+15}{(x+1)(x+3)}\, dx \quad \text{...(i)}$$

Let $\quad \frac{20x+15}{(x+1)(x+3)} = \frac{A}{(x+1)} + \frac{B}{(x+3)}$

$\Rightarrow \quad 20x + 15 = A(x+3) + B(x+1)$

$\Rightarrow \quad 20x + 15 = Ax + 3A + Bx + B = (A+B)x + (3A+B)$

On equating the coefficients of x and constant term both sides, we get

$$20 = A + B \quad \text{...(ii)}$$

and $$15 = 3A + B \quad \text{...(iii)}$$

On solving Eqs. (ii) and (iii), we get

$$A = -\frac{5}{2},\ B = \frac{45}{2}$$

$$\therefore \quad I = 5\int_1^2 1\, dx + \frac{5}{2}\int_1^2 \frac{1}{(x+1)}\, dx - \frac{45}{2}\int_1^2 \frac{1}{(x+3)}\, dx \quad \text{[from Eq. (i)]}$$

$$= \left[5x + \frac{5}{2}\log|x+1| - \frac{45}{2}\log|x+3|\right]_1^2$$

$$= \left[10 + \frac{5}{2}\log|3| - \frac{45}{2}\log|5| - 5 - \frac{5}{2}\log|2| + \frac{45}{2}\log|4|\right]$$

$$\Rightarrow \quad I = 5 + \frac{5}{2}\log\left|\frac{3}{2}\right| - \frac{45}{2}\log\left|\frac{5}{4}\right| \quad \left[\because m\log a - m\log b = m\log\left(\frac{a}{b}\right)\right]$$

Question 17 $\int_0^{\pi/4} (2\sec^2 x + x^3 + 2)\, dx$

Sol. Let $I = \int_0^{\pi/4} (2\sec^2 x + x^3 + 2)\, dx$

$$= 2\int_0^{\pi/4} \sec^2 x\, dx + \int_0^{\pi/4} x^3\, dx + 2\int_0^{\pi/4} 1\, dx$$

$$= 2[\tan x]_0^{\pi/4} + \frac{1}{4}[x^4]_0^{\pi/4} + 2[x]_0^{\pi/4}$$

$$= 2\tan\frac{\pi}{4} + \frac{1}{4}\left(\frac{\pi}{4}\right)^4 + 2\left(\frac{\pi}{4}\right) = 2 + \frac{\pi}{2} + \frac{\pi^4}{1024}$$

Question 18 $\int_0^{\pi} \left(\sin^2\frac{x}{2} - \cos^2\frac{x}{2}\right) dx$

Sol. Let $I = \int_0^{\pi} \left(\sin^2\frac{x}{2} - \cos^2\frac{x}{2}\right) dx = \int_0^{\pi} \frac{1-\cos x}{2}\, dx - \int_0^{\pi} \frac{1+\cos x}{2}\, dx$

$[\because \cos 2\theta = 2\cos^2\theta - 1 \text{ and } \cos^2 2\theta = 1 - 2\sin^2\theta]$

$$= \frac{1}{2}[x - \sin x]_0^{\pi} - \frac{1}{2}[x + \sin x]_0^{\pi} = \frac{1}{2}[\pi - \sin\pi - (0 - \sin\pi)]$$

$$- \frac{1}{2}[\pi + \sin\pi - (0 + \sin\pi)]$$

$$= \frac{1}{2}[\pi - 0] - \frac{1}{2}[\pi + 0] = \frac{\pi}{2} - \frac{\pi}{2} = 0$$

Quick Solution

Let $I = \int_0^{\pi} \left(\sin^2\frac{x}{2} - \cos^2\frac{x}{2}\right) dx = -\int_0^{\pi} \left(\cos^2\frac{x}{2} - \sin^2\frac{x}{2}\right) dx$

$= -\int_0^{\pi} \cos x\, dx$ $\quad [\because \cos 2x = \cos^2 x - \sin^2 x]$

$= -[\sin x]_0^{\pi} = -[\sin\pi - \sin 0] = 0$

Question 19 $\int_0^2 \frac{6x+3}{x^2+4}\, dx$

Sol. Let $I = \int_0^2 \frac{6x+3}{x^2+4}\, dx = \int_0^2 \frac{6x}{x^2+4}\, dx + \int_0^2 \frac{3}{x^2+4}\, dx$

Put $x^2 + 4 = t$

$\Rightarrow \quad 2x = \frac{dt}{dx} \Rightarrow dx = \frac{dt}{2x}$

For limits, when $x = 0$, $t = 0 + 4 = 4$

and when $x = 2$, $t = 4 + 4 = 8$

$\therefore \quad I = \int_4^8 \frac{6x}{t}\frac{dt}{2x} + \int_0^2 \frac{3}{x^2+4}\, dx = 3\int_4^8 \frac{1}{t}\, dt + 3\int_0^2 \frac{1}{x^2+2^2}\, dx$

$= 3[\log t]_4^8 + \frac{3}{2}\left[\tan^{-1}\frac{x}{2}\right]_0^2$ $\quad \left[\because \int \frac{dx}{a^2+x^2} = \frac{1}{a}\tan^{-1}\frac{x}{a} + C\right]$

$$= 3[\log(8) - \log(4)] + \frac{3}{2}\left[\tan^{-1}\frac{2}{2} - \tan^{-1}0\right]$$

$$= 3\log\left(\frac{8}{4}\right) + \frac{3}{2} \times \frac{\pi}{4} \qquad \left[\because \log b - \log a = \log\frac{b}{a}\right]$$

$$= 3\log 2 + \frac{3\pi}{8}$$

Question 20 $\int_0^1 \left(xe^x + \sin\frac{\pi \cdot x}{4}\right) dx$

◎ *Thinking Process* First integral solved by using the integration by parts and for second $\left(\int \sin ax\, dx = -\frac{\cos ax}{a}\right)$

Sol. Let $I = \int_0^1 \left(xe^x + \sin\frac{\pi \cdot x}{4}\right) dx = \int_0^1 xe^x\, dx + \int_0^1 \sin\left(\frac{\pi \cdot x}{4}\right) dx$

$$= [xe^x]_0^1 - \int_0^1 1 \cdot e^x\, dx + \left[\frac{-\cos\frac{\pi \cdot x}{4}}{\frac{\pi}{4}}\right]_0^1$$

$$= [xe^x - e^x]_0^1 - \frac{4}{\pi}\left[\cos\left(\frac{\pi \cdot x}{4}\right)\right]_0^1 = (e - e) - (0 - e^0) - \frac{4}{\pi}\left(\cos\frac{\pi}{4} - \cos 0\right)$$

$$= 0 - (-1) - \frac{4}{\pi}\left(\frac{1}{\sqrt{2}} - 1\right) = 1 - \frac{4}{\pi}\left(\frac{1-\sqrt{2}}{\sqrt{2}}\right) \times \frac{\sqrt{2}}{\sqrt{2}}$$

$$= 1 + \frac{2}{\pi}(2 - \sqrt{2}) = 1 + \frac{4}{\pi} - \frac{2\sqrt{2}}{\pi}.$$

Direction (Q. No. 21 and 22) Choose the correct answer.

Question 21 $\int_1^{\sqrt{3}} \frac{1}{1+x^2}\, dx$ equals

(a) $\frac{\pi}{3}$ (b) $\frac{2\pi}{3}$

(c) $\frac{\pi}{6}$ (d) $\frac{\pi}{12}$

Sol. (d) Let $I = \int_1^{\sqrt{3}} \frac{1}{1+x^2}\, dx = [\tan^{-1} x]_1^{\sqrt{3}}$

$$= \tan^{-1}\sqrt{3} - \tan^{-1} 1 \qquad \left(\because \int \frac{dx}{1+x^2} = \tan^{-1} x + C\right)$$

$$= \frac{\pi}{3} - \frac{\pi}{4} = \frac{4\pi - 3\pi}{12} = \frac{\pi}{12}.$$

Question 22 $\int_0^{2/3} \frac{1}{4+9x^2}\,dx$ equals

(a) $\frac{\pi}{6}$ (b) $\frac{\pi}{12}$

(c) $\frac{\pi}{24}$ (d) $\frac{\pi}{4}$

Sol. (c) Let $I = \int_0^{2/3} \frac{1}{4+9x^2}\,dx = \frac{1}{9}\int_0^{2/3} \frac{1}{\frac{4}{9}+x^2}\,dx = \frac{1}{9}\int_0^{2/3} \frac{1}{\left(\frac{2}{3}\right)^2+x^2}\,dx$

$$= \frac{1}{9}\cdot\frac{1}{2/3}\left[\tan^{-1}\left(\frac{x}{2/3}\right)\right]_0^{2/3} \quad \left[\because \int \frac{dx}{a^2+x^2} = \frac{1}{a}\tan^{-1}\frac{x}{a} + C\right]$$

$$= \frac{1}{6}\left[\tan^{-1}\left(\frac{3x}{2}\right)\right]_0^{2/3}$$

$$= \frac{1}{6}\left[\tan^{-1}\left(\frac{3}{2}\cdot\frac{2}{3}\right) - \tan^{-1}0\right] = \frac{1}{6}(\tan^{-1}1 - 0) = \frac{1}{6}\cdot\frac{\pi}{4} = \frac{\pi}{24}$$

Exercise 7.9

Direction (Q. No. 1 to 8) Evaluate the integrals using substitution.

Question 1 $\int_0^1 \frac{x}{x^2+1}\,dx$

Sol. Let $I = \int_0^1 \frac{x}{x^2+1}\,dx$

Put $x^2 + 1 = t \Rightarrow 2x = \frac{dt}{dx} \Rightarrow dx = \frac{dt}{2x}$

For limits when $x = 0 \Rightarrow t = 1$ and

when $x = 1 \Rightarrow t = 2$ $[\because t = x^2 + 1]$

$\therefore$ $I = \int_1^2 \frac{x}{t}\frac{dt}{2x} = \frac{1}{2}\int_1^2 \frac{1}{t}\,dt = \frac{1}{2}[\log|t|]_1^2 = \frac{1}{2}[\log|2| - \log|1|] = \frac{1}{2}\log 2$

$[\because \log 1 = 0]$

Mistake Alert Do not forget to change the limits of integration when substituting variable.

Question 2 $\int_0^{\pi/2} \sqrt{\sin\phi}\cos^5\phi\,d\phi$

Sol. Let $I = \int_0^{\pi/2} \sqrt{\sin\phi}\cos^5\phi\,d\phi = \int_0^{\pi/2} \sqrt{\sin\phi}\,(1-\sin^2\phi)^2\cos\phi\,d\phi$

$(\because \cos^2\theta + \sin^2\theta = 1)$

Put $\sin\phi = t \Rightarrow \cos\phi = \frac{dt}{d\phi} \Rightarrow \cos\phi\, d\phi = dt$

For limits, when $\phi = 0 \Rightarrow t = 0$ and when $\phi = \frac{\pi}{2} \Rightarrow t = 1$

$$\therefore \quad I = \int_0^1 \sqrt{t}(1-t^2)^2\,dt = \int_0^1 \sqrt{t}(t^4 + 1 - 2t^2)\,dt$$

$$= \int_0^1 (t^{9/2} + t^{1/2} - 2t^{5/2})\,dt$$

$$= \left[\frac{t^{\frac{9}{2}+1}}{\left(\frac{9}{2}+1\right)} + \frac{t^{\frac{1}{2}+1}}{\frac{1}{2}+1} - 2\left(\frac{t^{\frac{5}{2}+1}}{\frac{5}{2}+1}\right)\right]_0^1$$

$$= \left[\frac{2}{11}t^{\frac{11}{2}} + \frac{2}{3}t^{\frac{3}{2}} - \frac{4}{7}t^{\frac{7}{2}}\right]_0^1$$

$$= \left[\frac{2}{11} + \frac{2}{3} - \frac{4}{7}\right] - 0$$

$$= \frac{42 + 154 - 132}{11 \times 3 \times 7} = \frac{64}{231}$$

Question 3 $\int_0^1 \sin^{-1}\left(\frac{2x}{1+x^2}\right)dx$

◎ *Thinking Process* In angle of $\sin^{-1}$, we put $x = \tan\theta$ and use the identity $\sin^{-1}(\sin\theta) = \theta$ and change the limit also by using it and then integrate under proper limits.

Sol. Let $I = \int_0^1 \sin^{-1}\left(\frac{2x}{1+x^2}\right)dx$

Put $\tan\theta = x$

$\Rightarrow \sec^2\theta\, d\theta = dx$

For limits when $x = 0 \Rightarrow \theta = 0$ and when $x = 1 \Rightarrow \theta = \frac{\pi}{4}$ $(\because \theta = \tan^{-1}x)$

$$\therefore \quad I = \int_0^{\pi/4} \sin^{-1}\left(\frac{2\tan\theta}{1+\tan^2\theta}\right)\sec^2\theta\, d\theta$$

$$= \int_0^{\pi/4} \sin^{-1}(\sin 2\theta)\sec^2\theta\, d\theta \qquad \left(\because \sin 2\theta = \frac{2\tan\theta}{1+\tan^2\theta}\right)$$

$$= 2\int_0^{\pi/4} \underset{\text{I}}{\theta} \quad \underset{\text{II}}{{}^2\theta}\, d\theta$$

Now, applying rule of integration by parts taking θ as the first function and $\sec^2\theta$ as second function, we get

$$I = 2\left[\theta\int_0^{\pi/4}\sec^2\theta\,d\theta - \int_0^{\pi/4}\left\{\left(\frac{d}{d\theta}\theta\right)\int\sec^2\theta\,d\theta\right\}\right]$$

$$= 2[\theta\tan\theta]_0^{\pi/4} - 2\int_0^{\pi/4} 1\cdot\tan\theta\,d\theta] \qquad [\because \int\sec^2\theta\,d\theta = \tan\theta]$$

$$= 2[\theta\tan\theta + \log|\cos\theta|]_0^{\pi/4} \qquad [\because \int\tan\theta\,d\theta = -\log\cos\theta]$$

$$= 2\left\{\left(\frac{\pi}{4}\tan\frac{\pi}{4} + \log\left|\cos\frac{\pi}{4}\right|\right) - (0 + \log|\cos 0|)\right\}$$

$$= \frac{\pi}{2} + 2\log\frac{1}{\sqrt{2}} - 0 \qquad [\because \log 1 = 0]$$

$$= \frac{\pi}{2} + 2\log 2^{-1/2} = \frac{\pi}{2} - 2\times\frac{1}{2}\log 2 \qquad [\because \log m^n = n\log m]$$

$$= \frac{\pi}{2} - \log 2$$

Question 4 $\int_0^2 x\sqrt{x+2}\,dx$

Sol. Let $I = \int_0^2 x\sqrt{x+2}\,dx = \int_0^2 \{(x+2)-2\}\sqrt{x+2}\,dx$ [add and subtract 2]

$$= \int_0^2 \{(x+2)^{3/2} - 2(x+2)^{1/2}\}\,dx$$

$$= \left[\frac{(x+2)^{(3/2+1)}}{(3/2)+1} - \frac{2(x+2)^{1/2+1}}{(1/2)+1}\right]_0^2$$

$$= \frac{2}{5}[(x+2)^{5/2}]_0^2 - \frac{4}{3}[(x+2)^{3/2}]_0^2$$

$$= \frac{2}{5}[4^{5/2} - 2^{5/2}] - \frac{4}{3}[4^{3/2} - 2^{3/2}]$$

$$= \frac{2}{5}[2^5 - (\sqrt{2})^5] - \frac{4}{3}[2^3 - (\sqrt{2})^3]$$

$$= \frac{2}{5}[32 - 4\sqrt{2}] - \frac{4}{3}[8 - 2\sqrt{2}]$$

$$= \frac{8}{5}[8 - \sqrt{2}] - \frac{8}{3}[4 - \sqrt{2}]$$

$$= \left(\frac{64}{5} - \frac{32}{3}\right) + \left(\frac{8\sqrt{2}}{3} - \frac{8\sqrt{2}}{5}\right)$$

$$= \frac{32}{15} + \frac{16\sqrt{2}}{15} = \frac{16}{15}(2+\sqrt{2})$$

Quick Solution

Let $\quad I = \int_0^2 x\sqrt{x+2}\, dx$

Put $\quad x + 2 = t \Rightarrow dx = dt$

For limits, when $x = 0 \Rightarrow t = 2$ and when $x = 2 \Rightarrow t = 4$

$$\therefore \quad I = \int_2^4 (t-2)\sqrt{t}dt = \int_2^4 t^{3/2}dt - 2\int_2^4 t^{1/2}dt$$

$$= \frac{2}{5}[t^{5/2}]_2^4 - 2\times\frac{2}{3}[t^{3/2}]_2^4 = \frac{2}{5}[(4)^{5/2} - (2)^{5/2}] - \frac{4}{3}[(4)^{3/2} - (2)^{3/2}]$$

$$= \frac{2}{5}[2^5 - (\sqrt{2})^5] - \frac{4}{3}[2^3 - (\sqrt{2})^3] = \frac{2}{5}[32 - 4\sqrt{2}] - \frac{4}{3}[8 - 2\sqrt{2}]$$

$$= \frac{8}{5}[8 - \sqrt{2}] - \frac{8}{3}[4 - \sqrt{2}]$$

$$= \frac{32}{15} + 16\frac{\sqrt{2}}{5} = \frac{16}{15}(2 + \sqrt{2})$$

Question 5 $\int_0^{\pi/2} \frac{\sin x}{1 + \cos^2 x} dx.$

◎ **Thinking Process** Here, we put $\cos x = t$ for converting given integrand into standard form $\frac{1}{a^2 + x^2}$, also change the limit by using it and then integrate under the limits.

Sol. Let $I = \int_0^{\pi/2} \frac{\sin x}{1 + \cos^2 x} dx$

Put $\quad \cos x = t \Rightarrow -\sin x\, dx = dt \Rightarrow dx = \frac{dt}{-\sin x}$

For limits, when $x = 0 \Rightarrow t = \cos 0 = 1$ $\quad (\because t = \cos x)$

and when $x = \frac{\pi}{2} \Rightarrow t = \cos\frac{\pi}{2} = 0$

$$\therefore \quad I = \int_1^0 \frac{\sin x}{1 + t^2} \frac{dt}{(-\sin x)} dx = -\int_1^0 \frac{1}{1 + t^2} dt$$

$$= -\left[\frac{1}{1}\tan^{-1}\left(\frac{t}{1}\right)\right]_1^0$$

$$= -[\tan^{-1} t]_1^0 \quad \left(\because \int \frac{1}{a^2 + x^2} dx = \frac{1}{a}\tan^{-1}\frac{x}{a} + C\right)$$

$$= -[\tan^{-1}(0) - \tan^{-1}(1)]$$

$$= -\left(0 - \frac{\pi}{4}\right) = \frac{\pi}{4}$$

Question 6 $\int_0^2 \frac{1}{x+4-x^2}\,dx$

◎ *Thinking Process* Here, the given integrand connot integrate directly, so we convert the denominator in the standard form $\frac{1}{a^2 \pm x^2}$ and integrate under given limits.

Sol. Let $I = \int_0^2 \frac{1}{x+4-x^2}\,dx = \int_0^2 \frac{1}{x+4-x^2-\left(\frac{1}{2}\right)^2+\left(\frac{1}{2}\right)^2}\,dx$

$$= \int_0^2 \frac{1}{4+\frac{1}{4}-\left[\left(x^2-x+\frac{1}{4}\right)\right]}\,dx$$

$$= \int_0^2 \frac{1}{\frac{17}{4}-\left(x-\frac{1}{2}\right)^2}\,dx = \int_0^2 \frac{1}{\left(\frac{\sqrt{17}}{2}\right)^2-\left(x-\frac{1}{2}\right)^2}\,dx$$

$$= \frac{1}{2\cdot\frac{\sqrt{17}}{2}}\left[\log\left|\frac{\frac{\sqrt{17}}{2}+x-\frac{1}{2}}{\frac{\sqrt{17}}{2}-x+\frac{1}{2}}\right|\right]_0^2 \qquad \left(\because \int \frac{dx}{a^2-x^2} = \frac{1}{2a}\log\left|\frac{a+x}{a-x}\right|\right)$$

$$= \frac{1}{\sqrt{17}}\left[\log\left|\frac{\sqrt{17}+2x-1}{\sqrt{17}-2x+1}\right|\right]_0^2$$

$$= \frac{1}{\sqrt{17}}\left[\log\left|\frac{\sqrt{17}+3}{\sqrt{17}-3}\right| - \log\left|\frac{\sqrt{17}-1}{\sqrt{17}+1}\right|\right]$$

$$= \frac{1}{\sqrt{17}}\log\left|\frac{(\sqrt{17}+3)}{(\sqrt{17}-3)} \div \frac{(\sqrt{17}-1)}{(\sqrt{17}+1)}\right| \qquad \left(\because \log m - \log n = \log\frac{m}{n}\right)$$

$$= \frac{1}{\sqrt{17}}\log\left|\frac{(\sqrt{17}+3)(\sqrt{17}+1)}{(\sqrt{17}-3)(\sqrt{17}-1)}\right|$$

$$= \frac{1}{\sqrt{17}}\log\left|\frac{20+4\sqrt{17}}{20-4\sqrt{17}}\right| = \frac{1}{\sqrt{17}}\log\left|\frac{5+\sqrt{17}}{5-\sqrt{17}}\right|$$

To remove square root term from denominator, we multiply by its conjugate *i.e.*, $5+\sqrt{17}$ in both numerator and denominator.

$$= \frac{1}{\sqrt{17}}\log\left|\frac{(5+\sqrt{17})^2}{(5)^2-(\sqrt{17})^2}\right| \qquad [\because (a-b)(a+b) = a^2-b^2]$$

$$= \frac{1}{\sqrt{17}}\log\left|\frac{25+17+10\sqrt{17}}{25-17}\right|$$

$$= \frac{1}{\sqrt{17}}\log\left|\frac{42+10\sqrt{17}}{8}\right| = \frac{1}{\sqrt{17}}\log\left|\frac{21+5\sqrt{17}}{4}\right|$$

Question 7 $\int_{-1}^{1} \frac{1}{x^2+2x+5} dx$

Sol. Let $I = \int_{-1}^{1} \frac{1}{x^2+2x+5} dx = \int_{-1}^{1} \frac{1}{(x^2+2x+1)+4} dx$

$$= \int_{-1}^{1} \frac{1}{(x+1)^2+2^2} dx = \frac{1}{2}\left[\tan^{-1}\left(\frac{x+1}{2}\right)\right]_{-1}^{1} \quad \left[\because \int \frac{dx}{a^2+x^2} = \frac{1}{a}\tan^{-1}\frac{x}{a} + C\right]$$

$$= \frac{1}{2}\left[\tan^{-1}\left(\frac{2}{2}\right) - \tan^{-1}\left(\frac{0}{2}\right)\right] = \frac{1}{2}[\tan^{-1} 1] = \frac{1}{2} \times \frac{\pi}{4} = \frac{\pi}{8}.$$

Question 8 $\int_{1}^{2}\left(\frac{1}{x} - \frac{1}{2x^2}\right)e^{2x} dx$

Sol. Let $I = \int_{1}^{2}\left(\frac{1}{x} - \frac{1}{2x^2}\right)e^{2x} dx$

Let $2x = t \Rightarrow 2 = \frac{dt}{dx} \Rightarrow dx = \frac{1}{2}dt$

For limits, when $x = 1 \Rightarrow t = 2$

and when $x = 2 \Rightarrow t = 4$

$$\therefore \quad I = \frac{1}{2}\int_{2}^{4}\left(\frac{1}{t/2} - \frac{1}{2\frac{t^2}{4}}\right)e^t dt = \frac{1}{2}\int_{2}^{4}\left(\frac{2}{t} - \frac{2}{t^2}\right)e^t dt$$

$$= \int_{2}^{4}\left(\frac{1}{t} - \frac{1}{t^2}\right)e^t dt$$

Let $f(t) = \frac{1}{t} \Rightarrow f'(t) = \frac{-1}{t^2}$

$$\therefore \quad \int_{2}^{4}\left(\frac{1}{t} - \frac{1}{t^2}\right)e^t \, dt = \left(e^t \cdot \frac{1}{t}\right)_2^4$$

$$= \left(\frac{e^4}{4} - \frac{e^2}{2}\right) = \frac{e^2}{2}\left(\frac{e^2}{2} - 1\right)$$

Quick Solution

Let $I = \int_{1}^{2}\left(\frac{1}{x} - \frac{1}{2x^2}\right)e^{2x} dx = \int_{1}^{2} \frac{1}{x}e^{2x} dx - \int_{1}^{2} \frac{1}{2x^2}e^{2x} dx$

Evaluate the first integral by rule of integration by parts taking $\frac{1}{x}$ as the first function and e^{2x} as second function, we get

$$I = \left[\frac{1}{x}\cdot\frac{e^{2x}}{2}\right]_1^2 + \int_{1}^{2} \frac{1}{x^2}\cdot\frac{e^{2x}}{2} dx - \int_{1}^{2} \frac{1}{2x^2}e^{2x} dx$$

$$= \left[\frac{1}{x}\frac{e^{2x}}{2}\right]_1^2 = \frac{e^4}{4} - \frac{e^2}{2} = \frac{e^2}{2}\left(\frac{e^2}{2} - 1\right)$$

Direction (Q. Nos. 9 and 10) Choose the correct answer.

Question 9 The value of the integral $\int_{1/3}^{1} \frac{(x - x^3)^{\frac{1}{3}}}{x^4} dx$ is

(a) 6 (b) 0 (c) 3 (d) 4

Sol. (a) Let $I = \int_{1/3}^{1} \frac{(x - x^3)^{\frac{1}{3}}}{x^4} dx = \int_{1/3}^{1} \frac{(x^3)^{1/3}\left(\frac{x}{x^3} - \frac{x^3}{x^3}\right)^{1/3}}{x^4} dx$

[Multiply and divide the numerator by $(x^3)^{1/3}$]

$$= \int_{1/3}^{1} \frac{\left(\frac{1}{x^2} - 1\right)^{1/3}}{x^3} dx$$

Put $\frac{1}{x^2} = t \Rightarrow \frac{-2}{x^3} dx = dt \Rightarrow \frac{dx}{x^3} = \frac{dt}{(-2)}$

For limits, when $x = 1 \Rightarrow t = 1$ and when $x = \frac{1}{3} \Rightarrow t = 3^2 = 9$ $\left(\because t = \frac{1}{x^2}\right)$

$$\therefore \quad I = \int_9^1 (t-1)^{1/3} \frac{dt}{(-2)} = -\frac{1}{2}\left[\frac{(t-1)^{\frac{1}{3}+1}}{\frac{1}{3}+1}\right]_9^1$$

$$= -\frac{1}{2} \times \frac{3}{4}\left[(t-1)^{\frac{4}{3}}\right]_9^1 = -\frac{3}{8}\left[(1-1)^{\frac{4}{3}} - (9-1)^{\frac{4}{3}}\right]$$

$$= -\frac{3}{8}\left[0 - (2^3)^{\frac{4}{3}}\right] = -\frac{3}{8} \times (-16) = 6$$

Question 10 If $f(x) = \int_0^x t \sin t \, dt$, then $f'(x)$ is

(a) $\cos x + x \sin x$ (b) $x \sin x$ (c) $x \cos x$ (d) $\sin x + x \cos x$

◎ ***Thinking Process*** Fistly, we integrate the given function and then differentiate it to get the result.

Sol. (b) Given, $f(x) = \int_0^x t \sin t \, dt$

On integrating by parts, we get $f(x) = t\int_0^x \sin t dt - \int_0^x \left[\left(\frac{d}{dt} t\right) \int \sin t dt\right] dt$

$$= [t(-\cos t)]_0^x - \int_0^x (-\cos t) dt = [-t \cos t + \sin t]_0^x \Rightarrow f(x) = -x\cos x + \sin x$$

Now, on differentiating both sides w.r.t. x, we get

$$f'(x) = -[\{x(-\sin x)\} + \cos x] + \cos x = x\sin x - \cos x + \cos x = x\sin x$$

$\left[\text{Using the product rule} \frac{d}{dx}(u \cdot v) = u\frac{dv}{dx} + v\frac{du}{dx}\right]$

Exercise 7.10

Direction (Q. Nos. 1 to 19) By using the properties of definite integrals, evaluate the integrals.

Question 1 $\int_0^{\pi/2} \cos^2 x \, dx$

◎ ***Thinking Process*** Here, the given integrand cannot integrate directly, so we use the property of definite integral $\int_0^a f(x)\,dx = \int_0^a f(a-x)\,dx$ to convert it and then add it into given integrand to convert in simple form and then integrate.

Sol. Let $I = \int_0^{\pi/2} \cos^2 x \, dx$ ...(i)

$$\Rightarrow \quad I = \int_0^{\pi/2} \cos^2\left(\frac{\pi}{2} - x\right) dx \qquad \left(\because \int_0^a f(x)dx = \int_0^a f(a-x)dx\right)$$

$$\Rightarrow \quad I = \int_0^{\pi/2} \sin^2 x \, dx \qquad \text{...(ii)}$$

On adding Eqs. (i) and (ii), we get

$$2I = \int_0^{\pi/2} (\sin^2 x + \cos^2 x)\, dx$$

$$= \int_0^{\pi/2} 1 \, dx \qquad [\because \sin^2 x + \cos^2 x = 1]$$

$$\Rightarrow \quad 2I = [x]_0^{\pi/2} = \frac{\pi}{2} - 0 \Rightarrow I = \frac{\pi}{4}$$

Question 2 $\int_0^{\pi/2} \frac{\sqrt{\sin x}}{\sqrt{\sin x} + \sqrt{\cos x}} dx$

◎ ***Thinking Process*** Firstly, reduce the integrand into simplest form by using the property $\int_0^a f(x)\,dx = \int_0^a f(a-x)\,dx$, add them and integrate.

Sol. Let $I = \int_0^{\pi/2} \frac{\sqrt{\sin x}}{\sqrt{\sin x} + \sqrt{\cos x}} dx$ ...(i)

Then,

$$I = \int_0^{\pi/2} \frac{\sqrt{\sin\left(\frac{\pi}{2} - x\right)}}{\sqrt{\sin\left(\frac{\pi}{2} - x\right)} + \sqrt{\cos\left(\frac{\pi}{2} - x\right)}} dx$$

$$\left(\because \int_0^a f(x)\,dx = \int_0^a f(a-x)\,dx\right)$$

$$\Rightarrow \quad I = \int_0^{\pi/2} \frac{\sqrt{\cos x}}{\sqrt{\cos x} + \sqrt{\sin x}} dx \qquad \text{...(ii)}$$

$$\left[\because \sin\left(\frac{\pi}{2} - x\right) = \cos x \text{ and } \cos\left(\frac{\pi}{2} - x\right) = \sin x\right]$$

On adding Eqs. (i) and (ii), we get

$$2I = \int_0^{\pi/2} \frac{\sqrt{\sin x} + \sqrt{\cos x}}{\sqrt{\sin x} + \sqrt{\cos x}} dx$$

$$= \int_0^{\pi/2} 1\, dx = [x]_0^{\pi/2} = \frac{\pi}{2} - 0$$

$$\Rightarrow \qquad I = \frac{\pi}{4}$$

Question 3 $\displaystyle\int_0^{\pi/2} \frac{\sin^{\frac{3}{2}} x}{\sin^{\frac{3}{2}} x + \cos^{\frac{3}{2}} x} dx$

Sol. Let $\displaystyle I = \int_0^{\pi/2} \frac{\sin^{\frac{3}{2}} x}{\sin^{\frac{3}{2}} x + \cos^{\frac{3}{2}} x} dx$ ...(i)

$$\Rightarrow \quad I = \int_0^{\pi/2} \frac{\sin^{\frac{3}{2}}\left(\frac{\pi}{2} - x\right)}{\sin^{\frac{3}{2}}\left(\frac{\pi}{2} - x\right) + \cos^{\frac{3}{2}}\left(\frac{\pi}{2} - x\right)} dx \quad \left(\because \int_0^a f(x)dx = \int_0^a f(a-x)\,dx\right)$$

$$= \int_0^{\pi/2} \frac{\cos^{\frac{3}{2}} x}{\cos^{\frac{3}{2}} x + \sin^{\frac{3}{2}} x} dx \qquad \text{...(ii)}$$

$\left[\because \sin\left(\frac{\pi}{2} - x\right) = \cos x \text{ and } \cos\left(\frac{\pi}{2} - x\right) = \sin x\right]$

On adding Eqs. (i) and (ii), we get

$$2I = \int_0^{\pi/2} \frac{\sin^{\frac{3}{2}} + \cos^{\frac{3}{2}} x}{\sin^{\frac{3}{2}} x + \cos^{\frac{3}{2}} x} dx = \int_0^{\pi/2} 1\, dx = [x]_0^{\pi/2} = \frac{\pi}{2} - 0 \quad \Rightarrow \quad I = \frac{\pi}{4}$$

Question 4 $\displaystyle\int_0^{\pi/2} \frac{\cos^5 x}{\sin^5 x + \cos^5 x} dx$

Sol. Let $\displaystyle I = \int_0^{\pi/2} \frac{\cos^5 x}{\sin^5 x + \cos^5 x} dx$ ...(i)

$$\Rightarrow \quad I = \int_0^{\pi/2} \frac{\cos^5\left(\frac{\pi}{2} - x\right)}{\sin^5\left(\frac{\pi}{2} - x\right) + \cos^5\left(\frac{\pi}{2} - x\right)} dx \quad \left[\because \int_0^a f(x)\,dx = \int_0^a f(a-x)dx\right]$$

$$= \int_0^{\pi/2} \frac{\sin^5 x}{\cos^5 x + \sin^5 x} dx \qquad \text{...(ii)}$$

On adding Eqs. (i) and (ii), we get

$$2I = \int_0^{\pi/2} \frac{\cos^5 x + \sin^5 x}{\cos^5 x + \sin^5 x} dx$$

$$= \int_0^{\pi/2} 1\, dx = [x]_0^{\pi/2} = \frac{\pi}{2} - 0 \Rightarrow I = \frac{\pi}{4}$$

Question 5 $\int_{-5}^{5} |x+2| dx$

◎ *Thinking Process* Here, the given integrand is in the form of absolute function and we define the absolute function as $|x| = x, x \geq 0$ or $|x| = -x, x < 0$. Using it, we convert the given integrand in simple form and then integrate it.

Sol. Let $I = \int_{-5}^{5} |x + 2| dx$

It can be seen that $(x + 2) < 0$ on $[-5, -2)$ and $(x + 2) \geq 0$ on $[-2, 5]$.

$\therefore \quad I = \int_{-5}^{-2} -(x + 2) dx + \int_{-2}^{5} (x + 2) dx \quad \left[\because \int_a^b f(x) dx = \int_a^c f(x) dx + \int_c^b f(x) dx\right]$

$$\Rightarrow \quad I = -\left[\frac{x^2}{2} + 2x\right]_{-5}^{-2} + \left[\frac{x^2}{2} + 2x\right]_{-2}^{5}$$

$$= -\left[\frac{(-2)^2}{2} + 2(-2) - \frac{(-5)^2}{2} - 2(-5)\right] + \left[\frac{(5)^2}{2} + 2(5) - \frac{(-2)^2}{2} - 2(-2)\right]$$

$$= -\left[2 - 4 - \frac{25}{2} + 10\right] + \left[\frac{25}{2} + 10 - 2 + 4\right]$$

$$= -2 + 4 + \frac{25}{2} - 10 + \frac{25}{2} + 10 - 2 + 4 = 29$$

Question 6 $\int_{2}^{8} |x-5| dx$

Sol. Let $I = \int_2^8 |x - 5| dx$

It can be seen that $(x - 5) < 0$ on $[2, 5)$ and $(x - 5) \geq 0$ on $[5, 8]$.

$$\therefore \quad I = \int_2^5 \{-(x - 5)\} dx + \int_5^8 (x - 5) dx$$

$$\left[\because \int_a^b f(x)dx = \int_a^c f(x)dx + \int_c^b f(x)dx\right]$$

$$= \left[5x - \frac{x^2}{2}\right]_2^5 + \left[\frac{x^2}{2} - 5x\right]_5^8$$

$$= \left(25 - \frac{25}{2}\right) - \left(10 - \frac{4}{2}\right) + \left(\frac{64}{2} - 40\right) - \left(\frac{25}{2} - 25\right)$$

$$= \frac{25}{2} - 8 - 8 + \frac{25}{2} = 25 - 16 = 9$$

Question 7 $\int_0^1 x(1-x)^n\,dx$

◎ *Thinking Process* Here, we can use the property $\int_0^a f(x)\,dx = \int_0^a f(a-x)\,dx$ and splitting the integrand into two integrals which are easy to integrate.

Sol. Let $I = \int_0^1 x(1-x)^n\,dx$

$$\Rightarrow \quad I = \int_0^1 (1-x)\{1-(1-x)\}^n\,dx \quad \left[\because \int_0^a f(x)dx = \int_0^a f(a-x)dx\right]$$

$$= \int_0^1 (1-x)x^n\,dx = \int_0^1 (x^n - x^{n+1})dx$$

$$= \left[\frac{x^{n+1}}{n+1} - \frac{x^{n+2}}{n+2}\right]_0^1 = \left[\frac{1}{n+1} - \frac{1}{n+2}\right] - 0$$

$$= \frac{(n+2)-(n+1)}{(n+1)(n+2)} = \frac{1}{(n+1)(n+2)}$$

Question 8 $\int_0^{\pi/4} \log(1+\tan x)\,dx$

Sol. Let $I = \int_0^{\pi/4} \log(1+\tan x)\,dx \quad \ldots\text{(i)}$

$$\Rightarrow \quad I = \int_0^{\pi/4} \log\left[1+\tan\left(\frac{\pi}{4}-x\right)\right]dx \quad \left[\because \int_0^a f(x)dx = \int_0^a f(a-x)dx\right]$$

$$= \int_0^{\pi/4} \log\left(1+\frac{1-\tan x}{1+\tan x}\right)dx \quad \left[\because \tan(A-B) = \frac{\tan A - \tan B}{1+\tan A\tan B}\right]$$

$$= \int_0^{\pi/4} \log\left(\frac{2}{1+\tan x}\right)dx = \int_0^{\pi/4} \{\log 2 - \log(1+\tan x)\}\,dx \quad \ldots\text{(ii)}$$

$$\left[\because \log\left(\frac{m}{n}\right) = \log m - \log n\right]$$

On adding Eqs. (i) and (ii), we get

$$2I = \int_0^{\pi/4} \log 2\,dx$$

$$= \log 2\int_0^{\pi/4} 1\,dx = \log 2\,[x]_0^{\pi/4}$$

$$= (\log 2)\left(\frac{\pi}{4} - 0\right)$$

$$\Rightarrow \quad 2I = \frac{\pi}{4}\log 2$$

$$\Rightarrow \quad I = \frac{\pi}{8}\log 2$$

Question 9 $\int_0^2 x\sqrt{2-x}\,dx$

Sol. Let $$I = \int_0^2 x\sqrt{2-x}\,dx \quad \ldots(i)$$

Also, $$I = \int_0^2 (2-x)\sqrt{2-(2-x)}\,dx \quad \left[\because \int_0^a f(x)\,dx = \int_0^a f(a-x)dx\right]$$

$$= \int_0^2 (2-x)\sqrt{x}\,dx = \int_0^2 (2x^{1/2} - x^{3/2})\,dx$$

$$= \left[\frac{2x^{(1/2)+1}}{(1/2)+1} - \frac{x^{(3/2)+1}}{(3/2)+1}\right]_0^2 = \left[\frac{4}{3}x^{3/2} - \frac{2}{5}x^{5/2}\right]_0^2$$

$$= \frac{4}{3}\cdot 2^{3/2} - \frac{2}{5}\cdot 2^{5/2} - 0 = \frac{4}{3}2\sqrt{2} - \frac{2}{5}4\sqrt{2}$$

$$= \left(\frac{8}{3} - \frac{8}{5}\right)\sqrt{2} = \left(\frac{40-24}{15}\right)\sqrt{2} = \frac{16\sqrt{2}}{15}$$

Question 10 $\int_0^{\pi/2} (2\log\sin x - \log\sin 2x)\,dx$

Sol. Let $$I = \int_0^{\pi/2} (2\log\sin x - \log\sin 2x)\,dx$$

$$= \int_0^{\pi/2} (\log\sin^2 x - \log\sin 2x)\,dx \quad [\because m\log n = \log n^m]$$

$$= \int_0^{\pi/2} \log\left(\frac{\sin^2 x}{\sin 2x}\right)dx \quad \left[\because \log m - \log n = \log\frac{m}{n}\right]$$

$$= \int_0^{\pi/2} \log\left(\frac{\sin^2 x}{2\sin x\cos x}\right)dx \quad [\because \sin 2x = 2\sin x\cos x]$$

$$= \int_0^{\pi/2} \log\left(\frac{\tan x}{2}\right)dx = \int_0^{\pi/2} [\log(\tan x) - \log 2]dx$$

$$= \int_0^{\pi/2} \log(\tan x)\,dx - \int_0^{\pi/2} \log 2\,dx$$

Let $$I_1 = \int_0^{\pi/2} \log(\tan x)\,dx$$

$\therefore$ $$I = I_1 - (\log 2)\,[x]_0^{\pi/2} = I_1 - \left(\frac{\pi}{2} - 0\right)\log 2 \quad \ldots(i)$$

Now, $$I_1 = \int_0^{\pi/2} \log(\tan x)\,dx \quad \ldots(ii)$$

$\Rightarrow$ $$I_1 = \int_0^{\pi/2} \log\left(\tan\left(\frac{\pi}{2} - x\right)\right)dx \quad \left[\because \int_0^a f(x)dx = \int_0^a f(a-x)\right]dx$$

$\Rightarrow$ $$I_1 = \int_0^{\pi/2} \log(\cot x)\,dx \quad \ldots(iii)$$

On adding Eqs. (ii) and (iii), we get

$$2I_1 = \int_0^{\pi/2} (\log(\tan x) + \log(\cot x))\,dx$$

$$= \int_0^{\pi/2} \log(\tan x\cot x)\,dx \quad [\because \log m + \log n = \log(mn)]$$

$$= \int_0^{\pi/2} \log 1\,dx = 0 \Rightarrow I_1 = 0 \quad \left(\because \tan x = \frac{1}{\cot x}\right)$$

On putting the value of I_1 in Eq. (i), we get $I = 0 - \frac{\pi}{2}\log 2 = -\frac{\pi}{2}\log 2$

Question 11 Let $\int_{-\pi/2}^{\pi/2} \sin^2 x\, dx$

◎ *Thinking Process* Firstly, check the integrand function whether it is odd or even. If it is odd, then integral value is zero otherwise simplify $2\int_0^a f(x)\,dx$.

Sol. Let $I = \int_{-\pi/2}^{\pi/2} \sin^2 x\, dx$

Here, $f(x) = \sin^2 x$

$\Rightarrow \quad f(-x) = \sin^2(-x) = [\sin(-x)]^2 = (-\sin x)^2 = \sin^2 x = f(x)$

$\therefore$ $f(x)$ is an even function.

$$\therefore \quad I = \int_{-\pi/2}^{\pi/2} \sin^2 x\, dx = 2\int_0^{\pi/2} \sin^2 x\, dx$$

$$\left[\because \int_{-a}^{a} f(x)dx = 2\int_0^a f(x)dx, \text{ if } f(x) \text{ is an even function}\right]$$

$$= 2\int_0^{\pi/2} \left[\frac{1-\cos 2x}{2}\right]dx \qquad [\because \cos 2\theta = 1 - 2\sin^2\theta]$$

$$= \int_0^{\pi/2} (1-\cos 2x)\,dx = \left[x - \frac{\sin 2x}{2}\right]_0^{\pi/2}$$

$$= \left[\frac{\pi}{2} - \frac{\sin \pi}{2}\right] - (0-0) = \frac{\pi}{2} - 0 = \frac{\pi}{2}$$

Quick Solution

Let $I = \int_{-\pi/2}^{\pi/2} \sin^2 x dx$

Let $f(x) = \sin^2 x$

$\Rightarrow \quad f(-x) = [\sin(-x)]^2 = [-\sin x)^2 = \sin^2 x = f(x)$

$\therefore$ $f(x)$ is an even function

$$\therefore \quad I = 2\int_0^{\pi/2} \sin^2 x dx \qquad \ldots(i)$$

$$\therefore \quad I = 2\int_0^{\pi/2} \sin^2\left(\frac{\pi}{2} - x\right) \qquad \left(\because \int_0^a f(x)\,dx = \int_0^a f(a-x)\,dx\right)$$

$$= 2\int_0^{\pi/2} \cos x dx \qquad \ldots(ii)$$

On adding Eqs. (i) and (ii), we get

$$2I = 2\int_0^{\pi/2} (\sin^2 x + \cos^2 x)\,dx$$

$$= 2\int_0^{\pi/2} 1 \cdot dx = 2[x]_0^{\frac{\pi}{2}} = 2.\frac{\pi}{2}$$

$$\Rightarrow \quad I = \frac{\pi}{2}$$

Question 12 $\int_0^{\pi} \frac{x}{1+\sin x}\, dx$

Sol. Let $I = \int_0^{\pi} \frac{x}{1+\sin x}\, dx$ ...(i)

Then, $I = \int_0^{\pi} \frac{\pi - x}{1+\sin(\pi - x)}\, dx$ $\left[\because \int_0^a f(x)dx = \int_0^a f(a-x)dx\right]$

$\Rightarrow$ $I = \int_0^{\pi} \frac{\pi - x}{1+\sin x}\, dx$ ...(ii)

$[\because \sin(\pi - \theta) = \sin\theta]$

On adding Eqs. (i) and (ii), we get

$$2I = \int_0^{\pi} \frac{\pi}{(1+\sin x)}\, dx = \pi\int_0^{\pi} \frac{1}{(1+\sin x)}\, dx = \pi\int_0^{\pi} \frac{1-\sin x}{(1+\sin x)(1-\sin x)}\, dx$$

[multiply numerator and denominator by $(1-\sin x)$]

$\Rightarrow$ $2I = \pi\int_0^{\pi} \frac{1-\sin x}{1-\sin^2 x}\, dx = \pi\int_0^{\pi} \frac{1}{\cos^2 x}\, dx - \pi\int_0^{\pi} \frac{\sin x}{\cos^2 x}\, dx$

$[\because \sin^2\theta + \cos^2\theta = 1]$

$\Rightarrow$ $2I = \pi\int_0^{\pi} \sec^2 x\, dx - \pi\int_0^{\pi} \sec x \cdot \tan x\, dx$

$\Rightarrow$ $2I = \pi[\tan x - \sec x]_0^{\pi}$

$\Rightarrow$ $2I = \pi[\tan\pi - \sec\pi - (\tan 0 - \sec 0)]$

$\Rightarrow$ $2I = \pi[0 + 1 - 0 + 1]$

$\Rightarrow$ $2I = 2\pi \Rightarrow I = \pi$

Question 13 $\int_{-\pi/2}^{\pi/2} \sin^7 x\, dx$

Sol. Let $I = \int_{-\pi/2}^{\pi/2} \sin^7 x\, dx$

Let $f(x) = \sin^7 x$

$\Rightarrow$ $f(-x) = \sin^7(-x)$

$= [-\sin x]^7 = -\sin^7 x$

$\therefore$ $f(-x) = -f(x)$

So, $f(x)$ is an odd function.

$\therefore$ $I = \int_{-\pi/2}^{\pi/2} \sin^7 x\, dx = 0$ $[\because \int_{-a}^{a} f(x)dx = 0$, if $f(x)$ is an odd function$]$

Question 14 $\int_0^{2\pi} \cos^5 x\, dx$

Sol. Let $I = \int_0^{2\pi} \cos^5 x\, dx$

Let $f(x) = \cos^5 x$

$\therefore$ $f(2\pi - x) = [\cos(2\pi - x)]^5 = \cos^5 x = f(x)$

$\therefore \quad I = 2\int_0^{\pi} \cos^5 x dx$

$$\left(\because \int_0^{2a} f(x) = 2\int_0^a f(x) dx, \text{ if } f(2a - x) = f(x) \atop \int_0^{2a} f(x) dx = 0, \text{if } f(2a - x) = -f(x) = 2 \times 0 = 0\right)$$

Now, $f(\pi - x) = [\cos(\pi - x)]^5 = -\cos^5 x = -f(x)$

$\therefore \quad I = \int_0^{2\pi} \cos^5 x dx = 2 \times 0 = 0$

Question 15 $\int_0^{\pi/2} \dfrac{\sin x - \cos x}{1 + \sin x \cos x} dx$

Sol. Let $\quad I = \int_0^{\pi/2} \dfrac{\sin x - \cos x}{1 + \sin x \cos x} dx \quad$ ...(i)

$\Rightarrow \quad I = \int_0^{\pi/2} \dfrac{\sin\left(\frac{\pi}{2} - x\right) - \cos\left(\frac{\pi}{2} - x\right)}{1 + \sin\left(\frac{\pi}{2} - x\right)\cos\left(\frac{\pi}{2} - x\right)} dx \quad \left[\because \int_0^a f(x) dx = \int_0^a f(a - x) dx\right]$

$= \int_0^{\pi/2} \dfrac{\cos x - \sin x}{1 + \cos x \sin x} dx \quad$ ...(ii)

$$\left[\because \sin\left(\frac{\pi}{2} - x\right) = \cos x \text{ and } \cos\left(\frac{\pi}{2} - x\right) = \sin x\right]$$

On adding Eqs. (i) and (ii), we get

$$2I = \int_0^{\pi/2} \frac{0}{1 + \sin x \cos x} dx = 0 \Rightarrow I = 0$$

Question 16 $\int_0^{\pi} \log(1 + \cos x)\, dx.$

Sol. Let $\quad I = \int_0^{\pi} \log(1 + \cos x) dx$

$\Rightarrow \quad I = \int_0^{\pi} \log\{1 + \cos(\pi - x)\} dx \quad \left[\because \int_0^a f(x) dx = \int_0^a f(a - x) dx\right]$

$= \int_0^{\pi} \log(1 - \cos x) dx \quad [\because \cos(\pi - x) = -\cos x]$

$= \int_0^{\pi} \log\left\{2\sin^2\left(\frac{x}{2}\right)\right\} dx \quad \left[\because 1 - \cos x = 2\sin^2 \frac{x}{2}\right]$

$= \int_0^{\pi} \left\{\log 2 + 2\log\left(\sin\frac{x}{2}\right)\right\} dx \quad [\because \log(mn^2) = \log m + 2\log n]$

$= \int_0^{\pi} \log 2\, dx + 2\int_0^{\pi} \log\left(\sin\frac{x}{2}\right) dx$

In the second integral, put $\dfrac{x}{2} = t$

$\Rightarrow \quad dx = 2dt$

For limits when $x = 0$, $t = 0$ and when $x = \pi$, $t = \pi/2$

$$\therefore \quad I = \log 2[x]_0^{\pi} + 2\int_0^{\pi/2} \log(\sin t)\, 2dt$$

$$= (\log 2)(\pi - 0) + 4\left(-\frac{\pi}{2}\log 2\right)$$

$$\left(\because \int_0^{\pi/2} \log(\sin x)\, dx = -\frac{\pi}{2}\log 2\right)$$

$$= -\pi \log 2$$

Question 17 $\int_0^a \frac{\sqrt{x}}{\sqrt{x} + \sqrt{a-x}}\, dx$

◎ *Thinking Process* Here we reduce the integrand into simplest form, by using the property $\int_0^a f(x)\,dx = \int_0^a f(a-x)\,dx$ and then add them and integrate.

Sol. Let $I = \int_0^a \frac{\sqrt{x}}{\sqrt{x} + \sqrt{a-x}}\, dx$ ...(i)

$$\Rightarrow \quad I = \int_0^a \frac{\sqrt{a-x}}{\sqrt{a-x} + \sqrt{a-(a-x)}}\, dx \left[\because \int_0^a f(x)\,dx = \int_0^a f(a-x)\,dx\right]$$

$$= \int_0^a \frac{\sqrt{a-x}}{\sqrt{a-x} + \sqrt{x}}\, dx \quad \text{...(ii)}$$

On adding Eqs. (i) and (ii), we get

$$\Rightarrow \quad 2I = \int_0^a \frac{\sqrt{x} + \sqrt{a-x}}{\sqrt{a-x} + \sqrt{x}}\, dx \Rightarrow \quad 2I = \int_0^a 1\, dx$$

$$\Rightarrow \quad 2I = [x]_0^a = a - 0 = a \quad \Rightarrow \quad I = \frac{a}{2}$$

Question 18 $\int_0^4 |x - 1|\, dx$

Sol. Let $I = \int_0^4 |x - 1|\, dx$

It can be seen that, $(x - 1) < 0$ when $0 \le x < 1$ and $(x - 1) \ge 0$ when $1 \le x \le 4$

$$\therefore \quad I = \int_0^1 -(x-1)\,dx + \int_1^4 (x-1)\,dx \left[\because \int_a^b f(x)\,dx = \int_a^c f(x)\,dx + \int_c^b f(x)\,dx\right]$$

$$= \int_0^1 (1-x)\,dx + \int_1^4 (x-1)\,dx = \left[x - \frac{x^2}{2}\right]_0^1 + \left[\frac{x^2}{2} - x\right]_1^4$$

$$= \left(1 - \frac{1}{2}\right) - 0 + \left(\frac{4^2}{2} - 4\right) - \left(\frac{1}{2} - 1\right)$$

$$= \frac{1}{2} + 4 + \frac{1}{2} = 5$$

Question 19 Show that $\int_0^a f(x)g(x)dx = 2\int_0^a f(x)dx$, if f and g are defined as $f(x) = f(a-x)$ and $g(x) + g(a-x) = 4$.

Sol. Let $I = \int_0^a f(x)g(x)dx$ ...(i)

$\Rightarrow$ $$I = \int_0^a f(a-x)g(a-x)dx \quad \left[\because \int_0^a f(x)dx = \int_0^a f(a-x)dx\right]$$

$\Rightarrow$ $I = \int_0^a f(x)\{4 - g(x)\}dx = \int_0^a 4f(x)dx - \int_0^a f(x)g(x)dx$ ...(ii)

[$\because f(x) = f(a-x)$ and $g(x) + g(a-x) = 4$ (given)]

On adding Eqs. (i) and (ii), we get

$$2I = \int_0^a 4\,f(x)dx \Rightarrow I = 2\int_0^a f(x)dx.$$ **Hence Proved.**

Direction (Q. No. 20 and 21) Choose the correct answer.

Question 20 The value of $\int_{-\pi/2}^{\pi/2}(x^3 + x\cos x + \tan^5 x + 1)dx$ is

(a) 0 (b) 2
(c) π (d) 1

Sol. (c) Let $I = \int_{-\pi/2}^{\pi/2}(x^3 + x\cos x + \tan^5 x + 1)dx$

$\Rightarrow$ $$I = \int_{-\pi/2}^{\pi/2} x^3 dx + \int_{-\pi/2}^{\pi/2} x\cos x\,dx + \int_{-\pi/2}^{\pi/2} \tan^5 x dx + \int_{-\pi/2}^{\pi/2} 1dx$$

We know that, $\int_{-a}^{a} f(x)dx = \begin{cases} 2\int_0^a f(x)dx, & \text{if } f(x) \text{ is an even function} \\ 0, & \text{if } f(x) \text{ is an odd function} \end{cases}$

$\therefore$ $$I = 0 + 0 + 0 + 2\int_0^{\pi/2} 1dx.$$

[$\because x^3$, $x\cos x$ and $\tan^5(x)$ are odd functions.]

$\therefore$ $$I = 2[x]_0^{\pi/2} = \frac{2\pi}{2} = \pi$$

Question 21 The value of $\int_0^{\pi/2}\log\left(\frac{4+3\sin x}{4+3\cos x}\right)dx$ is

(a) 2 (b) $\frac{3}{4}$
(c) 0 (d) -2

Sol. (c) Let $I = \int_0^{\pi/2}\log\left(\frac{4+3\sin x}{4+3\cos x}\right)dx$ ...(i)

$\Rightarrow$ $$I = \int_0^{\pi/2}\log\left(\frac{4+3\sin(\pi/2-x)}{4+3\cos(\pi/2-x)}\right)dx \quad \left[\because \int_0^a f(x)dx = \int_0^a f(a-x)dx\right]$$

$$\Rightarrow \quad I = \int_0^{\pi/2} \log\left(\frac{4+3\cos x}{4+3\sin x}\right) dx \qquad \ldots(ii)$$

$$\left[\because \sin\left(\frac{\pi}{2}-x\right) = \cos x \quad \cos\left(\frac{\pi}{2}-x\right) = \sin x\right]$$

On adding Eqs. (i) and (ii), we get

$$2I = \int_0^{\pi/2} \left[\log\left(\frac{4+3\sin x}{4+3\cos x}\right) + \log\left(\frac{4+3\cos x}{4+3\sin x}\right)\right] dx$$

$$\Rightarrow \quad 2I = \int_0^{\pi/2} \log\left(\frac{4+3\sin x}{4+3\cos x} \times \frac{4+3\cos x}{4+3\sin x}\right) dx$$

$$[\because \log m + \log n = \log mn]$$

$$\Rightarrow \quad 2I = \int_0^{\pi/2} \log 1\, dx \Rightarrow 2I = \int_0^{\pi/2} 0\, dx \qquad (\because \log 1 = 0)$$

$$\Rightarrow \quad I = 0$$

Miscellaneous Exercise

Direction (Q. No.1 to 23) Integrate the functions.

Question 1 $\dfrac{1}{x-x^3}$

Sol. Let $I = \int \frac{1}{x-x^3} dx = \int \frac{1}{x(1-x^2)} dx = \int \frac{1}{x(1-x)(1+x)} dx \qquad \ldots(i)$

Let
$$\frac{1}{x(1-x)(1+x)} = \frac{A}{x} + \frac{B}{(1-x)} + \frac{C}{(1+x)}$$

$$\Rightarrow \quad 1 = A(1-x)(1+x) + B(x)(1+x) + C(x)(1-x)$$

$$\Rightarrow \quad 1 = A(1-x^2) + B(x+x^2) + C(x-x^2)$$

$$\Rightarrow \quad 1 = x^2(B-A-C) + x(B+C) + A$$

On equating the coefficients of x^2, x and constant term both sides, we get

$$-A+B-C=0, \quad B+C=0 \quad \text{and} \quad A=1$$

On solving these equations, we get $A = 1$, $B = \frac{1}{2}$ and $C = -\frac{1}{2}$

From Eq. (i), we get $\int \frac{1}{x(1-x^2)} dx = \int \frac{1}{x} dx + \frac{1}{2}\int \frac{1}{1-x} dx - \frac{1}{2}\int \frac{1}{1+x} dx$

$$= \log|x| - \frac{1}{2}\log|1-x| - \frac{1}{2}\log|1+x| + C$$

$$= \log|x| - \frac{1}{2}\log\{|1+x||1-x|\} + C$$

$$= \frac{1}{2}\log|x|^2 - \frac{1}{2}\log|1-x^2| + C = \frac{1}{2}\log\left|\frac{x^2}{1-x^2}\right| + C$$

Quick Solution

Let $\qquad I = \int \frac{1}{x(1-x^2)} dx$

Let $x = \sin\theta \Rightarrow dx = \cos\theta\, d\theta$

$$= \int \frac{\cos\theta \cdot d\theta}{\sin\theta(1-\sin^2\theta)} = \int \frac{\cos\theta\, d\theta}{\sin\theta \cos^2\theta} \qquad [\because \cos^2\theta + \sin^2\theta = 1]$$

$$= \int \frac{d\theta}{\sin\theta\cos\theta}$$

$$= 2\int \frac{d\theta}{2\sin\theta\cos\theta} = 2\int \frac{d\theta}{\sin 2\theta} \qquad \text{[Multiply and divide by 2]}$$

$$= 2\int \operatorname{cosec} 2\theta\, d\theta = 2 \cdot \left(\frac{\log|\tan\theta|}{2}\right) + C \qquad \left(\because \int \operatorname{cosec}\theta\, d\theta = \log\tan\frac{\theta}{2}\right)$$

$$= \log\left|\frac{\sin\theta}{\cos\theta}\right| = \log\left|\frac{\sin\theta}{\sqrt{1-\sin^2\theta}}\right|$$

$$= \log\left|\frac{x}{\sqrt{1-x^2}}\right| = \log\left(\frac{x^2}{1-x^2}\right)^{\frac{1}{2}}$$

$$= \frac{1}{2}\log\left(\frac{x^2}{1-x^2}\right) \qquad [\because \log x^m = m\log x]$$

Question 2 $\dfrac{1}{\sqrt{x+a}+\sqrt{x+b}}$

◎ **Thinking Process** First, we multiply the numerator and denominator both by the conjugate of denominator *i.e.*, $\sqrt{x+a}-\sqrt{x+b}$ to remove square root from denominator, then integrate the new integrand.

Sol. Let $I = \int \frac{1}{\sqrt{x+a}+\sqrt{x+b}} dx = \int \frac{1}{\sqrt{x+a}+\sqrt{x+b}} \times \frac{\sqrt{x+a}-\sqrt{x+b}}{\sqrt{x+a}-\sqrt{x+b}} dx$

$$= \int \frac{\sqrt{x+a}-\sqrt{x+b}}{(x+a)-(x+b)} dx = \frac{1}{a-b}\int \{(x+a)^{1/2} - (x+b)^{1/2}\} dx$$

$$= \frac{1}{a-b}\left\{\frac{(x+a)^{(1/2)+1}}{\frac{1}{2}+1} - \frac{(x+b)^{(1/2)+1}}{\frac{1}{2}+1}\right\} + C$$

$$= \frac{1}{a-b}\left\{\frac{(x+a)^{3/2}}{3/2} - \frac{(x+b)^{3/2}}{3/2}\right\} + C$$

$$= \frac{2}{3(a-b)}[(x+a)^{3/2} - (x+b)^{3/2}] + C$$

Question 3 $\frac{1}{x\sqrt{ax-x^2}}$

Sol. Let $I = \int \frac{1}{x\sqrt{ax-x^2}}\,dx$

Put $x = \frac{a}{t} \Rightarrow dx = \frac{-a\,dt}{t^2}$

$$\therefore \quad I = \int \frac{1}{\frac{a}{t}\sqrt{a\left(\frac{a}{t}\right) - \frac{a^2}{t^2}}}\left(\frac{-a}{t^2}\right)dt$$

$$= \int \frac{-a}{a \cdot a\sqrt{t-1}}\,dt$$

$$= -\frac{1}{a}\int (t-1)^{-1/2}dt = -\frac{1}{a}\cdot\frac{(t-1)^{(-1/2)+1}}{-(1/2)+1} + C$$

$$= -\frac{2}{a}\sqrt{t-1} + C = -\frac{2}{a}\sqrt{\frac{a}{x} - 1} + C \qquad \left(\because x = \frac{a}{t} \Rightarrow t = \frac{a}{x}\right)$$

$$= -\frac{2}{a}\sqrt{\frac{a-x}{x}} + C$$

Quick Solution

Let $I = \int \frac{1}{x\sqrt{ax-x^2}}\,dx$

$$= \int \frac{dx}{x \cdot x\sqrt{\frac{a}{x} - 1}} = \int \frac{dx}{x^2\sqrt{\frac{a}{x} - 1}} \qquad [\text{take } x^2 \text{ common from } \sqrt{ax - x^2}]$$

Let $\frac{a}{x} - 1 = t$

$$\frac{-a}{x^2}\,dx = dt$$

$$\frac{1}{x^2}\,dx = -\frac{1}{a}\,dt$$

$$\therefore \quad I = -\frac{1}{a}\int \frac{dt}{\sqrt{t}} = -\frac{1}{a}\left[\frac{t^{-\frac{1}{2}+1}}{-\frac{1}{2}+1}\right] = -\frac{1}{a}\cdot 2\sqrt{t}$$

$$= \frac{-2}{a}\sqrt{\frac{a}{x} - 1} = -\frac{2}{a}\sqrt{\frac{a-x}{x}} + C$$

Question 4 $\dfrac{1}{x^2(x^4+1)^{3/4}}$

Sol. Let $I = \int \dfrac{1}{x^2(x^4+1)^{3/4}}\,dx = \int \dfrac{1}{x^2\left\{x^4\left(1+\dfrac{1}{x^4}\right)\right\}^{3/4}}\,dx$

$$= \int \frac{1}{x^2.x^3\left(1+\dfrac{1}{x^4}\right)^{3/4}}\,dx = \int \frac{1}{x^5\left(1+\dfrac{1}{x^4}\right)^{3/4}}\,dx$$

Put $\quad 1+\dfrac{1}{x^4} = t \Rightarrow -\dfrac{4}{x^5}\,dx = dt \Rightarrow \dfrac{1}{x^5}\,dx = -\dfrac{dt}{4}$

$\therefore \quad I = \dfrac{1}{-4}\int \dfrac{1}{t^{3/4}}\,dt = -\dfrac{1}{4}\left[\dfrac{t^{1/4}}{1/4}\right] + C = -(1+x^{-4})^{1/4} + C$

Question 5 $\dfrac{1}{x^{1/2}+x^{1/3}}$

Sol. Let $I = \int \dfrac{1}{x^{1/2}+x^{1/3}}\,dx$

$\because$ LCM of 2 and 3 is 6.

$\therefore$ Put $\quad x^{1/6} = t \Rightarrow x = t^6 \Rightarrow dx = 6t^5\,dt$

$\therefore \quad I = \int \dfrac{6t^5}{(t^6)^{1/2}+(t^6)^{1/3}}\,dt = 6\int \dfrac{t^5}{t^3+t^2}\,dt$

$$= 6\int \frac{t^5}{t^2(t+1)}\,dt = 6\int \frac{t^3}{(t+1)}\,dt = 6\int\left(\frac{t^3+1-1}{t+1}\right)dt$$

$$= 6\int\left[\frac{(t+1)(t^2-t+1)}{t+1} - \frac{1}{t+1}\right]dt = 6\int\left\{t^2-t+1-\frac{1}{t+1}\right\}dt$$

$$= 6\left\{\frac{t^3}{3} - \frac{t^2}{2} + t - \log|t+1|\right\} + C$$

$$= 6\left\{\frac{(x^{1/6})^3}{3} - \frac{(x^{1/6})^2}{2} + (x^{1/6}) - \log|x^{1/6}+1|\right\} + C \quad [\because t = x^{1/6}]$$

$$= 2x^{1/2} - 3x^{1/3} + 6x^{1/6} - 6\log|x^{1/6}+1| + C$$

Question 6 $\dfrac{5x}{(x+1)(x^2+9)}$

◎ *Thinking Process* Firstly simplify it by using partial fraction method and then integrate.

Sol. Let $I = \int \dfrac{5x}{(x+1)(x^2+9)}\,dx$

Let $\quad \dfrac{5x}{(x+1)(x^2+9)} = \dfrac{A}{x+1} + \dfrac{Bx+C}{x^2+9}$

$$\Rightarrow \quad 5x = A(x^2 + 9) + (Bx + C)(x + 1)$$

$$\Rightarrow \quad 5x = Ax^2 + 9A + Bx^2 + Bx + Cx + C$$

$$= (A + B)x^2 + (B + C)x + (9A + C)$$

On equating the coefficients of x^2, x and constant term both sides, we get

$$A + B = 0, \quad B + C = 5, \quad 9A + C = 0$$

On solving these equations, we get

$$A = -\frac{1}{2}, B = \frac{1}{2} \text{ and } C = \frac{9}{2}$$

$$\therefore \quad \int \frac{5x}{(x+1)(x^2+9)} dx = \int \frac{\left(-\frac{1}{2}\right)}{(x+1)} dx + \int \frac{\frac{1}{2}x + \frac{9}{2}}{x^2 + 9} dx$$

$$= -\frac{1}{2}\int \frac{1}{x+1} dx + \frac{1}{2}\int \left(\frac{x+9}{x^2+9}\right) dx$$

$$= -\frac{1}{2}\log|x+1| + \frac{1}{2}\cdot\frac{1}{2}\int \frac{2x}{x^2+9} dx + \frac{9}{2}\int \frac{1}{x^2+9} dx$$

$$= -\frac{1}{2}\log|x+1| + \frac{1}{4}\log|x^2+9| + \frac{9}{2}\cdot\frac{1}{3}\tan^{-1}\left(\frac{x}{3}\right) + C$$

$$\left[\because \int \frac{dx}{a^2 + x^2} = \frac{1}{a}\tan^{-1}\left(\frac{x}{a}\right) + C\right]$$

$$= -\frac{1}{2}\log|x+1| + \frac{1}{4}\log|x^2+9| + \frac{3}{2}\tan^{-1}\left(\frac{x}{3}\right) + C$$

Question 7 $\dfrac{\sin x}{\sin(x-a)}$

Sol. Let $I = \int \frac{\sin x}{\sin(x-a)} dx = \int \frac{\sin\{(x-a)+a\}}{\sin(x-a)} dx$

$$= \int \frac{\sin(x-a)\cos a + \cos(x-a)\sin a}{\sin(x-a)} dx$$

$$[\because \sin(A+B) = \sin A\cos B + \cos A\sin B]$$

$$= \int \frac{\sin(x-a)\cos a}{\sin(x-a)} dx + \int \frac{\cos(x-a)\sin a}{\sin(x-a)} dx$$

$$= \cos a \int 1\, dx + \sin a \int \cot(x-a) dx$$

$$= (\cos a)x + \sin a \cdot \log|\sin(x-a)| + C$$

Question 8 $\dfrac{e^{5\log x}-e^{4\log x}}{e^{3\log x}-e^{2\log x}}$

Sol. Let $I=\int \dfrac{e^{5\log x}-e^{4\log x}}{e^{3\log x}-e^{2\log x}}dx=\int \dfrac{e^{\log x^5}-e^{\log x^4}}{e^{\log x^3}-e^{\log x^2}}dx$ $\quad [\because \log x = \log x^n]$

$$=\int \frac{x^5-x^4}{x^3-x^2}dx \qquad [\because e^{\log x}=x]$$

$$=\int \frac{x^4(x-1)}{x^2(x-1)}dx=\int x^2\,dx=\frac{1}{3}x^3+C$$

Question 9 $\dfrac{\cos x}{\sqrt{4-\sin^2 x}}$

Sol. Let $\quad I=\int \dfrac{\cos x}{\sqrt{4-\sin^2 x}}dx$

Put $\quad \sin x = t \Rightarrow \cos x\, dx = dt$

$\therefore \quad I=\int \dfrac{\cos x}{\sqrt{4-t^2}}\dfrac{dt}{\cos x}=\int \dfrac{1}{\sqrt{2^2-t^2}}dt=\sin^{-1}\left(\dfrac{t}{2}\right)+C$

$$\left[\because \int \frac{dx}{\sqrt{a^2-x^2}}=\sin^{-1}\left(\frac{x}{a}\right)+C\right]$$

$$=\sin^{-1}\left(\frac{\sin x}{2}\right)+C$$

Question 10 $\dfrac{\sin^8 x-\cos^8 x}{1-2\sin^2 x\cos^2 x}$

Sol. Let $I=\int \dfrac{\sin^8 x-\cos^8 x}{1-2\sin^2 x\cos^2 x}dx=\int \dfrac{\{(\sin^4 x)^2-(\cos^4 x)^2\}}{1-2\sin^2 x\cos^2 x}dx$

$$=\int \frac{(\sin^4 x-\cos^4 x)(\sin^4 x+\cos^4 x)}{1-2\sin^2 x\cos^2 x}dx \qquad [\because a^2-b^2=(a-b)(a+b)]$$

$$=\int \frac{(\sin^2 x-\cos^2 x)(\sin^2 x+\cos^2 x)[(\sin^2 x)^2+(\cos^2 x)^2]}{1-2\sin^2 x\cos^2 x}dx$$

$$=\int \frac{(\sin^2 x-\cos^2 x)1\{(\sin^2 x+\cos^2 x)^2-2\sin^2 x\cdot\cos^2 x\}}{1-2\sin^2 x\cos^2 x}dx$$

$$[\because \sin^2\theta+\cos^2\theta=1 \text{ and } a^2+b^2=(a+b)^2-2ab]$$

$$=\int \frac{-\cos 2x\{1-2\sin^2 x\cdot\cos^2 x\}}{1-2\sin^2 x\cos^2 x}dx \qquad [\because \cos 2\theta=\cos^2\theta-\sin^2\theta]$$

$$=-\int \cos 2x\,dx=-\frac{\sin 2x}{2}+C$$

Question 11 $\dfrac{1}{\cos(x+a)\cos(x+b)}$

Sol. Let $I = \int \dfrac{1}{\cos(x+a)\cos(x+b)}dx$

On multiplying and dividing by $\sin(a-b)$, we get

$$I = \frac{1}{\sin(a-b)}\int \frac{\sin(a-b)}{\cos(x+a)\cos(x+b)}dx$$

$\Rightarrow$ $$I = \frac{1}{\sin(a-b)}\int \frac{\sin[(x+a)-(x+b)]}{\cos(x+a)\cos(x+b)}dx$$

$$= \frac{1}{\sin(a-b)}\int \frac{\sin(x+a)\cos(x+b)-\cos(x+a)\sin(x+b)}{\cos(x+a)\cos(x+b)}dx$$

$[\because \sin(A-B) = \sin A\cos B - \sin B\cos A]$

$$= \frac{1}{\sin(a-b)}\int\left[\frac{\sin(x+a)}{\cos(x+a)} - \frac{\sin(x+b)}{\cos(x+b)}\right]dx$$

$$= \frac{1}{\sin(a-b)}\int[\tan(x+a)-\tan(x+b)]dx$$

$$= \frac{1}{\sin(a-b)}[-\log|\cos(x+a)| + \log|\cos(x+b)|] + C$$

$$= \frac{1}{\sin(a-b)}\log\left|\frac{\cos(x+b)}{\cos(x+a)}\right| + C \qquad \left(\because \log m - \log n = \log\frac{m}{n}\right)$$

Question 12 $\dfrac{x^3}{\sqrt{1-x^8}}$

Sol. Let $$I = \int \frac{x^3}{\sqrt{1-x^8}}dx = \int \frac{x^3}{\sqrt{1-(x^4)^2}}dx$$

Put $$x^4 = t \Rightarrow 4x^3 dx = dt \Rightarrow dx = \frac{dt}{4x^3}$$

$\therefore$ $$I = \int \frac{x^3}{\sqrt{1-t^2}}\frac{dt}{4x^3} = \frac{1}{4}\int\frac{1}{\sqrt{1-t^2}}dt$$

$$= \frac{1}{4}\sin^{-1}t + C \qquad \left[\because \int\frac{dx}{\sqrt{1-x^2}} = \sin^{-1}x + C\right]$$

$$= \frac{1}{4}\sin^{-1}(x^4) + C$$

Question 13 $\dfrac{e^x}{(1+e^x)(2+e^x)}$

Sol. Let $I = \int \dfrac{e^x}{(1+e^x)(2+e^x)}dx$

Put $e^x = t$

$\Rightarrow$ $e^x dx = dt$

$\therefore$ $$I = \int \frac{e^x}{(1+t)(2+t)} \frac{dt}{e^x} = \int \frac{1}{(1+t)(2+t)} dt$$

Let $$\frac{1}{(1+t)(2+t)} = \frac{A}{(1+t)} + \frac{B}{(2+t)}$$

$\Rightarrow$ $$1 = A(2+t) + B(1+t) = (2A+B) + t(A+B)$$

On equating the coefficients of t and constant term both sides, we get $A + B = 0$ and $2A + B = 1$

On solving both equations, we get $A = 1$ and $B = -1$

$\therefore$ $$I = \int \frac{1}{(1+t)} dt - \int \frac{1}{(2+t)} dt = \log|1+t| - \log|2+t| + C$$

$$= \log\left|\frac{1+t}{2+t}\right| + C = \log\left|\frac{1+e^x}{2+e^x}\right| + C$$

Question 14 $\dfrac{1}{(x^2+1)(x^2+4)}$

◎ ***Thinking Process*** It is not directly integrate so simplify it by the method of partial fraction and then integrate.

Sol. Let $I = \int \frac{1}{(x^2+1)(x^2+4)} dx$

Let $$\frac{1}{(x^2+1)(x^2+4)} = \frac{Ax+B}{x^2+1} + \frac{Cx+D}{x^2+4}$$

$\Rightarrow$ $$1 = (Ax+B)(x^2+4) + (Cx+D)(x^2+1)$$

$$= (A+C)x^3 + (B+D)x^2 + (4A+C)x + (4B+D)$$

On comparing the coefficients of x^3, x^2, x and constant term both sides, we get

$$A+C=0,\ B+D=0,\quad 4A+C=0 \text{ and } 4B+D=1$$

On solving these equations, we get $A=0, C=0, B=\frac{1}{3}$ and $D=-\frac{1}{3}$

$\therefore$ $$I = \int \frac{1}{(x^2+1)(x^2+4)} dx$$

$$= \frac{1}{3}\int \left(\frac{1}{(x^2+1)} - \frac{1}{(x^2+4)}\right) dx$$

$$= \frac{1}{3}\left\{\tan^{-1} x - \frac{1}{2}\tan^{-1}\left(\frac{x}{2}\right)\right\} + C$$

$$= \frac{1}{3}\tan^{-1} x - \frac{1}{6}\tan^{-1}\left(\frac{x}{2}\right) + C$$

Quick Solution

Let $I = \int \frac{1}{(x^2+1)(x^2+4)} dx$

Let $x^2 = y$

(we are not changing dx, so we will put $y = x^2$ before integration)

$\therefore \frac{1}{(x^2+1)(x^2+4)} = \frac{1}{(y+1)(y+4)}$

Let $\frac{1}{(y+1)(y+4)} = \frac{A}{y+1} + \frac{B}{y+4} \Rightarrow 1 = A(y+4) + B(y+1)$

Put $y = -4 \Rightarrow 1 = -3B \Rightarrow B = -\frac{1}{3}$ and $y = -1 \Rightarrow 1 = 3A \Rightarrow A = \frac{1}{3}$

$\therefore \frac{1}{(y+1)(y+4)} = \frac{1}{3(y+1)} - \frac{1}{3(y+4)}$

Now, $I = \int\left(\frac{1/3}{x^2+1} - \frac{1/3}{x^2+4}\right)dx = \frac{1}{3}\int\frac{1}{x^2+1}dx - \frac{1}{3}\int\frac{1}{x^2+2^2}dx$

$= \frac{1}{3}\tan^{-1}x - \frac{1}{3}\cdot\frac{1}{2}\tan^{-1}\frac{x}{2} = \frac{1}{3}\tan^{-1}x - \frac{1}{6}\tan^{-1}\frac{x}{2} + C$

Question 15 $\cos^3 x\, e^{\log \sin x}$

Sol. Let $I = \int \cos^3 x e^{\log \sin x} dx = \int (\cos x)^3 \sin x\, dx$ $[\because e^{\log x} = x]$

$= -\int (\cos x)^3(-\sin x)dx$

Put $\cos x = t \Rightarrow -\sin x\, dx = dt$

$\therefore I = -\int t^3 dt = -\frac{t^4}{4} + C = -\frac{\cos^4 x}{4} + C$

Question 16 $e^{3\log x}(x^4+1)^{-1}$

Sol. Let $I = \int e^{3\log x}(x^4+1)^{-1}dx = \int \frac{e^{\log x^3}}{(x^4+1)}dx = \int \frac{x^3}{(x^4+1)}dx$ $[\because e^{\log x} = x]$

Put $x^4 + 1 = t \Rightarrow 4x^3 dx = dt \Rightarrow dx = \frac{dt}{4x^3}$

$\therefore I = \int \frac{x^3}{t}\frac{dt}{4x^3} = \frac{1}{4}\int\frac{1}{t}dt = \frac{1}{4}\log|t| + C = \frac{1}{4}\log|x^4+1| + C$

Question 17 $f'(ax+b)[f(ax+b)]^n$

Sol. Let $I = \int f(ax+b)[f(ax+b)]^n dx$

Put $f(ax+b) = t \Rightarrow f'(ax+b)a\,dx = dt \Rightarrow dx = \frac{dt}{af'(ax+b)}$

$\therefore I = \int f(ax+b)t^n \frac{dt}{f'(ax+b)a}$

$= \frac{1}{a}\int t^n\, dt = \frac{1}{a}\left(\frac{t^{n+1}}{n+1}\right) + C = \frac{1}{a}\cdot\frac{[f(ax+b)]^{n+1}}{n+1} + C$

Question 18 $\dfrac{1}{\sqrt{\sin^3 x \sin(x+\alpha)}}$

Sol. Let $I = \int \dfrac{1}{\sqrt{\sin^3 x \sin(x+\alpha)}} dx$

$$= \int \frac{1}{\sqrt{\sin^3 x(\sin x \cos\alpha + \cos x \sin\alpha)}} dx$$

$[\because \sin(A+B) = \sin A \cos B + \cos A \sin B]$

$$= \int \frac{1}{\sqrt{\sin^4 x\,(\cos\alpha + \cot x \sin\alpha)}} dx$$

$$= \int \frac{1}{\sin^2 x\sqrt{\cos\alpha + \cot x \sin\alpha}} dx = \int \frac{\operatorname{cosec}^2 x}{\sqrt{\cos\alpha + \cot x \sin\alpha}} dx$$

Put $\cos\alpha + \cot x \sin\alpha = t$

$\Rightarrow \quad -\operatorname{cosec}^2 x \sin\alpha \, dx = dt$

$\Rightarrow \quad dx = \dfrac{dt}{-\operatorname{cosec}^2 x \sin\alpha}$

$\therefore \quad I = \dfrac{-1}{\sin\alpha}\displaystyle\int \frac{dt}{\sqrt{t}} = \frac{-1}{\sin\alpha}[2\sqrt{t}] + C$

$$= \frac{-1}{\sin\alpha}[2\sqrt{\cos\alpha + \cot x \sin\alpha}] + C = \frac{-2}{\sin\alpha}\sqrt{\cos\alpha + \frac{\cos x \sin\alpha}{\sin x}} + C$$

$$= \frac{-2}{\sin\alpha}\sqrt{\frac{\sin x \cos\alpha + \cos x \sin\alpha}{\sin x}} + C = -\frac{2}{\sin\alpha}\sqrt{\frac{\sin(x+\alpha)}{\sin x}} + C$$

$[\because \sin(A+B) = \sin A \cos B + \cos A \sin B]$

Question 19 $\sqrt{\dfrac{1-\sqrt{x}}{1+\sqrt{x}}}$

Sol. Let $I = \int \sqrt{\dfrac{1-\sqrt{x}}{1+\sqrt{x}}}\, dx$

Put $\sqrt{x} = \cos t$

$\Rightarrow \quad x = \cos^2 t \Rightarrow dx = 2\cos t\,(-\sin t)\,dt$

$\therefore \quad I = \displaystyle\int \sqrt{\frac{1-\cos t}{1+\cos t}}\,(-2\sin t \cos t)\,dt$

$\Rightarrow \quad I = -2\displaystyle\int \sqrt{\frac{2\sin^2 \frac{t}{2}}{2\cos^2 \frac{t}{2}}} \cdot 2\sin\frac{t}{2}\cos\frac{t}{2} \cdot \cos t\, dt$

$\left[\because 1-\cos x = 2\sin^2\frac{x}{2},\ 1+\cos x = 2\cos^2\frac{x}{2} \text{ and } \sin 2t = 2\sin t \cos t\right]$

$$= -4\int \sin^2\frac{t}{2} \cdot \cos t\, dt = -4\int \frac{1-\cos t}{2} \cdot \cos t\, dt$$

$$= -2\int (\cos t - \cos^2 t)\, dt = -2\int \left(\cos t - \frac{1+\cos 2t}{2}\right) dt$$

$$= -2\sin t + t + \frac{1}{2}\sin 2t + C$$

$$= -2\sin t + t + \frac{1}{2}\times 2\sin t\cdot\cos t + C$$

$$= -2\sqrt{1-\cos^2 t} + t + \frac{1}{2}[2\sqrt{1-\cos^2 t}\cdot\cos t] + C$$

$$= -2\sqrt{1-x} + \cos^{-1}\sqrt{x} + \sqrt{x}\sqrt{1-x} + C$$

$$[\because \sqrt{x} = \cos t \Rightarrow t = \cos^{-1}\sqrt{x}]$$

$$= -2\sqrt{1-x} + \cos^{-1}\sqrt{x} + \sqrt{x-x^2} + C$$

Questions 20 $\dfrac{2+\sin 2x}{1+\cos 2x}e^x$

Sol. Let $I = \int \dfrac{2+\sin 2x}{1+\cos 2x}e^x dx = \int \left[\dfrac{2}{1+\cos 2x} + \dfrac{\sin 2x}{1+\cos 2x}\right] e^x dx$

$$= \int\left[\frac{2}{2\cos^2 x} + \frac{2\sin x\cos x}{2\cos^2 x}\right]\cdot e^x dx$$

$$[\because 1+\cos 2x = 2\cos^2 x \text{ and } \sin 2x = 2\sin x\cos x]$$

$$= \int\left(\frac{1}{\cos^2 x} + \tan x\right)e^x dx = \int (\tan x + \sec^2 x)e^x dx$$

Let $f(x) = \tan x \Rightarrow f'(x) = \sec^2 x$

$\therefore$ $I = \tan x\, e^x + C$ $\quad [\because \int [f(x) + f'(x)]e^x dx = e^x f(x) + C]$

Question 21 $\dfrac{x^2+x+1}{(x+1)^2(x+2)}$

Sol. Let $I = \int \dfrac{x^2+x+1}{(x+1)^2(x+2)}dx$

The integrand $\dfrac{x^2+x+1}{(x+1)^2(x+2)}$ is a proper rational function.

$\therefore$ $$\frac{x^2+x+1}{(x+1)^2(x+2)} = \frac{A}{x+1} + \frac{B}{(x+1)^2} + \frac{C}{(x+2)} \quad \text{...(i)}$$

$\Rightarrow$ $x^2+x+1 = A(x+1)(x+2) + B(x+2) + C(x+1)^2$

$\Rightarrow$ $x^2+x+1 = A(x^2+3x+2) + B(x+2) + C(x^2+2x+1)$

$\Rightarrow$ $x^2+x+1 = (A+C)x^2 + (3A+B+2C)x + (2A+2B+C)$

On comparing the coefficients of like powers both sides, we get

$$A + C = 1,\quad 3A + B + 2C = 1 \quad\text{and}\quad 2A + 2B + C = 1$$

On solving these equations, we get

$$A = -2, B = 1 \quad\text{and}\quad C = 3$$

From Eq. (i), we get $\dfrac{x^2+x+1}{(x+1)^2(x+2)} = \dfrac{-2}{x+1} + \dfrac{1}{(x+1)^2} + \dfrac{3}{(x+2)}$

$$\therefore \quad \int \frac{x^2+x+1}{(x+1)^2(x+2)}\,dx = -2\int\frac{dx}{x+1} + \int\frac{dx}{(x+1)^2} + 3\int\frac{dx}{(x+2)}$$

$$= -2\log|x+1| - \frac{1}{(x+1)} + 3\log|x+2| + C$$

Question 22 $\tan^{-1}\sqrt{\dfrac{1-x}{1+x}}$.

◎ ***Thinking Process*** Firstly, put $x=\cos\theta$ and use the relation $1-\cos\theta = 2\sin^2\dfrac{\theta}{2}$ and $1+\cos\theta = 2\cos^2\dfrac{\theta}{2}$. It becomes $\tan^{-1}(\tan\theta)$ i.e. θ and then integrate it by integration by parts.

Sol. Let $I = \int \tan^{-1}\sqrt{\dfrac{1-x}{1+x}}\,dx$

Put $x = \cos\theta \quad dx = -\sin\theta\, d\theta$

$$\therefore \quad I = \int \tan^{-1}\sqrt{\frac{1-\cos\theta}{1+\cos\theta}}(-\sin\theta)\,d\theta = \int\tan^{-1}\sqrt{\frac{2\sin^2\left(\frac{\theta}{2}\right)}{2\cos^2\left(\frac{\theta}{2}\right)}}(-\sin\theta)\,d\theta$$

$$\left[\because 1-\cos x = 2\sin^2\frac{x}{2} \text{ and } 1+\cos x = 2\cos^2\frac{x}{2}\right]$$

$$= \int\tan^{-1}\left(\tan\frac{\theta}{2}\right)(-\sin\theta)\,d\theta = \frac{1}{2}\int\theta(-\sin\theta)\,d\theta \quad [\because \tan^{-1}(\tan\theta)=\theta]$$

[using integration by parts]

$$= \frac{1}{2}\{\theta\cos\theta - \int 1\cos\theta\,d\theta\} + C = \frac{1}{2}\theta\cos\theta - \frac{1}{2}\sin\theta + C$$

$$= \frac{1}{2}(\cos^{-1}x)x - \frac{1}{2}\sqrt{1-\cos^2\theta} + C = \frac{1}{2}x\cos^{-1}x - \frac{1}{2}\sqrt{1-x^2} + C$$

$$[\because \cos\theta = x \Rightarrow \theta = \cos^{-1}x]$$

Question 23 $\dfrac{\sqrt{x^2+1}[\log(x^2+1)-2\log x]}{x^4}$

Sol. Let $\quad I = \int\dfrac{\sqrt{x^2+1}[\log(x^2+1)-2\log x]}{x^4}\,dx$

$$= \int\frac{\sqrt{x^2+1}}{x^4}[\log(x^2+1) - \log x^2]\,dx \qquad (\because n\log x = \log x^n)$$

$$= \int\frac{\sqrt{x^2+1}}{x^4}\left[\log\left(\frac{x^2+1}{x^2}\right)\right]dx$$

$$= \int\frac{1}{x^3}\sqrt{\frac{x^2+1}{x^2}}\left[\log\left(1+\frac{1}{x^2}\right)\right]dx$$

Put $\quad \dfrac{x^2+1}{x^2}=t \quad \Rightarrow \quad 1+\dfrac{1}{x^2}=t$

$\Rightarrow \quad -\dfrac{2}{x^3}dx=dt \quad \Rightarrow \quad dx=\dfrac{-x^3}{2}dt$

$\therefore \quad I=\int \sqrt{t}\log t.\dfrac{1}{x^3}\left(-\dfrac{x^3dt}{2}\right)=-\dfrac{1}{2}\int (t)^{1/2}\log t\,dt$

On integrating by parts, we get

$$I=-\frac{1}{2}\left[\log t\cdot\int t^{1/2}dt-\int\left\{\left(\frac{d}{dt}\log t\right)\int t^{1/2}dt\right\}dt\right]$$

$$=-\frac{1}{2}\left[\log t\cdot\frac{t^{3/2}}{\frac{3}{2}}-\int\frac{1}{t}\cdot\frac{t^{3/2}}{\frac{3}{2}}\,dt\right]=-\frac{1}{2}\left[\frac{2}{3}\log t\cdot t^{3/2}-\frac{2}{3}\int t^{1/2}dt\right]$$

$$=-\frac{1}{2}\times\frac{2}{3}[\log t\cdot t^{3/2}-\int t^{1/2}dt]$$

$$=-\frac{1}{3}\left[\log t\cdot t^{3/2}-\frac{t^{3/2}}{\frac{3}{2}}\right]+C=-\frac{1}{3}t^{3/2}\left[\log t-\frac{2}{3}\right]+C$$

$$=-\frac{1}{3}\left(1+\frac{1}{x^2}\right)^{3/2}\left[\log\left(\frac{x^2+1}{x^2}\right)-\frac{2}{3}\right]+C$$

Direction (Q. No. 24 to 31) Evaluate the definite integrals.

Question 24 $\displaystyle\int_{\pi/2}^{\pi} e^x\left(\frac{1-\sin x}{1-\cos x}\right)dx.$

Sol. Let $\displaystyle I=\int_{\pi/2}^{\pi} e^x\left(\frac{1-\sin x}{1-\cos x}\right)dx=\int_{\pi/2}^{\pi} e^x\left(\frac{1-2\sin\left(\frac{x}{2}\right)\cos\left(\frac{x}{2}\right)}{2\sin^2\left(\frac{x}{2}\right)}\right)dx$

$\left(\because \sin x=2\sin\dfrac{x}{2}\cos\dfrac{x}{2} \text{ and } 1-\cos x=2\sin^2\dfrac{x}{2}\right)$

$\displaystyle =\int_{\pi/2}^{\pi} e^x\left(\frac{1}{2}\text{cosec}^2\frac{x}{2}-\cot\frac{x}{2}\right)dx=\int_{\pi/2}^{\pi} e^x\left(-\cot\frac{x}{2}+\frac{1}{2}\text{cosec}^2\frac{x}{2}\right)dx$

$\left[\text{Here, }\dfrac{d}{dx}\left(-\cot\dfrac{x}{2}\right)=\dfrac{1}{2}\text{cosec}^2\dfrac{x}{2} \text{ it is the form of } \int e^x\{f(x)+f'(x)\}\,dx=e^x f(x)\right]$

$\therefore \quad I=\left[e^x\left(-\cot\dfrac{x}{2}\right)\right]_{\pi/2}^{\pi}$

$=-e^{\pi}\cot\left(\dfrac{\pi}{2}\right)-\left[-e^{\pi/2}\cot\left(\dfrac{\pi}{4}\right)\right]=-e^{\pi}\cdot 0+e^{\pi/2}\cdot 1=e^{\pi/2}$

Question 25 $\int_0^{\pi/4} \frac{\sin x \cos x}{\cos^4 x + \sin^4 x} dx$

◎ *Thinking Process* Here, the given integrand cannot intergate directly, so we put $\sin^2 x = t$ and then convert it into the standard form $\frac{1}{x^2 + a^2}$ and then integrate under the proper limits.

Sol. Let $I = \int_0^{\pi/4} \frac{\sin x \cos x}{\cos^4 x + \sin^4 x} dx$

$$= \int_0^{\pi/4} \frac{\sin x \cos x}{(1 - \sin^2 x)^2 + (\sin^2 x)^2} dx \qquad [\because \cos^2 x = 1 - \sin^2 x]$$

Put $\sin^2 x = t \Rightarrow 2 \sin x \cos x \, dx = dt \Rightarrow dx = \frac{dt}{2 \sin x \cos x}$

For limits, when $x = 0 \Rightarrow t = 0$ and when $x = \frac{\pi}{4} \Rightarrow t = \frac{1}{2}$

$$\therefore \quad I = \int_0^{1/2} \frac{\sin x \cos x}{(1-t)^2 + t^2} \frac{dt}{2 \sin x \cos x}$$

$$= \frac{1}{2}\int_0^{1/2} \frac{1}{(1-t)^2 + t^2} dt = \frac{1}{2}\int_0^{1/2} \frac{1}{2t^2 - 2t + 1} dt$$

$$= \frac{1}{2} \cdot \frac{1}{2}\int_0^{1/2} \frac{1}{t^2 - t + \frac{1}{2}} dt = \frac{1}{4}\int_0^{1/2} \frac{1}{t^2 - t + \left(\frac{1}{2}\right)^2 - \left(\frac{1}{2}\right)^2 + \frac{1}{2}} dt$$

$$= \frac{1}{4}\int_0^{1/2} \frac{1}{\left(t - \frac{1}{2}\right)^2 + \left(\frac{1}{2}\right)^2} dt = \frac{1}{4} \cdot \frac{1}{\frac{1}{2}} \left[\tan^{-1}\left(\frac{t - \frac{1}{2}}{\frac{1}{2}} \right) \right]_0^{1/2}$$

$$= \frac{1}{2}[\tan^{-1} 0 - \tan^{-1}(-1)] = \frac{1}{2}\left[0 - \tan^{-1}\left(-\tan\frac{\pi}{4}\right)\right]$$

$$= -\frac{1}{2}\tan^{-1}\left[\tan\left(-\frac{\pi}{4}\right)\right] = -\frac{1}{2} \times \left(-\frac{\pi}{4}\right) = \frac{\pi}{8}$$

Quick Solution

$$I = \int_0^{\frac{\pi}{4}} \frac{\sin x \cos x}{\cos^4 x + \sin^4 x} dx = \int_0^{\frac{\pi}{4}} \frac{\frac{\sin x \cos x}{\cos^4 x}}{\frac{\cos^4 x}{\cos^4 x} + \frac{\sin^4 x}{\sin^4 x}} dx$$

[divide numerator and denominator by $\cos^4 x$]

$$= \int_0^{\frac{\pi}{4}} \frac{\tan x \cdot \sec^2 x}{1 + \tan^4 x} dx$$

$$\left(\because \frac{\sin x \cos x}{\cos^4 x} = \frac{\sin x}{\cos x} \cdot \frac{\cos x}{\cos x} \cdot \frac{1}{\cos^2 x} = \tan x \cdot \sec^2 x\right)$$

Put $\tan^2 x = t$

$$\Rightarrow \quad 2 \cdot \tan x \cdot \sec^2 x = \frac{dt}{dx}$$

$$\Rightarrow \quad \tan x \cdot \sec^2 x \, dx = \frac{1}{2} dt$$

For limits, if $x = 0 \Rightarrow t = \tan^2 0 = 0$ and if $x = \frac{\pi}{4} \Rightarrow t = \tan^2 \frac{\pi}{4} = 1$

$$\therefore \quad I = \frac{1}{2}\int_0^1 \frac{dt}{1+t^2} = \frac{1}{2}[\tan^{-1} t]_0^1$$

$$= \frac{1}{2}[\tan^{-1} 1 - \tan^{-1} 0] = \frac{1}{2} \cdot \left(\frac{\pi}{4} - 0\right) = \frac{\pi}{8}$$

Question 26 $\int_0^{\pi/2} \frac{\cos^2 x}{\cos^2 x + 4\sin^2 x} dx$

Sol. Let $I = \int_0^{\pi/2} \frac{\cos^2 x}{\cos^2 x + 4\sin^2 x} dx$ ...(i)

$$= \int_0^{\pi/2} \frac{\cos^2 x}{4 - 3\cos^2 x} dx \qquad [\because \sin^2 x = 1 - \cos^2 x]$$

$$= -\frac{1}{3}\int_0^{\pi/2} \frac{4 - 3\cos^2 x - 4}{4 - 3\cos^2 x} dx = -\frac{1}{3}\int_0^{\pi/2} \left(1 - \frac{4}{4 - 3\cos^2 x}\right) dx$$

$$= -\frac{1}{3}[x]_0^{\pi/2} + \frac{4}{3}\int_0^{\pi/2} \frac{\sec^2 x}{4\sec^2 x - 3} dx$$

[divide numerator and denominator in second integral by $\cos^2 x$]

$$= -\frac{\pi}{6} + \frac{4}{3}\int_0^{\pi/2} \frac{\sec^2 x}{4(1 + \tan^2 x) - 3} dx \qquad [\because 1 + \tan^2 x = \sec^2 x]$$

Put $\tan x = t \Rightarrow \sec^2 x \, dx = dt$

For limits, when, $x = 0 \Rightarrow t = 0$ and when $x = \left(\frac{\pi}{2}\right) \Rightarrow t = \infty$

$$\therefore \quad I = -\frac{\pi}{6} + \frac{4}{3}\int_0^{\infty} \frac{dt}{4(1+t^2) - 3} = -\frac{\pi}{6} + \frac{4}{3}\int_0^{\infty} \frac{dt}{4t^2 + 1}$$

$$= -\frac{\pi}{6} + \frac{4}{3} \times \frac{1}{4}\int_0^{\infty} \frac{dt}{t^2 + \left(\frac{1}{2}\right)^2} = -\frac{\pi}{6} + \frac{1}{3} \cdot 2\left[\tan^{-1} \frac{t}{\frac{1}{2}}\right]_0^{\infty}$$

$$\left[\because \int \frac{dx}{a^2 + x^2} = \frac{1}{a}\tan^{-1}\frac{x}{a} + C\right]$$

$$= -\frac{\pi}{6} + \frac{2}{3}[\tan^{-1} 2t]_0^{\infty} = -\frac{\pi}{6} + \frac{2}{3}[\tan^{-1} \infty - \tan^{-1} 0]$$

$$= -\frac{\pi}{6} + \frac{2}{3}\left[\frac{\pi}{2} - 0\right] = -\frac{\pi}{6} + \frac{\pi}{3} = \frac{\pi}{6}$$

Question 27 Let $I = \int_{\pi/6}^{\pi/3} \frac{\sin x + \cos x}{\sqrt{\sin 2x}} dx$

Sol. Let $I = \int_{\pi/6}^{\pi/3} \frac{\sin x + \cos x}{\sqrt{\sin 2x}} dx$

We know that, $(\sin x - \cos x)^2 = \sin^2 x + \cos^2 x - 2 \sin x \cos x$

$\Rightarrow \quad (\sin x - \cos x)^2 = 1 - \sin 2x$

$[\because \sin^2 x + \cos^2 x = 1 \text{ and } 2 \sin x \cos x = \sin 2x]$

$\Rightarrow \quad \sin 2x = 1 - (\sin x - \cos x)^2$

$\therefore \quad I = \int_{\pi/6}^{\pi/3} \frac{\sin x + \cos x}{\sqrt{1 - (\sin x - \cos x)^2}} dx$

Put $\sin x - \cos x = t$ ...(i)

$\Rightarrow \quad (\cos x + \sin x)\, dx = dt \Rightarrow dx = \frac{dt}{\cos x + \sin x}$

For limits, when $x = \frac{\pi}{6} \Rightarrow t = \sin\frac{\pi}{6} - \cos\frac{\pi}{6} = \frac{1}{2} - \frac{\sqrt{3}}{2}$

and when, $x = \frac{\pi}{3}, t = \sin\frac{\pi}{3} - \cos\frac{\pi}{3} = \frac{\sqrt{3}}{2} - \frac{1}{2}$

$\therefore \quad I = \int_{\frac{1-\sqrt{3}}{2}}^{\frac{\sqrt{3}-1}{2}} \frac{\sin x + \cos x}{\sqrt{1-t^2}} \frac{dt}{\cos x + \sin x} = \int_{\frac{1-\sqrt{3}}{2}}^{\frac{\sqrt{3}-1}{2}} \frac{dt}{\sqrt{1-t^2}}$

From here we can slove it in two ways

Ist method $I = \int_{\frac{1-\sqrt{3}}{2}}^{\frac{\sqrt{3}-1}{2}} \frac{1}{\sqrt{1-t^2}} dt = [\sin^{-1} t]_{\frac{1-\sqrt{3}}{2}}^{\frac{\sqrt{3}-1}{2}}$

$= \sin^{-1}\left(\frac{\sqrt{3}-1}{2}\right) - \sin^{-1}\left\{-\left(\frac{\sqrt{3}-1}{2}\right)\right\}$

Let $\sin^{-1}\left\{-\left(\frac{\sqrt{3}-2}{2}\right)\right\} = \theta \Rightarrow -\left(\frac{\sqrt{3}-1}{2}\right) = \sin\theta$

$\Rightarrow \quad \frac{\sqrt{3}-1}{2} = -\sin\theta \Rightarrow \frac{\sqrt{3}-1}{2} = \sin(-\theta)$

$\Rightarrow \quad \sin^{-1}\left(\frac{\sqrt{3}}{2} - 1\right) = -\theta$

$\Rightarrow \quad \theta = -\sin^{-1}\left(\frac{\sqrt{3}-1}{2}\right)$

$\therefore \quad I = \sin^{-1}\left(\frac{\sqrt{3}-1}{2}\right) - \sin^{-1}\left\{-\left(\frac{\sqrt{3}-1}{2}\right)\right\} = \sin^{-1}\left(\frac{\sqrt{3}-1}{2}\right) - \theta$

$= \sin^{-1}\left(\frac{\sqrt{3}-1}{2}\right) - \left\{-\sin^{-1}\left(\frac{\sqrt{3}-1}{2}\right)\right\}$

$= \left[\sin^{-1}\left(\frac{\sqrt{3}-1}{2}\right) + \sin^{-1}\left(\frac{\sqrt{3}-1}{2}\right)\right] = 2\sin^{-1}\left(\frac{\sqrt{3}-1}{2}\right)$

IInd method

$$\int_{\frac{1-\sqrt{3}}{2}}^{\frac{\sqrt{3}-1}{2}} \frac{1}{\sqrt{1-t^2}}\,dt = \int_{-\left(\frac{\sqrt{3}-1}{2}\right)}^{\frac{\sqrt{3}-1}{2}} \frac{1}{\sqrt{1-t^2}}\,dt$$

As $\frac{1}{\sqrt{1-(-t)^2}} = \frac{1}{\sqrt{1-t^2}}$, therefore $\frac{1}{\sqrt{1-t^2}}$ is an even function.

And we know that, if $f(x)$ is an even function, then

$$\int_{-a}^{a} f(x)\,dx = 2\int_0^a f(x)\,dx$$

$$\therefore \quad I = 2\int_0^{\frac{\sqrt{3}-1}{2}} \frac{dt}{\sqrt{1-t^2}} = [2\sin^{-1} t]_0^{\frac{\sqrt{3}-1}{2}} = 2\sin^{-1}\left(\frac{\sqrt{3}-1}{2}\right)$$

Question 28 $\int_0^1 \frac{1}{\sqrt{1+x}-\sqrt{x}}\,dx$

Thinking Process These such form of integrand is not solvable, so rationalize the integrand and integrate it.

Sol. Let $I = \int_0^1 \frac{1}{\sqrt{1+x}-\sqrt{x}}\,dx = \int_0^1 \frac{(\sqrt{1+x}+\sqrt{x})}{(\sqrt{1+x}-\sqrt{x})(\sqrt{1+x}+\sqrt{x})}\,dx$

[multiply numerator and denominator by $(\sqrt{1+x}+\sqrt{x})$]

$$= \int_0^1 \frac{(\sqrt{1+x}+\sqrt{x})}{1+x-x}\,dx = \int_0^1 [(1+x)^{1/2} + x^{1/2}]\,dx$$

$$= \left[\frac{(1+x)^{\frac{1}{2}+1}}{\frac{1}{2}+1} + \frac{x^{\frac{1}{2}+1}}{\frac{1}{2}+1}\right]_0^1 = \frac{2}{3}\left[(1+x)^{\frac{3}{2}} + x^{\frac{3}{2}}\right]_0^1$$

$$= \frac{2}{3}\left[2^{\frac{3}{2}} + 1^{\frac{3}{2}} - \left(1^{\frac{3}{2}} + 0\right)\right] = \frac{2}{3}(2\sqrt{2}) = \frac{4\sqrt{2}}{3}$$

Question 29 $\int_0^{\pi/4} \frac{\sin x + \cos x}{9+16\sin 2x}\,dx.$

Sol. Let $I = \int_0^{\pi/4} \frac{\sin x + \cos x}{9+16\sin 2x}\,dx$

We know that $(\sin x - \cos x)^2 = \sin^2 x + \cos^2 x - 2\sin x\cos x$

$\Rightarrow \quad (\sin x - \cos x)^2 = 1 - \sin 2x$

[$\because \sin^2 x + \cos^2 x = 1$ and $2\sin x\cos x = \sin 2x$]

$\Rightarrow \quad \sin 2x = 1 - (\sin x - \cos x)^2$

$$\therefore \quad I = \int_0^{\pi/4} \frac{\sin x + \cos x}{9+16[1-(\sin x - \cos x)^2]}\,dx$$

Put $\quad \sin x - \cos x = t$

$$\Rightarrow \qquad \cos x + \sin x = \frac{dt}{dx} \qquad \ldots(i)$$

$$\Rightarrow \qquad dx = \frac{dt}{\cos x + \sin x}$$

For limits, when, $x = 0, t = 0 - \cos 0 = -1$ and, when $x = \frac{\pi}{4}, t = \sin\frac{\pi}{4} - \cos\frac{\pi}{4} = 0$

$$\therefore \qquad I = \int_{-1}^{0} \frac{\sin x + \cos x}{9 + 16(1 - t^2)} \frac{dt}{\cos x + \sin x} = \int_{-1}^{0} \frac{1}{9 + 16(1 - t^2)} dt$$

$$= \int_{-1}^{0} \frac{1}{9 + 16 - 16t^2} dt$$

$$= \int_{-1}^{0} \frac{1}{25 - 16t^2} dt = \frac{1}{16}\int_{-1}^{0} \frac{1}{\left(\frac{5}{4}\right)^2 - t^2} dt$$

$$= \frac{1}{16} \cdot \frac{1}{2 \cdot \frac{5}{4}} \left[\log\left|\frac{\frac{5}{4} + t}{\frac{5}{4} - t}\right|\right]_{-1}^{0} \qquad \left(\because \int \frac{1}{a^2 - x^2} dx = \frac{1}{2a}\log\left|\frac{a + x}{a - x}\right| + C\right)$$

$$= \frac{1}{40}\left[\log\left|\frac{5 + 4t}{5 - 4t}\right|\right]_{-1}^{0} = \frac{1}{40}\left[\log 1 - \log\frac{1}{9}\right]$$

$$= \frac{1}{40}[\log 1 - (\log 1 - \log 9)] = \frac{1}{40}\log 9$$

$$\left[\because \log\left(\frac{m}{n}\right) = \log m - \log n\right]$$

Question 30 $\int_0^{\pi/2} \sin 2x \tan^{-1}(\sin x)\, dx$

Sol. Let $I = \int_0^{\pi/2} \sin 2x \tan^{-1}(\sin x)\, dx$

$$= \int_0^{\pi/2} 2\sin x \cos x \tan^{-1}(\sin x)\, dx \qquad [\because \sin 2x = 2\sin x \cos x]$$

Put $\sin x = t \Rightarrow \cos x\, dx = dt \Rightarrow dx = \frac{dt}{\cos x}$

For limits, when $x = 0 \Rightarrow t = \sin 0 \Rightarrow t = 0$ and when $x = \frac{\pi}{2} \Rightarrow t = \sin\frac{\pi}{2} = 1$

$$\therefore \qquad I = \int_0^1 2t \cos x \tan^{-1} t \frac{dt}{\cos x} = 2\int_0^1 t \cdot \tan^{-t} t\, dt$$

$$= 2\left(\left[(\tan^{-1} t)\frac{t^2}{2}\right]_0^1 - \int_0^1 \frac{1}{1 + t^2} \cdot \frac{t^2}{2} dt\right) \qquad \text{[using intergration by parts]}$$

$$= 2\left[\frac{\tan^{-1} 1}{2} - 0\right] - \int_0^1 \frac{t^2}{1 + t^2} dt$$

$$= 2\left(\frac{\pi}{8}\right) - \int_0^1 \frac{(1 + t^2) - 1}{1 + t^2} dt$$

$$= \frac{\pi}{4} - \int_0^1 \left(1 - \frac{1}{1+t^2}\right) dt = \frac{\pi}{4} - [t - \tan^{-1} t]_0^1$$

$$= \frac{\pi}{4} - [1 - \tan^{-1} 1 - (0 - 0)] = \frac{\pi}{4} - 1 + \frac{\pi}{4} = \frac{\pi}{2} - 1$$

Question 31 $\int_1^4 \{|x-1| + |x-2| + |x-3|\}\, dx$

◎ *Thinking Process* Firstly, define the absolute function as

$$|x-1| = \begin{cases} x-1, x \geq 1 \\ (x-1), x < 1 \end{cases}, |x-2| = \begin{cases} x-2, x \geq 2 \\ -(x-2), x < 2 \end{cases}, |x-3| = \begin{cases} x-3, x \geq 3 \\ -(x-3), x < 3 \end{cases}$$

and then it is easy to solve.

Sol. Let $I = \int_1^4 [|x-1| + |x-2| + |x-3|]\, dx$

$$= \int_1^2 (|x-1| + |x-2| + |x-3|)\, dx + \int_2^3 \{|x-1| + |x-2| + |x-3|\}\, dx + \int_3^4 \{|x-1| + |x-2| + |x-3|\}\, dx$$

$$= \int_1^2 \{x - 1 - (x-2) - (x-3)\}\, dx + \int_2^3 \{x - 1 + x - 2 - (x-3)\}\, dx + \int_3^4 (x - 1 + x - 2 + x - 3)\, dx$$

$$= \int_1^2 (-x+4)\, dx + \int_2^3 x\, dx + \int_3^4 (3x-6)\, dx$$

$$= \left[-\frac{x^2}{2} + 4x\right]_1^2 + \left[\frac{x^2}{2}\right]_2^3 + \left[\frac{3x^2}{2} - 6x\right]_3^4$$

$$= \left(\frac{-2^2}{2} + 8\right) - \left(\frac{-1}{2} + 4\right) + \frac{1}{2}(3^2 - 2^2) + \left(\frac{3}{2} \times 4^2 - 6 \times 4\right) - \left(\frac{3}{2} \times 3^2 - 6 \times 3\right)$$

$$= 6 - \frac{7}{2} + \frac{5}{2} + (24 - 24) - \left(-\frac{9}{2}\right) = \frac{12 - 7 + 5}{2} + 0 + \frac{9}{2} = \frac{19}{2}$$

Direction (Q. No. 32 to 37) Prove the following questions.

Question 32 $\int_1^3 \frac{1}{x^2(x+1)}\, dx = \frac{2}{3} + \log \frac{2}{3}$

Sol. Let $I = \int_1^3 \frac{1}{x^2(x+1)}\, dx$

By using partial fraction method

Let $$\frac{1}{x^2(x+1)} = \frac{A}{x} + \frac{B}{x^2} + \frac{C}{x+1} \quad \ldots\text{(i)}$$

$\Rightarrow$ $$1 = Ax(x+1) + B(x+1) + Cx^2 \quad \ldots\text{(ii)}$$

Substituting $x = 0, -1$ in Eq. (ii), we get

$$1 = B(0+1) \text{ and } 1 = C(-1)^2 \quad \Rightarrow \quad B = 1 \text{ and } C = 1$$

On equating the coefficients of x^2 both sides of Eq. (ii), we get

$$0 = A + C \Rightarrow A = -C = -1$$

$$\therefore \int_1^3 \frac{1}{x^2(x+1)} dx = \int_1^3 \left(-\frac{1}{x} + \frac{1}{x^2} + \frac{1}{x+1}\right) dx$$

$$= \left[-\log|x| - \frac{1}{x} + \log|x+1|\right]_1^3$$

$$= \left[\log\left|\frac{x+1}{x}\right| - \frac{1}{x}\right]_1^3 = \left(\log\left|\frac{4}{3}\right| - \frac{1}{3}\right) - \left(\log\left|\frac{2}{1}\right| - \frac{1}{1}\right)$$

$$= \left(\log\frac{4}{3} - \log 2\right) + \left(1 - \frac{1}{3}\right)$$

$$= \log\left(\frac{4}{3} \times \frac{1}{2}\right) + \frac{2}{3} \qquad \left[\because \log\left(\frac{m}{n}\right) = \log m - \log n\right]$$

$$= \log\frac{2}{3} + \frac{2}{3}$$

Hence Proved.

Questions 33 $\int_0^1 x e^x dx = 1$

Sol. Let $I = \int_0^1 x e^x dx$

Applying rule of integration by parts taking x as the first function and e^x as the second function, we get

$$I = x\int_0^1 e^x dx - \int_0^1 1.e^x dx = [xe^x - e^x]_0^1 = [e^x(x-1)]_0^1 = e(1-1) - e^0(0-1)$$

$$= 0 + 1 = 1$$

Hence Proved.

Question 34 $\int_{-1}^1 x^{17} \cos^4 x \, dx = 0$

Let $I = \int_{-1}^{1} x^{17} \cos^4 x \, dx$

Sol. Let $f(x) = x^{17}\cos^4 x,$

$\Rightarrow f(-x) = (-x)^{17}\cos^4(-x) = -x^{17}\cos^4 x = -f(x)$

Therefore, $f(x)$ is an odd function.

We known that if $f(x)$ is an odd function, then $\int_{-a}^{a} f(x)\, dx = 0$

$$\therefore \int_{-1}^1 x^{17}\cos^4 x \, dx = 0.$$

Hence Proved.

Question 35 $\int_0^{\pi/2} \sin^3 x \, dx = \frac{2}{3}$

Sol. Let $I = \int_0^{\pi/2} \sin^3 x \, dx = \int_0^{\pi/2} \sin^2 x \cdot \sin x \, dx$

$$= \int_0^{\pi/2} (1 - \cos^2 x)\sin x \, dx \qquad [\because \sin^2 x = 1 - \cos^2 x]$$

Put $\cos x = t \Rightarrow -\sin x \, dx = dt$

For limits, when $x = 0 \Rightarrow t = \cos 0 = 1$ and when $x = \frac{\pi}{2} \Rightarrow t = \cos\frac{\pi}{2} = 0$

$$\therefore \quad I = \int_1^0 (1 - t^2)(-dt)$$

$$= -\left[t - \frac{t^3}{3}\right]_1^0 = -\left\{(0-0) - \left(1 - \frac{1}{3}\right)\right\} = \frac{2}{3}$$ **Hence Proved.**

Quick Solution

Let $I = \int_0^{\pi/2} \sin^3 x\, dx = \frac{1}{4}\int_0^{\pi/2} (3\sin x - \sin 3x)dx$

$[\because \sin 3\theta = 3\sin\theta - 4\sin^3\theta]$

$$= \frac{1}{4}\left[-3\cos x + \frac{\cos 3x}{3}\right]_0^{\pi/2} = \frac{1}{4}\left[-3\cos\frac{\pi}{2} + \frac{1}{3}\cos\frac{3\pi}{2}\right] - \frac{1}{4}\left[-3\cos 0 + \frac{1}{3}\cos 0\right]$$

$$= \frac{1}{4}\left[-3 \times 0 + \frac{1}{3} \times 0\right] - \frac{1}{4}\left[-3 \times 1 + \frac{1}{3} \times 1\right] = 0 - \frac{1}{4}\left[-\frac{8}{3}\right] = \frac{2}{3}$$

Hence Proved.

Question 36 $\int_0^{\pi/4} 2\tan^3 x\, dx = 1 - \log 2$

Sol. Let $I = \int_0^{\pi/4} 2\tan^3 x\, dx = 2\int_0^{\pi/4} \tan^2 x \cdot \tan x\, dx$

$$= 2\int_0^{\pi/4} (\sec^2 x - 1)\tan x\, dx \qquad [\because 1 + \tan^2 x = \sec^2 x]$$

$$= 2\left[\int_0^{\pi/4} \sec^2 x \tan x\, dx - \int_0^{\pi/4} \tan x\, dx\right]$$

$$= 2\int_0^{\pi/4} (\tan x)\sec^2 x\, dx - 2\left[-\log|\cos x|\right]_0^{\pi/4}$$

Let, $\quad I_1 = \int (\tan x)\sec^2 x\, dx$

Put $\tan x = t \Rightarrow \sec^2 x\, dx = dt$

$$\therefore \quad I_1 = \int t\, dt = \frac{t^2}{2} = \frac{\tan^2 x}{2}$$

$$\therefore \quad I = 2\left[\frac{\tan^2 x}{2}\right]_0^{\pi/4} + 2\left[\log\left|\cos\frac{\pi}{4}\right| - \log|\cos 0|\right]$$

$$= \tan^2\left(\frac{\pi}{4}\right) - 0 + 2\log\left(\frac{1}{\sqrt{2}}\right) - \log 1 = 1 + 2\log 2^{-1/2} - 0$$

$(\because \log 1 = 0)$

$$= 1 - 2 \times \frac{1}{2}\log 2 = 1 - \log 2$$ **Hence Proved.**

Question 37 $\int_0^1 \sin^{-1} x\, dx = \frac{\pi}{2} - 1.$

Sol. Let $I = \int_0^1 \sin^{-1} x\, dx = \int_0^1 \sin^{-1} x \cdot 1\, dx$

Applying rule of integration by parts taking $\sin^{-1} x$ as the first function and 1 as second function, we get

$$I = [(\sin^{-1} x)x]_0^1 - \int_0^1 \frac{x}{\sqrt{1-x^2}} dx$$

Put $1 - x^2 = t \Rightarrow -2x\, dx = dt$

When $x = 0 \Rightarrow t = 1$ and when $x = 1 \Rightarrow t = 0$

$$\therefore I = [x \sin^{-1} x]_0^1 + \frac{1}{2}\int_1^0 \frac{dt}{\sqrt{t}} = [x \sin^{-1} x]_0^1 + \frac{1}{2}\left[\frac{t^{1/2}}{1/2}\right]_1^0 = 1 \sin^{-1}(1) + [-\sqrt{1}]$$

$$= \frac{\pi}{2} - 1$$

Hence Proved.

Direction (Q. No. 38 to 40) Choose the correct answer.

Question 38 $\int \frac{1}{e^x + e^{-x}} dx$ is equal to

(a) $\tan^{-1}(e^x) + C$

(b) $\tan^{-1}(e^{-x}) + C$

(c) $\log(e^x - e^{-x}) + C$

(d) $\log(e^x + e^{-x}) + C$

Sol. (a) $I = \int \frac{1}{e^x + e^{-x}} dx = \int \frac{1}{e^x + \frac{1}{e^x}} dx = \int \frac{e^x}{(e^x)^2 + 1} dx$

Put $e^x = t \Rightarrow e^x dx = dt$

$$\therefore \quad I = \int \frac{e^x}{(t^2+1)} \frac{dt}{e^x} = \tan^{-1}(t) + C = \tan^{-1} e^x + C \quad \left(\because \int \frac{dx}{1+x^2} = \tan^{-1} x + C\right)$$

Question 39 $\int \frac{\cos 2x}{(\sin x + \cos x)^2} dx$ is equal to

(a) $\frac{-1}{\sin x + \cos x} + C$

(b) $\log|\sin x + \cos x| + C$

(c) $\log|\sin x - \cos x| + C$

(d) $\frac{1}{(\sin x + \cos x)^2} + C$

Sol. (b) Let $I = \int \frac{\cos 2x}{(\sin x + \cos x)^2} dx = \int \frac{\cos^2 x - \sin^2 x}{(\sin x + \cos x)^2} dx$

$[\because \cos 2x = \cos^2 x - \sin^2 x]$

$$= \int \frac{(\cos x - \sin x)(\cos x + \sin x)}{(\sin x + \cos x)(\sin x + \cos x)} dx = \int \frac{\cos x - \sin x}{\sin x + \cos x} dx$$

Put $\sin x + \cos x = t \Rightarrow (\cos x - \sin x)\, dx = dt$

$$\therefore \quad I = \int \frac{1}{t} dt = \log|t| + C = \log|\sin x + \cos x| + C$$

Question 40 If $f(a+b-x)=f(x)$, then $\int_a^b x\, f(x)\, dx$ is equal to

(a) $\frac{a+b}{2}\int_a^b f(b-x)\, dx$ (b) $\frac{a+b}{2}\int_a^b f(b+x)\, dx$

(c) $\frac{b-a}{2}\int_a^b f(x)\, dx$ (d) $\frac{a+b}{2}\int_a^b f(x)\, dx$

Sol. (d) Let $I=\int_a^b x\, f(x)\, dx$ ...(i)

Then, by a property of definite integrals

$$I=\int_a^b (a+b-x)\, f(a+b-x)\, dx=\int_a^b (a+b-x)\, f(x)\, dx \quad \text{...(ii)}$$

$[\because f(a+b-x)=f(x), \text{(given)}]$

On adding Eqs. (i) and (ii), we get

$$2I=\int_a^b (a+b)\, f(x)\, dx \Rightarrow I=\frac{a+b}{2}\int_a^b f(x)\, dx$$

DIKSHA APP Questions

☐ Multiple Choice Questions

Q.1 Find $\int_1^2 [x]\, dx$, where $[x]$ is greatest integer function.

(a) 0 (b) 1

(c) 2 (d) 3

Sol. (b) Let $I=\int_1^2 [x]\, dx$

$\int_1^2 1\, dx$ $[\because [x]=1, \text{ when } 1\le x<2]$

$=[x]_1^2$

$=2-1=1$

Q.2 Integrate $\frac{2^x}{3^x}$

(a) $x\log 2 - x\log 3 + C$ (b) $\frac{\left(\frac{2}{3}\right)^x}{\log\left(\frac{2}{3}\right)}+C$

(c) $\frac{\left(\frac{3}{2}\right)^x}{\log\left(\frac{3}{2}\right)}+C$ (d) None of these

Sol. (b) Let $I = \int \frac{2^x}{3^x} dx = \int \left(\frac{2}{3}\right)^x dx$ $\left[\because \frac{(a)^n}{(b)^n} = \left(\frac{a}{b}\right)^n\right]$

$$= \frac{\left(\frac{2}{3}\right)^x}{\log\left(\frac{2}{3}\right)} + C \qquad \left[\because \int a^x = \frac{a^x}{\log a} + C\right]$$

Mistake Alert Students may incorrectly take $\int a^x = a^x \cdot \log a + C$

Instead of $\int a^x = \frac{a^x}{\log a} + C$

Q.3 $\int_0^1 \log\left(\frac{1-x}{x}\right) dx =$

(a) log 3 – log 5
(b) log 2 – log 3
(c) log 4 – log 5
(d) 0

Sol. (b) (d) Let $I = \int_0^1 \log\left(\frac{1-x}{x}\right) dx$

$$\Rightarrow \qquad I = \int_0^1 1 \cdot \log\left(\frac{1-x}{x}\right) dx$$

On taking $\log\left(\frac{1-x}{x}\right)$ as first function and 1 as second function and integrating by parts, we get

$$I = \left[\log\left(\frac{1-x}{x}\right) \cdot x\right]_0^1 - \int_0^1 \frac{1}{\frac{1-x}{x}}\left(\frac{-1}{x^2} - 0\right) \cdot x \, dx$$

$$= \left[x \cdot \log\left(\frac{1-x}{x}\right)\right]_0^1 + \int_0^1 \left(\frac{x}{1-x}\right) \cdot \frac{x}{x^2} \, dx$$

$$= \left[x \log\left(\frac{1-x}{x}\right)\right]_0^1 + \int_0^1 \frac{1}{1-x} dx$$

$$= \left[x \log\left(\frac{1-x}{x}\right)\right]_0^1 - [\log(1-x)]_0^1$$

$$= \left[1 \cdot \log\left(\frac{1-1}{1}\right) - 0\right] - [\log(1-1) - 0]$$

$$= 0$$

Quick Solution

Let $I = \int_0^1 \log\left(\frac{1-x}{x}\right)dx$ ...(i)

$= \int_0^1 \log\left(\frac{1-(1-x)}{1-x}\right)dx$ $\left[\because \int_0^a f(x)\,dx = \int_0^a f(a-x)\,dx\right]$

$= \int_0^1 \log\left(\frac{x}{1-x}\right)dx$ ...(ii)

On adding Eqs. (i) and (ii), we get

$$2I = \int_0^1 \log\left(\frac{1-x}{x} \times \frac{x}{1-x}\right)dx$$

$$= \int_0^1 \log(1)\,dx \Rightarrow 2I = 0 \Rightarrow I = 0$$

Q.4 $\int x^3 e^{x^4}\,dx$

(a) $\frac{1}{2}e^{x^4} + C$ (b) $\frac{1}{3}e^{x^4} + C$

(c) $\frac{1}{4}e^{x^4} + C$ (d) $\frac{1}{5}e^{x^4} + C$

Sol. (c) Let $I = \int x^3 e^{x^4}\,dx$

Put $x^4 = t \Rightarrow 4x^3 = \frac{dt}{dx}$

$\Rightarrow dx = \frac{dt}{4x^3}$

$\therefore I = \int x^3 e^t \times \frac{dt}{4x^3} = \frac{1}{4}\int e^t dt$

$= \frac{1}{4}e^t + C = \frac{1}{4}e^{x^4} + C$

Q.5 $\int \sqrt{1+x^2}\,dx$

(a) $\frac{x}{2}\sqrt{1+x^2} - \frac{1}{2}\log|x + \sqrt{1+x^2}| + C$

(b) $\frac{x}{2}\sqrt{1+x^2} + \frac{1}{2}\log|x + \sqrt{1+x^2}| + C$

(c) $\frac{x}{2}\sqrt{1+x^2} - \log|x + \sqrt{1+x^2}| + C$

(d) $\frac{x}{2}\sqrt{1+x^2} + \log|x + \sqrt{1+x^2}| + C$

Sol. (b) Let $I = \int \sqrt{1 + x^2}\, dx = \int \sqrt{1^2 + x^2}\, dx$

$$= \frac{x}{2}\sqrt{1^2 + x^2} + \frac{1^2}{2}\log|x + \sqrt{1^2 + x^2}| + C$$

$$\left[\because \int \sqrt{a^2 + x^2}\, dx = \frac{x}{2}\sqrt{a^2 + x^2} + \frac{a^2}{2}\log|x + \sqrt{x^2 + a^2}| + C\right]$$

$$\therefore \quad I = \frac{x}{2}\sqrt{1 + x^2} + \frac{1}{2}\log|x + \sqrt{1 + x^2}| + C$$

Q.6 Which of the expression is equal to $\int_0^{\pi/2} \log(\tan x)\, dx$

(a) $\int_0^{\pi/2} \log(\sin x)\, dx$ (b) $\int_0^{\pi/2} \log(\cos x)\, dx$

(c) $\int_0^{\pi/2} \log(\sec x)\, dx$ (d) $\int_0^{\pi/2} \log(\cot x)\, dx$

Sol. (d) Let $I = \int_0^{\pi/2} \log(\tan x)\, dx$

$$= \int_0^{\pi/2} \log\left(\tan\left(\frac{\pi}{2} - x\right)dx\right) \quad \left[\because \int_0^a f(x) \cdot dx = \int_0^a f(a - x)\, dx\right]$$

$$\therefore \quad I = \int_0^{\pi/2} \log(\cot x)\, dx \quad \left[\because \tan\left(\frac{\pi}{2} - x\right) = \cot x\right]$$

Q.7 $\int_1^2 e^x dx$

(a) e^x (b) $e(e + 1)$

(c) $e(e - 1)$ (d) None of these

Sol. (c) Let $I = I\int_1^2 e^x dx$

$$= [e^x]_1^2 = e^2 - e^1 = e(e - 1)$$

Q.8 $\int_1^2 \frac{1}{(x+1)(x+2)} dx$

(a) $\log 9 - \log 8$ (b) $\log(16) - \log(27)$

(c) $\log(32) - \log(25)$ (d) $\log(16) - \log(25)$

Sol. (a) Let $I = \int_1^2 \frac{1}{(x + 1)(x + 2)} dx$

Let $\frac{1}{(x + 1)(x + 2)} = \frac{A}{(x + 1)} + \frac{B}{(x + 2)}$

$\Rightarrow \quad 1 = A(x + 2) + B(x + 1) = Ax + 2A + Bx + B$

$\Rightarrow \quad 1 = (A + B)x + (2A + B)$

On equating the coefficients of x and constant term both sides, we get

$$A + B = 0, 2A + B = 1$$

On solving these equations, we get $A = 1, B = -1$

$$\therefore \quad \frac{1}{(x+1)(x+2)} = \frac{1}{(x+1)} + \frac{-1}{(x+2)}$$

$$\Rightarrow \quad \int_1^2 \frac{1}{(x+1)(x+2)}dx = \int \frac{1}{x+1}dx + \int_1^2 \frac{-1}{(x+2)}dx$$

$$= [\log(x+1)]_1^2 - [\log(x+2)]_1^2$$
$$= [\log 3 - \log 2] - [\log 4 - \log 3]$$
$$= \log 3 - \log 2 - \log 4 + \log 3$$
$$= 2\log 3 - \log 2 - \log 4$$
$$= \log 3^2 - (\log 2 + \log 4)$$
$$= \log 9 - \log(2 \cdot 4)$$
$$= \log 9 - \log 8$$

Q.9 $\int_0^{\pi/2} \frac{\sin x}{\sin x + \cos x} dx$

(a) 0 (b) $\frac{\pi}{6}$ (c) $\frac{\pi}{4}$ (d) $\frac{\pi}{3}$

Sol. (c) Let $I = \int_0^{\pi/2} \frac{\sin x}{\sin x + \cos x} dx$ ...(i)

$$\therefore \quad I = \int_0^{\pi/2} \frac{\sin\left(\frac{\pi}{2} - x\right)}{\sin\left(\frac{\pi}{2} - x\right) + \cos\left(\frac{\pi}{2} - x\right)} dx \qquad \left[\because \int_0^a f(x)dx = \int_0^a f(a-x)dx\right]$$

$$= \int_0^{\pi/2} \frac{\cos x}{\cos x + \sin x} dx \qquad \text{...(ii)}$$

$$\left[\because \sin\left(\frac{\pi}{2} - \theta\right) = \cos\theta \text{ and } \cos\left(\frac{\pi}{2} - \theta\right) = \sin\theta\right]$$

On adding Eqs. (i) and (ii), we get

$$2I = \int_0^{\pi/2} \left(\frac{\sin x}{\sin x + \cos x} + \frac{\cos x}{\cos x + \sin x}\right) dx$$

$$= \int_0^{\pi/2} \left(\frac{\sin x + \cos x}{\sin x + \cos x}\right) dx = \int_0^{\pi/2} 1\,dx = [x]_0^{\pi/2}$$

$$\Rightarrow \quad 2I = \frac{\pi}{2} - 0 \Rightarrow I = \frac{\pi}{4}$$

Q.10 $\int_{-1}^1 (x^3 - x)dx$

(a) $\frac{-3}{2}$ (b) 0

(c) $\frac{1}{4}$ (d) $\frac{3}{4}$

Sol. (b) Let $I = \int_{-1}^{1}(x^3 - x)dx$

$$= \left[\frac{x^4}{4} - \frac{x^2}{2}\right]_{-1}^{1} = \left(\frac{1}{4} - \frac{1}{2}\right) - \left(\frac{1}{4} - \frac{1}{2}\right) = \frac{1}{4} - \frac{1}{2} - \frac{1}{4} + \frac{1}{2} = 0$$

Q.11 $\int \sin x \cdot e^x dx$

(a) $\frac{1}{2}e^x(\sin x - \cos x) + C$ (b) $\frac{1}{2}e^x(\sin x + \cos x) + C$

(c) $\frac{1}{2}e^x(\cos x - \sin x) + C$ (d) $e^x(\sin x - \cos x) + C$

Sol. (a) Let $I = \int \sin x \cdot e^x dx$ ...(i)

On taking $\sin x$ as first function and e^x as second function and integrating by parts, we get

$$I = \sin x \int e^x dx - \int \left[\frac{d}{dx}\sin x \int e^x dx\right] dx$$

$$= \sin x \cdot e^x - \int \cos x e^x dx$$

$$= \sin x \cdot e^x - \left[\cos x \int e^x dx - \int \left\{\frac{d}{dx}\cos x \int \{e^x dx\} dx\right\}\right]$$

$$= \sin x \cdot e^x - [\cos x \cdot e^x + \int \sin x e^x dx]$$

$\Rightarrow$ $I = e^x(\sin x - \cos x) - I + C$ [from Eq. (i)]

$\Rightarrow$ $2I = e^x(\sin x - \cos x) + C$

$\Rightarrow$ $I = \frac{1}{2}e^x(\sin x - \cos x) + C$

Q.12 $\int \log x \, dx$

(a) $\frac{1}{x} + C$ (b) $\frac{-1}{x} + C$

(c) $x \log x + x + C$ (d) $x \log x - x + C$

Sol. (d) Let $I = \int 1 \cdot \log x \, dx$

On taking $\log x$ as first function and 1 as second function and integrating by parts, we get

$$I = \log x \int 1 dx - \int \left[\frac{d}{dx}\log x \int 1 dx\right] dx$$

$$= \log x \cdot x - \int \frac{1}{x} \cdot x \, dx$$

$$= \log x \cdot x - x + C$$

Mistake Alert Students may incorrectly take $\int \log x dx = \frac{1}{x} + C$ instead of $\int \log x \, dx = x \log x - x + C$

Q.13 $\int \cos(2x+3)dx =$

(a) $-2\sin(2x+3)+C$ (b) $2\sin(2x+3)+C$

(c) $\frac{\sin(2x+3)}{2}+C$ (d) $\frac{-\sin(2x+3)}{2}+C$

Sol. (c) Let $I = \int \cos(2x+3)dx$

$$= \frac{\sin(2x+3)}{2}+C$$

Q.14 Find $\int \sec x(\sec x+\tan x)dx$

(a) $\tan x + C$ (b) $\sec x + C$

(c) $\sec x + \tan x + C$ (d) None of the above

Sol. (c) Let $I = \int \sec x\,(\sec x + \tan x)dx$

$$= \int (\sec^2 x + \sec x\,\tan x)\,dx$$

$$= \tan x + \sec x + C$$

Q.15 $\int_a^b f(x)dx$ will not be equal to

(a) $\int_a^b f(y)dy$ (b) $-\int_b^a f(x)dx$

(c) $\int_a^b f(x)dy$ (d) $\int_a^b f(t)dt$

Sol. (c) $\int_a^b f(x)dx$ is not equal to $\int_a^b f(x)dy$.

☐ Subjective Type Questions

Q.1 Evaluate $\int_0^{\pi/2} \sin^2 x\,dx$

Sol. Let $I = \int_0^{\pi/2} \sin^2 x\,dx$ ...(i)

$$= \int_0^{\pi/2} \sin^2\left[\frac{\pi}{2}-x\right]dx \quad \left[\because \int_0^{\pi/2} f(x)dx = \int_0^a f(a-x)dx\right]$$

$\therefore$ $$I = \int_0^{\pi/2} \cos^2 x dx$$ ...(iii)

$$\left[\because \sin\left(\frac{\pi}{2}-x\right) = \cos x\right]$$

On adding Eqs. (i) and (ii), we get

$$2I = \int_0^{\pi/2} (\sin^2 x + \cos^2 x)dx = \int_0^{\pi/2} 1\,dx$$

$\Rightarrow$ $$2I = [x]_0^{\pi/2} = \frac{\pi}{2} - 0$$

$\Rightarrow$ $$I = \frac{\pi}{4}$$

Q.2 Find $\int_0^1 \frac{\tan^{-1} x}{1+x^2} dx$

Sol. Let $I = \int_0^1 \frac{\tan^{-1} x}{1+x^2} dx$

Put $\tan^{-1} x = t \Rightarrow \frac{1}{1+x^2} = \frac{dt}{dx}$

$$\Rightarrow \qquad \frac{dx}{1+x^2} = dt$$

For limits, when $x = 0$

$$\Rightarrow \qquad t = \tan^{-1}(0) = 0$$

and when $x = 1 \Rightarrow t = \tan^{-1}(1) = \frac{\pi}{4}$

$$\therefore \qquad I = \int_0^{\pi/4} t\, dt = \left[\frac{t^2}{2}\right]_0^{\pi/4}$$

$$= \frac{\left(\frac{\pi}{4}\right)^2}{2} - 0 = \frac{\pi^2}{32}$$

Application of Integrals

CHAPTER 08

Important Points

01 The area enclosed by the curve $y = f(x)$, the X-axis and the ordinates $x = a$ and $x = b$, is given by $\int_a^b |y|\, dx$.

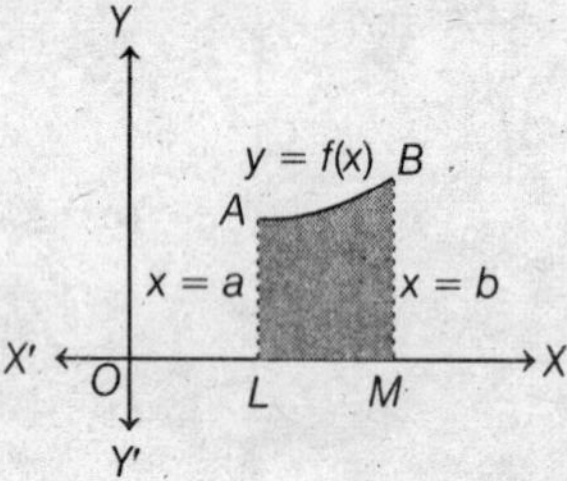

02 The area enclosed by the curve $x = f(y)$, the Y-axis and the abscissae $y = c$ and $y = d$ is given by $\int_c^d |x|\, dy$.

03 If the position of the curve under consideration is below the X-axis, then area bounded by the curve, X-axis and the ordinates $x = a$, $x = b$, is

$$\left|\int_a^b f(x)\,dx\right| \text{ or } \int_a^b |f(x)|\,dx$$

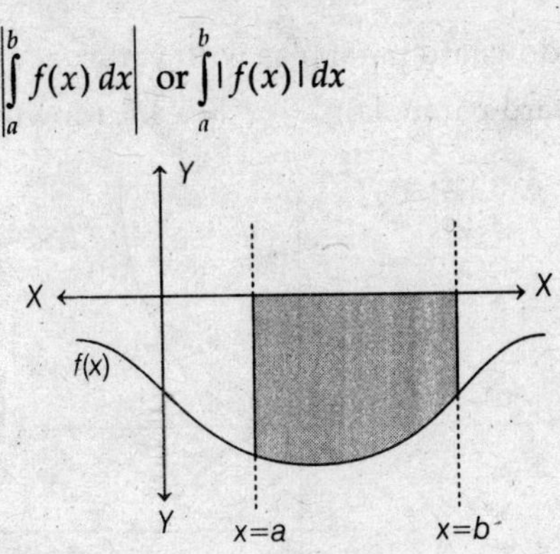

04 Some useful curves

(a) Circle with centre (0, 0) and radius r

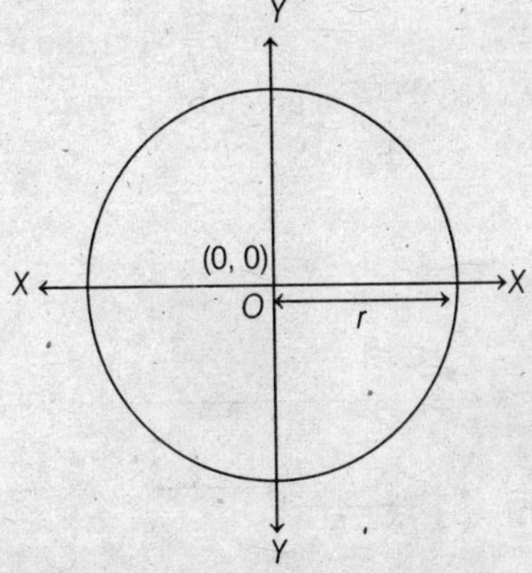

(b) Left handed and right handed parabolas with vertex at origin.
$y^2 = 4ax$ (right hand parabola),
$y^2 = -4ax$ (left hand parabola)

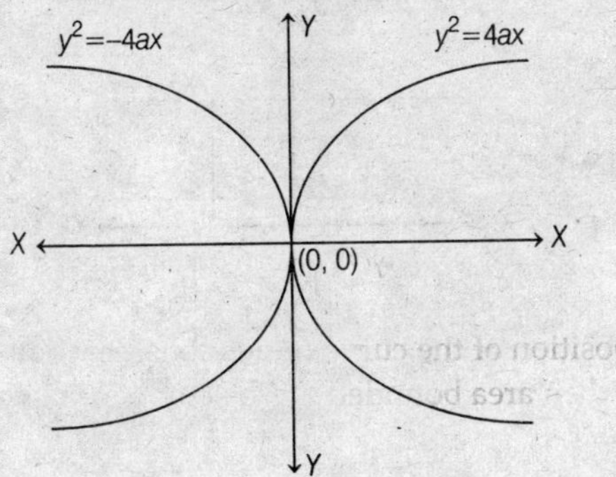

(c) Upward and downard parabolas with vertex at origin

$x^2 = 4ay$ (upward parabola), $x^2 = -4ay$ (downward parabola)

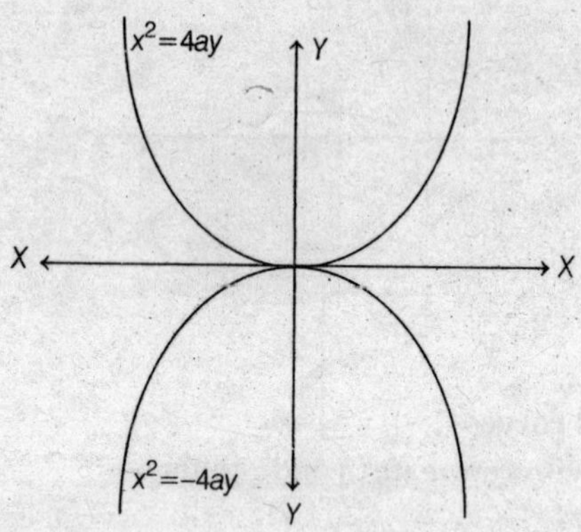

(d) Lines parallel to Y-axis

$$x = a, x = -b$$

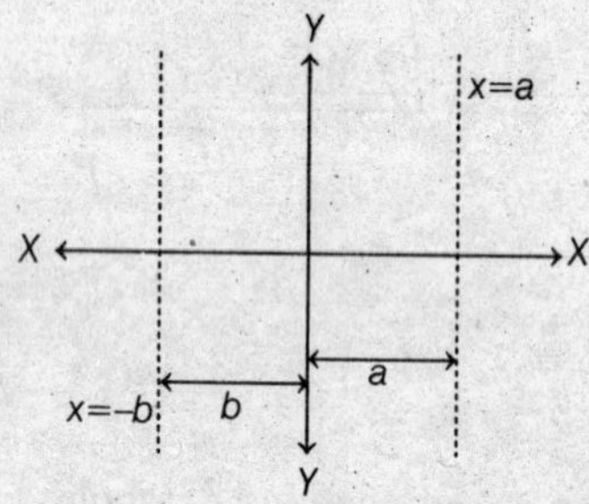

(e) Lines parallel to X-axis

$$y = a, y = -b$$

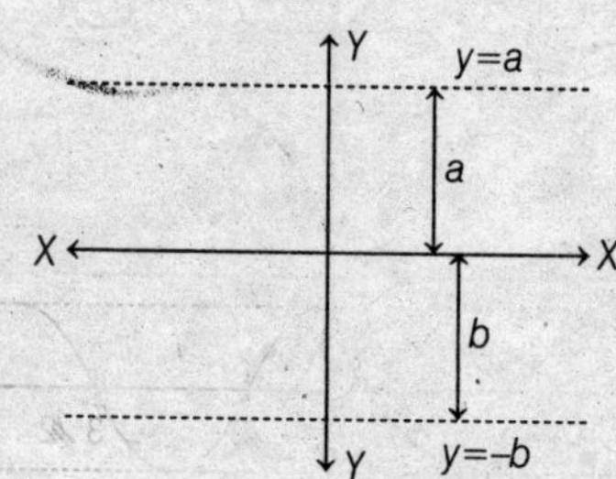

(f) Ellipse with centre (0,0)

$$\frac{x^2}{a^2} + \frac{y^2}{b^2} = 1$$

(i) Horizontal ellipse

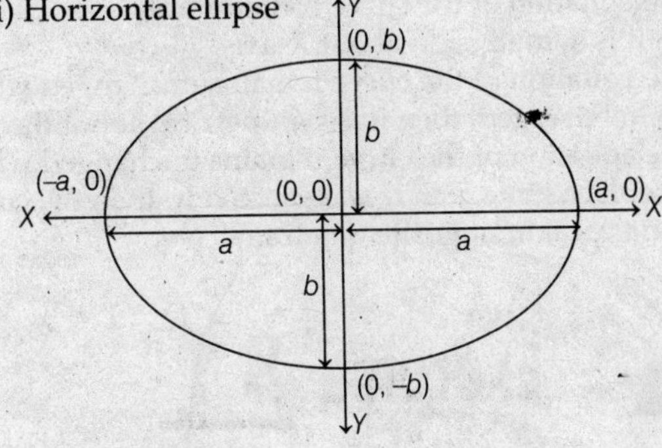

(ii) Vertical ellipse

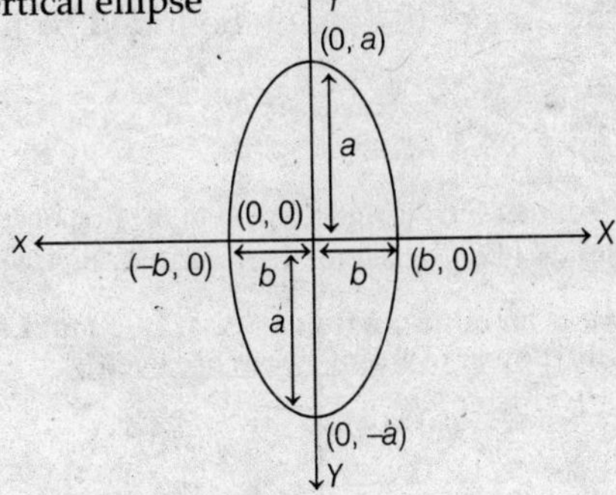

(g) $y = \sin x, \quad x \in [-2\pi, 2\pi]$

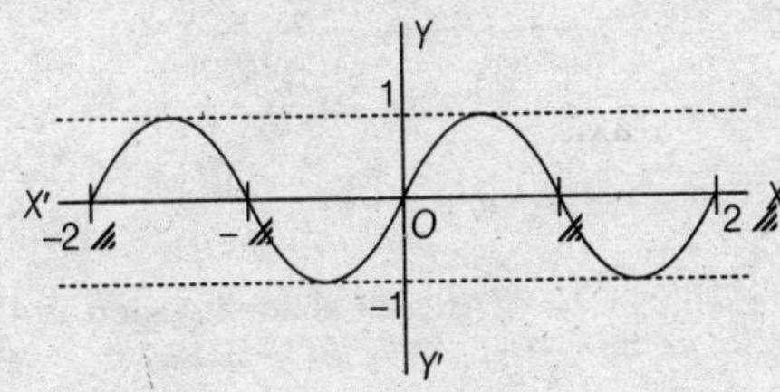

(h) $y = \cos x, \quad x \in [-2\pi, 2\pi]$

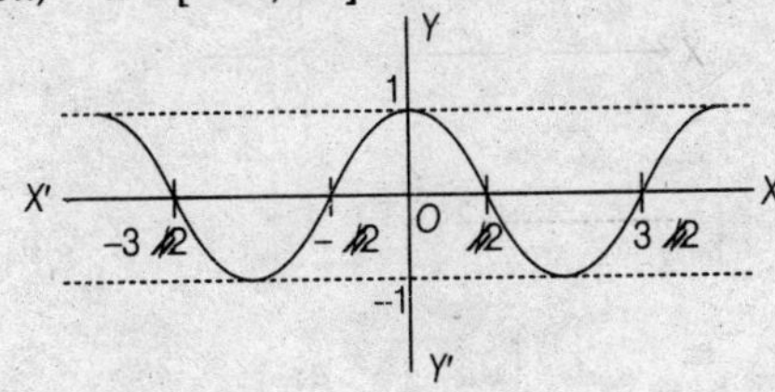

05 Curve sketching

(i) If the equation of the curve contains only even powers of x, then it is symmetrical about Y-axis.

(ii) If the equation of the curve contains only even powers of y, then it is symmetrical about X-axis.

(iii) If the equation of the curve remains unchanged when x and y are interchanged, then it is symmetrical about the line $y = x$.

(iv) If the equation of the curve remains unchanged when x and y are replaced by $-x$ and $-y$ respectively, then the curve is symmetrical in opposite quadrants.

Exercise 8.1

Question 1 Find the area of the region bounded by the ellipse $\frac{x^2}{16} + \frac{y^2}{9} = 1$.

◎ *Thinking Process* Firstly, find the area in the first quadrant and then multiply by four (as in one quadrant there will only be 1/4 part of the ellipse).

Sol. The given curve is an ellipse with centre at (0, 0) and symmetrical about X-axis and Y-axis. ($\because$ the power of x and y both are even).

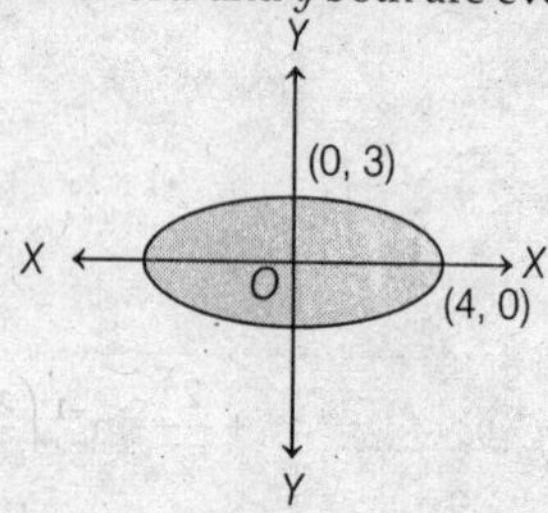

Area bounded by the ellipse = 4 × (Area of shaded region in the first quadrant only)

($\because$ By symmetry)

$$= 4 \times \int_{x=a}^{x=b} |y|\, dx = 4 \int_0^4 |y|\, dx = 4 \int_0^4 \frac{3}{4} \sqrt{16 - x^2}\, dx$$

$$\left(\because \frac{x^2}{16} + \frac{y^2}{9} = 1, \therefore |y| = \frac{3}{4} \sqrt{16 - x^2} \right)$$

$$= 3 \int_0^4 \sqrt{4^2 - x^2}\, dx = 3 \left[\frac{x}{2} \sqrt{4^2 - x^2} + \frac{4^2}{2} \sin^{-1}\left(\frac{x}{4}\right) \right]_0^4$$

$$\left[\because \int \sqrt{a^2 - x^2}\, dx = \frac{x}{2} \sqrt{a^2 - x^2} + \frac{a^2}{2} \sin^{-1}\left(\frac{x}{a}\right) + C \right]$$

$$= 3[2\sqrt{16-16} + 8\sin^{-1}(1) - 0 - 8\sin^{-1}(0)]$$

$$= 3[0 + 8\sin^{-1}(1) - 0] = 3 \times 8 \times \left(\frac{\pi}{2}\right) = 12\pi \text{ sq. units}$$

Note If we take elementary strip about either X or Y-axis, in both cases the area should be same.

Question 2 Find the area of the region bounded by the ellipse $\frac{x^2}{4} + \frac{y^2}{9} = 1.$

Sol. The given curve is an ellipse with centre at (0, 0) and symmetrical about X-axis and Y-axis.

Area bounded by the ellipse

$= 4 \times$ (Area of shaded region in the first quadrant only) ($\because$ By symmetry)

$$= 4 \times \int_{x=a}^{x=b} |y|\, dx$$

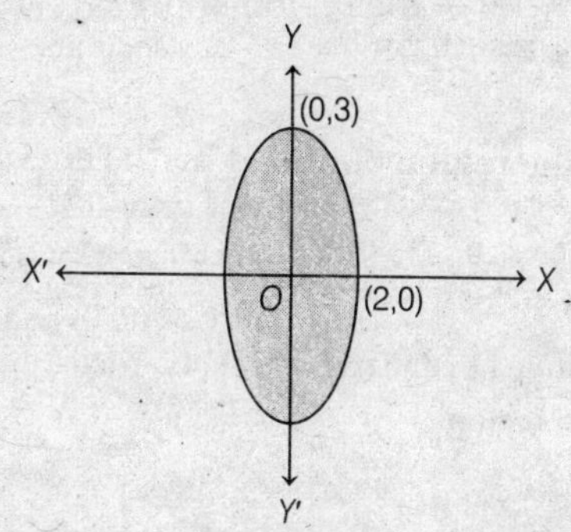

$$= 4\int_0^2 |y|\, dx = 4\int_0^2 \frac{3}{2}\sqrt{4-x^2}\, dx \qquad \left(\because \frac{x^2}{4} + \frac{y^2}{9} = 1, \therefore |y| = \frac{3}{2}\sqrt{4-x^2}\right)$$

$$= 6\int_0^2 \sqrt{2^2 - x^2}\, dx = 6\left[\frac{x}{2}\sqrt{2^2 - x^2} + \frac{2^2}{2}\sin^{-1}\left(\frac{x}{2}\right)\right]_0^2$$

$$\left[\because \int \sqrt{a^2 - x^2}\, dx = \frac{x}{2}\sqrt{a^2 - x^2} + \frac{a^2}{2}\sin^{-1}\left(\frac{x}{a}\right) + C\right]$$

$$= 6\{0 + 2\sin^{-1}(1) - 0\} = 6 \times 2 \times \left(\frac{\pi}{2}\right) = 6\pi \text{ sq. units}$$

Mistake Alert Do not forget to add the units of area after final results.

Direction (Q. Nos. 3 to 4) Choose the correct answer in the following.

Question 3 Area lying in the first quadrant and bounded by the circle $x^2 + y^2 = 4$ and the lines $x = 0$ and $x = 2$ is

(a) π (b) $\frac{\pi}{2}$ (c) $\frac{\pi}{3}$ (d) $\frac{\pi}{4}$

Sol. (a) The area bounded by the circle and the lines $x = 0$ and $x = 2$ in the first quadrant is represented in the figure by shaded region.

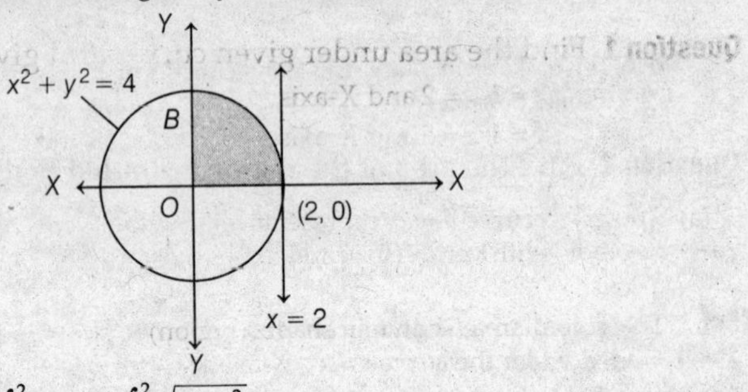

$$\text{Required area} = \int_0^2 |y| dx = \int_0^2 \sqrt{4 - x^2}\, dx$$

$$= \left[\frac{x}{2}\sqrt{4 - x^2} + \frac{4}{2}\sin^{-1}\left(\frac{x}{2}\right)\right]_0^2$$

$$= 0 + 2\sin^{-1}(1) - 0 = 2 \times \frac{\pi}{2} = \pi \text{ sq. units}$$

Question 4 Area of the region bounded by the curve $y^2 = 4x$, Y-axis and the line $y = 3$ is

(a) 2 (b) $\frac{9}{4}$ (c) $\frac{9}{3}$ (d) $\frac{9}{2}$

Sol. (b) The area bounded by the curve, $y^2 = 4x$, Y-axis and $y = 3$ is represented in the figure by shaded region.

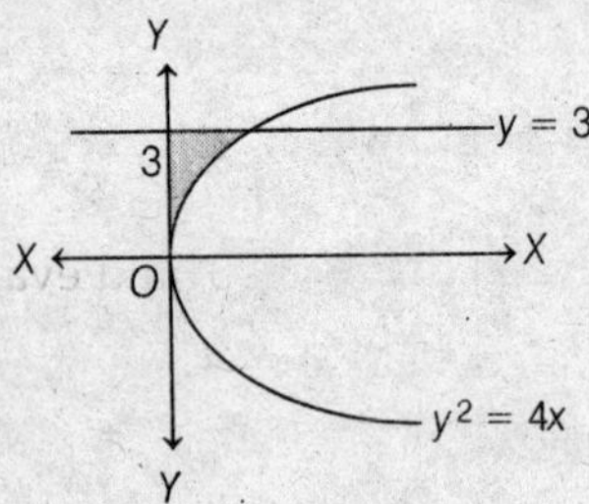

$$\therefore \text{Required area} = \int_0^3 |x|\, dy$$

$$= \int_0^3 \frac{y^2}{4} dy = \frac{1}{4}\left[\frac{y^3}{3}\right]_0^3$$

$$= \frac{1}{12}(3^3 - 0) = \frac{1}{12}(27) = \frac{9}{4} \text{ sq. units.}$$

Miscellaneous Exericse

Question 1 Find the area under given curves and given lines.

(a) $y = x^2$; $x = 1$, $x = 2$ and X-axis

(b) $y = x^4$; $x = 1$, $x = 5$ and X-axis.

Sol.

(a) The given curve $y = x^2$ represents an upward parabola with vertex (0, 0) and axis along Y-axis.

$\therefore$ Required area (shown in shaded region)
= Area under the curve $y = x^2$, X-axis
and $x = 1$, $x = 2$

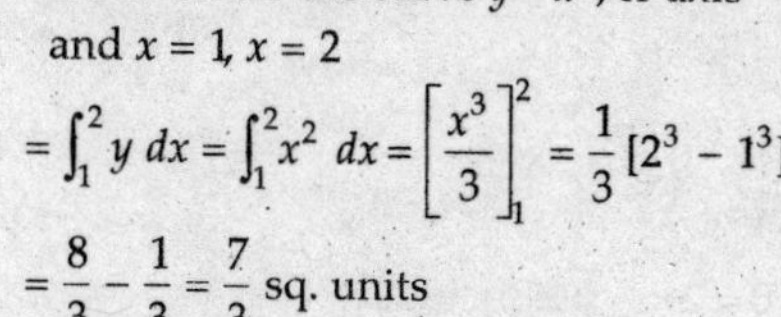

$$= \int_1^2 y\,dx = \int_1^2 x^2\,dx = \left[\frac{x^3}{3}\right]_1^2 = \frac{1}{3}[2^3 - 1^3]$$

$$= \frac{8}{3} - \frac{1}{3} = \frac{7}{3} \text{ sq. units}$$

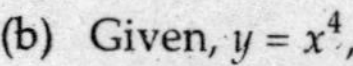

(b) Given, $y = x^4$,

Here, the power of x is even, so curve is symmetrical about Y-axis and passes through origin (0, 0).

$\therefore$ Required area = Area under the curve $y = x^4$, X-axis and $x = 1$, $x = 5$

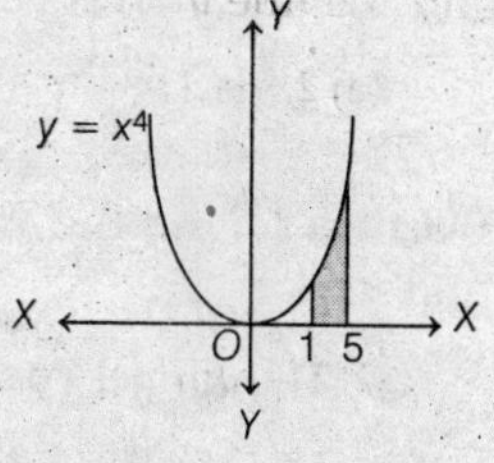

$$= \int_1^5 x^4 dx = \left[\frac{x^5}{5}\right]_1^5 = \frac{1}{5}[5^5 - 1]$$

$$= \frac{1}{5}(3125 - 1)$$

$$= \frac{3124}{5} = 624.8 \text{ sq. units}$$

Question 2 Sketch the graph of $y = |x + 3|$ and evaluate $\int_{-6}^{0} |x + 3|\,dx$.

Sol. We have, $y = |x + 3| = \begin{cases} -(x + 3) & \text{for } x < -3 \\ x + 3 & \text{for } x \geq -3 \end{cases}$

When $x < -3$, $y = -x - 3$

x	−4	−5	−6
y	1	2	3

When $x \geq -3$, $y = x + 3$

x	−1	−2	−3
y	2	1	0

Draw these points on the graph paper and we get the required figure.

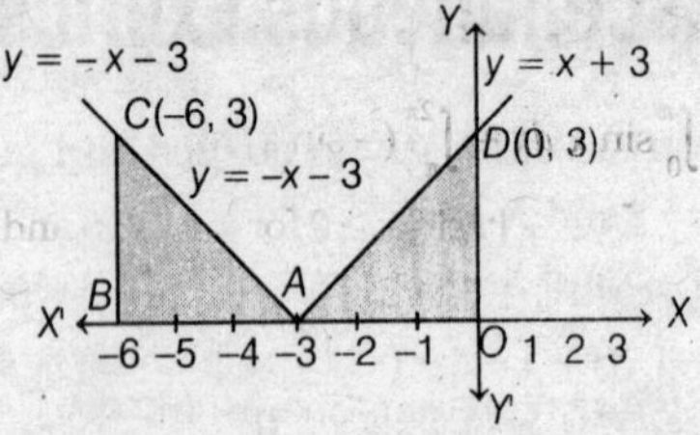

∴ Required area = Area of region ABC + Area of region OAD

$$= \int_{-6}^{-3} |x+3|\, dx + \int_{-3}^{0} |x+3|\, dx$$

$$= \int_{-6}^{-3} (-x-3)\, dx + \int_{-3}^{0} (x+3)\, dx$$

$$= \left[\frac{-x^2}{2} - 3x\right]_{-6}^{-3} + \left[\frac{x^2}{2} + 3x\right]_{-3}^{0} = \left[\left(\frac{-(-3)^2}{2} - 3\times(-3)\right) - \left(\frac{-(-6)^2}{2} - 3\times(-6)\right)\right]$$

$$+ \left[0 - \left(\frac{(-3)^2}{2} + 3\times(-3)\right)\right]$$

$$= \left[\left(\frac{-9}{2} + 9\right) - (-18+18)\right] + \left[9 - \frac{9}{2}\right]$$

$$= \frac{9}{2} + \frac{9}{2} = 9 \text{ sq. units}$$

Question 3 Find the area bounded by the curve $y = \sin x$ between $x = 0$ and $x = 2\pi$.

◎ ***Thinking Process*** Firstly, sketch the curve $y = \sin x$ between $x = 0$ and $x = 2\pi$ and integrate it by taking proper limit. Use the equation $y = |\sin x|$ for integration.

Sol. The graph of $y = \sin x$ can be drawn as

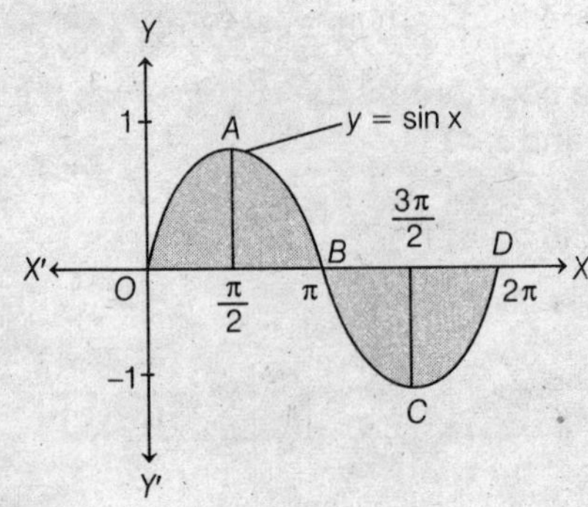

Required area = Area $(OABO)$ + Area $(BCDB)$

$$= \int_0^{\pi} |\sin x|\, dx + \int_{\pi}^{2\pi} |\sin x|\, dx$$

$$= \int_0^{\pi} \sin x\, dx + \int_{\pi}^{2\pi} (-\sin x)\, dx$$

$[\because \sin x \geq 0 \text{ for } x \in [0, \pi] \text{ and } \sin x \leq 0 \text{ for } x \in [\pi, 2\pi]]$

$$= [-\cos x]_0^{\pi} + [\cos x]_{\pi}^{2\pi} = -\cos\pi + \cos 0 + \cos 2\pi - \cos\pi$$

$$= -(-1) + 1 + 1 - (-1) = 4 \text{ sq. units}$$

Quick Solution

The graph of $y = \sin x$ can be drawn as

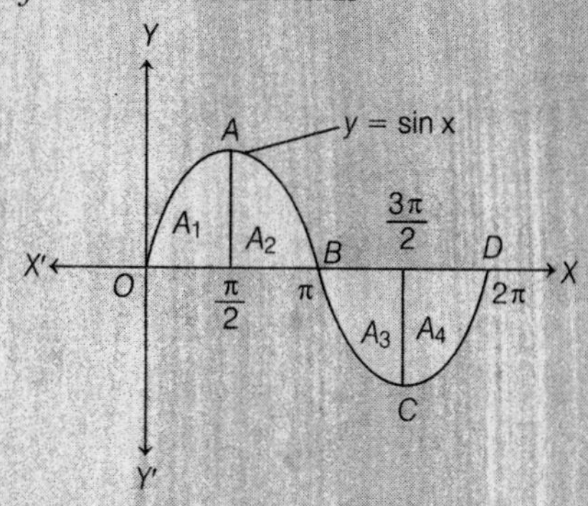

Required Area

$$= A_1 + A_2 + A_3 + A_4$$

$= 4A_1$ (all four areas are symmetry)

$$= 4\int_0^{\frac{\pi}{2}} \sin x\, dx = 4\,[-\cos x]_0^{\frac{\pi}{2}}$$

$$= 4\left[-\cos\frac{\pi}{2} - (-\cos 0)\right]$$

$$= 4\,[0 + 1] = 4 \text{ sq. units}$$

Direction (Q. Nos. 4 to 5) Choose the correct answer.

Question 4 Area bounded by the curve $y = x^3$, the X-axis and the ordinates $x = -2$ and $x = 1$ is

(a) -9

(b) $-\dfrac{15}{4}$

(c) $\dfrac{15}{4}$

(d) $\dfrac{17}{4}$

Sol. (d) Given curve is $y = x^3$

On putting $x = -x$ and $y = -y$, we get $y = x^3$

Therefore, the curve is symmetrical in opposite quadrant and passes through (0, 0).

$\therefore$ Required area

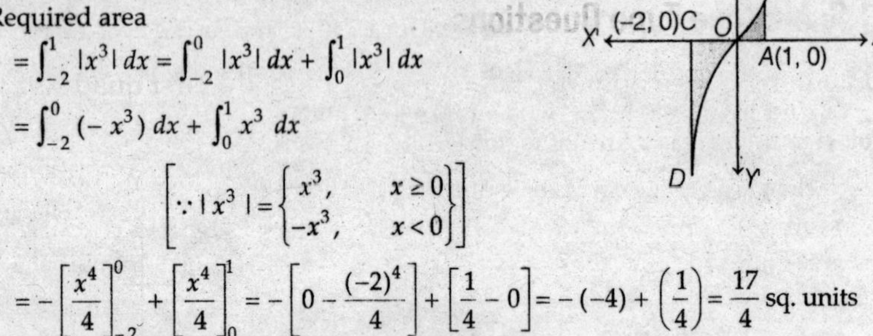

$$= \int_{-2}^{1} |x^3|\, dx = \int_{-2}^{0} |x^3|\, dx + \int_{0}^{1} |x^3|\, dx$$

$$= \int_{-2}^{0} (-x^3)\, dx + \int_{0}^{1} x^3\, dx$$

$$\left[\because |x^3| = \begin{cases} x^3, & x \geq 0 \\ -x^3, & x < 0 \end{cases}\right]$$

$$= -\left[\frac{x^4}{4}\right]_{-2}^{0} + \left[\frac{x^4}{4}\right]_{0}^{1} = -\left[0 - \frac{(-2)^4}{4}\right] + \left[\frac{1}{4} - 0\right] = -(-4) + \left(\frac{1}{4}\right) = \frac{17}{4} \text{ sq. units}$$

Question 5 The area bounded by the curve $y = x|x|$, X-axis and the ordinates $x = -1$ and $x = 1$ is given by

(a) 0

(b) $\frac{1}{3}$

(c) $\frac{2}{3}$

(d) $\frac{4}{3}$

Sol. (c) Given, $y = x|x| = \begin{cases} x^2, & x \geq 0 \\ -x^2, & x < 0 \end{cases}$

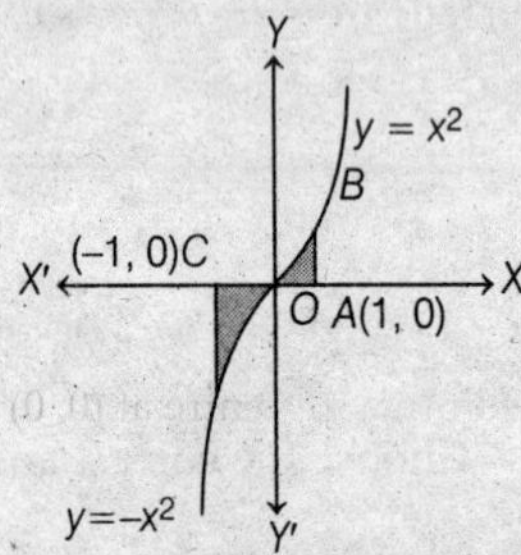

$\therefore$ Required area = 2 [Area under the curve $y = x^2$, between $x = 0$, $x = 1$

[$\because$ The curve is symmetrical in opposite quadrant]

$$= 2\int_{0}^{1} x|x|\, dx = 2\int_{0}^{1} x^2 dx$$

$$= 2\left[\frac{x^3}{3}\right]_{0}^{1} = \frac{2}{3}(1^3 - 0^3)$$

$$= \frac{2}{3} \text{ sq. units}$$

DIKSHA APP Questions

Subjective Type Questions

Q.1 Find the area bounded $x^2 = 4y$ and $y = 4$ in the first quadrant.

Sol. Required area = Area of region $OABO = \int_0^4 x\, dy$

$$= \int_0^4 2\sqrt{y}\, dy$$

$$= 2\left[\frac{y^{1/2+1}}{\frac{1}{2}+1}\right]_0^4$$

$$= 2 \times \frac{2}{3}\left[y^{3/2}\right]_0^4$$

$$= \frac{4}{3}[(4)^{3/2} - 0]$$

$$= \frac{4}{3}[(2^2)^{3/2}] = \frac{4}{3}[2^3] = \frac{32}{3} \text{ sq. units.}$$

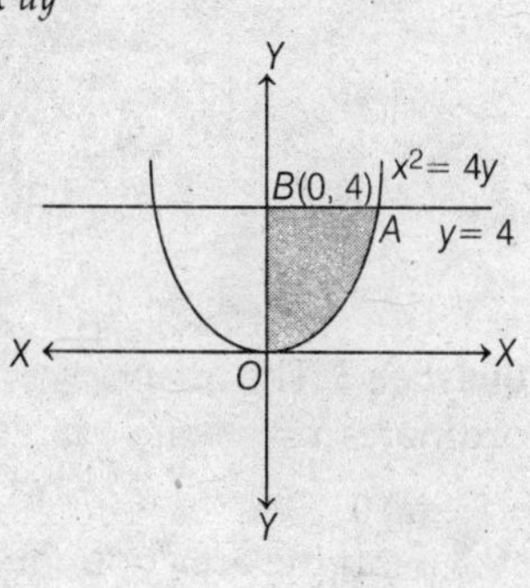

Mistake Alert Students may incorrectly take area $= \int_0^4 x\, dx$ instead of area $= \int_0^4 x\, dy$

Q.2 Find the area bounded by ellipse $9x^2 + 4y^2 = 36$

Sol. We have, $9x^2 + 4y^2 = 36$

$$\Rightarrow \frac{9x^2}{36} + \frac{4y^2}{36} = \frac{36}{36} \quad \text{[dividing by 36 on both sides]}$$

$$\Rightarrow \frac{x^2}{4} + \frac{y^2}{9} = 1$$

The given curve is an ellipse with centre at (0, 0) and symmetric about both axis.

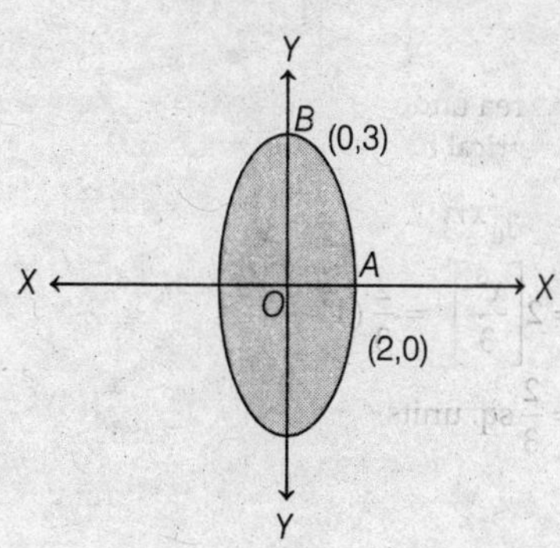

$\therefore$ Required area = 4 × area of region *OABO*

$$= 4\int_0^2 \frac{3}{2}\sqrt{4-x^2}\,dx$$

$$= 6\int_0^2 \sqrt{(2)^2-x^2}\,dx \qquad \left[\because \frac{x^2}{4}+\frac{y^2}{9}=1 \Rightarrow y=\frac{3}{2}\sqrt{4-x^2}\right]$$

$$= 6\left[\frac{x}{2}\sqrt{2^2-x^2}+\frac{2^2}{2}\sin^{-1}\frac{x}{2}\right]_0^2$$

$$\left[\because \int\sqrt{a^2-x^2} = \frac{x}{2}\sqrt{a^2-x^2}+\frac{a^2}{2}\sin^{-1}\frac{x}{a}+C\right]$$

$$= 6\left[\frac{2}{2}\sqrt{2^2-2^2}+2\sin^{-1}\frac{2}{2}-(0+2\sin^{-1}0)\right]$$

$$= 6\,[0+2\sin^{-1}(1)-0]$$

$$= 6\left(2\sin^{-1}\left(\sin\frac{\pi}{2}\right)\right) = 6\times 2\times\frac{\pi}{2}$$

$$= 6\,\pi \text{ sq. units}$$

Q.3 Find the area bounded by the curve $y^2=4x, x=1, x=4$ and X-axis.

Sol. Required area = 2 × Area of region *ABCDA*

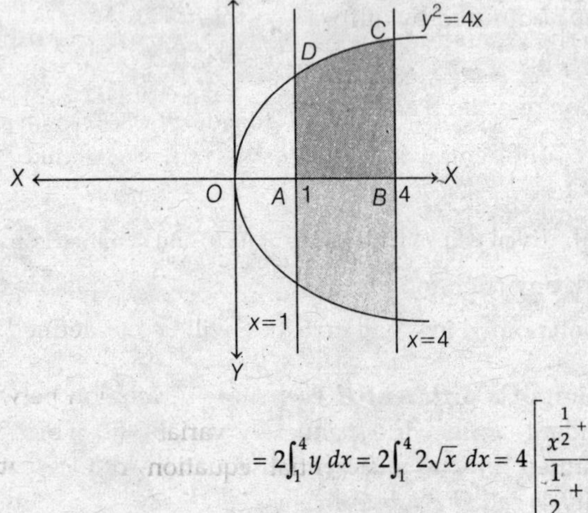

$$= 2\int_1^4 y\,dx = 2\int_1^4 2\sqrt{x}\,dx = 4\left[\frac{x^{\frac{1}{2}+1}}{\frac{1}{2}+1}\right]_1^4$$

$$= 4\times\frac{2}{3}[x^{3/2}]_1^4 = \frac{8}{3}[(4)^{3/2}-(1)^{3/2}] = \frac{8}{3}[2^3-1]$$

$$= \frac{8}{3}\times 7 = \frac{56}{3} \text{ Sq. units.}$$

Differential Equations

CHAPTER 09

Important Points

01 (i) **Order of a differential equation** The order of the highest order derivative occurring in the differential equation, is called its order.

(ii) **Degree of a differential equation** The highest power of the highest order derivative in the differential equation, is called its degree.

e.g., The equation $\left(\frac{d^3y}{dx^3}\right)^4 = 4 + \left(\frac{dy}{dx}\right)^3$ is a differential equation of order 3 and degree 4.

(iii) If any differential equation have any term like e^{d^ny/dx^n}, $\log\left(\frac{d^ny}{dx^n}\right)$, $\sin\left(\frac{d^ny}{dx^n}\right)$, $\cos\left(\frac{d^ny}{dx^n}\right)$

or with any trigonmetric function, then the equation will not be a polynomial in $\frac{dy}{dx}$ then degree will be not defined.

(iv) **Solution of a differential equation** A relation between the dependent and independent variables which when substituted in the differential equation reduces it to an identity, is called a solution.

02 Solving a Differential Equation

(i) **Equation in variable separable form** From $\frac{dy}{dx} = f(x, y)$, where variables are separable.

We express it in the form $f(x)\,dx = g(y)\,dy$.

Then, $\int g(y)\,dy = \int f(x)\,dx + C$

(ii) **Homogeneous differential equation**

A differential equation of the form $\frac{dy}{dx} = \frac{f(x, y)}{g(x, y)}$, where $f(x, y)$ and $g(x, y)$ are homeogeneous functions of x and y and are of the same order.

e.g., $\frac{dy}{dx} = \frac{(x^3 + y^3)}{x^2y}$, here $(x^3 + y^3)$ and x^2y both are homogeneous functions of degree 3.

Method for solving a homogeneous differential equation

Putting $y = vx$ and $\frac{dy}{dx} = v + x\frac{dv}{dx}$.

Now, we get a differential equation in which variables are separable and so we can solve it.

(iii) **Particular solution of a differential equation** The solution. obtained from the general solution, given, particular values to the arbitrary constants is called a particular solution. of the differential equation.

e.g., $y = a \sin x + b \cos x$ is the general solution of $\frac{d^2y}{dx^2} + y = 0$.

When $y(0) = 3$ and $y\left(\frac{\pi}{2}\right) = 5$, the particular solution becomes $y = 5 \sin x + 3 \cos x$.

(iv) **Linear differential equation** From $\frac{dy}{dx} + Py = Q$, where P and Q are constants or functions of x.

We find integrating factor IF $= e^{\int P\,dx}$.

Now, solution is

$$y \times (\text{IF}) = \int [Q \times (\text{IF})]\,dx. + C$$

(v) If a linear differential equation is of the form $\frac{dx}{dy} + Px = Q$, where P and Q are functions of y, then IF $= e^{\int P\,dy}$

Its solution is $x \times (\text{IF}) = \int \{Q \times (\text{IF.})\}\,dy + C$.

Exercise 9.1

Direction (Q. Nos. 1 to 10) Determine order and degree (when defined) of differential equations.

Thinking Process

(i) For order, see highest order derivative in the differential equation.
(ii) For degree,
(a) See that whether given, differential equation is polynomial in dy/dx or not.
(b) If it is a polynomial in dy/dx, then see to which power is the highest order derivative raised, that power is equal to degree.
(c) If it is not a polynomial in $\frac{dy}{dx}$, then its degee is not defined.

Question 1 $\frac{d^4y}{dx^4} + \sin(y''') = 0.$

Sol. We have, $\frac{d^4y}{dx^4} + \sin(y''') = 0 \Rightarrow y'''' + \sin(y''') = 0$

The highest order derivative which occurs in the given differential equation is y'''', therefore its order is 4.

As the given differential equation is not a polynomial equation in dy/dx (*i.e.*, y') therefore its degree is not defined.

Mistake Alert Whenever there is any of the term like $e^{\frac{d^ny}{dx^n}}$, $\log\left(\frac{d^ny}{dx^n}\right)$ and $\left(\frac{d^ny}{dx^n}\right)$ in the angle of any trigonometric function.

Then degree will be not defined.

Question 2 $y' + 5y = 0.$

Sol. We have, $y' + 5y = 0$

The highest order derivative which occurs in the given differential equation is y' and index of highest power is one, therefore the given differential equation is of order 1 and degree 1.

Question 3 $\left(\frac{ds}{dt}\right)^4 + 3s\frac{d^2s}{dt^2} = 0.$

Sol. We have, $\left(\frac{ds}{dt}\right)^4 + 3s\frac{d^2s}{dt^2} = 0$

The highest order derivative present in the given differential equation is d^2s/dt^2. and the index of its highest power is one. Hence, the given differential equation is of order 2 and degree 1.

Question 4 $\left(\frac{d^2y}{dx^2}\right)^2 + \cos\left(\frac{dy}{dx}\right) = 0.$

Sol. We have, $\left(\frac{d^2y}{dx^2}\right)^2 + \cos\left(\frac{dy}{dx}\right) = 0$

The highest order derivative present in the given differential equation is $\frac{d^2y}{dx^2}$, therefore, its order is 2.

But the given differential equation is not a polynomial equation in dy/dx. Hence, its degree is not defined.

Question 5 $\frac{d^2y}{dx^2} = \cos 3x + \sin 3x.$

Sol. We have, $\frac{d^2y}{dx^2} = \cos 3x + \sin 3x$

The highest order derivative which occurs in the given differential equation is $\frac{d^2y}{dx^2}$. Therefore, its order is two. It is a polynomial equation in $\frac{d^2y}{dx^2}$ and the power raised to $\frac{d^2y}{dx^2}$ is 1. Hence, its degree is one.

Question 6 $(y''')^2 + (y'')^3 + (y')^4 + y^5 = 0.$

Sol. We have, $(y''')^2 + (y'')^3 + (y')^4 + y^5 = 0$

The highest order derivative which occurs in the given differential equation is y'''. Therefore, its order is three. The given differential equation is a polynomial equation in y''', y'' and y'.

The highest power raised to y''' is 2. Hence, its degree is 2.

Question 7 $y''' + 2y'' + y' = 0.$

Sol. We have, $y''' + 2y'' + y' = 0$

The highest order derivative which occurs in the given differential equation is y'''. Therefore, its order is three. It is a polynomial equation in y''', y'' and y'. The highest power raised to y''' is 1. Hence, its degree is 1.

Question 8 $y' + y = e^x.$

Sol. We have, $y' + y = e^x$

The highest order derivative present in the given differential equation is y'. Therefore, its order is one. The given differential equation is a polynomial equation in y'. The highest power raised to y' is 1. Hence, its degree is 1.

Question 9 $y'' + (y')^2 + 2y = 0.$

Sol. We have $y'' + (y')^2 + 2y = 0$

The highest order derivative, present in the given differential equation is y''. Therefore, its order is two. The given differential equation is a polynomial equation in y'' and y' and the highest power raised to y'' is 1. Hence its degree is 1.

Question 10 $y'' + 2y' + \sin y = 0.$

Sol. We have $y'' + 2y' + \sin y = 0$

The highest order derivative, present in the differential equation is y''. Therefore, its order is two.

This is a polynomial equation in y'' and y' and the highest power raised to y'' is one. Hence, its degree is one.

Direction (Q. No. 11 and 12). Choose the correct answer.

Question 11 The degree of the differential equation

$$\left(\frac{d^2y}{dx^2}\right)^3 + \left(\frac{dy}{dx}\right)^2 + \sin\left(\frac{dy}{dx}\right) + 1 = 0 \text{ is}$$

(a) 3 (b) 2

(c) 1 (d) None of these

Sol. (d) The given differential equation is not a polynomial equation in $\frac{dy}{dx}$.

Therefore, its degree is not defined.

Question 12 The order of the differential equation

$$2x^2 \frac{d^2y}{dx^2} - 3\frac{dy}{dx} + y = 0 \text{ is}$$

(a) 2

(b) 1

(c) zero

(d) None of the above

Sol. (a) The highest order derivative present in the given differential equation is $\frac{d^2y}{dx^2}$. Therefore, its order is two.

Exercise 9.2

Direction (Q. Nos. 1 to 10) In each of the questions verify that the given function (explicit or implicit) is a solution of the corresponding differential equation.

Question 1 $y = e^x + 1$ and $y'' - y' = 0$.

◎ *Thinking Process* Differentiate the given function two times w.r.t. x and rearrange to verify given differential equation.

Sol. Given, $y = e^x + 1$

On differentiating both sides w.r.t. x, we get

$$y' = \frac{d}{dx}(e^x + 1) = e^x \quad \text{...(i)}$$

Again differentiating both sides of Eq. (i) w.r.t. x, we get

$$y'' = \frac{d}{dx}(e^x) = e^x \Rightarrow y'' = e^x$$

On substituting the values of y' and y'' in the given differential equation, we get

$$\text{LHS} = y'' - y' = e^x - e^x = 0 = \text{RHS}$$

Hence, $y = e^x + 1$ is a solution of the given differential equation.

Question 2 $y = x^2 + 2x + C$ and $y' - 2x - 2 = 0$.

Sol. Given, $y = x^2 + 2x + C$

On differentiating both sides w.r.t. x, we get

$$y' = \frac{d}{dx}(x^2 + 2x + C) \Rightarrow y' = 2x + 2$$

On substituting the value of y' in the given differential equation, we get

$$\text{LHS} = y' - 2x - 2 = 2x + 2 - 2x - 2 = 0 = \text{RHS}$$

Hence, $y = x^2 + 2x + C$ is a solution of the given differential equation.

Question 3 $y = \cos x + C$ and $y' + \sin x = 0$

Sol. Given, $y = \cos x + C$

On differentiating both sides w.r.t. x, we get

$$y' = -\sin x \quad \left(\because \frac{dy}{dx} = y'\right)$$

On substituting the value of y' in the given differential equation, we get

$$\text{LHS} = y' + \sin x$$
$$= -\sin x + \sin x = 0 = \text{RHS}$$

Hence, $y = \cos x + C$ is a solution of the given differential equation.

Question 4 $y=\sqrt{1+x^2}$ and $y'=\dfrac{xy}{1+x^2}$.

Sol. Given, $y=\sqrt{1+x^2}$

On differentiating both sides of this equation w.r.t. x, we get

$$y'=\frac{d}{dx}(\sqrt{1+x^2}) \Rightarrow y'=\frac{1}{2}(1+x^2)^{-\frac{1}{2}}(2x)$$

$$\Rightarrow \quad y'=\frac{2x}{2\sqrt{1+x^2}} \Rightarrow y'=\frac{x}{\sqrt{1+x^2}}$$

But we have to verify, $y'=\dfrac{xy}{1+x^2}$ ...(i)

On putting the values of y' and y in the given differential equation, we get

$$\text{LHS}=y'=\frac{x}{\sqrt{1+x^2}},$$

$$\text{and} \quad \text{RHS}=\frac{xy}{1+x^2}=\frac{x}{1+x^2}\times\sqrt{1+x^2}=\frac{x}{\sqrt{1+x^2}}$$

$$\therefore \quad \text{LHS}=\text{RHS}$$

Hence, $y=\sqrt{1+x^2}$ is a solution of the given differential equation.

Quick Solution

Given, $y=\sqrt{1+x^2}$

$$y'=\frac{1}{2\sqrt{1+x^2}}\frac{d}{dx}(1+x^2) \quad \text{(On differentiating w.r.t. 'x')}$$

$$=\frac{2x}{2\sqrt{1+x^2}}\times\frac{\sqrt{1+x^2}}{\sqrt{1+x^2}} \quad \text{(Multiply divide by } \sqrt{1+x^2}\text{)}$$

$$\Rightarrow \quad y'=\frac{x\sqrt{1+x^2}}{1+x^2} \Rightarrow y'=\frac{xy}{1+x^2} \quad (\because \sqrt{1+x^2}=y)$$

Hence, $y=\sqrt{1+x^2}$ is a solution of the given differential equation.

Question 5 $y=Ax$ and $xy'=y\ (x\neq 0)$.

Sol. Given, $y=Ax$

On differentiating both sides w.r.t. x, we get

$$y'=\frac{d}{dx}(Ax)$$

$$\Rightarrow \quad y'=A$$

On substituting the value of y' in the given differential equation, we get

$$\text{LHS}=xy'=x.A$$

$$=Ax=y=\text{RHS}$$

Hence, $y=Ax$ is a solution of the given differential equation.

Quick Solution

We have $y = Ax$

$\Rightarrow$ $$\frac{y}{x} = A$$

On differentiating w.r.t. 'x', we get $\frac{xy' - y}{x^2} = 0$ (using quitient rule)

$\Rightarrow$ $$xy' - y = 0 \Rightarrow xy' = y$$

Hence, $y = Ax$ is a solution of the given differential equation.

Question 6 $y = x\sin x$ and $xy' = y + x\sqrt{x^2 - y^2}$

$(x \neq 0$ and $x > y$ or $x < -y)$.

◎ *Thinking Process* Function y is the product of two functions. So, we use the product rule *i. e.*, $\frac{d}{dx}(u.v) = u\frac{dv}{dx} + v\frac{du}{dx}$.

Sol. Given, $y = x\sin x$

On differentiating both sides w.r.t. x, we get

$$y' = \frac{d}{dx}(x\sin x) \Rightarrow y' = \sin x \cdot \frac{d}{dx}x + x\frac{d}{dx}(\sin x)$$

(using product rule of differentiation)

$\Rightarrow$ $$y' = x\cos x + \sin x$$

On substituting the value of y and y' in the given differential equation, we get

$$\text{LHS} = xy' = x(x\cos x + \sin x) = x^2\cos x + x\sin x$$
$$= x^2\sqrt{1 - \sin^2 x} + y \quad (\because \cos^2 x = 1 - \sin^2 x \quad x\sin x = y)$$
$$= x^2\sqrt{1 - \left(\frac{y}{x}\right)^2} + y \quad = x\sqrt{x^2 - y^2} + y = \text{RHS}$$

Hence, $y = x\sin x$ is a solution of the given differential equation.

Question 7 $xy = \log y + C$ and $y' = \frac{y^2}{1 - xy}$ $(xy \neq 1)$.

Sol. Given, $xy = \log y + C$

On differentiating both sides w.r.t. x, we get

$$\frac{d}{dx}(xy) = \frac{d}{dx}(\log y + C) \Rightarrow y\frac{d}{dx}x + xy' = \frac{1}{y}y'$$

(using product rule of of differentiation in LHS)

$\Rightarrow$ $$xy' + y = \frac{1}{y}y' \Rightarrow xy'y + y^2 = y'$$

$\Rightarrow$ $$y^2 = y' - xy'y$$

$\Rightarrow$ $$y^2 = y'(1 - xy) \Rightarrow y' = \frac{y^2}{1 - xy}.$$ **Hence Proved.**

Hence, $xy = \log y + C$ is a solution of the given differential equation.

Question 8 $y-\cos y=x$ and $(y\sin y+\cos y+x)y'=y$.

Sol. Given, $y-\cos y=x$

On differentiating both sides w.r.t. x, we get

$$y'-\frac{d}{dx}(\cos y)=\frac{d}{dx}x \Rightarrow y'-(-\sin y)y'=1 \qquad \left(\because \frac{dy}{dx}=y'\right)$$

$$\Rightarrow \qquad y'(1+\sin y)=1 \Rightarrow y'=\frac{1}{1+\sin y}$$

On substituting the value of y' in the given differential equation, we get

$$\text{LHS}=(y\sin y+\cos y+x)y'=(y\sin y+y)\times\frac{1}{1+\sin y} \qquad (\because y=x+\cos y)$$

$$=y(1+\sin y)\times\frac{1}{1+\sin y}=y=\text{RHS}$$

Hence, $y-\cos y=x$ is a solution of the given differential equation.

Question 9 $x+y=\tan^{-1}y$ and $y^2y'+y^2+1=0$.

Sol. Given, $x+y=\tan^{-1}y$ ...(i)

On differentiating both sides w.r.t. x, we get

$$\frac{d}{dx}(x+y)=\frac{d}{dx}\tan^{-1}y \Rightarrow 1+y'=\frac{1}{1+y^2}(y') \qquad \left(\because \frac{dy}{dx}=y'\right)$$

$$\Rightarrow \quad (1+y')(1+y^2)=y' \Rightarrow 1+y^2+y'+y^2y'=y'$$

$$\Rightarrow \quad 1+y^2+y^2y'=0 \Rightarrow y'=\frac{-(1+y^2)}{y^2}$$

On substituting the value of y' in the given differential equation, we get

$$\text{LHS}=y^2\left\{\frac{-(1+y^2)}{y^2}\right\}+y^2+1=-(1+y^2)+(1+y^2)=0=\text{RHS}$$

Hence, $x+y=\tan^{-1}y$ is a solution of the given differential equation.

Question 10 $y=\sqrt{a^2-x^2}\ x\notin(-a,a)$ and $x+y\dfrac{dy}{dx}=0\ (y\neq 0)$.

Sol. Given, $y=\sqrt{a^2-x^2}$ ...(i)

On differentiating both sides w.r.t. x, we get

$$y'=\frac{d}{dx}\sqrt{a^2-x^2} \Rightarrow y'=\frac{1}{2}(a^2-x^2)^{\frac{1}{2}-1}\frac{d}{dx}(a^2-x^2)$$

$\Rightarrow$ On substituting the value of y' in the given differential equation, we get

$$\text{LHS}=x+yy'=x+\sqrt{a^2-x^2}\times\frac{-x}{\sqrt{a^2-x^2}}=x-x=0=\text{RHS} \qquad [\because y=\sqrt{a^2-x^2}]$$

$\therefore y=\sqrt{a^2-x^2}$ is a solution of the given differential equation.

Quick Solution

we have $y = \sqrt{a^2 - x^2}$

$\Rightarrow \quad y^2 = a^2 - x^2$ (Squaring Both side)

$\Rightarrow \quad 2y\dfrac{dy}{dx} = 0 - 2x$ (differentiating w.r.t 'x')

$\Rightarrow \quad y\dfrac{dy}{dx} + x = 0$

Direction (Q. No. 11 and 12). Choose the correct answer.

Question 11 The number of arbitrary constants in the general solution of a differential equation of fourth order are

(a) zero (b) 2 (c) 3 (d) 4

Sol. (d) We know that the number of constants in the general solution of a differential equation of order n is equal to its order. Therefore, the number of constants in the general equation of fourth order differential equation is four.

Question 12 The number of arbitrary constants in the particular solution of a differential equation of third order are

(a) 3 (b) 2 (c) 1 (d) zero

Sol. (d) In the particular solution of a differential equation of third order, there is no arbitrary constant because in the particular solution. of any differential equation, we removes all the arbitrary constant by substituting some particular values.

Exercise 9.3

Direction (Q. No. 1 to 10) For each of the differential equation in given question find the general Solution :

Question 1 $\dfrac{dy}{dx} = \dfrac{1 - \cos x}{1 + \cos x}$.

Thinking Process Firstly separating the variables x and y and then integrate to find a general solution.

Sol. Given, $\dfrac{dy}{dx} = \dfrac{1 - \cos x}{1 + \cos x}$

On separating the variables and integrating, we get

$$\int dy = \int \frac{1 - \cos x}{1 + \cos x}dx \Rightarrow y = \int \frac{2\sin^2(x/2)}{2\cos^2(x/2)}dx$$

$[\because 1 - \cos x = 2\sin^2(x/2) \text{ and } 1 + \cos x = 2\cos^2(x/2)]$

$\Rightarrow \quad y = \int \tan^2(x/2)\,dx$

$\Rightarrow \quad y = \int (\sec^2(x/2) - 1)\,dx \qquad [\because \sec^2 x - \tan^2 x = 1]$

$\Rightarrow \quad y = \int \sec^2(x/2)\,dx - \int 1\,dx \quad [\because \sec^2\theta - \tan^2\theta = 1]$

$\Rightarrow \quad y = 2\tan\frac{x}{2} - x + C. \quad [\because \int \sec^2 x\,dx = \tan x]$

which is the required general solution.

Question 2 $\frac{dy}{dx} = \sqrt{4-y^2}\ (-2 < y < 2)$

Sol. Given, $\frac{dy}{dx} = \sqrt{4-y^2}$

On separating the variables, we get $dx = \frac{dy}{\sqrt{4-y^2}}$

On integrating both sides, we get

$$\int \frac{dy}{\sqrt{2^2-y^2}} = \int dx \Rightarrow \sin^{-1}\frac{y}{2} = x + C \quad \left(\because \int \frac{1}{\sqrt{a^2-x^2}}dx = \sin^{-1}\frac{x}{a}\right)$$

$\Rightarrow \frac{y}{2} = \sin(x+C) \Rightarrow y = 2\sin(x+C)$, which is the required general solution.

Question 3 $\frac{dy}{dx} + y = 1, (y \neq 1).$

Sol. Given, $\frac{dy}{dx} + y = 1$

On separating the variables, we get

$$\frac{dy}{dx} = 1 - y$$

$$\Rightarrow \quad dx = \frac{dy}{1-y}$$

On integrating both sides, we get $\int \frac{dy}{(1-y)} = \int dx$

$\Rightarrow \quad -\log|1-y| = x - C \Rightarrow -x + C = \log|1-y|$

$\Rightarrow \quad |1-y| = e^{-x+C} \quad [\because \log_e x = m \Rightarrow e^m = x]$

$\Rightarrow \quad y - 1 = (\pm e^C)e^{-x} \Rightarrow y = 1 + Ae^{-x} \quad$ (where, $(A = \pm e^C)$)

which is the required general solution of the given differential equation.

Question 4 $\sec^2 x \tan y\, dx + \sec^2 y \tan x\, dy = 0.$

Sol. Given, $\sec^2 x \tan y dx + \sec^2 y \tan x dy = 0.$

On separating the variables, we get

$\Rightarrow \sec^2 x \tan y\, dx = -\sec^2 y \tan x\, dy \Rightarrow \frac{\sec^2 x}{\tan x}dx = -\frac{\sec^2 y}{\tan y}dy$

On integrating both sides, we get $\int \frac{\sec^2 x}{\tan x}dx = -\int \frac{\sec^2 y}{\tan y}dy$

Let $\quad \tan x = u \Rightarrow \sec^2 x = \frac{du}{dx} \Rightarrow dx = \frac{du}{\sec^2 x}$

and $\quad \tan y = v \Rightarrow \sec^2 y = \frac{dv}{dy} \Rightarrow dy = \frac{dv}{\sec^2 y}$

$$\int \frac{\sec^2 x}{u} \frac{du}{\sec^2 x} = -\int \frac{\sec^2 y}{v} \frac{dv}{\sec^2 y} \Rightarrow \int \frac{du}{u} = -\int \frac{dv}{v}$$

$\Rightarrow$ $\log|u| = -\log|v| + \log|C|$

$\Rightarrow$ $\log|\tan x| = -\log|\tan y| + \log|C|$

$\Rightarrow$ $\log|\tan x \tan y| = \log|C|$ $[\because \log m + \log n = \log mn]$

$\Rightarrow$ $\tan x \cdot \tan = C$ $(\because \log m = \log n \Rightarrow m = n)$

which is the required general solution.

Question 5 $(e^x + e^{-x})dy - (e^x - e^{-x})dx = 0.$

Sol. Given, $(e^x + e^{-x})dy - (e^x - e^{-x})dx = 0.$

$\Rightarrow$ $(e^x + e^{-x})dy = (e^x - e^{-x})dx$

On separating the variables, we get $dy = \left(\frac{e^x - e^{-x}}{e^x + e^{-x}}\right)dx$

On integrating both sides, we get $\int dy = \int \left(\frac{e^x - e^{-x}}{e^x + e^{-x}}\right)dx$

Let $e^x + e^{-x} = t \Rightarrow e^x - e^{-x} = \frac{dt}{dx} \Rightarrow dx = \frac{dt}{e^x - e^{-x}}$

$\therefore$ $\int dy = \int \frac{e^x - e^{-x}}{t} \frac{dt}{e^x - e^{-x}} = \int \frac{1}{t} dt$

$\Rightarrow$ $y = \log|t| + C \Rightarrow y = \log|e^x + e^{-x}| + C$

which is the required general solution.

Question 6 $\frac{dy}{dx} = (1 + x^2)(1 + y^2).$

Sol. Given, $\frac{dy}{dx} = (1 + x^2)(1 + y^2)$

On separating the variables, we get

$$\frac{dy}{1 + y^2} = (1 + x^2)dx \Rightarrow \frac{dy}{1 + y^2} = 1dx + x^2 dx$$

On integrating both sides, we get

$$\int \frac{dy}{1 + y^2} = \int dx + \int x^2 dx \Rightarrow \tan^{-1} y = x + \frac{x^3}{3} + C$$

which is the required general solution

Question 7 $y \log y \, dx - x \, dy = 0.$

Sol. Given, $y \log y \, dx - x dy = 0$

On separating the variables, we get

$$y \log y dx = x dy \Rightarrow \frac{1}{x} dx = \frac{1}{y \log y} dy$$

On integrating both sides, we get

$$\int \frac{1}{x} dx = \int \frac{1}{y \log y} dy$$

Let $\log y = t \Rightarrow \frac{1}{y} = \frac{dt}{dy} \Rightarrow dy = y\,dt$

$\therefore$ $\int \frac{1}{x}\,dx = \int \frac{1}{yt} y\,dt \Rightarrow \int \frac{1}{x}\,dx = \int \frac{1}{t}\,dt$

$\Rightarrow$ $\log|x| = \log|t| - \log|C| \Rightarrow \log|xC| = \log|\log y|$

$[\because \log m + \log n = \log mn]$

$\Rightarrow$ $Cx = \log y \Rightarrow y = e^{Cx}.$

$[\because \log_e x = m \Rightarrow e^m = x \text{ and } \log m = \log n \Rightarrow m = n]$

which is the required general solution.

Question 8 $x^5 \frac{dy}{dx} = -y^5.$

Sol. Given, $x^5 \frac{dy}{dx} = -y^5$

On separating the variables, we get $\frac{dy}{y^5} = -\frac{dx}{x^5}$

On integrating both sides, we get

$$\int \frac{dy}{y^5} = -\int \frac{dx}{x^5}$$

$\Rightarrow$ $\int y^{-5}\,dy = -\int x^{-5}\,dx$

$\Rightarrow$ $\frac{y^{-5+1}}{(-5+1)} = -\frac{x^{-5+1}}{(-5+1)} + C$ $\left(\because \int x^n\,dx = \frac{x^{n+1}}{n+1}\right)$

$\Rightarrow$ $\frac{y^{-4}}{-4} = -\frac{x^{-4}}{(-4)} + C$

$\Rightarrow$ $x^{-4} + y^{-4} = -4C$

$\Rightarrow$ $x^{-4} + y^{-4} = A$ [where, $A = -4C$]

which is the required general solution.

Question 9 $\frac{dy}{dx} = \sin^{-1} x.$

◎ *Thinking Process* Firstly, we separate the variables. Since, we cannot integrate $\sin^{-1} x$ directly. So, we apply the product rule of integration taking $\sin^{-1} x$ as first function and 1 as second function and then using the formula

$$\int u \cdot v\,dx = [u \cdot \int v\,dx - \int \left\{\frac{d}{dx}u\right\}(\int v\,dx)\,dx.$$

Sol. Given, $\frac{dy}{dx} = \sin^{-1} x$

On separating the variables, we get $dy = \sin^{-1} x\,dx$

On integrating both sides, we get $\int dy = \int \sin^{-1} x\,dx$

$\Rightarrow$ $y = \sin^{-1} x \int 1\,dx - \int \left[\frac{d}{dx}(\sin^{-1} x) \int 1\,dx\right] dx$ (using integration by parts)

($\sin^{-1} x \Rightarrow$ first function and $1 \Rightarrow$ second function)

$\Rightarrow \quad y = x\sin^{-1}x - \int\left[\frac{x}{\sqrt{1-x^2}}\right]dx$

Let $\quad 1 - x^2 = t \Rightarrow -2x = \frac{dt}{dx} = dx = \frac{dt}{-2x}$

$\therefore \quad y = x\sin^{-1}x + \int\frac{x}{\sqrt{t}}\frac{dt}{2x} \Rightarrow y = x\sin^{-1}x + \frac{1}{2}\cdot\frac{t^{-1/2+1}}{-1/2+1} + C$

$\Rightarrow \quad y = x\sin^{-1}x + \frac{2}{2}\sqrt{t} + C \Rightarrow y = x\sin^{-1}x + \sqrt{1-x^2} + C$

which is the required general solution.

Question 10 $e^x \tan y\, dx + (1 - e^x)\sec^2 y\, dy = 0.$

Sol. Given, $e^x \tan y\, dx + (1 - e^x)\sec^2 y\, dy = 0$

On separating the variables, we get $e^x \tan y\, dx = -(1 - e^x)\sec^2 y\, dy$

$\Rightarrow \quad \frac{e^x}{(e^x - 1)}dx = \frac{\sec^2 y}{\tan y}dy$

On integrating both sides, we get $\int\frac{e^x}{(e^x - 1)}dx = \int\frac{\sec^2 y}{\tan y}dy$

Let $\quad e^x - 1 = t \Rightarrow e^x = \frac{dt}{dx} = dx = \frac{dt}{e^x}$

and $\quad \tan y = v \Rightarrow \sec^2 y = \frac{dv}{dy} \Rightarrow dy = \frac{dv}{\sec^2 y}$

$\therefore \quad \int\frac{e^x}{t}\frac{dt}{e^x} = \int\frac{\sec^2 y}{v}\frac{dv}{\sec^2 y}$

$\Rightarrow \quad \log|t| = \log|v| - \log|C|$

$\Rightarrow \quad \log|e^x - 1| = \log|\tan y| - \log|C|$

$\Rightarrow \quad \log|C(e^x - 1)| = \log|\tan y| \quad [\because \log m + \log n = \log mn]$

$\Rightarrow \quad C(e^x - 1) = \tan y. \quad (\because \log m = \log n \Rightarrow m = n)$

which is the required general solution.

Direction (For Q. 11 to 14) For each of the differential equation in given question find a particular solution. satisfying the given condition.

Question 11 $(x^3 + x^2 + x + 1)\frac{dy}{dx} = 2x^2 + x : y = 1$ when $x = 0$.

◎ ***Thinking Process*** Separate the variables x and y and then integerate to find a general solution, then put the condition given in the general solution. To find values of arbitrary constant, and put the value of arbitrary constant in the general solution, to find the particular solution.

Sol. Given, $(x^3 + x^2 + x + 1)\frac{dy}{dx} = 2x^2 + x$

On separating the variables, we get $dy = \dfrac{2x^2 + x}{(x^3 + x^2 + x + 1)} dx$

On integrating both sides, we get

$$\int dy = \int \frac{2x^2 + x}{(x^3 + x^2 + x + 1)} dx \Rightarrow \int dy = \int \frac{2x^2 + x}{x^2(x + 1) + 1(x + 1)} dx$$

$$\Rightarrow \quad \int dy = \int \frac{2x^2 + x}{(x + 1)(x^2 + 1)} dx \Rightarrow y = \int \frac{2x^2 + x}{(x + 1)(x^2 + 1)} dx \quad \text{...(i)}$$

Let $\dfrac{2x^2 + x}{(x + 1)(x^2 + 1)} = \dfrac{A}{(x + 1)} + \dfrac{Bx + C}{(x^2 + 1)}$ [by partial fraction] ...(ii)

$$\Rightarrow \quad \frac{2x^2 + x}{(x + 1)(x^2 + 1)} = \frac{A(x^2 + 1) + (Bx + C)(x + 1)}{(x + 1)(x^2 + 1)}$$

$$\Rightarrow \quad 2x^2 + x = Ax^2 + A + Bx^2 + Bx + Cx + C$$

$$\Rightarrow \quad 2x^2 + x = x^2(A + B) + x(B + C) + (A + C)$$

On comparing the coefficients of x^2, x and constant terms on both sides, we get

$$A + B = 2, \quad B + C = 1 \quad \text{and} \quad A + C = 0$$

On solving these equations, we get

$$A = \frac{1}{2}, \ B = \frac{3}{2} \text{ and } C = -\frac{1}{2}$$

On substituting the values of A, B and C in Eq.(ii), we get

$$\frac{2x^2 + x}{(x + 1)(x^2 + 1)} = \frac{1}{2(x + 1)} + \frac{\frac{3}{2}x - \frac{1}{2}}{x^2 + 1}$$

$$\therefore \quad \int \frac{2x^2 + x}{(x^2 + 1)(x + 1)} dx = \frac{1}{2}\int \frac{1}{(x + 1)} dx + \int \frac{\frac{3}{2}x - \frac{1}{2}}{(x^2 + 1)} dx$$

Then from Eq. (i), we get

$$y = \frac{1}{2}\log|x + 1| + \frac{3}{2}\int \frac{x}{(x^2 + 1)} dx - \frac{1}{2}\int \frac{1}{(x^2 + 1)} dx$$

$$\Rightarrow \quad y = \frac{1}{2}\log|x + 1| + \frac{3}{2}\int \frac{x}{(x^2 + 1)} dx - \frac{1}{2}\tan^{-1} x$$

Let $\quad x^2 + 1 = t \Rightarrow 2x = \dfrac{dt}{dx} \Rightarrow dx = \dfrac{dt}{2x}$

$$\therefore \quad y = \frac{1}{2}\log|x + 1| + \frac{3}{2}\int \frac{x}{t}\frac{dt}{2x} - \frac{1}{2}\tan^{-1} x$$

$$\Rightarrow \quad y = \frac{1}{2}\log|x + 1| + \frac{3}{4}\int \frac{1}{t} dt - \frac{1}{2}\tan^{-1} x$$

$$\Rightarrow \quad y = \frac{1}{2}\log|x + 1| + \frac{3}{4}\log|t| - \frac{1}{2}\tan^{-1} x + C$$

$$\Rightarrow \quad y = \frac{1}{2}\log|x+1| + \frac{3}{4}\log|x^2+1| - \frac{1}{2}\tan^{-1}x + C$$

$$\Rightarrow \quad y = \frac{1}{4}[2\log|x+1| + 3\log|x^2+1|] - \frac{1}{2}\tan^{-1}x + C$$

$$\Rightarrow \quad y = \frac{1}{4}[\log\{(x+1)^2(x^2+1)^3\}] - \frac{1}{2}\tan^{-1}x + C \quad \text{...(iii)}$$

$[\because \log m^n = n\log m]$

When $x = 0$, then $y = 1$ on putting these values in Eq. (iii), we get

$$1 = \frac{1}{4}\log(1) - \frac{1}{2}\tan^{-1}(0) + C \Rightarrow 1 = \frac{1}{4}\times 0 - \frac{1}{2}\times 0 + C$$

$$C = 1$$

On putting $C = 1$ in Eq. (iii), we get

$$y = \frac{1}{4}[\log\{(x+1)^2(x^2+1)^3\}] - \frac{1}{2}\tan^{-1}x + 1$$

which is the required particular solution.

Question 12 $x(x^2-1)\frac{dy}{dx} = 1 : y = 0$ when $x = 2$.

Sol. We have, $x(x^2-1)\frac{dy}{dx} = 1$

On separating the variables, we get

$$dy = \frac{1}{x(x^2-1)}dx \Rightarrow dy = \frac{1}{x(x-1)(x+1)}dx$$

On integrating both sides, we get $\int dy = \int \frac{1}{x(x-1)(x+1)}dx$ ...(i)

Let $\frac{1}{x(x-1)(x+1)} = \frac{A}{x} + \frac{B}{x-1} + \frac{C}{x+1}$ (by partial fraction) ...(ii)

$$\Rightarrow \quad \frac{1}{x(x-1)(x+1)} = \frac{A(x-1)(x+1) + Bx(x+1) + Cx(x-1)}{x(x-1)(x+1)}$$

$$\therefore \quad 1 = A(x^2-1) + B(x)(x+1) + C(x)(x-1)$$

$$\Rightarrow \quad 1 = Ax^2 - A + Bx^2 + Bx + Cx^2 - Cx$$

$$\Rightarrow \quad 1 = x^2(A+B+C) + x(B-C) + (-A)$$

On comparing the coefficients of x^2, x and constant terms on both sides, we get

$$A + B + C = 0 \quad \text{...(iii)}$$

$$B - C = 0 \quad \text{...(iv)}$$

and $$-A = 1 \quad \text{...(v)}$$

On putting the value of A in Eq. (iii), we get

$$B + C = 1 \quad \text{...(vi)}$$

On adding Eqs. (iv) and (vi), we get $2B = 1 \Rightarrow B = \frac{1}{2}$

Then, from Eq. (iv), $C = \frac{1}{2}$

On putting the values of A, B and C in Eq. (ii), we get

Now, from eq. (i) we get $\dfrac{1}{x(x-1)(x+1)} = \dfrac{-1}{x} + \dfrac{1}{2(x-1)} + \dfrac{1}{2(x+1)}$

$$\int dy = -\int \frac{1}{x}dx + \frac{1}{2}\int \frac{1}{x-1}dx + \frac{1}{2}\int \frac{1}{x+1}dx$$

$$\Rightarrow \quad y = -\log|x| + \frac{1}{2}\log|(x-1)| + \frac{1}{2}\log|(x+1)| + C$$

$$\Rightarrow \quad y = -\frac{1}{2}\log(x^2) + \frac{1}{2}\log|(x-1)| + \frac{1}{2}\log|(x+1)| + C$$

$$\Rightarrow \quad y = \frac{1}{2}\left[\log\left|\left(\frac{(x-1)(x+1)}{x^2}\right)\right|\right] + C \quad \left(\because \log l + \log m - \log n = \log\frac{lm}{n}\right)$$

$$\Rightarrow \quad y = \frac{1}{2}\left[\log\left|\left(\frac{x^2-1}{x^2}\right)\right|\right] + C \qquad \text{...(vii)}$$

On putting $y = 0$ and $x = 2$ in Eq. (vii), we get

$$\therefore \quad 0 = \frac{1}{2}\left[\log\left|\left(\frac{2^2-1}{2^2}\right)\right|\right] + C \Rightarrow C = -\frac{1}{2}\log\left(\frac{3}{4}\right)$$

On substituting the value of C in Eq. (vii), we get

$$y = \frac{1}{2}\log\left|\left(\frac{x^2-1}{x^2}\right)\right| - \frac{1}{2}\log\left(\frac{3}{4}\right)$$

which is the required particular solution.

Quick Solution

We have $\quad x(x^2-1)\dfrac{dy}{dx} = 1$

$$\Rightarrow \quad dy = \frac{dx}{x(x^2-1)} \qquad \text{(On separating the variable)}$$

$$\Rightarrow \quad \int dy = \int \frac{dx}{x(x^2-1)} \qquad \text{(On integrating both sides)}$$

$$\Rightarrow \quad y = \int \frac{dx}{x(x^2-1)}$$

Put $x = \sec\theta \Rightarrow \cos\theta = \dfrac{1}{x}$

$$\frac{dx}{d\theta} = \sec\theta\tan\theta \Rightarrow dx = \sec\theta\tan\theta\, d\theta$$

$$\Rightarrow \quad y = \int \frac{\sec\theta\tan\theta\, d\theta}{\sec\theta(\sec^2\theta - 1)}$$

$$\Rightarrow \quad y = \int \frac{\tan\theta}{\tan^2\theta}\, d\theta$$

$$\Rightarrow \quad y = \int \cot\theta\, d\theta = \log\sin\theta$$

$$= \log\sqrt{1-\cos^2\theta} + C$$

Put $\cos\theta = \frac{1}{x}$, we get

$$y = \log\sqrt{1-\frac{1}{x^2}} + C$$

$$\Rightarrow \quad y = \frac{1}{2}\log\left(\frac{x^2-1}{x^2}\right) + C \quad \text{...(i)}$$

On putting $y = 0$ and $x = 2$ in (i) we get

$$0 = \frac{1}{2}\log\left(\frac{4-1}{4}\right) + C \Rightarrow C = -\frac{1}{2}\log\frac{3}{4}$$

On substituting the value of c in Eq. (i), we get

$$y = \frac{1}{2}\log\left(\frac{x^2-1}{x^2}\right) - \frac{1}{2}\log\frac{3}{4}$$

Which is the required solution.

Mistake Alert For partial fraction you have to factorise $x^2 - 1 = (x+1)(x-1)$

You can not take $(x^2 - 1)$ as quadratic factor.

Question 13 $\cos\left(\frac{dy}{dx}\right) = a, (a \in R): y = 1$ when $x = 0$.

Sol. Given, $\cos\left(\frac{dy}{dx}\right) = a \Rightarrow \frac{dy}{dx} = \cos^{-1} a$

On separating the variables, we get $dy = (\cos^{-1} a)\,dx$

On integrating both sides, we get $\int dy = \cos^{-1} a \int dx$

$$\Rightarrow \quad y = \cos^{-1} a(x) + C \quad \text{...(i)}$$

On putting $y = 1$ and $x = 0$, we get

$$1 = \cos^{-1}(a) \times 0 + C \Rightarrow C = 1$$

On substituting $C = 1$ in Eq. (i), we get

$$y = x\cos^{-1} a + 1 \Rightarrow \frac{y-1}{x} = \cos^{-1} a \Rightarrow \cos\left(\frac{y-1}{x}\right) = a.$$

which is the required particular solution.

Question 14 $\frac{dy}{dx} = y\tan x: y = 1$ when $x = 0$.

Sol. Given, $\frac{dy}{dx} = y\tan x$

On separating the variables, we get $\frac{1}{y}dy = \tan x\, dx$

On integrating both sides, we get

$$\int \frac{1}{y}dy = \int \tan x\, dx \Rightarrow \log|y| = \log|(\sec x)| + \log|C|$$

$$\Rightarrow \quad \log y = \log|(C\sec x)| \quad [\because \log m + \log n = \log mn]$$

$$\Rightarrow \quad y = C\sec x \quad (\because \log m = \log n \Rightarrow m = n) \quad \text{...(i)}$$

Now, put $y = 1$, when $x = 0$, we get

$$1 = C\sec 0 \Rightarrow 1 = C \times 1 \Rightarrow C = 1$$

On substituting $C = 1$ in Eq. (i), we get $y = \sec x$
which is the required particular solution.

Question 15 Find the equation of a curve passing through the point $(0, 0)$ and whose differential equation is $y' = e^x \sin x$.

Sol. The given differential equation of the curve is

$$y' = e^x \sin x \quad \text{or} \quad \frac{dy}{dx} = e^x \sin x$$

On separating the variables, we get

$$dy = e^x \sin x\, dx$$

On integrating both sides, we get

$$\int dy = \int e^x \sin x\, dx \quad \text{...(i)}$$

Let

$$I = \int \underset{\text{II}}{e^x} \underset{\text{I}}{\sin x}\, dx \quad \text{...(ii)}$$

$$\Rightarrow I = \sin x \int e^x dx - \int\left(\frac{d}{dx}(\sin x)\int e^x dx\right)dx \quad \text{(using integration by parts)}$$

$$= \sin x \int e^x dx - \int \underset{\text{I}}{\cos x} \cdot \underset{\text{II}}{e^x}\, dx$$

$$= \sin x . e^x - \left[\cos x . \int e^x dx - \int\left(\frac{d}{dx}(\cos x) \cdot \int e^x dx\right)dx\right]$$

[again integration by parts]

$$\Rightarrow I = \sin x \cdot e^x - [\cos x \cdot e^x - \int(-\sin x) \cdot e^x dx]$$

$$= \sin x \cdot e^x - e^x \cdot \cos x - \int e^x \cdot \sin x \cdot dx$$

$$\Rightarrow I = \sin x \cdot e^x - \cos x \cdot e^x - I \quad \text{[From Eq. (ii)]}$$

$$\Rightarrow 2I = e^x(\sin x - \cos x) \Rightarrow I = \frac{e^x(\sin x - \cos x)}{2} + C$$

On substituting this value in Eq. (i), we get

$$y = \frac{e^x(\sin x - \cos x)}{2} + C \quad \text{...(iii)}$$

Now, the curve passes through the point (0, 0) or we can say $x = 0$, $y = 0$.

$$\therefore \quad 0 = \frac{e^0(\sin 0 - \cos 0)}{2} + C \quad \text{[From Eq. (iii)]}$$

$$\Rightarrow \quad 0 = \frac{1(0 - 1)}{2} + C \Rightarrow C = \frac{1}{2}$$

On substituting $C = \frac{1}{2}$ in Eq. (iii), we get

$$y = \frac{e^x(\sin x - \cos x)}{2} + \frac{1}{2} \Rightarrow 2y = e^x(\sin x - \cos x) + 1$$

$$\Rightarrow \quad 2y - 1 = e^x(\sin x - \cos x)$$

Hence, the required equation of the curve is $2y - 1 = e^x(\sin x - \cos x)$.

Mistake Alert Be careful with constants; Always use the initial condition to find the value of C.

Question 16 For the differential equation $xy\frac{dy}{dx}=(x+2)(y+2)$, find the solution, curve passing through the point $(1,-1)$.

Sol. The given curve is $xy\frac{dy}{dx} = (x + 2)(y + 2)$ ...(i)

On separating the variables, we get $\frac{y}{y+2}dy = \frac{x+2}{x}dx$

On integrating both sides, we get

$$\int \frac{y}{y+2}dy = \int \frac{x+2}{x}dx \Rightarrow \int \left(\frac{y+2-2}{y+2}\right)dy = \int \frac{x+2}{x}dx$$

(adding an subtracting 2 in LHS)

$$\Rightarrow \int \frac{y+2}{y+2}dy - \int \frac{2}{y+2}dy = \int \frac{x}{x}dx + \int \frac{2}{x}dx$$

$$\Rightarrow \int dy - 2\int \frac{1}{y+2}dy = \int dx + 2\int \frac{1}{x}dx$$

$$\Rightarrow y - 2\log|y+2| = x + 2\log|x| + C \quad \text{...(ii)}$$

Now, the curve passes through the point $(1, -1)$.

So, put $x = 1$ and $y = -1$ in Eq. (ii), we get

$$-1 - 2\log|-1+2| = 1 + 2\log 1 + C$$

$$\Rightarrow -1 - 2\log 1 = 1 + 2\log 1 + C \Rightarrow C = -2 \quad [\because \log 1 = 0]$$

Hence, from Eq. (ii) we get

$$y - 2\log|y+2| = x + 2\log|x| - 2$$

$$\Rightarrow y - x + 2 = 2\log|x(y+2)| \quad [\because \log m + \log n = \log mn]$$

$$\Rightarrow y - x + 2 = \log[x^2(y+2)^2] \quad [\because \log m^n = n\log m]$$

which is the required equation of the curve.

Question 17 Find the equation of a curve passing through the point $(0,-2)$ given that at any point (x,y) on the curve, the product of the slope of its tangent and y coordinate of the point is equal to the x coordinate of the point.

Thinking Process

(i) Slope of a tangent is given by $\frac{dy}{dx}$.

(ii) Find differential equation according to the given condition. Integrate it to find a general solution.

(iii) Use the given point to find the value of arbitrary constant and then find the particular solution.

Sol. Let x and y be the x-coordinate and y-coordinate of the curve respectively.

We know that the slope of a tangent to the curve in the coordinate axis is given by the relation $\frac{dy}{dx}$.

According to given question, we get

Product of the slope of tangent with y-coordinate = x-coordinate

$$y \cdot \frac{dy}{dx} = x \quad \ldots(i)$$

On separating the variables, we get

$$y\,dy = x\,dx$$

On integrating both sides, we get $\int y\,dy = \int x\,dx \Rightarrow \frac{y^2}{2} = \frac{x^2}{2} + C$ ...(ii)

Now, the curve passes through the point $(0, -2)$, therefore

$$\frac{(-2)^2}{2} = 0 + C \Rightarrow C = \frac{4}{2} = 2$$

On substituting this value of C in Eq. (ii), we get

$$\frac{y^2}{2} = \frac{x^2}{2} + 2$$

$$\Rightarrow \quad x^2 - y^2 + 4 = 0$$

which is the required equation of the curve.

Question 18 At any point (x, y) of a curve, the slope of the tangent is twice the slope of the line segment joining the point of contact to the point $(-4, -3)$. Find the equation of the curve given that it passes through $(-2, 1)$.

Thinking Process Firstly, we find the slope of the line segment which passes through the points (x, y) and $(-4, -3)$ and then apply the given condition.

Sol. It is given that (x, y) is the point of contact of the curve and its tangent.

The slope of the line segment joining the points $(x_2, y_2) \to (x, y)$ and $(x_1, y_1) \to (-4, -3)$

$$= \frac{y - (-3)}{x - (-4)} = \frac{y + 3}{x + 4} \quad \left(\because \text{Slope of tangent} = \frac{y_2 - y_1}{x_2 - x_1}\right)$$

According to question (slope of tangent is twice the slope of the line), we must have, $\frac{dy}{dx} = 2\left(\frac{y + 3}{x + 4}\right)$

Now, separating the variables, we get

$$\frac{dy}{y + 3} = \left(\frac{2}{x + 4}\right)dx$$

On integrating both sides, we get

$$\int \frac{dy}{y+3} = \int \left(\frac{2}{x+4}\right) dx$$

$\Rightarrow \log|y+3| = 2\log|x+4| + \log|C| \Rightarrow \log|y+3| = \log|x+4|^2 + \log|C|$

$$\Rightarrow \quad \log\frac{|y+3|}{|x+4|^2} = \log|C| \qquad \left[\because \log m - \log n = \log\frac{m}{n}\right]$$

$$\Rightarrow \quad \frac{|y+3|}{|x+4|^2} = C \qquad \text{...(ii)}$$

The curve passes through the point (–2, 1), therefore

$$\Rightarrow \quad \frac{|1+3|}{|-2+4|^2} = C \Rightarrow C = 1$$

Substituting C = 1 in Eq. (ii), we get

$$\frac{|y+3|}{|x+4|^2} = 1 \Rightarrow y + 3 = (x+4)^2$$

which is the required equation of curve.

Question 19 The volume of spherical balloon being inflated changes at a constant rate. If initially its radius is 3 unit and after 3 seconds it is 6 unit. Find the radius of balloon after t seconds.

Sol. Let the rate of change of the volume of the balloon be k (where k, is constant)

$$\frac{d}{dt}(\text{volume}) = \text{constant}$$

$$\Rightarrow \quad \frac{d}{dt}\left(\frac{4}{3}\pi r^3\right) = k \qquad \left[\because \text{Volume of sphere} = \frac{4}{3}\pi r^3\right]$$

$$\Rightarrow \quad \left(\frac{4}{3}\pi\right)\left(3r^2\frac{dr}{dt}\right) = k$$

On separating the variables, we get

$$4\pi r^2\, dr = k\, dt \qquad \text{...(i)}$$

On integrating both sides, we get

$$4\pi\int r^2 dr = k\int dt$$

$$\Rightarrow \quad 4\pi\frac{r^3}{3} = kt + C \Rightarrow 4\pi r^3 = 3(kt + C) \qquad \text{...(ii)}$$

Now, at $t = 0$, $r = 3$, initially;

$$\therefore \quad 4\pi(3)^3 = 3(k \times 0 + C) \Rightarrow 108\pi = 3C \Rightarrow C = 36\pi$$

Also, when $t = 3$, $r = 6$, then from Eq. (ii)

$$4\pi(6)^3 = 3(k \times 3 + C) \Rightarrow 864\pi = 3(3k + 36\pi)$$

$$\Rightarrow \quad 3k = 288\pi - 36\pi = 252\pi \Rightarrow k = 84\pi$$

On substituting the values of k and C in Eq. (ii), we get

$$4\pi r^3 = 3[84\pi t + 36\pi] \Rightarrow 4\pi r^3 = 4\pi(63t + 27)$$

$$\Rightarrow \quad r^3 = 63t + 27 \Rightarrow r = (63t + 27)^{1/3}$$

which is the required radius of the balloon at time t.

Question 20 In a bank principal increases continuously at the rate of $r\%$ per year. Find the value of r if ₹ 100 double itself in 10 years ($\log_e 2 = 0.6391$).

Thinking Process Let the bank principal (P) increases at the rate of $r\%$ per year. Then, $\frac{dP}{dt} = r\%$ of $P \Rightarrow dP = \frac{rp}{100} dt$

Integrating it and put the given condition to get the result.

Sol. Let P, t and r represent the principal, time and rate of interest respectively.

It is given that the principal increases continuously at the rate of $r\%$ per year.

$$\therefore \quad \frac{dP}{dt} = r\% \text{of } P \Rightarrow \frac{dP}{dt} = \frac{rP}{100} \Rightarrow \frac{dp}{p} = \frac{r}{100} dt$$

(by separating the variables)

On integrating both sides, we get

$$\int \frac{dP}{P} = \int \frac{r}{100} dt \Rightarrow \log |P| = \frac{r}{100} t + C \quad \text{...(i)}$$

When $t = 0$ (initially), let $P = P_0$, then

$$\log |P_0| = 0 + C \Rightarrow C = \log |P_0|$$

On substituting the value of C in Eq. (i), we get

$$\log |P| = \frac{r}{100} t + \log |P_0|$$

$$\Rightarrow \quad \log |P| - \log |P_0| = \frac{r}{100} t \Rightarrow \log \left| \frac{P}{P_0} \right| = \frac{r}{100} t \quad \text{...(ii)}$$

It is given that when $t = 10$, then $P = 2P_0$, put in Eq. (ii), we get

$$\log \left| \frac{2P_0}{P_0} \right| = \frac{r(10)}{100} \Rightarrow r = 10 \log 2 = 10 \times 0.6931 \Rightarrow r = 6.931$$

Hence, the value of r is 6.93%.

Question 21 In a bank principal increases at the rate of 5% per year. An amount of ₹ 1000 is deposited with this bank, how much will it be worth after 10 years ($e^{0.5} = 1.648$)?

Sol. Let P and t be the principal and time respectively.

It is given that the principal increases continuously at the rate of 5% per year.

$$\text{So,} \quad \frac{dP}{dt} = 5\% \text{of } P \Rightarrow \frac{dP}{dt} = \frac{5}{100} P$$

On separating the variable, we get

$$\frac{dP}{P} = \frac{1}{20} dt$$

On integrating, we get

$$\int \frac{dP}{P} = \int \frac{1}{20} dt \Rightarrow \log |P| = \frac{1}{20} t + C \quad \text{...(i)}$$

When $t = 0$, $P = 1000$ (initially) then $\log 1000 = C$ ...(ii)

Put the value of C in Eq. (i), we get $\log|P| = \frac{1}{20}t + \log 1000$

$\Rightarrow$ $$\log\left|\left(\frac{P}{1000}\right)\right| = \frac{1}{20}t \quad \left[\because \log m - \log n = \log \frac{m}{n}\right]$$

When $t = 10$, then $\log\left|\frac{P}{1000}\right| = \frac{1}{20} \times 10 \Rightarrow \frac{P}{1000} = e^{1/2}$ $\quad [\because \log_e x = m \Rightarrow e^m = x]$

$\Rightarrow$ $$\frac{P}{1000} = e^{0.5} = 1.648 \Rightarrow P = 1000 \times 1.648 \Rightarrow P = 1648$$

Hence, after 10 years, the amount will worth ₹ 1648.

Question 22 In a culture the bacteria count is 100000. The number is increases by 10% in 2 hours. In how many hours will the count reach 200000, if the rate of growth of bacteria is proportional to the number present?

◎ **Thinking Process** Assume y be the count of bacteria at the end of t hours, then $\frac{dy}{dt} \propto y$ *i.e.*, $\frac{dy}{dt} = ky$. Integrate this relation further to get the answer.

Sol. Let y be the count of the bacteria at the end of t hours, then

$$\frac{dy}{dt} \propto y \Rightarrow \frac{dy}{dt} = ky,$$

where, k is constant of proportionality.

Now, separating the variables, we get $\frac{dy}{y} = k\,dt$

On integrating both sides, we get

$$\int \frac{dy}{y} = \int k\,dt \Rightarrow \log|y| = kt + C \quad \text{...(i)}$$

When $t = 0$, $y = 100000$ (initially) then $\log(100000) = C$ ...(ii)

and when $t = 2$, $y = 110000$, then $\log(110000) = 2k + C$ ...(iii)

$\because$ 10% increase in 100000

$$= 100000 + 10\% \text{ of } 100000$$
$$= 100000 + 10000$$
$$= 110000$$

On subtracting Eq. (ii) from Eq. (iii), we get

$$\log 110000 - \log 100000 = 2k \Rightarrow \log\frac{110000}{100000} = 2k \Rightarrow k = \frac{1}{2}\log\left(\frac{11}{10}\right)$$

On substituting the value of k and C in Eq. (i), we get

$$\log y = \frac{1}{2}\log\left(\frac{11}{10}\right)t + \log 100000$$

When $y = 200000$, then $\log 200000 = \frac{1}{2}\log\left(\frac{11}{10}\right)t + \log 100000$

$$\Rightarrow \log\left(\frac{200000}{100000}\right) = \frac{1}{2}\log\left(\frac{11}{10}\right)t \Rightarrow 2\log(2) = \log\left(\frac{11}{10}\right)t \Rightarrow t = \frac{2\log 2}{\log\left(\frac{11}{10}\right)}$$

Hence, in $\dfrac{2\log 2}{\log\left(\frac{11}{10}\right)}$ h the number of bacteria increases from 100000 to 200000.

Choose the correct answer.

Question 23 The general solution of the differential equation $\dfrac{dy}{dx} = e^{x+y}$ is

(a) $e^x + e^{-y} = C$ (b) $e^x + e^y = C$
(c) $e^{-x} + e^y = C$ (d) $e^{-x} + e^{-y} = C$

Sol. (a) Given, $\dfrac{dy}{dx} = e^{x+y} \Rightarrow \dfrac{dy}{dx} = e^x e^y$

Now, separating the variables, we get $e^{-y}dy = e^x dx$

On integrating both sides, we get

$$\int e^{-y}dy = \int e^x dx \Rightarrow \frac{e^{-y}}{-1} = e^x + A$$

$$\Rightarrow \quad e^x + e^{-y} = -A$$

$$\Rightarrow \quad e^x + e^{-y} = C, \text{ where } C = -A$$

Exercise 9.4

Direction (Q. No. 1 to 10) In each of the question show that the given differential equation is homogeneous and solve each of them.

Question 1 $(x^2 + xy)dy = (x^2 + y^2)dx.$

Thinking Process

(i) First check the homogeneous nature of the equation.

(ii) If it is homogeneous, then use the relations $y = vx$ and $\dfrac{dy}{dx} = v + x\dfrac{dv}{dx}$.

Sol. Given, differential equation is $\dfrac{dy}{dx} = \dfrac{x^2 + y^2}{x^2 + xy}$ ...(i)

Let $$f(x, y) = \frac{x^2 + y^2}{x^2 + xy}$$

On replaciang y by λy and x by λx, we get

$$f(\lambda x, \lambda y) = \frac{(\lambda x)^2 + (\lambda y)^2}{(\lambda x)^2 + \lambda x \cdot \lambda y}$$

$$= \frac{\lambda^2(x^2 + y^2)}{\lambda^2(x^2 + xy)} = \lambda^\circ f(x, y)$$

Since, power of λ is 0.

So, the given differential equation is homogeneous.

Let $$y = vx \Rightarrow \frac{dy}{dx} = v + x\frac{dv}{dx}$$

On putting the values of $\frac{dy}{dx}$ and y in Eq. (i), we get

$$v + x\frac{dv}{dx} = \frac{x^2 + x^2v^2}{x^2 + vx^2} \Rightarrow v + x\frac{dv}{dx} = \frac{x^2(1+v^2)}{x^2(1+v)}$$

$$\Rightarrow \quad x\frac{dv}{dx} = \frac{1+v^2}{1+v} - v \Rightarrow x\frac{dv}{dx} = \frac{1+v^2-v-v^2}{1+v} = \frac{1-v}{1+v}$$

$$\Rightarrow \quad \frac{1+v}{1-v}dv = \frac{dx}{x} \Rightarrow \frac{2-1+v}{1-v}dv = \frac{dx}{x}$$

$$\Rightarrow \quad \left(\frac{2}{1-v} - \frac{1-v}{1-v}\right)dv = \frac{dx}{x} \Rightarrow \left(\frac{2}{1-v} - 1\right)dv = \frac{dx}{x}$$

On integrating both sides, we get

$$\int \frac{2}{1-v}dv - \int 1dv = \int \frac{1}{x}dx$$

$$\Rightarrow \quad -2\log(1-v) - v = \log x - \log C$$

$$\Rightarrow \quad -v - 2\log(1-v) - \log x = -\log C$$

$$\Rightarrow \quad v + 2\log(1-v) + \log x = \log C$$

$$\Rightarrow \quad \frac{y}{x} + 2\log\left(1 - \frac{y}{x}\right) + \log x = \log C \qquad \left[\because v = \frac{y}{x}\right]$$

$$\Rightarrow \quad \frac{y}{x} + \log\left(\frac{x-y}{x}\right)^2 + \log x = \log C$$

$$\Rightarrow \quad \frac{y}{x} + \log(x-y)^2 - \log x^2 + \log x = \log C$$

$$\Rightarrow \quad \frac{y}{x} + \log(x-y)^2 - 2\log x + \log x = \log C$$

$$\Rightarrow \quad \frac{y}{x} + \log(x-y)^2 - \log x = \log C$$

$$\Rightarrow \quad \frac{y}{x} + \log\frac{(x-y)^2}{x} - \log C = 0 \Rightarrow \log\left(\frac{(x-y)^2}{x}\cdot\frac{1}{C}\right) = -\frac{y}{x}$$

$$\Rightarrow \quad (x-y)^2 = Cxe^{-\frac{y}{x}} \quad (\because \log_e x = m \Rightarrow x = e^m)$$

This is the required solution, of the given differential equation.

Question 2 $y' = \dfrac{x+y}{x}$.

Sol. Given, $y' = \dfrac{dy}{dx} = \dfrac{x+y}{x}$ ...(i)

Let $f(x, y) = \dfrac{x+y}{x}$

On replacing y by λy and x by λx, we get

$$f(\lambda x, \lambda y) = \frac{\lambda x + \lambda y}{\lambda x}$$

$$= \frac{\lambda(x + y)}{\lambda x}$$

$$= \lambda^{\circ} F(x, y)$$

Since, power of λ is 0.

So, the given differential equation is homogeneous.

Let $\quad y = vx \Rightarrow \frac{dy}{dx} = v + x\frac{dv}{dx}$

On putting values of $\frac{dy}{dx}$ and y in Eq. (i), we get

$$\therefore \quad v + x\frac{dv}{dx} = \frac{x + vx}{x} \Rightarrow v + x\frac{dv}{dx} = 1 + v \Rightarrow \frac{dv}{dx} = \frac{1}{x} \Rightarrow dv = \frac{dx}{x}$$

On integrating both sides, we get

$$\int dv = \int \frac{1}{x} dx \Rightarrow v = \log |x| + C \Rightarrow \frac{y}{x} = \log |x| + C \qquad [\because v = y/x]$$

$$\Rightarrow \quad y = x \log |x| + Cx.$$

This is the required solution of the given differential equation.

Question 3 $(x - y)\,dy - (x + y)\,dx = 0.$

Sol. Given, $(x - y)\,dy - (x + y)\,dx = 0$

$$\Rightarrow \quad (x - y)\,dy = (x + y)\,dx \Rightarrow \frac{dy}{dx} = \frac{x + y}{x - y} \qquad \ldots(i)$$

Let $\quad f(x, y) = \frac{x + y}{x - y}$

On replacing y by λy and x by λx, we get

$$f(\lambda x, \lambda y) = \frac{\lambda x + \lambda y}{\lambda x - \lambda y}$$

$$= \frac{\lambda(x + y)}{\lambda(x - y)}$$

$$= \lambda^{\circ} f(x, y)$$

Since, power of λ is 0.

Thus, the given differential equation is homogeneous.

Let $\quad y = vx \Rightarrow \frac{dy}{dx} = v + x\frac{dv}{dx}$

On putting values of $\frac{dy}{dx}$ and y in Eq. (i), we get

$$v + x\frac{dv}{dx} = \frac{x + vx}{x - vx} \Rightarrow v + x\frac{dv}{dx} = \frac{1 + v}{1 - v}$$

$$\Rightarrow \quad x\frac{dv}{dx} = \frac{1 + v}{1 - v} - v \Rightarrow x\frac{dv}{dx} = \frac{1 + v - v + v^2}{1 - v} \Rightarrow \frac{1 - v}{1 + v^2}\,dv = \frac{dx}{x}$$

On integrating both sides, we get

$$\int \frac{1-v}{1+v^2}dv = \int \frac{dx}{x} \Rightarrow \int \frac{1}{1+v^2}dv - \int \frac{v}{1+v^2}dx = \log|x| + C$$

Let $1+v^2 = t \Rightarrow 2v = \frac{dt}{dv} \Rightarrow dv = \frac{dt}{2v}$,

$$\therefore \quad \tan^{-1} v - \int \frac{v}{t} \times \frac{dt}{2v} = \log|x| + C$$

$$\Rightarrow \quad \tan^{-1} v - \frac{1}{2}\log|t| = \log|x| + C$$

$$\Rightarrow \quad 2\tan^{-1} v - [\log(1+v^2) + 2\log(x)] = 2C \qquad (\text{Put } t = 1+v^2)$$

$$\Rightarrow \quad 2\tan^{-1} v - \log[(1+v^2)x^2] = 2C$$

$$(n\log x = \log x^n \text{ and } \log a + \log b = \log(ab))$$

$$\Rightarrow \quad 2\tan^{-1}\frac{y}{x} - \log\left[\left(\frac{x^2+y^2}{x^2}\right)x^2\right] = 2C \qquad \left(\text{Put } v = \frac{y}{x}\right)$$

$$\Rightarrow \quad 2\tan^{-1}\frac{y}{x} - \log(x^2+y^2) = 2C \Rightarrow \tan^{-1}\frac{y}{x} - \frac{1}{2}\log(x^2+y^2) = C$$

This is the required solution of the given differential equation.

Question 4 $(x^2 - y^2)dx + 2xy\,dy = 0.$

Sol. We have, $(x^2 - y^2)dx + 2xydy = 0$

$$\Rightarrow \quad 2xy\,dy = (y^2 - x^2)dx \Rightarrow \frac{dy}{dx} = \frac{y^2 - x^2}{2xy} \qquad \ldots(i)$$

Let $f(x, y) = \dfrac{y^2 - x^2}{2xy}$

On replacing y by λy and x by λx, we get

$$f(\lambda x, \lambda y) = \frac{(\lambda y)^2 - (\lambda x)^2}{2.\lambda x.\lambda y}$$

$$= \frac{\lambda^2(y^2 - x^2)}{\lambda^2.2xy}$$

$$= \lambda^{\circ} f(x, y)$$

Since, the power of λ is 0.

Thus, the given differential equation is homogeneous.

So, put $y = vx \Rightarrow \frac{dy}{dx} = v + x\frac{dv}{dx}$, then Eq. (i) becomes

$$v + x\frac{dv}{dx} = \frac{v^2x^2 - x^2}{2x^2v} \Rightarrow v + x\frac{dv}{dx} = \frac{v^2 - 1}{2v}$$

$$\Rightarrow \quad x\frac{dv}{dx} = \frac{v^2 - 1}{2v} - v \Rightarrow x\frac{dv}{dx} = \frac{-1 - v^2}{2v} \Rightarrow \frac{2v}{v^2 + 1}dv = -\frac{dx}{x}$$

On integrating both sides, we get

$$\int \frac{2v}{v^2+1}dv + \int \frac{dx}{x} = 0$$

Let $\quad v^2 + 1 = t \Rightarrow 2v = \frac{dt}{dv} \Rightarrow dv = \frac{dt}{2v}.$

$\therefore \quad \int \frac{2v}{t} \times \frac{dt}{2v} + \int \frac{dx}{x} = 0$

$\Rightarrow \quad \log|t| + \log|x| = \log C \Rightarrow \log|(v^2+1)x| = \log C \qquad (\because t = 1 + v^2)$

$\Rightarrow \quad \log\left[\left(\frac{y^2+x^2}{x^2}\right)x\right] = \log C \Rightarrow \frac{y^2+x^2}{x} = C \qquad (\because v = y/x)$

$\Rightarrow \quad x^2 + y^2 = Cx.$

This is the required solution, of the given differential equation.

Question 5 $x^2 \frac{dy}{dx} = x^2 - 2y^2 + xy.$

Sol. Given, $\frac{dy}{dx} = \frac{x^2 - 2y^2 + xy}{x^2}$ ...(i)

Let $\quad f(x, y) = \frac{x^2 - 2y^2 + xy}{x^2}$

On replacing y by λy and x by λx, we get

$$f(\lambda x, \lambda y) = \frac{(\lambda x)^2 - 2(\lambda y)^2 + \lambda x \cdot \lambda y}{(\lambda x)^2}$$

$$= \frac{\lambda^2[x^2 - 2y^2 + xy]}{\lambda^2 . x^2}$$

$$= \lambda^\circ f(x, y)$$

Since, power of λ is zero.

Thus, the given differential equation is homogeneous.

So, put $\quad y = vx \Rightarrow \frac{dy}{dx} = v + x\frac{dv}{dx}$

Then, Eq. (i) becomes $v + x\frac{dv}{dx} = \frac{x^2 - 2x^2v^2 + x^2v}{x^2}$

$\Rightarrow \quad v + x\frac{dv}{dx} = 1 - 2v^2 + v \Rightarrow x\frac{dv}{dx} = 1 - 2v^2 \Rightarrow \frac{1}{1-2v^2}dv = \frac{1}{x}dx$

On integrating both sides, we get

$$\int \frac{1}{1-2v^2}dv = \int \frac{dx}{x} \Rightarrow \frac{1}{2}\int \frac{1}{\left(\frac{1}{\sqrt{2}}\right)^2 - v^2}dv = \int \frac{dx}{x}$$

$$\Rightarrow \quad \frac{1}{2}\cdot\frac{1}{2\cdot\frac{1}{\sqrt{2}}}\log\left|\frac{\frac{1}{\sqrt{2}}+v}{\frac{1}{\sqrt{2}}-v}\right| = \log|x| + C \quad \left[\because \int\frac{dx}{a^2-x^2} = \frac{1}{2a}\log\left|\frac{a+x}{a-x}\right| + C\right]$$

$$\Rightarrow \quad \frac{1}{2\sqrt{2}}\log\left|\frac{1+\sqrt{2}v}{1-\sqrt{2}v}\right| = \log|x| + C$$

$$\Rightarrow \quad \frac{1}{2\sqrt{2}}\log\left|\frac{1+\sqrt{2}\,\frac{y}{x}}{1-\sqrt{2}\,\frac{y}{x}}\right| = \log|x| + C \qquad \left(\text{put } v = \frac{y}{x}\right)$$

$$\Rightarrow \quad \frac{1}{2\sqrt{2}}\log\left|\frac{x+\sqrt{2}y}{x-\sqrt{2}y}\right| = \log|x| + C$$

This is the required solution of given differential equation.

Question 6 $x\,dy - y\,dx = \sqrt{x^2+y^2}\,dx.$

Sol. Given, $x\,dy = y\,dx + \sqrt{x^2+y^2}\,dx$

$$\Rightarrow \quad \frac{dy}{dx} = \frac{y+\sqrt{x^2+y^2}}{x} \qquad \text{...(i)}$$

Let $f(x, y) = \dfrac{y+\sqrt{x^2+y^2}}{x}$

On replacing y by λy and x by λx, we get

$$f(\lambda x, \lambda y) = \frac{\lambda y + \sqrt{(\lambda x)^2 + (\lambda y)^2}}{\lambda x}$$

$$= \frac{\lambda y + \sqrt{\lambda^2[x^2+y^2]}}{\lambda x} = \frac{\lambda y + \lambda\sqrt{x^2+y^2}}{\lambda x}$$

$$= \frac{\lambda[y+\sqrt{x^2+y^2}]}{\lambda x}$$

$$= \lambda^\circ f(x, y)$$

Since, power of λ is 0.

Thus, the given differential equation is homogeneous.

So, put $y = vx$

$$\Rightarrow \quad \frac{dy}{dx} = v + x\frac{dv}{dx}, \text{ then Eq. (i) becomes}$$

$$v + x\frac{dv}{dx} = \frac{vx + \sqrt{x^2+x^2v^2}}{x}$$

$$\Rightarrow \quad v + x\frac{dv}{dx} = \frac{x[v+\sqrt{1+v^2}]}{x} \Rightarrow v + x\frac{dv}{dx} = v + \sqrt{1+v^2}$$

$$\Rightarrow \quad \frac{1}{\sqrt{1+v^2}}\,dv = \frac{1}{x}\,dx$$

On integrating both sides, we get

$$\int \frac{1}{\sqrt{1+v^2}}\,dv = \int \frac{dx}{x} \Rightarrow \log\left(v+\sqrt{1+v^2}\right) = \log x + \log C$$

$$\left[\because \int \frac{dx}{\sqrt{x^2+a^2}} = \log\left|x+\sqrt{x^2+a^2}\right| + C\right]$$

$$\Rightarrow \quad \log\left[\frac{y}{x}+\sqrt{1+\left(\frac{y}{x}\right)^2}\right] = \log x + \log C \qquad \left(\text{Put } v = \frac{y}{x}\right)$$

$$\Rightarrow \quad \log\left[\frac{y}{x}+\sqrt{\frac{x^2+y^2}{x^2}}\right] = \log(xC) \qquad [\because \log m + \log n = \log mn]$$

$$\Rightarrow \quad \frac{y}{x}+\frac{\sqrt{x^2+y^2}}{x} = Cx \qquad [\because \log m = \log n \Rightarrow mn]$$

$$\Rightarrow \quad y+\sqrt{x^2+y^2} = Cx^2$$

which is the required solution.

Question 7 $\left\{x\cos\left(\frac{y}{x}\right)+y\sin\left(\frac{y}{x}\right)\right\} y\,dx = \left\{y\sin\left(\frac{y}{x}\right)-x\cos\left(\frac{y}{x}\right)\right\} x\,dy.$

Sol. Given, $\left\{x\cos\left(\frac{y}{x}\right)+y\sin\left(\frac{y}{x}\right)\right\} y\,dx = \left\{y\sin\left(\frac{y}{x}\right)-x\cos\left(\frac{y}{x}\right)\right\} x\,dy$

$$\Rightarrow \quad \frac{dy}{dx} = \frac{y\left\{x\cos\frac{y}{x}+y\sin\frac{y}{x}\right\}}{x\left\{y\sin\frac{y}{x}-x\cos\frac{y}{x}\right\}} \qquad \ldots(i)$$

Let $f(x, y) = \dfrac{y\left[x\cos\frac{y}{x}+y\sin\frac{y}{x}\right]}{x\left[y\sin\frac{y}{x}-x\cos\frac{y}{x}\right]}$

On replacing y by λy and x λx, we get

$$f(\lambda x, \lambda y) = \frac{\lambda y\left[\lambda x\cos\frac{\lambda y}{\lambda x}+\lambda y\sin\frac{\lambda y}{\lambda x}\right]}{\lambda x\left[\lambda y\sin\frac{\lambda y}{\lambda x}-\lambda x\cos\frac{\lambda y}{\lambda x}\right]} = \frac{\lambda y.\,\lambda\left[x\cos\frac{y}{x}+y\sin\frac{y}{x}\right]}{\lambda x\cdot\lambda\left[y\sin\frac{y}{x}-x\cos\frac{y}{x}\right]}$$

$$= \lambda^\circ f(x, y)$$

Since, power of λ is 0.

Thus, the given differential equation is homogeneous.

So, put $y = vx$

$$\Rightarrow \quad \frac{dy}{dx} = v + x\frac{dv}{dx}$$

$$\therefore \quad v + x\frac{dv}{dx} = \frac{vx\{x\cos v + vx\sin v\}}{x\{vx\sin v - x\cos v\}} \Rightarrow v + x\frac{dv}{dx} = \frac{v\{\cos v + v\sin v\}}{v\sin v - \cos v}$$

$$\Rightarrow \quad x\frac{dv}{dx} = \frac{v\cos v + v^2 \sin v}{v\sin v - \cos v} - v$$

$$\Rightarrow \quad x\frac{dv}{dx} = \frac{v\cos v + v^2 \sin v - v^2 \sin v + v\cos v}{v\sin v - \cos v} \Rightarrow x\frac{dv}{dx} = \frac{2v\cos v}{v\sin v - \cos v}$$

$$\Rightarrow \quad \left(\frac{v\sin v - \cos v}{v\cos v}\right)dv = \frac{2}{x}dx \Rightarrow \left(\tan v - \frac{1}{v}\right)dv = \frac{2}{x}dx$$

On integrating both sides, we get

$$\int\left(\tan v - \frac{1}{v}\right)dv = \int\frac{2\,dx}{x}$$

$$\Rightarrow \quad \int \tan v\,dv - \int\frac{1}{v}\,dv = 2\int\frac{1}{x}\,dx$$

$$\Rightarrow \quad -\log|\cos v| - \log|v| = 2\log|x| + C$$

$$\Rightarrow \quad \log|v\cos v| + 2\log|x| = -C \qquad (\because \log m + \log n = \log mn)$$

$$\Rightarrow \quad \log[(v\cos v)\,x^2] = -C \Rightarrow (v\cos v)\,x^2 = e^{-C}$$

$$[\because \log_e x = m \Rightarrow e^m = x]$$

$$\Rightarrow \quad x^2\,v\cos v = A \qquad (\text{where, } A = e^{-C})$$

$$\Rightarrow \quad x^2\,\frac{y}{x}\cos\frac{y}{x} = A \qquad \left(\because y = \frac{v}{x}\right)$$

$$\Rightarrow \quad xy\cos\frac{y}{x} = A$$

This is the required solution of the given differential equation.

Question 8 $x\dfrac{dy}{dx} - y + x\sin\left(\dfrac{y}{x}\right) = 0.$

Sol. Given, $\dfrac{dy}{dx} = \dfrac{y}{x} - \sin\dfrac{y}{x}$ ...(i)

Let $f(x, y) = \dfrac{y}{x} - \sin\dfrac{y}{x}$

On replacing y by λy and x by λx, we get

$$f(\lambda x, \lambda y) = \frac{\lambda y}{\lambda x} - \sin\frac{\lambda y}{\lambda x}$$

$$= \frac{\lambda y}{\lambda x} - \frac{\lambda}{\lambda}\sin\frac{\lambda y}{\lambda x} \qquad \text{[multiply and divide by } \lambda]$$

$$= \lambda^0\left[\frac{y}{x} - \sin\frac{y}{x}\right] = \lambda^0\,f(x, y)$$

Since, power of λ is 0.

Thus, the given differential equation is homogeneous.

So, put $\dfrac{y}{x} = v \Rightarrow y = vx$

$$\Rightarrow \quad \frac{dy}{dx} = v + x\frac{dv}{dx}$$

Then, Eq. (i) becomes $v + x\dfrac{dv}{dx} = v - \sin v \Rightarrow \operatorname{cosec} v\, dv = -\dfrac{1}{x}\, dx$

On integrating both sides, we get

$$\int \operatorname{cosec} v\, dv = -\int \frac{dx}{x}$$

$$\Rightarrow \quad \log|\operatorname{cosec} v - \cot v| = -\log|x| + A$$

$$\left(\because \int \operatorname{cosec} x\, dx = \log|\operatorname{cosec} x - \cot x|\right)$$

$$\Rightarrow \quad \log|(\operatorname{cosec} v - \cot v)| + \log|x| = A \Rightarrow \log|(\operatorname{cosec} v - \cot v)\, x| = A$$

$$\Rightarrow \quad |x(\operatorname{cosec} v - \cot v)| = e^A \Rightarrow x\left(\frac{1}{\sin v} - \frac{\cos v}{\sin v}\right) = e^A$$

$$\Rightarrow \quad x\left(\frac{1-\cos v}{\sin v}\right) = e^A \Rightarrow x(1-\cos v) = e^A \sin v$$

$$\Rightarrow \quad x\left(1 - \cos\left(\frac{y}{x}\right)\right) = C\sin\left(\frac{y}{x}\right) \qquad \left(\text{Put } C = e^A \text{ and } v = \frac{y}{x}\right)$$

This is the required solution of given differential equation.

Question 9 $y\, dx + x\log\left(\dfrac{y}{x}\right) dy - 2x\, dy = 0.$

Sol. Given, $y\, dx + x\log\left(\dfrac{y}{x}\right) dy - 2x\, dy = 0$

$$\Rightarrow \quad \frac{y}{x} + \log\left(\frac{y}{x}\right)\frac{dy}{dx} - 2\frac{dy}{dx} = 0$$

$$\Rightarrow \quad \frac{dy}{dx} = \frac{\frac{y}{x}}{2 - \log\frac{y}{x}} \qquad \text{...(i)}$$

Let

$$f(x, y) = \frac{\frac{y}{x}}{2 - \log\frac{y}{x}}$$

On replacing y by λy and x by λx, we get

$$f(\lambda x, \lambda y) = \frac{\frac{\lambda y}{\lambda x}}{2 - \log\frac{\lambda y}{\lambda x}} = \lambda^0\left[\frac{\frac{y}{x}}{2 - \log\frac{y}{x}}\right] = \lambda^0 f(x, y)$$

Since, power of λ is 0.

Thus, the given differential equation is homogeneous.

So, put $\dfrac{y}{x} = v$ i.e., $y = vx \Rightarrow \dfrac{dy}{dx} = v + x\dfrac{dv}{dx}$

Then, Eq. (i) becomes

$$v + x\frac{dv}{dx} = \frac{v}{2 - \log v}$$

$$\Rightarrow \quad x\frac{dv}{dx} = \frac{v}{2-\log v} - v$$

$$\Rightarrow \quad x\frac{dv}{dx} = \frac{v-2v+v\log v}{2-\log v}$$

$$\Rightarrow \quad x\frac{dv}{dx} = \frac{v\log v - v}{2-\log v} \Rightarrow \frac{2-\log v}{v\log v - v}\,dv = \frac{1}{x}\,dx$$

$$\Rightarrow \quad \frac{1-(\log v-1)}{v(\log v-1)}\,dv = \frac{1}{x}\,dx$$

$$\Rightarrow \quad \left(\frac{1}{v(\log v-1)} - \frac{(\log v-1)}{v(\log v-1)}\right) dv = \frac{1}{x}\,dx$$

On integrating both sides, we get

$$\int\left(\frac{1}{v(\log v-1)} - \frac{1}{v}\right) dv = \int\frac{dx}{x}$$

$$\Rightarrow \quad \int\frac{1}{v(\log v-1)}\,dv - \int\frac{1}{v}\,dv = \int\frac{dx}{x}$$

Let $\log v - 1 = t \Rightarrow \frac{1}{v}\,dv = dt$

$$\therefore \quad \int\frac{dt}{t} - \int\frac{1}{v}\,dv = \int\frac{dx}{x}$$

$$\Rightarrow \quad \log|t| - \log|v| = \log|x| + \log C$$

$$\Rightarrow \quad \log|\log v - 1| - \log|v| = \log|x| + \log C \qquad [\because t = \log v - 1]$$

$$\Rightarrow \quad \log|\log v - 1| - \log|v| - \log|x| = \log C$$

$$\Rightarrow \quad \log\left|\frac{\log v - 1}{vx}\right| = \log C \qquad \left[\because \log\frac{m}{n} = \log m - \log n\right]$$

$$\Rightarrow \quad \left|\frac{\log v - 1}{vx}\right| = C \Rightarrow \frac{\log v - 1}{vx} = C \Rightarrow \frac{\log\left(\frac{y}{x}\right) - 1}{y} = C \quad [\because v = y/x]$$

$$\Rightarrow \quad \log\left(\frac{y}{x}\right) - 1 = Cy$$

This is the required solution, of the given differential equation.

Question 10 $\left(1 + e^{\frac{x}{y}}\right)dx + e^{\frac{x}{y}}\left(1 - \frac{x}{y}\right)dy = 0.$

Sol. Given, $\left(1 + e^{\frac{x}{y}}\right)dx = e^{\frac{x}{y}}\left(\frac{x}{y} - 1\right)dy \Rightarrow \frac{dx}{dy} = \frac{e^{x/y}\left(\frac{x}{y} - 1\right)}{e^{x/y} + 1}$ ...(i)

Let, $f(x, y) = \dfrac{e^{x/y}\left(\dfrac{x}{y} - 1\right)}{e^{x/y} + 1}$

On replacing y by λy and x by λx, we get

$$f(\lambda x, \lambda y) = \frac{e^{\frac{\lambda x}{\lambda y}}\left(\dfrac{\lambda x}{\lambda y} - 1\right)}{e^{\lambda x/\lambda y} + 1}$$

$$= \frac{e^{\frac{x}{y}}\left(\dfrac{x}{y} - 1\right)}{e^{\frac{x}{y}} + 1} = f(x, y)$$

$$= \lambda^{\circ} f(x, y) \qquad [\because x^{\circ} = 1]$$

Since, power of λ is 0.

Therefore, the given differential equation is homogeneous.

So, put $\dfrac{x}{y} = v$ i.e., $x = vy \Rightarrow \dfrac{dx}{dy} = v + y\dfrac{dv}{dy}$

Then, Eq. (i) becomes

$$v + y\frac{dv}{dy} = \frac{e^v(v-1)}{e^v + 1} \Rightarrow y\frac{dv}{dy} = \frac{e^v(v-1)}{e^v+1} - v$$

$$\Rightarrow \quad y\frac{dv}{dy} = \frac{ve^v - e^v - ve^v - v}{e^v + 1}$$

$$\Rightarrow \quad \frac{e^v + 1}{e^v + v}\,dv = -\frac{1}{y}\,dy$$

On integrating both sides, we get

$$\int \frac{e^v + 1}{e^v + v}\,dv = -\int \frac{1}{y}\,dy$$

Put $\quad e^v + v = t \Rightarrow e^v + 1 = \dfrac{dt}{dv} \Rightarrow dv = \dfrac{dt}{e^v + 1}$

$$\therefore \quad \int \frac{e^v + 1}{t}\,\frac{dt}{e^v + 1} = -\log|y| + \log C$$

$$\Rightarrow \quad \log|t| + \log|y| = \log C \Rightarrow \log|e^v + v| + \log|y| = \log C \qquad [\because t = e^v + v]$$

$$\Rightarrow \quad \log|(e^v + v)\,y| = \log C \Rightarrow |(e^v + v)y| = C \Rightarrow (e^v + v)\,y = C$$

So, put $\quad v = \dfrac{x}{y}$, we get

$$\left(e^{x/y} + \frac{x}{y}\right)y = C \Rightarrow ye^{x/y} + x = C$$

This is the required solution of the given differential equation.

Mistake Alert If you have $\dfrac{x}{y}$ in the question then always let $\dfrac{x}{y} = v$

Direction (Q. Nos. 11 to 15) For each of the differential equation find the particular solution satisfying the given conditions.

Question 11 $(x+y)dy+(x-y)\,dx=0,\ y=1$ when $x=1$.

Sol. Given, $(x+y)\,dy=(y-x)\,dx \Rightarrow \dfrac{dy}{dx}=\dfrac{y-x}{(x+y)}$ ...(i)

Thus, the given differential equation is homogeneous.

So, put $\dfrac{y}{x}=v$ i.e., $y=vx \Rightarrow \dfrac{dy}{dx}=v+x\dfrac{dv}{dx}$

Then, Eq. (i) becomes $v+x\dfrac{dv}{dx}=\dfrac{vx-x}{x+vx}$

$$\Rightarrow \quad v+x\frac{dv}{dx}=\frac{x(v-1)}{x(1+v)} \Rightarrow v+x\frac{dv}{dx}=\frac{v-1}{1+v}$$

$$\Rightarrow \quad x\frac{dv}{dx}=\frac{v-1}{1+v}-v \Rightarrow x\frac{dv}{dx}=\frac{v-1-v-v^2}{1+v} \Rightarrow -x\frac{dv}{dx}=\frac{1+v^2}{1+v}$$

$$\Rightarrow \quad \frac{(v+1)}{1+v^2}\,dv=-\frac{1}{x}\,dx$$

On integrating both sides, we get

$$\int\frac{(v+1)}{1+v^2}\,dv=-\int\frac{dx}{x} \Rightarrow \int\frac{v}{1+v^2}\,dv+\int\frac{1}{1+v^2}\,dv=-\int\frac{dx}{x}$$

Put $\quad v^2+1=t \Rightarrow 2v=\dfrac{dt}{dv} \Rightarrow dv=\dfrac{dt}{2v}$

$$\therefore \quad \int\frac{v}{t}\times\frac{dt}{2v}+\int\frac{1}{1+v^2}\,dv=-\int\frac{dx}{x}$$

$$\Rightarrow \quad \frac{1}{2}\int\frac{1}{t}\,dt+\int\frac{1}{1+v^2}\,dv=-\int\frac{dx}{x}$$

$$\Rightarrow \quad \frac{1}{2}\log|t|+\tan^{-1}v=-\log|x|+C \qquad \left[\because \int\frac{1}{1+x^2}\,dx=\tan^{-1}x\right]$$

$$\Rightarrow \quad \frac{1}{2}\log|v^2+1|+\tan^{-1}v=-\log|x|+C \qquad [\because t=v^2+1]$$

$$\Rightarrow \quad \frac{1}{2}\log\left(\frac{y^2+x^2}{x^2}\right)+\log|x|+\tan^{-1}\left(\frac{y}{x}\right)=C \qquad \left(v=\frac{y}{x}\right)$$

$$\Rightarrow \quad \log\left(\frac{y^2+x^2}{x^2}\right)+2\log|x|+2\tan^{-1}\left(\frac{y}{x}\right)=2C$$

$$\Rightarrow \quad \log\left(\frac{y^2+x^2}{x^2}\right)+\log x^2+2\tan^{-1}\left(\frac{y}{x}\right)=2C$$

$$\Rightarrow \quad \log\frac{(y^2+x^2)x^2}{x^2}+2\tan^{-1}\left(\frac{y}{x}\right)=2C$$

$[\because \log a+\log b=\log(ab)]$

$$\Rightarrow \quad \log(x^2 + y^2) + 2\tan^{-1}\left(\frac{y}{x}\right) = A \qquad [\text{Put } 2C = A] \ldots\text{(ii)}$$

Given that when $x = 1$, $y = 1$

$$\therefore \quad \log 2 + \left(2 \times \frac{\pi}{4}\right) = A \Rightarrow A = \frac{\pi}{2} + \log 2 \qquad \left(\because \tan^{-1}(1) = \frac{\pi}{4}\right)$$

On putting the value of A in Eq. (ii), we get

$$\log(x^2 + y^2) + 2\tan^{-1}\left(\frac{y}{x}\right) = \frac{\pi}{2} + \log 2$$

This is the required solution of the given differential equation.

Question 12 $x^2 dy + (xy + y^2)\,dx = 0$, $y = 1$ when $x = 1$.

Sol. Given, $x^2 dy = -(xy + y^2)dx \Rightarrow \frac{dy}{dx} = -\frac{xy + y^2}{x^2}$

Thus, the given differential equation is homogeneous.

So, put $\frac{y}{x} = v$ i.e., $y = vx \Rightarrow \frac{dy}{dx} = v + x\frac{dv}{dx}$

Then, Eq. (i) becomes $v + x\frac{dv}{dx} = -\frac{x^2 v + x^2 v^2}{x^2}$

$$\Rightarrow \quad v + x\frac{dv}{dx} = -\frac{x^2(v + v^2)}{x^2} \Rightarrow v + x\frac{dv}{dx} = -(v + v^2)$$

$$\Rightarrow \quad x\frac{dv}{dx} = -(2v + v^2) \Rightarrow \frac{dv}{v^2 + 2v} = -\frac{1}{x}dx$$

On integrating both sides, we get

$$\int \frac{dv}{v^2 + 2v} = -\int \frac{dx}{x}$$

$$\Rightarrow \quad \int \frac{1}{v^2 + 2v + 1 - 1}dv = -\int \frac{dx}{x} \Rightarrow \int \frac{1}{(v+1)^2 - 1}dv = -\int \frac{dx}{x}$$

Let $\quad v + 1 = t \Rightarrow dv = dt$

$$\therefore \quad \int \frac{1}{t^2 - 1}dt = -\int \frac{dx}{x} \Rightarrow \frac{1}{2}\log\left|\frac{t-1}{t+1}\right| = -\log|x| + \log C$$

$$\left[\because \int \frac{dx}{x^2 - a^2} = \frac{1}{2a}\log\left|\frac{x-a}{x+a}\right| + C\right]$$

$$\Rightarrow \quad \frac{1}{2}\log\left|\frac{v+1-1}{v+1+1}\right| = -\log|x| + \log C \qquad [\because t = v + 1]$$

$$\Rightarrow \quad \frac{1}{2}\log\left|\frac{v}{v+2}\right| + \log|x| = \log C$$

$$\Rightarrow \quad \log\left|\frac{v}{v+2}\right| + 2\log|x| = 2\log C \Rightarrow \log\left|\left(\frac{v}{v+2}\right)x^2\right| = \log C^2$$

$$[n\log x = \log x^n, \log a + \log b = \log(ab)]$$

$$\Rightarrow \quad \log\left|\left(\frac{\frac{y}{x}}{\frac{y}{x}+2}\right)x^2\right| = \log C^2 \text{ (Put } v = \frac{y}{x}) \Rightarrow \frac{x^2y}{2x+y} = A \quad \ldots\text{(ii)}$$

[Let $C^2 = A$ and $\log m = \log n \Rightarrow m = n$]

When $x = 1, y = 1$

$$\therefore \quad \frac{1}{2+1} = A \Rightarrow A = \frac{1}{3}$$

On putting the value of A in Eq. (ii), we get

$$\frac{x^2y}{2x+y} = \frac{1}{3} \Rightarrow 3x^2\,y = 2x + y$$

This is the required solution of the given differential equation.

Question 13 $\left[x\sin^2\left(\frac{y}{x}\right) - y\right]dx + x\,dy = 0, y = \frac{\pi}{4}$ when $x = 1$.

Sol. Given, $\sin^2\left(\frac{y}{x}\right) - \frac{y}{x} + \frac{dy}{dx} = 0 \Rightarrow \frac{dy}{dx} = \frac{y}{x} - \sin^2\left(\frac{y}{x}\right)$ ...(i)

Thus, the given differential equation is homogeneous.

So, put $\quad \frac{y}{x} = v$

i.e., $\quad y = vx \Rightarrow \frac{dy}{dx} = v + x\frac{dv}{dx}$

Then, Eq. (i) becomes

$$v + x\frac{dv}{dx} = v - \sin^2 v \Rightarrow x\frac{dv}{dx} = -\sin^2 v \Rightarrow \text{cosec}^2\, v\, dv = -\frac{1}{x}dx$$

On integrating both sides, we get

$$\int \text{cosec}^2\, v\, dv = -\int \frac{dx}{x} \Rightarrow -\cot v = -\log|x| + C$$

$$\Rightarrow \quad \log|x| - \cot v = C \Rightarrow \log|x| - \cot\left(\frac{y}{x}\right) = C \quad \left(\text{Put } v = \frac{y}{x}\right) \ldots\text{(ii)}$$

When $x = 1, y = \frac{\pi}{4}$, then,

$$\log|1| - \cot\frac{\pi}{4} = C$$

$$\Rightarrow \quad C = 0 - 1 = -1$$

On putting the value of C in Eq. (ii), we get

$$\log|x| - \cot\left(\frac{y}{x}\right) = -1 \Rightarrow \log|x| - \cot\left(\frac{y}{x}\right) = -\log e \quad (\because 1 = \log e)$$

$$\Rightarrow \quad \cot\left(\frac{y}{x}\right) = \log|ex| \quad [\because \log m + \log n = \log mn]$$

This is the required solution of the given differential equation.

Question 14. $\frac{dy}{dx}-\frac{y}{x}+\operatorname{cosec}\left(\frac{y}{x}\right)=0,\ y=0$ when $x=1$.

Sol. Given, $\frac{dy}{dx}=\frac{y}{x}-\operatorname{cosec}\left(\frac{y}{x}\right)$ ...(i)

Thus, the given differential equation is homogeneous.

So, put $\frac{y}{x}=v$ i.e., $y=vx \Rightarrow \frac{dy}{dx}=v+x\frac{dv}{dx}$

Then, Eq. (i) becomes, $v+x\frac{dv}{dx}=v-\operatorname{cosec} v \Rightarrow x\frac{dv}{dx}=-\operatorname{cosec} v$

$$\Rightarrow \sin v\, dv=-\frac{1}{x}dx$$

On integrating both sides, we get

$$\int \sin v\, dv=-\int\frac{dx}{x} \Rightarrow -\cos v=-\log|x|+C$$

$$\Rightarrow \log|x|-\cos\left(\frac{y}{x}\right)=C \qquad \left[\text{Put } v=\frac{y}{x}\right] \text{...(ii)}$$

When $x=1$, then $y=0$, therefore $\log 1-\cos 0=C \Rightarrow C=0-1=-1$

On putting the value of C in Eq. (ii), we get $\log|x|-\cos\left(\frac{y}{x}\right)=-1$

$$\Rightarrow \log|x|+1=\cos\frac{y}{x} \Rightarrow \log|x|+\log e=\cos\left(\frac{y}{x}\right) \qquad [\because \log e=1]$$

$$\Rightarrow \log|ex|=\cos\left(\frac{y}{x}\right)$$

This is the required solution of the given differential equation.

Question 15 $2xy+y^2-2x^2\frac{dy}{dx}=0,\ y=2$ when $x=1$.

Sol. Given, $2x^2\frac{dy}{dx}=2xy+y^2 \Rightarrow \frac{dy}{dx}=\frac{2xy+y^2}{2x^2}$ ...(i)

Thus, the given differential equation is homogeneous.

So, put $\frac{y}{x}=v$ i.e., $y=vx \Rightarrow \frac{dy}{dx}=v+x\frac{dv}{dx}$

Then, Eq. (i) becomes $v+x\frac{dv}{dx}=\frac{2x^2v+x^2v^2}{2x^2}$

$$\Rightarrow v+x\frac{dy}{dx}=\frac{x^2(2v+v^2)}{2x^2} \Rightarrow v+x\frac{dv}{dx}=v+\frac{1}{2}v^2$$

$$\Rightarrow x\frac{dv}{dx}=\frac{1}{2}v^2 \Rightarrow \frac{2}{v^2}dv=\frac{1}{x}dx$$

On integrating both sides, we get

$$2\int v^{-2}dv=\int\frac{dx}{x} \Rightarrow 2\left(\frac{v^{-2+1}}{-2+1}\right)=\log|x|+C$$

$$\Rightarrow \quad 2\left(\frac{v^{-1}}{-1}\right) = \log|x| + C \Rightarrow -\frac{2}{v} = \log|x| + C$$

$$\Rightarrow \quad -\frac{2x}{y} = \log|x| + C \qquad \left(\because v = \frac{y}{x}\right) \ldots\text{(ii)}$$

When $x = 1$, then $y = 2$, therefore

$$\frac{-2 \times 1}{2} = \log 1 + C$$

$$\Rightarrow \quad -1 = 0 + C$$

$$\Rightarrow \quad C = -1$$

On, putting the value of C in Eq. (ii), we get

$$-\frac{2x}{y} = \log|x| - 1 \Rightarrow y = \frac{2x}{1 - \log|x|}$$

This is the required solution of the given differential equation.

Direction (Q. No 16 and 17) Choose the correct answer.

Question 16 A homogeneous equation of the form $\frac{dy}{dx} = h\left(\frac{x}{y}\right)$ can be solved by making the substitution

(a) $y = vx$ (b) $v = yx$ (c) $x = vy$ (d) $x = v$

Sol. (c) Since, given equation $\frac{dy}{dx} = h\left(\frac{x}{y}\right)$ is a homogeneous, so by the substitution $\frac{x}{y} = v$ i.e., $x = vy \Rightarrow \frac{dx}{dy} = v + y\frac{dv}{dy}$.

It becomes, $v + y\frac{dv}{dy} = hv \Rightarrow y\frac{dv}{dy} = v(h-1)$

$$\Rightarrow \quad \frac{1}{(h-1)v}\,dv = \frac{1}{y}\,dy$$

On integrating both sides, we get

$$\frac{1}{(h-1)}\int \frac{1}{v}\,dv = \int \frac{dy}{y}$$

$$\Rightarrow \quad \frac{1}{(h-1)}\log|v| = \log|y| + C$$

Question 17 Which of the following is a homogeneous differential equation?

(a) $(4x + 6y + 5)\,dy - (3y + 2x + 4)\,dx = 0$
(b) $xy\,dx - (x^3 + y^3)\,dy = 0$
(c) $(x^3 + 2y^2)\,dx + 2\,xy\,dy = 0$
(d) $y^2\,dx + (x^2 - xy - y^2)\,dy = 0$

Sol. (d) From the given options, we have.

(a) Given equation $(4x + 6y + 5)\, dy - (3y + 2x + 4)\, dx = 0$ can be rewritten as

$$\frac{dy}{dx} = \frac{3y + 2x + 4}{4x + 6y + 5} \Rightarrow \frac{dy}{dx} = \frac{x\left(3.\dfrac{y}{x} + 2 + \dfrac{4}{x}\right)}{x\left(4 + 6\dfrac{y}{x} + \dfrac{5}{x}\right)}$$

This equation is not homogeneous differential equation

(b) Given equations is $xy\, dx - (x^3 + y^3)\, dy = 0$

On separating the variables, we get

$$(x^3 + y^3)\, dy = xy\, dx \Rightarrow \frac{dy}{dx} = \frac{xy}{x^3 + y^3} \Rightarrow \frac{dy}{dx} = \frac{\dfrac{y}{x^2}}{1 + \left(\dfrac{y}{x}\right)^3}$$

This equation is not a homogeneous equation differential

(c) Given equation is $(x^3 + 2y^2)\, dx + 2\, xy\, dy = 0$

$$2xy\, dy = -(x^3 + 2y^2)\, dx$$

On separating the variables, we get

$$\frac{dy}{dx} = -\frac{x^3 + 2y^2}{2xy} \Rightarrow \frac{dy}{dx} = \frac{1 + \dfrac{2y^2}{x^3}}{\dfrac{2y}{x^2}}$$

This equation is not a homogeneous differential equation.

(d) Given equation $y^2\, dx + (x^2 - xy - y^2)\, dy = 0$

On separating the variable, we get

$$(x^2 - xy - y^2)\, dy = -y^2\, dx$$

$$\Rightarrow \quad \frac{dy}{dx} = -\frac{y^2}{x^2 - xy - y^2}$$

$$\Rightarrow \quad \frac{dy}{dx} = -\frac{\left(\dfrac{y}{x}\right)^2}{\left(1 - \dfrac{y}{x} - \left(\dfrac{y}{x}\right)^2\right)}$$

This equation is a homogeneous differential equation.

Exercise 9.5

Direction (Q. Nos. 1 to 12) For each of the given differential equation find the general solution.

Question 1 $\frac{dy}{dx}+2y=\sin x$

Thinking Process In a linear differential equation $\frac{dy}{dx}+Py=Q$

Firstly, find the Integrating Factor (IF) and then use the relation

$$y\cdot(\text{IF})=\int Q\times(\text{IF})\,dx+C$$

where, $(\text{IF})=e^{\int P\,dx}$

Sol. The given differential equation is $dy/dx+2y=\sin x$

On comparing with the form $dy/dx+Py=Q$, we get

$P=2$ and $Q=\sin x$.

$\therefore\quad \text{IF}=e^{\int Pdx}\Rightarrow e^{2\int 1dx}\Rightarrow \text{IF}=e^{2x}$

Hence, the solution is given by

$$y\cdot\text{IF}=\int Q\times\text{IF}\,dx+C\Rightarrow\ y\times e^{2x}=\int\sin x\cdot e^{2x}\,dx=I\text{ (say)}\qquad\text{...(i)}$$

$$\therefore\quad I=\sin x\int e^{2x}\,dx-\int\left[\frac{d}{dx}\sin x\int e^{2x}\,dx\right]dx\ \text{[Integration by parts]}$$

$$\Rightarrow\quad I=\sin x\,\frac{e^{2x}}{2}-\frac{1}{2}\int\cos x\,e^{2x}\,dx$$

$$\Rightarrow\quad I=\sin x\,\frac{e^{2x}}{2}-\frac{1}{2}\cos x\frac{e^{2x}}{2}+\frac{1}{2}\int\left[\frac{d}{dx}\cos x\int e^{2x}\,dx\right]dx$$

$$\Rightarrow\quad I=\sin x\,\frac{e^{2x}}{2}-\frac{1}{4}\cos x\,e^{2x}+\frac{1}{4}\int(-\sin x)\,e^{2x}\,dx$$

$$\Rightarrow\quad I=\sin x\,\frac{e^{2x}}{2}-\frac{1}{4}\cos x\,e^{2x}-\frac{1}{4}I+C$$

$$\Rightarrow\quad \frac{5I}{4}=\frac{e^{2x}}{4}(2\sin x-\cos x)+C\Rightarrow\quad I=\frac{e^{2x}}{5}(2\sin x-\cos x)+C$$

Therefore, Eq. (i) becomes

$$y\times e^{2x}=\frac{e^{2x}}{5}[2\sin x-\cos x]+C$$

$$\Rightarrow\quad y=\frac{1}{5}[2\sin x-\cos x]+e^{-2x}\,C$$

Which is the required general solution.

Question 2 $\frac{dy}{dx}+3y=e^{-2x}$.

Sol. The given differential equation is $\frac{dy}{dx}+3y=e^{-2x}$

On comparing with the form $\frac{dy}{dx}+Py=Q$, we get $P=3$ and $Q=e^{-2x}$

$$\therefore \quad \text{IF}=e^{\int P\,dx}\Rightarrow e^{\int 3\,dx}\Rightarrow \text{IF}=e^{3x}$$

The solution, of the given differential equation is given by

$$y\cdot \text{IF}=\int Q\times \text{IF}\,dx+C \Rightarrow y\times e^{3x}=\int e^{-2x}\cdot e^{3x}\,dx+C$$

$$\Rightarrow \quad ye^{3x}=\int e^{x}\,dx+C\Rightarrow ye^{3x}=e^{x}+C\Rightarrow y=e^{-2x}+Ce^{-3x}$$

Which is the required general solution.

Question 3 $\frac{dy}{dx}+\frac{y}{x}=x^2$.

Sol. The given differential equation is $\frac{dy}{dx}+\frac{y}{x}=x^2$

On comparing with the form $\frac{dy}{dx}+Py=Q$ we get $P=\frac{1}{x}$ and $Q=x^2$

$$\therefore \quad \text{IF}=e^{\int P\,dx}=e^{\int \frac{1}{x}dx}\Rightarrow \text{IF}=e^{\log|x|}=x \qquad [\because e^{\log x}=x]$$

The solution. of the given differential equation is given by

$$y\cdot \text{IF}=\int Q\times \text{IF}\,dx+C \Rightarrow yx=\int x^3\,dx+C \Rightarrow yx=\frac{x^4}{4}+C$$

Which is the required general solution.

Question 4 $\frac{dy}{dx}+y\sec x=\tan x\left(0\le x<\frac{\pi}{2}\right)$.

Sol. The given differential equation is $\frac{dy}{dx}+y\sec x=\tan x$

On comparing with the form $\frac{dy}{dx}+Py=Q$ we get

$$P=\sec x \text{ and } Q=\tan x$$

$$\therefore \quad \text{IF}=e^{\int P\,dx}=e^{\int \sec x\,dx}$$

$$\Rightarrow \quad \text{IF}=e^{\log|\sec x+\tan x|}=\sec x+\tan x \qquad \text{...(i)}$$

$$(\because e^{\log f(x)}=f(x))$$

The general solution of the given differential equation is given by

$$y\cdot \text{IF}=\int Q\times \text{IF}\,dx+C$$

$$\Rightarrow \quad y(\sec x+\tan x)=\int \tan x(\sec x+\tan x)\,dx+C$$

$$\Rightarrow \quad y(\sec x+\tan x)=\int \tan x\sec x\,dx+\int \tan^2 x\,dx+C$$

$$\Rightarrow \quad y(\sec x+\tan x)=\sec x+\int \sec^2 x\,dx-\int 1\,dx+C$$

$$(\because \tan^2 x=\sec^2 x-1)$$

$$\Rightarrow \quad y(\sec x+\tan x)=\sec x+\tan x-x+C$$

Which is the required general solution.

Question 5 $\cos^2 x \frac{dy}{dx} + y = \tan x \left(0 \le x < \frac{\pi}{2}\right)$.

Sol. The given differential equation is, $\cos^2 x \frac{dy}{dx} + y = \tan x$

On dividing by $\cos^2 x$ both sides, we get

$$\frac{dy}{dx} + y \sec^2 x = \tan x \sec^2 x$$

On comparing with the form $\frac{dy}{dx} + Py = Q$, we get

$$P = \sec^2 x \text{ and } Q = \tan x \sec^2 x$$

$$\therefore \quad \text{IF} = e^{\int P\,dx} = e^{\int \sec^2 x\,dx} = e^{\tan x} \quad \text{...(i)}$$

The general solution of the given differential equation is given by

$$y \cdot \text{IF} = \int Q \times \text{IF}\,dx + C \Rightarrow ye^{\tan x} = \int e^{\tan x} \cdot \tan x \sec^2 x\,dx$$

Put $\tan x = t \Rightarrow \sec^2 x = \frac{dt}{dx} \Rightarrow dx = \frac{dt}{\sec^2 x}$

$$\therefore \quad ye^{\tan x} = \int e^t \cdot t \sec^2 x \frac{dt}{\sec^2 x} \Rightarrow ye^{\tan x} = \int e^t \cdot t\,dt$$

$$\Rightarrow \quad ye^{\tan x} = e^t \cdot t - \int \left[\frac{d}{dt}(t) \cdot \int e^t\,dt\right] dt$$

(applying by parts 't' as first and 'e^t' as second function)

$$\Rightarrow \quad ye^{\tan x} = e^t \cdot t - \int e^t\,dt \Rightarrow y\,e^{\tan x} = e^t\,t - e^t + C$$

$$\Rightarrow \quad ye^{\tan x} = (\tan x - 1)\,e^{\tan x} + C \Rightarrow y = \tan x - 1 + Ce^{-\tan x}$$

Which is the required general solution.

Question 6 $x \frac{dy}{dx} + 2y = x^2 \log x$.

Sol. The given differential equation is $x \frac{dy}{dx} + 2y = x^2 \log x$

On dividing by x on both sides, we get

$$\frac{dy}{dx} + 2\frac{y}{x} = x \log x$$

On comparing with the form $\frac{dy}{dx} + Py = Q$, we get

$$P = \frac{2}{x} \text{ and } Q = x \log x$$

$$\therefore \quad \text{IF} = e^{\int P\,dx} = e^{2\int \frac{1}{x}\,dx} \Rightarrow \text{IF} = e^{2 \log|x|} = e^{\log x^2} = x^2 \qquad (\because e^{\log f(x)} = f(x))$$

The general solution of the given differential equation is given by

$$y \cdot \text{IF} = \int Q \times \text{IF}\,dx + C \Rightarrow x^2 y = \int x^2 \cdot x \log x\,dx + C$$

$$\Rightarrow \quad x^2 y = \int \underset{\text{II}}{x^3} \underset{\text{I}}{\log x}\,dx + C$$

$$x^2y = \log x \cdot \int x^3 - \int\left[\frac{d}{dx}\log x \int x^3\, dx\right] dx + C$$

$$\left[\text{Integration by parts } \int u \cdot v\, dx = u\int v dx - \int\left(\frac{d}{dx}(u)\int v\, dx\right) dx\right]$$

$$x^2y = \log x \cdot \frac{x^4}{4} - \int\left[\frac{1}{x} \times \frac{x^4}{4}\right] dx + C \Rightarrow x^2y = \log x \cdot \frac{x^4}{4} - \int \frac{x^3}{4}\, dx + C$$

$$x^2y = \frac{x^4}{4}\log x - \frac{x^4}{16} + C \Rightarrow y = \frac{x^2}{16}(4\log x - 1) + Cx^{-2}$$

hich is the required general solution.

uestion 7 $x\log x\dfrac{dy}{dx} + y = \dfrac{2}{x}\log x.$

ol. The given differential equation is, $x\log x\dfrac{dy}{dx} + y = \dfrac{2}{x}\log x$

n dividing by $x\log x$, on both sides, we get

$$\frac{dy}{dx} + \frac{y}{x\log x} = \frac{2}{x^2}$$

n comparing with the form $\dfrac{dy}{dx} + Py = Q$, we get $P = \dfrac{1}{x\log x}$ and $Q = \dfrac{2}{x^2}$

$$\text{IF} = e^{\int p\, dx} = e^{\int \frac{dx}{x\log x}}$$

t

$$\log x = t \Rightarrow \frac{1}{x} = \frac{dt}{dx} \Rightarrow dx = x\, dt$$

$$\text{IF} = e^{\int \frac{1}{t} dt} = e^{\log|t|} = t = \log x \qquad [\because t = \log x]$$

$$[\because e^{\log f(x)} = f(x)]$$

e general solution of the given differential equation is given by,

$$y \cdot \text{IF} = \int Q \times \text{IF}\, dx + C \Rightarrow y \cdot \log x = \int \frac{2}{x^2}\log x\, dx + C$$

$$y\log x = 2\int\left(\log x \cdot \frac{1}{x^2}\right) dx + C$$

$$= 2\left[\log x\int\frac{1}{x^2}\, dx - \int\left(\frac{d}{dx}(\log x)\int\frac{1}{x^2}\, dx\right) dx\right] + C \qquad \text{[integration by part]}$$

$$= 2\left[\log x\left(-\frac{1}{x}\right) - \int\left\{\frac{1}{x}\cdot\left(-\frac{1}{x}\right)\right\} dx\right] + C$$

$$= 2\left[-\frac{\log x}{x} + \int\frac{1}{x^2}\, dx\right] + C = 2\left[-\frac{\log x}{x} - \frac{1}{x}\right] + C$$

$$y\log x = -\frac{2}{x}(1 + \log x) + C$$

hich is the required general solution.

Question 8 $(1+x^2)\,dy + 2xy\,dx = \cot x\,dx.$ $(x \neq 0)$

Sol. The given differential equation is, $(1+x^2)\,dy + 2xy\,dx = \cot x\,dx$

$$\Rightarrow \quad (1+x^2)\,dy = dx\,(\cot x - 2xy) \Rightarrow \frac{dy}{dx} = \frac{\cot x - 2xy}{1+x^2}$$

$$\Rightarrow \quad \frac{dy}{dx} + \frac{2xy}{1+x^2} = \frac{\cot x}{1+x^2}$$

On comparing with the form $\frac{dy}{dx} + Py = Q$, we get

$$P = \frac{2x}{1+x^2} \text{ and } Q = \frac{\cot x}{1+x^2}$$

$$\therefore \quad \text{IF} = e^{\int P\,dx} = e^{\int \frac{2x}{1+x^2}dx}$$

Let $\quad 1+x^2 = t \Rightarrow 2x = \frac{dt}{dx} \Rightarrow dx = \frac{dt}{2x}$

$$\therefore \quad \text{IF} = e^{\int \frac{2x}{t} \times \frac{dt}{2x}} \Rightarrow \text{IF} = e^{\log|t|} = t = 1+x^2 \quad \ldots(\text{i})$$

$[\because e^{\log f(x)} = f(x)]$

The general solution of the given differential equation is given by

$$y \cdot \text{IF} = \int Q \times \text{IF}\,dx + C \Rightarrow (1+x^2)\,y = \int \left((1+x^2)\frac{\cot x}{(1+x^2)}\right) dx + C$$

$\Rightarrow \quad (1+x^2)\,y = \log|\sin x| + C \Rightarrow \quad y = \log|\sin x|\,(1+x^2)^{-1} + C\,(1+x^2)^{-1}$

Which is the required general solution.

Mistake Alert Student should be remember that when linean differential equation in the form of $\frac{dy}{dx} + Py = Q$ then Integrating factor $= e^{\int Pdx}$

Question 9 $x\frac{dy}{dx} + y - x + xy\cot x = 0\ (x \neq 0).$

Sol. The given differential equation is, $x\frac{dy}{dx} + y - x + xy\cot x = 0$

$$\Rightarrow \quad x\frac{dy}{dx} + y\,(1 + x\cot x) = x$$

On dividing by x both sides, we get

$$\frac{dy}{dx} + \frac{y(1+x\cot x)}{x} = 1$$

On comparing with the form $\frac{dy}{dx} + Py = Q$, we get

$$P = \frac{1+x\cot x}{x} \text{ and } Q = 1$$

$$IF = e^{\int P\,dx} = e^{\int\left(\frac{1}{x} + \cot x\right)dx} = e^{\log x + \log|\sin x|} = e^{\log(x \sin x)}$$

$(\because \log a + \log b = \log ab)$

$\Rightarrow$ $\quad IF = x \sin x$ $\quad (\because e^{\log ax} = ax)$ ...(i)

The general solution. of the given differential equation is given by

$$y \cdot IF = \int Q \times IF\,dx + C \Rightarrow y(x \sin x) = \int x \sin x\,dx + C$$

$\Rightarrow$ $y(x \sin x) = -x \cos x + \int \cos x\,dx + C$ (integration by parts)

$\Rightarrow$ $y(x \sin x) = -x \cos x + \sin x + C$

$\Rightarrow$ $$y = \frac{-x \cos x}{x \sin x} + \frac{\sin x}{x \sin x} + \frac{C}{x \sin x}$$

$\Rightarrow$ $$y = \frac{1}{x} - \cot x + \frac{C}{x \sin x}$$

Which is the required general solution.

Question 10 $(x + y)\dfrac{dy}{dx} = 1.$

◎ ***Thinking Process*** Given equation can be converted into linear equation by dividing $\frac{dy}{dx}$ and then solve it.

Sol. The given differential equation is $(x + y)\dfrac{dy}{dx} = 1 \Rightarrow \dfrac{dx}{dy} = (x + y)$

$$\frac{dx}{dy} - x = y$$

On comparing with the form $\frac{dx}{dy} + Px = Q$, we get

$$P = -1, Q = y$$

$$IF = e^{\int P\,dy} = e^{-\int 1\,dy} \Rightarrow IF = e^{-y}$$ ...(i)

The general solution of the given differential equation is given by

$$x \cdot IF = \int Q \times IF\,dy + C \Rightarrow x \cdot e^{-y} = \int e^{-y} \cdot y\,dy + C$$

$$xe^{-y} = y\int e^{-y}\,dy - \int\left[\frac{d}{dy}y\int e^{-y}\,dy\right]dy + C$$

(integration by parts)

$$xe^{-y} = -y(e^{-y}) + \int e^{-y}dy + C$$

$$xe^{-y} = -ye^{-y} - e^{-y} + C \Rightarrow x = -y - 1 + e^{y}C$$

$$x + y + 1 = Ce^{y}.$$

Which is the required general solution.

Quick Solution

We have $\frac{dy}{dx} = \frac{1}{x+y}$ ...

Put $x + y = t$

$\Rightarrow 1 + \frac{dy}{dx} = \frac{dt}{dx}$ (differentiating w.r.t.

$\Rightarrow \frac{dy}{dx} = \frac{dt}{dx} - 1$

From Eq. (i)

$\frac{dt}{dx} - 1 = \frac{1}{t} \Rightarrow \frac{dt}{dx} = \frac{1}{t} + 1$

$\Rightarrow \frac{t}{t+1} dt = dx$

On Integrating both side, we get

$\int \frac{t}{t+1} dt = \int dx$

$\Rightarrow \int \frac{t+1-1}{t+1} dt = x + c$ (adding and subtracting 1)

$\Rightarrow \int \left(1 - \frac{1}{t+1}\right) dt = x + c$

$\Rightarrow t - \log(t+1) = x + c$

$\Rightarrow x + y - \log(x+y+1) = x + c$ (Put $t = x + y$)

$\Rightarrow \log(x+y+1) = y - c$

$\Rightarrow x + y + 1 = e^{y-c} = e^{y} \cdot e^{-c}$ [$\because \log x = m \Rightarrow x =$

$\Rightarrow x + y + 1 = C \cdot e^{y}$ (e^{-c} is a constant say C)

Question 11 $y\,dx + (x - y^2)\,dy = 0.$

Sol. Given, differential equation is $y\,dx + (x - y^2)\,dy = 0 \Rightarrow y\,dx = (y^2 - x)\,dy$

$\Rightarrow \frac{dx}{dy} + \frac{x}{y} = y$

On comparing with the form $\frac{dx}{dy} + Px = Q$, we get $P = \frac{1}{y}, Q = y$

$\therefore$ $\text{IF} = e^{\int \frac{1}{y} dy} \Rightarrow \text{IF} = e^{\log|y|} = y$

[$\because e^{\log f(x)} = f$

The general solution of the given differential equation is given by

$x \cdot \text{IF} = \int Q \times \text{IF}\, dy + C \Rightarrow xy = \int (y \times y)\, dy + C \Rightarrow xy = \int y^2\, dy + C$

$\Rightarrow xy = \frac{y^3}{3} + C \Rightarrow x = \frac{y^2}{3} + \frac{C}{y}$

Which is the required general solution.

uestion 12 $(x+3y^2)\dfrac{dy}{dx}=y\,(y>0).$

ol. Given differential equation is $(x + 3y^2)\dfrac{dy}{dx} = y \Rightarrow y\dfrac{dx}{dy} = x + 3y^2$

n dividing by y both sides, we get

$$\frac{dx}{dy} = \frac{x}{y} + 3y \Rightarrow \frac{dx}{dy} - \frac{x}{y} = 3y$$

n comparing with the form $\dfrac{dx}{dy} + Px = Q$, we get

$$P = -\frac{1}{y}, Q = 3y$$

$$\text{IF} = e^{-\int \frac{1}{y}dy} \Rightarrow \text{IF} = e^{-\log y} = e^{\log(y)^{-1}} = y^{-1} = \frac{1}{y} \quad \ldots\text{(i)}$$

ne general solution of the given differential equation is given by

$$x \cdot \text{IF} = \int Q \times \text{IF}\, dy + C$$

$$x \cdot \frac{1}{y} = \int \frac{1}{y} \times 3y\, dy + C$$

$$\frac{x}{y} = 3y + C$$

$$x = 3y^2 + Cy$$

hich is the required general solution

irection (Q. Nos. 13 to 15) For each of the differential equation given the question find a particular solution satisfying the given condition.

uestion 13 $\dfrac{dy}{dx}+2y\tan x=\sin x,\ y=0$ when $x=\dfrac{\pi}{3}.$

ol. Given differential equation is $\dfrac{dy}{dx} + 2y \tan x = \sin x$,

n comparing with the form $\dfrac{dy}{dx} + Py = Q$, we get

$$P = 2\tan x, \text{ and } Q = \sin x$$

$$\text{IF} = e^{2\int \tan x\, dx} = e^{2\log|\sec x|} \Rightarrow \text{IF} = \sec^2 x \quad [\because e^{\log f(x)} = f(x)]$$

ne general solution is given by ...(i)

$$y \cdot \text{IF} = \int Q \times \text{IF}\, dx + C$$

$$y\sec^2 x = \int (\sin x \cdot \sec^2 x)\, dx + C$$

$$y\sec^2 x = \int \sin x \cdot \frac{1}{\cos^2 x}\, dx + C$$

$$y\sec^2 x = \int \tan x \sec x\, dx + C \Rightarrow y\sec^2 x = \sec x + C \quad \ldots\text{(ii)}$$

On putting, $y = 0$ and $x = \frac{\pi}{3}$ in Eq. (ii), we get

$$0 \times \sec^2 \frac{\pi}{3} = \sec \frac{\pi}{3} + C \Rightarrow 0 = 2 + C \Rightarrow C = -2$$

On putting the value of C in Eq. (ii), we get

$$y \sec^2 x = \sec x - 2 \Rightarrow y = \cos x - 2\cos^2 x$$

Hence, the required solution of the given differential equation is $y = \cos x - 2\cos^2 x$.

Question 14 $(1+x^2)\frac{dy}{dx} + 2xy = \frac{1}{1+x^2}$, $y = 0$ when $x = 1$.

Sol. Given differential equation is, $(1+x^2)\frac{dy}{dx} + 2xy = \frac{1}{1+x^2}$

On dividing by $(1+x^2)$ both sides, we get

$$\frac{dy}{dx} + \frac{2xy}{1+x^2} = \frac{1}{(1+x^2)^2}$$

On comparing with the form $\frac{dy}{dx} + Py = Q$, we get

$$P = \frac{2x}{1+x^2}, \text{ and } Q = \frac{1}{(1+x^2)^2}$$

$\therefore$ $$\text{IF} = e^{\int \frac{2x}{1+x^2} dx}$$

Put $$1 + x^2 = t \Rightarrow 2x = \frac{dt}{dx} \Rightarrow dx = \frac{dt}{2x}$$

$\therefore$ $$\text{IF} = e^{\int \frac{2x}{t} \times \frac{dt}{2x}} \Rightarrow \text{IF} = e^{\log|t|} = t \Rightarrow \text{IF} = 1 + x^2 \quad \ldots(i)$$

The general solution of the given differential equation is given by

$$y \cdot \text{IF} = \int Q \times \text{IF}\, dx + C$$

$$\Rightarrow y(1+x^2) = \int \left(\frac{1}{(1+x^2)^2} \times (1+x^2) \right) dx + C$$

$$\Rightarrow y(1+x^2) = \int \frac{1}{1+x^2} dx + C$$

$$\Rightarrow y(1+x^2) = \tan^{-1} x + C \quad \ldots(ii)$$

Now, $y = 0$ and $x = 1$, then

$$0(1+1) = \tan^{-1}(1) + C \Rightarrow 0 = \frac{\pi}{4} + C \Rightarrow C = -\frac{\pi}{4}$$

On putting the value of C in Eq. (ii), we get

$$(1+x^2)\, y = \tan^{-1} x - \frac{\pi}{4}$$

which is the required solution of the given differential equation.

Question 15 $\frac{dy}{dx} - 3y\cot x = \sin 2x, y = 2$ when $x = \frac{\pi}{2}\cdot$

Sol. Given differential equation is, $\frac{dy}{dx} - 3y\cot x = \sin 2x$

On comparing with the form $\frac{dy}{dx} + Py = Q$, we get

$$P = -3\cot x, Q = \sin 2x$$

$$\text{IF} = e^{-3\int \cot x\, dx} = e^{-3\log|\sin x|} = e^{\log|\sin x|^{-3}} \Rightarrow \text{IF} = \frac{1}{\sin^3 x} \quad \text{...(i)}$$

The general solution of the given differential equation is given by

$$y \times \text{IF} = \int Q \times \text{IF}\, dx + C$$

$$\Rightarrow \quad y \times \frac{1}{\sin^3 x} = \int \frac{1}{\sin^3 x} \sin 2x\, dx$$

$$\Rightarrow \quad y \times \frac{1}{\sin^3 x} = 2\int \frac{\sin x \cos x}{\sin^3 x} dx + C$$

$$\Rightarrow \quad \frac{1}{\sin^3 x} \times y = 2\int \frac{\cos x}{\sin^2 x} dx + C$$

$$\Rightarrow \quad \frac{y}{\sin^3 x} = 2\int \cot x \operatorname{cosec} x\, dx + C \Rightarrow \frac{y}{\sin^3 x} = -2\operatorname{cosec} x + C$$

$$\Rightarrow \quad y = -2\left(\frac{1}{\sin x} \times \sin^3 x\right) + C\sin^3 x \Rightarrow y = -2\sin^2 x + C\sin^3 x \quad \text{...(ii)}$$

Given, $y = 2$ and $x = \frac{\pi}{2}$, then from Eq. (ii), we get

$$2 = -2\sin^2\left(\frac{\pi}{2}\right) + C\sin^3\left(\frac{\pi}{2}\right) \Rightarrow 2 = -2 + C \Rightarrow C = 4$$

On putting the value of C in Eq. (ii), we get

$$y = -2\sin^2 x + 4\sin^3 x \Rightarrow y = 4\sin^3 x - 2\sin^2 x$$

Which is the required solution of the given differential equation.

Question 16 Find the equation of a curve passing through the origin, given that the slope of the tangent to the curve at any point (x, y) is equal to the sum of the coordinates of the points.

Sol. According to question, the differential equation is

$$\frac{dy}{dx} = x + y \Rightarrow \frac{dy}{dx} - y = x$$

On comparing with the form $\frac{dy}{dx} + Py = Q$, we get

$$P = -1 \text{ and } Q = x$$

$$\text{IF} = e^{-\int 1\, dx} \Rightarrow \text{IF} = e^{-x}$$

The general solution of the given differential equation is given by

$$y \cdot \text{IF} = \int Q \times \text{IF}\, dx + C \Rightarrow ye^{-x} = \int e^{-x} \cdot x\, dx + C$$

$\Rightarrow \quad y\,e^{-x} = x\int e^{-x}\,dx - \int\left[\frac{d}{dx}(x)\int e^{-x}\,dx\right]dx + C$ [Integration by parts]

$\Rightarrow \quad y\cdot e^{-x} = -\,xe^{-x} + \int e^{-x}\,dx + C$

$\Rightarrow \quad e^{-x}\,y = -\,xe^{-x} - e^{-x} + C$ ...(ii)

Since, the curve passing through the origin so put $x = 0$, $y = 0$ in Eq. (ii), we get

$$(0)\,e^{-0} = -\,0\,(e^{-0}) - e^{-0} + C \Rightarrow C = 1$$

On putting the value of C in Eq. (ii), we get

$$e^{-x}\,y = -\,xe^{-x} - e^{-x} + 1$$

$\Rightarrow \quad y = -\,x - 1 + e^{x} \Rightarrow x + y + 1 = e^{x}$

which is the required equation of curve.

Quick Solution

We have $\dfrac{dy}{dx} = x + y$ ... (i)

Put $x + y = t \Rightarrow 1 + \dfrac{dy}{dx} = \dfrac{dt}{dx}$ [On differentiating w.r.t.x]

$\Rightarrow \quad \dfrac{dy}{dx} = \dfrac{dt}{dx} - 1$

Put in (i) $\dfrac{dt}{dx} - 1 = t \Rightarrow \dfrac{dt}{dx} = t + 1 \Rightarrow \dfrac{dt}{t+1} = dx$

On integrating $\displaystyle\int \frac{dt}{t+1} = \int dx$

$\Rightarrow \quad \log(t + 1) = x + c$

$\Rightarrow \quad t + 1 = e^{x+c}$

Put, $t = x + y$ in above equation, we get

$\therefore \quad x + y + 1 = e^{x+c}$

$\Rightarrow \quad x + y + 1 = e^{x}.e^{c}$

$\Rightarrow \quad x + y + 1 = A\cdot e^{x}$ ...(ii)

As curve passing through origin. So, put $x = 0$, $y = 0$ in Eq (ii), we get

$$1 = A\cdot e^{0} \Rightarrow A = 1$$

On putting the value of A in Eq. (ii), we get $x + y + 1 = e^{x}$

Which is the required equation of curve.

Question 17 Find the equation of a curve passing through the point (0, 2) given that the sum of the coordinate of any point on the curve exceeds the magnitude of the slope of the tangent to the curve at that point by 5.

Sol. According to question, we have $x + y = \dfrac{dy}{dx} + 5$

or $\quad \dfrac{dy}{dx} + (-1)\,y = x - 5$ ...(

It is a linear differential equation of the form $\frac{dy}{dx} + Py = Q$

$\therefore$ $P = -1, Q = x - 5$ and $IF = e^{\int P\,dx} \Rightarrow = e^{\int(-1)\,dx} = e^{-x}$

The general solution of the curve is given by

$$y \cdot IF = \int Q \times IF\,dx + C \;\Rightarrow\; y \cdot e^{-x} = \int (x-5)e^{-x}\,dx + C$$

$$\Rightarrow \quad y \cdot e^{-x} = (x-5)\int e^{-x}\,dx - \int\left[\frac{d}{dx}(x-5)\cdot\int e^{-x}\,dx\right]dx + C$$

$$\Rightarrow \quad y \cdot e^{-x} = (x-5)(-e^{-x}) - \int(-e^{-x})\,dx + C$$

$$\Rightarrow \quad y \cdot e^{-x} = (5-x)\,e^{-x} - e^{-x} + C \qquad \text{...(ii)}$$

The curve passes through the point (0, 2), therefore

$$2e^{-0} = (5-0)\,e^{-0} - e^{0} + C \;\Rightarrow\; 2 = 5 - 1 + C \Rightarrow C = 2 - 4 = -2$$

On putting the value of C in Eq. (ii), we get

$$e^{-x}\,y = (5-x)\,e^{-x} - e^{-x} - 2 \Rightarrow y = 4 - x - 2\,e^{x}$$

which is the required equation of the curve.

Direction (Q. No 18 and 19) Choose the correct answer.

Question 18 The Integration Factor (IF) of the differential equation $x\frac{dy}{dx} - y = 2x^2$ is

(a) e^{-x} (b) e^{-y} (c) $\frac{1}{x}$ (d) x

Sol. (c) Given differential equation is $x\frac{dy}{dx} - y = 2x^2$

$$\Rightarrow \quad \frac{dy}{dx} + \left(-\frac{1}{x}\right)y = 2x$$

It is a linear differential equation of the form $\frac{dy}{dx} + Py = Q$

$$\therefore \quad P = -\frac{1}{x}, Q = 2x \text{ and } IF = e^{\int P\,dx}$$

$$\Rightarrow \quad IF = e^{\int\left(-\frac{1}{x}\right)dx} \Rightarrow IF = e^{-\log|x|} \Rightarrow IF = e^{\log|x|^{-1}} = \frac{1}{x}$$

Question 19 The Integrating Factor (IF) of the differential equation $(1-y^2)\frac{dx}{dy} + yx = ay\,(-1 < y < 1)$ is

(a) $\frac{1}{y^2-1}$ (b) $\frac{1}{\sqrt{y^2-1}}$

(c) $\frac{1}{1-y^2}$ (d) $\frac{1}{\sqrt{1-y^2}}$

Sol. (d) The given differential equation is $(1-y^2)\frac{dx}{dy} + yx = ay, -1 < y < 1$

(on dividing by $(1-y^2)$ both sides in the above equation)

$$\Rightarrow \quad \frac{dx}{dy}+\left(\frac{y}{1-y^2}\right)x=\frac{ay}{1-y^2}$$

It is a linear differential equation of the form $\frac{dx}{dy}+px=Q$

Here, $P=\frac{y}{1-y^2}, Q=\frac{ay}{1-y^2}$ and $\text{IF}=e^{\int\frac{y}{1-y^2}dy} \Rightarrow \text{IF}=e^{-\frac{1}{2}\int\frac{-2y}{1-y^2}dy}$

$$\Rightarrow \quad \text{IF}=e^{\frac{-1}{2}\log(1-y^2)} \Rightarrow \text{IF}=e^{\log(1-y^2)^{-1/2}}=(1-y^2)^{-1/2}=\frac{1}{\sqrt{1-y^2}}$$

Miscellaneous Exercise

Question 1 For each of the differential equations given below, indicate its order and degree (if defined)

(i) $\frac{d^2y}{dx^2}+5x\left(\frac{dy}{dx}\right)^2-6y=\log x$

(ii) $\left(\frac{dy}{dx}\right)^3-4\left(\frac{dy}{dx}\right)^2+7y=\sin x$

(iii) $\frac{d^4y}{dx^4}-\sin\frac{d^3y}{dx^3}=0$

Sol.

(i) The given differential equation is

$$\frac{d^2y}{dx^2}+5x\left(\frac{dy}{dx}\right)^2-6y=\log x \Rightarrow \frac{d^2y}{dx^2}+5x\left(\frac{dy}{dx}\right)^2-6y-\log x=0$$

As the order of the highest order derivative that occurs in the given differential equation is $\frac{d^2y}{dx^2}$. Thus, its order is 2. Also index of the highest order derivation $\frac{d^2y}{dx^2}$ is one. Hence, degree of the given differential equation is 1.

(ii) The given differential equation is

$$\left(\frac{dy}{dx}\right)^3-4\left(\frac{dy}{dx}\right)^2+7y=\sin x \Rightarrow \left(\frac{dy}{dx}\right)^3-4\left(\frac{dy}{dx}\right)^2+7y-\sin x=0$$

As the highest order derivative that occurs in the given differential equation is $\frac{dy}{dx}$, thus order of the equation is 1 and its degree is 3.

$\left(\because \text{The highest power of } \frac{dy}{dx}\text{, which occurs } \left(\frac{dy}{dx}\right)^3\right)$

(iii) The given differential equation is $\frac{d^4y}{dx^4} - \sin\left(\frac{d^3y}{dx^3}\right) = 0$

Since, the highest order derivative which occurs in the given differential equation is $\frac{d^4y}{dx^4}$. Thus, order of the given equation is 4, as $\sin\left(\frac{d^3y}{dx^3}\right)$ occurs in the equation is not a polynomial equation. Hence, degree is not defined.

Note In any differential equation, if a derivative is not in a polynomial equation, then we can find the order but degree cannot be determined.

Question 2 For each of the questions given below verify that the given function (implicit or explicit) is a solution of the corresponding differential equation.

(i) $xy = ae^x + be^{-x} + x^2 : x\frac{d^2y}{dx^2} + 2\frac{dy}{dx} - xy + x^2 - 2 = 0$

Thinking Process If given function is a solution of the given differential equation, then it will satisfy the differential equation. So, differentiate the given function y to find the value of $\frac{dy}{dx}, \frac{d^2y}{dx^2}$ and put these values in given differential equation.

Sol. We have $xy = ae^x + be^{-x} + x^2$

On differentiating w.r.t. 'x' we get

$$x \cdot \frac{dy}{dx} + y = ae^x + be^{-x} \cdot \frac{d}{dx}(-x) + 2x$$

$$x\frac{dy}{dx} + y = ae^x - be^{-x} + 2x$$

Again differentiating both sides w.r.t. 'x', we get

$$x\frac{d^2y}{dx^2} + \frac{dy}{dx} \cdot 1 + \frac{dy}{dx} = ae^x - be^{-x}(-1) + 2$$

$$\Rightarrow \quad x\frac{d^2y}{dx^2} + 2\frac{dy}{dx} = (ae^x + be^{-x}) + 2$$

$$\Rightarrow \quad x\frac{d^2y}{dx^2} + 2\frac{dy}{dx} = (xy - x^2) + 2 \quad \text{[using Eq. (i)]}$$

$$\Rightarrow \quad x\frac{d^2y}{dx^2} + 2\frac{dy}{dx} - xy + x^2 - 2 = 0$$

(ii) $y = e^x(a\cos x + b\sin x) : \frac{d^2y}{dx^2} - 2\frac{dy}{dx} + 2y = 0$

Thinking Process Firstly, shift e^x from RHS to LHS and then differentiate twice to eliminate the arbitrary constant.

Sol. Given, $y = e^x (a\cos x + b\sin x)$

On dividing by e^x both sides, we get

$$e^{-x} y = a\cos x + b\sin x \quad \text{...(i)}$$

On differentiating both sides w.r.t. x, we get

$$e^{-x}\frac{dy}{dx} - ye^{-x} = -a\sin x + b\cos x$$

Again, differentiating both sides with respect to x, we get

$$e^{-x}\frac{d^2y}{dx^2} - \frac{dy}{dx}e^{-x} - \left\{-ye^{-x} + e^{-x}\frac{dy}{dx}\right\} = -a\cos x - b\sin x$$

$$\Rightarrow \quad e^{-x}\frac{d^2y}{dx^2} - \frac{dy}{dx}e^{-x} + ye^{-x} - e^{-x}\frac{dy}{dx} = -(a\cos x + b\sin x)$$

$$\Rightarrow \quad e^{-x}\frac{d^2y}{dx^2} - 2e^{-x}\frac{dy}{dx} + ye^{-x} = -ye^{-x} \quad \text{[From Eq. (i)]}$$

$$\Rightarrow \quad e^{-x}\frac{d^2y}{dx^2} - 2e^{-x}\frac{dy}{dx} + 2ye^{-x} = 0$$

$$\Rightarrow \quad e^{-x}\left\{\frac{d^2y}{dx^2} - 2\frac{dy}{dx} + 2y\right\} = 0 \Rightarrow \frac{d^2y}{dx^2} - 2\frac{dy}{dx} + 2y = 0 \quad [\because e^{-x} \neq 0]$$

Hence, the given function is a solution of the corresponding differential equation.

Quick Solution

Given, $\quad y = e^x(a\cos x + b\sin x)$

$$\Rightarrow \quad \frac{dy}{dx} = e^x(-a\sin x + b\cos x) + (a\cos x + b\sin x)e^x$$

(On differentiating w.r.t. 'x')

$$\Rightarrow \quad \frac{dy}{dx} = e^x(-a\sin x + b\cos x) + y \quad \text{... (i)}$$

$$\Rightarrow \quad e^x(-a\sin x + b\cos x) = \frac{dy}{dx} - y \quad \text{... (ii)}$$

Again differentiating both sides of Eq. (i) w.r.t. 'x', we get

$$\Rightarrow \quad \frac{d^2y}{dx^2} = e^x(-a\cos x - b\sin x) + (-a\sin x + b\cos x)e^x + \frac{dy}{dx}$$

$$\Rightarrow \quad \frac{d^2y}{dx^2} = -e^x(a\cos x + b\sin x) + e^x(-a\sin x + b\cos x) + \frac{dy}{dx}$$

On puting $e^x(a\cos x + b\sin x) = y$ and $e^x(-a\sin x + b\cos x) = \frac{dy}{dx} - y$

(from (ii)), we get

$$\frac{d^2y}{dx^2} = -y + \frac{dy}{dx} - y + \frac{dy}{dx} \Rightarrow \frac{d^2y}{dx^2} - 2\frac{dy}{dx} + 2y = 0$$

Hence, the given function is a solution of the corresponding differential equation.

(iii) $y = x \sin 3x : \dfrac{d^2y}{dx^2} + 9y - 6\cos 3x = 0.$

Sol. Given, $y = x \sin 3x$ ...(i)

On differentiating both sides w.r.t. x, we get

$$\frac{dy}{dx} = x\frac{d}{dx}(\sin 3x) + \sin 3x\frac{d}{dx}(x) \quad \text{[using product rule of differentiation]}$$

$$\Rightarrow \quad \frac{dy}{dx} = x\cos 3x \times 3 + \sin 3x$$

Again, differentiating both sides w.r.t. x, we get

$$\frac{d^2y}{dx^2} = 3\left[x\frac{d}{dx}\cos 3x + \cos 3x\frac{d}{dx}(x)\right] + \frac{d}{dx}(\sin 3x)$$

$$\Rightarrow \quad \frac{d^2y}{dx^2} = 3\,[x\,(-\sin 3x \times 3) + \cos 3x] + \cos 3x \times 3$$

$$\Rightarrow \quad \frac{d^2y}{dx^2} = -9x\sin 3x + 3\cos 3x + 3\cos 3x$$

$$\Rightarrow \quad \frac{d^2y}{dx^2} = -9x\sin 3x + 6\cos 3x \Rightarrow \frac{d^2y}{dx^2} = -9y + 6\cos 3x$$

(using Eq. (i))

$$\Rightarrow \quad \frac{d^2y}{dx^2} + 9y - 6\cos 3x = 0$$

Hence, the given function is a solution of the corresponding differential equation.

(iv) $x^2 = 2y^2 \log y : (x^2 + y^2)\dfrac{dy}{dx} - xy = 0.$

Thinking Process It is a product of two functions.

Use the product rule of differentiation in RHS *i.e.*, $\dfrac{d}{dx}(u \cdot v) = u\dfrac{dv}{dx} + v\dfrac{du}{dx}$

Sol. Given, $x^2 = 2y^2 \log y$ ...(i)

On differentiating both sides w.r.t. x, we get

$$2x = 2\left[y^2 \times \frac{1}{y}\frac{dy}{dx} + \log y \times 2y\frac{dy}{dx}\right]$$

$$2x = 2\,\{y + 2y\log y\}\frac{dy}{dx} \Rightarrow x = (y + 2y\log y)\frac{dy}{dx}$$

On multiplying both sides by y, we get

$$xy = (y^2 + 2y^2\log y)\frac{dy}{dx} \Rightarrow xy = (y^2 + x^2)\frac{dy}{dx}$$

[using Eq. (i)]

$$(x^2 + y^2)\frac{dy}{dx} - xy = 0$$

Hence, the given function is a solution of the corresponding differential equation.

Question 3 Prove that $x^2 - y^2 = C(x^2 + y^2)^2$ is the general solution of differential equation $(x^3 - 3xy^2)\,dx = (y^3 - 3x^2y)\,dy$, where C is a parameter.

Thinking Process Firstly check the homogeneous nature of the given differential equation. If it is so, we put $y = vx$ and simplify it.

Sol. Given, differential equation can be rewritten as

$$\frac{dy}{dx} = \frac{x^3 - 3xy^2}{y^3 - 3x^2y} \quad \text{...(i)}$$

This is a homogeneous equation. So, put $y = vx$

$$\Rightarrow \quad \frac{d}{dx}(y) = \frac{d}{dx}(vx)$$

$$\Rightarrow \quad \frac{dy}{dx} = v + x\frac{dv}{dx}$$

Then, Eq. (i) becomes

$$v + x\frac{dv}{dx} = \frac{x^3 - 3x(vx)^2}{(vx)^3 - 3x^2(vx)}$$

$$\Rightarrow \quad v + x\frac{dv}{dx} = \frac{1 - 3v^2}{v^3 - 3v}$$

$$\Rightarrow \quad x\frac{dv}{dx} = \frac{1 - 3v^2}{v^3 - 3v} - v$$

$$\Rightarrow \quad x\frac{dv}{dx} = \frac{1 - 3v^2 - v^4 + 3v^2}{v^3 - 3v}$$

$$\Rightarrow \quad x\frac{dv}{dx} = \frac{1 - v^4}{v^3 - 3v}$$

$$\Rightarrow \quad \left(\frac{v^3 - 3v}{1 - v^4}\right) dv = \frac{dx}{x}$$

On integrating both sides, we get

$$\int \left(\frac{v^3 - 3v}{1 - v^4}\right) dv = \int \frac{dx}{x}$$

$$\Rightarrow \quad \int \left(\frac{v^3 - 3v}{1 - v^4}\right) dv = \log x + \log C \quad \text{...(ii}$$

$$\text{Now,} \quad \int \left(\frac{v^3 - 3v}{1 - v^4}\right) dv = \int \frac{v^3}{1 - v^4}\,dv - 3\int \frac{v}{1 - v^4}\,dv$$

$$\Rightarrow \quad \int \left(\frac{v^3 - 3v}{1 - v^4}\right) dv = I_1 - 3I_2, \quad \text{...(iii}$$

where, $I_1 = \int \frac{v^3}{1 - v^4}\, dv$

Put $1 - v^4 = t \Rightarrow -4v^3 = \frac{dt}{dv} \Rightarrow v^3\, dv = -\frac{dt}{4}$

$\therefore$ $I_1 = \int \frac{-dt}{4t} = -\frac{1}{4} \log t = -\frac{1}{4} \log (1 - v^4)$

and $I_2 = \int \frac{v dv}{1 - v^4} = \int \frac{v dv}{1 - (v^2)^2}$

Put $v^2 = z$

$\Rightarrow$ $v dv = \frac{dz}{2}$

$\therefore$ $I_2 = \frac{1}{2} \int \frac{dz}{1 - z^2} = \frac{1}{2 \times 2} \log \left| \frac{1 + z}{1 - z} \right| = \frac{1}{4} \log \left| \frac{1 + v^2}{1 - v^2} \right| \quad (\because z = v^2)$

$$\left(\because \int \frac{dx}{a^2 - x^2} = \frac{1}{2a} \log \left| \frac{a + x}{a - x} \right| \right)$$

On substituting the values of I_1 and I_2 in Eq. (iii), we get

$$\int \left(\frac{v^3 - 3v}{1 - v^4} \right) dv = -\frac{1}{4} \log (1 - v^4) - \frac{3}{4} \log \left| \frac{1 + v^2}{1 - v^2} \right|$$

Therefore, Eq. (ii) becomes

$$-\frac{1}{4} \log (1 - v^4) - \frac{3}{4} \log \left| \frac{1 + v^2}{1 - v^2} \right| = \log x + \log A$$

$\Rightarrow$ $$-\frac{1}{4} \log \left[(1 - v^4) \left(\frac{1 + v^2}{1 - v^2} \right)^3 \right] = \log Ax$$

$\Rightarrow$ $$-\frac{1}{4} \log \left[(1 - v^2)(1 + v^2) \times \frac{(1 + v^2)^3}{(1 - v^2)^3} \right] = \log Ax$$

$\Rightarrow$ $$\log \left[\frac{(1 + v^2)^4}{(1 - v^2)^2} \right]^{-\frac{1}{4}} = \log Ax \Rightarrow \left[\frac{(1 + v^2)^4}{(1 - v^2)^2} \right]^{-\frac{1}{4}} = Ax$$

$\Rightarrow$ $$\frac{(1 + v^2)^4}{(1 - v^2)^2} = (Ax)^{-4}$$

$\Rightarrow$ $$\frac{\left(1 + \frac{y^2}{x^2}\right)^4}{\left(1 - \frac{y^2}{x^2}\right)^2} = \frac{1}{A^4 x^4}$$

$$\Rightarrow \quad \frac{(x^2+y^2)^4}{x^4(x^2-y^2)^2} = \frac{1}{A^4x^4} \qquad (\because v = y/x$$

$$\Rightarrow \quad (x^2-y^2) = A^2(x^2+y^2)^2$$

$$\Rightarrow \quad x^2 - y^2 = A\ (x^2+y^2)^2 \text{ where, } A = A^2$$

Question 4. Find the general solution. of the differential equation

$$\frac{dy}{dx} + \sqrt{\frac{1-y^2}{1-x^2}} = 0.$$

Thinking Process The given differential equation can be converted into variable separable form and then integrate it to get the result.

Sol. Given, differential equation is $\frac{dy}{dx} + \sqrt{\frac{1-y^2}{1-x^2}} = 0$

$$\Rightarrow \quad \frac{dy}{dx} = -\frac{\sqrt{1-y^2}}{\sqrt{1-x^2}}$$

$$\Rightarrow \quad \frac{1}{\sqrt{1-y^2}}\,dy = -\frac{1}{\sqrt{1-x^2}}\,dx$$

On integrating both sides, we get

$$\int \frac{1}{\sqrt{1-y^2}}\,dy = -\int \frac{1}{\sqrt{1-x^2}}\,dx$$

$$\Rightarrow \quad \sin^{-1} y = -\sin^{-1} x + C \Rightarrow \sin^{-1} x + \sin^{-1} y = C$$

which is the required general solution.

Question 5 Show that the general solution of the differential equation $\frac{dy}{dx} + \frac{y^2+y+1}{x^2+x+1} = 0$ is given by $(x+y+1) = A(1-x-y-2xy$

where A is a parameter.

Sol. Given, differential equation is

$$\frac{dy}{dx} + \frac{y^2+y+1}{x^2+x+1} = 0$$

$$\Rightarrow \quad \frac{dy}{y^2+y+1} + \frac{dx}{x^2+x+1} = 0$$

On integrating both sides, we get

$$\int \frac{dy}{y^2+y+1} + \int \frac{dx}{x^2+x+1} = C$$

$$\Rightarrow \quad \int \frac{dy}{y^2+y+1+\left(\frac{1}{2}\right)^2-\left(\frac{1}{2}\right)^2} + \int \frac{dx}{x^2+x+1+\left(\frac{1}{2}\right)^2-\left(\frac{1}{2}\right)^2} =$$

$$\Rightarrow \quad \int \frac{dy}{\left(y+\frac{1}{2}\right)^2+\left(1-\frac{1}{4}\right)}+\int \frac{dx}{\left(x+\frac{1}{2}\right)^2+\left(1-\frac{1}{4}\right)}=C$$

$$\Rightarrow \quad \int \frac{dy}{\left(y+\frac{1}{2}\right)^2+\left(\frac{\sqrt{3}}{2}\right)^2}+\int \frac{dx}{\left(x+\frac{1}{2}\right)^2+\left(\frac{\sqrt{3}}{2}\right)^2}=C$$

$$\Rightarrow \quad \frac{2}{\sqrt{3}}\tan^{-1}\left(\frac{y+\frac{1}{2}}{\frac{\sqrt{3}}{2}}\right)+\frac{2}{\sqrt{3}}\tan^{-1}\left(\frac{x+\frac{1}{2}}{\frac{\sqrt{3}}{2}}\right)=C$$

$$\left[\because \int \frac{1}{a^2+x^2}dx=\frac{1}{a}\tan^{-1}\frac{x}{a}\right]$$

$$\Rightarrow \quad \tan^{-1}\left(\frac{2y+1}{\sqrt{3}}\right)+\tan^{-1}\left(\frac{2x+1}{\sqrt{3}}\right)=\frac{\sqrt{3}C}{2}=k \qquad \text{(say)}$$

$$\Rightarrow \quad \tan^{-1}\left[\frac{\frac{2y+1}{\sqrt{3}}+\frac{2x+1}{\sqrt{3}}}{1-\left(\frac{2y+1}{\sqrt{3}}\right)\left(\frac{2x+1}{\sqrt{3}}\right)}\right]=k$$

$$\left[\because \tan^{-1}x+\tan^{-1}y=\tan^{-1}\left(\frac{x+y}{1-xy}\right)\right]$$

$$\Rightarrow \quad \tan^{-1}\left[\frac{\frac{2y+1+2x+1}{\sqrt{3}}}{1-\left(\frac{4xy+2x+2y+1}{3}\right)}\right]=k$$

$$\Rightarrow \quad \frac{2\sqrt{3}\,(x+y+1)}{3-(4xy+2x+2y+1)}=\tan k$$

$$\Rightarrow \quad \frac{2\sqrt{3}\,(x+y+1)}{2\,(1-x-y-2xy)}=\tan k$$

$$\Rightarrow \quad x+y+1=\frac{1}{\sqrt{3}}\tan k\,(1-x-y-2xy)$$

Let, $A=\frac{1}{\sqrt{3}}\tan k$ is an arbitrary constant.

$$\Rightarrow \quad x+y+1=A\,(1-x-y-2xy).$$

Hence, the given result is proved.

Question 6 Find the equation of the curve passing through the point $\left(0, \frac{\pi}{4}\right)$ whose differential equation is $\sin x \cos y \, dx + \cos x \sin y \, dy = 0$

Sol. The differential equation of the given curve is

$$\sin x \cos y \, dx + \cos x \sin y \, dy = 0 \Rightarrow \frac{\sin x}{\cos x} dx + \frac{\sin y}{\cos y} dy = 0$$

$$\Rightarrow \quad \tan x \, dx + \tan y \, dy = 0$$

On integrating both sides, we get

$$\int \tan x \, dx + \int \tan y \, dy = \log C \Rightarrow \log(\sec x) + \log(\sec y) = \log C$$

$$\Rightarrow \quad \sec x \cdot \sec y = C \qquad \ldots\text{(i)}$$

The curve passes through the point $\left(0, \frac{\pi}{4}\right)$, therefore put $x = 0$, $y = \frac{\pi}{4}$, we get

$$\sec 0 \sec \frac{\pi}{4} = C \Rightarrow C = \sqrt{2}$$

On putting the value of C in Eq. (i), we get $\sec x \cdot \sec y = \sqrt{2}$

$$\Rightarrow \quad \sec x \cdot \frac{1}{\cos y} = \sqrt{2} \Rightarrow \cos y = \frac{\sec x}{\sqrt{2}}.$$

Hence, the required equation of the curve is $\cos y = \frac{\sec x}{\sqrt{2}}$.

Question 7 Find the particular solution of the differential equation $(1 + e^{2x})\, dy + (1 + y^2)\, e^x \, dx = 0$ given that $y = 1$ when $x = 0$.

Sol. Given, differential equation is $(1 + e^{2x})\, dy + (1 + y^2)\, e^x \, dx = 0$

On separating the variables, we get $\frac{dy}{1 + y^2} + \frac{e^x \, dx}{1 + e^{2x}} = 0$

On integrating both sides, we get $\int \frac{dy}{1 + y^2} + \int \frac{e^x \, dx}{1 + e^{2x}} = C$

Put $\quad t = e^x \Rightarrow e^x \, dx = dt \Rightarrow \tan^{-1} y + \int \frac{dt}{1 + t^2} = C$

$$\Rightarrow \quad \tan^{-1} y + \tan^{-1} t = C$$

$$\Rightarrow \quad \tan^{-1} y + \tan^{-1} e^x = C \qquad \ldots\text{(i)}$$

Now, put $\quad x = 0$ and $y = 1$

$$\therefore \quad \tan^{-1} 1 + \tan^{-1} e^0 = C \Rightarrow \frac{\pi}{4} + \frac{\pi}{4} = C \Rightarrow C = \frac{\pi}{2}$$

On putting the value of C in Eq. (i), we get

$$\tan^{-1} y + \tan^{-1} e^x = \frac{\pi}{2}$$

which is the required particular solution.

Question 8 Solve the differential equation

$$ye^{\frac{x}{y}}\,dx = \left(xe^{\frac{x}{y}} + y^2\right)dy\ (y \neq 0).$$

Thinking Process Firstly, check the homogeneous nature of the differential equation if it is homogeneous then put $x = vy$ and $\frac{dx}{dy} = v + y\frac{dv}{dy}$.

Sol. Given, differential equation is $ye^{\frac{x}{y}}\,dx = \left(xe^{\frac{x}{y}} + y^2\right)dy$

$$\Rightarrow \quad e^{\frac{x}{y}}\frac{dx}{dy} = \frac{x}{y}e^{\frac{x}{y}} + y \Rightarrow e^{\frac{x}{y}}\left(\frac{dx}{dy} - \frac{x}{y}\right) = y \qquad \ldots\text{(i)}$$

On putting $\quad \frac{x}{y} = v \Rightarrow x = vy \Rightarrow \frac{dx}{dy} = v + y\frac{dv}{dy}$

The Eq. (i) becomes

$$e^{v}\left(v + y\frac{dv}{dy}\right) - ve^{v} = y$$

$$\Rightarrow \quad e^{v}\,y\frac{dv}{dy} = y$$

$$\Rightarrow \quad e^{v}\frac{dv}{dy} = 1 \Rightarrow e^{v}\,dv = dy$$

On integrating both sides, we get

$$\int e^{v}\,dv = \int 1dy \Rightarrow e^{v} = y + C \Rightarrow e^{\frac{x}{y}} = y + C$$

Mistake Alert Don't put $\frac{y}{x} = v$

Question 9 Find a particular solution of the differential equation $(x-y)(dx+dy) = dx - dy$ given that $y = -1$, when $x = 0$.

Sol. Given, differential equation is $(x-y)(dx+dy) = dx - dy$

$$\Rightarrow \quad dx + dy = \frac{dx - dy}{x - y}$$

On integrating both sides, we get

$$\int (dx + dy) = \int \frac{dx - dy}{x - y} + C$$

Let $x - y = t \Rightarrow dx - dy = dt$

$$\therefore \quad x + y = \int \frac{dt}{t} + C$$

$$\Rightarrow \quad x + y = \log|t| + C$$

$$\Rightarrow \quad x + y = \log|x - y| + C \qquad \ldots\text{(i)}$$

It is given that when $x = 0, y = -1$, we get

$$\therefore \quad 0 + (-1) = \log(0+1) + C \Rightarrow C = -1$$

On substituting this value in Eq. (i), we get the required particular solution as $x + y = \log|x - y| - 1 \Rightarrow \log|x - y| = x + y + 1$

Question 10 Solve the differential equation

$$\left[\frac{e^{-2\sqrt{x}}}{\sqrt{x}} - \frac{y}{\sqrt{x}}\right]\frac{dx}{dy} = 1 \,(x \neq 0).$$

Sol. The given differential equation is $\left(\frac{e^{-2\sqrt{x}}}{\sqrt{x}} - \frac{y}{\sqrt{x}}\right)\frac{dx}{dy} = 1$

$$\Rightarrow \quad \frac{dy}{dx} = \frac{e^{-2\sqrt{x}}}{\sqrt{x}} - \frac{y}{\sqrt{x}}$$

$$\Rightarrow \quad \frac{dy}{dx} + \frac{1}{\sqrt{x}}y = \frac{e^{-2\sqrt{x}}}{\sqrt{x}}$$

On comparing with the form $\frac{dy}{dx} + Py = Q$, we get

$$P = \frac{1}{\sqrt{x}} \text{ and } Q = \frac{e^{-2\sqrt{x}}}{\sqrt{x}}.$$

$$\therefore \quad \text{IF} = e^{\int \frac{1}{\sqrt{x}} dx} \Rightarrow \text{IF} = e^{2x^{1/2}} = e^{2\sqrt{x}}$$

The general solution of the given differential equation is given by

$$y \cdot \text{IF} = \int Q \times \text{IF}\, dx + C$$

$$\Rightarrow \quad ye^{2\sqrt{x}} = \int e^{2\sqrt{x}} \times \frac{e^{-2\sqrt{x}}}{\sqrt{x}}\, dx + C$$

$$\Rightarrow \quad ye^{2\sqrt{x}} = \int \frac{1}{\sqrt{x}}\, dx + C$$

$$\Rightarrow \quad ye^{2\sqrt{x}} = 2\sqrt{x} + C$$

Question 11 Find a particular solution of the differential equation $\frac{dy}{dx} + y\cot x = 4x \operatorname{cosec} x \,(x \neq 0)$ given that $y = 0$ when $x = \frac{\pi}{2}$.

◎ **Thinking Process** The given differential equation can be easily compared to $\frac{dy}{dx} + Py = Q$, then find out IF and use the relation $y \cdot \text{IF} = \int Q \cdot \text{IF} + C$ to find general solution Use the given condition ($y = 0$ when $x = \frac{\pi}{2}$) to find particular solution.

Sol. Given differential equation is $\frac{dy}{dx} + y \cot x = 4x \operatorname{cosec} x$ ...(i)

On comparing with the form $\frac{dy}{dx} + Py = Q$, we get

$$P = \cot x \text{ and } Q = 4x \operatorname{cosec} x$$

$$\therefore \quad \text{IF} = e^{\int p\,dx} = e^{\int \cot x\,dx} \Rightarrow \text{IF} = e^{\log|\sin x|} = \sin x$$

The general solution of the given differential equation is given by

$$y \cdot \text{IF} = \int Q \times \text{IF}\,dx + C \Rightarrow y \sin x = \int 4x \operatorname{cosec} x \sin x\,dx + C$$

$$\Rightarrow \quad y \sin x = \int 4x\,dx + C$$

$$\Rightarrow \quad y \sin x = 4 \cdot \frac{x^2}{2} + C$$

$$\Rightarrow \quad y \sin x = 2x^2 + C \quad \text{...(ii)}$$

Now, $\quad x = \frac{\pi}{2}$ and $y = 0$.

$$\therefore \quad 0 \times \sin\frac{\pi}{2} = 2\left(\frac{\pi}{2}\right)^2 + C$$

$$\Rightarrow \quad C = -\frac{\pi^2}{2}$$

On putting the value of C in Eq. (ii), we get

$$y \sin x = 2x^2 - \frac{\pi^2}{2}$$

Which is the required particular solution of the given differential equation.

Question 12 Find a particular solution of the differential equation $(x+1)\frac{dy}{dx} = 2e^{-y} - 1$, given that $y = 0$ when $x = 0$.

Sol. Given, differential equation is $(x + 1)\frac{dy}{dx} = 2e^{-y} - 1$ ...(i)

On separating the variables, we get

$$\Rightarrow \quad \frac{dy}{2e^{-y} - 1} = \frac{dx}{x+1} \Rightarrow \frac{e^y\,dy}{2 - e^y} = \frac{dx}{x+1}$$

On integrating both sides, we get

$$\int \frac{e^y\,dy}{2 - e^y} = \int \frac{dx}{x+1} \quad \text{...(ii)}$$

Put $\quad 2 - e^y = t \Rightarrow -e^y = \frac{dt}{dy}$

$$\Rightarrow \quad e^y\,dy = -dt$$

Then Eq. (ii) becomes

$$\int \frac{-dt}{t} = \int \frac{dx}{x+1}$$

$$\Rightarrow \quad -\log|t| = \log|x+1| + \log C$$

$$\Rightarrow \quad -\log|2-e^y| = \log|C(x+1)| \Rightarrow \frac{1}{2-e^y} = C(x+1)$$

$$\left[\because -\log x = \log x^{-1} = \log\frac{1}{x}\right]$$

$$\Rightarrow \quad 2-e^y = \frac{1}{C(x+1)} \quad \text{...(iii)}$$

Now, at $x = 0$ and $y = 0$, $2 - 1 = \frac{1}{C} \Rightarrow C = 1$

On putting the value of C in Eq. (iii), we get

$$2-e^y = \frac{1}{(x+1)}$$

$$\Rightarrow \quad e^y = 2 - \frac{1}{x+1}$$

$$\Rightarrow \quad e^y = \frac{2x+2-1}{x+1}$$

$$\Rightarrow \quad e^y = \frac{2x+1}{x+1}$$

$$\Rightarrow \quad y = \log\left|\frac{2x+1}{x+1}\right|, (x \neq -1) \quad [\because \log_e x = m \Rightarrow e^m = x]$$

Which is the required particular solution of the given differential equation.

Direction (Q. No. 13 to 15). Choose the correct answer.

Question 13 The general solution of the differential equation $\frac{y\,dx - x\,dy}{y} = 0$ is

(a) $xy = C$ (b) $x = Cy^2$
(c) $y = Cx$ (d) $y = Cx^2$

Sol. (c) Given, differential equation is $\frac{y\,dx - x\,dy}{y} = 0$

$$\Rightarrow \quad y\,dx - x\,dy = 0 \Rightarrow \frac{1}{x}dx - \frac{1}{y}dy = 0$$

On integrating both sides, we get

$$\log|x| - \log|y| = \log k$$

$$\Rightarrow \quad \log\left|\frac{x}{y}\right| = \log k \Rightarrow \frac{x}{y} = k$$

$$\Rightarrow \quad y = \frac{1}{k}x \Rightarrow y = Cx \quad \left(\text{let } \frac{1}{k} = C\right)$$

Question 14 The general solution of a differential equation of the type $\frac{dx}{dy} + P_1 x = Q_1$ is

(a) $ye^{\int P_1 dy} = \int (Q_1 e^{\int P_1 dy}) dy + C$

(b) $ye^{\int P_1 dx} = \int (Q_1 e^{\int P_1 dx}) dx + C$

(c) $xe^{\int P_1 dy} = \int (Q_1 e^{\int P_1 dy}) dy + C$

(d) $xe^{\int P_1 dx} = \int (Q_1 e^{\int P_1 dx}) dx + C$

Sol. (c) The integrating factor of the given differential equation $\frac{dx}{dy} + P_1 x = Q_1$ is $e^{\int P_1 dy}$.

The general solution of the differential equation is given by

$$x \cdot \text{IF} = \int (Q \times \text{IF}) \, dx + C$$

$$\Rightarrow \quad ye^x = \int (-2xe^{-x} \times e^x) dx + C$$

$$\therefore \quad xe^{\int P_1 dy} = \int (Q_1 e^{\int P_1 dy}) \, dy + C$$

Question 15 The general solution of the differential equation $e^x dy + (ye^x + 2x) dx = 0$ is

(a) $xe^y + x^2 = C$
(b) $xe^y + y^2 = C$
(c) $ye^x + x^2 = C$
(d) $ye^y + x^2 = C$

Sol. (c) Given, differential equation is $e^x dy + (ye^x + 2x) \, dx = 0$

$$\Rightarrow \quad e^x \frac{dy}{dx} + ye^x + 2x = 0 \Rightarrow \frac{dy}{dx} + y = -2x e^{-x}$$

This is a linear differential equation of the form

$$\frac{dy}{dx} + Py = Q$$

On comparing, we get, $\quad P = 1$ and $Q = -2xe^{-x}$

$$\therefore \quad \text{IF} = e^{\int 1 \, dx} = e^x$$

The general solution of the given differential equation is given by

$$y \cdot \text{IF} = \int (\theta \times \text{IF}) + C$$

$$\Rightarrow \quad ye^x = \int (-2xe^{-x} \times e^x) dx + C$$

$$\Rightarrow \quad ye^x = -\int 2 \, x dx + C$$

$$\Rightarrow \quad ye^x = -x^2 + C \Rightarrow ye^x + x^2 = C$$

DIKSHA APP Questions

☐ Subjective Type Questions

Q.1 Find the order and degree of differential equation
$y = px + \sqrt{a^2 p^2 + b^2}$ where $p = \frac{dy}{dx}$

Sol. We have, $y = px + \sqrt{p^2 a^2 + b^2}$

$$\Rightarrow \quad y - px = \sqrt{p^2 a^2 + b^2}$$

On squaring both side, we get

$$\Rightarrow \quad (y - px)^2 = p^2 a^2 + b^2$$

$$\Rightarrow \quad y^2 + p^2 x^2 - 2pxy = p^2 a^2 + b^2$$

$$\Rightarrow \quad p^2(x^2 - a^2) - 2pxy + y^2 - b^2 = 0$$

$$\Rightarrow \quad \left(\frac{dy}{dx}\right)^2 (x^2 - a^2) - 2\frac{dy}{dx}xy + y^2 - b^2 = 0 \quad \left[\because p = \frac{dy}{dx} \text{(given)}\right]$$

The highest order derivative present in the given differential equation is $\frac{dy}{dx}$. Therefore order is one. Also, the given differential equation is a polynomial equation in $\frac{dy}{dx}$ and the highest power raised to $\left(\frac{dy}{dx}\right)$ is 2.

Hence, degree is 2.

Q.2 Show that the differential equation $x\frac{dy}{dx}\sin\frac{y}{x} + x - y\sin\frac{y}{x} = 0$ is homogeneous and find the particular solution when $x = 1$ and $y = \frac{\pi}{2}$.

Sol. The given differential equation is

$$x\frac{dy}{dx}\sin\frac{y}{x} + x - y\sin\frac{y}{x} = 0$$

On divide, by $x \cdot \sin\frac{y}{x}$, we get

$$\frac{dy}{dx} + \frac{x}{x\sin\frac{y}{x}} - \frac{y}{x} = 0$$

$$\Rightarrow \quad \frac{dy}{dx} = \frac{y}{x} - \frac{1}{\sin\frac{y}{x}}$$

$$\Rightarrow \quad \frac{dy}{dx} = \frac{y}{x} - \operatorname{cosec}\frac{y}{x} \quad \ldots(i)$$

Here, $f(x, y) = \frac{y}{x} - \text{cosec}\frac{y}{x}$

$\Rightarrow$ $f(\lambda x, \lambda y) = \frac{\lambda y}{\lambda x} - \text{cosec}\frac{\lambda y}{\lambda x} = \frac{y}{x} - \text{cosec}\frac{y}{x} = \lambda^0 f(x, y)$

Therefore, $f(x, y)$ is a homogeneous function of degree zero. So, the given differential equation is a homogeneous equation.

Let $y = vx$

On differentiating, both sides w.r.t. 'x' we get

$$\frac{dy}{dx} = v + x \cdot \frac{dv}{dx} \quad \text{... (iii)}$$

On substituting y and $\frac{dy}{dx}$ in equation (i), we get

$$v + x\frac{dv}{dx} = v - \text{cosec } v$$

$\Rightarrow$ $x\frac{dv}{dx} = -\text{cosec } v$

$\Rightarrow$ $\frac{dv}{\text{cosec}v} = -\frac{dx}{x}$

$\Rightarrow$ $\sin v \, dv = -\frac{dx}{x}$

On integrating both sides, we get

$$\int \sin v \, dv = -\int \frac{dx}{x}$$

$\Rightarrow$ $-\cos v = -\log x + C$

$\Rightarrow$ $\cos v = \log x - C$

Put $v = \frac{y}{x}$, we get

$\therefore$ $\cos\frac{y}{x} = \log x - C \quad \text{... (iv)}$

Put $x = 1$ and $y = \pi / 2$ in (iv), we get

$\Rightarrow$ $\cos\frac{\pi}{2} = \log 1 - C$

$\Rightarrow$ $C = 0$

Substituting $C = 0$ in (iv), we get

$$\cos\frac{y}{x} = \log x$$

which is the particular solution of the given differential equation.

Vector Algebra

CHAPTER 10

Important Points

01 (i) **Vector** A directed line segment is called a vector.

- A vector has a magnitude and direction.
- Any number is called a scalar.

If $\mathbf{a} = a\,\hat{\mathbf{i}} + b\,\hat{\mathbf{j}} + c\,\hat{\mathbf{k}}$, then $|\mathbf{a}| = \sqrt{a^2 + b^2 + c^2}$

(ii) **Zero or Null Vector** A vector whose initial and terminal points coincide is called a zero vector (Null vector) and denoted by **O**. Zero vector cannot be assigned a definite direction.

(iii) **Equal Vectors** Two vectors **a** and **b** are said to be equal, if they have the same magnitude and direction.

(iv) **Unit vector** A vector with unit length along any vector **a** is called a unit vector in the direction of **a** and it is denoted by $\hat{\mathbf{a}}$.

Thus, $\hat{\mathbf{a}} = \dfrac{\mathbf{a}}{|\mathbf{a}|}, |\hat{\mathbf{a}}| = 1$

(v) Let a vector $\mathbf{A} = a\hat{\mathbf{i}} + b\hat{\mathbf{j}} + c\hat{\mathbf{k}}$

Then, a, b, c are called direction ratios of **A**

and, $\dfrac{a}{|\mathbf{A}|}, \dfrac{b}{|\mathbf{A}|}, \dfrac{c}{|\mathbf{A}|}$ are called direction cosines

where $|A| = \sqrt{a^2 + b^2 + c^2}$

i.e., $\cos\alpha$, $\cos\beta$, $\cos\gamma$, respectively and their short name is l, m, n and sum of the square of Direction cosines is always one
i.e., $l^2 + m^2 + n^2 = 1$
Here α, β and γ are the angles made by the position vector A with the positive directions of the x, y and z-axes, respectively are called its direction angles.

(vi) **Collinear Vector** Two or more non-zero vectors are said to be collinear, if they are parallel to the same line. Two vectors **a** and **b** are collinear if $\mathbf{a} = \lambda\,\mathbf{b}$ for some scalar λ.

(vii) **Coplanar Vector** Three or more non-zero vectors are said to be coplanar, if they lie in the same plane.

(viii) **Negative of a Vector** *A* vector whose magnitude is the same as that of a given vector (say : **AB**) but direction is opposite to that of it is called negative of the given vector.
e.g., Vector **QP** is negative of the vector **PQ**
and written as **QP** = − **PQ**

(ix) **Coinitial Vectors** Two or more vectors having the same initial point are called coinitial vectors.

02 Addition of vectors

(i) **Triangle Law** If **OA** = **a** and **AB** = **b**, then

a + **b** = **OA** + **AB** = **OB**

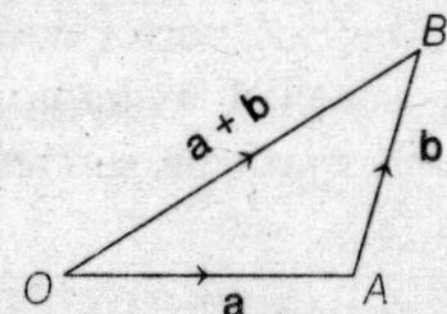

(ii) **Parallelogram Law** If two vectors **a** and **b** are represented in magnitude and direction by the two adjacent sides of a prarallelogram then their sum **c** is represented by the diagonal of the parallelogram which is coinitial with the given vectors.

OB = **c** = **a** + **b**

(iii) Properties of vector addition.

(a) For any two vectors **a** and **b**
a + **b** = **b** + **a** (commutative property)

(b) For any three vectors **a**, **b** and **c**
(**a** + **b**) + **c** = **a** + (**b** + **c**)
(Associative property)

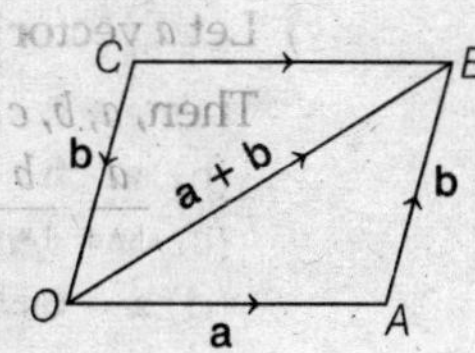

(c) For any vector **a** we have

$\mathbf{a} + \mathbf{o} = \mathbf{o} + \mathbf{a} = \mathbf{a}$

Here, the zero vector is called additive identity for vector addition.

03 **Multiplication of a Vector by a Scalar** Let **a** be any vector and k be any non-zero scalar. Then the product $k\mathbf{a}$ is defined as a vector whose magnitude is $|k|$ times that of **a** and the direction is same as that of **a** if k is positive and opposite as that of **a** if k is negative.

Properties of multiplication of a vector by a scalar:

For vectors **a**, **b** and scalars m, k, we have

(i) $k\mathbf{b} + m\mathbf{b} = (k+m)\mathbf{a}$ (ii) $k(m\mathbf{a}) = (km)\mathbf{a}$

(iii) $k(\mathbf{a}+\mathbf{b}) = k\mathbf{a} + k\mathbf{b}$

04 (i) **Position vector of a point** Let O be the origin and $\mathbf{OA} = \mathbf{a}$, we say that the position vector of A is **a**.

$\mathbf{AB}$ = (Position vector of B) − (Position vector of A)

(ii) **Section formula**

(a) Let A and B be two points with position vectors **a** and **b** respectively and let P be a point which divides AB internally in the ratio $m : n$. Then, position vector of

$$P = \frac{m\mathbf{b} + n\mathbf{a}}{m+n}$$

(b) Let A and B be two points with position vectors **a** and **b** respectively and let P be a point which divides AB externally in the ratio $m : n$. Then position vector of

$$P = \frac{m\mathbf{b} - n\mathbf{a}}{m-n}$$

If P is the mid-point of AB then position vector of $P = \dfrac{\mathbf{a}+\mathbf{b}}{2}$

(iii) **Component of a vector** If $\mathbf{a} = a_1\hat{\mathbf{i}} + a_2\hat{\mathbf{j}} + a_3\hat{\mathbf{k}}$, we say that the components of **a** along X-axis, Y-axis and Z-axis are a_1, a_2, a_3 respectively.

(iv) **Important results in components** For any two vectors $\mathbf{a} = a_1\hat{\mathbf{i}} + a_2\hat{\mathbf{j}} + a_3\hat{\mathbf{k}}$ and $\mathbf{b} = b_1\hat{\mathbf{i}} + b_2\hat{\mathbf{j}} + b_3\hat{\mathbf{k}}$ we define

(a) $\mathbf{a} + \mathbf{b} = (a_1 + b_1)\hat{\mathbf{i}} + (a_2 + b_2)\hat{\mathbf{j}} + (a_3 + b_3)\hat{\mathbf{k}}$

(b) $\mathbf{a} - \mathbf{b} = (a_1 - b_1)\hat{\mathbf{i}} + (a_2 - b_2)\hat{\mathbf{j}} + (a_3 - b_3)\hat{\mathbf{k}}$

(c) $\lambda\mathbf{a} = (\lambda a_1)\hat{\mathbf{i}} + (\lambda a_2)\hat{\mathbf{j}} + (\lambda a_3)\hat{\mathbf{k}}$, where λ is a scalar

(d) $\mathbf{a} = \mathbf{b} \Leftrightarrow a_1 = b_1, a_2 = b_2$ and $a_3 = b_3$

05 Dot product or Scalar product

Consider $\mathbf{a} = a_1\hat{\mathbf{i}} + a_2\hat{\mathbf{j}} + a_3\hat{\mathbf{k}}$ and $\mathbf{b} = b_1\hat{\mathbf{i}} + b_2\hat{\mathbf{j}} + b_3\hat{\mathbf{k}}$

Then dot product $\mathbf{a} \cdot \mathbf{b} = a_1b_1 + a_2b_2 + a_3b_3$

(i) If θ is the angle between **a** and **b**, then
$\mathbf{a} \cdot \mathbf{b} = |\mathbf{a}||\mathbf{b}| \cos \theta$

(ii) If θ is acute then $\mathbf{a} \cdot \mathbf{b} > 0$ and if θ is obtuse, then $\mathbf{a} \cdot \mathbf{b} < 0$

(iii) $\mathbf{a} \perp \mathbf{b} \Leftrightarrow \mathbf{a} \cdot \mathbf{b} = 0$

(iv) $\hat{\mathbf{i}} \cdot \hat{\mathbf{i}} = \hat{\mathbf{j}} \cdot \hat{\mathbf{j}} = \hat{\mathbf{k}} \cdot \hat{\mathbf{k}} = 1$ and $\hat{\mathbf{i}} \cdot \hat{\mathbf{j}} = \hat{\mathbf{j}} \cdot \hat{\mathbf{k}} = \hat{\mathbf{k}} \cdot \hat{\mathbf{i}} = 0$

(v) Projection of vector **a** on **b** is $\dfrac{\mathbf{a} \cdot \mathbf{b}}{|\mathbf{b}|}$

(vi) Vector projection of **a** on $\mathbf{b} = \left(\dfrac{\mathbf{a} \cdot \mathbf{b}}{|\mathbf{b}|^2}\right)\mathbf{b}$

(vii) Angle between two vector **a** and **b**

$$\Rightarrow \qquad \cos \theta = \frac{\mathbf{a} \cdot \mathbf{b}}{|\mathbf{a}| \cdot |\mathbf{b}|}$$

(viii) $\mathbf{a} \cdot \mathbf{b} = \mathbf{b} \cdot \mathbf{a}$

(ix) $\mathbf{a} \cdot (\mathbf{b} + \mathbf{c}) = \mathbf{a} \cdot \mathbf{b} + \mathbf{a} \cdot \mathbf{c}$

(x) $\mathbf{a} \cdot \mathbf{a} = |\mathbf{a}|^2 = a^2$, where a represents magnitude of vector **a**.

(xi) $(\mathbf{a} + \mathbf{b}) \cdot (\mathbf{a} - \mathbf{b}) = a^2 - b^2$, where a and b represent the magnitude of vectors **a** and **b**.

06 Cross product or Vector product

(i) If $\mathbf{a} = a_1\hat{\mathbf{i}} + a_2\hat{\mathbf{j}} + a_3\hat{\mathbf{k}}$ and $\mathbf{b} = b_1\hat{\mathbf{i}} + b_2\hat{\mathbf{j}} + b_3\hat{\mathbf{k}}$, then

$$\mathbf{a} \times \mathbf{b} = \begin{vmatrix} \hat{\mathbf{i}} & \hat{\mathbf{j}} & \hat{\mathbf{k}} \\ a_1 & a_2 & a_3 \\ b_1 & b_2 & b_3 \end{vmatrix}$$

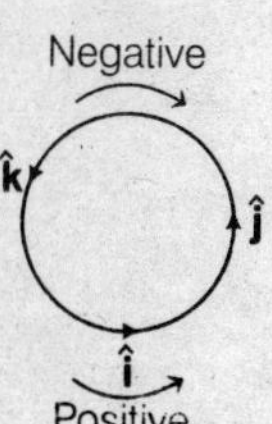

(ii) If θ is the angle between the vectors **a** and **b**, then
$\mathbf{a} \times \mathbf{b} = |\mathbf{a}||\mathbf{b}| \sin \theta \, \hat{\mathbf{n}}$, where, $\hat{\mathbf{n}}$ is a unit vector perpendicular to the plane of **a** and **b**.

(iii) A unit vector perpendicular to both **a** and **b** is given by $\hat{\mathbf{n}} = \dfrac{(\mathbf{a} \times \mathbf{b})}{|\mathbf{a} \times \mathbf{b}|}$.

(iv) Area of a parallelogram with adjacent sides $\mathbf{a}$ and $\mathbf{b} = |\mathbf{a} \times \mathbf{b}|$

(v) Area of a parallelogram with diagonals $\mathbf{a}$ and $\mathbf{b} = \frac{1}{2}|\mathbf{a} \times \mathbf{b}|$

(vi) Area of a quadrilateral $ABCD = \left|\frac{1}{2}(\mathbf{AC} \times \mathbf{BD})\right|$

(vii) Area of a $\Delta\, ABC = \frac{1}{2}|\mathbf{AB} \times \mathbf{AC}|$

(viii) $\mathbf{a} \parallel \mathbf{b} \Leftrightarrow \mathbf{a} \times \mathbf{b} = \mathbf{0}$

(ix) In terms of vector product, the angle

between two vectors $\mathbf{a}$ and $\mathbf{b}$

$$\sin\theta = \frac{|\mathbf{a} \times \mathbf{b}|}{|\mathbf{a}||\mathbf{b}|}$$

(x) $\mathbf{a} \times \mathbf{b} = -\mathbf{b} \times \mathbf{a}$

(xi) $\mathbf{a} \times (\mathbf{b} + \mathbf{c}) = \mathbf{a} \times \mathbf{b} + \mathbf{a} \times \mathbf{c}$

(xii) $\mathbf{a} \times \mathbf{a} = \mathbf{0}$

(xiii) $\hat{\mathbf{i}} \times \hat{\mathbf{j}} = \hat{\mathbf{k}},\ \hat{\mathbf{j}} \times \hat{\mathbf{k}} = \hat{\mathbf{i}},\ \hat{\mathbf{k}} \times \hat{\mathbf{i}} = \hat{\mathbf{j}}$ and $\hat{\mathbf{j}} \times \hat{\mathbf{i}} = -\hat{\mathbf{k}},\ \hat{\mathbf{k}} \times \hat{\mathbf{j}} = -\hat{\mathbf{i}},$
$\hat{\mathbf{i}} \times \hat{\mathbf{k}} = -\hat{\mathbf{j}}$

(xiv) $\hat{\mathbf{i}} \times \hat{\mathbf{i}} = 0, \hat{\mathbf{j}} \times \hat{\mathbf{j}} = 0, \hat{\mathbf{k}} \times \hat{\mathbf{k}} = 0$

Exercise 10.1

Question 1 Represent graphically a displacement of 40 km, 30° east of north.

Sol. The displacement is 30° east of north so, we have to draw a straight line making 30° with north.

Here, vector **OP** represents the displacement of 40 km, 30° east of north.

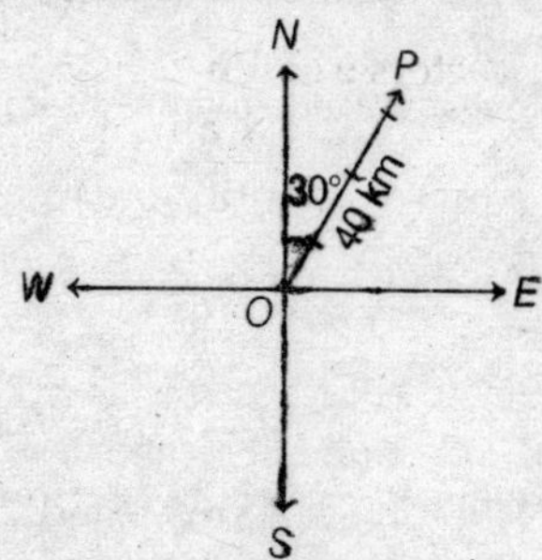

Question 2 Classify the following measures as scalars and vectors :

(i) 10 kg (ii) 2 m north-west (iii) 40°

(iv) 40 Watt (v) 10^{-19} Coulomb (vi) 20 m/s^2

Thinking Process

(i) A scalar is a quantity that has only magnitude and no direction.

(ii) A vector is a quantity that has both magnitude and direction.

Sol. (i) **Scalar** Here the unit involved is 'kg' which is the unit of mass and we know that mass is scalar so, 10 kg will also be a scalar.

(ii) **Vector** 2 m north-west is a vector quantity as it involves both magnitude (2 m) as well as direction (north-west).

(iii) **Scalar** 40° represents an angle and we know that angle is a scalar quantity as it involves only magnitude.

(iv) **Scalar** Here the unit involved is watt which is the unit of power which is a scalar quantity. So, 40 W is a scalar quantity as it involves only magnitude.

(v) **Scalar** 10^{-19} C is a scalar quantity as it involves only magnitude.

(vi) **Vector** Here the unit involved is m/s^2 which is the unit of acceleration and acceleration is a vector quantity. So, 20 m/s^2 is a vector quantity as it involves magnitude as well as direction.

Question 3 Classify the following as scalar and vector quantities:

(i) Time period (ii) Distance
(iii) Force (iv) Velocity
(v) Work done

Sol. (i) **Scalar** Time period is a scalar quantity as it involves only magnitude.

(ii) **Scalar** Distance is a scalar quantity as it involves only magnitude.

(iii) **Vector** Force is a vector quantity as it involves both magnitude as well as direction.

(iv) **Vector** Velocity is a vector quantity as it involves both magnitude as well as direction.

(v) **Scalar** Work done is a scalar quantity as it involves only magnitude.

Question 4 In figure (a square), identify the following vectors :

(i) Coinitial
(ii) Equal
(iii) Collinear but not equal.

a
d
b
c

Sol. (i) Vectors **a** and **d** are coinitial because they have the same initial point.

(ii) Vectors **b** and **d** are equal because they have the same magnitude and direction.

(iii) Vectors **a** and **c** are collinear but not equal. Although they are parallel, this is because their directions are not same.

Question 5 Answer the following as true or false :

(i) **a** and −**a** are collinear.
(ii) Two collinear vectors are always equal in magnitude.
(iii) Two vectors having same magnitude are collinear.
(iv) Two collinear vectors having the same magnitude are equal.

◎ *Thinking Process* Two or more vectors are said to be collinear if they are parallel to the same line, irrespective of their magnitudes and directions.

Sol. (i) **True** Vectors **a** and −**a** are parallel to the same line and hence collinear.

(ii) **False** Collinear vectors are those vectors that are parallel to the same line but they need not to be equal in magnitude.

(iii) **False** It is not necessary for two vectors having the same magnitude to be parallel to the same line.

(iv) **False** Two vectors are said to be equal, if they have the same magnitude and direction, regardless or the position of their initial points. Hence, two collinear vectors having the same magnitude need not be equal.

Exercise 10.2

Question 1 Compute the magnitude of the following vectors :

$$\mathbf{a} = \hat{\mathbf{i}} + \hat{\mathbf{j}} + \hat{\mathbf{k}}\,;\mathbf{b} = 2\hat{\mathbf{i}} - 7\hat{\mathbf{j}} - 3\hat{\mathbf{k}}\,;\mathbf{c} = \frac{1}{\sqrt{3}}\hat{\mathbf{i}} + \frac{1}{\sqrt{3}}\hat{\mathbf{j}} - \frac{1}{\sqrt{3}}\hat{\mathbf{k}}.$$

◎ *Thinking Process* The magnitude for a vector $\mathbf{a} = x\hat{\mathbf{i}} + y\hat{\mathbf{j}} + z\hat{\mathbf{k}}$ is given by $|\mathbf{a}| = \sqrt{x^2 + y^2 + z^2}$

Sol. Given, vector $\mathbf{a} = \hat{\mathbf{i}} + \hat{\mathbf{j}} + \hat{\mathbf{k}}$. On comparing with $\mathbf{a} = x\hat{\mathbf{i}} + y\hat{\mathbf{j}} + z\hat{\mathbf{k}}$ we get $x = 1, y = 1, z = 1$.

The magnitude of given vector is

$$|\mathbf{a}| = |\hat{\mathbf{i}} + \hat{\mathbf{j}} + \hat{\mathbf{k}}| = \sqrt{x^2 + y^2 + z^2} = \sqrt{1^2 + 1^2 + 1^2} = \sqrt{3}$$

Similarly magnitude of **b**

$$= |2\hat{\mathbf{i}} - 7\hat{\mathbf{j}} - 3\hat{\mathbf{k}}| \Rightarrow |\mathbf{b}| = \sqrt{2^2 + (-7)^2 + (-3)^2}$$

$$= \sqrt{4 + 49 + 9} = \sqrt{62}$$

and $$|\mathbf{c}| = \left|\frac{1}{\sqrt{3}}\hat{\mathbf{i}} + \frac{1}{\sqrt{3}}\hat{\mathbf{j}} - \frac{1}{\sqrt{3}}\hat{\mathbf{k}}\right|$$

$$= \sqrt{\left(\frac{1}{\sqrt{3}}\right)^2 + \left(\frac{1}{\sqrt{3}}\right)^2 + \left(-\frac{1}{\sqrt{3}}\right)^2} = \sqrt{\frac{1}{3} + \frac{1}{3} + \frac{1}{3}} = 1$$

Question 2 Write two different vectors having same magnitude.

Sol. Two vectors can have same magnitude, if the sum of the squares of coefficient of $\hat{\mathbf{i}}, \hat{\mathbf{j}}$ and $\hat{\mathbf{k}}$ is same. Let vectors $\mathbf{a} = (2\hat{\mathbf{i}} + 3\hat{\mathbf{j}} + \hat{\mathbf{k}})$ and $\mathbf{b} = (2\hat{\mathbf{i}} + 3\hat{\mathbf{j}} - \hat{\mathbf{k}})$ are different vectors having the same magnitude.

Magnitude of Ist vector $= \sqrt{(2)^2 + (3)^2 + (1)^2} = \sqrt{4 + 9 + 1} = \sqrt{14}$

and magnitude of IInd vector $= \sqrt{(2)^2 + (3)^2 + (-1)^2} = \sqrt{4 + 9 + 1} = \sqrt{14}$

i.e., they have same magnitude.

Here, infinite number of answers are possible.

Question 3 Write two different vectors having same direction.

◎ *Thinking Process* Two vectors can have the same directions, if their direction cosines (l, m, n) are same. Direction cosines for a vector $\vec{\mathbf{a}} = x\hat{\mathbf{i}} + y\hat{\mathbf{j}} + z\hat{\mathbf{k}}$ are given by $= \frac{x}{\sqrt{x^2 + y^2 + z^2}}$, $m = \frac{y}{\sqrt{x^2 + y^2 + z^2}}$,

$$n = \frac{z}{\sqrt{x^2 + y^2 + z^2}}$$

Sol. Let $\mathbf{a} = (\hat{\mathbf{i}} + \hat{\mathbf{j}} + \hat{\mathbf{k}})$ and $\mathbf{b} = (2\hat{\mathbf{i}} + 2\hat{\mathbf{j}} + 2\hat{\mathbf{k}})$.

For Ist vector $\mathbf{a} = \hat{\mathbf{i}} + \hat{\mathbf{j}} + \hat{\mathbf{k}}$

Comparing with $\mathbf{A} = x\,\hat{\mathbf{i}} + y\,\hat{\mathbf{j}} + z\,\hat{\mathbf{k}}$, we get $x = 1, y = 1, z = 1$

The direction cosines of **a** are given by

$$= \frac{1}{\sqrt{1^2 + 1^2 + 1^2}} = \frac{1}{\sqrt{3}}, m = \frac{1}{\sqrt{1^2 + 1^2 + 1^2}} = \frac{1}{\sqrt{3}}$$

and $$n = \frac{1}{\sqrt{1^2 + 1^2 + 1^2}} = \frac{1}{\sqrt{3}}$$

Similarly, the direction cosines of **b** are given by

$$= \frac{2}{\sqrt{2^2 + 2^2 + 2^2}} = \frac{2}{2\sqrt{3}} = \frac{1}{\sqrt{3}}, \quad m = \frac{2}{\sqrt{2^2 + 2^2 + 2^2}} = \frac{2}{2\sqrt{3}} = \frac{1}{\sqrt{3}}$$

and $$n = \frac{2}{\sqrt{2^2 + 2^2 + 2^2}} = \frac{2}{2\sqrt{3}} = \frac{1}{\sqrt{3}}$$

Here, we see that both have same direction cosines.

Hence, **both the vectors have same direction.**

Question 4 Find the value of x and y so that the vectors $2\hat{\mathbf{i}} + 3\hat{\mathbf{j}}$ and $x\hat{\mathbf{i}} + y\hat{\mathbf{j}}$ are equal.

◎ ***Thinking Process*** Two vectors are equal, if both have the same coefficients of $\hat{\mathbf{i}}$, $\hat{\mathbf{j}}$ and $\hat{\mathbf{k}}$ along with the sign.

Sol. Let $\mathbf{a} = 2\hat{\mathbf{i}} + 3\hat{\mathbf{j}}$ and $\mathbf{b} = x\hat{\mathbf{i}} + y\hat{\mathbf{j}}$ be two given vectors.

Comparing coefficients of $\hat{\mathbf{i}}$ and $\hat{\mathbf{j}}$ of both **a** and **b**, we have

$\Rightarrow$ $x = 2$ and $y = 3$

Question 5 Find the scalar and vector components of the vector with initial point $(2, 1)$ and terminal point $(-5, 7)$.

◎ ***Thinking Process*** A vector with initial point (x_1, y_1) and final point (x_2, y_2) is given by $(x_2 - x_1)\hat{\mathbf{i}} + (y_2 - y_1)\hat{\mathbf{j}}$.

Sol. Vector with initial point $A(2, 1)$ and final (terminal) point $B(-5, 7)$ can be given by

$$\mathbf{AB} = (x_2 - x_1)\hat{\mathbf{i}} + (y_2 - y_1)\hat{\mathbf{j}}$$
$$= (-5 - 2)\hat{\mathbf{i}} + (7 - 1)\hat{\mathbf{j}} = (-7)\hat{\mathbf{i}} + 6\hat{\mathbf{j}}$$

Hence, the required scalar components (coefficients of $\hat{\mathbf{i}}$ and $\hat{\mathbf{j}}$) are -7 and 6 while the vector components are $-7\hat{\mathbf{i}}$ and $6\hat{\mathbf{j}}$.

Question 6 Find the sum of the vectors $\mathbf{a} = \hat{\mathbf{i}} - 2\hat{\mathbf{j}} + \hat{\mathbf{k}}$, $\mathbf{b} = -2\hat{\mathbf{i}} + 4\hat{\mathbf{j}} + 5\hat{\mathbf{k}}$ and $\mathbf{c} = \hat{\mathbf{i}} - 6\hat{\mathbf{j}} - 7\hat{\mathbf{k}}$.

Thinking Process To find the sum of different vectors, different components ($\hat{\mathbf{i}}$, $\hat{\mathbf{j}}$ and $\hat{\mathbf{k}}$) are added separately.

Sol. Here, given $\mathbf{a} = \hat{\mathbf{i}} - 2\hat{\mathbf{j}} + \hat{\mathbf{k}}$, $\mathbf{b} = -2\hat{\mathbf{i}} + 4\hat{\mathbf{j}} + 5\hat{\mathbf{k}}$, $\mathbf{c} = \hat{\mathbf{i}} - 6\hat{\mathbf{j}} - 7\hat{\mathbf{k}}$

Sum of these vectors can be calculated by adding their $\hat{\mathbf{i}}$, $\hat{\mathbf{j}}$ and $\hat{\mathbf{k}}$ components.

$$\therefore \quad \mathbf{a} + \mathbf{b} + \mathbf{c} = (\hat{\mathbf{i}} - 2\hat{\mathbf{j}} + \hat{\mathbf{k}}) + (-2\hat{\mathbf{i}} + 4\hat{\mathbf{j}} + 5\hat{\mathbf{k}}) + (\hat{\mathbf{i}} - 6\hat{\mathbf{j}} - 7\hat{\mathbf{k}})$$
$$= (\hat{\mathbf{i}} - 2\hat{\mathbf{i}} + \hat{\mathbf{i}}) + (-2\hat{\mathbf{j}} + 4\hat{\mathbf{j}} - 6\hat{\mathbf{j}}) + (\hat{\mathbf{k}} + 5\hat{\mathbf{k}} - 7\hat{\mathbf{k}})$$
$$= 0\hat{\mathbf{i}} - 4\hat{\mathbf{j}} - \hat{\mathbf{k}} = -4\hat{\mathbf{j}} - \hat{\mathbf{k}}$$

Question 7. Find the unit vector in the direction of the vector $\mathbf{a} = \hat{\mathbf{i}} + \hat{\mathbf{j}} + 2\hat{\mathbf{k}}$.

Thinking Process Unit vector in the direction of given vector can be calculated by formula $\hat{\mathbf{a}} = \frac{\mathbf{a}}{|\mathbf{a}|}$ where, $|\mathbf{a}|$ = magnitude of given vector $\mathbf{a}$

Sol. Given, $\mathbf{a} = \hat{\mathbf{i}} + \hat{\mathbf{j}} + 2\hat{\mathbf{k}}$

On comparing with $\mathbf{x} = a\hat{\mathbf{i}} + b\hat{\mathbf{j}} + c\hat{\mathbf{k}}$, we get $a = 1, b = 1, c = 2$

$$\text{Magnitude of vector } \mathbf{a} = |\mathbf{a}| = \sqrt{a^2 + b^2 + c^2} = \sqrt{1^2 + 1^2 + 2^2} = \sqrt{6}$$

$\therefore$ The unit vector $\hat{\mathbf{a}}$ in the direction of vector $\mathbf{a} = \hat{\mathbf{i}} + \hat{\mathbf{j}} + 2\hat{\mathbf{k}}$ is given by $\hat{\mathbf{a}} = \frac{\mathbf{a}}{|\mathbf{a}|}$

$$= \frac{1}{\sqrt{6}}(\hat{\mathbf{i}} + \hat{\mathbf{j}} + 2\hat{\mathbf{k}}) = \frac{1}{\sqrt{6}}\hat{\mathbf{i}} + \frac{1}{\sqrt{6}}\hat{\mathbf{j}} + \frac{2}{\sqrt{6}}\hat{\mathbf{k}}$$

Question 8. Find the unit vector in the direction of vector **PQ**, where P and Q are the points (1, 2, 3) and (4, 5, 6), respectively.

Thinking Process In this question we are not given the vector, so first of all vector is to be calculated and then find the unit vector in the direction of given vector as in previous question.

A vector with initial point (x_1, y_1, z_1) and terminal point (x_2, y_2, z_2) is given by

$$(x_2 - x_1)\hat{\mathbf{i}} + (y_2 - y_1)\hat{\mathbf{j}} + (z_2 - z_1)\hat{\mathbf{k}}$$

Sol. The given points are $P(1, 2, 3)$ and $Q(4, 5, 6)$.

$$\therefore \quad x_1 = 1, y_1 = 2, z_1 = 3 \text{ and } x_2 = 4, y_2 = 5, z_2 = 6$$

So, vector $PQ = (x_2 - x_1)\hat{\mathbf{i}} + (y_2 - y_1)\hat{\mathbf{j}} + (z_2 - z_1)\hat{\mathbf{k}}$

$$= (4 - 1)\hat{\mathbf{i}} + (5 - 2)\hat{\mathbf{j}} + (6 - 3)\hat{\mathbf{k}} = 3\hat{\mathbf{i}} + 3\hat{\mathbf{j}} + 3\hat{\mathbf{k}}$$

$\therefore$ Magnitude of given vector

$$|\mathbf{PQ}| = \sqrt{3^2 + 3^2 + 3^2} = \sqrt{9+9+9} = \sqrt{27} = 3\sqrt{3}$$

Hence, the unit vector in the direction of **PQ**

$$= \frac{\mathbf{PQ}}{|\mathbf{PQ}|} = \frac{3\hat{\mathbf{i}} + 3\hat{\mathbf{j}} + 3\hat{\mathbf{k}}}{3\sqrt{3}} = \frac{3}{3\sqrt{3}}(\hat{\mathbf{i}} + \hat{\mathbf{j}} + \hat{\mathbf{k}})$$

$$= \frac{1}{\sqrt{3}}\hat{\mathbf{i}} + \frac{1}{\sqrt{3}}\hat{\mathbf{j}} + \frac{1}{\sqrt{3}}\hat{\mathbf{k}}.$$

Question 9 For given vectors, $\mathbf{a} = 2\hat{\mathbf{i}} - \hat{\mathbf{j}} + 2\hat{\mathbf{k}}$ and $\mathbf{b} = -\hat{\mathbf{i}} + \hat{\mathbf{j}} - \hat{\mathbf{k}}$, find the unit vector in the direction of the vector $\mathbf{a} + \mathbf{b}$.

◎ ***Thinking Process*** Firstly determine $a + b$ and $|a + b|$ then, unit vector of

$$\mathbf{a} + \mathbf{b} = \frac{\mathbf{a} + \mathbf{b}}{|\mathbf{a} + \mathbf{b}|}$$

Sol. The given vectors are $\mathbf{a} = 2\hat{\mathbf{i}} - \hat{\mathbf{j}} + 2\hat{\mathbf{k}}$ and $\mathbf{b} = -\hat{\mathbf{i}} + \hat{\mathbf{j}} - \hat{\mathbf{k}}$

$$\therefore \quad \mathbf{a} + \mathbf{b} = (2\hat{\mathbf{i}} - \hat{\mathbf{j}} + 2\hat{\mathbf{k}}) + (-\hat{\mathbf{i}} + \hat{\mathbf{j}} - \hat{\mathbf{k}})$$

Two vectors can be added by adding $\hat{\mathbf{i}}$, $\hat{\mathbf{j}}$ and $\hat{\mathbf{k}}$ components.

$$\therefore \quad \mathbf{a} + \mathbf{b} = [2\hat{\mathbf{i}} + (-\hat{\mathbf{i}})] + [(-\hat{\mathbf{j}}) + \hat{\mathbf{j}}] + [(2\hat{\mathbf{k}}) + (-\hat{\mathbf{k}})]$$

$$= (2\hat{\mathbf{i}} - \hat{\mathbf{i}}) + (-\hat{\mathbf{j}} + \hat{\mathbf{j}}) + (2\hat{\mathbf{k}} - \hat{\mathbf{k}}) = \hat{\mathbf{i}} + 0\hat{\mathbf{j}} + \hat{\mathbf{k}} = \hat{\mathbf{i}} + \hat{\mathbf{k}}$$

Comparing with $\mathbf{X} = x\hat{\mathbf{i}} + y\hat{\mathbf{j}} + z\hat{\mathbf{k}}$, we get $x = 1, y = 0, z = 1$

$$\therefore \quad \text{Magnitude } |\mathbf{a} + \mathbf{b}| = \sqrt{x^2 + y^2 + z^2} = \sqrt{1^2 + 0^2 + 1^2} = \sqrt{2}$$

Hence, the unit vector in the direction of $(\mathbf{a} + \mathbf{b})$,

$$\frac{(\mathbf{a} + \mathbf{b})}{|\mathbf{a} + \mathbf{b}|} = \frac{(\hat{\mathbf{i}} + \hat{\mathbf{k}})}{\sqrt{2}} = \frac{1}{\sqrt{2}}\hat{\mathbf{i}} + \frac{1}{\sqrt{2}}\hat{\mathbf{k}}$$

Question 10 Find a vector in the direction of vector $5\hat{\mathbf{i}} - \hat{\mathbf{j}} + 2\hat{\mathbf{k}}$ which has magnitude 8 unit.

◎ ***Thinking Process*** To find a vector in the direction of given vector, first of all we have to find unit vector in the direction of given vector, then multiply the given magnitude by the unit vector to obtain the required vector.

Sol. Let $\mathbf{a} = 5\hat{\mathbf{i}} - \hat{\mathbf{j}} + 2\hat{\mathbf{k}}$

On comparing with $\mathbf{X} = x\hat{\mathbf{i}} + y\hat{\mathbf{j}} + z\hat{\mathbf{k}}$, we get $x = 5$, $y = -1$, $z = 2$

$$\therefore \quad \text{Magnitude } |\mathbf{a}| = \sqrt{x^2 + y^2 + z^2} = \sqrt{5^2 + (-1)^2 + 2^2} = \sqrt{25 + 1 + 4} = \sqrt{30}$$

$\therefore$ Unit vector in the direction of given vector

$$\hat{\mathbf{a}} = \frac{\mathbf{a}}{|\mathbf{a}|} = \frac{5\hat{\mathbf{i}} - \hat{\mathbf{j}} + 2\hat{\mathbf{k}}}{\sqrt{30}}$$

Hence, the vector in the direction of vector $5\hat{\mathbf{i}} - \hat{\mathbf{j}} + 2\hat{\mathbf{k}}$ which has magnitude 8 units is given by (multiplying the unit vector by 8, we have the vector with magnitude 8 as the magnitude of unit vector is 1)

$$8\hat{\mathbf{a}} = 8\left(\frac{5\hat{\mathbf{i}} - \hat{\mathbf{j}} + 2\hat{\mathbf{k}}}{\sqrt{30}}\right) = \frac{40}{\sqrt{30}}\hat{\mathbf{i}} - \frac{8}{\sqrt{30}}\hat{\mathbf{j}} + \frac{16}{\sqrt{30}}\hat{\mathbf{k}}$$

Question 11 Show that the vectors $2\hat{\mathbf{i}} - 3\hat{\mathbf{j}} + 4\hat{\mathbf{k}}$ and $-4\hat{\mathbf{i}} + 6\hat{\mathbf{j}} - 8\hat{\mathbf{k}}$ are collinear.

◎ ***Thinking Process*** To prove the given two vectors $\mathbf{a}, \mathbf{b}$ to be collinear, we have to prove $\mathbf{a} = \lambda\mathbf{b}$ where λ is a numerical value.

Sol. Let $\mathbf{a} = 2\hat{\mathbf{i}} - 3\hat{\mathbf{j}} + 4\hat{\mathbf{k}}$ and $\mathbf{b} = -4\hat{\mathbf{i}} + 6\hat{\mathbf{j}} - 8\hat{\mathbf{k}}$

It is observed that $\mathbf{b} = -4\hat{\mathbf{i}} + 6\hat{\mathbf{j}} - 8\hat{\mathbf{k}} = -2(2\hat{\mathbf{i}} - 3\hat{\mathbf{j}} + 4\hat{\mathbf{k}}) = -2\mathbf{a}$

$\therefore$ $\mathbf{b} = \lambda\mathbf{a}$, where $\lambda = -2$

Vectors **a** and **b** have the same direction, therefore they are collinear.

Question 12 Find the direction cosine of the vector $\hat{\mathbf{i}} + 2\hat{\mathbf{j}} + 3\hat{\mathbf{k}}$.

◎ ***Thinking Process*** To find the direction cosines of a given vector, we have to find the unit vector in the direction of given vector.

Sol. Let $\mathbf{a} = \hat{\mathbf{i}} + 2\hat{\mathbf{j}} + 3\hat{\mathbf{k}}$

Then, $|\mathbf{a}| = \sqrt{1^2 + 2^2 + 3^2} = \sqrt{14}$

$\therefore$ $\hat{\mathbf{a}} = \dfrac{\mathbf{a}}{|\mathbf{a}|} \Rightarrow \hat{\mathbf{a}} = \dfrac{1}{\sqrt{14}}(\hat{\mathbf{i}} + 2\hat{\mathbf{j}} + 3\hat{\mathbf{k}})$

$\Rightarrow$ $\hat{\mathbf{a}} = \dfrac{1}{\sqrt{14}}\hat{\mathbf{i}} + \dfrac{2}{\sqrt{14}}\hat{\mathbf{j}} + \dfrac{3}{\sqrt{40}}\hat{\mathbf{k}}$

Hence, direction cosines of the given vector are $\dfrac{1}{\sqrt{14}}, \dfrac{2}{\sqrt{14}}, \dfrac{3}{\sqrt{14}}$.

($\because$ Direction cosines are the coefficients of $\hat{\mathbf{i}}, \hat{\mathbf{j}}, \hat{\mathbf{k}}$ of unit vector).

Direction cosine of $\mathbf{a} = x\hat{\mathbf{i}} + y\hat{\mathbf{j}} + z\hat{\mathbf{k}}$ are $\dfrac{x}{|\mathbf{a}|}, \dfrac{y}{|\mathbf{a}|}$ and $\dfrac{z}{|\mathbf{a}|}$.

Question 13 Find the direction cosines of the vector joining the points $A(1, 2, -3)$ and $B(-1, -2, 1)$, directed from A to B.

Sol. The given points are $A(1, 2, -3)$ and $B(-1, -2, 1)$.

i.e., $x_1 = 1, y_1 = 2, z_1 = -3$ and $x_2 = -1, y_2 = -2, z_2 = 1$

Vector $\mathbf{AB} = (x_2 - x_1)\hat{\mathbf{i}} + (y_2 - y_1)\hat{\mathbf{j}} + (z_2 - z_1)\hat{\mathbf{k}}$

$= (-1 - 1)\hat{\mathbf{i}} + (-2 - 2)\hat{\mathbf{j}} + [1 - (-3)]\hat{\mathbf{k}} = -2\hat{\mathbf{i}} - 4\hat{\mathbf{j}} + 4\hat{\mathbf{k}}$

On comparing with $\mathbf{X} = x\hat{\mathbf{i}} + y\hat{\mathbf{j}} + z\hat{\mathbf{k}}$, we get $x = -2, y = -4, z = 4$

Now, magnitude

$$|\mathbf{AB}|=\sqrt{x^2+y^2+z^2}=\sqrt{(-2)^2+(-4)^2+4^2}=\sqrt{4+16+16}=\sqrt{36}=6$$

Direction cosines of a vector $\mathbf{X}=x\hat{\mathbf{i}}+y\hat{\mathbf{j}}+z\hat{\mathbf{k}}$ are $\frac{x}{|\mathbf{X}|},\frac{y}{|\mathbf{X}|},\frac{z}{|\mathbf{X}|}$

$\therefore$ Direction cosines of **AB** are $\frac{-2}{6},\frac{-4}{6},\frac{4}{6}$ or $-\frac{1}{3},-\frac{2}{3},\frac{2}{3}$.

Question 14 Show that the vector $\hat{\mathbf{i}}+\hat{\mathbf{j}}+\hat{\mathbf{k}}$ is equally inclined to the axes OX, OY and OZ.

◎ ***Thinking Process*** To show that a vector is equally inclined with all the axes X, Y and Z or with OX, OY and OZ, we have to prove that direction cosines are equal.

Sol. Let $\mathbf{a}=\hat{\mathbf{i}}+\hat{\mathbf{j}}+\hat{\mathbf{k}}$

Then, magnitude of vector $\mathbf{a}=|\mathbf{a}|=\sqrt{1^2+1^2+1^2}=\sqrt{3}$

Therefore, the direction cosines of **a** are $\frac{x}{|\mathbf{a}|},\frac{y}{|\mathbf{a}|},\frac{z}{|\mathbf{a}|}$ *i.e.*, $\frac{1}{\sqrt{3}},\frac{1}{\sqrt{3}},\frac{1}{\sqrt{3}}$.

If **a** makes angles α, β and γ respectively with (positive) OX, OY and OZ.
Then, we have

$$\cos\alpha=1/\sqrt{3},\ \cos\beta=\frac{1}{\sqrt{3}}\text{ and }\cos\gamma=\frac{1}{\sqrt{3}},$$

($\because$ Direction cosines are the cosines of the angles made by $\hat{\mathbf{i}}$, $\hat{\mathbf{j}}$, $\hat{\mathbf{k}}$ components of the vector with X, Y and Z axes)

$$\Rightarrow \qquad \alpha=\beta=\gamma=\cos^{-1}\left(\frac{1}{\sqrt{3}}\right)$$

Hence, the given vector **a** is equally inclined with OX, OY and OZ.

Question 15. Find the position vector of a point R which divides the line joining two points P and Q whose position vectors are $\hat{\mathbf{i}}+2\hat{\mathbf{j}}-\hat{\mathbf{k}}$ and $-\hat{\mathbf{i}}+\hat{\mathbf{j}}+\hat{\mathbf{k}}$ respectively, in the ratio 2 : 1

(i) internally, (ii) externally.

◎ ***Thinking Process*** Use formula for internal division $\frac{m\mathbf{b}+n\mathbf{a}}{m+n}$ and use formula for external division $\frac{m\mathbf{b}-n\mathbf{a}}{m-n}$. where, m and n are the given ratio.

Sol. Position vectors of P and Q are given as

$$\mathbf{OP}=\hat{\mathbf{i}}+2\hat{\mathbf{j}}-\hat{\mathbf{k}}\text{ and }\mathbf{OQ}=-\hat{\mathbf{i}}+\hat{\mathbf{j}}+\hat{\mathbf{k}}$$

(i) PV of R [dividing (PQ) in the ratio $m:n$ internally]

$$=\frac{m(\mathbf{PV\ of\ }Q)+n(\mathbf{PV\ of\ }P)}{m+n}$$

$$= \frac{2(\textbf{PV of } Q) + 1(\textbf{PV of } P)}{2+1} \qquad \text{[here } m=2, n=1]$$

$$= \frac{1}{3}\{2(-\hat{\mathbf{i}} + \hat{\mathbf{j}} + \hat{\mathbf{k}}) + 1(\hat{\mathbf{i}} + 2\hat{\mathbf{j}} - \hat{\mathbf{k}})\}$$

$$= \frac{1}{3}(-\hat{\mathbf{i}} + 4\hat{\mathbf{j}} + \hat{\mathbf{k}}) = \left(-\frac{1}{3}\right)\hat{\mathbf{i}} + \left(\frac{4}{3}\right)\hat{\mathbf{j}} + \left(\frac{1}{3}\right)\hat{\mathbf{k}}$$

(ii) **PV** of R [dividing (PQ) in the ratio $2:1$ externally]

$$= \frac{m(\textbf{PV of } Q) - n(\textbf{PV of } P)}{m-n},$$

$$= \frac{2(\textbf{PV of } Q) - 1(\textbf{PV of } P)}{2-1} \qquad \text{[here } m = 2, n = 1]$$

$$= 2(-\hat{\mathbf{i}} + \hat{\mathbf{j}} + \hat{\mathbf{k}}) + (-1)(\hat{\mathbf{i}} + 2\hat{\mathbf{j}} - \hat{\mathbf{k}})$$

$$= (-3)\hat{\mathbf{i}} + 0\hat{\mathbf{j}} + 3\hat{\mathbf{k}} = -3\hat{\mathbf{i}} + 3\hat{\mathbf{k}}$$

Question 16 Find the position vector of the mid-point of the vector joining points $P(2,3,4)$ and $Q(4,1,-2)$.

Sol. The position vector of mid-point of the vector joining the points $P(2, 3, 4)$ and $Q(4, 1, -2)$ is given by

PV of the mid-point of $(PQ) = \frac{1}{2}(\text{PV of } P + \text{PV of } Q)$

$$= \frac{1}{2}[(2\hat{\mathbf{i}} + 3\hat{\mathbf{j}} + 4\hat{\mathbf{k}}) + (4\hat{\mathbf{i}} + \hat{\mathbf{j}} - 2\hat{\mathbf{k}})] = \frac{1}{2}(6\hat{\mathbf{i}} + 4\hat{\mathbf{j}} + 2\hat{\mathbf{k}}) = 3\hat{\mathbf{i}} + 2\hat{\mathbf{j}} + 1\hat{\mathbf{k}}$$

Question 17 Show that the points A, B and C with position vectors, $\mathbf{a} = 3\hat{\mathbf{i}} - 4\hat{\mathbf{j}} - 4\hat{\mathbf{k}}$, $\mathbf{b} = 2\hat{\mathbf{i}} - \hat{\mathbf{j}} + \hat{\mathbf{k}}$ and $\mathbf{c} = \hat{\mathbf{i}} - 3\hat{\mathbf{j}} - 5\hat{\mathbf{k}}$ respectively, form the vertices of a right angled triangle.

◎ ***Thinking Process*** If three points A, B, C form a right angle triangle, then $|\mathbf{AB}|^2 + |\mathbf{CA}|^2 = |\mathbf{BC}|^2$.

Sol. Position vectors of points A, B and C are respectively given as

$$\mathbf{a} = 3\hat{\mathbf{i}} - 4\hat{\mathbf{j}} - 4\hat{\mathbf{k}},\ \mathbf{b} = 2\hat{\mathbf{i}} - \hat{\mathbf{j}} + \hat{\mathbf{k}} \text{ and } \mathbf{c} = \hat{\mathbf{i}} - 3\hat{\mathbf{j}} - 5\hat{\mathbf{k}}$$

Now, $\quad \mathbf{AB} = \mathbf{b} - \mathbf{a} = (\text{PV of } B - \text{PV of } A)$

$\Rightarrow \quad = [(2\hat{\mathbf{i}} - \hat{\mathbf{j}} + \hat{\mathbf{k}}) - (3\hat{\mathbf{i}} - 4\hat{\mathbf{j}} - 4\hat{\mathbf{k}})] = -\hat{\mathbf{i}} + 3\hat{\mathbf{j}} + 5\hat{\mathbf{k}}$

On comparing with $X = x\hat{\mathbf{i}} + y\hat{\mathbf{j}} + z\hat{\mathbf{k}}$, we get

$$x = -1, y = 3, z = 5$$

Magnitude of **AB**, $|\mathbf{AB}| = \sqrt{x^2 + y^2 + z^2} = \sqrt{(-1)^2 + (3)^2 + (5)^2} = \sqrt{1 + 9 + 25} = \sqrt{35}$

$\therefore \quad |\mathbf{AB}|^2 = 35$

Similarly, $\mathbf{BC} = \mathbf{c} - \mathbf{b} = (\text{PV of } C - \text{PV of } B)$

$$= (\hat{\mathbf{i}} - 3\hat{\mathbf{j}} - 5\hat{\mathbf{k}}) - (2\hat{\mathbf{i}} - \hat{\mathbf{j}} + \hat{\mathbf{k}}) = -\hat{\mathbf{i}} - 2\hat{\mathbf{j}} - 6\hat{\mathbf{k}}$$

Similarly, $|\mathbf{BC}| = \sqrt{(-1)^2 + (-2)^2 + (-6)^2} = \sqrt{1+4+36} = \sqrt{41}$

$\Rightarrow$ $|\mathbf{BC}|^2 = 41$

and $\mathbf{CA} = \mathbf{a} - \mathbf{c} = (\text{PV of } A - \text{PV of } C)$

$\Rightarrow$ $= (3\hat{\mathbf{i}} - 4\hat{\mathbf{j}} - 4\hat{\mathbf{k}}) - (\hat{\mathbf{i}} - 3\hat{\mathbf{j}} - 5\hat{\mathbf{k}}) = 2\hat{\mathbf{i}} - \hat{\mathbf{j}} + \hat{\mathbf{k}}$

$$|\mathbf{CA}| = \sqrt{(2)^2 + (-1)^2 + (1)^2} = \sqrt{4+1+1} = \sqrt{6} \Rightarrow |\mathbf{CA}|^2 = 6$$

Now, $|\mathbf{AB}|^2 + |\mathbf{CA}|^2 = 35 + 6 = 41 = |\mathbf{BC}|^2$

Therefore, by Pythagoras theorem, ΔABC is a right angled triangle with right angle at A.

Question 18 In triangle ABC, which of the following is not true

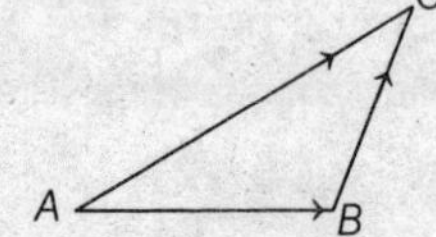

(a) $\mathbf{AB} + \mathbf{BC} + \mathbf{CA} = \mathbf{0}$

(b) $\mathbf{AB} + \mathbf{BC} - \mathbf{AC} = \mathbf{0}$

(c) $\mathbf{AB} + \mathbf{BC} - \mathbf{CA} = \mathbf{0}$

(d) $\mathbf{AB} - \mathbf{CB} + \mathbf{CA} = \mathbf{0}$

Sol. (c) By triangle law of vector addition,

$$\mathbf{AB} + \mathbf{BC} = \mathbf{AC} \text{ or } \mathbf{AB} + \mathbf{BC} = -\mathbf{CA}$$

Hence, the equation given in alternative (c) is incorrect.

Question 19. If $\mathbf{a}$ and $\mathbf{b}$ are two collinear vectors, then which of the following are incorrect

(a) $\mathbf{b} = \lambda\mathbf{a}$, for some scalar λ

(b) $\hat{\mathbf{a}} = \pm\hat{\mathbf{b}}$

(c) The respective components of $\mathbf{a}$ and $\mathbf{b}$ are not proportional.

(d) Both the vectors $\mathbf{a}$ and $\mathbf{b}$ have same direction but different magnitudes.

Sol. (c) Considering each option; Option (a) $b = \lambda a$ is correct, it is the condition for collinearity of two vectors.

Option (b) $\hat{\mathbf{a}} = \pm\hat{\mathbf{b}}$ is also correct, it shows that unit vectors in the direction of given vectors are either in the same direction or in opposite direction *i.e.*, they are collinear.

Option (c) is incorrect, if for two vectors the respective components are proportional, then their magnitude will be different but they will be collinear.

Option (d) is correct, because if the two vectors are collinear then they may have same directions or opposite directions. In both the cases they will be collinear, they may have different magnitude.

Exercise 10.3

Question 1 Find the angle between two vectors **a** and **b** with magnitudes $\sqrt{3}$ and 2 respectively, having $\mathbf{a}\cdot\mathbf{b}=\sqrt{6}$.

◎ *Thinking Process* To determine the angle between **a** and **b**, we can use the formula $\cos\theta=\dfrac{\mathbf{a}\cdot\mathbf{b}}{|\mathbf{a}||\mathbf{b}|}$

Sol. It is given that $|\mathbf{a}|=\sqrt{3}$, $|\mathbf{b}|=2$ and $\mathbf{a}\cdot\mathbf{b}=\sqrt{6}$

Let θ be the required angle, then

$$\cos\theta=\frac{\mathbf{a}\cdot\mathbf{b}}{|\mathbf{a}||\mathbf{b}|}=\frac{\sqrt{6}}{\sqrt{3}\times 2}=\frac{1}{\sqrt{2}}\Rightarrow\theta=\cos^{-1}\left(\frac{1}{\sqrt{2}}\right)=\cos^{-1}\left(\cos\frac{\pi}{4}\right)=\frac{\pi}{4}$$

Hence, the angle between the given vectors **a** and **b** is $\pi/4$.

Question 2 Find the angle between the vectors $\hat{\mathbf{i}}-2\hat{\mathbf{j}}+3\hat{\mathbf{k}}$ and $3\hat{\mathbf{i}}-2\hat{\mathbf{j}}+\hat{\mathbf{k}}$.

The angle between the two vectors **a** and **b** is given by $\cos\theta=\dfrac{\mathbf{a}.\mathbf{b}}{|\mathbf{a}||\mathbf{b}|}$. Here we are not given $\mathbf{a}\cdot\mathbf{b}$ (dot product) and magnitude of **a** and **b**, so first of all we have to find these required factors.

Sol. Let $\mathbf{a}=\hat{\mathbf{i}}-2\hat{\mathbf{j}}+3\hat{\mathbf{k}}$ and $\mathbf{b}=3\hat{\mathbf{i}}-2\hat{\mathbf{j}}+\hat{\mathbf{k}}$

Magnitude of **a**, $|\mathbf{a}|=\sqrt{1^2+(-2)^2+3^2}=\sqrt{1+4+9}=\sqrt{14}$

Magnitude of **b**, $|\mathbf{b}|=\sqrt{3^2+(-2)^2+1^2}=\sqrt{9+4+1}=\sqrt{14}$

Now, $\mathbf{a}\cdot\mathbf{b}=(\hat{\mathbf{i}}-2\hat{\mathbf{j}}+3\hat{\mathbf{k}})\cdot(3\hat{\mathbf{i}}-2\hat{\mathbf{j}}+\hat{\mathbf{k}})$

$$=1\cdot 3+(-2)\cdot(-2)+3\cdot 1=3+4+3=10$$

(Dot product of two vectors is equal to the sum of the products of their corresponding components.)

Let θ be the required angle between **a** and **b**, then

$$\cos\theta=\frac{\mathbf{a}\cdot\mathbf{b}}{|\mathbf{a}||\mathbf{b}|}=\frac{10}{\sqrt{14}\sqrt{14}}=\frac{10}{14}=\frac{5}{7}\Rightarrow\theta=\cos^{-1}\left(\frac{5}{7}\right)$$

$$\because (x_1\hat{\mathbf{i}}+y_1\hat{\mathbf{j}}+z_1\hat{\mathbf{k}})\cdot(x_2\hat{\mathbf{i}}+y_2\hat{\mathbf{j}}+z_2\hat{\mathbf{k}})=x_1x_2+y_1y_2+z_1z_2$$

Question 3 Find the projection of the vector $\hat{\mathbf{i}}-\hat{\mathbf{j}}$ on the vector $\hat{\mathbf{i}}+\hat{\mathbf{j}}$.

Sol. Let $\mathbf{a}=\hat{\mathbf{i}}-\hat{\mathbf{j}}$, $\mathbf{b}=\hat{\mathbf{i}}+\hat{\mathbf{j}}$

Projection of **a** on **b** is given by, $\dfrac{\mathbf{a}\cdot\mathbf{b}}{|\mathbf{b}|}=\dfrac{(\hat{\mathbf{i}}-\hat{\mathbf{j}})\cdot(\hat{\mathbf{i}}+\hat{\mathbf{j}})}{\sqrt{1^2+1^2}}=\dfrac{1\times 1+(-1)\times 1}{\sqrt{2}}=0$

Hence, the projection of vector **a** on **b** is 0.

Mistake Alert Sometime students are confused and use the formula for projection of **a** on **b** is $\frac{\mathbf{a}.\mathbf{b}}{|\mathbf{a}|}$ instead of $\frac{\mathbf{a}.\mathbf{b}}{|\mathbf{b}|}$.

Question 4 Find the projection of the vector $\hat{\mathbf{i}}+3\hat{\mathbf{j}}+7\hat{\mathbf{k}}$ on the vector $7\hat{\mathbf{i}}-\hat{\mathbf{j}}+8\hat{\mathbf{k}}$.

Sol. Let $\mathbf{a}=\hat{\mathbf{i}}+3\hat{\mathbf{j}}+7\hat{\mathbf{k}}$ and $\mathbf{b}=7\hat{\mathbf{i}}-\hat{\mathbf{j}}+8\hat{\mathbf{k}}$, then projection of **a** is given by

$$\frac{\mathbf{a}\cdot\mathbf{b}}{|\mathbf{b}|}=\left(\frac{(\hat{\mathbf{i}}+3\hat{\mathbf{j}}+7\hat{\mathbf{k}})\cdot(7\hat{\mathbf{i}}-\hat{\mathbf{j}}+8\hat{\mathbf{k}})}{\sqrt{7^2+(-1)^2+8^2}}\right)$$

$$=\left(\frac{1\times7+3\times(-1)+7\times8}{\sqrt{49+1+64}}\right)=\frac{7-3+56}{\sqrt{114}}=\frac{60}{\sqrt{114}}$$

Hence, the projection of vector $(\hat{\mathbf{i}}+3\hat{\mathbf{j}}+7\hat{\mathbf{k}})$ on $(7\hat{\mathbf{i}}-\hat{\mathbf{j}}+8\hat{\mathbf{k}})$ is $\frac{60}{\sqrt{114}}$.

Question 5 Show that each of the given three vectors is a unit vector : $\frac{1}{7}(2\hat{\mathbf{i}}+3\hat{\mathbf{j}}+6\hat{\mathbf{k}}), \frac{1}{7}(3\hat{\mathbf{i}}-6\hat{\mathbf{j}}+2\hat{\mathbf{k}}), \frac{1}{7}(6\hat{\mathbf{i}}+2\hat{\mathbf{j}}-3\hat{\mathbf{k}})$. Also, show that they are mutually perpendicular to each other.

Thinking Process To prove a vector is a unit vector, we have to prove that its magnitude is unity *i.e.*, 1. Two vectors **a** and **b** are perpendicular, if $\mathbf{a}\cdot\mathbf{b}=0$

Sol. Let $\mathbf{a}=\frac{1}{7}(2\hat{\mathbf{i}}+3\hat{\mathbf{j}}+6\hat{\mathbf{k}})=\frac{2}{7}\hat{\mathbf{i}}+\frac{3}{7}\hat{\mathbf{j}}+\frac{6}{7}\hat{\mathbf{k}}$

$$\mathbf{b}=\frac{1}{7}(3\hat{\mathbf{i}}-6\hat{\mathbf{j}}+2\hat{\mathbf{k}})=\frac{3}{7}\hat{\mathbf{i}}-\frac{6}{7}\hat{\mathbf{j}}+\frac{2}{7}\hat{\mathbf{k}}$$

and $$\mathbf{c}=\frac{1}{7}(6\hat{\mathbf{i}}+2\hat{\mathbf{j}}-3\hat{\mathbf{k}})=\frac{6}{7}\hat{\mathbf{i}}+\frac{2}{7}\hat{\mathbf{j}}-\frac{3}{7}\hat{\mathbf{k}}$$

Then, magnitude of **a**, $|\mathbf{a}|=\sqrt{\left(\frac{2}{7}\right)^2+\left(\frac{3}{7}\right)^2+\left(\frac{6}{7}\right)^2}=\sqrt{\frac{49}{49}}=1,$

$$\text{magnitude of } \mathbf{b},\ |\mathbf{b}|=\sqrt{\left(\frac{3}{7}\right)^2+\left(\frac{-6}{7}\right)^2+\left(\frac{2}{7}\right)^2}=\sqrt{\frac{49}{49}}=1$$

and magnitude of **c**, $|\mathbf{c}|=\sqrt{\left(\frac{6}{7}\right)^2+\left(\frac{2}{7}\right)^2+\left(\frac{-3}{7}\right)^2}=\sqrt{\frac{49}{49}}=1,$

Thus, each of the given three vectors is a unit vector.

Now,

$$\mathbf{a}\cdot\mathbf{b}=\left(\frac{2}{7}\hat{\mathbf{i}}+\frac{3}{7}\hat{\mathbf{j}}+\frac{6}{7}\hat{\mathbf{k}}\right)\cdot\left(\frac{3}{7}\hat{\mathbf{i}}-\frac{6}{7}\hat{\mathbf{j}}+\frac{2}{7}\hat{\mathbf{k}}\right)=\frac{2}{7}\times\frac{3}{7}+\frac{3}{7}\times\left(\frac{-6}{7}\right)+\frac{6}{7}\times\frac{2}{7}$$

$$=\frac{6}{49}-\frac{18}{49}+\frac{12}{49}=\frac{6-18+12}{49}=\frac{0}{49}=0$$

i.e., **a** and **b** are perpendicular to each other.

$$\mathbf{b}\cdot\mathbf{c}=\left(\frac{3}{7}\hat{\mathbf{i}}-\frac{6}{7}\hat{\mathbf{j}}+\frac{2}{7}\hat{\mathbf{k}}\right)\cdot\left(\frac{6}{7}\hat{\mathbf{i}}+\frac{2}{7}\hat{\mathbf{j}}-\frac{3}{7}\hat{\mathbf{k}}\right)$$
$$=\frac{3}{7}\times\frac{6}{7}+\left(\frac{-6}{7}\right)\times\frac{2}{7}+\frac{2}{7}\times\left(\frac{-3}{7}\right)$$
$$=\frac{18}{49}-\frac{12}{49}-\frac{6}{49}=\frac{18-12-6}{49}=\frac{0}{49}=0$$

i.e., **b** and **c** are perpendicular to each other.

$$\mathbf{c}\cdot\mathbf{a}=\left(\frac{6}{7}\hat{\mathbf{i}}+\frac{2}{7}\hat{\mathbf{j}}-\frac{3}{7}\hat{\mathbf{k}}\right)\left(\frac{2}{7}\hat{\mathbf{i}}+\frac{3}{7}\hat{\mathbf{j}}+\frac{6}{7}\hat{\mathbf{k}}\right)=\frac{6}{7}\times\frac{2}{7}+\frac{2}{7}\times\frac{3}{7}+\left(\frac{-3}{7}\right)\times\frac{6}{7}$$
$$=\frac{12}{49}+\frac{6}{49}-\frac{18}{49}=\frac{12+6-18}{49}=\frac{0}{49}=0$$

i.e., **c** and **a** are perpendicular to each other.

Hence, the given three vectors are mutually perpendicular to each other.

Question 6 Find $|\mathbf{a}|$ and $|\mathbf{b}|$, if $(\mathbf{a}+\mathbf{b})\cdot(\mathbf{a}-\mathbf{b})=8$ and $|\mathbf{a}|=8|\mathbf{b}|$.

Sol. Given, $(\mathbf{a}+\mathbf{b})\cdot(\mathbf{a}-\mathbf{b})=8$ and $|\mathbf{a}|=8|\mathbf{b}|$

$\Rightarrow$ $\mathbf{a}\cdot\mathbf{a}-\mathbf{a}\cdot\mathbf{b}+\mathbf{b}\cdot\mathbf{a}-\mathbf{b}\cdot\mathbf{b}=8$

$\Rightarrow$ $|\mathbf{a}|^2-|\mathbf{b}|^2=8$ $\quad(\because \mathbf{a}\cdot\mathbf{a}=|\mathbf{a}|^2$ and $\mathbf{a}\cdot\mathbf{b}=\mathbf{b}\cdot\mathbf{a})$

$\Rightarrow$ $(8|\mathbf{b}|)^2-|\mathbf{b}|^2=8\Rightarrow 63|\mathbf{b}|^2=8$ $\quad$(Given, $|\mathbf{a}|=8|\mathbf{b}|$)

$\Rightarrow$ $|\mathbf{b}|=\sqrt{\frac{8}{63}}=\frac{2}{3}\sqrt{\frac{2}{7}}$

Also, $\quad|\mathbf{a}|=8|\mathbf{b}|=8\left(\frac{2}{3}\sqrt{\frac{2}{7}}\right)=\frac{16}{3}\sqrt{\frac{2}{7}}$.

Question 7 Evaluate the product $(3\mathbf{a}-5\mathbf{b})\cdot(2\mathbf{a}+7\mathbf{b})$.

◎ ***Thinking Process*** To find the product, use $\mathbf{a}\cdot\mathbf{a}=|\mathbf{a}|^2$, $\mathbf{b}\cdot\mathbf{b}=|\mathbf{b}|^2$ and $\mathbf{a}\cdot\mathbf{b}=\mathbf{b}\cdot\mathbf{a}$.

Sol. We have, $(3\mathbf{a}-5\mathbf{b})\cdot(2\mathbf{a}+7\mathbf{b})$

$$=(3\mathbf{a})\cdot(2\mathbf{a}+7\mathbf{b})-(5\mathbf{b})\cdot(2\mathbf{a}+7\mathbf{b})$$
$$=6(\mathbf{a}\cdot\mathbf{a})+21(\mathbf{a}\cdot\mathbf{b})-10(\mathbf{b}\cdot\mathbf{a})-35(\mathbf{b}\cdot\mathbf{b})$$
$$=6|\mathbf{a}|^2+11(\mathbf{a}\cdot\mathbf{b})-35|\mathbf{b}|^2 \qquad (\because \mathbf{a}\cdot\mathbf{a}=|\mathbf{a}|^2 \text{ and } \mathbf{a}\cdot\mathbf{b}=\mathbf{b}\cdot\mathbf{a})$$

Question 8 Find the magnitude of two vectors **a and b** having the same magnitude and such that the angle between them is 60° and their scalar product is 1/2

Sol. Given, both the vectors have same magnitude *i.e.,* $|\mathbf{a}|=|\mathbf{b}|$ and scalar product of vectors, $\mathbf{a}\cdot\mathbf{b}=\frac{1}{2}$

Let θ be the angle between two vectors **a** and **b**, then

$$\cos\theta = \frac{\mathbf{a}\cdot\mathbf{b}}{|\mathbf{a}|\,|\mathbf{b}|} \Rightarrow \cos 60^\circ = \frac{\frac{1}{2}}{|\mathbf{a}|\,|\mathbf{a}|} \qquad [\because |\mathbf{a}| = |\mathbf{b}|]$$

$$\Rightarrow \quad \frac{1}{2} = \frac{1}{2|\mathbf{a}|^2} \Rightarrow |\mathbf{a}|^2 = 1 \Rightarrow |\mathbf{a}| = 1 \quad (\because |\mathbf{a}| \text{ can not be negative})$$

Thus, $|\mathbf{a}| = |\mathbf{b}| = 1$

Question 9 Find $|\mathbf{x}|$, if for a unit vector $\mathbf{a}$, $(\mathbf{x}-\mathbf{a})\cdot(\mathbf{x}+\mathbf{a}) = 12$.

Sol. Given, $|\mathbf{a}| = 1$ ($\because$ **a** is a unit vector)

and $(\mathbf{x}-\mathbf{a}).(\mathbf{x}+\mathbf{a}) = 12$

$\Rightarrow$ $\mathbf{x}\cdot\mathbf{x} + \mathbf{x}\cdot\mathbf{a} - \mathbf{a}\cdot\mathbf{x} - \mathbf{a}\cdot\mathbf{a} = 12$

$\Rightarrow$ $|\mathbf{x}|^2 - |\mathbf{a}|^2 = 12 \Rightarrow |\mathbf{x}|^2 - 1^2 = 12$

$\Rightarrow$ $|\mathbf{x}|^2 = 13 \Rightarrow |\mathbf{x}| = \sqrt{13}$

Question 10 If $\mathbf{a} = 2\hat{\mathbf{i}} + 2\hat{\mathbf{j}} + 3\hat{\mathbf{k}}$, $\mathbf{b} = -\hat{\mathbf{i}} + 2\hat{\mathbf{j}} + \hat{\mathbf{k}}$ and $\mathbf{c} = 3\hat{\mathbf{i}} + \hat{\mathbf{j}}$ such that $\mathbf{a} + \lambda\mathbf{b}$ is perpendicular to **c**, then find the value of λ.

◎ *Thinking Process* If **a** and **b** are perpendicular to each other then $\mathbf{a}\cdot\mathbf{b} = 0$

Sol. The given vectors are $\mathbf{a} = 2\hat{\mathbf{i}} + 2\hat{\mathbf{j}} + 3\hat{\mathbf{k}}$, $\mathbf{b} = -\hat{\mathbf{i}} + 2\hat{\mathbf{j}} + \hat{\mathbf{k}}$ and $\mathbf{c} = 3\hat{\mathbf{i}} + \hat{\mathbf{j}}$.

Now, $(\mathbf{a} + \lambda\mathbf{b}) \perp \mathbf{c}$ (Given)

$\Rightarrow$ $(\mathbf{a} + \lambda\mathbf{b})\cdot\mathbf{c} = 0$

($\because$ scalar product of two perpendicular vectors is zero)

$\Rightarrow$ $[(2\hat{\mathbf{i}} + 2\hat{\mathbf{j}} + 3\hat{\mathbf{k}}) + \lambda(-\hat{\mathbf{i}} + 2\hat{\mathbf{j}} + \hat{\mathbf{k}})]\cdot(3\hat{\mathbf{i}} + \hat{\mathbf{j}}) = 0$

$\Rightarrow$ $[(2-\lambda)\hat{\mathbf{i}} + (2+2\lambda)\hat{\mathbf{j}} + (3+\lambda)\hat{\mathbf{k}}]\cdot(3\hat{\mathbf{i}} + \hat{\mathbf{j}}) = 0$

$\Rightarrow$ $(2-\lambda)3 + (2+2\lambda)1 + (3+\lambda)0 = 0$

$\Rightarrow$ $6 - 3\lambda + 2 + 2\lambda = 0 \Rightarrow 8 - \lambda = 0 \Rightarrow \lambda = 8.$

Hence, the required value of λ is 8.

Question 11 Show that $|\mathbf{a}|\mathbf{b} + |\mathbf{b}|\mathbf{a}$ is perpendicular to $|\mathbf{a}|\mathbf{b} - |\mathbf{b}|\mathbf{a}$ for any two non-zero vectors **a** and **b**.

Sol. Let $\mathbf{p} = |\mathbf{a}|\,\mathbf{b} + |\mathbf{b}|\,\mathbf{a}$ and $\mathbf{q} = |\mathbf{a}|\,\mathbf{b} - |\mathbf{b}|\,\mathbf{a}$

Then, $\mathbf{p}\cdot\mathbf{q} = (|\mathbf{a}|\,\mathbf{b} + |\mathbf{b}|\,\mathbf{a}).(|\mathbf{a}|\,\mathbf{b} - |\mathbf{b}|\,\mathbf{a})$

$= |\mathbf{a}|^2(\mathbf{b}\cdot\mathbf{b}) - |\mathbf{a}|\,|\mathbf{b}|\,(\mathbf{b}\cdot\mathbf{a}) + |\mathbf{b}|\,|\mathbf{a}|\,(\mathbf{a}\cdot\mathbf{b}) - |\mathbf{b}|^2(\mathbf{a}\cdot\mathbf{a})$

$= |\mathbf{a}|^2|\mathbf{b}|^2 - |\mathbf{a}|\,|\mathbf{b}|\,(\mathbf{a}\cdot\mathbf{b}) + |\mathbf{a}|\,|\mathbf{b}|(\mathbf{a}\cdot\mathbf{b}) - |\mathbf{b}|^2|\mathbf{a}|^2 = 0$

$\Rightarrow$ $\mathbf{p} \perp \mathbf{q}$ ($\because$ If $\mathbf{c}\cdot\mathbf{d} = 0 \Rightarrow \mathbf{c}$ is perpendicular to **d**)

Hence, $|\mathbf{a}|\,\mathbf{b} + |\mathbf{b}|\,\mathbf{a}$ and $|\mathbf{a}|\,\mathbf{b} - |\mathbf{b}|\mathbf{a}$ are perpendicular to each other for any two non-zero vectors **a** and **b**.

Question 12 If $\mathbf{a} \cdot \mathbf{a} = 0$ and $\mathbf{a} \cdot \mathbf{b} = 0$, then what can be conclude about the vector $\mathbf{b}$?

Sol. It is given that $\mathbf{a} \cdot \mathbf{a} = 0$ or $|\mathbf{a}|^2 = 0 \Rightarrow |\mathbf{a}| = 0 \Rightarrow \mathbf{a} = \mathbf{0}$ *i.e.*, $\mathbf{a}$ is a zero vector because its magnitude is zero.

Hence, $\mathbf{a} \cdot \mathbf{b} = 0$ whatever $\mathbf{b}$ may $(\because \mathbf{a} = 0)$. This means that nothing can be concluded about $\mathbf{b}$ it can be any vector.

Question 13 If $\mathbf{a}$, $\mathbf{b}$, $\mathbf{c}$ are unit vectors such that $\mathbf{a} + \mathbf{b} + \mathbf{c} = \mathbf{0}$, then find the value of $\mathbf{a} \cdot \mathbf{b} + \mathbf{b} \cdot \mathbf{c} + \mathbf{c} \cdot \mathbf{a}$.

◎ ***Thinking Process*** As $\mathbf{a}$, $\mathbf{b}$ and $\mathbf{c}$ are unit vectors, so use $|\mathbf{a}| = |\mathbf{b}| = |\mathbf{c}| = 1$ and expand $(\mathbf{a} + \mathbf{b} + \mathbf{c}) \cdot (\mathbf{a} + \mathbf{b} + \mathbf{c})$ to get the value of $\mathbf{a} \cdot \mathbf{b} + \mathbf{b} \cdot \mathbf{c} + \mathbf{c} \cdot \mathbf{a}$.

Sol. Given, $|\mathbf{a}| = |\mathbf{b}| = |\mathbf{c}| = 1$ and $\mathbf{a} + \mathbf{b} + \mathbf{c} = \mathbf{0}$

We have, $$(\mathbf{a} + \mathbf{b} + \mathbf{c}) \cdot (\mathbf{a} + \mathbf{b} + \mathbf{c}) = 0$$

$$\Rightarrow \mathbf{a} \cdot (\mathbf{a} + \mathbf{b} + \mathbf{c}) + \mathbf{b} \cdot (\mathbf{a} + \mathbf{b} + \mathbf{c}) + \mathbf{c} \cdot (\mathbf{a} + \mathbf{b} + \mathbf{c}) = 0$$

$$\Rightarrow \mathbf{a} \cdot \mathbf{a} + \mathbf{a} \cdot \mathbf{b} + \mathbf{a} \cdot \mathbf{c} + \mathbf{b} \cdot \mathbf{a} + \mathbf{b} \cdot \mathbf{b} + \mathbf{b} \cdot \mathbf{c} + \mathbf{c} \cdot \mathbf{a} + \mathbf{c} \cdot \mathbf{b} + \mathbf{c} \cdot \mathbf{c} = 0$$

$$\Rightarrow |\mathbf{a}|^2 + |\mathbf{b}|^2 + |\mathbf{c}|^2 + 2(\mathbf{a} \cdot \mathbf{b} + \mathbf{b} \cdot \mathbf{c} + \mathbf{c} \cdot \mathbf{a}) = 0$$

$$(\because \mathbf{a} \cdot \mathbf{a} = |\mathbf{a}|^2 \text{ and } \mathbf{a} \cdot \mathbf{b} = \mathbf{b} \cdot \mathbf{a})$$

$$\Rightarrow 1 + 1 + 1 + 2(\mathbf{a} \cdot \mathbf{b} + \mathbf{b} \cdot \mathbf{c} + \mathbf{c} \cdot \mathbf{a}) = 0 \quad (\because |\mathbf{a}| = |\mathbf{b}| = |\mathbf{c}| = 1)$$

$$\Rightarrow 3 + 2(\mathbf{a} \cdot \mathbf{b} + \mathbf{b} \cdot \mathbf{c} + \mathbf{c} \cdot \mathbf{a}) = 0$$

$$\Rightarrow \mathbf{a} \cdot \mathbf{b} + \mathbf{b} \cdot \mathbf{c} + \mathbf{c} \cdot \mathbf{a} = -\frac{3}{2}$$

Question 14 If either $\mathbf{a} = \mathbf{0}$ or $\mathbf{b} = \mathbf{0}$, then $\mathbf{a} \cdot \mathbf{b} = 0$. But the converse need not to be true. Justify your answer with an example.

Sol. If $\mathbf{a} = 0 = 0\hat{\mathbf{i}} + 0\hat{\mathbf{j}} + 0\hat{\mathbf{k}}$ and $\mathbf{b}$ is non-zero *i.e.*, $\mathbf{b} = x\hat{\mathbf{i}} + y\hat{\mathbf{j}} + z\hat{\mathbf{k}}$

$$\therefore \quad \mathbf{a} \cdot \mathbf{b} = (0\hat{\mathbf{i}} + 0\hat{\mathbf{j}} + 0\hat{\mathbf{k}})(x\hat{\mathbf{i}} + y\hat{\mathbf{j}} + z\hat{\mathbf{k}}) = (0 \times x) + (0 \times y) + (0 \times z) = 0$$

So, if $\mathbf{a} = \mathbf{0}$ or $\mathbf{b} = \mathbf{0}$, then $\mathbf{a} \cdot \mathbf{b} = 0$

To prove that converse need not to be, for this we have to prove that for two non-zero vectors $\mathbf{a}$ and $\mathbf{b}$, $\mathbf{a} \cdot \mathbf{b}$ can be zero.

Let $\mathbf{a} = 2\hat{\mathbf{i}} + 4\hat{\mathbf{j}} + 3\hat{\mathbf{k}}$ and $\mathbf{b} = 3\hat{\mathbf{i}} + 3\hat{\mathbf{j}} - 6\hat{\mathbf{k}}$

Then, $$\mathbf{a} \cdot \mathbf{b} = 2 \cdot 3 + 4 \cdot 3 + 3 \cdot (-6) = 6 + 12 - 18 = 0$$

We now observe that $\vec{a} \neq \vec{0}$ and $\vec{b} \neq \vec{0}$ but $\vec{a} \cdot \vec{b} = 0$

Hence, the converse of the given statement need not to be true.

Question 15 If the vertices A, B, C of a triangle ABC have position vectors $(1, 2, 3)$, $(-1, 0, 0)$, $(0, 1, 2)$ respectively then find $\angle ABC$ ($\angle ABC$ is the angle between the vectors $\mathbf{BA}$ and $\mathbf{BC}$).

◎ ***Thinking Process*** Here, we have to find $\angle ABC$ *i.e.*, angle between $\mathbf{BA}$ and $\mathbf{BC}$, so first of all we have to calculate both vectors and after that we can find the angle between them by $\cos\theta = \dfrac{(\mathbf{BA}) \cdot (\mathbf{BC})}{|\mathbf{BA}||\mathbf{BC}|}$

Sol. The given point are $A(1, 2, 3)$, $B(-1, 0, 0)$ and $C(0, 1, 2)$.

Also, it is given that $\angle ABC$ is the angle between the vectors **BA** and **BC**.

Here, $\mathbf{BA} = \text{PV of } A - \text{PV of } B = (\hat{\mathbf{i}} + 2\hat{\mathbf{j}} + 3\hat{\mathbf{k}}) - (-\hat{\mathbf{i}} + 0\hat{\mathbf{j}} + 0\hat{\mathbf{k}})$

$= [\hat{\mathbf{i}} - (-\hat{\mathbf{i}}) + (2\hat{\mathbf{j}} - 0) + (3\hat{\mathbf{k}} - 0)] = 2\hat{\mathbf{i}} + 2\hat{\mathbf{j}} + 3\hat{\mathbf{k}}$

$|\mathbf{BA}| = \sqrt{(2)^2 + (2)^2 + (3)^2} = \sqrt{4+4+9} = \sqrt{17}$

$\mathbf{BC} = \text{PV of } C - \text{PV of } B$

$= (0\hat{\mathbf{i}} + 1\hat{\mathbf{j}} + 2\hat{\mathbf{k}}) - (-\hat{\mathbf{i}} + 0\hat{\mathbf{j}} + 0\hat{\mathbf{k}})$

$= [0 - (-\hat{\mathbf{i}}) + (1\hat{\mathbf{j}} - 0) + (2\hat{\mathbf{k}} - 0)] = \hat{\mathbf{i}} + \hat{\mathbf{j}} + 2\hat{\mathbf{k}}$

$|\mathbf{BC}| = \sqrt{(1)^2 + (1)^2 + (2)^2} = \sqrt{1+1+4} = \sqrt{6}$

Now, $\mathbf{BA} \cdot \mathbf{BC} = (2\hat{\mathbf{i}} + 2\hat{\mathbf{j}} + 3\hat{\mathbf{k}}) \cdot (\hat{\mathbf{i}} + \hat{\mathbf{j}} + 2\hat{\mathbf{k}})$

$= 2 \times 1 + 2 \times 1 + 3 \times 2 = 10$

and $\cos\theta = \dfrac{\mathbf{BA} \cdot \mathbf{BC}}{|\mathbf{BA}||\mathbf{BC}|} \Rightarrow \cos(\angle ABC) = \dfrac{10}{\sqrt{17}\sqrt{6}}$

$\Rightarrow \angle ABC = \cos^{-1}\left(\dfrac{10}{\sqrt{102}}\right)$

Question 16 Show that the points $A(1, 2, 7)$, $B(2, 6, 3)$ and $C(3, 10, -1)$ are collinear.

◎ ***Thinking Process*** For collinear, prove that $|\mathbf{AC}| = |\mathbf{AB}| + |\mathbf{BC}|$

Sol. The given points are $A(1, 2, 7)$, $B(2, 6, 3)$ and $C(3, 10, -1)$.

$\therefore \mathbf{AB} = \text{PV of } B - \text{PV of } A = (2\hat{\mathbf{i}} + 6\hat{\mathbf{j}} + 3\hat{\mathbf{k}}) - (1\hat{\mathbf{i}} + 2\hat{\mathbf{j}} + 7\hat{\mathbf{k}})$

$= (2-1)\hat{\mathbf{i}} + (6-2)\hat{\mathbf{j}} + (3-7)\hat{\mathbf{k}} = \hat{\mathbf{i}} + 4\hat{\mathbf{j}} - 4\hat{\mathbf{k}}$

Magnitude of **AB**, $|\mathbf{AB}| = \sqrt{(1)^2 + (4)^2 + (-4)^2} = \sqrt{1+16+16} = \sqrt{33}$

$\mathbf{BC} = \text{PV of } C - \text{PV of } B = (3\hat{\mathbf{i}} + 10\hat{\mathbf{j}} - 1\hat{\mathbf{k}}) - (2\hat{\mathbf{i}} + 6\hat{\mathbf{j}} + 3\hat{\mathbf{k}})$

$= (3-2)\hat{\mathbf{i}} + (10-6)\hat{\mathbf{j}} + (-1-3)\hat{\mathbf{k}} = \hat{\mathbf{i}} + 4\hat{\mathbf{j}} - 4\hat{\mathbf{k}}$

Magnitude of **BC**, $|\mathbf{BC}| = \sqrt{(1)^2 + (4)^2 + (-4)^2} = \sqrt{1+16+16} = \sqrt{33}$

$\mathbf{AC} = \text{PV of } C - \text{PV of } A = (3\hat{\mathbf{i}} + 10\hat{\mathbf{j}} - 1\hat{\mathbf{k}}) - (1\hat{\mathbf{i}} + 2\hat{\mathbf{j}} + 7\hat{\mathbf{k}})$

$= (3-1)\hat{\mathbf{i}} + (10-2)\hat{\mathbf{j}} + (-1-7)\hat{\mathbf{k}} = 2\hat{\mathbf{i}} + 8\hat{\mathbf{j}} - 8\hat{\mathbf{k}}$

Magnitude of **AC**, $|\mathbf{AC}| = \sqrt{2^2 + 8^2 + (-8)^2} = \sqrt{4+64+64} = \sqrt{132} = 2\sqrt{33}$

So, $|\mathbf{AB}| + |\mathbf{BC}| = \sqrt{33} + \sqrt{33} = 2\sqrt{33} = |\mathbf{AC}|$

$\therefore |\mathbf{AC}| = |\mathbf{AB}| + |\mathbf{BC}|$. Hence, the given points A, B and C are collinear.

Quick Solution

$\mathbf{AB} = \text{PV of } B - \text{P.V of } A$

$= (2\hat{\mathbf{i}} + 6\hat{\mathbf{j}} + 3\hat{\mathbf{k}}) - (\hat{\mathbf{i}} + 2\hat{\mathbf{j}} + 7\hat{\mathbf{k}})$

$= (2-1)\hat{\mathbf{i}} + (6-2)\hat{\mathbf{i}} - (3-7)\hat{\mathbf{k}} = \hat{\mathbf{i}} + 4\hat{\mathbf{j}} - 4\hat{\mathbf{k}}$

Similarly, $\mathbf{BC} = \text{PV of } C - \text{PV of } B = \hat{\mathbf{i}} + 4\hat{\mathbf{j}} - 4\hat{\mathbf{k}}$

Now, we can see that $\mathbf{AB} = \mathbf{BC}$. So, they are parallel and point B is common in it. So, A, B, C are collinear.

Question 17 Show that the vectors $2\hat{i} - \hat{j} + \hat{k}$, $\hat{i} - 3\hat{j} - 5\hat{k}$ and $3\hat{i} - 4\hat{j} - 4\hat{k}$ form the vertices of a right angled triangle.

◎ *Thinking Process* To prove a triangle right angled triangle, we have to prove that the sum of squares of two sides is equal to the square of the third side.

Sol. Let $A = 2\hat{i} - \hat{j} + \hat{k}$, $B = \hat{i} - 3\hat{j} - 5\hat{k}$ and $C = 3\hat{i} - 4\hat{j} - 4\hat{k}$

$\therefore$ Side $\mathbf{AB}$ = PV of B − PV of $A = (\hat{i} - 3\hat{j} - 5\hat{k}) - (2\hat{i} - \hat{j} + \hat{k})$

$$= \hat{i} - 3\hat{j} - 5\hat{k} - 2\hat{i} + \hat{j} - \hat{k} = -\hat{i} - 2\hat{j} - 6\hat{k}$$

$$|\mathbf{AB}| = \sqrt{(-1)^2 + (-2)^2 + (-6)^2} = \sqrt{1 + 4 + 36} = \sqrt{41}$$

$$\mathbf{BC} = \text{PV of } C - \text{PV of } B = (3\hat{i} - 4\hat{j} - 4\hat{k}) - (\hat{i} - 3\hat{j} - 5\hat{k})$$

$$= 3\hat{i} - 4\hat{j} - 4\hat{k} - \hat{i} + 3\hat{j} + 5\hat{k} = 2\hat{i} - \hat{j} + \hat{k}$$

$$|\mathbf{BC}| = \sqrt{2^2 + (-1)^2 + 1^2} = \sqrt{4 + 1 + 1} = \sqrt{6}$$

and $\mathbf{AC}$ = PV of C − PV of $A = (3\hat{i} - 4\hat{j} - 4\hat{k}) - (2\hat{i} - \hat{j} + \hat{k})$

$$= 3\hat{i} - 4\hat{j} - 4\hat{k} - 2\hat{i} + \hat{j} - \hat{k} = \hat{i} - 3\hat{j} - 5\hat{k}$$

and $$|\mathbf{AC}| = \sqrt{1^2 + (-3)^2 + (-5)^2} = \sqrt{1 + 9 + 25} = \sqrt{35}$$

Now, $$|\mathbf{BC}|^2 + |\mathbf{AC}|^2 = 6 + 35 = 41 = |\mathbf{AB}|^2$$

which shows that ABC is a right angled triangle.

Quick Solution

We have $\mathbf{A} = 2\hat{i} - \hat{j} + \hat{k}$, $\mathbf{B} = \hat{i} - 3\hat{j} - 5\hat{k}$,

$$\mathbf{C} = 3\hat{i} - 4\hat{j} - 4\hat{k}$$

$$\mathbf{AB} = \text{PV of } \mathbf{B} - \text{PV of } \mathbf{A} = (\hat{i} - 3\hat{j} - 5\hat{k}) - (2\hat{i} - \hat{j} + \hat{k}) = -\hat{i} - 2\hat{j} - 6\hat{k}$$

$$\mathbf{BC} = \text{PV of } \mathbf{C} - \text{PV of } \mathbf{B} = (3\hat{i} - 4\hat{j} - 4\hat{k}) - (\hat{i} - 3\hat{j} - 5\hat{k}) = 2\hat{i} - \hat{j} + \hat{k}$$

$$\mathbf{CA} = \text{PV of } \mathbf{A} - \text{PV of } \mathbf{C} = (2\hat{i} - \hat{j} + \hat{k}) - (3\hat{i} - 4\hat{j} - 4\hat{k}) = -\hat{i} + 3\hat{j} + 5\hat{k}$$

$$\mathbf{BC} \cdot \mathbf{CA} = (2\hat{i} - \hat{j} + \hat{k}) \cdot (-\hat{i} + 3\hat{j} + 5\hat{k}) = -2 - 3 + 5 = 0$$

$$\mathbf{BC} \cdot \mathbf{CA} = 0$$

Hence, **BC** is perpendicular to **CA**.

Thus, we can say that $\angle C = 90°$, Here ABC is a right angled triangle.

Question 18 If **a** is a non-zero vector of magnitude a and λ is a non-zero scalar, then λ **a** is unit vector if

(a) $\lambda = 1$ (b) $\lambda = -1$ (c) $a = |\lambda|$ (d) $a = 1/|\lambda|$

Sol. (d) Vector $\lambda \mathbf{a}$ is a unit vector, if $|\lambda \mathbf{a}| = 1$

Now, $$|\lambda \mathbf{a}| = 1 \Rightarrow |\lambda||\mathbf{a}| = 1 \Rightarrow |\mathbf{a}| = \frac{1}{|\lambda|}$$

$$\Rightarrow \quad a = \frac{1}{|\lambda|} \quad [\text{given } |\mathbf{a}| = a]$$

Exercise 10.4

Question 1. Find $|\mathbf{a} \times \mathbf{b}|$, if $\mathbf{a} = \hat{\mathbf{i}} - 7\hat{\mathbf{j}} + 7\hat{\mathbf{k}}$ and $\mathbf{b} = 3\hat{\mathbf{i}} - 2\hat{\mathbf{j}} + 2\hat{\mathbf{k}}$.

◎ *Thinking Process* If $\mathbf{a} = a_1\hat{\mathbf{i}} + b_1\hat{\mathbf{j}} + c_1\hat{\mathbf{k}}$ and $\mathbf{b} = a_2\hat{\mathbf{i}} + b_2\hat{\mathbf{j}} + c_2\hat{\mathbf{k}}$, then

$\mathbf{a} \times \mathbf{b} = \begin{vmatrix} \hat{\mathbf{i}} & \hat{\mathbf{j}} & \hat{\mathbf{k}} \\ a_1 & b_1 & c_1 \\ a_2 & b_2 & c_2 \end{vmatrix}$. We can find the value by expanding this determinant.

Sol. Given that $\mathbf{a} = \hat{\mathbf{i}} - 7\hat{\mathbf{j}} + 7\hat{\mathbf{k}}$ and $\mathbf{b} = 3\hat{\mathbf{i}} - 2\hat{\mathbf{j}} + 2\hat{\mathbf{k}}$

$$\therefore \quad \mathbf{a} \times \mathbf{b} = \begin{vmatrix} \hat{\mathbf{i}} & \hat{\mathbf{j}} & \hat{\mathbf{k}} \\ 1 & -7 & 7 \\ 3 & -2 & 2 \end{vmatrix} = (-14 + 14)\hat{\mathbf{i}} - (2 - 21)\hat{\mathbf{j}} + (-2 + 21)\hat{\mathbf{k}}$$

$$= 0\hat{\mathbf{i}} + 19\hat{\mathbf{j}} + 19\hat{\mathbf{k}}$$

$$\Rightarrow \quad |\mathbf{a} \times \mathbf{b}| = \sqrt{0^2 + (19)^2 + (19)^2} = \sqrt{2 \times (19)^2} = 19\sqrt{2}$$

Mistake Alert $\mathbf{a} \times \mathbf{a} \neq \mathbf{a} \cdot \mathbf{a}$

Question 2 Find a unit vector perpendicular to each of the vectors $\mathbf{a} + \mathbf{b}$ and $\mathbf{a} - \mathbf{b}$, where $\mathbf{a} = 3\hat{\mathbf{i}} + 2\hat{\mathbf{j}} + 2\hat{\mathbf{k}}$ and $\mathbf{b} = \hat{\mathbf{i}} + 2\hat{\mathbf{j}} - 2\hat{\mathbf{k}}$.

◎ *Thinking Process* Determine $\mathbf{a} + \mathbf{b}$ and $\mathbf{a} - \mathbf{b}$, then unit vector perpendicular to both $(\mathbf{a} + \mathbf{b})$ and $(\mathbf{a} - \mathbf{b})$ is given by $\pm \dfrac{(\mathbf{a} + \mathbf{b}) \times (\mathbf{a} - \mathbf{b})}{|(\mathbf{a} + \mathbf{b}) \times (\mathbf{a} - \mathbf{b})|}$.

Sol. Given that $\mathbf{a} = 3\hat{\mathbf{i}} + 2\hat{\mathbf{j}} + 2\hat{\mathbf{k}}$ and $\mathbf{b} = \hat{\mathbf{i}} + 2\hat{\mathbf{j}} - 2\hat{\mathbf{k}}$

$$\therefore \quad \mathbf{a} + \mathbf{b} = (3\hat{\mathbf{i}} + 2\hat{\mathbf{j}} + 2\hat{\mathbf{k}}) + (\hat{\mathbf{i}} + 2\hat{\mathbf{j}} - 2\hat{\mathbf{k}}) = 4\hat{\mathbf{i}} + 4\hat{\mathbf{j}} + 0\hat{\mathbf{k}}$$

$$\text{and} \quad \mathbf{a} - \mathbf{b} = (3\hat{\mathbf{i}} + 2\hat{\mathbf{j}} + 2\hat{\mathbf{k}}) - (\hat{\mathbf{i}} + 2\hat{\mathbf{j}} - 2\hat{\mathbf{k}}) = 2\hat{\mathbf{i}} + 4\hat{\mathbf{k}}$$

$$\text{Now,} \quad (\mathbf{a} + \mathbf{b}) \times (\mathbf{a} - \mathbf{b}) = \begin{vmatrix} \hat{\mathbf{i}} & \hat{\mathbf{j}} & \hat{\mathbf{k}} \\ 4 & 4 & 0 \\ 2 & 0 & 4 \end{vmatrix}$$

$$= \hat{\mathbf{i}}(16 - 0) - \hat{\mathbf{j}}(16 - 0) + \hat{\mathbf{k}}(0 - 8) = 16\hat{\mathbf{i}} - 16\hat{\mathbf{j}} - 8\hat{\mathbf{k}}$$

$$\Rightarrow \quad |(\mathbf{a} + \mathbf{b}) \times (\mathbf{a} - \mathbf{b})| = \sqrt{(16)^2 + (-16)^2 + (-8)^2}$$

$$= \sqrt{256 + 256 + 64} = \sqrt{576} = 24$$

$\therefore$ A unit vector, perpendicular to both $(\mathbf{a}+\mathbf{b})$ and $(\mathbf{a}-\mathbf{b})$

$$= \pm \frac{(\mathbf{a}+\mathbf{b})\times(\mathbf{a}-\mathbf{b})}{|(\mathbf{a}+\mathbf{b})\times(\mathbf{a}-\mathbf{b})|} = \pm \frac{16\hat{\mathbf{i}} - 16\hat{\mathbf{j}} - 8\hat{\mathbf{k}}}{24}$$

$$= \pm \frac{8(2\hat{\mathbf{i}} - 2\hat{\mathbf{j}} - \hat{\mathbf{k}})}{24} = \pm \frac{1}{3}(2\hat{\mathbf{i}} - 2\hat{\mathbf{j}} - \hat{\mathbf{k}})$$

$\therefore$ Required vector is either $\frac{2}{3}\hat{\mathbf{i}} - \frac{2}{3}\hat{\mathbf{j}} - \frac{1}{3}\hat{\mathbf{k}}$ or $-\frac{2}{3}\hat{\mathbf{i}} + \frac{2}{3}\hat{\mathbf{j}} + \frac{1}{3}\hat{\mathbf{k}}$.

Question 3 If a unit vector $\hat{\mathbf{a}}$, makes angles $\frac{\pi}{3}$ with $\hat{\mathbf{i}}$, $\frac{\pi}{4}$ with $\hat{\mathbf{j}}$ and an acute angle θ with $\hat{\mathbf{k}}$, then find θ and hence the components of $\mathbf{a}$.

◎ *Thinking Process* Suppose, a vector makes angles α, β and γ with $\hat{\mathbf{i}}$, $\hat{\mathbf{j}}$ and $\hat{\mathbf{k}}$ respectively, then use the relation $\cos^2\alpha + \cos^2\beta + \cos^2\gamma = 1$.

Sol. Let unit vector makes angle α, β and γ with $\hat{\mathbf{i}}$, $\hat{\mathbf{j}}$ and $\hat{\mathbf{k}}$ respectively, then

$$\alpha = \frac{\pi}{3}, \beta = \frac{\pi}{4} \text{ and } \gamma = \theta \qquad \text{(Given)}$$

$\therefore \quad \cos^2\frac{\pi}{3} + \cos^2\frac{\pi}{4} + \cos^2\theta = 1 \Rightarrow \left(\frac{1}{2}\right)^2 + \left(\frac{1}{\sqrt{2}}\right)^2 + \cos^2\theta = 1$

$\Rightarrow \quad \frac{1}{4} + \frac{1}{2} + \cos^2\theta = 1 \Rightarrow \cos^2\theta = 1 - \frac{3}{4} \Rightarrow \cos^2\theta = \frac{4-3}{4} = \frac{1}{4}$

$\Rightarrow \quad \cos\theta = \pm\frac{1}{\sqrt{4}} \Rightarrow \cos\theta = \pm\frac{1}{2}$

$\Rightarrow \quad \cos\theta = \frac{1}{2} \qquad \left[\cos\theta \neq -\frac{1}{2}, \because \theta \text{ is an acute angle}\right]$

$\Rightarrow \quad \theta = \cos^{-1}\left(\frac{1}{2}\right) = \cos^{-1}\left(\cos\frac{\pi}{3}\right)$

$\Rightarrow \quad \theta = \frac{\pi}{3}$ and components of $\mathbf{a} = \cos\frac{\pi}{3}, \cos\frac{\pi}{4}, \cos\frac{\pi}{3}. = \frac{1}{2}, \frac{1}{\sqrt{2}}, \frac{1}{2}$.

Note For acute angle, $\cos\theta > 0$ and for obtuse angle $\cos\theta < 0$.

Question 4 Show that $(\mathbf{a}-\mathbf{b})\times(\mathbf{a}+\mathbf{b}) = 2(\mathbf{a}\times\mathbf{b})$.

Sol. Given that $(\mathbf{a}-\mathbf{b})\times(\mathbf{a}+\mathbf{b}) = 2(\mathbf{a}\times\mathbf{b})$.

$$\text{LHS} = (\mathbf{a}-\mathbf{b})\times(\mathbf{a}+\mathbf{b}) = \mathbf{a}\times\mathbf{a} + \mathbf{a}\times\mathbf{b} - \mathbf{b}\times\mathbf{a} - \mathbf{b}\times\mathbf{b}$$
$$= \mathbf{0} + \mathbf{a}\times\mathbf{b} + \mathbf{a}\times\mathbf{b} - \mathbf{0} \qquad [\because \mathbf{a}\times\mathbf{a} = \mathbf{0} \text{ and } \mathbf{a}\times\mathbf{b} = -\mathbf{b}\times\mathbf{a}]$$
$$= 2(\mathbf{a}\times\mathbf{b}) = \text{RHS}$$

Hence Proved.

Question 5 Find λ and μ, if $(2\hat{\mathbf{i}} + 6\hat{\mathbf{j}} + 27\hat{\mathbf{k}})\times(\hat{\mathbf{i}} + \lambda\hat{\mathbf{j}} + \mu\hat{\mathbf{k}}) = \mathbf{0}$.

Sol. Given, $(2\hat{\mathbf{i}} + 6\hat{\mathbf{j}} + 27\hat{\mathbf{k}})\times(\hat{\mathbf{i}} + \lambda\hat{\mathbf{j}} + \mu\hat{\mathbf{k}}) = \mathbf{0}$

$$\Rightarrow \begin{vmatrix} \hat{\mathbf{i}} & \hat{\mathbf{j}} & \hat{\mathbf{k}} \\ 2 & 6 & 27 \\ 1 & \lambda & \mu \end{vmatrix} = \mathbf{0} \Rightarrow \hat{\mathbf{i}}(6\mu - 27\lambda) - \hat{\mathbf{j}}(2\mu - 27) + \hat{\mathbf{k}}(2\lambda - 6) = 0\hat{\mathbf{i}} + 0\hat{\mathbf{j}} + 0\hat{\mathbf{k}}$$

On comparing the corresponding components, we get

$$6\mu - 27\lambda = 0, -2\mu + 27 = 0, 2\lambda - 6 = 0 \Rightarrow 2\mu = 9\lambda, \mu = \frac{27}{2} \text{ and } \lambda = 3$$

Hence, $\lambda = 3$ and $\mu = \frac{27}{2}$

Question 6 Given that $\mathbf{a} \cdot \mathbf{b} = 0$ and $\mathbf{a} \times \mathbf{b} = 0$. What can you conclude about the vectors $\mathbf{a}$ and $\mathbf{b}$?

Sol. Given that $\mathbf{a} \cdot \mathbf{b} = 0$ and $\mathbf{a} \times \mathbf{b} = 0$

If $\mathbf{a} \cdot \mathbf{b} = 0$, then either $|\mathbf{a}| = 0$ or $|\mathbf{b}| = 0$ or $\mathbf{a} \perp \mathbf{b}$ (in case $\mathbf{a}$ and $\mathbf{b}$ are non-zero) and if $\mathbf{a} \times \mathbf{b} = 0$ then either $|\mathbf{a}| = 0$ or $|\mathbf{b}| = 0$ or $\mathbf{a} \parallel \mathbf{b}$ (in case $\mathbf{a}$ and $\mathbf{b}$ are non-zero)

But $\mathbf{a}$ and $\mathbf{b}$ cannot be perpendicular and parallel simultaneously.

Hence, $|\mathbf{a}| = 0$ or $|\mathbf{b}| = 0$

Question 7 Let the vectors $\mathbf{a}, \mathbf{b}, \mathbf{c}$ be given as $a_1 \hat{\mathbf{i}} + a_2 \hat{\mathbf{j}} + a_3 \hat{\mathbf{k}}$, $b_1 \hat{\mathbf{i}} + b_2 \hat{\mathbf{j}} + b_3 \hat{\mathbf{k}}$, $c_1 \hat{\mathbf{i}} + c_2 \hat{\mathbf{j}} + c_3 \hat{\mathbf{k}}$, then show that

$$\mathbf{a} \times (\mathbf{b} + \mathbf{c}) = \mathbf{a} \times \mathbf{b} + \mathbf{a} \times \mathbf{c}.$$

Sol. We have $\mathbf{a} = a_1\hat{\mathbf{i}} + a_2\hat{\mathbf{j}} + a_3\hat{\mathbf{k}}$,

$$\mathbf{b} = b_1\hat{\mathbf{i}} + b_2\hat{\mathbf{j}} + b_3\hat{\mathbf{k}} \text{ and } \mathbf{c} = c_1\hat{\mathbf{i}} + c_2\hat{\mathbf{j}} + c_3\hat{\mathbf{k}}$$

$$\mathbf{b} + \mathbf{c} = (b_1 + c_1)\hat{\mathbf{i}} + (b_2 + c_2)\mathbf{j} + (b_3 + c_3)\mathbf{k}$$

Now, $\mathbf{a} \times (\mathbf{b} + \mathbf{c}) = \begin{vmatrix} \hat{\mathbf{i}} & \hat{\mathbf{j}} & \hat{\mathbf{k}} \\ a_1 & a_2 & a_3 \\ b_1 + c_1 & b_2 + c_2 & b_3 + c_3 \end{vmatrix}$

$$= \hat{\mathbf{i}}\,[(b_3 + c_3)a_2 - (b_2 + c_2)a_3] - \hat{\mathbf{j}}\,[a_1(b_3 + c_3) - a_3(b_1 + c_1)] + \hat{\mathbf{k}}\,[a_1(b_2 + c_2) - a_2(b_1 + c_1)]$$

$$= \hat{\mathbf{i}}\,[a_2b_3 + a_2c_3 - a_3b_2 - a_3c_2] + \hat{\mathbf{j}}\,[a_3b_1 + a_3c_1 - a_1b_3 - a_1c_3] + \hat{\mathbf{k}}\,[a_1b_2 + a_1c_2 - a_2b_1 - a_2c_1]$$

$$\mathbf{a} \times \mathbf{b} = \begin{vmatrix} \hat{\mathbf{i}} & \hat{\mathbf{j}} & \hat{\mathbf{k}} \\ a_1 & a_2 & a_3 \\ b_1 & b_2 & b_3 \end{vmatrix} = \hat{\mathbf{i}}(a_2b_3 - a_3b_2) - \hat{\mathbf{j}}(a_1b_3 - a_3b_1) + \hat{\mathbf{k}}(a_1b_2 - a_2b_1)$$

$$= \hat{\mathbf{i}}(a_2b_3 - a_3b_2) + \hat{\mathbf{j}}(a_3b_1 - a_1b_3) + \hat{\mathbf{k}}(a_1b_2 - a_2b_1)$$

$$\mathbf{a} \times \mathbf{c} = \begin{vmatrix} \hat{\mathbf{i}} & \hat{\mathbf{j}} & \hat{\mathbf{k}} \\ a_1 & a_2 & a_3 \\ c_1 & c_2 & c_3 \end{vmatrix}$$

$$= \hat{\mathbf{i}}\,(a_2c_3 - a_3c_2) - \hat{\mathbf{j}}\,(a_1c_3 - a_3c_1) + \hat{\mathbf{k}}(a_1c_2 - a_2c_1)$$

$$= \hat{\mathbf{i}}\,(a_2c_3 - a_3c_2) + \hat{\mathbf{j}}\,(a_3c_1 - a_1c_3) + \hat{\mathbf{k}}(a_1c_2 - a_2c_1)$$

Now, $\mathbf{a} \times \mathbf{b} + \mathbf{a} \times \mathbf{c}$

$$= \hat{\mathbf{i}}\,(a_2b_3 - a_3b_2 + a_2c_3 - a_3c_2) + \hat{\mathbf{j}}\,(a_3b_1 - a_1b_3 + a_3c_1 - a_1c_3) + \mathbf{k}\,(a_1b_2 - a_2b_1 + a_1c_2 - a_2c_1)$$

$= \hat{\mathbf{i}}\,(a_2b_3 + a_2c_3 - a_3b_2 - a_3c_2) + \hat{\mathbf{j}}\,(a_3b_1 + a_3c_1 - a_1b_3 - a_1c_3) +$
$+ \hat{\mathbf{k}}\,(a_1b_2 + a_1c_2 - a_2b_1 - a_2c_1)$

$= a \times (b + a)$ **Hence, Proved.**

Question 8 If either $\mathbf{a} = \mathbf{0}$ or $\mathbf{b} = \mathbf{0}$, then $\mathbf{a} \times \mathbf{b} = \mathbf{0}$. Is the converse true? Justify your answer with an example.

Sol. If $\mathbf{a} = \mathbf{0}$ or $\mathbf{b} = \mathbf{0}$, then surely $\mathbf{a} \times \mathbf{b} = \mathbf{0}$.

However, the converse is not true *i.e.*, if $\mathbf{a} \times \mathbf{b} = \mathbf{0}$, then $\mathbf{a} = \mathbf{0}$ or $\mathbf{b} = \mathbf{0}$ may not hold. (**a** may be parallel to **b**).

We know $\mathbf{a} \times \mathbf{b} = ab\sin\theta$, if **a** and **b** are parallel, then $\theta = 0°$ and $\sin 0 = 0$.

$\therefore \qquad \mathbf{a} \times \mathbf{b} = \mathbf{0}$

As an example, consider the vectors $\mathbf{a} = \hat{\mathbf{i}}$, $\mathbf{b} = \hat{\mathbf{i}}$, then $\mathbf{a} \neq \mathbf{0}$ and also $\mathbf{b} \neq \mathbf{0}$ But $\mathbf{a} \times \mathbf{b} = \hat{\mathbf{i}} \times \hat{\mathbf{i}} = 0$

Another example

Let $\qquad \mathbf{a} = \hat{\mathbf{i}} + \hat{\mathbf{j}} + \hat{\mathbf{k}}$ and $\mathbf{b} = 4\hat{\mathbf{i}} + 4\hat{\mathbf{j}} + 4\hat{\mathbf{k}}$

Now, $\qquad \mathbf{a} \times \mathbf{b} = \begin{vmatrix} \hat{\mathbf{i}} & \hat{\mathbf{j}} & \hat{\mathbf{k}} \\ 1 & 1 & 1 \\ 4 & 4 & 4 \end{vmatrix} = (4-4)\hat{\mathbf{i}} - (4-4)\hat{\mathbf{j}} + (4-4)\hat{\mathbf{k}} = 0$

Thus, $\mathbf{a} \times \mathbf{b} = 0$ when $\mathbf{a} \neq \mathbf{0}$ and $\mathbf{b} \neq \mathbf{0}$

Note If $\mathbf{a} \times \mathbf{b} = 0$, then it is not necessary that either $\mathbf{a} = \mathbf{0}$ or $\mathbf{b} = 0$

Question 9 Find the area of the triangle with vertices $A(1, 1, 2)$, $B(2, 3, 5)$ and $C(1, 5, 5)$.

Thinking Process To determine the area of triangle, use formula $\Delta = \frac{1}{2}|\mathbf{AB} \times \mathbf{AC}|$.

Sol. The vertices of triangle ABC are given as $A(1, 1, 2)$, $B(2, 3, 5)$ and $C(1, 5, 5)$.

Now, $\qquad \mathbf{AB} = \text{PV of } B - \text{PV of } A = (2\hat{\mathbf{i}} + 3\hat{\mathbf{j}} + 5\hat{\mathbf{k}}) - (\hat{\mathbf{i}} + \hat{\mathbf{j}} + 2\hat{\mathbf{k}})$

$= (2-1)\hat{\mathbf{i}} + (3-1)\hat{\mathbf{j}} + (5-2)\hat{\mathbf{k}} = \hat{\mathbf{i}} + 2\hat{\mathbf{j}} + 3\hat{\mathbf{k}}$

and $\qquad \mathbf{AC} = \text{PV of } C - \text{PV of } A$

$= (\hat{\mathbf{i}} + 5\hat{\mathbf{j}} + 5\hat{\mathbf{k}}) - (\hat{\mathbf{i}} + \hat{\mathbf{j}} + 2\hat{\mathbf{k}})$

$= (1-1)\hat{\mathbf{i}} + (5-1)\hat{\mathbf{j}} + (5-2)\hat{\mathbf{k}} = 4\hat{\mathbf{j}} + 3\hat{\mathbf{k}}$

$\therefore \qquad \mathbf{AB} \times \mathbf{AC} = \begin{vmatrix} \hat{\mathbf{i}} & \hat{\mathbf{j}} & \hat{\mathbf{k}} \\ 1 & 2 & 3 \\ 0 & 4 & 3 \end{vmatrix} = \hat{\mathbf{i}}(6-12) - \hat{\mathbf{j}}(3-0) + \hat{\mathbf{k}}(4-0) = -6\hat{\mathbf{i}} - 3\hat{\mathbf{j}} + 4\hat{\mathbf{k}}$

Comparing with $\mathbf{X} = x\hat{\mathbf{i}} + y\hat{\mathbf{j}} + z\hat{\mathbf{k}}$, we get $x = -6$, $y = -3$, $z = 4$

$\therefore \qquad |\mathbf{AB} \times \mathbf{AC}| = \sqrt{x^2 + y^2 + z^2} = \sqrt{(-6)^2 + (-3)^2 + (4)^2}$

$= \sqrt{36 + 9 + 16} = \sqrt{61}$

Area of $\Delta ABC = \frac{1}{2}|\mathbf{AB} \times \mathbf{AC}| = \frac{1}{2} \times \sqrt{61} = \frac{\sqrt{61}}{2}$ sq unit.

Hence, the area of ΔABC is $\frac{\sqrt{61}}{2}$ sq unit.

Question 10 Find the area of the parallelogram whose adjacent sides are determined by the vectors $\mathbf{a} = \hat{\mathbf{i}} - \hat{\mathbf{j}} + 3\hat{\mathbf{k}}$ and $\mathbf{b} = 2\hat{\mathbf{i}} - 7\hat{\mathbf{j}} + \hat{\mathbf{k}}$.

Thinking Process To determine the area of parallelogram, use the formula, $|\mathbf{a} \times \mathbf{b}|$.

Sol. We know that the area of the parallelogram whose adjacent sides are **a** and **b** is $|\mathbf{a} \times \mathbf{b}|$.

Given, $\mathbf{a} = \hat{\mathbf{i}} - \hat{\mathbf{j}} + 3\hat{\mathbf{k}}$ and $\mathbf{b} = 2\hat{\mathbf{i}} - 7\hat{\mathbf{j}} + \hat{\mathbf{k}}$ are the adjacent sides of the parallelogram.

$$\therefore \quad \mathbf{a} \times \mathbf{b} = \begin{vmatrix} \hat{\mathbf{i}} & \hat{\mathbf{j}} & \hat{\mathbf{k}} \\ 1 & -1 & 3 \\ 2 & -7 & 1 \end{vmatrix} = \hat{\mathbf{i}}(-1+21) - \hat{\mathbf{j}}(1-6) + \hat{\mathbf{k}}(-7+2) = 20\hat{\mathbf{i}} + 5\hat{\mathbf{j}} - 5\hat{\mathbf{k}}$$

Comparing with $\mathbf{X} = x\hat{\mathbf{i}} + y\hat{\mathbf{j}} + z\hat{\mathbf{k}}$, we get $x = 20, y = 5, z = -5$

$$\therefore \quad |\mathbf{a} \times \mathbf{b}| = \sqrt{x^2 + y^2 + z^2} = \sqrt{(20)^2 + 5^2 + (-5)^2} = \sqrt{450} = \sqrt{225 \times 2}$$

$$= 15\sqrt{2}$$

Hence, the area of the given parallelogram is $15\sqrt{2}$ sq unit.

Question 11 Let the vectors **a** and **b** be such that $|\mathbf{a}| = 3$ and $|\mathbf{b}| = \frac{\sqrt{2}}{3}$, then $\mathbf{a} \times \mathbf{b}$ is a unit vector, if the angle between **a** and **b** is

(a) $\frac{\pi}{6}$ (b) $\frac{\pi}{4}$ (c) $\frac{\pi}{3}$ (d) $\frac{\pi}{2}$

Sol. (b) Given, $|\mathbf{a}| = 3$ and $|\mathbf{b}| = \frac{\sqrt{2}}{3}$.

Let θ be the angle between **a** and **b**.

Also, given $|\mathbf{a} \times \mathbf{b}| = 1$

$$\Rightarrow \quad |\mathbf{a}||\mathbf{b}|\sin\theta = 1 \Rightarrow 3 \times \frac{\sqrt{2}}{3} \times \sin\theta = 1 \quad \Rightarrow \quad \sin\theta = \frac{1}{\sqrt{2}} \Rightarrow \theta = \frac{\pi}{4}$$

Hence, $\mathbf{a} \times \mathbf{b}$ is a unit vector, if the angle between **a** and **b** is $\frac{\pi}{4}$.

Question 12 Area of a rectangle having vertices $A\left(-\hat{\mathbf{i}}+\frac{1}{2}\hat{\mathbf{j}}+4\hat{\mathbf{k}}\right)$, $B\left(\hat{\mathbf{i}}+\frac{1}{2}\hat{\mathbf{j}}+4\hat{\mathbf{k}}\right)$, $C\left(\hat{\mathbf{i}}-\frac{1}{2}\hat{\mathbf{j}}+4\hat{\mathbf{k}}\right)$ and $D\left(-\hat{\mathbf{i}}-\frac{1}{2}\hat{\mathbf{j}}+4\hat{\mathbf{k}}\right)$ is

(a) $\frac{1}{2}$ (b) 1 (c) 2 (d) 4

◎ *Thinking Process* To determine the area of rectangle, use the relation that if **a** and **b** are the adjacent sides of a parallelogram, then area of parallelogram $= |\mathbf{a}\times\mathbf{b}|$.

Sol. (c) The position vectors of vertices A, B, C and D of rectangle $ABCD$ are

$$A\left(-\hat{\mathbf{i}}+\frac{1}{2}\hat{\mathbf{j}}+4\hat{\mathbf{k}}\right), B\left(\hat{\mathbf{i}}+\frac{1}{2}\hat{\mathbf{j}}+4\hat{\mathbf{k}}\right), C\left(\hat{\mathbf{i}}-\frac{1}{2}\hat{\mathbf{j}}+4\hat{\mathbf{k}}\right) \text{ and } D\left(-\hat{\mathbf{i}}-\frac{1}{2}\hat{\mathbf{j}}+4\hat{\mathbf{k}}\right)$$

Now, $\mathbf{AB} = \text{PV of } B - \text{PV of } A = \left(\hat{\mathbf{i}}+\frac{1}{2}\hat{\mathbf{j}}+4\hat{\mathbf{k}}\right)-\left(-\hat{\mathbf{i}}+\frac{1}{2}\hat{\mathbf{j}}+4\hat{\mathbf{k}}\right)$

$$=[1-(-1)]\hat{\mathbf{i}}+\left(\frac{1}{2}-\frac{1}{2}\right)\hat{\mathbf{j}}+(4-4)\hat{\mathbf{k}}=2\hat{\mathbf{i}}$$

and $\mathbf{AD} = \text{PV of } D - \text{PV of } A = \left(-\hat{\mathbf{i}}-\frac{1}{2}\hat{\mathbf{j}}+4\hat{\mathbf{k}}\right)-\left(-\hat{\mathbf{i}}+\frac{1}{2}\hat{\mathbf{j}}+4\hat{\mathbf{k}}\right)$

$$=[-1-(-1)]\hat{\mathbf{i}}+\left(-\frac{1}{2}-\frac{1}{2}\right)\hat{\mathbf{j}}+(4-4)\hat{\mathbf{k}}=-\hat{\mathbf{j}}$$

$$\therefore \quad \mathbf{AB}\times\mathbf{AD}=\begin{vmatrix}\hat{\mathbf{i}} & \hat{\mathbf{j}} & \hat{\mathbf{k}}\\ 2 & 0 & 0\\ 0 & -1 & 0\end{vmatrix}=-2\hat{\mathbf{k}}$$

Area of rectangle $ABCD = |\mathbf{AB}\times\mathbf{AD}| = \sqrt{(-2)^2} = 2$ sq unit

Hence, the area of the rectangle is 2 sq. unit

Note If **a** and **b** are the adjacent sides of a parallelogram, then area $= |\mathbf{a}\times\mathbf{b}|$. If **a** and **b** are the diagonals of a parallelogram, then area $=\frac{1}{2}|\mathbf{a}\times\mathbf{b}|$

Miscellaneous Exercise

Question 1 Write down a unit vector in XY-plane, making an angle of 30° with the positive direction of X-axis.

Sol. Let **OP** make 30° with X-axis, 60° with Y-axis and 90° with Z-axis and it lies in XY-plane.

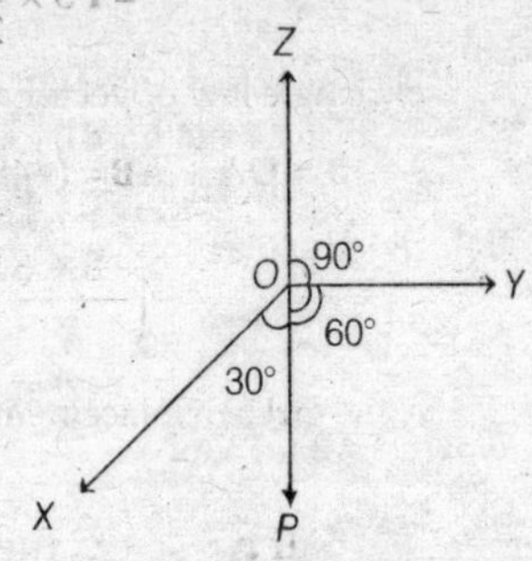

$\therefore$ Direction cosines of **OP** are $\cos 30°, \cos 60°$ and $\cos 90°$ *i.e.,* $\frac{\sqrt{3}}{2}, \frac{1}{2}, 0$. Thus, **OP** is $\frac{\sqrt{3}}{2}\hat{\mathbf{i}} + \frac{1}{2}\hat{\mathbf{j}}$,

$$|\mathbf{OP}| = \sqrt{\left(\frac{\sqrt{3}}{2}\right)^2 + \left(\frac{1}{2}\right)^2}$$

$$= \sqrt{\frac{3}{4} + \frac{1}{4}} = \sqrt{1} = 1$$

which is required unit vector in XY-plane.

Question 2 Find the scalar components and magnitude of the vector joining the points $P(x_1, y_1, z_1)$ and $Q(x_2, y_2, z_2)$.

Sol. The vector joining the points $P(x_1, y_1, z_1)$ and $Q(x_2, y_2, z_2)$ can be obtained by,

$$\mathbf{PQ} = \text{PV of } Q - \text{PV of } P = (x_2\hat{\mathbf{i}} + y_2\hat{\mathbf{j}} + z_2\hat{\mathbf{k}}) - (x_1\hat{\mathbf{i}} + y_1\hat{\mathbf{j}} + z_1\hat{\mathbf{k}})$$
$$= (x_2 - x_1)\hat{\mathbf{i}} + (y_2 - y_1)\hat{\mathbf{j}} + (z_2 - z_1)\hat{\mathbf{k}}$$

$\therefore$ Scalar components of **PQ** are $x_2 - x_1, y_2 - y_1, z_2 - z_1$.

$\therefore$ Magnitude of $|\mathbf{PQ}| = \sqrt{(x_2 - x_1)^2 + (y_2 - y_1)^2 + (z_2 - z_1)^2}$

Question 3 A girl walks 4 km towards west, then she walks 3 km in a direction 30° east of north and stops. Determine the girl's displacement from her initial point of departure.

Sol. Let O and B be the initial and final positions of the girl, respectively.

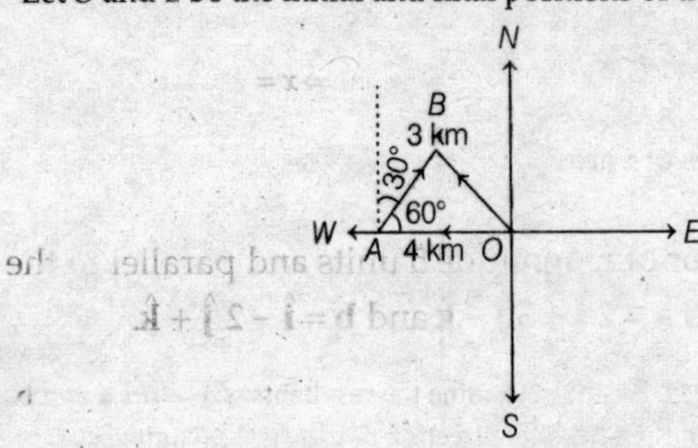

Then, the girl's position can be shown as in the figure. Now, we have $\mathbf{OA} = -4\hat{\mathbf{i}}$

$$\mathbf{AB} = \hat{\mathbf{i}}|\mathbf{AB}|\cos 60^\circ + \hat{\mathbf{j}}|\mathbf{AB}|\sin 60^\circ$$

($AB\cos 60^\circ$ is component of **AB**, along X-axis and $AB\sin 60^\circ$ is component of **AB** = along Y-axis)

$$= \hat{\mathbf{i}}\, 3 \times \frac{1}{2} + \hat{\mathbf{j}} 3 \times \frac{\sqrt{3}}{2} = \frac{3}{2}\hat{\mathbf{i}} + \frac{3\sqrt{3}}{2}\hat{\mathbf{j}}$$

By the triangle law of vector addition, we have

$$\mathbf{OB} = \mathbf{OA} + \mathbf{AB} = (-4\hat{\mathbf{i}}) + \left(\frac{3}{2}\hat{\mathbf{i}} + \frac{3\sqrt{3}}{2}\hat{\mathbf{j}}\right) = \left(-4 + \frac{3}{2}\right)\hat{\mathbf{i}} + \frac{3\sqrt{3}}{2}\hat{\mathbf{j}}$$

$$= \left(\frac{-8+3}{2}\right)\hat{\mathbf{i}} + \frac{3\sqrt{3}}{2}\hat{\mathbf{j}} = \frac{-5}{2}\hat{\mathbf{i}} + \frac{3\sqrt{3}}{2}\hat{\mathbf{j}}$$

Hence, the girl's displacement from her initial point of departure is $\frac{-5}{2}\hat{\mathbf{i}} + \frac{3\sqrt{3}}{2}\hat{\mathbf{j}}$

Question 4 If $\mathbf{a} = \mathbf{b} + \mathbf{c}$, then is it true that $|\mathbf{a}| = |\mathbf{b}| + |\mathbf{c}|$? Justify your answer.

Sol. In triangle ABC, let $\mathbf{CB} = \mathbf{a}$, $\mathbf{CA} = \mathbf{b}$ and $\mathbf{AB} = \mathbf{c}$

(as shown in the following figure)

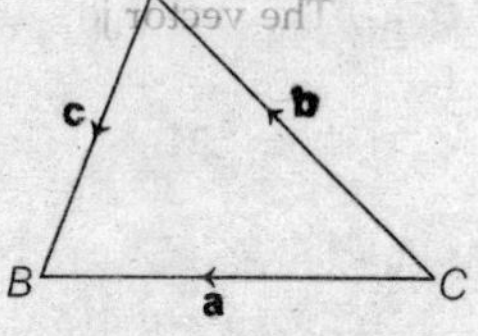

Now, by the triangle law of vector addition, we have $\mathbf{a} = \mathbf{b} + \mathbf{c}$

It is clearly known that $|\mathbf{a}|$, $|\mathbf{b}|$ and $|\mathbf{c}|$ represent the side of $\Delta\, ABC$.

Also, it is known that the sum of the lengths of any two sides of a triangle is greater than the third side.

$$\therefore \qquad |\mathbf{a}| < |\mathbf{b}| + |\mathbf{c}|$$

Hence, it is not true that $|\mathbf{a}| = |\mathbf{b}| + |\mathbf{c}|$.

Question 5 Find the value of x for which $x(\hat{\mathbf{i}} + \hat{\mathbf{j}} + \hat{\mathbf{k}})$ is a unit vector.

Sol. Given, $x(\hat{\mathbf{i}} + \hat{\mathbf{j}} + \hat{\mathbf{k}})$ is a unit vector, therefore $|x(\hat{\mathbf{i}} + \hat{\mathbf{j}} + \hat{\mathbf{k}})| = 1$

$$\Rightarrow \qquad |x\hat{\mathbf{i}} + x\hat{\mathbf{j}} + x\hat{\mathbf{k}}| = 1 \Rightarrow \sqrt{x^2 + x^2 + x^2} = 1$$

$$\Rightarrow \qquad \sqrt{3x^2} = 1 \Rightarrow \pm\sqrt{3}x = 1 \Rightarrow x = \pm\frac{1}{\sqrt{3}}$$

Hence, the required values of x are $\pm\frac{1}{\sqrt{3}}$.

Question 6 Find a vector of magnitude 5 units and parallel to the resultant of the vectors $\mathbf{a} = 2\hat{\mathbf{i}} + 3\hat{\mathbf{j}} - \hat{\mathbf{k}}$ and $\mathbf{b} = \hat{\mathbf{i}} - 2\hat{\mathbf{j}} + \hat{\mathbf{k}}$.

Thinking Process Firstly, determine the resultants of vectors **a** and **b**, vector $\mathbf{c} = \mathbf{a} + \mathbf{b}$ and then find the direction of **c** by finding unit vector in that direction and then multiplying it by $\pm$ 5, we can find the required vector.

Sol. Given, vectors $\mathbf{a} = 2\hat{i} + 3\hat{j} - \hat{k}$ and $\mathbf{b} = \hat{i} - 2\hat{j} + \hat{k}$

Let $\vec{c}$ be the resultant of **a** and **b**.

$\therefore \quad \mathbf{c} = \mathbf{a} + \mathbf{b} = (2\hat{i} + 3\hat{j} - \hat{k}) + (\hat{i} - 2\hat{j} + \hat{k}) \Rightarrow \mathbf{c} = 3\hat{i} + \hat{j} + 0\hat{k}$

On comparing with $\mathbf{X} = x\hat{i} + y\hat{j} + z\hat{k}$, we get

$$x = 3, y = 1 \text{ and } z = 0$$

$\therefore \quad |\mathbf{c}| = \sqrt{x^2 + y^2 + z^2} = \sqrt{3^2 + 1^2} = \sqrt{9 + 1} = \sqrt{10}$

$\therefore$ Unit vector in the direction of **c**, $\hat{\mathbf{c}} = \dfrac{\mathbf{c}}{|\mathbf{c}|} = \dfrac{3\hat{i} + \hat{j}}{\sqrt{10}}$

Hence, the vector of magnitude 5 units and parallel to the resultant of vectors **a** and **b** is $\pm 5\hat{\mathbf{c}} = \pm 5 \dfrac{1}{\sqrt{10}}(3\hat{i} + \hat{j}) = \pm \dfrac{3\sqrt{10}}{2}\hat{i} \pm \dfrac{\sqrt{10}}{2}\hat{j}$

Question 7 If $\mathbf{a} = \hat{i} + \hat{j} + \hat{k}$, $\mathbf{b} = 2\hat{i} - \hat{j} + 3\hat{k}$ and $\mathbf{c} = \hat{i} - 2\hat{j} + \hat{k}$ find a unit vector parallel to the vector $2\mathbf{a} - \mathbf{b} + 3\mathbf{c}$.

Sol. Given, $\mathbf{a} = \hat{i} + \hat{j} + \hat{k}$, $\mathbf{b} = 2\hat{i} - \hat{j} + 3\hat{k}$ and $\mathbf{c} = \hat{i} - 2\hat{j} + \hat{k}$

Let $\mathbf{v} = 2\mathbf{a} - \mathbf{b} + 3\mathbf{c} = 2(\hat{i} + \hat{j} + \hat{k}) - (2\hat{i} - \hat{j} + 3\hat{k}) + 3(\hat{i} - 2\hat{j} + \hat{k}) = 3\hat{i} - 3\hat{j} + 2\hat{k}$

Now, $\quad |\mathbf{v}| = |3\hat{i} - 3\hat{j} + 2\hat{k}| = \sqrt{3^2 + (-3)^2 + 2^2} = \sqrt{22}$

Hence, the unit vector along **v** is

$$\hat{\mathbf{v}} = \frac{\mathbf{v}}{|\mathbf{v}|} = \frac{3\hat{i} - 3\hat{j} + 2\hat{k}}{\sqrt{22}} = \left(\frac{3}{\sqrt{22}}\hat{i} - \frac{3}{\sqrt{22}}\hat{j} + \frac{2}{\sqrt{22}}\hat{k}\right)$$

Question 8. Show that the points $A(1, -2, -8)$, $B(5, 0, -2)$ and $C(11, 3, 7)$ are collinear and find the ratio in which B divides AC.

◎ *Thinking Process* Three vectors **A**, **B** and **C** are collinear iff $|\mathbf{AC}| = |\mathbf{AB}| + |\mathbf{BC}|$

Sol. The given points are $A(1, -2, -8)$, $B(5, 0, -2)$ and $C(11, 3, 7)$.

$$\mathbf{AB} = \text{PV of } B - \text{PV of } A = (5\hat{i} + 0\hat{j} - 2\hat{k}) - (\hat{i} - 2\hat{j} - 8\hat{k})$$
$$= (5 - 1)\hat{i} + (0 + 2)\hat{j} + (-2 + 8)\hat{k} = 4\hat{i} + 2\hat{j} + 6\hat{k}$$
$$|\mathbf{AB}| = \sqrt{4^2 + 2^2 + 6^2} = \sqrt{16 + 4 + 36} = \sqrt{56} = 2\sqrt{14}$$
$$\mathbf{BC} = \text{PV of } C - \text{PV of } B = (11\hat{i} + 3\hat{j} + 7\hat{k}) - (5\hat{i} + 0\hat{j} - 2\hat{k})$$
$$= (11 - 5)\hat{i} + (3 - 0)\hat{j} + (7 + 2)\hat{k} = 6\hat{i} + 3\hat{j} + 9\hat{k}$$
$$|\mathbf{BC}| = \sqrt{6^2 + 3^2 + 9^2} = \sqrt{36 + 9 + 81} = \sqrt{126} = 3\sqrt{14}$$
$$\mathbf{AC} = \text{PV of } C - \text{PV of } A = (11\hat{i} + 3\hat{j} + 7\hat{k}) - (\hat{i} - 2\hat{j} - 8\hat{k})$$
$$= (11 - 1)\hat{i} + (3 + 2)\hat{j} + (7 + 8)\hat{k} = 10\hat{i} + 5\hat{j} + 15\hat{k}$$
$$|\mathbf{AC}| = \sqrt{10^2 + 5^2 + 15^2} = \sqrt{100 + 25 + 225} = \sqrt{350} = 5\sqrt{14}$$

$\therefore \quad |\mathbf{AC}| = |\mathbf{AB}| + |\mathbf{BC}|$

Thus, the given points A, B and C are collinear.

For finding ratio, we have

A ——— B ——— C

$$|\mathbf{AB}| = 2\sqrt{14}$$
$$|\mathbf{BC}| = 3\sqrt{14}$$

So, we can say that $AB : BC = 2\sqrt{14} : 3\sqrt{14} = 2 : 3$

Question 9 Find the position vector of point R which divides the line joining two points $P(2\mathbf{a} + \mathbf{b})$ and $Q(\mathbf{a} - 3\mathbf{b})$ externally in the ratio 1 : 2. Also, show that P is the middle point of the line segment RQ.

Sol. It is given that $\mathbf{OP} = 2\mathbf{a} + \mathbf{b}, \mathbf{OQ} = \mathbf{a} - 3\mathbf{b}$

If a point divides the line joining point P and Q externally in the ratio $m:n$, then position vector of the point is $\dfrac{m(\text{PV of } Q) - n(\text{PV of } P)}{m-n}$

It is given that point R divides a line segment joining two points P and Q externally in the ratio 1 : 2.

Then, by using the section formula, we get

$$\text{Position vector of point } R = \frac{(\mathbf{a} - 3\mathbf{b}) \times 1 - (2\mathbf{a} + \mathbf{b}) \times 2}{1 - 2}$$
$$= \frac{\mathbf{a} - 3\mathbf{b} - 4\mathbf{a} - 2\mathbf{b}}{-1}$$
$$= \frac{-3\mathbf{a} - 5\mathbf{b}}{-1}$$
$$= 3\mathbf{a} + 5\mathbf{b}$$

$$\text{Now, position vector of mid-point of } RQ = \frac{\mathbf{OR} + \mathbf{OQ}}{2}$$
$$= \frac{(3\mathbf{a} + 5\mathbf{b}) + (\mathbf{a} - 3\mathbf{b})}{2}$$
$$= \frac{4\mathbf{a} + 2\mathbf{b}}{2}$$
$$= 2\mathbf{a} + \mathbf{b}$$

Also, the position vector of point $P = 2\mathbf{a} + \mathbf{b}$

which shows that P is mid-point of line segment RQ.

Question 10 The two adjacent sides of a parallelogram are $2\hat{\mathbf{i}} - 4\hat{\mathbf{j}} + 5\hat{\mathbf{k}}$ and $\hat{\mathbf{i}} - 2\hat{\mathbf{j}} - 3\hat{\mathbf{k}}$. Find the unit vector parallel to its diagonal. Also, find its area.

Sol. Let the adjacent sides of a parallelogram are $\mathbf{a} = 2\hat{\mathbf{i}} - 4\hat{\mathbf{j}} + 5\hat{\mathbf{k}}$ and $\mathbf{b} = \hat{\mathbf{i}} - 2\hat{\mathbf{j}} - 3\hat{\mathbf{k}}$.

There will be diagonals $\mathbf{v} = \mathbf{AC} = \mathbf{a} + \mathbf{b}$ and $\mathbf{u} = \mathbf{DB} = \mathbf{a} - \mathbf{b}$

($\because$ From the figure, it is clear that resultant of adjacent sides of a parallelogram is given by the diagonal)

$\therefore \quad \mathbf{v} = 2\hat{\mathbf{i}} - 4\hat{\mathbf{j}} + 5\hat{\mathbf{k}} + \hat{\mathbf{i}} - 2\hat{\mathbf{j}} - 3\hat{\mathbf{k}} = (2+1)\hat{\mathbf{i}} + (-4-2)\hat{\mathbf{j}} + (5-3)\hat{\mathbf{k}} = 3\hat{\mathbf{i}} - 6\hat{\mathbf{j}} + 2\hat{\mathbf{k}}$

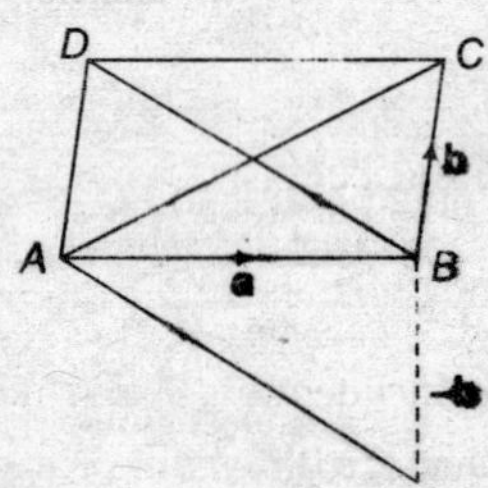

On comparing with $\mathbf{v} = x\hat{\mathbf{i}} + y\hat{\mathbf{j}} + z\hat{\mathbf{k}}$, we get

$$x = 3, y = -6, z = 2$$

$$\therefore \quad |\mathbf{v}| = \sqrt{x^2 + y^2 + z^2}$$

$$= \sqrt{(3)^2 + (-6)^2 + (2)^2}$$

$$= \sqrt{9 + 36 + 4}$$

$$= \sqrt{49} = 7$$

Thus, the unit vector parallel to the diagonal $\mathbf{v}$ is

$$\frac{\mathbf{v}}{|\mathbf{v}|} = \frac{3\hat{\mathbf{i}} - 6\hat{\mathbf{j}} + 2\hat{\mathbf{k}}}{7}$$

$$= \frac{3}{7}\hat{\mathbf{i}} - \frac{6}{7}\hat{\mathbf{j}} + \frac{2}{7}\hat{\mathbf{k}}$$

and $\quad \mathbf{u} = \mathbf{a} - \mathbf{b}$

$$\Rightarrow \quad \mathbf{u} = 2\hat{\mathbf{i}} - 4\hat{\mathbf{j}} + 5\hat{\mathbf{k}} - (\hat{\mathbf{i}} - 2\hat{\mathbf{j}} - 3\hat{\mathbf{k}})$$

$$\Rightarrow \quad \mathbf{u} = (2-1)\hat{\mathbf{i}} + (-4+2)\hat{\mathbf{j}} + (5+3)\hat{\mathbf{k}}$$

$$= \hat{\mathbf{i}} - 2\hat{\mathbf{j}} + 8\hat{\mathbf{k}}$$

On comparing with $\mathbf{Y} = x\hat{\mathbf{i}} + y\hat{\mathbf{j}} + z\hat{\mathbf{k}}$, we get

$$x = 1, y = -2, z = 8$$

$$\therefore \quad |\mathbf{u}| = \sqrt{x^2 + y^2 + z^2}$$

$$= \sqrt{1^2 + (-2)^2 + (8)^2} = \sqrt{69}$$

Thus unit vector parallel to diagonal **u**

$$= \frac{\hat{i} - 2\hat{j} + 8\hat{k}}{\sqrt{69}} = \frac{1}{\sqrt{69}}\hat{i} - \frac{2}{\sqrt{69}}\hat{j} + \frac{8}{\sqrt{69}}\hat{k}$$

Also, area of parallelogram $ABCD$, $|\mathbf{a} \times \mathbf{b}| = \begin{vmatrix} \hat{i} & \hat{j} & \hat{k} \\ 2 & -4 & 5 \\ 1 & -2 & -3 \end{vmatrix}$

$$= |\hat{i}(12 + 10) - \hat{j}(-6 - 5) + \hat{k}(-4 + 4)|$$
$$= |22\hat{i} + 11\hat{j} + 0\hat{k}|$$
$$= \sqrt{(22)^2 + (11)^2 + 0^2} = \sqrt{(11)^2(2^2 + 1^2)} = 11\sqrt{5} \text{ sq. unit}$$

Note If $\mathbf{d}_1$ and $\mathbf{d}_2$ are the diagonals of a parallelogram, then area of parallelogram $= \frac{1}{2}|\mathbf{d}_1 \times \mathbf{d}_2|$

Question 11 Show that the direction cosines of a vector equally inclined to the axes OX, OY and OZ are $\pm\left(\frac{1}{\sqrt{3}}, \frac{1}{\sqrt{3}}, \frac{1}{\sqrt{3}}\right)$

Sol. Let a vector be equally inclined to OX, OY and OZ and let it make an angle α with each of these three, then the direction cosines are $\cos\alpha$, $\cos\alpha$ and $\cos\alpha$.

$\therefore \quad \cos^2\alpha + \cos^2\alpha + \cos^2\alpha = 1 \quad (\because l^2 + m^2 + n^2 = 1)$

$\Rightarrow \quad 3\cos^2\alpha = 1$

$\Rightarrow \quad \cos^2\alpha = \frac{1}{3} \Rightarrow \cos\alpha = \pm\frac{1}{\sqrt{3}}$

Hence, the direction cosines of the vector which is equally inclined to the axes are either $\frac{1}{\sqrt{3}}, \frac{1}{\sqrt{3}}, \frac{1}{\sqrt{3}}$ or $-\frac{1}{\sqrt{3}}, -\frac{1}{\sqrt{3}}, -\frac{1}{\sqrt{3}}$.

Question 12 Let $\mathbf{a} = \hat{i} + 4\hat{j} + 2\hat{k}$, $\mathbf{b} = 3\hat{i} - 2\hat{j} + 7\hat{k}$ and $\mathbf{c} = 2\hat{i} - \hat{j} + 4\hat{k}$. Find a vector **d** which is perpendicular to both **a** and **b** and $\mathbf{c} \cdot \mathbf{d} = 15$.

Sol. The vector which is perpendicular to both **a** and **b** must be parallel to $\mathbf{a} \times \mathbf{b}$.

Now, $\mathbf{a} \times \mathbf{b} = \begin{vmatrix} \hat{i} & \hat{j} & \hat{k} \\ 1 & 4 & 2 \\ 3 & -2 & 7 \end{vmatrix} = \hat{i}(28 + 4) - \hat{j}(7 - 6) + \hat{k}(-2 - 12) = 32\hat{i} - \hat{j} - 14\hat{k}$

Let $\quad \mathbf{d} = \lambda(\mathbf{a} \times \mathbf{b}) = \lambda(32\hat{i} - \hat{j} - 14\hat{k})$

Also, $\quad \mathbf{c} \cdot \mathbf{d} = 15 \Rightarrow (2\hat{i} - \hat{j} + 4\hat{k}) \cdot \lambda(32\hat{i} - \hat{j} - 14\hat{k}) = 15$

$\Rightarrow \quad 2 \times (32\lambda) + (-1) \times (-\lambda) + 4 \times (-14\lambda) = 15$

$\Rightarrow \quad 64\lambda + \lambda - 56\lambda = 15 \Rightarrow 9\lambda = 15 \Rightarrow \lambda = \frac{15}{9} = \frac{5}{3}$

$\therefore$ Required vector, $\quad \mathbf{d} = \frac{5}{3}(32\hat{\mathbf{i}} - \hat{\mathbf{j}} - 14\hat{\mathbf{k}})$.

Note If **a** is perpendicular to both **b** and **c**, then **a** can be expressed as $\mathbf{a} = \lambda(\mathbf{b} \times \mathbf{c})$, where λ is a scalar constant.

Quick Solution

We have $\mathbf{a} = \hat{\mathbf{i}} + 4\hat{\mathbf{j}} + 2\hat{\mathbf{k}}$, $\mathbf{b} = 3\hat{\mathbf{i}} - 2\hat{\mathbf{j}} + 7\hat{\mathbf{k}}$

and $\quad \mathbf{c} = 2\hat{\mathbf{i}} - \hat{\mathbf{j}} + 4\hat{\mathbf{k}}$

Let $\quad \mathbf{d} = x\hat{\mathbf{i}} + y\hat{\mathbf{j}} + z\hat{\mathbf{k}}$

Now, $\quad \mathbf{a} \perp \mathbf{d} \Rightarrow \vec{a} \cdot \vec{d} = 0$

$\Rightarrow \quad (\hat{\mathbf{i}} + 4\hat{\mathbf{j}} + 2\hat{\mathbf{k}}) \cdot (x\hat{\mathbf{i}} + y\hat{\mathbf{j}} + z\hat{\mathbf{k}}) = 0$

$\Rightarrow \quad x + 4y + 2z = 0 \quad \ldots \text{(i)}$

and $\quad \mathbf{b} \perp \mathbf{d} \Rightarrow \mathbf{b} \cdot \mathbf{d} = 0$

$\Rightarrow \quad (3\hat{\mathbf{i}} - 2\hat{\mathbf{j}} + 7\hat{\mathbf{k}}) \cdot (x\hat{\mathbf{i}} + y\hat{\mathbf{j}} + z\hat{\mathbf{k}}) = 0$

$\Rightarrow \quad 3x - 2y + 7z = 0 \quad \ldots \text{(ii)}$

It is given that $\mathbf{c} \cdot \mathbf{d} = 15$

$\Rightarrow \quad (2\hat{\mathbf{i}} - \hat{\mathbf{j}} + 4\hat{\mathbf{k}}) \cdot (x\hat{\mathbf{i}} + y\hat{\mathbf{j}} + z\hat{\mathbf{k}}) = 15$

$\Rightarrow \quad 2x - y + 4z = 15 \quad \ldots\ldots \text{(iii)}$

From Eqs. (i) and (ii), we have

$$x + 4y + 2z = 0$$
$$3x - 2y + 7z = 0$$

By cross multiplication method, we get

$$\frac{x}{28 + 4} = \frac{-y}{7 - 6} = \frac{z}{-2 - 12} = k$$

$$\frac{x}{32} = \frac{y}{-1} = \frac{z}{-14} = k$$

$\Rightarrow \quad x = 32k, y = -k, z = -14k.$

Put x, y, z in Eq. (iii), we get

$$64k + k - 56k = 15$$

$\Rightarrow \quad 9k = 15$

$\Rightarrow \quad k = \frac{5}{3}$

Thus $\quad x = \frac{5}{3} \times 32, y = \frac{-5}{3}$ and $z = \frac{-70}{3}$

Hence, $\quad \mathbf{d} = \frac{5}{3}(32\hat{\mathbf{i}} - \hat{\mathbf{j}} - 14\hat{\mathbf{k}})$

Question 13 The scalar product of the vector $\hat{\mathbf{i}} + \hat{\mathbf{j}} + \hat{\mathbf{k}}$ with a unit vector along the sum of vectors $2\hat{\mathbf{i}} + 4\hat{\mathbf{j}} - 5\hat{\mathbf{k}}$ and $\lambda\hat{\mathbf{i}} + 2\hat{\mathbf{j}} + 3\hat{\mathbf{k}}$ is equal to one. Find the value of λ.

Sol. Let $\mathbf{a} = \hat{\mathbf{i}} + \hat{\mathbf{j}} + \hat{\mathbf{k}}$, $\mathbf{b} = 2\hat{\mathbf{i}} + 4\hat{\mathbf{j}} - 5\hat{\mathbf{k}}$ and $\mathbf{c} = \lambda\hat{\mathbf{i}} + 2\hat{\mathbf{j}} + 3\hat{\mathbf{k}}$

Now, $\mathbf{b} + \mathbf{c} = 2\hat{\mathbf{i}} + 4\hat{\mathbf{j}} - 5\hat{\mathbf{k}} + \lambda\hat{\mathbf{i}} + 2\hat{\mathbf{j}} + 3\hat{\mathbf{k}} = (2 + \lambda)\hat{\mathbf{i}} + 6\hat{\mathbf{j}} - 2\hat{\mathbf{k}}$

$\therefore \quad |\mathbf{b} + \mathbf{c}| = \sqrt{(2 + \lambda)^2 + (6)^2 + (-2)^2}$

$$= \sqrt{4 + \lambda^2 + 4\lambda + 36 + 4} = \sqrt{\lambda^2 + 4\lambda + 44}$$

The unit vector along $(\mathbf{b} + \mathbf{c})$, *i.e.*, $\dfrac{\mathbf{b} + \mathbf{c}}{|\mathbf{b} + \mathbf{c}|} = \dfrac{(2 + \lambda)\hat{\mathbf{i}} + 6\hat{\mathbf{j}} - 2\hat{\mathbf{k}}}{\sqrt{\lambda^2 + 4\lambda + 44}}$

Given, scalar product of $(\hat{\mathbf{i}} + \hat{\mathbf{j}} + \hat{\mathbf{k}})$ with this unit vector is 1.

$$\therefore \quad (\hat{\mathbf{i}} + \hat{\mathbf{j}} + \hat{\mathbf{k}}) \cdot \frac{\mathbf{b} + \mathbf{c}}{|\mathbf{b} + \mathbf{c}|} = 1$$

$$\Rightarrow \quad (\hat{\mathbf{i}} + \hat{\mathbf{j}} + \hat{\mathbf{k}}) \cdot \frac{(2 + \lambda)\hat{\mathbf{i}} + 6\hat{\mathbf{j}} - 2\hat{\mathbf{k}}}{\sqrt{\lambda^2 + 4\lambda + 44}} = 1 \Rightarrow \frac{1(2 + \lambda) + 1(6) + 1(-2)}{\sqrt{\lambda^2 + 4\lambda + 44}} = 1$$

$$\Rightarrow \quad \frac{(2 + \lambda) + 6 - 2}{\sqrt{\lambda^2 + 4\lambda + 44}} = 1 \Rightarrow \lambda + 6 = \sqrt{\lambda^2 + 4\lambda + 44}$$

$$\Rightarrow \quad (\lambda + 6)^2 = \lambda^2 + 4\lambda + 44$$

$$\Rightarrow \quad \lambda^2 + 12\lambda + 36 = \lambda^2 + 4\lambda + 44$$

$$\Rightarrow \quad 8\lambda = 8 \quad \Rightarrow \lambda = 1.$$

Hence, the value of λ is 1.

Question 14 If **a**, **b**, **c** are mutually perpendicular vectors of equal magnitudes, show that the vector $(\mathbf{a} + \mathbf{b} + \mathbf{c})$ is equally inclined to **a**, **b** and **c**.

◎ ***Thinking Process*** If **a**, **b** and **c** are mutually perpendicular vectors, then $\mathbf{a} \cdot \mathbf{b} = \mathbf{b} \cdot \mathbf{c} = \mathbf{c} \cdot \mathbf{a} = 0$.

Sol. Given, $\mathbf{a} \cdot \mathbf{b} = \mathbf{b} \cdot \mathbf{c} = \mathbf{c} \cdot \mathbf{a} = 0$ ($\because$ **a**, **b**, **c** are mutually perpendicular)

It is also given that $|\mathbf{a}| = |\mathbf{b}| = |\mathbf{c}|$ ($\because$ All the vectors have same magnitude)

Let vector $(\mathbf{a} + \mathbf{b} + \mathbf{c})$ be inclined to **a**, **b** and **c** at angles α, β and γ respectively.

Then, we have

$$\cos\alpha = \frac{(\mathbf{a} + \mathbf{b} + \mathbf{c}) \cdot \mathbf{a}}{|\mathbf{a} + \mathbf{b} + \mathbf{c}|\,|\mathbf{a}|} = \frac{\mathbf{a} \cdot \mathbf{a} + \mathbf{b} \cdot \mathbf{a} + \mathbf{c} \cdot \mathbf{a}}{|\mathbf{a} + \mathbf{b} + \mathbf{c}|\,|\mathbf{a}|}$$

$$= \frac{\mathbf{a} \cdot \mathbf{a} + 0 + 0}{|\mathbf{a} + \mathbf{b} + \mathbf{c}|\,|\mathbf{a}|} = \frac{|\mathbf{a}|^2}{|\mathbf{a} + \mathbf{b} + \mathbf{c}|\,|\mathbf{a}|} \qquad [\because \mathbf{b} \cdot \mathbf{c} = \mathbf{c} \cdot \mathbf{a} = 0]$$

$$= \frac{|\mathbf{a}|}{|\mathbf{a} + \mathbf{b} + \mathbf{c}|}$$

$$\cos\beta = \frac{(\mathbf{a} + \mathbf{b} + \mathbf{c}) \cdot \mathbf{b}}{|\mathbf{a} + \mathbf{b} + \mathbf{c}|\,|\mathbf{b}|} = \frac{\mathbf{a} \cdot \mathbf{b} + \mathbf{b} \cdot \mathbf{b} + \mathbf{c} \cdot \mathbf{b}}{|\mathbf{a} + \mathbf{b} + \mathbf{c}|\,|\mathbf{b}|}$$

$$= \frac{\mathbf{b}\cdot\mathbf{b} + 0 + 0}{|\mathbf{a}+\mathbf{b}+\mathbf{c}||\mathbf{b}|} = \frac{|\mathbf{b}|^2}{|\mathbf{a}+\mathbf{b}+\mathbf{c}||\mathbf{b}|} \qquad [\because \mathbf{a}\cdot\mathbf{b} = \mathbf{c}\cdot\mathbf{b} = 0]$$

$$= \frac{|\mathbf{b}|}{|\mathbf{a}+\mathbf{b}+\mathbf{c}|}$$

$$\cos\gamma = \frac{(\mathbf{a}+\mathbf{b}+\mathbf{c})\cdot\mathbf{c}}{|\mathbf{a}+\mathbf{b}+\mathbf{c}||\mathbf{c}|} = \frac{\mathbf{a}\cdot\mathbf{c}+\mathbf{b}\cdot\mathbf{c}+\mathbf{c}\cdot\mathbf{c}}{|\mathbf{a}+\mathbf{b}+\mathbf{c}||\mathbf{c}|}$$

$$= \frac{\mathbf{c}\cdot\mathbf{c} + 0 + 0}{|\mathbf{a}+\mathbf{b}+\mathbf{c}||\mathbf{c}|} = \frac{|\mathbf{c}|^2}{|\mathbf{a}+\mathbf{b}+\mathbf{c}||\mathbf{c}|} \qquad [\because \mathbf{a}\cdot\mathbf{c} = \mathbf{b}\cdot\mathbf{c} = 0]$$

$= \dfrac{|\mathbf{c}|}{|\mathbf{a}+\mathbf{b}+\mathbf{c}|}$. Now, as $|\mathbf{a}| = |\mathbf{b}| = |\mathbf{c}|$, therefore, $\cos\alpha = \cos\beta = \cos\gamma$

$\therefore \qquad \alpha = \beta = \gamma$

Hence, the vector $(\mathbf{a}+\mathbf{b}+\mathbf{c})$ is equally inclined to $\mathbf{a}$, $\mathbf{b}$ and $\mathbf{c}$.

Quick Solution

We have a, b and c are mutually perpendicular vectors

$\therefore \qquad \mathbf{a}\cdot\mathbf{b} = \mathbf{b}\cdot\mathbf{c} = \mathbf{c}\cdot\mathbf{a} = 0$

and a, b and c have equal magnitude

then, $|a| = |b| = |c| = k$ (say)

Now, $\qquad |\mathbf{a}+\mathbf{b}+\mathbf{c}|^2 = |\mathbf{a}| + |\mathbf{b}| + |\mathbf{c}| + 2(\mathbf{a}\cdot\mathbf{b}+\mathbf{b}\cdot\mathbf{c}+\mathbf{c}\cdot\mathbf{a})$

$\qquad = k^2 + k^2 + k^2 + 0 = 3k^2$

$\Rightarrow \qquad |\mathbf{a}+\mathbf{b}+\mathbf{c}| = \sqrt{3}k$

Now, angle between $\mathbf{a}$ and $\mathbf{a}+\mathbf{b}+\mathbf{c}$ (say α)

$$\cos\alpha = \frac{\mathbf{a}\cdot(\mathbf{a}+\mathbf{b}+\mathbf{c})}{|\mathbf{a}||\mathbf{a}+\mathbf{b}+\mathbf{c}|} = \frac{|\mathbf{a}|^2 + \mathbf{a}\cdot\mathbf{b}+\mathbf{a}\cdot\mathbf{c}}{\mathbf{k}\cdot\sqrt{3}\mathbf{k}} \qquad (\mathbf{a}\cdot\mathbf{a} = |\mathbf{a}|^2)$$

$$= \frac{k^2}{\sqrt{3}\,k^2} = \frac{1}{\sqrt{3}}$$

Similarly, $\cos\beta = \dfrac{1}{\sqrt{3}}$ and $\cos\gamma = \dfrac{1}{\sqrt{3}}$

$\therefore \cos\alpha = \cos\beta = \cos r = \dfrac{1}{\sqrt{3}} \Rightarrow \alpha = \beta = r$

Thus, $\mathbf{a}$, $\mathbf{b}$, $\mathbf{c}$ are equally inclined to $\mathbf{a}+\mathbf{b}+\mathbf{c}$

Question 15 Prove that $(\mathbf{a}+\mathbf{b})\cdot(\mathbf{a}+\mathbf{b}) = |\mathbf{a}|^2 + |\mathbf{b}|^2$, if and only if $\mathbf{a}$, $\mathbf{b}$ are perpendicular, given $\mathbf{a} \neq \mathbf{0}$, $\mathbf{b} \neq \mathbf{0}$.

Thinking Process To expand $(\mathbf{a}+\mathbf{b})\cdot(\mathbf{a}+\mathbf{b})$, use $\mathbf{a}\cdot\mathbf{a} = |\mathbf{a}|^2$, $\mathbf{b}\cdot\mathbf{b} = |\mathbf{b}|^2$ and $\mathbf{a}\cdot\mathbf{b} = \mathbf{b}\cdot\mathbf{a}$.

Sol. Given, $\qquad (\mathbf{a}+\mathbf{b})\cdot(\mathbf{a}+\mathbf{b}) = |\mathbf{a}|^2 + |\mathbf{b}|^2$

$\Leftrightarrow \qquad \mathbf{a}\cdot(\mathbf{a}+\mathbf{b}) + \mathbf{b}\cdot(\mathbf{a}+\mathbf{b}) = |\mathbf{a}|^2 + |\mathbf{b}|^2$

$\Leftrightarrow \qquad \mathbf{a}\cdot\mathbf{a} + \mathbf{a}\cdot\mathbf{b} + \mathbf{b}\cdot\mathbf{a} + \mathbf{b}\cdot\mathbf{b} = |\mathbf{a}|^2 + |\mathbf{b}|^2$

$\Leftrightarrow \qquad |\mathbf{a}|^2 + 2\mathbf{a}\cdot\mathbf{b} + |\mathbf{b}|^2 = |\mathbf{a}|^2 + |\mathbf{b}|^2$

$\Leftrightarrow \quad 2\mathbf{a}\cdot\mathbf{b}=0$ [$\because \mathbf{a}\cdot\mathbf{b}=\mathbf{b}\cdot\mathbf{a}$ (scalar product is commutative)]

$\Leftrightarrow \quad \mathbf{a}\cdot\mathbf{b}=0$

$\therefore$ **a** and **b** are perpendicular. [given $\mathbf{a}\neq 0, \mathbf{b}\neq 0$]

Direction (Q.No. 16 to 19) Choose the correct answer.

Question 16 If θ is the angle between two vectors **a** and **b**, then $\mathbf{a}\cdot\mathbf{b}\geq 0$ only when

(a) $0<\theta<\frac{\pi}{2}$ (b) $0\leq\theta\leq\frac{\pi}{2}$

(c) $0<\theta<\pi$ (d) $0\leq\theta\leq\pi$

Sol. (b) It is given that $\mathbf{a}\cdot\mathbf{b}\geq 0$

We know that $\mathbf{a}\cdot\mathbf{b}=|\mathbf{a}||\mathbf{b}|\cos\theta\geq 0\Rightarrow\cos\theta\geq 0$, [$|\mathbf{a}|$ and $|\mathbf{b}|$ are positive]

$\Rightarrow \quad 0\leq\theta\leq\frac{\pi}{2}$

Question 17 Let **a** and **b** be two unit vectors and θ is the angle between them. Then, **a** + **b** is a unit vector, if

(a) $\theta=\frac{\pi}{4}$ (b) $\theta=\frac{\pi}{3}$

(c) $\theta=\frac{\pi}{2}$ (d) $\theta=\frac{2\pi}{3}$

Sol. (d) Let **a** and **b** be two unit vectors and θ be the angle between them.

Then, $|\mathbf{a}|=|\mathbf{b}|=1$

Now, $(\mathbf{a}+\mathbf{b})$ is a unit vector if

$$|\mathbf{a}+\mathbf{b}|=1\Rightarrow(\mathbf{a}+\mathbf{b})^2=1$$

$\Rightarrow \quad (\mathbf{a}+\mathbf{b})\cdot(\mathbf{a}+\mathbf{b})=1$

$\Rightarrow \quad \mathbf{a}\cdot\mathbf{a}+\mathbf{a}\cdot\mathbf{b}+\mathbf{b}\cdot\mathbf{a}+\mathbf{b}\cdot\mathbf{b}=1$

$\Rightarrow \quad |\mathbf{a}|^2+|\mathbf{b}|^2+2\mathbf{a}\cdot\mathbf{b}=1$ [$\because \mathbf{a}\cdot\mathbf{b}=\mathbf{b}\cdot\mathbf{a}$]

$\Rightarrow \quad 1^2+1^2+2\mathbf{a}\cdot\mathbf{b}=1$

$\Rightarrow \quad \mathbf{a}\cdot\mathbf{b}=-\frac{1}{2}\Rightarrow|\mathbf{a}||\mathbf{b}|\cos\theta=-\frac{1}{2}$

$\Rightarrow \quad 1\times 1\times\cos\theta=-\frac{1}{2}\Rightarrow\cos\theta=-\frac{1}{2}\Rightarrow\theta=\frac{2\pi}{3}$

Question 18 The value of $\hat{\mathbf{i}}\cdot(\hat{\mathbf{j}}\times\hat{\mathbf{k}})+\hat{\mathbf{j}}\cdot(\hat{\mathbf{i}}\times\hat{\mathbf{k}})+\hat{\mathbf{k}}\cdot(\hat{\mathbf{i}}\times\hat{\mathbf{j}})$ is

(a) zero (b) -1

(c) 1 (d) 3

Sol. (c) We have, $\hat{\mathbf{i}}\cdot(\hat{\mathbf{j}}\times\hat{\mathbf{k}})+\hat{\mathbf{j}}\cdot(\hat{\mathbf{i}}\times\hat{\mathbf{k}})+\hat{\mathbf{k}}\cdot(\hat{\mathbf{i}}\times\hat{\mathbf{j}})$

$$=\hat{\mathbf{i}}\cdot(\hat{\mathbf{i}})+\hat{\mathbf{j}}\cdot(-\hat{\mathbf{j}})+\hat{\mathbf{k}}\cdot(\hat{\mathbf{k}})(\because \hat{\mathbf{j}}\times\hat{\mathbf{k}}=\hat{\mathbf{i}},\hat{\mathbf{i}}\times\hat{\mathbf{k}}=-\hat{\mathbf{j}},\hat{\mathbf{i}}\times\hat{\mathbf{j}}=\hat{\mathbf{k}})$$

$$=1-1+1=1$$

Question 19 If θ is the angle between any two vectors **a** and **b**, then $|\mathbf{a}\cdot\mathbf{b}| = |\mathbf{a}\times\mathbf{b}|$ when θ is equal to

(a) zero (b) $\frac{\pi}{4}$ (c) $\frac{\pi}{2}$ (d) π

Sol. (b) We have $|\mathbf{a}\cdot\mathbf{b}| = |\mathbf{a}\times\mathbf{b}| \Rightarrow |\mathbf{a}|\,|\mathbf{b}|\cos\theta = |\mathbf{a}|\,|\mathbf{b}|\sin\theta$

$\Rightarrow \quad \cos\theta = \sin\theta$ [$|\mathbf{a}|$ and $|\mathbf{b}|$ are positive]

$\Rightarrow \quad \tan\theta = 1$

$\Rightarrow \quad \theta = \frac{\pi}{4}$

DIKSHA APP Questions

□ Multiple Choice Questions

Q.1 If $\mathbf{a}\times\mathbf{b} = \mathbf{b}\times\mathbf{c} \neq 0$ then for any scalar λ.

(a) $\mathbf{a}+\mathbf{b} = \lambda(\mathbf{c}-\mathbf{b})$ (b) $\mathbf{b}+\mathbf{c} = \lambda\mathbf{a}$

(c) $\mathbf{a}+\mathbf{b} = \lambda\mathbf{c}$ (d) $\mathbf{a}+\mathbf{c} = \lambda\mathbf{b}$

Sol. (d) We have $\mathbf{a}\times\mathbf{b} = \mathbf{b}\times\mathbf{c}$

$\Rightarrow \quad \mathbf{a}\times\mathbf{b} - \mathbf{b}\times\mathbf{c} = 0$

$\Rightarrow \quad \mathbf{a}\times\mathbf{b} + \mathbf{c}\times\mathbf{b} = 0$ $(\because \mathbf{b}\times\mathbf{c} = -\mathbf{c}\times\mathbf{b})$

$\Rightarrow \quad (\mathbf{a}+\mathbf{c})\times\mathbf{b} = 0$ (By distributive low)

$\Rightarrow$ $\mathbf{a}+\mathbf{c}$ is parallel to **b**

$\Rightarrow \quad \mathbf{a}+\mathbf{c} = \lambda\mathbf{b}$

Q.2 If $\mathbf{a} = 2\hat{i}+3\hat{j}-5\hat{k}$, $\mathbf{b} = m\hat{i}+n\hat{i}+12\hat{k}$ and $\mathbf{a}\times\mathbf{b} = 0$, then $(m, n) =$

(a) $\left(\frac{-24}{5}, \frac{-36}{5}\right)$ (b) $\left(\frac{-24}{5}, \frac{36}{5}\right)$ (c) $\left(\frac{24}{5}, \frac{-36}{5}\right)$ (d) $\left(\frac{24}{5}, \frac{36}{5}\right)$

Sol. (a) We have $\mathbf{a} = 2\hat{i}+3\hat{j}-5\hat{k}$

and $\mathbf{b} = m\hat{i}+n\hat{j}+12\hat{k}$

Also $\mathbf{a}\times\mathbf{b} = 0$

$\therefore \quad |\mathbf{a}\times\mathbf{b}| = |\mathbf{a}|\,|\mathbf{b}|\sin\theta = 0$

$\Rightarrow \quad \sin\theta = 0$

$\Rightarrow$ **a** and **b** are parallel to each other.

$\Rightarrow \quad \theta = 0$

Now, direction ratic of $\mathbf{a} = 2, 3, -5$ and direction ratio of $\mathbf{b} = m, n, 12$

If **a** and **b** are parallel then ratio of their direction ratio will be equal.

So, $\frac{2}{m} = \frac{3}{n} = \frac{-5}{12} \Rightarrow m = \frac{-24}{5}$ and $n = \frac{-36}{5}$

Q.3 The non-zero vectors **b** and **c** are related by $\mathbf{a} = 8\mathbf{b}$ and $\mathbf{c} = -7\mathbf{b}$, then the angle between **a** and **c** is

(a) 0 (b) π (c) $\frac{\pi}{4}$ (d) $\frac{\pi}{2}$

Sol. (b) Given, $\mathbf{a} = 8\mathbf{b}$ and $\mathbf{c} = -7\mathbf{b}$

Here, $\mathbf{a} = 8\mathbf{b}$ shows that **a** and **b** are parallel and in same direction.
and $\mathbf{c} = -7\mathbf{b}$ shows that **c** and **b** are parallel and in opposite direction.

$\therefore$ We can say that **a** and **c** are parallel but opposite direction.

Hence angle between **a** and **c** is 'π'.

Q.4 If $|\mathbf{a}| = 8$ then $|(-5)\mathbf{a}| =$

(a) −40 (b) 40 (c) −80 (d) 80

Sol. (b) Given, $|\mathbf{a}| = 8$

Now, we know that $|k\mathbf{a}| = |k|\,|\mathbf{a}|$

So $$|(-5)\,\mathbf{a}| = |-5|\,|\mathbf{a}| = 5\,|\mathbf{a}| = 5 \times 8 = 40$$

Q.5 Let **a**, **b** are two unit vectors such that $\mathbf{a} \times \mathbf{b}$ is also a unit vector, then the angle between **a** and **b** is

(a) 0 (b) $\frac{\pi}{3}$ (c) π (d) $\frac{\pi}{2}$

Sol. (d) Given, $|\mathbf{a}| = |\mathbf{b}| = 1$ and $|\mathbf{a} \times \mathbf{b}| = 1$

$$\therefore \quad |\mathbf{a}|\,|\mathbf{b}| \sin\theta = 1 \Rightarrow 1 \cdot 1 \cdot \sin\theta = 1$$

$$\Rightarrow \quad \sin\theta = 1 \Rightarrow \theta = \frac{\pi}{2}$$

Q.6 A unit vector perpendicular to both $\hat{i} + \hat{j}$ and $\hat{j} + \hat{k}$ is

(a) $\hat{i} - \hat{j} + \hat{k}$ (b) $\pm\frac{\hat{i} + \hat{j} + \hat{k}}{\sqrt{3}}$ (c) $\hat{i} + \hat{j} - \hat{k}$ (d) $\pm\frac{\hat{i} - \hat{j} + \hat{k}}{\sqrt{3}}$

Sol. (d) Let $\mathbf{a} = \hat{i} + \hat{j}$ and $\mathbf{b} = \hat{j} + \hat{k}$

A vector perpendicular to both **a** and **b** is always parallel to $\mathbf{a} \times \mathbf{b}$

Now, $$\mathbf{a} \times \mathbf{b} = \begin{vmatrix} \hat{i} & \hat{j} & \hat{k} \\ 1 & 1 & 0 \\ 0 & 1 & 1 \end{vmatrix}$$

$$= \hat{i}(1-0) - \hat{j}(1-0) + \hat{k}(1-0) = \hat{i} - \hat{j} + \hat{k}$$

Unit vector along $\mathbf{a} \times \mathbf{b} = \pm\frac{\mathbf{a} \times \mathbf{b}}{|\mathbf{a} \times \mathbf{b}|} = \pm\frac{\hat{i} - \hat{j} + \hat{k}}{\sqrt{(1)^2 + (-1)^2 + (1)^2}} = \pm\frac{\hat{i} - \hat{j} + \hat{k}}{\sqrt{3}}$

☐ Subjective Type Questions

Q.1 Let **a**, **b** and **c** be three vectors such that $\mathbf{a} \neq 0$ and $\mathbf{a} \times \mathbf{b} = 2\mathbf{a} \times \mathbf{c}$, $|\mathbf{a}| = |\mathbf{c}| = 1$, $|\mathbf{b}| = 4$ and $|\mathbf{b} \times \mathbf{c}| = \sqrt{15}$, $\mathbf{b} - 2\mathbf{c} = \lambda\mathbf{a}$ then find the value of λ

Sol. Given, $\mathbf{a} \times \mathbf{b} = 2\,\mathbf{a} \times \mathbf{c}$, $|\mathbf{a}| = |\mathbf{c}| = 1$, $|\mathbf{b}| = 4$

and $|\mathbf{b} \times \mathbf{c}| = \sqrt{15}$, $\mathbf{b} - 2\mathbf{c} = \lambda\,\mathbf{a}$

Now, $\mathbf{b} - 2\mathbf{c} = \lambda\mathbf{a}$

$|\mathbf{b} - 2\mathbf{c}| = |\lambda\mathbf{a}|$

$\Rightarrow |\mathbf{b} - 2\mathbf{c}|^2 = \lambda^2|\mathbf{a}|^2$

$\Rightarrow (\mathbf{b} - 2\mathbf{c})\cdot(\mathbf{b} - 2\mathbf{c}) = \lambda^2|\mathbf{a}|^2 \quad (\because \mathbf{a}\cdot\mathbf{a} = |\mathbf{a}|^2)$

$\Rightarrow \mathbf{b}\cdot\mathbf{b} - 2\mathbf{b}\cdot\mathbf{c} - 2\mathbf{c}\cdot\mathbf{b} + 4\cdot\mathbf{c}\cdot\mathbf{c} = \lambda^2|\mathbf{a}|^2$

$\Rightarrow |\mathbf{b}|^2 - 4\mathbf{b}\cdot\mathbf{c} + 4|\mathbf{c}|^2 = \lambda^2|\mathbf{a}|^2 \quad \ldots(i)$

Also, given $|\mathbf{b} \times \mathbf{c}| = \sqrt{15}$

$\Rightarrow |\mathbf{b}||\mathbf{c}|\cdot\sin\theta = \sqrt{15}$

$\Rightarrow 4\cdot 1\cdot\sin\theta = \sqrt{15}$

$\Rightarrow \sin\theta = \dfrac{\sqrt{15}}{4}$

$\Rightarrow \cos\theta = \sqrt{1 - \sin^2\theta} = \dfrac{1}{4}$

From Eq. (i), $(4)^2 - 4\cdot|\mathbf{b}|\cdot|\mathbf{c}|\cos\theta + 4\cdot(1)^2 = \lambda^2\cdot(1)^2$

$\Rightarrow 16 - 4\times 4\times 1\times\dfrac{1}{4} + 4 = \lambda^2$

$\Rightarrow 16 - 4 + 4 = \lambda^2 \Rightarrow \lambda^2 = 16 \Rightarrow \lambda = \pm 4$

Q.2 Let **a**, **b** and **c** be three vectors such that $\mathbf{a} + \mathbf{b} + \mathbf{c} = 0$, $|\mathbf{a}| = 1$, $|\mathbf{b}| = 2$ and $|\mathbf{c}| = 3$ then find $\mathbf{a}\cdot\mathbf{c} + \mathbf{b}\cdot\mathbf{c} + \mathbf{c}\cdot\mathbf{a}$.

Sol. Given, $\mathbf{a} + \mathbf{b} + \mathbf{c} = 0$, $|\mathbf{a}| = 1$, $|\mathbf{b}| = 2$ and $|\mathbf{c}| = 3$

Now, $|\mathbf{a} + \mathbf{b} + \mathbf{c}|^2 = (\mathbf{a} + \mathbf{b} + \mathbf{c})\cdot(\mathbf{a} + \mathbf{b} + \mathbf{c})$

$\Rightarrow 0 = \mathbf{a}\cdot\mathbf{a} + \mathbf{a}\cdot\mathbf{b} + \mathbf{a}\cdot\mathbf{c} + \mathbf{b}\cdot\mathbf{a} + \mathbf{b}\cdot\mathbf{b}$

$+ \mathbf{b}\cdot\mathbf{c} + \mathbf{c}\cdot\mathbf{a} + \mathbf{c}\cdot\mathbf{b} + \mathbf{c}\cdot\mathbf{c}$

$\Rightarrow 0 = |\mathbf{a}|^2 + |\mathbf{b}|^2 + |\mathbf{c}|^2 + 2(\mathbf{a}\cdot\mathbf{b} + \mathbf{b}\cdot\mathbf{c} + \mathbf{c}\cdot\mathbf{a})$

$\Rightarrow 0 = (1)^2 + (2)^2 + (3)^2 + 2(\mathbf{a}\cdot\mathbf{b} + \mathbf{b}\cdot\mathbf{c} + \mathbf{c}\cdot\mathbf{a})$

$\Rightarrow 2(\mathbf{a}\cdot\mathbf{b} + \mathbf{b}\cdot\mathbf{c} + \mathbf{c}\cdot\mathbf{a}) = -14.$

$\Rightarrow \mathbf{a}\cdot\mathbf{b} + \mathbf{b}\cdot\mathbf{c} + \mathbf{c}\cdot\mathbf{a} = -7$

Q.3 If $\mathbf{a} \times \mathbf{b} = \mathbf{c} \times \mathbf{d}$ and $\mathbf{a} \times \mathbf{c} = \mathbf{b} \times \mathbf{d}$ then prove that $\mathbf{a} - \mathbf{d}$ is parallel to $\mathbf{b} - \mathbf{c}$, where $\mathbf{a} \neq \mathbf{d}$ and $\mathbf{b} \neq c$

Sol. We have, $\mathbf{a} \times \mathbf{b} = \mathbf{c} \times \mathbf{d}$ ...(i)

and $\mathbf{a} \times \mathbf{c} = \mathbf{b} \times \mathbf{d}$ ... (ii)

On substracting Eq. (ii) From Eq. (i), we get

$\Rightarrow \quad \mathbf{a} \times \mathbf{b} - \mathbf{a} \times \mathbf{c} = \mathbf{c} \times \mathbf{d} - \mathbf{b} \times \mathbf{d}$

$\Rightarrow \quad \mathbf{a} \times (\mathbf{b} - \mathbf{c}) = (\mathbf{c} - \mathbf{b}) \times \mathbf{d}$ (By distributive law)

$\Rightarrow \mathbf{a} \times (\mathbf{b} - \mathbf{c}) - (\mathbf{c} - \mathbf{b}) \times \mathbf{d} = 0$

$\Rightarrow \mathbf{a} \times (\mathbf{b} - \mathbf{c}) + (\mathbf{b} - \mathbf{c}) \times \mathbf{d} = 0$ $(\because \mathbf{c} - \mathbf{b} = -(\mathbf{b} - \mathbf{c})$

$\Rightarrow \mathbf{a} \times (\mathbf{b} - \mathbf{c}) - \mathbf{d} \times (\mathbf{b} - \mathbf{c}) = 0$ $(\because \mathbf{a} \times \mathbf{b} = -\mathbf{b} \times \mathbf{a})$

$\Rightarrow \quad (\mathbf{a} - \mathbf{d}) \times (\mathbf{b} - \mathbf{c}) = 0$ (By distributive law)

$\Rightarrow \quad \mathbf{a} - \mathbf{d} = 0$ or $\mathbf{b} - \mathbf{c} = \mathbf{0}$ or $\mathbf{a} - \mathbf{d} = \lambda(\mathbf{b} - \mathbf{c})$

We have given that $\mathbf{a} \neq \mathbf{d}$ and $\mathbf{b} \neq \mathbf{c}$

$\therefore \quad \mathbf{a} - \mathbf{d} = \lambda(\mathbf{b} - \mathbf{c})$

Hence, $\mathbf{a} - \mathbf{d}$ is parallel to $\mathbf{b} - \mathbf{c}$.

Q.4 Let, $\mathbf{a}$, $\mathbf{b}$ and $\mathbf{c}$ be three vectors such that $|\mathbf{a}| = 3$, $|\mathbf{b}| = 4$ and $|\mathbf{c}| = 5$ and each one of them being perpendicular to the sum of other two, then prove that $|\mathbf{a} + \mathbf{b} + \mathbf{c}| = 5\sqrt{2}$

Sol. Given, $|\mathbf{a}| = 3$, $|\mathbf{b}| = 4$ and $|\mathbf{c}| = 5$

Also, given, each one of them is perpendicular to sum of other two

i.e., $\mathbf{a} \perp \mathbf{b} + \mathbf{c} \Rightarrow \mathbf{a} \cdot (\mathbf{b} + \mathbf{c}) = 0$ ... (i)

$\mathbf{b} \perp \mathbf{a} + \mathbf{c} \Rightarrow \mathbf{b} \cdot (\mathbf{a} + \mathbf{c}) = 0$ ... (ii)

$\mathbf{c} \perp \mathbf{a} + \mathbf{b} \Rightarrow \mathbf{c} \cdot (\mathbf{a} + \mathbf{b}) = 0$ ...(iii)

On adding Eqs. (i), (ii) and (iii), we get

$$2(\mathbf{a} \cdot \mathbf{b} + \mathbf{b} \cdot \mathbf{c} + \mathbf{c} \cdot \mathbf{a}) = 0 \quad \text{...(iv)}$$

Now $|\mathbf{a} + \mathbf{b} + \mathbf{c}|^2 = (\mathbf{a} + \mathbf{b} + \mathbf{c}) \cdot (\mathbf{a} + \mathbf{b} + \mathbf{c})$ $(\because \mathbf{a} \cdot \mathbf{a} = |\mathbf{a}|^2)$

$= \mathbf{a} \cdot \mathbf{a} + \mathbf{a} \cdot \mathbf{b} + \mathbf{a} \cdot \mathbf{c} + \mathbf{b} \cdot \mathbf{a} + \mathbf{b} \cdot \mathbf{b} + \mathbf{b} \cdot \mathbf{c}$

$+ \mathbf{c} \cdot \mathbf{a} + \mathbf{c} \cdot \mathbf{b} \cdot + \mathbf{c} \cdot \mathbf{c}$

$= |\mathbf{a}|^2 + |\mathbf{b}|^2 + |\mathbf{c}|^2 + 2(\mathbf{a} \cdot \mathbf{b} + \mathbf{b} \cdot \mathbf{c} + \mathbf{c} \cdot \mathbf{a})$

$= (3)^2 + (4)^2 + (5)^2 + 0$ [using Eq. (iv)]

$\Rightarrow \quad |\mathbf{a} + \mathbf{b} + \mathbf{c}|^2 = 50$

$\Rightarrow \quad |\mathbf{a} + \mathbf{b} + \mathbf{c}| = 5\sqrt{2}$ **Hence Proved.**

Q.5 Let $P(2,-1,4)$ and $Q(4,3,2)$ be two points and R be on PQ such that $3PQ = 5QR$ then co-ordinate of R is

(a) $\left(\frac{14}{5}, \frac{3}{5}, \frac{16}{5}\right)$ (b) $\left(\frac{16}{5}, \frac{7}{5}, \frac{14}{5}\right)$

(c) $(6, -7, 18)$ (d) $\left(-1, \frac{7}{2}, \frac{13}{2}\right)$

Sol. Given, $P = (2, -1, 4)$ and $Q = (4, 3, 2)$

P R Q

Also, $3PQ = 5QR$

$$\Rightarrow \quad 3(PR + QR) = 5QR$$

$$\Rightarrow \quad 3PR + 3QR = 5QR \Rightarrow 3PR = 2QR$$

$$\Rightarrow \quad \frac{PR}{QR} = \frac{2}{3} \Rightarrow PR : QR = 2 : 3$$

By using section formula we get

$$\mathbf{R} = \frac{2 \cdot \mathbf{OQ} + 3 \cdot \mathbf{OP}}{2 + 3}$$

$$= \frac{2(4\hat{\mathbf{i}} + 3\hat{\mathbf{j}} + 2\hat{\mathbf{k}}) + 3(2\hat{\mathbf{i}} - \hat{\mathbf{j}} + 4\hat{\mathbf{k}})}{5}$$

$$= \frac{8\hat{\mathbf{i}} + 6\hat{\mathbf{j}} + 4\hat{\mathbf{k}} + 6\hat{\mathbf{i}} - 3\hat{\mathbf{j}} + 12\hat{\mathbf{k}}}{5}$$

$$= \frac{14\hat{\mathbf{i}} + 3\hat{\mathbf{j}} + 16\hat{\mathbf{k}}}{5} = \frac{14}{5}\hat{\mathbf{i}} + \frac{3}{5}\hat{\mathbf{j}} + \frac{16}{5}\hat{\mathbf{k}}$$

Hence, the coordinates of R is $\left(\frac{14}{5}, \frac{3}{5}, \frac{16}{5}\right)$.

Three-Dimensional Geometry

CHAPTER 11

Important Points

Lines

01 Direction Cosines and Direction Ratios of a Line

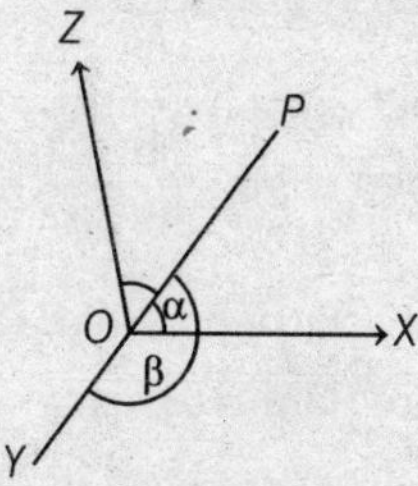

(i) **Direction cosines** If a line make angles α, β, γ with X-axis, Y-axis and Z-axis respectively, then $l = \cos\alpha$, $m = \cos\beta$ and $n = \cos\gamma$ are called the direction cosines of the line.

(ii) We always have $l^2 + m^2 + n^2 = 1$.

(iii) **Direction ratios** Any three numbers which are proportional to the direction cosines of a line are called the direction ratios of the line.

(iv) If a, b and c are direction ratios of a line, then $\frac{l}{a} = \frac{m}{b} = \frac{n}{c} = k$ (say) where, k is constant

$\Rightarrow l = ak$, $m = bk$ and $n = ck$

(v) If a, b, c are the direction ratios of a line, then

$$l = \frac{a}{\sqrt{a^2 + b^2 + c^2}}, \; m = \frac{b}{\sqrt{a^2 + b^2 + c^2}} \text{ and } n = \frac{c}{\sqrt{a^2 + b^2 + c^2}}$$

(vi) In any line, direction cosines are unique but direction ratios are not unique.

02 Equation in Vector Form

(i) Equation of a line through a given point A with position vector $\mathbf{a}$ and parallel to a given vector $\mathbf{b}$ is given by $\mathbf{r} = \mathbf{a} + \lambda\mathbf{b}$, where λ is a scalar.

(ii) The vector equation of a line passing through two points with position vectors $\mathbf{a}$ and $\mathbf{b}$ is given by $\mathbf{r} = \mathbf{a} + t(\mathbf{b} - \mathbf{a})$, where t is a scalar.

03 Equation in Cartesian Form

(i) The equations of a line passing through a point $A(x_1, y_1, z_1)$ and having direction ratios a, b, c are $\dfrac{x - x_1}{a} = \dfrac{y - y_1}{b} = \dfrac{z - z_1}{c}$.

(ii) The equations of a line passing through two points $A(x_1, y_1, z_1)$ and $B(x_2, y_2, z_2)$ are $\dfrac{x - x_1}{x_2 - x_1} = \dfrac{y - y_1}{y_2 - y_1} = \dfrac{z - z_1}{z_2 - z_1}$.

04 Angles between two lines

(a) **Vector form**

If θ is the angle between two lines $\mathbf{r} = \mathbf{a} + t\mathbf{b}$ and $\mathbf{r} = \mathbf{c} + s\mathbf{d}$, then $\cos\theta = \dfrac{\mathbf{b}\cdot\mathbf{d}}{|\mathbf{b}|\cdot|\mathbf{d}|}$.

(i) If two lines are perpendicular, than $\mathbf{b}\cdot\mathbf{d} = 0$

(ii) If two lines are parallel, then $b = \lambda d$

(b) **Cartesion form**

(i) Let L_1 and L_2 be two lines passing through the origin and with direction ratios a_1, b_1, c_1 and a_2, b_2, c_2 then

$$\cos\theta = \left|\frac{a_1a_2 + b_1b_2 + c_1c_2}{\sqrt{a_1^2 + b_1^2 + c_1^2}\sqrt{a_2^2 + b_2^2 + c_2^2}}\right|$$

(ii) If θ is the angle between two lines with direction cosines l_1, m_1, n_1 and l_2, m_2, n_2, then

$$\cos\theta = l_1 l_2 + m_1m_2 + n_1n_2.$$

(iii) Two lines with direction ratios a_1, b_1, c_1 and a_2, b_2, c_2 are perpendicular *i.e.* if $\theta = 90°$, then $a_1a_2 + b_1b_2 + c_1c_2 = 0$ and parallel *i.e* if $\theta = 0$, then $\dfrac{a_1}{a_2} = \dfrac{b_1}{b_2} = \dfrac{c_1}{c_2}$.

05 Shortest Distance between Two Skew-Lines

(a) **Vector form**

Let the equations of L_1 and L_2 be

$\mathbf{r} = \mathbf{a}_1 + \lambda \mathbf{b}_1$ and $\mathbf{r} = \mathbf{a}_2 + \mu \mathbf{b}_2$

Then, shortest distance PQ between these two skew-lines is $\text{SD} = \dfrac{|(\mathbf{a}_2 - \mathbf{a}_1) \cdot (\mathbf{b}_1 \times \mathbf{b}_2)|}{|\mathbf{b}_1 \times \mathbf{b}_2|}$

(b) **Cartesian Form**

Let L_1 and L_2 be two skew-lines with equations

$$L_1: \frac{x - x_1}{a_1} = \frac{y - y_1}{b_1} = \frac{z - z_1}{c_1} \text{ and } L_2: \frac{x - x_2}{a_2} = \frac{y - y_2}{b_2} = \frac{z - z_2}{c_2}$$

Then the shortest distance between these lines is

$$\left| \frac{\begin{vmatrix} x_2 - x_1 & y_2 - y_1 & z_2 - z_1 \\ a_1 & b_1 & c_1 \\ a_2 & b_2 & c_2 \end{vmatrix}}{\sqrt{(b_1 c_2 - b_2 c_1)^2 + (c_1 a_2 - c_2 a_1)^2 + (a_1 b_2 - a_2 b_1)^2}} \right|$$

06 Distance between parallel lines

(i) If two lines L_1 and L_2 are parallel, then they are coplanar.

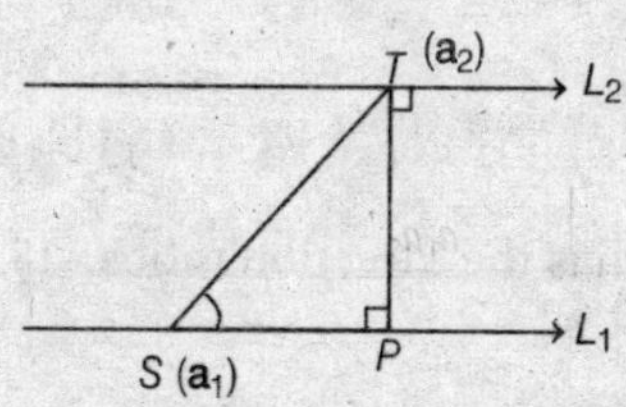

(ii) The shortest distance TP between parallel lines

$L_1: \mathbf{r} = \mathbf{a}_1 + \lambda \mathbf{b}$ and $L_2: \mathbf{r} = \mathbf{a}_2 + \mu \mathbf{b}$ is

$$\text{SD or } d = |\mathbf{PT}| = \left| \frac{\mathbf{b} \times (\mathbf{a}_2 - \mathbf{a}_1)}{|\mathbf{b}|} \right|$$

Exercise 11.1

Questions 1 If a line makes angles 90°, 135°, 45° with the positive X, Y and Z-axes respectively, find its direction cosines.

Thinking Process Let a line makes angles α, β and γ with the positive x, y and z-axes respectively. Then, direction cosines of a line are $\cos\alpha$, $\cos\beta$ and $\cos\gamma$.

Sol. Let direction cosines of the line be l, m and n with the X, Y, and Z-axes respectively, and given that

$$\alpha = 90°, \beta = 135° \text{ and } \gamma = 45°$$

Then, $l = \cos\alpha = \cos 90° = 0,\ m = \cos\beta = \cos 135° = -1/\sqrt{2}$

and $n = \cos\gamma = \cos 45° = 1/\sqrt{2}$

Therefore, the direction cosines of the line are $0, -\frac{1}{\sqrt{2}}$ and $\frac{1}{\sqrt{2}}$.

Question 2 Find the direction cosines of a line which makes equal angles with the coordinate axes.

Thinking Process If the direction cosines of a line are l, m and n, then use the relation $l^2 + m^2 + n^2 = 1$ and simplify it.

Sol. Let the line makes an angle α with each of the three coordinate axes, then its direction cosines are

$$l = \cos\alpha,\ m = \cos\alpha,\ n = \cos\alpha$$

We know that $l^2 + m^2 + n^2 = 1$

$\Rightarrow \cos^2\alpha + \cos^2\alpha + \cos^2\alpha = 1$ $[\because l = m = n = \cos\alpha]$

$\Rightarrow 3\cos^2\alpha = 1 \Rightarrow \cos^2\alpha = \frac{1}{3} \Rightarrow \cos\alpha = \pm\frac{1}{\sqrt{3}}$

$\therefore$ Direction cosines of the line are either $\frac{1}{\sqrt{3}}, \frac{1}{\sqrt{3}}, \frac{1}{\sqrt{3}}$ or $-\frac{1}{\sqrt{3}}, -\frac{1}{\sqrt{3}}, -\frac{1}{\sqrt{3}}$.

Question 3. If a line has the direction ratios –18, 12, –4, then what are its direction cosines?

Thinking Process If a, b and c are the direction ratios of a line then direction cosines are

$$\frac{a}{\sqrt{a^2+b^2+c^2}}, \frac{b}{\sqrt{a^2+b^2+c^2}}, \frac{c}{\sqrt{a^2+b^2+c^2}}$$

Sol. Given, direction ratios are –18, 12, –4.

Here $a = -18$, $b = 12$ and $c = -4$, then direction cosines of a line are

$$\left(\frac{a}{\sqrt{a^2+b^2+c^2}}, \frac{b}{\sqrt{a^2+b^2+c^2}}, \frac{c}{\sqrt{a^2+b^2+c^2}}\right)$$

$$= \left(\frac{-18}{\sqrt{(-18)^2 + (12)^2 + (-4)^2}}, \frac{12}{\sqrt{(-18)^2 + (12)^2 + (-4)^2}}, \frac{-4}{\sqrt{(-18)^2 + (12)^2 + (-4)^2}} \right)$$

$$= \left(\frac{-18}{\sqrt{484}}, \frac{12}{\sqrt{484}}, \frac{-4}{\sqrt{484}} \right) = \left(\frac{-18}{22}, \frac{12}{22}, \frac{-4}{22} \right) = \left(-\frac{9}{11}, \frac{6}{11}, \frac{-2}{11} \right)$$

Thus, the direction cosines are $-\frac{9}{11}, \frac{6}{11}$ and $\frac{-2}{11}$.

Question 4 Show that the points (2, 3, 4), (–1, –2, 1), (5, 8, 7) are collinear.

◎ ***Thinking Process*** Firstly we determine the direction ratio of joining two points *i.e.*, *AB*, *BC*, *CA* if they are proportional, then points are collinear.

Sol. Let the given points be *A*, *B* and *C* respectively, then $A(2, 3, 4)$, $B(-1, -2, 1)$ and $C(5, 8, 7)$.

We know that the direction ratios of line joining the points, (x_1, y_1, z_1) and (x_2, y_2, z_2) are given by $(x_2 - x_1, y_2 - y_1, z_2 - z_1)$.

Then, direction ratios of *AB* are $(-1-2, -2-3, 1-4) \Rightarrow (-3, -5, -3)$

and direction ratios of *AC* are $(5-2, 8-3, 7-4) \Rightarrow (3, 5, 3)$

As $\frac{-3}{3} = \frac{-5}{5} = \frac{-3}{3}$, therefore the direction ratios of *AB* and *AC* are proportional.

Hence, *AB* and *AC* are parallel, but they have a point *A* in common, therefore *AB* and *AC* are along the same line *i.e.*, *A*, *B* and *C* are collinear.

Question 5 Find the direction cosines of the sides of the triangle whose vertices are (3, 5, –4), (–1, 1, 2) and (–5, –5, –2).

Sol. Let the vertices of the triangle be $A(3, 5, -4)$, $B(-1, 1, 2)$ and $C(-5, -5, -2)$ respectively.

The direction ratios of side *AB* are $(-1-3, 1-5, 2-(-4)) = (-4, -4, 2+4)$, *i.e.*, $(-4, -4, 6)$.

A(3, 5, –4)
B(–1, 1, 2)
C(–5, –5, –2)

[$\because$ If $A(x_1, y_1, z_1)$ and $B(x_2, y_2, z_2)$ then DR's of $AB = (x_2 - x_1, y_2 - y_1, z_2 - z_1)$]

Then, magnitude of *AB*,

$$|AB| = \sqrt{(-4)^2 + (-4)^2 + (6)^2}$$
$$= \sqrt{16 + 16 + 36} = \sqrt{68} = 2\sqrt{17}$$

Therefore, the direction cosines of *AB* are

$$\frac{-4}{2\sqrt{17}}, \frac{-4}{2\sqrt{17}}, \frac{6}{2\sqrt{17}} \Rightarrow \frac{-2}{\sqrt{17}}, \frac{-2}{\sqrt{17}}, \frac{3}{\sqrt{17}}$$

[$\because$ If *a*, *b*, *c* are direction ratios, then direction cosines are $\frac{a}{\sqrt{a^2 + b^2 + c^2}}, \frac{b}{\sqrt{a^2 + b^2 + c^2}}, \frac{c}{\sqrt{a^2 + b^2 + c^2}}$]

Similarly, the direction ratios of side *BC* are $[-5-(-1), -5-1, -2-2]$ *i.e.*, $(-4, -6, -4)$.

Magnitude of BC, $|BC| = \sqrt{(-4)^2 + (-6)^2 + (-4)^2} = \sqrt{68} = 2\sqrt{17}$

Therefore, the direction cosines of BC are

$$\frac{-4}{2\sqrt{17}}, \frac{-6}{2\sqrt{17}}, \frac{-4}{2\sqrt{17}} \Rightarrow \frac{-2}{\sqrt{17}}, \frac{-3}{\sqrt{17}}, \frac{-2}{\sqrt{17}}$$

The direction ratios of side CA are (3 (–5), –5 (–5), –4 –(–2) *i.e.,* (8, 10, –2).

$$|CA| = \sqrt{(8)^2 + (10)^2 + (-2)^2} = \sqrt{64 + 100 + 4} = \sqrt{168} = 2\sqrt{42}$$

Therefore, the direction cosines of CA are

$$\frac{8}{2\sqrt{42}}, \frac{10}{2\sqrt{42}}, \frac{-2}{2\sqrt{42}} \Rightarrow \frac{4}{\sqrt{42}}, \frac{5}{\sqrt{42}}, \frac{-1}{\sqrt{42}}$$

Exercise 11.2

Question 1 Show that the lines with direction cosines $\frac{12}{13}, \frac{-3}{13}, \frac{-4}{13}; \frac{4}{13}, \frac{12}{13}, \frac{3}{13}; \frac{3}{13}, \frac{-4}{13}, \frac{12}{13}$ are mutually perpendicular.

Thinking Process The two lines, with direction cosines l_1, m_1, n_1 and l_2, m_2, n_2 are perpendicular to each other, if $l_1 l_2 + m_1 m_2 + n_1 n_2 = 0$

Sol.

(i) For first two lines with direction cosines, $\frac{12}{13}, \frac{-3}{13}, \frac{-4}{13}$ and $\frac{4}{13}, \frac{12}{13}, \frac{3}{13}$,

We have

$$l_1 l_2 + m_1 m_2 + n_1 n_2 = \frac{12}{13} \times \frac{4}{13} + \left(\frac{-3}{13}\right) \times \frac{12}{13} + \left(\frac{-4}{13}\right) \times \frac{3}{13} = \frac{48}{169} - \frac{36}{169} - \frac{12}{169} = 0$$

Therefore, the lines are perpendicular.

(ii) For second and third lines with direction cosines, $\frac{4}{13}, \frac{12}{13}, \frac{3}{13}$ and $\frac{3}{13}, \frac{-4}{13}, \frac{12}{13}$, we have

$$l_1 l_2 + m_1 m_2 + n_1 n_2 = \frac{4}{13} \times \frac{3}{13} + \frac{12}{13} \times \left(\frac{-4}{13}\right) + \frac{3}{13} \times \frac{12}{13} = \frac{12}{169} - \frac{48}{169} + \frac{36}{169} = 0$$

Therefore, the lines are perpendicular.

(iii) For third and first lines with directions cosines, $\frac{3}{13}, \frac{-4}{13}, \frac{12}{13}$ and $\frac{12}{13}, \frac{-3}{13}, \frac{-4}{13}$,

we have $l_1 l_2 + m_1 m_2 + n_1 n_2 = \frac{3}{13} \times \frac{12}{13} + \left(\frac{-4}{13}\right) \times \left(\frac{-3}{13}\right) + \frac{12}{13} \times \left(\frac{-4}{13}\right)$

$$= \frac{36}{169} + \frac{12}{169} - \frac{48}{169} = \frac{36}{169} - \frac{36}{169} = 0$$

Therefore, the lines are perpendicular.

Hence, all the lines are mutually perpendicular.

Question 2 Show that the line through the points $(1,-1,2)$, $(3,4,-2)$ is perpendicular to the line through the points $(0,3,2)$ and $(3,5,6)$.

◎ *Thinking Process* Two lines having direction ratios (a_1, b_1, c_1) and (a_2, b_2, c_2) are perpendicular if and only if $a_1a_2 + b_1b_2 + c_1c_2 = 0$, use this to solve above problem.

Sol. Let the given points are $A(1, -1, 2)$, $B(3, 4, -2)$, $C(0, 3, 2)$ and $D(3, 5, 6)$
Now, direction ratios of AB are $(3-1, 4-(-1), -2-2) = (2, 4+1, -4) = (2, 5, -4)$
and direction ratios of CD are $(3-0, 5-3, 6-2)$ or $(3, 2, 4)$.
We know that two lines AB and CD with direction ratios, a_1, b_1, c_1 and a_2, b_2, c_2 are perpendicular if $a_1a_2 + b_1b_2 + c_1c_2 = 0$

$$\therefore \quad 2 \times 3 + 5 \times 2 + (-4) \times 4 = 6 + 10 - 16 = 0$$

Therefore, the lines AB and CD are perpendicular.

Question 3 Show that the line through the points $(4, 7, 8)$, $(2, 3, 4)$ is parallel to the line through the points $(-1,-2,1)$, $(1,2,5)$.

◎ *Thinking Process* Let direction ratios 's of two lines are (a_1, b_1, c_1) and (a_2, b_2, c_2), then conditions of parallel lines are $\frac{a_1}{a_2} = \frac{b_1}{b_2} = \frac{c_1}{c_2}$.

Sol. Let the given points be $A(4, 7, 8)$, $B(2, 3, 4)$, $C(-1, -2, 1)$ and $D(1, 2, 5)$.
Direction ratios of AB (a_1, b_1, c_1) are $(2-4), (3-7), (4-8) \Rightarrow (-2, -4, -4)$

$$\therefore \quad a_1 = -2, b_1 = -4, c_1 = -4$$

Direction ratios of CD (a_2, b_2, c_2) are $(1+1), (2+2), (5-1) \Rightarrow (2, 4, 4)$

$$\therefore \quad a_2 = 2, b_2 = 4, c_2 = 4$$

AB is parallel to CD if $\Rightarrow \frac{a_1}{a_2} = \frac{b_1}{b_2} = \frac{c_1}{c_2}$

We have, $$\frac{a_1}{a_2} = \frac{-2}{2} = -1,\ \frac{b_1}{b_2} = \frac{-4}{4} = -1 \text{ and } \frac{c_1}{c_2} = \frac{-4}{4} = -1$$

$$\therefore \quad \frac{a_1}{a_2} = \frac{b_1}{b_2} = \frac{c_1}{c_2}.$$

Hence, $AB \parallel CD$.

Question 4 Find the equation of the line which passes through the point $(1, 2, 3)$ and is parallel to the vector $3\hat{i} + 2\hat{j} - 2\hat{k}$.

◎ *Thinking Process* The equation of line passing through **a** and parallel to **b** is $\mathbf{r} = \mathbf{a} + \lambda \mathbf{b}$

Sol. It is given that the line passes through the point $A(1, 2, 3)$. Therefore, the position vector of A is $\mathbf{a} = \hat{\mathbf{i}} + 2\hat{\mathbf{j}} + 3\hat{\mathbf{k}}$ and parallel to vector $\mathbf{b} = 3\hat{\mathbf{i}} + 2\hat{\mathbf{j}} - 2\hat{\mathbf{k}}$.
It is known that the line which passes through point **a** and parallel to **b** is given by $\mathbf{r} = \mathbf{a} + \lambda \mathbf{b}$, where λ is a constant.

$$\therefore \quad \mathbf{r} = \hat{\mathbf{i}} + 2\hat{\mathbf{j}} + 3\hat{\mathbf{k}} + \lambda(3\hat{\mathbf{i}} + 2\hat{\mathbf{j}} - 2\hat{\mathbf{k}}) \qquad \text{(Vector form)}$$

Cartesian form The equation of line passing through (x_1, y_1, z_1) which are (1, 2, 3) and direction ratios, a, b, c which are 3, 2, –2

$$\Rightarrow \quad \frac{x-x_1}{a}=\frac{y-y_1}{b}=\frac{z-z_1}{c} \Rightarrow \frac{x-1}{3}=\frac{y-2}{2}=\frac{z-3}{-2}$$

This is the cartesian form of required equation of the line.

Question 5 Find the equation of the line in vector and in cartesian form that passes through the point with position vector $2\hat{i}-\hat{j}+4\hat{k}$ and is in the direction $\hat{i}+2\hat{j}-\hat{k}$.

Sol. It is given that the line passes through the point with position vector $\mathbf{a}=2\hat{\mathbf{i}}-\hat{\mathbf{j}}+4\hat{\mathbf{k}}$ and in the direction of $\mathbf{b}=\hat{\mathbf{i}}+2\hat{\mathbf{j}}-\hat{\mathbf{k}}$.

It is known that a line through a point with position vector **a** and parallel to **b** *i.e.*, in direction of **b** is given by the equation, $\mathbf{r}=\mathbf{a}+\lambda\mathbf{b}$.

$$\therefore \quad \mathbf{r}=2\hat{\mathbf{i}}-\hat{\mathbf{j}}+4\hat{\mathbf{k}}+\lambda(\hat{\mathbf{i}}+2\hat{\mathbf{j}}-\hat{\mathbf{k}})$$

This is the required equation of the line in vector form.

Let $\quad \mathbf{r}=x\hat{\mathbf{i}}+y\hat{\mathbf{j}}+z\hat{\mathbf{k}}$

$$\therefore \quad x\hat{\mathbf{i}}+y\hat{\mathbf{j}}+z\hat{\mathbf{k}}=(\lambda+2)\hat{\mathbf{i}}+(2\lambda-1)\hat{\mathbf{j}}+(-\lambda+4)\hat{\mathbf{k}}$$

On comparing both sides, we get

$$\begin{pmatrix} x=\lambda+2 \Rightarrow x-2=\lambda \\ y=2\lambda-1 \Rightarrow y+1=2\lambda \\ z=-\lambda+4 \Rightarrow z-4=-\lambda \end{pmatrix}$$

Eliminating λ, we obtain the cartesian form equation as

$$\frac{x-2}{1}=\frac{y+1}{2}=\frac{z-4}{-1}$$

This is the required equation of the given line in Cartesian form.

Question 6 Find the cartesian equation of the line which passes through the point $(-2, 4, -5)$ and parallel to the line given by $\frac{x+3}{3}=\frac{y-4}{5}=\frac{z+8}{6}$.

Thinking Process The equation of line passing through $(x_1, y_1\ z_1)$ and parallel to given line whose direction ratio is (a_1, b_1, c_1), is $\frac{x-x_1}{a_1}=\frac{y-y_1}{b_1}=\frac{z-z_1}{c_1}$.

Sol. It is given that the line passes through the point (–2, 4, – 5) and is parallel to

$$\frac{x+3}{3}=\frac{y-4}{5}=\frac{z+8}{6}$$

The direction ratios of the line $\frac{x+3}{3}=\frac{y-4}{5}=\frac{z+8}{6}$, are (3, 5, 6)

We know that the equation of the line passes through the point (x_1, y_1, z_1) and with direction ratios a, b, c, is given by $\frac{x-x_1}{a}=\frac{y-y_1}{b}=\frac{z-z_1}{c}$

Therefore, the equation of the line (in cartesian form) passes through (–2, 4, – 5) and having direction ratios (3, 5, 6) is

$$\frac{x-(-2)}{3}=\frac{y-4}{5}=\frac{z-(-5)}{6} \Rightarrow \frac{x+2}{3}=\frac{y-4}{5}=\frac{z+5}{6}$$

which is the required equation of line.

Question 7 The cartesian equation of a line is $\frac{x-5}{3}=\frac{y+4}{7}=\frac{z-6}{2}$. Write its vector form.

Thinking Process The line passing through position vector **a** and in the direction of the vector **b** is given by the equation, $r = \mathbf{a} + \lambda \mathbf{b}$, .

Sol. The given cartesian equation is $\frac{x-5}{3}=\frac{y+4}{7}=\frac{z-6}{2}$.

The above line passes through the point (5, – 4, 6). The position vector of this point is $\mathbf{a} = 5\hat{\mathbf{i}} - 4\hat{\mathbf{j}} + 6\hat{\mathbf{k}}$. Also, the direction ratios of the given line are 3, 7 and 2. This means that the line is in the direction of vector, $\mathbf{b} = 3\hat{\mathbf{i}} + 7\hat{\mathbf{j}} + 2\hat{\mathbf{k}}$.

It is known that the line through position vector **a** and in the direction of the vector **b** is given by the equation, $\mathbf{r} = \mathbf{a} + \lambda \mathbf{b}$, $\lambda \in R$

$$\therefore \quad \mathbf{r} = 5\hat{\mathbf{i}} - 4\hat{\mathbf{j}} + 6\hat{\mathbf{k}} + \lambda(3\hat{\mathbf{i}} + 7\hat{\mathbf{j}} + 2\hat{\mathbf{k}})$$

This is the required equation of the given line in vector form.

Quick Solution

We have $\frac{x-5}{3}=\frac{y+4}{7}=\frac{z-6}{2}=\lambda$ (let)

$$x-5=3\lambda \Rightarrow x=5+3\lambda$$
$$y+4=7\lambda \Rightarrow y=-4+7\lambda$$
$$z-6=2\lambda \Rightarrow z=6+2\lambda$$
$$\therefore \quad \mathbf{r}=x\hat{\mathbf{i}}+y\hat{\mathbf{j}}+z\hat{\mathbf{k}}=5\hat{\mathbf{i}}+3\lambda\hat{\mathbf{i}}+(-4\hat{\mathbf{j}}+7\lambda\hat{\mathbf{j}})+(6\hat{\mathbf{k}}+2\lambda\hat{\mathbf{k}})$$
$$\mathbf{r}=(5\hat{\mathbf{i}}-4\hat{\mathbf{j}}+6\hat{\mathbf{k}})+\lambda(3\hat{\mathbf{i}}+7\hat{\mathbf{j}}+2\hat{\mathbf{k}})$$

This is required equation of line in the vector form.

Question 8 Find the angle between the following pairs of lines :

(a) $\mathbf{r} = 2\hat{i} - 5\hat{j} + \hat{k} + \lambda(3\hat{i} + 2\hat{j} + 6\hat{k})$ and $\mathbf{r} = 7\hat{i} - 6\hat{k} + \mu(\hat{i} + 2\hat{j} + 2\hat{k})$

(b) $\mathbf{r} = 3\hat{i} + \hat{j} - 2\hat{k} + \lambda(\hat{i} - \hat{j} - 2\hat{k})$ and $\mathbf{r} = 2\hat{i} - \hat{j} - 56\hat{k} + \mu(3\hat{i} - 5\hat{j} - 4\hat{k})$.

Thinking Process The angle between the pairs of lines $\mathbf{r} = \mathbf{a}_1 + \lambda \mathbf{b}_1$ and $\mathbf{r} = \mathbf{a}_2 + \lambda \mathbf{b}_2$ is $\cos\theta = \left|\frac{\mathbf{b}_1 \cdot \mathbf{b}_2}{|\mathbf{b}_1||\mathbf{b}_2|}\right|$.

Sol.

(a) Let θ be the acute angle between the given lines, then

$$\cos\theta = \left|\frac{\mathbf{b}_1 \cdot \mathbf{b}_2}{|\mathbf{b}_1||\mathbf{b}_2|}\right|$$

The given lines are respectively parallel to the vectors $\mathbf{b}_1 = 3\hat{\mathbf{i}} + 2\hat{\mathbf{j}} + 6\hat{\mathbf{k}}$ and $\mathbf{b}_2 = \hat{\mathbf{i}} + 2\hat{\mathbf{j}} + 2\hat{\mathbf{k}}$.

$\therefore \quad |\mathbf{b}_1| = \sqrt{3^2 + 2^2 + 6^2} = \sqrt{9+4+36} = \sqrt{49} = 7,$

$|\mathbf{b}_2| = \sqrt{1^2 + 2^2 + 2^2} = \sqrt{1+4+4} = \sqrt{9} = 3$

and $\quad \mathbf{b}_1 \cdot \mathbf{b}_2 = (3\hat{\mathbf{i}} + 2\hat{\mathbf{j}} + 6\hat{\mathbf{k}}).(\hat{\mathbf{i}} + 2\hat{\mathbf{j}} + 2\hat{\mathbf{k}})$

$= 3 \times 1 + 2 \times 2 + 6 \times 2 = 3 + 4 + 12 = 19$

$$\therefore \quad \cos\theta = \left|\frac{\mathbf{b}_1 \cdot \mathbf{b}_2}{|\mathbf{b}_1||\mathbf{b}_2|}\right| = \frac{19}{7 \times 3} = \frac{19}{21} \Rightarrow \theta = \cos^{-1}\left(\frac{19}{21}\right)$$

(b) Let θ be the acute angle between the given lines, then

$$\cos\theta = \left|\frac{\mathbf{b}_1 \cdot \mathbf{b}_2}{|\mathbf{b}_1||\mathbf{b}_2|}\right|$$

The given lines are respectively parallel to the vectors $\mathbf{b}_1 = \hat{\mathbf{i}} - \hat{\mathbf{j}} - 2\hat{\mathbf{k}}$ and $\mathbf{b}_2 = 3\hat{\mathbf{i}} - 5\hat{\mathbf{j}} - 4\hat{\mathbf{k}}$.

$\therefore \quad |\mathbf{b}_1| = \sqrt{(1)^2 + (-1)^2 + (-2)^2} = \sqrt{1+1+4} = \sqrt{6},$

$|\mathbf{b}_2| = \sqrt{(3)^2 + (-5)^2 + (-4)^2} = \sqrt{9+25+16} = \sqrt{50} = 5\sqrt{2}$

and $\quad \mathbf{b}_1 \cdot \mathbf{b}_2 = (\hat{\mathbf{i}} - \hat{\mathbf{j}} - 2\hat{\mathbf{k}}) \cdot (3\hat{\mathbf{i}} - 5\hat{\mathbf{j}} - 4\hat{\mathbf{k}})$

$= 1 \times 3 + (-1)(-5) + (-2)(-4) = 3 + 5 + 8 = 16$

$$\therefore \cos\theta = \left|\frac{\mathbf{b}_1 \cdot \mathbf{b}_2}{|\mathbf{b}_1||\mathbf{b}_2|}\right| = \frac{16}{\sqrt{6} \times 5\sqrt{2}} = \frac{16}{10\sqrt{3}} = \frac{8}{5\sqrt{3}} \Rightarrow \quad \theta = \cos^{-1}\left(\frac{8}{5\sqrt{3}}\right)$$

Question 9 Find the angle between the following pair of lines

(a) $\dfrac{x-2}{2} = \dfrac{y-1}{5} = \dfrac{z+3}{-3}$ and $\dfrac{x+2}{-1} = \dfrac{y-4}{8} = \dfrac{z-5}{4}$.

(b) $\dfrac{x}{2} = \dfrac{y}{2} = \dfrac{z}{1}$ and $\dfrac{x-5}{4} = \dfrac{y-2}{1} = \dfrac{z-3}{8}$.

Thinking Process Firstly, find direction ratios of both lines *i.e.*, (a_1, b_1, c_1) and (a_2, b_2, c_2) and then, use formula $\cos\theta = \dfrac{a_1a_2 + b_1b_2 + c_1c_2}{\sqrt{a_1^2 + b_1^2 + c_1^2}\sqrt{a_2^2 + b_2^2 + c_2^2}}$ and simplify it.

Sol. (a) Here, the equation of given lines are

$$\frac{x-2}{2} = \frac{y-1}{5} = \frac{z+3}{-3} \text{ and } \frac{x+2}{-1} = \frac{y-4}{8} = \frac{z-5}{4}$$

We know that if $\dfrac{x-x_1}{a_1} = \dfrac{y-y_1}{b_1} = \dfrac{z-z_1}{c_1}$ be a line then its dr's are (a_1, b_1, c_1)

$\therefore$ Direction ratios of given lines are (2, 5, –3) and (–1, 8, 4).

Let θ be the acute angle between the given lines, then

$$\cos\theta = \frac{a_1a_2 + b_1b_2 + c_1c_2}{\sqrt{a_1^2 + b_1^2 + c_1^2}\sqrt{a_2^2 + b_2^2 + c_2^2}}$$

$$\Rightarrow \quad \cos\theta = \frac{2\times(-1) + 5\times 8 + (-3)\times 4}{\sqrt{2^2 + 5^2 + (-3)^2}\sqrt{(-1)^2 + 8^2 + 4^2}}$$

$$= \frac{-2 + 40 - 12}{\sqrt{4 + 25 + 9}\sqrt{1 + 64 + 16}}$$

$$= \frac{26}{\sqrt{38}\sqrt{81}} = \frac{26}{9\sqrt{38}} \Rightarrow \theta = \cos^{-1}\left(\frac{26}{9\sqrt{38}}\right)$$

(b) Here, the equation of given lines are

$$\frac{x}{2} = \frac{y}{2} = \frac{z}{1} \text{ and } \frac{x-5}{4} = \frac{y-2}{1} = \frac{z-3}{8}$$

We know that if $\frac{x - x_1}{a_1} = \frac{y - y_1}{b_1} = \frac{z - z_1}{c_1}$ be a line, then its dr's are (a_1, b_1, c_1)

$\therefore$ Direction ratios of two lines are (2, 2, 1) and (4, 1, 8).

Let θ be the acute angle between the given lines, then

$$\cos\theta = \frac{a_1a_2 + b_1b_2 + c_1c_2}{\sqrt{a_1^2 + b_1^2 + c_1^2}\sqrt{a_2^2 + b_2^2 + c_2^2}}$$

$$\Rightarrow \quad \cos\theta = \frac{2\times 4 + 2\times 1 + 1\times 8}{\sqrt{2^2 + 2^2 + 1^2}\sqrt{4^2 + 1^2 + 8^2}}$$

$$= \frac{8 + 2 + 8}{\sqrt{4 + 4 + 1}\sqrt{16 + 1 + 64}} = \frac{18}{\sqrt{9}\sqrt{81}} = \frac{18}{3\times 9} = \frac{2}{3}$$

$$\Rightarrow \quad \theta = \cos^{-1}\left(\frac{2}{3}\right)$$

Question 10 Find the values of p so that the lines $\frac{1-x}{3} = \frac{7y-14}{2p} = \frac{z-3}{2}$ and $\frac{7-7x}{3p} = \frac{y-5}{1} = \frac{6-z}{5}$ are at right angles.

Thinking Process (Q. No. 10-11) Two lines are at right angles, if $a_1a_2 + b_1b_2 + c_1c_2 = 0$, where (a_1, b_1, c_1) and (a_2, b_2, c_2) are the dr's of the lines.

Sol. Equation of the given lines can be written in standard form

$$\frac{x-1}{-3} = \frac{y-2}{\frac{2p}{7}} = \frac{z-3}{2} \text{ and } \frac{x-1}{-\frac{3p}{7}} = \frac{y-5}{1} = \frac{z-6}{-5}$$

Direction ratios of these lines are respectively $-3, \frac{2p}{7}, 2$ and $\frac{-3p}{7}, 1, -5$

Two lines with direction ratios a_1, b_1, c_1 and a_2, b_2, c_2 are perpendicular to each other, if $a_1a_2 + b_1b_2 + c_1c_2 = 0$.

$\therefore \quad (-3)\left(\frac{-3p}{7}\right)+\left(\frac{2p}{7}\right)(1)+(2)(-5)=0$

$\Rightarrow \quad \frac{9p}{7}+\frac{2p}{7}-10=0$

$\Rightarrow \quad \frac{11p}{7}=10 \Rightarrow p=\frac{70}{11}.$

Thus, the value of $p=\frac{70}{11}$

Mistake Alert For making a line in standard form be ensure that coefficient of variable should be 1.

Question 11 Show that the lines $\frac{x-5}{7}=\frac{y+2}{-5}=\frac{z}{1}$ and $\frac{x}{1}=\frac{y}{2}=\frac{z}{3}$ are perpendicular to each other.

Sol. The equations of the given lines are $\frac{x-5}{7}=\frac{y+2}{-5}=\frac{z}{1}$ and $\frac{x}{1}=\frac{y}{2}=\frac{z}{3}$.

Direction ratios of the given lines are 7, – 5, 1 and 1, 2, 3.

Two lines with direction ratios, a_1, b_1, c_1 and a_2, b_2, c_2 are perpendicular to each other, if

$$a_1a_2+b_1b_2+c_1c_2=0$$

$\therefore \quad (7)(1)+(-5)(2)+(1)(3)=7-10+3=0$

Therefore, the given lines are perpendicular.

Question 12. Find the shortest distance between the lines
$r=(\hat{i}+2\hat{j}+\hat{k})+\lambda(\hat{i}-\hat{j}+\hat{k})$ and $r=(2\hat{i}-\hat{j}-\hat{k})+\mu(2\hat{i}+\hat{j}+2\hat{k})$.

Thinking Process (Q. No. 12-15) From the equation of two lines find $\mathbf{a}_1, \mathbf{b}_2$ and $\mathbf{a}_2, \mathbf{b}_2$, then put in formula $\frac{(\mathbf{b}_1\times\mathbf{b}_2).(\mathbf{a}_2-\mathbf{a}_1)}{|\mathbf{b}_1\times\mathbf{b}_2|}$ to get the shortest distance between the lines.

Sol. The given equations are $\mathbf{r}=\hat{\mathbf{i}}+2\hat{\mathbf{j}}+\hat{\mathbf{k}}+\lambda(\hat{\mathbf{i}}-\hat{\mathbf{j}}+\hat{\mathbf{k}})$

and $\quad \mathbf{r}=2\hat{\mathbf{i}}-\hat{\mathbf{j}}-\hat{\mathbf{k}}+\mu(2\hat{\mathbf{i}}+\hat{\mathbf{j}}+2\hat{\mathbf{k}})$

which is of the form $\mathbf{r}=\mathbf{a}_1+\lambda\,\mathbf{b}_1$ and $\mathbf{r}=\mathbf{a}_2+\mu\,\mathbf{b}_2$

where $\quad \mathbf{a}_1=\hat{\mathbf{i}}+2\hat{\mathbf{j}}+\hat{\mathbf{k}}, \mathbf{b}_1=\hat{\mathbf{i}}-\hat{\mathbf{j}}+\hat{\mathbf{k}}$

and $\quad \mathbf{a}_2=2\hat{\mathbf{i}}-\hat{\mathbf{j}}-\hat{\mathbf{k}}, \mathbf{b}_2=2\hat{\mathbf{i}}+\hat{\mathbf{j}}+2\hat{\mathbf{k}}$

Now, $\mathbf{a}_2-\mathbf{a}_1=(2\hat{\mathbf{i}}-\hat{\mathbf{j}}-\hat{\mathbf{k}})-(\hat{\mathbf{i}}+2\hat{\mathbf{j}}+\hat{\mathbf{k}})=\hat{\mathbf{i}}-3\hat{\mathbf{j}}-2\hat{\mathbf{k}}$

and $\quad \mathbf{b}_1\times\mathbf{b}_2=\begin{vmatrix}\hat{\mathbf{i}} & \hat{\mathbf{j}} & \hat{\mathbf{k}}\\ 1 & -1 & 1\\ 2 & 1 & 2\end{vmatrix}=\hat{\mathbf{i}}(-2-1)-\hat{\mathbf{j}}(2-2)+\hat{\mathbf{k}}(1+2)=-3\hat{\mathbf{i}}+3\hat{\mathbf{k}}$

$\Rightarrow \quad |\mathbf{b}_1\times\mathbf{b}_2|=\sqrt{(-3)^2+(3)^2}=\sqrt{9+9}=\sqrt{18}=3\sqrt{2}$

Now, shortest distance = $\left|\frac{(\mathbf{b}_1 \times \mathbf{b}_2) \cdot (\mathbf{a}_2 - \mathbf{a}_1)}{|\mathbf{b}_1 \times \mathbf{b}_2|}\right|$

$$= \frac{|(-3\hat{\mathbf{i}} + 3\hat{\mathbf{k}}) \cdot (\hat{\mathbf{i}} - 3\hat{\mathbf{j}} - 2\hat{\mathbf{k}})|}{3\sqrt{2}} = \frac{|(-3) \times 1 + 0 \times (-3) + 3 \times (-2)|}{3\sqrt{2}}$$

$$= \frac{9}{3\sqrt{2}} = \frac{3 \times \sqrt{2}}{\sqrt{2} \times \sqrt{2}} = \frac{3\sqrt{2}}{2} \text{ units}$$

Therefore, the shortest distance between the two lines is $\frac{3\sqrt{2}}{2}$ units.

Question 13 Find the shortest distance between the lines

$$\frac{x+1}{7} = \frac{y+1}{-6} = \frac{z+1}{1} \text{ and } \frac{x-3}{1} = \frac{y-5}{-2} = \frac{z-7}{1}$$

Sol. The given lines are

$$\frac{x+1}{7} = \frac{y+1}{-6} = \frac{z+1}{1}$$

and $$\frac{x-3}{1} = \frac{y-5}{-2} = \frac{z-7}{1}.$$

On comparing with

$$\frac{x-x_1}{a} = \frac{y-y_1}{b} = \frac{z-z_1}{c} \text{ we get}$$

For Ist line dr's = (7, – 6, 1) and passes through (–1, – 1, – 1) then equation of given line (in vector form) is

$$\mathbf{r}_1 = -\hat{\mathbf{i}} - \hat{\mathbf{j}} - \hat{\mathbf{k}} + \lambda(7\hat{\mathbf{i}} - 6\hat{\mathbf{j}} + \hat{\mathbf{k}})$$

Similarly, $$\mathbf{r}_2 = 3\hat{\mathbf{i}} + 5\hat{\mathbf{j}} + 7\hat{\mathbf{k}} + \mu(\hat{\mathbf{i}} - 2\hat{\mathbf{j}} + \hat{\mathbf{k}})$$

which are of the form $\mathbf{r}_1 = \mathbf{a}_1 + \lambda \mathbf{b}_1$ and $\mathbf{r}_2 = \mathbf{a}_2 + \mu \mathbf{b}_2$

where, $$\mathbf{a}_1 = -\hat{\mathbf{i}} - \hat{\mathbf{j}} - \hat{\mathbf{k}}, \mathbf{b}_1 = 7\hat{\mathbf{i}} - 6\hat{\mathbf{j}} + \hat{\mathbf{k}}$$

and $$\mathbf{a}_2 = 3\hat{\mathbf{i}} + 5\hat{\mathbf{j}} + 7\hat{\mathbf{k}}, \mathbf{b}_2 = \hat{\mathbf{i}} - 2\hat{\mathbf{j}} + \hat{\mathbf{k}}$$

Now, $$\mathbf{a}_2 - \mathbf{a}_1 = (3\hat{\mathbf{i}} + 5\hat{\mathbf{j}} + 7\hat{\mathbf{k}}) - (-\hat{\mathbf{i}} - \hat{\mathbf{j}} - \hat{\mathbf{k}}) = 4\hat{\mathbf{i}} + 6\hat{\mathbf{j}} + 8\hat{\mathbf{k}}$$

and $$\mathbf{b}_1 \times \mathbf{b}_2 = \begin{vmatrix} \hat{\mathbf{i}} & \hat{\mathbf{j}} & \hat{\mathbf{k}} \\ 7 & -6 & 1 \\ 1 & -2 & 1 \end{vmatrix} = \hat{\mathbf{i}}(-6+2) - \hat{\mathbf{j}}(7-1) + \hat{\mathbf{k}}(-14+6) = -4\hat{\mathbf{i}} - 6\hat{\mathbf{j}} - 8\hat{\mathbf{k}}$$

$$|\mathbf{b}_1 \times \mathbf{b}_2| = \sqrt{(-4)^2 + (-6)^2 + (-8)^2}$$

$$= \sqrt{16 + 36 + 64} = \sqrt{116} = 2\sqrt{29}$$

$\therefore$ SD between the given lines is given by

$$d = \frac{|(\mathbf{b}_1 \times \mathbf{b}_2).(\mathbf{a}_2 - \mathbf{a}_1)|}{|\mathbf{b}_1 \times \mathbf{b}_2|} = \frac{|(-4\hat{\mathbf{i}} - 6\hat{\mathbf{j}} - 8\hat{\mathbf{k}}).(4\hat{\mathbf{i}} + 6\hat{\mathbf{j}} + 8\hat{\mathbf{k}})|}{2\sqrt{29}}$$

$$= \frac{|(-4) \times 4 + (-6) \times 6 + (-8) \times 8|}{2\sqrt{29}} = \frac{|-16 - 36 - 64|}{2\sqrt{29}}$$

$$= \frac{116}{2\sqrt{29}} = \frac{58}{\sqrt{29}} = 2\sqrt{29} \text{ units.}$$

Question 14 Find the shortest distance between the lines whose vector equations are $\mathbf{r} = (\hat{i} + 2\hat{j} + 3\hat{k}) + \lambda(\hat{i} - 3\hat{j} + 2\hat{k})$
and $\mathbf{r} = (4\hat{i} + 5\hat{j} + 6\hat{k}) + \mu(2\hat{i} + 3\hat{j} + \hat{k})$.

Sol. The given lines are $\mathbf{r} = \hat{\mathbf{i}} + 2\hat{\mathbf{j}} + 3\hat{\mathbf{k}} + \lambda(\hat{\mathbf{i}} - 3\hat{\mathbf{j}} + 2\hat{\mathbf{k}})$

and $\mathbf{r} = 4\hat{\mathbf{i}} + 5\hat{\mathbf{j}} + 6\hat{\mathbf{k}} + \mu(2\hat{\mathbf{i}} + 3\hat{\mathbf{j}} + \hat{\mathbf{k}})$

It is known that the shortest distance between the lines $\mathbf{r} = \mathbf{a}_1 + \lambda\mathbf{b}_1$ and $\mathbf{r} = \mathbf{a}_2 + \mu\mathbf{b}_2$ is given by $\dfrac{|(\mathbf{b}_1 \times \mathbf{b}_2).(\mathbf{a}_2 - \mathbf{a}_1)|}{|\mathbf{b}_1 \times \mathbf{b}_2|}$

On comparing the given equations with $\mathbf{r} = \mathbf{a}_1 + \lambda\,\mathbf{b}_1$ and $\mathbf{r} = \mathbf{a}_2 + \mu\,\mathbf{b}_2$, we obtain

$$\mathbf{a}_1 = \hat{\mathbf{i}} + 2\hat{\mathbf{j}} + 3\hat{\mathbf{k}}, \ \mathbf{b}_1 = \hat{\mathbf{i}} - 3\hat{\mathbf{j}} + 2\hat{\mathbf{k}}$$

and $$\mathbf{a}_2 = 4\hat{\mathbf{i}} + 5\hat{\mathbf{j}} + 6\hat{\mathbf{k}}, \ \mathbf{b}_2 = 2\hat{\mathbf{i}} + 3\hat{\mathbf{j}} + \hat{\mathbf{k}}$$

Here, $$\mathbf{a}_2 - \mathbf{a}_1 = (4\hat{\mathbf{i}} + 5\hat{\mathbf{j}} + 6\hat{\mathbf{k}}) - (\hat{\mathbf{i}} + 2\hat{\mathbf{j}} + 3\hat{\mathbf{k}}) = 3\hat{\mathbf{i}} + 3\hat{\mathbf{j}} + 3\hat{\mathbf{k}}$$

Also, $$\mathbf{b}_1 \times \mathbf{b}_2 = \begin{vmatrix} \hat{\mathbf{i}} & \hat{\mathbf{j}} & \hat{\mathbf{k}} \\ 1 & -3 & 2 \\ 2 & 3 & 1 \end{vmatrix} = \hat{\mathbf{i}}(-3 - 6) - \hat{\mathbf{j}}(1 - 4) + \hat{\mathbf{k}}(3 + 6) = -9\hat{\mathbf{i}} + 3\hat{\mathbf{j}} + 9\hat{\mathbf{k}}$$

$\Rightarrow$ $$|\mathbf{b}_1 \times \mathbf{b}_2| = \sqrt{(-9)^2 + (3)^2 + (9)^2} = \sqrt{81 + 9 + 81} = \sqrt{171} = 3\sqrt{19}$$

$\therefore$ Required shortest distance

$$d = \frac{|(\mathbf{b}_1 \times \mathbf{b}_2).(\mathbf{a}_2 - \mathbf{a}_1)|}{|\mathbf{b}_1 \times \mathbf{b}_2|}$$

$$= \frac{|(-9\hat{\mathbf{i}} + 3\hat{\mathbf{j}} + 9\hat{\mathbf{k}}).(3\hat{\mathbf{i}} + 3\hat{\mathbf{j}} + 3\hat{\mathbf{k}})|}{3\sqrt{19}}$$

$$= \frac{|-9 \times 3 + 3 \times 3 + 9 \times 3|}{3\sqrt{19}}$$

$$= \frac{-27 + 9 + 27}{3\sqrt{19}} = \frac{9}{3\sqrt{19}} = \frac{3}{\sqrt{19}} \text{ units}$$

Therefore, the shortest distance between the two given lines is $\dfrac{3}{\sqrt{19}}$ units.

Question 15. Find the shortest distance between the lines whose vector equations are

$\mathbf{r} = (1-t)\hat{i} + (t-2)\hat{j} + (3-2t)\hat{k}$ and $\mathbf{r} = (s+1)\hat{i} + (2s-1)\hat{j} - (2s+1)\hat{k}$.

Sol. Equation of the given lines of the form

$$\mathbf{r} = (\hat{\mathbf{i}} - 2\hat{\mathbf{j}} + 3\hat{\mathbf{k}}) + t(-\hat{\mathbf{i}} + \hat{\mathbf{j}} - 2\hat{\mathbf{k}}) \text{ and } \mathbf{r} = (\hat{\mathbf{i}} - \hat{\mathbf{j}} - \hat{\mathbf{k}}) + s(\hat{\mathbf{i}} + 2\hat{\mathbf{j}} - 2\hat{\mathbf{k}})$$

Compare these with $\mathbf{r} = \mathbf{a}_1 + t\mathbf{b}_1$ and $\mathbf{r} = \mathbf{a}_2 + s\mathbf{b}_2$

$$\mathbf{a}_1 = \hat{\mathbf{i}} - 2\hat{\mathbf{j}} + 3\hat{\mathbf{k}},\ \mathbf{b}_1 = -\hat{\mathbf{i}} + \hat{\mathbf{j}} - 2\hat{\mathbf{k}} \text{ and } \mathbf{a}_2 = \hat{\mathbf{i}} - \hat{\mathbf{j}} - \hat{\mathbf{k}},$$
$$\mathbf{b}_2 = \hat{\mathbf{i}} + 2\hat{\mathbf{j}} - 2\hat{\mathbf{k}}$$

Now, $\mathbf{a}_2 - \mathbf{a}_1 = (\hat{\mathbf{i}} - \hat{\mathbf{j}} - \hat{\mathbf{k}}) - (\hat{\mathbf{i}} - 2\hat{\mathbf{j}} + 3\hat{\mathbf{k}}) = \mathbf{j} - 4\hat{\mathbf{k}}$

and
$$\mathbf{b}_1 \times \mathbf{b}_2 = \begin{vmatrix} \hat{\mathbf{i}} & \hat{\mathbf{j}} & \hat{\mathbf{k}} \\ -1 & 1 & -2 \\ 1 & 2 & -2 \end{vmatrix} = (-2+4)\hat{\mathbf{i}} - (2+2)\hat{\mathbf{j}} + (-2-1)\hat{\mathbf{k}}$$
$$= 2\hat{\mathbf{i}} - 4\hat{\mathbf{j}} - 3\hat{\mathbf{k}}$$

$\Rightarrow$ $$|\mathbf{b}_1 \times \mathbf{b}_2| = \sqrt{(2)^2 + (-4)^2 + (-3)^2} = \sqrt{4 + 16 + 9} = \sqrt{29}$$

$\therefore$ Required shortest distance

$$d = \frac{|(\mathbf{b}_1 \times \mathbf{b}_2) \cdot (\mathbf{a}_2 - \mathbf{a}_1)|}{|\mathbf{b}_1 \times \mathbf{b}_2|} = \frac{|(2\hat{\mathbf{i}} - 4\hat{\mathbf{j}} - 3\hat{\mathbf{k}}) \cdot (\hat{\mathbf{j}} - 4\hat{\mathbf{k}})|}{\sqrt{29}} = \frac{|-4 + 12|}{\sqrt{29}} = \frac{8}{\sqrt{29}} \text{ units.}$$

Miscellaneous Exercise

Question 1. Find the angle between the lines where direction ratios are (a, b, c) and $(b-c, c-a, a-b)$.

Sol. The direction ratios of the two lines are (a, b, c) and $(b-c, c-a, a-b)$.

Let θ be the acute angle between the two lines, then

$$\cos\theta = \left| \frac{a(b-c) + b(c-a) + c(a-b)}{\sqrt{a^2 + b^2 + c^2}\sqrt{(b-c)^2 + (c-a)^2 + (a-b)^2}} \right|$$

$$\left[\because \cos\theta = \left| \frac{a_1a_2 + b_1b_2 + c_1c_2}{\sqrt{a_1^2 + b_1^2 + c_1^2}\sqrt{a_2^2 + b_2^2 + c_2^2}} \right| \right]$$

$$= \left| \frac{ab - ac + bc - ab + ca - bc}{\sqrt{a^2 + b^2 + c^2}\sqrt{(b-c)^2 + (c-a)^2 + (a-b)^2}} \right| = 0$$

$\Rightarrow$ $$\cos\theta = 0 \Rightarrow \theta = \frac{\pi}{2} = 90^\circ$$

Thus, the angle between the lines is 90°.

Question 2. Find the equation of a line parallel to X-axis and passing through the origin.

Thinking Process A line parallel to X-axis and passing through the origin is X-axis itself.

Sol. Let A be a point on X-axis. Therefore, the coordinates of A are given by $(a, 0, 0)$, where $a \in R$.

Direction ratios of X-axis are $K, 0, 0$

Direction ratios of OA are $(a-0), 0, 0 = a, 0, 0$

The equation of OA is given by, $\frac{x-0}{a} = \frac{y-0}{0} = \frac{z-0}{0} \Rightarrow \frac{x}{1} = \frac{y}{0} = \frac{z}{0} = a$

Question 3. If the lines $\frac{x-1}{-3} = \frac{y-2}{2k} = \frac{z-3}{2}$ and $\frac{x-1}{3k} = \frac{y-1}{1} = \frac{z-6}{-5}$ are perpendicular, then find the value of k.

Mistake Alert Firstly, determine the direction ratios of given lines and put in formula $a_1a_2 + b_1b_2 + c_1c_2 = 0$ and get the result.

Sol. Direction ratio of the given two lines are respectively $(-3, 2k, 2)$ and $(3k, 1, -5)$.

It is known that two lines with direction ratios, a_1, b_1, c_1 and a_2, b_2, c_2 are perpendicular, if $a_1 a_2 + b_1 b_2 + c_1 c_2 = 0$

$$\therefore \quad (-3) \times (3k) + (2k) \times 1 + 2 \times (-5) = 0$$

$$\therefore \quad -9k + 2k - 10 = 0 \Rightarrow 7k = -10 \Rightarrow k = \frac{-10}{7}$$

Therefore, for $k = \frac{-10}{7}$, the given lines are perpendicular to each other.

Thinking Process In the process of finding direction ratio of a line in a cartesian form, the coefficient of x, y, z should be '+1'.

Question 4. Find the shortest distance between the lines

$$\mathbf{r} = 6\hat{i} + 2\hat{j} + 2\hat{k} + \lambda(\hat{i} - 2\hat{j} + 2\hat{k}) \text{ and } \mathbf{r} = -4\hat{i} - \hat{k} + \mu(3\hat{i} - 2\hat{j} - 2\hat{k}).$$

Thinking Process The shortest distance between the lines $\mathbf{r} = \mathbf{a}_1 + \lambda \mathbf{b}_1$ and $\mathbf{r} = \mathbf{a}_2 + \lambda \mathbf{b}_2$ is $d = \frac{|(\mathbf{b}_1 \times \mathbf{b}_2) \cdot (\mathbf{a}_2 - \mathbf{a}_1)|}{|\mathbf{b}_1 \times \mathbf{b}_2|}$

Sol. Given lines are $\mathbf{r} = 6\hat{\mathbf{i}} + 2\hat{\mathbf{j}} + 2\hat{\mathbf{k}} + \lambda(\hat{\mathbf{i}} - 2\hat{\mathbf{j}} + 2\hat{\mathbf{k}})$ ...(i)

and $\mathbf{r} = -4\hat{\mathbf{i}} - \hat{\mathbf{k}} + \mu(3\hat{\mathbf{i}} - 2\hat{\mathbf{j}} - 2\hat{\mathbf{k}})$ ...(ii)

It is known that the shortest distance between two lines $\mathbf{r} = \mathbf{a}_1 + \lambda\, \mathbf{b}_1$ and $\mathbf{r} = \mathbf{a}_2 + \mu\, \mathbf{b}_2$ is given by $d = \frac{|(\mathbf{b}_1 \times \mathbf{b}_2).(\mathbf{a}_2 - \mathbf{a}_1)|}{|\mathbf{b}_1 \times \mathbf{b}_2|}$ ...(iii)

Comparing $\mathbf{r} = \mathbf{a}_1 + \lambda\mathbf{b}_1$ and $\mathbf{r} = \mathbf{a}_2 + \mu\mathbf{b}_2$ to Eqs. (i) and (ii), we obtain

$$\mathbf{a}_1 = 6\hat{\mathbf{i}} + 2\hat{\mathbf{j}} + 2\hat{\mathbf{k}}, \mathbf{a}_2 = -4\hat{\mathbf{i}} - \hat{\mathbf{k}},\ \mathbf{b}_1 = \hat{\mathbf{i}} - 2\hat{\mathbf{j}} + 2\hat{\mathbf{k}} \text{ and } \mathbf{b}_2 = 3\hat{\mathbf{i}} - 2\hat{\mathbf{j}} - 2\hat{\mathbf{k}},$$

Now, $\mathbf{a}_2 - \mathbf{a}_1 = (-4\hat{\mathbf{i}} - \hat{\mathbf{k}}) - (6\hat{\mathbf{i}} + 2\hat{\mathbf{j}} + 2\hat{\mathbf{k}}) = -10\hat{\mathbf{i}} - 2\hat{\mathbf{j}} - 3\hat{\mathbf{k}}$

Also, $\mathbf{b}_1 \times \mathbf{b}_2 = \begin{vmatrix} \hat{\mathbf{i}} & \hat{\mathbf{j}} & \hat{\mathbf{k}} \\ 1 & -2 & 2 \\ 3 & -2 & -2 \end{vmatrix} = \hat{\mathbf{i}}(4+4) - \hat{\mathbf{j}}(-2-6) + \hat{\mathbf{k}}(-2+6) = 8\hat{\mathbf{i}} + 8\hat{\mathbf{j}} + 4\hat{\mathbf{k}}$

$\therefore \quad |\mathbf{b}_1 \times \mathbf{b}_2| = \sqrt{8^2 + 8^2 + 4^2} = \sqrt{64 + 64 + 16} = \sqrt{144} = 12$

Substituting all the values in Eq. (iii), we obtain

$$d = \left|\frac{(8\hat{\mathbf{i}} + 8\hat{\mathbf{j}} + 4\hat{\mathbf{k}}) \cdot (-10\hat{\mathbf{i}} - 2\hat{\mathbf{j}} - 3\hat{\mathbf{k}})}{12}\right| = \frac{|-80 - 16 - 12|}{12} = \frac{108}{12} = 9 \text{ units.}$$

Question 5. Find the vector equation of the line passing through the point (1, 2, –4) and perpendicular to the two lines

$$\frac{x-8}{3} = \frac{y+19}{-16} = \frac{z-10}{7} \text{ and } \frac{x-15}{3} = \frac{y-29}{8} = \frac{z-5}{-5}.$$

◎ ***Thinking Process*** Any equation of line passing through the point (x_1, y_1, z_1) with the direction ratio a, b, c is $\frac{x-x_1}{a} = \frac{y-y_1}{b} = \frac{z-z_1}{c}$.

Sol. Any line passing through (1, 2, –4) can be written as

$$\frac{x-1}{a} = \frac{y-2}{b} = \frac{z+4}{c} \quad \ldots\text{(i)}$$

where, a, b, c are the direction ratios of line (i).

Now, the line (i) be perpendicular to the lines

$$\frac{x-8}{3} = \frac{y+19}{-16} = \frac{z-10}{7}$$

and $$\frac{x-15}{3} = \frac{y-29}{8} = \frac{z-5}{-5}$$

In above having direction ratios are (3, –16, 7) and (3, 8, –5) respectively. Which is perpendicular with the Eq. (i).

$\therefore \quad 3a - 16b + 7c = 0 \quad \ldots\text{(ii)}$

and $\quad 3a + 8b - 5c = 0 \quad \ldots\text{(iii)}$

By cross-multiplication, we have

$$\frac{a}{80-56} = \frac{b}{15+21} = \frac{c}{24+48}$$

$$\Rightarrow \quad \frac{a}{24} = \frac{b}{36} = \frac{c}{72}$$

$$\Rightarrow \quad \frac{a}{2} = \frac{b}{3} = \frac{c}{6} = \lambda \quad \text{(say)}$$

$\therefore \quad a = 2\lambda, b = 3\lambda$ and $c = 6\lambda$

The equation of required line which is passes through the point (1, 2, –4) and parallel to vector $2\hat{\mathbf{i}} + 3\hat{\mathbf{j}} + 6\hat{\mathbf{k}}$ is $\mathbf{r} = (\hat{\mathbf{i}} + 2\hat{\mathbf{j}} - 4\hat{\mathbf{k}}) + \lambda(2\hat{\mathbf{i}} + 3\hat{\mathbf{j}} + 6\hat{\mathbf{k}})$.

DIKSHA APP Questions

☐ Multiple Choice Questions

Q.1 If the direction cosines of a line are $\frac{k}{3}, \frac{k}{3}, \frac{k}{3}$ the value of k is

(a) 0 (b) $0 < k < 1$
(c) 13 (d) $\pm\sqrt{3}$

Sol. (d) Given, the direction cosine are $\frac{k}{3}, \frac{k}{3}, \frac{k}{3}$

i.e., $\cos\alpha = \frac{k}{3}, \cos\beta = \frac{k}{3}, \cos\gamma = \frac{k}{3}$

We know that

$$\cos^2\alpha + \cos^2\beta + \cos^2\gamma = 1$$

$$\Rightarrow \frac{k^2}{9} + \frac{k^2}{9} + \frac{k^2}{9} = 1$$

$$\Rightarrow 3k^2 = 9$$

$$\Rightarrow k^2 = 3$$

$$\Rightarrow k = \pm\sqrt{3}$$

Q.2 The perpendicular distance of the point $P(1, -1, 2)$ from the line $\frac{x+1}{2} = \frac{y-2}{-3} = \frac{z+2}{4}$ is

(a) 7 (b) 5
(c) $\sqrt{6}$ (d) 0

Sol. (d) We have line $\frac{x+1}{2} = \frac{y-2}{-3} = \frac{z+2}{4}$

If we draw a perpendicular line from P to line let the point be Q.

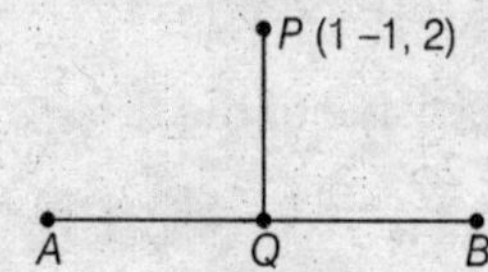

For point Q

$$\frac{x+1}{2} = \frac{y-2}{-3} = \frac{z+2}{4} = \lambda \text{ (say)}$$

$$\Rightarrow x = 2\lambda - 1, y = -3\lambda + 2, z = 4\lambda - 2$$

So, point $Q = (2\lambda - 1, -3\lambda + 2, 4\lambda - 2)$

$\therefore$ $\quad \mathbf{PQ}$ = Position Vector of Q – position vector of P

$$= (2\lambda - 1 - 1)\,\hat{\mathbf{i}} + (-3\lambda + 2 + 1)\,\hat{\mathbf{j}} + (4\lambda - 2 - 2)\,\hat{\mathbf{k}}$$
$$= (2\lambda - 2)\,\hat{\mathbf{i}} + (-3\lambda + 3)\,\hat{\mathbf{j}} + (4\lambda - 4)\,\hat{\mathbf{k}}$$

Direction ratios of given line AB are 2, –3, 4

Clearly, we can see that **PQ** is perpendicular to line **AB**

$\Rightarrow$ **PQ** $\cdot$ (Direction ratio of AB) = 0

$$\Rightarrow \quad (2\lambda - 2)\,2 + (-3\lambda + 3)(-3) + (4\lambda - 4)\,4 = 0$$
$$\Rightarrow \quad 4\lambda - 4 + 9\lambda - 9 + 16\lambda - 16 = 0$$
$$\Rightarrow \quad 29\lambda - 29 = 0$$
$$\Rightarrow \quad \lambda = 1$$

Put the value of λ in point Q, we get

$$Q = (1, -1, 2)$$

Now, P and Q are same i.e., point P lies on the line AB. Hence, distance is zero.

Q.3 A line makes α, β, γ with x-axis, y-axis and z-axis respectively then $\cos 2\alpha + \cos 2\beta + \cos 2\gamma =$

(a) 2 (b) 1 (c) –1 (d) –2

Sol. (c) If a line makes α, β, γ with x, y, z-axis respectively then $\cos\alpha$, $\cos\beta$ and $\cos\gamma$ are direction cosine of line.

We know that

$$\cos^2\alpha + \cos^2\beta + \cos^2\gamma = 1$$

$$\frac{1 + \cos 2\alpha}{2} + \frac{1 + \cos 2\beta}{2} + \frac{1 + \cos 2\gamma}{2} = 1 \qquad \left(\begin{aligned} &\cos 2\alpha = 2\cos^2\alpha - 1 \\ &\Rightarrow \cos^2\alpha = \frac{1 + \cos 2\alpha}{2} \end{aligned}\right)$$

$$\Rightarrow \quad 3 + \cos 2\alpha + \cos 2\beta + \cos 2\gamma = 2$$
$$\Rightarrow \quad \cos 2\alpha + \cos 2\beta + \cos 2\gamma = -1$$

Q.4 Find the direction cosine of the line

$$\frac{x + 2}{2} = \frac{2y - 5}{3}, z = -1.$$

(a) $\frac{4}{5}, \frac{3}{5}, 0$ (b) $\frac{5}{6}, \frac{7}{6}, 1$ (c) $\frac{3}{7}, \frac{4}{7}, 0$ (d) $\frac{1}{7}, \frac{3}{7}, 2$

Sol. (a) We have an equation of line

$$\therefore \quad \frac{x + 2}{2} = \frac{2y - 5}{3}, z = -1$$

So, equation can be written as $\dfrac{x + 2}{2} = \dfrac{2y - 5}{3} = \dfrac{z + 1}{0}$

$$\Rightarrow \quad \frac{x+2}{2} = \frac{y-\frac{5}{2}}{\frac{3}{2}} = \frac{z+1}{0}$$

Thus direction ratio of line is 2, $\frac{3}{2}$, 0 or 4, 3, 0.

$\therefore$ Direction cosines are $= \frac{4}{\sqrt{4^2+3^2+0^2}}, \frac{3}{\sqrt{4^2+3^2+0^2}}, \frac{0}{\sqrt{4^2+3^2+0^2}}$

$$= \frac{4}{5}, \frac{3}{5}, 0$$

Q.5 The line joining the points (–2, 1, –8) and (a, b, c) is parallel to the line whose direction ratios are 6, 2, 3, the value of a, b, c are

(a) 4, 3, –5 (b) 3, 2, $\frac{-13}{2}$

(c) 9, 5, – 2 (d) None of these

Sol. (a) Let $A = (-2, 1, -8)$ and $B = (a, b, c)$

Direction ratios of AB = Position Vector of B – position vector of A

$$= (a-(-2)), (b-1), (c-(-8)) = (a+2), (b-1), (c+8)$$

Now, we have given that AB is parallel to the direction ratios of 6, 2, 3.

So, the ratio of direction ratios will be equal.

$$\Rightarrow \quad \frac{a+2}{6} = \frac{b-1}{2} = \frac{c+8}{3} \quad \ldots(i)$$

If we put $a = 4$, $b = 3$ and $c = -5$

$$\Rightarrow \quad \frac{4+2}{6} = \frac{3-1}{2} = \frac{-5+8}{3} \Rightarrow 1 = 1 = 1 \text{ satisfy equation (i)}$$

Q.6 A line makes the same angle θ with each of x-axis and z-axis and β makes with y-axis is such that $\sin^2\beta = 3\sin^2\theta$ then $\cos^2\theta =$

(a) $\frac{2}{5}$ (b) $\frac{1}{5}$ (c) $\frac{3}{5}$ (d) $\frac{2}{3}$

Sol. (c) A line makes θ with x and z-axis and β with y-axis then $\cos\theta$, $\cos\beta$ and $\cos\theta$ will be direction cosines then

$$\cos^2\theta + \cos^2\beta + \cos^2\theta = 1 \Rightarrow 2\cos^2\theta = 1 - \cos^2\beta$$

$$\Rightarrow \quad 2\cos^2\theta = \sin^2\beta \quad \ldots(i)$$

$$(\because 1 - \cos^2\beta = \sin^2\beta)$$

$$\Rightarrow \quad 2\cos^2\theta = 3\sin^2\theta \quad [\because \sin^2\beta = 3\sin^2\theta]$$

$$\Rightarrow \quad 2\cos^2\theta = 3(1-\cos^2\theta) \Rightarrow 5\cos^2\theta = 3 \Rightarrow \cos^2\theta = \frac{3}{5}$$

Q.7 A line makes α, β, γ with x-axis, y-axis and z-axis respectively. If $\alpha + \beta = 90°$ then $\gamma =$

(a) 0 (b) 90°

(c) 180° (d) None of these

Sol. (b) If a line makes α, β, γ with x, y, z-axis respectively then $\cos\alpha$, $\cos\beta$ and $\cos\gamma$ will be directions cosine of line.

We know that

$$\cos^2\alpha + \cos^2\beta + \cos^2\gamma = 1 \quad \text{...(i)}$$

It is given that $\alpha + \beta = 90°$

$\Rightarrow \quad \beta = (90° - \alpha)$

On putting the value of β in Eq. (i), we get

$\Rightarrow \quad \cos^2\alpha + \cos^2(90° - \alpha) + \cos^2\gamma = 1$

$\Rightarrow \quad \cos^2\alpha + \sin^2\alpha + \cos^2\gamma = 1 \quad (\because \cos(90° - \alpha) = \sin\alpha)$

$\Rightarrow \quad 1 + \cos^2\gamma = 1 \quad (\because \sin^2\theta + \cos^2\theta = 1)$

$\Rightarrow \quad \cos^2\gamma = 0 \Rightarrow \cos\gamma = 0$

$\Rightarrow \quad \gamma = 90°$

Q.8 A line makes α, β, γ with x-axis, y-axis and z-axis respectively and $\cos\alpha = \frac{14}{15}$ and $\cos\beta = \frac{1}{3}$ then $\cos\gamma =$

(a) $\pm\frac{2}{15}$ (b) $\frac{1}{5}$ (c) $\pm\frac{1}{15}$ (d) None

Sol. (a) If a line makes α, β, γ with x, y, z-axis, then $\cos\alpha$, $\cos\beta$ and $\cos\gamma$ will be direction cosines of line.

We know that

$\cos^2\alpha + \cos^2\beta + \cos^2\gamma = 1$

Put $\cos\alpha = \frac{14}{15}$ and $\cos\beta = \frac{1}{3}$ (given), we get

$\Rightarrow \quad \left(\frac{14}{15}\right)^2 + \left(\frac{1}{3}\right)^2 + \cos^2\gamma = 1$

$\Rightarrow \quad \cos^2\gamma = 1 - \frac{196}{225} - \frac{1}{9}$

$$= \frac{225 - 196 - 25}{225}$$

$\Rightarrow \quad \cos^2\gamma = \frac{4}{225}$

$\Rightarrow \quad \cos\gamma = \pm\frac{2}{15}$

Q.9 If $\frac{1}{2}, \frac{1}{3}, n$ are the direction cosines of a line, then $n =$

(a) $\frac{\sqrt{23}}{6}$ (b) $\frac{23}{6}$ (c) $\frac{2}{3}$ (d) $\frac{1}{6}$

Sol. (a) Given, $\frac{1}{2}, \frac{1}{3}$ and n are direction cosines of a line.

We know that the sum of square of direction cosine is 1.

$$\therefore \quad \left(\frac{1}{2}\right)^2 + \left(\frac{1}{3}\right)^2 + n^2 = 1$$

$$\Rightarrow \quad n^2 = 1 - \frac{1}{4} - \frac{1}{9}$$

$$= \frac{36 - 9 - 4}{36}$$

$$\Rightarrow \quad n^2 = \frac{23}{36}$$

$$\Rightarrow \quad n = \pm \frac{\sqrt{23}}{6}$$

Q.10 Direction ratios of the line which is perpendicular to the lines with direction ratios –1, 2, 2 and 0, 2, 1 are

(a) 1, 1, 2 (b) 2, –1, 2 (c) –2, 1, –2 (d) 2, 1, –2

Sol. (c) We have direction ratio of two line.

So, $l_1 = -1, 2, 2$ and $l_2 = 0, 2, 1$

Direction ratio of a line which is perpendicular to l_1 and l_2 can be find by cross product of direction ratios of given line.

Then direction ratio of required line

$$= \begin{vmatrix} \hat{i} & \hat{j} & \hat{k} \\ -1 & 2 & 2 \\ 0 & 2 & 1 \end{vmatrix}$$

$$= \hat{i}(2 - 4) - \hat{j}(-1 - 0) + \hat{k}(-2 - 0)$$

$$= -2\hat{i} + \hat{j} - 2\hat{k}$$

Hence, direction ratios are –2, 1, –2.

Linear Programming

CHAPTER 12

Important Points

01 Linear Programming

It is a method used in decision making in business for obtaining the maximum or minimum values of a linear expression subject to the satisfying certain given inequations. This linear expression is known as the objective function and the linear inequations are known as linear constraints.

02 Linear Constraints In business or industry we want to make the best use of our limited resources, be these in the form of money, labour, expenses etc. The limitations on the resources can often be expressed in the form of linear inequalities, known as linear constraints.

e.g., $$a_1x + b_1y (\leq = \geq) c_1$$

03 Objective Function A linear function of the involved variables, which we want to maximize or minimize subject to the given linear constraints, is known as an objective function.

e.g., $$Z = Px + Qy$$

04 Optimal Value of an Objective Function The maximum or minimum value of the objective function within the feasible region is known as its optimal value.

05 Feasible Solution A set of values of the variables satisfying all the constraints is known as a feasible solution.

Note Any point outside the feasible region is called an infeasible solution

06 **Optimal Solution** A feasible solution which leads to an optimal value of the objective function is known as an optimal solution.

Let our objective function is $z = ax + by$ and let M and m respectively denote the largest and smallest values of these points.

(a) When the feasible region is bounded, M and m are the maximum and minimum values of z.

(b) In case the feasible region is unbounded.

(i) M is the maximum value of Z, if the open half plane determined by $ax + by > M$ has no point in common with the feasible region. Otherwise Z has no maximum value.

(ii) Similarly m is the minimum value of Z, if the open half plane determined by $ax + by < m$ has no point in common with the feasible region. Otherwise Z has no minimum value.

07 **Optimization Techniques** The process of obtaining the optimal values are called optimization techniques.

08 **Linear Programming Problem (LPP)** A general linear programming consists of maximizing or minimizing an objective function subject to certain given constraints.

09 **Corner Point** A corner point of a feasible region is a point in the region which is the intersection of two boundary lines.

10 (i) Let R be the feasible region (convex polygon) for a linear programming problem and let $Z = ax + by$ be the objective function. When Z has an optimal value (maximum or minimum), where the variables x and y are subject to constraints described by linear inequalities, this optimal value must occur at a corner point (vertex) of the feasible region.

(ii) Let R be the feasible region for a linear programming problem and let $Z = ax + by$ be the objective function. If R is bounded, then the objective function Z has both a maximum and a minimum value on R and each of these occurs at a corner point (vertex) of R.

Graphical Method of Solving Linear Programming Problem (LPP)

Working Rules

Step 1 Identify the unknown in the given LPP.
Denote them by x and y.

Step 2 Formulate the objective function in terms of x and y.

Be sure whether it is to be maximized or minimized.

Step 3 Translate all the constraints in the form of linear inequations.

Step 4 Solve these inequations simultaneoulsy. Mark the common area by shaded region. This is called the feasible region.

Step 5 Find the coordinates of all the vertices of the feasible region.

Step 6 Find the value of the objective function at each and every vertex of the feasible region.

Step 7 Find the values of x and y for which the objective function $Z = ax + by$ has maximum or minimum value (as the case may be).

Exercise 12.1

Solve the following linear programming problems graphically.

Question 1. Maximize $Z = 3x + 4y$, subject to the constraints: $x + y \leq 4$, $x \geq 0$ and $y \geq 0$.

(Q. Nos. 1 to 10)

Thinking Process

(a) Frame equation from the given constraints and plot these equations on the graph.

(b) Find the feasible region and find the corner points.

(c) Find the value of Z at those points and see at which point Z is minimum/maximum.

Sol. Our problem is to maximize $Z = 3x + 4y$ ...(i)

Subject to constraints $x + y \leq 4$ ...(ii)

$x \geq 0, \quad y \geq 0$ ...(iii)

Firstly, draw the graph of the line $x + y = 4$

x	0	4
y	4	0

On putting (0, 0) in the inequality $x + y \leq 4$, we get

$$0 + 0 \leq 4 \Rightarrow 0 \leq 4 \text{ (which is true)}$$

So, the half plane is towards the origin. Since, $x, y \geq 0$

So, the feasible region lies in the first quadrant.

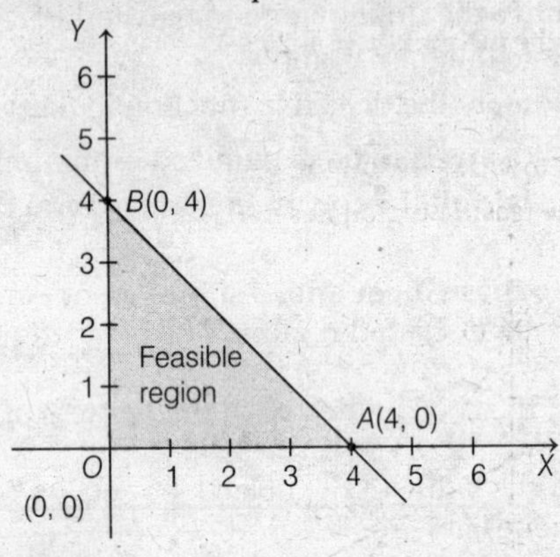

∴ Feasible region is $OABO$.

The corner points of the feasible region are $O(0, 0)$, $A(4,0)$ and $B(0, 4)$. The values of Z at these points are as follows:

Corner point	$Z = 3x + 4y$
$O(0, 0)$	0
$A(4, 0)$	12
$B(0, 4)$	16 → Maximum

Therefore, the maximum value of Z is 16 at the point $B(0, 4)$.

Note While plotting the graph, please be careful about the inequalities in which direction we have to plot this.

Question 2. Minimize $Z = -3x + 4y$, subject to constraints are $x + 2y \leq 8$, $3x + 2y \leq 12$, $x \geq 0$ and $y \geq 0$.

Sol. Our problem is to minimize

$$Z = -3x + 4y \quad \text{...(i)}$$

Subject to constraints

$$x + 2y \leq 8 \quad \text{...(ii)}$$
$$3x + 2y \leq 12 \quad \text{...(iii)}$$
$$x \geq 0, \quad y \geq 0 \quad \text{...(iv)}$$

Firstly, draw the graph of the line, $x + 2y = 8$

x	0	8
y	4	0

On putting (0, 0) in the inequality $x + 2y \leq 8$, we get

$$0 + 0 \leq 8 \Rightarrow 0 \leq 8 \quad \text{(which is true)}$$

So, the half plane is towards the origin.

Secondly, draw the graph of the line, $3x + 2y = 12$

x	0	4
y	6	0

On putting (0, 0) in the inequality $3x + 2y \leq 12$, we have
$3 \times 0 + 2 \times 0 \leq 12$

$\Rightarrow \quad 0 \leq 12$ (which is true)

So, the half plane is towards the origin.

Since, $x, y \geq 0$, So the feasifle region lies in the first quadrant.

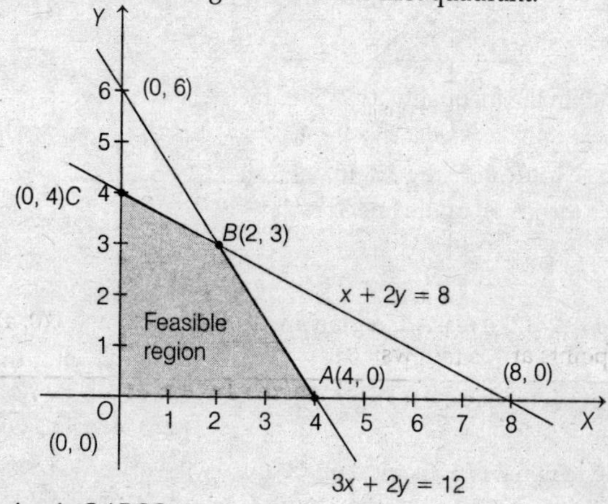

$\therefore$ Feasible region is $OABCO$.

On solving equations

$x + 2y = 8$ and $3x + 2y = 12$, we get $x = 2$ and $y = 3$

$\therefore$ Intersection point B is (2, 3).

The corner points of the feasible region are $O(0, 0)$, $A(4, 0)$, $B(2, 3)$ and $C(0, 4)$. The values of Z at these points are as follows:

Corner point	$Z = -3x + 4y$
$O(0, 0)$	0
$A(4, 0)$	$-12 \rightarrow$ Minimum
$B(2, 3)$	6
$C(0, 4)$	16

Therefore, the minimum value of Z is -12 at the point $A(4, 0)$.

Note To check the region of an inequality using the origin, substitute (0, 0) into the inequality. If true, shade toward the origin; if false, shade away from it.

Question 3 Maximize $Z = 5x + 3y$, subject to constraints are $3x + 5y \le 15$, $5x + 2y \le 10$, $x \ge 0$ and $y \ge 0$.

Sol. Our problem is to maximize $Z = 5x + 3y$ ...(i)

Subject to constraints $3x + 5y \le 15$ ...(ii)

$5x + 2y \le 10$ ...(iii)

$x \ge 0, y \ge 0$ ...(iv)

Firstly, draw the graph of the line $3x + 5y = 15$

x	0	5
y	3	0

On putting (0, 0) in the inequality $3x + 5y \le 15$, we have

$0 \times 0 \le 5 \Rightarrow 0 \le 15 \Rightarrow 0 \le 15$ (which is true)

So, the half plane is towards the origin.

Secondly, draw the graph of the line $5x + 2y = 10$

x	0	2
y	5	0

On putting (0, 0) in the inequality $5x + 2y \le 10$, we have

$0 + 0 \le 10 \Rightarrow 0 \le 10$ (which is true)

So, the half plane is towards the origin.

Since, $x, y \ge 0$

So, the feasible region lies in the first quadrant.

On solving given equations $3x + 5y = 15$ and $5x + 2y = 10$,

we get $x = \frac{20}{19}, y = \frac{45}{19}$

Coordinates of point B $\left(\frac{20}{19}, \frac{45}{19}\right)$.

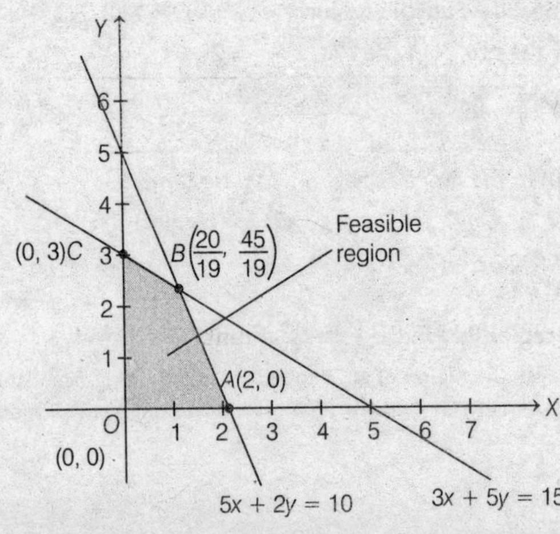

$\therefore$ Feasible region is $OABCO$.

The corner points of the feasible region are $O(0, 0)$, $A(2, 0)$, $B\left(\frac{20}{19}, \frac{45}{19}\right)$ and $C(0, 3)$

The values of Z at these points are as follows

Corner point	$Z = 5x + 3y$
$O(0, 0)$	0
$A(2, 0)$	10
$C(0, 3)$	9
$B\left(\frac{20}{19}, \frac{45}{19}\right)$	$\frac{235}{19} \to$ Maximum

Therefore, the maximum value of Z is $\frac{235}{19}$ at the point $B\left(\frac{20}{19}, \frac{45}{19}\right)$.

Question 4 Minimize $Z = 3x + 5y$, subject to constraints are $x + 3y \geq 3$, $x + y \geq 2$ and $x, y \geq 0$.

Sol. Our problem is to minimize $Z = 3x + 5y$ ...(i)

Subject to constraints

$$x + 3y \geq 3 \quad \text{...(ii)}$$
$$x + y \geq 2 \quad \text{...(iii)}$$
$$x \geq 0, y \geq 0 \quad \text{...(iv)}$$

Firstly, draw the graph of the line $x + 3y = 3$

x	0	3
y	1	0

On putting (0, 0) in the inequality $x + 3y \geq 3$, we have

$0 + 3 \times 0 \geq 3 \Rightarrow 0 \geq 3$ (which is false)

So, the half plane is away from the origin.

Secondly, draw the graph of the line $x + y = 2$

x	0	2
y	2	0

On putting (0, 0) in the inequality $x + y \geq 2$, we have

$0 + 0 \geq 2 \Rightarrow 0 \geq 2$ (which is false)

So, the half plane is away from the origin.

Since, $x, y \geq 0$

So, the feasible region lies in the first quadrant.

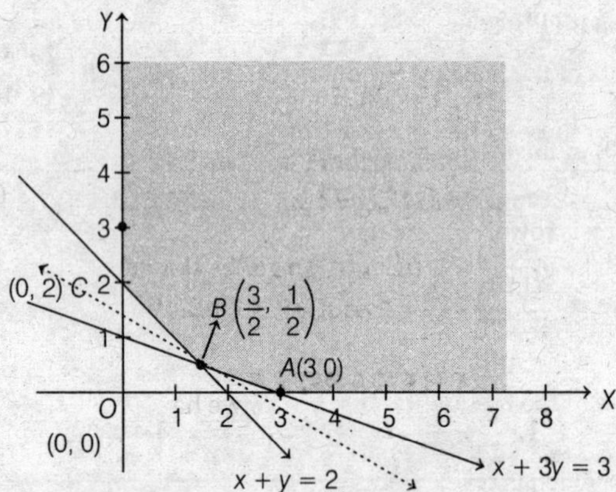

It can be seen that the feasible region is unbounded.

On solving equations $x + y = 2$ and $x + 3y = 3$, we get $x = \frac{3}{2}$ and $y = \frac{1}{2}$

$\therefore$ Intersection point $B\left(\frac{3}{2}, \frac{1}{2}\right)$

The corner points of the feasible region are $A(3, 0)$, $B\left(\frac{3}{2}, \frac{1}{2}\right)$ and $C(0, 2)$.

The values of Z at these points are as follows:

Corner point	$Z = 3x + 5y$
$A(3, 0)$	9
$B\left(\frac{3}{2}, \frac{1}{2}\right)$	$7 \rightarrow$ Minimum
$C(0, 2)$	10

As the feasible region is unbounded therefore, $z = 7$ may or may not be the minimum value of Z. For this, we draw the graph of the inequality, $3x + 5y < 7$ and check whether the resulting half plane has points in common with the feasible region or not. It can be seen that the feasible region has no common point with $3x + 5y < 7$. Therefore, the minimum value of Z is 7 at $\left(\frac{3}{2}, \frac{1}{2}\right)$.

Note For unbounded feasible region, m is the minimum value of Z using the counterpoint method. if the open half plane determined by $ax + by < m$ has no point in common with the feasible region. Otherwise, z has no minimum value.

Question 5 Maximize $Z = 3x + 2y$, subject to constraints are $x + 2y \le 10$, $3x + y \le 15$ and $x, y \ge 0$.

Sol. Our problem is to maximize, $Z = 3x + 2y$ ...(i)

Subject to constraints $x + 2y \le 10$ ...(ii)

$3x + y \le 15$ ...(iii)

$x \ge 0, y \ge 0$ ...(iv)

Firstly, draw the graph of the line $x + 2y = 10$

x	0	10
y	5	0

On putting (0, 0) in the inequality $x + 2y \leq 10$, we have

$$0 + 2 \times 0 \leq 10 \Rightarrow 0 \leq 10 \quad \text{(which is true)}$$

So, the half plane is towards the origin.

Secondly, draw the graph of the line $3x + y = 15$

x	0	5
y	15	0

On putting (0, 0) in the inequality $3x + y \leq 15$, we have

$3 \times 0 + 0 \leq 15$

$\Rightarrow \quad 0 \leq 15$ (which is true)

So, the half plane is towards the origin.

Since, $x, y \geq 0$

So, the feasible region lies in the first quadrant.

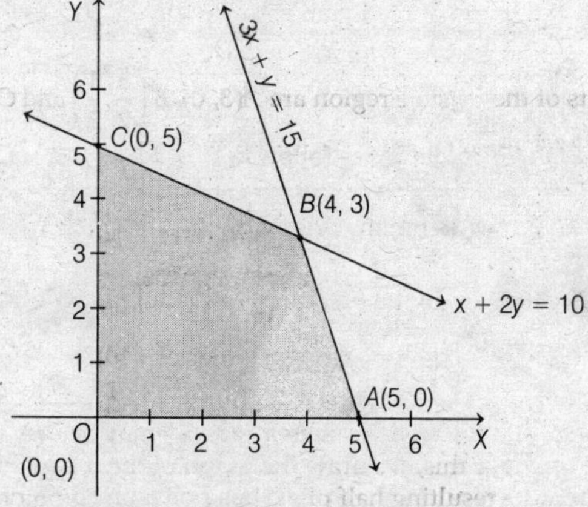

On solving equations $x + 2y = 10$ and $3x + y = 15$, we get

$$x = 4 \text{ and } y = 3$$

$\therefore$ Intersection point B (4, 3).

$\therefore$ Feasible region is $OABCO$.

The corner points of the feasible region are O (0, 0), A(5, 0), B(4, 3) and C(0, 5). The values of Z at these points are as follows:

Corner point	$Z = 3x + 2y$
O(0, 0)	0
A(5, 0)	15
B(4, 3)	18 → Maximum
C(0, 5)	10

Therefore, the maximum value of Z is 18 at the point B(4, 3).

Question 6 Minimize $Z = x + 2y$, subject to constraints are $2x + y \geq 3$, $x + 2y \geq 6$ and $x, y \geq 0$. Show that the minimum of Z occurs at more than two points.

Sol. Our problem is to minimize

$$Z = x + 2y \quad \text{...(i)}$$

Subject to the constraints are

$$2x + y \geq 3 \quad \text{...(ii)}$$

$$x + 2y \geq 6 \quad \text{...(iii)}$$

$$x \geq 0, y \geq 0 \quad \text{...(iv)}$$

Firstly, draw the graph of the line $2x + y = 3$

x	0	3/2
y	3	0

On putting (0, 0) in the inequality $2x + y \geq 3$, we have

$2 \times 0 + 0 \geq 3 \Rightarrow 0 \geq 3$ (which is false)

So, the half plane is away from the origin.

Secondly, draw the graph of the line $x + 2y = 6$

x	0	6
y	3	0

On putting (0, 0) in the inequality $x + 2y \geq 6$, we have

$0 + 2 \times 0 \geq 6 \Rightarrow 0 \geq 6$ (which is false)

So, the half plane is away from the origin.

Since, $x, y \geq 0$

So, the feasible region lies in the first quadrant.

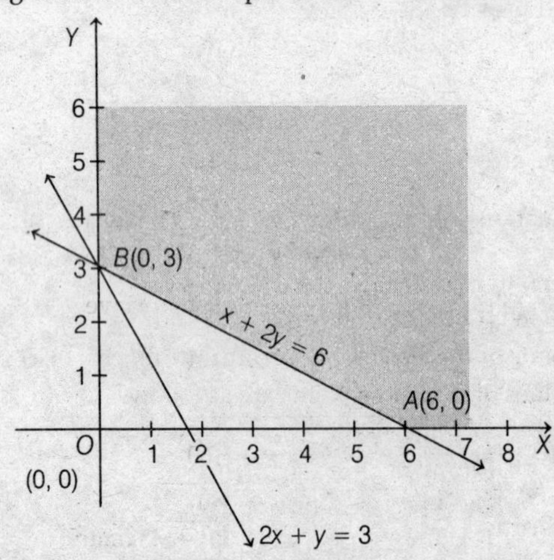

The intersection point of the lines $x + 2y = 6$ and $2x + y = 3$ is $B(0, 3)$.
The corner points of the feasible region are $A(6, 0)$ and $B(0, 3)$. The values of Z at these points are as follows:

Corner point	$Z = x + 2y$
$A(6, 0)$	6
$B(0, 3)$	6

As the feasible region is unbounded therefore $z = 6$ may or may not be the minimum value of Z.

For this we draw the inequality $x + 2y < 6$ and check whether the resulting half plane has points in common with the feasible region or not.

It can be seen the feasible region has no common point with $x + 2y < 6$.

It can be seen that the value of Z at points A and B is same. If we take any other point such as (2, 2) on line $x + 2y = 6$, then $Z = 6$. Thus, the minimum value of Z occurs for more than 2 points. Therefore, the value of Z is minimum at every point on the line, $x + 2y = 6$.

Note If the optimal value of the objective function is the same at two corner points of the feasible region, then the optimal value of the objective function will also be the same at every point on the line segment joining these two corner points.

Question 7 Minimize and maximize $Z = 5x + 10y$ subject to constraints are $x + 2y \le 120$, $x + y \ge 60$, $x - 2y \ge 0$ and $x, y \ge 0$.

Sol. Our problem is to minimize and maximize

$$Z = 5x + 10y \quad \ldots(i)$$

Subject t· ·onstraints $x + 2y \le 120$ ...(ii)

$$x + y \ge 60 \quad \ldots(iii)$$

$$x - 2y \ge 0 \quad \ldots(iv)$$

$$x \ge 0, y \ge 0 \quad \ldots(v)$$

Firstly, draw the graph of the lines $x + 2y = 120$

x	0	120
y	60	0

On putting (0, 0) in the inequality $x + 2y \le 120$, we have

$$0 + 2 \times 0 \le 120$$

$\Rightarrow$ $0 \le 120$ (which is true)

So, the half plane is towards the origin.

Secondly, draw the graph of the line $x + y = 60$

x	0	60
y	60	0

On putting (0, 0) in the inequality $x + y \geq 60$, we have

$$0 + 0 \geq 60 \Rightarrow \quad 0 \geq 60 \qquad \text{(which is false)}$$

So, the half plane is away from the origin.

Thirdly, draw the graph of the line $x - 2y = 0$

x	0	10
y	0	5

On putting (5, 0) in the inequality $x - 2y \geq 0$, we have

$$5 - 2 \times 0 \geq 0$$

$$\Rightarrow \qquad 5 \geq 0 \qquad \text{(which is true)}$$

So, the half plane is towards the X-axis. Since, $x, y \geq 0$

So, the feasible region lies in the first quadrant.

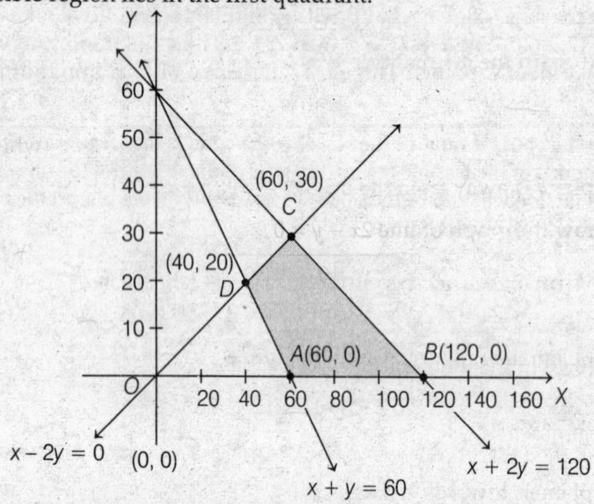

∴ Feasible region is $ABCDA$.

On solving equations $x - 2y = 0$ and $x + y = 60$, we get D (40, 20)

and on solving equations $x - 2y = 0$ and $x + 2y = 120$, we get C(60, 30).

The corner points of the feasible region are A(60, 0), B(120, 0), C(60, 30) and D(40, 20). The values of Z at these points are as follows:

Corner point	$Z = 5x + 10y$
A(60, 0)	300 → Minimum
B(120, 0)	600 → Maximum
C(60, 30)	600 → Maximum
D(40, 20)	400

The minimum value of Z is 300 at A (60, 0) and the maximum value of Z is 600 at all the points on the line segment joining the points (120, 0) and (60, 30).

Question 8 Minimize and maximize $Z = x + 2y$ subject to constraints are $x + 2y \geq 100, 2x - y \leq 0, 2x + y \leq 200$ and $x, y \geq 0$.

Sol. Our problem is to minimize and maximize

$$Z = x + 2y \quad \ldots(i)$$

Subject to constraints are $x + 2y \geq 100$ ...(ii)

$$2x - y \leq 0 \quad \ldots(iii)$$

$$2x + y \leq 200 \quad \ldots(iv)$$

$$x \geq 0, y \geq 0 \quad \ldots(v)$$

Firstly, draw the graph of the line $x + 2y = 100$

x	0	100
y	50	0

On putting (0, 0) in the inequality $x + 2y \geq 100$, we have

$$0 + 2 \times 0 \geq 100$$

$\Rightarrow$ $0 \geq 100$ (which is false)

So, the half plane is away from the origin.

Secondly, draw the graph of line $2x - y = 0$

x	0	10
y	0	20

On putting (5, 0) in the inequality $2x - y \leq 0$, we have

$$2 \times 5 - 0 \leq 0$$

$\Rightarrow$ $10 \leq 0$ (which is false)

So, the half plane is towards Y-axis.

Thirdly, draw the graph of line $2x + y = 200$

x	0	100
y	200	0

On putting (0, 0) in the inequality $2x + y \leq 200$, we have

$$2 \times 0 + 0 \leq 200$$

$\Rightarrow$ $0 \leq 200$ (which is true)

So, the half plane is towards the origin. Since, $x, y \geq 0$

So, the feasible region lies in the first quadrant.

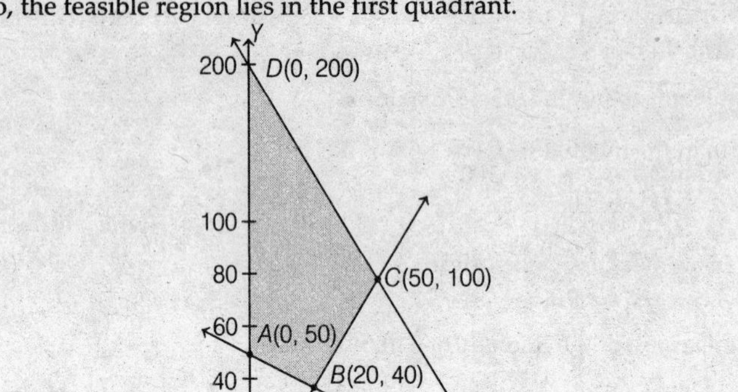

On solving equations $2x - y = 0$ and $x + 2y = 100$, we get $B(20, 40)$ and on solving the equations $2x - y = 0$ and $2x + y = 200$, we get $C(50, 100)$.

$\therefore$ Feasible region is $ABCDA$.

The corner points of the feasible region are $A(0, 50)$, $B(20, 40)$, $C(50, 100)$ and $D(0, 200)$. The values of Z at these points are as follows:

Corner point	$Z = x + 2y$
$A(0, 50)$	100 $\rightarrow$ Minimum
$B(20, 40)$	100 $\rightarrow$ Minimum
$C(50, 100)$	250
$D(0, 200)$	400 $\rightarrow$ Maximum

The maximum value of Z is 400 at $D(0, 200)$ and the minimum value of Z is 100 at all the points on the line segment AB joining $A(0, 50)$ and $B(20, 40)$.

Question 9 Maximize $Z = -x + 2y$, subject to the constraints are $x \geq 3$, $x + y \geq 5$, $x + 2y \geq 6$ and $x, y \geq 0$.

Sol. Our problem is to maximize $Z = -x + 2y$ ...(i)

Subject to constraints are $x \geq 3$ ...(ii)

$x + y \geq 5$ ...(iii)

$x + 2y \geq 6$ ...(iv)

$x \geq 0, y \geq 0$ ...(v)

Firstly, draw the graph of the line $x + y = 5$

x	0	5
y	5	0

On putting (0, 0) in the inequality $x + y \geq 5$, we have

$$0 + 0 \geq 5$$

$\Rightarrow$ $\quad 0 \geq 5$ (which is false)

So, the half plane is away from the origin.

Secondly, draw the graph of line $x + 2y = 6$

x	0	6
y	3	0

On putting (0, 0) in the inequality $x + 2y \geq 6$, we have

$$0 + 2 \times 0 \geq 6$$

$\Rightarrow$ $\quad 0 \geq 6$ (which is false)

So, the half plane is away from the origin.

Since, $\quad x \geq 3, y \geq 0$

So, the feasible region lies in the first quadrant.

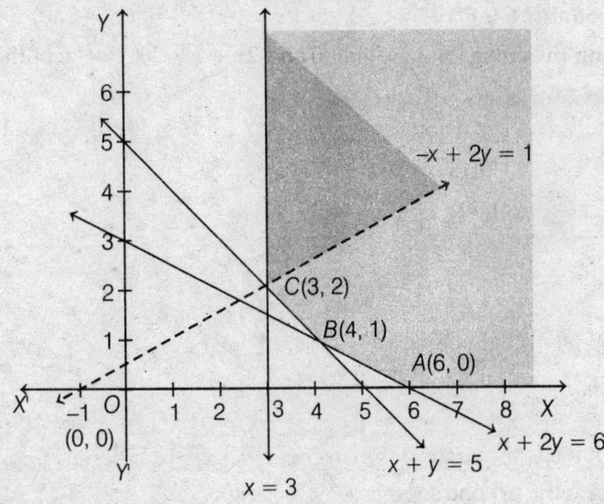

The points of intersection of lines $x = 3$ and $x + y = 5$ is $C(3, 2)$ and lines $x + 2y = 6$ and $x + y = 5$ is $B(4, 1)$.

It can be seen that the feasible region is unbounded.

The corner points of the feasible region are $A(6, 0)$, $B(4, 1)$ and $C(3, 2)$. The values of Z at these points are as follows:

Corner point	$Z = -x + 2y$
$A(6, 0)$	-6
$B(4, 1)$	-2
$C(3, 2)$	$1 \leftarrow$ Maximum

As the feasible region is unbounded therefore, $Z = 1$ may or may not be the maximum value. For this, we graph the inequality, $-x + 2y > 1$ and check whether the resulting half plane has points in common with the feasible region or not.

The resulting feasible region has points in common with the feasible region. Therefore, $Z = 1$ is not the maximum value.

Hence, Z has no maximum value.

Question 10 Maximize $Z = x + y$, subject to constraints are $x - y \leq -1, -x + y \leq 0$ and $x, y \geq 0$.

Sol. Our problem is to maximize $Z = x + y$ ...(i)

Subject to constraints are $x - y \leq -1$ ...(ii)

$-x + y \leq 0$ ...(iii)

$x \geq 0, y \geq 0$ ...(iv)

Firstly, draw the graph of the line $x - y = -1$

x	0	-1
y	1	0

On putting (0, 0) in the inequality $x - y \leq -1$, we have

$$0 - 0 \leq -1$$

$\Rightarrow$ $0 \leq -1$ (which is false)

So, the half plane is away from the origin.

Secondly, draw the graph of the line $-x + y = 0$

x	0	1
y	0	1

On putting (2, 0) in the inequality $-x + y \leq 0$, we have

$$-2 + 0 \leq 0$$

$\Rightarrow$ $-2 \leq 0$ (which is true)

So, the half plane is towards the X-axis.

Since, $x, y \geq 0$

So, the feasible region lies in the first quadrant.

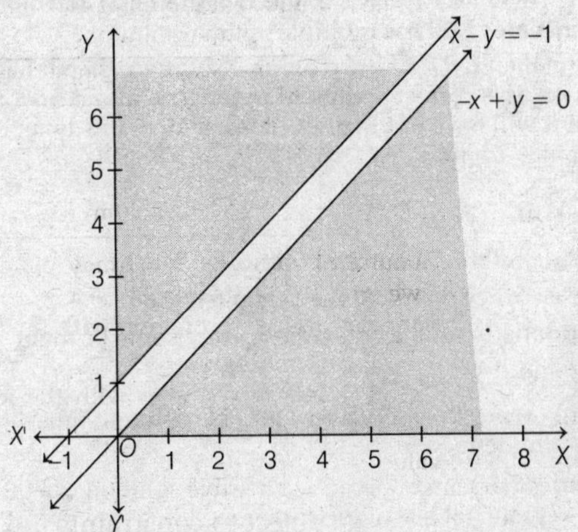

From the above graph, it is clearly shown that there is no common region. Hence, there is no feasible region and thus Z has no maximum value.

Mistake Alert If there is no common region, then we do not determine the minimum/maximum value.

DIKSHA APP *Questions*

☐ Multiple Choice Questions

Q.1 A objective function in a linear programming problem is

(a) constraints (b) to be maximised or minimised

(c) relation between variables (d) None of the above

Sol. (b) A objective function in L.P.P. is to be maximised or minimised.

Q.2 Which of the following statements is correct ?

(a) Every LP problem has at least one optimal solution.

(b) Every LP problem has a unique solution.

(c) If an LP problem has two optimal solutions, then it has infinitely many solutions.

(d) If a feasible region is unbounded, then LP problem has no solution.

Sol. (c) For option (a) every L.P.P. has atleast one optimal solution it is not correct because some times we does not have any optimal solution.

For option (b) every L.P.P. has a unique solution, it is also not correct because sometimes LPP has multiple optimal solution.

For option (c) if an L.P.P. has two optimal solution, then it has infinity many solution, it is correct because if optimal solutions are on A and B points, then it will have optimal solutions at all points lying on the line segment joining A and B.

Q.3 A feasible solution of LPP

(a) must satisfy all the constraints simultaneously

(b) must be a corner points of the feasible region

(c) need not satisfty all the constraints, only some of them

(d) Both (a) and (b)

Sol. (a) Statement (a) is correct because a feasible solution must adhere to every constraint defined in the LPP.

Statement (b) is not correct because a feasible solution can be any point in the feasible region, not just at the corners.

Statement (c) is not correct because a solution that does not satisfy all constraints is not a feasible solution.

Q.4 The value of the objective function is maximum under linear constraints

(a) all the centre of feasible region

(b) at (0, 0)

(c) at any vertex of feasible region

(d) the vertex which is maximum distance from (0, 0)

Sol. (c) The value of objective function can be maximum at any vertex of the feasible region.

Probability

CHAPTER 13

Important Points

01 Random experiment An experiment in which all possible outcomes are known in advance and the exact outcome in any specific trial of the experiment is unpredictable, is known as a random experiment.

02 Sample space The set of all outcomes in a random experiment is called a sample space, it is denoted by S.

03 Event Any subset of sample space S is called an event.

Since, $\phi \subset S$, so ϕ is an event, called an impossible event.

Since, $S \subseteq S$, so S is an event, called a sure event.

04 Complementary events Let E be an event.

Then, $\overline{E}$ is an event, called the complement of E.

05 Mutually exclusive events Two events A and B are said to be mutually exclusive, if $A \cap B = \phi$.

06 Independent events Two events are said to be independent, if the occurrence of one does not depend upon the occurrence or non-occurrence of the other.

If E_1 and E_2 are independent events, then $P(E_1 \cap E_2) = P(E_1)\, P(E_2)$. Also, their complement events are independent.

07 Probability In a random experiment, let S be the sample space and let E be the event. Then,

$$P(E) = \frac{\text{Number of distinct elements in } E}{\text{Number of distinct elements in } S} = \frac{n(E)}{n(S)}$$

$$= \frac{\text{Number of outcomes favourable to } E}{\text{Number of all possible outcomes}}$$

Results on Probability

01 If E is an event and S is the sample space, then

(i) $0 \le P(E) \le 1$ (ii) $P(\phi) = 0$ (iii) $P(S) = 1$

02 $P(\overline{E}) = 1 - P(E)$

03 **Addition theorem** For any events A, B and C, we have

(i) $P(A \cup B) = P(A) + P(B) - P(A \cap B)$

(ii) $P(A \cup B \cup C) = P(A) + P(B) + P(C) + P(A \cap B \cap C)$
$$-[P(A \cap B) + P(B \cap C) + P(C \cap A)]$$

(iii) $P(A \cap \overline{B}) = P(A) - P(A \cap B)$

(iv) $P(\overline{A} \cap B) = P(B) - P(A \cap B)$

(v) $P(\overline{A} \cap \overline{B}) = 1 - P(A \cup B)$

(iv) $P(\overline{A} \cup \overline{B}) = 1 - P(A \cap B)$

04 If A and B are mutually exclusive events, then
$$P(A \cup B) = P(A) + P(B)$$

05 **Conditional Probability** The probability of the event A is called conditional probability of A given that B has already occurred and is denoted by $P\left(\frac{A}{B}\right)$

(a) $P\left(\frac{A}{B}\right) = \frac{P(A \cap B)}{P(B)}$, $B \ne \phi$ i.e. $P(B) \ne 0$

(b) $P\left(\frac{B}{A}\right) = \frac{P(A \cap B)}{P(A)}$, $A \ne \phi$ i.e. $P(A) \ne 0$

(c) $P\left(\frac{\overline{A}}{B}\right) = \frac{P(\overline{A} \cap B)}{P(B)} = \frac{P(B) - P(A \cap B)}{P(B)}$
$$= 1 - \frac{P(A \cap B)}{P(B)} = 1 - P\left(\frac{A}{B}\right)$$

(d) $P\left(\frac{A}{\overline{B}}\right) = \frac{P(A \cap \overline{B})}{P(\overline{B})} = \frac{P(A) - P(A \cap B)}{1 - P(B)}$

(e) $P\left(\frac{\overline{A}}{\overline{B}}\right) = \frac{P(\overline{A} \cap \overline{B})}{P(\overline{B})} = \frac{1 - P(A \cap B)}{1 - P(B)}$

06 Multiplication theorem of Probability

(a) $P(A \cap B) = P(A) \cdot P\left(\frac{B}{A}\right)$

(b) $P(A \cap B \cap C) = P(A) \cdot P\left(\frac{B}{A}\right) \cdot P\left(\frac{C}{A \cap B}\right)$

Theorem of total probability Let E_1, E_2 ...... E_n be a partition of the sample space S_1 and suppose that each of the events E_1, E_2 ...... E_n has non zero probability of occurrence. Let A be any event associated with S, then

$P(A) = P(E_1)P(A/E_1) + P(E_2)P(A)/E_2) + \ldots + P(E_n)P(A/E_n)$

$= \sum_{j=1}^{n} P(E_j)P(A/E_j)$

Bayes' theorem If $E_1, E_2, E_3, \ldots, E_n$ form a set of mutually exclusive and exhaustive events and E is any other event, then

$$P\left(\frac{E_i}{E}\right) = \frac{P\left(\frac{E}{E_i}\right).P(E_i)}{\sum_{i=1}^{n} P\left(\frac{E}{E_i}\right).P(E_i)}$$

Exercise 13.1

Question 1 Given that E and F are events such that $P(E) = 0.6$, $P(F) = 0.3$ and $P(E \cap F) = 0.2$, find $P\left(\frac{E}{F}\right)$ and $P\left(\frac{F}{E}\right)$.

◎ *Thinking Process* (Q.Nos.1 to 3) Using the relation for conditional probability $P\left(\frac{A}{B}\right) = \frac{P(A \cap B)}{P(B)}$ and simplify it.

Sol. It is given that $P(E) = 0.6$, $P(F) = 0.3$ and $P(E \cap F) = 0.2$

$\therefore$ We know that $P\left(\frac{E}{F}\right) = \frac{P(E \cap F)}{P(F)} = \frac{0.2}{0.3} = \frac{2}{3}$

and $P\left(\frac{F}{E}\right) = \frac{P(F \cap E)}{P(E)} = \frac{0.2}{0.6} = \frac{1}{3}$

Question 2 Compute $P\left(\frac{A}{B}\right)$, if $P(B) = 0.5$ and $P(A \cap B) = 0.32$.

Sol. It is given that $P(B) = 0.5$ and $P(A \cap B) = 0.32$

$\therefore \quad P\left(\frac{A}{B}\right) = \frac{P(A \cap B)}{P(B)} = \frac{0.32}{0.5} = \frac{32}{50} = \frac{16}{25}$

Question 3 If $P(A)=0.8$, $P(B)=0.5$ and $P\left(\frac{B}{A}\right)=0.4$, find

(i) $P(A \cap B)$ (ii) $P\left(\frac{A}{B}\right)$

(iii) $P(A \cup B)$

Sol. (i) Given, $P(A)=0.8, P(B)=0.5$ and $P\left(\frac{B}{A}\right)=0.4$

$$\therefore \quad \frac{P(A \cap B)}{P(A)} = 0.4 \qquad \left[\because P\left(\frac{B}{A}\right)=\frac{P(A \cap B)}{P(A)}\right]$$

$$\Rightarrow \quad \frac{P(A \cap B)}{0.8} = 0.4 \quad \Rightarrow \quad P(A \cap B) = 0.8 \times 0.4 = 0.32$$

(ii) $P\left(\frac{A}{B}\right) = \frac{P(A \cap B)}{P(B)} = \frac{0.32}{0.5} = \frac{32}{50} = 0.64$

(iii) We know that $P(A \cup B) = P(A) + P(B) - P(A \cap B)$

$$= 0.8 + 0.5 - 0.32 = 1.3 - 0.32 = 0.98$$

Question 4 Evaluate $P(A \cup B)$, if $2P(A) = P(B) = \frac{5}{13}$ and $P\left(\frac{A}{B}\right) = \frac{2}{5}$.

◎ *Thinking Process* First use the formula $P\left(\frac{A}{B}\right) = \frac{P(A \cap B)}{P(B)}$ and then find $P(A \cup B)$ by using the formula, $P(A \cup B) = P(A) + P(B) - P(A \cap B)$

Sol. Given, $2P(A) = P(B) = \frac{5}{13}$ and $P\left(\frac{A}{B}\right) = \frac{2}{5}$

$$\therefore \quad P(A) = \frac{5}{26} \text{ and } P(B) = \frac{5}{13}$$

Now, $P\left(\frac{A}{B}\right) = \frac{P(A \cap B)}{P(B)} \Rightarrow \frac{2}{5} = \frac{P(A \cap B)}{\frac{5}{13}}$

$$\Rightarrow \quad P(A \cap B) = \frac{2}{5} \times \frac{5}{13} = \frac{2}{13}$$

Again, $P(A \cup B) = P(A) + P(B) - P(A \cap B)$

$$= \frac{5}{26} + \frac{5}{13} - \frac{2}{13}$$

$$= \frac{5 + 10 - 4}{26} = \frac{11}{26}$$

Question 5 If $P(A)=\frac{6}{11}$, $P(B)=\frac{5}{11}$ and $P(A\cup B)=\frac{7}{11}$, find

(i) $P(A\cap B)$ (ii) $P\left(\frac{A}{B}\right)$

(iii) $P\left(\frac{B}{A}\right)$

Sol.

(i) Given, $P(A\cup B)=\frac{7}{11}$, $P(A)=\frac{6}{11}$ and $P(B)=\frac{5}{11}$

We know that $P(A\cup B)=P(A)+P(B)-P(A\cap B)$

$$\Rightarrow \quad \frac{7}{11}=\frac{6}{11}+\frac{5}{11}-P(A\cap B)\Rightarrow P(A\cap B)=\frac{6}{11}+\frac{5}{11}-\frac{7}{11}=\frac{4}{11}$$

(ii) We know that $P\left(\frac{A}{B}\right)=\frac{P(A\cap B)}{P(B)} \Rightarrow P\left(\frac{A}{B}\right)=\frac{\frac{4}{11}}{\frac{5}{11}}=\frac{4}{11}\times\frac{11}{5}=\frac{4}{5}$

$\left(\because P(B)=\frac{5}{11} \text{ given}\right)$

(iii) We know that $P\left(\frac{B}{A}\right)=\frac{P(B\cap A)}{P(A)}$

$$\Rightarrow \quad P\left(\frac{B}{A}\right)=\frac{\frac{4}{11}}{\frac{6}{11}}=\frac{4}{11}\times\frac{11}{6}=\frac{4}{6}=\frac{2}{3}. \qquad [\because P(A\cap B)=P(B\cap A)]$$

Direction (Q. Nos. 6 to 9) Determine $P\left(\frac{E}{F}\right)$.

Question 6. A coin is tossed three times

(i) E : head on third toss, F : head on first two tosses

(ii) E : atleast two heads, F : atmost two heads

(iii) E : atmost two tails, F : atleast one tail

◎ **Thinking Process** Frame a set containing all the possible outcomes of all the events given in individual questions.
Then, find $P(E)$, $P(F)$ and $P(E\cap F)$ using the set of outcomes.
Further use the relation, $P\left(\frac{E}{F}\right)=\frac{P(E\cap F)}{P(F)}$.

Sol. When a coin is tossed three times, the sample space S contains $2^3=8$ equally likely sample points.

$$\therefore \quad S=\{HHH, HHT, HTH, HTT, THH, THT, TTH, TTT\}$$

(i) Here, E : set of events in which head occurs on third toss and F : set of events in which heads occur on first two tosses,

$\therefore$ $E = \{HHH, THH, HTH, TTH\}$, $F = \{HHH, HHT\}$

and $E \cap F = \{HHH\}$

Hence, $P(E) = \dfrac{\text{Number of favourable outcomes}}{\text{Total number of outcomes}} = \dfrac{4}{8} = \dfrac{1}{2}$

Similarly, $P(F) = \dfrac{2}{8} = \dfrac{1}{4}$ and $P(E \cap F) = \dfrac{1}{8}$

$$\therefore \quad P\left(\frac{E}{F}\right) = \frac{P(E \cap F)}{P(F)} = \frac{\frac{1}{8}}{\frac{1}{4}} = \frac{1}{8} \times \frac{4}{1} = \frac{1}{2}$$

(ii) Here, E : set of events in which atleast two heads occur and F : set of events in which at most two heads occur.

$\therefore$ $E = \{HHH, HHT, HTH, THH\}$,

[Here, we consider the cases of two and three heads, as the condition given is atleast not atmost]

$F = \{TTT, THT, TTH, HTT, HHT, HTH, THH\}$

and $(E \cap F) = \{HHT, HTH, THH\}$

Hence, $P(E) = \dfrac{\text{Number of favourable outcomes}}{\text{Total number of outcomes}} = \dfrac{4}{8} = \dfrac{1}{2}$

Similarly, $P(F) = \dfrac{7}{8}$ and $P(E \cap F) = \dfrac{3}{8}$

$$\therefore \quad P\left(\frac{E}{F}\right) = \frac{P(E \cap F)}{P(F)} = \frac{\frac{3}{8}}{\frac{7}{8}} = \frac{3}{8} \times \frac{8}{7} = \frac{3}{7}$$

(iii) Here, E : set of events in which atmost two tails occur and F : set of events in which atleast one tail occurs.

$\therefore$ $E = \{HHH, HHT, HTH, THH, HTT, THT, TTH\}$

(Here, we can consider the cases of the two tails, one tail and no tail because the condition is atmost not atleast)

$F = \{TTT, THT, TTH, HTT, HHT, HTH, THH\}$

(Here, we can consider the cases of one or more tails because the condition given is atleast not atmost.)

and $(E \cap F) = \{HHT, HTH, THH, HTT, THT, TTH\}$

Now, $P(E) = \dfrac{\text{Number of favourable outcomes}}{\text{Total number of outcomes}} = \dfrac{7}{8}$

Similarly, $P(F) = \dfrac{7}{8}$ and $P(E \cap F) = \dfrac{6}{8}$

$$\therefore \quad P\left(\frac{E}{F}\right) = \frac{P(E \cap F)}{P(F)} = \frac{6/8}{7/8} = \frac{6}{7}$$

Mistake Alert In atmost two tails zero tail will be included.

Question 7 Two coins are tossed once, where

(i) E : tail appears on one coin, F : one coin shows head.

(ii) E : no tail appears, F : no head appears.

Sol. If two coins are tossed once, then the sample space $S = \{HH, HT, TH, TT\}$

(i) E = Set of events having tail on one coin $= \{HT, TH\}$,
F = Set of events having one coin showing head $= \{HT, TH\}$
and $E \cap F = \{HT, TH\}$

$\therefore P(E) = \frac{2}{4} = \frac{1}{2}, P(F) = \frac{2}{4} = \frac{1}{2}$ and $P(E \cap F) = \frac{2}{4} = \frac{1}{2}$

$$\therefore \quad P\left(\frac{E}{F}\right) = \frac{P(E \cap F)}{P(F)} = \frac{\frac{1}{2}}{\frac{1}{2}} = 1$$

(ii) E = Set of events having no tail $= \{HH\}$,
F = Set of events having no head $= \{TT\}$ and $E \cap F = \phi$

$\therefore \quad P(E) = \frac{1}{4}, P(F) = \frac{1}{4}$ and $P(E \cap F) = \frac{0}{4} = 0.$

$$\therefore P\left(\frac{E}{F}\right) = \frac{P(E \cap F)}{P(F)} = \frac{0}{1/4} = 0$$

Question 8 A die is thrown three times,
E : 4 appears on the third toss
F : 6 and 5 appears, respectively on first two tosses.

Sol. If a die is thrown three times, then the number of elements in the sample space will be $6 \times 6 \times 6 = 216$.

The sample space is $S = \{(x, y, z) : x, y, z \in \{1, 2, 3, 4, 5, 6\}\}$.

Here, E : set of events in which 4 appears on the third toss and
F : Set of events in which 6 and 5 appears respectively on first two tosses

$$E = \begin{Bmatrix} (1, 1, 4), (1, 2, 4), (1, 3, 4), (1, 4, 4), (1, 5, 4), (1, 6, 4) \\ (2, 1, 4), (2, 2, 4), (2, 3, 4), (2, 4, 4), (2, 5, 4), (2, 6, 4) \\ (3, 1, 4), (3, 2, 4), (3, 3, 4), (3, 4, 4), (3, 5, 4), (3, 6, 4) \\ (4, 1, 4), (4, 2, 4), (4, 3, 4), (4, 4, 4), (4, 5, 4), (4, 6, 4) \\ (5, 1, 4), (5, 2, 4), (5, 3, 4), (5, 4, 4), (5, 5, 4), (5, 6, 4) \\ (6, 1, 4), (6, 2, 4), (6, 3, 4), (6, 4, 4), (6, 5, 4), (6, 6, 4) \end{Bmatrix}$$

$\Rightarrow n(E) = 36$

$$F = \{(6, 5, 1), (6, 5, 2), (6, 5, 3), (6, 5, 4), (6, 5, 5), (6, 5, 6)\} \Rightarrow n(F) = 6$$

and $\quad E \cap F = \{(6, 5, 4)\} \Rightarrow n(E \cap F) = 1$

$$\therefore \quad P(E) = \frac{\text{Number of favourable outcomes}}{\text{Total number of outcomes}} = \frac{36}{216} = \frac{1}{6}$$

Similarly, $P(F) = \frac{6}{216} = \frac{1}{36}$ and $P(E \cap F) = \frac{1}{216}$

Required probability, $P\left(\frac{E}{F}\right)=\frac{P(E\cap F)}{P(F)}$

$$=\frac{\frac{1}{216}}{\frac{1}{36}}=\frac{1}{216}\times\frac{36}{1}=\frac{1}{6}.$$

Question 9 Mother, father and son line up at random for a family picture

E : son on one end, F : father in middle

Sol. If mother (m), father (f) and son (s) line up for the family picture, then the sample space will be $S=\{mfs, msf, fms, fsm, smf, sfm\}\Rightarrow n(S)=6$ which contains 6 equally likely sample events.

Here, E : = set of events having son on one end and F : set of events having father in the middle.

$\therefore E=\{mfs, fms, smf, sfm\}$, $F=\{mfs, sfm\}$ and $E\cap F=\{mfs, sfm\}$

$\Rightarrow \quad n(E)=4, n(F)=2, n(E\cap F)=2$

Now, $P(E)=\frac{\text{Number of favourable outcomes}}{\text{Total number of outcomes}}=\frac{4}{6}=\frac{2}{3}$,

Similarly, $P(F)=\frac{2}{6}=\frac{1}{3}$ and $P(E\cap F)=\frac{2}{6}=\frac{1}{3}$

We know that $P\left(\frac{E}{F}\right)=\frac{P(E\cap F)}{P(F)}=\frac{\frac{1}{3}}{\frac{1}{3}}=1$

Question 10. A black and a red dice are rolled.

(i) Find the conditional probability of obtaining a sum greater than 9, given that the black die resulted in a 5.

(ii) Find the conditional probability of obtaining the sum 8, given that the red die resulted in a number less than 4.

◎ ***Thinking Process*** Frame a set S containing all the possible outcomes of rolling a fair die.

Use relation $P\left(\frac{A}{B}\right)=\frac{P(A\cap B)}{P(E)}$.

Sol. Let the first observation be from the black die and second from the red die.

When two dice (one black and another red) are rolled, the sample space $S=6\times 6=36$ (equally likely sample events).

(i) Let E : set of events in which sum greater than 9 i.e., sum should be 10, 11, 12 and F : set of events in which black die resulted in a 5.

$E=\{(6,4),(4,6),(5,5),(5,6),(6,5),(6,6)\}\Rightarrow n(E)=6$,

$F=\{(5,1),(5,2),(5,3),(5,4),(5,5),(5,6)\}\Rightarrow n(F)=6$

and $\quad E \cap F = \{(5, 5), (5, 6)\} \Rightarrow n(E \cap F) = 2$

$$\therefore \quad P(E) = \frac{\text{Number of favourable outcomes}}{\text{Total number of outcomes}} = \frac{6}{36} = \frac{1}{6}$$

Similarly, $P(F) = \frac{6}{36} = \frac{1}{6}$ and $P(E \cap F) = \frac{2}{36} = \frac{1}{18}$

The conditional probability of obtaining a sum greater than 9, given that the black die resulted in a 5, is given by $P\left(\frac{E}{F}\right)$

$$\therefore \quad P\left(\frac{E}{F}\right) = \frac{P(E \cap F)}{P(F)} = \frac{1/18}{1/6} = \frac{1}{18} \times \frac{6}{1} = \frac{1}{3}.$$

(ii) Let E : set of events having 8 as the sum of the observations,
F : set of events in which red die resulted in a number less than 4

$$\therefore \quad E = \{(2, 6), (3, 5), (4, 4), (5, 3), (6, 2)\} \Rightarrow n(E) = 5,$$

$$F = \begin{Bmatrix} (1, 1), (1, 2), (1, 3), (2, 1), (2, 2), (2, 3) \\ (3, 1), (3, 2), (3, 3), (4, 1), (4, 2), (4, 3) \\ (5, 1), (5, 2), (5, 3), (6, 1), (6, 2), (6, 3) \end{Bmatrix} \Rightarrow n(F) = 18$$

and $\quad E \cap F = \{(5, 3), (6, 2)\} \Rightarrow n(E \cap F) = 2$

Now, $\quad P(E) = \frac{\text{Number of favourable outcomes}}{\text{Total number of outcomes}} = \frac{5}{36}$

Similarly, $P(F) = \frac{18}{36} = \frac{1}{2}$ and $P(E \cap F) = \frac{2}{36} = \frac{1}{18}$

$$\therefore \text{Required probability} = P\left(\frac{E}{F}\right) = \frac{P(E \cap F)}{P(F)} = \frac{\frac{1}{18}}{\frac{1}{2}} = \frac{1}{18} \times \frac{2}{1} = \frac{1}{9}$$

Question 11 A fair die is rolled. Consider events $E = \{1, 3, 5\}$, $F = \{2, 3\}$ and $G = \{2, 3, 4, 5\}$. Find

(i) $P\left(\frac{E}{F}\right)$ and $P\left(\frac{F}{E}\right)$ (ii) $P\left(\frac{E}{G}\right)$ and $P\left(\frac{G}{E}\right)$

(iii) $P\left(\frac{E \cup F}{G}\right)$ and $P\left(\frac{E \cap F}{G}\right)$

◎ ***Thinking Process*** (Q. Nos. 11 to 17) Firstly, frame a set S cantaining all possible outcomes, then find the conditional probability using $P\left(\frac{A}{B}\right) = \frac{P(A \cap B)}{P(B)}$.

Sol. We have $E = \{1, 3, 5\}$, $F = \{2, 3\}$, $G = \{2, 3, 4, 5\}$

$$S = \{1, 2, 3, 4, 5, 6\}$$

(i) Here, $E \cap F = \{3\}$

Now, $P(E) = \dfrac{\text{Number of favourable outcomes}}{\text{Total number of outcomes}} = \dfrac{3}{6} = \dfrac{1}{2}$

Similarly $P(F) = \dfrac{2}{6} = \dfrac{1}{3}$ and $P(E \cap F) = \dfrac{1}{6}$

$$\therefore \quad P\left(\frac{E}{F}\right) = \left(\frac{P(E \cap F)}{P(F)}\right) = \frac{\frac{1}{6}}{\frac{1}{3}} = \frac{1}{2}$$

and $$P\left(\frac{F}{E}\right) = \frac{P(E \cap F)}{P(E)} = \frac{\frac{1}{6}}{\frac{1}{2}} = \frac{1}{3}$$

(ii) Here, $E \cap G = \{3, 5\}$

$$P(E) = \frac{\text{Number of favourable out comes}}{\text{Total Number of out comes}} = \frac{3}{6} = \frac{1}{2}$$

Similarly, $P(G) = \dfrac{4}{6} = \dfrac{2}{3}$ and $P(E \cap G) = \dfrac{2}{6} = \dfrac{1}{3}$

$$\therefore \quad P\left(\frac{E}{G}\right) = \frac{P(E \cap G)}{P(G)} = \frac{\frac{1}{3}}{\frac{2}{3}} = \frac{1}{2}$$

and $$P\left(\frac{G}{E}\right) = \frac{P(E \cap G)}{P(E)} = \frac{\frac{1}{3}}{\frac{1}{2}} = \frac{2}{3}$$

(iii) Here, $E \cup F = \{1, 2, 3, 5\}$

and $(E \cup F) \cap G = \{2, 3, 5\}$

Now, $P(G) = \dfrac{\text{Number of favourable outcomes}}{\text{Total Number of outcomes}} = \dfrac{4}{6} = \dfrac{2}{3}$

Similarly, $P((E \cup F) \cap G) = \dfrac{3}{6} = \dfrac{1}{2}$

$$\therefore \quad P\left(\frac{E \cup F}{G}\right) = \frac{P((E \cup F) \cap G)}{P(G)} = \frac{\frac{1}{2}}{\frac{2}{3}} = \frac{3}{4}$$

Now, $E \cap F = \{3\}$

and $((E \cap F) \cap G) = \{3\}$

$$\therefore P((E \cap F) \cap G) = \frac{\text{Number of favourable outcomes}}{\text{Total Number of outcomes}} = \frac{1}{6}$$

Now, $$P\left(\frac{E \cap F}{G}\right) = \frac{P((E \cap F) \cap G)}{P(G)} = \frac{\frac{1}{6}}{\frac{2}{3}} = \frac{1}{4}$$

Question 12 Assume that each child born is equally likely to be boy or a girl. If a family has two children, what is the conditional probability that both are girls given that

(i) the youngest is a girl? (ii) atleast one is a girl?

Sol. Let b and g represent the boy and the girl child, respectively. If a family has two children, the sample space will be

$$S = \{bb, bg, gb, gg\}$$

which contains four equally likely sample points *i.e.*, $n(S) = 4$

(i) Let E : both children are girls, then $E = \{gg\} \Rightarrow n(E) = 1$,

F : the youngest is a girl, then $F = \{bg, gg\} \Rightarrow n(F) = 2$

and $E \cap F = \{gg\} \Rightarrow n(E \cap F) = 1$

$\therefore$ $$P(E) = \frac{1}{4},\ P(F) = \frac{2}{4} = \frac{1}{2} \text{ and } P(E \cap F) = \frac{1}{4}$$

Now, Required probability $= P\left(\frac{E}{F}\right) = \frac{P(E \cap F)}{P(F)} = \frac{1/4}{2/4} = \frac{1}{2}$

(ii) Let F : atleast one is a girl, then $F = \{bg, gb, gg\} \Rightarrow E \cap F = \{gg\}$

$\Rightarrow$ $$n(F) = 3, n(E \cap F) = 1$$

$\therefore$ Required probability $= P\left(\frac{E}{F}\right) = \frac{P(E \cap F)}{P(F)} = \frac{1/4}{3/4} = \frac{1}{3}$

Question 13. An instructor has a question bank consisting of 300 easy true/false questions, 200 difficult true/false question, 500 easy multiple choice questions and 400 difficult multiple choice questions. If a question is selected at random from the test bank, what is the probability that it will be an easy question given that it is a multiple choice question?

Sol. Total number of questions = 300 + 200 + 500 + 400 = 1400.

Let E be the event that selected question is an easy question

Then, $$n(E) = 500 + 300 = 800$$

$\therefore$ $$P(E) = \frac{\text{Number of favourable outcomes}}{\text{Total number of outcomes}} = \frac{800}{1400} = \frac{4}{7}$$

Let F be the event that selected question is a multiple choice question.

Then, $n(F)=500+400=900$

Now, $P(F)=\dfrac{\text{Number of favourable outcomes}}{\text{Total number of outcomes}}=\dfrac{900}{1400}=\dfrac{9}{14}$

and $P(E\cap F)=\dfrac{500}{1400}=\dfrac{5}{14}$

$\therefore$ $P\left(\dfrac{E}{F}\right)=\dfrac{P(E\cap F)}{P(F)}=\dfrac{5/14}{9/14}=\dfrac{5}{9}$

Question 14 Given that the two numbers appearing on throwing two dice are different. Find the probability of the events 'the sum of numbers on the dice is 4'.

Sol. When dice is thrown, number of observations in the sample space $S=6\times 6=36$ (equally likely sample events) *i.e.*, $n(S)=36$

Let E : set of numbers in which the sum of the numbers on the dice is 4,

F : set of numbers in which numbers appearing on the two dice are different

Then, $E=\{(1,3),(2,2),(3,1)\}\Rightarrow n(E)=3$

and $F=\begin{Bmatrix}(1,2),(1,3),(1,4),(1,5),(1,6)\\(2,1),(2,3),(2,4),(2,5),(2,6)\\(3,1),(3,2),(3,4),(3,5),(3,6)\\(4,1),(4,2),(4,3),(4,5),(4,6)\\(5,1),(5,2),(5,3),(5,4),(5,6)\\(6,1),(6,2),(6,3),(6,4),(6,5)\end{Bmatrix}$

$\Rightarrow$ $n(F)=30$

Here, F contains all points of S except $\{(1,1),(2,2),(3,3),(4,4),(5,5),(6,6)\}$.

$\therefore$ $E\cap F=\{(1,3),(3,1)\}$

Now, $P(E)=\dfrac{\text{Number of favourable outcomes}}{\text{Total number of outcomes}}=\dfrac{3}{36}=\dfrac{1}{12}$

Similarly, $P(F)=\dfrac{30}{36}=\dfrac{5}{6}$ and $P(E\cap F)=\dfrac{2}{36}=\dfrac{1}{18}$

Hence, the required probability $=P\left(\dfrac{E}{F}\right)=\dfrac{P(E\cap F)}{P(F)}=\dfrac{\frac{1}{18}}{\frac{5}{6}}=\dfrac{1}{15}$

Question 15 Consider the experiment of throwing a die, if a multiple of 3 comes up throw the die again and if any other number comes, toss a coin. Find the conditional probability of the event the coin shows a tail, given that atleast one die shows a 3.

Sol. The outcomes of the given experiment can be represented by the following set.

The sample space of the experiment is,

$$S = \begin{Bmatrix} (3, 1), (3, 2), (3, 3), (3, 4), (3, 5), (3, 6) \\ (6, 1), (6, 2), (6, 3), (6, 4), (6, 5), (6, 6) \\ (1, H), (1, T), (2, H), (2, T), (4, H) \\ (4, T), (5, H), (5, T) \end{Bmatrix}$$

$$n(S) = 20$$

Let E : the coin shows a tail, F : atleast one die shows up a 3,

$$E = \{(1, T), (2, T), (4, T), (5, T)\}, \Rightarrow n(E) = 4$$

$$F = \{(3, 1), (3, 2), (3, 3), (3, 4), (3, 5), (3, 6), (6, 3)\} \Rightarrow n(F) = 7$$

$\Rightarrow$ $E \cap F = \phi$, because there is no common elements.

$$\therefore \quad P(E) = \frac{\text{Number of favourable outcomes}}{\text{Total number of outcomes}}$$

$$= \frac{n(E)}{n(S)} = \frac{4}{20} = \frac{1}{5}$$

Similarily, $P(F) = \dfrac{n(F)}{n(S)} = \dfrac{7}{20}$

and $\quad P(E \cap F) = \dfrac{n(E \cap F)}{n(S)} = \dfrac{0}{20} = 0$

Hence, the required probability $= P\left(\dfrac{E}{F}\right) = \dfrac{P(E \cap F)}{P(F)} = \dfrac{0}{\frac{7}{20}} = 0.$

Direction (Q. Nos. 16 and 17) In each of the questions choose the correct answer.

Question 16 If $P(A) = \dfrac{1}{2}$, $P(B) = 0$, then $P\left(\dfrac{A}{B}\right)$ is

(a) zero (b) $\dfrac{1}{2}$

(c) not defined (d) 1

Sol. (c) It is given that $P(A) = \dfrac{1}{2}$ and $P(B) = 0$

$$\therefore \quad P\left(\frac{A}{B}\right) = \frac{P(A \cap B)}{P(B)} = \frac{P(A \cap B)}{0} = \infty$$

$\Rightarrow \quad P\left(\dfrac{A}{B}\right)$ is not defined.

Question 17 If A and B are events such that $P\left(\frac{A}{B}\right) = P\left(\frac{B}{A}\right)$, then

(a) $A \subset B$ but $A \neq B$ (b) $A = B$ (c) $A \cap B = \phi$ (d) $P(A) = P(B)$

Sol. (d) Here, $P\left(\frac{A}{B}\right) = P\left(\frac{B}{A}\right)$

$\therefore \quad \frac{P(A \cap B)}{P(B)} = \frac{P(B \cap A)}{P(A)} \Rightarrow P(A) = P(B) \quad [\because P(A \cap B) = P(B \cap A)]$

Exercise 13.2

Question 1. If $P(A) = \frac{3}{5}$ and $P(B) = \frac{1}{5}$, find $P(A \cap B)$, if A and B are independent events.

Sol. Given, $P(A) = \frac{3}{5}$ and $P(B) = \frac{1}{5}$

As, A and B are independent events, therefore

$$P(A \cap B) = P(A) \times P(B) = \frac{3}{5} \times \frac{1}{5} = \frac{3}{25}.$$

Note If A and B are independent events, then $P(A \cap B) = P(A)\, P(B)$.

Question 2 Two cards are drawn at random and without replacement from a pack of 52 playing cards. Find the probability that both the cards are black.

Sol. There are 26 black cards in a pack of 52 cards.

Let E : first card drawn is black, F : second card drawn is black

$\therefore \quad P(E) = \frac{\text{Number of favourable outcomes}}{\text{Total number of outcomes}} = \frac{26}{52} = \frac{1}{2},$

and $\quad P(F/E) = \frac{25}{51}$

(After drawing one black, there will be 25 black cards and total 51 cards)

$\therefore \quad$ Required probability $P(E \cap F) = P(F/E)\, P(E) = \frac{1}{2} \times \frac{25}{51} = \frac{25}{102}$

Question 3 A box of oranges is inspected by examining three randomly selected oranges drawn without replacement. If all the three oranges are good, the box is approved for sale otherwise it is rejected. Find the probability that a box containing 15 oranges out of which 12 are good and 3 are bad one will be approved for sale.

Thinking Process Find the respective probabilities of drawing out good orange from the box. Since, the events of drawing good oranges are independent, then product of the three probabilities equals the probability of a box getting approved for sale.

Sol. Let A, B and C be the respective events that the first, second and third drawn orange is good.

Therefore, probability that first drawn orange is good, $P(A) = \frac{12}{15}$

Therefore, probability of getting second orange good, $P(B/A) = \frac{11}{14}$

($\because$ The oranges are not replaced so number of good oranges left is 11and total 14)

Similarly, probability of getting third orange is good, $P\left(\frac{C}{AB}\right) = \frac{10}{13}$

($\because$ The oranges are not replaced so number of good oranges left is 10 and total 13)

The box is approved for sale, if all the three oranges are good.

Thus, probability of getting all the three oranges good= $P(A) \cdot P(B/A) \cdot P\left(\frac{C}{AB}\right)$

$$= \frac{12}{15} \times \frac{11}{14} \times \frac{10}{13}$$

Therefore, the probability that the box is approved for sale = $\frac{44}{91}$.

Question 4 A fair coin and an unbiased die are tossed. Let A be the event 'head appears on the coin' and B be the event '3 on the die'. Check whether A and B are independent events or not.

Sol. If a fair coin and an unbiased die are tossed, then the sample space S is given by,

$$S = \begin{Bmatrix} (H, 1), (H, 2), (H, 3), (H, 4), (H, 5), (H, 6) \\ (T, 1), (T, 2), (T, 3), (T, 4), (T, 5), (T, 6) \end{Bmatrix} \Rightarrow n(S) = 12$$

Also, A: head appears on the coin and B: 3 appears on the die.

$\therefore \quad A =$

$= \{(H, 1), (H, 2), (H, 3), (H, 4), (H, 5), (H, 6)\}$,

$B =$ the $= \{(H, 3), (T, 3)\}$

$\Rightarrow \quad A \cap B = \{(H, 3)\} \Rightarrow n(A) = 6, \quad n(B) = 2, \quad n(A \cap B) = 1$

Hence, $\quad P(A) = \frac{6}{12} = \frac{1}{2}$, $P(B) = \frac{2}{12} = \frac{1}{6}$ and $P(A \cap B) = \frac{1}{12}$

Now, $P(A) \times P(B) = \frac{1}{2} \times \frac{1}{6} = \frac{1}{12} = P(A \cap B)$

Therefore, A and B are independent events.

Question 5 A die marked 1, 2, 3 in red and 4, 5, 6 in green is tossed. Let A be the event, 'number is even' and B be the event, 'number is red'. Are A and B independent?

Sol. When a die is thrown, the sample space $S = \{1, 2, 3, 4, 5, 6\}$.

Also, A : number is even and B : number is red

$\therefore \quad A = \{2, 4, 6\}, B = \{1, 2, 3\}$ and $A \cap B = \{2\}$.

$\Rightarrow \quad n(A) = 3, n(B) = 3, n(A \cap B) = 1$

Now, $\quad P(A) = \frac{3}{6} = \frac{1}{2}, P(B) = \frac{3}{6} = \frac{1}{2}, \quad P(A \cap B) = \frac{1}{6}$

and $P(A) \times P(B) = \frac{1}{2} \times \frac{1}{2} = \frac{1}{4} \neq \frac{1}{6} = P(A \cap B)$

$\Rightarrow \quad P(A \cap B) \neq P(A) P(B)$

Thus, A and B are not independent events.

Question 6 Let E and F be events with $P(E) = \frac{3}{5}$, $P(F) = \frac{3}{10}$ and $P(E \cap F) = \frac{1}{5}$. Are E and F independent?

Sol. Given, $P(E) = \frac{3}{5}, P(F) = \frac{3}{10}$ and $P(E \cap F) = \frac{1}{5}$

Now, $\quad P(E) \cdot P(F) = \frac{3}{5} \times \frac{3}{10} = \frac{9}{50} \neq \frac{1}{5} = P(E \cap F)$,

Therefore, E and F are not independent events.

Question 7 Given that the events A and B are such that $P(A) = 1/2$, $P(A \cup B) = 3/5$ and $P(B) = p$. Find p, if they are

(i) mutually exclusive (ii) independent

Sol. Given, $P(A) = \frac{1}{2}, P(A \cup B) = \frac{3}{5}$ and $P(B) = p$

(i) When A and B are mutually exclusive, then

$$A \cap B = \phi \Rightarrow P(A \cap B) = 0$$

$\therefore \quad P(A \cup B) = P(A) + P(B) - P(A \cap B) \Rightarrow \frac{3}{5} = \frac{1}{2} + p - 0$

$\Rightarrow \quad p = \frac{3}{5} - \frac{1}{2} = \frac{6-5}{10} = \frac{1}{10}$

(ii) When A and B are independent events, then

$$P(A \cap B) = P(A) \cdot P(B) = \frac{1}{2} p \qquad \left(\because P(A) = \frac{1}{2}, P(B) = p \text{ given}\right)$$

Now, $\quad P(A \cup B) = P(A) + P(B) - P(A) \times P(B)$

$\Rightarrow \quad \frac{3}{5} = \frac{1}{2} + p - \frac{1}{2} p \Rightarrow \frac{3}{5} - \frac{1}{2} = \frac{2p - p}{2}$

$\Rightarrow \quad \frac{p}{2} = \frac{6-5}{10} \Rightarrow p = \frac{2}{10} = \frac{1}{5}$

Note • Two events A and B are mutually exclusive, if $P(A \cap B) = 0$ or $A \cap B = \phi$.

• Two events A and B are independent, if $P(A \cap B) = P(A) P(B)$

Question 8 Let A and B be independent events with $P(A) = 0.3$ and $P(B) = 0.4$. Find

(i) $P(A \cap B)$ (ii) $P(A \cup B)$

(iii) $P\left(\frac{A}{B}\right)$ (iv) $P\left(\frac{B}{A}\right)$

Sol. Given, $P(A) = 0.3$ and $P(B) = 0.4$

(i) If A and B are independent events, then

$$P(A \cap B) = P(A) \times P(B) = 0.3 \times 0.4 = 0.12$$

(ii) We know that,

$$P(A \cup B) = P(A) + P(B) - P(A \cap B) = P(A) + P(B) - P(A)\,P(B)$$

$$= 0.3 + 0.4 - 0.3 \times 0.4 = 0.7 - 0.12 = 0.58$$

(iii) We know that, $P\left(\frac{A}{B}\right) = \frac{P(A \cap B)}{P(B)} = \frac{P(A)\,P(B)}{P(B)}$

$$\Rightarrow \quad P\left(\frac{A}{B}\right) = \frac{0.12}{0.4} = 0.3$$

(iv) We know that, $P\left(\frac{B}{A}\right) = \frac{P(B \cap A)}{P(A)} = \frac{P(B)\,P(A)}{P(A)}$

$$\Rightarrow \quad P\left(\frac{B}{A}\right) = \frac{0.12}{0.3} = 0.4$$

Question 9 If A and B are two events such that $P(A) = \frac{1}{4}$, $P(B) = \frac{1}{2}$ and $P(A \cap B) = \frac{1}{8}$, find P (not A and not B).

◎ ***Thinking Process*** Firstly use the relation $P(A \cap B) = P(A) \times P(B)$ and then use $P(\overline{A} \cap \overline{B}) = P(\overline{A}) \times P(\overline{B})$

Sol. We have, $P(A) = \frac{1}{4}, P(B) = \frac{1}{2}, \; P(A \cap B) = \frac{1}{8}$

$$\Rightarrow \quad P(A') = 1 - P(A) = 1 - \frac{1}{4} = \frac{3}{4}$$

and $\quad P(B') = 1 - P(B) = 1 - \frac{1}{2} = \frac{1}{2}$

As, $\quad P(A \cap B) = \frac{1}{8} = \frac{1}{4} \times \frac{1}{2} = P(A) \times P(B).$

Therefore, A and B are independent events.

$\Rightarrow A'$ and B' are also independent events

$\Rightarrow P(A' \cap B') = P(A')\,P(B')$

$\therefore P$ (not A and not B) $= P(A' \cap B') = P(A')P(B') = \frac{3}{4} \times \frac{1}{2} = \frac{3}{8}$

Quick Solution

We have, $P(A) = \frac{1}{4}, P(B) = \frac{1}{2}, P(A \cap B) = \frac{1}{8}$

$$P(\text{not } A \text{ and not } B) = (\overline{A} \cap \overline{B})$$
$$= 1 - P(A \cup B)$$
$$= 1 - (P(A) + P(B) - P(A \cap B)$$
$$= 1 - \left(\frac{1}{4} + \frac{1}{2} - \frac{1}{8}\right)$$
$$= 1 - \left(\frac{2+4-1}{8}\right) = 1 - \frac{5}{8} = \frac{3}{8}$$

Note If A and B are independent events, then A' and B' are also independent events.

Question 10 Events A and B are such that $P(A) = \frac{1}{2}$, $P(B) = \frac{7}{12}$ and $P(\text{not } A \text{ or not } B) = \frac{1}{4}$. State whether A and B are independent?

Sol. Given, P (not A or not B) = $P(A' \text{ or } B') = \frac{1}{4} = P(A' \cup B')$

$$\Rightarrow \quad P(A' \cup B') = \frac{1}{4} \Rightarrow P[(A \cap B)'] = \frac{1}{4} \qquad [\because P(A' \cup B') = P(A \cap B)']$$

$$\Rightarrow \quad 1 - P(A \cap B) = \frac{1}{4} \Rightarrow P(A \cap B) = 1 - \frac{1}{4} = \frac{3}{4} \qquad \ldots(i)$$

Also, $\quad P(A) \times P(B) = \frac{1}{2} \times \frac{7}{12} = \frac{7}{24} \neq \frac{3}{4} \qquad \left[\text{given}, P(A) = \frac{1}{2}, P(B) = \frac{7}{12}\right]$

$$\Rightarrow \quad P(A) \times P(B) \neq P(A \cap B)$$

$\therefore$ A and B are not independent events.

Question 11 Given two independent events A and B such that $P(A) = 0.3$, $P(B) = 0.6$. Find

(i) $P(A \text{ and } B)$ (ii) $P(A \text{ and not } B)$

(iii) $P(A \text{ or } B)$

(iv) P (neither A nor B)

◎ ***Thinking Process*** If A and B are two independent events, then A' and B, A and B', A' and B' are all independent events.

Sol. Given, $P(A) = 0.3$ and $P(B) = 0.6$

Also, A and B are independent events.

(i) $P(A \text{ and } B) = P(A \cap B) = P(A) \times P(B) = 0.3 \times 0.6 = 0.18$

[$\because$ A and B are independent]

(ii) $P(A \text{ and not } B) = P(A \cap B') = P(A) \times P(B')$

[$\because A$ and B are independent, $\therefore A$ and B' are also independent]

$= P(A)[1 - P(B)]$

$= (0.3)(1 - 0.6)$

$= 0.3 \times 0.4 = 0.12$

(iii) $P(A \text{ or } B) = P(A \cup B)$

$= P(A) + P(B) - P(A \cap B)$

$= P(A) + P(B) - P(A) \times P(B)$

$= 0.3 + 0.6 - 0.3 \times 0.6$

$= 0.9 - 0.18 = 0.72$

(iv) P (neither A nor B) $= P(A' \text{ and } B')$

$= P(A' \cap B') = P(A \cup B)'$ [$\because P(A' \cap B') = P(A \cup B)'$]

$= 1 - P(A \cup B)$

$= 1 - 0.72 = 0.28$ (using parts (iii))

Quick Solution

P (neither A nor B) $= P(A' \cap B') = P(A')\,P(B')$

($\because A$ and B are independent, $\therefore A'$ and B' are also independent)

$= [1 - P(A)][1 - P(B)] = (1 - 0.3)(1 - 0.6) = 0.7 \times 0.4 = 0.28$

Question 12 A die is tossed thrice. Find the probability of getting an odd number atleast once.

◎ **Thinking Process** The probability of getting an odd number atleast once $= 1 -$ probability of getting an odd number in none of the throws.

Sol. When a die is thrown, there are 3 odd numbers on the die out of 6 numbers.

$\therefore$ Probability of getting an odd number

$$= \frac{\text{Number of favourable outcomes}}{\text{Total number of outcomes}} = \frac{3}{6} = \frac{1}{2}$$

Probability of getting an even number

$$= 1 - \text{probability of getting an odd number} = 1 - \frac{1}{2} = \frac{1}{2}$$

Probability of getting an even number when the die is tossed thrice

$$P(E) = \frac{1}{2} \times \frac{1}{2} \times \frac{1}{2} = \frac{1}{8}$$

Therefore, probability of getting an odd number atleast once

$= 1 -$ Probability of getting an odd number in none of the throws

$$= 1 - P(E) = 1 - \frac{1}{8} = \frac{7}{8}$$

Question 13 Two balls are drawn at random with replacement from a box containing 10 black and 8 red balls. Find the probability that

(i) both balls are red

(ii) first ball is black and second is red

(iii) one of them is black and other is red

◎ ***Thinking Process*** If balls are drawn with replacement it means number of balls will be same in each draw so they will be independent event.

Sol. Total number of balls = 18, number of red balls = 8 and number of black balls = 10

$\therefore$ Probability of drawing a red ball $= \frac{\text{Number of red balls}}{\text{Total number of balls}} = \frac{8}{18} = \frac{4}{9}$

Similarly, probability of drawing a black ball

$$= \frac{\text{Number of black balls}}{\text{Total number of balls}} = \frac{10}{18} = \frac{5}{9}$$

(i) Probability of getting both red balls = P (both balls are red)

= P (a red ball is drawn at first draw and again a red ball at second draw)

$$= \frac{4}{9} \times \frac{4}{9} = \frac{16}{81}$$

(ii) P (probability of getting first ball is black and second is red)

$$= \frac{5}{9} \times \frac{4}{9} = \frac{20}{81}$$

(iii) Probability of getting one black and other red ball

= P(first ball is black and second is red)

+ P (first ball is red and second is black)

$$= \frac{5}{9} \times \frac{4}{9} + \frac{4}{9} \times \frac{5}{9} = \frac{40}{81}$$

Question 14 Probability of solving specific problem independently by A and B are $\frac{1}{2}$ and $\frac{1}{3}$, respectively. If both try to solve the problem independently, find the probability that

(i) the problem is solved

(ii) exactly one of them solves the problem

Sol. Given, probability of solving the problem by A, $P(A) = \frac{1}{2}$

and probability of solving the problem by B, $P(B) = \frac{1}{3}$

$\therefore$ Probability of not solving the problem by $A = P(A') = 1 - P(A) = 1 - \frac{1}{2} = \frac{1}{2}$

and probability of not solving the problem by

$$B = P(B') = 1 - P(B) = 1 - \frac{1}{3} = \frac{2}{3}$$

(i) P(the problem is solved) = P (at least one solve problem)

$$= P(A \cup B) = P(A) + P(B) - P(A \cap B)$$

$$= P(A) + P(B) - P(A) \cdot P(B)$$

($\because$ A and B are independent events)

$$= \frac{1}{2} + \frac{1}{3} - \frac{1}{2} \times \frac{1}{3} = \frac{1}{2} + \frac{1}{3} - \frac{1}{6} = \frac{2}{3}$$

(ii) P (exactly one of them solve the problem) = $P(A)\, P(B') + P(A')P(B)$

$$= \frac{1}{2} \times \frac{2}{3} + \frac{1}{2} \times \frac{1}{3} = \frac{1}{3} + \frac{1}{6} = \frac{2+1}{6} = \frac{3}{6} = \frac{1}{2}$$

Question 15 One card is drawn at random from a well-shuffled deck of 52 cards. In which of the following cases are the events E and F independent?

(i) E : the card drawn is a spade, F : the card drawn is an ace

(ii) E : the card drawn is black, F : the card drawn is a king

(iii) E : the card drawn is a king or queen,
F : the card drawn is a queen or jack.

Sol.

(i) In a deck of 52 cards, 13 cards are spades and 4 cards are aces.

Given, E: the card drawn is a spade $\Rightarrow$ $n(E) = 13$,
and F: the card drawn is an ace $\Rightarrow n(F) = 4$
and $n(S) = 52$

Here, $P(E) = P$ (card drawn is spade) $= \dfrac{n(E)}{n(S)} = \dfrac{13}{52} = \dfrac{1}{4}$

$$P(F) = P\text{ (card drawn is an ace)} = \frac{4}{52} = \frac{1}{13}$$

Also, $E \cap F$ in the deck of cards, only 1 card is an ace of spades.

$$\Rightarrow \quad P(E \cap F) = \frac{n(E \cap F)}{n(S)} = \frac{1}{52}$$

Now, $P(E) \times P(F) = \dfrac{1}{4} \times \dfrac{1}{13} = \dfrac{1}{52} = P(E \cap F)$

Therefore, the events E and F are independent.

(ii) In a deck of 52 cards, 26 cards are black and 4 cards are kings.

Given, E : the cards drawn is black $\Rightarrow n(E) = 26$
F : the cards drawn is king $\Rightarrow n(F) = 4$

Also, $n(S) = 52$

$$P(E) = P\text{ (card drawn is black)} = \frac{n(E)}{n(S)} = \frac{26}{52} = \frac{1}{2}$$

and $P(F) = P$ (card drawn is a king) $= \dfrac{n(E)}{n(S)} = \dfrac{4}{52} = \dfrac{1}{13}$

Also, $E \cap F$: card drawn is a black king there are two black king one of spade and other of club.

$$\Rightarrow \qquad P(E \cap F) = \frac{n(E \cap S)}{n(S)} = \frac{2}{52} = \frac{1}{26}$$

Now, $P(E) \times P(F) = \frac{1}{2} \times \frac{1}{13} = \frac{1}{26} = P(E \cap F) \Rightarrow P(E \cap F) = P(E)P(F)$

Therefore, the events E and F are independent.

(iii) In a deck of 52 cards, 4 cards are kings, 4 cards are queens and 4 cards are jacks.

$P(E) = P$ (card drawn is a king or a queen)

$$= P \text{ (King)} + P \text{ (Queen)} = \frac{4}{52} + \frac{4}{52} = \frac{8}{52} = \frac{2}{13}$$

and $P(F) = P$ (cards drawn is a queen or a jack)

$$= P \text{ (Queen)} + P \text{ (Jack)} = \frac{4}{52} + \frac{4}{52} = \frac{8}{52} = \frac{2}{13}$$

Also, $E \cap F$: card drawn is a queen $\Rightarrow P(E \cap F) = \frac{4}{52} = \frac{1}{13}$

Now, $P(E) \times P(F) = \frac{2}{13} \times \frac{2}{13} = \frac{4}{169} \neq P(E \cap F) \Rightarrow P(E \cap F) \neq P(E)\, P(F)$

Therefore, the events E and F are not independent.

Question 16 In a hostel, 60% of the students read Hindi newspaper, 40% read English newspaper and 20% read both Hindi and English newspapers. A student is selected at random,

(i) Find the probability that he/she reads neither Hindi nor English newspapers.

(ii) If he/she reads Hindi newspaper, find the probability that she reads English newspaper.

(iii) If he/she reads English newspaper, find the probability he/she reads Hindi newspaper.

Sol. Let H : Set of students reading Hindi newspaper and E : set of students reading English newspaper.

Let $n(S) = 100$

Then, $n(H) = 60$, $n(E) = 40$ and $n(H \cap E) = 20$

$$\therefore \qquad P(H) = \frac{n(H)}{n(S)} = \frac{60}{100} = \frac{3}{5},\ P(E) = \frac{n(E)}{n(S)} = \frac{40}{100} = \frac{2}{5}$$

and

$$P(H \cap E) = \frac{n(H \cap E)}{n(S)} = \frac{20}{100} = \frac{1}{5}$$

(i) Required probability $= P$ (student reads neither Hindi nor English newspaper)

$$= P(H' \cap E') = P(H \cup E)' = 1 - P(H \cup E)$$

$$= 1 - [P(H) + P(E) - P(H \cap E)] = 1 - \left[\frac{3}{5} + \frac{2}{5} - \frac{1}{5}\right] = \frac{1}{5}$$

(ii) Required probability $= P$(a randomly chosen student reads English newspaper, if he/she reads Hindi newspaper)

$$\therefore \quad P\left(\frac{E}{H}\right) = \frac{P(E \cap H)}{P(H)} = \frac{\frac{1}{5}}{\frac{3}{5}} = \frac{1}{3}$$

(iii) Required probability $= P$ (student reads Hindi newspaper when it is given that reads English newspaper)

$$\therefore \quad P\left(\frac{H}{E}\right) = \frac{P(H \cap E)}{P(E)} = \frac{\frac{1}{5}}{\frac{2}{5}} = \frac{1}{2}$$

Direction (Q. Nos. 17 and 18) Choose the correct answer.

Question 17 The probability of obtaining an even prime number on each die when a pair of dice is rolled is

(a) 0 (b) $\frac{1}{3}$ (c) $\frac{1}{12}$ (d) $\frac{1}{36}$

Thinking Process In numbers, the even prime number is only 2, use this result and simplify it.

Sol. (d) When a pair of dice is rolled once, the sample space contains $6 \times 6 = 36$ elements.

i.e., $n(S) = 36$

We know that the only even prime number is 2.

Let E be the event of getting an even prime number on each die, $E = (2, 2)$

i.e., $n(E) = 1$

Required probability $= P$ (an even prime on each die)

$$= \frac{n(E)}{n(S)} = \frac{1}{36}$$

Question 18 Two events A and B are said to be independent, if

(a) A and B are mutually exclusive

(b) $P(A' \cap B') = [1 - P(A)][1 - P(B)]$

(c) $P(A) = P(B)$

(d) $P(A) + P(B) = 1$

Sol. (b) A and B are independent, if $P(A \cap B) = P(A)\, P(B)$

$$\therefore P(A' \cap B') = P(A \cup B)' = 1 - P(A \cup B) = 1 - [P(A) + P(B) - P(A \cap B)]$$

$$[\because P(A \cup B)' = 1 - P(A \cup B)]$$

$$= 1 - P(A) - P(B) + P(A)\, P(B) \quad [\because P(A \cap B) = P(A) \cdot P(B)]$$

$$= (1 - P(A)) - P(B)(1 - P(A))$$

$$= (1 - P(A))(1 - P(B))$$

Exercise 13.3

Question 1 An urn contains 5 red and 5 black balls. A ball is drawn at random, its colour is noted and is returned to the urn. Moreover, 2 additional balls of the colour drawn are put in the urn and then a balls is drawn at random. What is the probability that the second ball is red?

◎ ***Thinking Process*** The event that the second ball is red will contain two cases

(i) If first ball drawn is red, then two more red balls are added. Then, the number of red balls increases by 2 and the probability of second ball being red also increases.

(ii) If first ball drawn is black, then two more black balls are added and no change in number of red balls. The total number of balls increases by 2 and the probability of second ball being red decreases.

The required probability will be the sum of probabilities of above two cases.

Sol. The urn contains 5 red and 5 black balls.

i.e., $n(R)=5, n(B)=5 \quad \text{and} \quad n(S)=10$

Let a red ball be drawn in the first attempt

$$\therefore \quad P\text{ (drawing a red ball)} = \frac{n(R)}{n(S)} = \frac{5}{10} = \frac{1}{2}$$

If two red balls are added to the urn, then the urn contains 7 red and 5 black balls *i.e.*, $n(R)=7, n(B)=5 \quad \text{and} \quad n(S)=12$

$$\therefore \quad P\text{ (drawing a red ball)} = \frac{n(R)}{n(S)} = \frac{7}{12}$$

Let a black ball be drawn in the first attempt

Then, $n(R)=5, n(B)=5 \quad \text{and} \quad n(S)=10$

$$\therefore P\text{ (drawing a black ball in the first attempt)} = \frac{n(B)}{n(S)} = \frac{5}{10} = \frac{1}{2}$$

If two black balls are added to the urn, then the urn contains 5 red and 7 black balls.

i.e., $n(R)=5, n(B)=7$ and $n(S)=12$

$$\therefore P\text{ (drawing a red ball)} = \frac{n(R)}{n(S)} = \frac{5}{12}$$

Therefore, probability of drawing second ball as red is

$$= \frac{1}{2} \times \frac{7}{12} + \frac{1}{2} \times \frac{5}{12} = \frac{1}{2}\left(\frac{7}{12} + \frac{5}{12}\right)$$

$$= \frac{1}{2} \times 1 = \frac{1}{2}$$

Question 2 A bag contains 4 red and 4 black balls, another bag contains 2 red and 6 black balls. One of the two bags is selected at random and a ball is drawn from the bag which is found to be red. Find the probability that the ball is drawn from the first bag.

◎ *Thinking Process* Event that the ball drawn is red can be under two cases

(i) ball was drawn from first bag.

(ii) ball was drawn from second bag. Then, use Baye's theorem

Sol. Let E_1 : first bag is selected, E_2 : second bag is selected

Then, E_1 and E_2 are mutually exclusive and exhaustive.

Moreover, $P(E_1) = P(E_2) = \frac{1}{2}$

and E : ball drawn is red.

$$\therefore \quad P\left(\frac{E}{E_1}\right) = P\text{ (drawing a red ball from first bag)} = \frac{4}{8} = \frac{1}{2}$$

$$\text{and} \quad P\left(\frac{E}{E_2}\right) = P\text{ (drawing a red ball from second bag)} = \frac{2}{8} = \frac{1}{4}$$

$$\therefore \text{ Required probability} = P\left(\frac{E_1}{E}\right) = \frac{P\left(\frac{E}{E_1}\right)P(E_1)}{P\left(\frac{E}{E_1}\right)P(E_1) + P\left(\frac{E}{E_2}\right)P(E_2)}$$

$$= \frac{\frac{1}{2}\times\frac{1}{2}}{\frac{1}{2}\times\frac{1}{2}+\frac{1}{2}\times\frac{1}{4}} = \frac{\frac{1}{4}}{\frac{1}{4}+\frac{1}{8}} = \frac{\frac{1}{4}}{\frac{2+1}{8}} = \frac{\frac{1}{4}}{\frac{3}{8}} = \frac{1}{4}\times\frac{8}{3} = \frac{2}{3}$$

Question 3 Of the students in a college, it is known that 60% reside in hostel and 40% are day scholars (not residing in hostel). Previous years results report that 30% of all students who reside in hostel attain *A* grade and 20% of day scholars attain *A* grade in their annual examination. At the end of the year, one student is chosen at random from the college and he has an *A* grade, what is the probability that the student is a hostler?

◎ *Thinking Process* (Q.Nos. 3 to 8) If $E_1, E_2, \dots, E_n$ form a set of mutually exclusive and exhaustive events and E is any other event, then by Bayes' theorem,

$$P\left(\frac{E_i}{E}\right) = \frac{P(E/E_i)\cdot P(E_i)}{\sum_{r=1}^{n} P(E/E_i)\cdot P(E_i)}$$

Sol. Let E_1 : the event that the student is residing in hostel

E_2 : the event that the student is not residing in the hostel.

and : a student attains A grade,

Then, E_1 and E_2 are mutually exclusive and exhaustive. Moreover,

$$P(E_1) = 60\% = \frac{60}{100} = \frac{3}{5} \text{ and } P(E_2) = 40\% = \frac{40}{100} = \frac{2}{5}$$

Then,
$$P\left(\frac{E}{E_1}\right) = 30\% = \frac{30}{100} = \frac{3}{10} \text{ and } P\left(\frac{E}{E_2}\right) = 20\% = \frac{20}{100} = \frac{2}{10}$$

By using Bayes' theorem, we get

$$P\left(\frac{E_1}{E}\right) = \frac{P\left(\frac{E}{E_1}\right)P(E_1)}{P\left(\frac{E}{E_1}\right)P(E_1) + P\left(\frac{E}{E_2}\right)P(E_2)}$$

$$= \frac{\frac{3}{10} \times \frac{3}{5}}{\frac{3}{10} \times \frac{3}{5} + \frac{2}{10} \times \frac{2}{5}} = \frac{9}{9+4} = \frac{9}{13}$$

Question 4 In answering a question on a multiple choice test a student either knows the answer or guesses. Let 3/4 be the probability that he knows the answer and 1/4 be the probability that he guesses. Assuming that a student who guesses at the answer will be correct with probability 1/4. What is the probability that a student knows the answer given that he answered it correctly?

Sol. Let E_1 : the event that the student knows the answer and

E_2 : the event that the student guesses the answer.

Therefore E_1 and E_2 are mutually exclusive and exhaustive.

$$\therefore \quad P(E_1) = \frac{3}{4} \text{ and } P(E_2) = \frac{1}{4}$$

Let E : the answer is correct.

The probability that the student answered correctly, given that he knows the answer, is 1 i.e.,
$$P\left(\frac{E}{E_1}\right) = 1$$

and the probability that the students answered correctly, given that the he guessed, is $\frac{1}{4}$ *i.e.,*
$$P\left(\frac{E}{E_2}\right) = \frac{1}{4}.$$

By using Bayes' theorem, we get

$$P\left(\frac{E_1}{E}\right) = \frac{P\left(\frac{E}{E_1}\right)P(E_1)}{P\left(\frac{E}{E_1}\right)P(E_1) + P\left(\frac{E}{E_2}\right)P(E_2)}$$

$$= \frac{1 \times \frac{3}{4}}{1 \times \frac{3}{4} + \frac{1}{4} \times \frac{1}{4}} = \frac{\frac{3}{4}}{\frac{3}{4} + \frac{1}{16}} = \frac{\frac{3}{4}}{\frac{12+1}{16}} = \frac{3}{4} \times \frac{16}{13} = \frac{12}{13}$$

Mistake Alert If two events are not mutually exclusive/exhaustive, then you do not use Baye's theorem.

Question 5 A laboratory blood test is 99% effective in detecting a certain disease when it is in fact present. However, the test also yields a false positive result for 0.5% of the healthy person tested (*i.e.*, if a healthy person is tested, then with probability 0.005, the test will imply he has the disease). If 0.1% of the population actually has the disease, what is the probability that a person has disease given that his test result is positive?

Sol. Let E_1 : the event that the person has disease, E_2 : the events that the person is healthy.

Then, E_1 and E_2 are mutually exclusive and exhaustive.

Moreover, $P(E_1) = 0.1\% = \frac{0.1}{100} = 0.001$ and $P(E_2) = 1 - 0.001 = 0.999$

and E : the event that test is positive,

$$\therefore \quad P\left(\frac{E}{E_1}\right) = P\text{(result is positive given the person has disease)}$$

$$= 99\% = \frac{99}{100} = 0.99$$

and probability that a person does not have disease and test result is positive,

$$P\left(\frac{E}{E_2}\right) = 0.5\% = \frac{0.5}{100} = 0.005$$

By using Bayes' theorem, we get

$$P\left(\frac{E_1}{E}\right) = \frac{P\left(\frac{E}{E_1}\right)P(E_1)}{P\left(\frac{E}{E_1}\right)P(E_1) + P\left(\frac{E}{E_2}\right)P(E_2)}$$

$$= \frac{0.001 \times 0.99}{0.001 \times 0.99 + 0.999 \times 0.005} = \frac{0.00099}{0.00099 + 0.004995}$$

$$= \frac{0.00099}{0.005985} = \frac{990}{5985} = \frac{110}{665} = \frac{22}{133}$$

Question 6 There are three coins. One is a two headed coin (having head on both faces), another is a biased coin that comes up heads 75% of the time and third is an unbiased coin. One of the three coins is chosen at random and tossed, it shows head, what is the probability that it is was the two headed coin?

Sol. Let E_1 : the event that the coin chosen is two headed,

E_2 : the event that the coin chosen is biased,

E_3 : the event that the coin chosen is unbiased

$\Rightarrow E_1, E_2, E_3$ are mutually exclusive and exhaustive events. Moreover,

$$P(E_1) = P(E_2) = P(E_3) = \frac{1}{3}$$

and E : tosses coin shows up a head,

$\therefore P\left(\frac{E}{E_1}\right) = P$ (coin showing heads, given that it is a two headed coin) = 1,

$P\left(\frac{E}{E_2}\right) = P$ (coin showing heads, given that it is a biased coin)

$$= 75\% = \frac{75}{100} = \frac{3}{4}$$

and $P\left(\frac{E}{E_3}\right) = P$ (coin showing heads, given that it is an unbiased coin) $= \frac{1}{2}$

The probability that the coin is two headed, given that it shows head, is given by $P\left(\frac{E_1}{E}\right)$.

By using Bayes' theorem, we get

$$P\left(\frac{E_1}{E}\right) = \frac{P\left(\frac{E}{E_1}\right)P(E_1)}{P\left(\frac{E}{E_1}\right)P(E_1) + P\left(\frac{E}{E_2}\right)P(E_2) + P\left(\frac{E}{E_3}\right)P(E_3)}$$

$$= \frac{1 \times \frac{1}{3}}{1 \times \frac{1}{3} + \frac{3}{4} \times \frac{1}{3} + \frac{1}{2} \times \frac{1}{3}} = \frac{1}{1 + \frac{3}{4} + \frac{1}{2}}$$

$$= \frac{1}{\frac{4+3+2}{4}} = \frac{4}{9}$$

Question 7 An insurance company insured 2000 scooter drivers, 4000 car drivers and 6000 truck drivers. The probability of accidents are 0.01, 0.03 and 0.15, respectively. One of the insured persons meets with an accident. What is the probability that he is a scooter driver?

Sol. There are 2000 scooter drivers, 4000 car drivers and 6000 truck drivers.

Total number of drivers = 2000 + 4000 + 6000 = 12000

Let E_1 : the event that insured person is a scooter driver, E_2 : the event that insured person is a car driver

and E_3 : the event that insured person is a truck driver.

Then, E_1, E_2, E_3 are mutually exclusive and exhaustive events. Moreover,

$$P(E_1) = \frac{\text{Number of scooter drivers}}{\text{Total number of drivers}} = \frac{2000}{12000} = \frac{1}{6},$$

$$P(E_2) = \frac{\text{Number of car drivers}}{\text{Total number of drivers}} = \frac{4000}{12000} = \frac{1}{3},$$

and $$P(E_3) = \frac{\text{Number of truck drivers}}{\text{Total number of drivers}} = \frac{6000}{12000} = \frac{1}{2},$$

Let E : the events that insured person meets with an accident,

$$\therefore \quad P\left(\frac{E}{E_1}\right) = P\text{ (scooter driver met with an accident)} = 0.01 = \frac{1}{100},$$

$$P\left(\frac{E}{E_2}\right) = P\text{ (car driver met with an accident)} = 0.03 = \frac{3}{100}$$

and $$P\left(\frac{E}{E_3}\right) = P\text{ (truck driver met with an accident)} = 0.15 = \frac{15}{100}$$

The probability that the driver is a scooter driver, given he met with an accident, is given by $P\left(\frac{E_1}{E}\right)$.

By using Bayes' theorem, we get

$$P\left(\frac{E_1}{E}\right) = \frac{P\left(\frac{E}{E_1}\right)P(E_1)}{P\left(\frac{E}{E_1}\right)\cdot P(E_1) + P\left(\frac{E}{E_2}\right)P(E_2) + P\left(\frac{E}{E_3}\right)P(E_3)}$$

$$= \frac{\frac{1}{6} \times \frac{1}{100}}{\frac{1}{6} \times \frac{1}{100} + \frac{1}{3} \times \frac{3}{100} + \frac{1}{2} \times \frac{15}{100}} = \frac{\frac{1}{6}}{\frac{1}{6} + 1 + \frac{15}{2}} = \frac{1}{1 + 6 + 45} = \frac{1}{52}$$

Question 8 A factory has two machines A and B. Past record shows that machine A produced 60% of the item of output and machine B produced 40% of the items. Further, 2% of the items produced by machine A and 1% produced by machine B were defective. All the items are put into one stockpile and then one item is chosen at random from this and is found to be defective. What is the probability that it was produced by machine B?

Sol. Let E_1 : the event that the item is produced by machine A and E_2 : the event that the item is produced by machine B.

Then, E_1 and E_2 are mutually exclusive and exhaustive events. Moreover,

$$P(E_1) = 60\% = \frac{60}{100} = \frac{3}{5}$$

and $$P(E_2) = 40\% = \frac{40}{100} = \frac{2}{5}.$$

Let E : the event that the item chosen is defective,

$\therefore$ $$P\left(\frac{E}{E_1}\right) = P\text{ (machine } A \text{ produced defective items)} = 2\% = \frac{2}{100}$$

$$P\left(\frac{E}{E_2}\right) = P\text{ (machine } B \text{ produced defective items)} = 1\% = \frac{1}{100}$$

The probability that the randomly selected item was from machine B, given that it is defective, is given by $P\left(\frac{E_2}{E}\right)$.

By using Bayes' theorem, we get

$$P\left(\frac{E_2}{E}\right) = \frac{P\left(\frac{E}{E_2}\right)P(E_2)}{P\left(\frac{E}{E_1}\right)P(E_1) + P\left(\frac{E}{E_2}\right)P(E_2)} = \frac{\frac{1}{100} \times \frac{2}{5}}{\frac{2}{100} \times \frac{3}{5} + \frac{1}{100} \times \frac{2}{5}} = \frac{\frac{2}{500}}{\frac{6}{500} + \frac{2}{500}}$$

$$= \frac{2}{6+2} = \frac{1}{4}$$

Question 9 Two groups are competing for the position on the board of directors of a corporation. The probability that the first and the second groups will win are 0.6 and 0.4, respectively. Further, if the first group wins the probability of introducing a new product is 0.7 and the corresponding probability is 0.3, if the second group wins. Find the probability that the new product introduce was by the second group.

◎ ***Thinking Process*** Assume E_1 : first group wins, E_2 : second group wins, E : new product was introduced.

Then, the probability that new product was introduced by second group is $P\left(\frac{E_2}{E}\right)$ which can be found out by using Bayes' theorem.

Sol. Let E_1 : the event that the first group wins and E_2 : the event that the second group wins.

Then, E_1 and E_2 are mutually exclusive and exhaustive events.

$\therefore$ $$P(E_1) = 0.6 = \frac{6}{10} \text{ and } P(E_2) = 0.4 = \frac{4}{10}$$

Let E : the event that the new product is introduced.

$$\therefore \quad P\left(\frac{E}{E_1}\right) = P\text{(introducing a new product, if the first group wins)}$$
$$= 0.7 = \frac{7}{10}$$

and $$P\left(\frac{E}{E_2}\right) = P\text{(introducing a new product, if the second group wins)}$$
$$= 0.3 = \frac{3}{10}$$

The probability that the new product is introduced by the second group is given by $P\left(\frac{E_2}{E}\right)$.

By using Baye's theorem, we obtain

$$P\left(\frac{E_2}{E}\right) = \frac{P\left(\frac{E}{E_2}\right)P(E_2)}{P\left(\frac{E}{E_1}\right)P(E_1) + P\left(\frac{E}{E_2}\right)P(E_2)}$$

$$= \frac{\frac{3}{10} \times \frac{4}{10}}{\frac{7}{10} \times \frac{6}{10} + \frac{3}{10} \times \frac{4}{10}} = \frac{12}{42 + 12} = \frac{12}{54} = \frac{2}{9}$$

Question 10. Suppose, a girl throws a die. If she gets a 5 or 6, she tosses a coin three times and notes the number of heads. If she gets 1, 2, 3 or 4 she tosses a coin once and notes whether a head or tail is obtained. If she obtained exactly one head, what is the probability that she threw 1, 2, 3 or 4 with the die?

Sol. Let E_1 : the event that 5 or 6 is shown on die

and E_2 : the event that 1, 2, 3, or 4 is shown on die.

Then, E_1 and E_2 are mutually exclusive and exhaustive events.

and $n(E_1)=2, n(E_2)=4$

Also, $n(S)=6$

$$\therefore \quad P(E_1) = \frac{2}{6} = \frac{1}{3} \text{ and } P(E_2) = \frac{4}{6} = \frac{2}{3}$$

Let E : The event that exactly one head show up,

$$\therefore \quad P\left(\frac{E}{E_1}\right) = P\text{(exactly one head show up when coin is tossed thrice)}$$

$$= P\{HTT, THT, TTH\} = \frac{3}{8} \quad (\because \text{ total number of events} = 2^3 = 8)$$

and $P\left(\frac{E}{E_2}\right) = P$ (head shows up when coin is tossed once) $= \frac{1}{2}$

The probability that the girl threw, 1, 2, 3 or 4 with the die, if she obtained exactly one head, is given by $P\left(\frac{E_2}{E}\right)$.

By using Bayes' theorem, we obtain

$$P\left(\frac{E_2}{E}\right) = \frac{P\left(\frac{E}{E_2}\right)P(E_2)}{P\left(\frac{E}{E_1}\right)P(E_1) + P\left(\frac{E}{E_2}\right)P(E_2)}$$

$$= \frac{\frac{1}{2}\times\frac{2}{3}}{\frac{3}{8}\times\frac{1}{3}+\frac{1}{2}\times\frac{2}{3}} = \frac{\frac{1}{3}}{\frac{1}{8}+\frac{1}{3}} = \frac{8}{3+8} = \frac{8}{11}$$

Question 11 A manufacturer has three machine operators *A*, *B* and *C*. The first operator *A* produces 1% defective items, where as the other two operators *B* and *C* produce 5% and 7% defective items, respectively. *A* is on the job for 50% of the time, *B* on the job for 30% of the time and *C* on the job for 20% of the time. A defective item is produced, what is the probability that it was produced by *A*?

Sol. Let E_1 : the event that item is produced by machine *A*,

E_2 : the event that item is produced by machine *B*

and E_3 : the event that item is produced by machine *C*

Here, E_1, E_2 and E_3 are mutually exclusive and exhaustive events. Moreover,

$$P(E_1) = 50\% = \frac{50}{100},\ P(E_2) = 30\% = \frac{30}{100} \text{ and } P(E_3) = 20\% = \frac{20}{100}$$

Let E : The event that item chosen is found to be defective,

$\therefore$ $P\left(\frac{E}{E_1}\right) = P$ (defective items produced by *A*) $= \frac{1}{100}$

$P\left(\frac{E}{E_2}\right) = P$ (defective items produced by *B*) $= \frac{5}{100}$

and $P\left(\frac{E}{E_3}\right) = P$ (defective items produced by *C*) $= \frac{7}{100}$

By using Bayes' theorem, we obtain

$$P\left(\frac{E_1}{E}\right) = \frac{P\left(\frac{E}{E_1}\right)P(E_1)}{P\left(\frac{E}{E_1}\right)P(E_1) + P\left(\frac{E}{E_2}\right)P(E_2) + P\left(\frac{E}{E_3}\right)P(E_3)}$$

$$= \frac{\frac{1}{100} \times \frac{50}{100}}{\frac{1}{100} \times \frac{50}{100} + \frac{5}{100} \times \frac{30}{100} + \frac{7}{100} \times \frac{20}{100}}$$

$$= \frac{50}{50 + 150 + 140}$$

$$= \frac{50}{340} = \frac{5}{34}$$

Question 12 A card from a pack of 52 cards is lost. From the remaining cards of the pack, two cards are drawn and are found to be diamonds. Find the probability of the lost card being a diamond.

Sol. Let E_1 : the event that lost card is a diamond $\Rightarrow n(E_1) = 13$

E_2 : lost card is not a diamond $\Rightarrow n(E_2) = 52 - 13 = 39$

And, $n(S) = 52$

Then, E_1 and E_2 are mutually exclusive and exhaustive events.

$$\therefore \quad P(E_1) = \frac{13}{52} = \frac{1}{4} \text{ and } P(E_2) = \frac{39}{52} = \frac{3}{4}$$

Let E : the events that two cards drawn from the remaining pack are diamonds, Now, when one diamond card is lost, there are 12 diamond cards out of a total of 51 cards. The cards can be drawn out of 12 diamond cards in ${}^{12}C_2$ ways. Similarly, 2 diamond cards can be drawn out of 51 cards in ${}^{51}C_2$ ways. Then probability of getting two cards, when one diamond card is lost, is given by $P\left(\frac{E}{E_1}\right)$.

$$\therefore \quad P\left(\frac{E}{E_1}\right) = \frac{{}^{12}C_2}{{}^{51}C_2} = \frac{\frac{12 \times 11}{1 \times 2}}{\frac{51 \times 50}{1 \times 2}} = \frac{12 \times 11}{51 \times 50}$$

Now, when not a diamond cad is lost, then there are 13 diamond cards out of a total of 51 cards. The cards can be drawn out of 13 diamond cards in ${}^{13}C_2$ ways. Similarly, two diamond cards can be drawn out of 51 cads in ${}^{51}C_2$ ways. Then, probability of getting two cards, when the card is lost, which is not a diamond is given by $P\left(\frac{E}{E_2}\right)$

$$\therefore \quad P\left(\frac{E}{E_2}\right) = \frac{{}^{13}C_2}{{}^{51}C_2} = \frac{\frac{13 \times 12}{1 \times 2}}{\frac{51 \times 50}{1 \times 2}}$$

$$= \frac{13 \times 12}{51 \times 50}$$

By using Bayes' theorem, we obtain

$$P\left(\frac{E_1}{E}\right)=\frac{P\left(\frac{E}{E_1}\right)P(E_1)}{P\left(\frac{E}{E_1}\right)P(E_1)+P\left(\frac{E}{E_2}\right)P(E_2)}=\frac{\frac{12\times 11}{51\times 50}\times\frac{1}{4}}{\frac{12\times 11}{51\times 50}\times\frac{1}{4}+\frac{13\times 12}{51\times 50}\times\frac{3}{4}}$$

$$=\frac{12\times 11}{12\times 11+13\times 12\times 3}=\frac{132}{132+468}=\frac{132}{600}=\frac{11}{50}$$

Note Whenever more than one items will be drawn simultaneously than we should use ${}^nC_r=\frac{n!}{r!(n-r)!}$.

Question 13 Probability that A speaks truth is 4/5. A coin is tossed, A reports that a head appears. The probability that actually there was head is

(a) $\frac{4}{5}$ (b) $\frac{1}{2}$

(c) $\frac{1}{5}$ (d) $\frac{2}{5}$

Sol. (a) Let E_1 : the event that coin comes up with a head,

E_2 : the event that coin comes up with a tail.

Then, E_1 and E_2 are mutually exclusive and exhaustive events. Moreover,

$$P(E_1)=P(E_2)=\frac{1}{2}$$

E : The event that A speaks truth

$\therefore$ $P\left(\frac{E}{E_1}\right)=P$ (head comes up and A speaks truth) $=\frac{4}{5}$

and $P\left(\frac{E}{E_2}\right)=P$ (tail comes up and A speaks lie) $=\frac{1}{5}$

The probability that there is actually a head is given by $P\left(\frac{E_1}{E}\right)$.

By using Bayes' theorem, we obtain

$$P\left(\frac{E_1}{E}\right)=\frac{P\left(\frac{E}{E_1}\right)P(E_1)}{P\left(\frac{E}{E_1}\right)P(E_1)+P\left(\frac{E}{E_2}\right)P(E_2)}=\frac{\frac{4}{5}\times\frac{1}{2}}{\frac{4}{5}\times\frac{1}{2}+\frac{1}{5}\times\frac{1}{2}}=\frac{4}{4+1}=\frac{4}{5}$$

Mistake Alert Don't Let $E_1\rightarrow A$ speaks truth, $E_2\rightarrow A$ speaks lie.

Question 14. If A and B are two events such that $A \subset B$ and $P(B) \neq 0$, then which of the following is correct?

(a) $P\left(\frac{A}{B}\right) = \frac{P(A)}{P(B)}$ (b) $P\left(\frac{A}{B}\right) < P(A)$ (c) $P\left(\frac{A}{B}\right) \geq P(A)$ (d) None of these

Sol. (c) If $A \subset B$, then $A \cap B = A$

$$\therefore \quad P(A \cap B) = P(A)$$

We know that $P\left(\frac{A}{B}\right) = \frac{P(A \cap B)}{P(B)} = \frac{P(A)}{P(B)}$

But $P(B) \leq 1$

$$\therefore \quad P\left(\frac{A}{B}\right) \geq P(A).$$

Miscellaneous Exercise

Question 1 A and B are two events such that $P(A) \neq 0$. Find $P\left(\frac{B}{A}\right)$ if

(i) A is a subset of B (ii) $A \cap B = \phi$

◎ **Thinking Process** If $A \subset B$, then $P(A \cap B) = P(A)$, use this result and simplify it.

Sol. It is given that, $P(A) \neq 0$

(i) Given, A is a subset of B *i.e* ($A \subset B$)

$$\Rightarrow \quad A \cap B = A$$

$$\Rightarrow \quad P(A \cap B) = P(A)$$

$$\therefore \quad P\left(\frac{B}{A}\right) = \frac{P(B \cap A)}{P(A)} = \frac{P(A)}{P(A)} = 1$$

(ii) Here, $A \cap B = \phi \Rightarrow P(A \cap B) = 0$

$$\therefore \quad P\left(\frac{B}{A}\right) = \frac{P(B \cap A)}{P(A)} = \frac{0}{P(A)} = 0$$

Question 2 A couple has two children.

(i) Find the probability that both children are males, if it is known that atleast one of the children is male.

(ii) Find the probability that both children are females if it is known that the elder child is a female.

Sol. Here, the sample space is $S = \{bb, bg, gb, gg\}$ where b stands for a boy and 'g' for a girl; first letter standing for elder child and second for the younger child.

$$\therefore \quad n(S) = 4$$

(i) Let E : both the children are males

F : atleast one of the children is a male

$\therefore \quad E = \{bb\}, F = \{bg, gb, bb\}$

$\Rightarrow \quad n(F) = 3$

and $\quad E \cap F = \{bb\} = E$

$\Rightarrow \quad n(E \cap F) = n(E) = 1$

$$\therefore \text{Required probability} = P\left(\frac{E}{F}\right) = \frac{P(E \cap F)}{P(F)} = \frac{P(E)}{P(F)} = \frac{1/4}{3/4} = \frac{1}{3}$$

(ii) Let E : both the children are females and

and F : elder child is a female elder means who born first

$\therefore \quad E = \{gg\}, F = \{gb, gg\}$ and $E \cap F = \{gg\} = E$

$\Rightarrow \quad n(E) = 1, n(F) = 2$ and $n(E \cap F) = 1$

$$\therefore \text{Required probability} = P\left(\frac{E}{F}\right) = \frac{P(E \cap F)}{P(F)} = \frac{P(E)}{P(F)} = \frac{1/4}{2/4} = \frac{1}{2}$$

Question 3 Suppose that 5% of men and 0.25% of women have grey hair. A grey haired person is selected at random. What is the probability of this person being male? Assume that there are equal number of males and females.

Sol. Let E_1 : the event that selected person is a male and E_2 : the event that selected person is a female.

E_1 and E_2 are mutually exclusive and exhaustive events. Moreover,

$$P(E_1) = P(E_2) = \frac{1}{2}$$

[$\because$ it is given, there are equal number of males and females.]

Let E : the event that selected person is grey haired.

$$\therefore \quad P\left(\frac{E}{E_1}\right) = \frac{5}{100} = \frac{1}{20} \text{ and } P\left(\frac{E}{E_2}\right) = \frac{0.25}{100} = \frac{1}{400}$$

By using Bayes' theorem

$$\text{Required probability} = P\left(\frac{E_1}{E}\right) = \frac{P\left(\frac{E}{E_1}\right)P(E_1)}{P\left(\frac{E}{E_1}\right)P(E_1) + P\left(\frac{E}{E_2}\right)P(E_2)}$$

$$= \frac{\frac{1}{20} \times \frac{1}{2}}{\frac{1}{20} \times \frac{1}{2} + \frac{1}{400} \times \frac{1}{2}}$$

$$= \frac{\frac{1}{20}}{\frac{1}{20} + \frac{1}{400}} = \frac{\frac{1}{20}}{\frac{21}{400}} = \frac{20}{21}$$

Question 4 Suppose that 90% of people are right handed. What is the probability that atmost 6 of random sample of 10 people are right handed?

Sol. A person can be either right handed or left handed. It is given that 90% of the people are right handed.

Therefore, $p = \frac{90}{100} = \frac{9}{10}$

and $q = 1 - p = 1 - \frac{9}{10} = \frac{1}{10}$, $n = 10$

Clearly, X has a binomial distribution with $n = 10$, $p = \frac{9}{10}$ and $q = \frac{1}{10}$

$\therefore$
$$P(X = r) = {}^nC_r\, p^r\, q^{n-r} = {}^{10}C_r \left(\frac{9}{10}\right)^r \left(\frac{1}{10}\right)^{10-r}$$

Required probability $= P(X \le 6)$

$$= P(X = 0) + P(X = 1) + P(X = 2) + P(X = 3) + P(X = 4) + P(X = 5) + P(X = 6)$$

$$= {}^{10}C_0\, p^0 q^{10} + {}^{10}C_1\, p^1 q^9 + {}^{10}C_2\, p^2 q^8 + {}^{10}C_3\, p^3 q^7 + {}^{10}C_4\, p^4 q^6 + {}^{10}C_5\, p^5 q^5 + {}^{10}C_6\, p^6 q^4$$

$$= q^{10} + 10pq^9 + \frac{10 \times 9}{1 \times 2} p^2 q^8 + \frac{10 \times 9 \times 8}{1 \times 2 \times 3} p^3 q^7 + \frac{10 \times 9 \times 8 \times 7}{1 \times 2 \times 3 \times 4} p^4 q^6 + \frac{10 \times 9 \times 8 \times 7 \times 6}{1 \times 2 \times 3 \times 4 \times 5} p^5 q^5 + \frac{10 \times 9 \times 8 \times 7}{1 \times 2 \times 3 \times 4} p^6 q^4$$

$$= q^{10} + 10pq^9 + 45p^2 q^8 + 120p^3 q^7 + 210p^4 q^6 + 252p^5 q^5 + 210p^6 q^4$$

$$= \left(\frac{1}{10}\right)^{10} + 10\left(\frac{9}{10}\right)\left(\frac{1}{10}\right)^9 + 45\left(\frac{9}{10}\right)^2\left(\frac{1}{10}\right)^8 + 120\left(\frac{9}{10}\right)^3\left(\frac{1}{10}\right)^7 + 210\left(\frac{9}{10}\right)^4\left(\frac{1}{10}\right)^6 + 252\left(\frac{9}{10}\right)^5\left(\frac{1}{10}\right)^5 + 210\left(\frac{9}{10}\right)^6\left(\frac{1}{10}\right)^4$$

$$= \frac{1 + 90 + 45 \times 9^2 + 120 \times 9^3 + 210 \times 9^4 + 252 \times 9^5 + 210 \times 9^6}{10^{10}}$$

Question 5 If a leap year is selected at random, what is the chance that it will contain 53 Tuesday?

◎ *Thinking Process* In a leap year, there are 366 days having 52 weeks and 2 extra days.

Sol. In a leap year, there are 366 days *i.e.*, 52 weeks and 2 days.

In 52 weeks, there are 52 Tuesday.

Therefore, the probability that the leap year will contain 53 Tuesday is equal to the probability that from the remaining 2 days one will be Tuesday.

For the remaining 2 days there are following 7 cases

(i) Sunday and Monday
(ii) Monday and Tuesday
(iii) Tuesday and Wednesday
(iv) Wednesday and Thursday
(v) Thursday and Friday
(vi) Friday and Saturday
(vii) Saturday and Sunday

Out of these seven possibilities, only two *i.e.*, (ii) and (iii) are favourable to the events '53 Tuesday'.

$\therefore$ Total number of cases = 7 and favourable cases = 2.

Hence, required probability $= \frac{2}{7}$.

Question 6 Suppose we have four boxes *A*, *B*, *C* and *D* containing coloured marbles as given below

Box	Marble colour		
	Red	White	Black
A	1	6	3
B	6	2	2
C	8	1	1
D	0	6	4

One of the boxes has been selected at random and a single marble is drawn from it. If the marble is red what is the probability that it was drawn from box *A*? box B?, box C?

◎ *Thinking Process* (Q. Nos. 6 and 7) If events are mutually exclusive and exhaustive, then Bayes' theorem is

$$P\left(\frac{E_i}{E}\right) = \frac{P\left(\frac{E}{E_i}\right)P(E_i)}{\sum_{i=1}^{n} P\left(\frac{E}{E_i}\right)P(E_i)}$$

Sol. Let E_1 : the event that box A is selected, E_2 : the event that box B is selected, E_3 : the event that box C is selected and E_4 : the event that box D is selected,

$\therefore E_1, E_2, E_3, E_4$ are mutually exclusive and exhaustive. Moreover,

$$P(E_1) = P(E_2) = P(E_3) = P(E_4) = \frac{1}{4}.$$

Let E : ball drawn is red,

$$\therefore \quad P\left(\frac{E}{E_1}\right) = \frac{1}{1+6+3} = \frac{1}{10},$$

$$P\left(\frac{E}{E_2}\right) = \frac{6}{6+2+2} = \frac{6}{10},$$

$$P\left(\frac{E}{E_3}\right) = \frac{8}{8+1+1} = \frac{8}{10}$$

and
$$P\left(\frac{E}{E_4}\right) = \frac{0}{0+6+4} = 0$$

By using Bayes' theorem

$P(\text{ball is drawn from box } A) = P\left(\frac{E_1}{E}\right)$

$$= \frac{P\left(\frac{E}{E_1}\right)P(E_1)}{P\left(\frac{E}{E_1}\right)P(E_1) + P\left(\frac{E}{E_2}\right)P(E_2) + P\left(\frac{E}{E_3}\right)P(E_3) + P\left(\frac{E}{E_4}\right)P(E_4)}$$

$$= \frac{\frac{1}{10}\times\frac{1}{4}}{\frac{1}{10}\times\frac{1}{4}+\frac{6}{10}\times\frac{1}{4}+\frac{8}{10}\times\frac{1}{4}+0\times\frac{1}{4}}$$

$$= \frac{\frac{1}{40}}{\frac{1}{4}\left(\frac{1}{10}+\frac{6}{10}+\frac{8}{10}+0\right)} = \frac{\frac{1}{40}}{\frac{1}{4}\times\frac{15}{10}} = \frac{\frac{1}{40}}{\frac{15}{40}} = \frac{1}{15}$$

P (ball is drawn from box B)

$$= P\left(\frac{E_2}{E}\right) = \frac{P\left(\frac{E}{E_2}\right)P(E_2)}{P\left(\frac{E}{E_1}\right)P(E_1) + P\left(\frac{E}{E_2}\right)P(E_2) + P\left(\frac{E}{E_3}\right)P(E_3) + P\left(\frac{E}{E_4}\right)P(E_4)}$$

$$= \frac{\frac{6}{10}\times\frac{1}{4}}{\frac{1}{10}\times\frac{1}{4}+\frac{6}{10}\times\frac{1}{4}+\frac{8}{10}\times\frac{1}{4}+0\times\frac{1}{4}}$$

$$= \frac{\frac{6}{40}}{\frac{1}{4}\left(\frac{1}{10}+\frac{6}{10}+\frac{8}{10}+0\right)}$$

$$= \frac{\frac{6}{40}}{\frac{1}{4}\times\frac{15}{10}} = \frac{\frac{6}{40}}{\frac{15}{40}} = \frac{6}{40}\times\frac{40}{15} = \frac{2}{5}$$

and P (ball is drawn from box C)

$$= P\left(\frac{E_3}{E}\right) = \frac{P\left(\frac{E}{E_3}\right)P(E_3)}{P\left(\frac{E}{E_1}\right)P(E_1) + P\left(\frac{E}{E_2}\right)P(E_2) + P\left(\frac{E}{E_3}\right)P(E_3) + P\left(\frac{E}{E_4}\right)P(E_4)}$$

$$= \frac{\frac{8}{10}\times\frac{1}{4}}{\frac{1}{10}\times\frac{1}{4}+\frac{6}{10}\times\frac{1}{4}+\frac{8}{10}\times\frac{1}{4}+0\times\frac{1}{4}}$$

$$= \frac{\frac{8}{40}}{\frac{1}{4}\left(\frac{1}{10}+\frac{6}{10}+\frac{8}{10}+0\right)} = \frac{\frac{8}{40}}{\frac{1}{4}\times\frac{15}{10}} = \frac{\frac{8}{40}}{\frac{15}{40}}$$

$$= \frac{8}{40}\times\frac{40}{15} = \frac{8}{15}$$

Question 7 Assume that the chances of a patient having a heart attack is 40%. It is also assumed that a meditation and yoga course reduces the risk of heart attack by 30% and prescription of certain drug reduces its chances by 25%. At a time a patient can choose any one of the two options with equal probabilities. It is given that after going through one of the two options the patient selected at random suffers a heart attack. Find the probability that the patient followed a course of meditation and yoga?

Sol. Let E_1 : the event that the patient follows meditation and yoga and

and E_2 : the event that the patient uses drug.

It is given at a time a patient can choose anyone of two options, with equal probabilities

$\therefore E_1$ and E_2 are mutually exclusive events and $P(E_1) = P(E_2) = \frac{1}{2}$

Let E : the event that the selected patient suffers a heart attack

$\therefore$ $$P\left(\frac{E}{E_1}\right) = \frac{40}{100}\left(1 - \frac{30}{100}\right) = \frac{28}{100}$$

and $$P\left(\frac{E}{E_2}\right) = \frac{40}{100}\left(1 - \frac{25}{100}\right) = \frac{30}{100}$$

$\therefore P$ (patient who suffers heart attack follows meditation and yoga)

$$= P\left(\frac{E_1}{E}\right) = \frac{P\left(\frac{E}{E_1}\right)P(E_1)}{P\left(\frac{E}{E_1}\right)P(E_1) + P\left(\frac{E}{E_2}\right)P(E_2)}$$

$$= \frac{\frac{28}{100} \times \frac{1}{2}}{\frac{28}{100} \times \frac{1}{2} + \frac{30}{100} \times \frac{1}{2}}$$

$$= \frac{\frac{14}{100}}{\frac{14}{100} + \frac{15}{100}} = \frac{\frac{14}{100}}{\frac{14 + 15}{100}}$$

$$= \frac{14}{100} \times \frac{100}{29} = \frac{14}{29}$$

Mistake Alert Student confuse in $P(E_1 / E)$ and $P(E / E_1)$. This leads to errors in applying Bayes' theorem.

Question 8 If each element of a second order determinant is zero or one, what is the probability that the values of the determinant is positive? (Assume that the individual entries of the determinant are chosen independently, each value being assumed with probability $\frac{1}{2}$).

Sol. A second order determinant has four entries which may be 0 or 1.

Total number of determinants = $2^4 = 16$

The only positive determinants are $\begin{vmatrix} 1 & 0 \\ 0 & 1 \end{vmatrix}$, $\begin{vmatrix} 1 & 0 \\ 1 & 1 \end{vmatrix}$ and $\begin{vmatrix} 1 & 1 \\ 0 & 1 \end{vmatrix}$.

Since, each entry of the above determinant can be selected with probability $\frac{1}{2}$, $\therefore$

Required probability.

$$= 3\left(\frac{1}{2} \times \frac{1}{2} \times \frac{1}{2} \times \frac{1}{2}\right) = \frac{3}{16}.$$

Quick Solution

Here, total number of cases = 16

Favourable number of cases = 3

$\therefore$ Required probability $= \dfrac{3}{16}$

Question 9 An electronic assembly consists of two subsystems, say A and B. From previous testing procedures, the following probabilities are assumed to be known

$$P\,(A \text{ fails}) = 0.2,\ P\,(B \text{ fails alone}) = 0.15,\ P\,(A \text{ and } B \text{ fail}) = 0.15$$

Evaluate the following probabilities

(i) $P\,(A \text{ fails}/B \text{ has failed})$ (ii) $P\,(A \text{ fails alone})$

Sol. Let the event in which A fails and B fails be denoted by A' and B'

$$P(A') = 0.2,\ P(A' \cap B') = 0.15$$

$$P(B \text{ fails alone}) = P(B') - P(A' \cap B')$$

$\therefore$ $$0.15 = P(B') - 0.15$$

$\Rightarrow$ $$P(B') = 0.30$$

(i) $P(A \text{ fails}/B \text{ has failed}) = P(A'/B') = \dfrac{P\,(A' \cap B')}{P(B')} = \dfrac{0.15}{0.30} = 0.5$

(ii) $P(A \text{ fails alone}) = P(A \text{ fails}) - P\,(\text{Both } A \text{ and } B \text{ fails})$

$$= P(A') - P(A' \cap B') = 0.2 - 0.15 = 0.05$$

Question 10 Bag I contains 3 red and 4 black balls and bag II contains 4 red and 5 black balls. One ball is transferred from bag I to bag II and then ball is drawn from bag II. The ball so drawn is found to be red in colour. Find the probability that the transferred ball is black.

Sol. Let E_1 : red ball is transferred from bag I to bag II

and E_2 : black ball is transferred from bag I to bag II

$\therefore$ E_1 and E_2 are mutually exclusive and exhaustive events.

$\therefore$ $$P(E_1) = \frac{3}{3+4} = \frac{3}{7} \text{ and } P(E_2) = \frac{4}{3+4} = \frac{4}{7}$$

Let E be the event that the ball drawn is red. When a red ball is transferred from bag I to II.

$$P\left(\frac{E}{E_1}\right) = \frac{4+1}{(4+1)+5} = \frac{5}{10} = \frac{1}{2}$$

When a black ball is transferred from bag I to II.

$$P\left(\frac{E}{E_2}\right) = \frac{4}{4+(5+1)} = \frac{4}{10} = \frac{2}{5}$$

$$\therefore \text{Required probability} = P\left(\frac{E_2}{E}\right) = \frac{P\left(\frac{E}{E_2}\right)P(E_2)}{P\left(\frac{E}{E_1}\right)P(E_1) + P\left(\frac{E}{E_2}\right)P(E_2)}$$

$$= \frac{\frac{2}{5} \times \frac{4}{7}}{\frac{1}{2} \times \frac{3}{7} + \frac{2}{5} \times \frac{4}{7}} = \frac{\frac{8}{35}}{\frac{3}{14} + \frac{8}{35}}$$

$$= \frac{\frac{8}{35}}{\frac{105 + 112}{14 \times 35}} = \frac{8 \times 14}{217} = \frac{16}{31}$$

Question 11 If A and B are two events such that $P(A) \neq 0$ and $P\left(\frac{B}{A}\right) = 1$, then

(a) $A \subset B$ (b) $B \subset A$

(c) $B = \phi$ (d) $A = \phi$

Sol. (a) Given, $P(A) \neq 0$

and $P\left(\frac{B}{A}\right) = 1$

$\Rightarrow$ $P\left(\frac{B}{A}\right) = \frac{P(A \cap B)}{P(A)} = 1 \Rightarrow P(A \cap B) = P(A)$

$\Rightarrow$ $A \cap B = A \Rightarrow A \subset B$

Question 12 If $P\left(\frac{A}{B}\right) > P(A)$, then which of the following is correct?

(a) $P\left(\frac{B}{A}\right) < P(B)$ (b) $P(A \cap B) < P(A)\,P(B)$

(c) $P\left(\frac{B}{A}\right) > P(B)$ (d) $P\left(\frac{B}{A}\right) = P(B)$

Sol. (c) Given, $P\left(\frac{A}{B}\right) > P(A)$

$\Rightarrow$ $\frac{P(A \cap B)}{P(B)} > P(A)$

$\Rightarrow$ $P(A \cap B) > P(A) \cdot P(B)$

$\Rightarrow$ $\frac{P(A \cap B)}{P(A)} > P(B)$

$\Rightarrow$ $P\left(\frac{B}{A}\right) > P(B)$ $\left[\because P\left(\frac{B}{A}\right) = \frac{P(A \cap B)}{P(A)}\right]$

Question 13 If A and B are any two events such that $P(A) + P(B) - P(A \text{ and } B) = P(A)$, then

(a) $P\left(\frac{B}{A}\right) = 1$

(b) $P\left(\frac{A}{B}\right) = 1$

(c) $P\left(\frac{B}{A}\right) = 0$

(d) $P\left(\frac{A}{B}\right) = 0$

Sol. (b) Given, $P(A) + P(B) - P(A \text{ and } B) = P(A)$

$\Rightarrow \quad P(A) + P(B) - P(A \cap B) = P(A)$

$\Rightarrow \quad P(B) - P(A \cap B) = 0 \Rightarrow P(B) = P(A \cap B)$

$\Rightarrow \quad 1 = \frac{P(A \cap B)}{P(B)}$

$\Rightarrow \quad 1 = P\left(\frac{A}{B}\right) \qquad \left[\because P\left(\frac{A}{B}\right) = \frac{P(A \cap B)}{P(B)}\right]$

DIKSHA APP Questions

☐ Multiple Choice Questions

Q.1 A and B are two events cuch that $P(A \cup B) = \frac{3}{4}$, $P(A \cap B) = \frac{1}{4}$, $P(\overline{A}) = \frac{2}{3}$ then $P(\overline{A} \cap B) =$

(a) $\frac{5}{12}$ (b) $\frac{3}{8}$

(c) $\frac{5}{8}$ (d) $\frac{7}{4}$

Sol. (a) We have, $P(A \cup B) = \frac{3}{4}$, $P(A \cap B) = \frac{1}{4}$ and $P(\overline{A}) = \frac{2}{3}$

$\therefore \quad P(A) = 1 - P(\overline{A})$

$\Rightarrow \quad P(A) = 1 - \frac{2}{3} = \frac{1}{3}$

Now, we know that

$$P(A \cup B) = P(A) + P(B) - P(A \cap B)$$

$$\Rightarrow \quad \frac{3}{4} = \frac{1}{3} + P(B) - \frac{1}{4}$$

$$\Rightarrow \quad P(B) = \frac{3}{4} + \frac{1}{4} - \frac{1}{3} = 1 - \frac{1}{3} = \frac{2}{3}$$

Now, $P(\overline{A} \cap B) = P(B) - P(A \cap B)$

$$= \frac{2}{3} - \frac{1}{4} = \frac{8-3}{12} = \frac{5}{12}$$

Q.2 The probability that A speaks truth is $\frac{4}{5}$ and for B is $\frac{3}{4}$, then probability that they contradict each other when asked to speak on a fact.

(a) $\frac{4}{5}$ (b) $\frac{1}{5}$

(c) $\frac{7}{20}$ (d) $\frac{3}{20}$

Sol. (c) Given, probability of A speaks truth $= \frac{4}{5} \Rightarrow P(A) = \frac{4}{5}$

and probability of B speaks truth $= \frac{3}{4} \Rightarrow P(B) = \frac{3}{4}$

If they are contradicting for the same fact, then either A speaks truth and B speaks lie or A speaks lie and B speaks truth.

$\therefore$ Required probability

$$= P(A) \cdot P(\overline{B}) + P(B) \cdot P(\overline{A})$$

$$= P(A)(1 - P(B)) + P(B)(1 - P(A)) \quad \left[\begin{array}{l}\because P(\overline{A}) = 1 - P(A) \\ \text{and } P(\overline{B}) = 1 - P(B)\end{array}\right]$$

$$= \frac{4}{5}\left(1 - \frac{3}{4}\right) + \frac{3}{4}\left(1 - \frac{4}{5}\right)$$

$$= \frac{4}{5} \times \frac{1}{4} + \frac{3}{4} \times \frac{1}{5} = \frac{7}{20}$$

Q.3 It is given that event A and B are such that $P(A) = \frac{1}{4}$, $P(A/B) = \frac{1}{2}$ and $P(B/A) = \frac{2}{3}$, then $P(B) =$

(a) $\frac{2}{3}$ (b) $\frac{1}{2}$

(c) $\frac{1}{6}$ (d) $\frac{1}{3}$

Sol. (d) We have, $P(A) = \frac{1}{4}, P\left(\frac{A}{B}\right) = \frac{1}{2}$ and $P\left(\frac{B}{A}\right) = \frac{2}{3}$

Now, $P\left(\frac{B}{A}\right) = \frac{P(A \cap B)}{P(A)} = \frac{2}{3}$

$$\Rightarrow \quad P(A \cap B) = \frac{2}{3} \cdot P(A)$$

$$= \frac{2}{3} \times \frac{1}{4} = \frac{1}{6}$$

and, $P\left(\frac{A}{B}\right) = \frac{P(A \cap B)}{P(B)} = \frac{1}{2}$ (given)

On putting $P(A \cap B) = \frac{1}{6}$, we get

$$\frac{\frac{1}{6}}{P(B)} = \frac{1}{2}$$

$$\Rightarrow \quad \frac{1}{6} = \frac{1}{2} \cdot P(B)$$

$$\Rightarrow \quad P(B) = \frac{1}{3}$$